MANAGEMENT OF ORGANIZATIONAL BEHAVIOR

John A. Wagner III
John R. Hollenbeck
Michigan State University

Prentice Hall, Inc.
Englewood Cliffs, New Jersey 07632

Library of Congress Cataloging-in-Publication Data

WAGNER, JOHN A.,
  Management of organizational behavior/John A. Wagner III, John
R. Hollenbeck.
      p. cm.
  Includes index.
  ISBN 0-13-556648-7
  1. Organizational behavior   2. Organizational behavior—Case
studies.   I. Hollenbeck, John R.   II. Title.
HD58.7.W24 1992
658.3—dc20   91–34368
                                                      CIP

To Mary Jane, Allison, and Jillian Elizabeth Wagner
and
Harold J. Hollenbeck

Acquisition Editor: *Alison Reeves*
Development Editor: *Virginia Otis Locke*
Production Editor: *Esther S. Koehn*
Copy Editor: *Shirley Stone*
Designer: *Lorraine Mullaney*
Cover Designer: *Butler/Udell Design*
Photo Research: *Anita Duncan* and *Teri Stratford*
Page Layout: *Martin J. Behan*
Prepress Buyer: *Trudy Pisciotti*
Manufacturer Buyer: *Robert Anderson*
Supplements Editor: *David M. Scholder*
Marketing Manager: *Sandra Steiner*

Printed in the United States of America
10 9 8 7 6 5 4 3 2

ISBN 0-13-556648-7

Prentice-Hall International (UK) Limited, *London*
Prentice-Hall of Australia Pty. Limited, *Sydney*
Prentice-Hall Canada Inc., *Toronto*
Prentice-Hall Hispanoamericana, S.A., *Mexico City*
Prentice-Hall of India Private Limited, *New Delhi*
Prentice-Hall of Japan, Inc., *Tokyo*
Simon & Schuster Asia Pte. Ltd., *Singapore*
Editora Prentice-Hall do Brasil, Ltda., *Rio de Janeiro*

BRIEF CONTENTS

iii

CONTENTS

PART I
INTRODUCTION

6 DECISION MAKING 159

7 MOTIVATION AND PERFORMANCE 197

8 SATISFACTION AND STRESS 241

PART III
INTERPERSONAL, GROUP, AND INTERGROUP RELATIONS

10 INTERPERSONAL PROCESSES AND COMMUNICATION 329

13 POWER, POLITICS, AND CONFLICT 457

14 MANAGING GROUP AND INTERGROUP RELATIONS: ORGANIZATION DEVELOPMENT I 503

PART IV
THE ORGANIZATIONAL CONTEXT

15 STRUCTURING THE ORGANIZATION 545

16 ORGANIZATION DESIGN 589

17 JOB DESIGN 637

18 MANAGING THE ORGANIZATION: STRATEGY, CULTURE, AND ORGANIZATION DEVELOPMENT II 681

PART V
SUMMARY AND CAPSTONE

19 INTERNATIONAL DIMENSIONS: ORGANIZATIONAL BEHAVIOR ABROAD 731

PREFACE

Organizational behavior is the study of human behavior in the workplace. This real-world focus makes OB a discipline that embraces both research and the practical application of research findings. Some OB texts tend to emphasize research; some focus on practical applications. Still others try to cover both areas by dotting their explorations of theory and research with applications material. Professors of organizational behavior have long struggled with the issue of whether theory and practice can be presented together effectively.

We think they can. The value of OB research is measured by its usefulness in the real world of business and industry. And what makes OB research useful is having the right tools to apply its theories and concepts. When we started writing this book we set ourselves two primary aims: first, to cover the field of OB with complete accuracy and second, to offer you, the student, solid guidance and practice in using the theories and concepts that we discuss. With these two goals before us, we created a set of tools that will help you acquire the skills and expertise you'll need to be effective managers in the complex world of work.

SMART THINKING: LINKING THEORY AND PRACTICE

Learning a handful of theories in rote fashion might not be too difficult, but it would probably be tedious, and it definitely would not be very useful. Learning theories and how to apply them may be more challenging at the outset but ultimately it is much more worthwhile. The key to the successful application of theory is critical thinking, smart thinking. To help you think critically about the material in this book, both now, as you study it, and later, as you manage organizational behavior in the workplace, we have incorporated several special features into our text: diagnostic issues and questions, diagnostic frameworks, exercises and cases, and in-text examples.

Diagnostic Issues and Questions

The first three chapters of this book are designed to orient you to the field of organizational behavior and to our particular focus on learning how to manage human behavior in organizations. With Chapter 4, we move into the core part of our book, in which each chapter starts out with a section called "Diagnostic Issues." These issues, like traditional learning objectives, will alert you to the significant concerns of each chapter and will guide you in applying the diagnostic approach we outline in Chapter 1, helping you target and solve real-world problems.

At the end of each chapter you will find a set of "Diagnostic Questions" that have several functions. First, they supplement the chapter's review questions in helping you to summarize the important issues covered in the chapter. Second, they supplement the study questions at the ends of cases, guiding you through the process of assembling the facts of a case, diagnosing the problem, and prescribing appropriate action. Finally, these questions offer you valuable guidelines that you'll use throughout your career in analyzing problems/situations and prescribing and implementing effective solutions.

Problem-solving is a big part of a manager's daily job. The tools you'll acquire in studying this book and in participating in classwork will help you build the foundation for a successful management career.

Diagnostic Frameworks

One problem students of organizational behavior often confront is having to learn many different theories of a given phenomenon without any guidance as to what to accept or reject. To eliminate this source of confusion we've created what we call diagnostic frameworks, or informal models that show you how each of several equally valid theories fit together. Even though a theory may fail to explain something completely, it may still have something useful to contribute when combined with other theories. We think you will find that these frameworks will help you organize complex material, learn it more efficiently, and remember it better. Chapters that present such frameworks include Chapter 7, "Motivation and Performance," Chapter 12, "Leadership," and Chapter 16, "Organization Design."

Exercises and Cases

This book's cases and exercises offer students solid practice in applying each chapter's concepts and theories. The cases will help you think about what you would actually do in a particular situation, based on what you've learned. They will also give you a chance to practice using some of the diagnostic questions in working toward solutions of the problems they pose.

The exercises we've selected for this book, which are designed to be performed in the classroom, are realistic models of problems that managers encounter on the job. For this reason they'll give you meaningful practice in applying your knowledge.

Examples

As you read the chapters of our book, you will find a wealth of examples of real people and of companies that are familiar to you. These examples help make the text's theories and concepts more concrete. We present some of these examples in a sentence or two in the course of explaining a particular aspect of a theory. More complex examples are discussed at greater length, in the stories that open each of our chapters or in the "In Practice" series of boxes. And you'll find other examples in the captions that describe the book's photographs of people on the job.

Integrating Ethical and International Dimensions

Because both ethics in business and industry and the international aspects of management are so important, we have integrated our coverage of these topics into the text. Throughout the book, "Management Issues" boxes discuss such subjects as responsibility for the *Exxon Valdez* oil spill, surveillance of employees without their knowledge, and the complex notion of comparable worth. For example, Chapter 9 discusses Canadian employers' struggle to figure out how to compensate jobs that are of equal worth but that are paid widely varying wages.

In many chapters you will find an "International OB" box that in some cases introduces a concept expanded on in the last chapter of the book. These boxes explore such issues as the way work groups are formed in different national cultures, the Japanese notion of *karoshi*, or death from overwork, and the rise of innovation in Taiwan. A box in Chapter 6, for example, traces the evolution of Taiwanese industry from copying foreign designs to creating new ones.

A Structure That Emphasizes Applications

We have structured our book to provide more than one level of application. As we've said, each of our chapters uses diagnostic issues and questions, in-text examples, opening stories, and end-of-chapter cases and exercises to help you apply what you've learned. In addition, in each major part of the book a concluding chapter expands on the applications already described and introduces you to a formal, applied OB field. Chapter 9, on managing individuals, discusses the applied field of human resources management (HRM). Chapter 14, on managing groups, discusses the applied field of organization development (OD). Chapter 18, on managing the organization, discusses the applied field of strategic management (SM) and returns to the topic of OD, this time at the organization-wide level. The last part of the book presents a single chapter in capstone fashion, exploring the challenge of applying OB concepts throughout the world.

THE DEVELOPMENT PROCESS

When we set out to write this book, we wanted to balance theory with practice. We wanted to cover micro and macro OB equally. We wanted the book to be completely accurate. And we wanted our book to be useful, employing a diagnostic perspective throughout. Prentice Hall's market research and development divisions helped us in many ways to achieve our goals. Initially, we worked with market research in creating a detailed questionnaire to survey OB instructors' thoughts on the distinctive features we planned for our book as well as on other general issues.

Out of the nearly 1500 professors of organizational behavior who received this questionnaire, to our great delight, over a third responded. Prentice Hall's market researchers fed this material into a database that tabulated the information and compared the data across variables. This feedback helped us refine our first draft of the book.

Next, a full-time in-house development editor was assigned to our project. This editor's job was to read our manuscript as if she were a student taking a course in OB for the first time. Combining the results of this experience with her editing skills, the editor helped us present the material clearly and interestingly.

Intensive rounds of reviews and reviewer conferences further advanced the development process. During the development of our first two drafts, Prentice Hall obtained over 50 reviews of our manuscript by peers and colleagues. At each stage, several reviewers met with us face to face to discuss issues and ideas. The insights and comments of these reviewers were invaluable in producing the final draft.

The long, intensive process of development has been well worth the effort. We are proud that, with the help of Prentice Hall and our many reviewers, we have provided you with an excellent, clearly written textbook. We are proud to have realized our vision of an accurate and engaging book that will help present and future managers think smart and work effectively.

SUPPLEMENTS PACKAGE

The tools that we've included in this textbook are those we think the most critical for students to acquire. However, a number of highly effective supplements are available to those who want to add a particular emphasis to one or another aspect of the course. Items that are designed strictly for the professor, such as the Test Item File, the Instructor's Manual, and Transparency Masters, are discussed in the preface to the Annotated Instructor's Edition. Following are the items that are of interest to both professors and students.

ABC News/Prentice Hall Video Library for Management of Organizational Behavior. Carefully selected videos from ABC News's award-winning programs bring the real world to life. This library provides a video for each chapter of the text, emphasizing the application of OB concepts. Teaching notes for integrating the videos with the text are included in the Applications Pack that we'll describe shortly.

Management Live! The Video Book; The Video Collection. Developed by Bob Marx, Peter Frost, and Todd Jick, this creative, video-based experiential workbook is available at a discounted price when shrinkwrapped to *Management of Organizational Behavior*. The companion *Video Collection* is available on adoption of the shrinkwrapped package (one per department). It contains exercises, readings, and self-assessment materials on eighteen topics of interest to managers and people studying to become managers. These materials are enhanced by video clips contained in *The Video Collection*. An *Instructor's Manual* to accompany the *Book/Video Collection* is available.

Acumen, Educational Version 2.0. Designed for use on an IBM-compatible personal computer, *Acumen* is a managerial assessment and development program that enables you to evaluate your managerial strengths and weaknesses by responding to 120 statements. The program then compares your graphic, personalized profile with a cross-section of professional managers and gives you a detailed report that suggests ways of improving your skills. Like *Management Live!*, *Acumen: Educational Version* is available at a discounted price when ordered shrinkwrapped to this text.

Applications Pack with Video Guide. The applications pack includes additional exercises and cases that can be used with *Management of Organizational Behavior* as well as teaching notes for both. It also includes teaching notes for the ABC/PH video library, the *Management Live!* video collection and book, and *Acumen*.

Management and Organizational Behavior: A Contemporary View, sponsored by The New York Times and Prentice Hall. This collection of timely newspaper articles gives students current information about topics discussed in the text. The articles come from one of the world's most distinguished newspapers, *The New York Times*, and demonstrate the vital connection between what you learn in the classroom and what is happening in the world about you.

ACKNOWLEDGMENTS

Our book has been influenced by the ideas and suggestions of many people. First, we would like to thank the instructors who reviewed and commented on initial drafts and helped us refine our ideas: Murray R. Baruch, University of Iowa; Robert A. Bolda, University of Michigan-Dearborn; Robert Bontempo, Columbia University; Joel Brockner, Columbia University; Donald Conlon, University of Delaware; Gerald R. Ferris, University of Illinois; Douglas M. Fox, Western Connecticut State University; Terry L. Gaston, Southern Oregon State College; Barrie Gibbs, Simon Fraser University; Stephen G. Green, Purdue University; James L. Hall, Santa Clara University; Nell Hartley, Robert Morris College; Diane Hoadley, University of South Dakota; Russell E. Johannesson, Temple University; Ralph Katerberg, University of Cincinnati; Kenneth A. Kovach, George Mason University; Charles Kuehl, University of Missouri, St. Louis; Vicki LaFarge, Bentley College; Edwin A. Locke, University of Maryland; Gail H. McKee, Roanoke College; Linda L. Neider, University of Miami; Aaron Nurick, Bentley College; Daniel Ondrack, University of Toronto; Christine Pearson, University of Southern California; Gary N. Powell, University of Connecticut; Gerald L. Rose, University of Iowa; Joseph G. Rosse, University of Colorado, Boulder; Carol Sales, Brock University, Ontario; Mel E. Schnake, Valdosta State College; Randall G. Sleeth; E. M. Teagarden, Dakota State University; Lucian Spataro, Ohio University; Gary L. Whaley, Norfolk State University; and David G. Williams, West Virginia University.

Second, we would like to acknowledge the special input we received from the reviewers who examined our text in depth and, meeting with us twice, helped us fine-tune its chapters: Hrach Bedrosian, New York University; Jeannette Davy, Arizona State University; Howard E. Mitchell, Wharton School, University of Pennsylvania; Ronald R. Sims, College of William and Mary; Roger Volkema, American University; Deborah L. Wells,

Creighton University; and Wayne M. Wormley, Drexel University. All of these individuals deserve special thanks for the time and effort they devoted to their task.

Third, we would like to thank the people at Prentice Hall whose patience and guidance enabled us to complete the task of writing a college textbook: Alison Reeves, assistant vice president and executive editor, who introduced us to Prentice Hall and managed our project from beginning to end, and her assistant, Diane Peirano; Garret White, publisher of the business and economics team; Virginia Otis Locke, senior editor, who helped us turn dry, wordy prose into clear, engaging text and forced us to live up to the promises made in this preface; Raymond Mullaney, vice president and editor in chief, who managed our book's development, and his assistant, Asha Rohra; Esther S. Koehn, supervisory production editor, who oversaw the entire production process and brought all of the words, diagrams, and pictures together into a meaningful whole; Sandra M. Steiner, marketing manager, and her assistant, Elizabeth Gamboa; Lorraine Mullaney, designer, who created the book's beautiful design; William Ethridge, editorial director; Jeanne Hoeting, production manager; Frances Russello, managing editor; Christine Wolf, design supervisor; Lorinda Morris-Nantz, director of photo archives; Anita Duncan and Teri Stratford, photo researchers; David Scholder, supplements editor; Bob Anderson, manufacturing buyer; Trudy Pisciotti, pre-press buyer; Elizabeth Robertson, scheduler; Kama Siegel, assistant editor; Lourdes Brun and Frances Falk, former assistants; and Dennis Hogan, former publisher of the business and economics team, who took a chance and signed a contract with first-time textbook authors.

Finally, we owe special thanks to our families, who put up with our occasional absences and our constant preoccupation with the task of writing this book. Without their support and understanding the book would not exist.

We conclude with a special invitation to you, our newest student. We want to know how you like our book and how you feel about the field of organizational behavior. We encourage you to contact us with your ideas, especially your suggestions for making future editions of our book even better. Please write to us at:

Michigan State University
Graduate School of Business Administration
Department of Management
East Lansing, Michigan 48824–1121

John A. Wagner III
John R. Hollenbeck

ACKNOWLEDGMENT OF ILLUSTRATIONS

CHAPTER 15

545, 546 Alen MacWeeney/Onyx; **555** Bartholomew/Gamma-Liaison; **561** Red Morgan; **563** © R. Ian Lloyd, Singapore; **571** Ann States/SABA.

CHAPTER 16

589, 590 Courtesy of General Motors; **594** Gerry Gropp/Sipa Press; **607** Charles Archambault; **615** Richard Howard; **619** Les Stone/Sygma.

CHAPTER 17

637, 638 Courtesy of National Bevpak, a subsidiary of National Beverage Corp.—Ann States/SABA; **650** National Bicycle Industrial Co.; **661** Courtesy of Volvo Cars of North America; **665** Courtesy of Chad Industries, Orange, California.

CHAPTER 18

681, 682 Courtesy of USX Corporation; **686** Robert Holmgren; **692** Steve Winter/Gamma-Liaison; **698** Steven Pumphrey; **702** © Celestial Seasonings Inc., Boulder, Colorado.

CHAPTER 19

731, 732 Caroline Parsons; **735** Nikolai Ignatiev/Matrix; **746** Karen Kasmauski; **754** Bill Gentile/Sipa Press.

CHAPTER 1

ORGANIZATIONAL BEHAVIOR

Restoring American competitiveness is one of the goals of General Motor's new Saturn division, which aims to build a small car not only as good as Japanese cars but better. GM's poor reputation in the small-car field began to spread in 1970 with the Chevrolet Vega, which was poorly engineered and subject to breakdowns, and moved steadily downhill into the 1990s, when other automakers outdistanced the company in the marketplace. The Saturn models, like the sports touring sedan seen here, have got off to a slow start largely because of the company's determination to ensure both workers' motivation and a high quality product. Such things as teaching employees to inspect their own work and changing engine-mount specifications in mid-production caused delays, but for Saturn president Richard LeFauvre, building a reputation for excellence is worth it: "You absolutely have to bite the bullet on quality."

Although there's no free lunch, one thing comes awfully close: productivity. When it's growing, businesses can do the impossible. Companies can hand out raises, slash prices, and increase profits—sometimes all at once. . . . But for all its potential, productivity has not been living up to its promise lately. Output per worker has been growing, on average, less than 1 percent a year since 1973, compared with a rate of more than 2 percent in the 1960s. . . . [This lag] is clearly a culprit in America's declining competitiveness. U.S. trade rivals are scoring faster productivity growth, and America now ranks near the bottom among industrialized countries.[1]

This quote from a 1987 issue of *Business Week* is as true today as it was a few years ago. Companies throughout North America continue to face the choice of improving productivity or losing ground to aggressive competitors. Imagine yourself as a manager in such a company. Initial assessments indicate that lagging productivity is due to poor employee motivation, and your boss tells you to solve this problem. Your future with the company—and possibly the future of the company itself—may depend on whether you can find a way to improve employee motivation.

To help you decide what to do, you call in four highly recommended management consultants. After analyzing your company's situation, the first consultant states that many of today's jobs are so simple, monotonous, and uninteresting that they thwart employee motivation and fulfillment. As a result, employees become so bored and resentful that productivity falls off. The consultant recommends that you redesign your firm's jobs, making them more complex, stimulating, and fulfilling.

Consultant number two performs her own assessment of your company. As she reviews her findings, she agrees that monotonous work can reduce employee motivation. She says, however, that the absence of clear, challenging goals is an even greater threat to motivation and productivity. She goes on to say that such goals provide performance targets that draw attention to the work to be done and focus employee effort on successful performance. Therefore, the second consultant advises that you solve your company's productivity problem by implementing a program of formal goal setting.

Next, the third consultant conducts an investigation and concedes that both job design and goal setting can improve employee motivation. She suggests, however, that you consider a contingent payment program instead. She explains that contingent payment means paying employees according to their performance instead of giving them fixed salaries or hourly wages. For instance, salespeople may be paid commissions on their sales, production employees may be paid piece-rate wages according to their productivity, or executives may be paid bonuses according to their firm's profitability. The consultant's formal report points out that contingent payment programs change the way wages are *distributed* but not necessarily the *amount* of wages paid to the work force as a whole.

Finally, the fourth consultant examines your situation and agrees that any of the three approaches might work but describes another technique that is often used to deal with motivational problems—allowing employees to participate in decision making. He suggests that such participation gives employees a sense of belongingness or ownership that energizes productivity, and he recites an impressive list of companies—among them, General Motors, IBM, General Electric—that have recently established participatory programs.

[1] Joan Berger, "Productivity: Why It's the Number One Underachiever," *Business Week*, April 20, 1987, pp. 54–55.

In 1989, 58,000 Boeing machinists went out on strike, convinced by their union that wage increases were more desirable than the company's traditional year-end bonuses. Although bonuses don't contribute to benefits like pensions, organizational behavior research indicates that pay for performance is probably the most effective motivator in the workplace. How would you reconcile this finding with union demands for regular, guaranteed pay increases?
Source: *"Bonus Battles,"* Fortune, *November 6, 1989, p. 9.*

Later, alone in your office, you consider the four consultants' reports and conclude that you should probably recommend all four alternatives—just in case one or two of the consultants are wrong. However, you also realize that your company can afford the time and money needed to implement only one of the four approaches. What do you do? Which alternative should you choose?

According to a recent review of research comparing the effectiveness of these alternatives, if you chose the first one, job redesign, productivity would probably rise by about 9 percent.[2] An increase of this size would save your job, keep your company afloat, and probably earn you the company president's eternal gratitude. If you chose the second alternative, goal setting, productivity would probably increase by around 16 percent. This outcome would save your job and your company and might even put you in the running for a promotion. If you chose the third alternative, contingent payment, you could dust off that vice president nameplate hidden in your desk drawer and prepare for a bigger office. Productivity could be expected to increase by approximately 30 percent, ensuring you an executive position with the company until retirement.[3]

But what about the fourth alternative, employee participation in decision making? How might this approach affect productivity where low performance is attributable to poor motivation? Given that contemporary managers are increasingly choosing participatory programs to solve motivation problems, it stands to reason that this alternative should work at least as well as the other three. Surprisingly, however, participation usually has virtually no effect on productivity. It is likely to improve performance only when combined with one or more of the other three alternatives.[4] Consequently, as the manager in our story, if you chose participation you might soon be looking for a new job.

[2] Edwin A. Locke, Dena B. Feren, Vickie M. McCaleb, Karyll N. Shaw, and Anne T. Denny, "The Relative Effectiveness of Four Methods of Motivating Employee Performance," in *Changes in Working Life,* ed. K. D. Duncan, Michael M. Gruneberg, and D. Wallis, (Chichester, England: John Wiley, 1980), pp. 363–88.

[3] One study suggests that productivity might rise even more dramatically, increasing by more than 100 percent under certain situations and over extended periods of time. See John A. Wagner III, Paul A. Rubin, and Thomas J. Callahan, "Incentive Payment and Nonmanagerial Productivity: An Interrupted Time Series Analysis of Magnitude and Trend," *Organizational Behavior and Human Decision Processes* 42 (1988), 47–74.

[4] Locke et al., "Relative Effectiveness"; John A. Wagner III and Richard Z. Gooding, "Shared Influence and Organizational Behavior: A Meta-Analysis of Situational Variables Expected to Moderate Participation-Outcome Relationships," *Academy of Management Journal* 30 (1987), 524–41. For an explanation of why research findings do not support the popular idea that participation is effective, see Wagner and Gooding, "Effects of Societal Trends on Participation Research," *Administrative Science Quarterly* 32 (1987), 241–62.

IN PRACTICE

OB Gains in Leading Business Schools

Boxes like this one appear throughout this book to illustrate the significance of OB in today's management world. In this vein, if we haven't yet convinced you of the importance of studying OB, consider changes that have recently taken place at the University of Chicago. Long a haven for statistical business approaches, Chicago is developing courses on such OB topics as communication and team building. For Chicago, the change is the result of a soul searching that started when a group of students began challenging the school's numbers-oriented curriculum.

According to the dean of Chicago's business school, John P. Gould, faculty and alumni as well as students became concerned when Chicago rated only eleventh in a national survey of top business schools. A subsequent internal study revealed that Chicago's program had underemphasized the skills needed to manage people. To correct this deficiency, the study recommended new courses in areas such as leadership and management.

Chicago is not alone in making such changes. Dean John H. McArthur recently recruited leading OB scholars from other universities to redirect Harvard Business School toward a new emphasis on the management of people at work. Dean Donald Jacobs of Northwestern University's J. L. Kellogg School saw his MBA program ascend to the top in a national poll after he built a strong OB curriculum. If trends in business school curricula are reliable indicators, expertise in OB is critically important in today's business world.*

* David Greising, "Chicago's B-School Goes Touchy-Feely," *Business Week*, November 27, 1989, p. 140; Bruce Nussbaum and Alex Beam, "Remaking the Harvard B-School, *Business Week*, March 24, 1986, pp. 54–58; and John A. Byrne, "The Best B-Schools," *Business Week*, November 28, 1988, pp. 76–80.

How realistic is this story? Is the predicament it portrays an everyday problem? Echoing the quotation that opened this chapter, experts in the United States have recently bemoaned the fact that American firms' productivity levels are declining compared with foreign competitors. These writers point to "people problems" as an important cause of this situation.[5]

As the "In Practice" box indicates, top U.S. business schools are taking ideas like this seriously. U.S. politicians running for office have even recommended laws or policies that would mandate workplace efforts to improve employee motivation and performance.[6]

[5] Norman Jonas, "No Pain, No Gain: How America Can Grow Again," *Business Week*, April 20, 1987, pp. 68–69; William J. Hampton, "Why Image Counts: A Tale of Two Industries," *Business Week*, June 8, 1987, pp. 138 40; John A. Byrne, "How the Best Get Better," *Business Week*, September 14, 1987, pp. 98–99; Bruce Nussbaum, "Needed: Human Capital," *Business Week*, September 19, 1988, pp. 100–103; and Christopher Farrell and John Hoerr, "ESOPs: Are They Good for You?" *Business Week*, May 15, 1989, pp. 116–23.

[6] See Richard Fly, Douglas Harbrecht, Howard Gleckman, and Lee Walczak, "The Duke and the Democrats," *Business Week*, July 25, 1988, pp. 22–34.

American managers' increasing concern with employee satisfaction and performance owes a great deal to research in organizational behavior and management. A recent M.I.T. study, for example, suggests that better "people management" practices have enabled Japanese firms to sell higher-quality products at lower prices. Toshiba's annual corporate baseball tournament, by reinforcing company spirit, enhances employees' loyalty and commitment.
Source: *"Pacific Rim,"* Fortune, 1989, p. 15.

Most of the theories and concepts presented in this book are based on research conducted in North America. As a result, these ideas should be used as management tools only in the U.S., Canada, and other countries with similar cultural backgrounds. In other regions throughout the world, local cultural values encourage forms of organizational behavior that differ from the American norm. Chapter 19 examines many of these differences in detail and discusses how to translate material from this book for use abroad. If you are especially interested in international management, we suggest that you read Chapter 19 before proceeding to the central chapters of this book.

In addition to Chapter 19, we have included boxes like this one throughout the book to help you contrast American practices with the way things are done in other countries. These boxes indicate important ways in which organizational behavior varies throughout the world, reminding you of significant international differences.

One such difference concerns the effects of money and participation on work motivation. Although participation has little effect on motivation in the U.S., experience at Saab-Scania, Volvo, and other western European companies indicates that participation *does* have a strong, positive effect on performance in Sweden, Norway, and Germany. Conversely, money has a strong effect on motivation in North America, but workers in Sweden are hardly influenced by incentive payment. How can these differences be explained?

In part they seem to be the consequence of national laws throughout Europe that require that workers be allowed to participate in running their place of work. Owing to these laws, European workers have been participating in decision making for years. They perceive participation as an interesting, rewarding part of their jobs. In contrast, the U.S. does not have any major laws requiring workplace participation, and American workers often have little experience in employee participation, Thus many American employees really don't care whether they participate in making decisions. In sum, American and European workers value participation differently.

The different effects of money on motivation in America

For these workers in Dresden, Germany, participation in decision making is an important motivating factor, but apparently it is not for many United States workers. Money aside, how would you reconcile this apparent lack of interest in making decisions on the job with such American traditions as self-government and the rights of the individual?

and western Europe may also reflect the high income taxes collected in countries like Sweden. Offering Swedish employees more money for greater productivity is not much of an incentive, because they must pay up to 70 percent of any additional income in national income taxes. Little is left over as a reward for working harder. For Americans, however, only about 30 percent of incentive wages are consumed by national income taxes. Consequently, monetary rewards are valued differently by American and European employees.*

* Jonathan Kapstein and John Hoerr, "Volvo's Radical New Plant: 'The Death of the Assembly Line'?" *Business Week*, August 28, 1989, pp. 92–93; and Fred E. Emery and Einar Thorsrud, *Democracy at Work* (Leiden, Netherlands: Kroese, 1976).

Thus poor employee motivation is a widespread problem. American managers are painfully aware of the need to improve motivation at work and are struggling to find a way to do it. Our opening story is indeed realistic.

Without the kind of information that the study of organizational behavior provides, managers have no basis for accepting any one consultant's advice or for choosing one particular way to solve people problems instead of another. As a result, managers often make unsound decisions and wait for changes in productivity that never materialize. Fortunately, however, expertise in the field of organizational behavior can provide the insight necessary to avoid making these sorts of mistakes. It is the purpose of this book to provide you with this expertise, introducing you to the field of organizational behavior and helping you to develop the skills you will need to perform as an informed, effective manager. The theories and models we will discuss are meant primarily for application in North America. However, as the "International OB" box indicates, we will also discuss how things are done in other parts of the world so as to give you basic knowledge about international differences in the management of organizational behavior.

WHAT IS ORGANIZATIONAL BEHAVIOR?

organizational behavior (OB) A field of study that endeavors to understand, explain, predict, and change human behavior as it occurs in the organizational context.

Organizational behavior (OB) is a field of study that endeavors to understand, explain, predict, and change human behavior as it occurs in the organizational context. This definition has three corollaries:

1. OB focuses on observable behaviors, such as talking with coworkers, running equipment, or preparing a report. It also deals with internal states — thinking, perceiving, deciding, and similar hidden processes that accompany visible actions.
2. OB studies the behavior of people both as individuals and as members of groups and organizations.
3. OB also analyzes the "behavior" of groups and organizations per se. Neither groups nor organizations "behave" in the same sense that people do. In the organizational context, however, some events occur that cannot be explained in terms of individual behavior. These events must be examined in terms of group or organizational variables.

The approach this book takes to the topic of OB is indicated by its title—*Management of Organizational Behavior*. As the second half of the title, *Organizational Behavior*, suggests, we will introduce and explain the key theories and concepts that make up the field of OB. However, consistent with the first half of the title, *Management of*, we will also focus on the managerial uses of OB, that is, on making OB's concepts and theories useful to those of you who are or will soon be managers.

A MODEL OF SKILL ACQUISITION

Can a textbook really help managers learn how to use OB theories? Can classroom experiences actually help managers become better at their jobs? Managing is something that can be learned only by doing, isn't it? Many managers and potential managers doubt that books and classes on management can help people learn how to manage. Perhaps you share this doubt. However, the five-stage **skill-acquisition model** shown in Table 1–1 indicates how books and classroom activities *can* contribute to the development of effective management skills.[7]

[7] Based on information presented in Hubert L. Dreyfus and Stuart E. Dreyfus with Tom Athanasiou, *Mind over Machine: The Power of Human Intuition and Expertise in the Era of the Computer* (New York: Free Press, 1986). For an extended managerial example based on this model, see Robert E. Quinn, *Beyond Rational Management: Mastering the Paradoxes and Competing Demands of High Performance* (San Francisco: Jossey-Bass, 1988).

skill-acquisition model A five-stage model of the process of developing expertise in a particular behavior.

TABLE 1-1
How Managers Learn Management Skills

STAGE	GENERAL DESCRIPTION	MANAGEMENT ANALOGY
Novice	Behaving mechanically. Following elementary rules and procedures.	Practicing applying textbook theories in case analyses and experiential exercises.
Advanced Beginner	Memorizing elementary rules. Using rules under various conditions. Developing circumstantial rules.	Discovering workplace cues that indicate applicability of textbook theories.
Competence	Developing "rules of thumb" and the ability to focus on important information.	Developing personalized models of how to solve management problems effectively.
Proficiency	Developing the ability to read situations unconsciously and respond intuitively.	Developing the ability to respond intuitively to particular management problems.
Expertise	Developing the ability to respond intuitively in a wide variety of situations.	Developing the ability to respond intuitively to a wide range of management problems.

Stage 1: Novice

novice The stage of skill development in which people learn elementary rules and procedures that, followed mechanically, result in actions resembling skilled behaviors.

Developing skills of any kind begins with a **novice** stage. Novices are beginners who learn rules and procedures that when followed consciously and mechanically result in actions resembling skilled behaviors. For example, novice drivers learn a step-by-step procedure to pass slower cars. Pull up behind the car, check your rearview mirror to be sure no one is passing you, edge out to check for oncoming traffic, accelerate around the slower car, pull back into the lane only after you can see in your rearview mirror the whole front end of the car you have passed. By following this procedure carefully, a new driver can mimic the behavior of experienced drivers and pass slower cars without causing a wreck.

Similarly, novice managers and OB students like you can learn basic rules and procedures by studying textbook theories. You can discover how to use these rules and procedures as you complete case analyses or experiential exercises. A case is a narrative depicting an organizational situation. To perform a *case analysis*, you use textbook theories to identify problems in the case and formulate solutions. For example, you may read a chapter on work motivation in this book and use the theories you learn to analyze a case illustrating motivation problems. In performing case analyses, you learn how to use OB theories as tools to solve real-world problems.

An *experiential exercise* is an activity—often completed in a classroom—in which you learn by doing. For instance, after reading a chapter on motivation, you might complete a questionnaire assessing your own needs and motives. You might also work with classmates to determine how to award incentive payment to the members of a fictitious work group. Experiential exercises like these reinforce textbook theories and provide personal insight into how to use them.

Case analyses and experiential exercises give novice managers the chance to practice using textbook information about OB and management much as behind-the-wheel training enables novice drivers to practice textbook driving skills. When students work on cases and exercises in groups they can share what they know and help one another out. In these ways novices learn that theories provide "what-to-do" guidance that can help them cope with management problems in a skillful—though at this point mechanical—manner.

Stage 2: Advanced Beginner

advanced beginner The stage of skill development in which people learn to base behaviors on an expanded set of rules that include both the elementary rules of novices and circumstantial rules discovered through experience.

As novices continue to learn theories and practice applying them, repetition reinforces the rules of skillful behavior, and it becomes easier to follow these rules. At the same time, as they apply rules in different circumstances, novices learn that they cannot follow the same rules in every situation. As they enter the **advanced beginner** stage, they learn to base behaviors on an expanded set of rules that now include both textbook rules and the circumstantial rules that experience has suggested.

By practicing under different road conditions, advanced beginner drivers learn to allow greater distance between cars when, for example, passing at higher speeds or driving in stormy weather. Similarly, entry-level managers advance their skills by learning that certain workplace cues indicate when particular textbook theories should be used as managerial tools and when they should not. For instance, after a year or two of experience a manager might discover that a company's low productivity is caused by a variety of factors besides poor motivation—faulty equipment, inadequate supervision, defective raw materials. He could then conclude that motivation theories would not help him solve productivity problems caused by these other factors.

Stage 3: Competence

competence The stage of skill development in which people replace basic rules with advanced rules of thumb that can be altered to fit a wide range of circumstances.

As advanced beginners continue to gain experience and learn additional circumstantial rules, the number of rules they must remember becomes potentially overwhelming. At this point, advanced beginners develop **competence**. Instead of mechanically following rules, they formulate complex rules of thumb that can be altered to fit a broad range of circumstances. For example, instead of having a different rule for each driving condition, competent drivers develop personal theories about how to pass other cars that can be quickly adjusted to fit varying circumstances. Similarly, managers develop competence by relying less on the mechanical application of textbook theories and more on experimenting with new combinations of theories and new ways of assessing their applicability. Thus a competent manager might develop a personalized model of how to manage productivity by combining several OB theories of motivation with first-hand knowledge about factory automation and advice from others about the effectiveness of different supervisory styles.

In gaining competence, people learn how to focus on important information. In part, this ability comes from personal trial-and-error learning. Advice and guidance from other experienced individuals can also help sharpen competence. Textbook theories contribute to the development of competence, because they continue to influence the makeup of competent individuals' personal theories. Lessons learned as a novice are not forgotten, even as people grow more skilled.

Stage 4: Proficiency

proficiency The stage of skill development in which people learn how to read situations instinctively and respond to familiar circumstances intuitively, deliberating consciously only in unusual situations.

Competence, which is characterized by conscious thought and deliberate reasoning, develops into **proficiency** when people learn how to read situations instinctively and respond to familiar circumstances intuitively. Proficiency comes from experiencing the same situation so many times that the behaviors required to deal with it become automatic. Once proficiency is achieved, conscious deliberation is required only in unusual situations.

Proficient drivers approaching slower vehicles on a rainy day know intuitively if they are driving too fast and reduce their speed without thinking. However, a proficient driver experienced only in warm-weather driving must think about what to do when encountering snowy conditions for the first time. Proficiency reverts to conscious rule following until the driver learns how to drive on snow. Similarly, proficient managers do not have to think about which theories to use to solve familiar productivity problems—they know what to do. If poor productivity is caused by an unknown or unfamiliar factor, however, even the most proficient manager must consciously consider different ways of diagnosing the situation and attacking the problem. In doing this he may need to go back to textbook rules and theories.

Stage 5: Expertise

expertise The stage of skill development in which individuals develop the ability to act intuitively in a wide variety of situations, rarely needing to deliberate consciously.

Expertise, the final stage of skill development, involves the ability to act intuitively in a wider variety of situations than the proficient manager can handle. Proficient individuals develop expertise as they become accustomed to so many different situations that few if any are novel enough to trigger conscious deliberation. Expert drivers often have little conscious awareness of their vehicles or driving conditions but retain complete intuitive awareness of the "feel" of the road. They can maintain a steady speed or react to changing conditions without needing to think about what to do. Expert managers develop a similar intuitive understanding that replaces conscious thought. They do not have to think specifically about motivation, supervision, or other such factors to solve a problem with, say, productivity. Instead, their gut instincts tell them that only certain factors cause the sort of low productivity they confront and that only a particular type of program will lead to acceptable improvement. Expert managers know what needs to be done without having to think about it.

THE DIAGNOSTIC MODEL

diagnostic model A four-step model that describes how managers perceive and solve problems and that is both a learning tool and an on-the-job guide.

Expertise and the intuition it involves are based on a combination of personal experience and advice from others. But expertise is also anchored in the textbook theories learned as a novice. An important implication of this statement is that becoming an expert manager can begin with classroom training in which you learn and apply textbook theories to experiential exercises and case analyses. For this reason, exercises and cases are featured throughout this book. Particularly useful to you in analyzing cases will be the **diagnostic model** that is the foundation of our book and that we discuss next (see also Table 1–2).[8]

Description

description Collecting information about a situation without attempting to explain either the cause of the situation or the motives of the people involved in it.

Description is the simple collection of information about a situation. No attempt is made at this point to explain either the cause of the situation or the motives of the people involved in it. Managers can obtain descriptive information in several ways. For instance, they can make personal observations. A manager can walk through a plant to estimate the amount of inventory on hand, observe production speed, and count the number of employees at work. Observation provides quick, first-hand information, but it cannot furnish data about widespread conditions

---

[8] Our diagnostic model is partly based on information presented in Judith R. Gordon, *A Diagnostic Approach to Organizational Behavior*, 2nd ed. (Allyn & Bacon, 1987) and is derived from the action research model presented in Wendell French, "Organization Development Objectives, Assumptions, and Strategies," *California Management Review* 12 (Winter 1969), 23–34. We will discuss the action research model in greater detail in Chapter 14.

TABLE 1-2
Using the Diagnostic Model in Case Analysis

STEP	MANAGERIAL ACTION	CASE ANALYSIS COUNTERPART
Description	Collection information about a situation without explaining causes or motives.	Reading a case and identifying relevant information.
Diagnosis	Determinining basic causes; identifying and stating the major problem.	Using classroom theories and concepts to identify a problem in the case.
Prescription	Specifying an appropriate solution.	Using the same theories and concepts to develop a case solution.
Action	Implementing the solution, evaluating its consequences.	Specifying the actions needed to implement the proposed solution.

or general situations. To acquire information about what employees think and feel about their work, managers can also distribute questionnaires throughout their firms. The major strength of this method is that it allows access to a wider range of opinions than can be collected through personal observation. However, questionnaires lack flexibility, because people can respond to only a limited number of items. In a third method, the face-to-face interview, a manager can ask questions as they come to mind, and interviewees can ask questions of their own. The major limitation of interviewing is the amount of time it requires. Managers must spend a lot of time interviewing different individuals to get a sense of what is going on in an organization, and employees must stop working at their normal jobs to participate in interview sessions. Fourth and last, written documents such as annual reports, office memoranda, personnel files, and production records can both provide new data and verify information acquired through the other three sources.

As you read this book, you can sharpen your descriptive skills by studying the cases carefully and teasing out the facts of each case. Remember that not all of the information presented in a case is relevant to the solution of a particular problem. Just as managers must separate relevant facts from irrelevant details, in performing a case analysis you must begin by deciding the relevance of different pieces of information and determining what to do where information is unavailable.

Diagnosis

diagnosis Looking for the causes of a troublesome situation and summarizing them in a problem statement.

In the step called **diagnosis**, managers look for the causes of the situation described and attempt to summarize them in a *problem statement*. Depending on their level of skill, managers rely on a mix of textbook theories, experience, and intuition as they diagnose the situation before them.

To begin developing your own diagnostic skills, you should study each theory presented in this book to develop a basic understanding of the variables and relationships it describes. Next, practice using the theory as a tool to help define the problem in a case. Then, as you become comfortable applying the theory, try combining it with several others to develop the type of expanded theory used by advanced beginners. For example, you might combine theories of employee

MANAGEMENT ISSUES

Do Companies Have Social Responsibilities?

Management often involves hard decisions with no obvious right or wrong answers. Some of these decisions pose ethical dilemmas in which social values conflict with personal well-being or organizational interests. Consider Perrier's decision to pull potentially tainted Perrier water off the market rather than maintain the short-term profitability of the company and its retailers. Other decisions involve issues of social responsibility in which a company must identify its obligations as a "citizen" in society and decide how to fulfill them. For example, should a business firm leave unemployment programs to the government or try to help society by hiring and training the hard-core unemployed? Other issues concern the practice of management itself. For example, what right do managers have to tell others what to do?

To get you thinking about these kinds of issues, we have included boxes like this one throughout the book. We hope you will consider the issues they raise with care and discuss them with your classmates and instructor.

One basic issue is the idea of social responsibility itself. Should businesses even concern themselves with social responsibility? For one manager's answer to this question, consider remarks made by Henry Ford II while he was the head of Ford Motor Company:

> Like governments and universities and other institutions, business is much better at some tasks than at others. Business is especially good at all the tasks that are necessary for economic growth and development. To the extent that the problems of society can be solved by providing more and better jobs, higher incomes of more people and a larger supply of goods and services, the problems can best be solved by relying heavily on business.
>
> On the other hand, business has no special competence in solving many other urgent problems. Businesspeople, for example, know little about the problems involved in improving the education of ghetto children, the quality of ghetto family life, the relations between police and minority citizens or the administration of justice. Solutions to problems such as these will be more effective if they are left to political, educational, and social agencies. In short, our society will be served best if each of its specialized institutions concentrates on doing what it does best, and refuses either to waste its time or to meddle in tasks it is poorly qualified to handle.*

** Henry Ford II, *The Human Environment and Business* (New York: Weybright & Talley, 1970), pp. 30–31.*

Many corporate leaders today disagree with Henry Ford about the role of business in dealing with society's problems. Almost all of the 206 CEOs of Fortune and Service 500 companies polled recently by Fortune *magazine believe that corporations must help educate and train workers, and many companies have already developed such programs.*
Sources: *Andrew Erdman, "How to Make Workers Better,"* Fortune, *October 22, 1990.*

Ford is saying that businesses have an obligation to make and use profits to promote economic well-being, and that government agencies should not interfere in this regard. Do you agree with this opinion? From Ford's viewpoint, who is responsible for equal opportunity and affirmative action—businesses that need talented employees of all races or government agencies charged with protecting the rights of all citizens? What do you think about Ford's assertion that different types of agencies and organizations should specialize in dealing with different kinds of social problems?†

† For additional information about this issue, see "The 'Responsible' Corporation: Benefactor or Monopolist?" Fortune, November 1973, pp. 56–58; Eli Goldston, "New Prospects for American Business," Daedalus 15 (Winter 1969), 78–79; and Milton Friedman, Capitalism and Freedom (Chicago: University of Chicago Press, 1962).

---

motivation, leadership, and job design to try to explain the causes of poor employee performance. Such personalized theories will help you to develop your skills further and to understand the complexity of many organizational problems.

Prescription

prescription Developing a solution responding to a problem statement identified through diagnosis.

Prescription involves developing a solution to the problem one has identified through diagnosis. Organizational problems are often multifaceted, and there is usually more than one way to solve a given problem. Therefore, successful managers usually consider several reasonable alternatives before choosing one to deal with a troublesome situation. Whether they review these alternatives mechanically, consciously, or intuitively depends, of course, on the level of skill they have achieved.

For the student, prescription involves following the theories she has applied during problem definition through to their logical conclusions. For instance, the same theory of employee motivation you use to diagnose a productivity problem may also suggest ways to reduce or eliminate the problem. The more theories you apply during diagnosis, the more comprehensive your final solution will be. Thus as you develop into an advanced beginner, the solutions you devise are likely to become increasingly thorough and more effective.

Action

action Stipulating the specific actions needed to implement a prescribed solution.

Action involves implementing a proposed solution. In this step, managers must stipulate the specific actions needed to solve a particular problem. This step will require you, as a student, to indicate the actions required to implement and assess your proposed solution. Your action plan should specify a sequence of steps that indicate what needs to be done, who will do it, when it will be done, and how its effectiveness will be measured.

Planning actions is a value-laden process. Which actions are morally correct? Which ones are not? Managers considering various actions must constantly raise such questions of social responsibility. As the "Management Issues" box indicates, different managers have different ideas about what is right and what is wrong, what is responsible and what is irresponsible. We urge you to think about the ethical implications of the actions you propose, both now as a student of organizational behavior and in the future as a manager.

In sum, the five-stage skill-acquisition model shows you how you can shape your management skills by studying the contents of this book, and the four-step diagnostic model shows you how you can apply your knowledge to case analyses and managerial decision making. These models will help you get the most out of this book, not only as you read it today but as you refer back to it on the job.

Using the Diagnostic Approach

As you study the core chapters of this book, you will find yourself most of the time in one phase or another of our diagnostic model. As Chapter 3 points out, the steps of the model parallel the stages of the scientific method of research, and both model and method inform our approach to the topics of this book. First and foremost, they compel us to ask questions. To describe we need to ask, What are the basic data? To diagnose we need to ask, How are different factors related to each other? To prescribe we need to ask, How will these factors interact in different circumstances? And to take action we need to implement a plan and be ready to evaluate its success—by asking more questions.

To lead you into this information-seeking mode, we have begun each of our core chapters with a "Diagnostic Issues" section that previews for you the questions the chapter undertakes to answer. When you have finished the chapter you will be able to answer not only these initial questions but the more detailed and specific "Diagnostic Questions" that precede the chapter's exercise and cases. The diagnostic questions flesh out the earlier ones and help you apply what you have learned to analyzing the cases. For those of you who will become managers, these questions will also be invaluable guides to on-the-job problem solving.

THE CONTINGENCY PERSPECTIVE

contingency perspective The view that no single theory, procedure, or set of rules is useful in every situation and that each situation determines the usefulness of different management approaches.

Both the skill acquisition model and the diagnostic model suggest that managers draw on a variety of theories in order to cope with different situations. They also propose that managers have to determine which theory to apply in each specific situation. Thus these models both embody the **contingency perspective**, the view that no single theory, procedure, or set of rules is useful in every situation. Instead, according to the contingency perspective, the usefulness of a particular management approach depends on the situation being managed.

For the student and the beginning manager this view is sometimes more confusing than helpful. Too often, textbooks present a long list of theories and then leave the student without guidance in choosing a theory to follow in one or another managerial problem situation. We have tried in our book not only to describe the important theories and concepts of the field but to show you how to diagnose the surrounding situation and choose which specific theory to apply.

CHARTING THE FIELD OF ORGANIZATIONAL BEHAVIOR

Given that OB theories can be useful to managers, what exactly is the field of organizational behavior all about? How is it similar to the field of management? How do OB and management differ? OB traces its origins to the late 1940s, when a group of researchers in psychology, sociology, and other social sciences decided to work together to develop a new, comprehensive body of organizational research.[9] Despite the intentions of its founders, however, the field of OB has resisted unification. It is now divided into two distinct subfields: micro organizational behavior, deriving from psychology and the behavioral sciences, and macro organizational behavior, deriving largely from economics, sociology, and political science.

Micro Organizational Behavior

micro organizational behavior The subfield of OB concerned with understanding the behaviors of individuals working alone or in small groups.

Micro organizational behavior is concerned mainly with understanding the behaviors of individuals working alone or in small groups.[10] Four subfields of psychology were the principal contributors to micro OB. *Experimental psychology* provided theories of learning, motivation, perception, and stress. *Clinical psychology* furnished models of personality and human development. *Industrial psychology* offered theories of employee selection, workplace attitudes, and performance assessment. And *social psychology* supplied theories of socialization, leadership, and group dynamics. Owing to this heritage, micro OB has a distinctly psychological orientation.[11] Among the questions it examines are, What motivates employees to perform their jobs? What effects do differences in ability have on employee performance? Why do some employees feel satisfied with their jobs while others experience stress? What makes leaders effective? How can group performance be improved?

[9] Larry L. Greiner, "A Recent History of Organizational Behavior," in *Organizational Behavior*, ed. Steven Kerr (Columbus, Ohio: Grid Publishing, 1979) pp. 3–14.

[10] Larry L. Cummings, "Toward Organizational Behavior," *Academy of Management Review* 3 (1978), 90–98.

[11] Ibid.

Macro Organizational Behavior

macro organizational behavior The subfield of OB that focuses on understanding the actions of a group or an organization as a whole.

Macro organizational behavior focuses on understanding the "behaviors" of groups and organizations. The origins of macro OB can be traced to four principal disciplines: *Sociology* provided theories of structure, social status, and institutional relations. *Political science* offered theories of power, conflict, bargaining, and control. *Anthropology* contributed theories of symbolism, cultural influence, and comparative analysis. And *economics* furnished theories of competition and efficiency. Research on macro OB considers questions such as, How is power acquired and retained? How can conflicts be resolved? What mechanisms can be used to coordinate work activities? Why do we have different forms of organizational structure? How should an organization be structured in order to cope with surrounding circumstances?[12]

Related Domains of Research

Besides the two OB subfields, three other domains of research also focus on organizational topics. In general, these additional domains of human resource management, organization development, and strategic management arose from the same scientific disciplines as OB. Their origins, however, can also be traced to the field of management. Thus in contrast to OB's theoretical orientation, they emphasize *doing* things to shape behaviors in organizations, such as developing programs, facilitating change, and assessing results.

human resource management A domain of organizational research that focuses on devising practical, effective ways to manage employee behaviors.

Human Resource Management. **Human resource management** (HRM) is similar to micro OB; they share a common focus on the behavior of individuals. In fact, HRM studies often incorporate theories of micro OB. For example, incentive-payment programs devised in HRM are often based on micro OB theories of employee motivation. However, the two domains differ in one important respect. In contrast to micro OB's emphasis on theory development, HRM focuses mainly on devising practical, effective ways to manage employee behaviors. HRM researchers study different ways to select employees, to train and evaluate them, and to compensate them for their performance.[13]

organization development An area of organizational research that develops techniques to instill cooperation and manage change.

Organization Development. **Organization development** (OD) is an area of practical research that develops techniques to instill cooperation and manage change.[14] Some OD techniques focus on the personal development of individual organization members. A few others are concerned with the effectiveness of entire organizations. Most OD techniques, however, emphasize group and intergroup relations, highlighting ways in which cooperation can be strengthened and conflict resolved within and between groups. Thus there is a great deal of overlap between OD and micro OB research on behavior in small groups. In addition, there is significant overlap between OD and macro OB studies of group behavior. Yet

[12] Robert H. Miles, *Macro Organizational Behavior* (Santa Monica, Calif: Goodyear, 1980); Richard L. Daft and Richard M. Steers, *Organizations: A Micro/Macro Approach* (Glenview, Ill: Scott, Foresman, 1986).

[13] Wayne F. Cascio, *Applied Psychology in Personnel Management*, 2nd cd. (Englcwood Cliffs, N.J.: Prentice Hall, 1989); and George T. Milkovich, *Personnel and Human Resource Management: A Diagnostic Approach* (Plano, Texas: Business Publications, 1985).

[14] Richard Beckhart, *Organizational Development: Strategies and Models* (Reading, Mass.: Addison-Wesley, 1969); and Wendell L. French and Cecil H. Bell, Jr., *Organization Development: Behavioral Science Interventions for Organization Improvement*, 4th ed. (Englewood Cliffs, N.J.: Prentice Hall, 1990).

OD's emphasis on the development of effective management techniques differs from the accent on theory development that characterizes both subfields of OB.

strategic management A domain of organizational research concerned with defining an organization's purpose and planning how to achieve organizational objectives.

Strategic Management. Like macro OB, **strategic management (SM)** focuses more on organizations than on individuals. However, in contrast to macro OB's concern with developing theories that explain organizational events, SM addresses the development of techniques to manage organizations.[15] For example, SM research provides advice about how to set organizational goals, determine competitive postures, and choose which business opportunities to pursue. Thus SM is the practical counterpart of macro OB.

Fitting the Domains Together

We have now identified five relatively distinct domains of current organizational research. Separating these domains are differences in *level of analysis* and *primary orientation*, as you can see in Figure 1-1. The vertical dimension in the figure, **level of analysis**, differentiates among the domains according to whether their primary focus is on the *individual*, the *group*, or the *organization*. The horizontal dimension, **primary orientation**, classifies the domains according to whether their main focus is on *theory* or *application*.

level of analysis A dimension that classifies the five areas of organizational research according to whether their primary focus is on the behaviors of individuals, of groups, or of organizations.

primary orientation A dimension that classifies the five areas of organizational research according to whether their main focus is on abstract theories or practical techniques.

Some commentators have suggested that the five domains pictured in Figure 1-1 should be permitted—or even required—to remain separated from one another.[16] For organizational researchers intent on developing in-depth expertise,

[15] H. Igor Ansoff, *Corporate Strategy* (New York: McGraw-Hill, 1965); Kenneth R. Andrews, *The Concept of Corporate Strategy* (Homewood, Ill: Richard D. Irwin, 1980); and Arthur A. Thompson, Jr., and A. J. Strickland III, *Strategic Management: Concepts and Cases*, 4th ed. (Plano, Texas: Business Publications, 1987).

[16] Cummings, "Toward Organizational Behavior," p. 90.

FIGURE 1-1

Subfields of Organizational Behavior and Domains of Related Research

The field of organizational behavior is divided into two subfields, micro organizational behavior and macro organizational behavior. Closely associated with these two subfields are three other domains of organizational research: human resource management, organization development, and strategic management.

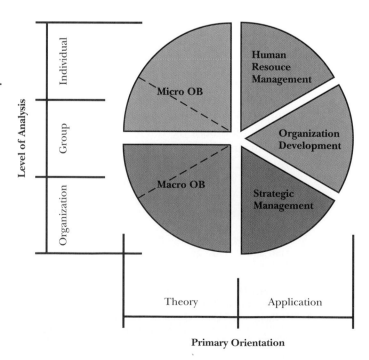

16

this suggestion makes sense; keeping the five domains separate makes it easier to specialize in a narrow area of knowledge. For present or future managers, however, knowing how to cope with a wide variety of situations is usually more important than being a specialist in any one area. From this perspective, separating the five domains and specializing in only one or two of them means that useful information may be omitted. Thus although this is primarily a book on OB, we also include special chapters on HRM, OD, and SM to provide the breadth of practical knowledge required to develop effective management skills.

OVERVIEW OF THE BOOK

Besides charting the five domains of organizational research, Figure 1-1 also diagrams the contents of this book. The following chapters strike a balance between the two orientations indicated in the figure, both theory and application. They also span all three levels of analysis shown in the figure by considering issues pertaining to individuals, groups, and organizations.

Part I consists of three introductory chapters, including this one, that overview the field of organizational behavior, survey the general topic of management, and briefly outline research methods in organizational behavior. You may read one, two, or all three of these chapters, depending on the focus of your course and the teaching goals of your instructor. Part II, on individuals in organizations, is composed of five chapters that introduce you to various theories about people's behavior in the work setting and a sixth chapter that focuses on the application of these theories to work-related issues. As you can see, this part of the book encompasses the upper left and upper right segments of Figure 1-1. In Part III of the book, on groups in organizations, four chapters present concepts of interpersonal, group, and intergroup behavior and a fifth chapter shows you how these concepts can be applied in managing groups in the organizational setting. Thus this part covers the two middle segments in Figure 1-1. Part IV, on the organizational context, is made up of three chapters that focus on the structure and design of organizations and the jobs that comprise them and a fourth chapter that applies this material to the management of entire organizations. This part, which focuses on change in the organizational context, encompasses the lower left and lower right segments of Figure 1-1. Part V consists of a single, capstone chapter that examines the challenges of applying OB theories throughout the world.

Summary

Organizational behavior is a field of research that helps predict, explain, and understand behaviors occurring in and among organizations. Learning how to use knowledge about OB for managerial purposes begins by studying textbook theories and using them to perform case analyses and experiential exercises. The five-stage *skill acquisition model* and the four-step *diagnostic model* provide helpful guidance for students engaged in this process of initial learning. The latter model in particular, through its steps of *description*, *diagnosis*, *prescription*, and *action*, facilitates the analysis of case material in this book and of real-world, on-the-job managerial problems. In common, both models share grounding in the *contingency perspective*, which suggests that the usefulness of a particular theory or concept depends on the situation being managed.

Organizational behavior's two subfields, *micro organizational behavior* and *macro organizational behavior*, reflect differences among the scientific disciplines that contributed to the founding of this field of study. Micro OB is concerned primarily with individual behavior and the behaviors of people in small groups. Macro OB focuses on the behaviors of people in larger groups and on the "behaviors" of organizations as entities.

Closely related to these subfields of OB are three other domains of organizational study, each of which is primarily concerned with the application of knowledge derived from OB subfields. *Human resources management* uses data from micro OB studies. *Strategic management* makes use of data from macro OB studies. *Organization development* uses data from both micro and macro OB studies.

The *primary orientation* of micro and macro OB is theoretical, whereas human resources management, strategic management, and organization development are applications oriented. The *levels of analysis* at which the latter three fields operate are the individual, the group, and the organization, respectively.

REVIEW QUESTIONS

1.   What is the field of organizational behavior? What kinds of behavior does it examine? Why does it include examination of the "behaviors" of groups and organizations?

2.   What are the five stages of skill development? What role do textbook theories and concepts play during each of these stages? How will the information you learn from this book affect your development as a manager?

3.   What are the four steps of the diagnostic model? How can using this model help you develop managerial skills? Why is it important for you to refer to textbook theories at each step? How can you use your creativity in performing the diagnostic procedure?

4.   What is the contingency perspective of management? In what ways is this perspective related to the skill-development process and diagnostic model?

5.   What are the two subfields of OB? What are each of them about? Why have they developed separately? Why is it important for you to know about both of them?

6.   Name the three domains of organizational research that are closely linked to OB. How is each of these domains linked to one or both subfields of OB? How do they differ from one another?

7.   Explain how the two dimensions, level of analysis and primary orientation, map the five areas of organizational research examined in this book. Why is it important to have chapters on practical management—HRM, OD, SM—in a book on OB?

CHAPTER 2

MANAGEMENT AND MANAGERS

According to Lee Iacocca, his mother—who came to the United States through Ellis Island—taught him to revere the Statue as a symbol of the American way of life. Iacocca himself has become a symbol of expert management in American business, although the company he rescued from bankruptcy in the late 1970s continues to be beset by problems. Recently, Iacocca initiated an extensive cost-cutting program and reorganized product development into vehicle rather than component-part teams. He also created the Bet Your Check program in which 2000 top managers put as much as 10 percent of their salaries in escrow on the assurance of doubling their money if they delivered budget cuts on time. They did, and the company paid out $15.4 million.
Source: *Alex Taylor III, "Can Iacocca Fix Chrysler—Again?"* Fortune, *April 8, 1991, pp. 50–54.*

Chrysler Corporation is hitting the road with a six-city promotional tour in which Chairman Lee A. Iacocca will tout his cars and his company. . . The number three U. S. auto maker will show off current and future products during the tour, which begins on February 21. . . In each city—New York, Chicago, Atlanta, Dallas, Los Angeles, and Washington, D.C.—Mr. Iacocca will preside over news conferences and receptions for financial analysts, money managers, dealers, and other invited guests . . . [who] will hobnob with Mr. Iacocca and other top company officials, "plus a smattering of vice presidents, group directors, and managers," said a company spokesperson. . . This will be the first time in several years that Mr. Iacocca has made so public a pitch for the company he heads. . . According to the spokesperson, Chrysler has been planning the tour "literally for months." "People are raising questions about Chrysler's viability," he said. "We want to give a positive answer to that question, and we're going to bring out our top salesman to do it."[1]

Chrysler's Lee Iacocca is living proof that successful managers sometimes become "executive celebrities."[2] Designer of the Ford Mustang—the first and most successful "muscle car" of the 1960s—Iacocca joined Chrysler in 1978, when the firm was on the brink of failure. Iacocca soon won public attention by negotiating $1.5 billion worth of federal loan guarantees and secured his reputation by repaying these loans well before the 1990 deadline. Recognizing Iacocca's management expertise and growing worldwide reputation, President Ronald Reagan asked him to head the Statue of Liberty-Ellis Island Centennial Commission. Leading Democrats promoted Iacocca as a potential presidential candidate in 1984 and 1988, but he declined to run. In perhaps the ultimate expression of executive celebrity, Iacocca appeared in a 1985 episode of "Miami Vice." Back in the business world, Iacocca's image as a triumphant manager was clinched when Chrysler purchased Jeep/American Motors from the French auto maker Renault and, with Japan's Mitsubishi Corporation, began the Diamond-Star joint venture to build Plymouth Lasers and Mitsubishi Eclipses.[3]

Although the general public has come to admire Lee Iacocca, few people who are not managers know much about the topic of management. Could you tell someone what management is? How current management practices have developed? What managers do? Probably not. Yet modern societies depend on the well-being of thousands of organizations ranging from industrial giants like Chrysler to local businesses like the corner grocery store. All of these organizations depend on competent management. Ignorance about management would doom a society like ours to failure. Therefore, it is critical that you know what management is and what managers do. This chapter is a primer on management thought. It begins by defining the concept of management and then considers several schools of thought about management and managers. The chapter con-

[1] Melinda Grenier Guiles, "Iacocca Roadshow Will Try to Make Point Chrysler Isn't Down and Out Despite Woes," *Wall Street Journal*, January 24, 1990, p. B4.

[2] Judith H. Dobrzynski and Jo Ellen Davis, "Business Celebrities," *Business Week*, June 23, 1986, pp. 100–105.

[3] Lee Iacocca and William Novak, *Iacocca: An Autobiography* (New York: Bantam Books, 1984); William J. Hampton, "Chrysler's Next Act," *Business Week*, November 3, 1986, pp. 66–72; and Dobrzynski and Davis, "Business Celebrities."

cludes by discussing what managers actually do, focusing on the skills the and the roles they fill as they perform their jobs.

DEFINING MANAGEMENT

What is management? Stated simply, it is a process of influencing people's behaviors in organizations. To define management in greater detail, let's begin by considering a closely related question: What is an organization?

Three Attributes of Organizations

organization An assembly of people and materials brought together to accomplish a purpose that would be beyond the means of individuals working alone.

An **organization** is an arrangement of people and materials brought together to accomplish a purpose that would be beyond the means of individuals working alone. Three attributes enable an organization to achieve this feat: a mission, division of labor, and distribution of authority.

mission An organization's purpose or reason for being.

Mission. Each organization works toward a specific **mission**, which is its purpose or reason for being. As you can see in Table 2-1, a statement of mission identifies the primary goods or services the organization produces and the markets it hopes to serve. An organization's mission helps hold it together by giving members a shared sense of direction.

T A B L E 2-1
Some Statements of Mission

COMPANY	MISSION
Hershey Foods Corp.	Hershey Foods Corporation's basic business mission is to become a major, diversified food company. . . . A basic principle which Hershey will continue to embrace is to attract and hold customers with products and services of consistently superior quality and value.
Polaroid Corp.	Polaroid designs, manufactures, and markets worldwide a variety of products based on its inventions, primarily in the photographic field. These include instant photographic cameras and films, light polarizing filters and lenses, and diversified chemical, optical, and commercial products. The principal products of the company are used in amateur and professional photography, industry, science, medicine, and education.
MCI Communications, Inc.	MCI's mission is leadership in the global telecommunications services industry. Profitable growth is fundamental to that mission, so that we may serve the interests of our stockholders and our customers.
Litton Industries, Inc.	Litton is a technology-based company applying advanced electronics products and services to business opportunities in defense, industrial automation, and geophysical markets. Research and product engineering emphasis is on developing advanced products which the company manufactures and supplies worldwide to commercial, industrial, and government customers.

Source: Excerpted from recent annual stockholder reports.

division of labor The process and result of breaking difficult work into smaller tasks.

Division of Labor. In every organization, difficult work is broken into smaller tasks. Such **division of labor** can enhance *efficiency* because it simplifies tasks and makes them easier to perform. You can see a classic example of this effect in an analysis of the task of pin making by the eighteenth-century economist Adam Smith:

> One man draws out the wire, another straightens it, a third cuts it, a fourth points it, a fifth grinds it at the top for receiving a head. To make the head requires two or three more operations. [Using a division of labor such as this,] ten persons could make among them upward of forty-eight thousand pins a day. But if they had all wrought separately and independently they certainly could not each of them have made twenty; perhaps not one pin in a day.[4]

The division of labor enables organized groups of people to accomplish tasks that would be beyond their physical or mental capacities as individuals. Few people, for example, can build a car by themselves, but companies like Chrysler turn out thousands of cars each year by dividing the complex job of building a car into simple assembly-line tasks.

hierarchy of authority A pyramidal distribution of authority in which managers higher in the pyramid can tell managers in lower positions what to do.

Hierarchy of Authority. The **hierarchy of authority** is a third attribute of every organization. In very small organizations, the authority to issue commands, make decisions, and enforce obedience may be shared equally among all members. More often, however, authority is distributed among members in a hierarchical pattern such as the one shown in Figure 2-1. At the top of this hierarchy, the chief executive officer (CEO) has the authority to issue orders to every other member of the organization and to expect these orders to be obeyed. At successively lower levels, managers direct the activities of people beneath them but are constrained by the authority of managers above them.

[4] Adam Smith, *An Inquiry into the Nature and Causes of the Wealth of Nations*, 5th ed. (Edinburgh: Adam and Charles Black, 1859), p. 3.

Ford Motor Co. long wanted to enter the luxury-car market dominated by German companies and jumped at the opportunity to acquire Britain's prestigious Jaguar, which had fallen on hard times. Jaguar (left) had been spending an incredible 100 man-hours to produce a single car and was forced early in 1990 to recall most of the cars sold over the past two years because of defects that could cause fire to break out. Ford plans to improve the Jaguar to compete with the highly successful BMW and Daimler-Benz Mercedes (right), which are made on automated assembly lines.
Sources: Fortune, *January 29, 1990, p. 96; Paul Ingrassia and Jacqueline Mitchell, "Jaguar Recalling Majority of Cars Sold Over 2 Years,"* The Wall Street Journal, *February 21, 1990.*

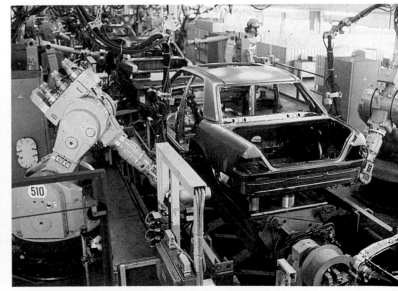

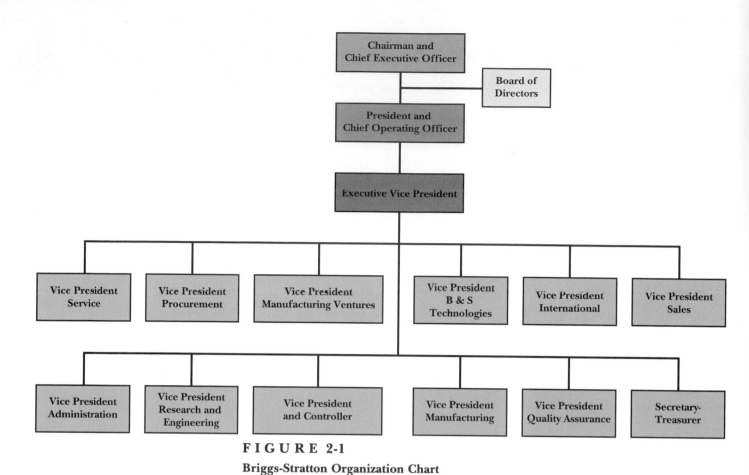

FIGURE 2-1

Briggs-Stratton Organization Chart

An organization chart is a graphic representation of a firm's hierarchy of authority. The organization chart in this figure shows the top and middle management of Briggs-Stratton, a manufacturer of small gasoline engines used in lawn mowers, snow blowers, and similar equipment. Note that the company is divided *horizontally* into various functional departments—such as manufacturing and sales—whose efforts are unified through authority relations that extend *vertically* between vice presidents and the CEO.

Source: The 1987 annual report of the Briggs-Stratton Company.

A Functional Definition

The three attributes of organizations that we have discussed help clarify the role of management in organizational life. In a sense, the first two are in conflict. The mission assumes the integration of effort, whereas the division of labor produces a differentiation of effort. As a result, an organization's members are simultaneously pushed together and pulled apart. It is managerial authority that reconciles this conflict by balancing the two opposing attributes. This balancing act is what managers do and what management is all about.

management A process of planning, organizing, directing, and controlling organizational behaviors in order to accomplish a mission through the division of labor.

Management is thus a process of planning, organizing, directing, and controlling organizational behaviors in order to accomplish a mission through the division of labor. This definition incorporates several important ideas. First, management is a process, an ongoing flow of activities. It is not something that can be accomplished once and for all. Second, managerial activities affect the behaviors of both an organization's members and the organization itself. Third, to accom-

FIGURE 2-2
The Four Management Functions

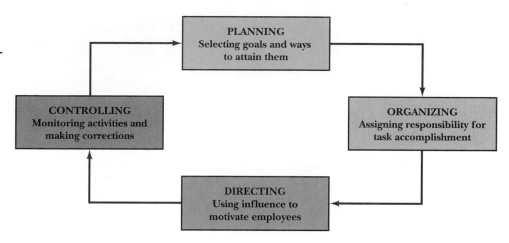

plish a firm's mission requires organization. If the mission could be accomplished by individuals working alone, neither the firm nor its management would be necessary. Let us look next at the four functions of management: planning, organizing, directing, and controlling (see also Figure 2-2).

planning The management function of deciding what to do in the future; setting goals and establishing the means to attain them.

Planning. **Planning** is a forward-looking process of deciding what to do. Managers who plan try to anticipate the future. They set goals and objectives for a firm's performance and identify the actions required to attain these goals and objectives. For example, managers at Sears planned a policy of increasing business by offering "everyday low prices." General Electric's managers were planning when they decided to have Black and Decker make GE steam irons.

In planning, managers set three types of goals and objectives:

1. *Strategic goals* are the outcomes that the organization as a whole expects to achieve in the pursuit of its mission.
2. *Functional* or *divisional objectives* are the outcomes that units within the firm are expected to achieve.
3. *Operational objectives* are the specific, measurable results that the members of an organizational unit are expected to accomplish.[5]

As shown in Figure 2-3, these three types of goals and objectives fit into an interdependent hierarchy. The focus of lower-order objectives is shaped by the content of higher-level goals, and, achieving higher-level goals depends on the fulfillment of lower-level objectives.

Goals and objectives are targets for organizational behavior. They help managers plan and implement a sequence of actions that will lead to goal attainment. For example, the sales objectives on which Sears based its pricing policy became performance targets for local stores and regional operations. Goals and objectives also serve as benchmarks of the success or failure of organizational behavior. When they review past performance, managers can judge effectiveness by assessing goal achievement. Thus GE's managers assessed the success of their decision to outsource steam iron production by comparing actual revenue and cost data with the profitability goals they had set.

organizing The management function of developing a structure of interrelated tasks and allocating people and resources within this structure.

Organizing. In **organizing**, managers develop a structure of interrelated tasks and allocate people and resources within this structure. Organizing begins with dividing an organization's labor and designing tasks that will lead to the achieve-

[5] Herbert Simon, *Administrative Behavior: A Study of Decision Making Processes in Administrative Organization* 3rd. ed. (New York: Free Press, 1976), pp. 257–78.

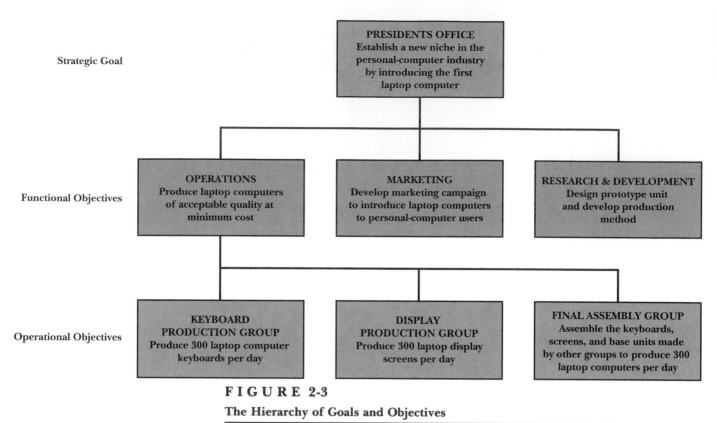

Strategic Goal

PRESIDENTS OFFICE
Establish a new niche in the
personal-computer industry
by introducing the first
laptop computer

Functional Objectives

OPERATIONS
Produce laptop computers
of acceptable quality at
minimum cost

MARKETING
Develop marketing campaign
to introduce laptop computers
to personal-computer users

RESEARCH & DEVELOPMENT
Design prototype unit
and develop production
method

Operational Objectives

KEYBOARD
PRODUCTION GROUP
Produce 300 laptop computer
keyboards per day

DISPLAY
PRODUCTION GROUP
Produce 300 laptop display
screens per day

FINAL ASSEMBLY GROUP
Assemble the keyboards,
screens, and base units made
by other groups to produce 300
laptop computers per day

FIGURE 2-3

The Hierarchy of Goals and Objectives

An organization's strategic goals set boundaries within which functional objectives are established. In turn, functional objectives shape the objectives of operational units. Thus accomplishing operational objectives contributes to the attainment of functional objectives and strategic goals.

ment of organizational goals and objectives. In companies like General Motors, Boeing, and IBM, assembly lines are designed and built during this phase. Managers must next determine who will perform these tasks. But first they must analyze the tasks to determine the knowledge, skills, and abilities needed to perform them successfully. They can then select qualified employees or train other employees who lack the necessary qualifications.

organizational unit A recognizable group of employees responsible for completing its own particular functional and/or operational objectives.

Grouping tasks and the people who perform them into **organizational units** is another step in the organizing process. One type of organizational unit, a *department*, is formed by people who perform the same type of work. For instance, all employees who market an organization's goods or services can form a marketing department. Another type of unit, a *division*, is formed by people who do the company's work in the same geographic territory, who work with similar kinds of clients, or who make or provide the same type of good or service. For example, the Ford Motor Company has a European division that does business in Europe. General Dynamics has a division that specializes in military contracts. General Electric's consumer electronics division markets only household appliances.

directing The management function of encouraging and guiding employees' efforts toward the attainment of organizational goals and objectives.

Directing. **Directing** encourages member effort and guides it toward the attainment of organizational goals and objectives. Directing is partly a process of communicating goals and objectives to members. Managers must announce, clarify, and promote targets toward which effort should be directed. For example, Steve Jobs is directing when he meets with the employees of Next Computer Company to publicize sales objectives. Directing is also a process of learning

Is Management the Same Thing as Domination?

Many experts have proposed that organization is best understood as a process of domination. Since the beginning of recorded time, by banding together for political, military, or other purposes, groups of people have succeeded in bending others to their will.

Where there is organization there is usually management. Do managers then dominate the people they supervise? Certainly the earliest managers wielded absolute power over those who worked under them. Think, for example, of the Egyptian rulers under whose direction the pyramids were built. The planning, organization, direction, and control that were required to supervise the construction of the Great Pyramid at Giza seem almost to overshadow any modern effort at managing the work of others. More important, the slaves and laborers who performed the actual work were pressed into service and probably received little more than food and lodging in return for their Herculean efforts.

But surely today, you may say, workers can choose whether or not they wish to work for a particular organization, under a particular kind of management. Unions have greatly improved the working conditions and pay of many employees. Workers are increasingly given a voice in their own manage-

ment. In some cases small groups of workers actually function without a direct supervisor. This does not sound as if workers are being dominated.

Critics suggest, however, that management relations that result in the majority working in the interests of the few are the hallmark of domination. They point out that over the course of history whether it was the building of pyramids or the maintenance of an army or the running of a multinational corporation—sometimes even the management of a family business—the lives and hard labor of many people have been used to serve the interests of a privileged few.*

Do you agree or disagree with the idea that management is a process of dominating others and controlling their behaviors? Why do you agree? Disagree? Is dominating or controlling others necessarily bad? Inherently good? What implications do your answers have for your future behavior as a manager?

* Gareth Morgan, *Images of Organization* (Beverly Hills, CA: Sage, 1986); Stewart Clegg and David Dukevley, *Organization, Class, and Control* (London, England: Routledge & Kegan Paul, 1980); and Loven Baritz, *The Servants of Power* (Middletown, Conn.: Wesleyan University Press, 1960).

---

employees' desires and interests and of ensuring that these desires and interests are satisfied in return for successful goal-oriented performance. When Sam Walton of Wal-Mart chats with employees about their jobs and the products they're selling, he is being more than a friendly person—he's directing. Directing may also require managers to use personal expertise or charisma to inspire employees to overcome obstacles that might appear insurmountable. Lee Iacocca is the perfect example of a manager performing this sort of directing. In all instances, directing is a process in which managers *lead* their subordinates, influencing them to work together to achieve organizational goals and related objectives. It is this influence-using aspect of management direction that has sometimes led critics to remark that management is the same thing as domination (see "Management Issues" box).

controlling The management function of evaluating the performance of an organization or organizational unit to determine whether it is progressing in the desired direction.

Controlling. Controlling involves evaluating the performance of an organization and its units to see whether the firm is progressing in the desired direction. In typical performance evaluation, managers compare an organization's actual results with the desired results described in the organization's goals and objectives. For example, GE might compare its actual profitability with the profitability objectives set for outsourcing. To make this sort of evaluation, members of the organization must collect and assess performance information. A firm's accounting personnel first gather data about the costs and revenues of organizational activities. Marketing representatives may provide additional data about sales volume or the organization's position in the marketplace. Finance specialists then appraise organizational performance by determining whether the ratio of costs to revenues meets or surpasses a target level.

If evaluation reveals a significant difference between goals and actual performance, the control process enters a phase of *correction*. In this phase, managers return to the planning stage, redeveloping goals and objectives, and indicating how differences between goals and outcomes can be reduced. Then the cycle begins again, with new efforts at planning, organizing, directing, and controlling.

SCHOOLS OF MANAGEMENT THOUGHT

Our definition of management is based on a wealth of management thoughts and practices, many of which are thousands of years old. Consider the following:

1. As early as 3000 B.C., the Sumerians formulated missions and goals for government and commercial enterprises.
2. Between 3000 and 1000 B.C, the Egyptians successfully organized the efforts of thousands of workers to build the Pyramids.
3. Between 800 B.C and about 300 A.D. the Romans perfected the use of hierarchical authority.
4. Between 450 A.D. and the late 1400s, Venetian merchants developed commercial laws and invented double-entry bookkeeping.
5. In the early 1500s, at the request of an Italian prince, Niccolo Machiavelli prepared an analysis of power that is still widely read.
6. At about the same time, the Catholic Church perfected a governance structure involving the use of standardized procedures.

Truly modern management practices did not begin to develop, however, until the industrial revolution of the 1700s and 1800s. Inventions like James Watt's steam engine and Eli Whitney's cotton gin created new forms of mass production that made existing modes of administration obsolete. The field of industrial engineering—which arose to invent and improve workplace machinery—began to address the selection, instruction, and coordination of industrial employees. Toward the end of the industrial revolution, managers and engineers throughout North America and Europe focused on developing general theories of management.

1890–1940: The Scientific Management School

Management theories initially took the form of *management principles* intended to provide managers with practical advice about managing their firms. Most of these principles were written by practicing managers or others closely associated with the management profession. Among the first principles to be widely read were those of the **scientific management school**.

scientific management school
The school of management thought that focuses on increasing the efficiency of production processes in order to enhance organizational profitability.

All principles of scientific management reflected the idea that through proper management an organization could achieve profitability and long-term survival in the competitive world of business. Thus, theorists in the scientific management school devoted their attention to describing proper management and determining the best way to achieve it.

Frederick W. Taylor. The founder of scientific management, Frederick W. Taylor (1856–1915) developed his principles of scientific management as he rose from laborer to chief engineer at the Midvale Steel Works in Philadelphia, Pennsylvania. Shown in Table 2-2, these principles focused on increasing the efficiency of the workplace by differentiating managers from nonsupervisory workers and systematizing the jobs of both.

According to Taylor, the profitability of an organization could be assured only by finding the "one best way" to perform each job. Managers could teach workers this technique and use a system of rewards and punishments to encourage its use. Consider Taylor's work to improve the productivity of coal shovelers at the Bethlehem Steel Company. As he observed these workers, Taylor discovered that a shovel load of coal could range from 4 to 30 pounds depending on the density of the coal being carried. By experimenting with a group of workers, Taylor discovered that shovelers could move the most coal in a day without suffering undue fatigue if each load of coal weighed 21 pounds. He then developed a variety of different shovels, each of which would hold approximately 21 pounds of coal of a particular density. After Taylor taught workers how to use these shovels, each shoveler's daily yield rose from 16 tons to 59. Moreover, the average wage per worker increased from $1.15 to $1.88 per day. Bethlehem Steel was able to reduce the number of shovelers in its yard from about 500 to 150, saving the firm about $80,000 per year.

Taylor's ideas influenced management around the world. In a 1918 article for the newspaper *Pravda*, Russian Communist Party founder Lenin even recommended that Taylor's scientific management be used throughout the USSR. In the U.S., Taylor's principles had such a dramatic effect on management that in 1912 he was called to testify before a special committee of the House of Representatives. Union employees and employers all objected to Taylor's idea that employers and employees should share the economic gains of scientific management and wanted Congress to do something about it. Nevertheless, with the newspaper publicity he gained from his appearance, Taylor found even wider support for his ideas and was soon joined in his work by other specialists.

Other Contributors. The husband-and-wife team of Frank (1868–1924) and Lillian Gilbreth (1878–1972), followed in Taylor's footsteps in pursuing the "one best way" to do any job. The Gilbreths are probably best known for their invention of "motion study," a procedure in which jobs are reduced to their most basic movements. A sample listing of these basic movements, each of which is called a *therblig* (Gilbreth spelled backward without inverting the *th*), is shown in Table 2-3. They also invented the microchronometer, a clock with a hand capable of

| **T A B L E 2-3** | | | |
Therblig Motions			
Search	Transport loaded	Dissemble	Transport empty
Find	Position	Inspect	Rest to relieve fatigue
Select	Assemble	Pre-position	Other unavoidable delay
Grasp	Use	Release load	Avoidable delay
Plan			

measuring time to the 1/2000 of a second. Using this instrument, analysts could precisely determine the time required by each of the movements needed to perform a job.

Another contributor to scientific management, Henry Gantt (1861–1919) developed a task-and-bonus wage plan that paid workers a bonus besides their regular wages if they completed their work in an assigned amount of time. Gantt's plan also provided bonuses for supervisors. Each supervisor's bonus was determined by the number of subordinates who met deadlines. If all subordinates finished on time, the supervisor received an additional bonus.[6] Gantt also invented the Gantt chart, a bar chart used by managers to compare actual with planned performance.[7] Present-day scheduling methods such as the program evaluation and review technique (PERT) are based on this invention.

Harrington Emerson (1853–1931), a third contributor to scientific management, applied his own list of twelve principles to the railroad industry in the early 1900s.[8] Among Emerson's principles were recommendations to establish clear objectives, seek advice from competent individuals, manage with justice and fairness, standardize procedures, reduce waste, and reward workers for efficiency. Late in his life, Emerson became interested in the selection and training of employees, stressing the importance of explaining scientific management to employees during their initial training. Emerson reasoned that sound management practices could succeed only if every member of the firm understood them.

1900–1950: The Administrative Principles School

At about the same time that Taylor and his colleagues were formulating their principles of scientific management, another group of theorists was developing the **administrative principles school**. In contrast to scientific management's emphasis on reducing the costs of production activities, this second school focused on increasing the efficiency of administrative procedures.

administrative principles school The school of management thought that deals with streamlining administrative procedures in order to encourage internal stability and efficiency.

Henri Fayol. Considered the father of modern management thought, Henri Fayol (1841–1925) developed his principles of administration in the early 1900s while serving as chief executive of a French mining and metallurgy firm, Commentry-Fourchambault-Decazeville, known as "Comambault." Fayol was the first to identify the four functions of management we have already discussed: planning, organizing, directing, and controlling.[9] He also formulated the fourteen principles shown in Table 2-4 to help administrators perform their jobs.

[6] Henry L. Gantt, "A bonus system of rewarding labor, *ASME Transactions* 23 (1901), 341–72; and *Work, Wages, and Profits* (New York: Engineering Magazine Company, 1910), pp. 18–29.

[7] Henry L. Gantt, *Organizing for Work* (New York: Harcourt, Brace, and Howe, 1919), pp. 74–97.

[8] Harrington Emerson, *The Twelve Principles of Efficiency* (New York: Engineering Magazine Company, 1912), pp. 59–367.

[9] Henri Fayol, *General and Industrial Management*, trans. Constance Storrs (London: Sir Isaac Pitman & Sons, 1949), pp. 19–43.

TABLE 2-4
Fayol's Fourteen Principles of Management

PRINCIPLE	DESCRIPTION
Division of work	A firm's work should be divided into specialized, simplified tasks. Matching task demands with work force skills and abilities will improve productivity. The management of work should be separated from its performance.
Authority and responsibility	Authority is the right to give orders, and responsibility is the obligation to accept the consequences of using authority. No one should possess one without the other.
Discipline	Discipline is performing a task with obedience and dedication. It can be expected only when a firm's managers and subordinates agree on the specific behaviors that subordinates will perform.
Unity of command	Each subordinate should receive orders from only one hierarchical superior. The confusion of having two or more superiors would undermine authority, discipline, order, and stability.
Unity of direction	Each group of activities directed toward the same objective should have only one manager and only one plan.
Individual versus general interests	The interests of individuals and the whole organization must be treated with equal respect. Neither can be allowed to supersede the other.
Remuneration of personnel	The pay received by employees must be fair and satisfactory to both them and the firm. Pay should be in proportion to personal performance, but employees' general welfare must not be threatened by unfair incentive-payment schemes.
Centralization	Centralization is the retention of authority by managers. It should be used when managers desire greater control. Decentralization should be used, however, if subordinates' opinions, counsel, and experience are needed.
Scalar chain	The scalar chain is a hierarchical string extending from the uppermost manager to the lowest subordinate. The line of authority follows this chain and is the proper route for organizational communications.
Order	Order, or "everything in its place," should be instilled whenever possible because it reduces wasted materials and efforts. Jobs should be designed and staffed with order in mind.
Equity	Equity means enforcing established rules with a sense of fair play, kindliness, and justice. Equity should be guaranteed by management, because it increases members' loyalty, devotion, and satisfaction.
Stability of tenure	Properly selected employees should be given the time needed to learn and adjust to their jobs. The absence of such stability undermines organizational performance.
Initiative	Members should be allowed the opportunity to think for themselves because this motivates performance and adds to the organization's pool of talent.
Esprit de corps	Managers should harmonize the interests of members by resisting the urge to split up successful teams. They should rely on face-to-face communication to detect and correct misunderstandings immediately.

Fayol believed that the number of management principles that might help improve an organization's operation is potentially limitless. He considered his principles to be flexible and adaptable, labeling them principles rather than laws or rules in order to avoid any idea of rigidity, as there is nothing rigid or absolute in [management] matters; everything is a question of degree. The same principle is hardly ever applied twice in exactly the same way, because we have to allow for different and changing circumstances, for human beings who are equally different and changeable, and for many other variable elements. The principles, too, are flexible, and can be adapted to meet every need; it is just a question of knowing how to use them.[10]

For Fayol, management was more than mechanical rule following. It required the sort of intuition and skillful application we have discussed in Chapter 1.

Max Weber. Max Weber (1864–1920) was a German sociologist who, though neither manager nor management consultant, had a major effect on twentieth-century management thought. Like Fayol, Weber was interested in the efficiency of different kinds of administrative arrangements. To figure out what makes organizations efficient, Weber analyzed the Egyptian empire, the Prussian army, the Roman Catholic church, and other large organizations that had functioned efficiently over long periods of time. Based on these analyses, Weber developed his model of **bureaucracy**, an idealized description of an efficient organization.

According to Weber, bureaucratic organizations are characterized by six important traits. First, employees of these organizations are selected and promoted solely on the basis of *technical competence*. Managers are appointed rather than elected and can be removed if they lack the expertise to perform their jobs correctly.

Second, bureaucratic organizations link superiors and subordinates through a *hierarchy of authority* in order to facilitate managerial control. The holder of each lower position in the hierarchy reports to, and is controlled by, the person in the position directly above.

Third, the tasks, responsibilities, and authority of the employees of bureaucratic organizations are defined by specific *rules and regulations* that give employees consistent, impartial guidance about how to behave on the job.

Fourth, bureaucratic organizations use a systematic *division of labor*. Employees carry out the work specified in their job descriptions, and other employees do not interfere so long as the work is performed in accordance with relevant job specifications.

Fifth, all administrative decisions, activities, and rules are set down in *written documentation*. Bureaucratic record keeping makes rules and decisions accessible to all employees. It also facilitates evaluation of existing rules and provides a source of information that can guide future decision making.

The sixth and last characteristic of bureaucratic organizations is *ownership or control by each organization* of its property, positions, and affairs. The rights and control associated with the positions in the organization's hierarchy belong to the organization and not to the employees occupying the positions.[11]

Weber's bureaucratic model, summarized in Table 2-5, provides for both the differentiation (through the division of labor and task specialization) and the integration (by the hierarchy of authority and written rules and regulations) necessary to get a specific job done. Weber believed that any organization with

bureaucracy An idealized description of an efficient organization based on clearly defined authority, formal record keeping, and standardized procedures.

---

[10] Henri Fayol, *Industrial and General Administration*, trans. J. A. Coubrough (Geneva, Switzerland: International Management Institute, 1930), p. 19.

[11] H. H. Gerth and C. Wright Mills, trans., *From Max Weber: Essays in Sociology* (New York: Oxford University Press, 1946); Nicos P. Mouzelis, *Organisation and Bureaucracy: An Analysis of Modern Theories* (Chicago: Aldine 1967); and Talcott Parsons, trans., *Max Weber: The Theory of Social and Economic Organization* (New York: Free Press, 1947).

TABLE 2-5
Features of Bureaucratic Organizations

FEATURE	DESCRIPTION
Selection and promotion criteria	Expertise is the primary criterion. Friendship or other favoritism is explicitly rejected.
Hierarchy of authority	Superiors have the authority to direct subordinates' actions. They are responsible for ensuring that these actions are in the bureaucracy's best interests.
Rules and regulations	Unchanging regulations provide the bureaucracy's members with consistent, impartial guidance.
Division of labor	Work is divided into tasks that can be performed by the bureaucracy's members in an efficient, productive manner.
Written documentation	Records provide consistency and a basis for evaluation of bureaucratic procedures.
Separate ownership	Members cannot gain unfair or undeserved advantage through ownership.

Source: Based on information presented in H. H. Gerth and C. Wright Mills, trans., *From Max Weber: Essays in Sociology* (New York: Oxford University Press, 1946).

bureaucratic characteristics would be efficient. He also noted, though, that work in a bureaucracy could become so simple and undemanding that employees might grow dissatisfied and, as a result, less productive.

Other Contributors. A number of other management experts have contributed to the administrative principles school. James Mooney (1884–1957), was vice-president and director of General Motors and president of General Motors Overseas Corporation during the late 1920s when he created his principles of organization.[12] Mooney's *coordinative principle* highlighted the importance of organizing the tasks and functions in a firm into a coordinated whole. He defined coordination as the orderly arrangement of group effort to provide unity of action in the pursuit of a common mission. Mooney's *scalar principle* identified the importance of scalar, or hierarchical, chains of superiors and subordinates as a means of integrating the work of different employees. Finally, Mooney's *functional principle* stressed the importance of functional differences, such as marketing, manufacturing, and accounting. He noted how work in each functional area both differs from and interlocks with the work of other areas.

Lyndall Urwick (1891–1983), another writer in the administrative principles school, was a British military officer and director of the International Management Institute in Geneva, Switzerland. Urwick made his mark by consolidating the ideas of Fayol and Mooney with those of Taylor.[13] From Taylor, Urwick adopted the idea that systematic, rigorous investigation should inform and support the management of employees. Urwick also used Fayol's fourteen principles to guide managerial planning and control and Mooney's three principles of organization to structure his discussion of organizing. Urwick's synthesis thus bridged Taylor's scientific management and the administrative principles approach, and integrated the work of others within the framework of the four functions of management with which you are now familiar.

[12] James D. Mooney and Alan C. Reiley, *Onward Industry: The Principles of Organization and Their Significance to Modern Industry* (New York: Harper & Brothers, 1931); revised and published as James D. Mooney, *The Principles of Organization* (New York: Harper & Brothers, 1947).

[13] Lyndall Urwick, *The Elements of Administration* (New York: Harper & Brothers, 1944).

Mary Parker Follett (1868–1933), who became interested in industrial management in the 1920s, was among the first proponents of what became known as *industrial democracy*. Follett proposed that, to promote cooperation and attention to a company's overall mission and goals, every employee should have an ownership interest in the company.[14] As you will see, Follett's work contributed to the human relations school, which we describe next. Follett, who advanced a number of administrative principles, suggested that because organizational problems typically stem from a variety of interdependent factors, they tend to resist simple solutions. Here again she anticipated later theorists, contributing to the contingency perspective that we introduced in Chapter 1 and discuss in this chapter in more detail.

1930–1970: The Human Relations School

Although members of both the scientific management and administrative principles schools advocated the scientific study of management, they rarely evaluated their ideas in any formal way. This situation changed in the middle 1920s when university researchers began to use scientific methods to test existing management thought.

The Hawthorne Studies. The now-famous *Hawthorne studies*, performed in 1924 at Western Electric's Hawthorne plant near Chicago, were among the earliest attempts to use scientific techniques to examine human behavior at work.[15] This three-stage series of experiments was undertaken to assess the effects of varying physical conditions and management practices on workplace efficiency. The design of these studies reflected the Hawthorne research team's grounding in the scientific management school of thought.[16] The first-stage experiment tested the effects of workplace lighting on productivity. One group of employees (the test group) was exposed to varying intensities of illumination. A second group (the control group) worked under a constant degree of illumination. The researchers expected to find that among the workers exposed to varying lighting conditions productivity would also vary and that productivity would peak when an optimal level of lighting was reached. They also predicted that the control group's performance would not change because their lighting conditions remained constant. Unexpectedly, the productivity of *both* groups rose. Only after workplace illumination was reduced to the level of moonlight did the test group's productivity drop significantly! These results led the researchers to conclude that it was not illumination alone that affected worker productivity. Reviewing their findings, they hypothesized that changes in social conditions, that is, the increased attention the workers received from researchers, might underlie the observed rise in productivity in both groups.

To investigate this possibility, the Hawthorne researchers conducted three more experiments. First, over a two-year period, they observed the performance of a group of women who assembled telephone relays. In this group, tasks were

[14] Henry C. Metcalf and Lyndall Urwick, eds., *Dynamic Administration: The Collected Papers of Mary Parker Follett* (New York: Harper & Row, 1940). Also see Judith Garwood, "*A Review of Dynamic Administration: The Collected Papers of Mary Parker Follett*," *New Management* 2 (1984), 61–62.

[15] Alex Carey, "The Hawthorne Studies: A Radical Criticism," *American Sociological Review* 33 (1967), 403–16.

[16] L. J. Henderson, T. N. Whitehead, and Elton Mayo, "The Effects of Social Environment," in *Papers on the Science of Administration*, ed. Luther Gulick and L. Urwick (New York: Institute of Public Administration, 1937), pp. 143–58; Elton Mayo, *The Human Problems of an Industrial Civilization* (Cambridge, Mass.: Harvard University Press, 1933); F. J. Roethlisberger and William J. Dickson, *Management and the Worker* (Cambridge, Mass.: Harvard University Press, 1939).

simplified, working hours were shortened, rest breaks were permitted, friendlier supervision was instituted, and an incentive-payment system was introduced. Next, the researchers convened a second group of five women, also assembling relays, and put them on the same simplified tasks and incentive-payment plan, but without the special working hours, rest periods, and friendly supervision given the first group. Finally, a third group of women who performed a mica-splitting task were exposed to the same working hours, rest periods, and friendly supervision given the first group of relay assemblers but were not put on the incentive-payment system.

Reviewing the results of this second group of experiments, the researchers concluded that the productivity increases they observed probably resulted from a change in the workers' attitudes owing to the new, more friendly supervisory style instituted in the first and third experimental groups. From a series of interviews with the subjects of the second group of experiments, the researchers learned that each group had apparently influenced the productivity of its members by enforcing informal agreements about what a fair day's work should be.

Finally, the Hawthorne researchers conducted an experiment that focused on the productivity of a group of nine men who assembled terminal banks for telephone exchanges. After implementing an incentive system in which each man was paid according to the number of pieces of work he completed, the researchers found that the group developed agreements about what constituted a day's work. Based on these agreements, both underproducing "chiselers" and overproducing "rate busters" were punished by social isolation, even occasional physical violence. The researchers concluded that social factors—specifically, workers' adherence to group norms to ensure the continued satisfaction of social needs—explained the results observed across all the Hawthorne studies.

Interestingly, much later reanalyses of the Hawthorne data not only found weaknesses in the studies' methods and techniques but suggested yet another possible cause of the results obtained. As shown in Table 2-6, these later investigators discovered that incentive pay rather than social factors improved productivity in the relay assembly experiments. They also concluded that the net

---

T A B L E 2-6
The Hawthorne Studies

EXPERIMENT	MAJOR CHANGES	RESULTS
Stage I		
Illumination study	Lighting conditions	Improved productivity at nearly all levels of illumination
Stage II		
First relay-assembly test	Job simplification, shorter work hours, rest breaks, friendly supervision, incentive pay	Thirty percent productivity improvement
Second relay-assembly test	Incentive pay	Twelve percent productivity improvement
Mica-splitting test	Shorter work hours, rest breaks, friendly supervision	Fifteen percent productivity improvement
Stage III		
Interview program	—	Discovery of presence of informal productivity norms
Bank-wiring-room test	Incentive pay	Emergence of productivity norms

effects of social factors could not even be correctly determined because other important elements of the work situation (the tasks being performed, rest periods, working hours) had been modified at the same time that social factors had been changed.[17] Consequently, conclusions reached by the original Hawthorne researchers are subject to doubt.

Douglas McGregor. Even though they were flawed in important respects, the Hawthorne studies raised serious questions about the efficiency-oriented focus of the scientific management and administrative principles schools. Most important, they stimulated debate about the importance of human satisfaction and personal development at work. The **human relations school** of management thought grew out of this debate, redirecting attention away from improving efficiency and toward increasing employee growth, development, and satisfaction.[18]

In 1960, Douglas McGregor (1906–1964), one spokesperson for the human relations school, contrasted the philosophy of the human relations approach with the efficiency orientation of the scientific management and administrative principles schools of management.[19] McGregor's **Theory X** incorporated the key assumptions about human nature shown in Table 2-7. McGregor suggested that theorists and managers holding these assumptions would describe management as follows:

1. Managers are responsible for organizing the elements of productive enterprise—money, materials, equipment, people—solely in the interest of economic efficiency.
2. The manager's function is to motivate workers, direct their efforts, control their actions, and modify their behavior to fit the organization's needs.
3. Without such active intervention by managers, people would be passive or even resistant to organizational needs; they must be persuaded, rewarded, and punished for the good of the organization.[20]

According to McGregor, the scientific management and administrative principles schools promoted a "hard" version of Theory X. They favored overcoming employees' resistance to organizational needs with strict discipline and economic rewards or sanctions. McGregor added that a "soft" version of Theory X seemed to underlie the Hawthorne studies. The Hawthorne researchers appeared to regard satisfaction and social relations mainly as rewards to employees who followed orders.

Theory Y, a contrasting philosophy of management that McGregor attributed to theorists, researchers, and managers from the human relations school, is based on the second set of assumptions shown in Table 2-7. McGregor indicated

---

human relations school The school of management thought that emphasizes increasing employee growth, development, and satisfaction.

Theory X A managerial point of view that assumes that nonmanagerial employees have little interest in attaining organizational goals and must therefore be motivated to fit the needs of the organization.

Theory Y A managerial point of view that assumes that nonmanagerial employees will readily direct behavior toward organizational goals if given the opportunity to do so.

---

[17] Carey, "Hawthorne Studies"; R. H. Franke and J. D. Kaul, "The Hawthorne Experiments: First Statistical Interpretation," *American Sociological Review* 43 (1978), 623–43; and A. J. M. Sykes, "Economic Interests and the Hawthorne Researchers," *Human Relations* 18 (1965), 253–63.

[18] Examples from the body of research stimulated by the Hawthorne studies include Lester Coch and John R. P. French, Jr., "Overcoming Resistance to Change," *Human Relations* 1 (1948), 512–33; Leonard Berkowitz, "Group Standards, Cohesiveness, and Productivity," *Human Relations* 7 (1954), 509–14; and Stanley E. Seashore, *Group Cohesiveness in the Industrial Work Group* (Ann Arbor: University of Michigan Survey Research Center, 1954).

[19] Douglas McGregor, "The Human Side of Enterprise," *Management Review* 56 (1957), 22–28 and 88–92; Douglas McGregor, *The Human Side of Enterprise* (New York: McGraw-Hill, 1960).

[20] Adapted from McGregor, "The Human Side of Enterprise," p. 23.

TABLE 2-7
Theory X and Theory Y Assumptions

Theory X assumptions
1. The average human being has an inherent dislike of work and will avoid it if possible.
2. Because they dislike work, most people must be coerced, controlled, directed, or threatened with punishment before they will put forth effort toward the achievement of organizational objectives.
3. The average human being prefers to be directed, wishes to avoid responsibility, has relatively little ambition, and wants security above all.

Theory Y Assumptions
1. Expending physical and mental effort at work is as natural as play and rest. The average human being does not inherently dislike work.
2. External control and the threat of punishment are not the only means to direct effort toward organizational objectives. People will exercise self-direction and self-control in the service of objectives to which they feel committed.
3. Commitment to objectives is a function of the rewards associated with their achievement. The most significant rewards—the satisfaction of ego and self-actualization needs—can be direct products of effort directed toward organizational objectives.
4. Avoidance of responsibility, lack of ambition, and emphasis on security are not inherent human characteristics. Under proper conditions, the average human being learns not only to accept but to seek responsibility.
5. Imagination, ingenuity, creativity, and the ability to use these qualities to solve organizational problems are widely distributed among people.

Source: Based on information presented in Douglas McGregor, *The Human Side of Enterprise* (New York: McGraw-Hill, 1960), pp. 33–34 and 47–48.

Summarizing Theory Y some 30 years after McGregor first proposed it, Dupont's CEO Edgar Woolard (center) says, "Employees have been underestimated. You have to start with the premise that people at all levels want to contribute and make the business a success." Woolard initiated the Adopt a Customer program in which blue-collar workers visit customers once a month, learn their needs, and literally serve as their representatives on the factory floor. Source: *Brian Dumaine, "Creating a New Company Culture,"* Fortune, *January 15, 1990.*

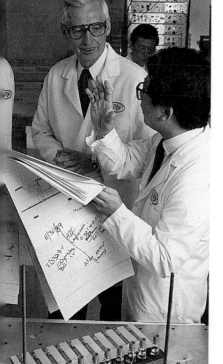

that individuals holding Theory Y assumptions would view the task of management as follows:

1. Managers are responsible for organizing the elements of productive enterprise—money, materials, equipment, people—in the interest of economic ends.

2. Because people are motivated to perform, have potential for development, can assume responsibility, and are willing to work toward organizational goals, managers are responsible for enabling people to recognize and develop these basic capacities.

3. The essential task of management is to arrange organizational conditions and methods of operation so that working toward organizational objectives is also the best way for people to achieve their own personal goals.[21]

Thus, unlike Theory X managers, who try to control their employees, Theory Y managers try to help employees learn how to manage themselves.

Other Contributors. Many management theorists, including Abraham Maslow (Chapter 7) and Frederick Herzberg (Chapter 17) embraced McGregor's Theory Y perspective in their work, discussing how personal autonomy and group participation might encourage employee growth, development, and satisfaction at work. We will discuss the ideas of these contributors to the human relations school later in the book.

1960–Present: The Open Systems School

The concern with employee satisfaction and development broadened to include a focus on organizational growth and survival with the emergence in the 1960s

---

[21] Adapted from McGregor, "The Human Side of Enterprise," pp. 88–89.

open systems school The school of management thought that characterizes every organization as a system that is open to the influence of the surrounding environment.

of the **open systems school**. According to this school of thought, every organization is a *system*—a unified structure of interrelated subsystems—and it is *open*, or subject to the influence of the surrounding environment. Together, these two ideas form the central tenet of the open systems approach. Organizations whose subsystems can cope with the surrounding environment can continue to do business, whereas organizations whose subsystems cannot cope do not survive. John Deere exemplifies a company whose subsystems—financial management, marketing and sales, human resource development—helped it survive in the competitive heavy-equipment industry of the 1980s. International Harvester is a company from the same industry whose subsystems failed to cope effectively; it no longer exists.

Daniel Katz and Robert L. Kahn. In one of the founding works of the open systems school, Daniel Katz and Robert Kahn identified the process shown in Figure 2-4 as essential to organizational growth and survival.[22] This process consists of the following sequence of events:

1. Every organization imports *inputs*, such as raw materials, production equipment, human resources, and technical know-how from the surrounding environment. For instance, Shell Oil Company hires employees and, from sources around the world, acquires unrefined oil, refinery equipment, and knowledge about how to refine petroleum products.

2. Some of these inputs are used to transform other inputs during a process of *throughput*. At Shell, employees use refinery equipment and know-how to transform unrefined oil into petroleum products like gasoline, kerosene, and diesel fuel.

3. The transformed resources are exported as *outputs*—saleable goods or services—to the environment. Petroleum products from Shell's refineries are loaded into tankers and transported to service stations throughout North America.

4. Outputs are exchanged for new inputs, and the cycle repeats. Shell sells its products and uses the resulting revenues to pay its employees and purchase additional oil, equipment, and know-how.

FIGURE 2-4
The Open Systems View of Organizations

[22] Daniel Katz and Robert L. Kahn, *The Social Phychology of Organizations* (New York: Wiley, 1966).

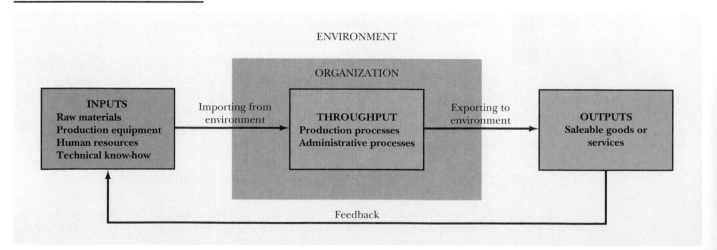

According to Katz and Kahn, organizations continue to grow and survive only as long as they import more inputs from the environment than they expend in producing the outputs exported back to the environment. *Information inputs* that signal how the environment and organization are functioning can help determine whether the organization will continue to survive; *negative feedback* indicates potential failure and the need to change the way things are being done.

Fred Emery and Eric Trist. In Katz and Kahn's model, the environment surrounding an organization is both the origin of needed resources and the recipient of transformed products. Accordingly, organizational survival depends on sensing the environment and adjusting to its demands. Describing environments and the demands they make so as to improve this sensing and adjustment was the goal of Fred Emery and Eric Trist, two early theorists of the open systems school.[23]

After noting that every organization's environment is itself composed of a collection of more or less interconnected organizations—supplier companies, competitors, and customer firms—Emery and Trist proposed four basic kinds of environments. The first kind, which they labeled *placid random environments*, are loosely interconnected and relatively unchanging. Organizations in such environments operate independently of each other, and one firm's decision to change the way it does business has little effect on the others. They are usually small—for example, landscape maintenance companies, construction firms, and industrial job shops—and can usually ignore each other and still stay in business by catering to local customers.

Placid clustered environments are more tightly interconnected. Here firms are grouped together into stable industries. Environments of this sort require organizations to cope with the actions of a *market*—a fairly constant group of suppliers, competitors, and customers. As a result, companies in these environments develop strategic moves and countermoves in response to competitors' actions. Grocery stores in the same geographic region often do business in this type of environment, using coupon discounts, in-store specials, and similar promotions to lure customers away from each other.

Disturbed reactive environments are as tightly interconnected as placid clustered environments but are less stable. Changes that occur in the environment itself have forceful effects on every organization. For instance, new competitors from overseas, increasing automation, and changing consumer tastes in the U.S. automobile market revolutionized the American auto industry in the 1970s and 1980s. As a result, GM, Ford, and Chrysler had to change their way of doing business, and a fourth long-time manufacturer, American Motors, ceased to exist. In such circumstances, organizations must respond not only to competitors' actions but to changes in the environment itself. It is very difficult to plan how to respond to these changes because their very nature makes future situations and actions hard to predict.

Turbulent fields are extremely complex and changeful. Companies operate in multiple markets. Public and governmental actions can alter the nature of an industry virtually overnight. Technologies advance at lightning speed. Finally, the amount of information needed to stay abreast of industrial trends is overwhelming. It is virtually impossible for organizations facing such uncertainty to do business in any consistent way. Instead, they must remain flexible, ready to adapt themselves to whatever circumstances unfold. Today's computer and communications industries exemplify this sort of environment.

[23] Fred E. Emery and Eric Trist, "The Causal Texture of Organizational Environments." *Human Relations* 18 (1965), 21–32; and *Towards a Social Ecology* (London: Plenum, 1973).

Other Contributors. As you can see, Emery and Trist hold that organizations must respond in different ways to different environmental conditions. Tighter environmental interconnections require greater awareness about environmental conditions, and more sweeping environmental change requires greater flexibility and adaptability. In Chapter 16, when we discuss designing organizations to fit environmental conditions, we will explore the ideas of open systems theorists including Paul Lawrence, Robert Duncan, and Jay Galbraith, who have stressed the need for organizations to adjust to their environments.

A Contingency Framework

As we pointed out in Chapter 1, the contingency perspective suggests that no single theory, perspective, or school of thought is entirely correct. There is no single best way to manage or even to think about the process of management. From this viewpoint, none of the four schools of management thought tells the whole story about management. Instead, as shown in Figure 2-5, each contributes valuable insights that supplement the others' contributions. The scientific management school focuses on making a profit in the *external* world by increasing the *efficiency* of production activities. The administrative principles school emphasizes improving *internal* operations by increasing the *efficiency* of administration. The human relations school concerns developing the *flexibility* to respond to the individual needs of members *inside* the organization. The open systems school focuses on developing the *flexibility* to respond to changes in the *external* environment.[24]

Parallels are evident among the schools. The scientific management and administrative behavior schools both promote attention to efficiency and stability. The human relations and open systems schools share a common emphasis on

[24] Our classification scheme is based on research conducted by Robert E. Quinn and associates. See, for example, Robert E. Quinn and John Rohrbaugh, "A Spatial Model of Effectiveness Criteria: Towards a Competing Values Approach to Organizational Analysis," *Management Science* 29 (1983), 363–77; Quinn, *Beyond Rational Management: Mastering the Paradoxes and Competing Demands of High Performance* (San Francisco: Jossey-Bass, 1988), pp. 50–54; and Quinn, Sue R. Faerman, Michael P. Thompson, and Michael R. McGrath, *Becoming a Master Manager: A Competency Framework* (New York: John Wiley, 1990), pp. 2–12.

FIGURE 2-5

The Four Schools of Management Thought

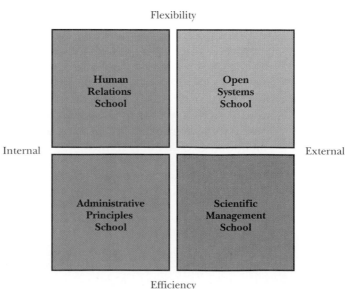

flexibility and change. The administrative principles and human relations schools focus on characteristics and procedures within the organization. The open systems and scientific management schools emphasize the importance of dealing with demands on the organization from external sources.

Each school of thought also has an opposite. The human relations school, with its emphasis on human growth and satisfaction, stands in stark contrast to the scientific management school's emphasis on employee efficiency and task simplification. The focus of the open systems school on adapting to environmental circumstances contrasts sharply with the administrative principles school's concern with developing stable, internally efficient operations. These differences reflect dilemmas that managers face every day. Shall we stimulate task performance or employee satisfaction? Shall we structure the organization to promote efficiency or flexibility? Shall we design jobs to encourage satisfaction or maximize profitability? We will discuss choice points like these throughout this book. For now, we conclude our discussion of management thought by repeating that in dealing with management dilemmas, no single approach is either always right or always wrong. Managers must make hard choices, but the perspectives offered by all four schools can help them weigh the alternatives and decide what to do.

WHAT DO MANAGERS DO?

Managers are people who plan, organize, direct, and control in order to manage organizations and organizational units. They are found in virtually every organization, from Exxon to the Girl Scouts (see "In Practice" box). Managers establish the directions to be pursued, allocate people and resources among tasks, supervise individual, group, and organizational performance, and assess progress toward goals and objectives. In order to fulfill these functions, they perform specific jobs, use a variety of skills, and play particular roles.

Managerial Jobs

Although all managers are responsible for the same functions, not all of them perform exactly the same jobs. Instead, as Figure 2-6 on page 43 shows, most organizations have three kinds of managers: top managers, middle managers, and supervisory managers. Figure 2-7 on page 43 illustrates the specific mix of planning, organizing, directing, and controlling performed by each of the three types of managers.[25]

Top Managers. *Top managers*, who are responsible for managing the entire organization, include *chairperson*, *president*, *chief executive officer*, *executive vice president*, and *chief operating officer*. The job of these managers consists mainly of performing the planning activities needed to develop the organization's mission and strategic goals. Top managers also perform organizing and controlling activities resulting from strategic planning. In controlling, they assess progress toward the attainment of strategic goals by monitoring information about activities occurring both within the firm and in its surrounding environment. Top management's responsibilities include making adjustments in the organization's overall direction on the basis of information reviewed in controlling procedures. Because strategic planning, organizing, and controlling require a great deal of time, top managers have little

manager A person who is responsible for planning, organizing, directing, and controlling behavior in organizations. *Top managers* are responsible for the entire firm; *middle managers* manage an organizational unit; *supervisory managers* manage the employees who do the firm's basic work.

[25] Luis R. Gomez-Mejia, Joseph E. McCann, and Ronald C. Page, "The Structure of Managerial Behaviors and Rewards," *Industrial Relations* 24 (1985), 147–54.

Lessons from a Nonprofit Manager

Not all successful managers are concerned about making a profit. Frances Hesselbein, former national executive director of Girl Scouts of the U.S.A., had other goals in mind as she reframed and pursued her organization's mission: to help each scout reach her highest potential.

Hesselbein, who was first lured into the Girl Scouts in the 1950s as a volunteer troop leader, moved up gradually to a full-time, paid position as a local Council director and then, in 1976, to national executive director of the organization.

A formidable challenge greeted Hesselbein. The Girl Scouts had seemingly lost touch with the society it served. Largely a white, middle-class group, it had failed to take note of important changes in its environment. Teenagers were losing interest in the Scouts, and adult volunteers were hard to find. Hesselbein undertook a major reexamination of the Girl Scouts' mission. "We kept asking ourselves very simple questions," she says. "What is our business? Who is the customer? And what does the customer consider value? Whether you're the Girl Scouts, IBM, or AT&T, you have to manage for a mission. . . . When you are clear about your mission, corporate goals and operating objectives flow from it."

Hesselbein gave the business more focus. She installed a planning system, reorganized the national staff, and introduced management training for both paid staff and volunteers. In keeping with her mission, she undertook market studies to determine how to help today's young girls to fulfill their best potential. She found that the Scouts needed to emphasize science, the environment, and business. "Math Whiz" and "Computer Fun" badges took the place of the traditional awards for household skills.

She championed "equal access" for all girls, and as a result the percentage of Girl Scouts from minority groups has tripled in the past ten years. Emphasizing again the mission of the organization, she told her staff that every girl in the country should be able to identify with the scout epitomized in the scouting handbook. "If I'm a Navajo child on a reservation, a newly arrived Vietnamese child, or a young girl in rural Appalachia, I have to be able to open that book and find myself. That's a very powerful message that 'I'm not an outsider,' that 'I can be part of something big.' "

Hesselbein's belief that everyone in the organization—scouts, volunteers, employees—must be free to develop to her fullest potential is exemplified in her innovative organization chart. Instead of the traditional pyramid with layers of increasing hierarchical power and influence, she designed a cir-

Reemphasizing the mission and purpose of the Girl Scouts has led to a revitalization of the organization and a new interest in the Scouts on the part of girls from all groups of society. Badges are now awarded for achievement in scientific and technological subjects, reflecting the entry of women into fields long dominated by men, and the percentage of Scouts who are from minority groups has tripled.

cular management structure with herself at the hub of the wheel-like diagram. "We don't talk about moving up or down," she says. "We move across. It's how we liberate the creative spirits of people."

Since leaving the Scouts, Hesselbein has become a leading speaker on management. Ranked as one of today's foremost managers by experts on leadership, she has made a videotape for management training at IBM and Motorola and also addresses classes at the Harvard Business School. As indicated by Hesselbein's accomplishments, good management practices—planning, organizing, directing, and controlling—can contribute to the success of non-profit firms just as they advance the fortunes of profit-oriented companies.*

* John A. Byrne, "Profiting from the Nonprofits: Much Can Be Learned from Some of the Best-Run Organizations Around," *Business Week*, March 26, 1990, pp. 66–74; Sally Helgesen, "The Pyramid and the Web," *The New York Times*, May 27, 1990, p. 13.

---

time to spend in directing subordinates' behavior. Typically, they delegate responsibility for directing such behavior to managers lower in the hierarchy of authority.

Middle Managers. *Middle managers* are usually responsible for the performance of a particular organizational unit and for implementing top managers' strategic

FIGURE 2-6

Types of Managers

Top managers occupy positions at the top of their organization's hierarchy of authority and are responsible for managing the entire organization. *Middle managers*, found immediately below, oversee a department or division. *Supervisory managers* are at the base of the hierarchy of authority, where they manage non-supervisory employees.

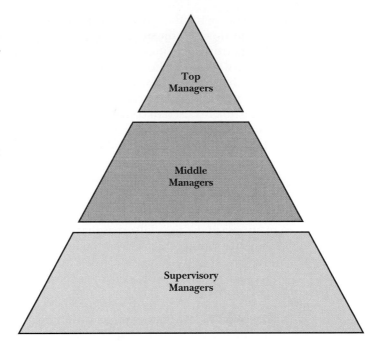

plans. During strategic implementation, each middle manager helps establish functional or divisional objectives that will guide unit performance toward targets established by strategic plans. Middle managers may also set operational objectives to be pursued at lower levels in the unit. They organize and direct unit members toward accomplishing functional or divisional objectives, and they control unit behavior by determining whether objectives are successfully attained. Labels such as *vice president*, *director* or *manager* are usually a part of a middle manager's title—for example, vice president of finance, director of personnel relations, manager of consumer affairs.

Supervisory Managers. *Supervisory managers*, often called *superintendents*, *supervisors*, or *foremen*, are charged with overseeing the nonsupervisory employees who perform the organization's basic work. Of the three types of managers, supervisory

FIGURE 2-7

Managerial Functions and Types of Managers

Planning is the most important function of top managers; middle managers fulfill all four management functions about equally; directing is the most important function of supervisory managers.

Source: Based on information presented in Luis Gomez-Mejia, Joseph E. McCann, and Ronald C. Page, "The Structure of Managerial Behaviors and Rewards," Industrial Relations 24 (1985), 147–54.

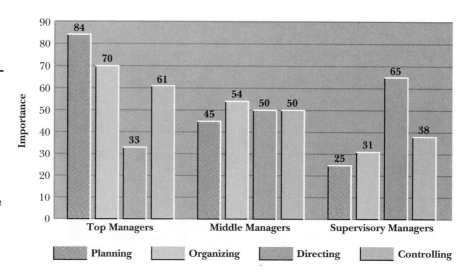

managers spend the greatest amount of time directing employees. Except for small, on-the-job adjustments, supervisory managers seldom perform planning and organizing activities. These activities are normally performed by the middle manager who has authority over the supervisory manager. Supervisory managers initiate the upward flow of information that middle and top managers use to control organizational behavior. They may also distribute many of the rewards or punishments used to control nonsupervisory employees' behaviors. Their ability to control subordinates' activities is limited, however, to the authority delegated to them by middle management.

Managerial Skills

Not surprisingly, the skills that managers must have to succeed in their jobs are largely determined by the combination of planning, organizing, directing, and controlling that they must perform. As diagrammed in Figure 2-8, each level of management has its own skill requirements.[26]

conceptual skills Management skills involving the ability to perceive an organization or organizational unit as a whole, to understand how its labor is divided into tasks and reintegrated by the pursuit of common goals or objectives, and to recognize important relationships between the organization or unit and its environment.

human skills Management skills involving the ability to work effectively as a group member and to build cooperation among the members of an organization or unit.

Conceptual Skills. Conceptual skills include the ability to perceive an organization or organizational unit as a whole, to understand how its labor is divided into tasks and reintegrated by the pursuit of common goals or objectives, and to recognize important relationships between the organization or unit and the environment that surrounds it. Conceptual skills involve a manager's ability to *think* and are most closely associated with planning and organizing. Thus, these skills are used quite frequently by top managers, who are responsible for organizationwide strategic endeavors.

Human Skills. Human skills include the ability to work effectively as a group member and to build cooperation among the members of an organization or unit. Managers with well-developed human skills can create an atmosphere of trust and security in which people can express themselves without fear of punishment or humiliation. Such managers, who are adept at sensing the desires,

[26] Robert L. Katz, "Skills of an Effective Administrator," *Harvard Business Review* 52 (1974), 90–102.

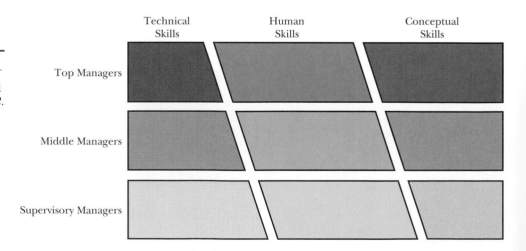

interests, and viewpoints of others, can often foresee others' likely reactions to prospective courses of action. Because all management functions require that managers interact with other employees to acquire information, make decisions, implement changes, and assess results, top, middle, and supervisory managers all need strong human skills.

technical skills Management skills involving an understanding of the specific knowledge, procedures, and tools used to make the goods or services produced by an organization or unit.

Technical Skills. Technical skills involve an understanding of the specific knowledge, procedures, and tools used to make the goods or services produced by an organization or unit. Of the three managerial skills, technical skills are the most practical and down to earth. For example, a marketing manager must have skills in selling. An accounting supervisor must have bookkeeping skills. A supervisor of maintenance mechanics may need to have welding skills. To managers at the top or middle of an organization's hierarchy of authority, these skills are the least important. Technical skills are critical to managerial success only for supervisory managers overseeing employees who use technical skills in their work.

Managerial Roles

managerial role Behaviors expected of managers in performing their jobs. Managers promote good interpersonal relations in the *interpersonal* role, receive and send information to others in the *informational* role, and determine the firm's direction in the *decisional* role.

Like skills, **managerial roles** vary from one manager to another. As shown in Table 2-8, these roles cluster together in three general categories: interpersonal, informational, and decisional roles.[27]

[27] The list of ten roles described in this section is adapted from Henry Mintzberg, *The Nature of Managerial Work* (New York: Harper & Row, 1973). Other researchers who have described similar managerial roles include Sune Carlson, *Executive Behavior* (Stockholm: Stromsberg, 1951), and Rosemary Stewart, *Managers and Their Jobs* (London: MacMillan, 1967).

TABLE 2-8
The Ten Roles of Managers

ROLE	DESCRIPTION
Interpersonal Roles	
Figurehead	Representing the organization or unit in ceremonial and symbolic activities
Leader	Guiding and motivating employee performance
Liaison	Linking the organization or unit with others
Informational Roles	
Monitor	Scanning the environment for information that can enhance organizational or unit performance
Disseminator	Providing information to subordinates
Spokesperson	Distributing information to people outside of the organization or unit
Decisional Roles	
Entrepreneur	Initiating changes that improve the organization or unit
Disturbance handler	Adapting the organization or unit to changing conditions
Resource allocator	Distributing resources within the organization or unit
Negotiator	Bargaining or negotiating to sustain organizational or unit survival

Source: Based on information presented in Henry Mintzberg, *The Nature of Managerial Work* (New York: Harper & Row, Publishers, 1973).

Interpersonal Roles. In three distinct *interpersonal roles*, managers create and maintain interpersonal relations to ensure the well-being of their organizations or units. Managers represent their organizations or units to other people in the *figurehead role*, which involves such ceremonial and symbolic activities as greeting visitors, attending awards banquets, and cutting ribbons to open new facilities. In the *leader role*, they motivate and guide employees by issuing orders, setting performance goals, and training subordinates. Managers create and maintain links between their organizations or units and others in the *liaison role*. For example, a company president may meet with the presidents of other companies at an industrial association conference.

Informational Roles. Because they serve as the primary authority figures of the organizations or units they supervise, managers have unique access to both internal and external information networks. In *informational roles* managers receive and transmit information within these networks. In the *monitor role*, managers scan the environment surrounding their organizations or units, seeking information to enhance performance. Activities in this role can range from reading periodicals and reports to trading rumors with managers in other firms or units. In the *disseminator role*, managers pass information to subordinates who would otherwise have no access to it. To disseminate information, managers may hold meetings with subordinates, write them memoranda, or telephone them. In the *spokesperson role*, managers distribute information to people outside of their organizations or units through annual stockholder reports, speeches, memos, and various other means.

Decisional Roles. In *decisional roles*, managers determine the direction to be taken by their organizations or units. In the *entrepreneur role*, managers must make decisions about improvements in the organizations or units for which they are responsible. Such decisions often entail initiating change. For example, a manager who hears about a new product opportunity may decide to commit the firm to producing it. She may also decide to delegate the responsibility for managing the resulting project to others. The *disturbance handler role* also involves change-oriented decisions. Managers acting in this role must often try to adapt to change beyond their personal control. For example, they may have to handle such problems as conflicts among subordinates, the loss of an important customer, or damage to the firm's building or plant.

In the *resource allocator role*, managers decide what specific resources will be acquired and who will receive them. Such decisions often involve important tradeoffs. For instance, if a manager decides to acquire personal computers for sales clerks, he may have to deny manufacturing department employees a piece of equipment. As part of the resource allocation process, priorities may be set, budgets established, and schedules devised. Finally, in the *negotiator role*, managers engage in formal bargaining or negotiations to acquire the resources needed for the survival of their organizations or units. In this role, for example, managers may negotiate with suppliers about delivery dates or bargain with union representatives about employee wages.

Differences Among Managers. Just as the mix of functions managers perform and the skills they use differ from one managerial job to another, so do the roles

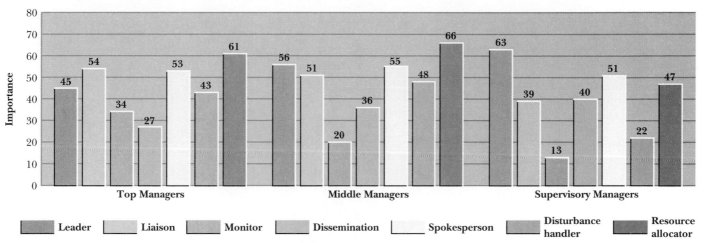

FIGURE 2-9

Managers' Jobs and the Roles They Fill

When researchers asked top, middle, and supervisory managers about the importance of the roles they perform, their answers revealed the data illustrated here. Note that the roles of figurehead, entrepreneur, and negotiator were not included in this survey.

Source: Based on information presented in Allen I. Kraut, Patricia R. Pedigo, D. Douglas McKenna, and Marvin D. Dunnette, "The Role of the Manager: What's Really Important in Different Management Jobs," Academy of Management Executive 3(1989), 286–93.

managers fill. Figure 2-9 shows, for example, that the roles of liaison, spokesperson, and resource allocator are most important in the jobs of top managers, reflecting top management's responsibilities for planning, organizing, and controlling the strategic direction of the firm. In addition, monitor activities are more important for top managers than for others because they must scan the environment for pertinent information.

Among middle managers, leader, liaison, disturbance handler, and resource allocator roles are the most important. These roles are in keeping with middle management's job of organizing, directing, and controlling the functional or divisional units of the firm. The role of disseminator is also important in middle managers' jobs because they are responsible for explaining and implementing the strategic plans of top management.

For supervisory managers, the leader role is the most important. They spend most of their time directing non-supervisory personnel. They also act as spokespersons who disseminate information within their groups and serve as liasons that connect their groups with the rest of the organization. In addition, they acquire and distribute the resources their groups need to do their jobs.

THE NATURE OF MANAGERIAL WORK

To further analyze the classification of managerial roles we've just discussed, Henry Mintzberg observed a group of top managers at work for several weeks. Listing major activities and the time it took to perform

FIGURE 2-10

The Manager's Day

Source: Reproduced with the author's permission from Henry Mintzberg, The Nature of Managerial Work (New York: Harper & Row, Publishers 1973), p. 39.

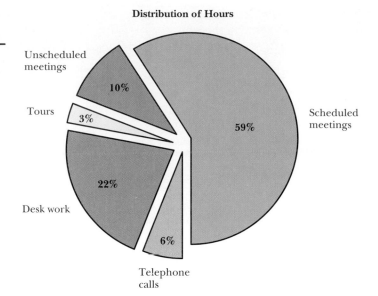

Distribution of Hours

them, Mintzberg found that his managers spent by far the most time in scheduled meetings. When combined with unscheduled meetings, this activity accounted for almost 70 percent of the managers' time. As Figure 2-10 shows, the managers were left with barely a fifth of the day for desk work, and about a tenth for telephone calls and company tours.

Mintzberg also recorded the amount of time consumed by each instance of each activity. Scheduled meetings averaged a little over an hour in length and ranged from under 10 minutes to over 2 hours. Unscheduled meetings were normally shorter, lasting from a few minutes to about an hour and averaging approximately 12 minutes each. Periods of desk work and tours to inspect the company averaged around 11 to 15 minutes each and were fitted in between scheduled meetings and unscheduled interruptions. Telephone calls were almost always quite short, averaging about 6 minutes apiece.

Based on his observations, Mintzberg concluded that managers work in short bursts rather than in long, uninterrupted sessions. They frequently lack the time to complete rigorous planning, organizing, directing, and controlling. Instead, managing is often more a process of making erratic, *incremental adjustments* than one of following a routine, well-planned course of action.[28] Managing is a fast-paced, active profession.

SUMMARY

Management is a process of *planning, organizing, directing,* and *controlling* the behavior of others that makes it possible for an *organization* using a *division of labor* to accomplish a *mission* beyond the means of individuals working alone.

Theorists from four schools of thought have attempted to explain or improve management practices. Members of the *scientific management school* have tried to increase the efficiency of production processes in order to enhance marketplace

[28] James Brian Quinn, *Strategies for Change: Logical Incrementalism* (Homewood, Ill: Richard D. Irwin, 1980), p. 18.

profitability. Proponents of the *administrative principles school* have focused on enhancing the efficiency of administrative procedures. Researchers in the *human relations school* have put the emphasis on nurturing the growth and satisfaction of organization members. Theorists in the *open systems school* have highlighted the importance of coping with the surrounding environment.

Managers differ in terms of where they fit in the *hierarchy of authority*. These differences affect managers' jobs, influencing the *skills* they use, the behaviors they engage in, and the *roles* they fill. The job of manager is fast paced and allows the manager little time to devote to any single activity.

REVIEW QUESTIONS

1. How does an organization enable its members to accomplish a purpose beyond the means of individuals working alone? Why aren't organizations formed to achieve purposes that people can accomplish individually?

2. What is an organization's mission? Its division of labor? Its hierarchy of authority? How do these three organizational attributes clarify the role of management?

3. Describe the work of a manager in performing each of the four basic management functions: planning, organizing, directing, and controlling. How does planning affect organizing? How does organizing affect directing? How does directing affect controlling? How does controlling affect later planning?

4. What is the central idea underlying work in the scientific management school? What advice would an expert in this school give managers? Give an example of the kind of change an expert in scientific management might recommend if he or she were asked to improve the efficiency of your class.

5. How does the administrative principles school differ from the scientific management school? What is a management principle? How does it differ from a law or rule? What is a bureaucracy? Give an example of an organization that is extremely bureaucratic. Of an organization that is not very bureaucratic.

6. What does the human relations school focus attention on? According to Douglas McGregor, what sort of perspective do members of this school have on management? The Hawthorne researchers differed from members of the human relations school in what important respect?

7. What are the two key ideas underlying the open systems school? What central tenet do they support? Explain the cycle of events described by Katz and Kahn. According to your description, why is it important for managers to be able to diagnose environmental conditions and adapt their organizations to environmental changes as they occur?

8. Explain the contingency model formed by the four schools of management thought described in this chapter. If you were a manager having problems with employee satisfaction, which school of thought would you consult for advice? If you were concerned about efficiency, which schools of thought could probably help you out?

9. What do managers do? What are the three kinds of managers? How do hierarchical differences affect the job of being a manager? How do the management jobs at various levels fit together, connecting the whole organization with each of its parts?

10. What kinds of skills do all managers use to perform their jobs? Which of these skills are you learning about as you read this book? Which skill becomes

more important as managers move up the hierarchy of authority? Which one stays about the same? Which one loses importance?

11.   What roles do managers perform? What effect do hierarchical differences have on the roles of managers?

12.   Describe the job of being a manager. How realistic is the television portrayal of managers as doing little more than sitting behind desks, making decisions, and telling people what to do? How might this portrayal be made more realistic?

CHAPTER 3

THINKING CRITICALLY ABOUT ORGANIZATIONS: RESEARCH METHODS

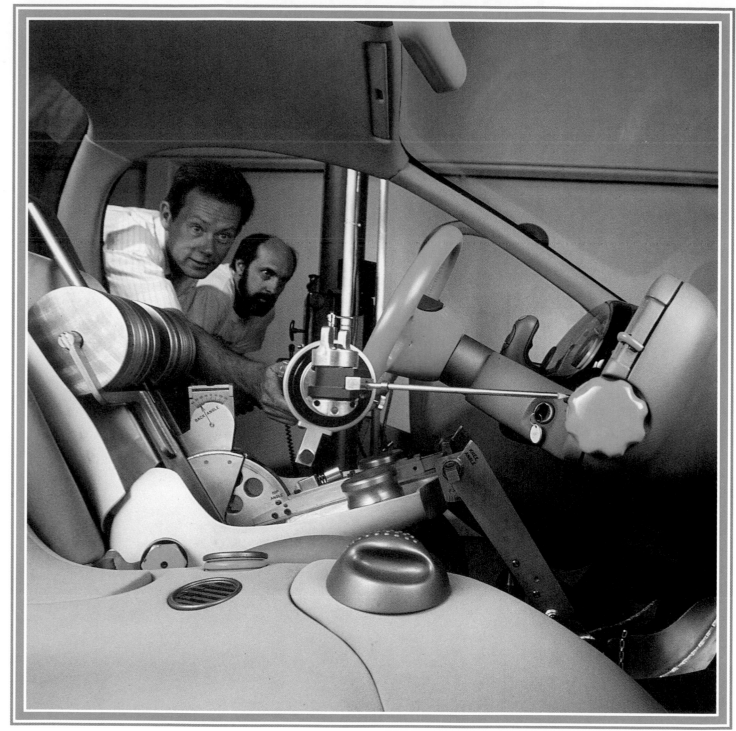

Is the United States number one? Is it in danger of losing its economic leadership? According to J. D. Power & Associates Inc., U.S. auto makers may not yet realize that their arch rival, Japan, is into a "second phase of quality," researching refinements of design and function that Japanese firms hope will win consumer approval. At Nissan, for example, engineers turn the results of anthropological research on what people want in cars into features that give cars a comfortable feel, such as computer-driven hydraulics that cushion jolts and level a car during quick stops and sharp cornering.

Source: "A New Era for Auto Quality," Business Week, *October 22, 1990.*

> **"I** know it may sound un-American, but I don't believe that we were born to be number one. America won't be number one forever as a genetic or historic right. I think that it is entirely conceivable that the United States could lose its world economic leadership. It is no longer unthinkable that we could just fade away. Remember that Britain kept saying that productivity stagnation was unacceptable even as her position steadily deteriorated. I think that unless this nation decides to do something about the problems that have generated our productivity stagnation, we will fade away.[1]"

This statement on productivity in America paints a grim picture of our current economic situation. It also underlines our need for more and better knowledge about the effective management of organizations and the people who form them. The complexity and volatility of the modern world have raised the stakes associated with managerial success or failure as they have increased the challenge to organizations and entire societies.

The performance of a firm depends to a great extent on the competence of its managers, and the manager's job is essentially one of directing the behavior of others. This fact is recognized by the increasing tendency of firms to evaluate managers' performance on the basis of their success in handling behavioral problems with the firm. General Electric, for example, now assesses its managers' performance with an employee relations index in which all eight indicators of success or failure deal with employee behaviors like performance on the job, absenteeism, and the initiation of formal grievance procedures.[2]

RESEARCH IN ORGANIZATIONAL BEHAVIOR

Clearly, knowledge about organizational behavior has become increasingly critical to a manager's performance and to her long-term career success. Given this need for knowledge, it is not surprising that writers in this field often claim to have the information that managers need to excel at their jobs. Mitroff and Mohrman comment that "in this environment U.S. businesses often fall prey to every new management fad promising a painless solution, especially when it is presented in a neat, bright package."[3] Indeed, the demand for this knowledge has created a veritable cottage industry of "pop" management books; consider the "excellence" books—the best-selling *In Search of Excellence*, by Tom Peters and Robert Waterman, and its sequel, *A Passion for Excellence*, by Peters and Nancy Austin.[4]

Initially, Peters and Waterman outlined eight principles that they said distinguished excellent firms from others. Peters and Austin reduced this list to four. Since the appearance of these two books, many business firms have reportedly been attempting to conform their practices to one or the other set of principles.

If these and other similar books have already provided managers with all the answers they need, why do we devote an entire chapter in this textbook to

---

[1] Reprinted from P. Galagan, "Staying Alive: Jack Grayson on the American Productivity Crisis," *Training and Development Journal* (1984), 59–62.

[2] H. F. Merrihue and R. A. Katzell, "ERI—Yardstick of Employee Relations," *Harvard Business Review* 33 (1955), 91–99.

[3] I. I. Mitroff and S. A. Mohrman, "The Slack Is Gone: How the United States Lost Its Competitive Edge in the World Economy," *Academy of Management Executives* (1987), 69.

[4] Tom J. Peters and Robert Waterman, *In Search of Excellence* (New York: Harper and Row, 1982); and Tom J. Peters and Nancy Austin, *A Passion for Excellence* (New York: Random House, 1985).

research in organizational behavior? Let's take a closer look at some of the answers provided by Peters and his colleagues.

The widespread acceptance of the excellence books led researchers Michael Hitt and Duane Ireland, to attempt to replicate Peters' work.[5] Employing more rigorous research techniques and a sample of 185 firms (which included all those studied by Peters and Waterman as well as many others), Hitt and Ireland came to some startling conclusions. First, comparing market returns, they found no significant differences between the so-called excellent firms and others. Second, Hitt and Ireland discovered that the firms designated excellent were no more likely to report following the excellence principles than were other firms. Finally, these researchers found that whether or not firms were designated excellent, there was no relationship between their market performance and their adherence to the principles formulated by Peters and his associates.

Concluding their report, Hitt and Ireland comment that "excellent firms identified by Peters and Waterman may have not been excellent performers, and they may have not applied the excellence principles to any greater extent than did the general population of firms. Additionally, the data call into question whether these excellence principles are in fact related to performance."[6] Hitt and Ireland note that ultimately the problem with the "excellence" books is not so much that their message is wrong—even their authors did not intend that managers should follow their guidelines blindly. Rather, the problem lies in the fact that practicing managers are so intent in their search for answers that they often uncritically adopt the first useful-looking material they find, failing to survey and evaluate the wide range of research data available.

To avoid this quick-fix mentality, Hitt and Ireland offer several suggestions. First, they urge managers to keep current with the literature in the field of management and to pay particular attention to journal articles that translate research findings into practical guidelines. Second, they warn managers to be skeptical when simple solutions are offered, analyzing such solutions (and their supposed evidence) thoroughly. Third, Hitt and Ireland suggest that managers make sure that the concepts they apply are based on science rather than advocacy. They also urge managers to experiment with new solutions themselves whenever possible.

The purpose of this chapter is to help dispel the quick-fix mentality by focusing on Hitt and Ireland's three recommendations. We will begin by examining the nature of the scientific process in order to show you not only how you can use others' research findings but how you can conduct your own experiments. Next, we will show you how to be skeptical in evaluating the claims made by those who propose solutions to your problems. Finally, we will describe some of the scientific sources you can turn to in seeking answers to your managerial questions.

People who teach organizational behavior and management skills often lament the fact that there is not enough dialogue between practicing managers and researchers. This kind of dialogue can develop only when managers and researchers understand each other's work and appreciate its value for their own efforts. Practicing managers need to know what organizational behavior researchers do and why they do it the way they do. Researchers need to know what practitioners' most pressing problems are so that they can study issues that managers view as significant. It is in large part because we feel it is so important to create and encourage this kind of ongoing practitioner–researcher dialogue that we have included this chapter on research methods in our book.

---

[5] M. A. Hitt and R. D. Ireland, "Peters and Waterman Revisited: The Unended Quest for Excellence," *Academy of Management Executives* 2 (1987), 91–98.

[6] Ibid., p. 95.

EXPLORING THE SCIENTIFIC PROCESS

As part of their solution for restoring the United States's competitive edge, Mitroff and Mohrman note that what managers need is not simple solutions to complex problems but "a method for helping [them] debate and thereby assess the proposed attributes of excellence."[7] The purpose of this section is to describe one such method—the scientific method. Let us begin by comparing the scientific method to other ways of discovering truth.

Ways of Knowing

How do we come to know things? When we say we know that there are nine planets in our solar system, how do we know this is true? When we say that dropping atomic bombs on Nagasaki and Hiroshima caused the end of World War II in the Pacific, how do we know this is true? When we say we know that providing workers with specific and difficult goals leads them to perform better than just telling them to do their best, how do we know this is true? Finally, when we say we know that an organization's structure must match its technology and its environment, how do we know this is true?

Traditional Ways of Knowing. Philosophers of science have explored many ways of arriving at knowledge.[8] Figure 3-1 suggests that some ways of acquiring knowledge are more reliable than others. Thus among the traditional ways of knowing, personal experience and rationalism are more satisfactory than tenacity, intuition, and authority, and science is the most reliable of all. Let's look first at the traditional sources of knowledge.

By *tenacity* we mean believing that something is true simply because we have always believed it to be true. Many superstitions and prejudices are based on this method of knowing. *Intuition* means arriving at knowledge without relying on either reason or inference. This method is based on an appeal to propositions

---

[7] Mitroff and Mohrman, "Slack is Gone," p. 69.

[8] See, e.g., J. Buchler, *Philosophical Writings of Peirce* (New York: Dover, 1955); M. Cohen and E. Nagel, *An Introduction to Logic and the Scientific Method* (New York: Harcourt, 1954); M. Polyani, *Personal Knowledge* (Chicago: University of Chicago Press, 1958); L. B. Christenson, *Experimental Methodology* (Boston; Allyn & Bacon, 1977).

FIGURE 3-1

Ways of Knowing

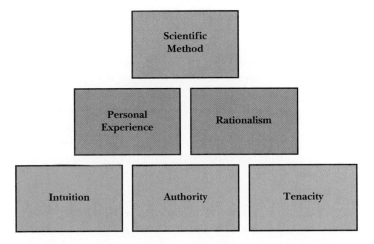

felt to be obvious and indisputable. Recall, for example, Thomas Jefferson's assertion in the introduction to the Declaration of Independence that "we hold these truths to be self-evident." By the method of *authority*, we may believe a statement or proposition to be true because it is made by a person whom we respect or who we feel is an expert on the topic. For example, if a doctor tells a pregnant woman her baby must be delivered by Caesarean section, the woman is likely to believe what he says.

Although most of us base some of our knowledge on these three methods, clearly they are not always reliable ways of coming to know something.[9] Two people or two groups often hold tenaciously to opposite beliefs; self-evident truths are often more evident to some than to others; authorities often give conflicting advice on the same issue. The main problem with these three methods is that they do not allow for reconciling the disagreements that inevitably arise.

We find the same problem with the fourth traditional way of knowing—*personal experience*. This is probably the most widespread source of knowledge for most of us. Most people tend to believe information they acquire through interacting with other people and the world at large and to conclude that their experience reflects truth. Again, different people may have different experiences that point to different truths. Even more problematic, people's perceptions and memories of their experiences are often biased, inaccurate, or distorted over time. Finally, even if we disregard inaccuracies of perception or memory, the fact remains that any one person can experience only a tiny fraction of all possible situations: thus the knowledge she acquires by personal experience will necessarily be extremely limited.

The last traditional method of attaining knowledge is *rationalism*, or the notion that we can acquire knowledge if we use the correct reasoning procedure. Logical deductions form the basis for such knowledge. For example, in mathematics, if A is greater than B and B is greater than C, logic tell us that A is greater than C. Once we step outside the world of mathematics, however, this kind of logic breaks down. Suppose, for example, that a baseball team—we'll call it Team A—beats another team, Team B, and Team B beats Team C; can we say that therefore Team A will beat Team C? No, because there are too many factors and too much variability over time in events like a baseball game or a company's advertising campaign. Such events involve many different individuals and many different conditions.

scientific method An objective method of expanding knowledge characterized by an endless cycle of theory building, hypothesis formation, data collection, empirical hypothesis testing, and theoretical modification.

objectivity In science, the degree to which a set of scientific findings are independent of any one person's opinion about them.

Scientific Method. The problems and pitfalls of these more traditional ways of knowing, and in particular their subjectivity, led to the development of the **scientific method**. As Charles Sanders Peirce has stated, "To satisfy our doubts . . . it is necessary that a method should be found by which our beliefs may be determined by nothing human, but by some external permanency. . . . The method must be such that the ultimate conclusion of every man shall be the same. Such is the method of science."[10]

Thus **objectivity**, which measures the degree to which scientific findings are independent of any one person's opinion about them, stands as the major difference between the scientific approach to knowledge and the other approaches described so far. Science as an enterprise is *public* in the sense that methods and results obtained by one scientist are shared with others. It is also *self-correcting*, in the sense that erroneous findings can be isolated through the replication of one scientist's work by another scientist. And it is *cumulative*, in the sense that one scientist's experiment often builds on the work of another. These features

---

[9] E. F. Stone, *Research Methods in Organizational Behavior* (Santa Monica, Calif.: Goodyear, 1978).
[10] Buchler, *Philosophical Writings of Peirce*, p. 18.

of the scientific method make it ideal as a means of generating reliable knowledge, and it is no coincidence that the physical, natural, and social sciences receive so much emphasis in today's colleges and universities. For all these reasons, it will be useful for us, in this chapter, to explore the nature of the scientific process more closely. We will look first at the major goals or purposes of science and then at how the scientific method is structured to achieve these objectives.

THE PURPOSES OF SCIENCE

The basic goal of science is to help us understand the world around us. Science defines the understanding it seeks as the ability to describe, explain, predict, and control the subjects of its inquiry. We will examine each of these objectives.

Description. The purpose of some research is simply *description*, that is, drawing an accurate picture of a particular phenomenon or event. In Chapter 2, for example, we presented data from Mintzberg's study of managerial roles (see Table 2-8). The purpose of Mintzberg's research was simply to find out what managers actually do on the job on a daily basis.[11] In Chapter 4, we will review descriptive research that attempts to describe the major dimensions of intelligence, or cognitive ability. In Chapter 17, we will look at descriptive research that seeks the dimensions best suited to describe the nature of jobs. The development of scientific knowledge usually begins with descriptive work. The ultimate criterion for evaluating all descriptive research is the fidelity with which it reflects the real world.

Explanation. The ultimate goal of science is *explanation*—stating why some relationship exists. Some might argue that as long as we can describe, predict and control things, why go any further? For example, if a manager in the insurance business knows that people with college degrees sell more life insurance than people with high school degrees, why does she need to know more than this? Why not just hire all college graduates for sales positions? Well, if researchers can uncover the reason for college graduates' greater success, the manager may be able to bring about the desired outcome (selling more insurance) in a more efficient or cost-effective way.

For example, suppose that college-educated salespeople outperform those without higher education not because of their years of study per se but because, on average, they are more self-confident, and self-confidence sells. If this were the case, the manager might be able to get the same high success rate by hiring, at lower salaries, high-school-educated people who are high in self-confidence or by hiring such persons and training them to boost their self-confidence. You can see that if we know the exact reason why something occurs we can usually explain and control it much more efficiently.

Prediction. *Prediction*, or stating what will happen in the future, is the primary goal of many scientific studies. Prediction requires that we know the relationships between certain conditions and outcomes. For example, in Chapter 8, we will look at research that attempts to predict who will leave organizations and who will stay. In Chapter 10, we will review studies that predict when decisions are made best by groups and when they are best left to individuals. In Chapter 18,

[11] H. A. Mintzberg, "Structured Observation as a Method to Study Managerial Work," *Journal of Management Studies* 7 (1970), 87–104.

we will discuss studies that attempt to predict strategic choices of various kinds of organizations. When we cannot accurately predict what will happen in a given situation, we have generally failed to understand it.

Control. Studies that focus on prediction often lead to further research in which the goal is to *control* the situation. Predictive studies often uncover relationships between antecedents and outcomes, and if it is possible to manipulate the antecedents, it may be possible to control the outcomes. In Chapter 8, for example, we will review studies that show that by manipulating pay practices, one can also manipulate how hard individuals will work. In Chapter 10, we will discuss research that shows how group communication patterns can be controlled by manipulating how chairs are arranged around a table. In Chapter 17, we will show how changing the design of work will lead to changes in worker attitudes. It is in the area of control that the interests of scientists and practitioners most clearly converge.

As we have seen already, managers in organizations are responsible for controlling the behaviors of others. Thus the more information a study provides on how control can be achieved, the more useful the study is to practicing managers. Indeed, research guided by the other three objectives is often perceived by managers as "academic" and not worthwhile. But as you have seen, studies dealing with control often are the by-products of earlier descriptive, explanatory and predictive studies. Without good descriptive, explanatory and predictive research, we would probably never do much successful research aimed at control.

The four objectives of science are often pursued by researchers in the order given above, that is, starting out with description and proceeding through control. Despite this fact, the four goals do not explicitly build on each other in any tight hierarchical fashion. That is, you can sometimes predict things that you cannot explain. For example, before Copernicus, people could predict the passage of day to night even though they could not explain why this occurred. Today, someone with little background in auto mechanics or chemistry may be able to control engine knocking by using higher octane fuel but not have any idea why this works.

The Interplay of Theory and Data

We have concluded that the scientific method is the best available means for arriving at knowledge, and we have laid out the goals, or purposes, of scientific inquiry. Now we need to consider precisely what scientific method entails. Figure 3-2 represents our conception of scientific inquiry and depicts science as a con-

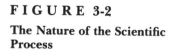

FIGURE 3-2

The Nature of the Scientific Process

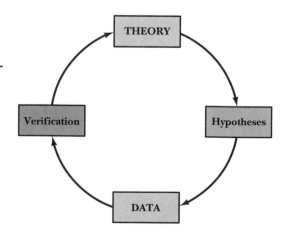

theory A set of interrelated constructs, definitions, and propositions that present a systematic view of phenomena by specifying relations among variables.

hypothesis A specific, testable prediction, derived typically from a theory, about the relationship between two variables.

verification A stage in the scientific process in which scientists assess the degree to which hypotheses based on theories match empirical data.

implicit theories Loose, informal theories about phenomena that people rarely test in a rigorous, empirical fashion.

tinuous process that links theory, which resides in the world of abstract ideas, with data, which reside in the world of concrete facts. A theory is translated into real-world terms by the process of stipulating hypotheses, and real-world data are translated back into the realm of ideas through the process of verification. These processes then form a chain, and any one scientific study is only as strong as its weakest link. Moreover, if one link breaks apart (e.g., if the theory is not appropriately expressed in the hypotheses) then the whole process breaks down.

Kerlinger defines a **theory** as "a set of interrelated constructs, definitions, and propositions that present a systematic view of a phenomenon by specifying relations among variables."[12] With your understanding of the purposes of science and this definition of theory, can you see why theory plays such a central role in the scientific process? A good theory, through its constructs and definitions, should provide us with a clear description of a part of the real world. Moreover, by specifying relations among variables, a theory facilitates both prediction and control. Finally, a theory's systematic nature allows us to explain the relationships described. The remaining chapters of this book are filled with theories that attempt to help you understand how to manage the behavior of people in organizations.

Theory is only half of the scientific process, however. The other half deals with *data*, or real-world facts. Theories, to have any practical utility, cannot remain solely in the world of ideas. The scientific process requires that theories prove themselves in the world of data. Through a process of deduction, **hypotheses**, or specific predictions about the relationships between certain conditions in the real world, are generated. These hypotheses are related to the theory in the sense that if the theory is correct, then what the hypotheses predict should be found in the real world.

Here is where data enter the scientific process. Once hypotheses are formulated, data can be collected, and the hypothesized and actual patterns of results can be compared. Then, through the process of **verification**, this comparison can be used to check the accuracy of the theory—to judge the extent to which it is true. If there is very little correspondence between the hypothesized results and the actual findings, the theory must be rejected. The process must begin all over again, with the generation of a new theory. If there is only some correspondence between the projected and actual findings, the theory may need to be changed in some way so as to be consistent with the data. If there is almost complete correspondence between the hypothesized results and the actual findings, we may be tempted to claim that we have proven that the theory is true. Such a conclusion would not be warranted, however, unless we could establish that all other possible explanations for the results (explanations not accounted for by the theory) had been eliminated. Because this is almost never possible, we usually refer to data that correspond closely with a hypothesis as "supporting" rather than "proving" the theory.

Thus the scientific process relies on the constant interplay of theory and data. One without the other is no better than neither at all. For example, in the Middle Ages, an elaborate theory of body chemistry led early physicians to practice bloodletting, in which they applied leeches to various parts of the human body in an effort to heal various illnesses. The problem was that no one ever tested the theory to see if those who were treated in this fashion actually were better off than those who were not. Had such data been collected, people would have realized that the theory was false. Scientific knowledge requires both theory and data, and great mistakes can be made when one is divorced from the other.

Good Theories. One doesn't have to be a scientist to have a theory. Indeed, in our daily lives, we all develop informal or **implicit theories** about the world

[12] F. N. Kerlinger, *Foundations of Behavioral Research* (New York: Holt, Rinehart & Winston, 1986), p. 9.

explicit theories Internally consistent, formal theories that are subject to empirical test.

around us. We arrive at these theories through our personal experience and are often unaware that they exist. Many of these implicit theories can be lumped together under the general heading of common sense. Scientific theories are usually developed more formally. We will refer to these as **explicit theories** in order to distinguish them from implicit theories. As you will see throughout this book, much of what we are trying to do when we discuss the diagnostic stage of our overall model is to get you to replace your implicit theories with explicit theories that have been supported by research. However, explicit theories are not always better than implicit theories. Moreover, there are often multiple explicit theories that deal with a given subject, and some may be better than others. How do we judge whether a theory is good?

John B. Miner has offered several good criteria for judging the worth of theories.[13] First and foremost, a theory should contribute to the objectives of science: it should be useful in describing, explaining, predicting, or controlling important things. Most theories, whether implicit or explicit, meet this test.

Second, a theory must be logically consistent within itself. Here is where many implicit theories (and some explicit ones) fall short. For example, common sense tells us that "fortune favors the brave." On the other hand, common sense also tells us that "fools rush in where angels fear to tread," which has the opposite implication. Again common sense tells us that "two heads are better than one," but it also tells us that "too many cooks spoil the broth." As you can see, common sense, and many of the implicit theories on which it is based, is not good theory at all because it contradicts itself.

Third, it is also important that a theory be consistent with known facts. For example, many people have an implicit theory that "a happy worker is a productive worker." In fact, a vast amount of research shows that satisfaction and performance are actually unrelated.[14] Any theory that stated directly or implied that these two variables are related would not be a good theory.

A fourth criterion by which to evaluate a theory is its consistency with respect to future events. The critical notion here is not simply that the theory predicts but that it makes *testable* predictions. A prediction is testable if it can be refuted by data. A theory that predicts all possible outcomes says nothing at all. For example, if a theory states that a particular leadership style can increase, decrease, or leave employee performance unchanged, it has really said nothing about the relationship between that leadership style and worker performance.

Finally, simplicity is a desirable characteristic of a theory. Highly complex and involved theories are not only more difficult to test but more difficult to apply. Therefore, a theory that uses only a few concepts to predict and explain some outcome is preferable to one that does the same thing with more concepts. Theoretical simplicity, however, is hard to maintain. Theories are by their nature oversimplifications of the real world. The inductive nature of the scientific process, which requires that a theory be consistent with real-world data, inevitably pushes simple theories toward increasing complexity over time. A good theory is one that can walk the fine line between being too simple (when it will fail to predict events with any accuracy) and being too complex (when it is no longer testable or useful for any purpose).

Good Data. Because science deals with the interplay of theory and data, good data are just as important as good theory. Most of the data for testing theories are gathered through measures of the theory's important concepts. There are

---

[13] J. B. Miner, *Theories of Organizational Behavior* (Hinsdale, Ill.: Dryden Press, 1980).
[14] M. T. Iaffaldono and P. M. Muchinsky, "Job Satisfaction and Performance: A Meta-Analysis," *Psychological Bulletin* 97 (1985), 251–73.

several characteristics that make some measures, and therefore some data, better than others.

First, the measures of the theoretical concepts that we are interested in must possess **reliability**; that is, they must be free of random errors and thus present a consistent, stable reflection of the underlying concept. Suppose, for example, that you were applying for graduate school and the person who was interviewing you was interested in your scholastic aptitude because he felt this measure was predictive of success in graduate school. Imagine, then, that to assess your aptitude the interviewer handed you two dice and asked you to toss them, at the same time suggesting that a high score would mean you had high aptitude and a low score that you had low aptitude. At this point, you would probably start wondering about the aptitude of the interviewer, as dice tossing is obviously a very poor measure of scholastic aptitude. Aside from this fact, one of the main problems with dice as a measure is that they generate completely random, unreliable numbers. That is, you could get a high score today, and tomorrow you could get a low score. There would be little consistency or agreement in your scholastic aptitude from one measurement to the next. Thus the unreliability of this measure makes it virtually worthless.

This is an extreme and obvious case, but consider the following. It was once believed that interviewers, after talking to job applicants in an unstructured way for about 30 minutes, could provide ratings reflecting the suitability of these people for the jobs for which they were being considered. Research showed, however, that these ratings were about as unreliable as the dice-tossing example cited above.[15] That is, an interviewer would rate an applicant high one day and then after some passage of time rate the same applicant differently another day. In making important decisions like admitting an applicant to graduate school, most institutions rely heavily on test scores like the Graduate Record Exam (GRE), the Graduate Management Admissions Test (GMAT), and the Law School Admissions Test (LSAT). Although these tests are not perfectly reliable (i.e., students taking them repeatedly will not get the exact same score each time), they do exhibit a high degree of consistency on retesting.

reliability The degree to which a measure of an individual, group, organizational, or environmental attribute is free from random error and thus replicable.

[15] R. Arvey and M. Campion, "The Employment Interview: A Summary and Review of Recent Research," *Personnel Psychology* 34 (1982), 281–322.

When people are conducting applied research, the speed with which data can be collected is often very important. Information needs to be brought to bear on problems before it's too late. When Frito-Lay issued hand-held Fujitsu computers to all its salespeople, the quality of the information about the company's products and its competitors' that fed into Frito-Lay's Dallas headquarters skyrocketed. In two days, for example, the company was able to revitalize a sales promotion that was lagging in some stores of a Von's chain in Los Angeles. Under its old system, the company might not have noticed the difference between store sales for weeks, too late to do anything about the problem.

Source: *"Managing,"* Fortune, *September 24, 1990, pp. 116–18.*

validity The degree to which a measure of an individual, group, organizational, or environmental attribute does what it is intended to do.

criterion-related validation Establishing validity by showing that a measure predicts some variable that, based on theory, it should predict.

content validation Establishing validity by showing that, according to expert judges, the measure samples the appropriate material.

construct validation Establishing validity by showing that a measure of a concept is congruent with the theory and data that support the concept.

standardization In the context of scientific measurement, the practice of ensuring that all people measure the same variables with the same instruments applied in the same manner.

Second, the measures of a theory's concepts must possess **validity**; that is, they must assess what they were meant to assess. To see if the GMAT is valid, for example, we might want to test whether those who perform better on the test actually perform better in graduate school. This means of testing validity is called **criterion-related validation**, because we test whether the measure predicts some criterion (e.g., grade point average) that it is supposed to be able to predict. We can also assess validity by having recognized experts on the concept the test is designed to measure rate the extent to which the test items actually represent that concept. This is called **content validation**, because we test whether the content of the test is appropriate according to experts on the subject.

In **construct validation** we assess the degree to which the measure actually taps some abstract concept. The most complex form of validation, construct validation requires all the steps associated with criterion-related and content validation as well as other tests. Among the latter tests, one of the most important is designed to show that the test is not contaminated, that is, that it does not measure something that it is *not* supposed to measure. For example, if we were trying to measure scholastic aptitude with a handwritten essay test and could show that students with poor handwriting consistently got lower grades than students with good handwriting (especially if we knew that the content of all the students' answers was the same) we would conclude that this measure was contaminated. It lacks construct validity because it is measuring something (i.e., handwriting ability) that it is not supposed to be measuring.

Reliability and validity are closely related. Reliability is necessary for validity, but it is not sufficient, because we could develop highly reliable measures that might not prove valid. For example, we could probably measure people's height reliably, but this measure would have little validity as a measure of scholastic aptitude (i.e., it could not predict who would do well in graduate school). Reliability is necessary for validity though, because an unreliable measure cannot pass any of the tests necessary for establishing validity. An unreliable measure does not relate well even to itself. Thus it is virtually impossible for such a measure to relate well to anything else. So the next time you see "Lottery Dice," which generate random numbers in the hope of allowing you to predict winning lottery numbers (numbers that are generated randomly), save your money.

A third desirable property of the measures of a theory's concepts is **standardization**. Standardization in the context of measurement means that everyone who measures the construct uses the same instrument in the same way. That is, the measures used to obtain data should ideally be common and the procedures for administering the measure well established. Holding reliability and validity constant, data obtained from standardized procedures are preferable to data obtained from procedures or measures that are unique to a particular situation. Jum Nunnally notes that because of the time and effort required to develop measures that are reliable and valid, a great deal of *efficiency* can be achieved by using existing standardized measures.[16]

Standardized measures provide two other advantages. First, they are far more likely than other measures to achieve *objectivity*. Because everyone uses the same procedures, the results of measurement are much less likely to be affected by who happens to be doing the assessing. Second, standardized measures facilitate the *communication* and *comparison* of results across situations. You could construct a scale to measure job satisfaction in your own company, but even if you did succeed in developing a reliable and valid measure (a difficult task), you could not compare the satisfaction level in your company to that in other companies. The Job Descriptive Index (JDI), for example, which is discussed in detail in

---

[16] Jum C. Nunnally, *Psychometric Theory* (New York: McGraw-Hill, 1978), p. 4.

Chapter 8, is a standardized measure of job satisfaction that has been used in hundreds of companies. For most standardized measures, a wealth of existing data allow you to compare your company to other companies that have measured the concept in which you are interested in the same way.

For these and other reasons, you would be foolish to try to develop your own measures for every situation. At worst, you would come up with measures that lack reliability and validity, and at best you would be reinventing the wheel. Moreover, even if the new wheel you developed were reliable and valid, it would not be comparable to the wheel that everyone else was using. For this reason, throughout this book we will provide you either with specific, standardized measures of various concepts or with the sources from which such measures can be obtained. It is possible, of course, that on some occasion you will need to test new concepts or develop measures that are unique to your situation. Such cases, however, will be the exception rather than the rule. Many of the measures you will need are already available.

Causal Inferences

From an applied perspective, the beauty of the scientific method is its ability to isolate the probable causes for various outcomes. Once causes are identified, they can often be manipulated to bring about the specific outcomes we want. Good theory and good data take us a long way toward this objective, but they are not sufficient for making causal inferences. Making causal inferences depends not only on how the data are obtained but also on when the data are obtained and on what is done with the data once they are collected.

Criteria for Inferring Cause

According to philosopher John Stuart Mill (1806–1873), in order to establish that one thing causes another, we must be able to establish three things: the temporal precedence of one thing over the other; the covariation, or relationship between, the two things in question; and the absence of alternative explanations for the observed results.

temporal precedence The degree to which any measured cause actually precedes an effect in time.

Temporal Precedence. The first step is establishing **temporal precedence**, which simply means that the cause must occur before the effect. That is relatively easy to determine, although sometimes you can fool yourself if you are not precise. For example, some professors think that giving tests causes students to study. This notion is technically incorrect, for it has the effect (studying) occurring *before* the proposed cause (giving the test). More precisely, it is probably the fear of failing the test that causes studying, not the test itself.

covariation The degree to which two variables are associated with each other; the degree to which changes in one are related to changes in the other.

Covariation. Mill's second criterion for inferring cause is **covariation**, which simply means that the cause and effect are related. For example, if we believe that providing day care for employees' children causes less worker absenteeism, then there should be a relationship between company day care services and low employee absenteeism.

There are several ways to assess covariation, all of which rely on statistical methods. As this is not a statistics book, we will limit our discussion here to two simple but widely applicable statistical techniques. The first, known as a test of

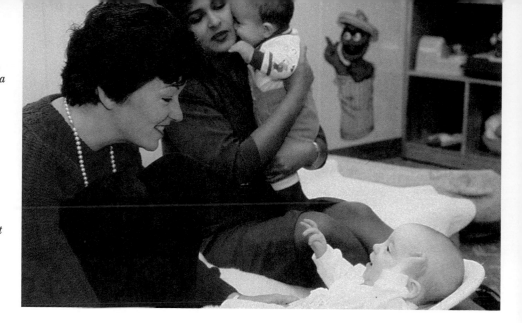

correlation coefficient A statistic that assesses the degree of relationship between two variables.

mean differences, compares the mean, or average, scores of two groups on a measure of the proposed causal factor. Table 3-1 presents data on absenteeism for two groups of workers: Ten work in Plant A, where there is an in-house day-care center, and ten work in Plant B, where there are no on-site provisions for day care. As you can see, the level of absenteeism is much higher for Plant B than Plant A. This simple analysis of mean differences suggests that day-care provision and absenteeism are in fact related. As we will see, however, more rigorous approaches will enable us to refine our conclusions. We might also test for mean differences between numbers of absences at Plant A before and after the establishment of the day care center (see Table 3-2). If the average absenteeism rates were higher before putting in the day-care center than they were after it was in place, we might again conclude (before engaging in more rigorous analyses) that there is a relationship between providing day care and lower absenteeism.

A second means of establishing covariation is through the use of the **correlation coefficient**. This statistic, a number that ranges from $+1.0$ to -1.0, is an expression of the relationship between two things. A $+1.0$ correlation means that there is a perfect positive relationship between the two measures in question. That is, as the value of one increases, the value of the other increases to the same

TABLE 3-1
Absence Data at Two Hypothetical Plants

| | NUMBER OF ABSENCES | |
EMPLOYEE	Plant A (with day care)	Plant B (without day care)
01	10	12
02	11	11
03	8	13
04	11	8
05	3	16
06	4	14
07	3	10
08	2	4
09	1	2
10	5	3
Average	5.8	9.3

TABLE 3-2
Absence Data for One Hypothetical Plant at Two Different Times

	NUMBER OF ABSENCES AT PLANT A	
EMPLOYEE	Before Day Care	After Day Care
01	12	10
02	14	11
03	10	8
04	12	11
05	6	3
06	8	4
07	4	3
08	2	2
09	1	1
10	6	5
Average	7.5	5.8

relative degree. A correlation of -1.0 reflects a perfect negative relationship between the two measures in question. Here, as the value of one increases, the value of the other decreases, again to the same relative degree. Finally, a correlation of .00 indicates that there is no relationship whatever between the measures, so that as the value of one increases, the value of the other can be anything—high, medium, or low. To give you a feel for other values of the correlation coefficient, Figure 3-3 shows plots of 5 different correlation values, $+1.0$, $+.50$, $+.20$, .00 and $-.50$. As you can see, the sign of the correlation reveals whether the relationship is positive or negative, and the absolute value of the correlation reveals the magnitude of the relationship.

Let's go back to our employees at Plants A and B. In Table 3-3, in addition to the data on day care and rates of absenteeism we also show data on the ages of all the workers. We could use the correlation coefficient to answer the question, Is there a relationship between age and absenteeism? In fact, the correlation between age and absenteeism for these data is $-.50$, indicating that older workers are absent less often than younger ones. If one were to plot these data on a graph, where x is the horizontal axis and y the vertical axis, it would look just like the figure shown in Figure 3-3e.

One important question that must be answered at this point is how big a difference in means or how big a correlation is big enough to conclude that there is a relationship. Even if there is no relationship between day care and absenteeism, it is unlikely that the means for the two different groups will be exactly the same. Similarly, even if age is not related to absenteeism, it is unlikely that the observed correlation is exactly .00. What if this correlation is .10? Does that mean we have established a relationship? What about correlations of .40 or .70?

Common sense probably tells you that .10 is not going to be big enough, and that .70 probably is big enough. In fact, as is often the case, common sense may let you down here. The fact is that in some cases .10 may be big enough and in other cases .70 may *not* be big enough. The precise answer to this question is generally provided by tests of **statistical significance**.

statistical significance A numerical index of the probability that a relationship detected between two variables could be explained by luck or chance.

A relationship is said to be statistically significant when there is a very small probability (often set at 5 percent, or 1 in 20) that a relationship that size could be attained through chance alone. For example, you know already that dice tossing generates a random set of numbers. You should also be aware now that random numbers do not correlate well with anything, including other sets of random numbers. Yet if you were to toss dice ten times today and ten times tomorrow and then calculate the correlation, you would find that it was not .00 exactly.

FIGURE 3-3

Plots Depicting Various Levels of Correlation between Variables

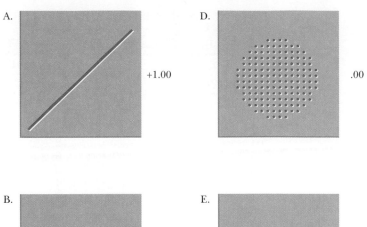

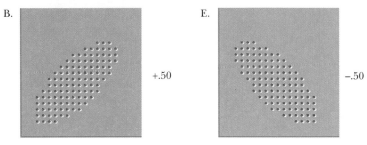

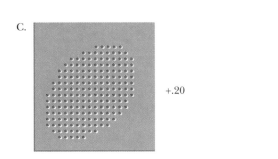

TABLE 3-3
Absence and Age Data at Two Hypothetical Plants

EMPLOYEE	PLANT A (DAY CARE)		PLANT B (NO DAY CARE)	
	No. of Absences	Age	No. of Absences	Age
01	10	27	12	27
02	11	31	11	34
03	8	30	13	31
04	11	26	8	25
05	3	40	16	33
06	4	61	14	35
07	3	52	10	25
08	2	47	4	40
09	1	46	2	52
10	5	41	3	46
Average	5.8	40.1	9.3	34.6

Rather, it would probably be some small number like .02, .11 or −.13 just by chance alone. In fact, if you were to try this experiment for 100 days you would get 100 correlations that, though they would have a mean of zero, would not all be zero.

Of these 100 correlations, how many of them would be as large as .10? The answer is many of them—many more than 5 percent. Many of them would also be as large as .40, and again, more than 5 percent. On the other hand, few and less than 5 percent would be as large as .70. Thus one would conclude that the .70 is a statistically significant correlation but that the .10 and .40 are not. So far, common sense is performing well; statistical significance is a function of the size of the relationship.

There is one additional consideration beyond the size of the relationship that is critical to statistical significance, however, and that is *sample size*. If instead of performing our 100–trial experiment by tossing the dice ten times each day we tossed the dice ten thousand times each day we would observe quite a different set of correlations. Now almost all of the correlations would be .00. Few would be as large as .10, and none would be as large as .40 or .70. With this many tosses, all the chance elements that went into the previous nonzero correlations would be canceled out over the ten thousand trials in a way that could not happen in just ten tosses. Thus here even a correlation as small as .10 would be statistically significant. Table 3-4 shows the size of the correlation needed to achieve statistical significance for various sample sizes. We have already shown that .10 is large enough for a sample of 10,000. One thing this table shows is that .70 is not large enough if the sample is only 5. The moral of this story is that it is hard to detect statistically significant relationships when sample sizes are small, and this makes it hard to establish covariation in certain kinds of contexts. We have used a small sample in our day-care example to make it easier to present some basic concepts. Real experiments with this small number of subjects, however, are generally uninformative.

We must stress that both covariation and temporal precedence must be shown to infer cause—one without the other is insufficient. For example, suppose data on "supervisors' consideration for employees" were collected at Plants A and B at the *same time* that the data on absenteeism were collected. We might very well find a negative correlation between consideration and absenteeism and be tempted to conclude that lack of consideration on the part of supervisors causes high absenteeism. Here we have covariation but not temporal precedence. Under these conditions, we cannot conclude that lack of consideration caused high absenteeism; for all we know, the high rates of absenteeism could have caused supervisors to be less considerate. In general, when all data are collected at the same time, it is virtually impossible to establish causation. About all one can do under these circumstances is establish covariation.

T A B L E 3-4
Magnitude of Correlation Needed to Achieve Statistical Significance

NUMBER OF SUBJECTS	CORRELATION NEEDED
5	.75
10	.58
20	.42
40	.30
100	.19

Eliminating Alternative Explanations. Once we have established both covariation and temporal precedence, it would seem that we are only one step away from establishing that something actually caused something else. Unfortunately, Mill's third criterion for establishing cause, the *elimination of alternative explanations*, is more like "one giant leap" than like "one small step." In our continuing example, if we are to infer that providing day care caused lower absenteeism, we must also show that there was not some other factor that actually caused the low rates of absenteeism. Most real-world situations are so complex, however, that it is often very difficult to rule out other possible explanations for the results one obtains. Indeed, this one problem, more than any other, is what makes it so much more difficult to conduct research in the social sciences than in the physical sciences. In the physical sciences, experimenters can use things like lead shields and vacuum chambers to protect the variables they are examining from outside influences.

This kind of tight control is harder to achieve in social science research, and indeed, some alternative explanations are so common that they are given special names. For example, the **selection threat** is the danger that we may claim that A caused B because of mean differences between groups when what really happened was that the groups were not the same to begin with.[17] Returning to our continuing example, if we had only the data on absenteeism in the two plants (the data in Table 3-1), because of the lower mean rate of absenteeism in the plant with day care we might have concluded that providing the day care caused the lower absenteeism. We have additional data, however, that show that age was negatively related to absenteeism, and it happens that workers in Plant A are older than those in Plant B. In fact, if we were to control for age by comparing only workers who were the same age (e.g., in the 35–65 range), we would find that for people in the same age groups there were no differences in absenteeism between the plants. Thus because the two groups selected for study were not the same to begin with, it would have been incorrect to conclude that providing day care led to low absenteeism. In fact, that was not the case at all. Rather, older workers are absent less often; the workers in Plant A are older than those in Plant B; and therefore the difference in absenteeism across the plants is apparently not due to the day care but to age.

At this point you may be saying "So what—what difference does it make?" It makes a huge difference if based on your incorrect judgment as to what caused what, your company invested a lot of money in providing day-care facilities on a corporationwide basis. This large investment would be based on your conclusion that day care would pay for itself through lower absenteeism. But because day care was actually irrelevant to absenteeism, this investment would be completely lost, and many people would be left wondering what happened.

The selection threat will be a problem any time you are comparing two groups that differed from each other even before you started out. Any time you compare two groups you are subject also to the **mortality threat**. In this situation, the groups may be comparable at the start, but because over time different kinds of people may leave each group, at the end the groups are no longer comparable. Suppose, for example, that you were on the staff of a college that wanted to set up a program to improve the chances that on graduation, undergraduate business majors would be accepted into the country's top MBA programs. You create two groups that are equal from the outset in terms of "commitment to pursue the MBA degree" and put one group of 50 students into the proposed program but do nothing with the other group of 50 students. Finally, the program that you and your colleagues devise is a long and difficult one that includes several advanced courses and requires students to write many term papers and to give a number of oral presentations.

selection threat A threat to validity created when experimental and control groups differ from each other before an experimental manipulation.

mortality threat A threat to validity created when subjects who drop out of an experimental group differ on some significant characteristic or characteristics from those who drop out of the control group.

---

[17] T. D. Cook and D. T. Campbell, *Quasi-Experimentation: Design Analysis Issues for Field Settings* (Chicago: Rand McNally, 1979), p. 53.

You might very well find that because of the difficulty of the program, only 25 of the original 50 students actually complete it. If you were then to compare these 25 to the original, control group of 50 students who did not enter the program, you would probably find that those who completed the program were more frequently admitted to the best graduate schools than those who were in the control group. However, you would be incorrect to assume that it was the program that was the cause. If the 25 students who dropped out of the program were low in "commitment to pursue the MBA degree," the experimental and control groups were not equal in the end, because only those high in commitment remained in the experimental group, while people of high, medium, and low commitment remained in the control group.

history threat A threat to validity created when some important variable other than the one manipulated experimentally changes during an experiment.

The **history threat** is common in before-and-after studies. In this situation, the real cause is not the change you made but something else that happened at the same time. Returning to our old example, what if we had no data from Plant B and simply compared the mean number of absences for Plant A *before* day care with the mean number of absences *after* day-care (see Table 3-2)? We might see a lower average rate of absenteeism after we put in a day-care center than before and be tempted to infer that the center caused lower absenteeism. Accordingly, we might recommend that the program be extended to all other plants in the corporation, despite its high cost.

Suppose, however, that we obtained the "before" measure during the summer months and the "after" measure during the winter. It's possible that people find more reasons to be absent in the summer than in the winter; thus it could be the weather rather than the day-care center that caused the difference in absenteeism rates. Again, if we were to extend the day-care program throughout the corporation, we would find that it would not reduce absenteeism and would be left wondering why.

instrumentation threat A threat to validity created by artificial changes in the measurement device used to assess an experimental effect.

The history threat will be a problem any time you make before and after comparisons in the absence of a control group. Another common threat in this situation, the **instrumentation threat**, is the danger that a change from before to after will reflect not what you did but a change in the measurement instrument itself. For example, assume that you are the manager of a real estate sales agency that in 1972 initiated a strategy of advertising on television. You notice that sales volume in terms of absolute dollars increases steadily for the next three years. In 1975, though, television advertising prices get too high, and you switch to advertising in newspapers. You then notice that sales volume in terms of absolute dollars decreases steadily for the next two years. Detecting a pattern, in 1977 you reinstate television advertising and are happy to find that sales volume increases steadily for the next three years.

Who among us would not be tempted, given this experience, to conclude that television advertising causes increased sales in the real estate industry? We could all be wrong, however. Figure 3-4 shows the Consumer Price Index (CPI) for the years 1972 to 1980. The CPI is a measure of inflation, that is, the relative value of the U.S. dollar. You can see that the value of the dollar itself changes from one year to the next. For this reason, sales volume measured in dollars may change despite unchanging levels of real estate sales. Thus it could be that the form of advertising has no impact whatsoever on real estate sales and that the changing value of our measure of it (which is based on dollars) led us to the wrong inference.

Designing Observations to Infer Cause

Earlier we noted that obtaining good data is an issue not only of how but of when. Both the timing and the frequency of data collection affect our ability to

FIGURE 3-4

Changes in Inflation Over Time

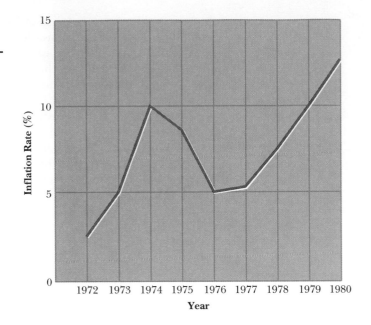

make causal interpretations. Deciding on the timing of measurement is a large part of research design.

Faulty Designs. Consider the two *faulty designs* shown in Figure 3-5. In the One Group Before-After design (Fig 3-5A), data are collected both before and after some event or treatment. If the after score ($CD2$) is different from the before score ($CD1$), it is assumed that the treatment (represented by Δ) caused the difference. The reason this is a faulty design is that both the history threat and the instrumentation threat are possible alternative explanations for the results. If in our day-care example, for instance, we collected data from only one plant, once in the summer and once in the winter, we would be using this type of faulty design. Were this the case, we would be open to the two threats.

FIGURE 3-5

Two Faulty Research Designs

A. One Group Before-After

CD_1	Δ	CD_2
Collect data at Time 1	Change situation	Collect data at Time 2

B. After Only With Unequal Groups

Change situation for A		Collect data from A
Δ		CD_A
		CD_B
Do Not change situation for B		Collect data from B

70

In the After Only with Unequal Groups design (Fig. 3-5B), data are collected from two different groups, one of which receives some experimental treatment while the other does not. The reason this design is faulty is that we do not know that the groups were equal before the treatment or during the treatment, and thus both the selection and mortality threats are alternative explanations for the results. If in our day-care example, we collected data from both Plant A and Plant B without making sure that the people in those plants were similar (e.g., were the same age on average), we would have this kind of faulty design. Our research design would thus be subject to the two threats to validity.

Improved Designs. There are several ways to design studies that can help eliminate some of these threats. Let's take the One Group Before-After design, where our major threats are history and instrumentation. Here we are somewhat better off if we add a control group, turning the design into the Two Group Before-After design shown in Figure 3-6A. This design allows us to test whether the two groups were equal to begin with by comparing CD_{1A} with CD_{1B}. That is, in our day-care example, was the rate of absenteeism in Plants A and B similar before the treatment—the day-care center—was put in place? This design also allows us to test whether some historical factor other than the treatment could have caused the results. That is, if the real cause was time of the year (summer versus winter), we could expect a decrease in absenteeism in Plant B as we moved from Time 1 to Time 2, even though no day-care center was established there.

The Two Group After-Only with Randomization model shown in Figure 3-6B is an even better design. It is just like the one shown in Figure 3-5B with one major exception: subjects are randomly assigned to groups. **Random assignment** of subjects to conditions means that each person has an equal chance of being placed in either the experimental or control group. This random arrangement can be achieved by pulling names out of a hat, flipping coins, tossing dice or using a random numbers table from a book on statistics. For example,

random assignment A method of increasing the validity of a study by ensuring that each subject has an equal probability of being assigned to any one experimental condition. Random assignment eliminates the *selection threat*.

F I G U R E 3-6
Two Improved Research Designs

A. Two Group Before-After

Collect data from Group A at Time 1	Change situation for A	Collect data from at Time 2
CD_{1A} CD_{1B}	Δ	CD_{2A} CD_{2B}
Collect data from Group B at Time 1	Do not change situation for B	Collect data from B at Time 2

B. Two Group After Only   With Randomization

Randomly assign subjects to Groups A and B	Change situation for Group A	Collect data from Group A
R	Δ	CD_A CD_B
	Do not change situation for Group B	Collect data from Group B

in our day-care study, if at the outset we could simply have assembled the twenty workers at the two plants and then tossed a coin to see who would go to which plant, the odds are that when we were finished the two resulting groups would have been equal in age, that is, each group would have had roughly the same number of people of a given age.

In fact, the real value of randomization is that it not only equates groups on factors (like age) that we expect to influence our results, but it equates groups on virtually all factors. Thus in our day-care study, if we randomized the groups at the outset, we could be fairly confident that they would be equated not only on age but on other things, such as height and weight. You might not think that a person's height or weight would relate to absenteeism, but some research actually has found a relationship between absenteeism and weight.[18] Even if we were unaware of this relationship when we started the day-care study, it is nice to know that randomization solved a potential problem for us. Because of randomization's ability to rule out both anticipated and unanticipated selection threats, one should randomly assign subjects to treatments whenever possible.

Because randomization is not always possible, we often need other tools to rule out selection threats. For example, suppose that when we start our day-care experiment we know that workers at the two plants are not evenly distributed in terms of age, and we also know that age affects absenteeism. In the real world, we could not randomly move people from plant to plant; we would have to work with existing groups.

What, then, can we do to rule out age as the alternative explanation for our results? We have several choices. First, we could use *homogeneous groups*, that is, groups that do not differ on age. For example, we might compare absenteeism in the two plants but only among workers in the 25–35-year-old bracket. Thus, as you can see from Table 3-3, we would compare Subjects 1, 2, 3, and 4 in Plant A with Subjects 1, 2, 3, 4, 5, 6, and 7 in Plant B. With this sample, if we still found lower absenteeism in Plant A than in Plant B, we could not attribute the difference to age because all subjects were roughly the same age.

We could also equate groups by *matching subjects*. For example, we might use only the subjects in Plant A for whom there are corresponding subjects in Plant B, or subjects who are within two years of each other in age. Thus, looking again at Table 3-3, we could match subjects 1, 3, 5, 7, and 9 in Plant A with Subjects 1, 4, 8, 9, and 10 in Plant B. Again, if we found that absenteeism was lower in one plant than another we could not attribute this result to age because we equated the groups on this factor.

Finally, we could also *build the threat into the design*. By this we mean that we could simply treat age as another possible factor affecting rate of absenteeism and examine its effect at the same time that we examine the effect of day care. One advantage of building alternative explanations into your design is that it allows you to test for **interactions**. An interaction exists when the relationship between the treatment (e.g., the day-care center) and the outcome (e.g., absenteeism) depends upon some other variable (e.g., age). Figure 3-7 shows what we might find if we built the alternative explanation of age into our day-care study. As you can see, among the younger group day care does lower absenteeism somewhat, but among the older group it has no effect at all. Thus the relation between day care and absenteeism depends on the factor of age. Day care lowers absenteeism among younger workers who are likely to have young children but not among older workers, whose children are grown.

At this point you can see how many factors must be considered in designing studies that allow us to infer causality. Clearly the more variables we can control

interaction An experimental outcome in which the relationship between two variables changes depending on the presence or absence of some third variable.

[18] K. R. Parkes, "Relative Weight, Smoking and Mental Health as Predictors of Sickness and Absence from Work," *Journal of Applied Psychology* 72 (1987), 275–87.

FIGURE 3-7

The Effect of Age and Day-Care
Facilities on Absenteeism

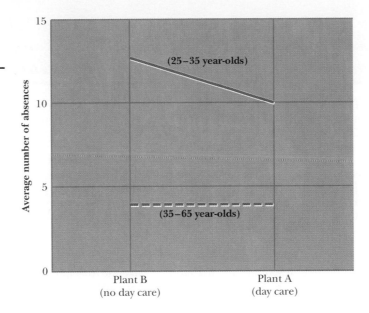

the tighter our research design and the more likely it is that our results will be significant. As the "Management Issues" box shows, however, the best designed studies sometimes manipulate people in ways that are open to attack on ethical grounds.

GENERALIZING RESEARCH RESULTS

Research is usually conducted with one sample, in one setting, across one time period. Often, however, we wish to know whether the results obtained in a unique sample-setting-time period would be the same had the study been conducted in some other sample-setting-time period. Such **generalizability** is sometimes of interest when we are conducting research, but it is always of interest when we evaluate research findings to see whether what worked for the investigators can be applied in a real-world setting.

generalizability The degree to which the result of a study conducted in one sample-setting-time configuration can be replicated in other sample-setting-time configurations.

Sample, Setting, and Time

Our day-care example provides a good illustration of how results might not generalize across different samples. Recall that the results of our study eventually showed that day care reduced absenteeism among workers in the 25–35-year-old group but not in the older group. An astute manager who studied our results would be unlikely to recommend establishing a day-care center for her company without further investigation, because the data indicate that it lowers absenteeism rates in only one small group of workers.

Suppose, however, that we had used a design where we homogenized our subjects on age (i.e., used only those in the 25–35 bracket). In this case, we would have reported simply that providing day care reduced absenteeism. A manager who read these results and then, based on our experiment, instituted a day-care center in a company where most of the workers were between 35 and 65 years old would find that the results of our work did not generalize to his situation.

MANAGEMENT ISSUES·

Ethical Issues in Organizational Behavior Research

Are hiring decisions based solely on an objective examination of applicants' credentials, or are these decisions biased by the race of the applicant? This is a question of critical importance for both organizations and the larger society. You will not be surprised to find, therefore, that this question has been examined in scientific research.

Let's look at a study in which resumés of non-existent "paper people" were sent to the personnel managers of 240 organizations.* These bogus resumés portrayed the educational attainments and work experiences of two applicants who were exactly the same on every dimension presented in the resumes *except race*. One half of the organizations were randomly selected to receive the resumé describing an African-American job applicant. The other half were sent the resumé describing a white candidate.

The addressees, who were responsible for sending out interview invitations to applicants submitting resumés, were asked to send any correspondence to an address that actually belonged to the research team. The researchers, Newman and Krzystofiak, collected the correspondence and checked to see if black and white candidates with identical resumés had an equal probability of receiving an invitation to interview with the companies in their sample.

This was a well-designed, tightly-controlled study that was well suited to ask the research question posed at the outset of this box. Given that it was a good research design, should we ask any other questions about it? Yes. We now need to ask, was this study ethical?

Consider, first, the personnel managers of the organizations selected for study. These are busy people who have enough work to do without pouring over resumés and sending correspondence to people who do not actually exist. Moreover, the managers did not ask to be in this research study, and in fact were unaware that they were even participating in research. Is this the research equivalent of a crank phone call?

Consider, too, other real applicants for the position in question. Most organizations go through employee selection in steps. First one group of applicants, let's say 10, are invited in for interviews based on their resumes. Perhaps five of these are called back for additional interviews. Finally, one applicant is selected. Suppose the bogus resumé was rated higher than the legitimate resumé of a real person? Then that individual, who otherwise would have obtained an interview, would have been eliminated from further consideration because of the research study.

Does the scientific-social value of this study outweigh its costs to personnel managers? Does the value of the study to the *researcher's career* outweigh its potential negative effects on some *job applicant's career*?

Before you pronounce your verdict consider an additional twist. Newman and Krzystofiak actually told some of the managers that they were part of a study. This allowed the researchers to compare managers who knew they were involved in research with those who did not. The results of this study were striking. African-American applicants were treated either equally or preferentially by managers who were aware of the research but were rated lower by managers who were not aware that they were being studied.

This study highlights some of the intricate issues involved in making decisions about the ethics of organizational research. In general, professional associations of researchers like the Academy of Management or the Society of Industrial/Organizational Psychology strongly recommend that all research subjects give informed consent to participation in research. In the study in question, however, informed consent from all subjects—the personnel managers—could change the "truth" of the findings.

Similar issues arise in studies where subjects know they are involved in research but are deceived as to its true nature. Professional guidelines clearly stipulate that honesty is the best policy when dealing with subjects. It does not seem to make sense that the first step some researchers take in their quest for "truth" is to deceive the very people asked to join in the project. Still, an abundance of sound empirical research shows that subjects who are aware of the exact nature of studies respond differently from subjects who are naive.†

It appears very difficult, if not impossible, to devise hard and fast rules for resolving ethical dilemmas like these. But professional researchers do lean on some general prescriptions. First, deception or lack of informed consent in research should be absolute last resorts. Second, researchers must demonstrate that (a) the problem under study is of critical importance, (b) there is a high probability that without the use of deception the study's validity will be compromised, (c) the subjects are not likely to be emotionally upset nor to sustain any long-term harm when the deception is revealed, (d) the researcher takes responsibility for removing any detrimental side effects of the study, and (e) the researcher fairly compensates the subjects for their time and efforts. Most universities have "Human Subject Committees" who review all faculty research proposals. For researchers not affiliated with academic institutions, however, there may be no such checks and balances.

Do you think the professional guidelines now in place are adequate to ensure the ethical nature of behavioral and social science research? If not, what other rules might be imposed? What if anything can we do about the independent, nonuniversity-affiliated researcher?

---

* J. Newman and F. Krzystofiak, "Self-Reports Versus Unobtrusive Measures: Balancing Method Variance and Ethical Concerns in Employment Discrimination Research," *Journal of Applied Psychology* 64 (1979), 82–85.

† J. H. Resnick and T. Schwartz, "Ethical Standards as an Independent Variable in Psychological Research," *American Psychologist* 28 (1973), 134–39.

This is one of the major drawbacks of making groups homogeneous; it limits one's ability to generalize results across other types of samples.

We may also be concerned about generalizing research results across settings. For example, suppose that the plants in our original study were both located in rural settings. Assume further that it is more difficult to obtain high-quality day care in rural settings than in urban settings. Someone reading our study who manages a plant in an urban area might establish a day-care center in her plant only to find that because child care is not a problem for her workers, the center has no effect on absenteeism. Here again, our results would not generalize to another setting.

Finally, we might also be concerned about whether our results would generalize across time. For example, suppose that we had conducted our study at a time when there was a huge labor shortage; that is, when many more jobs were available than there were people to fill them. At such a time, unemployment rates would be low, both parents might well be working, and many people who might in other circumstances serve as day-care providers would very likely be working at different and perhaps higher-paying jobs. Thus when we conducted our study, there may have been a great demand for day-care services but a small supply. By providing our own day-care services, we solved a major problem for our workers with small children, and this ultimately led to lower absenteeism rates.

Now let's move forward ten years, say, to a time when there is a labor surplus. Unemployment is high, there is a good chance that one parent is not working, and anyone capable of setting up a day-care center is open for business. In this situation, because the demand for day care is small and the supply of day-care services large, company-sponsored day care does not provide a needed service to employees, and so there is no relationship between providing day care and lowering absenteeism. Here our results do not generalize across time.

Facilitating Generalization

You may be wondering if there are any findings that are generalizable given the many factors that might differ from one unique sample-setting-time to another. From a researcher's perspective, can anything be done to increase the ability to generalize? The answer to both of these questions is yes. Technically, one can safely generalize from one sample to another if the original sample of people we study is *randomly selected* from the larger population of people to which we wish to generalize.

As an example of random selection, you may have noticed that in presidential elections the television networks usually declare a winner when less than 10 percent of the actual results are available. Making the wrong call here might be very embarrassing, so why are the networks taking such a big risk? They are not. The key to their success is that when they poll people who have just finished voting, they do so randomly. In this way they ensure that the small percentage of people they poll are by all odds very similar to the larger group of voters. In fact, this is a case in which the researchers are so sure that their results will generalize that they have no fear whatsoever in publicly declaring a winner way in advance of the results, even though there are huge costs associated with being wrong. Just as the ability to generalize to other people can be assured with random selection of subjects, generalizing from one setting or time to another can be assured only if we randomly sample settings and time periods.

Although random selection is the only way to ensure the ability to generalize, from a practical perspective it is often very difficult to achieve. Studies that employ

The research that has been going into the development of the new Globex system, being tested here by Reuters employees, may ultimately lead to major changes in the way traders in the world's futures markets do business. This new electronic trading system and others like it are making it possible to trade around the clock on a worldwide basis. Rapid technological changes like these highlight the issue of generalizability. Will research-based techniques developed for jobs in this century be equally useful in 21st-century jobs? Source: *David Zigas and Gary Weiss with Ted Holden and Richard A. Melcher, "A Trading Floor on Every Screen,"* Business Week, *November 5, 1990.*

random selection are usually huge in scale, requiring a large number of investigators and a great deal of money. More often, in the real world of research, the ability to generalize a finding is achieved not by one big experiment but by many small experiments, using the same measures, in which results are replicated over and over again in a host of different sample-setting-time configurations.[19] For example, in Chapter 7 we will discuss some research results that generalize very well—the repeated finding that high performance is more likely to result from setting specific and difficult goals than from offering vague goals like "do your best."

As we have noted, although generalizing results to other samples-settings-times is always of interest in evaluating research, it is not always interesting to the original researchers. Often research is conducted strictly to test or build theories. Here investigators may be less interested in what *does* happen than in what *can* happen.[20] For example, in Chapter 8, when we discuss stress, we will look at research that shows people can learn to control some of their own physiological processes, such as heart rate and blood pressure, when hooked up to special devices that give them feedback on these processes. One can think of few real-world samples-settings-times that would correspond to the situation in which subjects in this kind of research find themselves. That is not the point of this research, however. Its purpose is to test a theory that states that human beings can voluntarily control supposedly involuntary physiological responses when provided with the right feedback. There is nothing inherent in this theory that suggests it would not work with college sophomores in a laboratory setting at some specific time period. Thus, if the results fail to support the theory, the theory must be either rejected or modified and retested, and the fact that neither subjects, settings, nor times were randomized is completely irrelevant. With this kind of research, the ultimate aim is not to make the laboratory setting more like the real world but to make the real world more like the lab—that is, to change the real world in ways that benefit us all.

LINKING OB SCIENCE AND PRACTICE

Unless you intend to work as a staff member in a research capacity for some organization, you will probably have only a few opportunities to do much real experimentation yourself. As a practicing manager, how-

[19] Cook and Campbell, *Quasi-Experimentation.*
[20] D. G. Mook, "In Defense of External Invalidity," *American Psychologist* 38 (1983), 379–87.

TABLE 3-5
**The Ten Most Influential Journals
in Organizational Behavior**

Micro Organizational behavior
1. *Journal of Applied Psychology*
2. *Organizational Behavior and Human Decision Processes*
3. *Personnel Psychology*
4. *Journal of Vocational Behavior*
5. *Journal of Occupational Psychology*

Macro Organizational behavior
1. *Administrative Science Quarterly*
2. *Academy of Management Journal*
3. *Academy of Management Review*
4. *Human Relations*
5. *Administration and Society*

Source: G. R. Salancik, "An Index of Subgroup Influence in Dependent Networks," *Administrative Science Quarterly 31* (1986), 207–11.

ever, you should know that there is a wealth of research just waiting to be discovered. Table 3-5 provides a list of the major scientific journals that publish theory and research related to topics in this book. These journals are rank ordered, within the categories of micro and macro organizational behavior (see Chapter 1 for a refresher on this distinction), by their influence in the field. A high ranking means that the findings reported in that journal tend to be more widely cited in the organizational sciences than are those in lower ranked journals.

A great deal of the research conducted in this area is performed by people working in university settings. Thus you may also be able to uncover research on the topics that interest you by contacting university faculty who publish a good deal of research on topics related to organizational behavior. Table 3-6 lists universities where OB researchers are particularly interested in micro organi-

TABLE 3-6
Research Productivity: The Top Forty Institutions in Micro Organizational Behavior

1. University of Houston	21. University of Pennsylvania
2. Ohio State University	22. University of South Carolina
3. University of Washington	23. University of Tennessee
4. Pennsylvania State University	24. University of California at Los Angeles (UCLA)
5. Michigan State University	25. Wayne State University
6. University of Illinois (Champaign)	26. Texas Christian University
7. University of Maryland	27. Bowling Green University
8. Purdue University	28. Florida International University
9. University of Georgia	29. Baruch College
10. University of Alberta	30. Colorado State University
11. University of California (Berkeley)	31. New York University
12. University of Kansas	32. Temple University
13. Virginia Polytechnic Institute	33. Old Dominion University
14. Iowa State University	34. Kansas State University
15. University of Michigan	35. University of Western Ontario
16. Northwestern University	36. Case Western Reserve
17. University of Minnesota	37. University of Texas (Austin)
18. University of Akron	38. Dartmouth College
19. Illinois State University	39. Flinders University
20. George Washington University	40. Howard University

Source: G. S. Howard, S. E. Maxwell, S. M. Berra, and M. E. Sernitzke, "Institutional Research Productivity in Industrial/ Organization Psychology," *Journal of Applied Psychology 70* (1985), 233–36.

T A B L E 3-7
Research Productivity: The Top 40 Institutions in Macro and Micro Organizational Behavior

1. Harvard University	21. University of California at Los Angeles
2. Columbia University	22. University of Minnesota
3. Massachusetts Institute of Technology	23. Northwestern University
4. University of California (Berkeley)	24. University of Maryland
5. Stanford University	25. Michigan State University
6. New York University	26. Boston University
7. Ohio State University	27. Arizona State University
8. Indiana University at Bloomington	28. University of South Carolina
9. Texas A&M University	29. Carnegie-Mellon University
10. University of Illinois (Champaign)	30. University of Chicago
11. University of Pennsylvania	31. Georgia Institute of Technology
12. Pennsylvania State University	32. University of Georgia
13. University of Houston	33. University of North Carolina
14. University of Michigan (Ann Arbor)	34. University of Pittsburgh
15. University of Washington	35. University of Cincinnati
16. University of Southern California	36. University of Nebraska (Lincoln)
17. Cornell University	37. University of Missouri (Columbia)
18. Purdue University	38. University of Alabama (Birmingham)
19. University of Wisconsin (Madison)	39. Auburn University
20. Virginia Polytechnic Institute	40. University of Illinois (Chicago)

Source: M. J. Stahl, T. L. Leap, and Z. Z. Wei, "Publication of Leading Management Journals as a Measure of Institutional Research Productivity," *Academy of Management Journal 31* (1988), 707–19.

zational behavior; Table 3-7 lists universities where investigators do both micro and macro OB research.

The Scientific and Diagnostic Models

In Chapter 1, we outlined the diagnostic model that we follow in Chapters 4 through 19 of this book. In this chapter, we have described the scientific model, which produced much of the information we discuss in the remaining chapters of this text. The two models can be compared by matching the four stages of the diagnostic model with the four objectives of the scientific method. The first objective of science and the first stage of the diagnostic model match exactly: *description*. In describing a situation, which is the first stage in diagnostic problem solving, it is generally a good idea to use methods of data collection that are reliable, valid, and standardized. In the model's second stage, diagnosis, we are concerned with determining the underlying causes for some situation. Diagnosis corresponds directly with the scientific goal of *understanding*. Here is where theories can be most useful, by separating key factors from irrelevant ones. The third diagnostic stage, *prescription*, corresponds to the scientific objective of *prediction* in that both require us to predict what may happen in the future. Finally, the *action* stage of the diagnostic model corresponds to the scientific goal of *control*: If our prescriptions and predictions are correct, we should be able to manipulate our environment in order to bring about the ends we seek. In implementing our actions, however, we must keep in mind the various threats to our ability to make valid causal inferences and, as far as possible, arrange our observations to eliminate these threats. This is critical, because if we mistakenly assume that a change in some outcome was due to our actions when in reality the change was due to something else, we may try this action again in the future only to find out how wrong we were.

The Scientist-Practitioner Model

We hope that by this point we have convinced you of the need to think about managing organizational behavior from a scientific point of view. Even though you may not actually conduct research yourself, you will find it invaluable to familiarize yourself with the wealth of scientific evidence available on topics that will be crucial to you, your employer, and your employees. Although this research may not provide you with all the answers, it will most assuredly give you something to think about and perhaps provide new slants on old problems. In addition, as a manager, you will be constantly bombarded by people claiming to be able to solve your problems (for a sizeable fee, of course). It is important that you be able to examine their claims with a critical eye, so that you won't be the victim of every fad that comes across your desk. The critical perspective provided from thinking scientifically will make you less likely to fall for this year's "quick fix of the century."

SUMMARY

It is important to generate reliable and valid knowledge in the area of organizational behavior. Traditional ways of ascertaining knowledge, such as rationalism, personal experience and reliance on authorities have many limitations. The advantage of science relative to these more traditional means is its *objectivity*, and science as an enterprise tends to be public, self-correcting and cumulative. The major goals of science are the description, explanation, prediction and control of various phenemona. These goals are achieved through an interplay of *theory* and *data*, whereby ideas contained in theories are expressed in testable *hypotheses*, which are then compared to actual data. The correspondence (or lack thereof) between the hypothesized results and the actual results are then used to verify, refute, or modify the theory. There are many similarities between the scientific method of inquiry and the diagnostic model laid out in Chapter 1.

Good theories are characterized by simplicity, self-consistency, and consistency with known facts, and they should contribute to the objectives of science. To be useful, data for testing theories should be *reliable* and *valid*, and there are many advantages to using established *standardized* measures.

At the core of many theories is the idea of establishing causes. Cause can be inferred only when one establishes *temporal precedence* and *covariation* and when all *alternative explanations* have been eliminated. This last is often the most troublesome aspect of research in the social sciences, and some kinds of threats like *selection, mortality, instrumentation*, and *history threats* are especially problematic. These threats can be partially ameliorated through research designs that use control groups and make these comparable to experimental groups through *randomization, matching* or *homogenization*.

To *generalize* the findings from one study—with a specific sample, in a specific setting, and during a specific time period—to another context it is necessary to randomly select samples, settings, and time periods. This is rarely achieved in the social sciences. However, if over time experimental results have repeatedly been confirmed in different samples and settings and at different times, it may be possible to generalize such findings.

REVIEW QUESTIONS

1. Many theories can be shown to follow a similar pattern. They start out simply, grow increasingly complex as empirical tests on the theory proliferate, and then die out or are replaced by new theories. Look back at the criteria for

a good theory and discuss why this pattern is so common. In your discussion, specify possible conflicts or inconsistencies among the "criteria for a good theory."

2.   Objectivity is one of the hallmarks of scientific inquiry. Yet all scientists can be shown to have their own subjective beliefs and biases surrounding the phenomena they study. Indeed, some scientists are motivated to do their work because of passionate beliefs about these phenomena. Discuss whether this kind of passion is an asset or a liability to the scientist. Discuss further how science can be an objective exercise when everyone who practices it can be shown to have biases. What prevents a passionate scientist from cheating or distorting results in favor of his beliefs?

3.   Experiments in organizations usually involve people other than the experimenters, that is, managers or employees. What are some of the ethical responsibilities of an experimenter with respect to these people? Is it ethical, for example, for an experimenter to use one group of employees as a control group when she strongly suspects that the treatment given to the experimental group will enhance their chances for success, promotion, or satisfaction? If the experimenter is afraid that explaining the nature of the experiment will cause people to act differently than they would otherwise (and hence ruin the experiment), is it ethical for her to deceive them about the study's true purpose?

4.   Philosopher of science Murray S. Davis once remarked that "the truth of a theory has very little to do with its impact." (See his 1978 article, "That's Interesting! Towards a Phenomenology of Sociology and a Sociology of Phenomenology," *Philosophy of the Social Sciences* 1, 309–44.) History, according to Davis, shows that the impact of a theory depends more on how interesting the theory is perceived to be by practitioners and scientists than on how much truth it holds. We listed criteria for good theories in this chapter; list what you think are criteria for "interesting" theories. Where do these two lists seem to conflict most, and what can be done by scientists and the practitioners they serve to generate theories that are both interesting and truthful?

C H A P T E R 4

ABILITY AND PERSONALITY

When Toyota Motor Corporation decided to establish manufacturing operations in the United States, it paid careful attention to individual differences in hiring its workers. With the slogan, "Investing in the individual," it set about building good will among Americans through its support of diverse aspects of the U.S. culture and society. The Toyota USA Foundation granted some $87,000 to the Chesapeake Bay Foundation to support student trips and teacher training in the biology and environment of the Bay watershed. Toyota has also "adopted" a high school in Torrance, California, and will support its students and programs by donating funds to the school and by encouraging company employees to volunteer their time in tutoring students and giving them career guidance.

Sources: Toyota Motor Corporation and Chesapeake Bay Foundation, 1991; Fortune, March 25, 1991.

In 1987, Toyota Motor Corporation became one of the first Japanese-owned firms to open up manufacturing operations in the United States. Many American businesses were amazed by the intensity of the selection procedures used by Toyota in staffing their new plant in Lexington, Kentucky. Applicants for even the lowest paying job on the shop floor went through a minimum of 14 hours of assessment procedures. Other applicants endured over 25 hours of testing for individual differences. William Osos, a regional official for the United Auto Workers, contrasted this procedure with his own experience in applying for work at an American-owned plant, where "you wrote down what work you had done before, and that was the end of it. If you knew somebody who worked in the plant and put in a good word for you that helped."[1]

DIAGNOSTIC ISSUES

In Chapter 1, when we introduced the diagnostic model we said we would begin each core chapter by reintroducing this model and by showing you how the questions it generates can help you to learn the material in the chapter. Like the sections that open all the other chapters, this first one raises questions that arise out of each of the model's stages. When you finish the chapter, you will be able not only to answer these questions but to use the more detailed "Diagnostic Questions" at the end of the chapter to analyze the book's cases and solve real problems on the job.

What sorts of questions about human abilities and personality characteristics does our diagnostic model lead us to raise? To begin with, How can we *describe* the major dimensions of human abilities? How do these abilities affect performance on various tasks? What are some of the important differences between people in terms of mental ability? How do these differences relate to performance on particular tasks? How can we *diagnose* the effects on a situation of people's varying social traits? Can a person's traits change because of the job she holds? Why are there sometimes big differences between a person's maximum performance level and the level she typically displays? How can we *prescribe* who should be assigned tasks that must be learned very quickly? How can we predict who will improve on the job and who will not? Can we prescribe what sorts of jobs different people are best suited for on the basis of measures of their personality characteristics? Finally, what *actions* can we take to measure human abilities and personality characteristics most effectively? How can we use information on these qualities to improve performance and enhance satisfaction?

THE MIRROR IMAGE FALLACY

Ralph Waldo Emerson once wrote that "the wise man shows his wisdom in separation, in gradation, and his scale of creatures and of merits is as wide as nature. . . . The foolish have no range in their scale, but suppose that every man is as every other man."

This passage gets to the heart of our chapter. Although most of us would readily acknowledge the truth of Emerson's statement, many people have a persistent tendency to assume that people are basically alike. This belief that the whole world is "just like me," called the **mirror image fallacy**, is attractive because

mirror image fallacy The false belief that all people are alike or that others share one's own abilities, beliefs, motives, or predispositions.

---

[1] R. Koenig, "Toyota Takes Pains and Time, Filling Jobs at Its Kentucky Plant," *The Wall Street Journal*, December 1, 1987, p. 21.

Attention to individual differences may become more and more important as companies around the world become increasingly globalized. Fitting into a particular corporate culture in one's own society is often hard enough (see Chapter 18). Succeeding in an organizational culture that is based on the customs of a different country can be twice as difficult. According to William Ahern (left), a vice president at Mitsui Taiyo Kobe Bank in New York City, American employees of Japanese firms must be culturally aware and "keep their egos in check." Scott Whitlock, executive vice president of American Honda Motors agrees. Honda is a company for team players, he says, one where people achieve with others, not by themselves.
Source: *"Managing,"* Fortune, *December 3, 1990.*

it makes the world seem much easier to manage. For example, if an owner of a firm believes that everyone in her company shares her abilities, interests, beliefs, and values, she will consider it an easy task to organize and encourage her employees to pursue a common goal. Because the mirror image fallacy *is* a fallacy, however, she will soon find that the myriad differences among the people she employs will make her task far from easy.

As we will see, when the mirror image belief is allowed expression in the real world of management it can become very dangerous. First and foremost, it often leads people to make incorrect diagnoses, attributing to other factors many problems that are in fact due to individual differences. For example, if two people do not seem to be getting along, a manager who holds the mirror image belief may assume that some misperception or miscommunication has caused the problem and that clearing the communication channels will solve the problem. Often, however, each person in a conflict has a very clear picture of the other's position but simply has different values and interests. Just making it easier for two such people to communicate would have little problem-solving potential, and could even inflame matters. For example, in 1988, when Geraldo Rivera tried to bring members of the Congress of Racial Equality together with the Skinheads of the National Resistance and other extremist groups, a melee ensured in which Rivera's nose was broken.

Suppose a highly competent engineer with degrees from several of the best engineering schools is promoted to a position that requires him to manage engineers with somewhat less aptitude and education. If the managing engineer holds the mirror image fallacy, he may attribute poor performance among his subordinates to a lack of either effort or motivation rather than to a lack of ability (a problem he personally never faced). As a result, he might promise subordinates large raises for improving the quality of their work or threaten them with termination. These methods might well increase subordinates' desire to improve, but if their problems stem from lack of ability rather than lack of effort the manager's efforts will meet with failure.

The mirror image fallacy can also cause a failure to anticipate problems. The people responsible for the security of the marine barracks in Lebanon that was hit by a devastating terrorist bomb in 1983 plainly admitted that there was no provision for defending against that type of attack. The thought of such a suicidal mission was so utterly foreign to Western decisionmakers that it was unforeseen.

Foreign competition has heightened this need to anticipate problems. Clearly, Toyota executives are not assuming that all American workers are alike or that American workers are like Japanese workers. To realize the full potential of a labor force, managers must ensure that the right people are in the right places. The person who is best for one job will not necessarily be best for another. The increasing complexity of the world around us has forced businesses to make a greater effort to assess the unique abilities and personality characteristics needed to fill today's specialized jobs. Needless to say, matching the right people to the right jobs takes time, and it is difficult for firms that don't spend this time to compete with firms that do. Competition becomes extremely keen when firms share the same labor pool; some firms take the best employees, and others must make do with what's left.

SELECTION AND PLACEMENT

personnel selection The process by which an organization decides who will and who will not be allowed to work for an organization.

Organizations that take advantage of individual differences do so through either selection or placement. **Selection** is the process of choosing some applicants and rejecting others. It controls individual differences by

84

personnel placement The process by which an organization assigns new employees to specific jobs.

determining who enters the organization. **Placement** is the process of assigning individuals who have been selected to jobs. The distinction between these two processes is quite important. First, organizations in tight labor markets—that is, where there are few applicants for many positions—may not be able to reject many applicants. The only way to take advantage of individual differences, then, is through placement opportunities. The "baby bust" of the early 1970s has led experts to predict that this kind of tight labor market will confront most firms in the year 2000.

Second, although selection decisions provide competitive advantages to individual companies, accurate selection does not necessarily help the economy as a whole. That is, unless there is widespread unemployment, even the poorest applicants will be selected by some firm, and their lack of productivity will be reflected in the general economy. On the other hand, if effective placement would allow these individuals to be placed in jobs they could do well, the overall health of the economy would improve.[2]

HUMAN ABILITIES

Differences among individuals have been recognized for many thousands of years. But the systematic study of such variation and its application to matters of social concern did not begin until the nineteenth century.

Darwin and Galton

The study of individual differences can be traced directly to the work of the English naturalist Charles Darwin (1809–1882). Darwin's theory of evolution, which suggested that human beings are animals, legitimized the scientific study of the human being. Before Darwin, human beings were thought of as qualitatively different from animals and thus as subject to philosophic and theologic, but not scientific, inquiry.

In addition, Darwin's theory of natural selection and his notion of the "survival of the fittest" illustrated that even small, within-species differences can have important implications. For example, Darwin showed that although to the casual observer one finch may look just like any other, specific characteristics of different varieties of finch serve to adapt these birds to particular environments. As a result, when Darwin switched the customary environments of finches with long, curved bills (for eating out of flowers) and finches with short, stout bills (for eating off the hard ground), the mismatched birds died rapidly.

Expanding on Darwin's work, Sir Francis Galton (1822–1911) proposed that there might be important within-species differences in human beings that could have major implications for survival. Galton devoted his life to measuring and studying these differences, giving particular attention to their possible genetic origin. At the time that he conducted his research, the then new field of psychology was focusing largely on the mental makeup of the "average person." Galton's work ensured that the new area of study would not ignore individual differences.

physical ability Ability to perform a task involving body movement, strength, endurance, dexterity, force, or speed.

Physical and Psychomotor Abilities

Nonmental tests of individual differences are usually of two types.[3] One type measures general **physical abilities**, such as the ability to lift a weight. The other

---

[2] G. F. Dreher and P. R. Sackett, *Perspectives on Employee Status and Selection* (Homewood, Ill.: Irwin, 1984), p. 23.

[3] M. D. Dunnette, "Aptitudes, Abilities, and Skills" in *Handbook of Industrial and Organizational Psychology*, ed. Dunnette (Chicago: Rand McNally, 1976).

TABLE 4-1
Fleishman's Major Physical Abilities

1. Static strength	Maximizes force that can be exerted against external objects (e.g., lifting weights).
2. Dynamic strength	Muscular endurance in exerting force continuously or repeatedly (e.g., pull-ups).
3. Explosive strength	Ability to mobilize energy effectively in bursts (e.g., standing broad jump).
4. Trunk strength	Dynamic strength limited to leg muscles (e.g., leg lifts).
5. Dynamic flexibility	Ability to stretch trunk and muscles (e.g., twist-and-touch floor test).
6. Gross body coordination	Ability to coordinate action of several parts of the body while the body is in motion (e.g., jump rope test).
7. Gross body equilibrium	Ability to maintain balance (e.g., walking a balance beam).
8. Stamina	Capacity to sustain maximum effect requiring cardiovascular exertion (e.g., a one-mile run).

Source: E. A. Fleishman, *The Structure and Measurement of Physical Fitness* (Englewood Cliffs, N.J.: Prentice-Hall, 1964). pp. 31–42.

psychomotor ability Ability to perform a task involving coordination between physical and mental functions.

type assesses **psychomotor abilities**, or abilities that require the precise coordination of sensory information, such as sight or sound, with physical movements, such as threading a needle. Edwin Fleishman, a leading researcher in the area of human abilities, has conducted a number of studies of physical and psychomotor abilities and has been able to reduce a long list to 17 primary dimensions (see Tables 4-1 and 4-2).

Although a thorough analysis of a job is needed to determine whether it requires a particular physical capacity, in general, the abilities listed in Table 4-1 are most frequently needed in jobs of three types: the protective services, such as municipal police, fire, and prison-corrections departments; construction and other physically demanding industries; and professional athletics.

If police, fire, or correctional personnel lack the necessary physical abilities, they or the persons they seek to protect may be injured. Testing for the kinds of physical abilities listed in Table 4-1 is much more common now than in the past, when height and weight criteria substituted for specific abilities. Because height and weight measures are considered to discriminate unfairly against women and the members of some minority groups they are rarely used today.

Physical ability tests are also used to select employees for work such as construction, where jobs require physical strength and agility. Such tests can predict not only job performance but job-related injuries. For example, research by Chaffin has shown that the incidence of lower-back injury can be predicted by tests of physical strength.[4] This is a significant finding, since back-related disability claims have been rising at 14 times the rate of the population over the last ten years. Because employers are increasingly picking up the bill for employees' medical costs (and because lower-back pain is such a widespread and recurring affliction), tests that allow one to predict health problems for a job applicant are extremely cost effective. General Dynamics Corporation's electric boat unit has actually developed specific physical examinations designed to screen out individuals at risk for back-pain problems.

[4] D. B. Chaffin, "Human Strength Capability and Low Back Pain," *Journal of Occupational Medicine* 16 (1974), 248–54.

TABLE 4-2
Fleishman's Major Psychomotor Abilities

1. **Control precision**	Tasks requiring finely controlled muscular adjustments (e.g., moving a lever to a precise setting).
2. **Multi-limb coordination**	The ability to coordinate the movements of limbs simultaneously (e.g., packing a box with both hands).
3. **Response orientation**	The ability to make correct and accurate movements in relation to a stimulus under highly accelerated conditions (e.g., reaching and flicking a switch when a warning horn sounds).
4. **Reaction time**	The speed of a person's response when a stimulus appears (e.g., pressing a key in response to a bell).
5. **Speed of arm movement**	The speed of gross arm movements where accuracy is not required (e.g., gathering trash and throwing it into a large pile).
6. **Rate control**	The ability to make continuous motor adjustments relative to a moving target that changes in speed and direction (e.g., holding a rod on a moving rotor).
7. **Manual dexterity**	Skillful arm and hand movements in handling rather large objects under speeded conditions (e.g., rapidly placing blocks of different shapes into the correct holes of a special board).
8. **Finger dexterity**	Skillful manipulations of small objects with the fingers (e.g., attaching nuts and bolts).
9. **Arm-hand steadiness**	The ability to make precise arm-hand positioning movements that do not require strength (e.g., threading a needle).

Source: E. A. Fleishman, *The Structure and Measurement of Physical Fitness* (Englewood Cliffs, N.J.: Prentice-Hall, 1964). pp. 67–78.

Finally, tests of physical and motor abilities are used in professional athletics, where performance is highly dependent on physical characteristics. In this field of work, people over a certain age may have difficulty developing some of the necessary skills. Moreover, when training is provided, the gap between individuals who differ in some physical ability tends to get even larger.[5] Highly standardized tests (e.g., the 40-yard dash) are used in these areas, because it is often necessary to compare individuals from widely different geographic regions.

The motor ability tests shown in Table 4-2 have been most useful for predicting success in three broad types of occupation: vehicle operators (e.g., truck drivers, fork-lift operators); industrial employees (e.g., assembly-line workers, packagers); and people engaged in crafts and trades (e.g., carpenters, plumbers, electricians, mechanics).[6]

Cognitive Abilities

Binet and Spearman. Although Galton referred to his tests as mental tests, psychologists today classify most of his measurements under physical or pyschomotor abilities. It was actually Alfred Binet (1857–1911) who in 1905 created the first test of intelligence, or cognitive ability. Binet's first test attempted to distinguish between poor students who could benefit from remedial education and poor

---

[5] I. L. Goldstein, *Training: Program Development and Evaluation* (Belmont, Calif.: Brooks, Cole, 1986), p. 20.
[6] E. E. Ghiselli, *The Validity of Occupational Aptitude Tests* (New York: John Wiley, 1966), p. 38.

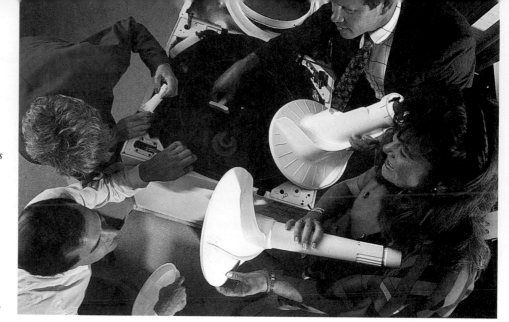

In the service industry, the need to meet an increasing variety of customer needs has heightened job complexity and led companies to alter their employee selection programs. In the past, answering telephone inquiries was not considered that demanding a job, but today companies are raising their requirements for these positions. For example, to staff its highly regarded telephone answer center, General Electric now recruits college graduates with good general cognitive ability, interpersonal skills, and sales experience. The company puts the recruits through six weeks of training in which they learn precisely how GE's machines function. Taking apart a washing machine and putting it back together can help a GE Answer Center phone representative explain to a caller how to operate the appliance or to make minor repairs. Source: "Selling," Fortune, December 5, 1990, pp. 43–44.

students who could not. Today, virtually all students in higher education have taken tests of cognitive ability, and many of these modern tests bear a close resemblance to Binet's initial effort. Tests of cognitive ability are also used increasingly in the business sector, as industries search for people who can learn quickly and who can solve complex problems.

Whereas Binet's work was highly practical, the British psychologist Charles Spearman (1863–1945) took a more scholarly approach, submitting many of the things that Binet took for granted to scientific test. For example, Binet assumed that intelligence was one dimensional, that is, that all his tests and items measured the same thing. As a result, Binet always reported intelligence test results in the form of one score.

Spearman set out to test this presumption of unidimensionality, and after years of collecting data and building mathematical models he concluded that all tests of intelligence were made up of two dimensions. The first, a generalized intelligence, he called "g"; the second was a unique dimension associated with each test. Today it is widely accepted that intellectual ability is multifaceted. We are more likely to characterize someone as "good with words, but bad with numbers," than "of average intelligence." This kind of distinction is especially critical in today's business climate, where increasing specialization demands a high level of one or two specific skills for most jobs rather than an average level of a broad set of abilities.

general cognitive ability The totality of an individual's mental capacity, summing across specific mental abilities such as verbal comprehension, quantitative aptitude, reasoning ability, and deductive ability.

General Cognitive Ability. Although mental abilities are not one dimensional, we do generally find positive relationships among people's performance on different kinds of mental tests. Thus scores across different types of tests are often summed and treated as an index of general intelligence. Specialists often substitute the term **general cognitive ability** for *intelligence* because the former term is more precise and because it conjures up less controversy over such issues as the role of genetic factors in mental ability. The term *intelligence* is used imprecisely in the lay community where the high social value placed on it complicates discussions of things like age, sex, and racial differences.

Specific Dimensions of Cognitive Ability. Although there is a common core among the many different kinds of mental tests, several dimensions of mental ability are sufficiently unique that they are worth assessing in their own right.

Moreover, because certain specific jobs require more of one type of mental ability than others, we may want to select out data on this particular ability from information on less relevant aspects of mental ability.

According to Jum Nunnally, seven primary dimensions of cognitive, or mental, ability stand out in terms of both their generality and their usefulness as predictors of performance in the real world. Figure 4-1 displays some sample test items that assess each of these dimensions.

The first two dimensions illustrated in the figure are probably the most familiar to you. **Verbal ability** reflects the degree to which a person can understand and use written and spoken language. **Quantitative ability** reflects the person's ability to perform all kinds of arithmetic problems. This includes not only the four major functions of addition, subtraction, multiplication, and division but square root, rounding procedures, and the multiplication of positive and negative values. Although a high-school education should ensure that job applicants will have at least minimal levels of these skills, many employers who engage in testing find this is not always the case. For example, Prudential Life Insurance found that many of the applicants they tested, although they held high-school diplomas, were performing at the third-grade level in math and reading proficiency. Because these deficiencies were found disproportionately within various minority groups, and because Prudential could hardly afford to hire people with such minimal skills, Prudential went into the business of remedial education. In a precedent-setting agreement with the U.S. Department of Labor, the company spent $3 million to offer 260 hours of classroom training to some of the people it had rejected for jobs. Although extravagantly funded, the goal of this program was quite modest: to bring people who had completed the twelfth grade up to ninth-grade level of competency in math and reading.[7]

Different kinds of analytical skills are associated with Nunnally's third and fourth dimensions. **Reasoning ability** is the ability to invent solutions to many different types of problems. Although items tapping reasoning sometimes employ numbers, they should not be confused with simple measures of quantitative ability. At the heart of a reasoning problem is the need to invent a solution or grasp a principle, not make computations. **Deductive ability** is the ability to use logic and to evaluate the implication of an argument. This ability also encompasses detecting the relationship between two elements and drawing analogies between them.

Two dimensions of mental ability rely on the interaction between visual ability and mental skills. **Spatial visualization** reflects a person's ability to imagine how an object would look if its position in space were changed. It also reflects the ability to make an accurate determination of the spatial arrangement of objects with respect to one's own body. Such an ability is important, for example, to an airplane pilot, who should be able to detect changes in a plane's position just by looking at changes in the horizon seen through the cockpit window. **Perceptual ability** is the ability to recognize visual details rapidly as well as to recognize similarities and differences between two different objects of perception. Many jobs that require attention to detail, such as that of a copy editor, a quality-control technician, or a clerical worker, demand this sort of skill.

Finally, *memory*, Nunnally's last dimension of mental ability, is the ability to recall material that was mentally processed in the past. Rote memory may be tested with lists like the one described in Figure 4-1. Memory may also be tested by asking a subject to read a paragraph and then answer questions about its content. Visual memory may be tested by asking subjects to recall images or pictures they have viewed.

---

[7] *Time*, "School Days at Prudential High," September 3, 1985, p. 60.

verbal ability A specific type of cognitive ability that deals with the comprehension and use of language.

quantitative ability A specific form of cognitive ability that deals with the understanding and application of mathematical rules and operations.

reasoning ability An individual's capacity to invent solutions to many different types of problems.

deductive ability An individual's capacity to use logic and to evaluate the implications of various arguments.

spatial visualization An individual's capacity to mentally manipulate objects in space and time.

perceptual ability An individual's capacity to quickly and accurately recognize visual details.

FIGURE 4-1

Sample Items that Test Specific Facets of Mental Ability

1. Verbal Ability	Which of the following words means most nearly *the same* as ABERRATION? (a) conception (b) discussion (c) abhorrence (d) deviation (e) humiliation Which of the following words means most nearly *the opposite* of AMICABLE? (a) nauseous (b) unfriendly (c) obscene (d) penetrating (e) fondness
2. Quantitative Ability	Mrs. Jones deposits $700.00 in a bank that pays 3 percent interest per year. How much money will she have at the end of the year? (a) $21.00 (b) $679.00 (c) $702.10 (d) $721.00 (e) $910.00 What is the value of r after it has been decreased by 16 2/3 percent? (a) $1/6\ r$ (b) $1/3\ r$ (c) $5/6\ r$ (d) $6/7\ r$ (e) $7/6\ r$
3. Reasoning Ability	_____ is to prison as Smithsonian is to _____ (a) Alcatraz – Museum (b) Guard – Washington, D. C. (c) Warden – Warhol (d) Criminal – Washinton D.C. (e) Guard – Museum Which design belongs in E—a, b, c, d, or e?
4. Deductive Ability	The post office is bigger than the book store. The movie theater is smaller than the library. The town hall is the same size as the library. The book store is larger than the movie theater. Which of the following statements is true? (a) The movie theater is smaller than the post office. (b) The town hall is larger than the book store. (c) The library is larger than the post office. (d) The book store is smaller than the library. (e) The post office is larger than the town hall. Balloons sell at 6 for 12 cents. How much will 2 1/2 dozen cost? (a) 48 cents (b) 52 cents (c) 60 cents (d) 64 cents (e) 50 cents
5. Spatial Ability	Place a check next to every alternative that can be obtained by a rotation of the first figure.
6. Perceptual Ability	Which of the five pairs of numbers is an exact duplicate? (a) 253234 253324 (b) 756876 756786 (c) 986978 986978 (d) 356534 355634 (e) 275641 275461
7. Memory	Here is a list of cities and zip codes. Study this list for one minute, memorizing as many pairs of cities/zip codes as you can. At the end of one minute, hand in the list and then on a separate sheet of paper write down as many city/zip code pairs as you can recall. Dayton 08810 Plainsboro 08536 Layton 07851 Hazelet 07730 Westfield 07090 Runnemede 08078

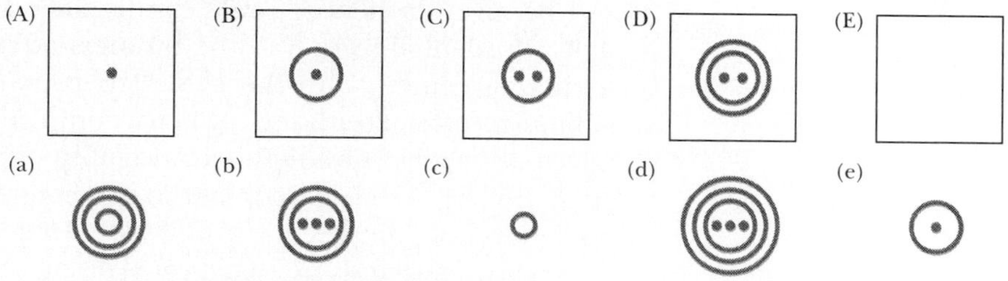

Cognitive Ability Tests

The usefulness of mental ability tests in predicting task performance has been investigated in both academic and organizational contexts.

General Tests. In academic settings, researchers have found high correlations between tests like the Scholastic Aptitude Test (SAT) and first-year-college grade point average, or GPA (correlations in the .50s), as well as overall rank in class (correlations in the .60s).[8] These tests are more predictive for students in the physical sciences or math than in the humanities or the social sciences. They are less predictive of success in graduate school (correlations in the .30s), because most applicants for graduate school score relatively high in mental ability and are therefore a somewhat homogeneous group.

There is a great deal of evidence to suggest that general cognitive ability is also predictive of success in the world of work.[9] Research by Jack Hunter has shown that in virtually any job where planning, judgment, and memory are used in day-to-day performance, individuals high in cognitive ability will generally outperform those who are low in this ability. Other research has shown that the relationship between general mental ability and job performance increases as the job gets more complex in terms of decision making, planning, problem solving, and analyzing information.[10] General cognitive ability is important even for jobs not characterized by such complexity if these jobs require the person to learn something new. Individuals high in general cognitive ability will learn the job more quickly than others. In low-complexity jobs, experience over time often wipes out this initial difference between high- and low-ability individuals, as Figure 4-2 demonstrates.[11] That is, as months on the job increase, the initial performance differences attributable to differences in ability decrease. Thus general cognitive ability is important in two respects. It relates both to learning the job

[8] A. R. Jenson, *Bias in Mental Testing* (New York: Free Press, 1980), p. 313.

[9] J. E. Hunter, "Cognitive Ability, Cognitive Aptitudes, Job Knowledge, and Job Performance," *Journal of Vocational Behavior* 29 (1986), 340–62.

[10] R. L. Gutenberg, R. D. Arvey, H. G. Osburn, and R. P. Jeanneret, "Moderating Effects of Decision-Making/Information Processing Dimensions on Test Validities," *Journal of Applied Psychology* 68 (1983), 600–608.

[11] F. L. Schmidt, J. E. Hunter, A. N. Outerbridge, and S. Goff, "Joint Relation of Experience and Ability With Job Performance: Test of Three Hypotheses," *Journal of Applied Psychology* 73 (1988), 46–57.

FIGURE 4-2

General Cognitive Ability and Experience on the Job as Determinants of Performance

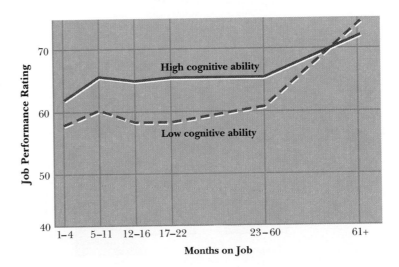

and to performing the job when the job requires the person to deal continually with new situations.

Specific Tests. In certain specific jobs, tests of specific mental ability can add greatly to the predictive power of tests of general intelligence.[12] For example, spatial visualization is critical for draftsmen and personnel in technical positions, and it is an important component in jobs that require mechanical skills, such as machinist, forklift operator, and warehouse worker. Perceptual ability is important in positions such as accountant, bookkeeper, stenographer, proofreader, typist, and general office clerk. Verbal ability and reasoning are critical to success in executive, administrative, and professional positions. Numerical ability is important in jobs such as accountant, payroll clerk, and salesperson and in many types of supervisory jobs.

At the outset of this chapter we distinguished between selection and placement. The use of general mental ability tests is most appropriate in selection because of the wide variety of jobs to which this ability is relevant. All applicants can be rank ordered in terms of general cognitive ability and then assigned to jobs, with the assumption that "more is better" regardless of the nature of the job. The use of specific ability tests facilitates placement. The key here is to place individuals with different strengths in jobs requiring different specific abilities. The assumption is that there are few people who cannot do some job well, and thus a high level of overall firm performance can be obtained from the correct matching procedure.

Figure 4-3 illustrates how various kinds of ability combine to affect task performance. General cognitive ability is the main influence on general job knowledge. It influences both how fast a person can learn the job, and how readily the person can adapt to changing circumstances when on the job. Job complexity affects the relationship between general cognitive ability and general job knowledge because the more complex the job in terms of decision making, planning, and judgment, the more learning and improvising the job requires. In simple jobs, the impact of general cognitive ability is less, and experience on the job can often substitute for lesser mental ability.

---

[12] G. K. Bennett, H. G. Seashore, and A. G. Wesman, *Administrators Handbook for the Differential Aptitude Test*, Psychological Corporation (San Antonio, Texas: Harcourt, Brace, Jovanovich, 1982), p. 55.

FIGURE 4-3

How Abilities Combine to Form Total Job Capability

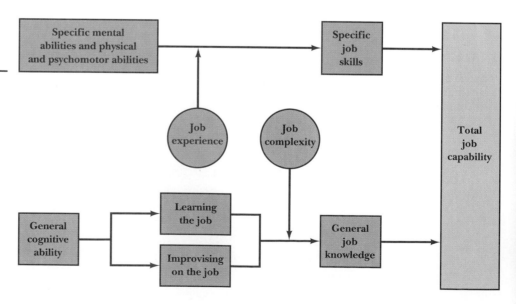

Specific facets of mental, physical, and motor ability in general relate to specific aspects of a task. Whereas general cognitive ability will almost always be relevant, the importance of specific abilities can be determined only by a detailed job analysis. Experience is shown in Figure 4-3 as a moderator of the relationship between specific abilities and specific job skills because initial individual differences on these characteristics tend to increase as people develop more experience or are further trained.[13] Specific job skills combine with general job knowledge to create the individual's total job capability.

HUMAN PERSONALITY

Whereas abilities deal with the things an individual can or cannot do, personality deals with what a person is like. It is useful to distinguish between these two broad aspects of individual differences for several reasons. First, the two have relatively distinct histories. Second, there is more controversy over personality measurement methods than over methods of measuring ability. Finally, the evidence for the usefulness of ability measures as predictors of performance is clearer than the corresponding evidence for personality measures.

Freud and Guilford

The great impact of Darwin's theories was felt not only by researchers on human abilities but by early psychologists who were interested in the study of personality. In the wake of Darwin's theory of evolution, which implied a great deal of common ground between human beings and animals, it was not surprising that many early approaches to the study of personality described consistencies in human behavior as instincts. Unfortunately, just as unique dimensions piled up in research on intelligence, "instincts" piled up in the area of personality research. In fact, by the 1920s, over 800 different classes of instincts had been proposed![14] Clearly, such a major violation of the principle of theoretical simplicity (see Chapter 3) required a more economical approach. For many, this approach was Sigmund Freud's.

Freud, an Austrian physician and psychiatrist and the founder of psychoanalysis, proposed that all behavior is powered by two unconscious drives, or instincts: the *life instinct* and the *death instinct*. The former represented a striving for creative and constructive aims, and the latter represented a striving toward destructive outcomes. Freud accounted for individual differences in personality by suggesting that different people dealt with their fundamental drives in different ways. He postulated that the *ego* mediates between these two opposing forces, constantly trying to strike a compromise between them.

According to Freud, because many of the compromises arrived at fail to satisfy either drive, and because many of the desires stemming from both instincts are socially unacceptable, people use **defense mechanisms** to deflect this inner turmoil (see Table 4-3). Unhealthy, or neurotic, people, he said, expend so much energy erecting defense mechanisms that they have little left for productive work or satisfying relationships. Freud conceived of a healthy person as one who could successfully "love and work."

defense mechanism In Freudian psychology, a kind of mental operation by which individuals rechannel the energies linked to socially unacceptable urges.

[13] L. S. Gottfredson, "Societal Consequences of the g Factor in Employment," *Journal of Vocational Behavior* 29 (1986), 379–411.

[14] L. L. Berbard, *Instincts* (New York: Holt, 1924), p. 91.

T A B L E 4-3
Major Ego Defense Mechanisms

Denial	Protecting the self from unpleasant realities by refusing to perceive them.
Repression	Preventing painful or dangerous thoughts from entering consciousness.
Displacement	Releasing pent-up feelings, usually of hostility, and directing them toward persons who are perceived as less dangerous than the individuals toward whom the feelings were originally directed.
Reaction formation	Preventing dangerous desires from being expressed by exaggerating attitudes and behaviors that are in direct opposition to such desires.
Sublimation	Substituting nonsexual, socially acceptable, usually creative activities for the expression of frustrated sexual desires.
Regression	Reverting to behaviors that are typical of an earlier stage of life, when one has fewer responsibilities and, generally, a lower level of aspiration.

Freudian theory has been widely criticized and not without reason. First, because it proposes unconscious states and drives, it is almost impossible to test empirically. Whatever supporting evidence there is for the theory comes out of psychotherapy sessions and thus relies on the memory of a therapist who is not objective and who could misinterpret subjects' responses. These criticisms notwithstanding, Freud left an indelible mark on the study of personality. Many current theories still employ the concept of unconscious causes of behavior, and many of our present methods of personality measurement claim to tap unconscious drives. In addition, although most people believe that Freud overemphasized the role of sexual factors, the role of early childhood experiences in personality development is now widely recognized.

Many recent approaches to personality owe less to Freud, however, than they do to J. P. Guilford and his associates.[15] By the 1950s, when Guilford began his research, the notion of instincts had given way to the notion of traits. Personality traits were similar to instincts in that they reflected simple behavioral consistencies (e.g., if a person exhibited a tendency to be curious across many situations, the trait of curiosity was invented as a means to describe this characteristic). No claim was made, however, that traits were strictly inherited. Guilford, like Spearman, used mathematical models to uncover the dimensions that underlay the many different characteristics that others had described. Table 4-4 describes ten of the major dimensions of personality identified by Guilford.

As we noted before, whereas ability refers to what individuals can and cannot do, personality refers to what people are like. The fact that many personality characteristics are described in everyday language—for example, aggressiveness, sociability, impulsiveness—is both good news and bad news. It is good news because most people can readily perceive individual differences in these qualities and can see how such variations might affect particular situations. It is bad news because terms adopted from everyday language are usually not very precise. This can create considerable difficulty in understanding, communicating, and using information obtained from scientific measures of personality. In the next three sections of this chapter, we will try to help clarify this point by describing some

---

[15] J. P. Guilford, *Personality* (New York: McGraw-Hill, 1959); R. B. Cattell, *The Scientific Analysis of Personality* (Baltimore: Penguin, 1965); and H. J. Eysenck, *The Structure of Personality* (London: Methuen, 1960).

TABLE 4-4
Guilford's Major Dimensions of Personality

	CHARACTERISTICS OF PERSONS SCORING HIGH ON DIMENSION
General activity	Need to be doing something all the time. Possess seemingly endless energy.
Restraint	Seem overcontrolled, stiff, and lacking in spontaneity. Very deliberate in actions; not impulsive.
Ascendance	Self-assured and ambitious. Like leadership and control over other people.
Sociability	Enjoy face-to-face dealings with others. Confident in social situations.
Emotional stability	Even tempered and not easily upset. Low scorers are seen as moody and over-emotional.
Objectivity	Possess a realistic view of self and others. Not easily hurt by others' remarks and sometimes insensitive to others' feelings.
Friendliness	Want to please others and avoid confrontation. Cooperative, agreeable, and easy to be with.
Thoughtfulness	Introspective and reflective about self. Prefer tasks that involve deep, prolonged, analytic thinking.
Personal relations	Tolerant of other people and accepting of rules and customs.
Masculinity	Behave in stereotypically male fashion. Low scorers are considered motherly, protective, and sensitive.

Source: Adapted from J. P. Guilford, *Personality* (New York: McGraw-Hill Book Co., 1959), pp. 51–53.

general and specific characteristics of personality, some ways of measuring these characteristics scientifically, and some of the existing evidence for the usefulness of measuring these characteristics in organizational contexts.

A Classification System

Given the vast number of personality characteristics that are described in the scientific literature, we need some type of classification scheme in order to understand both the characteristics themselves and their interrelationships. Nunnally assigns all the various facets of personality to five categories: (a) social traits, (b) motives, (c) personal conceptions, (d) emotional adjustment, and (e) personality dynamics.[16] In the following sections, we will describe each of these classes. We will also show specific examples of measures used in the real world to measure specific characteristics. If you see how a characteristic is actually measured in the real world, you will get a better idea of what it means.

social traits Behavior patterns that an individual typically displays when interacting with others in social contexts.

Social Traits. **Social traits** are behavior patterns that people typically manifest when interacting with others in social contexts. Social traits, which often represent the surface layer of personality, reflect the way a person appears to others.

One widely recognized approach to individual differences, based on the work of Carl Jung and translated into measures by Katherine Myers and Isabel Briggs, focuses on personal style.[17] Jung identified two basic personality types; introverts, who are shy and withdrawn, and extroverts, who are outgoing, ag-

[16] J. C. Nunnally, *Psychometric Theory* (New York: McGraw Hill, 1978), p. 546.

[17] D. B. Myers and K. C. Briggs, *Myers-Briggs Type Indicators* (Princeton, N.J.: Educational Testing Service, 1962).

gressive, and dominant. These personality types are matched by four problem-solving orientations or personal styles.

On one dimension, Myers and Briggs distinguish *feeling-type* individuals from *thinking-type* individuals. Feeling types are characterized as "sensitive to other peoples' feelings," "sympathetic," "disliking confrontation," and "warm and personable." Thinking types are characterized as "unemotional and hard-hearted," "logical and analytical," and "uninterested in relating" to other, nonthinking type individuals. As an example of this distinction, note the self-description of ex-college professor, millionaire real-estate developer Clay Hamner, who states, "I don't feel, I think. It would never occur to me to ask someone how they feel. I'm a tough touch for people who don't know me."[18]

Myers and Briggs also differentiate between *sensor types* and *intuitive types*. Sensor-type people are characterized by "emphasizing action and wanting to get things done," "being highly precise in action and language," and "hard-charging." Intuitive types "emphasize conceptions and theories," "engage in long-range planning," and "are oriented to problem solving but not necessarily to application." Clay Hamner lined up a $105 million purchase of The Pantry in two days. He bought options on 1,500 acres near Atlanta for the Gwinnett Progress Center, over the telephone, sight unseen. He bought and then sold the Hotel Europa in Chapel Hill within 24 hours.

Table 4-5 shows some of the occupations for which Myers and Briggs feel these four types are best suited. Note how their classification system clearly predicts *both* occupations of a personality like Clay Hamner.

A social trait measure recently developed specifically for the work context is the Employee Reliability Scale.[19] According to this scale, low-reliability employees are characterized by (a) hostility toward rules, (b) thrill-seeking impulsiveness, (c) social insensitivity, and (d) alienation, or a feeling of detachment from others. Studies using this scale have found that high scores on this measure are related to supervisory ratings such as good attitudes, teamwork, punctuality, adaptability, and sales productivity. Low scores are related to turnover, high absenteeism rates, high equipment-repair records, and a greater incidence of reported injuries.

Finally, companies are becoming increasingly interested in the honesty of their prospective employees. As the Management Issues Box indicates, there has been an increase in the use of paper and pencil measures of honesty, particularly since polygraph, or lie detector, tests were outlawed.

---

[18] "Feats of Clay," *Business/North Carolina*, August 1989, pp. 23–31.

[19] J. Hogan and R. Hogan, "How to Measure Employee Reliability," *Journal of Applied Psychology* 74 (1988), 273–79.

T A B L E 4-5
Myers-Briggs' Personal Styles and Compatible Occupations

TYPE	OCCUPATION
Thinking	Lawyer, engineer, teacher, computer programmer
Feeling	Writer, nurse, social worker, psychologist
Sensation	Accountant, pilot, salesperson, physician, land developer
Intuitive	Scientist, artist, corporate planner, inventor

Source: Based on D. B. Myers and K. C. Briggs, *Myers-Briggs Type Indicators* (Princeton, N.J.: Educational Testing Service, 1962), pp. 15–35.

MANAGEMENT ISSUES

Testing Employee Honesty

Jerry Pardue, vice-president of loss prevention for Super D Drugs, Inc., a Southeastern chain, noticed with horror a few years ago that shrinkage—retailing jargon for stolen goods—was rising dramatically. Mr. Pardue wanted to see if paper-and-pencil honesty tests could screen out thieves among job applicants.

He had quite a surprise. By his own calculations the tests have helped Super D save about $400,000 a year by reducing shrinkage. Absenteeism rates, substance abuse, lateness, and other forms of counterproductive behavior are down too. "As soon as we started using these tests to screen employees, the integrity of the work force improved all around" Pardue said.*

The passage of the Employee Polygraph Protection Act in 1988 prohibits the use of physiological lie detectors in most instances. Since then, many employers, like Super D Drugs, have turned to paper-and-pencil honesty tests as a means of ensuring integrity in the work force. An indication of this trend can be seen in the growth rate of the $25 million testing industry, roughly 20 percent annually.

Can these kinds of tests actually weed out thieves and other undesirable elements from an employer's work force? Although there is certainly a lot of anecdotal evidence like our story about Super D Drugs, there is very little independent research to support either advocates or critics of this kind of testing. The evidence we have is generally positive, but it is based on studies performed by the testing companies themselves, and thus obviously subject to bias. Independent studies are difficult to perform because of the proprietary nature of the answer keys that go along with the tests. Setting this problem aside, researchers who have taken test results at face value, have found the validity of these tests is not sufficiently high to meet the "reasonable doubt" standards of our justice system.† Thus one could call into question the ethics of using these tests on job applicants who have been accused of no crime.

Another drawback is that the tests have relatively high rejection rates; 40 to 70 percent of applicants fail the tests. In many of the industries in which these kinds of tests are popular, such as retailing and the restaurant business, there are few applicants relative to the number of available positions. Moreover, the laws of many states (e.g., Massachusetts and Rhode Island) limit the use of these tests. Although no federal laws prohibit these tests as yet, the fact that Congress has appropriated funds to study "integrity" tests suggests that federal legislation is under consideration.

Ironically, some reviewers have noted that "it is not uncommon to encounter questionable, if not blatantly deceptive, sales tactics"‡ in the very aggressive marketing of some integrity tests. Thus organizations considering the use of integrity tests should not take the integrity of the testers for granted. This is one area in which you may need to do your own research to see what works and does not work for your own company.

† K. R. Murphy, "Detecting Infrequent Deception," *Journal of Applied Psychology* 72 (1987), 611–14.

‡ P. R. Sackett, L. R. Burris and C. Callahan, "Integrity Testing in Personnel Selection: An Update," *Personnel Psychology* 42 (1989), 491–528.

* C. H. Deutsch, "Pen-and-Pencil Integrity Tests," *New York Times*, February 11, 1990, p. D1.

---

motive A reflection of an individual's underlying drives, needs, and values

Motives. **Motives** reflect an individual's underlying drives, needs, and values. In general, motives are below the surface; that is, they reside within the person. Because this class of personality variables lies at the core of many theories of motivation, we will explore the specific topic of drives and needs in Chapter 7. Here we will look at some common measures of personal values.

The Minnesota Importance Questionnaire (MIQ), widely used in the work context, assesses personal values. It measures the importance that an individual places on various features of the work situation, classified into the following six categories:

1. *Autonomy*: Authority and responsibility
2. *Pleasant working conditions*: Being in a work situation that includes variety and activity
3. *Achievement*: The opportunity to use valued abilities and to be promoted
4. *Recognition*: Enjoying high social status and the respect of others
5. *Altruism*: Doing work that is consistent with moral values and providing needed social services
6. *Management responsibilities*: Managing other people and implementing company policies and practices

The MIQ is typically used in conjunction with another measure called the Occupational Reinforcer Pattern (ORP). The ORP, which is administered to current jobholders, asks which of the characteristics assessed by the MIQ actually describe the job for which applicants who have taken the test are being considered. Thus the two instruments are used together in an effort to match the applicants who favor a particular set of values with the job that most closely fits those values. Research has shown that when there is a close fit between values and job, job satisfaction will be greater and the risk of turnover will be less.[20]

personal conceptions A person's thoughts, attitudes, and beliefs about his social and physical environment.

locus of control The extent to which an individual believes that his own actions influence the environment.

Personal Conceptions. Personal conceptions reflect the way a person thinks about the social and physical environment. They reflect the person's major beliefs and her personal outlook on a variety of issues.

One widely used formulation is Julian Rotter's **locus of control**. Locus of control refers to the extent to which a person believes that his own actions influence his environment and the events that affect him. *Internals* believe that they control their own destiny. *Externals* believe that their lives are controlled by fate and other forces beyond their control. Some sample items from Rotter's measure of locus of control are shown in Table 4-6.

A major review of the organizational behavior literature on locus of control draws several conclusions about individuals who differ on this personality characteristic.[21] First, internals tend to be more easily motivated than externals, because they seek out and conform to rules that tie rewards to high performance. Thus internals work much better than externals under incentive systems. Second, internals tend to be self-motivated and to prefer participative approaches by supervisors, whereas externals want more directive supervision. This difference seems to spill over to other situations; for example, in leadership roles, internals

[20] E. Betz, "Need Reinforcer Correspondence as a Predictor of Satisfaction," *Personnel and Guidance Journal* 47 (1969), 878–83.
[21] P. E. Spector, "Behavior in Organizations as a Function of Employee Locus of Control," *Psychological Bulletin* 91 (1982), 482–97.

T A B L E 4-6
Items From the Rotter Internal-External Locus of Control Scale

1. a. Many of the unhappy things in people's lives are partly due to bad luck.
   b. People's misfortunes result from the mistakes they make.
2. a. In the long run, people get the respect they deserve in this world.
   b. Unfortunately, an individual's worth often passes unrecognized no matter how hard he tries.
3. a. No matter how hard you try, some people just won't like you.
   b. People who can't get others to like them don't understand how to get along with others.
4. a. Becoming a success is a matter of hard work; luck has little or nothing to do with it.
   b. Getting a good job depends mainly on being in the right place at the right time.
5. a. The average citizen can have an influence in governmental decisions.
   b. This world is run by the few people in power, and there is not much the little guy can do about it.
6. a. Many times I feel that I have little influence over the things that happen to me.
   b. It is impossible for me to believe that chance or luck plays an important role in my life.

Note: For each numbered item the respondent must choose the statement that best describes him or her. You can see how an internal-external pattern can emerge.
Source: Based on Julian Rotter, "Generalized Expectancies For Internal versus External Locus of Control," *Psychological Monographs* 80 (1966), 1–44.

98

use more democratic approaches than do externals. Finally, internals seem better at collecting and processing information. Thus they seem to perform better on complex tasks even when general mental ability is held constant.

authoritarianism A set of personality characteristics that include ethnocentrism and strong tendencies to overvalue authority, to stereotype others, and to be suspicious and distrustful of people in general.

Research on another personal conception, **authoritarianism**, began in the aftermath of World War II as social scientists tried to understand the psychological forces that made the creation of the Nazi political system possible.[22] In particular, investigators wanted to know whether certain personality types were especially susceptible to Fascist, antidemocratic propaganda. The result of their efforts was the F scale (*F* stood for "fascism"), which identifies the "authoritarian" personality type, the person who is susceptible to this kind of influence. People who have high scores on the F scale can be characterized as follows:

> They believe that obedience and respect for authority should be the individual's primary values.
> They are ethnocentric: they believe in their own superiority and the superiority of the subgroup to which they belong. They distrust outsiders.
> They are superstitious. They often stereotype others and reject introspection and analysis.
> They feel that they live in a hostile environment full of threatening people.

People who score high on the F scale tend to be rigid in their approach to problem solving and generally score low on measures of creativity. They tend to follow written rules and procedures very closely and to be highly conformist. In general, they follow superiors' orders without question, and they are very apt to use punishment when dealing with subordinates. In the light of the recent emphasis on ethical issues in the business world, authoritarian people are undesirable candidates for key positions in any organization. By their nature, they are too susceptible to the lures of acting unethically.

emotional adjustment A class of personality variables that deal with the extent to which a person experiences affective distress or engages in socially unacceptable behaviors.

Type A behavior pattern A set of personality characteristics that include aggressiveness, competitiveness, and the tendency to work under self-induced time pressures.

Emotional Adjustment. Emotional adjustment deals with the extent to which a person experiences emotional distress or engages in socially unacceptable behavior. A person is said to be emotionally *maladjusted* if such distress prevents her from functioning properly in the environment or if it affects her health in a deleterious way.

Commonly seen in the business setting, especially among managers, is what has been called the **Type A behavior pattern**.[23] People with a Type A personality are characterized as aggressive and competitive. They set high standards for themselves and others and put themselves under constant time pressure.[24] Type B's, on the other hand, are free of such feelings of urgency. We discuss the Type A behavior pattern here as a maladjustment, because a tremendous amount of evidence links this characteristic to coronary heart disease. For example, one study of over 3,000 people found that individuals classified as Type A were twice as likely to suffer a fatal heart attack as those classified as Type B.[25] Another study showed that over 70 percent of coronary heart disease sufferers were Type A's.[26]

---

[22] T. W. Adorno, E. Frenkel-Brunswick, D. J. Levinson, and B. J. Sanford, *The Authoritarian Personality* (New York: Harper, 1950).

[23] J. H. Howard, D. A. Cunningham, and P. A. Rechnitzer, "Health Patterns Associated with Type A Behavior: A Managerial Population," *Journal of Human Stress* 2 (1976), 24–31.

[24] K. A. Mathews, "Psychological Perspectives on the Type A Behavior Pattern," *Psychological Bulletin* 91 (1982), 293–323.

[25] R. Rosenman and M. Friedman, "The Central Nervous System and Coronary Heart Disease," *Hospital Practice* 6 (1971), 87–97.

[26] C. D. Jenkins, "Psychologic and Social Precursors of Coronary Disease," *New England Journal of Medicine* 284 (1971), 244–55; 307–17.

Dealing with Type A behavior becomes a complex matter when we add one more ingredient to the mix. That is, Type A's tend to outperform Type B's on most tasks that require persistence and endurance. It would seem, then, that attempts to eliminate Type A personalities from an organization would risk destroying the firm's ability to accomplish its mission.

We are learning more, however, about this personality characteristic. A recent study of college professors with Type A personalities, for example, found that job performance was most influenced by just one part of the behavior pattern, that dealing with goal setting and time pressures. The negative emotional consequences of the behavior pattern sprang out of its aggressive and competitive components.[27] Thus the Type A pattern is a kind of two-edged sword; we might wield this sword to the advantage of the organization if we could just find individuals who were strong in some of its aspects but weak in others.

One of the most widely used personality assessment devices, the Minnesota Multiphasic Personality Inventory (MMPI) is designed to differentiate among various types of psychological disturbance, such as depression and paranoid behavior. Some of these dimensions are shown in Table 4-7. As a manager in a business organization, you would rarely encounter anyone whose scores on the MMPI were "clinically elevated," or high enough to indicate serious mental disorder and the need for specific treatment. However, research suggests that only mildly elevated levels of these kinds of characteristics can affect performance on complex tasks that demand a great deal of attention.[28] The reason is that even at low levels, these kinds of distress tend to distract a person from any task.

personality dynamics A class of personality characteristics that deal with the integration and organization of traits, motives, personal conceptions, and adjustment.

self-esteem the degree to which a person believes that she is a worthwhile and deserving individual.

Personality Dynamics. **Personality dynamics** constitute the most complex group of personality characteristics. This group deals with the principles by which all the other four classes are integrated and organized. Personality dynamics explain how all the other types of characteristics are put together to form the "whole person."

One such personality dynamic is referred to as the self-concept, and one of the most important aspects of the self-concept is self-esteem. **Self-esteem** (SE) describes the extent to which the person believes that he is a worthwhile and deserving individual. People with high self-esteem differ from people with low self-esteem in terms of all four sets of personality characteristics we have discussed—social traits, motives, personal conceptions, and emotional adjustment.[29]

[27] M. S. Taylor, E. A. Locke, C. Lee, and M. E. Gist, "Type A Behavior and Faculty Research Productivity: What are the Mechanisms?" *Organizational Behavior and Human Performance* 34 (1984), 402–18.

[28] Ruth Kanfer, Personal Communication, April 17, 1989.

[29] J. Brockner, *Self-Esteem at Work* (Lexington, Mass.: Lexington Books, 1988), p. 144.

T A B L E 4-7
Some Dimensions of Maladjustment Measured by the MMPI

Depression	Sadness, despondency, feelings of worthlessness.
Paranoia	Extreme suspiciousness and distrust of others; belief that others intend one harm.
Hypomania	Hyperactivity; inability to concentrate on things for any length of time.
Psychasthenia	Being subject to strong fears and compulsions.
Psychopathic deviance	Lacking a conscience, having little regard for the feelings of others, and getting into trouble frequently.

With regard to social traits, high-SE individuals are less interested in seeking approval from others, less likely to model others, and less affected by others' feedback. Also, because they accept and feel good about themselves, high SE's tend to be more accepting of others. With regard to motives, high SE's are driven to meet their own self-set goals, which tend to be high and resistant to change. With regard to personal conceptions, high SE's tend to have an internal locus of control and to expect to succeed, regardless of the context. Finally, high self esteem tends to be correlated with emotional adjustment.

Interestingly, research does not always show high-self-esteem people to be better performers. In fact, they are less competent performers under some conditions, as when a little self-doubt is needed to spur the search for additional information.[30] Most studies suggest, however, that people with high self-esteem choose occupations that are compatible with their needs, and self-esteem is generally positively related to job satisfaction.[31]

To understand how the five sets of personality characteristics we have discussed work together, we might picture the personality as a ship. The visible social traits determine what the ship looks like above the waterline. The hidden motives form the ship's propeller, making it move. Personal conceptions form the compass. They locate the ship in its surroundings. Personality dynamics, which can be seen as the ship's rudder, determine the direction in which the ship will move.

What about emotional adjustment? When it's good, the ship sails smoothly. Maladjustment, however, can be seen as a crack in the hull. Atttention must be shifted from the ship's purpose—reaching its destination—to repairing the damage. In terms of the human personality, when people experience serious emotional distress they are likely to divert their energies from productive activity to concern with and attempts to solve the problems that beset them. If the crack in the ship's hull cannot be repaired—if a person cannot solve his problems—the entire enterprise is in trouble.

Measuring Personality Characteristics

We did not need a separate section on measurement when discussing human abilities because, for the most part, testing in this area is relatively straight forward and uncontroversial. There is much less consensus on the best way to measure personality characteristics. In fact, there continues to be substantial debate about the many measurement techniques that have been developed. In this section, we will look briefly at the types of measures employed in this area and at the advantages and disadvantages of each.

self-inventory A measure of personality characteristics that asks the individual to describe herself by means of standardized responses to questionnaire items.

Self-Inventories. By far the most frequently employed personality measure is the **self-inventory**, a paper-and-pencil test in which people are asked to describe themselves by answering questions. Most such inventories present people with a series of descriptions of personality characteristics and ask them to indicate, in a yes-no or agree-disagree format, whether each description applies to them. Although many such measures are developed by using the same mathematical models used by Spearman, these tests differ fundamentally from ability tests in that the items on personality measures have no right or wrong answers.

[30] H. M. Weiss and P. A. Knight, "The Utility of Humility: Self-Esteem, Information Search, and Problem Solving Efficiency," *Organizational Behavior and Human Performance* 25 (1980), 216–23.

[31] E. A. Locke, "The Nature and Causes of Job Satisfaction," in *Organizational and Industrial Psychology*, ed. M. D. Dunnette, (Chicago: Rand McNally, 1976), pp. 515–612.

The main advantage of the personality inventory is that it is quick and efficient—it can measure a large number of characteristics with a minimum of expense. Moreover, experts in the area of personality assessment generally agree that it is the best general approach to measuring personality. There are some drawbacks, however, to self-inventories.[32]

The main problem, referred to as **social desirability bias**, is that a person's responses may reflect not what she is actually like but what she would like you to think she is like. For example, in one study a researcher asked people to rate 140 items on the extent to which the items were socially desirable, that is, to indicate whether most people would think that having a given characteristic was good rather than bad.[33] The same researcher then asked another group of people to respond to the items and found a very high (.87) correlation between the rated desirability of the item and the likelihood that people would say yes when asked if it applied to them. This result could come about in several ways. Of course, it could be that most people actually have the desirable qualities they attribute to themselves. Most researchers think, however, that people who respond in this manner are just not being frank. It could also be that people simply do not know themselves very well and think they are providing factual responses when they are not. Both lack of self-knowledge and lack of frankness will present an inaccurate picture of an individual's personality.

Note that this type of bias cannot affect ability tests. That is, even though a person might wish to pass himself off as having strong mathematical ability, if he is actually weak in this ability, he will be unable to make a good showing. The social-desirability problem, probably more than any other, has fueled the perceived need for other approaches to measuring personality.

Observational Techniques. The observational technique asks one person to describe another. This kind of test may be conducted in a contrived setting, as when an interviewer talks with a person he has never met before and then makes a judgment as to what the person is like. Or observations may be made in everyday situations: a researcher may ask people who should know a particular person well (e.g., best friends, former boss, co-workers) to describe him. This method runs into trouble, however, because observers' judgments depend on their own abilities or personality characteristics, and different observers may make different judgments about the same person. This is especially likely when the observer has had only limited opportunity to interact with the person being rated. Suppose, for example, that a university professor is asked by a student's prospective employer to describe the student's personality, when the student has never participated in class discussions or met with the teacher outside of class. Under these conditions, the person doing the rating hasn't the vaguest idea of what the person being rated is truly like.

The employment interview is a good example of an observational technique for measuring personality. For example, at Mobil Oil Company, interviewers are trained to look for ten characteristics—among them initiative and flexibility—that signal a good fit with the company culture. Thomas Padden, a manager of the heavy-products staff at Mobil suggests that in looking for initiative the interviewer does not simply check off the number of extra-curricular activities the person reports, but tries to uncover the nature of those activities. For example, the interviewer might ask someone who listed "member of student government" whether he typed the minutes of the group's meetings or negotiated with college

[32] Nunnally, *Psychometric Theory*.

[33] A. L. Edwards, *The Measurement of Personality Traits by Scales and Inventories* (New York: Holt, 1970).

trustees. Either of these jobs might have been part of student government, but only one of them has implications for initiative.[34]

Projective Tests. You will recall that a significant difference between Freud's and Guilford's approaches to personality lay in Freud's assumption that important aspects of personality reside in the unconscious and that as a result the person is not aware of them. If Freud was right, the self-inventory is not a valid method of personality measurement. In addition, if people approach the world from behind the shield of the defense mechanisms described in Table 4-3, it is unlikely that untrained observers can offer us very helpful information about what a person is really like. In fact, although they reject many of Freud's other ideas, some personality researchers insist that most people have little consciousness, or awareness, of their true personalities. Thus because this belief casts doubt on the utility of self-inventories and untrained observations as measurement methods, some other technique must be used. For these researchers, projective measures of personality are the solution.

Projective measurement techniques are based on the notion that when people are presented with an ambiguous situation, one that is open to many different interpretations, they will project aspects of their own personalities into such situations. Thus in asking people to provide meaning to a vague stimulus of some sort, the **projective test** theoretically induces them to reveal themselves to a trained observer. Among the several types of projective measures, the Rorschach ink-blot test is probably the most famous. In this test, a person is shown a series of patterns (literally created by spreading ink on a surface and then blotting it) and asked to tell the interviewer what she sees in these patterns, or what images they call to her mind. In the Thematic Apperception Test (TAT), another widely used projective device, people are asked to write stories about pictures of people in different types of social situations. The stories are then judged in terms of the presence of several themes, such as the need for power, achievement, or affiliation.

Although there are scattered findings that particular techniques are useful for particular purposes, the evidence in general suggests that projective techniques do not provide valid measures of personality.[35] Because most of these techniques depend heavily on the subjective opinion of the test administrator, few projective devices are well standardized. Indeed, some investigators have suggested that the interpretations of these tests reveal more about the examiner than about the examinee. For example, one study showed that examiners who were rated as hostile by their colleagues were more likely than others to interpret subjects' ink-blot responses as reflecting hostility.[36] This kind of problem severely reduces the reliability of judgments across different measurements. For example, different judges may evaluate the same person in different ways.

In view of the many weaknesses in the measurement techniques we have discussed, how should we go about measuring personality? Our classification of personality characteristics can help us fit measurement methods to a number of the characteristics we are interested in. For example, social traits, which often represent the surface layer of personality, reflect the way a person appears to others. This class of variables therefore might be best assessed through observations by other people.

projective test A measure of personality in which individuals are asked to assign meaning to an ambiguous stimulus. Unconscious aspects of the personality are inferred from the person's responses.

---

[34] "The New Job Interview: Show Thyself," *Wall Street Journal*, December 4, 1989, p. B4.

[35] D. C. McClelland and R. E. Boyatzis, "Leadership Motive Patterns and Long-Term Success," *Journal of Applied Psychology* 67 (1982), 737–43.

[36] J. Masling, "The Influence of Personal and Situational Variables in Projective Testing," *Psychological Bulletin* 57 (1960), 65–85.

Personal conceptions represent an individual's beliefs, and these are probably best assessed by self-reports. Self-reports may also be appropriate to measure motives, which reflect an individual's underlying drives and needs. However, to guard against social desirability bias, we might want to use projective measures in addition to self-inventories. It is generally a good idea, in attempting to assess personality, to use multiple methods. If the judgments derived from multiple measures are not in agreement, you may be hard pressed to determine which is correct. On the other hand, if such judgments are in agreement, you can be reasonably confident that the picture painted of the individual truly reflects that individual rather than the painter, the brush, or the canvas.

Usefulness of Personality Testing

Many companies, including General Motors, American Cyanamid, J. C. Penney, and Westinghouse, rely heavily on personality assessment programs to evaluate and promote employees. Many other firms use such programs as screens for initial hiring. For example, American Multi Cinema (AMC), the third largest theater chain in America, looks for individuals with "kinetic energy, emotional maturity, and the ability to deal with large numbers of people in a fairly chaotic situation."[37] Despite their widespread use in industry, however, the usefulness of personality measures in the explanation and prediction of human behavior has been criticized on several counts.

In Chapter 3 we discussed the difference between construct validity and criterion-related validity. Many of the measures of personality characteristics that we have examined have been attacked on the grounds of not achieving either type of validity. In terms of the constructs themselves, Walter Mischel has stated that "the assumption of massive behavioral similarity across diverse situations is untenable."[38] Rather, according to Mischel, people act differently in different situations. If someone could exhibit an internal locus of control when dealing with friends and family problems but exhibit an external locus of control when dealing with problems at work, does it even make sense to talk about a generalized notion of this concept?

With regard to criterion-related validity, after reviewing studies of the use of personality measures in personnel selection, Guion and Gottier concluded that "it is difficult, in the face of this summary, to advocate with a clear conscience the use of personality measures in most situations as a basis for making employment decisions about people."[39] This same conclusion was reached more recently by Landy.[40] The low criterion validity of personality measures is particularly noticeable when we compare the validity of these measures with tests of cognitive or physical abilities needed to perform a particular function. Even as predictors of work attitudes, personality variables have served mainly as accessories to other theories and have rarely accounted for a great deal of variance in employee reactions to work.[41] As a whole, especially in organizational contexts, personality variables have simply not had a great history of success in terms of predicting the kinds of outcomes managers are most interested in.

Despite these criticisms, others have held that the problem with research on personality in organizational contexts is not with the conceptions of personality

---

[37] "Can You Pass the Job Test?" *Newsweek*, May 5, 1986, pp. 46–51.

[38] Walter Mischel, *Personality and Assessment* (New York: John Wiley, 1968), p. 295.

[39] R. M. Guion and R. F. Gottier, "Validity of Personality Measures in Personnel Selection," *Personnel Psychology* 18 (1965), 135–64.

[40] F. J. Landy, *The Psychology of Work Behavior*, 4th ed. (New York: Free Press, 1985), p. 186.

[41] T. R. Mitchell, "Organizational Behavior," in *Annual Review of Psychology*, vol. 30, ed. M. R. Rosenzweig and L. W. Porter (Palo Alto, Calif.: Annual Reviews Institute, 1979), p. 70–119.

characteristics themselves. The problem, they have argued, lies in the way theory and data have been used. In the first place, the fact that most organizational research is conducted at one level of a single organization influences the degree to which individual differences in personality can be observed. According to these investigators, the recruitment-selection-training-retention cycle characteristic of most organizations tends to produce a group of employees who are rather similar in personal style. People who are widely different from the status quo, according to this perspective, either (a) are not attracted to the organization in the first place, (b) are never hired, (c) conform if they do get in, or (d) quit or are fired if they fail to conform. This restriction in range precludes the strong manifestation of differences attributable to personality.[42] A similar problem exists in laboratory studies where participants are often students of the same age and social class, come from the same geographic area, and may be majoring in the same subject. Some research suggests that personality characteristics serve as better predictors when the person being observed is exposed to different tasks and contexts, and all of his responses are summed across all observations.[43]

Other defenders of the role of personality characteristics have criticized the methodology of organizational personality research. Howard Weiss and Seymour Adler, for example, have noted that most research is either cross-sectional (i.e., all the data are collected at one time) or of relatively short duration.[44] The subtle influences of personality on behavior are probably best captured in longitudinal research that follows people over relatively long periods of time. Indeed, one study that runs counter to the vast majority of the literature on personality has shown that predictability on the basis of personality characteristics increases over time.[45] In some rare cases, successful predictions on the basis of such characteristics have been made as far as twenty years into the future.[46] Weiss and Adler also note that the theoretical rationale for including most personality variables in studies is weaker than it is for including situational variables such as goals or incentives.

Thus there is no consensus on how to measure personality characteristics. Moreover, the evidence for the predictive value of many of these measures is not impressive. This poor showing is probably best attributed to a lack of conceptual development regarding which characterisitics are likely to predict which outcomes and in what ways.

The five-fold breakdown we use here to classify different approaches to personality may help us bring everything together. First, in terms of the sheer volume of personality characteristics, this breakdown may make it easier for you to evaluate proposals for new characteristics. It may also help you to appreciate the relationship of a new personality characteristic to established ones.

Figure 4-4 offers a conceptual base from which to understand personality's effect on work outcomes. Personality dynamics, especially as revealed through motives and personal conceptions, probably have their greatest impact on motivation, in that they provide and direct the person's available energy for performing the task. Certain social traits, on the other hand, act more like specific facets of mental ability and physical or motor skills in that they are requirements for specific aspects of the job. For example, extroversion and an outgoing per-

---

[42] B. Schneider, "Interactional Psychology and Organizational Behavior," in *Research in Organizational Behavior*, ed. B. M. Staw and L. L. Cummings (Greenwich, Conn.: JAI Press, 1983), pp. 49–81.

[43] Seymour Adler and Howard M. Weiss, "Criterion Aggregation in Personality Research: Self-Esteem and Goal Setting" (Paper presented at the Ninetieth Annual Convention of the American Psychological Association, Washington, D.C., 1983).

[44] H. M. Weiss and S. Adler, "Personality and Organizational Behavior," in *Research in Organizational Behavior*, pp. 191–236.

[45] J. R. Hinrichs, "An Eight Year Follow-Up of a Management Assessment Center," *Journal of Applied Psychology* 63 (1978), 596–601.

[46] McClelland and Boyatzis, "Leadership Motive Patterns," p. 742.

FIGURE 4-4

How Personality Characteristics Combine to Affect Motivation, Skills, and Concentration

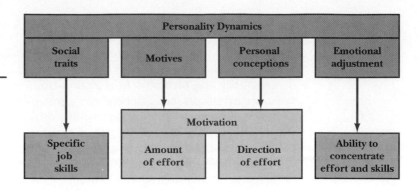

sonality may have a direct positive effect on how well a salesperson can do her job. Finally, the degree to which a person can concentrate her attention on the task at hand will be a function of her adjustment. Even a mild degree of maladjustment may distract attention from the task and thus from performance, especially in complex jobs.

ABILITY AND PERSONALITY IN TASK PERFORMANCE

Performance is a function of the interaction between ability and motivation, particularly as the latter is influenced by personality factors (see Figure 4-5). The relation between ability and motivation seems quite clear. Even if you have the ability to do a particular job you may not do it well unless you are motivated to do it. Conversely, you may have all the motivation in the world but if you lack the ability you will not do well. The relations between these two factors and the many varying personality characteristics that we have been able only to sample here—for instance, thinking versus intuiting or having high or low self-esteem—are much more complicated and often difficult to assess.

There is certainly anecdotal evidence to support the notion that personality characteristics interact with motives and abilities to affect performance. See, for example, the "In Practice" box, which describes the role of the commander of

FIGURE 4-5

How Abilities and Personality Characteristics Combine to Affect Job Performance

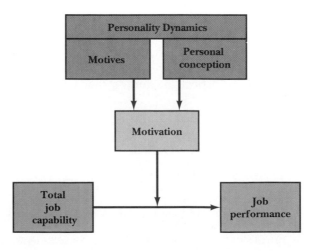

The General's Resume

It was perhaps one of the most complex jobs ever designed. The head of the Allied Forces assembled to retake Kuwait had to orchestrate a war machine made up of forces from 28 different nations. This included 675,000 troops, hundreds of ships, and thousands of airplanes and tanks that had to work in a tightly coordinated fashion. What were the abilities, experiences, and personality characteristics of the man assigned the task, General H. Norman Schwarzkopf, and how did these match the task's requirements?

First and foremost, the leader of this effort needed a high degree of cognitive ability. Schwarzkopf's IQ is over 170 and he graduated in the top 10 percent of his class at West Point. When he was head of the U.S. Central Command in North Africa Schwarzkopf foresaw the Arab aggression in the Middle East. In fact, by 1983 he had already designed contingency plans (later called Operation Desert Storm) for a campaign to retake a Gulf state from an invading force. A mere five days before Saddam Hussein launched his attack in August 1990, Schwarzkopf and his staff were actually running an exercise predicated on the possibility that Iraq might overrun Kuwait. "Initially," said one British Commander, "we were taken aback by his gung-ho appearance, but in a very short time we came to realize that here was a highly intelligent soldier—a skilled planner."

Managing the diversity of the allied coalition also required interpersonal skills and sensitivity of the highest order. Schwarzkopf had to manage the four branches of the U.S. military, which are often rivals, as well as the forces of 28 foreign nations. Many of these countries, like Syria and Britain, were not on the best of terms with each other. Schwarzkopf's early years in Iran, where his father worked for the Central Intelligence Agency, gave him a sensitivity to Middle Eastern traditions and values. And when his family later moved to Europe, he attended foreign schools and learned German and French. These early experiences, along with his own later military assignments abroad helped prepare him for managing the multinational forces arrayed against Iraq.

Finally, Schwarzkopf's high self-esteem and need for achievement fitted him well for command. He decided to become a general when he was ten years old and friends from his West Point days still marvel at his single-minded ambition. According to a former roommate, retired General Leroy Suddath, Schwarzkopf "saw himself as a successor to Alexander the Great, and we didn't laugh when he said it."* Indeed, Schwarzkopf's abiding certitude and bristling self-assurance,

* Stormin' Norman on Top, *Time*, February 4, 1991, pp. 28–30.

General Norman Schwarzkopf brought to his role as Allied commander not only a mix of high intelligence, strong interpersonal skills, sensitivity to others, and a broad range of experience but an ability to obsess long enough to plan an effective strategy tempered by the knowledge of when enough is enough. "I thought about this plan every waking and sleeping moment," he says, and he made repeated modifications in his strategy. "But there comes a point where. . . . You say, OK, that's it." The effectiveness of Schwarzkopf's strategy and his implementation of it brought the war in the Persian Gulf to a close with a very small number of casualties. A miracle, he said. "but it will never be miraculous for the families of those people." Source: *Tom Mathews with C. S. Manegold and Thomas M. DeFrank, "A Soldier of Conscience,"* Newsweek, *March 11, 1991.*

in combination with his commanding physical presence—6'4", 245 lbs.—immediately strikes observers.

Schwarzkopf, a student of military history, has focused particularly on the Battle of Cannae, where in 216 Hannibal crushed the forces of Rome in the first real war of annihilation. History may record Operation Desert Storm as a mismatch of forces in the same class as that at Cannae. This battlefield mismatch, however, was also due in part to the excellent match between Schwarzkopf's abilities, experiences, personality, and the job he was assigned.

the Allied Forces in the Persian Gulf War. But we also have a considerable amount of empirical evidence.[47] Consider the findings of one study, diagrammed in Figure 4-6, which examined the relative success of salespersons who varied in terms of both ability and self-esteem. As you can see, salespeople who were not very skilled made low commissions regardless of whether their self-esteem was low or high.

[47] J. R. Hollenbeck and E. M. Whitener, "Reclaiming Personality Traits for Personnel Selection: Self-

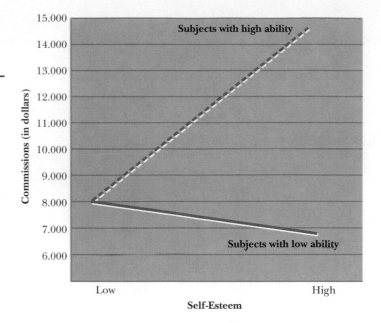

For the salespeople who were extremely skilled, however, self-esteem made a big difference. High-ability people with low self-esteem made no more in sales commissions than the low-ability salespeople did. On the other hand, high-ability people with high self-esteem earned nearly twice as much in commissions as those with low self-esteem.

Here again ability is the bottom line. If you lack the ability to do the job you won't do well. But if you have the ability to do the job, other factors may affect how well you do it. Together with other research that has supported the interactive relationship between ability and personality,[48] these studies suggest that measures of personality characteristics can indeed be useful if they are used in conjunction with measures of ability.

A good example of how ability and motivation interact can be seen in the increasing "foreignization" of U.S. schools of engineering. Becoming an engineer, especially at the Ph.D. level, takes both a high degree of cognitive ability and a lot of motivation, for years of training are required. Moreover, because yearly stipends for graduate training are so low ($12,000–$15,000) and opportunities for engineers with four-year degrees are numerous, most high-ability U.S. students opt for jobs in private industry, foregoing future training. High-ability foreigners who make it to the U.S. are much more motivated to pursue the Ph.D., despite poor funding. As a result, according to Iowa State University president, Gordon Eaton, soon 75 to 93 percent of the faculties of U.S. engineering schools will be foreign born.[49]

Interestingly, recent research has suggested that it is useful to distinguish between measures of a person's maximum level of performance and that person's typical level of performance. For example, in a study of cash-register operators, Paul Sackett and his colleagues obtained both a measure of typical performance (an objective measure of average daily processing speed) and a measure of max-

Esteem as an Illustrative Case," *Journal of Management* 14 (1988), 81–91 and J. R. Hollenbeck, A. P. Brief, E. M. Whitener and K. Pauli, "A Note on the Interaction of Personality and Aptitude in Personnel Selection," *Journal of Management* 14 (1988), 441–50.

[48] E. G. French, "The Interaction of Achievement Motivation and Ability in Problem Solving Success," *Journal of Abnormal and Social Psychology* 7 (1958), 306–9; and D. Kipnis, "A non-cognitive correlate of performance among Lower Aptitude Men," *Journal of Applied Psychology* 46 (1962), 76–80.

[49] *Time*, "Wanted: Fresh, Homegrown Talent," January 11, 1987, p. 65.

imum performance (a timed test of speed based on a standardized package of 25 items). When the data were analyzed, these researchers found that there was in fact very little relationship between an operator's maximum and typical performance.

This distinction may help untangle the effects of personality and ability on performance. Sackett and colleagues note that "it is reasonable to view the maximum performance measure as highly ability loaded, whereas motivational factors play a larger role in long term typical performance."[50]

Figure 4-7, which combines and expands on Figures 4-3, 4-4, and 4-5, summarizes what we have discussed in this chapter. The diagram shows that both maximum and typical performance levels are a function of one's motivation and total job capability. When both motivation and capability are high, typical performance will come very close to maximum performance, but when motivation is low, typical performance will be something substantially less than maximum performance. Typical performance will also be significantly less than maximum performance if emotional maladjustment detracts from the individual's ability to concentrate on the task. Finally, the figure reveals that other aspects of personality—social traits, motives, and personal conceptions—can influence the in-

[50] P. R. Sackett, S. Zedeck and L. Fogli, "Relations Between Measures of Typical and Maximum Performance," *Journal of Applied Psychology* 73 (1988), 482–86.

FIGURE 4-7

How Individual Differences Combine to Affect Performance

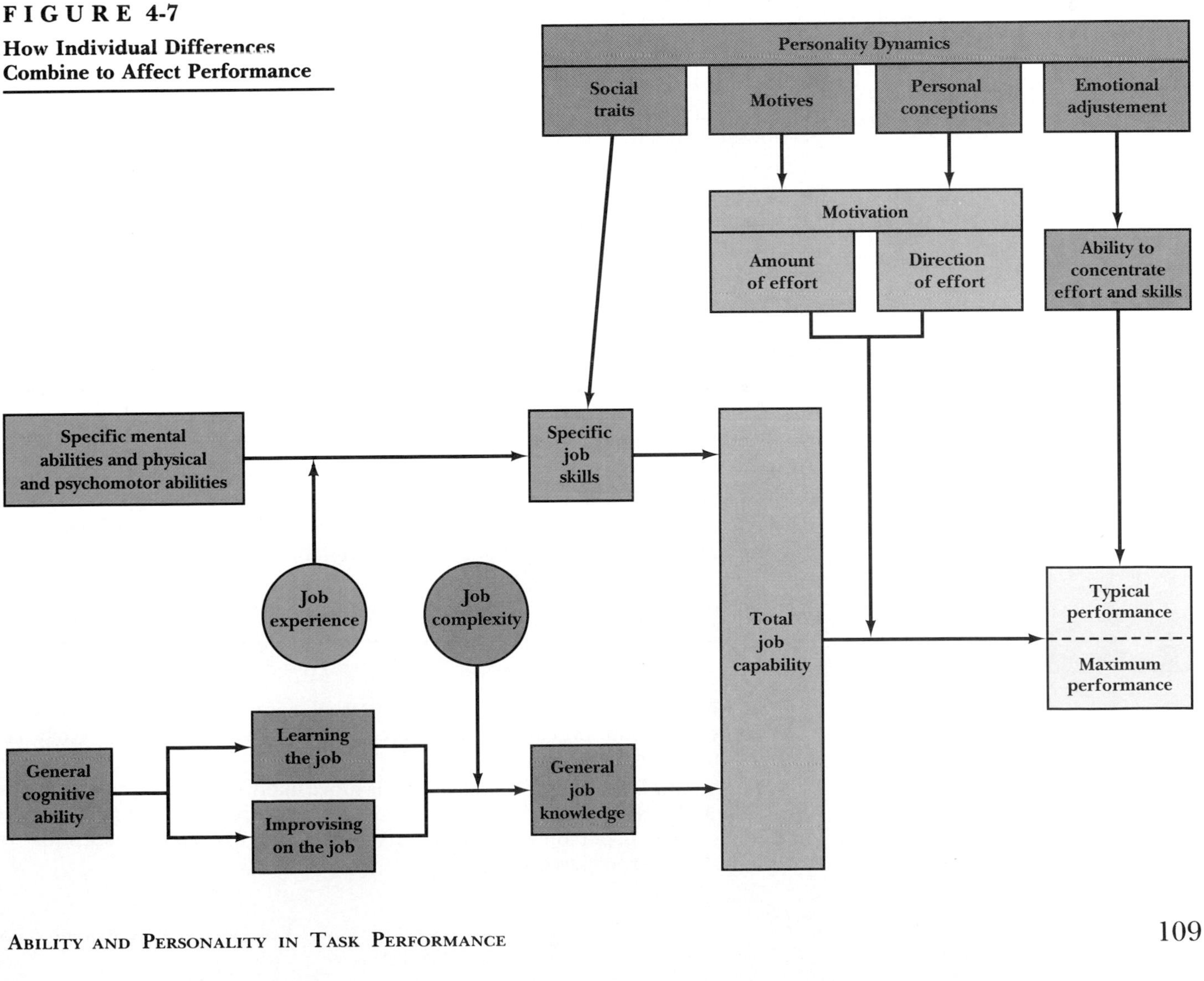

dividual's motivation in terms of both the person's level of effort and the way he will expend that effort.

An individual's total job capability is a function of her general job knowledge and her specific job skills. Specific job skills are primarily a function of specific facets of mental ability as well as specific physical and motor abilities that may be needed for particular jobs. Although personality plays a smaller role here, certain social traits may be required for certain jobs.

Finally, general cognitive ability (see the lower left-hand portion of Figure 4-7) influences general job knowledge by helping the individual to learn the job and to improvise on the job when nonroutine circumstances crop up. Job complexity moderates the relationship between general cognitive ability and job knowledge. As the job becomes more complex in terms of planning, decision making, and judgment, general cognitive ability becomes more important. For jobs that are low in complexity, general cognitive ability is less important. As the figure shows, under these conditions job experience becomes a more important influence on job knowledge.

Thus individual differences affect the behaviors of people in many ways. The manager who ignores these differences or assumes that everyone else is just like him is making a very big mistake that could be costly not only to him but to his company and his co-workers.

SUMMARY

Individuals differ on a number of different dimensions, and successfully taking advantage of this fact is essential to the effective control of organizational behavior. For example, individuals differ in their *physical* and *psychomotor abilities*, and there are many job situations in which people who lack the necessary abilities perform poorly and put themselves and others at risk for injuries. *General cognitive ability* is another characteristic on which individuals differ and one that has important implications for a much wider variety of jobs. Indeed, this characteristic is relevant for any job that requires planning and complex decision making on a daily basis. General cognitive ability also relates to both learning the job and adapting to new situations. Specific facets of cognitive ability, such as *verbal ability*, *quantitative ability*, *deduction*, *reasoning*, *spatial skills*, and *perceptual ability*, are important supplements to general cognitive ability for certain types of jobs.

Individuals also differ in personality characteristics. These differences in *social traits*, *motives*, *personal conceptions*, *emotional adjustment*, and *personality dynamics* often spill over into job-performance differences and have important implications for coordination and control. There is controversy, however, about how to measure personality, and the evidence for the utility of this kind of measure is not as strong as the evidence for the usefulness of ability measures. Further research on the use of personality measures in conjunction with ability measures and on the interaction between personality characteristics and typical versus maximum performance may provide stronger evidence for the usefulness of assessing personality in the organizational context.

REVIEW QUESTIONS

1. In what ways are the underlying beliefs of companies that use rigorous testing and selection processes much like the underlying beliefs of early researchers like Darwin, Galton, and Binet?

2. Do you think the mirror image fallacy is more likely to affect our assessments of others' abilities or of their personalities? Are there particular dimensions of ability or classes of personality characteristics that are especially susceptible to this kind of mistaken perception? Explain your answer.

ABILITY AND PERSONALITY

3. Think of someone you know who was highly successful in her chosen field. What were the important personal characteristics that led to this person's success? Now think of what would have happened if that person had chosen a different line of work. Do you think the person would have been successful no matter what she ventured into, or can you imagine lines of work for which she was poorly suited? How does your answer to this question relate to the selection-versus-placement distinction?

4. Think of someone who is turned down for a job and told that he was rejected because of (a) his performance on a paper-and-pencil cognitive ability test, (b) an interviewer's assessment of his intelligence and self-esteem, (c) a projective test of his need for affiliation and need for achievement, (d) his responses to a personality inventory, or (e) his answers on a paper-and-pencil honesty test. What differential reactions would you expect from this person? Explain your answer.

5. One of the authors knows of a firm that hands out several different kinds of tests to prospective employees but never actually scores them before making employment decisions. What message is indirectly being sent to applicants by firms that employ rigorous selection testing, and how might the intention to send such a message explain this company's behavior?

6. Some nations, for instance Japan, have federally controlled education, which results in educational standardization. They also promote a clear hierarchy of primary schools, secondary schools, and universities, arranged in order of their prestige and quality. Other nations, including the United States, leave control over education to state and local authorities. How might this difference in education policies lead to differential needs on the part of employers in the area of personnel testing?

DIAGNOSTIC QUESTIONS

 When attempting to come to grips with individual differences in resolving organizational problems, it may help to ask the following diagnostic questions.

1. Are there any special features of this job that call for high levels of specific physical or motor abilities? Does the jobholder possess these abilities?

2. Are there any features of this job that require specific facets of mental ability? Does the jobholder possess these abilities?

3. How much cognitive ability does the jobholder have? How will this influence the speed with which he will learn the job?

4. How much improvising will the person have to do on this job? Does the jobholder have enough general cognitive ability to adapt to changing circumstances?

5. If the jobholder lacks general cognitive ability, does he have sufficient work experience to make up for this deficiency?

6. How complex is this job? If it is highly complex, does the jobholder have enough cognitive ability to handle this complexity?

7. Are there any features of this job that require certain types of social traits? Does the holder of this job possess those traits?

8. What motives seem to drive this person? How do these motives influence the amount of energy that she brings to the task?

9. What are the major personal conceptions that guide this person? How do they influence the way he directs his energy?

10. Are there any signs of personality maladjustments that may be hindering this person's ability to concentrate on the task?

11. What is the relation between the person's typical and maximum level of performance?

12. How do we know what abilities and personality characteristics this jobholder possesses? How should we go about measuring these if we are unsure?

EXERCISE 4-1

MEASURING PERSONALITY DIFFERENCES[1]

JOHN E. OLIVER, *Valdosa State College*
GARY B. ROBERTS, *Kennesaw College*

Individual differences in personality characteristics such as social traits and personal conceptions affect the way people think, feel, and behave. The behavior of people in organizations is particularly likely to be affected by the four dimensions of *uncertainty avoidance*, *empathy-aggression*, *individualism-collectivism*, and *power distance*. If you have already read Chapter 19, you will recognize these as the dimensions Hofstede uses to differentiate organizational behaviors across cultures. In the exercise for that chapter we will take another look at these dimensions of human behavior.

In this exercise, after assessing yourself in terms of these four dimensions, you'll meet with class members who have assessed themselves as similar to you. You'll share your self-perceptions and learn how the four characteristics can affect people's satisfaction and performance in organizations. Then you'll meet with students who have assessed themselves as different from you and learn how individual differences can affect the way people work together.

STEP ONE: PRE-CLASS PREPARATION

To prepare for class, read the entire exercise. Next, find out where you stand on the four behavioral dimensions by completing the Personality Dimensions Questionnaire (Exhibit 4-1). As you respond to the questions, keep in mind that *there are no right or wrong answers*. This is a measure of individual differences, not a test of ability or knowledge. Just respond as honestly as you can. When you've completed the questionnaire, score your answers using the key at the end of this exercise.

STEP TWO: DISCUSSIONS IN SIMILAR GROUPS

The class session will begin by dividing into groups of people who have similar scores on the Personality Dimensions Questionnaire. Your instructor will set up four types of groups—one type to represent each of the four dimensions. You'll join a group for the dimension on which you get the highest total. Thus if your highest score is on power distance, you'll join a PD group. Suppose, however, that you have two or more scores—say

empathy-aggression and power distance—that are equally high. In this case, you would join either a PD or an EA group, depending on which one has the fewest members. The total number of groups will vary, of course, depending on the size of your class, but in general each group should have between four and six members.

Do not be concerned about your actual scores on the four dimensions. It's not necessarily good to be high on one, or low on another. What we're interested in here is how people who are *either alike* or *different from* each other interact and work together.

The task of every group is to answer the following questions:

1. Given that we have all rated ourselves similarly on X dimension, what do we think about this predisposition that we share? Are there good things about it? Are there bad things about it?
2. How does having this predisposition and the corresponding strengths and weaknesses that we've defined affect our behavior in the group? Our satisfaction with the group interaction?

Important: If your class will do Exercise 19-1 later in the term, be sure to make a list of the members of your group and to keep notes on your discussions in this step of Exercise 4-1. Later, in Exercise 19-1 you'll reconvene in the same groups to continue these discussions.

STEP THREE: DISCUSSIONS IN DISSIMILAR GROUPS

Now the class should divide into new groups of four to six members in which each of the four dimensions is represented by at least one high-scoring member. These

---

[1] The text of this exercise is adapted with the authors' permission from an exercise entitled "Personality Traits and Organizational Cultures: Two one-hour experiential learning exercises." The Personality Dimensions Questionnaire appearing in this exercise was developed by John Wagner and is based on dimensions described in Geert Hofstede, *Culture's Consequences: International Differences in Work-Related Values* (Beverly Hills, CA: Sage, 1980).

EXHIBIT 4-1
Personality Dimensions Questionnaire

Indicate whether you agree with each of the following statements by circling the appropriate number: 1 = Strongly Disagree, 2 = Disagree, 3 = Slightly Disagree, 4 = Neither Agree Nor Disagree, 5 = Slightly Agree, 6 = Agree, 7 = Strongly Agree.

1. I enjoy going to new and unfamiliar places.

   [1] [2] [3] [4] [5] [6] [7]

2. In an organization, subordinates should be allowed to participate in decision making.

   [1] [2] [3] [4] [5] [6] [7]

3. People are more likely to succeed in life if they are dominant and aggressive.

   [1] [2] [3] [4] [5] [6] [7]

4. Working alone is better than working in a group.

   [1] [2] [3] [4] [5] [6] [7]

5. People are more likely to succeed in life if they are compassionate and understanding.

   [1] [2] [3] [4] [5] [6] [7]

6. People in a group should do their best to cooperate with each other instead of trying to work things out on their own.

   [1] [2] [3] [4] [5] [6] [7]

7. People with power should have more status and prestige.

   [1] [2] [3] [4] [5] [6] [7]

8. Safety and security are the most important things in life.

   [1] [2] [3] [4] [5] [6] [7]

9. People in a group should be willing to make sacrifices for the sake of the group's welfare.

   [1] [2] [3] [4] [5] [6] [7]

10. I sympathize with people who are victims.

    [1] [2] [3] [4] [5] [6] [7]

11. Not knowing what is going to happen next makes me feel anxious and uncomfortable.

    [1] [2] [3] [4] [5] [6] [7]

12. Employees should be able to express disagreement with their managers.

    [1] [2] [3] [4] [5] [6] [7]

13. I admire people who are achievers.

    [1] [2] [3] [4] [5] [6] [7]

14. People like me want managers to make all the decisions.

    [1] [2] [3] [4] [5] [6] [7]

15. A group is more productive when its members do what they personally want to do rather than what the group wants them to do.

    [1] [2] [3] [4] [5] [6] [7]

16. I like not knowing what will happen tomorrow.

    [1] [2] [3] [4] [5] [6] [7]

---

groups should begin by having each member report the results of the Step Two discussions. After everyone in the group understands all four dimensions and their corresponding advantages and disadvantages, the group should answer the following questions:

1. Are there areas of unavoidable conflict among the four dimensions? How might such conflicts be managed?
2. Do the four dimensions complement each other in any way? Do some dimensions' advantages make up for other dimensions' disadvantages?

Then the group should select a spokesperson to present a five-minute summary of these answers to the rest of the class.

STEP FOUR: GROUP REPORTS AND CLASS DISCUSSION

In this last step, the spokespersons will present their summaries, and the class should look for similarities and differences among the conclusions that the various Step Three groups have reached. Your instructor will then share his or her personal observations of how the members of the similar and dissimilar groups worked together. Finally, the class should discuss how the individual differences examined in this exercise may affect organizational behavior. Here are some questions to consider in this discussion:

1. Did you see the advantages and disadvantages you associated with the different dimensions actually

influence work in the groups created in Step Three? What positive things happened? What negative things occurred?

2. What might be done to help people with different characteristics, attitudes, and beliefs work together? In what ways might the four personality dimensions examined here influence the management of organizational behavior?

CONCLUSION

Knowledge of individual differences such as those examined in this exercise can inform personnel selection and placement practices. Intelligently applied, it can help reduce absenteeism and turnover, and it can strengthen communication, motivation, and cooperation in organizations. Remember, though, that before we can use our knowledge about individual differences we must measure these differences properly, and our measures must be both reliable and valid. Otherwise, our personnel decisions may be inaccurate and subject to criticism or even legal action. Finally, it is crucial to keep in mind that many factors influence attitudes and performance at work: general and specific abilities, intelligence, job knowledge, personality characteristics,

and motivation (see Chapter 7) also have important effects on organizational behavior.

SCORING KEY

1. For questionnaire items 1, 2, 4, 5, 10, 12, 15, 16, subtract the number you circled from 8; the result is your score on each of these items. For example, if you circled the number (5) on item 1, your score for that item is 3.

    For questionnaire items 3, 6, 7, 8, 9, 11, 13, and 14, the number you circled is your item score.

2. Add your scores for items 1, 8, 11, and 16 and write the total here: _____. This is your score on *uncertainty avoidance* (UA).

3. Add your scores together for items 3, 5, 10, and 13 and write the total here: _____. This is your score on *empathy-aggression* (EA).

4. Add your scores together for items 4, 6, 9, and 15 and write the total here: _____. This is your score on *individualism-collectivism* (IC).

5. Add your scores together for items 2, 7, 12, and 14 and write the total here: _____. This is your score on *power distance* (PD).

DIAGNOSING ORGANIZATIONAL BEHAVIOR

John Matthews was a young executive at the divisional level of a large corporation. John, like a number of other young men in business throughout the United States, had been selected by higher-ups in his firm to attend a two-and-a-half-week executive development retreat.

The retreat was held at a remote camp in northern Minnesota. Although all of the necessary facilities for an enjoyable vacation were present, the structure and demands of the retreat left little time for relaxing and enjoying the surroundings. John was among 60 male executives who were registered to attend the retreat. They would spend 15 days living, working, and competing with one another.

ORGANIZATION AND ACTIVITIES

The 60 participants were broken down into 5 groups of 12. Each group was provided with a group leader. This leader was a senior corporate executive who had

CASE 4-1

EXECUTIVE RETREAT: A CASE OF GROUP FAILURE*
DONALD D. WHITE, *University of Arkansas*

previously attended the retreat. For 15 days, the men were involved in a variety of academic and athletic activities.

Selected sessions of the retreat were designated for "educational activities." The men participated in seminar sessions designed to deepen their understanding of central management decision making. These sessions involved a limited amount of lecture by either the group leader or a visitor. However, the majority of time devoted to academic pursuits was spent in case studies and a business game. Athletically, a good deal of the men's time was spent in physical fitness training and athletic competition. Finally, a few sessions were conducted along the lines of sensitivity training. (Chapter 14 discusses this method of group intervention).

Although a considerable amount of time was spent in intra-group activities, inter-group competition was

* Reprinted with the author's permission.

also fostered. In particular, groups competed athletically and through the business game.

The remaining portions of this case represent the reflections of John Matthews on his experiences at the executive retreat.

FIRST IMPRESSIONS

It is hard to express the emotions or thoughts that were going through my mind, let alone the minds of others, when I first met the members of my group. Until now, I had been working with business acquaintances in my company's San Francisco office. When I learned of my selection for the retreat and the manner in which it would be conducted, I wondered what my new associates would be like. Would we all remain for the full two and one-half weeks of the retreat? Would I be able to take the criticisms of others? How would our group do athletically and academically? And would the other members of my group resent the fact that I could not participate in the sporting events due to an old knee injury? Subconsciously, I had been establishing the criteria by which I would accept others and they would accept me.

During the first group meeting, I tried to learn the backgrounds of others who were with me. I went through the following process. I tried to find out where the others were from, what their education was, and the kind of experience they had accumulated. I discovered that the level at which one had worked within a firm together with whether or not he had held down a "home office" job were important because they created identification and solidarity between individuals; i.e., financial officers interacted with other financial officers, production managers with production managers, marketing people with others from marketing departments, and so forth. Our group leader made sure that he allowed enough time for all of us to meet each other before he walked in the door.

The group leader was the faculty member who had over-all responsibility for administrative functions in the group. He also graded papers and presentations, conducted all of our counseling sessions and was the all-around nursemaid for the group. Our leader, Mark, was a top-level corporate executive out of New York. This posed an immediate threat to some in the group when they first met him. After a few minutes of informal chitchat, Mark called everyone into a seminar room.

Mark made a low-key introduction of himself and the retreat. He emphasized that to be a success individually at "the camp," everyone had to cooperate and function as a group. He explained that no group always dominated intellectually or athletically. He related that his last group was not especially great in academics or

athletics yet their cumulative scores both in tests and games enabled them to become the top group at the retreat. This allowed certain privileges over other groups. The point Mark kept trying to make was that the men could no longer think of themselves as individuals. "The school theme" he said, "is 'Think—Communicate—Cooperate' and I suggest that you too adopt it as your guiding principle while you are here."

GROUP MEMBERS

The following are my recollections of the other members in our group.

Wally was an older member of the group and became the group student leader. He was a middle-level manager in a large company and had no formal technical training. This may have made him reluctant to assume a leadership role in the group. He appeared to be afraid of hurting other people's feelings even though his actions usually were justified.

Dave also did not have formal technical training; however, he was one of the few who had experience as a corporate president. He was an average student and speaker and above average in his writing ability. He appeared to be obsessed with sex. He called his wife every night, "studied" *The Art of Sensual Response*, and occasionally sniffed some musk oil which he had bought for his wife.

Jim was a financial analyst. He was one of two bachelors and was considered to be the playboy of the group. His goal was just to finish the retreat and get back to his home office.

Bob was a manager of production and operations for a leading producer of men's apparel. He, too, was a bachelor and considered himself to be a "ladykiller." To most of us he appeared to be conceited and boisterous. He claimed to be an authority on most subjects. He was also suspected of cheating in the 25-Mile Jogging Club (cheating on anything was strictly forbidden).

Larry was a director of public relations for a major steel producer. He had a liberal arts background and turned out to be our only distinguished graduate. Although he participated in everything, he never really assumed a leadership role and his contribution to the section was minimal. He was the only one (with the exception of me) who was not able to run a mile and a half in 12 minutes. He was a good speaker but a below average writer.

Rich was an internal financial consultant. He attended Harvard Business School and was later to be considered as one of the better executive prospects at the retreat. He was a good speaker and writer. Although he was very outspoken, he did make a lot of sense. He assumed the leader's role in two major exercises; however, he never did maintain his hold as leader over the group.

Wayne was a personnel director. He was an average student, writer, and speaker. He never did assume a leader's role, possibly because he was the most naive member of the group.

Ollie was a marketing manager and was considered the "country boy" of the group. He was an average student, good speaker, and good writer. He performed many odd jobs for us and was successful in leading us to two victories in athletics.

Gary was an executive vice president for a pipeline supplier whom I thought, at the beginning, would emerge as the leader of the group. He was poor academically, an average writer, and a good speaker. His additional duty was that of athletic chairman. Although he encouraged everyone to run 25 miles (25-Mile Club) during this period, he himself failed to achieve this goal.

Burrell was a personnel and public relations manager. He also was considered to be among the more promising men at the retreat. He was a fair speaker and an average writer. His additional duties were academic chairman and basketball coach. He was the type of guy that, if something were to go wrong, he would be in the middle of it.

Paul was manager for engineering for an electronics manufacturer. He had to spend three days of the first week of the retreat in the infirmary with a virus. This may have been one of the reasons why he was always trying to promote group functions when he got back. One thing I remember in particular about Paul is that he was always complaining about the "developmental rotation" program in his company. The program placed technically trained managers in functional areas other than their own for up to six months to provide them with career broadening. He saw the program as a threat to his own career but failed to see it as a threat to "general managers with no technical expertise." Over-all, Paul was an average speaker, writer, and student.

I, John, did not have formal education for my job as division director of industrial relations. I was an average student and writer and above average speaker. I considered myself to be a harmonizer of the group. I was the only member who was excused from sports because of an injury. Although I disagreed many times with decisions that were made, I usually went along with the group to the end.

The group members lived in three locations during the school. Living in Cabin I were Dave, Wally, Jim, Bob, John, and Larry. Wayne, Burrell, and Paul lived in Cabin II, while Ollie, Rich, and Gary lived in Cabin III. Bob and John generally walked to seminar sessions together as did Wally and Larry, Wayne, Burrell, and Paul and Ollie, Rich, and Gary. Dave and Jim walked separately to the sessions. Rich and Burrell studied together regularly. Larry, Rich, and Paul generally studied together.

GROUP ORGANIZATION AND ACTIVITIES

For convenience, Mark arranged the seating alphabetically around the table (see Exhibit 4-2). There was only one exception; Wally, the designated leader by virtue of age and experience, sat near the front. Following some brief introductions and a few administrative actions, goals of the group were established.

After much haggling about the goals, which ranged from totally idealistic to extremely pragmatic, the group decided on the following goals:

1. Everyone in the group would strive to complete the program and would seek to assure that our group was ranked first among various competing groups.
2. We would strive to be the best in sports.
3. Everyone would run at least 25 miles.
4. We would strive to maintain a harmonious atmosphere in the group.

Of immediate importance to the group was developing athletically rather than academically. (In final group ratings, athletics ranked a very close second to academics in total possible points that could be scored.) In fact, it wasn't until the latter part of the school that the section would come together in academics.

A couple of incidents that occurred during the retreat illustrated the extent of the group's success.

Toward the end of the first week, an entire afternoon was set aside for self-evaluation. The session resembled a sensitivity-training group session. Most groups had lunch followed with a little beer drinking to "loosen things up." After our loosening up we started our discussion. Several comments were made that should have provoked a fiery discussion, but for some reason they never did.

I don't believe we were open that afternoon. We looked at our leadership in academics, but none of us was willing to tell Burrell that he had a weak academic program. None of use would tell Gary that our athletics program was bad and that our group looked worse than most other groups with whom we competed. We all knew these things, but were unwilling to place the blame on anyone. Our group leader must have been totally frustrated at the end of the day. How could a group,

EXHIBIT 4-2
Seating Arrangement, First Day

which had such high goals and such mediocre results, have allowed such an opportunity to pass by?

A few days later another group project was scheduled. An obstacle course, intriguingly called "Project X," consisted of a series of tasks to be performed by six people at a time. It was supposed to test the group's ability to recognize the problem, decide on a solution, and carry it out in a 15-minute period. During the break, we tallied our score, 0 for 5. Mark seemed very upset. It was the first time he got upset with the entire group. Larry commented on the episode:

> We didn't see "Project X" or even the rest of the retreat as a life or death situation. In a retreat where no one fails to graduate, it can hardly be considered as a threat to anyone's career if these group goals go unaccomplished.

Personally, I saw us as a group of individuals in search of a real leader. We were all strong in our own individual specialities in our own organizations, but couldn't muster up the same vitality and enthusiasm to carry forth this synthetically designed group toward goal achievement. Although we wouldn't openly admit it, we were not committed to our goals. Yet, even though we lacked this commitment, we still maintained the goals. Going back to the afternoon encounter session, someone suggested that we revise our goals in light of our successes and failures to date. Even though it was impossible to achieve the original goals set, they still were unchanged!

The seating as depicted in Exhibit 4-3 was the arrangement for the last few days.

EXHIBIT 4-3
Seating Arrangement, Last Few Days

1. These individuals finished in top third of class.
2. These individuals never changed their seats.
3. Gary and John sat next to each other during the last seven days.
4. Wally never did assume the leader's position at the end of the table except when he led the two seminars.

Our group finished the two-and-one-half-week session having accomplished the following: Out of 12 individuals, one finished as a distinguished graduate and a total of three finished in the top third of the class. Ollie made the observation, "Lacking strong leadership in education, we each went our separate ways in trying to wade through all the material."

Our second goal also shared defeat. At the beginning of the program it was felt that our group had a chance to do well in sports. During practice sessions, we appeared to be relatively good. However, practice sessions reflected one characteristic of the group. Generally, we were disorganized, and there was always a lot of joking going on. I believed this carried over to the games and resulted in less than full commitment to winning. Gary would get frustrated and try to motivate the team at times, but his sudden surge of spirit usually was short-lived.

The third goal also fell short of being successfully accomplished. Only six of the members of our group actually finished the 25 miles. Another important factor regarding the 25-Mile Club centered on the ethics of one individual. Bob had been suspected of not running all the miles that he logged. At first Wally and Larry had suspected this, as later all the group members living around Bob did. One member noted, "We all felt that Wally should have confronted him with our suspicions." However, because the evidence against Bob was circumstantial, Wally didn't formally say anything to Bob about the incident. One change that did develop out of the episode was that the entire group ceased to listen to or trust Bob once they suspected his cheating.

The group came closest to achieving the final goal that involved the maintenance of harmonious relationships between one another. An example of this was our mutual respect for each other's territory. As one member stated it, "When Paul went to the hospital, his seat remained vacant even though we didn't have permanently assigned seats. When he returned, everyone made a special effort to make him feel a part of the group. Even when we suspected Bob of not really completing his running, we tried not to make too big a deal out of it."

Personally, I think I got a lot out of the retreat. I learned a lot in the academic sessions and even discovered some things about myself that I hadn't realized before. But, truthfully, I never figured out our group. Sometimes I think it was a near disaster.

When you have read this case, look back at the chapter's diagnostic questions and choose the ones that apply to the case. Then use those questions with the ones that follow in your case analysis.

1. What abilities did each member of John Matthews' group have? How did group members complement one another in terms of their abilities? How did they clash?

2. What abilities did the group's tasks require? Did any of the members have these abilities? Could members without these abilities develop them while working on the group tasks?

3. Did the group members' personalities help or hurt the group's performance? If, on the basis of their personality characteristics, you were to choose which people to keep in the group and which to dismiss, who would you keep? Why?

CASE 4-2

FREIDA MAE JONES

Read Chapter 5's Case 5-1, "Freida Mae Jones." Next, look back at Chapter 4's diagnostic questions and choose the ones that apply to that case. Then use those questions with the ones that follow in your case analysis.

1. What job-related abilities does Freida Mae Jones have? What are her personal strengths? What are her weaknesses?

2. Does Freida have the abilities needed to do the work currently assigned to Paul Koehn? What abilities does such work require?

3. What can a company do to ensure that promotions and job assignments are based on job-relevant abilities? Do you think the Industrialist World Bank of Boston has done this?

CASE 4-3

THE LORDSTOWN PLANT OF GENERAL MOTORS

Read Chapter 17's Case 17-1, "The Lordstown Plant of General Motors." Next, look back at Chapter 4's diagnostic questions and choose the ones that apply to that case. Then use those questions with the ones that follow in this first analysis of the case.

1. How did the backgrounds of the Lordstown employees differ from those of workers in other GM plants? What abilities distinguished Lordstown workers from the others?

2. What abilities did the jobs at Lordstown require? Did these match the abilities of the work force? What were the results of the match or mismatch?

3. Do you think GM used the same management practices at Lordstown as at other assembly plants? If it did, should it have instead adapted its approach to local conditions at Lordstown?

CHAPTER 5

PERCEPTION AND JUDGMENT

Even before its invasion of Kuwait, Iraq was a former ally of the Soviet Union and certainly was not a pro-western nation. Nevertheless, James Guerin, former CEO of International Signal and Control Group PLC, apparently helped Iraq acquire cluster bombs, bombs that could later have been deployed against the Allied Forces in the Persian Gulf War. When this and other questionable business transactions were revealed, Guerin, who had generally been perceived as an outstanding citizen, was regarded quite differently by people who thought they knew him. How would you reconcile two such different perceptions of the same person? How would you determine which is correct?

James Guerin, founder and CEO of International Signal and Control Group PLC, was considered a patriot, a rock of integrity, and a "true man of God." Guerin taught Bible classes, sang in the church choir, and gave more than $10 million dollars to charity. In Lancaster, Pennsylvania, where he started a backyard business that later grew into a huge conglomerate selling products all over the world, local residents perceived him as a man of "high moral character" and the region's premier philanthropist. Guerin showered money on all kinds of charities, including churches, colleges, relief organizations, and the Urban League. At the pinnacle of Guerin's career he sold his company in 1989 to Ferranti International PLC for $670 million. The purchase appeared particularly attractive to Ferranti because Guerin had obtained a $460 million contract to sell missiles to Pakistan.

Unfortunately, investigators soon found a more disturbing side to this family man. Painting a classic Jekyll-and-Hyde portrait of Guerin, these reports uncovered an alleged labyrinth of secret dealings including a covert, U.S.-backed intelligence project in South Africa and an elaborate scheme for moving monies among companies in Panama, Switzerland, and South Africa. The purpose of this scheme was to create the impression that the Pakistani deal which apparently was never finalized, had generated considerable revenues. When word of this scheme reached the press, Ferranti stock took a 25 percent drop, and many Lancaster residents were left scratching their heads. As one of Guerin's former employees stated, "I feel a great sense of loss and astonishment. The person I am reading about is just not the person I knew"[1]

We human beings have five senses through which we experience the world around us; sight, hearing, touch, smell, and taste. Barring extrasensory perception (ESP), which some believe we possess, these five are the only avenues through which we can acquire information about our environment. *Perception* is the process by which individuals select, organize, store, and interpret the information gathered from these senses. *Judgment* is the process whereby this perceived information is retrieved and used to evaluate various aspects of the environment. More often than not, these two connected processes of perception and judgment work well for us in our daily lives.

Indeed, the usual trustworthiness of these two processes sometimes leads people to accept their own perceptions and judgments without question. Such blind faith can lead to **phenomenal absolutism**, or the belief that one's perceptions are a perfect reflection of reality.

phenomenal absolutism The belief that one's perceptions reflect reality perfectly.

In chapter 4, we tried to discredit the idea of the mirror image fallacy. In this chapter we will take the same approach to the notion of phenomenal absolutism. People react to what they *perceive*, and their perceptions do not necessarily reflect objective reality. Those who believe in phenomenal absolutism rarely bother checking to see whether their perceptions correspond to reality. Because of the mirror image fallacy they tend to assume that most others share their perceptions and that those who do not are in error. This is a major problem, because as the difference between perceived and objective reality increases, so too does the opportunity for disaster, as evidenced in our opening story.

You can begin to appreciate the vast possibilities for perceptual distortion by considering some well-known illusions. Figure 5-1 shows several simple perceptual illusions that very often fool naive subjects into making the wrong judgments. Try your luck.

[1] Reprinted from E.T. Pound and A. Pasztor, "Shadowy Trail: American Arms Dealer Was Amazing Success, or So Ferranti Believed," *Wall Street Journal*, January 23, 1990, p. 1.

FIGURE 5-1

**Four Common Perceptual
Illusions**

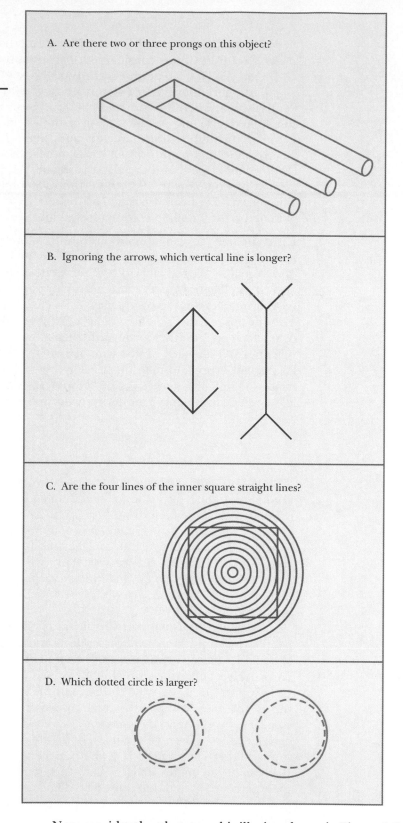

A. Are there two or three prongs on this object?

B. Ignoring the arrows, which vertical line is longer?

C. Are the four lines of the inner square straight lines?

D. Which dotted circle is larger?

Now consider the photographic illusion shown in Figure 5-2. Although three men in panel A appear to be of very different heights, in actuality they are about the same size. This illusion is based on the observer's assumption that the men are in a rectangular room that has four walls of the same height and windows that are equal in size. In fact, as you can see from panel B, the room is not rectangular, and the walls vary in height. The right rear corner of the room is much closer to the observer than the left rear corner. The floor-to-ceiling height

FIGURE 5-2

A Perceptual Illusion Based on Faulty Assumptions

Reprinted from I. Kaufman and I. Rock, "The Moon Illusion," Sciencific American, 1962, p. 27–28.

A

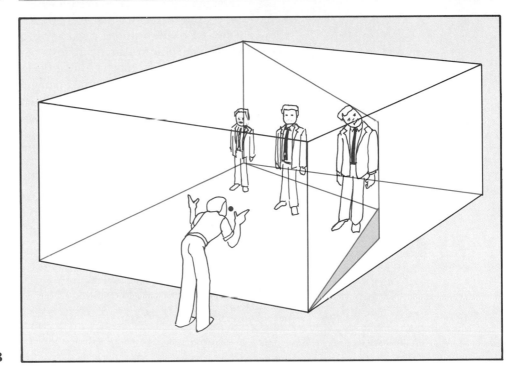

B

of the walls at that corner is also less than at any other corner of the room. The room is constructed so that if one looks through a specially placed peephole in the front wall, the image cast on the retina is of a normally shaped room. As a result, it is the people who appear strange.

Here's an illusion you can experiment with on the next clear evening when there is a full moon. Observe the moon (a) as it appears on the horizon and then (b) as it appears overhead. Even though we know that the size of the moon is constant, most people see its size at the horizon as two to three times its size when it is right above them. For an explanation of this curious illusion, take a look at I. Kaufman and I. Rock's article on "The Moon Illusion" (*Scientific American*, 1962, 204, pp 120–30).

Perceptual illusions involve more than just the sense of sight; try this next experiment. Fill three bowls with water. Put hot water in one, room-temperature water in the second, and ice water in the third. Place your right hand in the hot water and your left hand in the ice water. After about ninety seconds, remove both hands and put them both in the bowl containing the water at room temperature. Despite the objective fact that the temperature in the water in the second bowl is uniform, your two hands will experience it differently.

Although vision is probably the sense that we rely on most, the most compelling illusions are those that get several of our senses "working against us." For example, the StarTours adventure at Disneyland creates the illusion of movement (and quite fast movement) by deceiving three of our senses: vision, hearing, and touch.

DIAGNOSTIC ISSUES

The diagnostic model draws attention to several questions in the area of perception. For example, in terms of *description*, do managers and those they manage see eye to eye on whether the managers engage in specific behaviors? As the results from a study by Rensis Likert indicate (see Table 5-1), they may not.[2] Do subordinates even agree among themselves about their managers' behaviors? Some research suggests that there is almost as much disagreement here as between managers and subordinates.[3] Can we *diagnose* why, when confronted with identical data, some managers see the problem one way whereas others see it differently? Research by Dearborne and Simon, for example, has shown that managers' departments (for example, sales, accounting, production) strongly influence their perceptions and judgment of case problems.[4]

Can we *predict* when steps taken to solve certain problems actually worsen the problems because of the perceptions they create? For example, research by Madeline Heilman has shown that affirmative action programs designed to help advance women and minority workers often cause misperceptions on the part of these groups. Heilman found that women who were told they were hired based

[2] Rensis Likert, *New Patterns in Management*. (New York: McGraw-Hill, 1961).

[3] G. Graen and J. F. Cashman, "The Role Making Model of Leadership in Formal Organizations: A Developmental Approach," in *Leadership Frontiers*, ed. J. G. Hunt and L. L. Larson (Kent State, Ohio: Kent State University Press, 1975), p. 161.

[4] D. C. Dearborne and H. A. Simon. "Selective Perception: A Note on Departmental Identification of Executives." *Sociometry* 21 (1958), 142.

The StarTours adventure at Disney World alters the perceptions of 30 to 40 people at a time by simulating movement through space. As the "passengers" in this spaceship watch such things as an attack on an enemy ship on a screen in front of them, the flight simulator in which they're seated rotates in several directions, giving them a very intense feeling that what they are experiencing is real.

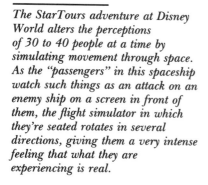

TABLE 5-1
Supervisors' and Subordinates' Views of Supervisors' Praise for Good Work

FORM OF RECOGNITION	FREQUENCY WITH WHICH SUPERVISORS SAY THEY GIVE RECOGNITION "VERY OFTEN"	FREQUENCY WITH WHICH EMPLOYEES SAY SUPERVISORS GIVE RECOGNITION "VERY OFTEN"
"A pat on the back"	82%	13%
Sincere and thorough praise	80	14
Training for better job	64	9
Special privileges	52	14
More interesting work	51	5
Added responsibility	48	10

Source: Adapted from R. Likert, *New Patterns in Management* (New York: McGraw-Hill Book Co., 1961), p. 71.

partly on their sex perceived themselves as less qualified and their performance as lower than it actually was.[5] Finally, what *action* can managers take when those they supervise contest and reject managerial perceptions? For example, in the five years between 1982 and 1987, over eight thousand lawsuits were brought by terminated employees who disagreed with managerial assessments of their performance. In over 80 percent of these cases, the ex-employees were vindicated and received settlements that averaged over a half-million dollars.[6] What actions can managers take to avoid these kinds of settlements and convince others—judges or juries—that these managers' perceptions were valid?

PERCEPTUAL ACCURACY

Judging other people's performance is one of the primary functions of a manager. In learning how to make such judgments as accurately as possible, it is useful to distinguish among different kinds of accuracy because some are more difficult to achieve than others, and each is needed for a different purpose. Four kinds of accuracy can be identified: elevation accuracy, differential elevation accuracy, stereotype accuracy, and differential accuracy.[7]

Table 5-2 shows the "true" scores (i.e., the objective level of performance) of five hypothetical employees on five characteristics. A score of 1 represents a very low standing on the characteristic, and a score of 9 reflects a very high standing. Table 5-3 presents a supervisor's evaluations of each employee on each dimension. Comparing the true, or objective, scores shown in Table 5-2 with the supervisor's ratings shown in Table 5-3—which are, of course, based on the supervisor's perceptions—will help us illustrate the four types of perceptual accuracy.

Elevation accuracy, deals with how high or low the ratings are in general, (hence the term *elevation*).

elevation accuracy The degree to which a rater's assessment of an entire group of people, across a number of different dimensions, reflects the group's true standing on those dimensions.

[5] M. C. Heilman and D. O. Repper, "Intentionally Favored, Unintentionally Harmed? Impact of Sex-Based Preferential Selection on Self-Perceptions and Self-Evaluations," *Journal of Applied Psychology* 72 (1987), 62–68.

[6] J. B. Copeland, "The Revenge of the Fired," *Newsweek*, February 16, 1987, p. 49.

[7] L. J. Cronbach, "Processes Affecting Scores on 'Understanding of Others' and 'Assumed Similarity,'" *Psychological Bulletin* 52 (1955), 177–93.

TABLE 5-2
"True" Scores of Five Workers on Five Different Characteristics

PERSON	TRAITS Job Knowledge	Interpersonal	Initiative	Creativity	Loyalty	TOTAL SCORE FOR PERSON
Bob	7	2	8	5	7	29
John	8	3	7	6	3	27
Steve	9	1	8	4	5	27
Carol	8	3	9	5	4	29
Dean	8	1	8	5	6	28
Average rating for group on characteristic	8	2	8	5	5	

TOTAL SCORE FOR GROUP

140

TABLE 5-3
Supervisor's Ratings of Five Workers on Five Different Characteristics

PERSON	TRAITS Job Knowledge	Interpersonal	Initiative	Creativity	Loyalty	TOTAL RATING FOR PERSON
Bob	9	2	7	6	7	31
John	6	2	8	7	2	25
Steve	7	3	4	2	7	23
Carol	4	2	5	3	2	16
Dean	8	1	8	5	6	28
Average rating for group on characteristic	6.8	2	6.4	4.6	4.8	

TOTAL RATING FOR GROUP

123

This measure reflects the degree to which the sum of all true values added up across both employees and dimensions (this sum is shown in the triangle in Table 5-2) matches the corresponding sum arrived at by the supervisor (shown in the triangle in Table 5-3). This could be thought of as the group's total score. When the two values differ substantially, a type of inaccuracy called leniency-severity may be operating. A leniency bias occurs when a supervisor rates all members of the group on all dimensions higher than they deserve. A severity bias reflects the opposite kind of error. In the data provided here, the supervisor appears to show severity rather than leniency, for the summed ratings in Table 5-3 are lower than the summed true scores in Table 5-2.

Elevation accuracy is particularly important when we need to compare individuals or groups rated by different supervisors. Suppose, for example, that two groups of employees have equal total true scores (in the triangle) but that the very lenient supervisor of one group rates its members significantly higher on the target characteristics, whereas the very tough supervisor of the other group rates its members as quite low. Imagine now that the organization in question has a pay-for-performance plan that rewards people based on their supervisors' ratings. The implementation of this plan might be perceived as quite unfair by those working under the severe supervisor, and over time this inaccuracy could lead to substantial conflict.

differential elevation accuracy The extent to which a rater's assessment of one individual, across a number of dimensions, reflects that person's true standing on those dimensions.

The second type of accuracy, **differential elevation accuracy**, reflects the degree to which the supervisor's ratings are accurate with respect to how high or low individuals are across all dimensions (hence the term *differential elevation*). This determination has implications for the accuracy of rank orders. This type of accuracy deals with how well the sum of each employee's true scores, shown in circles in the last column of Table 5-2, matches the same value as judged by the supervisor, shown in circles in the last column of Table 5-3.

Differential elevation accuracy is important in distinguishing among employees within the same group. Suppose, for example, that Bob, John, Steve, Carol, and Dean, whose scores and ratings are shown in Tables 5-2 and 5-3, were all candidates for promotion to a single, new position. Suppose further that the five dimensions assessed in the tables were considered equally important. Based on the supervisor's ratings, Bob would get the new job. Based on the true scores, however, Bob and Carol are equally qualified and, in fact, all five are very close on the five dimensions measured.

One rating error that has occurred here may be the similar-to-me bias. Our tendency to be attracted to people who are similar to us sometimes colors our ratings of others. Supervisors may unknowingly overestimate well-liked subordinates and, across all dimensions, assign excessively high ratings. Suppose, for example, that the supervisor whose ratings are shown in Table 5-3 is a male. The fact that his ratings of Carol are much lower than her true scores, might lead to charges of sexism and could severely damage the supervisor's credibility.

stereotype accuracy The extent to which a rater's assessment of a group of people, on a single dimension, reflects the group's true standing on that dimension.

The third type of accuracy, **stereotype accuracy**, deals with how accurately the supervisor describes the group as a whole in terms of its strengths and weaknesses.

The term *stereotype* has negative connotations because many stereotypes based on sex or race are innaccurate. However, we use the term here more broadly, recognizing that some group stereotypes may be accurate. For example, it is generally accurate to describe offensive linemen in football as bigger but slower than wide receivers.

Moreover, in the present context, the term *stereotype* focuses attention on general characteristics of a group as a whole rather than any individual within the group. The degree to which the group's true, or average, score on a given dimension (see squares at the bottom of each column in Table 5-2) matches the average rating on that dimension assigned the group by the supervisor (see squares at the bottom of each column in Table 5-3) gives us an index of stereotype accuracy. In this example, the supervisor assesses interpersonal skills accurately but is way off the mark in evaluating job knowledge and initiative.

This kind of accuracy is important when we are trying to diagnose group characteristics. Suppose that we were considering adopting some form of group training. The group described in Table 5-2 is strong in the areas of job knowledge and initiative (scores of 8 out of a possible 9), but weak in interpersonal skills (score of only 2). As we've already noted, the supervisor has accurately perceived this weakness, but he has underestimated the group's strength in initiative. Such a misperception could lead us to devise group training that would waste time focusing on developing skills the group already possessed.

T A B L E 5-4
The Four Kinds of Perceptual Accuracy

RANGE OF RATING	SUBJECT OF RATING	
	Group	Individual
Across several dimensions	Elevation	Differential elevation
On one dimension	Stereotype	Differential

differential accuracy The extent to which a rater's assessment of one individual, on one single dimension, is reflective of the person's true standing on that one dimension.

The most difficult type of accuracy to achieve, **differential accuracy**, is the extent to which the supervisor correctly assesses different employees on different dimensions (hence the term *differential* accuracy). As you can see from Tables 5-2 and 5-3, this fourth type of accuracy is the degree to which the true score for each individual on each specific dimension matches the supervisor's corresponding rating (as examples, see the numbers in the diamonds in columns 2 and 3 of Tables 5-2 and 5-3). This kind of accuracy is important in diagnosing an individual employee's strengths and weaknesses, as we would need to do if we were considering entering him or her in a career development program.

For example, suppose Steve's grasp of his assignment, willingness to take on new projects, and consistent hard work have come to the attention of a company executive and she has suggested that he be considered for career development. As you can see, Steve's score on job knowledge is the highest of anyone's, and his score on initiative is also very high. He is one of the lowest, however, on interpersonal skills, a dimension on which his supervisor overrates him. Moreover, the supervisor seriously underestimates Steve on initiative and underestimates his job knowledge as well. Steve probably will not be recommended for the career development program if a decision is based on his supervisor's ratings, in particular, of low initiative. If the decision is based on Steve's true ratings, however, the company might decide to give him some help in improving his interpersonal skills and then move him into the program.

Differential accuracy requires a great deal of perceptual skill on the part of the supervisor, and for reasons we will discuss later in this chapter, it is very difficult to achieve. Fortunately, for some decisions this type of accuracy is not always necessary. For example, if the dimensions being assessed are equally important and the ratings are to be used for merit-pay-raise decisions, differential elevation accuracy is all that is needed. If decisions are to be made about which group or team in the company is performing the best and should serve as a model for others, making this identification requires only elevation accuracy. If some type of team development is being planned, then only stereotype accuracy is needed to ensure that the right kind of training program is selected. But if decisions are being made about the strengths and weaknesses of an individual employee, differential accuracy must be achieved. Table 5-4 shows how the four types of accuracy differ in terms of the level at which the rating is made, and the dimensional specificity of the rating.

THE PERCEPTUAL PROCESS

In the next five sections of this chapter we describe a model of the perceptual process that is adapted from the work of Robert Lord.[8] In examining each stage in this process, we will identify and describe the types of factors that

[8] Robert Lord, "An Information Processing Approach to Social Perceptions, Leadership and Behavioral Measurement in Organizations," in *Research in Organizational Behavior*, vol. 7, ed. B. M. Staw and L. L. Cummings (Greenwich, Conn.: JAI Press, 1985), pp. 87–128.

bias accuracy. We will also suggest ways of combatting these biases in order to maximize perceptual accuracy.

Before we explore our perceptual framework and learn what kinds of factors get in the way of perceptual accuracy, let us consider for a moment how human beings process information from the environment. Basically, we process such information in one of two ways, by controlled or by automatic processing. In **controlled processing**, perceivers are aware of the fact that they are processing information. **Automatic processing**, on the other hand, is characterized by a lack of awareness on the part of the perceiver. For example, an interviewer actively listening to a job applicant's answers to specific questions and taking notes is processing information in a controlled mode. However, at the same time that she is listening and taking notes, the interviewer may perceive certain nonverbal behaviors of the applicant (such as not maintaining eye contact, profuse sweating, or other signs of nervousness). Even if the interviewer isn't conscious of these behaviors at the time and makes no formal notes about them, they may still enter into her mind through automatic processing. These impressions, although unrecorded formally, may affect the interviewer's judgment of the job applicant later, when she must make a formal decision about that person. Moreover, because the original perceptions were processed automatically, the interviewer may not be aware of all the information that is affecting the judgment she makes. We will see that in many different stages of the perceptual process, automatic processing greatly increases the likelihood of perceptual inaccuracies.

Figure 5-3 presents a model of the perception and judgment process that will guide our discussion in the next few sections. As the figure shows, there is a stimulus in the objective environment that must be subjectively processed by the observer. After this information is processed, a judgment is eventually reported, and, as the dotted lines indicate, the subjective judgment and the environmental stimulus match if the perception is accurate. Decisions and behaviors based on accurate perceptions are likely to be effective in dealing with the stimulus. Behaviors and decisions that are inaccurate, however, are usually ineffective.

But how do we get to an accurate judgment, one that can yield useful choices and actions? That is the topic of this chapter. As Figure 5-3 shows, before information reaches the stage at which a final judgment is made, it moves through four distinct stages of the perceptual process: attention, organization, interpretation, and retrieval. Let's start with the attention stage. Our five senses are constantly bombarded with so much information that we cannot process even a fraction of it. In the *attention stage* all available information is filtered, with the result that only a tiny portion of it is actually allowed inside the system for further processing. Despite this filtering process, the complexity of the incoming information is still so great that in the second, *organization stage*, it must be further simplified. Specific bits of information are grouped into more meaningful chunks, which reduces processing requirements. In the third, *interpretation stage*, the per-

controlled processing A manner of information processing in which the perceiver is aware that he is processing information.

automatic processing A manner of information processing in which the perceiver is not aware that he is processing information.

FIGURE 5-3

A Five-stage Model of the Perception and Judgment Process

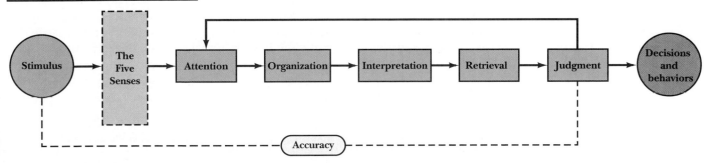

ceiver assigns meaning to the information and attempts to determine its implications. In the *retrieval stage*, the fourth stage of the perceptual process, information must be retrieved from memory. Because the input of information and its recall for specific use may sometimes be separated by weeks, months, or even years, much information is probably lost. In the *judgment stage*, whatever information can be retrieved is used to make needed decisions.

ATTENTION STAGE

As we have said earlier, in the **attention stage** the incredible amount of available information is filtered so that some enters the system and some does not. Of all the information that does enter the system, the observer can attend consciously to only a subset. Thus the controlled mode of processing can be used for only a small fraction of the incoming information. As a result, some of what enters the system does so automatically, so that the person may not be aware of its presence.

Although information that is not processed in a controlled manner usually has little effect on subsequent evaluations, this is not always the case. For example, in the initial phase of one experiment, subjects were given a mild electric shock whenever a certain word appeared on a screen placed before them. Over time the subjects began to associate this word with the shock. In the second phase of the same experiment, words were flashed on the screen so rapidly that they could not be read. Despite the fact that subjects could not tell what the words were, they gave evidence of fear as measured by physiological arousal (increased heart rate, amount of perspiration) whenever the threatening word appeared.[9] Perceptions like this that enter the system in an automatic rather than a controlled fashion are often referred to as **subliminal perceptions**.

Although we cannot overlook the effects of subliminal perceptions, controlled perceptions dominate judgment. Moreover, because perceptions cannot be processed in a controlled mode without conscious attention to them, the *external* and *internal* factors that draw attention to certain objects are worth noting.

External Factors

Certain characteristics of objects influence the degree to which these objects capture our attention. The intensity of a stimulus, its contrast with other stimuli in the environment, its familiarity or novelty are all factors that affect our attention. These factors often counterbalance each other and combine in complex ways.

Intensity refers to the overall impact that the external object has on the sensing person. Intense objects are more likely to capture one's attention. For example, although shouting at someone may not be polite, it is probably more likely to capture the person's attention than speaking in a normal tone of voice. Why do you suppose a bright red light is used for traffic "stop" signals? It is because this color has been shown to make the biggest impact physiologically on our visual receptors and hence is most likely to be noticed. Bigger things are also more likely to catch your eye than smaller things, because they excite a greater number of your visual receptors.

attention stage The stage in the information processing cycle in which the individual decides what will be processed and what will be ignored.

subliminal perception Information that is enco[...] perceiver without his or [...] awareness.

[9] R. S. Corteen and B. Wood, "Autonomic Responses to Shock-Associated Words in an Unattended Channel," *Journal of Experimental Psychology* 94 (1972), 308–13.

On the 1988 presidential campaign trail, George Bush answered questions about new taxes so many times he sought an answer that would really drive home his point: "Read my lips—no new taxes." The words "read my lips" have become so familiar that people now use it whenever they want to get the attention of others. Here a supporter of the 1990 Civil Rights Act is using the perceptual principle of frequency to try to get President Bush's attention.

Counterbalanced against the notion of intensity, however, is the notion of *contrast*. As one television commercial correctly noted, "If you want to capture someone's attention, just whisper." Similarly, if you looked first at this sentence when you turned to this page, you have just demonstrated that contrast sometimes wins out over size or intensity in drawing one's attention. Thus in a sea of intense stimuli, a less intense stimulus can sometimes succeed in capturing our attention.

In general, the greater the *frequency* with which people encounter a given stimulus or the greater its familiarity, the more likely it is that they will attend to it. Thus the more often students complain about a particular aspect of a course, the more likely the teacher is to pay attention to their concerns. The more often a particular recording is played on the radio, the more likely it is that people will become aware of the tune.

Counterbalanced against frequency, is the notion of novelty. We may encounter a given stimulus so often that we begin to ignore it. Something that is totally new to our experience, on the other hand, may arouse our interest and draw our attention. Thus *novelty*, or the extent to which a stimulus is seen as new and different, is also important. Advertisers, who are professional attention getters, try to mix frequency and novelty together by repeating a fundamental theme with a minor innovation. During the very solemn lighting of the Olympic torch at the 1988 Summer Games, the producer of ABC television's Olympics coverage was heard to say: "Fine, but I wanted a Bud Light." Clearly this one advertising campaign's use of repetition (always ending with the same line) in combination with novelty (the same line capping many different setups) had captured the attention of at least one viewer.

Internal Factors

The perceiver's *expectations* of an object will often affect his evaluation of that object. One reason for this reaction is that attention is more easily drawn to objects that confirm our expectations. A good example can be seen in Eden and Shani's study of tank crews in the Israeli army.[10] In this study, the researchers told one set of tank commanders that test data indicated that some members of the crews assigned to them had exceptional ability. The tank commanders were also told

[10] D. Eden and A. B. Shani, "Pygmalian Goes to Boot Camp: Expectancy, Leadership and Trainee Performance," *Journal of Applied Psychology* 67 (1982), 194–99.

that some of the soldiers assigned to them were, according to the tests, only average. In reality, the soldiers were assigned to commanders randomly so that the two groups were equally able. Nevertheless, when asked later to rate the performance of their men, the commanders reported that the performance of the "exceptional" soldiers was better than the performance of soldiers who were said to be "average." The researchers explained their findings by noting that the commanders "naturally lavished more attention on individuals for whom they harbored more positive expectancies."[10] Thus expectations become a self-fulfilling prophecy in that they help bring about exactly what they predict.

The *needs and interests* of perceivers themselves can also influence attention. For example, when you are reading a newspaper, a story about a robbery that occurred on your street is much more likely to grab your attention than a story on overall trends in the U.S. crime rate. A news story on a surge in interest rates that many readers might ignore might attract a great deal of attention among workers in construction. For construction firms, high interest rates mean low demand for services and can even cause firms to go out of business.

perceptual defense The process by which an individual avoids processing information that is potentially threatening.

One way in which needs and interests influence perceptions is by **perceptual defense**, in which a person completely blocks out a stimulus that is highly threatening to him. He simply does not perceive it. Studies have shown, for example, that when words are presented under speeded viewing conditions, subjects have a harder time recognizing threatening words (e.g., *rape*, *kill*) than nonthreatening words (e.g., *rake* or *mill*).[11]

Earlier we discussed the study by Heilman on the effects of granting preferential treatment to women and minorities on the perceptions of those who were favored. Given the influence of needs and interests on perceptions, it is not hard to anticipate the effect of such practices on those who are placed at a disadvantage.

[11] E. McGinnies, "Emotionality and Perceptual Defense," *Psychological Review* 56 (1949), 244–51.

TABLE 5-5

Differences in the Views of Black and White Americans on Opportunities for Blacks

		BLACKS	WHITES
Perceptual Differences	Do black Americans have the same opportunities as whites?		
1	In housing?		
	Yes	22%	48%
	No	75	47
2	In education?		
	Yes	38	73
	No	59	24
3	In employment?		
	Yes	26	59
	No	71	37
Judgmental Differences			
4	Should colleges admit some students whose records would not normally qualify them for admission?		
	Yes	33	15
5	Should businesses set a goal of hiring a minimum number of black employees?		
	Yes	62	32

Source: Adapted from "Attitudes in Black and White," *Time*, February 2, 1987, p. 37.

Consider the results of an opinion survey of blacks and whites shown in Table 5-5. As you can see, there were marked differences in the way blacks and whites perceived and judged current opportunities for African Americans in the United States. These differences are probably best explained by the fact that each group is attending to different things. Given these differences in perceptual input, it is not surprising that the two sides come to markedly different judgments with respect to questions 4 and 5 in the Table. Working out these kinds of perceptual differences may be essential before true progress can be made in the area of civil rights.

Making Attention More Efficient

Clearly there are many ways a human observer can fail to portray her environment accurately. Before we look at some methods of improving our powers of attention, we should note one thing. There is no free lunch when it comes to increasing the accuracy of perceptions. Most of the solutions we will discuss require a controlled mode of information processing. As we noted at the outset, human observers can process only one thing at a time in this mode, and therefore time devoted to increasing accuracy of perceptions subtracts from time available for other aspects of the observer's job. Thus if we expect supervisors to provide detailed and accurate judgments of a subordinate's effectiveness, we must also understand that this responsibility will take time away from other dimensions of their jobs. Moreover, we should keep the four types of perceptual accuracy in mind. The kind of accuracy needed for one type of decision may be easier to achieve than the accuracy needed for another kind of decision.

Because one of the major problems at the attention stage is simply the amount of information available for processing, one way to improve accuracy is by *increased frequency of observations*. That is, we can increase the observer's exposure to the thing being observed. By making more observations, an observer may gather more information and thus heighten the accuracy of her perceptions.[12]

Because a second major problem at the attention stage is the representativeness of the information, the manner in which observations are obtained should also be considered. If we obtain observations by *random sampling* (see Chapter 3), we increase the probability that these observations will be accurate. If a supervisor observes a group of workers only at a given time on a given day or makes observations only when problems develop, the behaviors she observes may not truly reflect what is happening in this group.

The opportunity to observe employee work behaviors frequently, randomly, and secretively has increased rapidly with technological developments in the field of surveillance. In fact, this opportunity has increased so dramatically that some are beginning to raise ethical issues with regard to monitoring practices. Some of these practices and the ethical issues involved are described in the "Management Issues" box.

Finally, because observers have a tendency to ignore information that is inconsistent with their expectations, it is often good advice to actively *seek information that is inconsistent* with, or that disconfirms, one's current beliefs. For example, if in the past you have judged a particular worker as someone who "can't do anything right," approach the observation of that person from the opposite direction. That is, systematically search for things that the person *does* do right. You might surprise yourself.

---

[12] W. C. Borman, "Exploring the Upper Limits of Reliability and Validity of Performance Ratings," *Journal of Applied Psychology* 63 (1978), 135–44.

MANAGEMENT ISSUES
The Brave New World of Employee Surveillance

Nurses at Holy Cross Hospital in Silver Springs, Maryland, were surprised when they discovered that the silver box with red lights hanging on their locker room wall was actually a video camera. They were shocked when they learned that the pictures taken by this camera, which captured the nurses in various stage of undress, were being broadcast over the hospital's closed-circuit TV network. Although the hospital later claimed that the pictures were viewed only by the hospital's (male) chief of security, this did little to alleviate the nurses' outrage. Moreover, few outside observers of this incident felt that the hospital's stated purpose of trying to track disappearing narcotics justified its behavior.

Incidents like this are becoming widespread. The DuPont Company, for example, now uses hidden long-distance cameras to monitor its loading docks. At Delta Airlines, computers track which salespeople write the most reservations. At Management Recruiters, Inc., in Chicago, supervisors surreptitiously watch computerized schedules to see which interviewers talk to the most job candidates. Supervisors at the Internal Revenue Service can "tap into" telephone conversations between IRS agents and taxpayers calling for information.

Firms are not reluctant to use the data captured by these electronic devices in making decisions. Safeway Stores, for example, has installed dashboard computers on its 800 trucks. The computers record driving speed, idling time, and when and how long a truck is stopped. According to George Sveum, secretary of Teamsters Local 350 in Martinez, California, Safeway tries to suspend or discharge up to 20 drivers a year using this computerized data.

The increased use of computerized employee monitoring has been a product of two forces. First, there has always been a need to observe employees' work behaviors, and recent developments in surveillance technology have simply made this easier and less obtrusive. The second force is the increasing number of court cases dealing with "negligent hiring," where employers are held liable for the mistakes or crimes of employees. These two developments have led to a serious erosion of employee rights to privacy.

Finding the right balance between these rights and the employer's right and responsibility to monitor workers will be

Pilferage at loading docks, whether inland or on the waterfront, has always been a difficult problem to control. Now, with hidden cameras that have telephoto lenses and that can make continuous and constant observations, it is very difficult to get away with such theft. But for many people this means of surveillance raises ethical issues. Has the worker a right to privacy on the job? Is there a differnce between having a foreman watching you constantly or an executive vice president strolling by your desk several times a day and having your every action recorded by an electronic eye?

a difficult process. Undoubtedly it will play itself out in the courts and legislatures. Although current federal and state laws permit most forms of eavesdropping and electronic monitoring in the workplace, growing public awareness of such practices may lead to remedial legislation that provides employees with some assurance of privacy.*

* J. Rothfeder, M. Galen and L. Driscoll, "Is Your Boss Spying on You?: High Tech Snooping in 'the Electronic Sweatshop,'" *Business Week*, January 15, 1990, pp. 74–75.

ORGANIZATION STAGE

organization stage The stage in the information processing cycle in which many discrete bits of information are chunked into higher-level, abstract concepts.

Even though much information is automatically filtered out at the attention stage, the remaining information is still too abundant and too complex to be easily understood and stored. Because human perceivers can process only a few bits of information at a time in a controlled fashion, in the **organization stage** we further simplify and organize these incoming data. One method is to "chunk" several discrete pieces of information into a single piece of information that can be processed more easily.

134

To show you how effective this kind of chunking can be, imagine your reaction if someone were to ask you to memorize a string of 40 numbers. You might very well doubt your capacity to memorize this many numbers regardless of how much time you were given. Your doubts are probably misplaced, however, because if asked, you could probably write down (a) your social security number, (b) your telephone number with area code, (c) your license plate number, (d) the month, date, and year of your birth, (e) your current zip code, and (f) your height and weight. You might say, "Well, yes, but these are only six numbers," but note that *a* and *b* have 9 digits each, *c* and *d* have 6, and *e* and *f* probably have 5; this comes to a grand total of 40 digits! The fact that we think of these as six numbers rather than forty shows how we mentally chunk things together. The fact that by the chunking process we can memorize many more than forty numbers (think of all the telephone numbers, zip codes, birthdays, and so on that you can recall) attests to the efficiency of this type of organizing process.

When we do this kind of chunking with non-numerical information we refer to the chunks as schema. **Schema** are cognitive structures that group discrete bits of perceptual information in an organized fashion.[13] In general, two types of schema are particularly important to understanding the processing of social-interpersonal information: scripts and prototypes.

schema Cognitive structures that group discrete bits of perceptual information in an organized fashion. (The term *schema* is used for both singular and plural forms.)

Scripts

Suppose you are chatting with a friend and ask him, "So what did you do Friday night?" Imagine, then, that he replies, "I put on my best suit. I got in my car. I drove downtown and picked up a young woman at her apartment. We drove to an expensive restaurant. We had drinks. We made polite conversation. We ordered something to eat. We ate our dinner. We got back in my car. I drove the young woman back to her apartment. I walked her to her door. I stole a kiss. I got back in my car. I drove back home." You might say, "In other words, you went out on a date," and he might respond "Yes." Note how in the last two exchanges you and your friend chunked a 14-bit sequence into a one-word schema: *date*. Schemas that involve sequences of actions are called **scripts**, for the very good reason that they resemble the material from movies or plays.

script A schema that involves well-known sequences of action

Assume that your friend went on to report that he had dinner at his parents' house on Thursday, studied with friends on Wednesday, went to a college basketball game on Tuesday, and washed and waxed his car on Monday. You can probably envision scripts for all five activities that your friend engaged in Monday through Friday and in doing so chunk over a hundred bits of information into five tight pieces. This kind of efficiency makes scripts highly useful from an information-processing point of view.

Now imagine that from your friend's report of his date last night, you form the judgment that he probably does not have the money to go to a movie tonight. To your surprise, he says he can indeed go, because "last night didn't cost me a dime, my date paid for the dinner." Herein lies the problem with scripts, namely, that a given script may have different meanings for different people. Note that nowhere in your friend's 14-point description of his date did he mention how the bill was paid. You simply assumed that he paid because that is part of *your* script for a date—one that some might call sexist and outdated!

Thus while the kind of simplification that is granted by scripts is vital for efficient information processing, one should not lose sight of the fact that in scripting such sequences we may be adding things to the event that never took place or deleting things that did happen. Clearly there are numerous events in

[13] U. Neisser, *Cognition and Reality* (San Francisco: W. H. Freeman, 1976), p. 112.

organizations that prompt different scripts in different people's minds. Things such as taking a client to lunch, preparing a written report, or disciplining a subordinate, may involve sequences of behavior for some organizational members that are not the same as the sequences envisioned by others. Clarifying these scripts is essential if perceptual accuracy is the goal.

Prototypes

prototype One type of schema that involves a unified configuration of personal characteristics that are used to classify persons into "types."

Just as there are schema for simplifying events, there are also schema for simplifying the description of persons. **Prototypes** are schema that enable us to chunk information about people's characteristics.

For example, if you asked your precise friend what the person he dated was like, he might report that she was spirited, exuberant, outgoing, boisterous, and warm. "You mean she's an extrovert," you say. Here again we see multiple bits of information chunked into one word that is meant to carry a detailed description of a person. Like scripts, however, prototypes sometimes carry excess baggage and thus may not reflect the person accurately. You may recall how during the 1988 presidential election George Bush repeatedly labeled Michael Dukakis an "old-fashioned, liberal democrat" and a "card-carrying member of the American Civil Liberties Union." The purpose of this strategy was to get the voters to categorize Dukakis as a certain type of person, one whom many people would find unsuitable as a president of the United States.

In the area of organizational behavior, the leader prototype is an important one. Most managers want others to perceive them as leaders. What characteristics are likely to cause people to categorize someone in this way? According to research conducted by Robert Lord, the leader prototype is made up of the 12 characteristics shown in Table 5-6 and listed in descending order of importance. People who exhibit a majority of these characteristics will be seen as leaders. Moreover, according to Lord, people generally assume that anyone who is a leader must have these characteristics.

With a concept as broad as *leader*, there is a tendency to make distinctions among various kinds of leaders. Lord and his colleagues have found that there are specific prototypes for many kinds of leaders, including military, religious, business, political, labor, and minority leaders, to name just a few.

Prototypes can be negative. For example, the expression "empty suit" emerged in the business world in the late 1980s as a label for a particular type of manager. Specifically, an "empty suit" was a manager with a great deal of style and a "dress-for-success" image but little in the way of substance, skill, or deeply rooted values.[14]

[14] W. Kiechel, "How to Spot an Empty Suit," *Fortune*, November 20, 1989, p. 22.

T A B L E 5-6
Major Characteristics of the "Leader" Prototype (in descending order of importance)

1. Intelligent	5. Aggressive	9. Decisive
2. Outgoing	6. Determined	10. Dedicated
3. Understanding	7. Industrious	11. Educated
4. Articulate	8. Caring	12. Well dressed

Source: R. G. Lord, R. J. Foti, and D. DeVader. "A Test of Leadership Categorization Theory: Internal Structure, Information Processing, and Leadership Perceptions," *Organizational Behavior and Human Performance* 34 (1984), 343–78.

Stereotyping. Not all prototypes are useful. A *stereotype* is a widely held generalization about a group of people. Often it is a prototype organized around a person's race, sex, age, ethnic origin, socioeconomic group, or other sociocultural characteristics: for example, African-Americans, women, the elderly, Hispanic-Americans, blue-collar workers, homosexuals. In one study business students displayed a clear stereotype of the elderly.[15] Among other things, students described this group as less creative, less able to do physically demanding work, less able to change or be innovative. These perceptions led the students to make other negative judgments about elderly workers. For instance, they expressed the belief that these workers would be less likely than younger workers to benefit from training and development. Given the increasing age of our national work force, such stereotypes need to be examined closely.

Stereotypes are not confined to students. Many people feel that businesses systematically discriminate against older workers by forcing them into early retirement programs. For example, Richard E. Wilson, a former vice-president of Monarch Paper Company was demoted to a warehouse-maintenance job that included clean-up duty and other menial tasks, after failing to accept an early retirement "offer." A federal jury awarded Wilson $3.2 million and judged that the company was guilty of age bias. The jury suggested that the company's heavy-handed offer was part of a plan to eliminate older managers and replace them with younger ones.[16]

In some cases, workers are actually punished for not living up to widely shared stereotypes. For example, despite the fact that she had won a $34-million government contract, Ann B. Hopkins was not promoted to partner in the prestigious accounting firm of Price Waterhouse. Male colleagues criticized Hopkins for being "too macho" and suggested that she needed "a course at charm school."[17] The U.S. Supreme Court found this type of sex stereotyping a violation of the Civil Rights Act and awarded Hopkins a large settlement.

halo error A rating error wherein a rater's judgment about a specific behavior is colored by her overall evaluation of the person she is rating.

Halo error. Another type of perceptual bias, the **halo error**, occurs when a rater's judgment about specific facets of behavior are colored by his overall evaluation of the person he is rating.

For example, Figure 5-4 reproduces an instructor evaluation form in which students are asked to answer one general question and ten specific questions about an instructor's performance. Presumably, the ten dimensions tapped in the specific questions are unrelated. That is, it is assumed that a person might be very enthusiastic but not well organized. Similarly it is assumed that an instructor may be able to outline the direction of the course adequately but may not be very good at stimulating class discussion. Despite these assumptions by persons who constructed the rating form, actual ratings obtained from students often make it look as if the ten factors were highly interrelated.

For example, in filling out the questionnaire, Student A gave the instructor a "superior" ("S") on all eleven items. This instance of halo error suggests that the student's overall impression of his instructor has created a positive bias in his ratings of the specific dimensions of performance. That is, the student has developed a prototype of what a good instructor is, judges this person to be a good instructor, and therefore rates the person high on every single dimension. Clearly, if raters make no distinctions with respect to the specific dimensions in which we are interested, we have a major threat to differential accuracy. In this case, the

---

[15] B. Rosen and T. H. Jerdee, "The Influence of Age Stereotypes on Managerial Decisions," *Journal of Applied Psychology* 61 (1976), 428–32.

[16] E. G. Olson, "The Workplace Is High on the High Court's Docket," *Business Week*, October 10, 1988, pp. 88–89.

[17] Ibid.

QUESTIONNAIRE ITEMS

Overall Evaluation

1. How would you rate this instructor overall?

Specific Evaluation

2. Instructor's enthusiasm
3. Instructor's interest in teaching
4. Instructor's organization of the course material
5. Instructor's stimulation of class discussion
6. Adequacy of the course outline
7. Instructor's use of examples
8. Ease of taking notes during instructor's presentation
9. Instructor's concern for students' learning
10. Appropriateness of instructor's pace
11. Instructor's receptiveness to students' ideas

STUDENTS EVALUATIONS

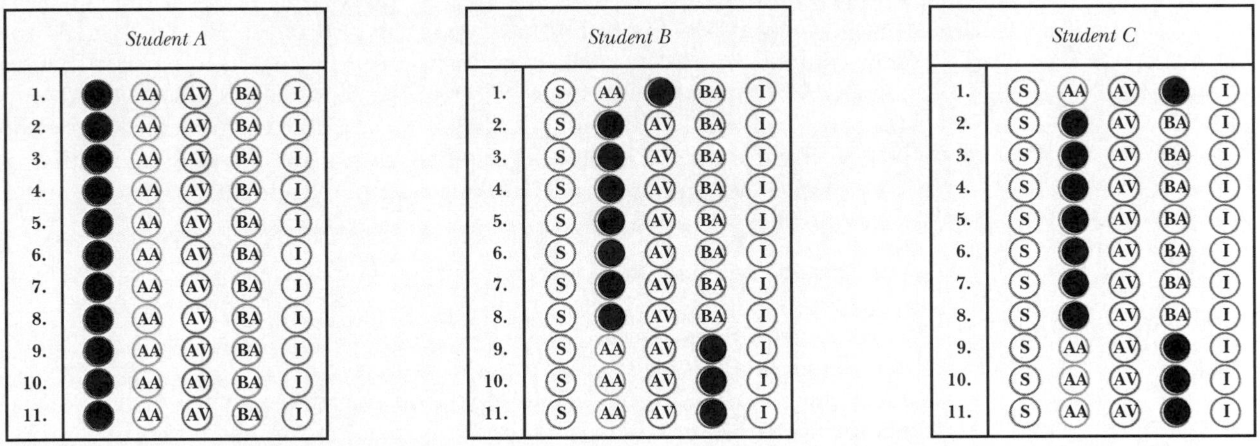

KEY:	S	Superior–exceptionally good course or instructor
	AA	Above Average–better than the typical course or instructor
	AV	Average–typical course or instructor
	BA	Below Average–not as good as the typical course or instructor
	I	Inferior–exceptionally poor course or instructor

FIGURE 5-4

Hypothetical Student Evaluations of Instructors

halo error undermines any attempt to help instructors improve in areas in which they are weak.

What makes the halo error such an intractable problem, however, is that we often do not know how much true relationship there is among the dimensions in which we are interested. Consider a recent study of major league baseball players.[18] In this study, several dimensions of player performance (e.g., batting average, runs batted in, stolen bases, fielding errors) were measured objectively. Subjects were then asked to rate several well-known players on these dimen-

[18] S. W. J. Kozlowski and M. P. Kirsch, "The Systematic Distortion Hypothesis, Halo, and Accuracy: An Individual Level Analysis," *Journal of Applied Psychology* 72 (1987), 252–61.

sions. The ratings did indicate a relationship among the dimensions. If a player was rated high on one dimension (e.g., hitting), for example, he tended to be rated high on others (e.g., fielding and running) even though the dimensions appear to tap different abilities.

Do these results reflect a halo error? No, because the true relationship among the dimensions was even greater than the ratings indicated. The raters did not show *enough* halo. Whereas hitting and fielding may *seem* to be different things, the objective data show that these two aspects of performance actually are related to each other. Separating illusory halo from true halo is not an easy matter. Before securing ratings one needs to think seriously about how and when one dimension of performance may be related to another.

Improving Perceptual Organization

The main problem at the organization stage is oversimplification of the information that we attend to. Given the limited information-processing skills that human beings have, it is unrealistic to expect people to completely give up the use of schemas. It is a good idea, on the other hand, to *elaborate prototypes and stereotypes*, that is, to make people aware of the prototypes and stereotypes they hold of other people. It is also a good idea to get observers to *abandon particular prototypes or scripts* that seem to lead them astray, and perhaps to replace these with other scripts and prototypes that will be accurate and still helpful in simplifying data.

When a person must work with social groups that differ from her own, it may be useful for her to *increase her exposure to different social groups*. This approach may go a long way toward helping the person develop more accurate prototypes. Research on expert-novice differences in all kinds of domains shows that experts differ from novices not because they ignore developing prototypes but because they develop more complex, detailed prototypes that are more accurate.[19] Thus as people develop experience with people and situations that are unfamiliar to them, their processes of organization become more complex and better able to reflect the underlying reality. Actively *searching for disconfirming prototype information*, is particularly useful in this regard.

INTERPRETATION STAGE

interpretation stage The stage in the information processing cycle in which meaning is attached to the relation among abstract concepts.

Organizing discrete observations into scripts and prototypes is a first step toward making sense of what one perceives. However, the processes that occur during organization merely set the stage with identifiable actors and actions. Still further processing must occur to make complete sense of the incoming data, and much of it occurs at the **interpretation stage**. Here the perceiver tries to go beyond merely identifying "who is doing what with whom" and tries to uncover the reasons behind the actions. Often the same objective behavior can lead to quite different judgments depending on how the perceiver answers the question, "Why?" For example, the behavior of working late at the office each night could be interpreted in different ways by different people. One observer might see such behavior as a sign of an employee's drive and ambition, but another observer might see it as a sign that the person cannot keep up with the work that is assigned. It is easy to see how these two people who view the same behavior can come to quite different conclusions.

[19] L. T. DeFong and C. J. Ferguson-Hessler, "Information Processing Differences in Experts and Novices," *Journal of Applied Social Psychology, 21* 19–27.

Projection

projection A bias in the interpretation of information wherein the perceiver assumes that his own motivations explain the behaviors of others.

One common way in which observers interpret the behaviors of others is to use themselves as a point of reference. In this context particularly you can see that interpretation can involve both controlled and automatic processing. In **projection**, people project their own thoughts and feelings onto other people, often unconsciously. That is, they assume, often incorrectly, that others share their own feelings or motivations.

A good example of the projection process can be found in Richard Mowday's study of government employees. Mowday was interested in organizational turnover as viewed by employees who stayed with an organization. Reminding employees that several of their coworkers had left the organization in recent years, he asked them why the other people had left. The subjects of the study were given the choice of three explanations. The first was that the former employees left because they were dissatisfied with their jobs. The second was that they were not dissatisfied but left to take better jobs. The third was they left both because they were dissatisfied and because they received better offers.

The results of this study indicated that employees who liked their own jobs and their organization were much less likely to believe that turnover resulted from others' dissatisfaction. Those who were themselves dissatisfied with their jobs and the organization, however, embraced dissatisfaction as an explanation for turnover and tended to downplay the possibility that better offers were the reason.

Thus projection can become a means of self-justification. Satisfied workers can defend their decisions to stay with the organization by viewing it as a good place to work and believing that those who left did so for reasons other than job dissatisfaction. The dissatisfied workers, on the other hand, can cite this turnover as proof that there is something wrong with their jobs or the organization.

Projection can also act as a means of self-protection. More often than not it is their socially undesirable characteristics that observers project onto others. For example, a person who is overly cynical may be quick to point to the moral failures of famous religious or political leaders in an effort to quell the anxieties she has about her own moral stance. Projecting negative traits in this fashion has a way of dragging one's perceptions of the world to a very low level. Everyone is seen in terms of his basest impulses. When combined with the potential for self-fulfilling prophecies, projection can seriously distort one's organization of information and can make one's entire world seem a desolate place.

Attribution

attribution The process whereby observers decide what caused the behavior of another person.

Attributions are the causal factors that observers use to explain the behaviors of other people. Attribution theory tries to explain how people decide among possible explanations for various outcomes such as high or low task performance. The explanations that observers arrive at have a great impact on subsequent evaluations and judgments in that even a successful performance can be turned into a loss if a certain kind of attribution is made.

Types of attributions. In general, those who have studied attribution have focused on four possible explanations for a person's success or failure on a task, depending on the *stability* of the cause (i.e., either stable or unstable) and the *locus of causality* (i.e., internal or external to the person.)[20] As shown in Figure

[20] B. Weiner, I. Freize, A. Kukla, L. Reed, S. Rest, and R. M. Rosenbaum, "Perceiving the Causes of Success and Failure" in *Attribution: Perceiving the Causes of Behavior*, ed. E. Jones, D. Kanouse, H. Kelley, R. Nesbitt, S. Valins, and B. Weiner (Morristown, N.J.: General Learning Press, 1971), pp. 45–61.

FIGURE 5-5

**Four Types of Attributions
of Task Success or Failure**

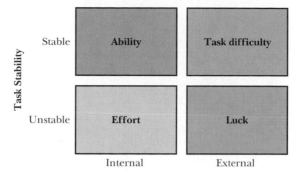

5-5, these four types of attributions are ability, effort, task difficulty, and luck. Ability is a potential cause of performance that is stable (it is not expected to change much over time) and internal (it is a characteristic of the performer). Effort is also a characteristic that is internal to the performer, but unlike ability, it may fluctuate from time to time. External causes include task difficulty (e.g., the performer was successful because it was an easy task) and luck. Task difficulty tends to be a stable dimension, whereas luck is unstable.

Results of attribution. For any given instance of success or failure, the explanation that the observer chooses from these four possibilities will greatly influence the judgments he eventually renders. At the end of the 1987 professional football season, the coach of the rarely successful Cincinnati Bengals, Sam Wyche, found many sportswriters calling for his resignation. Wyche did not resign, and in the following year he lead the Bengals to the top and earned the team a spot in the Super Bowl.

You might think that such an outstanding performance would have been enough to get the critics off Wyche's back, but you would be wrong. Despite this objective achievement, some sportswriters still held fast to their earlier published judgments about the coach's lack of ability. How could they possibly do this? Attribution theory explains this nicely. Some writers pointed to the fact that 1988 was an off year for most teams in the league and that winning in that year was thus a relatively easy task. Others said that the Bengals had a lot of lucky breaks in a lot of close ball games. Note that by explaining the Bengals' success in terms of external factors (task difficulty and luck) that were beyond Wyche's control, these observers were able to question his ability despite the objective fact that his team posted more wins than the other 27 teams in the league.

But attributions can also work the other way. Someone who fails miserably at a task can still be held in high regard if her failure is attributed to external factors. In general, it is only when internal attributions are made that there is a strong relationship between a performer's success or failure on the one hand and a rater's opinion of that performer on the other. Some research even suggests that some types of internal attributions are better than others. For example, success that is perceived to be a function of effort is viewed more positively than success that is seen as due to ability, because the former is more directly under the person's control. The complex relationships between success and failure and ratings as a function of attributions are illustrated in Figure 5-6.

These attributions are important from a diagnostic point of view because they affect decisions regarding problem solving. If failure is attributed to lack of ability, then selecting different applicants or retraining the current jobholders is the solution. If lack of effort is the explanation, selecting different applicants or

FIGURE 5-6
Relation Between Performance
Evaluations, Task
Accomplishment, and Attribution

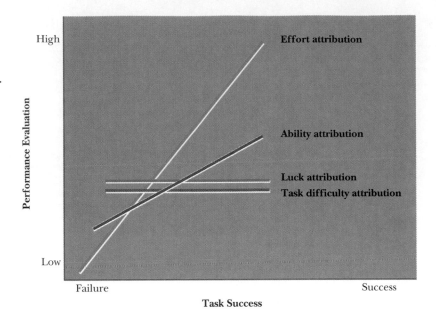

increasing jobholders' motivation is the answer. If failure is due to task difficulty, redesigning the task may be the best option.

Choosing attributions. What are some of the factors that lead observers to choose one type of attribution over another? Observers sometimes arrive at attributional decisions as a result of *self-serving biases*. That is, observers may choose the attributions that present the observers themselves in the best light. When rating their own performance, observers tend to attribute their successes to internal causes and their failures to external causes. Some interesting research by Bettman and Weitz illustrates this tendency. In their study of over 150 corporate annual reports, these investigators found that unfavorable organizational outcomes were likely to be attributed to external factors (e.g., market slowdowns, high interest rates, bad weather, foreign competition), whereas favorable outcomes were usually explained in terms of factors for which the firm was responsible (e.g., new marketing campaigns, new-product development, introduction of new technology).[21]

Self-serving biases influence attributions people make with regard to others' behavior in just the opposite way. Others' successes are explained by situational factors, while others' failures are attributed to internal factors.[22] Given these tendencies, it is easy to see how there can be a great deal of controversy in organizations over one person's merit as compared with another's, even when there is agreement on the objective facts of success and failure.

Causal determination is a complex process, and self-serving interests are not the only determinant of attributional choice. Other important factors include consensus, consistency, and distinctiveness.[23] *Consensus* refers to the extent to which everyone else experiences the same outcome (or engages in the same behavior) as the person being observed. If everybody who ever takes on the task fails, observers are much more prone to blame the task than the task performer.

[21] J. R. Bettman and B. A. Weitz, "Attributions in the Board Room: Causal Reasoning in Corporate Annual Reports," *Administrative Science Quarterly* 28 (1983), 165–83.

[22] H. H. Kelley and J. L. Michela, "Attribution Theory and Research," *Annual Review of Psychology* 12 (1980), 457– 501.

[23] Kelley, "Attribution in Social Interaction," (Morristown, N.J.: General Learning Press, 1971), p. 71.

PERCEPTION AND JUDGMENT

IN PRACTICE

Who Was Responsible for the Exxon Valdez Disaster?

The grounding of the *Exxon Valdez* and resulting oil spill resulted in the devastation of 117 miles of coastline in Prince William Sound and along the Gulf of Alaska. The spill had a terrible effect on both plant and animal life (over 30,000 seagulls alone were killed), and severely damaged the economy of the surrounding areas. The spill was also costly for Exxon, which eventually paid over $2 billion for the cleanup. Last, but certainly not least, was the effect the event had on the ship's captain, Joseph Hazelwood, who was faced with the possibility of seven years in prison and fines of over $50,000. Answering the question of why this disaster took place, as well as determining what can be done to prevent another such disaster is critical, yet difficult.

According to Hazelwood's lawyers, the Coast Guard, which has responsibility to monitor ships in Prince William Sound, failed to warn the *Exxon Valdez* before it went aground. Hazelwood's attorneys also noted that Third Mate Gregory Cousins, who was in charge of the ship when it crashed, was qualified to run the vessel in Hazelwood's absence. Lastly, the widely held notion that the captain was drunk at the time of the accident was also disputed by Hazelwood's lawyers.*

Let us look at what two other people have had to say, both about the cause of the disaster and about what actions should be taken to prevent a reoccurrence. The first speaker is Oliver Holmes, Exxon tanker captain, retired after 43 years of service:

The Cause: "It is a wrong against his many friends and former colleagues at Exxon to portray him [Hazelwood] as victim rather than cause of that tragedy. Overlooked in many news accounts is the master's complex responsibility for his ship's safety at all times. If Captain Hazelwood had done what he was duty bound to do, there would have been no grounding. . . . The questions about double hulled ships, crew fatigue or shorthandedness; about the failure of the U.S. Coast Guard; . . . about the master's paperwork; even the questions about alcohol are either irrelevant or subordinate to the real cause of the grounding.

*P. A. Witteman, "Fall Guy or Villain?" *Time*, February 26, 1990, p. 34.

The Remedy: "Perhaps the company's worst mistake has been its good-humored toleration of soreheads and crybabies. I believe that Captain Hazelwood was influenced by these people in his petty defiance of company operating procedures. In any case, Exxon shore staff apparently overlooked many of Captain Hazelwood's infractions and certainly was remarkably kind to him in helping him through various personal problems."†

Lawrence Rawl, chairman of the board at Exxon, was asked what he felt was the cause of the oil spill and, in particular, whether Exxon's huge personnel cutbacks in the 1980s put company safety and maintenance in jeopardy:

The Cause: "I think, in the end, the Alaska oil spill was caused by compounded human failure. In Louisiana [where an Exxon refinery exploded], that was legitimately an act of God. . . . As for Arthur Kill [site of 500,000-gallon spill off New York City], that was an act of God ripping that pipeline, but the way it was handled afterward was human error. . . . [As to cutbacks] . . . I don't have the answer, but I'm dissatisfied with sitting tight and hoping the bad luck goes away, because if you've got bad luck, you've missed something somewhere."

The Remedy: "We haven't reduced people at the lower level . . . but somewhere between the top of the house and the bottom there are employees who need more training, as well as managers who have to do a better job of evaluating people. What's motivating these people on the docks and in the ships? Are they upset? Is there too much time pressure? Maybe we'll have an industrial psychologist talk to them. We're not rushing people when they're moving oil. We want them to slow down."

The central question in the trial of Joseph Hazelwood was whether one man could be singled out for blame in the worst oil spill in U.S. history. In the end, a grand jury ruled he could not, and Captain Joseph Hazelwood was acquitted.

†O. Holmes, "Captain Hazelwood: The Safety Device that Failed," *The Wall Street Journal*, January 12, 1990, p. 1.

Consistency is the extent to which the person being observed obtains the same outcome (or engages in the same behavior) at different times. If the performer either succeeds or fails every time she attempts the task, then observers are likely to make internal attributions. Finally, *distinctiveness* is the extent to which the person achieves the same result on widely different tasks. If the person being rated succeeds or fails on whatever assignment is handed down, observers are much more likely to make internal attributions. Imagine how difficult it would be to criticize Sam Wyche if his success in 1988 had been followed up with similar success in 1989 and then in 1990—especially if he had switched teams.

In many cases, however, an incident occurs only one time, greatly complicating the process of determining the real cause. The "In Practice" box, for example, shows how three different people generated different attributions in order to account for the cause of the *Exxon Valdez* oil spill.

Increasing the Objectivity of Interpretations

Many interpretations that observers make can influence their self-perceptions. For this reason, an insecure, overly sensitive rater is not a reliable witness. An observer who has a high degree of *self-acceptance*—who knows and accepts her strengths and weaknesses—will have less psychological need to project negative characteristics onto others. The need to employ self-serving attributional biases will also be less in a rater who has high self-acceptance than in one who is low on this characteristic.

Because interpretation is so much "in the eye of the beholder," it is also a good idea to compare your interpretation of a person or a situation with others' interpretations. This process, called *reality testing*, is most useful when the people whose interpretations you are comparing with your own have attended to different information and perhaps developed prototypes that differ from yours.[24] Also, if other raters' needs and yours differ, the potential for self-serving biases is reduced even further. Following this reasoning, many firms insist on obtaining not only supervisor's ratings of an employee but peers', or coworkers', ratings as well.[25]

RETRIEVAL STAGE

retrieval stage The stage of the information processing cycle in which the observer tries to recall information about past events.

You can probably see by the time we reach the **retrieval stage,** that there may be little resemblance between the information that originally was available in the objective environment and that which is moving through the subjective perceptual system. Furthermore, in the real world, there is almost always a considerable delay between entering information into memory and retrieving it. Indeed for information to be retrieved, it must have been originally memorized. Memorizing information is typically a controlled rather than an automatic process, and therefore not all that is interpreted will necessarily be recalled. For example, think of how easy it is to *interpret* what is written on this page, compared to how difficult it is to *memorize* what is on it.

Moreover, not all that is stored will always be retrievable; there is a tendency for memory to decay overtime. A critical question is whether memory decay is selective or random. Most research suggests that such decay is quite selective. For example, studies by James Phillips and his colleagues show that people are likely to forget information that is inconsistent with the scripts or prototypes that were used to organize the information.[26] Look back at Table 5-5 where the prototypical traits of a leader are presented. If someone viewed as a leader possesses some characteristics that are unleaderlike, there is a good chance that after the passage of time, people will forget these characteristics. Or, a person who became a leader despite a low level of education might be recalled as having had a more extensive educational background than she did. Indeed, the most

---

[24] M. K. Johnson and C. L. Raye, "Reality Monitoring," *Psychological Review* 88 (1981), 67–85.

[25] D. Cederbloom and J. W. Lounsbury, "An Investigation of User Acceptance of Peer Evaluations," *Personnel Psychology* 33 (1980), 567–79.

[26] J. S. Phillips and R. G. Lord, "Schematic Information Processing and Perceptions of Leadership in Problem Solving Groups," *Journal of Applied Psychology* 67 (1982), 486–92.

worrisome aspect of Phillips's research is his finding that people were as likely to "recall" prototypical traits that were never there as they were to recall traits that were there.[27]

Once established in someone's memory, a prototype can persist for a long time. For example, Fred Malek, the president of Northwest Airlines, has struggled for 20 years with a mistake he made in 1971. Working for an embattled and, some say, paranoid Richard Nixon, Malek was asked to generate a list of Jews in the Bureau of Labor Statistics. Nixon apparently believed that a consortium of Jewish economists was twisting economic data to embarrass him. Although he ignored the order at first, Malek eventually complied. This fact first came out in the 1981 book *The Final Days* by Bob Woodward and Carl Bernstein, but it was in 1988 when the *Washington Post* put the story on the front page that Malek was forced to resign as head of the Republican National Committee. Even though the Anti-Defamation League has formally accepted Malek's apologies, and its national director, Abraham Foxman, has said "enough is enough," the memory of that earlier event still seems to haunt Malek's career.

Point of View

One indication of the selectivity of retrieval can be found in studies that have asked subjects to take different points of view in recalling past information. For example, in one study subjects were asked to read a description of a house and then, at the retrieval stage, to recall as much as possible about the house. One set of subjects was asked to do this from the point of view of a prospective house buyer, whereas the other group were asked to take on the perspective of a burglar. Different details of the house were recalled depending on which perspective the subject took.[28] This shows clearly how memory involves a backward search from a current perspective to a desired piece of information.

Similar point-of-view effects can be found within organizations in the area of performance appraisal. Performance information is collected for different purposes and the purpose of an evaluation seems to affect the kind of information that managers are able to recall. In one study, managers who took the point of view of a coach and were asked to do an evaluation to aid employee development were able to recall much more specific behavioral information than managers who were asked to take the point of view of a judge whose ratings would determine merit raises.[29] Another study that showed the same kind of effect suggests that stereotypes have a greater influence on ratings when they are used in making administrative decisions than when the information is collected for other reasons. In this study, raters who held traditional stereotypes about women were much more likely to show bias in their ratings of female employees when the decision dealt with pay raises than when the ratings were collected for "research purposes."[30]

[27] J. S. Phillips, "The Accuracy of Leadership Ratings: A Categorization Perspective," *Organizational Behavior and Human Performance* 33 (1984), 125–38.

[28] R. C. Anderson and J. W. Pichert, "Recall of Previously Unrecallable Information Following a Shift in Perspective," *Journal of Verbal Learning and Verbal Behavior* 17 (1981), 1–12.

[29] S. Zedeck and W. F. Cascio, "Performance Appraisal Decisions as a Function of Rater Training and Purpose of the Appraisal," *Journal of Applied Psychology* 67 (1982), 752–58.

[30] G. H. Dobbins, R. L. Cardy and D. M. Truxillo, "The Effects of Purpose of Appraisal and Individual Differences in Stereotypes of Women on Sex Differences in Performance Ratings: A Laboratory and Field Study," *Journal of Applied Psychology* 73 (1988), 551–58.

Performance Cues

Another indication of the selectivity of the retrieval process comes from research on the "performance-cue effect."[31] In these studies, subjects are placed in groups and assigned a task. After performing the task for some period of time, the groups are given feedback on how well they have performed in comparison with other groups. Half of the groups are then selected randomly and told they performed very well, and the rest are told they performed poorly. The groups are then asked to describe group processes and the effectiveness of their leaders. Despite the fact that the two sets of groups actually performed at the same levels on similar tasks, group members invariably recall different processes, depending on the feedback they received. Groups who are told they did well recall positive aspects of leadership and group processes, whereas just the opposite occurs in groups who are told they did poorly.

This type of bias shows how dangerous it is to rely on retrospective reports of what certain individuals or companies did to achieve their success (recall our discussion of the "excellence" books in Chapter 3). In looking back on their success, individuals may recall things selectively, deleting things that may have been important and adding things that may never have occurred. Knowledge of the outcome may create serious biases in terms of what is recalled and what is forgotten. Thus the trustworthiness of the retrieval process should not go unquestioned. As we said in Chapter 3, it is important to collect information from multiple sources, using a number of different methods.

Increasing the Accuracy of Retrieval

One way to reduce demands on one's ability to recall information accurately is to maintain physical records of incidents or behaviors. Such logs, or *behavioral diaries*, can then be consulted whenever important judgments need to be made. In this way we can short-circuit our tendency to selectively recall some incidents and not others. For example, the results of one study on diary keeping found that raters who regularly recorded critical incidents of employee effectiveness showed much less evidence in their ratings of leniency and halo bias. The level of agreement among diary-keeping raters was also higher than the level of agreement among raters who relied on memory alone.[32]

Because recalling information from different points of view or for different purposes seems to elicit different information, having observers take *multiple perspectives* can increase the overall amount of information that is available for making judgments. Thus a rater might try to take the point of view of the person being rated, of her coworkers, or of her clients. Just going through this process will force the rater to consider the fact that other people's opinions may differ from hers and may force her to recall information that though perhaps buried, is yet retrievable.

JUDGMENT STAGE

In the final **judgment stage** of the process, the information available for use—the data that have survived to this stage in the perceptual process—must be condensed into one or more judgments. Turn back to Figure 5-4,

judgment stage The stage of the information processing cycle in which recalled information is weighted and aggregated to come up with a single overall judgment.

[31] M. C. Rush and L. L. Beauvais, "A Critical Analysis of Format Induced Versus Subject Imposed Bias in Leadership Ratings," *Journal of Applied Psychology* 66 (1981), 722–27.

[32] H. J. Bernardin and C. S. Walters, "Effects of Rater Training and Diary-Keeping on Psychometric Error in Rating," *Journal of Applied Psychology* 62 (1977), 64–69.

which shows three students' evaluations of an instructor on ten specific dimensions of performance and one overall judgment. Note that Student B's overall judgment is not the average of her ten specific ratings. Rather, it is more negative than her average rating and can probably be traced to the fact that this student thought that some dimensions were more important than others. This weighing process may differ for different people. For example, Student C, whose ratings of the instructor on the ten specific dimensions were identical to Student B's ratings came up with a different overall rating. It might be a little discouraging to find that even though Students B and C agreed on all ten specific points, they rendered different overall judgments when summarizing their perceptions. Thus, perceptual differences can result when raters apply different degrees of importance to various dimensions.

Not only can different raters give different weights to various pieces of information, but the same individual may apply different weights in rating different people. Suppose that Students B and C are actually the same person, and that B represents the student's rating of an instructor in a quantitative course where, for example, "organization" is weighted more heavily than "stimulation of discussion," whereas C represents a rating of a more qualitative course to which the student applies an opposite pattern of emphasis. Or, consider the possibility that the same person could apply different patterns of emphasis at different points in time. For example,"organization" might be viewed as more important for a freshman class, and "stimulation of class discussion" more important in an upper-level, elective course.

Effects of Earlier Judgments

If you look back at Figure 5-3 you will see that it shows an arrow going from the judgment stage back to the beginning of the perceptual process. This arrow represents the dynamic nature of the entire perception and judgment cycle. That is, not only do perceptions give rise to judgments, but judgments influence subsequent perceptions. As we will see, the **assimilation effect** is the tendency for present judgments to be biased in the direction of past judgments. Two of the ways in which assimilation can occur are priming and the confirmation bias.

assimilation effect The tendency for present judgments to be biased in the direction of past judgments.

priming Forcing raters to recall a specific set of events so that subsequent judgments will be biased by what is recalled.

Priming. Research shows that the ease with which information can be recalled affects the degree to which it is used in forming judgments.[33] **Priming** raters simply means forcing them to recall one set of events and then very soon afterward asking them to make a judgment to which the information just retrieved may be relevant. Because the primed information was so recently recalled, it is easier to retrieve than other information and thus is likely to be used in forming the required judgment.

For example, suppose that a sales manager has just received a call from an irate customer who is upset about a salesperson's behavior. Further, suppose that the salesperson's annual performance appraisal is being conducted that same day. The manager may give this very recent, or primed, information a lot more weight in the annual review than she will give experiences with this salesperson that accrued earlier in the year. Past judgments may act the same way in influencing future perceptions and judgments. Indeed, one of the first things a rater often thinks of when making an evaluation is, How did I evaluate this in the past?

[33] A. Tversky and D. Kahneman, "Availability: A Heuristic for Judging Frequency and Probability," *Cognitive Psychology* 5 (1973), 207–32.

Confirmation bias. Assimilation can also be brought about through **confirmation bias**, the tendency for raters to seek out information that reaffirms their earlier judgments while discounting evidence that runs counter to earlier impressions.[34] This kind of bias seems particularly prevalent when ratings are made public, because raters often feel compelled to confirm past judgments so as to appear to be consistent.[35] Thus whereas priming seems to affect primarily the retrieval part of the perception process, confirmation bias seems largely to affect what observers attend to and how they interpret it.

Making Better Judgments

One way to improve the observers' accuracy is to *simplify and reduce the number of judgments* that are required, so that there is less subjective processing. Asking the rater to be a witness of behavior, rather than a judge of others' intentions or personality characteristics simplifies the task considerably. It reduces the need to make complex inferences and interpretations.

Also, emphasis should be placed on asking raters to form judgments only on those behaviors or dimensions that they have had *ample opportunity to observe*. Asking an interviewer to infer the intelligence of a job applicant after talking to him for 30 minutes is asking a lot. There are better means of collecting this kind of information, and it is more useful to focus on things that can be observed in the context of an interview, such as the degree to which a person can express herself verbally or the ease with which she handles a somewhat stressful situation.

Third, the overall context in which the evaluation is made should not be overlooked. People will make more accurate judgments in a *supportive climate*, that is, when they are given positive feedback for making accurate judgments, especially if those judgments are harsh and likely to engender negative reactions on the part of the person being rated. For example, a study by Margaret Padgett showed that in one organization, 70 percent of the supervisors intentionally inflated their ratings of subordinates, particularly when a rater felt that subordinates would react negatively to poor ratings. Raters did not feel free, in these circumstances, to be honest.[36] Such intentional biasing of ratings is most trou-

[34] J. Darley and R. Fazio, "Expectancy Confirmation Processes in the Social Interaction Sequence," *American Psychologist* 35 (1980), 867–81.

[35] M. Bazerman, R. Beekun and F. Schoorman, "Performance Evaluation in a Dynamic Context: A Laboratory Study of the Impact of Prior Commitment to the Ratee," *Journal of Applied Psychology* 67 (1982), 873–76.

[36] M. Padgett, "Performance Appraisal in Context: Motivational Influences on Performance Ratings" (Paper Presented at the Annual Meeting of the National Academy of Management, Washington, D.C., August 1989, p. 11).

One way to improve the accuracy of human judgment is to simplify the perceptual task. Advertising agencies like Romann and Tannenholz enlist the help of consumers in testing brands of various products. This group is testing the tastes of different toothpastes. By focusing their attention on a single aspect of a specific product, testers may be able to provide more accurate ratings of a number of brands.
Source: Fortune, *December 3, 1990, p. 40.*

blesome, for it is hard enough to get accurate ratings when everyone is trying his best. If raters feel that accuracy is not in their own best interests, how can we strive to improve perceptual accuracy?

SUMMARY

A thorough understanding of the perceptual process, that is, the process by which people encode and make sense out of the complex world around them, is critical to those who would manage organizational behavior. The very existence of perceptual illusions documents the fact that what we perceive is not always a very close approximation of objective reality. Accurately perceiving one's environment enhances the ability to both describe and diagnose current organizational problems. It also helps to ensure that the prescriptions and actions taken to solve those problems are directed toward the correct source. Accuracy in the perception of persons is especially critical. This type of perceptual accuracy takes four forms: *elevation accuracy*, *differential elevation accuracy*, *stereotype accuracy*, and *differential accuracy*. Different kinds of organizational problems require different kinds of accuracy. It is important to recognize this because some types of accuracy are easier than others to achieve.

Perceptual processing is either *controlled* or *automatic* and moves through five stages: *attention*, *organization*, *interpretation*, *retrieval* and *judgment*. At the *attention stage*, a small subset of all the information that is available to the five senses is selected for processing. The degree to which any stimulus attracts attention is a complex function of characteristics of the object and of the perceiver. At the *organization stage*, information is simplified. Complex behavioral sequences are converted into *scripts*, and people are represented by *prototypes*. A number of biases, including *stereotyping* and the *halo error*, can creep into this complex process. In the *interpretation stage* the condensed information is then interpreted, as perceivers employ *projection* or make *attributions* that allow them to understand why some object or person is as it is. If the information processed is not used immediately, it is stored in memory and later recovered in the *retrieval stage*. There is a tendency to lose information that is inconsistent with scripts and prototypes. Finally, at the *judgment stage*, the information processed in the four prior stages is used to come up with an evaluation of an object, person, or event. This evaluation, once made, often affects decisions, behaviors, and subsequent perceptions.

REVIEW QUESTIONS

1.   Which of the four types of perceptual accuracy require the greatest amount of controlled information processing? Which might be achieved through less energy-consuming, automatic information-processing strategies?

2.   List a set of traits that would make up the prototype for a yuppie, a hippie, an absent-minded professor, and a card-carrying member of the American Civil Liberties Union. Recalling Chapter 4, is your list dominated by ability or personality characteristics? What category of abilities (physical, psychomotor, cognitive) or personality characteristics (social traits, motives, personal conceptions, emotional adjustment, personality dynamics) is most heavily represented? What does this tell you about how prototypes are developed and in what ways they are most likely to be accurate?

3.   Sometimes the same behavioral episode in an organization—for example a fight among coworkers, a botched work assignment, or an ineffective meeting—

can be organized perceptually along the lines of a script or a prototype. How might the decision to use one or the other of these schemas affect things that occur later in the judgment process, such as attribution and memory recall?

4. Think of four kinds of perceptual biases. Do each of these biases affect the diagnostic approach to problem solving (description-diagnosis-prescription-action) in the same way, or are some more problematic at certain stages than others?

5. Subliminal advertising is restricted by law. There are limits on the number of images that a television viewer can be exposed to over certain specified time intervals. What is the basis for this legislation? In what ways is this kind of advertising categorically different from other subtle types of influence that are not restricted?

DIAGNOSTIC QUESTIONS

 The following questions attempt to capture some of the major points of this chapter. They are designed to help you to diagnose perceptual problems in analyzing both case studies in this book and on-the-job problems now or in the future.

1. On whose perceptions do you rely to describe and diagnose organizational problems? How might the choice of this person affect the description and diagnosis provided?

2. Which of the four types of accuracy is required for specific organizational decisions that must be made based on perceptual data? Such decisions include promotion decisions and decisions about group or individual training.

3. What characteristics of persons or objects that you have to evaluate "pull" your attention? How do these characteristics affect your judgments regarding these persons or objects?

4. What kinds of expectations do you have for persons or objects that you need to evaluate? How might these expectations affect your judgment?

5. What are some of the major events in your organization that you conceive in terms of scripts? How might your version of these scripts differ from others' views of the same scripts?

6. What are some of the major prototypes that exist for persons in your organization? How accurate are these prototypes?

7. What stereotypes do you hold of persons from particular social groups in your organization? Are these stereotypes accurate?

8. Are your reasons for interpreting other people's actions self-serving? Do you project any of your own socially undesirable characteristics onto others?

9. Do you keep external records of important past events, or do you rely exclusively on your own memory for important information?

10. Do you take the point of view of a judge or a coach when evaluating others? How might each of these views affect your judgments?

11. How are your present judgments influenced by judgments that you or others have made in the past?

12. Which of the many ways to increase perceptual accuracy are most practical for your organization? How might different means of enhancing accuracy be more or less appropriate for different organizational needs (e.g., interviewing, performance appraisal, problem diagnosis)?

LEARNING THROUGH EXPERIENCE

EXERCISE 5-1

SIX STYLES OF THINKING[1]

JANET MILLS, *Boise State University*

Perception and judgment processes involve many different styles of thinking, some more logical and analytical, others emotional or speculative. According to Edward deBono,[2] when we try to organize and interpret sensory data, different modes of thinking—for example, reasoning, intuiting, questioning observing—may

crowd in all at once. To prevent the confusion that can result, deBono proposes that we teach people to do one kind of thinking at a time. To help you develop your thinking skills, this exercise introduces you to deBono's six styles of thinking (see Exhibit 5-1) and lets you practice using one style of thinking at a time.

[1] Adapted with the author's permission from an exercise entitled "Six Thinking Hats: An Exercise to Combat Confusion and Develop Thinking Skills."

[2] Edward deBono, *Six Thinking Hats* (Boston, MA: Little, Brown and Company, 1985).

EXHIBIT 5-1
Six Styles of Thinking

STYLE OF THINKING	WHAT IT IS	WHAT IT ISN'T
Factual-Literal	Neutral Objective Rational Mechanical	Argumentative Interpreting Extrapolating Opinion giving Persuading
Emotional-Intuitive	Emotional Based on gut reactions, hunches, intuition, personal taste, aesthetic preference	Justifying Explaining Accounting for Logical Consistent
Logical-Negative	Looking for problems Fault finding Objecting to alternatives Criticizing Focusing on risks and dangers Confronting factual-literal thinking	Emotional Argumentative Subjective
Speculative-Positive	Looking for opportunities Constructive Optimistic Focusing on benefits Emphasizing practical value Using dreams and visions Probing, exploring Finding logical support Making things happen	Emotional Intuitive Naive Unrealistic
Innovative-Creative	Developmental Fertile, nurturing Generating alternatives Getting new ideas Approaching old problems in new ways Being absurd, humorous, playful	Logical Judgmental Negative
Controlled-Regulated	Managing thinking Planning and organizing Monitoring and controlling Giving all types of thinking their turn Formally structuring thinking	Persuading Advocating Criticizing

STEP ONE: PRE-CLASS PREPARATION

In class you will use deBono's thinking styles to make an important decision. To prepare for this class work, study Exhibit 5-1 to familiarize yourself with the six styles of thinking. Then read the rest of the exercise so you will know what to do.

STEP TWO: THINKING IN A SINGLE STYLE

Your instructor will divide your class into groups of four to six members each and will assign each group one of deBono's thinking styles. (Any number of groups may be formed, so long as the total number of groups is a multiple of six.) Each group should then review the thinking style it has been assigned, describing the style in detail and giving examples of thinking in that style. Next, the group should try thinking in its assigned style as it undertakes the following assignment:

> This term your class will perform exercises allowing you to experience personally many of the challenges of being a manager. Although you created temporary groups to perform the exercise in Chapter 4, you should now divide into permanent groups of four to six members each that will remain together for the rest of the term. The decision you must make today is, How should these groups be formed? At the end of today's session, your decision will actually be implemented, and permanent groups will be organized.

Before leaving this step, every member of each group should be completely familiar with the group's thinking style and be able to illustrate its use to others.

STEP THREE: THINKING IN MULTIPLE STYLES

Your instructor will now reorganize the class into new groups made up of one person from each of the six different kinds of thinking-style groups. In these mixed-style groups you will again reach a decision about how

to form permanent groups. It is important that as you complete this step you use the thinking style you learned in Step One. Once your group has made a decision, choose a spokesperson to report it to the class and to describe the way it was made. The spokesperson's presentation should last about five minutes.

STEP FOUR: CLASS DISCUSSION AND PERMANENT GROUP FORMATION

As each group's spokesperson reports on its decision, all decisions should be listed on a chalk board, flip chart, or overhead projector transparency. After every group has presented its decision, the class as a whole must reach a final decision and form its permanent groups.

During this final judgment process, you should discuss questions like the following:

1. In what ways is each of the six thinking styles useful? What drawbacks are associated with each style?
2. Were any of the styles more powerful than others in influencing the decisions reached in Step Three? Were any of the styles virtually ignored?
3. Did any of the styles conflict with others? How did the groups deal with such conflicts?
4. What challenges do differences among the six styles create for managers engaged in decision making? How can the benefits of the various thinking styles be balanced against their costs?

CONCLUSION

Managing organizational behavior involves thinking processes that begin with perception and culminate in judgment and decision making. As this exercise illustrates, no single style of thinking is likely to be adequate during the entire process. Managers must be able to use different thinking styles, each to its best advantage. As Edward deBono suggests, the way to do this may be to use one style of thinking at a time.

DIAGNOSING ORGANIZATIONAL BEHAVIOR

Freida Mae Jones was born in her grandmother's Georgia farmhouse on June 1, 1949. She was the sixth of George and Ella Jones's ten children. Mr. and Mrs. Jones moved to New York City when Freida was four because they felt that the educational and career opportunities

CASE 5-1

FREIDA MAE JONES*

MARTIN R. MOSER, *University of Lowell*

for their children would be better in the North. With the help of some cousins, they settled in a five-room apartment in the Bronx. George worked as a janitor at Lincoln Memorial Hospital, and Ella was a part-time housekeeper in a nearby neighborhood. George and Ella were conservative, strict parents. They kept a close watch on their children's activities and demanded they be home by a certain hour. The Jones believed that because they were black, the children would have to perform and behave better than their peers to be successful. They believed that their children's education would be the most important factor in their success as adults.

Freida entered Memorial High School, a racially integrated public school, in September 1963. Seventy percent of the student body was Caucasian, 20 percent black, and 10 percent Hispanic. About 60 percent of the graduates went on to college. Of this 60 percent, 4 percent were black and Hispanic and all were male. In the middle of her senior year, Freida was the top student in her class. Following school regulations, Freida met with her guidance counselor to discuss her plans upon graduation. The counselor advised her to consider training in a "practical" field such as housekeeping, cooking, or sewing, so that she could find a job.

George and Ella Jones were furious when Freida told them what the counselor had advised. Ella said, "Don't they see what they are doing? Freida is the top-rated student in her whole class and they are telling her to become a manual worker. She showed that she has a fine mind and can work better than any of her classmates and still she is told not to become anybody in this world. It's really not any different in the North than back home in Georgia, except that they don't try to hide it down South. They want her to throw away her fine mind because she is a black girl and not a white boy. I'm going to go up to her school tomorrow and talk to the principal."

As a result of Mrs. Jones's visit to the principal, Freida was assisted in applying to ten Eastern colleges, each of which offered her full scholarships. In September 1966, Freida entered Werbley College, an exclusive private women's college in Massachusetts. In 1970, Freida graduated summa cum laude in history. She decided to return to New York to teach grade school in the city's public school system. Freida was unable to obtain a full-time position, so she substituted. She also enrolled as a part-time student in Columbia University's Graduate School of Education. In 1975 she had attained her Master of Arts degree in Teaching from Columbia but could not find a permanent teaching job. New York City was laying off teachers and had instituted a hiring freeze because of the city's financial problems.

Feeling frustrated about her future as a teacher, Freida decided to get an MBA. She thought that there was more opportunity in business than in education. Churchill Business School, a small, prestigious school located in upstate New York, accepted Freida into its MBA program.

Freida completed her MBA in 1977 and accepted an entry-level position at the Industrialist World Bank of Boston in a fast-track management development program. The three-year program introduced her to all facets of bank operations, from telling to loan training and operations management. She was rotated to branch offices throughout New England. After completing the program she became an assistant manager for branch operations in the West Springfield branch office.

During her second year in the program, Freida had met James Walker, a black doctoral student in business administration at the University of Massachusetts. Her assignment to West Springfield precipitated their decision to get married. They originally anticipated that they would marry when James finished his doctorate and could move to Boston. Instead, they decided he would pursue a job in the Springfield-Hartford area.

Freida was not only the first black but also the first woman to hold an executive position in the West Springfield branch office. Throughout the training program Freida felt somewhat uneasy although she did very well. There were six other blacks in the program, five men and one woman, and she found support and comfort in sharing her feelings with them. The group spent much of their free time together. Freida had hoped that she would be located near one or more of the group when she went out into the "real world." She felt that although she was able to share her feelings about work with James, he did not have the full appreciation or understanding of her co-workers. However, the nearest group member was located one hundred miles away.

Freida's boss in Springfield was Stan Luboda, a fifty-five-year-old native New Englander. Freida felt that he treated her differently than he did the other trainees. He always tried to help her and took a lot of time (too much, according to Freida) explaining things to her. Freida felt that he was treating her like a child and not like an intelligent and able professional.

"I'm really getting frustrated and angry about what is happening at the bank," Freida said to her husband. "The people don't even realize it, but their prejudice comes through all the time. I feel as if I have to fight all the time just to start off even. Luboda gives Paul Koehn more responsibility than me and we both started at the same time, with the same amount of training. He's meeting customers alone and Luboda has accompanied me to each meeting I've had with a customer."

"I run into the same thing at school," said James. "The people don't even know that they are doing it. The other day I met with a professor on my dissertation committee. I've known and worked with him for over three years. He said he wanted to talk with me about a memo he had received. I asked him what it was about and he said that the records office wanted to know about my absence during the spring semester. He said that I had to sign some forms. He had me confused with Martin Jordan, another black student. Then he realized that it wasn't me, but Jordan he wanted. All I could think was that we all must look alike to him. I was angry. Maybe it was an honest mistake on his part, but whenever something like that happens, and it happens often, it gets me really angry."

"Something like that happened to me," said Freida. "I was using the copy machine, and Luboda's secretary was talking to someone in the hall. She had just gotten a haircut and was saying that her hair was now like Freida's—short and kinky—and that she would have to talk to me about how to take care of it. Luckly, my back was to her. I bit my lip and went on with my business. Maybe she was trying to be cute, because I know she saw me standing there, but comments like that are not cute, they are racist."

"I don't know what to do," said James. "I try to keep things in perspective. Unless people interfere with my progress, I try to let it slide. I only have so much energy and it doesn't make sense to waste it on people who don't matter. But that doesn't make it any easier to function in a racist environment. People don't realize that they are being racist. But a lot of times their expectations of black people or women, or whatever, are different because of skin color or gender. They expect you to be different, although if you were to ask them they would say that they don't. In fact, they would be highly offended if you implied that they were racist or sexist. They don't see themselves that way."

"Luboda is interfering with my progress," said Freida. "The kinds of experiences I have now will have a direct effect on my career advancement. If decisions are being made because I am black or a woman, then they are racially and sexually biased. It's the same kind of attitude that the guidance counselor had when I was in high school, although not as blatant."

In September 1980, Freida decided to speak to Luboda about his treatment of her. She met with him in his office. "Mr. Luboda, there is something that I would like to discuss with you, and I feel a little uncomfortable because I'm not sure how you will respond to what I am going to say."

"I want you to feel that you can trust me," said Luboda. "I am anxious to help you in any way I can."

"I feel that you treat me differently than you treat the other people around here," said Freida. "I feel that you are overcautious with me, that you always try to help me, and never let me do anything on my own."

"I always try to help the new people around here," answered Luboda. "I'm not treating you any differently than I treat any other person. I think that you are being

a little too sensitive. Do you think that I treat you differently because you are black?"

"The thought had occurred to me," said Freida. "Paul Koehn started here the same time that I did and he has much more responsibility than I do." (Koehn was already handling accounts on his own, while Freida had not yet been given that responsibility.)

"Freida, I know you are not a naive person," said Luboda. "You know the way the world works. There are some things which need to be taken more slowly than others. There are some assignments for which Koehn has been given more responsibility than you, and there are some assignments for which you are given more responsibility than Koehn. I try to put you where you do the most good."

"What you are saying is that Koehn gets the more visible, customer contact assignments and I get the behind-the-scenes running of the operations assignments," said Freida. "I'm not naive, but I'm also not stupid either. Your decisions are unfair. Koehn's career will advance more quickly than mine because of the assignments that he gets."

"Freida, that is not true," said Luboda. "Your career will not be hurt because you are getting different responsibilities than Koehn. You both need the different kinds of experiences you are getting. And you have to face the reality of the banking business. We are in a conservative business. When we speak to customers we need to gain their confidence, and we put the best people for the job in the positions to achieve that end. If we don't get their confidence they can go down the street to our competitors and do business with them. Their services are no different than ours. It's a competitive business in which you need every edge you have. It's going to take time for people to change some of their attitudes about whom they borrow money from or where they put their money. I can't change the way people feel. I am running a business, but believe me I won't make any decisions that are detrimental to you or to the bank. There is an important place for you here at the bank. Remember, you have to use your skills to the best advantage of the bank as well as your career."

"So what you are saying is that all things being equal, except my gender and my race, Koehn will get different treatment than me in terms of assignments," said Freida.

"You're making it sound like I am making a racist and sexist decision," said Luboda. "I'm making a business decision utilizing the resources at my disposal and the market situation in which I must operate. You know exactly what I am talking about. What would you do if you were in my position?"

When you have read this case, look back at the chapter's diagnostic questions and choose the ones that apply to the case. Then use those questions with the ones that follow in your case analysis.

1. Were Stan Luboda's perceptions of Freida Mae Jones accurate? What perceptual bias might explain the way Stan treated Freida? Might this same sort of bias explain his secretary's comments?

2. How might Stan's perceptual bias have affected his judgment of Freida's ability to do the same work as Paul Koehn? How did that judgment affect Freida's ability to put her knowledge and skills to the fullest use?

3. How can biases like those illustrated in this case undermine the performance of an organization? What can a firm do to improve its managers' perceptual accuracy? Why do such actions make good sense, both socially and financially?

CASE 5-2

WORLD INTERNATIONAL AIRLINES, INC.*

P. D. JIMERSON, *General Mills, Inc.*
DAVID L. FORD, *University of Texas at Dallas*

BACKGROUND

World International Airlines is a foreign-based multinational commercial air carrier. The corporate offices for its western hemisphere operations are located in New York City, New York. The company employs many hundreds of multilingual and multicultural employees, since its operations maintain World International terminals in South America, Central America, Mexico, the United States and Canada, all of which comprise the western hemisphere territory. In all of the continents the district managers, whose territory may involve several countries or, in the case of the United States, several states, are usually multilingual Europeans. The assistant managers are usually nationals of the country. The general manager of the western hemisphere is a native Spaniard while the personnel manager is a Spanish-American. Both the general manager and personnel manager are multilingual and multicultural. While many air carriers in the western hemisphere have experienced strikes and work stoppages in the past, there is no history of strikes having ever occurred at World International Airlines.

The present general manager is a man in his mid-fifties. He has worked his way up to the top of the western hemisphere's organization. He has hand-picked all of the men who are district managers in each of the

* Reprinted with the authors' permission.

aforementioned countries. He knows over 90 percent of the company's employees in the New York offices on a personal basis and is well liked by all of his subordinates. On one occasion when he was away attending a National Training Laboratories-sponsored workshop in California, the employees from the New York offices surprised him with a huge birthday cake, complete with the decorations and even champagne. His job performance has earned him influence and power in Spain. In addition, the present general manager's educational background is more along the classical line typical of many Spaniards in his socio-economic class (i.e., law, engineering, etc.) as opposed to a more applied business and management education background.

CHANGE IN SENIOR PERSONNEL CREATES PROBLEMS

The company is in a state of flux. The present general manager, John Nepia, is scheduled to be transferred to Barcelona, Spain and a new man, Stephen Esterant, has been sent to replace him. The present general manager has had little or no input into the selection of the new general manager. However, the incoming general manager has an outstanding record in the eastern hemisphere, and it is rumored that he is being groomed for something big. Coupled with this impending change in senior personnel is the fact that international flights are currently in a state of flux since a review committee is currently deliberating on a new rate structure.

John Nepia was scheduled to depart New York on April 30. Stephen Esterant arrived March 20. There was to be at least a 30-day transition period before the departure of Mr. Nepia. Problems on the setting of the international rate structure became acute on or about April 20. Mr. Nepia's departure was delayed and termed indefinite, since he was actively participating in the rate-setting negotiation with the FAA (Federal Aviation Administration).

During the transition period Stephen was to make himself acquainted with all of the district general managers as well as the rank and file employees. Stephen visited all of the district offices; he met and talked with district managers, sales personnel and operations personnel, and he made comments wherever he felt that company policy was not being followed. He seldom found anything worthy of praise if it did not comply with established company policy.

The first sign of difficulty came when the corporate chauffeur in New York asked to speak to John Nepia, the outgoing general manager. The outgoing general manager had maintained a policy of being accessible to any of the company's employees. The driver explained the following:

> I been with this company for five years now. I like my work and I like my job. But I don't believe that I should get less respect because I'm a driver. I don't like the idea of having to drive Mr. Esterant's wife and her friends around on a shopping trip in downtown New York. I don't think it's part of my responsibility to walk his dog or carry his wife's packages. I realize that I *work* for him, but I refuse to be treated as though I were his *servant*. I decided that if this treatment continues on his part, I will have to find out what grievance procedure is available and file an official complaint.

John Nepia was quick to assure the driver that the matter would be looked into and he would get in touch with him as soon as he knew more about the situation.

Other rumblings came from the operations employees. They contended that Stephen Esterant was thoughtless, unappreciative and distant in his interactions with them. They further believed that he felt and acted "too damn superior." For example, one of the operative employees related the following story. "Once Stephen visited the baggage-handling area at Chicago where a new computerized routing system was being tested. He had worked with a similar system before and immediately spotted some procedures which would increase the efficiency of operation. He proceeded to tell the employees that they didn't know what they were doing and questioned their intelligence."

The most recent sign of major discord came when the district managers sent a plea to John Nepia begging him to implore Spain to recall the new general manager. In their opinion, morale had suffered greatly, and Stephen was the direct cause.

The outgoing general manager and Jason DuBryne, the director of personnel, were good and long-time friends. They had survived many crises together. Therefore, John called in his trusted friend to seek advice and ponder their problem and their possible courses of action.

Jason was considered by many of the employees to be a firm, but fair administrator. He often prided himself on the fact that he was always available to talk to and help his people. He was often consulted by members of the firm concerning interpersonal matters. These consultations often concerned private as well as corporate issues.

During their meeting, the personnel manager acknowledged to John that the situation was indeed grave; however, at no point in the conversation did he indicate what his personal beliefs were concerning the problem. He stated that he did not believe that the heir apparent was technically incompetent. He also suggested the possibility that the heir apparent just did not understand the way of doing business in the western hemisphere. The meeting ended with John Nepia deciding that a conversation with Stephen Esterant was needed.

THE NEW GENERAL MANAGER'S VIEWPOINT

Stephen Esterant was named to head the western hemispheric operations of World International Airlines, Inc. as a reward for his outstanding service as a district manager in Spain. He was told that he was selected because he had been able to bring district offices into compliance with company operations policy and to maintain or increase sales volume at the same time.

Stephen had served in five other district posts prior to receiving this promotion. He was 32 years old and married to a lovely woman who was a member of a wealthy and influential family in Spain. In fact, Stephen's wife's family was one of a few wealthy families owning a substantial portion of World International Airlines stock. Stephen was a man who knew what he wanted and he knew how to get it. He moved briskly about his affairs asking no favors *from* anyone and giving no favors *to* anyone. He appeared to be the coming star in the organization.

Stephen Esterant received a memo from John Nepia requesting that he meet with him and Jason DuBryne, the personnel director, about a matter of apparent great importance. En route to the meeting he pondered over what would possibly be discussed. He, of course, had a few items on his own agenda. Since coming to New York, Stephen had become aware of several problems involved in his becoming the new general manager. He was displeased by the apparent lack of respect given to him by his subordinates as well as the "cocky" attitude of the hourly employees. He was sure that John and Jason were aware of the attitude problems and yet he could not understand why they had not dealt with these matters sooner and in a stronger manner. From Stephen's point of view, there was a need to run a tight ship, as he had done in the eastern hemisphere. He obviously had a distaste for the hourly employees' practice of calling managers by their first names and a lack of deference to those in authority, as was often done not only in the New York offices, but also throughout the rest of the western hemisphere operations. He also wanted to tell John and Jason that he needed to have them run less interference for him. Since he was soon to be general manager, he believed that he should start to handle inter-group conflict and decide about policy disputes so that the organization could easily recognize its new boss and leader. He resolved that if the opportunity arose in the meeting, he would raise these issues with John and Jason.

As he reached the door to John's office, Stephen turned the knob and jauntily entered the office to meet with John Nepia and Jason DuBryne, not really knowing what to expect.

When you have read this case, look back at the chapter's diagnostic questions and choose the ones that apply to the case. Then use those questions with the ones that follow in your case analysis.

1. How accurate were Stephen Esterant's perceptions of western hemisphere employees? What perceptual bias did he display? How did this bias affect his behavior?

2. Was Stephen the only person in this case whose perceptions were faulty? How accurate were the western-hemisphere employees' perceptions of Stephen? Did they display any perceptual biases?

3. What short-term action should John Nepia have taken to resolve the problems developing between Stephen and other airline employees? What long-term actions should the company have taken to prevent similar future problems?

CASE 5-3

PRECISION MACHINE TOOL

Read Chapter 6's Case 6-1, "Precision Machine Tool." Next, look back at Chapter 5's diagnostic questions and choose the ones that apply to that case. Then use those questions with the ones that follow in this first analysis of the case.

1. John Garner and Tom Avery reacted very differently to the prospect of selling their company to Ako Wang. Based on what you have learned in Chapter 5, explain why.

2. In what ways were each man's perceptions accurate? What inaccuracies, if any, can you identify? Did they show any perceptual biases? Which of the two men's perceptions do you think were the least biased? Why?

3. John and Tom had to evaluate alternatives, decide what to do, and then contact Ako Wang to inform him of their decision. As they went through these steps, how best could they have controlled for perceptual biases?

C H A P T E R 6

DECISION MAKING

According to Donald Regan, President Reagan's former chief of staff, Nancy Reagan's insistence on consulting astrologer Joan Quigley before any important decisions were made about the president's activities began "to interfere with the normal conduct of the presidency." Regan says in his memoir that for a time he kept a calendar on his desk with "good" days highlighted in green, "bad" in red, and "iffy" in yellow. That way he could remember when "it was propitious to move the President of the U.S. from one place to another, or schedule him to speak in public, or commence negotiations with a foreign power."
Source: *Barret Seaman, "Good Heavens!" Time, May 16, 1988, 25; Donald T. Regan, "For the Record," Time, May 16, 1988, pp. 26–36.*

In May of 1988, much of the world was shocked to learn that for some years decisions about the schedule of the President of the United States had been made at least partially in consultation with San Francisco astrologer Joan Quigley. In 1981 Quigley showed Ronald Reagan's wife, Nancy, that astrological charts could have predicted extreme danger for the president on March 30 of that year—the day that John Hinckley, Jr., attempted to assassinate the president. Obsessed with her fear for her husband's safety and convinced of Quigley's power to protect him, Nancy Reagan resolved that from that day on, no presidential public appearance would be confirmed without Quigley's seal of approval. Over just one four month interval, Quigley forbade the president's public exposure on 47 days. Moreover, she characterized three of those four months as generally "bad."[1]

Many insiders consider the president's schedule the single most potent tool of the White House because it determines what the most powerful person in the Western world is going to do, with whom, and when. The fact that such important decisions as the timing of the 1987 Geneva summit talks were being influenced by an astrologer immediately captured the attention of the entire world. Most people have little respect for astrological interpretations and predictions, seeing them as baseless advice found in some newspapers—usually next to the comics. In a letter to the editor of *Time* magazine one person declared, "No wonder our government is in such confusion. It is ruled by a man who is ruled by his wife who is ruled by a friend who is ruled by the stars."[2]

Interestingly, in all the ensuing uproar, there was very little criticism of the actual decisions that were made. For example, no one ever claimed that the time ultimately selected for the Geneva summit was bad in any way. Rather, it was the nonrational way in which decisions were being reached that produced the controversy. Astrology was seen as totally irrational, and people felt that if any decisions ought to be based on rationality, certainly decisions about the schedule of the president of the United States should be among them.

DIAGNOSTIC ISSUES

In this chapter you will see that our diagnostic model brings to light many questions about the process of decision making. One of the most important is, What key factors enable us to *describe* and distinguish effective decisions from ineffective decisions? What factors differentiate between effective and ineffective decision-making processes? How can we *diagnose* a situation in which different ways of seeing a problem lead to different prospective solutions? Can we explain why a decision maker sticks to a failing course of action in the face of consistently negative feedback?

How can we *prescribe* whether an organizational decision maker should rely on past practices or whether he should opt for more innovative choices? Can we determine when a decision maker should lean toward risky decisions and when he should be cautious? Finally, what *actions* can a manager take to control biases in the decision-making process and to enhance the quality of decisions made? What actions can create a climate that is conducive to creative decision making?

[1] Adapted from "For the Record," *Time Magazine*, May 16, 1988, p 29.
[2] *Time*, June 5, 1989, p 5.

EVALUATING DECISION MAKING

Making decisions is an essential part of the job of any manager or executive. Although the nature of the decision depends on the manager's area of expertise, such as marketing or production, the responsibility for choosing among different courses of action is something that all managers share. Managerial decisions often have a great impact not only on an organization's future but on the future of all the people who depend on the organization or are in some way affected by its actions—customers, suppliers, competitors, even the general public. Thus the decisions made by key people in many organizations are often closely scrutinized.

Certainly the outcome of a decision is the ultimate basis for judging its effectiveness. However, many factors can affect that outcome, and it is often a long time before the outcome is known. Thus the decision-making process itself is often of great interest.

Outcomes

Let's look first at some of the factors that affect our evaluation of a decision's ultimate *outcome*. First and perhaps most obvious is *decision quality*, or the degree to which the chosen course of action is ultimately seen as the best among all those available. Also of considerable importance is *decision timeliness*. The right decision at the wrong time is no better than a wrong decision. In addition, because in most organizational contexts decisions are implemented by people other than the decision makers, *decision acceptance* by others is one of the important criteria by which decisions come to be judged. A manager who makes high-quality decisions but who cannot demonstrate the quality of the decision to the people who must put its results into effect will be no more successful than a manager who makes low-quality decisions.

Processes

distributive justice An individual's perception of the fairness of his reward in comparison with the rewards given others.

procedural justice Perceived fairness of the process by which reward allocations have been made.

In evaluating decision quality, people are influenced by the *decision-making process*—by how just they feel a decision is and by how fairly they feel the decision was arrived at. Theorists in the area of decision making distinguish between two kinds of perceived justice; distributive justice and procedural justice. **Distributive justice** is the fairness of the amount of a reward as perceived by its recipient and as compared with rewards given to others.

Procedural justice, on the other hand, is the fairness of the way in which rewards are allocated as perceived by the recipients of the rewards.

Some research suggests that procedural justice is more important than distributive justice. For example, a study of 2,800 federal employees found that level of job satisfaction was more strongly related to employees' concerns about *the way their salaries were determined* than to their actual pay levels.[3]

Perceptions of procedural justice are critically important when distributive justice is seen as low. In one study, workers who were underpaid in comparison with other employees reacted negatively—for example, they displayed poor work attitudes and were often absent—when pay decisions seemed based on arbitrary

[3] S. Alexander and M. Ruderman, "The Role of Procedural and Distributive Justice in Organizational Behavior," *Social Justice Research* 3, (1987), 117–98.

reasons.[4] On the other hand, when these same workers were led to believe that pay differentials were based on differences in performance, no such negative reactions took place.

These and other studies suggest that the public's reaction to the manner in which decisions were made about President Reagan's schedule was not an isolated phenomenon. On the contrary, it reflected a real concern that decisions affecting individuals and groups in our society be based on rational processes rather than on irrational or arbitrary judgments. In this chapter we examine the positive and negative features of a rational decision-making model and consider some practical examples of how this model can be used. After exploring several factors that interfere with our ability to make purely rational decisions, we examine a decision-making model that recognizes the difficulty—sometimes the impossibility—of making rational decisions. We conclude with a look at some processes that fuel creative decision making.

rational decision-making model A model in which decisions are made systematically and based consistently on the principle of economic rationality.

economic rationality The belief underlying rational decision-making models that people attempt to maximize their individual economic outcomes.

FIGURE 6-1

The Rational Decision-Making Process

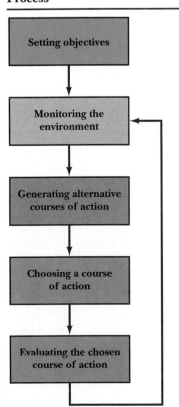

RATIONAL DECISION MAKING

Because of its ties to classic economic theories of behavior, the **rational decision-making model** is often referred to as the rational-economic model. One of the most important of this model's key assumptions is that of **economic rationality**, or the notion that people attempt to maximize their individual economic outcomes. The model also assumes that people will consistently, logically, and in a precise, mathematical way pursue this goal of economic maximization through the five steps we describe next (see also Figure 6-1).

Setting Objectives

The first step in the rational decision-making process involves *setting objectives*, or goals. For example, the manager of a dairy farm may set a goal of increasing sales by 10 percent over the coming year. Similarly, a student may set a goal of attaining a 3.0 grade point average (GPA) over the next semester. The rational model assumes that it is possible to specify objectives in terms of outcomes that can be easily observed and measured.[5]

The objectives established in the first stage of the decision-making process not only determine the target one is aiming for but provide standards with which the objective situation can be compared. As we will see in the next section, decisions can be reassessed and adjustments made whenever the situation appears to deviate from these preset standards.

Monitoring the Environment

Although setting a goal is a decision in itself, from the perspective of the rational decision-making model, a substantive decision is not made until some problem or prospect related to the established goal appears. Thus, in the second stage of the decision-making process *monitoring the environment* is necessary to see how

[4] J. Greenberg, "Reactions to Procedural Injustice in Payment Distributions: Do the Ends Justify the Means?" *Journal of Applied Psychology* 72 (1988), 55–61.
[5] L. S. Baird, R. W. Beatty and C. E. Schneier, *The Performance Appraisal Sourcebook* (Amherst, Mass.: Human Resource Development Press, 1982), p. 37.

When he became chairman of American Airlines, Bob Crandall set two major goals for the company: to become the leading air carrier in the U.S. and to derive 30 percent of its revenues from international traffic by 2000. By 1990 American had achieved the first goal and was well on its way to the next: the international share of its traffic had grown from 8 to 20 percent in just 8 years. Crucial to American's rise in both domestic and overseas markets was cost cutting. By emphasizing internal growth it avoided the high cost of labor that accompanies mergers and acquisitions. By flying into smaller cities on its new international routes, it has saved both itself and its passengers money and the hassle of crowds and delays. Source: *Kenneth Labich, "American Takes on the World,"* Fortune, *September 24, 1990, pp. 40–48.*

well the individual or group responsible for meeting the goal is progressing toward it. This scanning can lead to several different outcomes. First, matters could proceed pretty much as the decision maker anticipated, and thus no new decisions would be required. In this case, the decision maker would simply "stay the course," continuing to engage in the behaviors and practices that are already in place.

A second possibility is that a problem, or *threat*, may arise in the environment, making the goal impossible to reach. The manager of the dairy farm, for example, may notice that a competing farm has started to advertise, and that his own farm's sales have decreased by 20 percent during the first quarter of the year. Or our student may discover that one of her courses is much more difficult than she thought it would be when she receives a failing grade on the first quiz. Such unanticipated events make staying the course an illogical reaction, and in each situation some different course of action must be decided upon.

Monitoring the environment may also reveal an unanticipated prospect of a favorable nature, or an *opportunity*, that would enhance the probability of goal attainment. For example, the dairy farm manager may have an opportunity to supply the local elementary schools and may have to decide whether to expand his operations in this direction. The student may learn that she can get extra credit in one of her classes if she participates in a research project and thus may have to decide whether to invest time in this activity.

Interestingly, research indicates that most real-world managers are more sensitive to perceived threats than to perceived opportunities. In fact, managers often infer a threat when information is ambiguous, and they sometimes ignore information that suggests an opportunity.[6] For example, when other small companies began developing clones or replicas of IBM personal computers (PCs), IBM first saw the competition from these numerous, tiny companies as a threat. Over time, however, IBM executives came to see the situation as an opportunity. An environment in which many smaller companies were producing IBM-compatible equipment with a considerable time lag would clearly be preferable to one in which major competitors like Apple were doing their own thing.

Generating Alternatives

The rational decision-making model requires that all potential solutions to a problem be identified before a decision is made. Without *generating alternatives*,

[6] S. E. Jackson and J. E. Dutton, "Discerning Threats and Opportunities," *Administrative Science Quarterly* 33 (1988), 370–87.

historical decision model A method of generating alternatives for current decisions by reviewing processes that were used in the past.

or examining all possible courses of action, we can never be sure we are choosing the best alternative. According to Paul Nutt, managers can choose possible actions in three major ways: they can use historical models, off-the-shelf processes, or nova techniques.

Nutt's research revealed that **historical decision models**, or actions taken in the past, are the most commonly used sources for generating alternatives. As Table 6-1 shows, he found that managers consult such sources almost half the time. There are several kinds of historical model. Very often we select from among *provincial models*; that is, we consider doing almost exactly what some other single firm or individual has already done. For example, when the material management system (a system for making purchases and managing raw-material inventories) of one of Nutt's subject companies failed, the company chose simply to make a carbon copy of the system used by its most successful competitor.

In the *enriched model*, a variation of the historical model, decision makers may visit several different plants or facilities that have dealt with the same problem and use what they learn from these site visits in generating alternatives. Thus if a university is thinking about restructuring its MBA program, it may send representatives to a number of different schools to explore the ways their programs are structured.

A third category of the historical model is the *pet idea*. In this variation, managers who have dealt at other times or in other places with the problem that now confronts them renew the alternatives they considered before. For example, Frank Lorenzo, former chairman of Texas Air, Continental Air, and Eastern Airlines, on more than one occasion chose bankruptcy in order to void or renegotiate noncompetitive union labor contracts. Each time he faced the same problem he used the same, highly controversial tactic.

off-the-shelf decision model A method of generating alternatives for current decisions by consulting agents external to the organization that have standardized, ready-made alternatives.

In the second most widely used method of generating alternatives, the **off-the-shelf decision model**, decision makers use outside consultants who provide ready-made solutions. Sometimes a firm may seek only one proposal, but in other instances it may invite outside firms to bid competitively for the opportunity to solve the problem. For example, a firm with high turnover in its managerial ranks may fear that its executive salaries are no longer competitive. Rather than prepare its own wage-and-salary survey, the company may turn to consulting firms like

---

TABLE 6-1
Methods Managers Use to Generate Alternative Courses of Action

METHOD		FREQUENCY OF USE (%)
Historical models		41
Provincial	20	
Enriched	6	
Pet idea	15	
Off-the-shelf processes		30
Extended (multiple proposals)	7	
Truncated (single proposal)	23	
Nova techniques		15
Internal staff	8	
External consultants	7	
Unclassified		14

Source: P. C. Nutt, "Types of Organizational Decision Processes," *Administrative Science Quarterly* 29 (1984), 14–50.

the Hay Group, Management Compensation Services, or Growth Resources, Inc. Because making salary surveys is the consulting firm's bread and butter, these firms may be able to do a better job at less cost than the firm could do on its own.

When a problem has never been confronted before, historical and off-the-shelf methods may be inappropriate, and managers may use **nova techniques** to generate new ideas. Nova techniques seek ideas from many sources: the organization's own staff, outside consultants, or managers' colleagues in other firms. The key is to generate innovative ideas without reference to the practices of others.

Nutt's research, as reflected in Table 6-1, clearly suggests that managers tend to copy the ideas of others or to search for ready-made solutions to problems rather than generate new ideas. This tendency can probably be attributed to the speed and certainty associated with the first two approaches. Developing innovative approaches usually takes more time, and the outcome is harder to predict.

Choosing a Course of Action

The fourth step proposed by the rational decision-making model involves comparing all the alternatives that one has selected and choosing the one that seems most likely to lead to goal accomplishment. The final choice is determined by a cost-benefit, or **utility maximization**, approach. That is, the decision maker selects the alternative that leads to the maximum payoff.

Utility maximization is complicated by the fact that one cannot always be certain of the outcome associated with a particular choice. That is, there is not always a 100 percent probability that a given choice will lead to a given outcome. One's degree of certainty about the outcome of an alternative can be seen as falling somewhere along a continuum that ranges from *certainty* through a condition of *risk* to *uncertainty* (see Figure 6-2).

In some situations, you can be confident that a particular choice will lead to a particular outcome. For example, you can be assured that if you place $1,000 in a guaranteed savings account, the value of your money will grow each year by the rate of interest offered you by the savings institution.

In other cases, you cannot be sure of an outcome but you can try to assess the risk involved. Suppose you were to bet your $1,000 on a racehorse that gave odds of ten to one. Although you could not predict the precise outcome, you could be sure that one of two things would happen. Either the horse would win the race and you would win $9,000 ($10,000 less your investment of $1,000) or the horse would lose the race and you would lose your original bet.

An important characteristic of decisions made under the condition of risk is that we can compute **expected values** that permit us to compare alternatives with each other.

An expected value is derived by multiplying each possible outcome of a particular alternative by the probability that that outcome will occur. Table 6-2 shows the calculation of the expected values associated with each of three alternative investment opportunities. Clearly, Alternative 3 is the best overall investment in terms of expected value.

nova technique A method of generating alternatives by seeking new and innovative solutions.

utility maximization A process by which a decision maker selects the one alternative that leads to the highest possible payoff.

expected value The projected value of an outcome that has less than a 100 percent probability of occurring. The expected value is derived mathematically by multiplying each possible outcome of a particular course of action by the probability that that outcome will occur.

FIGURE 6-2

A Continuum of Uncertainty in Decision-Making Situations

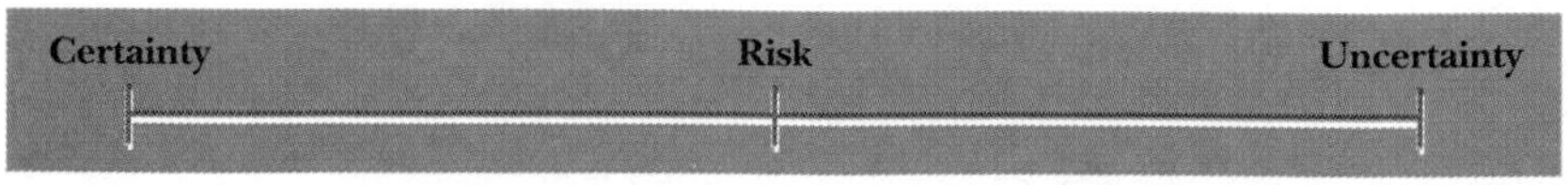

Certainty	Risk	Uncertainty

TABLE 6-2
Calculating Expected Values and Comparing Alternatives

Alternative 1
$1,000 investment with

50% chance of returning $0
50% chance of returning $3,000

Expected value = (.50)(0) + (.50)(3,000)
= $1,500

Alternative 2
$1,000 investment with

33.3% chance of returning $0
33.3% chance of returning $1,000
33.3% chance of returning $3,000

Expected value = (.333)(0) + (.333)(1,000) + (.333)(3,000)
= $1,332

Alternative 3
$1,000 investment with

25% chance of returning $0
25% chance of returning $500
25% chance of returning $1,000
25% chance of returning $5,000

Expected value = (.25)(0) + (.25)(500) + (.25)(1,000) + (.25)(5,000)
= $1,625

Evaluating Actions

According to the rational decision-making model, once a decision is selected and implemented, we must check periodically to see if the results of the decision are in line with the original goals. If the feedback from the environment suggests that the goals are being reached, the decision maker will stay with his chosen course of action. If results deviate from what is expected, however, the entire decision-making process may begin anew. Thus decision making according to this model is a dynamic process designed to be self-correcting over time.

THREATS TO RATIONAL DECISION MAKING

Rationality in decision making is neither easily nor commonly achieved. In Chapter 5 we used perceptual illusions to show that perception is not nearly as straightforward as it seems. Here we will use what we might call decision-making illusions to show why rationality is not so easy to achieve. Credit for documenting the existence of these illusions goes to Kahneman and Tversky, who first documented the existence of several of the illusions we examine here: loss aversion, availability bias, base rate bias, and regression to the mean.

Loss Aversion

As a prelude to this discussion, read the paragraph in Table 6-3 and decide what strategy you would choose if you were the sales executive faced with the situation described. If you decided to go with Strategy 1 and save the 200 accounts for sure, you are not alone. In fact, research with managers and nonmanagers alike

The development of a new technology by a competitor threatens the viability of your organization because it may mean the loss of 600 accounts. You have two available strategies to counter this new technology. Your advisors make it clear that if you choose Strategy 1, 200 accounts will be saved. If you choose Strategy 2, there is a one-third chance that 600 accounts will be saved and a two-thirds chance that none will be saved. Which strategy would you choose?

Source: Adapted from A. Twersky and D. Kahneman, "The Framing of Decisions and the Psychology of Choice," *Science* 211 (1981), 453–58.

shows that this choice is preferred roughly three to one over the more risky Strategy 2.

Now turn to a similar decision situation, shown in Table 6-4, and decide what strategy you would use under these circumstances. If this time you chose Strategy 2, again you are not alone. Research shows that this choice is preferred roughly four to one over Strategy 1.[7]

The surprising thing about these results, though, is that the problems described are virtually identical. Read the paragraphs in Tables 6-3 and 6-4 once more. You can see that Strategy 1 is the same in both tables. The only difference is that in Table 6-3, it is expressed in terms of accounts *saved* (200 out of 600) whereas in Table 6-4 it is expressed in terms of accounts *lost* (400 out of 600). Clearly, if 200 are saved, 400 are lost and vice versa.

Strategy 2 is also the same in both situations, expressed in terms of accounts saved in one table and accounts lost in the other. If you compute expected values for all four strategies (refer to Table 6-2 for help in doing this), you will confirm that both situations have the same expected values. Why then is Strategy 1 preferred when the situation is described as it is in Table 6-3 and Strategy 2 preferred when the situation is outlined as in Table 6-4?

Because the expected values in these problem situations are all the same, none of the choice strategies presented are bad. Thus let's consider the decision situations outlined in Table 6-5. Most people show the same pattern of preference when presented with these decision choices, even though in each case, in terms of expected value one choice is clearly superior to the other. In Decision 1, most people choose the sure gain (a), even though the expected value for the risky gain (b) is clearly higher. Similarly, in Decision 2, most people take the risk on the larger loss (d), even though the expected value associated with the sure loss (c) is higher.

[7] A. Twersky and D. Kahneman, "The Framing of Decisions and the Psychology of Choice," *Science* 211 (1981), 453–58.

The development of a new technology by a competitor threatens the viability of your organization because it may mean the loss of 600 accounts. You have two available strategies to counter this new technology. Your advisors make it clear that if you choose Strategy 1, 400 accounts will be lost. If you choose Strategy 2, there is a one-third chance that no accounts will be lost and a two-thirds chance that all would be lost. Which strategy would you choose?

Source: Adapted from A. Twersky and D. Kahneman, "The Framing of Decisions and the Psychology of Choice," *Science* 211 (1981), 453–58.

> **T A B L E 6-5**
> **Decision Strategies with an Expected Value-Attractiveness Discrepancy**
>
> Examine the decision situations that follow and choose one of the two alternatives offered for each.
>
> *Decision 1*
> a. A sure gain of $240
> b. A 25 percent chance of winning $1,000 and a 75 percent chance of winning nothing
>
> *Decision 2*
> a. A sure loss of $740
> b. A 75 percent chance of losing $1,000 and a 25 percent chance of losing nothing
>
> *Source*: Adapted from A. Tversky and D. Kahneman, "The Framing of Decisions and the Psychology of Choice," *Science* 211 (1981), 453–58.

loss aversion bias The tendency of most decision makers to weigh losses more heavily than gains, even when the absolute value of each is equal.

Research indicates that, in general, people have a slight preference for sure outcomes over risky ones. Studies also indicate, however, that people hate losing, and this **loss aversion bias** affects their decision making even more strongly than their preference for nonrisky situations. Thus, when given a choice between a sure gain and a risky gain, most people will take the sure thing and avoid the risk (showing the minor aversion to risk). When given a choice between a sure loss and a risky loss, however, most people will avoid the sure loss and take a chance on not losing anything (showing the major aversion to loss).

We can see this preference for risk over loss in many real-world situations. For example, in the early 1980s oil companies like Shell Oil and Amoco Oil found themselves faced with the increasing costs of managing credit-card accounts. To make up for the added cost of managing these accounts, these firms began to charge customers differentially depending on whether they paid cash for gasoline or used their credit cards. Initially, some companies described this extra charge as a credit surcharge (a sure loss). Their customers were outraged. Other companies advertised a discount for cash (a sure gain), and their customers thought this was great! Needless to say, nobody talks about credit surcharges anymore, and everyone offers discounts for cash.

Availability Bias

availability bias The tendency in decision makers to judge the likelihood that something will happen by the ease with which they can recall examples of it.

Let's explore another kind of bias in decision making. In a typical passage of English prose, does the letter *k* occur more often as the first or the third letter in a word? Twice as many people confronted with this problem choose first over third, although the fact is that *k* appears in the third spot almost twice as often as in the first. This phenomenon can be explained in terms of the **availability bias**, which means that people have a tendency to judge the likelihood that something will happen by the ease with which they can call examples to mind. Most people assume that *k* is more common at the beginning of words simply because it is easier to remember words beginning with *k* than words that have *k* as their third letter.

You can see the availability bias at work in the way people think about death, illness, and disasters. In general, people vastly overestimate the numbers of deaths caused by vividly imaginable events like an airplane crash and underestimate deaths caused by illness like emphysema or stroke. Deaths caused by sudden disasters are more easily called to mind because they are so vivid and so public, often making the first page of newspapers across the country. Death caused by illness, on the other hand, is generally private and thus less likely to be recalled.

Companies that employ risky technologies, such as nuclear power plants, must deal with the availability bias continuously. Ironically, some things they do to allay people's fears actually make things worse. For example, going over disaster scenarios and detailing what would be done in case of a nuclear accident actually makes residents of a community more fearful. Indeed, research shows that the more detail presented, the more vivid the picture becomes, the greater the probability of a disaster appears, and the more strongly people resist having such a plant in their community.[8]

The power of either the loss aversion bias or the availability bias is great in isolation, but when the two are combined, many decision makers find them impossible to resist. The insurance industry, for example, is financed almost solely through the compelling nature of this combination. Suppose you pay $300 for home owners' insurance that will pay your beneficiary $100,000 in case of a disaster. This is a terrible bet, because the odds that such a disaster will occur are less than .003 (i.e., 300/100,000). Nevertheless, because we often see fires on television news broadcasts (vividness plus frequency), and because one's home, if owned, represents such a huge investment (loss of great proportions), people are more than happy to make such bets.

Base Rate Bias

To understand a third type of decision bias, consider the decision-making problem described in Table 6-6. By now you are probably ready to guess that the answer that seems obviously correct—that the cab was a Blue—is actually wrong. You are right. In fact, the odds are much better that the cab was a Green. Figure 6-3 shows you mathematically why that is so.

If there were 100 cabs in the city, 85 would be Greens and 15 would be Blues. This is the base rate, that is, the initial probability given no other piece of information. On the premise—established in Table 6-6—that the witness (who provides an additional piece of information over and above the base rate) would be right 80 percent of the time, let us see what would happen in each possible scenario. If the cab in the accident was actually a Blue, the witness would identify it correctly as a Blue 12 times (.80 × 15 = 12) and would incorrectly identify it as a Green 3 times (.20 × 15 = 3). If the car was a Green, however, the witness would correctly identify it as a Green 68 times (.80 x 85) and misidentify it as a Blue 17 times (.20 x 85). Thus the odds are much greater that the witness's identification of the cab as a Blue was a misidentification of a Green cab (which

[8] P. Slovic, B. Fischhoff and S. C. Lichtenstein, "Cognitive Processes and Societal Risk Taking," in *ORI Research Bulletin*, vol. 16, (Eugene: Oregon Research Institute, 1974), pp. 16–76.

TABLE 6-6
Identifying a Hit-and-Run Driver

A cab was involved in a hit-and-run accident.

Two taxicab companies serve the city: the Green Company operates 85 percent of the cabs, and the Blue Company operates the remaining 15 percent.

A witness identifies the hit-and-run cab as blue. When the court tests the witness's reliability under circumstances similar to those on the night of the accident, he correctly identifies the color of a cab 80 percent of the time and misidentifies it 20 percent of the time.

Which cab company was most probably involved in the hit-and-run accident?

Source: A. Tversky and D. Kahneman, "The Framing of Decisions and the Psychology of Choice," *Science* 211 (1981), 453–58.

FIGURE 6-3

How to Test the Witness's
Accuracy in the Hit-and-Run-
Driver Case

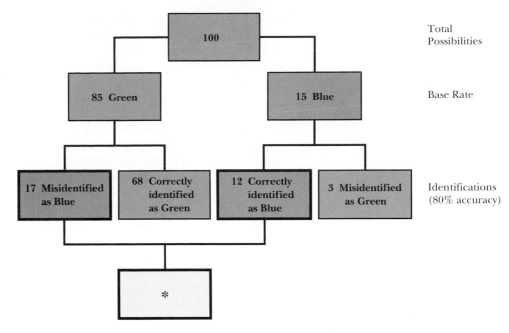

*The probability is greater that the cab was a misidentified Blue (17 out of 100) than a correctly identified Blue (12 out of 100).

base rate bias The tendency in decision makers to ignore the underlying objective probability or base rate, that a particular outcome will follow a particular course of action.

happens 17 out of 100 times) than a correct identification of a Blue cab (which happens only 12 out of 100 times).

The reason why virtually everyone who approaches this problem naively gets it wrong is that we put too much weight on the evidence provided by the witness and not enough weight on the evidence provided by the base rate. That is what is meant by the term **base rate bias**. People tend to ignore the background information in this sort of case and to feel that they are dealing with something unique. In one example, decision makers will discount the evidence of how few cars are actually blue, and instead put more confidence in human judgment about the color of the car. Ignoring the base rate leads to misplaced confidence in decision making.

The problem of misplaced confidence is particularly pronounced when more than one probabilistic event is involved. As you might guess, this is more often than not the case in actual business ventures. Suppose, for example, that a house builder contracts to have a house completed by the end of the year. Assume further that her chances of accomplishing four specific tasks in time to meet this deadline are as follows:

TASK	PROBABILITY
Get permits	excellent (90%)
Get financing	very good (80%)
Get materials	excellent (90%)
Get subcontractors to complete their work	very good (80%)

Reviewing these data, our builder might well conclude that there is a good to excellent chance that she can complete the project in the time specified in the contract. In fact, the odds that this will happen are only about 50-50. Multiplying the 4 probabilities together (.9 x .8 x .9 x .8 = .52) gives us just over 50 percent, which is hardly a good to excellent chance. The axiom known as Murphy's Law states that anything that can go wrong will go wrong. This may be a tad pessimistic, but in a long series of events, the odds are quite good that any one event *will* go wrong, and sometimes it takes just one mishap to destroy an entire venture. Any business executive who is putting together a deal where the ultimate outcome depends on a series of discrete events, none of which are sure things, must keep this fact in mind.

Again, combining two biases can have a particularly powerful effect. The lottery industry gets people to make bad bets by combining the tendency to ignore the base rate with the availability bias. People's tendency to think that their chances of winning are greater than they are is fueled by marketing that provides vivid, graphic examples of the joy of winning the lottery. For example, you may have seen publicity pictures of lottery winners holding up ridiculous, four-foot checks. Moreover, winners are announced every day or every weekend, making it appear as if winning happens all the time. Publishing the names of losers, of course, would require producing a document the size of an encyclopedia every day.

The scope of such operations (state-run lotteries generate over $17 billion a year nationally)[9] shows how intelligent, hard-working people can be tricked into making poor decisions. Indeed, in some communities people have questioned the ethics of the government's involvement in what is actually gambling. Other people have suggested that lotteries are in effect a regressive tax on people who do not understand probability theory. This latter criticism is understandably linked with the observation that, seen as a fixed-rate tax, the purchase of a weekly lottery ticket hurts the poor much more than it hurts people of middle- to-upper income levels.

Regression toward the Mean

Table 6-7 presents another decision problem that confounds almost all naive subjects. Read over this exhibit and decide which stock you would like to purchase. By this time, you are probably so sensitized to being misled that you do not even want to be in the same room with the stock that has gone up five years in a row, let alone hold it. In fact, one study has shown that if over a fifty-year span, an investor continually bought only the stocks that had declined the most in value over each preceding five-year period he would have earned 30 percent above the average market return in each succeeding five-year period.[10] Nevertheless, most naive subjects jump on the continually rising stock because they fail to recognize a phenomenon called **regression toward the mean**.

regression toward the mean The phenomenon whereby in a series of events that is influenced by complex factors, any single extraordinary event is almost sure to be followed by a more ordinary event.

To understand this phenomenon, you must realize that in any series of events that is influenced by a complex array of factors, any single extraordinary event is almost sure to be followed by a more ordinary event. That is, extraordinary events are more often than not preceded by events that are closer (i.e., they regress) to average (i.e., the mean). Because most people fail to appreciate this

[9] Tom Callahan, "Did Pete Do It? What Are the Odds?" *Time*, July 26, 1989, p. 92.

[10] L. Thaler and W. De Bront, "Regression to the Mean on the New York Stock Exchange," working paper, University of Wisconsin at Madison.

T A B L E 6-7
Regression toward the Mean at the New York Stock Exchange

Two stocks exist, one of which has decreased in value five consecutive years, and one that has increased in value for five consecutive years. Assuming you had to purchase and hold the stock for the next five years, which would you choose?

Source: A. Tversky and D. Kahneman, "The Framing of Decisions and the Psychology of Choice," *Science* 211 (1981), 453–58.

---

phenomenon, their decision making is biased. One of the authors once saw an insurance company almost abandon what was actually an effective incentive system—providing travel prizes to the top salesperson—because experience revealed that the winner's performance was always poorer in the following year. Given the complex number of factors that go into a final sales figure, this kind of variation is to be expected. Undoubtedly some of the lucky breaks that help make an incredibly successful year simply do not repeat themselves the next year. This is also the reason why in sports like baseball, repeating as the champion is considered one of the most difficult feats to accomplish.

Escalation of Commitment

For a final demonstration of biased decision making, imagine the following scenario. You are on the ground floor of a building and have two minutes to get to a job interview on the fourth floor. You can either take the elevator, which can whisk you to the fourth floor in a matter of seconds, or you can take the stairs, which can get you to your destination in a few minutes. The elevator is the obvious choice, but this is a twenty-story building, and you don't know where the elevator is at the moment. You push the button, and nothing happens. You could immediately take to the stairs, but you decide to wait. After a few seconds you again look at the stairs and consider giving up on the elevator. But the elevator will surely arrive the moment you head up the stairs, so you continue to wait. Still no elevator appears, and you realize that you probably should have taken the stairs in the first place. By now, however, if you are going to have a chance of arriving on time you must continue to wait for the elevator. On the other hand, being a little late is better than being quite late. You reconsider the stairs. You conclude, "What the heck, I've waited this long, what's a little more time," and continue to wait. The elevator does not appear, and in a fit of disgust, you rush to the stairs, sprinting the four flights while thinking up excuses for why you are late and wondering, "Was that the elevator I just heard?"

escalation of commitment
Investing additional resources in failing courses of action that are not justified by any foreseeable payoff.

If you can imagine your frustration in this situation, you have a feel for another threat to rationality in decision making called **escalation of commitment**. Escalation of commitment is a process in which people invest more and more heavily in an apparently losing course of action in order to justify their earlier decisions. Usually the investments that are made once this process gets started are disproportionate to any gain that could conceivably be realized. Consider the following memo sent by Undersecretary of State George Ball to President Lyndon Johnson prior to U.S. involvement in the Vietnam War:

> The decision you face now is crucial. Once large numbers of U.S. troops are committed to direct combat, they will begin to take heavy casualties in a war they are ill-equipped to fight in a non-cooperative if not downright hostile countryside. Once we suffer large casualties, we will have started a well-nigh irreversible process. Our involvement will be so great that we cannot—without national humiliation—stop short of achieving our complete objectives. Of the two possibilities, I think humiliation would be more likely than achievement of our objectives—even after we have paid terrible costs.[11]

Even in the face of evidence that costs are actually outstripping benefits, a decision maker may feel many different kinds of pressure to continue to act in accord with a particular decision.[12] For psychological reasons, the decision maker

---

[11] B. M. Staw, "The Escalation of Commitment to a Failing Course of Action," *Academy of Management Review* 6 (1981), 577–87.

[12] B. M. Staw and J. Ross, "Behavior in Escalation Situations," in *Research in Organizational Behavior*, ed. B. M. Staw and L. L. Cummings (Greenwich, Conn.: JAI Press, 1987), pp. 12–47.

may not want to appear inconsistent by changing course. He may not want to admit that he has made a mistake. Moreover, particularly where feedback is ambiguous or complex, perceptual distortions like the expectation effect we discussed in Chapter 5 can make the picture appear more hopeful than it really is. Because one cannot make perfect predictions regarding future outcomes, there is always the hope that staying the course will pay off. Moreover, the decision maker may have been rewarded in past situations for sticking it out. Although rare, such experiences are usually quite memorable (availability bias). The experience of giving up when it is appropriate is often not rewarded, at least in the short run, and thus is something people like to forget. Finally, sometimes a decision maker throws out cost-benefit analyses altogether, and develops a win-at-any-cost mentality. The quest to prove himself completely takes over, and the decision maker comes to resemble Captain Ahab in his obsessive pursuit of Moby Dick.

FACTORS THAT PREVENT RATIONALITY

The illusions we have discussed make rational decision making difficult but not impossible. Often, however, the complexity of real-world decision situations literally makes rationality impossible. Our exploration of the factors that prevent rational decision making will lead us to our discussion, in the next section, of a decision making model that acknowledges these barriers to rationality.

Nobel laureate Herbert A. Simon has remarked that "the capacity of the human mind for formulating and solving complex problems is very small compared with the size of the problems whose solution is required for objectively rational behavior in the real world."[13]

Simon's comment on the limits of human intelligence is not so much a condemnation of human beings as it is an acknowledgement of the complexity of the environment in which human beings must operate. Indeed, according to Simon and to others who have followed his lead, the complexity of the real world will typically overwhelm the decision maker at each step of the rational decision making process, making rationality completely impossible.

Lack of Goal Consensus

A problem at the outset of the decision-making process is that rational decisions can be made only when there is general agreement on the goals to be pursued. In large organizations, such goal consensus is very hard to achieve. Neither individuals nor organizations consistently rank desired outcomes in the same way, and in complex organizations the only shared goals are those that are so vague as to be almost meaningless. For example, the public goal of a firm may be the "benefit of humankind through the development of technology." This is a fine goal around which everyone in the firm may rally. However, it is vague and provides no guidance on exactly how it is to be achieved. In running the day-to-day operations of the firm, the goal is worthless, and if there are disagreements among organizational members about specific objectives there is no way to proceed in any rational manner.

Let's return for a moment to our story about the president's astrologer. Every member of the president's cabinet probably has a different idea of how

[13] J. G. March and H. A. Simon, *Organizations* (New York: John Wiley, 1958), p. 10.

There was goal consensus among
political and military leaders of
Desert Storm: the goal was to get
Iraq out of Kuwait. The media
and general public often discussed
a second possible goal, to destroy
both Saddam Hussein and Iraq.
Because not all members of the
multinational coalition would have
subscribed to this secondary goal,
it never became formalized.
Without such consensus, no
rational decision could be taken.

the president should spend his time, as does probably every White House staffer and every member of Congress. Indeed, probably no single agreed-upon rank ordering could ever be established for what the president of the United States should be trying to accomplish on a given day. Lack of goal consensus implies that there is no one best solution, and some problems that the President has to face will engender harsh negative reactions regardless of the stance he takes. For example, whether he supports or opposes abortion, he will enrage one group of people. Either the right-to-life group or the pro-choice group will picket the White House. In such a no-win situation, perhaps the president's best alternative is to keep a low profile and focus his attention instead on an issue that may engender more consensus. For example, most people cringe at the thought of burning the American flag (goal consensus). As a result, public-relations-minded staff tried to direct President Bush toward a constitutional amendment to ban flag burning.

In business organizations, too, different departments and different individuals have different ideas about what goals should be pursued. Because this lack of goal consensus characterizes most organizations, the political processes of bargaining and compromise are more commonly used to reach decisions than are analytical processes in which people try to maximize their gains by the use of techniques like linear programming. Although this kind of mathematical formulation is appropriate for some well-defined organizational problems, like scheduling routine purchases, it doesn't work for the kind of complex, often ill-defined problems that top managers continually must face.

Increasingly, the curricula of business schools, which train future managers, are being criticized for an excessive emphasis on quantitative methods. Experienced executives complain that graduates must be more than flesh-and-blood calculators, and many schools have responded. For example, the University of Chicago's Graduate School of Business, which we mentioned in Chapter 1, has recently overhauled its MBA programs, eliminating the numbers-oriented focus. Although the dean of the school, John Gould, insists that "we're going to keep our pocket protectors," he also has insisted on instituting seminars focusing on the "softer skills" of negotiation tactics and team building.[14]

Problems in Monitoring the Environment

Monitoring the environment, although crucial to identifying threats and opportunities, is not easy. *Time constraints*, for example, may interfere with accurate monitoring. Returning again to our opening example, many problems cross the president's desk that demand immediate action. In these cases, there is no time to engage in surveys to determine where the public at large stands on the issue. In addition, one may get *equivocal feedback*: Some evidence may suggest that a threat or opportunity is developing, whereas other information may be contradictory. Soviet initiatives on nuclear arms talks, for example, were perceived by some of the president's staff as genuine attempts to move toward world peace. Others, however, pointed to Soviet support of leftist groups throughout Latin America as contradicting that impression.

Means-End Relations

In rational decision making we encounter a problem when we try to generate possible courses of action and then try to select the most promising one. Managers

[14] D. Greising, "Chicago's B-School Goes Touchy Feely," *Business Week*, February 12, 1990, p. 61.

In monitoring the organizational environment, it helps to have what a recent Fortune *article called the "laser-like focus" of Home Depot. Bernard Marcus (left), CEO and cofounder of the chain of do-it-yourself warehouse stores, says he wants to be the power retailer in any of his product categories. When the Swedish home furnishings chain IKEA bounded into the United States market with five stores, Home Depot had to make a fast and tough decision. On average, IKEA stores devote 200,000 square feet to furniture, whereas Home Depot warehouses gave their unfinished wood furniture departments only 2000 to 7000 square feet. With a much greater selection, IKEA could sell more and keep its prices even lower than Home Depot's. Home Depot decided to close its furniture section and to use the space to expand its selection of floor tiles and wallpaper.*
Source: *Susan Caminiti, "The New Champs of Retailing,"* Fortune, *September 24, 1990, pp. 85–86.*

often cannot anticipate what actions will lead to what consequences. Because, as Simon points out, most real-world decisions are characterized by uncertainty, managers cannot even speculate on the odds. Under these conditions, one cannot compute expected values, and thus there is no common metric with which to compare various alternatives. This problem occurs especially with nonprogrammed decisions, that is, decisions that are called for only infrequently. In making these kinds of decisions, no one ever develops enough experience to assess the probabilities associated with any alternative easily. For example, how was the president able to decide what he should do in response to the democratization of the Soviet Union? This was an unprecedented event in history for which there was no clear knowledge of what actions might lead to what results.

Although the necessity to make nonprogrammed decisions sometimes creates paralysis, programmed decisions, on the other hand, often become so institutionalized that one wonders if any rational thought is ever given to them. For example, the president routinely makes time in his schedule to call the winning coach of the Super Bowl game, and he meets yearly with college athletes who win national championships in major sports. Nobody sits down each year and compares the time spent doing this with every other possible thing the president could be doing at these times. These are simply practices that have been carried out as long as most people can remember, and tradition rather than analytical thought dictates the decision.

You should also note that managers are not free to choose among all the choices they may generate. The term **bounded discretion**, first suggested by Herbert Simon, refers to the fact that the list of alternatives that any decision maker generates is restricted by social, legal, and moral norms. As Figure 6-4 indicates, the discretionary area within which acceptable choices can be made is bounded on all sides by the limits imposed by (a) unofficial social norms, (b) organizational rules and policies, (c) moral and ethical norms, and (d) legal re-

bounded discretion The recognition that the alternatives offered to a decision maker are bounded by social, legal, moral, and organizational restrictions.

DECISION MAKING

FIGURE 6-4

The Concept of Bounded
Discretion

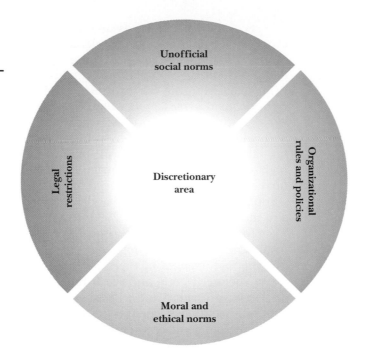

strictions. The boundaries between each of these sets of limitations and the discretionary area are not clear-cut, and as a result decision makers do not always know whether an alternative is in or out of bounds.

Moreover, recent litigation has blurred these boundaries even further. One recent phenomenon that has certainly caught the eyes of executives is personal liability for organizational decisions. Such liability may even extend to include criminal wrongdoing. For example, a New York jury found two executives at Pymm Thermometer Company guilty of assault and reckless endangerment for exposing a worker (who later developed brain damage) to poisonous metal. Similarly, in Illinois, Cook County attorneys successfully prosecuted three senior executives of Film Recovery Systems, Inc., on murder and reckless conduct charges after one of their workers died from inhaling cyanide fumes. These examples make it clear that managers must conform their decisions to societal norms, and that failure to do so may result in very negative consequences both for them and for their organizations.[15]

Noisy Environments

Finally, the idea proposed by the rational decision-making model that once a course of action has been initiated, it can be evaluated by checking its outcome against the original objective must be questioned. In complex environments, where many factors other than the chosen alternative can influence the outcome, making what seems to be the right choice may not lead invariably to the desired outcome. In fact, in *noisy environments*, where the link between actions and outcomes is tenuous, decision makers often place too much value on what happens in any given instance. This can lead them to assign too much importance to their own actions in bringing about the observed results and thus may inhibit their ability to learn from their experience.

[15] S. B. Garland, "This Safety Ruling Could Be Hazardous to Employers' Health," *Business Week*, February 12, 1989, p. 34.

For example, let us assume that in 2000 there will be a fax machine in every home and office, and the demand for overnight mail delivery will be close to zero. If one knew this was going to be the case, then a 1993 decision by a corporate manager to sell off overnight-mail-delivery firms and instead invest in firms manufacturing fax machines would be a good decision. It would be the right decision *in the long run* but 1993 might be too soon to put it in place. For example, the transition process from a time when relatively few have fax machines to the day when they are in every home and office may not be smooth. Moreover, fax sales for 1994 might be off for some unstable, unforeseen reason (such as high interest rates that limit business expansions). If overnight-delivery revenues hold constant that year, the corporate decision maker may very well question the wisdom of her earlier decision and be tempted to reverse it—a decision that could cost millions if the world in 2000 turned out to be as described above.

In noisy environments, one can make sense of action-outcome links only by making many observations of the same outcomes after the same actions. After multiple occurrences of the same sequence of events, the random influences factor themselves out, and the true nature of the action-outcome link becomes clear. Unfortunately, most decision makers in noisy environments fail to stick with one action long enough to sort out the effects of the chosen action on the outcome from the effects of random influences. This lack of consistency in decision making makes people move from one action to another without ever learning much about the action-outcome link associated with any one specific action.[16]

ADMINISTRATIVE DECISION MAKING

There are many contexts in organizations where the use of the rational decision-making model serves as a valuable decision aid. It is particularly useful in routine decision making where everyone agrees on the desired outcomes and the best methods for attaining those outcomes. But because of the many factors that make the rational decision-making model useless in some contexts, alternatives to the model have been developed. We will look next at one of the most widely cited alternatives.

Simon's **administrative decision-making model**, as outlined in Figure 6-5, a move away from the rational decision-making model, was an attempt to paint a more realistic picture of the way organizations make decisions.[17] According to Simon, although the rational decision-making model may be useful in outlining what organizations *should* do if strict rationality were possible, the administrative model provides a better picture of what effective organizations *actually* do when strict rationality is impossible. Simon's model differs from the rational model in four fundamental ways.

administrative decision-making model A model in which decisions pursuant to negotiated goals are made based on satisficing rather than maximizing outcomes, through a sequential consideration of alternatives.

Satisficing versus Optimizing

According to Simon, optimal solutions require that the decision arrived at be better than all other possible decisions. For all the reasons we have discussed, that is simply not possible most of the time. So instead of striving for this impossible goal, organizations try to find **satisficing** solutions to the problems they confront.

satisficing Settling for a decision alternative that meets some minimum level of acceptability, as opposed to trying to maximize utility by considering all possible alternatives.

[16] B. Brehmer, "Response Consistency in Probabilistic Inference Tasks," *Organizational Behavior and Human Performance* 22 (1978), 103–15.

[17] March and Simon, *Organizations*, 1958, pp. 10–12.

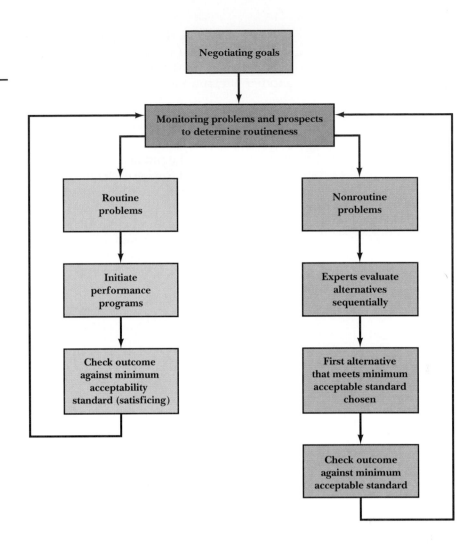

Satisficing means settling for an alternative that meets some minimum level of acceptability. Needless to say, it is much easier to achieve this goal than to try for an optimal solution, which requires that the alternative chosen be superior to all possible alternatives. Indeed, Simon likens it to the comparison between finding *a* needle in a haystack (satisficing) and finding the *biggest, sharpest* needle in the haystack (optimizing).

Considering Alternatives Sequentially

In searching for satisficing solutions, organizations further simplify the process by *considering alternatives sequentially* rather than simultaneously. That is, instead of first generating all possible alternatives and then comparing and contrasting them, each alternative is evaluated one at a time against the criteria for a satisficing outcome. The first alternative generated that is satisfactory is chosen, and the organization moves on to other problems.

For example, a firm needing to downsize (reduce its total number of employees) is faced with over a dozen means of bringing about this outcome. Rather than try to compare the expected results for every possible means with every other possible means (a step that may even be impossible if the firm has never tried to downsize before), the firm may just look at an early retirement program and think, that may do the trick. If the company puts such a program in place and it achieves the desired results, no further alternatives need be considered. If the plan does *not* work, some other reasonable alternative, like a hiring freeze, may be implemented. If this course of action fails, it may be followed by yet another attempt, such as closing down antiquated plants.

Performance Programs

performance programs Scripts that detail exactly what actions are to be taken by a job incumbent when confronted with a standard problem or situation.

Because many of the problems that an organization encounters are routine, new decisions need not be made each time these problems arise. Instead, organizations develop **performance programs**, or scripts that detail exactly what is to be done in a given situation. Typically these programs are set in motion without any conscious thought as to whether they are the best means of accomplishing the objective. For example, when a fire gong rings at a fire station, it immediately triggers a great deal of smoothly coordinated activity, and there is no need for any one firefighter to spend much time thinking about what he should do next.

Developing Experts

discretion An area of latitude wherein the decision maker can use her own judgment in developing and deciding among alternative decisions.

Even though we can develop programs that help simplify a task for an employee, uncertainty in the environment makes it impossible to develop perfectly detailed scripts that will be applicable everywhere. Thus there is still a need for **discretion**, or individual authority to change or modify performance programs while they are being carried out. The range of discretion tends to be limited to tightly defined areas, and experts are developed who become the decision makers for such areas. The advantage of using experts in decision making is that people with special expertise in an area can devise more accurate and more detailed scripts.

In this way complexity is handled by breaking it up into discrete, more manageable chunks that can be handled by a single individual. Thus as we will discuss in Chapters 15–17, an organization may be divided into departments (e.g., personnel) which are divided into units (e.g., personnel selection) which are divided into areas (first-line managerial selection) which are divided into job categories (college recruiter) which are divided into individual jobs (western regional interviewer). The occupant of an individual job typically focuses in on one very narrow area of organizational problem solving.

Failing to differentiate and delegate in this fashion can lead to a situation where one person is simply trying to do much and, in the process, not accomplishing anything. For example, many considered the disastrous $1.2 billion losses recorded by the Bank of New England Corporation (BNE) in the fourth quarter of 1989 to be just this kind of failure. Many claimed that CEO Walter Connolly became involved in many decisions that most bankers would delegate to low-level loan specialists. As the former president of a BNE subsidiary noted, "Walter Connolly could very successfully run a $6 billion institution. . . . When he tried to keep his hands on everything in a $30 billion bank, nothing got done."[18]

As the "In Practice" box illustrates, the combination of expertise and autonomy is often the perfect solution to managing complexity—even the complexity inherent in the management of diversified businesses within a large corporation.

Coupling Programs and Experts

If we break up jobs into small parts, we reduce the burden on any one individual, but then we must integrate each person's contribution with everyone else's.

[18] L. Jereski, "A Stomach for the Bank That Ate New England," *Business Week*, February 5, 1990, p. 68.

In the late 1980s many firms grew through acquisition strategies. That is, rather than grow through internal development, they simply bought out smaller firms and added them to their corporate portfolios. Most corporations employing this strategy found that buying these companies was a lot easier than managing them. The tremendous complexity of managing multiple businesses that were sometimes unrelated to each other often overwhelmed corporate leadership. This happened particularly often when corporate leadership had the financial expertise to put the deal together but lacked the technical expertise necessary to run the business that was purchased. More recently, however, corporations growing by acquisitions have recognized the need for technical expertise and have obtained it from an obvious, but long overlooked source: former owners.

The traditional approach was to "clean house." Former owners departed, and the acquiring corporation brought in a totally new management team. Increasingly, however, corporations are employing former owners as experts and giving them considerable decision-making autonomy.

RPM Inc. of Medina, Ohio is one holding company that has employed this practice successfully for a long time. In fact, in just over two decades Chairman Thomas Sullivan persuaded 25 business owners to sell their companies to him and then to run them as independent divisions of RPM. Retaining former owners and keeping them happy and productive is not an easy task, yet RPM has managed this time and time again.

RPM's formula for success is quite straightforward. Rather than merge or relocate the firms he purchases, Sullivan almost always leaves them in place. Owners are retained and given a share of the firms' earnings. Decision making is highly decentralized; each owner produces an annual plan that is evaluated and refined by RPM top management. The former owners and corporate staff then meet face-to-face and iron out any differences in the original and revised plans. The resulting plans are an effective combination of the former owners' technical expertise and RPM's financial discipline. The plans are often more daring than those typically produced by a large, unwieldy corporation yet more in line with market realities than they might be if drawn up by free-wheeling entrepreneurs.

RPM's strategy has reaped huge benefits. At year end 1989, the firm reported earnings of $24.2 million, nearly five times the $5.1 million earned ten years earlier. Moreover, despite numerous economic swings, RPM's earnings and sales have increased for 24 years in a row. This huge growth has been achieved with the addition of only two headquarters staff members since 1976. This latter fact alone stands as a testament to the effectiveness of managing complexity through the use of decentralized decision-making experts.*

* Source: M. Selz, "RPM Bases Success on Keeping Owners of the Firms It Buys," *Wall Street Journal,* June 19, 1990, p. B1.

Chunking does not change the fact that organization members are interrelated, and it is unrealistic to think that one expert can operate unaffected by others or that one set of programs can be activated independently of others. In integrating groups, the complexity of planning is greatly simplified by **loosely coupling** the different parts, that is, weakening the effect that one subgroup has on another so that each can plan and operate almost as if the other were not there.

loosely coupling Managing interrelatedness across different functional areas by not allowing the actions or decisions of one functional unit to have an overly large or immediate impact on the actions or decisions of other functional units.

For example, a production department's work is greatly facilitated by having steady operations, that is, operations that do not fluctuate a great deal over time. Yet the sales department may be subject to wild swings in consumer demand that need to be met quickly. These two departments can make decisions more easily if inventories can be used as buffers. That is, by letting products accumulate in inventories, the production department can go on operating (for a while at least) as if there is a steady demand for the product, even if sales are down. Later, when demand may exceed production capacity, the sales group can sell out of inventories without making rush demands on the production process.

Comparing Models

Figure 6-5 makes it possible to compare the administrative decison-making model with the rational decision-making model. As the figure shows, although the administrative model is also a goal-driven model, it recognizes that day-to-day operational goals are rarely givens and instead come about only through negotiation

Archer Daniels Midland (ADM) has gained a reputation for innovation. It keeps turning out an expanding variety of products made from three basic resources: corn, wheat, and oilseeds. Currently the company makes vegetable oil, animal feed, vodka, flour, caramel coloring, sorbitol (used in making Vitamin C supplements), corn syrup, and ethanol. In an impressive show of creativity, the company married the low-margin product ethanol with an increasingly profitable one, high fructose corn syrup (HFCS), producing both with the same milling process. This process turns out ethanol in the winter, when some cities already require the use of this clean-burning but still costly motor fuel. In the summer, when people consume more soft drinks, the mill switches to high fructose corn syrup (HFCS), which is fast becoming the sweetener of choice in the soft drink industry.
Source: *Ronald Henkoff, "Oh, How the Money Grows at ADM,"* Fortune, *October 8, 1990, pp. 105–116.*

preparation A stage in the creative decision making process in which the person accumulates information needed to solve a problem.

and compromise. Once goals are set, the decision maker monitors the environment and analyzes any problems that arise, to determine if they are programmed or nonprogrammed in nature. If a problem is routine, a well-established performance program is executed to deal with it. If a satisficing solution is found the process is complete. If the problem is nonroutine, however, possible solutions are analyzed sequentially, and sometimes experts are called in to help evaluate alternatives. The first reasonable alternative is then implemented, and if it results in a satisficing solution, the process is complete. Otherwise, a second reasonable alternative is attempted, and then the process continues until a satisficing solution is reached.

CREATIVITY IN DECISION MAKING

One elusive quality essential to organizational decision making is creativity. We will define **creative decisions** as choices that are new and unusual but effective. Neither the rational nor the administrative decision-making process gets at the issue of how creative decisions are produced. Indeed, there are elements in both models that make the generation of creative solutions to problems less, rather than more, likely. For example, strictly following the rational decision-making model's historical method or off-the-shelf methods of generating alternatives (See Table 6-1) will rarely result in innovation. In fact, these methods will probably lead to innovation only by chance or by mishap.[19]

The need for creative solutions to problems becomes especially important as the environment changes more and more rapidly. In such environments, old solutions to problems become outdated relatively quickly, and firms that can shift most readily to new and effective operations gain a huge competitive advantage. The "International OB" box illustrates the lengths to which some countries will go to encourage this kind of activity. In this section we will emphasize the creativity process and how organizations can enhance creativity by selecting appropriate people and altering the workplace environment.

The Creative Process

Studies of people engaged in the creative process or of the decision-making processes of people who were famous for their creativity suggest that a discernible pattern of events leads up to most innovative solutions. Most creative episodes can be broken down into the four distinct stages shown in Figure 6-6: preparation, incubation, insight, and verification.

Contrary to what most people think, creative solutions to problems rarely come out of the blue. Indeed, anyone waiting around for an idea to pop into her head more than likely will be waiting a long time. Although creative ideas do sometimes come about serendipitously, this seems to be the exception more than the rule. More often than not, innovations are first sparked by a problem or perceived need. Because creative decision making is in this way like other decision-making processes,[20] it should not surprise you to know that **preparation**, the first stage in the creative process, involves assembling materials. Analogous to the rational model's "generating alternatives" stage, preparation is character-

[19] T. S. Kuhn, *The Structure of Scientific Revolutions* (Chicago: University of Chicago Press, 1962), pp. 22–39.
[20] D. G. Marquis, "The Anatomy of Successful Innovations," *Managing Advancing Technology* 1 (1972), 34–48.

DECISION MAKING

From Imitators to Innovators: The Taiwan Conversion

For many years, the Taiwanese were more than happy to copy products that had already been developed in the West or in Japan. A large supply of cheap labor and a relatively weak currency allowed the Taiwanese to make a comfortable living simply by producing inexpensive clones of others' toys, electronics and athletic equipment. Today, however, this practice is a less viable option. Since 1986, the cost of labor has increased almost 40 percent, and the value of the New Taiwan dollar has risen to as high as 50 percent of the U.S. dollar. No longer able to compete on the basis of producing at low cost, Taiwanese firms have had to develop other avenues of competition. Long-standing practices have been abandoned, and creativity and innovation have become the pillars of the future Taiwan economy.

The Taiwan government has played an important role in moving the country from imitation to innovation, and the country's new methods of success are studied and copied by other Pacific Rim nations such as South Korea and Indonesia. One of Taiwan's first steps was to increase expenditures for research and development (R&D). In fact, this type of investment has doubled in just the last five years. Typically, R&D funding goes to projects that can be shared by many small companies.

Second, through tax laws, the Taiwanese government encourages companies to substitute machines for workers. Quite purposefully, it is encouraging labor-intensive businesses to move overseas. Low-tech factories are being closed, and instead Taiwan firms, with government aid, are purchasing small Silicon Valley enterprises. The new thinking is also evidenced by Taiwan's stepped-up foreign investments, including roughly $1 billion in mainland China, which is still officially at war with Taiwan.

When they cannot buy entire businesses, Taiwan companies are not afraid to pirate key personnel. For example, Bobo Wang, a young and rising star in the Xerox Corporation was recently lured to Taiwan. The government set Wang up in a Silicon Valley-like industrial park, ideally situated between the capital city and two of the area's finest engineering schools. The park had cheap rent, clean water, and affordable electricity. The payoff came in 1990, when Microtek, the company founded by Wang, hit the market with a new machine that feeds not only black-and-white but color photographs into a computer for processing. The machine was highly coveted by desktop publishers, and in six months little Microtek sold 11,000 of them at almost $3,000 each.

Besides adding relocated Asian-Americans to their staffs, Taiwanese companies maintain close ties with U.S. markets by such means as sending key personnel to U.S. seminars and workshops. Microtek and many other firms keep a staff of technical people in the United States to monitor trends. These companies encourage staff members to visit other countries for exposure to different ideas.

Most Taiwan companies are, like Microtek, small, entrepreneurial, and able to move quickly into new areas. As Robert Hsieh, Microtek's head of office automation notes, "We move fast. . . . Japan has committees, committees, and committees to decide something. We can jump right on things because all I need is one signature." Although small size and lack of brand-name familiarity are handicaps, it looks as though creative solutions to these problems will be forthcoming soon.*

* *Source*: D. Darlin, "Unlikely Leader: Taiwan, Long Noted for Cheap Imitations, Becomes an Innovator," *Wall Street Journal*, June 1, 1990, p. 1.

---

ized by plain, old-fashioned hard work. In attempting to solve the problem, the creative person immerses himself in all existing solutions to the problem, usually to the point of saturation.

The second stage, **incubation**, differs greatly from steps in other decision-making models. Rather than come to a decision immediately after assembling

incubation A stage in the creative decision-making process in which the person apparently stops attending to the problem at hand.

FIGURE 6-6

Steps in the Creative Decision-Making Process

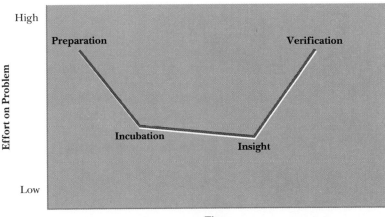

and evaluating the relevant material, creative decision makers enter a period during which they seem not to expend any visible effort on the problem. Sometimes, out of frustration or sheer exhaustion they may give up working on the problem temporarily and turn to other things.

It has been suggested that when people seem to give up on a problem in this way they are actually continuing to work on it but on an unconscious level. Allusions to "unconscious" processes like this, however, are in large part signs that although research has been able to identify the stage of incubation, it has been unsuccessful so far in explaining what really goes on during this stage.

After a person spends some time in the incubation stage, the solution to the problem typically manifests itself in a flash of inspiration, or **insight**. Usually, the person is engaged in some other task when this insight comes to her. This third stage in the creative decision-making process is a very delicate one because insights tend to be ephemeral. They can disappear as quickly as they appear. It is because insights can come at any time that many truly creative people have a habit of carrying a notebook or of jotting ideas down on whatever piece of paper is available to make sure an idea is not lost. Arthur Laffer, for example, is supposed to have sketched the basic ideas of supply-side economics on the back of a cocktail napkin at a Washington, D.C., bar. This theory served as the intellectual underpinning for "Reaganomics" which dominated public policy decisions in the 1980s.

The fourth stage of the creative decision-making process is **solution verification**. Here, the solution formulated in the insight stage is tested more rigorously to determine its usefulness for solving the problem. This stage in creative decision making is very much like the rational decision-making model's stage of evaluating action.

Typically, the verification process takes a lot of time. In fact, it resembles the preparation stage in the amount of hard work it requires. This is primarily because people, particularly if they have a lot invested in traditional ideas and methods, resist change. They have to be convinced to try a new approach, and we can rarely convince them without independently verifying the new findings.

Creative People

Certain characteristics of individuals seem to be associated with creative endeavor. First, there seems to be a modest relationship between creativity and general cognitive ability (see Chapter 4) and the specific capacities of reasoning and deduction. According to J.P. Guilford, some minimum threshold of intelligence seems to be necessary for creative work. As shown in Figure 6-7, however, once we get above that minimum threshold, general intelligence becomes less critical. In terms of the creative process, a severe lack of cognitive ability would probably impair one's ability to get immersed in information about the problem. Once the threshold is reached, however, hard work is probably more important than raw intelligence for creative achievement.

It appears that such personality characteristics as interests, attitudes, and motivation are more important than intelligence in distinguishing creative people from the general population. One common characteristic of creative people is that they set high goals for themselves which may make them dissatisfied with the status quo and current solutions to problems.[21] High levels of aspiration may also explain why creative people often do not seem to feel any particular loyalty to an employer and are instead highly mobile, moving from company to com-

---

insight A stage in the creative decision-making process in which the solution to a problem manifests itself in a flash of inspiration.

solution verification A stage in the creative decision-making process wherein the person tests the efficacy of a proposed novel solution.

---

[21] D. W. MacKinnon, "Assessing Creative Persons," *Journal of Creative Behavior* 1 (1967), 303–4.

FIGURE 6-7

The Relationship between
Cognitive Ability and Creativity

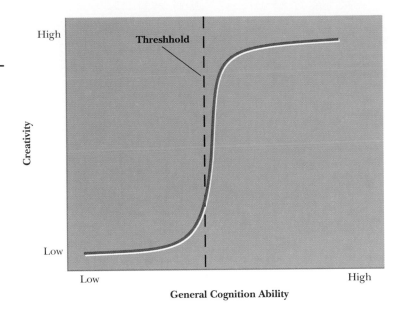

pany.[22] Like most valued commodities, creative talent is highly sought after. Thus it is often hard for a company to hold on to its creative people.

It has also been suggested that the creative person is *persistent* and has a high energy level.[23] These characteristics are probably particularly useful in the stages of preparation and verification, which demand hard work for long periods of time. Persistent people will stick with something despite obstacles and setbacks, and people with a lot of energy can continue to work hard for long periods of time. Both these qualities may help creative people to assemble more relevant information and to test their ideas more exhaustively.

Self-acceptance and independence also seem to relate to creativity.[24] These characteristics probably are needed most in the verification stage, where maintaining one's confidence in the face of criticism and even ridicule becomes important.

Finally, *age* seems to be related to creativity. In a seminal study of people recognized for their creativity, one consistent finding was that regardless of the field in which the person did his or her work (the fields studied included mathematics, physics, biology, chemistry, medicine, music, painting, and sculpture), creativity peaked between the ages of 30 and 40 (see Figure 6-8).[25]

Creativity-Inducing Situations

Selecting people who have characteristics that seem to be related to creativity is not the only option organizations have for increasing innovativeness. Providing *specific and difficult goals* and *firm deadlines* actually seems to stimulate creative achievement. Although they can be taken too far, in general, time pressures seem to aid rather than hinder the creative process. This also seems to be true of

[22] T. Rotundi, "Organizational Identification: Issues and Implications," *Organizational Behavior and Human Performance* 13 (1975), 95–109.

[23] E. Randsepp, "Are You a Creative Manager?" *Management Review* 58 (1978), 15–16.

[24] H. G. Gough, "Techniques for Identifying the Creative Research Scientist," *Conference on the Creative Person* (Berkeley: University of California, Institute of Personality Assessment, 1961).

[25] H. C. Lehman, *Age and Achievement* (Princeton, N.J.: Princeton University Press, 1953, pp. 50–61.

FIGURE 6-8

The Relationship between Age and Creativity

From J. P. Guilford, "Some Misperceptions Regarding Measurement of Creative Talents," Journal of Creative Behavior 5 *(1971), 86–99.*

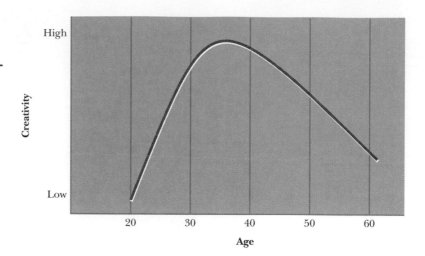

budgetary pressures. Perhaps one reason is that these kinds of constraints limit the use of historical options or "off-the-shelf" solutions. Consequently, the organization is forced to come up with innovative, nova-type techniques.[26]

Some firms even set goals for creativity. As an example, 3M company, based in Minneapolis, has set a goal that 25 percent of its total revenues should come from new products developed in the past five years. Currently those revenues are running closer to 30 percent, and 3M insists that nearly 70 percent of its annual $12 billion in sales comes from ideas that originated from the work force.[27]

Although a bit trite, there is some truth in the old saying that "necessity is the mother of invention," and creativity often springs from organizations that have their backs to the wall. For example, David Luther, senior vice-president and corporate director of quality at Corning notes that "desperation is a good motive. . . . Customers came to us and said if we didn't change, they'd go somewhere else."[28] This point of view can also be seen in the "International OB" box referred to earlier, which illustrates the way changes in the economy in Taiwan forced businesses to think along more creative lines.

Certain characteristics of what is called the *organizational culture* (see Chapter 18) may also be related to creativity. First, the degree to which organizations recognize and reward creativity is of paramount importance.[29] Although you might think otherwise, unfortunately, many organizations place more emphasis on following existing written rules and procedures than on experimenting with new procedures.

A culture that promotes creativity must ensure not only that innovativeness is reinforced but that experimentation leading to failure is not punished. Executives like James Burke, CEO of Johnson and Johnson, attempt to create a climate where the risks of innovation are minimized. Burke, in fact, has gone so far as to tell his employees, "We won't grow unless you take risks. . . . Any successful company is riddled with failures. There's just no other way to do it."[30] Although they needn't reward every failure, companies that want to encourage innovation might consider giving an award for "the best failed experiment." Recognition of this sort would drive home the point that the organization values risk taking and trying new approaches more than it fears mistakes.

[26] G. Zaltman, R. Duncan and J. Holbek, *Innovations and organizations* (New York: John Wiley, 1969), p. 191.

[27] T. Curry, J. E. Gallagher and W. McWhirter, "Let's Get Crazy," *Time*, June 11, 1990, pp. 41–42.

[28] Ibid.

[29] H. A. Shepard, "Innovation-Resisting and Innovation- Producing Organizations," *Journal of Business* 40 (1967), 470–77.

[30] W. Guzzardi, "The National Business Hall of Fame," *Fortune*, 121 (1990), pp. 17–29.

Finally, since much creativity comes out of collaborative efforts among different individuals, organizations should promote *internal diversity and exposure* among organizational members. If all the people in a group have the same interests, experiences, strengths, and weaknesses, they will be less likely to generate new ideas than if they are of divergent backgrounds and capabilities. We will have more to say about this in Chapter 11 when we discuss group decision making.

Moreover, because different organizations do different things in different places, exposing people to varying kinds of experiences, such as foreign assignments, professional development seminars, or extended leaves may help shake up overly routine decision-making processes. The notion that difference and variety encourage creative thinking receives some support from the finding that organizations that emphasize external recruiting seem to be more innovative than firms that promote from within.[31] This does not mean that organizations should completely abandon promote-from-within policies. However, the value of mixing new and long-tenured employees in fostering a climate of creativity may be considerable.

SUMMARY

Both the outcomes of decisions and the processes by which decisions are made are of interest to managers of organizational behavior. The *rational decision-making model* proceeds through five steps wherein the decision maker sets objectives, monitors the environment to determine progress toward those objectives, generates alternative courses of action when problems are detected, chooses a course of action, and finally, evaluates the chosen course of action for its ability to accomplish the original objectives. Many types of programmed decisions such as setting production standards and determining inventory levels, can be handled by this model. Other kinds of problems, however, may exceed our capacity for rational analysis. Moreover, illusions, or threats, like *loss aversion*, *availability bias*, and *escalation of commitment* can seriously interfere with rational decision making. For a whole host of nonprogrammed decisions, rational decision making simply is not possible. With nonprogrammed decisions, few of the assumptions required for deriving optimal solutions are met. Under these conditions, the *administrative decision-making model* provides a more accurate depiction of the decision-making process. The administrative model emphasizes *satisficing* rather than *optimizing* and also differs from the rational model by suggesting that alternatives be evaluated sequentially. The creative process in decision making proceeds through the four stages of *preparation*, *incubation*, *insight* and *verification of solutions*. Both personal (cognitive ability, persistence, energy level, age) and situational (organizational goals, culture, diversity) characteristics affect creativity in the workplace.

REVIEW QUESTIONS

1.   Compare and contrast the decision-making process associated with rational decision making, administrative decision making, and creative decision making. At what points do these three models diverge most? What implications does this have for decision makers who employ one model when they should be employing the other?

[31] B. Schneider and N. Schmitt, *Staffing Organizations* (Glenview, Ill: Scott, Foresman, 1986), p. 71.

2.   Assume for a moment that over time, the price of a stock is not stationary, but ever increasing. Is a bias that ignores the base rate or regression to the mean really a bias in this context? Can you think of other instances in which what looks like a decision-making bias may actually facilitate decision making?

3.   Suppose that managerial jobs can be distinguished by the kinds of decision processes required. For example, some jobs call for rational decision making, others require administrative decision-making processes, and still others require creative decision processes. If you were a recruiter, what personal characteristics would you look for in staffing these three kinds of positions? Do you think it is possible to find one individual who would be comfortable with all three kinds of processes? If so, what characteristics would this person display?

4.   Escalation of commitment to a failing course of action has been widely researched and it is easy to call to mind many examples of this kind of mistake. The flip side of this mistake, however, is giving up too soon, which has not been studied much and for which it is hard to think of examples. Why can't we recall such events? How might researchers in this area be victims of "availability bias"?

5.   Recall the distinctions drawn in this chapter between certainty, risk, and uncertainty, and think of a decision you made recently that conformed to each of these conditions. Which of these conditions is most pervasive for managers? What weight in causing these conditions would you assign to (a) organizational level, that is, top, middle, or supervisory management; (b) the individual manager's experience or cognitive ability; (c) the nature of the organization's industry; and (d) characteristics of the manager's subordinates?

DIAGNOSTIC QUESTIONS

In analyzing an organization's decision-making process, the following set of diagnostic questions may be useful.

1.   Are ineffective decisions actually poor-quality decisions? Or is the ineffectiveness a result of poor timing and low acceptance of decisions by those needed to carry them out?

2.   Is the process by which decisions are made likely to be scrutinized? What can be done to convince people that the process is not arbitrary?

3.   Does the organization have clear goals and objectives, so that analytical solutions can be developed? Or is the organization characterized by a lack of goal consensus, thus requiring a bargaining solution?

4.   Can the organization detect threats and opportunities in the environment accurately? Does it tend to see things in terms of one rather than the other of these phenomena?

5.   When deciding on a course of action, does the organization tend to rely more on past practice or on experimentation?

6.   Is the organization's environment best characterized by risk or uncertainty? How does this environmental characteristic affect decision-making processes?

7.   Does the organization employ standard mathematical solutions to routine or programmable problems where they are appropriate?

8.   Do factors such as loss aversion or availability bias influence the organization's decisions adversely?

9.   Do organizational members understand the concepts of base rate and regression to the mean? Do they take account of these influences in making decisions?

10.   Do organizational decision makers stick to a single course of action too long (as in escalation of commitment)? Or do decision makers switch from one decision to another too quickly, making it impossible to learn in "noisy environments"?

11.   Does the organization employ experts? Does it use these forces successfully, through loose coupling, successfully integrating these people with its own staff?

12.   Does the organization seek creativity? What does it do to select people or design situations so as to enhance creativity?

EXERCISE 6-1

DECISION-MAKING HEURISTICS AND BIASES*

ARIEL S. LEVI, *Wayne State University*
LARRY E. MAINSTONE, *University of Michigan*

Managers often work under complex, changing circumstances that require rapid and accurate decision making. They must constantly process information, diagnose problems, think creatively, and develop solutions under conditions of substantial uncertainty. Technical aids that facilitate decision making like computerized information systems and diagnostic decision trees can be helpful, but they cannot substitute for human judgment.

In making judgments of all kinds, we often violate some fundamental laws of logic and probability. Why do we do this? Because we use *heuristics*, or mental strategies for processing the information we need to make a decision. Heuristics are really rules of thumb. For example, a common heuristic is, When it's cloudy, carry an umbrella. Heuristics can produce accurate results. If it rains, you'll be glad you have the umbrella. On the other hand, they can also bias decision making. If you carry an umbrella and it doesn't rain, you will be sorry. The biases that we have discussed in this chapter—loss aversion, availability, base rate, and regression to the mean—are all rooted in the use of heuristics.

This exercise focuses on those decision making processes in which people collect and mentally combine information to make estimates and evaluations of people, objects, and events. To make you more aware of heuristic biases and to stimulate class discussion about how to control their effects, we will show you how several heuristics work and how they influence judgment and decision making.

STEP ONE: PRE-CLASS PREPARATION

To prepare for class, read this entire exercise and then write down your responses to the four problems that follow. Try your hardest to come up with the best answer to each one. The first problem will be familiar to you, for we discussed it in this chapter.

1. A cab company was involved in a hit-and-run accident at night. Two cab companies, the Green and the Blue, operate in the city. You have the following information:
   A. 85 percent of the cabs in the city are Green and 15 percent are Blue.
   B. A witness identified the cab as a Blue cab. The court tested her ability to identify cabs under night visibility conditions. When presented with a sample of cabs (half Blue and half Green), the witness made correct identifications in 80 percent of the cases and erred in 20 percent.
   Question: The probability that a Blue cab was involved in the accident is _____ percent.

2. Bill is 34 years old. He is intelligent, compulsive, unimaginative, and sedentary. In school, he was strong in mathematics but weak in science and social studies.
   Rank order the following statements by their probability of being correct, using 1 for the most probable and 8 for the least probable.
   Ranking
   _____ A. Bill is a physician who plays poker for a hobby.
   _____ B. Bill is an architect.
   _____ C. Bill is an accountant.
   _____ D. Bill plays jazz for a hobby.
   _____ E. Bill surfs for a hobby.
   _____ F. Bill is a television reporter.
   _____ G. Bill is an accountant who plays jazz for a hobby.
   _____ H. Bill climbs mountains for a hobby

3. In an average year in the United States, do more people die of fire or drowning? Circle the letter that indicates your answer:
   A. Fire
   B. Drowning
   C. About the same

4. Many professional athletes believe that to be pictured on the cover of *Sports Illustrated* is bad luck because one's performance is likely to decline during the weeks and months afterward. Do you think there is any basis for this belief? If so, what is it?

_____

_____

_____.

* Adapted with the authors' permission from an exercise entitled "A Group-Based Procedure for Revealing Judgmental Heuristics and Biases." Related information is reported in Ariel S. Levi and Larry E. Mainstone, "A Strategy for Teaching about Judgmental Bias and Methods for Improving Judgment," *Organizational Behavior Teaching Review*, 10 (1985), 9–24.

STEP TWO: COMPARING INDIVIDUAL AND GROUP ANSWERS

The class should divide into groups of four to six members each. If you formed permanent groups in Exercise 5-1, you should assemble in those same groups. In each group you should begin by discussing the four problems just presented and reach agreement on an answer for each one. Next, compare your group's answers with those you and other members reached working alone. Then select a spokesperson to compile this information and prepare a brief presentation for the entire class. The spokesperson should discuss the means and distributions of individual responses to each question, the group's response to each question, and the way the group reached agreement. For example, did the group take a majority vote or was it persuaded by one dominant individual?

STEP THREE: GROUP PRESENTATIONS AND DISCUSSION

The spokespersons should take no more than five minutes each to report their group's results to the rest of the class. The class should try to uncover reasons for any differences between individual responses and group agreements and for any differences among different groups' responses.

Next, your instructor will reveal the best answers for the four questions and will discuss the heuristics and biases that the problems illustrate.

STEP FOUR: GROUP JUDGMENT TASKS

Once everyone understands the heuristics and biases discussed in Step Three, the judgment groups should reconvene and choose the best answer to each of the following four problems.

1. As of 1985, approximately what percentage of the male working-age population in Japan was guaranteed lifetime employment? _____ percent.
2. Film critics have noted that sequels like "The Godfather III" or "Ghostbusters II" are usually of lower quality than their predecessor films. Sequels are usually financially less successful as well. Critics sometimes accuse the film studios of trying to "milk" a good idea. Do you think this is a valid criticism and, if so, how do you explain the phenomenon?

_____
_____
_____.

3. A panel of psychologists have interviewed and administered personality tests to 30 engineers and 70 lawyers, all successful in their fields. The following is one of the descriptions written about these 100 people, based on the results of the tests.

> Joan is a 45-year-old woman. She is married and has four children. She is generally conservative, careful, and ambitious. She shows no interest in political or social issues and spends most of her time on her many hobbies which include camping, sailing, and mathematical puzzles.

Question: The probability that Joan is an engineer is _____ percent.

4. Rank order the following events by their probability of occurrence this year, using 1 for the most probable and 4 for the least probable.

Ranking

_____ A. The industrial midwest will gain in economic strength.

_____ B. The industrial midwest will decline in economic strength.

_____ C. The fortunes of the major U.S. automakers will improve.

_____ D. While the fortunes of the major U.S. automakers will improve, the industrial midwest will decline in economic strength because of the continued exodus of companies to the Sun Belt.

After reaching agreement on how to answer the four problems, each group should again appoint a spokesperson to report on the group's four answers and how they were reached.

STEP FIVE: GROUP REPORTS AND CLASS DISCUSSION

After each spokesperson has presented a report and the class has discussed similarities and differences between the groups' answers, your instructor again will reveal the best answers and discuss relevant heuristics and biases. The class should then discuss the problems raised by heuristics and biases, paying special attention to the following questions:

1. Some people won't admit they have biases. Others react defensively when their biases are pointed out. Are biases a sign of abnormality? Of low intelli-

gence? Of not trying hard enough to make the right decision?

2. Are group judgments generally more accurate than individual judgments? Or can groups impair accuracy? What factors might determine whether groups improve or impair accuracy?

3. What real-world organizational examples can you think of that illustrate each of the biases you learned about in this exercise? Do any of these examples show the effects of more than one bias?

4. NASA has made several monumental errors in recent years, including the decision to launch Challenger despite warnings from the space shuttle's designer and the decision to orbit the Hubble Space Telescope without adequately checking the focus of its mirrors. Based on what you have learned from this exercise, what advice would you give NASA to help it avoid similar mistakes in the future?

CONCLUSION

Managers need to learn about heuristics and biases for several reasons. First, heuristic-based biases are pervasive. They affect many organizational phenomena ranging from performance appraisal to strategic planning. Second, because these biases often operate unconsciously, neither intelligence, expertise, nor motivation to be accurate can protect us against them. Once we become aware of these biases, however, we can learn to step back each time and ask ourselves whether one or more of them have led us to misdiagnose a problem, make a poor decision, or fail to respond effectively to a crisis or opportunity. As organizational work and decision making become more complicated and challenging, bias-free managerial judgment becomes more and more important.

DIAGNOSING ORGANIZATIONAL BEHAVIOR

CASE 6-1

PRECISION MACHINE TOOL*

JANET BARNARD, *Rochester Institute of Technology*

John Garner, president of Precision Machine Tool, watched the elegantly tailored Mr. Wang leave the office after making his disturbing proposition. Of course, John had known that his own production people were working with Suzuki Machines on developing specifications for a machining center that would help solve Precision's nagging quality problems. Negotiations were winding down and the Japanese firm's price quotation was expected. Ako Wang's name on today's appointment calendar, therefore, was no surprise. From past dealings with Asian firms, John had expected the traditional old-world formalities that precede the closing of a sale for a major piece of capital equipment. In fact, he had braced himself for the usual rich combination of urbane courtesy and sharp technology. The United States machine tool industry has a strong bias to "buy American," and Precision was no exception.

This morning Wang had performed as expected, but this time Suzuki wasn't intent on making a sale. True, the proposal on John's desk contained a purchase document, but it wasn't a quotation for a $250,000 heavy-duty machining center. Instead, it was a formal invitation to discuss the purchase of Precision Machine Tool by Suzuki Machines.

"Lorraine," John spoke into the intercom on his desk, "see if you can find Tom and ask him to come up."

While waiting for his partner, John stood by the window that overlooked a big machining bay on the floor below. Even through the heavy insulated glass he could hear the ceaseless clamor of the big machines that were making high-precision parts for the lathes that Precision produced and sold to the automobile industry to use in their factories. John watched as an operator checked the control panel of a new cobalt-blue lathe that stood among the aging machines on the shop floor. The hulking lathe was state-of-the-art machine technology, precise and sophisticated—with a manufacturer's nameplate that read, "Suzuki/Made in Japan."

The machine tool industry is unique in that it uses its own products to make its own products, and much of Precision's old equipment was becoming dulled by decades of use. In a desperate move to stem customer complaints about quality, they had bought the computer-controlled Japanese lathe to use for making parts for the machines they produced. To buy foreign-made machinery went against the grain, but many domestic toolmakers were buying imported machines because they were more efficient to operate, gave a higher quality of output, and were cheaper than American-made equipment. For some toolmakers it was the alternative to joining the 20 percent of the nation's machine tool companies that had gone out of business recently.

John turned away from the window and took a sales printout from a desk drawer. His company was in better shape than many of the medium-sized toolmakers, but that wasn't saying a lot. Sales were down 30 percent. Booked orders were weak, and quality rejects due to the aging and long-used equipment ate into profits. Precision was a victim of recession in the automobile industry. Like many other machine toolmakers, it had never fully recovered. John looked up as his partner entered the office.

Tom Avery flung himself into the chair that had been occupied by Ako Wang. Precision's works manager was a big man, blunt and outspoken, and a first-class tool design engineer. Tom ran the manufacturing and materials management end of the business and, with John, had founded Precision Machine Tool. His reaction to John's news about Wang's proposition was expressed in a single word that was short, direct, and explosively negative.

Despite excess capacity in American plants, Japan's share of the American machine tool market was increasing and was hotly resented by the domestic industry. The fire was currently being fueled by Japan's determination to increase exports of cars to the United States now that the voluntary quota system had expired. There was no corresponding assurance that there would be any increase in the trickle of American goods that were allowed to enter Japan. As a result the decrease in American market share could be significant in an industry linked so closely with automobiles and steel. Employment would be hard hit as well, and Precision's 312 employees were down 22 percent.

"That was my first reaction, too, Tom. But I think we should think this through." John held up his hand to silence his partner as Tom leaned forward, scowling. "Let me go on for a minute. Our industry is in its worst crisis since the Depression. Sure, Precision's done better than some, but our sales are down to $16 million and you know what the reject rate is doing to costs. Orders have softened steadily, Tom, and that's what worries me most. We've had a reputation for top-quality machine tools from the time we opened our shop.

"Precision Machine Tool has always been synonymous with precision quality. We're losing that, Tom." John went over to the bay window. "Sixty percent of our equipment is old, some of it more than 20 years. Accuracy of these machines is unreliable, they're expensive to operate, and not worth any more rebuilding. We're in a spiral, Tom; without profits, we can't afford to modernize the plant. And with obsolete machines, we can't compete with foreign imports, not in price and not in quality."

The late 1970s were the apex of the domestic machine tool industry. There was a record backlog in orders that couldn't be filled because of inadequate production capacity. Industrial customers waited two years for machine tool orders they needed today. The domestic industry was too busy to notice that several years before, Japan had identified machine tools as a growth industry and started subsidizing modern factories. Now was the time to cash in. American manufacturers were turning overseas for fast delivery of high-quality, inexpensive machines and machine tools to use in their production processes. During the 1980–1981 recession in the automobile industry, American tool firms had little capital for investment. When the economy recovered, they were left behind in the marketplace. Lately, subsidiaries of big Japanese toolmakers began to appear in the United States, along with an occasional Japanese acquisition of a domestic firm.

"What are you telling me, John? That you want to sell out?" Tom's voice was tight. "This is the most exciting industry around right now. We've got the wonders of automation to sell these days, the futuristic manufacturing systems. You want them all to be Japanese, John? Or West German, or Korean, or everything but American? You want to get out of the race just when we've survived the cash crunch from buying the new equipment we do have? That Japanese lathe, for starters."

It had taken Tom a long time to accept the idea of using an imported machine in their own production process, but the harshness in his voice was gone as he said, "Listen, John. You're a financial expert, but I know that yesterday's production gives us yesterday's dollars. Why not get rid of this patch-and-mend philosophy and shop for some real capital to modernize the plant? The U.S. capabilities for producing the computer software that meshes the tools together is superior to anybody's. We've got access to that, John, and all Precision needs is modern machines to get the edge we need to stay in the race." Tom waited. He knew that John was a financial conservative, dedicated to financing capital improvements from profits.

John turned from the window and sat down in the chair across from his partner. Tom knew as well as he did that it wasn't a matter of catching up with the competition; it would be necessary to leapfrog over a moving target. A big capital investment meant a big debt, and interest rates would tend to be high for a firm in the troubled machine tool industry. Precision would become highly leveraged and could risk ruin. There were too many "ifs." What if there were a downturn in the economy . . . or if too many customers were irrevocably lost during the transition . . . or if foreign toolmakers slashed prices to protect their market share . . . or if software companies outside the machine tool industry won important orders in the area of software expertise where American toolmakers had the edge? It was ironic, but John knew that Tom would infinitely prefer bankruptcy to selling out to foreign competition.

"All right, Tom," John took a deep breath. "Look at *this* scenario, and think about it for a minute. If we wanted to go the retrenchment route, maybe it makes sense to sell a line of imports to help us finance some new equipment. I don't like the idea any better than you do, but it would be temporary, Tom, and it's profitable. They wouldn't have to be Asian. The dollar's strong, and we might be able to buy West German machine tools at a price that would give us a good markup." John stopped, expecting Tom's outburst that was as vehement as his response to the Wang proposition.

Both of the men, especially Tom, had always been severely critical of the strategy of some of the hard-up domestic toolmakers who acted as distributors of imported machines and machine tools, or who bought imported products and customized them for special-order customers. John had to agree with the tone of derision and contempt in Tom's words. Selling imported machine tools in direct competition with your own industry was quite different from using a couple of pieces of imported equipment to beef up your own production process in a crisis.

Not only could the practice spell doom for the domestic industry, but the knife cut a lot deeper. One of the opportunity costs of selling foreign goods is that while a manufacturer is doing it he tends not to improve his own technology and capabilities. The machine tool industry is at the core of modern manufacturing, and the country that controls state-of-the-art machines and machine tools has the advantage of being able to make better cars and aircraft and drilling equipment—and ballistic missiles.

It was inconsistent that an industry that had spent so much time and resources trying to get the federal government to provide protection from foreign competition by limiting imports was itself buying those same imports. Buying foreign was repugnant, John knew that, but it was a trade-off. Was it worth it?

"What are our options, Tom?" John's voice was quiet. "Is it better to commit ourselves to a debt that could wipe us out? Is it better to fold? Whatever we do, we've both got to buy into it, right? We always have." Tom smiled, and John knew that they were both remembering the early days of Precision Machine Tool when they operated on a shoestring and sat down together every Thursday to decide what bills they could afford to pay.

Things seemed more complex now, and even more uncertain. During the life of Precision, its industry had experienced a revolutionary change in products, and the past ten years had been either feast or famine for

domestic machine tools. Now the race to build the factories of the future would be won by the nation that had the most efficient computerized operations to produce the cheapest, most reliable products. For the owners of Precision Machine Tool, the price paid for falling behind was high, and the risks in trying to stay in the race was great.

Precision's key executives had to take a number of complex variables into account in making their decision. Important economic and political factors impacted Precision's ability to compete in its industry. Foreign competition and foreign technologies posed a serious threat both to the machine tool industry and to the future of domestic manufacturing. Personal attitudes and values as well influenced John and Tom in their task.

Lorraine sent out for sandwiches and coffee, and as the afternoon passed the two men examined the future of their industry and their place in it. When they parted late that night, their decision had been made—and they agreed to meet in John's office the next morning at ten for his telephone call to Ako Wang.

When you have read this case, look back at the chapter's diagnostic questions and choose the ones that apply to the case. Then use those questions with the ones that follow in your case analysis.

1. At which step of the rational decision making process are John Garner and Tom Avery now? How would you characterize their decision making up to this point?

2. What threats to rational decision making are evident? Are there factors that make rational decision making impossible? What specific steps should John and Tom take to complete the process of deciding whether to sell or not?

3. If they follow your suggestion, what decision do you think the two will make? In the long run, how satisfactory do you expect this decision to be. Why?

CASE 6-2
BOB COLLINS*

RICHARD E. DUTTON, *University of South Florida*
RODNEY C. SHERMAN, *University of South Florida*

Bob Collins was employed by the Mansen Company, a division of Sanford, Barnes, Inc., a diversified company engaged mainly in the manufacture and sale of men's and women's apparel. The Miami plant of the Mansen Company is the largest of the 19 manufacturing loca-

---

* Reprinted with the authors' permission.

tions and has, in its organization, an industrial engineering unit.

As department head of industrial engineering in the Miami plant, Jim Douglas also has the responsibility for all industrial engineering functions in the Florida Region. This includes three smaller plants within a 275-mile radius of Miami. Jim reports to the Miami plant manager, Mr. Scott, for local projects and to the Florida regional manager, Mr. Glenn, for projects of a regional nature. Mr. Glenn has been regional manager for many years, but only for the previous 23 months had this been his sole responsibility. Prior to this time, he was also the manager of the Miami plant, and he was still a dominant personality in the plant, partially because of Mr. Scott's indecisiveness.

Assisting Jim in Miami are two other industrial engineers, Bob Collins and Mark Douglas (see Exhibit 6-1). Mark was hired in September, 1992, soon after his release from the army, and had been with Mansen about 27 months. Bob had been with the company for about 21 months since leaving his last position because of a conflict there regarding a heavy workload and a schedule requiring some night work. Bob had freely given this information during his preemployment interview, but no effort had been made to uncover the past employer's version of the situation.

Jim holds an associate degree in industrial engineering from a two-year technical school, while both Bob and Mark have bachelor's degrees, in history and

business, respectively. All three men are army veterans. Jim and Mark served as enlisted men for nine and two years, respectively, Jim becoming a staff sergeant and Mark, a sergeant. Bob served as an officer for four years, reaching the rank of captain. Bob had displayed a talent for creative and imaginative thinking in regard to mechanical development and was assigned a majority of the projects that delved into the creation, installation, and improvement of mechanical innovations and devices. In addition, he and the local head of mechanical development, Ned Larson, worked together on many of their own original ideas, both in the planning and development.

CURRENT SITUATION

One day Bob came upon an interoffice memo, in Jim's incoming mail box, containing a question from Mr. Glenn about a mechanical project on which Bob was working. Feeling that he could save time for Jim, he picked up the memo, read it, and proceeded to Mr. Glenn's office to answer the question. When he returned, he simply put the memo back in Jim's mail box and went on with other work.

Later in the day Jim returned to the office to answer his mail and came upon Mr. Glenn's memo. Jim sought out Bob and the following conversation ensued:

Jim: Bob, I've got a short note here from Mr. Glenn asking about the status of the cuff machine project I gave you. Where do we stand on that now?

Bob: Well, as I mentioned before, all we have to build is the automatic stacking device and then we should have the machine about ready to go. Some of the parts won't be in until the first of the next week, but it should only take a day after that to finish.

Jim: Okay, that's good. How about answering this memo to Mr. Glenn and we'll have him up-to-date on this thing?

Bob: I already have. I saw the memo earlier and went on in and brought him up on how the project stands.

Jim: Did you get a copy of this too?

Bob: No, I saw yours and decided to save you time so I went ahead and answered his question.

Jim: You mean you got this out of my box?

Bob: Yeah, I saw it as I was coming to my desk and decided to go ahead and get it out of the way.

Jim: Oh well, I'll just hold on to this for a while then.

Several days later, Jim and Bob were discussing one of Bob's new ideas, and the discussion became very

---

EXHIBIT 6-1

Partial Organization Chart—The Mansen Company

Regional Manager
Mr. Glenn

Plant Manager
Mr. Scott

Industrial Engineering
Department Head
Jim Douglas

Bob Collins   Mark Douglas

---

heated when Jim rejected the idea as too expensive, in both time and money.

Jim: And another thing, Bob, I don't want you going through my mail box again. What's in there is none of your business unless I assign it to you.

Bob: I was just trying to do you a favor and get the memo answered. If you don't want me to do that, then I won't.

Jim: You would have answered eventually, but I don't want you to do these things unless I tell you to. I'm in charge of the department, and I have to know what's going on. That reminds me of another thing. From now on, you tell me about all of the projects you're working on. I don't want any more secret projects being worked on without my knowing it. I feel pretty stupid when Mr. Scott or Mr. Glenn asks me a question about something I've never even heard of. From now on, you tell me about your ideas, and if we can work it into the schedule we will; otherwise it will have to wait until we can get to it. This also means not going to Mr. Glenn with your ideas first, and then telling me that he thinks it's a good idea and should be developed. I'll approve the ideas first, and then we'll check with him if necessary.

Bob: I know you're talking about the new sleeve hemming stacker, and I just happened to mention it to Mr. Glenn this morning at coffee break, and he wanted to know more about it. I had to tell him about it when he asked.

Jim: That's right. In that case you couldn't have done anything else, but from now on make sure you've cleared these ideas with me before going to him.

Mark came into the office, and the discussion was ended.

The following day, Bob and Mark were leaving the office together, and Bob told Mark about his discussion with Jim.

Bob: Mark, I'm so mad at Jim I'd like to quit and walk out of here right now. I know darn well I could make more money somewhere else and wouldn't have to put up with Jim. You know what really gets me down is the thousands of dollars that I can prove I've saved the company, and I can't get a decent raise. I know Jim is making about $36,000, and I feel I'm worth as much as he is, but I do realize that they have to pay him more because he's a department head. However, he's not worth the amount of difference in our salaries. I feel I should be able to get at least $1,000 a year more than I'm get-

ting now, but the "Book" won't allow that much of a raise at one time. And besides that, I'd feel more like putting out more for the company. As it is, I want to do my best, but it's hard to feel that way when you aren't fairly paid for your work.

Mark: You know what chances you've got of getting that kind of a raise! What started all of this anyway?

Bob: Well, I was telling Jim about my idea for the fronts presser and he turned it down, just like he's done most of my ideas.

Mark: Did he tell you why he turned it down?

Bob: Said it would be too expensive and would take too much time. Mark, it would save us a penny a dozen which would be about $5,000 a year; they're just time studies to try and satisfy some operator who doesn't really want to work.

Mark: I know. My projects are like that too, and he turned down my idea for revamping the boxing department. You know what a bottleneck that has been. My first estimate, which was conservative, was savings of $50,000 a year plus being able to get out our weekly production. We're not anywhere near that now and spending twice the amount of money we need to. This would also allow the warehouse to have half of the present boxing area. But Jim says it can't be done because there would have to be too much coordination between departments, and that it would take someone with more authority than we have to make it work. I told him if we were to work up the proposal and send it to Mr. Scott, he couldn't pass up those savings on a system that's workable. Of course, you know how Scott hates to make decisions, but if Mr. Glenn knew about it, it would be our main project until it was installed. You know how he likes those dollar signs.

Bob: Yeah, I know. Jim doesn't seem to understand that these little projects don't save us any money and yet he turns down ideas that will save us thousands of dollars a year. You know he doesn't know anything about mechanical development. And besides that, when you try to explain something to him and he doesn't understand it, he says it won't work. But I know that he takes some of these ideas and mentions them to Mr. Scott and Mr. Glenn and takes credit for them. I don't like that one little bit, and I'm going to tell him so one of these days. Then, after telling me my idea for the fronts presser wasn't any good, he chewed me out for going through his mail box. That happened a couple of days ago. When I tried to do him a favor by answering a question Mr. Glenn had asked in a memo, he got all upset. He didn't know anything about it anyway, so what's the difference?

Mark: Well, do you think it was right to go through his mail?

Bob: Well, I just happened to see the subject of the memo and I knew it was concerned with my project so I went ahead and answered the question. I didn't go through his mail; the memo was right on top, and I just happened to see it on my way to my desk.

Mark: Yes, but you *did* get into his personal mail box and went ahead without him knowing about it. Do you see what I mean, Bob? I mean he *is* the head of the department, and he needs to know what goes on within the department.

Bob: But he doesn't have to know *everything* I'm working on. It's none of his business. Most of the things Ned and I do are our own ideas, and he doesn't have a thing to do with them—he doesn't even understand them. Anyway, he told me he didn't want me working on any "secret" projects, that I was to tell him about all of my ideas before I did anything with them. Well, I'll tell you, I'm going ahead and do the projects he assigns me, but I'm *still* going to work on my own ideas whenever I get a chance. Here comes Mr. Scott, I'll see you later.

After closing hours that night and after Bob had left, Jim and Mark were still in the office.

Jim: Mark, did Bob tell you about our little discussion yesterday afternoon?

Mark: He said you had a few words.

Jim: Bob's just getting too big for his own britches. If he doesn't like something I say or do, he acts like a little child. Goes around pouting and gloomy for two or three days. He's just going to have to learn that he's not running the department, although I'm sure he feels he could do a better job than I'm doing. But the thing is that he can't take any criticism. Some of his ideas are good, but others are just too far out and we don't have the time for them. He's going to have to realize that we have other things to do besides mechanical development. I know a lot of our projects cost us more to carry out than can be saved in terms of dollars, but if we can show an operator what is being done is right—or if it's wrong—admit the error and correct the situation, then that can be worth as much as saving several thousand of dollars a year. Al-though we are becoming increasingly auto-mated, we have to remember that people are still our main source of production and that without their cooperation, we're out of business. Besides, mechanical development isn't even his job, but because he has had some good ideas, I've let him work with Ned on them. I know he's sensitive, and that he is worth a lot to the company because some of his ideas are worth-while, but if he doesn't change his ways, I'm going to have to talk to Mr. Glenn about letting him go. I've got to run this department, and we can't do our best when he acts up like he does.

When you have read this case, look back at the chapter's diagnostic questions and choose the ones that apply to the case. Then use those questions with the ones that follow in your case analysis.

1. As the case suggests, Bob Collins has displayed a talent for creative and imaginative thinking. Has Jim Douglas taken full advantage of this talent?

2. Jim is thinking about disciplining Bob for going through Jim's mail. Might Bob's actions be responsive to Jim's failure to recognize Bob's creative abilities? What alternatives to discipline might Jim consider?

3. What should Jim do to manage Bob's creativity more effectively? In general, what special requirements does the task of managing creative employees like Bob place on managers like Jim?

CASE 6-3

NURSE ROSS

Read Chapter 10's Case 10-1, "Nurse Ross." Next, look back at Chapter 6's diagnostic questions and choose the ones that apply to that case. Then use those questions with the ones that follow in this first analysis of the case.

1. What factors in this case make rational decision making impossible? How can the management of Benton Hospital make a satisfactory decision as to how to integrate the ward and clinic facilities?

2. Compare the approach you have just recommended with the one actually followed. What differences can you detect? Did these differences contribute to any of the problems that confronted Nurse Ross?

3. Is there anything Dr. Peake could have done when he first arrived to eliminate or modify the factors that are blocking rational decision making? Would such actions have affected your recommendations? How?

MOTIVATION AND PERFORMANCE

Although many retail apparel chains filed for bankruptcy in the late 1980s and early 1990s, Phillips-Van Heusen entered the retailing industry for the first time in 1987 and was soon doing better than ever. One reason was the extraordinary $1 million bonus plan for top managers that Larry Phillips, PVH chairman, dreamed up (see opening story). Phillips (left) and PVH president Bruce Klatsky (center) encouraged their senior executives to find new markets for PVH's shirts, sweaters, and casual shoes, such as the J. C. Penney Co., with whom they confer here. PVH also established its own Profiles stores, where a new sweater collection with PVH's own label was sold for the first time. PVH's incentive program has not only motivated top managers' performance but has encouraged their cooperation in such ventures as Profiles, thus sharpening the company's focus on its goals and objectives.
Source: *Christopher Knowlton, "11 Men's Million-Dollar Motivators," Fortune, April 9, 1990, pp. 8–10.*

What would you do with a million dollars? This is a hypothetical question that we have probably all been asked at one time or another. For 11 executives at Phillips-Van Heusen (PVH), however, it was not a hypothetical question. The corresponding question, What would you do *for* a million dollars, was also very real to them. A million dollars was exactly what each of these executives would receive if the company's earnings per share grew at a 35 percent compound annual rate during the four years ending in January 1992. The first $500,000 came in installments for meeting four year-end goals; the next $500,000 would come as the kicker for meeting the final goal.

This unique incentive plan was the brainchild of Lawrence S. Phillips, PVH's chairman. In the words of one Wall Street analyst this program "has been critical to the success, evolution, and expanding growth of Phillips-Van Heusen." Like many innovative programs, this one was born out of necessity. One long-standing problem faced by PVH was that the demand for men's apparel was susceptible to wide, cyclical swings associated with the notoriously fickle retail industry. The need to solve this recurrent problem became immediate in 1987, when another problem emerged. In an attempt to ward off an outside takeover attempt from a Dallas-based investment firm, PVH was forced to take drastic defensive maneuvers. These maneuvers left the company with $150 million in debt and a devastated stock price of $8, down from $28 less than a year earlier. To solve these problems, Phillips decided that it was "important that we tackle, very aggressively, both the expansion of our third-party [wholesale] business and the creation of our own retail unit."

The only problem with this two-pronged strategy was that the wholesale group and the retail group became potential competitors with each other. Thus there was a strong need to foster camaraderie and cooperation among these units. This unique incentive plan, based upon *organization-wide*, rather than divisional results, was the solution.

The results were evident almost immediately. Soon after the announcement of the plan, the division heads began to meet more frequently and to discuss their operations more openly. Clever cooperative efforts emerged, such as a joint venture between the "sweater" and "shirt" groups to combine sales by offering color-coordinated combinations. A feeling of mutual dependency and team spirit began to emerge. For example, after failing to meet one of the interim goals because of poor returns from the retail group, Michael Blitzer, president of PVH Retail announced with conviction that "you can be damn sure those ten guys are not going to look me in the eye two years from now and tell me that I blew their million dollars." Thus the PVH plan showed not only that money still motivates but that when used creatively, it can reinforce a team-oriented culture that rivets attention on team goals.[1]

The concept of motivation is central to the understanding of human behavior. For example, in everyday life, homicide detectives conducting criminal investigations must establish not only that a suspect had the opportunity to commit a murder but that the person had a specific *motive* for the crime. Indeed, the failure to establish a suspect's motivation is often considered a fatal flaw in attempts to prosecute criminal cases. Our greatest actors have often said that the success of their performances on stage or on screen depends largely on their ability to

[1] Based on C. Knowlton, "11 Men's Million Dollar Motivator," *Fortune*, April 9, 1990, pp. 8–10.

understand the motivation of the characters they portray. In preparing for their roles, they often go to great lengths to research and read as much as they can about their characters, including their personality characteristics and the kinds of circumstances in which they find themselves.

Understanding the reasons behind behaviors and related attitudes is also critical to managerial success. Managing behaviors in the workplace effectively requires the ability to predict human reactions and to prescribe and take appropriate actions. Managing organizational behavior is thus greatly aided by theories that help us understand people's motives. The purpose of this chapter is to introduce and discuss several theories of motivation.

Given the managerial importance of understanding human motivation, it should come as no surprise that there are a large number of well-developed theories of motivation. In general, each of these theories defines **motivation** as the reason or reasons behind an individual's action. Although there are over 100 definitions of motivation in the literature, almost all hold that motivation deals with the factors that initiate, direct, and sustain human behavior over time.[2]

Unfortunately, the sheer number of definitions and theories of motivation can obscure understanding rather than encourage it. We will try to avoid this problem in three ways. First, we begin our discussion of motivation with a brief overview of several dimensions that reduce some of the dissimilarities among theories of motivation. Second, rather than try to cover every theory of motivation, we will focus our attention on just six; expectancy theory, need theory, reinforcement theory, self-efficacy theory, goal-setting theory, and equity theory. Third, we will develop a diagnostic model to make it clear how the theories interrelate. In doing this, we will show how certain theories are best at describing certain aspects of motivation.

motivation The factors that initiate, direct, and sustain human behavior over time.

DIAGNOSTIC ISSUES

In the area of work motivation and performance, the diagnostic model evokes many critical questions. To begin with, how do we *describe* the many varying needs and values that characterize different people? How do we describe the ways in which people learn that certain behaviors will lead to certain outcomes? Can we *diagnose* the reasons why some people perform poorly no matter how hard they try? Can we explain why some people approach their jobs with confidence in their ability to perform well whereas others are plagued by fear and self-doubt?

Can we *prescribe* the kinds of rewards that will enhance motivation and avoid those that won't? Can we prescribe how people evaluate what is fair and what is unfair? Can we predict which employees will feel fairly treated and which will not? Finally, what *actions* can we take to enhance performance? Should we set performance goals? How should these goals be set?

CLASSIFYING THEORIES OF MOTIVATION

content theories Theories of motivation that attempt to specify what sorts of events or outcomes motivate behavior.

The theories we will discuss in this chapter can be differentiated in several ways. First, we can distinguish between content theories and process theories of motivation. **Content theories** like the need and goal-setting

---

[2] J. P. Campbell, M. P. Dunnette, E. E. Lawler, and K. E. Weick, *Managerial Behavior, Performance and Effectiveness* (New York: McGraw-Hill, 1970), p. 77; and F. J. Landy and W. S. Becker, "Motivation

process theories Theories of motivation that attempt to specify how different kinds of events or outcomes motivate behavior.

theories try to answer the question of *what* motivates behavior—what sorts of events or outcomes cause people to behave as they do. **Process theories** like the equity and expectancy theories try to answer the question of *how* events and outcomes interact to motivate people's behavior.

The theories discussed in this chapter can also be differentiated by the degree to which their descriptions of motivation include *cognition* as an important element. Cognition here refers to the process of consciously thinking about personal actions and the probable outcomes associated with those actions. Cognitive theories like expectancy theory and self-efficacy theory suggest that motivation is heavily influenced by conscious thought and purposeful choice. Need and other "acognitive" theories emphasize unconscious drives. These theories suggest that people may not be aware of some of the factors that influence their behavior. Certain learning theories also downplay cognitive factors. These theories describe human behavior essentially as a consequence of the rewards and punishments an individual has received in the past. According to this view, human actions are more mechanical reactions than the product of conscious choice.

Finally, the *breadth* of a theory refers to its generality, its ability to explain different types of behavior. "Narrow" theories attempt to specify in great detail the antecedents of one or a few specific behaviors and attitudes. Goal-setting theory, for example, deals almost solely with performance. Self-efficacy theory deals primarily with persistence on a task. Other theories, such as the expectancy and equity theories, are "broad" theories because they can be used to explain a wide variety of behaviors including performance, persistence, job choice, work attitudes, absenteeism, and turnover.

A DIAGNOSTIC MODEL OF MOTIVATION AND PERFORMANCE

The diagnostic model of motivation developed in this chapter is an elaboration of Vroom's *expectancy theory*,[3] particularly as it was extended by Porter and Lawler and supplemented by several other theories.

Expectancy Theory

expectancy theory A broad, cognitive, process theory of motivation that explains behavior as a function of expectancies, instrumentalities, and valences.

Expectancy theory is a broad, cognitive, process theory of motivation. It is broad because it explains a diverse set of personal outcomes, most notably, a person's desire to perform and the level of effort the person is willing to exert. The theory is cognitive because it places a strong emphasis on personal thoughts and judgment processes. Finally, it is a process theory because it focuses on how motivation occurs. These features, together with the considerable literature that supports the theory's predictions, make it an excellent base for an integrative approach.[4]

The three major components underlying expectancy theory are the concepts of valence, instrumentality, and expectancy. Sometimes the first letters of these words are used to form the term "VIE" theory.

Theory Reconsidered," in *Research in Organizational Behavior*, ed. L. L. Cummings and B. M. Straw (Greenwich, Conn.: JAI Press, 1988), p. 101.

[3] V. H. Vroom, *Work and Motivation* (New York: John Wiley, 1964), pp. 55–71; and L. W. Porter and E. E. Lawler, *Managerial Attitudes and Performance* (Homewood, Ill.: Richard D. Irwin, 1968), pp. 107–39.

[4] T. R. Mitchell, "Expectancy Models of Job Satisfaction, Occupational Choice, and Effort: A Theoretical, Methodological, and Empirical Appraisal," *Psychological Bulletin* 81 (1974), 1053–77.

valence The amount of satisfaction an individual anticipates receiving from a particular outcome.

Valence. The concept of **valence** is based on the assumption that at any given time, a person prefers certain outcomes to others. Valence is a measure of the attraction a given outcome holds for an individual, or the satisfaction she anticipates receiving from a particular outcome.

Outcomes can have positive, negative, or zero valence. An outcome is said to have a positive valence when a person would rather attain it than not attain it. For example, in our opening story, for a group of top-management executives in their early 40s, almost all of whom started at PVH in entry-level positions as merchandising assistants or store clerks, $1 million would surely have a very positive valence. If a person prefers *not* to attain the outcome, the outcome is said to have a negative valence. For example, not wanting to have to look other PVH executives in the eye after being responsible for their losing $1 million clearly had negative valence for the head of PVH's retail unit. When a person is indifferent to attaining an outcome, the outcome is assigned a valence of zero. PVH CEO Phillips has noted that "this company has no corporate baloney tied to it. Nobody here gets a car or a country club paid for. This is a very straight, down-to-earth company."[5] Clearly, Phillips is saying that these kinds of perks should have no valence for anyone who wants to work for him.

It is important to distinguish between valence and value. Valence refers to *anticipated* satisfaction. *Value* represents the *actual* satisfaction a person experiences from attaining a desired outcome. Vroom has noted that "An individual may desire an object but derive little satisfaction from its attainment—or he may strive to avoid an object which he later finds to be quite satisfying. At any given time there might be quite a discrepancy between the anticipated satisfaction from an outcome (i.e., its valence) and the actual satisfaction that it provides (i.e., its value)."[6] Thus when we are trying to understand someone's motivation, we must determine his valence for a particular outcome, not the value he will place on that outcome.

instrumentality A person's subjective belief about the relationship between performing a behavior and receiving an outcome.

Instrumentality. The second major component of expectancy theory is instrumentality. **Instrumentality** refers to a person's subjective belief about the relationship between performing a behavior and receiving an outcome. This belief is sometimes referred to as a performance-outcome expectation. Determining

[5] Knowlton, "Million-Dollar Motivator," p. 8.
[6] Vroom, *Work and Motivation*, p. 27.

A well motivated work force for whom work accomplishment has a high valence can make a big difference in bottom-line results. Recently, a team of Federal Express clerks spotted and solved a billing problem that was costing the company $2.1 million a year.
Source: *Brian Dumaine, "Who Needs a Boss?" Fortune, May 7, 1990, pp. 50–52.*

how a person perceives instrumentalities is important because a person's desire to perform a particular behavior is likely to be strong only when both valence and instrumentality are perceived as acceptably high. Thus we need to know more than the satisfaction an individual expects as the consequence of attaining a particular outcome. We also need to know what the person believes she must do in order to obtain that outcome. Thus, the key to the motivation of the PVH executives is not that a million dollars may be available to them but that this bonus will be forthcoming only if they accomplish their objectives.

expectancy A person's beliefs regarding the link between his efforts and his performance.

Expectancy. The third element of expectancy theory consists of the concept for which the theory is named: expectancy. **Expectancies** refer to beliefs regarding the link between making an effort and actually performing well, or effort-performance expectations. Whereas knowledge about valences and instrumentalities tells us what an individual *wants to do*, we cannot know what the individual will *try to do* without knowing his expectancies. According to Vroom, "Whenever an individual chooses between alternatives which involve uncertain outcomes, it seems clear that his behavior is affected not only by his preferences among these outcomes, but also by the degree to which he believes these outcomes to be probable."[7]

Money, prestige, and performing an enjoyable task may have high valence for most of us. Furthermore, we may see that playing basketball in the National Basketball Association is instrumentally related to achieving all three of these outcomes. Despite these high levels of valence and instrumentality, however, few of us are likely to try out for a professional team, because we doubt we could make the team.

In the same way, although executives at PVH wanted the $1 million bonus and clearly understood what they needed to do to get it, their motivation could still have been low if they felt that the goal was impossible because of factors outside their control. For example, although the PVH group met its first interim goal, it did not meet its second. A plague of bad luck and world events conspired against them. First, much of the manufacturing of sweaters had been outsourced to China, and the Tiananmen Square riots severely affected these operations. Other work was outsourced to Puerto Rico, where damage from Hurricane Hugo forced the closing of two other sweater mills. Finally, in the same disastrous year, the largest purchasers of PVH clothing, Federal Department Stores and Allied Department Stores, filed for bankruptcy. If PVH executives had seen these events as destroying all hope of reaching their objectives—they did not—the $1 million bonus would no longer have served as an incentive.

Thus expectancy theory defines motivation in terms of desire and effort, and sees the achievement of desired outcomes as an interactive function of valences, instrumentalities, and expectancies. Desire comes about only when both valence and instrumentality are high, and effort comes about only when all three are high.

Supplemental Theories

There are two primary reasons why we need to supplement expectancy theory with five other motivation theories. First, a number of other theories deal in much more detail with certain specific components of motivation. Therefore, they help to elaborate expectancy theory constructs. For example, need theories provide important insights into how valences are developed and how they can change over time. Learning theories explain how perceptions of instrumentality come

[7] Ibid., p. 17.

about. Self-efficacy theory describes the origin of effort-performance expectancies as well as the ways in which they are maintained.

Second, we need to extend expectancy theory to explain outcomes other than desire and effort. For example, to predict performance, expectancy theory needs information about human ability (see Chapter 4) and about how people set goals. In order to predict satisfaction levels, we need to know what equity theory tells us about social comparisons. Thus along with expectancy theory, our diagnostic model will also incorporate ideas from the need, learning, self-efficacy, goal-setting, and equity theories.

Overview of the Model

To develop our diagnostic model of motivation and performance we will use a 6–5–4 heuristic. That is, the model contains *six components* put together in *five steps* to explain *four outcomes*.

One of our six components, "abilities," has already been explained in Chapter 4, and will be only briefly touched on here. Three of the remaining five are valence, instrumentality, and expectancy. These have already been defined, but we will elaborate on each using need, learning, and self-efficacy theories. The remaining two components are accuracy of role perceptions, and equity, particularly as these are delineated in goal-setting theory and equity theory.

The model's five steps are the key places where components combine to influence outcomes. These steps build on each other progressively. For example, as we have already suggested, the components of valence and instrumentality combine to determine desire. Desire then combines with another component, expectancy, to determine effort.

The four outcomes of interest to us are desire, effort, performance, and satisfaction. Because we are also interested in how these outcomes might affect variables like valence and instrumentality, in our fifth step we will look at valences,

FIGURE 7-1

A Diagnostic Model of Motivation and Performance

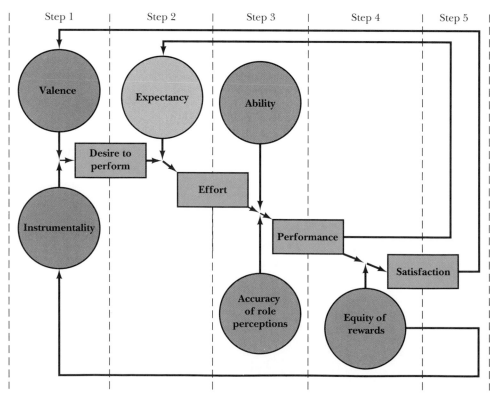

instrumentalities, and expectancies at Time 2 as a function of satisfaction levels at Time 1.

Figure 7-1 presents our model of motivation and performance graphically. As you can see, the six components are shown in circles, the four outcomes are shown in rectangles, and the five steps in which these are combined are indicated by vertical lines. In line with expectancy theory, the first two steps of the model suggest that valence and instrumentality combine to influence desire to perform, and desire and expectancy combine to determine effort. In the third step, effort combines with ability and accuracy of role perceptions to influence performance. In the fourth step, performance and equity of rewards combine to influence satisfaction. In the fifth and last step, the dynamics of the model become apparent. The levels of satisfaction, rewards, and performance feed back to influence valences, instrumentalities, and expectancies, respectively. With this overview in mind, we will describe and illustrate each component of the model and show why the components interact as we have suggested.

VALENCE: NEED THEORIES

Given the central role played by valence in determining motivation, it seems critically important that we understand how an individual's valences are determined. As you know from your own personal experience, people differ greatly in their personal preferences. For example, one person may decide to be a missionary, another to become a stockbroker, and each may be quite satisfied with the choice. We would not expect Mother Teresa and Ivan Boesky to share the same valences. Need theories are especially helpful in understanding not only how valences originate but why they differ among people.

Maslow's Need Hierarchy

Abraham Maslow was a clinical psychologist and a pioneer in the development of *need theories*. Little existed in the way of empirical, scientific studies of motivation in Maslow's day. He based his own theory on 25 years of experience treating individuals of varying degrees of psychological health.

Maslow's need theory A theory of motivation that suggests that behavior is driven by the urge to fulfill five fundamental needs: physiological and safety needs love, esteem, and self-actualization.

prepotency The notion arising from Maslow's theory that higher-order needs can influence motivation only if lower-order needs are largely satisfied.

Maslow's need theory proposed the existence of five distinct types of needs: physiological, safety, love, esteem, and self-actualization. These needs, according to Maslow, are genetically based and characteristic of all human beings. Moreover, he argued, these five needs are arranged in the hierarchy shown in Figure 7-2 and influence motivation on the basis of need **prepotency**. Prepotency means that needs residing higher in the hierarchy can influence motivation only if needs that are lower are largely satisfied.

At the lowest level of Maslow's hierarchy are the *physiological needs*, such as hunger and thirst. According to Maslow, these physiological needs possess the greatest initial prepotence. If they are unfulfilled, no other needs can influence an individual's motivation. Maslow said that when a person's needs for things like food are unfulfilled,

> Capacities that are not useful for this purpose lie dormant, or are pushed into the background. The urge to write poetry, the desire to acquire an automobile, the interest in American history, the desire for a new pair of shoes are, in the extreme case, forgotten or become of secondary importance. For the [person] who is extremely and dangerously hungry, no other interests exist but food.[8]

[8] A. H. Maslow, "A Theory of Human Motivation," *Psychological Reports* 50 (1943), 370–96.

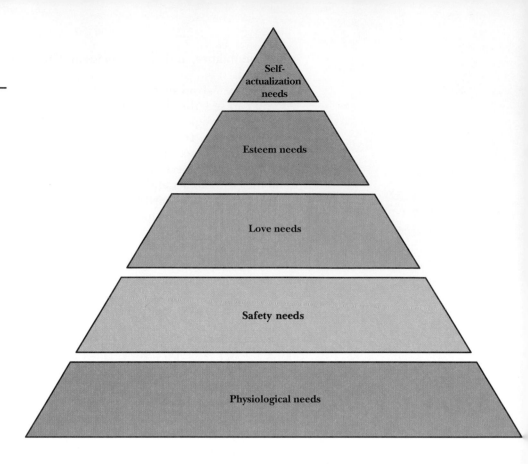

On the other hand, once physiological needs are mostly gratified, they no longer serve as strong motivating elements. Under these conditions, the second-level, *safety needs*, increase in strength. Safety needs have to do with acquiring objects and relationships that protect their possessor from future threats, especially threats to the person's ability to satisfy physiological needs.

If both physiological and safety needs are mostly fulfilled, *love needs* become prepotent. Maslow used the term *love* in a broad sense to refer to preferences for affection from others as well as a sense of community or belongingness. The need for friends, family, and colleagues falls within this category. Maslow classified sexual desires among the physiological needs.

At the fourth level of needs in Maslow's hierarchy are *esteem needs*. Maslow grouped two distinct kinds of esteem within this category. Social esteem consists of the respect, recognition, attention, and appreciation of others. Self-esteem reflects an individual's own feelings about personal adequacy. Consequently, esteem needs can be satisfied partly from sources outside an individual and partly from sources within.

The last set of needs, at the top of Maslow's hierarchy, are the *self-actualization needs*. Maslow felt that if all needs beneath self-actualization were fulfilled, a person could be considered generally satisfied. He also suggested that "since in our society, basically satisfied people are the exception, we do not know much about self-actualization, either experimentally or clinically." For this reason, perhaps, Maslow failed to define this category of needs precisely. In general, these needs seem to involve an individual's desire to realize her full potential. In Maslow's words, self-actualization ". . . might be phrased as the desire to become more and more what one is, to become everything that one is capable of becoming."[9]

[9] Ibid.

The way the need for self-actualization expresses itself varies among people. It may lead one individual to strive to be an ideal teacher. In another person, it may be expressed athletically. In still another, it may be expressed in artistic endeavors. Unlike all the other needs identified by Maslow, self-actualization needs can never be fully satisfied. Hence, the picture of human motivation drawn by Maslow is one of constant striving as well as constant deprivation of one sort or another.

Perhaps because of its simplicity, Maslow's theory has been widely accepted by managers and management educators. It is of interest because of its place in history as one of the earliest motivation models and as a precursor to more modern theories of motivation. Maslow, however, failed to provide researchers with clear-cut measures of his concepts, and his theory has not received much empirical support. In a comprehensive review of studies testing Maslow's theory, Wahba and Bridwell concluded that there was little evidence for (a) Maslow's hierarchical classification scheme of five different types of needs, (b) his deprivation-domination hypothesis, which proposed that unfulfilled needs should dominate others, or (c) his gratification-activation hypothesis, which asserted that gratified needs activate higher-order needs.[10]

Alderfer's ERG Theory

ERG theory A theory of motivation developed by Alderfer that suggests that behavior is dirven by the urge to fulfill three essential needs: existence, relatedness, and growth.

Largely in response to the lack of research support for Maslow's need hierarchy, Alderfer attempted to reformulate the theory.[11] Rather than five levels of needs, Alderfer proposed three: existence, relatedness, and growth. The first initial of each of these needs furnished the name for the **ERG theory** that resulted.

At the base of Alderfer's ERG theory are *existence needs*, which incorporate Maslow's physiological needs as well as those safety needs satisfied by the possession of material objects. In the middle of Alderfer's theory are *relatedness needs*, which include safety needs satisfied by the presence of other people as well as love needs and needs for social esteem. Finally, at the top of Alderfer's theory are *growth needs*, which encompass needs for self-esteem and self-actualization.

In proposing fewer levels of need, Alderfer's theory is more economical than Maslow's. It is also more flexible in that it allows for the possibility that several needs may affect motivation simultaneously. Alderfer agreed with Maslow that need importance progresses up the hierarchy one step at a time. He argued, however, that individuals frustrated by failed attempts to satisfy some higher-level need will often regress and reaffirm the importance of lower-level needs. Alderfer constructed the instrument shown in Table 7-1 to measure satisfaction with each of his three types of needs. Research has supported the hypothesized three dimensions of this instrument as well as its reliability and construct validity. Moreover, predictions based on Alderfer's theory have received greater research support than those based on Maslow's theory.[12]

[10] M. A. Wahba and L. G. Bridwell, "Maslow Reconsidered: A Review of Research on the Need Hierarchy," *Organizational Behavior and Human Performance* 15 (1976), 121–40.

[11] C. P. Alderfer, "An Empirical Test of a New Theory of Human Needs," *Organization Behavior and Human Performance* 4 (1969) 142–75; and *Existence, Relatedness and Growth: Human Needs in Organizational Settings*, (New York: Free Press, 1972), p. 27.

[12] C. P. Alderfer, R. E. Kaplan, and K. K. Smith, "The Effect of Variation in Relatedness Need Satisfaction on Relatedness Desires" *Administrative Science Quarterly* 19 (1974), 507–32; and J. P. Wanous and A. Zwany, "A Cross-Sectional Test of Need Hierarchy Theory," *Organizational Behavior and Human Performance* 18 (1977), 78–97.

TABLE 7-1
Some Items from Alderfer's ERG Measure of Need Satisfaction

Existence Needs

Pay:
1. Compared to the rates for similar work here my pay is good.
2. Compared to similar work in other places my pay is poor.
3. I do not make enough money from my job to live comfortably.
4. Compared to the rates for less demanding jobs my pay is poor.
5. My pay is adequate to provide for the basic things in life.
6. Considering the work required, the pay is what it should be.

Fringe Benefits:
1. Our fringe benefits do not cover many of the areas they should.
2. The fringe benefit program here gives nearly all the security I want.
3. The fringe benefit program here needs improvement.
4. Compared to other places, our fringe benefits are excellent.

Relatedness Needs

Respect from Superiors:
1. My boss will play one person against another.
2. My boss takes account of my wishes and desires.
3. My boss discourages people from making suggestions.
4. It's easy to talk with my boss about my job.
5. My boss does not let me know when I could improve my performance.
6. My boss gives me credit when I do good work.
7. My boss expects people to do things his way.
8. My boss keeps me informed about what is happening in the company.

Respect from Peers:
1. My co-workers are uncooperative unless it's to their advantage.
2. I can count on my co-workers to give me a hand when I need it.
3. I cannot speak my mind to my co-workers.
4. My co-workers welcome opinions different from their own.
5. My co-workers will not stick out their necks for me.

Belongingness (Love):
1. I have developed close friendships in my job.
2. I have an opportunity in my job to help my co-workers quite a lot.

Status (Esteem):
1. I have the feeling that my job is regarded as important by other people.
2. My job gives me status.

Growth
1. I seldom get the feeling of learning new things from my work.
2. I have an opportunity to use many of my skills at work.
3. In my job I have the same things to do over and over.
4. My job requires that a person use a wide range of abilities.
5. My job requires making one or more important decisions every day.
6. I do not have the opportunity to do challenging things at work.

Source: C. P. Alderfer, "An Empirical Test of a New Theory of Human Needs," *Organization Behavior and Human Performance* 4 (1969).

Murray's Theory of Manifest Needs

Henry Murray's *theory of manifest needs,* developed before Maslow's theory, defined needs as recurrent concerns for particular goals or end states.[13] Each need was made up of two components. The first dealt with the object toward which the need was directed. The second was concerned with the intensity or the strength of the need for that particular object. Murray proposed over twenty needs, several of which are described in Table 7-2.

Because Murray's needs are not arranged in any hierarchical fashion, the theory has considerable flexibility. Like Alderfer, Murray held that an individual could be motivated by more than one need at a time, and he also suggested that at times, needs could conflict with each other. Unlike Maslow, who viewed needs as innate and genetically determined, Murray regarded needs as learned.

[13] H. A. Murray, *Explorations in Personality* (New York: Oxford University Press, 1938).

T A B L E 7-2
Some of Murray's Manifest Needs

Achievement	To do one's best, to be successful, to accomplish tasks requiring skill and effort, to be a recognized authority, to accomplish something important, to do a difficult job well
Deference	To get suggestions from others, to find out what others think, to follow instructions and do what is expected, to praise others, to accept leadership of others, to conform to custom
Order	To keep things neat and orderly, to make advance plans, to organize details of work, to have things arranged so they run smoothly without change
Autonomy	To be able to come and go as desired, to say what one thinks about things, to be independent of others in making decisions, to do things without regard for what others may think
Affiliation	To be loyal to friends, to participate in friendly groups, to form strong attachments, to share things with friends, to write letters to friends, to make as many friends as possible
Succorance	To have others provide help when in trouble, to seek encouragement from others, to have others be kindly and sympathetic, to receive a great deal of affection from others
Dominance	To argue for one's point of view, to be a leader in groups to which one belongs, to persuade and influence others, to supervise and direct the actions of others
Nurturance	To help friends when they are in trouble, to treat others with kindness and sympathy, to forgive others and do favors for them, to show affection and have others confide in one
Change	To do new and different things, to travel, to meet new people, to have novelty and change in daily routine, to try new and different jobs, to participate in new fads and fashions
Endurance	To keep at a job until it is finished, to work hard at a task, to work at a single job before taking on others, to stick at a problem even though no apparent progress is being made
Aggression	To attack contrary points of view, to tell others off, to get revenge for insults, to blame others when things go wrong, to criticize others publicly, to read accounts of violence.

Source: H. A. Murray, *Explorations in Personality* (New York: Oxford University Press, 1938), pp. 152–205.

To measure the needs proposed in his theory, Murray developed the Thematic Apperception Test (TAT). As you may recall from Chapter 4, the TAT is a projective test in which a person views an ambiguous picture and makes up a story about it. The person is asked to include in her story such information as, What is going on in the picture? Who is involved? What led up to the situation portrayed? What are the people pictured thinking and feeling? What will happen next? What will the outcome be? The projective test assumes that people will project their own thoughts and feelings onto an ambiguous stimulus, unconsciously revealing their own needs.

McClelland's Theory of Achievement Motivation

Just as Alderfer's theory grew out of Maslow's, Murray's work was extended and expanded upon by others. Most notably, David McClelland developed a theory of motivation that has focused particularly on the need for achievement (nAch).[14]

[14] D. C. McClelland, *The Achieving Society* (Princeton, N.J.: Van Nostrand Press, 1963).

How do you nurture achievement motivation, find innovative uses for natural products, and save the rain forests of the Amazon all in one fell swoop? If you're Cultural Survival Enterprises, you help indigenous people form cooperatives to harvest and sell rain forest products. CSE's biggest product is Rainforest Crunch, a confection made with cashews and Brazil nuts that's sold as a candy as well as an ingredient in Ben & Jerry's Rainforest Crunch Ice Cream. CSE puts the profit from this and other endeavors into the hands of forest residents, enabling them to resist selling out to miners, loggers, and cattle-ranchers.
Source: *"Ideas for 1991,"* Fortune, January 14, 1991, p 42.

According to McClelland certain types of situations are preferred by people with a high need for achievement and tend to elicit achievement striving from these people. These types of situations often offer the opportunity to take personal responsibility. They may also permit people to receive personal credit for the consequences of their actions.

People with a high need for achievement also prefer situations characterized by the availability of clear and unambiguous feedback about personal performance. Task difficulty is yet another situational characteristic important to high nAch individuals. According to McClelland, such people prefer tasks of intermediate difficulty—where the probability of success is close to 50-50—to tasks that are too easy or too difficult. Finally, situations that have a future orientation or permit the development of novel or innovative solutions are attractive to achievement-oriented people.

The four need theories we have discussed are just a few of the many theories that contribute to the complexity of the valence construct. Many things other than pay have valence for workers, a fact that is being increasingly recognized by both management and organized labor. Thus we see labor contracts pushed by the United Auto Workers that trade pay for job security. We see employers like the Park Plaza Hotel in Boston providing employer-financed housing aid for its workers. And we see many employers providing company-sponsored day care.[15]

INSTRUMENTALITY: LEARNING THEORIES

The understanding of valence contributed by need theories provides us with only one piece of the motivation puzzle—what human beings want. In order to understand behavior, we need to know not just what outcomes people want but what they believe will lead to the attainment of desired outcomes.

[15] P. C. Judge, "U.A.W. Faces Test at Mazda Plant," *New York Times*, March 27, 1990, p. D1; and A. R. Karr, "Housing Benefits for Workers Expected to Get Boost from Change in Labor Law," *Wall Street Journal*, April 9, 1990, p. 3.

These beliefs are referred to as instrumentalities in expectancy theory. Learning theories help clarify how relationships between behaviors and rewards come to be perceived. They also provide information that allows us to estimate the character, permanence, and strength of these relationships and are thus another useful supplement to expectancy theory.

The notion that human beings generally behave so as to maximize pleasure and minimize pain, first formulated by the ancient Greek philosophers as the concept of **hedonism**, is part of virtually all modern theories of motivation. It is especially conspicuous in learning theories, all of which attempt to explain behavior in terms of the associations people form between performance and the receipt of some pleasurable or painful outcome. We will look at three types of learning theory: classical conditioning; reinforcement theory, or operant conditioning; and social learning theory.

Classical Conditioning

Does the name Pavlov ring a bell? It might, because it was Ivan Pavlov, a Russian physiologist working early in this century, whose research on conditioning a dog to salivate at the sound of a bell led him to formulate the theory of classical conditioning. **Classical conditioning** creates associations between an **unconditioned stimulus**, something that is known to consistently produce a certain response, and a **conditioned stimulus**, something that has never produced that response. When a conditioned and an unconditioned stimulus are repeatedly presented to a subject at the same time, the subject eventually comes to make the same response to the conditioned stimulus that he originally made to the unconditioned stimulus.

For example, in his experiments at the Soviet Military Academy, Pavlov found that he could make hungry dogs salivate at the sound of a bell (the conditioned stimulus), if in prior conditioning processes, the bell was paired with the presentation of food (the unconditioned stimulus). Later, in the United States, John Watson demonstrated the role played by classical conditioning in human learning by consistently presenting a young child with white, furry objects at the same time as he made a frightening loud noise. As a result, the child became afraid of all white, furry objects.[16]

Classical conditioning provides insights into the way people form associations between different stimuli even when there is no outwardly obvious relationship between them. Managers need to be sensitive to this type of learning so they can avoid becoming aversive conditioned stimuli themselves. For example, a well-intentioned manager who takes up his boss's time only when a problem develops may unwittingly be teaching his boss to expect nothing but problems when the manager approaches. As management consultant Jane Halpert notes, "If every time you see a person, he's bringing you bad news, you tend to want to avoid him."[17] It would be a good idea for this manager to develop a relationship with his supervisor that entails something other than discussion of problem situations.

Reinforcement Theory

Reinforcement theory, or as it is also referred to, operant conditioning, grew out of E. L. Thorndike's work on the *law of effect*. According to Thorndike,

hedonism The belief that human beings generally behave so as to maximize pleasure and minimize pain.

classical conditioning Learning that occurs when a neutral stimulus, through repeated pairing with a stimulus that elicits a specific response, comes to elicit that same response.

unconditioned stimulus A stimulus that naturally and invariably produces a given response.

conditioned stimulus A stimulus that is initially neutral but when repeatedly paired with an unconditioned stimulus, elicits the response associated with the latter stimulus.

---

[16] J. B. Watson and R. Raynor, "Conditioned Emotional Reactions," *Journal of Experimental Psychology* 20 (1920), 1–14.

[17] W. Kiechel, "Breaking Bad News to the Boss," *Forbes*, April 9, 1990, pp. 70–71.

Of several responses made to the same situation, those which are accompanied or closely followed by satisfaction to the animal will, other things being equal, be more firmly connected with the situation, so that, when it recurs, they will be more likely to recur; those that are accompanied or closely followed by discomfort to the animal will, other things being equal, have their connections with that situation weakened, so that when it recurs, they will be less likely to recur. The greater the satisfaction or discomfort, the greater is the strengthening or weakening of the bond."[18]

reinforcement theory A theory of motivation that suggests that people are motivated to engage in or avoid certain behaviors because of past rewards and punishments associated with those behaviors.

The learning process described in reinforcement theory differs substantially from the one depicted in classical conditioning. **Reinforcement theory** proposes that a subject comes to make a specific response because that response has been reinforced by a specific outcome. For example, if a pigeon receives a pellet of food every time it pecks a particular spot on the wall of its cage, in time it will peck that spot repeatedly in order to receive the **positive reinforcement** of food. Here, the unconditioned stimulus and the conditioned stimulus are essentially the same (food), and they both *follow* the conditioned response (pecking). In classical conditioning, however, the unconditioned stimulus and the conditioned stimulus are presented to the subject at the same time, and *precede* the conditioned response. Pavlov's bell, for example, became a sign of food to the dog and thus came to elicit a conditioned (salivary) response.

positive reinforcement The increase in a response that occurs when engaging in the response leads to obtaining a pleasurable stimulus.

The term *operant conditioning*, more or less synonymous with reinforcement learning, got its name from the fact that in this type of learning the subject must perform some operation in order to receive the reinforcing outcome. Thus the subject plays an active role in responding. The pigeon must perform a specific behavior in order to receive his reward. In classical conditioning, however, a more or less automatic response comes to be made to a stimulus that never elicited that response before. Consider our manager's boss, for example, who begins to respond automatically with apprehension when the manager appears at his door.

extinction The gradual disappearance of a response that occurs after the cessation of positive reinforcement.

Extinction occurs in both types of learning. For example, if our manager starts talking with his supervisor about such things as improvements in production and new ideas, as we suggested, his supervisor will form a new, positive association with him and the negative one will weaken and eventually extinguish. Suppose we stop giving our pigeon food pellets when he pecks at the accustomed spot. Eventually, the pecking response too will extinguish; the pigeon will give it up in the absence of reinforcement.

Companies are becoming increasingly interested in basing pay specifically on performance. They are recognizing the potential rewards of linking the reinforcer of pay directly with the response they want to reinforce, or successful job performance. One GTE spokesperson has noted that "our philosophy is reward for performance. . . . Inflation isn't a factor as it was a generation ago." Similarly, compensation specialists at Gantos Corporation note that they are "aware of the inflation rate" but believe that paying for performance is "the most equitable, sensible way."[19]

negative reinforcement The increase in a response that occurs when engaging in the response leads to the removal of an aversive stimulus.

punishment A decrease in a response that occurs when engaging in the response leads to receiving an aversive stimulus.

Negative reinforcement and punishment are two other ways to influence behavior. In **negative reinforcement**, the likelihood that a person will engage in a particular behavior is increased because the behavior is followed by the removal of something the person dislikes. In **punishment**, the likelihood of a given behavior is decreased because it is followed by something that the person dislikes. The distinctions among positive reinforcement, extinction, negative reinforcement, and punishment are shown in Figure 7-3. The figure shows reinforcement theory's ability to explain how to strengthen and weaken behaviors as well as its ability to predict the effects of rewards that have positive or negative valences.

[18] E. L. Thorndike, *The Elements of Psychology* (New York: Seiler, 1911), p. 244.

[19] "Labor Letter," *Wall Street Journal*, March 6, 1990, p. 1.

FIGURE 7-3

Effects of Methods of Reinforcement on Behavioral Response

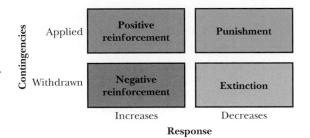

Managers in organizations sometimes contend that they cannot make use of reinforcement theory because they do not have enough resources to give positive reinforcements. For example, they cannot always raise salaries or award bonuses as they might like. What Figure 7-3 makes clear is that positive reinforcement is only one of a number of ways to increase the frequency of a desired behavior. Managers can also employ negative reinforcement to increase a response. They can find something about the job that people do not like and, when employees engage in desired behaviors, remove it. For example, a sales manager who wants to increase sales and who knows that salespeople hate to complete paperwork associated with their work might offer to shift the responsibility for completing paperwork to others if the salespeople increase their productivity. The sales force's enthusiasm for selling might increase noticeably as a result.

As Figure 7-3 clearly shows, punishment suppresses an incorrect response. Unfortunately, however, punishment does nothing to increase the frequency of correct responses. Moreover, although punishment may appear to eliminate an unwanted behavior, its effect is only temporary.[20] A final drawback in the use of punishment is that it often leads to undesirable side effects. Most commonly, these take the form of negative emotional reactions from those who have been punished. Negative reactions are especially likely to occur when punishment is rendered publicly rather than privately. We will have more to say about organizations' use of discipline programs in Chapter 9.

Another important factor in the usefulness of reinforcement theory is the *schedule of reinforcement* used to pace the delivery of reinforcing outcomes. There are five different kinds of schedules: continuous, fixed ratio, variable ratio, fixed interval, and variable interval. In a *fixed-ratio schedule*, reinforcement is given after the occurrence of a fixed number of target behaviors. For example, under a piece-rate payment plan a worker might earn one dollar for every ten products produced. *Continuous reinforcement* is a special case of fixed ratio reinforcement in which there is one-to-one correspondence between the occurrence of a behavior and the receipt of a reward (e.g., one dollar for every product produced). Under fixed-ratio or continuous schedules, initial learning tends to occur rapidly and the behavior, once learned, is typically exhibited quite often thereafter. On the negative side, however, behaviors reinforced in this fashion tend to extinguish quite rapidly if reinforcing outcomes are withheld.

Behaviors are much more resistant to extinction when reinforced on a *variable-ratio* schedule. This schedule is similar to the fixed-ratio schedule in that the receipt of an outcome is contingent on the number of behaviors exhibited. On a variable-ratio schedule, however, the number of responses required to obtain an outcome is not the same every time. Thus, an employee working under a variable ratio piece-rate payment system would earn one dollar for every 10 products produced on average, but his actual earnings might be contingent on producing a different number of items from one time to the next. The number of produced products needed to obtain a reward might be 8 in one case, 12 in

[20] R. L. Solomon, "Punishment," *American Psychologist* 19 (1964), 239–53.

another, and 3 in yet another. Notably, slot machines produce rewards in this manner, and anyone who has observed people playing these machines will attest to their ability to motivate high rates of behavior despite little reinforcement.

Interval schedules differ from ratio schedules in that time rather than the number of behaviors determines rewards. On a *fixed-interval* schedule, individuals receive initial reinforcement after exhibiting a target behavior, and reinforcement continues after a predetermined time interval that does not vary from one reinforcement episode to the next. Because the receipt of outcomes is tied to the passage of time rather than to personal performance, the number of target behaviors encouraged by this type of schedule is typically quite low. Nevertheless, fixed-interval schedules are used quite often in business. Hourly pay reflects the passage of time but is unrelated to whether employees have behaved productively while at work.

A *variable-interval* schedule, which provides greater resistance to extinction, also gears the distribution of outcomes to the passage of time. However, unlike fixed-interval schedules, the amount of time between the receipt of outcomes differs from one reinforcement episode to the next. For example, a production supervisor who visits a remote work station sometimes once a week, sometimes once a month, sometimes twice a month, is using a variable-interval schedule. This schedule increases the probability that employees at the remote station will work at a constant rate; they never know when the supervisor might show up. Compare this situation to that of employees managed by a supervisor whose arrival can be predicted precisely because she uses a fixed-interval schedule.

Although they differ in important respects, all the reinforcement schedules we have discussed have one thing in common. They are initially activated by the occurrence of a particular behavior. When we want to encourage a complex behavior that might not occur on its own the process of shaping can be helpful.

shaping Bringing about a desired behavior by rewarding successive approximations to that behavior.

Shaping means rewarding successive approximations to a desired behavior. For example, it is virtually impossible for someone who has never played golf to pick up a club and execute a perfect drive the first time. Moreover, left on her own to try and try again with no instruction, a novice golfer is unlikely ever to exhibit the correct behavior. In shaping, rather than wait for the correct behavior to occur on its own, one begins by rewarding close approximations. Then over time, rewards are held back until the person gets closer and closer to the right behavior. Thus a golf instructor might at first reward a novice golfer for holding the club with the right grip. To obtain a second reward, the novice may be required not only to display the correct grip but to stand at the right distance from the ball. To obtain additional rewards, the novice may have to do both of these things and perform the appropriate backswing, and so on. In this way, initially simple behaviors are shaped into a complex desired behavior.

Social Learning

social-learning theory A theory of motivation originated by Bandura that suggests that behavior is often driven by the desire of an observer to model the behavior of some other person.

Social-learning theory, as proposed by Albert Bandura, is a theory of observational learning that holds that most people learn behaviors by observing others and then *modeling* the behaviors they perceive to be effective. This sort of observational learning contrasts markedly with the process of learning through direct reinforcement.

For example, suppose a worker observes a colleague who, after giving bad news to her manager, is punished. Strict reinforcement theory would suggest that when confronted with the same task, the observing worker will be neither more nor less prone to be the bearer of bad tidings because she has received no direct reinforcement herself. Social-learning theory suggests otherwise, however. Despite the fact that the worker may never have directly experienced the fate of her colleague, she will nonetheless learn by observation that this boss "shoots the messenger." She will doubtless conclude that the best response in such situations is to keep quiet. Even though the manager would probably never agree that problems should be covered up, this may be the precise message sent by his behavior.

It is important to distinguish social learning, or modeling, from simple imitation or mimicry. When we imitate or mimic others, we simply copy their behaviors. When we model our behaviors on others, however, we are very selective. Before we decide to imitate a model, we consider such things as our own abilities and the effectiveness of the model's behavior in the situation surrounding her. For example, a study of pairs of lower-level supervisors and their direct subordinates showed that subordinates attempting to succeed on the job did not always imitate the values and behaviors of their direct supervisors. In fact they imitated only those supervisors whom they perceived as competent and successful. Also, subordinates who were low in self-esteem were much more likely to model supervisor behaviors than those who possessed higher self-esteem. Thus, rather than simply imitating their supervisors, the subordinates first tried to discern whether their supervisors were worth imitating. They also considered whether they could do better on their own.[21]

Besides its focus on learning by observation, social-learning theory proposes that people can reinforce or punish their own behaviors; that is, they can engage in *self-reinforcement*. According to Bandura, a self-reinforcing event occurs when (a) tangible rewards are readily available for the taking, (b) people deny themselves free access to those rewards, and (c) they allow themselves to acquire the rewards only after achieving difficult self-set goals.[22] Consider the behavior of many novelists. Once alone and seated at their typewriters, a considerable number of authors refuse to take a break until they have written a certain number of pages. Obviously, these people can get up and leave any time they wish. However, they deny themselves the reward of a rest until they have accomplished their self-set goal.[23] Research has indicated that self-reinforcement can be used to help people stop smoking, overcome drug addiction, cure obesity, improve study habits, enhance scholastic achievement, and reduce absenteeism.[24]

[21] H. M. Weiss, "Subordinate Imitation of Supervisory Behavior," *Organizational Behavior and Human Performance* 19 (1977), 89–105; "Social Learning of Work Values in Organizations," *Journal of Applied Psychology* 63 (1978), 711–18; Weiss and J. B. Shaw, "Social Influences on Judgments on Tasks," *Organizational Behavior and Human Performance* 24 (1979), 126–40; and T. L. Rakestraw and Weiss, "The Interaction of Social Influences and Task Experience on Goals, Performance and Performance Satisfaction," *Organizational Behavior and Human Performance* 27 (1981), 326–44.

[22] A. Bandura, "Self-Reinforcement: Theoretical and Methodological Considerations," *Behaviorism* 4 (1976), 135–55.

[23] I. Wallace, "Self-Control Techniques of Famous Novelists," *Journal of Applied Behavioral Analysis* 10 (1977), 515–25.

[24] F. H. Kanfer and J. S. Phillips, *Learning Foundations of Behavior Therapy* (New York: John Wiley, 1970), p. 59; Kanfer, "Self-Regulation: Research, Issues, and Speculation," in *Behavior Modification in Clinical Psychology* ed. C. Neuringer and J. Michael (New York: Appleton-Century-Crofts, 1974), pp. 178–220; M. J. Mahoney, N. G. Moura, and T. C. Wade, "The Relative Efficacy of Self-Reward, Self-Punishment, and Self-Monitoring Techniques for Weight Loss," *Journal of Consulting and Clinical Psychology* 40 (1973), 404–7; C. S. Richards, "When Self-Control Fails: Selective Bibliography of Research on the Maintenance Problems in Self-Control Treatment Programs," *JSAS: Catalog of Selected Documents in Psychology* 8 (1976), 67–68; E. L. Glynn, "Classroom Applications of Self-Determined Reinforcement," *Journal of Applied Behavioral Analysis* 3 (1970), 123–30; and C. A. Frayne and G. P. Latham, "Application of Social Learning Theory to Employee Self-Management of Attendance," *Journal of Applied Psychology* 72 (1987), 387–92.

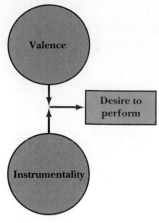

F I G U R E 7-4

Step 1. The Desire to Perform as a Function of Valence and Instrumentality

self-efficacy The judgments people make about their ability to execute courses of action required to deal with prospective situations.

STEP 1: DESIRE TO PERFORM AS A FUNCTION OF VALENCE AND INSTRUMENTALITY

Valence and instrumentality are the first two parts of our diagnostic model of motivation. As shown in Figure 7-4, these two concepts combine to influence the desire to perform. People will be motivated to perform at a high level so long as they perceive that receiving high-valence outcomes is contingent upon strong personal performance. Our understanding of the process depicted in Figure 7-4 is based in part on need theories, which help explain what outcomes individuals will perceive as having a positive valence. In addition, because reinforcement theories explain how people learn about contingencies, they also provide insight into the process that makes people want to perform. As the "In Practice" box suggests, when valence and instrumentality issues are not dealt with satisfactorily, employees' desire to perform their jobs may plummet to zero.

EXPECTANCY: SELF-EFFICACY THEORY

Although actually part of Bandura's social-learning theory, self-efficacy is an important topic in its own right.[25] **Self-efficacy** refers to the judgments people make about their ability to execute courses of action required to deal with prospective situations. People high in self-efficacy feel they can master, or have mastered, some specific task. As you can see, self-efficacy is a perception and may be accurate or faulty.

Self-efficacy differs from self-esteem in that it is usually more task specific or situation specific. For example, an artist may have a positive self-image generally but may feel little self-efficacy when confronted with the need to repair his car. Self-efficacy also differs from the concept of locus of control discussed in Chapter 5. An internal locus of control implies that a person perceives that his actions are responsible for the outcomes he receives. It does not, however, imply that the person perceives himself as having the ability to actually execute the actions required to obtain desired outcomes. To underscore this distinction, Bandura reserved the term *efficacy-based futility* for individuals who have both an internal locus of control *and* low self-efficacy.[26]

Self-Efficacy and Behavior

Self-efficacy perceptions strongly influence human behavior. In Bandura's words:

> People avoid activities that they believe exceed their coping capabilities, but they undertake and perform assuredly those that they judge themselves capable of managing. . . . Judgments of self-efficacy also determine how much effort people will expend and how long they will persist in the face of obstacles or aversive experiences. When beset with difficulties people who entertain serious doubts about their capabilities slacken their efforts or give up altogether, whereas those who have a strong sense of efficacy exert greater effort to master the challenges.[27]

[25] A. Bandura, "Self-Efficacy Mechanism in Human Behavior," *American Psychologist* 37 (1982), 122–47.

[26] Ibid.

[27] Ibid.

Valences, Instrumentalities, and the Boeing Strike

Most tasks required to construct a modern aircraft, such as riveting, wiring, metal binding, wing assembly, and cockpit installation, are done in large hangars. These hangars seem cavernous when they are absolutely still, as the Boeing hangars were in October, 1989, when 58,000 workers walked off their jobs.

The Boeing strike had implications for more than one employer or one industry. Indeed, the strike became symbolic of organized labor's crucial fight against bonuses as substitutes for pay raises. This practice was unheard of in the late 1970s. By 1990, however, 42 percent of all American workers covered by union agreements were receiving such bonuses. This early battle between union and management helps illustrate the usefulness of the valence and instrumentality concepts. It also showcases the process of social exchange in a context where foreign competition is intense and where failure to reach an agreement could mean economic suicide for one or both parties.

Valences deal with needs. The notion of substituting bonuses for raises first emerged to meet the needs of employers. Unlike raises, bonuses do not count toward pensions, vacations, sick pay, or overtime. And they do not compound or accumulate year after year. In the early 1980s a wave of deregulation and an influx of foreign competition put almost unbearable pressures on many U.S. manufacturing firms. Companies pleaded hardship and turned to their unions for relief. In many cases the unions agreed to forego yearly wage raises, in return for yearly bonuses.

Boeing employees were willing to agree to such provisions because it was obvious that the company had fallen on hard times. Moreover, the bonuses met the needs of many Boeing employees. In the early 1980s, Boeing's work force was one of the youngest in America and for them, a big year-end bonus (given out ten days before Christmas) was "like winning the lottery."

Times and needs change, however. In 1989, Boeing was no longer in danger as a company. In fact, when the strike occurred, Boeing was enjoying its most profitable period ever, having piled up orders to build 1,600 planes for $80 billion. Executive salaries, which were often tied to stock performance, increased dramatically. Moreover, in the intervening period, despite union concessions, Boeing had engaged in several layoffs that reduced the company's size at one point to less than a quarter of what it had been in the 1970s. This experience, coupled with the aging of Boeing's work force, made needs for security and long-term economic growth more im-

portant than the instant gratification associated with hefty bonuses. The economic impact of the bonuses was detailed in a union circular, which showed that since 1983, Boeing had paid bonuses equal to 31 percent of each worker's gross pay. The circular explained that if the same 31 percent had been in the form of wages, compounding (i.e., accumulation) alone would have given employees three times as much income.

Boeing's management resisted union demands. Their long-term plan was to move the entire work force toward a system that included not only bonuses but also annual profit-sharing payments. The latter would rise during good times, and disappear during the inevitable bad times. Management saw both these payments as "rewards for profitability and hard work." But while management was attempting to make performance instrumental to receiving high pay, the unions were interested in setting some instrumentalities of their own. In particular, the contingency they set for accepting this kind of flexible pay in place of raises was an agreement by management to forgo all future layoffs.

Thus needs, valences, and instrumentalities drive the behaviors of both employers and employees. Moreover, these factors change over time, so that a solution that was once viable may no longer be successful. Approaches to worker motivation that fail to take these facts into consideration are as empty as the hangars at Boeing in 1989.*

* Based on L. Uchitelle, "Boeing's Fight over Bonuses: Trend Threatens Traditional Raises," *New York Times*, October 12, 1989, p. D1.

Sources of Self-Efficacy

Given the effect that feelings of self-efficacy can have on behavior, it is important to know where these feelings come from. In his research, Bandura has identified four different sources of self-efficacy beliefs. First, self-efficacy can be based on a person's *past accomplishments*. Past instances of successful behavior increase personal feelings of self-efficacy, especially when these successes seem attributable to unchanging factors such as personal ability or a manageable level of task difficulty. Conversely, past instances of failure tend to reduce personal feelings of self-efficacy. However, if these failures can be attributed to causes over which one has no control, such as bad luck, or that one has the power to change, such as effort, then relatively high self-efficacy beliefs can be maintained even in the face of failure.

The link between self-efficacy theory and social-learning theory is made clear in Bandura's second source of self-efficacy beliefs: *observation of others*. Merely watching someone else perform successfully on a task may increase an individual's sense of self-efficacy with respect to the same task. In his research, Bandura often cured children who had irrational fears of dogs with a treatment in which the fearful children repeatedly observed other children of the same age and sex approaching and petting dogs. After repeated observations, the self-efficacy of the fearful children increased to the point where they were able to approach and pet the dogs themselves.

It is important to note that characteristics of the observer and model can influence the effects of observation on feelings of self-efficacy. For instance, the observer must judge the model to be both credible and similar to the observer (in terms of personal characteristics like ability and experience) if observation is to influence efficacy perceptions.

A third source of self-efficacy is *verbal persuasion*. Convincing people that they can master a behavior will under some circumstances increase their perceptions of self-efficacy. The characteristics of the source and the target of the communication, however, can affect the influence that persuasion has on self-efficacy perceptions. Again, people who are perceived as credible and trustworthy are most able to influence others' self-efficacy perceptions through verbal persuasion.

Self-efficacy training is gaining wide acceptance in business and industry. For example, Dale Carnegie and Associates reports that companies enrolled over 170,000 people in their "you-can-do-it" training courses in the last decade alone. More and more blue-collar workers are enrolling in such courses. At a Ford Motor Company stamping plant in Buffalo, New York, for instance, a joint labor-management training center has as many as three Carnegie classes a day. Carnegie CEO Stewart Levine explains, "We focus on the critical skills of self-confidence, so that [people] on the assembly line can make decisions, even though they're thousands of miles away from the CEO."[28]

Logical verification is another source of self-efficacy perceptions. By logical verification, people can generate perceptions of self-efficacy at a new task if they can perceive a logical relationship between the new task and a task they have already mastered. Suppose, for example, that a highly competent secretary is worried she will not be able to master a word processor. If the secretary can be convinced that the word processor is nothing more than a glorified typewriter, which she knows very well how to handle, her perceived self-efficacy as a word processor may well increase.

STEP 2: EFFORT AS A FUNCTION OF DESIRE AND EXPECTANCY

In Step 1 we stated that the desire to perform is influenced by both valence and instrumentality. Now we can state that effort is a function of desire to perform and expectancy. In other words, the level of effort a person will

---

[28] A. Bernstein, "How to Work the Line and Influence People," *Business Week*, May 7, 1990, pp. 140–41.

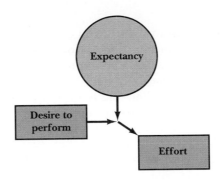

put forth is determined by three components of our model: valence, instrumentality, and expectancy.

Self-efficacy theory is particularly useful as an explanation of how expectancies are formed and how they can be changed. However, as Figure 7-5 suggests, a person's belief that she can perform possesses no motivational value unless she truly desires to excel. Similarly, simply wanting to excel will not bring about high levels of effort unless the person has some belief that it is possible to do so.

Our diagnostic model of motivation now consists of the three basic components of expectancy theory: valences, instrumentalities, and expectancies. This so-called VIE theory is quite useful in understanding how people are motivated to perform and how they decide what effort they will put forth. Porter and Lawler have argued, however, that to fully understand performance we must supplement this theory with additional components.[29] In the next section we will examine one such component: the effect of setting specific goals on the accuracy with which people perceive their tasks.

goal-setting theory A theory of motivation originated by Locke that suggests that behavior is driven by goals and aspirations, such that specific and difficult goals lead to higher levels of achievement.

ACCURACY OF ROLE PERCEPTIONS: GOAL-SETTING THEORY

Role perceptions are people's beliefs about what they are supposed to be accomplishing on the job and how. Role perceptions are accurate when people facing a task know what needs to be done, how much needs to be done, and who will have the responsibility to do it. Role accuracy of this sort guarantees that the energy devoted to task accomplishment will be directed toward the right activities and outcomes. At the same time, it decreases the amount of energy wasted on unimportant goals and activities. Goal-setting theory can help us understand how to enhance the accuracy of role perceptions.

Important Goal Attributes

Employees are often told, "Do your best." This axiom is a standard instruction intended to guide job performance in everyday situations. Yet, research by Edwin Locke, the leading advocate of **goal-setting theory**, and numerous other organizational scientists, has consistently demonstrated that vague instructions like this can actually undermine personal performance. In contrast, over 100 studies have provided evidence supporting the assertion that performance is enhanced by goals that are both specific and difficult. In summarizing these studies, Locke and several of his colleagues concluded that "the beneficial effect of goal setting on task performance is one of the most robust and replicable findings in the

[29] Porter and Lawler, "Managerial Attitudes."

psychological literature."[30] As you can see from Table 7-3, setting specific goals has improved performance in a wide variety of jobs.

Although initially Locke defined a goal as simply "what the individual is trying to do,"[31] he has long emphasized that specific and difficult goals lead to higher performance than vague or simple goals. According to Locke, specific and difficult goals seem to promote greater effort and to enhance persistence. Moreover, they are likely to encourage people to develop effective task strategies. Their primary virtue, however, is that they direct attention.

By directing our attention to specific desired results, goals clarify both what is important and what level of performance is needed. Goal setting is most effective when teamed with feedback so that progress can be monitored. Because goals clarify what needs to be done they lead to accurate role perceptions. For example, for the executives at Phillips-Van Heusen, any result could have been considered consistent with the goal of "do your best." However, these top managers were told that they had to move the stock price to $28 per share by January 1, 1992. This was a much more specific goal and open to much less interpretation. In addition, PVH provided clear feedback on progress toward this goal. The stock price was charted on a bulletin board placed in the reception area at corporate headquarters, where PVH executives could hardly fail to notice it.

Goal Commitment and Participation

goal commitment A person's willingness to put forth effort in accomplishing goals and unwillingness to lower or abandon goals.

Another factor that affects performance is the extent to which a person feels committed to a goal. Specific and difficult goals lead to increased performance only when there is high **goal commitment**. The requirement that people be committed to goals makes the managerial use of goal-setting programs somewhat exacting, because goals that are particularly difficult are typically met with less personal commitment. Taken to an extreme, there is a good chance that people will view a goal that is set excessively high as impossible and thus will reject it altogether.

Fortunately, research has examined several ways to increase commitment to difficult goals. One important factor is the degree to which the goals are public rather than private. For example, in one study, students for whom difficult GPA goals were made public (posted on a bulletin board) showed higher levels of

---

[30] Edwin A. Locke, "Toward a Theory of Task Motivation and Incentives," *Organizational Behavior and Human Performance* 3 (1968), 145.

[31] Locke, "Task Motivation," p. 159. For a later review, see Locke, K. N. Shaw, L. Saari, and G. P. Latham, "Goal Setting and Task Performance: 1968–1980," *Psychological Bulletin* 80 (1981), 125–52. For research on the focusing affects of goals, see Locke and J. F. Bryan, "The Directing Function of Goals in Performance," *Organizational Behavior and Human Performance* 4 (1969), 35–42.

T A B L E 7-3
Jobholders Who Have Improved Performance in Goal-Setting Programs

Telephone servicepersons	Marine recruits
Baggage handlers	Union bargaining representatives
Typists	Bank managers
Salespersons	Assembly-line workers
Truck loaders	Animal trappers
College students	Maintenance technicians
Sewing machine operators	Dock workers
Engineering research scientists	Die casters
Loggers	

commitment to those goals than students whose goals were kept private. So one way to commit yourself to a course of action is to tell people what goal you are working toward.

This study also found a significant positive relationship between need for achievement and goal commitment. Moreover, the relationship between need for achievement and commitment was especially strong when the goals were set by the subjects themselves, as opposed to when they were assigned to the subjects by an outside party. Figure 7-6 depicts this complex relationship between goal origin (self-set vs. assigned by others), need for achievement, and goal commitment.

The complex relationship found in this study is typical of research in the area of goal setting. Prior to studies like this one, it was widely assumed that participation in the goal-setting process would invariably enhance performance and commitment. That is, it was thought that the more input people had in establishing their goals, the more committed they would be to them. This common-sense notion has not held up well in scientific studies, however. Many contemporary studies have failed to find significant differences between participative goal-setting groups and assigned-goal groups in terms of either goal commitment or performance. Generally speaking, studies that have found positive effects for participation have been able to do so only within limited subsamples of research participants.[32] Thus although commitment is important in enhancing the effect of goals on performance, participation does not guarantee commitment.

Goals and Strategies

As Table 7-3 shows, goal setting has been used to increase performance on a variety of jobs. Yet most of the early research on goal setting consisted of studies that focused attention on relatively simple tasks. That was not an accident or an oversight; it was quite intentional. In characterizing his pioneering research on goal setting, Locke stated that "the research to be reported here involves pre-

[32] G. P. Latham, M. Erez, and E. A. Locke, "Resolving Scientific Disputes through the Joint Design of Crucial Experiments by the Antagonists: Application to the Erez-Latham Dispute Regarding Participation in Goal Setting," *Journal Of Applied Psychology* 73 (1978), 753–72.

F I G U R E 7-6

Effect of Need for Achievement and Type of Goal on Goal Committment

High need for achievement leads to high goal commitment, but only when people set their own goals.

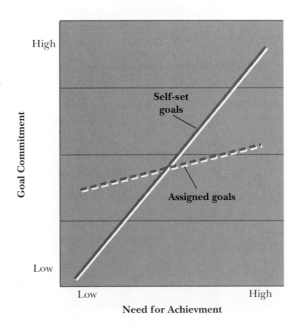

dominantly simple tasks in which learning complex new skills and making long-term plans and strategies is not necessary to achieve goals."[33]

More recent research has extended goal-setting theory into more complex task domains, however, and in these situations, the links between goals, effort, and performance are not so direct. A review of these later studies indicated that while goals have positive effects for all tasks, the magnitude of the effect is stronger for simple tasks than for complex tasks.[34] Figure 7-7 shows how the effect of goal difficulty on performance decreases as task complexity increases.

The primary reason why the goal-setting effect for complex tasks is not as straightforward as it is for simple tasks involves task strategies. With complex tasks, the *task strategies* or plans of action that people devise have a big impact on the outcome of their efforts. This impact can obscure and in some rare cases even wipe out goal-setting effects.

Research on goal setting and task strategies by Christopher Earley and his colleagues suggests that whereas setting specific and difficult goals may lead to increased strategy development, there is no guarantee that the resulting strategies will always be effective.[35] Moreover, because developing strategies consumes time that might otherwise be devoted to task performance, there may be situations where goals actually hinder performance. Accordingly, Earley has shown that specific and difficult goals may be least effective for "tasks in which (a) performance is primarily a function of strategy rather than task effort, (b) there are many available strategies, (c) the optimal strategy is neither obvious nor readily identified, and (d) little opportunity to test hypotheses retrospectively exists."[36]

[33] Locke, "Task Motivation," p. 161.

[34] R. E. Wood, E. A. Locke, and A. J. Mento, "Task Complexity as a Moderator of Goal Effects: A Meta-Analysis," *Journal of Applied Psychology* 72 (1987), 416–25.

[35] P. C. Earley and B. C. Perry, "Work Plan Availability and Performance: An Assessment of Task Strategy Priming on Subsequent Task Completion," *Organizational Behavior and Human Decision Processes* 39 (1987), 279–302; and Earley, P. Wajnaroski, and W. Prest, "Task Planning and Energy Expended: Exploration of How Goals Influence Performance," *Journal of Applied Psychology* 72 (1987), 107–14.

[36] P. C. Earley, T. Connolly, and G. Ekegren, "Goals, Strategy Development and Task Performance: Some Limits on the Efficacy of Goal Setting," *Journal of Applied Psychology* 74 (1989), 24–33.

FIGURE 7-7

Goal Difficulty, Task Complexity, and Performance

When tasks are relatively simple, there is a close relation between the difficulty of the goal and the person's performance. That is, a person will work hard to achieve a difficult goal but may make less effort to reach an easy one. When tasks are complex, however, the relation between goal difficulty and performance changes. A person trying to achieve a difficult goal in a highly complex task may not be able to sustain the level of performance that he can on a simpler task.

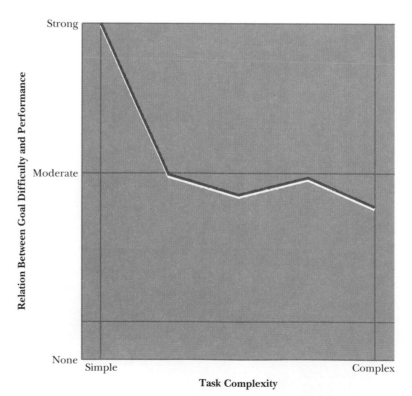

Although research on performance strategies has yielded findings that complicate the results of other goal-setting studies, this research is helpful in delineating the specific role-clarifying effect of goals. In simple tasks, where the *means* to perform a task are clear, specific and difficult goals lead to higher performance because they clarify the *ends* toward which task performance should be directed. In complex tasks, however, the *means* are not clear. Individuals performing such tasks do not know how to go about them in the best way, so merely clarifying the *ends* sought is unlikely to enhance performance. In sum, goals can clarify the ends to which role-related performance should be directed and may even promote strategy-development efforts. Goals alone offer no guidance about how to attain these ends, however, and thus need to be teamed with effective strategies.

ABILITY AND EXPERIENCE REVISITED

Predicting task performance from goals is also contingent upon the abilities of the jobholder. We discussed abilities at great length in Chapter 4, so here we will focus only on how such individual differences interact with goal setting and task strategies.

Three things are worth noting. First, it should be obvious that people lacking requisite abilities cannot perform a complex task even under the most favorable goal-related circumstances. Second, there are some subtle relations among goal setting, attention, and cognitive capacity that affect task performance. Recall that one of the ways in which goal setting affects performance is by directing attention to the kinds of results that are desired. Kanfer and Ackerman have developed a model that recognizes that different people have different amounts of cognitive ability to bring to bear on a task, and that this limits how much they can attend to at any one time.[37] Because it diverts attention from the task to the goal, goal setting may be particularly damaging to people who have low ability or who are still learning the task. Such people need to devote all their attention to the task, and goal setting for them is unlikely to enhance performance.

Finally, it should be noted that individuals high in ability are more likely to develop effective strategies. For one thing, high-ability people, especially those high in reasoning and deduction, can often figure out good strategies prior to working on the task. Second, individuals high in cognitive ability learn more quickly and are therefore more likely to deduce effective strategies through trial-and-error.[38]

Thus, although motivation is critical to performance, the lessons learned in Chapter 4 about the importance of ability should not be forgotten. For all but the most simple of tasks, there is no substitute for ability.

STEP 3: PERFORMANCE AS A FUNCTION OF EFFORT, ACCURACY OF ROLE PERCEPTIONS, AND ABILITY

At last, in this third step, we can see how motivation and other factors combine to determine performance (see Figure 7-8). Specifically, performance will be high when a person (a) puts forth significant effort, (b) has the ability to exhibit the right behaviors and (c) focuses her effort properly.

[37] R. Kanfer and P. L. Ackerman, "Motivation and Cognitive Abilities: An Integrative/Aptitude-Treatment Interaction Approach to Skill Acquisition," *Journal of Applied Psychology* 74 (1989), 657–90.

[38] J. Shapiro, "Goal Setting, Cognitive Ability, and Task Strategy," Master's Thesis, Michigan State University, 1990, p. 79.

FIGURE 7-8

**Step 3. Performance as a
Function of Effort, Accuracy
of Role Perceptions, and Ability**

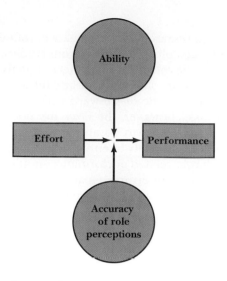

Proper focus is achieved by making role requirements clear, that is, by clarifying the ends sought through goal setting and by clarifying the means to be used in achieving these goals through the development of task strategies.

EVALUATION OF REWARDS: EQUITY THEORY

Motivation, we have seen, is a complex and dynamic process in which valences, instrumentalities, expectancies, role perceptions, and abilities interact to affect performance. Now we will add another component to our diagnostic model—the effect of rewards for successful performance on the individual's satisfaction. Equity theory seems particularly useful in examining the intricate relations among motivation, performance, and rewards.

Equity, Equality, and Social Comparisons

equity theory A theory of motivation originated by Adams that suggests that behavior is motivated by the desire to reduce guilt or anger associated with social exchanges that are perceived to be unfair.

Equity theory is a theory of social exchange that describes the process by which people determine whether they have received fair treatment. More specifically, as shown in Figure 7-9, equity theory holds that people make judgments about fairness by forming a ratio of their perceived investments (or inputs) and perceived rewards (or outcomes). They then compare this ratio to a similar ratio reflecting the perceived costs and benefits of some other person. If these ratios are not equal, the situation is perceived as unfair. For example, is it fair for the CEO of a savings and loan institution that lost $120 million to make $4.8 million in salary? That is precisely what happened for CenTrust Bank of Miami chairman, David Paul. He was ousted, however, after an investigation by federal regulators who were given tips by disgruntled employees.[39]

[39] J. Fierman, "The People Who Set the CEO's Pay," *Fortune*, March 12, 1990, pp. 58–66.

FIGURE 7-9

**Algabraic Expression of How
People Make Equity Comparisons**

$$\frac{I_{person}}{O_{person}} = \frac{I_{Reference\ person}}{O_{Reference\ person}}$$

Equity theory does not require that outcomes or inputs be equal for equity to exist. A person receiving fewer desirable outcomes than someone else may still feel fairly treated if he sees himself as contributing fewer inputs than the other person.

Adams identified a number of possible inputs and outcomes that might be incorporated in equity comparisons (see Table 7-4). Two crucial issues complicate the use of Adams's theory. First, equity judgments are based on individual perceptions of inputs and outcomes, and perceptions of the same inputs or outcomes may differ markedly from one person to the next. For instance, an employer may be less impressed with an employee's experience than the employee himself, and the employee may not see the status of his job the same way the employer does. Second, the importance associated with a particular input or outcome differs from one person to the next. Thus, one employee might consider pay an extremely important outcome whereas another might place greater emphasis on job security. Without even realizing it, an employer who was unaware of differences like these could easily create inequity by treating two people identically.

Responses to Inequity

According to Adams, after a person perceives inequity, she experiences an unpleasant emotional state of either anger or guilt. When people perceive themselves as receiving a greater share of outcomes than they deserve, they may feel guilty. Indeed, a significant amount of the early research on equity theory dealt with the guilt-bearing *over-compensation effect*. In these studies, some workers who were led to believe they were overpaid proceeded to produce at higher levels out of guilt.[40] About the $1 million bonus offer, one PVH executive stated flat out, "I can honestly say that I was embarrassed by it. I don't know that I deserve it."[41]

But results like these are not so common. Research has shown that perceived inequities associated with the *under-compensation effect* are far more frequent and more potent. Moreover, perceiving oneself as at the low end of the equity comparison results in anger, a much stronger reaction. With respect to the huge salaries of upper-level executives, for example, one middle-level financial analyst notes that "it disturbs me when someone on high dictates that no matter how hard you work or what you do, you're only going to get a 6% increase, and if

[40] J. S. Adams and W. B. Rosenbaum, "The Relationship of Worker Productivity to Cognitive Dissonance about Wage Inequities," *Journal of Applied Psychology* 46 (1962), 161–64.

[41] Knowlton, "Million-Dollar Motivator," p. 10.

T A B L E 7-4
Inputs and Outcomes in Equity Theory

INPUTS	OUTCOMES
Education	Pay
Intelligence	Satisfying supervision
Experience	Seniority benefits
Training	Fringe benefits
Skill	Status symbols
Social status	Job perquisites
Job effort	Working conditions
Personal appearance	
Health	
Possession of tools	

---

you don't like it you can take a hike. Yet whatever they have negotiated for themselves—10%, 20%, or 30%—is a different issue."[42]

Whether guilt or anger, the tension associated with inequity motivates the person to do something to reduce the inequity. Adams specified six possible reactions. First, the individual might *alter personal inputs*, either increasing them or decreasing them depending upon the type of inequity perceived. In situations characterized by the over-compensation effect described above, an increase in effort inputs might be expected in response to the receipt of an outcome that was greater than expected. The analogous response in situations of undercompensation would be a decrease in personal inputs. Someone feeling underpaid on a job might put forth less effort.

A second response to inequity is to try to *alter personal outcomes*. Individuals who feel they are relatively underpaid according to the market may demand raises and threaten to leave or strike. An area of increased activity recently is the renegotiation of so-called two-tier labor contracts. These contracts, like the substitution of bonus for pay raise we discussed in the "In Practice" box, were born in the recession-ridden early 1980s. In an effort to keep foundering employers alive, unions agreed that although current workers' wages would not be lowered, all newly hired employees would be brought in at a lower wage rate. These employees would be on a different pay scale that would leave them forever underpaid relative to current employees, who were on the higher tier. As one disgruntled, second-tier American Airlines pilot put it, "We like to describe it as mortgaging the unborn."[43] Interest in these kinds of plans peaked in 1985, when 11 percent of union employees were covered by such agreements. As the business climate improved, second-tier employees, who soon began to outnumber first-tier employees, fought to dismantle this inequitable solution. By 1990, this pressure brought the 11 percent figure down to 6 percent, and according to James Martin, a leading researcher in this area, such provisions "are going to be fairly rare" by 2000.[44]

A third way of responding to inequity is to use what is called *cognitive distortion*, that is, rationalizing the results of one's comparisons. For example, if a manager feels she is overpaid for her effort, rather than increase that effort she may rationalize the imbalance by overvaluing her inputs. For example, a relatively overpaid worker may exaggerate the importance of her level of education.

People can also distort their perceptions of outcomes. In one equity-theory study, subjects who were underpaid for a particular task justified this underpayment by stating that the task they were working on was more enjoyable than the task performed by research participants who were overpaid, even though their tasks were identical.

Yet another means of eliminating an inequity via cognitive distortion is to change the reference person. A salesperson who brings in less revenue than his peers may claim, "You can't compare me with them because I have a different territory." By this statement, he seeks to disqualify his peers as reference persons.

A fourth way to restore equity is to take some action that will *change the behavior of the reference person*. Workers who in the eyes of their peers perform too well on piece-rate systems often earn the derogatory title of *rate buster* (see Chapter 2). Research has shown that if name calling of this sort fails to constrain personal productivity, more direct tactics may be invoked. In one study, for instance, the researchers coined the term *binging* to refer to a practice in which

Suppose an employee seeks equity through a more challenging job challenge rather than through a higher salary? John Allegretti (center), a trainee at the Hyatt Regency hotel chain, couldn't wait for the eight years or more that it takes to become a manager in the hotel business. When Hyatt found out that Allegretti was considering a job with a waste-recycling company, it found a way to keep him on board. The company asked him to head a project to reduce waste at its Chicago hotel. Allegretti built this project into a new waste-consulting company, called International ReCycle Co. Inc., that now has 24 clients in 8 states.
Source: *James E. Ellis, "Feeling Stuck at Hyatt? Create a New Business,"* Business Week, *December 10, 1990, p. 195.*

[42] A. Bennett, "Caught in the Middle: Managers Don't Mind that the CEO Makes a Lot of Money, but Raise Questions About Fairness," *The Wall Street Journal*, April 18, 1990, p. 9.

[43] R. Tomsho, "Employers and Unions Feeling Pressure to Eliminate Two-Tier Labor Contracts," *Wall Street Journal*, April 20, 1990, p. 25.

[44] Ibid.

INTERNATIONAL OB

Establishing Equity Overseas

If you were given a chance to work in any city in the world, what city would you choose? San Francisco? London? New York? San Diego? Paris? Hong Kong? How about Khartoum, in Sudan? Many Americans might hesitate at the thought of working in Khartoum, and after doing a little homework, they might refuse outright. In 1989, the United States State Department designated Khartoum the most difficult place in the world to live and work.*

What might North Americans find objectionable about Khartoum? To begin with, Sudan, of which Khartoum is the capital city, is a developing nation, and it stills lacks many of the technological advances that Americans have come to take for granted. In 1989, many phones in the city had not worked for years. Live power lines drooped over pot-holed roads and dirt paths. The city was also plagued by labor unrest. For example, in one month alone, bank workers, bus drivers, electricians, pilots, doctors, pharmacists, postal workers, engineers, and university staff were all on strike.

Sudan borders on two countries that have experienced considerable political unrest, Chad and Ethiopia. It also borders on Libya, whose leader, Muammar Qadaffi, is considered by many to be unstable and potentially dangerous. The Sudan government itself has had repeatedly to fend off rebel insurgents, and the re-emergence of civil war is an ever present threat.

Like several African countries, Sudan has oil and several ports on the Persian Gulf. American companies thus have a legitimate reason to do business in the country. So a very realistic question is, What would an American organization have to offer an employee to get him to work in Sudan? As large corporations continue to internationalize, compensation issues associated with overseas assignments, particularly to hardship posts, have become salient. Approaching these problems from an equity perspective highlights two of the major problems in this area: keeping expatriates whole, and keeping local country nationals satisfied.

Keeping expatriates whole means enabling United States personnel stationed abroad to maintain the same standard of living that they enjoy at home. Organizations try to do this by adding an incentive component and an equalization component to the job.† The *incentive component*, essentially a bonus, takes the form of a percentage increment in salary. The U.S. State Department, for example, recommends a 25 percent premium for Khartoum. The *equalization component* is an additional payment to adjust for differentials in buying power of an employee's base salary in one country versus another. Equalization payments typically include allowances, for housing, private school for children, and taxes (expatriates are taxed by both the United States and the host nation). It also includes a cost-of-living allowance to adjust for price differences on such necessities as food.

With the addition of both incentive and equalization components, compensation for overseas jobs can be quite high. This raises more problems: how to justify such high salaries for Americans when local country nationals (LCNs) are doing similar work yet being paid less. Further, many U.S. firms overseas employ third-country nationals (TCNs), or people who are neither U.S. citizens nor citizens of the country where they work. No incentive or equalization payments are made to TCNs. Among both LCNs and TCNs who compare themselves with U.S. expatriates, the possibility for perceptions of inequity and exploitation is great.‡

To minimize these problems, organizations employ two strategies. Sometimes they try to limit awareness of pay differences by keeping salary information secret or to mask the issue by paying people in different currencies. Or they may make an expatriate job a relatively short-term consulting assignment that includes training LCNs and TCNs. As organizations become increasingly experienced in internationalization, other more creative solutions to the inequity problems posed by expatriates, LCNs, and TCNs will probably evolve. A clear understanding of equity theory should help future managers to achieve such solutions.

† G. T. Milkovich and J. M. Newman, *Compensation*, (Richard D. Irwin, Homewood IL, 1990), p. 545.

‡ D. Darlin, "When in Rome," *The Wall Street Journal*, May 3, 1988, p. 1.

* R. Winslow, "How Khartoum Won No. 1 Ranking as a Hardship Post," *The Wall Street Journal*, April 26, 1989, p. 1.

---

workers periodically punched suspected rate busters in the arm until they reduced their level of effort.

Finally, if all else fails, equity can be secured by *leaving an inequitable situation* altogether. Turnover and absenteeism are common means of dealing with perceptions of unfairness in the workplace. Research emphasizes that it is the perception of unfairness, not absolute level of pay, that causes such escape behaviors. In many cases, workers receiving low pay in an absolute sense have very good attendance records because they also perceive their inputs as being low.[45]

[45] M. Patchen, *The Choice of Wage Comparisons* (Englewood Cliffs, N.J.: Prentice-Hall, 1961), p. 38.

Choosing among Responses. Given all these methods of reducing inequity, it is not surprising that equity theory is frequently criticized for its failure to specify how equity is most likely to be restored. As the "International OB" box points out, the increasing globalization of business and industry is putting ever greater pressure on us to figure out how to maintain equity among people from different countries and with different training and backgrounds.

Adams has offered some guidelines, however, as to how people behave in the face of inequity. First, an individual will attempt to maximize highly valued outcomes. Second, inputs that are costly or difficult to increase will rarely be altered. Third, the person will resist both distortions and real changes in inputs and outcomes that are central to his self-concept. Fourth, it is easier for a person to mentally distort the inputs and outcomes of others than his own inputs and outcomes. Fifth, people will leave a relationship only when the magnitude of the inequity is large and there are no other means of eliminating it. Sixth, the longer someone has used another as an object of comparison, the more resistant he will be to changing to another reference person.

STEP 4: SATISFACTION AS A FUNCTION OF PERFORMANCE AND EQUITY

Figure 7-10 incorporates the implications of equity theory into our model of human motivation. As the figure shows, the level of satisfaction experienced by the individual will be a function of both the person's performance and the perceived equity of the rewards she receives for that performance. The rewards will contribute to high levels of satisfaction only when the person perceives them as equitable. We will have more to say about job satisfaction in our next chapter.

STEP 5: MOTIVATIONAL COMPONENTS AS A FUNCTION OF PRIOR OUTCOMES

The fifth and final step needed to complete our model deals with the feedback loops that make the model dynamic over time. Let's look back at Figure 7-1, which shows three such feedback loops. First, there is a feedback loop going from level of satisfaction back to valence. Recall that valence, as a construct, deals with anticipated satisfaction, not realized satisfaction. The feedback loop allows for the possibility that an outcome a person thought might be valent might not bring him much real satisfaction when he actually receives it. His valence for such an outcome would then decrease relative to what it was at an earlier time.

Another feedback loop goes from rewards experienced after performance to instrumentalities. This loop is meant to suggest that the receipt of rewards at

FIGURE 7-10

Step 4. Satisfaction as a Function of Performance and Equity of Rewards

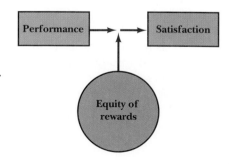

one time will affect the person's perceived instrumentalities at later times. If high performance is not followed by equitable rewards, extinction of the performance response could take place. High performance followed by equitable rewards, on the other hand, may be positively reinforcing.

Finally, there is also a feedback loop from performance to expectancy. This loop affirms the fact that expectancies and self-efficacy are based at least partially on prior performance. All else equal, successful performance strengthens self-efficacy and leads to high expectancies. Failing at a task, however, generally leads to lower levels of self-efficacy.

These three feedback loops in our model of motivation create the possibility that motivation can change over time. For example, Figure 7-1 suggests that a highly motivated person might lose motivation for any of three reasons. First, a person starting out with high expectancies might discover during job performance that she cannot perform nearly as well as she thought. Decreased self-efficacy would reduce expectancy perceptions and lower motivation would probably result. Second, a person might discover that performing well on a job does not lead to the desirable outcomes he initially expected. His motivation could be expected to diminish as projected instrumentalities fail to materialize. Third, experience with the rewards received from performing a job might lead a person to discover faults with initial valences. That is, rewards expected to yield satisfaction do not do so. Motivation might drop owing to the absence of desirable rewards if no other performance-contingent rewards were available.

SUMMARY

Our diagnostic model of *motivation* and *performance* is based on *expectancy theory* and incorporates notions from five other theories of motivation including *need theory*, *learning theory*, *self-efficacy theory*, *goal-setting theory*, and *equity theory*. The model focuses on explaining four outcomes. The first, desire to perform, is a function of *valences* and *instrumentalities*. A person's desire to perform well will be high when valent rewards are associated with high performance. The second outcome, *effort*, is a function of desire to perform and *expectancy*. Effort will be forthcoming only when individuals want to perform well and when they believe they can do so. The third outcome, *performance*, is a function of effort, *accurate role perceptions*, and *ability*. Performance will be high only when individuals with the requisite abilities and knowledge of desired goals and strategies put forth their best effort. The model also shows how *satisfaction*, the fourth outcome, is a product of past performance and the perceived *equity of rewards* received for performing well. The dynamic nature of the motivation process is revealed in the way present levels of satisfaction, perceived equity of rewards, and performance affect future levels of valence, instrumentality, and expectancy.

REVIEW QUESTIONS

1.   Recent research suggests that personality characteristics, like individual needs, may be determined more by genetic factors than we have thought. Take each of the four different need theories described in this chapter and discuss whether this new evidence supports, contradicts or is irrelevant to that theory.

2.   Specific, difficult goals have been suggested to enhance performance, but researchers have also shown that performance will be high only when expectancies are high. We might think that as goals become increasingly difficult, expectations

for accomplishing these goals would decrease. Can you resolve this apparent contradiction between goal-setting theory and expectancy theory?

3.   Free agents in baseball are players whose contracts with current teams have expired. They put themselves on the "auction block" at the end of their option year (the last year of their current contract) and offer their services to the highest bidder. Some experts have suggested that, according to expectancy theory, a player's performance will be higher in the option year than in the year following his signing of a new contract. Others have suggested that, according to equity theory, performance will be higher after the new contract is signed. Why might these theories make different predictions in this case, and which do you feel is right?

4.   Imagine that you work for Phillips-Van Heusen and that your immediate supervisor is one of the 11 executives vying for the million-dollar bonus. How do you think this incentive would affect your boss's attitude toward your work? How would you feel if he got the bonus and you got your normal raise for that year? Analyze this situation using equity theory and describe what steps you think should be taken to reduce feelings of inequity among PVH employees other than the 11 top managers.

5.   Analyst Daniel Shore once called motivation researchers "servants of power" because their research was often used to manipulate lower-level workers. Is trying to motivate people necessarily exploitative? Are there any conditions under which providing external motivation might be exploitative? Which theories of motivation do you feel are exploitive? Which ones are not?

DIAGNOSTIC QUESTIONS

When you are trying to diagnose a situation in which motivation may be a problem, the following questions can guide your inquiry:

1.   What are the most important needs of the person I am trying to motivate?

2.   What contingencies has this person learned over the course of his or her reinforcement history?

3.   How can I make the receipt of outcomes that have positive valence for this person contingent upon performing at a high level?

4.   What outcomes that have negative valence for this person can I remove, contingent upon performance at a high level?

5.   Does the person I am trying to motivate believe that he or she can perform well? If not, what can I do to increase the person's self-efficacy perceptions?

6.   Does the person I am trying to motivate actually have the ability to accomplish the tasks that he or she is attempting to perform?

7.   Does the person I am trying to motivate have specific, difficult performance goals in mind?

8.   Is the person I am trying to motivate committed to goals?

9.   Does the person I am trying to motivate know the best strategies for accomplishing these goals?

10.   Who is the reference person for the person I am trying to motivate?

11.   Are the rewards I am giving equitable with respect to this reference person?

12.   If the person I am trying to motivate was initially higher in motivation than he or she is at present, which of the three feedback loops in the diagnostic model accounts for the loss in motivation?

EXERCISE 7-1
MANAGING MOTIVATION: AN EXERCISE IN POSITIVES AND NEGATIVES[1]

JANET MILLS, *Boise State University*
MELVIN MCKNIGHT, *Northern Arizona University*

What can managers do to improve workplace performance? One approach is to review the model and theories of motivation presented in this chapter and to identify some *positive* steps that one can take to improve employee motivation. Another, more unusual approach would be to review the models we've discussed, identify *negative* factors that discourage employee motivation, and take steps to eliminate or avoid these factors. In this exercise you will have a chance to experiment with both of these approaches as you consider situations involving motivational issues that you have experienced and think about how you might motivate employees who will be working for you in the future.

_____

_____

_____.

STEP ONE: PRE-CLASS PREPARATION

In class you are going to work together to develop lists of adjectives that describe what it is like to be motivated. To prepare for this class, think of a recent situation in which you were highly motivated and intensely involved in what you were doing. The situation can be from any context, including school, work, sports, hobbies, or travel. Try to remember the situation so vividly that you can "see" it in your mind. Now, list 10 to 15 words or phrases that describe how you felt in the situation. Such words or phrases might include "being challenged," "feeling stressed," or "wanting to prove I could do it."

_____

_____

_____

_____

_____.

Next, think of another recent situation in which you lacked motivation—in which you were bored, apathetic, turned off. Again, picture the situation vividly and list 10 to 15 words or phrases that describe your experience. These words or phrases might include "having no choice," "feeling resentful," or "feeling rejected."

_____

_____

STEP TWO: SHARING POSITIVE AND NEGATIVE EXPERIENCES

The class should divide into groups of 4 to 6 members each (if you have already formed permanent groups, reassemble in those same groups again). In each group, members should take turns discussing each of the highly motivated situations they have recalled and should share their lists of words and phrases that describe how they felt in these situations. A spokesperson should keep a master list of all of the words and phrases reported during this discussion. After everyone has had a turn, group members should take turns discussing the situations in which they lacked motivation and should share their lists of descriptive words and phrases. The spokesperson should again keep a master list.

STEP THREE: DEVELOPING MOTIVATIONAL PROGRAMS

The instructor should reconvene the class and ask each spokesperson to read the master lists developed during Step Two. As the spokespersons read their lists, your instructor will record the words and phrases on a chalk board or flipchart. He or she should make two lists: one, positive list for motivated situations and another negative list for unmotivated situations. After both lists are completed, your instructor will break the class up again into groups and will assign half of the groups Task A and the other half Task B:

Task A: Imagine that you manage a staff of 20. Productivity and satisfaction are at an acceptable level—neither especially high nor especially low. Your objective is to interfere with productivity and satisfaction by weakening employees' motivation.

[1] Adapted with the authors' permission from a paper entitled "Two Exercises for Teaching about Motivation."

You have one week to do this. Describe what specific actions you would take to accomplish this objective and explain how and why your actions would work.

Task B: Imagine that you manage a staff of 20. Productivity and satisfaction are at an acceptable level—neither especially high nor especially low. Your objective is to improve productivity and satisfaction by strengthening employees' motivation. You have one week to do this. Describe what specific actions you would take to accomplish this objective and explain how and why your actions would work.

All group members should record the group's recommendations, and a spokesperson should be appointed to report back to the class. After the two sets of groups have each completed their tasks (that is, one set of groups have performed Task A and the other Task B) and if time permits, your instructor will ask the groups to perform the second task (either Task B or Task A). As each group completes its second task its members should again record the group's recommendations, and a spokesperson should be ready to present a summary to the class.

STEP FOUR: CLASS DISCUSSION

The class should reconvene and each spokesperson should summarize the results of Step Three. As group summaries are given, the instructor and the class should work together to develop a master list of negative actions that would weaken employee motivation and positive actions that would strengthen it. After all groups have completed their reports, the class should discuss the results of this exercise, focusing on the following questions:

1. Which negative actions designed to weaken motivation would probably have the greatest effect? Why? Which negative actions would probably have the least effect? Why?

2. Which positive actions designed to strengthen motivation would probably have the greatest effect? Why? Which positive actions would probably have the least effect? Why?

3. Combine the strongest positive and negative actions together to form a list of motivational "dos" and "don'ts." How might managers use this list? What kinds of motivational programs does it suggest?

CONCLUSION

Motivating employees is a process of energizing them to perform their work in a productive, satisfying manner. On a daily basis, managers face the task of determining how to motivate employee performance in the most effective way. To accomplish this task, it is important that managers know not only what to do but also what *not* to do. Clearly, the axiom "one can know a thing best only by also knowing its opposite" applies to the issue of employee motivation.

DIAGNOSING ORGANIZATIONAL BEHAVIOR

CASE 7-1

THE PRODUCTION OF KCDE-TV*

C. PATRICK FLEENOR, *Seattle University*

KCDE-TV is one of two television stations in Tuttle, a city of 100,000 population, with a metropolitan area population of 175,000.

KCDE-TV (and radio) for some time had serious morale problems, especially in the television production department. KCDE employed 85 people in six departments: general office; data processing; news; engineering; radio; and television production. The television production group formed the single largest department, about 20 people. The functional areas of the production department are: announcing, directing, switching, camera operating, and video tape operating. See Exhibit 7-1 for description of these functions.

As is the case with many small to medium-sized stations, KCDE was looked upon as a training ground by many members of both management and staff. This was a reason offered by management on occasion for not granting a raise to an employee. It was suggested to the employee that if he wished to remain at KCDE he had better accept his present wage as the maximum for the foreseeable future. He then would find it necessary to move on to a bigger city if he expected to be paid more for the same job. The turnover, especially in the radio and production departments, was high.

Each employee negotiated his own salary with management since there was no union representation. There were no published salary ranges, but staff members knew that approximate ranges in 1990 were as follows:

Announcers	$1,650–$2,000/mo.
Directors	1,650–1,800
Switchers	1,200–1,300
Video Tape Operators	1,200–1,300
Cameramen	800–1,200

The salaries were based on a 48-hour, six day week. Much conversation among the crew members centered around what they all agreed was a low pay scale. As one of the crew members put it regularly in conversation: "No where else can you work a six-day week, a night shift, and virtually every holiday for such lousy money."

Benefits were another sore point. The company made group insurance available, but there was no retirement program. Though providing paid vacations, the company paid the vacationing employee for two 40-hour weeks. The two-week paycheck then was less by sixteen hours of overtime what the employee was acustomed to.

Working conditions with regard to physical comfort and safety were adequate and about average for the industry.

It was a common feeling among the crew members that they were being "used" to one degree or another by management. The men knew that many general office workers for the city's major private employers and the state government were making more money than they, working better hours and shorter weeks. Adding salt to the wound was the feeling that the television job required infinitely more creative ability then the general office workers needed or had. At the same time, most felt their jobs were intrinsically interesting, and far more challenging than office or administrative work.

Great animosity was directed toward the assistant general manager of the station. His previous post was chief engineer of the station, where he was tagged with the nickname "Overkill" by some members of the engineering department. This name was inspired by his tendency to over-react to situations. On one occasion he had fired an employee for smoking in the television control room. Though parts of the studio and control areas were posted against smoking, members of the staff looked upon this regulation as trivial. Care was taken not to smoke only when the assistant general manager was in the immediate area.

More than once, "Overkill" threatened to have a vital piece of equipment removed, ". . . unless you guys take better care of it." The threats were obviously hollow, since the station couldn't operate without the equipment. He had been heard to refer to the operating crew and the engineering department, or various members as "coolies."

The leader of the production department itself was not spared the crew's wrath. Every member of the crew looked upon Gary Brown, the production supervisor, as, as one of the switchers put it, "a miserable, two-timing s.o.b." More than one of the men had had the experience of making a request for a raise, only to find some weeks later that the production supervisor had "forgotten to take it up," or to be counseled that "this just isn't the right time to ask." It had been observed by everyone on the production staff that Gary often delivered different versions of a story to upper management than he gave to his subordinates. It was generally felt that he always sided with management, especially "Overkill," rather than backing his subordinates.

The general manager of the station, Gordon Frederick, was a retired military officer and an ex-mayor of the city. He was active in political causes and was out of town frequently, leaving the day-to-day operation of the station to the assistant general manager. Most of the staff members looked upon Frederick as being a slightly befuddled autocrat since he conducted regular "inspections" when in the building, and indulged a fetish for small detail, such as seeing that the flags were removed from the flagpole in front of the building promptly at sunset. He was responsible for, and for the most part the author of, a booklet of company rules and regulations called the Blue Book. In the Blue Book were voluminous descriptions of each job title within the organization, and page upon page of rules pertaining to coffee breaks, use of company telephones, and virtually every other activity within the building.

The Blue Book was treated with varying degrees of contempt by most staff members, and with utter contempt by the production department. Those who had been in the military service insisted parts of the Blue Book text were lifted wholesale from military manuals. It was felt that the book's only value was to management, in that some obscure regulation could be used to chastise an employee, while other rules were totally ignored. For example, the Blue Book stated that the company had a policy against members of the same family being employed. However, Overkill's son Steve worked as a full-time cameraman, one of the director's wives worked in the office, and the husband of the TV program director served as a technician.

The Blue Book also contained rules for communication between departments, the management feeling being that the rank and file of one department should not communicate directly with their counterparts in other departments in matters of operations. For example, if a newsman became upset at a cameraman,

director, or any other member of the production staff in connection with a newscast, he was to inform the news director, who would then take the matter up with the production supervisor. This rule was totally ignored.

Though the Blue Book delineated a very rigid chain of command, it was fairly common for orders to the production crew to come from "Overkill," the program director, or Brown, the production supervisor. On occasion, in the case of an equipment failure or similar emergency, these orders would conflict, resulting in confusion until the three decided upon a common plan.

Job security was felt to be nonexistent. Many of the workers felt directly threatened by "Overkill" and verbally expressed their fear of his capricious behavior.

Seemingly arbitrary changes of shift upset some of the men. In early Spring of 1990, one of the directors was moved to the position of video tape operator. Though his salary was left at its old level, this move involved a real loss of prestige. No explanation was given to members of the crew. A cameraman was promoted directly to the position of director, by-passing several switchers. Again, there was no explanation.

Sabotage, in the name of "games," became quite common among the operating crew. It was not too unusual for a film projector to be mis-threaded, causing the film to be torn to ribbons when the projector was started, resulting in program down-time. Program sets would occasionally topple over during a video taping session, or microphones would refuse to work. One favorite trick was the tripping of master light breakers for the control room areas. Another was pounding on the wall of an area where an announcer was on the air. One of the more ingenious acts involved the wiring of a prop telephone on the tv news set. The phone was then rung during a newscast, causing the newsman to "break up." Though members of management never appeared to suspect sabotage, its occurrence was by no means rare.

Also in the Spring of 1990, Ron E., the announcer, came to work for KCDE radio. The television and radio control areas were adjacent to one another, and some of the announcers worked both radio and television. There was a great deal of social contact between employees of both sides.

At the end of his first pay period, Ron became tremendously upset. His check totaled about $100 less for the two-week period than he thought it would be. According to Ron, the radio station manager had hired him at $1900 a month, but his first check was paid at the rate of $1700 a month. Ron promptly complained to his supervisor, and the matter was taken to the general manager. He informed Ron that the radio station manage did not have the authority to hire an announcer at such a salary as Ron had been promised. There was no offer to compromise on the salary. Frederick offered to pay Ron's moving expenses back to the city he had left just weeks before. Ron's answer was, "And what the hell am I supposed to do for a job if I do return?" Feeling he had no choice, Ron accepted the lower salary.

In May, about a month after the salary episode, Ron began questioning other employees about the possibility of unionizing the station. His idea was met with great enthusiasm by the members of the production department. More than one of them indicated that though they did not like unions, they liked the management of KCDE even less. The few holdouts expressed fear for their jobs, but no one expressed any pro-management thoughts.

Several meetings were held with union representatives and the union formally notified Mr. Frederick of their intention to organize the production department. This action was met with disbelief on the part of Frederick, followed soon by a meeting to stress to employees that "the door is always open, and you know we're interested in your problems." Union "horror" stories soon followed, accompanied by a frigid atmosphere and veiled threats by both sides. Rumor generation reached very high levels.

In early August, Ron E., was fired for "inattention to duties." He filed an unfair labor practices suit against the station management with the National Labor Relations Board. The filing of the suit served to freeze the unionization proceedings until the suit was resolved.

In the meantime, Frederick, Brown and "Overkill" turned to a well known management consulting firm for help in analysis of the organizational and personnel problems.

When you have read this case, look back at the chapter's diagnostic questions and choose the ones that apply to the case. Then use those questions with the ones that follow in your case analysis.

1. How does KCDE-TV's practice of paying low wages affect employees' equity perceptions? Does your answer to this question help explain the morale problems evident among the station's employees?

2. From the point of view of employee motivation, how have the station's managers made a bad situation even worse? In answering this question, review the actions of "Overkill," Gary Brown, and Gordon Frederick, and consider employee reactions of each of these people.

3. What does the station's treatment of Ron E. tell you about the way KCDE-TV manages its employees? If you were asked to join this company as a new general manager, what would you do first to improve employee motivation? What long-term actions would you initiate?

CASE 7-2

CONNORS FREIGHT LINES*
RICHARD PETERSON, *University of Washington*

Connors Freight Lines is a large, interstate trucking concern serving the north, central, and western states. Its head office is in Fargo, North Dakota, and it has forty-three terminals, with Chicago at one extreme and Los Angeles at the other. The La Crosse, Wisconsin, terminal has been in existence for sixty of the company's seventy-five years and enjoys a fair reputation competitively.

The technical organization of the La Crosse plant consists of a fleet of twenty-seven pickup trucks, ten town-tractors, two fork-lifts, and a cart line hookup track to facilitate loading. This branch is housed at a typical freight terminal which is superior to most other trucking firms, from the technical standpoint, although considered only "adequate" from the standpoint of its social organization. Since the plant is located well away from the business district, most drivers and dock workers bring their lunches, and a small lunchroom is provided for their convenience, where they can also buy coffee or milk. This lunchroom is furnished with long tables and benches, measures approximately 15' x 20' and will comfortably seat about twenty-four workers.

The formal organization of the company, which employs approximately 180 people, consists of the terminal manager, Ralph Preston, and his assistant terminal manager, Jason Hobbs. Exhibit 7-2 shows the company organizational structure.

Although the company appears successful enough in solving its external problems, the high rate of absenteeism, the generally low morale among the truckers, and their relatively short tenure of employment are puzzling internal problems that have vexed management for the past several years. The truck drivers at Connors are strongly union-oriented which results in feelings of mixed loyalties. To some extent, therefore, an undercurrent of conflict is felt in this area by the company as well as by the workers.

It is part of the company's policy to select its supervisors from the ranks of the drivers. This assures them of men who are experienced with the specific job and its problems. In theory, at least, this also rewards the employee with the advancement from a job at worker-level to a position within the organization. Upon becoming a supervisor, the employee is no longer a union member, so he works overtime without any pay

* Reprinted with the author's permission.

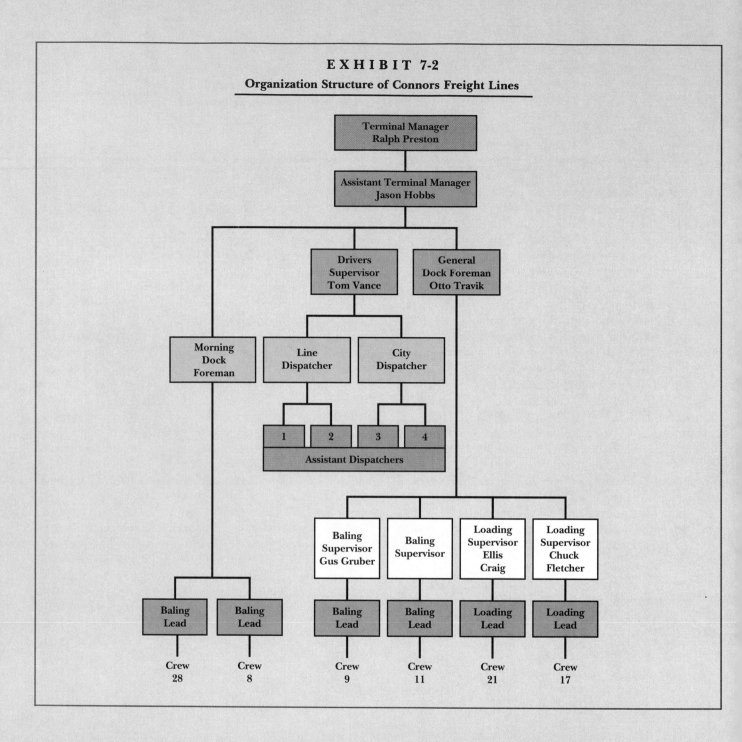

EXHIBIT 7-2

Organization Structure of Connors Freight Lines

and forfeits his seniority standing. The new supervisor is now salaried, with his base income slightly higher than that which he had earned as a driver on straight time. He no longer wears work clothes as his job is considered a "clean" one, and it would seem that some increase in prestige should also accompany this advancement.

Workers of supervisory caliber at Connors have not been too plentiful among the ranks of truck drivers, and the high rate of turnover aggravates this further. The drivers fall mainly into three categories (1) family

men in their 30s and 40s who are settled in their job and, because of various circumstances, have decided to make a career of it; (2) young fellows in their twenties who have a few years of college and must earn money in order to continue toward a degree; and (3) young fellows for whom it is simply "a job," and who in time will probably make up the bulk of the first group or drift on to other employment elsewhere.

Chuck Fletcher would belong in the second of these categories. At 25, he had three years of college but was still uncertain about his field of interest so decided to work a while, keep his eyes open, and do some thinking. Son of parents who were both college graduates, he was well above average in intelligence. Other truckers on his shift both liked and respected him, as did the members of management that had come to know him. He had worked for Connors for two years, spending half his shift on the dock, loading, and the other half as a driver.

Because of the nature of the freighting business, there is a great need for overtime help, since prompt movement of freight is a large part of the "product" which the company sells. Chuck maintained a good attitude about this added work load which was lightened somewhat by his paychecks, reflecting the regular union demand for overtime pay. Not all workers showed as good an attitude toward this overtime work even with the added pay, and several among the top 5 percent in seniority who were given a choice as to overtime work, flatly refused any work other than the regular 8-hour shift, regardless of compensation.

There is a fairly intricate technique involved in the correct loading of trucks and trailers so that the weight is kept under the maximum allowed in highway regulations and is distributed evenly and correctly. The more fragile or perishable items must be given special attention and the merchandise loaded with logic in respect to the order of its being unloaded at the delivery point. Chuck caught on quickly to these loading techniques and soon attracted the attention of the dock foreman, Otto Travik. In a conversation with Chuck's loading supervisor, Ellis Craig, Travik suggested that Craig "keep his eye on" Chuck, with the idea of possibly bringing him into management in the future when an opening might occur within the organization. Craig, who was aware of Chuck's ability to get along well with other workers and knew him as a hard worker, agreed that he was "worth watching."

In January 1991 at one of the regular Wednesday morning staff meetings, Hobbs, the assistant terminal manager, mentioned that a sales job would soon open up, and that they planned to move Al Johnson into this spot. Johnson's move to Sales would then leave a supervisor's job open on the loading dock. Preston, the terminal manager, asked for suggestions as to who might best fill this spot. Thomas Vance, the drivers' supervisor, suggested Ford Wheeler, who had been working on day shift, was thirty-five years old, and a former school teacher. Preston agreed that Wheeler was a good prospect, but Travik and Craig suggested they consider Chuck Fletcher for the position. Qualifications of both men when then compared and discussed and the decision left open, pending more thought on the two candidates, and the actual job opening.

At about this time, Craig said to Fletcher one day:

"I know you like the shift you're on, but would you consider cancelling your bid on it and taking the St. Paul loading job that's driving me crazy? I know the late night shift is a crummy one, but this would be the chance you've wanted to learn to drive the heavy-duty trucks. Vance is our official qualifier, and he's on that shift, so I'm sure by coming to work early you could qualify inside of a month. I'll help expedite the whole thing if you'll help me out on this. After all, the annual bids come up in five months, so if you don't like the job, you can always re-bid. And keep this under your hat—there's going to be a supervisor's job open before too long, and if you make good on this job I think your chances for it would be excellent."

Chuck thought about the St. Paul loading job. He didn't like the night shift, and the job was an especially "dirty" one, but he took it for two reasons: he had been hoping for a chance at supervision, and he also had wanted time to learn to drive the heavy-duty rigs both for the increased pay diesel drivers drew and also because it offered him a challenge.

At a staff meeting in June, 1991, after other articles of business were out of the way, the conversation ran something like this:

Preston: There is now a definite need for a new supervisor, and I hope you have all been keeping this situation in mind and giving it earnest thought. What are your suggestions?

Vance: I still think Ford Wheeler is your boy.

Preston: Yes, I've been seriously considering him. Checked into his background from his job application and I was really quite impressed. Do the rest of the workers respect him? Would they work for him?

Craig: I don't feel he has any of the workers' respect! For one thing he's lazy, and we'll be setting the poor example that all you have to do to get ahead in the organization is do nothing. On the other hand, there's Fletcher who really is liked by the other workers, and respected too. In the time he has worked for me he has shown himself a hard worker, often doing more than is required. For a couple of months he's been coming to work an hour early to practice driving heavy-duty trucks on his own time and hoping to get qualified—and by the way, Vance, he's been ready for his test for some time—he shows a great desire to do a thorough job and accepts more than his share of responsibility. To me, this adds up to material for a good company man.

Vance: Hell! He's a union boy straight down the line. Don't you remember how he initiated two valid grievances against us last year? There has even been some talk of his being named shop steward. But Wheeler, now, has a college degree as a school teacher. He can hardly wait to shake loose from the union.

Preston remembered seeing Fletcher many times, and in all kinds of weather, out practicing driving the diesel rig in the loading zones before his shift time. In checking over Fletcher's job application he found it almost as good as Wheeler's, considering the differences in their ages.

After some further discussion Preston decided in favor of Fletcher. The supervisory position was offered to him on the usual 90-day provision which would allow either him or the company to terminate the arrangement at the end of that time, with no loss of status or seniority on his part. After a few days of consideration, Fletcher accepted the new assignment and went to work as a supervisor of the same crew with which he had been working previously.

Preston gave Fletcher a short "welcoming" talk before his first day in the new job, and in it he covered three main points. He first suggested that Fletcher try to be tactful in his initiation of ideas, maybe even to the point of making his cooperating supervisors sometimes think that the idea came from them. Secondly, he stressed the importance of demanding respect from his crew. "If the occasion demands a reprimand, see that it's done in some private place where others can't see or hear you. Otherwise you both lose face. It must be kept private between you and your man." That led to the third point, that of not being too familiar with the workers on your crew. "It's not really any of our business what you do off the job, but it'd be best if you don't hobnob with your men," Preston had said.

Soon afterwards, at Craig's invitation, Fletcher joined the bowling team of which both Preston and Vance were members. He and Craig, with whom he had always had a good relationship, were becoming close friends since he had been made supervisor. They'd usually go somewhere for a couple of beers together on the nights after bowling.

One night Fletcher was off on his game. After some ribbing from Vance and Preston, he mentioned to Craig how tired he was from so much overtime, "tired and disgusted" was the way he put it. He told Craig that earlier that day he had overheard Preston "chewing out old Gus Gruber" down in the steel bay, and the incident had both embarrassed and disappointed Fletcher. Craig, at that time, was planning a vacation to the East coast with his family and invited Fletcher to come with them. Chuck said he knew he needed a rest and a change

of scenery, but he was short of funds. Last year he had gone up to Canada with some of the men from his crew, but that was when he was getting paid for overtime.

Craig previously had included Fletcher on a couple of family outings and at one time, when the men were alone, they got to talking shop as usual. Fletcher seemed discouraged about the attitude of his crew. "We have always gotten along so well before, but now there's no more kidding. No one hardly cracks a smile and I keep getting jibes like 'Gettin' rich on your overtime, Chuck?' or 'How do you like your new raise by now?'

Part of his interest in taking the supervising job was that he hoped he'd find ways of easing the obvious friction between management and labor, and this development was really discouraging.

The weekly staff meetings, which were attended by all management personnel, were the occasions when affairs concerning the company's technical and social organization and welfare were brought up for discussion. A variety of issues were constantly being introduced, listened to, considered and many were acted upon promptly. At the third staff meeting Chuck himself made the suggestion that the company might see fit to supply work aprons to the workers, adding that these were not expensive items when bought in quantity, and that the gesture of goodwill on the part of the company might help to improve the rather poor relations between it and the workers. This suggestion was listened to but not acted upon.

Another suggestion was made by Fletcher within the next few weeks: that of switching of lunchrooms between the workers and supervisors. The lunchroom reserved for the twelve supervisors was twice the size of the one into which forty-five drivers were crowded at peak times to have their lunches, and this necessitated several of them sitting on the floor or standing to eat. This suggestion, too, was not acted upon, although Craig and Travik both thought it was "worth considering."

Within a short space of time, however, the company was gratified by the outcome of two other suggestions which Fletcher made in work operations. One of these resulted in substantial savings to the company, and the second, in a greater profit. The first was accomplished by Fletcher's simplifying of a certain loading procedure and organizing it in such a way that two men from another crew, ordinarily required for extra help at this time, were no longer needed. Dispensing with this usual short-handing of the second crew enabled it to finish its own loading on schedule, resulting in more efficient moving of freight on the two jobs and less need for overtime on both.

At about this time, two company officials from Fargo were visiting the terminal and Preston took them on a tour of the docks. As they passed the loading area,

Fletcher looked up and nodded. Farther on, as they circled the dock, one of the officials said, "Where is this new supervisor, Fletcher, that you've mentioned a few times lately?"

Preston replied, "Oh, he's the fellow in the red shirt we just passed down there at the north end. I'll introduce him to you at coffee break if he comes up."

The second instance in which Fletcher's suggestion worked to the company's advantage took place toward the end of the ninety-day trial period. It was not presented at the staff meeting but to Hobbs in person one day when he happened to be out on the dock as Fletcher came on shift. Fletcher's attitude, which had always been friendly and respectful, seemed to have changed in recent weeks, and Hobbs, who had become confident that Fletcher was proving to be good supervisory material, was a little puzzled by his apparently growing coolness.

Hobbs: Good morning, Fletcher.

Fletcher: Good morning, Mr. Hobbs. May I speak to you a minute when you have the time?

Hobbs: Sure. Right now is as good a time as any.

Fletcher: It's about the St. Paul run. While I was on the St. Paul-loading job I realized that on the last schedule to St. Paul at night there was always more freight moving from La Crosse to St. Paul than returned from St. Paul to La Crosse. We'd always need a 'double' heading east and then always have to haul back one 'empty.'

A college friend of mine is the son of a truck farmer over east of the Mississippi, and I was talking to him the other day. I think we could arrange for a full load of produce to be picked up near Winona. Then we'd have a full paying load in both directions.

I've already said something to Vance about it yesterday but didn't hear anything from him so thought I'd let you know. The arrangements could be made easily. I'll give you the farmer's name, if you're interested. It's all up to you, of course.

Hobbs thought Fletcher seemed a bit abrupt, but the suggestion pleased and impressed him as it did Preston when he was told about it later in the day.

On Thursday of the last week of the ninety-day trial period, Fletcher came into the office of the assistant manager and told Hobbs that he was going to exercise his option and ask to be returned to worker status the following Monday.

Hobbs was surprised by this unexpected turn of events, but said, "Well, we'll live up to our side of the bargain. I'm sure Mr. Preston will want to hear your reasons for this decision, though. He has some free time

at two o'clock. Could you come in and see him then?"

In Preston's office later:

Preston: What's this I hear about your request to be returned to your old job as trucker?

Fletcher: Yes, I've decided to hang it up. The long hours are getting me down.

Preston: Well, you knew what the hours were like when you took the job. Aren't they the same ones you worked as a driver?

Fletcher: Yes. Well, I thought perhaps I could expedite a few things and maybe shorten them a little, I guess.

Preston: Well, are you sure you gave this "expediting" your best efforts?

Fletcher: Yes, sir I did. Until I got to the point where I felt I was knocking my head against a stone wall.

Preston: Are you sure it's the long hours, or are there some other reasons?

Fletcher: Well, the money and the shift, coupled with the long hours.

Preston: Well, we think you were doing a fine job, and we are already taking steps in these areas you're dissatisfied with. In two weeks we hope to add one new supervisor and possibly two to cut down hours worked by the supervisors.

Fletcher: Well, that would make it a lot easier all right . . .

Preston: And there will be an opening in Dispatch in the not-too-distant future that would be a day-shift job rather than a night one.

Fletcher: That would be a real improvement . . .

Preston: So that just leaves the problem of money. How much more would you say you'd need to make it worth your while to stay on?

Fletcher: A hundred dollars a month, sir.

Preston: Hmm, well, I think we can probably make some kind of arrangements that will make you more contented. I'll check with the head office and let you know on Monday.

Fletcher: All right. Fine. You can let me know.

After Fletcher left his office, Preston said to Hobbs, "I think the head office will go for an eighty-five dollar raise anyway, and that will probably be enough to hold Fletcher here. Put a note in his locker-box stating we will meet his demands, but don't state a definite amount of money. I have to talk to the head office first."

Hobbs: That's still a lot of money. Do you realize that would make him the sixth highest paid man in this terminal? He'll be jumping over eight men.

Preston: Fletcher has already saved the company more than he'll make in a year on that produce haul alone, and he has come up with quite a number of ideas that have helped us out. He's a thinking boy and that's the kind we need. He has a bright future and I want to keep him with us.

The Monday morning mail contained the following note addressed to Preston:

Dear Mr. Preston:

Please accept this notice of my resignation from the company, to be effective in two weeks.

I have thought it over carefully and this is the only possible solution.

Thank you for your generous offer, even though I cannot accept it.

Sincerely,
Charles S. Fletcher

When you have read this case, look back at the chapter's diagnostic questions and choose the ones that apply to the case. Then use those questions with the ones that follow in your case analysis.

1. What motivated Chuck Fletcher when he was doing his initial job at Connors Freight Lines, on Otto Travik's loading dock? What motivated him to perform so well on the St. Paul loading job? What changed when Chuck moved into the supervisory job?

2. Explain Chuck's letter of resignation. Why did he decide to quit instead of continuing in his position as supervisor? Is there anything the company could do to get him to change his mind? If there is, can the company take such action and should it?

3. What should Connors do to ensure that the kinds of problems described in this case do not happen again in the future?

CASE 7-3

CHANCELLOR STATE UNIVERSITY

Read Chapter 9's Case 9-2, "Chancellor State University." Next, look back at Chapter 7's diagnostic questions and choose the ones that apply to that case. Then use those questions with the ones that follow in this first analysis of the case.

1. What effect is the salary compression problem at Chancellor State University likely to have on the motivation of faculty members?

2. University teaching is a profession in which it is fairly easy to move from one institution to another. Which faculty members would be the most likely to become so dissatisfied with the situation at Chancellor State as to leave? Which would be least likely to leave? How might the university's salary compression problem and its effect on faculty members affect students?

3. What can Fred Kennedy do to cope with his department's morale problems? What rewards other than salary could he use to motivate his faculty's performance? How should such rewards be administered?

CHAPTER 8

SATISFACTION AND STRESS

Despite its ongoing battle with its Seattle employees' union and a recent loss in earnings, Nordstrom made ambitious plans for the five-year period beginning in 1990. This one-time family shoe store with a legendary reputation for service expects to add 20 new stores in 13 states with the goal of 80 stores and sales of $5 billion by 1995. The retailer's owners, all members of the Nordstrom family, say they aren't worried about complaints from disgruntled employees or union threats to picket new stores. They are concerned, however, about the chain's earnings. Although Nordstrom carries less debt than many of its competitors, management says it will cut back the number of planned openings if earnings don't improve.

Source: Dori Jones Yang and Laurie Zinn, "Will 'The Nordstrom Way' Travel Well?" Business Week, September 3, 1990, pp. 82–83.

She had worked weeks without a day off and pulled 15-hour shifts without a break. She had stockpiled service awards and customer thank-you notes. Yet she thought she was going to be fired, and she wasn't alone. In fact, according to employment counselor Alice Snyder, she was "the fourth person from that store that I've seen this week." "That store" was Nordstrom, the Seattle-based clothing store, and the strung-out workers who marched through Snyder's office suffering from ulcers, colitis, hives, and hand tremors were among a growing army of "Nervous Nordies." Worn down by the relentless pressure associated with working at Nordstrom, workers "were dropping like flies," according to Patty Bemis, a one-time top salesperson.

According to disgruntled employees, the sources of stress at Nordstrom were many. There were constant threats of job loss for failing to meet quotas. For example, the manager of a cosmetics department told employees that if the goals she had set for them were not met within 60 days, they would be fired. Moreover, the numbers of hours that employees were expected to put in created problems away from the job. "It reminds me of a cult the way they program you to devote your life to Nordstrom," noted Cheri Validi, a four-year salesperson in women's clothing. Some employees felt deprived by their work requirements of basic needs like sleep and nutrition. Lori Lucas, who developed an ulcer while working for Nordstrom said, "I'd be up til 3 A.M. doing my letters and doing my manager's books. Before you know it, your whole life is Nordstrom. But you couldn't complain because . . . the next thing you know, you're out the door."

Pressure at Nordstrom reportedly extended into such areas as dress and demeanor. Becoming a Nordie involved getting "a certain look," and managers were said to have strong-armed new salesclerks into purchasing expensive new wardrobes—all from Nordstrom. Management was also accused of using "Secret Shoppers"—people dressed to look like customers—to determine whether salespersons were smiling enough.

According to employees, the atmosphere at Nordstrom created a cut-throat mentality. Some salespeople engaged in "sharking" activities. They might hog the cash register, taking all the "walk-up" business for themselves. Or they would cut deals with temporary, non-commission salespeople, getting the latter to generate false sales records. Some even went so far as to use rival employees' ID numbers when customers returned merchandise.

In early 1990, workers' complaints began to have severe negative consequences for Nordstrom. First, tips from disgruntled workers led to an investigation by the Washington State Department of Labor and Industry. The investigation found that the firm had systematically violated state law by failing to pay employees for a variety of off-the-clock duties. The agency ordered Nordstrom to pay back wages—as much as $30 to $40 million—or face legal action.

Lawsuits brought by individuals also cost the firm large sums of money. Cindy Nelson was fired reportedly because five of her coworkers accused her of sharking. She sued for "wrongful discharge" and "failure to receive due process," and a King County Superior Court jury made Nordstrom offer her a $180,000 award for damages.

All of these developments led to a deterioration in the firm's image, and Nordstrom stock tumbled $3.25 (from roughly $33.00 to $29.75) in one week alone. Profits fell too. In fact, for 1989, the firm reported a decline in profits for the first time since it went public in 1971.[1]

[1] S. C. Faludi, "At Nordstrom Stores, Service Comes First— But At a Price," *Wall Street Journal*, February 20, 1990, p. 1.

Because most organizations are not in the job-satisfaction business, it is sometimes difficult to make employers see the importance of recognizing workers' attitudes and feelings about their work. Establishing this recognition is made more difficult by research that fails to support a clear relationship between job satisfaction and job performance.[2] Working in organizations has several important effects on organizational members that cannot be overlooked—even by those interested only in financial profits. Some managers who would not think of failing to maintain their physical equipment and resources give little thought to their human resources, and the consequences can be disastrous.

This chapter focuses on the attitudes and emotions that people experience in the workplace. We will start by defining job satisfaction and job stress, and we will then show how cognitive appraisal theory ties these two constructs together. Then, to convince you of the importance of attitudes and emotions at work, we will examine the consequences of dissatisfaction and stress. We will examine the cost of such problems both in human terms and in terms of dollars and cents. Next, we will review the major sources of dissatisfaction and stress in work environments. Finally, we will discuss methods and techniques to eliminate dissatisfaction and stress or to help employees cope with these unpleasant phenomena.

DIAGNOSTIC ISSUES

As in preceding chapters, the diagnostic model calls attention to a host of important issues in the area of job satisfaction and job stress. Can we *describe* the kinds of situations in which people experience too much stress? Are there common symptoms that tell us when people may be having problems with stress? How can we *diagnose* why some people seem quite satisfied with their work while others seem dissatisfied? What explains the fact that some workers are generally satisfied but others aren't, no matter what kinds of jobs they hold? How can we explain why some jobs that seem quite simple to perform actually cause high levels of dissatisfaction and stress?

Can we *prescribe* which individuals should be assigned to jobs that are stress-inducing and which individuals should not? Are there measures of job satisfaction that can help predict rates of absenteeism and turnover? Finally, what *actions* can managers take to eliminate dissatisfaction and stress? If they can't remove all the stressful aspects of a job, what can they do to help people cope with stress? What can employees do for themselves, when away from work to cope with work-related stress?

DEFINING SATISFACTION AND STRESS

Satisfaction and stress are closely related but separate concepts. In this chapter, we will show what they have in common as well as what is unique to each.

Satisfaction

job satisfaction The perception that one's job enables one to fulfill important job values.

Job satisfaction is a pleasurable feeling that "results from the perception that one's job fulfills or allows for the fulfillment of one's important job values."[3] There

---

[2] M. T. Iaffaldono and P. M. Muchinsky, "Job Satisfaction and Job Performance: A Meta-Analysis," *Psychological Bulletin* 97 (1985), 251–73.

[3] E. A. Locke, "The Nature and Causes of Job Dissatisfaction," in *Handbook of Industrial/Organizational Psychology*, ed. M. D. Dunnette (Chicago: Rand McNally, 1976), pp. 901–69.

is a considerable amount of research on the topic. Reviewing this literature in 1976, Edwin Locke estimated that there were over 3,000 articles or studies dealing with job satisfaction. More recent reviews show that this interest is still alive and well.[4]

Key Components. There are three key components of our definition of job satisfaction: values, importance of values, and perception. First, job satisfaction is a function of values. In his 1976 review, Locke defined *values* as "what a person consciously or unconsciously desires to obtain."[5]

Locke, however, distinguished between values and needs. Needs, he said, are best thought of as "objective requirements" of the body that are essential for maintaining life, such as the needs for oxygen and for water. Values, on the other hand, are "subjective requirements" that exist in the person's mind. Needs are innate, and all people have the same needs. People learn values, however, and thus their values differ widely. As you can see, Locke's values include many of the higher-order needs we discussed in Chapter 7, such as the need for self-actualization.

The second important component of our job satisfaction is *importance*. People differ not only in the values they hold but in the importance they place on those values, and these differences are critical in determining the degree of their job satisfaction. One person may value job security above all else. Another may be most concerned with the opportunity to travel. Yet another person may be most interested in doing work that is fun or that helps others.

The last important component of our definition of job satisfaction is *perception*. Satisfaction is based on our perception of the present situation and our values. That is, will the job help me obtain what I want? Remember that perceptions may not be completely accurate reflections of objective reality. When they are not, we must look at the person's perception of the situation—not the actual situation—to understand her reactions.

Thus the three components of values, importance, and perception help us define job satisfaction. A person will be satisfied with a job when her *perception* of what the job offers exceeds her values, and the more *important* those values are to her the more intense her satisfaction will be.

Conceptualizing job satisfaction in terms of the value-perception-importance triad reveals the many different ways that people can become satisfied or dissatisfied with work. Table 8-1 shows three sets of examples. In the first example, Bill and Susan, both of whom work on the same job and perceive the job in the same way, wind up having different levels of satisfaction. That's because they have different values and place importance on different things. The second example pairs Bill with Sherry, who works on a different job. Although both these people share the same values and importance ratings, their jobs make their perceptions different and thus they have different levels of satisfaction. Finally, in the third example, we compare two people who differ on all three dimensions but are equally satisfied in their work.

Measuring Job Satisfaction. Most attempts to measure workers' satisfaction levels rely on self-reports. Some measures, like the Job Descriptive Index (JDI), emphasize aspects of work, such as pay, work itself, supervision, coworkers. Other measures, like the Faces Scale, emphasize overall satisfaction. Table 8-2 shows several items from these two measures.

[4] M. T. Iaffaldono and P. M. Muchinsky, "Job Satisfaction and Job Performance."
[5] Locke, "Job Dissatisfaction."

T A B L E 8-1
Hypothetical Examples of Varying Levels of Satisfaction

EXAMPLE 1	PERCEPTION	VALUE	IMPORTANCE	SATISFACTION
Bill	Job provides opportunity to travel.	Likes to travel.	Considered important.	Very satisfied.
Susan	Job provides opportunity to travel.	Dislikes travel.	Considered unimportant.	Not satisfied.
EXAMPLE 2				
Bill	Job provides opportunity to travel.	Likes to travel.	Considered important.	Very satisfied.
Sherry	Job does not allow one to travel.	Likes to travel.	Considered important.	Not satisfied.
EXAMPLE 3				
Bill	Job provides opportunity to travel.	Likes to travel.	Considered important.	Very satisfied.
John	Job provides high job security.	Likes high job security.	Considered important.	Very satisfied.

The JDI and the Faces Scale are useful measures for the manager who wants to assess the satisfaction levels of all his employees. They are easy to use across the board because the JDI requires minimal reading skills and the Faces Scale requires none. The tests' reliability and validity have been supported by many studies.[6] Because there is a wealth of data on the use of these measures, it is easy to compare their results in one firm with their results at another.

Stress

The term stress has been used widely and with varying meanings over the years. Indeed, researchers and practitioners alike have lamented the imprecision with which this term is used.[7] We will adopt the definition provided by Joseph McGrath, a leading researcher in this area, who defined **stress** as an unpleasurable emotional state resulting from the perception that a situational demand one feels it is important to meet exceeds one's capacity. As in the case of satisfaction, we will find it easier to understand the nature of stress if we break this definition into three key components. We'll look first at perception of the demand, then at importance, and finally at perception of one's capacity.

The first component, *perception of the demand*, emphasizes that stress involves the interaction between the person and his environment. It is the person's perception that something is happening "out there," not objective reality, that creates

stress An unpleasurable emotional state resulting from the perception that a situational demand exceeds one's capacity and that it is very important to meet the demand.

[6] S. M. Johnson, P. C. Smith and C. M. Tucker, "Response Format of the Job Descriptive Index: Assessment of Reliability and Validity by the Multitrait-Multimethod Matrix," *Journal of Applied Psychology* 67 (1982), 500–505.

[7] R. L. Kahn, "Some Propositions toward a Researchable Conceptualization of Stress," in *Social and Psychological Factors in Stress*, ed. J. E. McGrath (New York: Holt, Rinehart & Winston, 1970), pp. 19–37.

T A B L E 8-2
Examples of Items Taken from Various Measures of Organizational Attitudes

JOB SATISFACTION FROM THE JOB DESCRIPTIVE INDEX

Pay	Work Itself	Supervision	Coworkers	Response (Circle One)
Income adequate for personal expenses	Fascinating	Hard to please	Slow	Yes ? No
Satisfactory pay levels	Boring	Asks my advice	Talks too much	Yes ? No
Less than I deserve	Routine	Annoying	Unpleasant	Yes ? No
Underpaid	Challenging	Quick tempered	Loyal	Yes ? No
Income provides for luxuries	Endless	Stubborn	Smart	Yes ? No

JOB SATISFACTION FROM THE FACES SCALE

Consider all aspects of your job. Circle the face which best describes your feelings about your job in general.

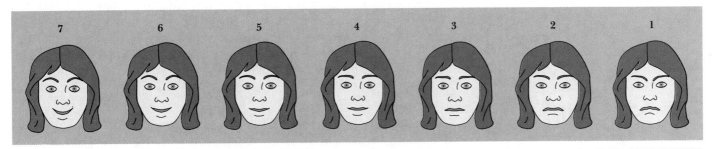

The faces were created by R. B. Dunham and J. B. Herman and published in the *Journal of Applied Psychology, 60,* 629–631, copyright 1975 by the American Psychological Association. Reprinted with permission of the publisher and authors.

the potential for stress. For example, unfounded rumors about a factory closing will create stress, even though no real threat exists. On the other hand, if management actually is planning to close a factory but keeps its meetings to discuss its plan secret, workers will experience no stress.

The second component, *importance*, is critical for the same reason it is critical to our definition of satisfaction. Unless a demand threatens some important value, it will not cause stress. The rumored plant closing may not create stress for a worker who is about to retire in two weeks. Interestingly, a demand need not be perceived as negative as to create stress. Stress can also be associated with demands that have positive consequences (i.e., opportunities). This kind of stress is sometimes referred to as **eustress**. A manager notified that she is being considered for a promotion is likely to feel more stressed than she did before she learned of the opportunity. Even if she knows that at worst, she will be right where she is now, the possibility of failing to secure a potential gain can invoke stress.

Finally, the third component, *perception of one's capacity to meet the demand*, highlights the notion that the person must interpret the demand in terms of his perceived ability to handle it. Clearly, if a person perceives that he can cope easily with a demand, he feels no stress. But what if the person is overwhelmed by the demand, seeing no possible chance that he can meet it? If we assume that his stress will be very high we will be wrong. Research shows that stress is actually highest when the perceived difficulty of the demand closely matches the person's perceived capacity to meet the demand. The reason is that as the difficulty level and the ability level get closer and closer, the outcome becomes increasingly uncertain. It is this uncertainty that creates the stress, not the fear of a negative outcome.

eustress A particular kind of stress created when an individual is confronted with an opportunity.

Perhaps one of the best examples of this process can be seen in McGrath's research with baseball teams.[8] In these studies, researchers measured the stress levels of members of teams rated both "good" and "poor" before and during games. When were the players most stressed? You might think that stress would be high for members of poor teams matched against good teams because the former would be afraid of losing. But that is not what happened. In this situation there was very little uncertainty about the outcome and neither side showed much stress. The poor teams knew they couldn't beat the good teams and were resigned to their fate. On the other hand, poor teams showed a great deal of stress when they played other poor teams. Here the level of uncertainty was high. They didn't know what the outcome might be. Similarly, good teams showed signs of high stress only when playing other good teams.

The same types of relationships were found for individual players. Stress measures taken in the "on-deck" circle (the place where the next batter waits), indicated that stress was highest when the batter and the pitcher were equal in ability. Poor hitters showed very little stress when facing excellent pitchers. These same hitters, however, showed high levels of stress when confronted with poor pitchers. Thus it seems quite clear that stress is as much a product of uncertainty of outcome as it is of the outcome itself.

Cognitive Appraisal Theory

Cognitive appraisal theory provides a useful framework for integrating the two similar yet different constructs of satisfaction and stress. This theory is also valuable because it shows how each of these emotions is linked to physiological, cognitive, and behavioral outcomes. In the next three sections, we will overview cognitive appraisal theory and show how it distinguishes satisfaction from stress and relates these concepts to each other. We will also show how the theory relates these emotions to physiological, cognitive, and behavioral responses.

Overview of Cognitive Appraisal Theory. In Chapter 5, we saw how important perception is in determining peoples' understanding of objective reality. As we have seen in this chapter, perceptions are key components in our definitions of satisfaction and stress. Two leading psychologists, Arnold and Lazarus have emphasized the role of perception in the formation of emotional reactions.[9] The cognitive appraisal theory of satisfaction and stress summarized in Figure 8-1 is based on the work of these two researchers. As we will see, cognitive appraisal theory emphasizes the interplay between cognitive, emotional, behavioral, and physiological responses. It highlights emotions like satisfaction and stress as complex, mind-body interactions.

The first step shown in Figure 8-1 is *perception*. The person perceives a demand in the external environment. In the next step, of **primary appraisal**, the person judges whether the demand is good or bad, an opportunity or a threat. A positive appraisal will lead to *satisfaction*, and processing will stop. But a negative appraisal will lead to *dissatisfaction*, an unpleasant state that the person wants to escape. He will then make a **secondary appraisal**, in which he assesses his *ability to cope* with the environmental demand. If he judges himself able to cope and succeeds in doing so, the appraisal process stops. If the person is uncertain about

primary appraisal In cognitive appraisal theory, the first stage in a person's assessment of the environment in which she judges whether some object in the environment is good or bad, beneficial or harmful, an opportunity or a threat.

secondary appraisal In cognitive appraisal theory, the second stage in a person's assessment of the environment in which he judges his capacity to cope with perceived threats or opportunities in the environment.

[8] J. E. McGrath, "Stress and Behavior in Organizations," in *Handbook of Industrial/Organizational Psychology*, pp. 1315–73.

[9] M. B. Arnold, *Emotion and Personality* (New York: Columbia University Press, 1960); and R. S. Lazarus, "Emotions and Adaptation: Conceptual and Empirical Relations," in *Nebraska Symposium on Motivation*, ed. W. J. Arnold (Lincoln: University of Nebraska Press, 1968).

248

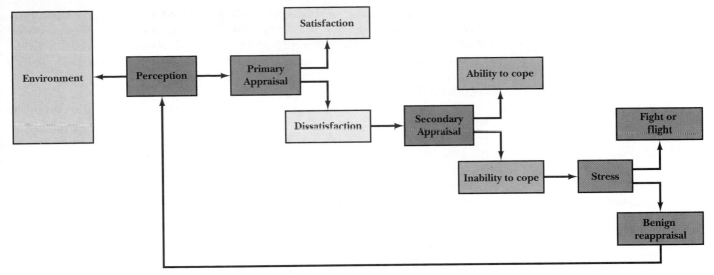

FIGURE 8-1

Satisfaction and Stress in the Cognitive Appraisal Theory of Emotion

fight or flight response A response to stress in which a person confronts and overcomes a stressful demand or escapes it by leaving the scene.

benign reappraisal A response to stress in which the person reassesses an apparently threatening environmental demand and modifies his original perception of it.

his *ability to cope*, however, he will experience *stress*. Stress is even more unpleasant than dissatisfaction, and to get rid of it the person will try to eliminate the environmental demand. In primarily behavioral actions, he can **fight**, or remove the stressor (e.g., a manager can fire an insubordinate employee), or he can take **flight**, simply leaving the scene (e.g., a person can walk away from someone who is annoying her). Alternatively, in **benign appraisal**, a person can use cognitive means to change his goals or values so as to adjust his perception of the environmental demand.

All strong emotions are accompanied by some sort of physiological response. A student who's just been admitted to her first-choice medical school may feel her heart racing as she sprints to the phone to call her family. In general, however, it is the negative emotions that are accompanied by the most intense physiological reactions. As we will see, it is particularly important to understand the relations between such reactions and our experience of stress. In our model, this experience reflects a more complex judgment of an environmental demand than do either satisfaction or dissatisfaction. When we feel stressed we are judging not only that a demand is threatening but that we can't deal with it. Our emotional response is also more complex, typically including such unpleasant feelings as anger and fear. In the next three sections, we will explore the links between emotions and physiological response, emotions and cognitive-behavioral responses, and the increasingly common syndrome of job burnout.

Emotions and Physiological Responses: The General Adaptation Syndrome. As Darwin's theory of evolution (see Chapter 4) made clear, there are many similarities between human beings and lower animals. You may not be surprised to learn that at the biological level, the physiological changes that occur in a deer when it realizes a mountain lion is closing in are not very different from the changes that occur in a human being who is similarly threatened.

Indeed, the body's physiological reaction to any threat is an adaptive process that probably once had great survival value. When threatened, the body produces chemicals that cause the blood pressure to rise and that divert the blood from the skin and digestive organs to the muscles. Blood fats are then released to provide a burst of energy and to enhance blood clotting in case of injury. These changes are adaptive in the sense that they ready the person either to physically fight or to flee some threat.[10] Unfortunately, these same physiological changes

[10] D. H. Funkenstein, "The Physiology of Fear and Anger," *Scientific American* 192 (1955), 74–80.

occur today in response to threats regardless of whether increased physical capacity is adaptive. For example, workers who hold jobs with many demands over which they have little control (e.g., middle managers) are three times more likely to suffer from high blood pressure than other workers. The increased physical capacity purchased with high blood pressure is not going to help these workers cope with the demands they face.[11]

When the threat facing the individual is prolonged over time, other changes begin that prepare the body for a long battle. The body begins to conserve resources by retaining water and salts. Extra gastric acid is produced to increase the efficiency of digestion in the absence of blood (which has been diverted away from internal organs). The body begins to act as if it is under seige.[12]

general adaptation syndrome
The theory developed by Hans Selye that the body's response to stress occurs in three distinct stages: alarm, resistance and exhaustion.

Hans Selye, a prominent physician and researcher, developed the theory of the **general adaptation syndrome**, which has been useful in explicating the relationship between stress and physical-physiological or psychosomatic symptoms. According to Selye, the body's reaction to prolonged stress occurs in three stages: alarm. resistance, and exhaustion (see Figure 8-2).

In the first, *alarm stage*, the person identifies the threat. Whether this threat is physical (e.g., a threat of bodily injury) or psychological (e.g., a threat to self-esteem), the same physiological changes ensue. You have probably noticed that people suffering from diverse illnesses often share such common symptoms as headache, fatigue, aching muscles, and loss of appetite.

In the *resistance stage* the organism seems to become resilient to the pressures created by the original stressor. All the symptoms that occurred in the alarm stage disappear, even though the stressor itself is still in place. This resistance seems to be accomplished through increased levels of hormones secreted by the pituitary gland and the adrenal cortex.

If exposure to the threatening stressor continues, the person reaches the *exhaustion stage*, when he can no longer maintain resistance. Pituitary gland and adrenal cortex activity slows down and the person can no longer adapt to the continuing stress. Many of the physiological symptoms that originally appeared

[11] R. Winslow, "Study Uncovers New Evidence Linking Strain on the Job and High Blood Pressure," *Wall Street Journal*, April 11, 1990, p. B18.

[12] D. Foley, "How to Avoid 'the Perfect Day for a Heart Attack,'" *Prevention*, Sept. 6, 1986, pp. 54–58.

FIGURE 8-2

The General Adaptation Syndrome

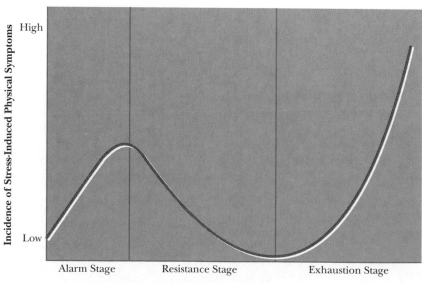

SATISFACTION AND STRESS

Now manager of a franchise owned by ProForma Business Products, Keith Beck left his position as manager of executive placement and development at Mervyn's, a nationwide department store chain because he had "mentally resigned from the company." Burnout in Beck's case came after he was passed over for a promotion and then had to help lay off hundreds of employees when the company, facing intense retailing competition, closed a regional base in Dallas and then fired 600 employees from the company's California headquarters.
Source: "Executive Life," Fortune, December 17, 1990, pp. 52–56.

job burnout A condition of emotional, physical, and mental exhaustion resulting from prolonged exposure to intense, job-related stress.

in the alarm stage now reappear. The stage of exhaustion is rarely reached, and in fact, stress continued beyond the resistance stage can lead to severe physical damage, even to death.

Emotions and Behavioral-Cognitive Responses. Let's look again at the final stage of our cognitive appraisal theory of satisfaction and stress, where the person confronts two basic alternatives. In a primarily behavioral response, she can fight or she can flee from the stressor. Or, in a primarily cognitive response, she can reappraise the situation and modify her original perceptions.

For example, in a fight response, a Nordstrom salesperson who is frightened of losing her job may begin to work 15 hours a day, seven days a week to meet the pressing demands of her sales quota. Or, she may choose a flight response; she may remove herself from the situation by applying for work with another employer. In general, people try behavioral means of eliminating threats first because they actually change an unpleasant environment. In some cases, however, behavioral responses may not be possible. For example, the person may not be able to work any harder or may not have other employment opportunities.

We have called the cognitive mode of response to a threatening stimulus *benign reappraisal* because in this mode the person simply rearranges her values and perceptions. Although the original threat persists, the stress goes away. For example, another Nordstrom employee reappraised the consequences of losing her job: "I remember thinking I'm making less than $20,000 a year, why am I killing myself? Nordstrom was the most unfair place I ever worked."[13] This worker simply reappraised the thought of being fired from Nordstrom and concluded that it might not be that negative after all.

Job Burnout. In some cases, benign reappraisal may be as difficult as fighting or fleeing. One extreme form of job stress has been labeled **job burnout**. Burnout is a condition of emotional, physical, and mental exhaustion resulting from prolonged exposure to intense, job-related stress. The term was coined to refer to a particular pattern of stress development that occurs in the human services sector of the economy.[14] Burnout is prevalent in occupations that require a great deal of contact with people who are in serious need of help. Candidates for burnout include social workers, nurses, teachers, public defenders, doctors, and police officers.

Two defining characteristics of a burned-out worker are a feeling of *low personal accomplishment* from not being able to meet all the needs of the people one serves, and *emotional exhaustion*, which stems from the never-ending demands of those in need. The unique problem faced by human services workers, however, is their inability, in the face of unsuccessful fight-flight responses, to benignly reappraise their situation. It is difficult for a physician trained in the art of healing others to simply dismiss the death of a longtime patient with a "win some, lose some" attitude.

The third and perhaps most revealing characteristic of a burned-out worker is *depersonalization*. In depersonalization the worker begins to treat persons as objects. For example, a doctor may refer to a patient as "the bleeding ulcer in room 305." Depersonalization seems to become particularly pronounced when the person in question feels she is not being supported by colleagues or supervisors.[15]

[13] Ibid.

[14] H. J. Freudenberger, "Staff Burnout," *Journal of Social Issues*, 30 (1974), 159–64.

[15] S. E. Jackson, R. L. Schwab and R. S. Schuler, "Toward an Understanding of the Burnout Phenomenon," *Journal of Applied Psychology* 71 (1986), 630–40; and D. W. Russell, E. Altmaier and V. Van Velzen, "Job-Related Stress, Social Support and Burnout Among Classroom Teachers," *Journal of Applied Psychology* 72 (1987), 269–79.

Stress and Need-Value Conflicts

One last point should be made about cognitive appraisal theory. The model as outlined in Figure 8–1 implies a relatively strong, negative relationship between job satisfaction and job stress. Considerable research has borne out this prediction, and for the most part, it is accurate to say that chronic dissatisfaction leads to stress.[16] Is it ever possible for someone who is basically satisfied with his work to develop stress and stress-related symptoms? The answer is yes.

Earlier we distinguished needs (objective, bodily requirements) from values (subjective, mental desires and wishes). There is usually a close correspondence between one's needs and one's values, but that is not always the case. Pursuing values that are misaligned with needs may lead to momentary satisfaction but ultimately damage a person. Thus an executive who is burning the candle at both ends may love her job but may still feel stressed. Moreover, the job she loves so much could very well make her emotionally sick in the long run. In this example, the value for achieving more and more at work may be at variance with the body's need for nutrition or sleep. Such a person might show symptoms of stress without necessarily feeling dissatisfied with the job itself.

COSTS OF DISSATISFACTION AND STRESS

As we have noted already, because the explicit goals of most firms are financial or consumer oriented rather than worker oriented, it is sometimes difficult to convince managers of the need to monitor and act on problems of dissatisfaction and stress. In this section we will examine the costs, in both financial and human terms, of neglecting this critical area of management.

Health Problems

As we have already seen, work-related attitudes and emotions have a great impact on workers' health and well-being. A fact of organizational life in the 1990s is that employing organizations bear much of the cost for employee health care. A Department of Labor survey, for example, has shown that 96 percent of medium and large firms provide health insurance for all employees.[17] The term *fringe benefit* hardly applies to health insurance today. It is virtually impossible to attract good talent to one's organization if such insurance is not part of the package. Although wages have risen over the last 30 years, the spiraling costs of medical fees of doctors, hospitals, and other health care personnel and facilities have increased the cost of patient insurance three times as much as wage increases.[18]

Besides paying for general health insurance, employers are increasingly finding themselves held liable for specific incidents of stress-related illness. The Occupational Safety and Health Act of 1970 (OSHA) and many state laws hold employing organizations accountable "for all diseases arising out of and in the course of employment."[19] Because research has shown a strong link between stress and mental disorders, it was possible for an overworked advertising ex-

[16] C. Cooper and R. Payne, *Stress at Work* (London: John Wiley, 1978), p. 39.

[17] U.S. Department of Labor, *Employee Benefits 1985* (Washington, D.C.: Chamber of Commerce, 1984).

[18] D. W. Belcher and T. J. Atchison, *Compensation Administration* (Englewood Cliffs, N.J.: Prentice Hall, 1987), p. 57.

[19] *Analysis of Workers' Compensation Laws* (Washington, D.C.: U.S. Chamber of Commerce, 1985), p. 3.

IN PRACTICE

Employer Health Care: Asset or Liability?

It is becoming quite clear that business managers need to do something to bring the rising costs of health care under control. However, the traditional means of cost cutting used by employers is coming under closer scrutiny, and many are now asking whether the cure for high costs might not be worse than the disease.

Typically, to reduce business-related health-care costs firms have hired outside insurers. These insurers build custom-designed health plans in which a selected group of "preferred" doctors work for lower fees. These health maintenance organizations (HMOs) or preferred provider organizations (PPOs) have been effective in the short-term management of costs, but some observers are beginning to question their long-term effectiveness. These observers' concerns center on two issues: employer liability for physician malpractice, and the long-term ineffectiveness of inexpensive treatments for mental health problems.

There has always been a concern that cost cutting through HMOs and PPOs might diminish the quality of health care. The fact, however, that businesses themselves can be held liable for problems arising out of this cost cutting is a recent phenomenon. That is, if the company's health plan is deficient or if a preferred provider engages in malpractice, the company can be sued. Employers are particularly vulnerable when they offer huge discounts to employees who opt for the HMO or PPO and pass on their costs to employees who prefer to stay with plans that allow them to choose their own physicians. The Employee Retirement Income Securities Act of 1974 created a fiduciary responsibility for anyone who offers employee benefits, including health care. The interpretation of this act's provision that the employer must act as a "prudent person" forms the core of many lawsuits against executives who act as fiduciaries in selecting health-care providers.

Two other traditional cost-cutting practices that can lead to trouble deal with utilization reviews and physician incentives. *Utilization review* is a term that really means stingier use of medical care. For example, bed rest at home may be substituted for a long stay in the hospital. If these general rules deny the patient the care he needs, problems arise. For example, in 1986, after Lois Wickline's doctors performed car-diovascular surgery on her leg they advised her to stay in the hospital eight days to recuperate. The state of California's medical program said four was enough. Wickline's leg became infected, however, and subsequently had to be amputated. One state court awarded her $500,000, and another stated bluntly that "third-party payers can be held accountable when cost-limitation programs corrupt medical judgments."*

Physician incentives are programs that give bonuses to doctors contingent upon reducing costs. One way a physician can reduce patient costs is to neglect to refer him to expensive specialists. Here too, where such incentives promote malpractice, those offering the incentives can be held liable.

Traditional cost cutting programs are being attacked from a different angle in the area of mental health. Specifically, some observers are now questioning whether short-term cost-cutting maneuvers may actually increase long-term costs for mental health problems. Treatment for such afflictions as depression, job-related stress, and drug and alcohol abuse account for up to 20 percent of employers' health costs, and that makes these types of treatment a prime target for cost cutters. But a recent study conducted at McDonnell-Douglas indicates that the best financial returns are obtained when people suffering from these kinds of disorders are given the best possible service.

For example, a crucial feature of McDonnell-Douglas's program is the requirement that the whole family be included in any treatment program. In almost all cases, this arrangement results in higher first-year costs, but it turns out to be one of the most important aspects of long-term recovery and cost management. For example, when families were included in chemical dependency treatment programs for McDonnell-Douglas employees, treatment costs were on average $8,400 less in each of the second through the fifth years of treatment than they were for families who were not involved in first-year treatment. For psychiatric patients, the cost difference in follow-up years was $11,000. Thus the message from studies like these is that quality health care and cost-effective health care may not be mutually exclusive alternatives.

* M. Galen, "Are Companies Cutting Too Close to the Bone?" *Business Week*, October 30, 1989, pp. 143–44.

---

ecutive who was the victim of a nervous breakdown to successfully sue his employer.[20] Indeed, stress-induced mental disorders are the fastest rising category of occupational disease, and the number of lawsuits involving organizations and allegedly stress-damaged employees is increasing at a rapid rate.

Studies have also revealed a link between job stress and actual physical disorders like coronary heart disease, which is one of the major causes of death in this country. As employers are held increasingly liable for the onset of this disease and others such as hypertension and ulcer, the financial cost of stress becomes a major problem. As the "In Practice" box indicates, although there is

[20] R. Poe, "Does Your Job Make You Sick?" *Across the Board* 9 (1987), 34–43.

often a tradeoff between employee health benefits and company liability, some companies are finding ways to provide quality health care that are also cost effective.

Absenteeism and Turnover

Dissatisfaction and stress not only create direct costs for organizations in terms of health care programs. They also are the source of indirect costs, most notably in the form of absenteeism and turnover. Dissatisfaction is one of the major reasons for absenteeism, a very costly organizational problem. In the early 1980s, for example, executives at General Motors announced that absenteeism was costing the company a billion dollars every year. Among the 500,000 members of the United Auto Workers (UAW) employed by GM, casual absenteeism—the failure of employees to report to work as scheduled—was 5 percent. Thus on any given day, 25,000 people were absent. With 250 scheduled workdays in a year, this added up to 6,250,000 lost workdays, or 50 million hours. The average wage at GM was roughly $10 an hour plus $5 an hour in fringe benefits that were paid whether or not an employee showed up for work. Each hour lost cost GM $5 in fringe benefits and $15 for a temporary replacement—a total of $20 an hour. Multiply this $20 figure by the 50 million lost hours, and you will see why GM considered casual absenteeism a billion-dollar problem.[21]

Replacing workers who leave the organization voluntarily is also a costly undertaking. One high-tech company, Hewlett-Packard, estimates that the cost of replacing one middle-level manager is $40,000.[22] And replacement costs are not the only issue here. If people who leave an organization are better performers than those who stay, turnover lowers the productivity of the remaining work force. This kind of "negative employee flow" is most likely to affect complex jobs that take a long time to learn.[23] Under these conditions, companies lose the investment they have made in employee development. In the worst cases, disgruntled, experienced employees take jobs with competitors. A company's investment in employee development not only is lost but actually winds up as an investment in a competing firm that gains access to a lot of knowledge of the first firm's operations.

Dissatisfaction is also a major cause of declining organizational commitment. **Organizational commitment** is the degree to which people identify with the organization that employs them. Commitment implies a willingness to put forth a great deal of effort on the organization's behalf and an intention to stay with the organization for a long time.

The subject of organizational commitment has been attracting a great deal of attention of late. Many employers fear that staffing policies they pursued in the 1980s may have killed company loyalty in the 1990s. A decade ago, to cope with ferocious global competition, deregulation, hostile takeovers, and unprecedented levels of corporate debt, many firms were forced to slash labor costs through massive layoffs. According to the Department of Commerce, 4.7 million workers who had held their jobs for more than three years have been dismissed since 1983. For example, in 1989, during one two-month period, Chrysler, Kodak, Campbell's Soup, Sears, and RJR Nabisco let 13,000 workers go. Between 1980 and 1989, General Motors fired over 150,000 workers. As chief economist for the AFL-CIO Rudy Oswald notes, "Workers have a right to be upset and angry.

organizational commitment
Identification with one's employer that includes the willingness to work hard on behalf of the organization and the intention to remain with the organization for an extended period of time.

[21] C. R. Deitsch and D. A. Ditts, "Getting Absent Workers Back on the Job: The Case at General Motors," *Business Horizons* 11 (1981), 52–53.

[22] W. R. Wilhelm, "Helping Workers to Self-Manage Their Careers," *Personnel Administrator* 28 (1983), 83–89.

[23] J. W. Boudreau and C. J. Berger, "Decision-Theoretic Utility Analysis Applied to Employee Separations and Acquisitions," *Journal of Applied Psychology* 70 (1985), 581–619.

They have been bought and sold and have seen their friends and relations fired and laid off in large numbers. There is little bond between employers and workers anymore."[24] Evidence provided by surveys of American workers bolster this claim. When asked, "Compared with ten years ago, are employees today more loyal or less loyal to their companies?" 63 percent said less, and only 22 percent said more. A full 50 percent of those responding said it was likely that they would change employers in the next five years. Thus, just when American businesses are trying to inculcate a new sense of worker participation and involvement, many of their employees are looking to reduce their levels of commitment and dependency.

Sample items from the most frequently used measure of organizational commitment are shown in Table 8-3. Job satisfaction and organizational commitment are positively, but not perfectly, related.[25] A person can be high on one, yet low on the other. For example, professional workers like lawyers, teachers, or journalists are particularly likely to say they love their work, but would be just as happy doing it for one employer as for another.

Performance Failures

Severe levels of stress can affect a person's concentration on his job. At very high levels of stress a person simply stops concentrating on the task and focuses instead on the stress. In jobs requiring attention to detail, performance may suffer as stress goes beyond a tolerable level. Interestingly, very low levels of stress can have similar effects on task concentration. When a job is so undemanding that workers become bored, they are likely to daydream and to focus on nonjob factors, which also lowers performance. The inverted-U relationship between stress and job performance is depicted in Figure 8-3.

Widespread dissatisfaction among a firm's employees can diminish the firm's reputation in the labor market. The best applicants (those with the most ability)

[24] J. Castro, "Where Did All the Gung-Ho Go?" *Time*, September 11, 1989, pp. 52–55.

[25] L. J. Williams and J. T. Hazer, "Antecedents and Consequences of Satisfaction and Commitment on Turnover Models: A Reanalysis Using Structural Equations Modeling," *Journal of Applied Psychology* 71 (1986), 219–27.

TABLE 8-3
Items Measuring Organizational Commitment

I find that my values and this organization's values are very similar.	<u>Agree</u> or Disagree
I am proud to tell others that I work for this organization.	<u>Agree</u> or Disagree
I could just as well be working for a different organization as long as the type of work was similar.	Agree or <u>Disagree</u>
This organization really inspires the very best in me in terms of job performance.	<u>Agree</u> or Disagree
It would take very little change in my present circumstances to cause me to leave this organization.	Agree or <u>Disagree</u>
I am extremely glad that I chose this organization to work for over others I was considering at the time I joined.	<u>Agree</u> or Disagree

Note: Underlined responses indicate a committed employee.
Source: Based on Mowday, Steers, and Porter.

FIGURE 8-3

The Inverted-U Relationship between Stress and Performance

Moderate amounts of stress tend to have an energizing effect. As you can see, performance is generally highest when people are under some degree of pressure. But where there's no stress at all or too much of it performance breaks down, as people become bored and inattentive or completely overwhelmed.

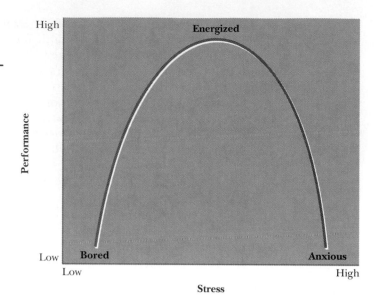

gravitate toward the most desirable employers. Employers perceived as undesirable end up with labor-pool "leftovers." For example, one of the best sources of recruits for an employer in terms of subsequent performance and turnover are *walk-ins*.[26] Walk-ins are people who go out of their way to apply to an organization even though no formal openings have been advertised. These walk-ins usually do their homework and know both the company and themselves very well. This applicant self-selection leads to a good person-organization fit. For similar reasons, another excellent source of recruits is referrals by current, satisfied employees. Thus firms with poor reputations as employers find it difficult, if not impossible, to recruit the best applicants. Indeed, sometimes, the only way such firms can staff their positions is to pay higher wages than the competition. Competition for job applicants will likely become even more intense in the next 20 years, as the United States goes through an impending labor shortage. So few firms can afford to have a bad reputation in the labor pool.

Human Costs

It would be quite unfair to imply that the only reason organizations care about employee attitudes and emotions is their need to save money. Some managers feel morally responsible for maintaining a reasonably high level of satisfaction among workers. One executive has put it this way: "I have over 500 people who spend 60 percent of their waking hours in my plant five, six, sometimes seven days a week, and I don't know how much time traveling to and from work and thinking about their jobs. If they're basically unhappy with their work, that means I'm responsible for one helluva lot of human misery, particularly if they go home and take it out on their families."[27]

Indeed, research has borne out this executive's worst fears. A significant correlation has been found between job stress and domestic violence such as spouse or child abuse. In particular, wife abuse has been related to sex-related

---

[26] P. J. Decker and E. T. Cornelius, "A Note of Recruiting Sources and Job Survival Rates," *Journal of Applied Psychology* 64 (1974), 463–64; and D. P. Schwab, "Recruiting and Organizational Participation," in *Personnel Management*, ed. K. M. Rowland and G. R. Ferris (Boston: Allyn & Bacon, 1982), pp. 103–28.

[27] H. J. Reitz, *Behavior in Organizations* (Homewood, Ill.: Irwin-Dorsey, 1981), p. 202.

status inconsistency. That is, abuse is most likely to occur with underachieving husbands who hold jobs that are lower in socioeconomic status than the jobs held by their wives. Wife abuse is also common among men who have lost their jobs.[28]

Alcohol and drug abuse have also been related to job-induced stress.[29] Thus many employers develop employee assistance programs (EAPs) to help workers with personal problems that have often been triggered or made worse by events or conditions in the workplace. Whether one wishes to approach the topic from a financial or a moral perspective, there is simply no escaping the importance of work attitudes and job-related stress.

Identifying Symptoms of Dissatisfaction and Stress

Because of the varied and important costs associated with employee dissatisfaction and stress, the identification of such problems should be a major part of the job description of every manager. In some cases, employees themselves report problems in these areas. Often, however, employees are afraid to admit that they cannot meet some of the demands their jobs impose on them. Similarly, workers dissatisfied with some facet of their job may censor themselves to avoid sounding like chronic complainers. Finally, the attitudes of some workers may have got so bad that they may see reporting dissatisfaction as a waste of time.

For this reason, it is critical for managers to monitor the kinds of physiological, cognitive, or behavioral responses that we discussed earlier for clues to underlying levels of dissatisfaction and stress. It is also a good idea for managers to be aware of well-known sources of dissatisfaction and stress. As we will see in the next section, many of these sources have been documented empirically by organizational researchers.

SOURCES OF DISSATISFACTION AND STRESS

There are many areas within organizations from which dissatisfaction and stress can arise. According to the conceptual scheme depicted in Figure 8-4, behavior in organizations (*ABC*) can be thought of as the interaction of three separate systems. First, there is the *physical and technological environment* (A) in which behavior takes place. Second, there is the *social environment* (B), or interpersonal relations among organizational members. Third, there is the *person* (C) whose behaviors and reactions are of interest to us.

Dissatisfaction and stress can originate in any of these three systems but more commonly arise in the overlapping areas shown in the figure. The *behavior settings* (AB), where the physical and social environments overlap, are the physical surroundings as they affect workers. Hence, they deal with factors such as crowding or privacy. In the *organization tasks* (AC) person and physical environment come together. The task is simply what the person's job is, that is, his formal function in carrying out the organization's mission. Finally, the *organization role*, (BC), which involves an interaction between the person and the social environment, includes the behavioral expectations that other people in the organization

[28] J. Barling and A. Rosenbloom, "Work Stressors and Wife Abuse," *Journal of Applied Psychology* 71 (1986), 346–50; C. A. Hornung, B. C. McCullough, and T. Sugimoto, "Status Relationships in Marriage: Risk Factors in Spouse Abuse," *Journal of Marriage and Family* 43 (1981), 675–92; and M. A. Straus, R. J. Gelles and S. K. Steinmetz, *Behind Closed Doors* (New York: Anchor, 1981), p. 21.

[29] H. Peyser, "Stress and Alcohol," in *Handbook of Stress*, ed. L. Goldberger and S. Breznitz (New York: Free Press, 1982), pp. 135–171.

FIGURE 8-4

**Sources of Dissatisfaction
and Stress**

*Adapted from J. E. McGrath, "Stress
and Behavior in Organizations," in
Handbook of Industrial/
Organizational Psychology, ed. M. D.
Dunnette (Chicago: Rand McNally,
1976).*

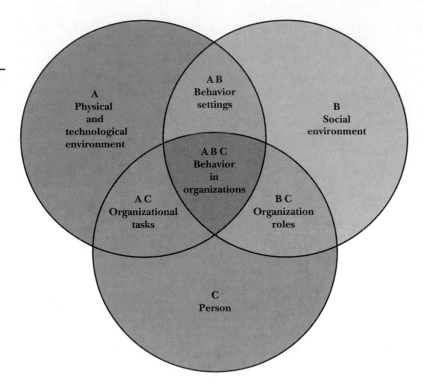

have for the person. These expectations include not only the things specified in the organization's formal definition of the job but many things that are not. For example, a production supervisor's subordinates may come to expect her consistently to show an interest in their families and to advise them on personal problems, even though the supervisor's job description requires her only to deal with problems that arise on the job. Expectations for role behaviors develop gradually. They are subject to negotiation between the person and other organization members who have a stake in how the person performs the job.[30] With this discussion as our framework, let us look more closely at each of the six areas where dissatisfaction and stress can originate.

Physical-Technological Environment

Although the Hawthorne research discussed in Chapter 2 had the effect of moving investigators away from studying the physical environment, we have documented evidence that some physical factors can engender negative emotional reactions in workers. For example, studies have shown that *extremes in temperatures* can affect job attitudes as well as performance and decision making. Research has also shown that there are different optimal *lighting requirements* for different tasks, and perceived darkness has been found to correlate significantly with job dissatisfaction.[31]

[30] D. R. Ilgen and J. R. Hollenbeck, "The Structure of Work: Job Design and Roles," in *Handbook of Industrial/Organizational Psychology*, 2nd ed., ed. M. D. Dunnette (San Diego: Contemporary Psychology Press).

[31] G. B. Meese, M. I. Lewis, D. P. Wyon, and R. Kok, "A Laboratory Study of the Effects of Thermal Stress on the Performance of Factory Workers," *Ergonomics* 27 (1982), 19–43; H. D. Ellis, "The Effect of Cold on Performance of Serial Choice Reaction Time and Various Discrete Tasks," *Human Factors* 24 (1982), 589–98; D. G. Hayward, "Psychological Factors in the Use of Light and Lighting in Buildings," in *Designing for Human Behavior: Architecture and the Behavioral Sciences*, ed. J. Lang, C. Burnette, W. Moleski and D. Vachon (Stroudsburg, Pa.: Dowden, Hutchinson, and Ross, 1974), pp. 120–29; and G. R. Oldham and N. L. Rotchford, "Relationships Between Office Characteristics and Employee Reactions: A Study of the Physical Environment," *Administrative Science Quarterly* 28 (1983), 542–56.

Can sick-building syndrome be prevented or cured? Architectural designer Paul Bierman-Lytle of New Canaan, Connecticut, believes it can, and he searches all over the world for building and decorating materials that are nonhazardous, such as formaldehyde-free plywood from Finland. Bierman-Lytle believes that manufacturers of paint and other materials will eventually develop environmentally safe products, but in the meantime he plans to open a chain of stores that will carry products he has judged safe.
Source: "Environment," Fortune, July 2, 1990, p. 88.

functional attraction Satisfaction with other persons in the workplace that comes about because these other people help one attain valued work outcomes.

entity attraction Satisfaction with other persons in the workplace that comes about because these people share one's fundamental values, attitudes or philosophy.

Moreover, research on how people perceive tasks shows that physical features of the environment such as *cleanliness, working outdoors,* and *health hazards* are very important in the way people perceive their tasks.[32] These factors often have more important effects on attitudes at work than do the more psychologically based factors that we will discuss later.[33] The fact that many jobs are seen as physically unattractive is reflected in the "compensating differentials," or extra pay, that employers must often give to workers who hold such jobs.

More recent research has focused on some very subtle characteristics of the physical environment. In fact, researchers have coined the term *sick building syndrome* to refer to physical structures whose indoor air is contaminated by invisible pollutants. Ironically, as buildings have become better insulated, this syndrome has become more common. With today's office technology, fumes from copier machine liquids, carbonless paper, paint, rugs, synthetic draperies, wall paneling, and cleaning solvents are held in a building's inside air and endlessly recycled. In addition, to conserve energy, many firms turn off air conditioning and heating systems on weekends. The stagnant air provides fertile breeding grounds for mold and bacteria, which are spewed forth into the work area come Monday morning.

Sometimes problems like these get so bad that workers take matters into their own hands. In June of 1988, 70 workers picketed the headquarters of the Environmental Protection Agency in Washington, charging that the air inside the building was so contaminated that it caused burning eyes, fatigue, dizziness, and breathing difficulty. In California, one worker won $600,000 in a lawsuit that claimed that formaldehyde fumes in a new office building caused him to lose consciousness and suffer permanent brain damage. Restoring the air purity in contaminated structures can be costly. At the Veterinary Teaching Hospital at the University of Florida, for example, it cost $6 million to clean up a brand-new building that cost only $10 million to build.[34]

Social Environment

Two primary sets of people in the organization serve as potential sources of satisfaction or frustration for the employee: supervisors and coworkers. There are two major ways in which these people can engender positive or negative reactions in a worker. First, the employee may be satisfied with her supervisor or coworkers because these people help her attain some valued outcome. This attitude is referred to as **functional attraction.**

On the other hand, a person may also be attracted to others because their values, attitudes, or philosophy are fundamentally similar to his. This attraction is referred to as **entity attraction.** The fact that people can make such a distinction is evident when people say they like their manager as a supervisor but not as a person. The greatest degree of satisfaction with supervisors and coworkers will be found where both kinds of attraction are at work. Thus, many organizations try to foster a culture of shared values among employees. We will discuss organizational culture in Chapter 18. For now we will simply note that although generating a strong unitary culture throughout an entire organization is difficult, significant increases in satisfaction can be achieved even if only direct supervisors and subordinates come to share some values.[35] Managers must take care, however,

[32] E. F. Stone and H. G. Gueutal, "An Empirical Derivation of the Dimensions along Which Characteristics of Jobs are Perceived," *Academy of Management Journal* 28 (1985), 376–96.

[33] S. J. Zacarro and E. F. Stone, "Incremental Validity of an Empirically Based Measure of Job Characteristics," *Journal of Applied Psychology* 73 (1988), 245–52.

[34] A. Toufexis, "Got That Stuffy, Run-Down Feeling," *Time,* June 6, 1988, p.

[35] B. M. Meglino, E. C. Ravlin, and C. L. Adkins, "A Work Values Approach to Corporate Culture: A Field Test of the Value Congruence Process and Its Relationship to Individual Outcomes," *Journal of Applied Psychology* 74 (1989), 424–33.

lest workers think that management is encouraging the development of entity attraction among a firm's employees simply because it wants something from them.

Social support is the active provision to a person, by other people in her environment, of sympathy and caring. Many writers have suggested that social support from supervisors and coworkers can buffer employees from stress. The notion behind **buffering** is illustrated in Figure 8-5 where, as you can see, the presence of people who are supportive can lower the incidence of stress-related symptoms under conditions of high stress. Our evidence for this effect has come largely from research in medical contexts that shows that recovery and rehabilitation from illness proceed better when the patient is surrounded by caring friends and family.[36]

The concept of buffering, however, is somewhat controversial. For example, although one organizational behavior study showed that student nurses who received social support were much better able to perform their jobs in the face of stress than nurses who received little support,[37] a second study found just the opposite. In the latter study, social support actually made the effects of some stressors more powerful.[38] For example, nurses who had strong social support actually found role conflict more stressful than did nurses who lacked social support. This could have been because the nurses' families, friends, and other supporters placed additional role-related demands on them. A third study, this time of workers in the construction industry, found that social support had little effect on stress one way or the other.[39] Despite the conflicting evidence regarding social support as a buffer, one important thing on which all three studies agreed is that social support is an independent predictor of stress and dissatisfaction.

social support A surrounding environment in which people are sympathetic and caring.

buffering The notion that certain positive factors in the person's environment can limit the capacity of other factors to create dissatisfaction and stress.

[36] R. E. Mitchell, A. G. Billings, and R. M. Moos, "Social Support and Well-Being: Implications for Prevention Programs," *Journal of Primary Prevention* 11 (1982), 77–98.

[37] K. R. Parkes, "Occupational Stress Among Student Nurses: A Natural Experiment," *Journal of Applied Psychology* 67 (1982), 784–96.

[38] G. M. Kaufman and T. A. Beerh, "Interactions between Job Stressors and Social Support: Some Counter-Intuitive Results," *Journal of Applied Psychology* 71 (1986), 522–30.

[39] G. C. Ganster, M. R. Fusilier, and B. T. Mayes, "Role of Social Support in the Experience of Stress at Work," *Journal of Applied Psychology* 71 (1986), 102–11.

FIGURE 8-5

How Social Support May Buffer Stress

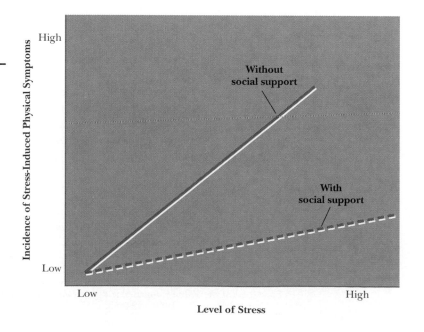

That is, holding type of stressor constant, people receiving support were less stressed and dissatisfied. Social support may be a good thing in and of itself, but it may not be the remedy for stress that many have proposed.

Behavior Settings

Looking again at Figure 8-4 we see that at the intersection of physical and social environments is the behavior setting. Two important and interrelated aspects of the behavior setting are social density and privacy. **Social density** is a measure of crowding. It is calculated by dividing the number of people in a given area by the number of square feet in that area. **Privacy**, on the other hand, is the freedom to work without either observation by others or unnecessary interruption. Research with clerical workers has shown that job satisfaction decreases as social density increases.[40] Moreover, social density is a particular problem when it is compounded by lack of privacy, as when workers' stations are not enclosed by walls or partitions. Research by Greg Oldham and Yitzak Fried found that neither crowding nor lack of partitions alone predicted turnover in university office staff, but when workers were both crowded and without privacy, turnover was exceptionally high.[41]

These findings have significant implications for organizations with **open-office plans**. In the late 1960s, open-office plans enjoyed enormous popularity among design professionals in Western countries. The open-office plan is characterized by an absence of the interior walls and partitions that more conventional designs used to define private work spaces. Typically in open-office plans, all office personnel, from clerks to managers, are located in one large open space. Advocates of this approach hoped that open designs would increase communication and thus improve work efficiency and lower operating costs.

Research on open-office designs suggests that these hopes have gone largely unrealized, primarily because of problems with crowding and lack of privacy. Firms that have moved away from open offices and have returned to more conventional designs have increased work satisfaction either by giving workers more space and thus decreasing social density or by installing partitions and thus providing real privacy.[42] Moreover, crowding and privacy are not the sole issues. Other research shows that the egalitarian nature of open offices leads some employees, particularly managerial and professional staff, to resent the loss of perceived status attached to having a private office.[43]

The Person

Because both stress and dissatisfaction ultimately reside within a person, it is not surprising that many who have studied these outcomes have focused on individual difference variables. The term **negative affectivity**, for example, describes a dimension of subjective distress that includes such unpleasant mood states as

social density An index of crowding, typically calculated as the number of people occupying an area divided by the number of square feet in that area.

privacy The freedom to work unobserved by others and without undue interruption.

open-office plan A physical work environment that minimizes interior walls and partitions.

negative affectivity A person's tendency to often experience feelings of subjective distress such as anger, contempt, disgust, guilt, fear, and nervousness.

[40] R. I. Sutton and A. Rafaeli, "Characteristics of Work Stations as Potential Occupational Stressors," *Academy of Management Journal* 30 (1987), 260–76.

[41] G. R. Oldham and Y. Fried, "Employee Reactions to Workspace Characteristics," *Journal of Applied Psychology* 72 (1987), 75–84.

[42] G. R. Oldham, "Effects of Change in Workspace Partitions and Spatial Density on Employee Reactions: A Quasi-Experiment," *Journal of Applied Psychology* 73 (1988), 253–60.

[43] M. D. Zalesny and R. V. Farace, "Traditional versus Open Offices: A Comparison of Sociotechnical, Social Relations, and Symbolic Meaning Perspectives," *Academy of Management Journal* 30 (1987), 240–59.

anger, contempt, disgust, guilt, fear, and nervousness.[44] Table 8-4 shows some items that are used to assess individual differences on some aspects of negative affectivity.

People who are generally high in negative affectivity tend to focus on both their own negative qualities and those of others. Such people are also more likely to experience significantly higher levels of distress than are individuals who are low on this dimension. Being familiar with the concept of negative affectivity is important for two reasons. First, this notion highlights the fact that some people bring stress and dissatisfaction with them to work. Such people may be relatively dissatisfied regardless of what steps are taken by the organization or the manager. For example, research by Barry Staw and his colleagues showed that degree of negative affectivity in early adolescence predicted overall job satisfaction in adulthood.[45] These investigators also found significant correlations between work attitudes measured over a five-year period even when workers changed employers or occupations.[46] This too points to an underlying personal predisposition to negative affectivity.

Second, negative affectivity influences both a person's perception of a situation (e.g., a task, a supervisor) and her perception of her level of stress. Thus one needs to be cautious in interpreting the relation between situation and stress when both factors are measured by the employee's perceptions. A study by Arthur Brief and his colleagues found that what appeared to be a strong relationship between job stress and health complaints, was in reality quite weak.[47] As Figure

[44] D. Watson, L. A. Clark, and A. Tellegen, "Development and Validation of Brief Measures of Positive and Negative Affect: The PANAS Scales," *Journal of Personality and Social Psychology* 54 (1988), 1063–70.

[45] B. M. Staw, N. E. Bell, and J. A. Clausen, "The Dispositional Approach to Job Attitudes: A Lifetime Longitudinal Test," *Administrative Science Quarterly* 31 (1986), 56–78.

[46] Staw and J. Ross, "Stability in the Midst of Change: A Dispositional Approach to Job Attitudes," *Journal of Applied Psychology* 70 (1985), 469–80.

[47] A. P. Brief, M. J. Burke, J. M. George, B. S. Robinson, and J. Webster, "Should Negative Affectivity Remain an Unmeasured Variable in the Study of Job Stress," *Journal of Applied Psychology* 73 (1988), 193–200.

TABLE 8-4
Items from a Measure of Negative Affectivity

This scale consists of a number of words that describe different feelings and emotions. Please indicate to what extent you have the following feelings _____ .*

Read each item in the second and third columns and then write the number from the scale in the first column that corresponds to your answer in the space next to that word.

1	**Very slightly or not at all**	_____ interested	_____ irritable
		_____ distressed	_____ alert
		_____ excited	_____ ashamed
2	**A little**	_____ upset	_____ inspired
		_____ strong	_____ nervous
3	**Moderately**	_____ guilty	_____ determined
		_____ scared	_____ attentive
4	**Quite a bit**	_____ hostile	_____ jittery
		_____ enthusiastic	_____ active
5	**Extremely**	_____ proud	_____ afraid

* By filling in the blank with such instructions as "at this moment," "today," or "generally," we can use this scale to measure feeling states at particular times or over different time periods.

FIGURE 8-6

Influence of Negative Affectivity on Both Self-Reports of Stress and Health Complaints

The relation between employees' reports of stress and their reports of health problems is tenuous, as the broken line in B indicates. Negative affectivity, or the tendency to experience frequent feelings of distress, may be the cause of both reported stress and reported health problems.

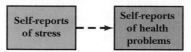

A Apparent Causal Relationship

B Actual Causal Relationship

8-6 indicates, negative affectivity caused both the perceptions of being stressed *and* the health complaints, thus inflating the stressor-health complaint relationship.

Although the origins of negative affectivity are not completely known, interesting research by Richard Arvey suggests that a genetic component may be involved.[48] Arvey studied identical twins who had been separated at birth and reared apart. Thirty-four pairs of such twins were located and assessed on general job satisfaction as well as satisfaction with intrinsic and extrinsic aspects of their jobs. Amazingly, there was a significant correlation between twin pairs' ratings on general satisfaction and intrinsic satisfaction. Despite the fact that these twins were reared apart and were working in different jobs, the work attitudes they expressed were very similar.

A second critical individual-difference variable, one we looked at in Chapter 4, is the Type A behavior pattern. The unrealistic expectations of the impatient, ambitious, and overly aggressive Type A person makes him particularly susceptible to dissatisfaction and stress. This susceptibility may also account for the Type A person's 2-to-1 risk ratio, compared to the Type B person, for developing coronary heart disease. Research suggests that the aggressiveness and hostility of the Type A pattern are its most damaging aspects.[49]

Although the focus of this chapter is on stress induced by the job, one must recognize that stress can originate in events outside of work. This nonjob-related stress cannot simply be turned off when people enter the plant gates or office doors. Table 8-5 presents a list of various life-change events that are sources of stress. On this scale, 100 represents the most stressful event, and 11 the least stressful. Typically, subjects are asked to check off any event that has occurred in their lives in the preceding 12 months and to sum the corresponding values. In one of the original studies using this scale, people with scores between 0 and 150 usually reported good health in the year that followed. People who scored over 300, however, had a 70 percent chance of contracting a major illness the following year. It must be admitted that subsequent research has not always documented strong relations between scores on this scale and subsequent illness.

[48] R. D. Arvey, T. J. Bouchard, N. L. Segal, and L. M. Abraham, "Job Satisfaction: Genetic and Environmental Components," *Journal of Applied Psychology* 74 (1989), 187–93.

[49] R. B. Williams, "Type A Behavior Pattern and Coronary Heart Disease: Something Old and Something New," *Behavioral Medicine Update* 6 (1984), 29–33.

T A B L E 8-5
The Stress-Inducing Impact of Some Work and Nonwork Related Events

LIFE EVENT	SCALE VALUE	LIFE EVENT	SCALE VALUE
Death of spouse	100	Change in responsibilities at work	29
Divorce	73	Son or daughter leaving home	29
Marital separation	65	Trouble with in-laws	29
Jail term	63	Outstanding personal achievement	28
Death of a close family member	63	Spouse begins or stops work	26
Major personal injury or illness	53	Begin or end school	26
Marriage	50	Change in living conditions	25
Fired from work	47	Revision of personal habits	24
Marital reconciliation	45	Trouble with boss	23
Retirement	45	Change in work hours or conditions	20
Major change in health of family		Change in residence	20
member	44	Change in schools	20
Pregnancy	40	Change in recreation	19
Sex difficulties	39	Change in church activities	19
Gain of a new family member	39	Change in social activities	18
Business readjustment	39	Mortgage or loan less than $10,000	17
Change in financial state	38	Change in sleeping habits	16
Death of a close friend	37	Change in number of family	
Change to a different line of work	36	get-togethers	15
Change in number of arguments		Change in eating habits	15
with spouse	35	Vacation	13
Mortgage over $10,000	31	Christmas	12
Foreclosure of mortgage or loan	30	Minor violations of the law	11

Source: L. O. Ruch and T. H. Holmes, "Scaling of Life Change: Comparison of Direct and Indirect Methods,"
Journal of Psychosomatic Research (June 1971), p. 213.

Moreover, some hardy individuals can experience a whole host of these life events without showing any signs of stress.[50] Interestingly, as you have probably noticed, the life event scale lists a number of events that seem quite positive, such as marriage, vacation, and outstanding personal achievement. Why do you suppose such events cause stress?

Organizational Tasks

In spite of the influence of dispositional levels, nothing predicts a person's level of satisfaction or stress better than the nature of her job.[51] Table 8-6 shows a list of some of the most and least stressful jobs. Innumerable aspects of tasks have been linked to dissatisfaction and stress. Moreover, as you will see in Chapter 14, some elaborate theories relating task characteristics to worker reactions have been formulated and extensively tested. In general, the key factors that determine satisfaction and stress are task complexity, physical strain, and task meaningfulness.

[50] T. H. Holmes and R. H. Rahe, "The Social Readjustment Rating Scale," *Journal of Psychosomatic Research* 40 (1967), 213– 18; D. V. Perkins, "The Assessment of Stress Using Life Change Scales," in *Handbook of Stress*, ed. L. Goldberger and S. Breznitz (New York: Free Press, 1982), pp. 320–31; and S. C. Kobasa, "Stressful Life Events, Personality, and Health: An Inquiry into Hardiness," *Journal of Personality and Social Psychology* 35 (1983), 1–11.

[51] B. A. Gerhart, "How Important Are Dispositional Factors as Determinants of Job Satisfaction? Implications for Job Design and Other Personnel Programs," *Journal of Applied Psychology* 72 (1987), 493–502.

TABLE 8-6	
Jobs Characterized as High and Low in Stress	
HIGH-STRESS JOBS	**LOW-STRESS JOBS**
Manager	Farm laborer
Foreman	Craft worker
Nurse	Stock handler
Waitress	College professor
Air traffic controller	Heavy-equipment operator

Task Complexity. Although some tasks are too complex, it is very common to find a strong positive relationship between *task complexity* and satisfaction. The boredom generated by simple, repetitive jobs that are not mentally challenging leads to frustration for the worker. This frustration manifests itself in the form of dissatisfaction, stress and, ultimately, tardiness, absenteeism, and turnover.[52]

Boredom created by lack of task complexity can also hinder performance on certain types of jobs. For example, airport security personnel, air traffic controllers, operators in nuclear power stations, medical technicians, and inspectors on production floors all belong in a class of jobs that require *vigilance*. Workers on these jobs must continually monitor equipment and be prepared to respond to critical events. However, because such events are so rare these jobs are exceedingly boring, and boredom results in poor concentration. Ultimately, this inattention results in performance breakdowns of often serious dimensions.

For example, in 1985, TWA flight 847 from Athens to Rome was hijacked and forced to land in Beirut, beginning an ordeal that lasted 17 days. The hijackers had been able to pass a dozen hand grenades and handguns through airport security. This performance lapse was attributed by experts to a breakdown in vigilance on the part of security personnel, who up until that day had never personally encountered a smuggling incident.

Interestingly, some research indicates that on tasks requiring vigilance, some of what are typically referred to as "disabilities" can often enhance performance. Some basic research has shown that blind subjects do better than sighted people on auditory vigilance tasks, and that deaf people do better than hearing subjects on visual vigilance tasks. Judging from these results, businesses might serve themselves well by hiring the "disabled" for jobs that entail certain types of vigilance.[53]

The Department of Labor (DOL), which keeps vital statistics on thousands of jobs in the United States, rates all jobs in terms of three dimensions of complexity: interaction with other people, use of data, and actions. Table 8-7 shows the numerical rating system used by the DOL in rating jobs, and Table 8-8 shows some actual DOL ratings of jobs with which you may be familiar. An examination of these two tables should give you a feel for at least one system of defining complexity.

Physical Strain. Another important determinant of work satisfaction is how much physical strain and exertion the job involves.[54] This factor is sometimes overlooked in this age of technology, where much of the physical strain associated with jobs has been removed by automation. Indeed, the very fact that technology

[52] L. W. Porter and R. M. Steers, "Organizational, Work and Personal Factors in Employee Absenteeism and Turnover," *Psychological Bulletin* 80 (1973), 151–76.

[53] J. S. Warm and W. N. Dember, "Awake at the Switch," *Psychology Today*, April 1986, pp. 46–50.

[54] Locke, "Job Dissatisfaction."

TABLE 8-7
U.S. Department of Labor's Rating System for Evaluating Task Complexity*

PEOPLE	DATA	ACTIONS
0 Mentor	0 Synthesize	0 Set up
1 Negotiate	1 Coordinate	1 Precision work
2 Instruct	2 Analyze	2 Operate/Control
3 Supervise	3 Compile	3 Drive
4 Divert	4 Compute	4 Manipulate
5 Persuade	5 Copy	5 Tend
6 Speak/Signal	6 Compare	6 Feed
7 Serve		7 Handle
8 Take instruction		

* Lower numbers indicate greater complexity.

continues to advance highlights the degree to which physical strain is universally considered an undesirable work characteristic. Many jobs, however, can still be characterized as physically demanding.

Task Meaningfulness. Finally, it is also important for the worker to believe that his work has value. The Peace Corps recruits applicants by describing its work as "the toughest job you will ever love." Similar recruiting advertisements for Catholic priests note that "the pay is low but the rewards are infinite." Indeed, there are over one million volunteer workers in the U.S. alone who perform their jobs almost exclusively because of the meaning attached to the work. Some of these jobs are low in complexity and high in physical exertion. People who do them, however, view themselves as performing a worthwhile service. This perception overrides the other two factors and ultimately contributes to high levels of satisfaction.

Organization Roles

organization role The total set of expectations that people who interact with an organizational member have for that person and his performance of his job.

Look back at Figure 8-4. As you can see, the **organization role** occurs at the intersection of the social environment and the person (BC). The person's role in the organization can be defined as the total set of expected behaviors that both the person and other people who make up the social environment have for the

TABLE 8-8
U.S. Department of Labor Ratings of Job Complexity for Some Common Jobs

	PEOPLE	DATA	ACTIONS	AVERAGE RATING
Optometrist	0	1	1	1
Nuclear engineer	6	0	1	2
Psychological counselor	0	1	7	3
Photo journalist	6	0	2	3
Airplane pilot	6	2	2	3
Elementary school teacher	2	2	7	4
Auto mechanic	8	3	1	4
Food concession manager	6	1	7	5
Welder	8	4	2	5
Bicycle assembler	8	2	7	5
Tree pruner	8	6	4	6
Ticket taker	8	6	7	7

role incumbent.[55] As we noted earlier, these behaviors include all the formal aspects of the job as well as the expectations of coworkers, supervisors, clients, or customers. These expectations have a great impact on how the person responds to the work. Three of the most researched aspects of roles are role ambiguity, role conflict, and role scope.

role ambiguity Lack of clarity about the expectations of a person's role in an organization.

Role Ambiguity. **Role ambiguity** refers to the level of uncertainty or lack of clarity surrounding expectations about the person's role in the organization. It is an indication that the person in the role does not have enough information about what is expected of her. What should she do? How should she do it? Role ambiguity can also stem from a lack of information about the rewards for performing well and the punishments for failing to do the right thing or for doing things the wrong way. For example, imagine that you were in a class where an instructor assigned a term paper but neglected to tell you (a) what topics were pertinent, (b) how long the paper should be, (c) when it was due, (d) how it would be evaluated, and (e) how much it was worth toward the final course grade. Would you feel stress under these circumstances?

role conflict Conflict or incompatibility between the demands facing a person who occupies a particular role.

Role Conflict. **Role conflict** is the recognition of incompatible or contradictory demands that face the person who occupies the role. Role conflict can occur in many different forms. *Intersender role conflict* occurs when two or more people in the social environment convey mutually exclusive expectations. For example, a middle manager may find that upper management wants severe reprimands for worker absenteeism but that the workers themselves expect consideration of their needs and personal problems.

Intrasender role conflict occurs when one person in the social environment holds two competing expectations. A research assistant for a magazine editor may be asked to write a brief but detailed summary of a complex and lengthy article from another source. In trying to accomplish this task, the assistant may experience considerable distress over what to include and what to leave out of the summary.

A third form of role conflict is called *interrole conflict*. Most of us occupy multiple roles, and the expectations for our different roles may conflict. A parent who has a business trip scheduled during his daughter's first piano recital will feel torn between the demands of two roles.

Finally, *person-role conflict* arises when the role occupant's own expectations for the role conflict with the expectations of others in her role set. For example, a new college instructor who values research but is told to disregard this aspect of his job and to concentrate solely on teaching might experience this type of conflict. Sometimes organizations can avoid such conflict through selection procedures. In fact, some colleges recruit only professors who have little interest in research, actively discouraging research activity.

role scope The total number of expectations that exist for the person occupying a particular role.

Role Scope. **Role scope** refers to the absolute number of expectations that exist for the person occupying the role. In role overload, too many expectations or demands are placed on the role occupant, and in role underload we have the opposite problem. Because researchers have focused primarily on jobs with high role scope, they have tended to look at the negative consequences of jobs that are too challenging. Jobs that are too high in role scope also demand a tremendous amount of time from incumbents, and as you can see from the "Management Issues" box, there is considerable danger in this.

[55] S. E. Jackson and R. S. Schuler, "A Meta-Analysis and Conceptual Critique of Research on Role Ambiguity and Role Conflict in Work Settings," *Organizational Behavior and Human Decision Processes* 36 (1987), 16–78.

INTERNATIONAL OB

Karoshi—*One Japanese Import that Americans May Not Want*

Other than nationality, what do the heads of a major Japanese robotics firm, a large Japanese publishing house, and Japan's leading communications empire have in common? According to the Japanese press, all three died from *karoshi*. To the millions of Japanese upper- and middle-level managers who work in perpetual overdrive, *karoshi* is a well-known term for "death by overwork."* On the average, Japanese managers work over 500 hours more a year than those in West Germany, and over 250 hours more than American managers. Yet just at a time when American firms are importing more and more types of Japanese management practices, the widespread problems with *karoshi*, the dark side of the Japanese economic miracle, seem to question the wisdom of adopting *all* Japanese business practices.

Is *karoshi* being imported into the United States? Surveys seem to indicate yes. In a recent poll, 77 percent of 206 CEOs from the Fortune 500 and Service 500 companies indicated that "large U.S. companies will have to push their managers harder if we are to compete successfully with the Japanese." Moreover, whereas 62 percent of the CEOs agreed that managers are working longer hours today than ten years ago, a whopping 91 percent disagreed with the notion that "companies are pushing managers too hard." Texaco CEO James Kinnear summarized the feelings of the respondents, when he stated that "heads of companies must set objectives and monitor employee performance—and if that leads to longer hours, then so be it!" Winston Wallin, CEO of Medtronics, one of the few dissenters, noted that "executives who work 80 hours a week are not likely to have the breadth of knowledge that they ought to have. Managers are likely to be more creative if they have a little balance in their lives."†

Back in Japan, however, the tide may be turning Wallin's way. The government recently announced a $2 million study of *karoshi*, and some of the major firms are forcing their man-

agers to take time off. The Sony Corporation announced in 1990 that all employees would be required to take a vacation of a week or two, whether they wanted it or not. Moreover, as part of a nationwide drive toward a five-day week, Japanese banks now close down on Saturdays. Of course, old ways die hard, and several prominent institutions have spread the word that employees are expected to make up the lost time by tacking on more hours during the week.

The willingness of the younger Japanese managers to adhere to such expectations, however, is decreasing. Executives say that new hires are shying away from working on Sundays, and that young Japanese managers insist on having time to be with their families. These managers are more likely to agree with the sentiments expressed in a book entitled *Karoshi*—supposedly a set of reflections written in the appointment calendar of an advertising agency executive who died of this syndrome. In one passage, he notes that "people become inured to the ease of a slavelike existence. They are bought by money. They are bound by time. The slaves of the past most likely had time to eat with their own families."

---

* D. E. Sanger, "Tokyo Tries to Find Out if 'Salarymen' Are Working Themselves to Death," *New York Times*, March 19, 1990, p. A8.
† S. Solo, "Stop Whining and Get Back to Work," *Fortune*, March 12, 1990, pp. 49–51.

Assessing the problems that people experience with regard to their roles on the job (see Table 8-9) is only the first step. Getting rid of the sources of stress or finding ways to cope with them is the next task and, as we will see, it is often a challenging one.

ELIMINATING OR COPING WITH DISSATISFACTION AND STRESS

Given the huge direct and indirect costs associated with dissatisfaction and stress in organizations, it is not surprising that a great many ways to deal with stress have been proposed. Some have received more research sup-

TABLE 8-9
Some Items That Measure Role Problems

Role conflict
1. Having to work under conflicting guidelines
2. Having to work with two or more groups of people who expect different things from you
3. Having conflicting demands from people at work
4. Not knowing exactly what your responsibilities are
5. Having to do things you feel should be done differently
6. Being uncertain about how much authority you have

Role ambiguity
7. Not knowing how you must perform to do your work well
8. Being uncertain whether you have divided your time properly between the work you have to do
9. Doing work where you can't always be certain what's expected of you
10. Doing work where it's hard to get all the necessary information, resources, or materials
11. Feeling that you don't have all the necessary skills to do your job well

Role underload
12. Working on tasks that could be done by someone less qualified
13. Doing work that is repetitive or boring
14. Working on things you feel are not absolutely necessary or helpful

Role overload
15. Working under continuous time pressure
16. Working hard to meet deadlines

port than others. The 12 specific approaches we discuss are organized according to whether they attempt to eliminate stress and dissatisfaction at the source or merely deal with the physiological and behavioral symptoms associated with stress. Clearly, interventions aimed at the source are preferable to those aimed only at the symptoms. Because it is not always possible to eliminate stressors, however, research on symptom-based approaches is valuable. Figure 8-7 shows the 12 interventions associated with the stages of the overall dissatisfaction-stress model that constitute their targets: primary appraisal, secondary appraisal, stress, fight-flight, and benign reappraisal.

Targeting the Primary Appraisal

Organizational interventions that aim at the primary appraisal focus on the stressors themselves. These methods attempt to change characteristics of either tasks or roles.

FIGURE 8-7

Stress-Reduction Interventions that Target Stages of the Cognitive Appraisal Theory of Emotion

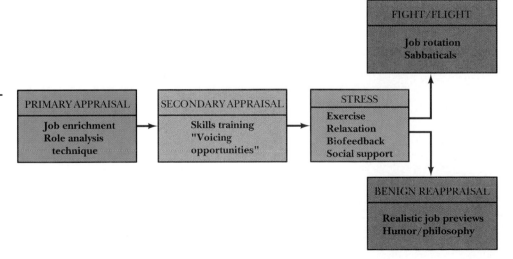

Job enrichment. Because the nature of the task is such a strong influence on dissatisfaction and stress, some of the most effective means of reducing negative reactions to work focus on the task. *Job enrichment* methods include many techniques designed to add complexity and meaning to a person's work. As the term *enrichment* suggests, this kind of intervention is directed at jobs that are boring because of their repetitive nature or low scope. Although enrichment is not universally successful in bringing about improved employee reactions to work, it can be very useful. In Chapter 17 we will discuss a number of job enrichment techniques.

Role Analysis Technique. Role problems rank right behind job problems in creating distress. *Role analysis technique* is designed to clarify role expectations for a jobholder by improving communication between her and her *role set*, or the supervisors, coworkers, subordinates, and other employees with whom she interacts regularly.

In role analysis, both jobholder and role set members are asked to write down their expectations. These people are then gathered together to review their lists. All expectations are written down so that ambiguities can be removed and conflicts identified. Where there are conflicts, the group as a whole tries to decide how these conflicts should be resolved. When this kind of analysis is done throughout an organization, instances of overload and underload may be discovered, and role requirements may be traded off, so that more-balanced roles can be developed. Compared to job enrichment, there has not been a great deal of research on role analysis. What little research there is suggests that this technique may be a useful means for reducing role pressures. We will discuss role analysis technique in greater detail in Chapter 14.

Targeting the Secondary Appraisal

Interventions that target the secondary appraisal aim at teaching the person how to cope with the demands that are creating the stress or dissatisfaction.

Skills Training. The key to the secondary appraisal process is to remove the person's self-doubt about his ability to do what he must to eliminate the stressor. *Skills training* is one way of accomplishing this end. For example, training in time management and goal prioritization has been successful in reducing managers' physiological stress symptoms such as rapid pulse rate and high blood pressure.[56] Subjects in one study first decided on their most important work values. They were then taught how to pinpoint goals, how to identify roadblocks to successful goal accomplishment, and how to seek the collaboration of coworkers in achieving these goals. Other research points to the importance of good job skills in overcoming stress. Lois Tetrick and James LaRocco found that the greater job incumbents' ability to predict, understand, and control events occurring on the job, the less stress they experienced. Moreover, being able to understand and control these events weakened the effect of perceived stress on job satisfaction.[57] Thus increasing a person's management and technical skills increases his capacity for resolving stressful situations.

[56] N. S. Bruning and D. R. Frew, "Effects of Exercise, Relaxation, and Management Skills Training on Physiological Stress Indicators: A Field Experiment," *Journal of Applied Psychology* 72 (1987), 515–21.

[57] L. E. Tetrick and J. M. LaRocca, "Understanding, Prediction and Control as Moderators of the Relationship Between Perceived Stress, Satisfaction and Pyschological Well-Being," *Journal of Applied Psychology* 72 (1987), 538–48.

Voicing and Participating in Decision Making. A person's ability to handle dissatisfying or stressful work experiences is also enhanced when he feels he has an opportunity to air his problems. The formal opportunity to complain to the organization about one's work situation has been referred to as **voice**.[58] Work by Dan Farrell and his colleagues has shown that voicing provides employees with an active, constructive outlet for their work frustrations.[59] Research with nurses shows that the provision of such voice mechanisms as grievance procedures, employee attitude surveys, and question-and-answer sessions between employees and management all lead to better worker attitudes and less turnover.[60]

One step beyond voicing opinions is the chance to take action or make decisions based on one's opinions. *Participation in decision making* (PDM) provides opportunities for workers to provide input into important organizational decisions that involve their work. In a field experiment that randomly assigned subjects to PDM and non-PDM conditions, Susan Jackson found that PDM in the form of bimonthly information-sharing meetings among nursing staff and nursing supervisors resulted in reduced role conflict and ambiguity. In turn there was less emotional stress and absenteeism and fewer nurses resigned. Figure 8-8 depicts the process suggested by this study. Many organizations that use PDM have adopted *quality circles* as an approach to improving productivity and quality of work life. Quality circles (which will be discussed in more detail in Chapter 17) take advantage of the extensive knowledge of a company's operations that lower-level workers have often developed. Typically they are groups of three to thirty workers who meet for about an hour every week or two on company time to discuss production problems or problems with product quality. Although these groups are performance oriented, one hoped-for side effect is the enhancement of employee satisfaction.

voice The formal opportunity to complain to the organization about one's work situation.

Targeting the Symptoms of Stress

In some situations, neither roles, tasks, nor individual capacities can be altered sufficiently to reduce dissatisfaction and stress. Here we must aim our interventions at the symptoms of stress. Although clearly not as desirable as eliminating the stressors themselves, eliminating the symptoms is better than nothing. Some interventions that fall in this category focus exclusively on physiological reactions to stress.

---

[58] A. O. Hirshman, *Exit Voice and Loyalty* (Cambridge, Mass.: Harvard University Press, 1970), p. 51.

[59] D. Farrell, "Exit, Voice, Loyalty and Neglect as Responses to Job Dissatisfaction: A Multidimensional Scaling Study," *Academy of Management Journal* 26 (1983), 596–607.

[60] D. G. Spencer, "Employee Voice and Employee Retention," *Academy of Management Journal* 29 (1986), 488–502.

FIGURE 8-8

How Participation in Decision Making Affects Stress and Withdrawal from Work

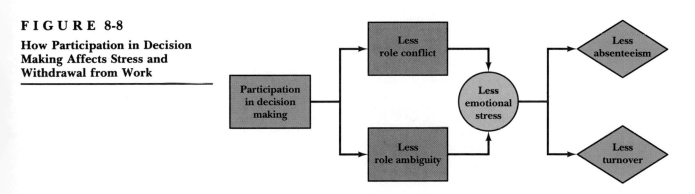

Exercise Programs. Physical conditioning, particularly in the form of *aerobic exercise*, helps make a person more resistant to the physiological changes, such as high blood pressure, that accompany stress reactions. CTI, a Knoxville-based manufacturer of medical equipment, and Southwestern Bell are but two of the many companies that hold aerobic exercise classes for their employees. Other firms organize group hikes and cross-country ski trips. Tenneco, a diversified manufacturing company even provides its employees, free of charge, with a gym that occupies 25,000 square feet. Here one can find basketball and racquetball courts, a workout area, a glass-enclosed running track with piped-in music and $200,000 worth of exercise and body-building equipment. Tenneco chairman, James Ketelsen, feels that the $3 million it takes to run the center is well worth it. He comments: "Our testing process discovered problems that could have been fatal. I'm sure we've saved some lives. How do you put a value on that?"[61] Research strongly supports the fact that this kind of program can be successful in reducing stress-related symptoms.[62] Other programs not only focus on encouraging positive behaviors, like exercise but also aim at discouraging negative behaviors that make the person less resistant to stress, like smoking or over eating.[63] Research by Katherine Parkes shows that both these factors are significantly associated with sickness and absenteeism and increase the negative impact of existing stressors on absenteeism and stress reactions.[64]

Relaxation Programs. Another approach to treating stress symptoms is to employ *relaxation techniques*. When under a severe amount of stress (as when preparing a fight or flight response), many of the body's muscle systems tighten. Relaxation programs focus on eliminating tenseness in most of the major muscle groups, including the hand, forearm, back, neck, face, foot, and ankle. Relaxing all these major muscle groups lowers blood pressure and pulse rate and reduces other physiological stress manifestations. One experiment that dealt with relaxation therapy in a social service agency found that subjects who were randomly assigned to such therapy reported less anxiety than did control subjects.[65]

Some forms of relaxation therapy, such as *meditation*, include mental concentration as well as tension reduction. In one popular form of meditation, transcendental meditation (TM), the person sits comfortably, relaxing all muscle groups, concentrating on a single thought, and repeating a special sound (a *mantra*) for 20 minutes. Advocates of TM have made claims that it can cure everything from physical disease to male-pattern baldness. Although many of these claims must be taken lightly, there is evidence from organizational research that TM can reduce heart rate, blood pressure, and oxygen consumption.[66]

biofeedback A technique that uses machines to monitor bodily functions thought to be involuntary, such as heart beat and blood pressure, so that a person can learn to regulate these functions.

Biofeedback. It was once thought that people had no voluntary control over physiological responses. **Biofeedback** machines that allow a person to monitor her own physiological reactions have changed all that.[67] Indeed, with the right

[61] M. Freudenheim, "Assessing the Corporate Fitness Craze," *New York Times*, March 18, 1990, p. D1.

[62] Bruning and Frew, "Exercise, Training, and Management Skills Training."

[63] K. D. Brownell, A. J. Stunkard, and P. E. McKeon, "Weight Reduction at the Worksite: A Promise Partially Fulfilled," *American Journal of Psychiatry* 142 (1985), 47–52.

[64] K. R. Parkes, "Relative Weight, Smoking and Mental Health as Predictors of Sickness and Absence from Work," *Journal of Applied Psychology* 72 (1987), 275–86.

[65] D. C. Ganster, B. T. Mayes, W. E. Sime, and G. D. Tharp, "Managing Organizational Stress: A Field Experiment," *Journal of Applied Psychology* 67 (1982), 533–42.

[66] D. Kuna, "Meditation at Work," *Vocational Guidance Quarterly* 12 (1975), 342–46.

[67] N. E. Miller, "Learning of Visceral and Glandular Responses," *Science* 163 (1969), 1271–78.

feedback, some people can learn to control brain waves, muscle tension, heart rate, and even body temperature. Biofeedback training teaches people to recognize when these physiological reactions are taking place as well as how to lower the levels of these symptoms when under stress. A biofeedback program set up by Equitable Life Insurance, for example, led to an 80 percent reduction in visits to the company's health center for stress-related problems.[68]

Social Support Groups. Because, as we have seen, a supportive environment can reduce stress, many organizations encourage team sports both at work and in off hours. The hope behind softball and bowling leagues is that group cohesiveness and support for individual group members will be increased through socializing and team effort. Although management certainly cannot ensure that every stressed employee will develop friends, it can make it easier for employees to interact.

Targeting Flight Reactions

Other means of coping with stress that cannot be eliminated at the source focus on flight reactions. (Remember, in the fight reaction the person attacks the source of the stress directly.) These interventions allow a person time away from the stressful environment.

job rotation A process whereby an individual is systematically moved from one job to another over the course of time.

Job Rotation. Does it surprise you to learn that air traffic controllers at Chicago's O'Hare airport are restricted to 90–minute work periods? They are required to rest for a period of time before returning to their stations. Many employers employ **job rotation** in much the same way. Although one may not feel capable of handling the stress or putting up with the dissatisfying aspects of a particular job indefinitely, it is often possible to do so temporarily. Rotation is supported by the resistance stage notion proposed in Selye's general adaptation syndrome, which we discussed earlier. Thus, during the Vietnam War, soldiers would "rotate stateside," or return to the U.S., after a tour of duty lasting for a specified time period. The idea behind this policy was that the stress of combat would be easier to manage if the soldier knew it would be over in the foreseeable future.

Job rotation in more conventional organizations can do even more than simply spread out the stressful aspects of a particular job. It can also increase the complexity of the work and provide valuable cross-training in jobs so that any one person eventually comes to understand many different jobs. This makes for a more flexible work force and increases the workers' appreciation for the other tasks that must get done in order for the organization to complete its mission. We will discuss job rotation and its consequences again in Chapter 17.

Sabbaticals. At the upper executive level, more and more organizations are also providing *sabbaticals*. These are extended periods of time away from work, lasting anywhere from six months to a year. The purpose of these leaves is to reenergize a person and provide a new perspective on life and work that can be achieved only when the whole process is viewed from a distance. The chairman of Apple Computers, John Sculley, took off for six months. Sculley claims that while building a barn he came up with an entirely new vision of the strategic direction his company should take over the next ten years.

[68] J. S. Manuso, "Executive Stress Management," *Personnel Administrator* 24 (1979), 23–26.

Targeting Benign Reappraisal

Finally, there are also interventions that focus on making cognitive adjustments to stressful environments.

Realistic Job Previews. If the negative aspects of a job cannot be changed, managers should be up front with prospective jobholders about the nature of the work. Many companies are hesitant to admit to the undesirable aspects of a job when trying to recruit workers, for fear that nobody will take the job. Fooling someone into taking a job, however, is not good for the company or the person. Similarly, a fancy job title, like executive assistant, for a job that is more accurately described as typist is self-defeating. These practices raise peoples' expectations unjustly. The firm winds up attracting people to the job who would not be at all interested in joining the company if they knew what was truly involved in the work. The ultimate result is increased turnover. *Realistic job previews* (RJPs) lower expectations and are likely to attract workers whose values will more closely match the actual job situation (see also Chapter 14). When these people do go on the job and begin to experience its negative aspects, they are likely to see them as not so bad, saying, "I knew the job was difficult when I took it."

Steve Premack and John Wanous reviewed 21 separate realistic job preview experiments and found that although previews have not been 100 percent effective, there is certainly evidence that they can reduce subsequent turnover. Audiovisual presentations in these previews make them especially useful.[69]

Humor and Philosophical Approaches. Cognitively reappraising a situation through the use of *humor* is also an effective means of making an environment seem less threatening. A number of professional comedians have come from family backgrounds that were filled with stress and uncertainty. Humor for them was a means of diffusing and minimizing such stress.

Humor is also useful for managing one's image. For example, President Reagan had a full-time joke writer, Landon Parvin, on his staff. According to Parvin, for every Reagan speech he would "put together three to six pages of one-liners" that "relied mostly on self-deprecatory humor." Because it was thought that voters might be afraid that the President was too old, his age was the frequent target of Parvin's jokes. For example, speaking to the Washington Press Corps, Reagan noted that the Press Corps was founded in 1919 and quipped, "It feels just like yesterday." When giving a talk to the 105th annual meeting of the American Bar Association, Reagan said, "It isn't true that I attended the first meeting."[70] Obviously, the tactic here is to get people laughing about age, a potentially worrisome issue. If we can laugh about it, how serious an issue can it really be? This is benign reappraisal in its purest form.

Reappraisal can also take the form of changes in one's *personal philosophy* on life. A manager whose career seems to have come to a dead end may simply adopt the stance that "family should come first anyway." By devaluing career goals, he feels less troubled by his inability to accomplish those goals. Indeed, the notion of being born again to a new set of values, whether they be religious or otherwise, is a way of untying oneself from a dissatisfying past life. If this past life brought only dissatisfaction and stress, the substitution of a new set of values can certainly do no harm.

[69] S. L. Premack and J. P. Wanous, "A Meta-Analysis of Realistic Job Preview Experiments," *Journal of Applied Psychology* 70 (1985), 706–19.
[70] E. M. Miller, "Working Hard for the Last Laugh, *Time*, August 15, 1983, p. 16.

SUMMARY

Among the great variety of attitudes and emotions generated in the workplace, the most important constructs are *job satisfaction* and occupational *stress*. Job satisfaction is a pleasurable emotional state resulting from the perception that a job helps one attain valued outcomes. Occupational stress, an unpleasant emotional state, comes from the perceived uncertainty that one can meet the demands of a job when attaining important, valued outcomes is at stake. *Cognitive appraisal theory* is useful in comparing and contrasting these two constructs. Satisfaction is a product of the *primary appraisal*, whereas stress is a product of the *secondary appraisal*. There are multiple responses to stress, including physiological responses (high blood pressure, rapid pulse rates), behavioral responses (e.g., *fight or flight*), and cognitive reactions (e.g., *benign reappraisal*). These stress reactions have important consequences for organizations, particularly in the financial costs of health care, absenteeism and turnover, and performance failure. There are six discrete sources from which dissatisfaction and stress originate: These sources include the *physical-technical environment*, the *social environment*, the *behavior setting*, the *person*, the *organizational task*, and the *organizational role*. A dozen different intervention programs are aimed at eliminating the stress-inducing event, enabling the person to eliminate or cope with the stressor or, failing these efforts, eliminating the symptoms of stress. Some of these are *job enrichment*, *skills training*, *biofeedback*, *job rotation*, and *realistic job previews*.

REVIEW QUESTIONS

1.   Recall from Chapter 2 some of the many roles a manager must play in her organization. Which of these roles do you think create the most stress, and which are probably the least stressful? Which role do you think most managers derive their greatest satisfaction from? Compare your answers to these three questions and speculate on the relationship between satisfaction and stress for managerial employees.

2.   Reexamine the scale of life-change events presented in Table 8–5. Do you think that on a year-to-year basis more stress is created by on-the-job or off-the-job events? Do you think that more stress is generated by positive events or negative events? Can you think of particular years in a person's life when both positive and negative sources of stress are likely to be exceedingly high?

3.   Organizational turnover is generally considered a negative outcome, and many organizations spend a great deal of time, money, and effort trying to reduce turnover. Can you think of any situations where an increase in turnover might be just what an organization needs? What are some steps that organizations might take to enhance functional types of turnover? Do you think mass firings of ineffective workers are likely to enhance overall organization effectiveness, or do you think that they would have deleterious effects on the firm's ability to recruit the most desirable applicants?

4.   We saw in this chapter that characteristics like negative affectivity and the Type A behavior pattern are associated with aversive emotional states including dissatisfaction and stress. Do you think these tendencies are learned, or genetically determined? If these tendencies are learned, from reinforcement theory perspective, what reinforcers might sustain the behaviors associated with these characteristics? Although by their nature these characteristics seem associated with aversive outcomes, from an operant perspective, something must be reinforcing them for them to persist over time.

5.   If off-the-job stress begins to spill over and create on-the-job problems, what do you think are the rights and responsibilities of the manager in helping the employee overcome these problems? If employees are engaged in unhealthy, off-the-job behavior patterns such as smoking, overeating, or alcohol abuse, what

are the rights and responsibilities of the employer to change these behaviors? Are intrusions into such areas an invasion of privacy? Is it a benevolent-paternalistic move on the part of the employer? Or is it simply a prudent financial step taken to protect the firm's investment?

DIAGNOSTIC QUESTIONS

In evaluating an organization to determine where and when dissatisfaction and stress may be problems and how to go about resolving these problems, the following diagnostic questions may prove a useful start.

1. Why might the organization be concerned about dissatisfaction and stress? What costly health-related or behavioral problems linked to stress are evident?

2. Are the values that the organization expects its members to uphold consistent with the members' own values and needs?

3. Are any aspects of the physical environment (such as noise, darkness, hazards) causing stress among organizational members?

4. Are any aspects of the social environment (such as hostile coworkers or supervisors) causing stress among organizational members?

5. Are any aspects of the behavioral settings (such as crowding or lack of privacy) causing stress among organizational members?

6. Do certain characteristics of organization members contribute to stress problems at work (e.g., negative affectivity or the Type A behavior pattern)?

7. How can the jobs that need to be performed by organization members be described in terms of complexity, meaning, and physical demand? How might characteristics of the jobs relate to dissatisfaction and stress?

8. How clear and unambiguous are the role expectations that are being sent to various organization members? How might the ambiguity of some expectations relate to stress?

9. Is the organization most interested in eliminating the sources of stress, or is it willing (or forced) to deal only with stress-related symptoms?

10. How can overly simple jobs in the organization be enriched? How can jobs characterized by too many conflicting role requirements be simplified?

11. Do employees have outlets for registering complaints? Do they have any influence in decisions that affect how they conduct their jobs?

12. What types of programs would be most useful in handling stress-related physiological symptoms that arise in this organization?

EXERCISE 8-1
ROLES: UNDERSTANDING SOURCES
OF STRESS*
Patrick Doyle, St. Lawrence College

All of us fulfill various roles in our lives. Each of these roles is a set of expectations about good or appropriate behaviors that people hold for us because we occupy a specific social position. When people's expectations for us in one of our roles conflict with the way we see ourselves in that role, or when expectations associated with one role conflict with expectations associated with another that we must fulfill, we tend to experience stress.

To reduce stress we must first recognize its causes. In order to do this we must identify the different roles we hold and recognize the expectations associated with each one. Suppose, for example, that you are a student in the business school, and that you are married and have several children. You are treasurer of your school's management club, and you are also a part-time employee in the campus bookstore. All of these roles and the people with expectations about your role performance could be diagrammed as shown in Exhibit 8-1. Starting at the upper left of this diagram, your instructors will expect you to attend class and do your home-

work. Your boss at the bookstore will expect you to be at your job on time and to perform the tasks you are assigned. Your parents will expect you to telephone them occasionally and to do well in school. Your spouse will expect you to be a companion and help support the family. The members of your club will expect you to keep accurate records of club revenues and expenses. And your children will expect you to spend time with them and to show an interest in their activities.

You can imagine potential conflicts among these varying role expectations. One such conflict could be expressed as shown in the illustration at the top of the next page.

Group discussions can often help identify ways of resolving such conflicts. For example, a family discussion might lead to the suggestion that you plan to take part in family activities earlier in the term, when school-

* Adapted from: J. William Pfeiffer, *The 1986 Annual: Developing Human Resources* (San Diego, CA: University Associates, Inc., 1986). Used with permission.

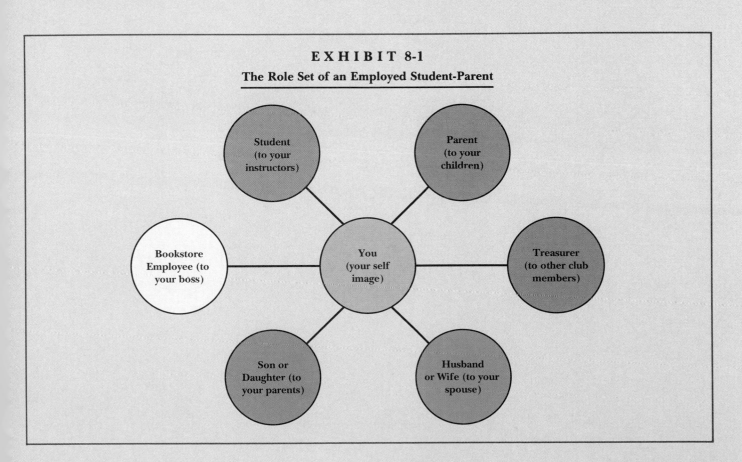

EXHIBIT 8-1

The Role Set of an Employed Student-Parent

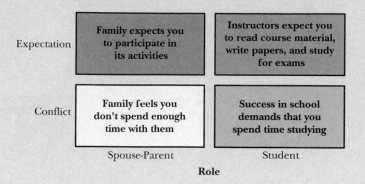

	Spouse-Parent	Student
Expectation	Family expects you to participate in its activities	Instructors expect you to read course material, write papers, and study for exams
Conflict	Family feels you don't spend enough time with them	Success in school demands that you spend time studying

Role

In class you are going to discuss the roles you actually occupy and consider how to reduce any stress that you feel as a result of conflicting role expectations. To prepare for this discussion, begin by completing the Roles Diversity Sheet in Exhibit 8-2. Be sure to identify *at least* four different roles. Next, fill in the Roles Characteristics Sheet in Exhibit 8–3, listing each of the roles you identified in the Role Diversity Sheet and, for each role, identifying the people who provide you with role expectations and the expectations themselves. Then, think about which pairs of expectations you have listed might conflict and list these, one on each side of the top portion of the Role Conflict-Resolution Sheet in Exhibit 8-4. In the bottom portion of the sheet, list any ways you can think of that you might cope with these conflicts or resolve them.

work demands are somewhat lighter, and focus more energy on coursework as the term progresses and you have projects to complete and final exams to take.

Reducing role-related stress requires you not only to identify the causes of stress but to modify role expectations and resolve conflicts among your different roles. This exercise gives you the opportunity to develop these kinds of skills so that you can use them to manage the stress in your life.

STEP TWO: PRE-CLASS PREPARATION

The class should divide into groups of four to six members each (if you formed permanent groups in an earlier

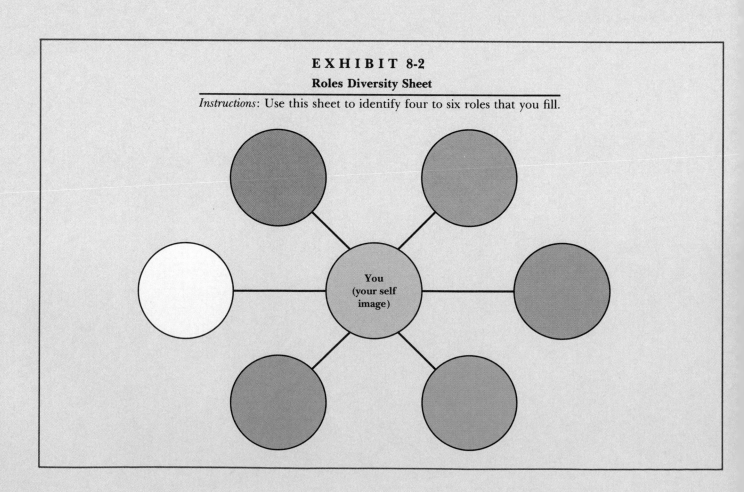

EXHIBIT 8-2

Roles Diversity Sheet

Instructions: Use this sheet to identify four to six roles that you fill.

You
(your self image)

EXHIBIT 8-3
Roles Characteristics Sheet

List the roles you have identified as follows: First, list these roles in descending order, according to how comfortable you feel in them; the most comfortable first, the least comfortable last. Then, for each role, list the people who provide you with expectations for that role and describe those expectations.

ROLES	EXPECTATIONS

EXHIBIT 8-4

Roles Conflict-Resolution Sheet

Given the roles that you have listed, what expectations are likely to conflict?

EXPECTATIONS THAT CONFLICT

What are some potential ways to resolve these conflicts?

POTENTIAL RESOLUTIONS

SATISFACTION AND STRESS

exercise, reassemble in those same groups). Each group member should begin by describing one of the conflicts identified in Step One, being sure to include descriptions of the roles involved, the people holding expectations for those roles, and the expectations themselves.

After every group member has described a conflict, the group should discuss potential ways to reduce the stress caused by each of the conflicts identified. To begin this discussion, members should refer to potential solutions identified during Step One and should provide each other with feedback about those solutions. The group should then search for about additional ways to solve the role conflicts of its members.

If time permits, group members may describe additional conflicts and ask the group to consider how to solve them. Throughout Step Two a spokesperson should take notes and be prepared to summarize the group's discussion for the class as a whole.

STEP THREE: CLASS DISCUSSION

The instructor should convene the entire class. As each group spokesperson summarizes a group's discussion, the instructor should list all role conflicts and potential solutions the group finds acceptable on a blackboard, flipchart, or transparency projector. The class should look for similarities and contrasts among the results of Step Two, being sure to discuss the following questions:

1. What is the most common type of role-related stress experienced by members of this class? The second most common type? The third most common type? What expectations are causing each kind of stress? From whom do these expectations originate?

2. For each type of stress, what seem to be the most effective methods of stress reduction? Did any approaches seem promising initially but fail ultimately to be useful?

3. What kind of support might you need from others around you to implement the stress reduction approaches you've identified? What obstacles stand in your way? What are the benefits of adopting one or more of these approaches? How might they change your life?

CONCLUSION

Stress originating in conflicts among role expectations is ever present in modern organizations and everyday life. It is important, therefore, that you have the skills needed to identify role conflicts and to decide what to do about them. The process of charting roles, recognizing expectations, and identifying potential conflicts and solutions might seem overly complicated and time consuming. However, the costs of failing to deal with role conflict are even greater: prolonged stress can cause severe physical and psychological illness, limiting your ability to lead a satisfying and productive life.

DIAGNOSING ORGANIZATIONAL BEHAVIOR

CASE 8-1
NO RESPONSE FROM MONITOR TWENTY-THREE*
ROBERT D. JOYCE, *Innovative Management*

Loudspeaker: IGNITION MINUS 45 MINUTES.

Paul Keller tripped the sequence switches at control monitor 23 in accordance with the countdown instruction book just to his left. All hydraulic systems were functioning normally in the second stage of the spacecraft booster at checkpoint 1 minus 45. Keller automatically snapped his master control switch to GREEN and knew that his electronic impulse along with hundreds of others from similar consoles within the Cape Kennedy complex signaled continuation of the countdown.

Free momentarily from data input, Keller leaned back in his chair, stretched his arms above his head, and then rubbed the back of his neck. The monitor lights on console 23 glowed routinely.

It used to be an incredible challenge, fantastically interesting work at the very fringe of man's knowledge about himself and his universe. Keller recalled his first day in Brevard County, Florida, with his wife and young daughter. How happy they were that day. Here was the future, the good life . . . forever. And Keller was going to be part of the fantastic, utopian future.

Loudspeaker: IGNITION MINUS 35 MINUTES.

* Reprinted with the publisher's permission from Robert D. Joyce, *Encounters in Organizational Behavior* (New York: Pergamon Press, 1972), pp. 168–72.

Keller panicked! His mind had wandered momentarily, and he lost his place in the countdown instructions. Seconds later he found the correct place and tripped the proper sequence of switches for checkpoint 1 minus 35. No problem. Keller snapped master control to GREEN and wiped his brow. He knew he was late reporting and would hear about it later.

Damn! he thought, I used to know countdown cold for seven systems monitors without countdown instructions. But now . . . you're slipping Keller . . . you're slipping, he thought. Shaking his head, Keller reassured himself that he was overly tired today . . . just tired.

Loudspeaker: IGNITION MINUS 30 MINUTES.

Keller completed the reporting sequence for checkpoint 1 minus 30, took one long last drag on his cigarette, and squashed it out in the crowded ashtray. Utopia! Hell! It was one big rat race and getting bigger all the time. Keller recalled how he once naively felt that his problems with Naomi would disappear after they left Minneapolis and came to the Cape with the space program. Now, 10,000 arguments later, Keller knew that there was no escape.

Only one can of beer left, Naomi? One stinking lousy can of beer, cold lunchmeat, and potato salad? Is that all a man gets after 12 hours of mental exhaustion?

Oh, shut up, Paul! I'm so sick of you playing Mr. Important. You get leftovers because I never know when you're coming home . . . your daughter hardly knows you . . . and you treat us like nobodies . . . incidental to your great personal contribution to the Space Age.

Don't knock it, Naomi. That job is plenty important to me, to the Team, and it gets you everything you've ever wanted . . . more! Between this house and the boat, we're up to our ears in debt.

Now don't try to pin our money problems on me, Paul Keller. You're the one who has to have all the same goodies as the scientists earning twice your salary. Face it, Paul. You're just a button-pushing technician regardless of how fancy a title they give you. You can be replaced, Paul. You can be replaced by any S.O.B. who can read and punch buttons.

Loudspeaker: IGNITION MINUS 25 MINUTES.

A red light blinked ominously indicating a potential hydraulic fluid leak in subsystem seven of stage two. Keller felt his heartbeat and pulse rate increase. Rule 1 . . . report malfunction immediately and stop the count. Keller punched POTENTIAL ABORT on the master control.

Loudspeaker: THE COUNT IS STOPPED AT IGNITION MINUS 24 MINUTES 17 SECONDS.

Keller fumbled with the countdown instructions. Any POTENTIAL ABORT required a cross-check to separate an actual malfunction from sporadic signal error. Keller began to perspire nervously as he initiated standard cross-check procedures.

"Monitor 23, this is Control. Have you got an actual abort, Paul?" The voice in the headset was cool, but impatient, "Decision required in 30 seconds."

"I know, I know," Keller mumbled, "I'm cross-checking right now."

Keller felt the silence closing in around him. Cross-check one proved inconclusive. Keller automatically followed detailed instructions for cross-check two.

"Do you need help, Keller?" asked the voice in the headset.

"No, I'm O.K."

"Decision required," demanded the voice in the headset. "Dependent systems must be deactivated in 15 seconds."

Keller read and reread the console data. It looked like a sporadic error signal . . . the system appeared to be in order.

"Decision required," demanded the voice in the headset.

"Continue count," blurted Keller at last. "Subsystem seven fully operational." Keller slumped back in his chair.

Loudspeaker: THE COUNT IS RESUMED AT IGNITION MINUS 24 MINUTES 17 SECONDS.

Keller knew that within an hour after lift off, Barksdale would call him in for a personal conference. "What's wrong lately, Paul?" he would say. "Is there anything I can help with? You seem so tense lately." But he wouldn't really want to listen. Barksdale was the kind of person who read weakness into any personal problems and demanded that they be purged from the mind the moment his men checked out their consoles.

More likely Barksdale would demand that Keller make endless practice runs on cross-check procedures while he stood nearby . . . watching and noting any errors . . . while the pressure grew and grew.

Today's performance was surely the kiss of death for any wage increase too. That was another of Barksdale's methods of obtaining flawless performance . . . which would surely lead to another scene with Naomi . . . and another sleepless night . . . and more of those nagging stomach pains . . . and yet another imperfect performance for Barksdale.

Loudspeaker: IGNITION MINUS 20 MINUTES.

The monitor lights at console 23 blinked routinely.

"Keller," said the voice in the earphone. "Report, please."

"Control, this is Wallace at monitor 24. I don't believe Keller is feeling well. Better send someone to cover fast!"

Loudspeaker: THE COUNT IS STOPPED AT IGNITION MINUS 19 MINUTES 33 SECONDS.

"This is Control, Wallace. Assistance has been dispatched and the count is on temporary hold. What seems to be wrong with Keller?"

"Control, this is Wallace, I don't know. His eyes are open and fixed on the monitor, but he won't respond to my questions. It could be a seizure or . . . a stroke."

When you have read this case, look back at the chapter's diagnostic questions and choose the ones that apply to the case. Then use those questions with the ones that follow in your case analysis.

1. Explain Paul Keller's behavior at monitor 23. Why did he have trouble remembering and following countdown instructions? Why did he fail to answer Wallace's questions?

2. How were Keller's problems at home related to his behavior at work? Why did he have trouble sleeping? What might explain his stomach pains?

3. What should Barksdale do about Keller and his problems? Can an organization like NASA do anything to identify employees like Paul and to help them cope with their problems before they become serious?

CASE 8-2

CAMERAN MUTUAL INSURANCE COMPANY*

ROBERT J. COX, *Salt Lake Community College*

Cameran Mutual Insurance Company is a large national insurance company that has been in business since the early 1900s. The company is best known for its loss prevention service and for its workers compensation policies. The company also takes pride in personal sales and service to its industrial insurance accounts.

Recently, Mrs. Kay was referred to a local insurance office in Salt Lake City, Utah, where she had applied for a job. She had a college degree in sociology, some business background, five years' experience with public relations-type jobs, and an excellent reputation at her previous jobs for being reliable, dependable, and a hard worker. She was well qualified for the job except

* Reprinted with the author's permission.

for her lack of technical knowledge about the insurance business. However, she typed up a resume and made an appointment for a job interview.

The job interview was long and intense. First, the potential supervisor, Mrs. Perry, interviewed her for 30 minutes. Afterwards, she was required to fill out an application form. Upon completion of the form she was called back into the office to talk with the district sales manager, Mr. Landers. At the conclusion of this interview she was asked to fill out a more in-depth questionnaire that required far more detailed information. Finally, she was asked to come into the office for a third interview. While Mrs. Kay was a bit overwhelmed by the length of interviews and the personal data required on the forms, she was nevertheless flattered by the personal attention and felt that the extra time and depth of concern was a good omen for her chances of securing the job for which she applied. In this final interview, both Mrs. Perry and Mr. Landers asked, "What is your major goal in life? If you had a chance to do anything over again in your life what would it be? Do you have any objections to working with people who smoke? If you get this job, what do you think you would dislike the most?" Such questions caught her off guard, but somehow she felt she responded favorably in the eyes of the interrogators.

The job was described in the interview as being the "right-hand" assistant to the sales manager, Mr. Landers. It would be Mrs. Kay's job to fill in whenever he was out of the office: to prepare rates as specified by the underwriters, prepare reports, collect data for policies, handle phone calls, file, type, and perform other duties assigned by the sales manager and the supervisor of sales assistance, and even to handle some duties assigned by the district sales manager and underwriters. Since she'd need to be licensed by the state to sell policies, the company would pay for the on-the-job training and also the cost of the license fee.

Early that afternoon, Mrs. Kay was informed that, provided her references and other job information checked out, she would have the job and would start her job training the following Monday. She would be working very closely with the woman whom she would be replacing, Mrs. Mone. Mrs. Mone had agreed to stay on for the next three weeks to help with the orientation process.

Mrs. Kay arrived at work early Monday morning so she could become oriented to the office. She met Mr. Johnson, the Claims Manager, Mr. Metts, the Loss Prevention Manager, and several other workers in the office. When Mr. Landers arrived, Mrs. Kay was asked to fill out additional legal and administrative forms, including government licensing forms, a bonding contract, and insurance forms. She was then oriented to many of the company policies and benefits. She learned that raises were to be based upon the quality and quantity of work she performed, not on seniority. There was a mandatory probation period of three months, and then she would be eligible for insurance and sick leave benefits. There were also educational benefits that included full financial reimbursement for all classes dealing with insurance and reimbursement for half the price of the books used. There were also many additional benefits offered.

After a rather formal introduction to most of the workers in the office, Mrs. Kay was shown to her desk and told to start "on-the-job reading" of manuals in a prescribed manner. She started her studies in insurance with an introduction and description of the loss prevention program. Because this particular office served Utah, Wyoming, and Montana, it was necessary for some part of the staff to be out of the office much of the time, leaving a large amount of clerical work to be done by those who stayed in the office, including Mrs. Mone (who handled both technical assistance and routine clerical responsibilities).

During the course of the day there was time for Mrs. Kay to observe office functions and procedures. She also watched, with growing interest, the relationship between Mr. Landers and Mrs. Mone. Mrs. Kay was rather surprised at the behavior of Mr. Landers. Without any apparent provocation, except for a minor mistake, Landers burst into a fit of rage belittling Mrs. Mone in front of all the other workers. Mrs. Mone was apparently accustomed to her supervisor's behavior because she put up with his temper tantrum and did not get upset over the incident.

Later that day, Mrs. Kay talked briefly with Mrs. Mone about Mr. Landers. She said, "Well, you see, everybody in the company below the level of Executive Vice President has two or more bosses. For example, you will have Mr. Landers and Mrs. Perry as your main supervisors. Later on, you'll learn that the handling of many of your accounts and your bosses' accounts will be subject to the judgment and releases of the underwriting department. In a sense, you'll be taking on a third boss." She talked further about Mr. Landers. "Mr. Landers tends to get angry without regard to who is at fault. You'll also find out that there will be occasions where Mrs. Perry will direct you to do one thing, and Mr. Landers will tell you to do almost the complete opposite. There will also be occasions when they will both direct you to do the same chore, but they will use different terminology for the specific tasks they want you to accomplish. I've tried to find assigned tasks in the procedural manuals, but many times I've found that I've had to ask either Mr. Landers or Mrs. Perry for directions to complete the task, only to find that Mr. Landers gets angry, and Mrs. Perry is out of her office. Just don't let him bully you around. If you are right

(and you'd better be sure you are), stick to your guns and you'll come out o.k."

Reflection on the day's activities caused Mrs. Kay to feel good about the people she'd be working with, but she still felt a little apprehensive about Mr. Landers. Getting into her car, she immediately sensed the day's accumulation of the cigarette smoke that had adhered to her clothes and hair. It was soon apparent that the smoking of the other employees made her physically ill. This surprised her a bit since she had smoked up until four years before.

The next day, accustomed to arriving a few minutes early for work, Mrs. Kay arrived at 8:15 A.M., just fifteen minutes before work was to begin. She straightened out her desk and then pondered over the events of the previous day. When the clock reached 8:30 A.M. she started immediately into her studies. She later talked to the Claims Manager, Mr. Johnson, who informed her of his departmental functions. This helped her grasp how she fit into the picture of this office.

Mr. Landers instructed Mrs. Mone to spend at least an hour a day teaching Mrs. Kay the clerical duties. No specific hour was mentioned; however, and at three o'clock that afternoon, Mr. Landers again verbally assaulted Mrs. Mone because she hadn't instructed Mrs. Kay on the clerical duties. Twenty other people in the office looked on and listened to the argument. Mrs. Kay felt sympathetic toward Mrs. Mone and wondered if this was the way that she would be treated by Mr. Landers. She talked with another technical-clerical person, Sherry Olsen, who told Mrs. Kay that every time that Mrs. Mone stood up to Mr. Landers she felt like applauding. She added, "If he ever yells at you, don't feel embarrassed because all of the staff knows how he reacts and we're all used to it."

At the end of the day, Mrs. Kay put on her coat and prepared to go home. The instant she sat in the car, the nauseating smell of stale tobacco recaptured her attention. The odor became very strong, and almost overwhelmed her. This added to the anxiety that she already felt. There were several heavy smokers in the office, and the office had very little ventilation. It was quite easy to accumulate smoke in her clothes. Arriving home, supressed feelings rose to the surface and she became very tempermental, even hostile. This was contrary to her nature, but she supposed that the anxieties in acquiring a new job, the irritating physical effects of the office smoke, and the problems of working with a very temperamental boss had finally taken their toll. Family members unfortunately were most convenient and subject to the venting of her frustrations.

That night she pondered over the events of the past two days. She tried to weigh the benefits and drawbacks of her new job. Could she do it? She would receive a fair salary with good benefits, on-the-job training, and have opportunities for advancement. However, there were obvious complications. Much would be expected of her: a much heavier work load than most new employees carry, the "pool hall" working conditions, and a very temperamental boss worried her. Could she expect to have much impact on working conditions or her boss? Would there be a way of implementing new office procedures or practices?

When you have read this case, look back at the chapter's diagnostic questions and choose the ones that apply to the case. Then use those questions with the ones that follow in your case analysis.

1. Why did Mrs. Kay find the smell of cigarette smoke on her clothing so disagreeable? Why did she become temperamental at home after her second day at Cameran Mutual Insurance Company? What attitudes about work might be symptomized by these feelings and behaviors?

2. How might having two or three bosses affect an employee's attitudes toward her work? Her ability to perform satisfactorily? How would you advise Cameran management on this issue?

3. Under the circumstances described, how long would you expect Mrs. Kay to remain with Cameran Insurance? Why? What improvements, if any, would you recommend in the way the company's management treats employees?

CASE 8-3

CONNORS FREIGHT LINES

Review this case, which appears in Chapter 7. Next, look back at Chapter 8's diagnostic questions and choose the ones that apply to the case. Then use those questions with the ones that follow in your case analysis.

1. Was Chuck Fletcher dissatisfied with his supervisory job? Why? What symptoms do you see in this case that seem to signal his dissatisfaction? What factors might be causing this dissatisfaction?

2. Was Chuck's supervisory job stressful? What clues suggest that Chuck was experiencing stress? What sources of stress can you identify?

3. What actions might Connors Freight Lines take to reduce the dissatisfaction and stress experienced by supervisors like Chuck? Are there things the company currently does that it should stop doing? Are there things it doesn't do that it should start doing?

C H A P T E R 9

MANAGING INDIVIDUALS IN ORGANIZATIONS

Whether you are a line manager and supervise employees who do the organization's work or a staff manager in human resources, selecting and placing applicants in the company's jobs, knowing some simple rules of the game can save you and your company a lot of heartache. One of these is, Know and respect one another's expertise and call on it when you need to. If Larry Buck's supervisor (see opening story) had referred his caller to human resources rather than trying to handle the inquiry himself, Hall & Co. might not have been out $2 million.

Larry Buck's boss, an executive at Frank B. Hall and Company, an insurance firm in Houston, worked 50 hours a week keeping up to speed on insurance matters and had little time to keep track of what was happening in human resources. He certainly could not be expected to have the expertise in this area that members of the company's personnel department doubtless possessed. Thus, what happened one day in 1987 is not so surprising. The recently dismissed Buck, angry about his treatment by Hall and Company, hired a private investigator who telephoned Buck's former boss and represented himself as an executive of another insurance company. The private investigator pretended that he was interested in hiring Buck. Asked by the investigator what kind of person Buck was, the Hall and Company manager told the detective exactly what he thought: "Buck was a Jekyll and Hyde person, a classic sociopath."

An outraged Buck sued his former employer for malicious slander and libel and won before the U.S Supreme Court. Hall and Company had to pay Buck over $600,000 in lost wages and a $1,300,000 penalty, for a grand total of close to two million dollars. Local or long distance, this is a high price for a three-minute telephone call! Moreover, it was an unnecessary expense, for the litigation could have been avoided if Buck's former manager had known what was standard operating procedure for his company's personnel department.[1] There is an increasing tendency among former employees to bring suits against past employers who provide damaging references. The old rule "if you can't say anything nice about a person, don't say anything at all" is common procedure for today's human resource staff. A company staff member responding to a referral request should share only information about the duties of the job the person in question was performing. If compelled to describe the person, the staff member should share only information that is objectively verifiable.

Organizations often distinguish between line managers and staff managers. Line managers oversee the creation, production, and distribution of organizational products or services. Staff managers provide advice, assistance, and guidance to line managers in certain functional specialty areas (e.g., accounting and finance). Although executives and line managers need to be informed in all the functional areas of staff expertise, in the area of organizational behavior, the link between managers and the human resources, or personnel, department is of paramount importance.

The functional specialty area of personnel/human resources (P/HR) deals with enhancing the effectiveness of the organization's employees.[2] P/HR departments handle employee recruitment, employee selection, training of employees, worker surveys, employee compensation, and collective bargaining. The increasingly litigious nature of our society has made it necessary also for P/HR specialists to keep up to date on legislative and litigation issues in the area of human resources. Most public or private organizations that employ at least 150 people find that the complexity of the problems in this area are sufficient to create a separate department to carry out these activities.[3]

[1] Based on "The Revenge of the Fired," *Newsweek*, February 16, 1987, pp. 46–47.
[2] G. T. Milkovich and J. W. Boudreau, *Personnel/Human Resource Management: A Diagnostic Approach* (Plano, Texas: Business Publications, 1988), pp. 3–4.
[3] H. G. Heneman, D. P. Schwab, J. A. Fossum, and L. D. Dyer, *Personnel/Human Resource Management* (Homewood, Ill.: Richard Irwin, 1986), p. 17.

TABLE 9-1
Areas of Overlap among Personnel Directors and Executives*

	MANAGERS			PERSONNEL DIRECTORS		
	Setting Policy	Advising	Controlling	Setting Policy	Advising	Controlling
Employment testing	55%	81%	42%	50%	50%	46%
Performance appraisal	60	83	48	51	56	44
Affirmative action programs	71	61	65	76	79	63
Developing pay structures	56	51	42	36	26	29
Incentive systems	45	63	36	53	71	46
Training	53	71	43	52	56	40
Punishment and discipline	59	85	37	58	57	44
Career planning	62	73	44	65	70	51
Average percent	58	71	45	55	58	45

* Entries represent percentage of respondents who deal regularly with the area represented.
Source: H. C. White and M. N. Wolfe, "The Role Desired for Personnel Administration," *Personnel Administrator* 25 (1980), 90–91.

Because this book is addressed to current and future executives and line managers and not to personnel specialists, it would be inappropriate to go into the details of P/HR here. There is, however, a great deal of overlap in the interests and needs of line managers and personnel specialists. Thus effective understanding and communication between them is critical in managing a company's human resources. The Hall and Company experience is a good example. Their P/HR group surely knew the dangers of providing negative information about a former employee. Better communication between P/HR and Larry Buck's manager could have saved the company two million dollars that day in Houston.

Research conducted with groups of managers and P/HR specialists suggests that eight primary areas of OB and P/HR overlap. These eight areas are listed in Table 9-1, which shows the nature and level of involvement for each group in each of the eight areas. Clearly, line managers and executives are heavily involved in all areas.

As you will see, the practices of P/HR specialists are often based on the theories of organizational behavior described in this section of the book. Thus this chapter serves a dual purpose. It shows you how organizational behavior and human resources management interrelate, and it further illustrates the way many of the concepts and theories we have explored in the preceding five chapters find application in industry. Table 9-2 also fulfills two purposes. It tells you which earlier chapter each of the major sections in this chapter relates to, and in so doing, it provides you with an outline of this chapter.

TABLE 9-2
How Organizational Behavior and Human Resource Management Mesh

ORGANIZATIONAL BEHAVIOR	HUMAN RESOURCE MANAGEMENT
Human attributes (Chapter 4)	Employment testing
Perception and judgment (Chapter 5)	Performance appraisal
Administrative decision making (Chapter 6)	Affirmative action programs
Equity theory (Chapter 7)	Developing pay structures
Expectancy theory (Chapter 7)	Incentive systems
Reinforcement theory (Chapter 7)	Training and discipline programs
Cognitive appraisal theory (Chapter 8)	Career development

DIAGNOSTIC ISSUES

Applying the diagnostic model to human resources management highlights several important issues for managers. For starters, can we *describe* areas of organizational behavior that are of interest both to line managers and to the human resources staff? Can we develop systems for analyzing and describing jobs that will make recruitment and selection of employees more efficient? What *diagnostic* techniques can help us explain why selection and promotion procedures that seem fair sometimes fail to create a racially integrated workforce? How can we distinguish between situations in which merit raises and profit-sharing will be useful and situations in which pay-for-performance plans may prove disastrous?

How can we *prescribe* which job applicants will perform well and which will struggle unsuccessfully? What can we do to ensure that employees will respond positively to performance appraisals? What *actions* can we take to create a pay structure that will be viewed as fair? What can we do to change the behaviors of workers who engage in counterproductive activities?

TESTING EMPLOYEES' ABILITIES

One constantly recurring problem in organizations is deciding whom to hire for various job openings when there are many more applicants than positions. Without a crystal ball, one cannot look into the future and know which applicants will become high performers and which will fail. Using certain kinds of tests, however, employers can forecast these outcomes with a fair degree of accuracy and thereby increase organizational effectiveness. Moreover, effective testing and screening programs help individual job applicants—even those who are rejected. If applicants who are turned away would have been unsuccessful if hired, steering them into other occupations for which they are better qualified contributes to their own development.[4] Testing may also be useful in encouraging unsuccessful applicants to go back and improve their skills and qualifications through further education.[5] Thus for both employer and applicant, predicting job success accurately is important.

We will now look at two models of testing that are widely used in predicting job success—aptitude testing and skill testing. Both forms of testing are based on the theories of human attributes that we discussed in Chapter 4. As you study this section, you may want to refer back to that discussion.

Aptitude Testing

aptitude testing Measuring broad, general abilities of job applicants.

In Chapter 4, we noted that there were basically eight major physical abilities, nine major psychomotor abilities, eight major mental abilities, and five categories of personality characteristics (see Tables 4-4, 4-5, and 4-6 and Figure 4-4). **Aptitude testing** is illustrated in Figure 9-1. First, we perform a job analysis to determine which human attributes are most relevant to good performance on the job in which we are interested. Next we purchase any one of a number of existing tests that measure these particular human attributes. Then in our initial "test of the tests," we administer them to a group of job applicants. We keep the scores a secret (so as not to create expectation effects—see Chapter 5) from those who

[4] G. F. Dreher and P. R. Sackett, *Perspectives of Employee Staffing* (Homewood, Ill.: Richard Irwin, 1984), p. 57.

[5] B. Schneider and N. Schmitt, *Staffing Organizations* (Glenview, Ill.: Scott, Foresman, 1986), p. 91.

FIGURE 9-1
The Process of Aptitude Testing

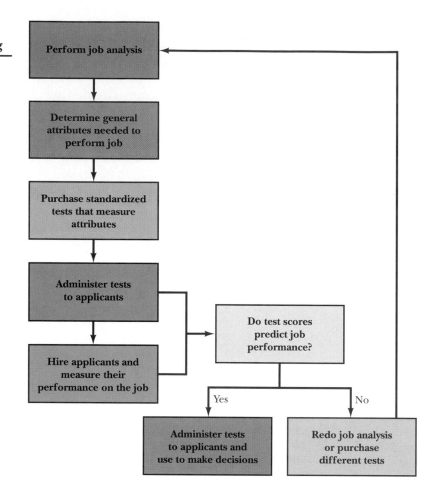

will be appraising the actual performance of whoever gets the job. In this trial period, the tests are not generally used for making selection decisions, because we have not yet proven their predictive value.

After a period of time, we look for a relationship between success on the tests and success on the job. That is usually done by calculating the correlation coefficient (see Chapter 3) between the original test scores and scores derived from a performance appraisal discussed later in this chapter. If there is a relationship, we can conclude that the tests are valid. (You may recall from Chapter 3 that this is referred to as criterion-related validity.) Once we have validated our tests in this fashion we can start to use them to help us decide which applicants to accept and which to reject for a particular job. Of course, if there is no re-

The Aetna Institute for Corporate Education, headed by Badi Foster, former Harvard education professor, teaches Hartford inner-city residents to do basic math, write an acceptable memo, and compose a business letter. To be admitted to this program, would-be job applicants must pass an aptitude test, be drug-free, and have positive self-esteem. Foster admits his program can't handle all the inner-city educational problems. But it has made a small dent: two years after Aetna Life launched this program 47 people had completed the course and were hired by the company.
Source: Joel Dreyfuss, "Get Ready for the New Work Force," Fortune, April 23, 1990.

lationship between the test scores and on-the-job performance, we may have to reanalyze the job or obtain new tests and go through the procedure again.

An example of aptitude testing is the Graduate Management Admissions Test (GMAT), which most prestigious MBA programs require applicants to take. An analysis of the task that confronts an MBA student clearly indicates the need for verbal and quantitative ability, two broad facets of ability tapped by this test. Because individuals who perform well on the test have the abilities required for the position, it should come as no surprise that the test predicts success in MBA programs.[6]

Many employers also use tests of verbal and quantitative ability, such as the Differential Aptitude Test or the Employee Aptitude Survey.[7] This kind of testing is called aptitude testing because the same attribute (and even the same test) may be used to select people for different jobs. That is, general mental ability may be needed for a whole host of jobs in an organization, and anyone applying for any of these jobs may be tested with the same instrument. Indeed, tests of general mental aptitude have been successfully validated across a wide variety of job categories.[8]

Skill Testing

skill testing Measuring narrow, job-specific abilities of job applicants.

Skill testing ties the test specifically to the job in question. One test or set of tests is designed to fit each position. The process underlying this method, shown in Figure 9-2, rests on the assumption that the best predictor of future behavior is

[6] A. Jenson, *Bias in Mental Testing* (New York: Free Press, 1980), p. 239.

[7] G. K. Bennett, H. G. Seashore and A. G. Wesman, *Differential Aptitude Tests: Administrator's Handbook* (New York: Psychological Corporation, 1982), p. 55; and F. L. Ruch and W. W. Ruch, *Employee Aptitude Survey: Technical Report* (Los Angeles: Psychological Services, 1980), p. 2.

[8] J. E. Hunter, "Cognitive Abilities, Cognitive Aptitudes, Job Knowledge, and Performance," *Journal of Vocational Performance* 29 (1986), 411–14.

FIGURE 9-2

The Process of Skill Testing

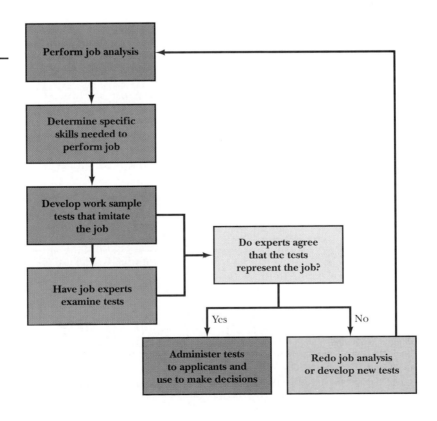

work sample tests Tests that present job applicants with realistic simulations of actual job problems and ask them to indicate how they would handle them.

situational interview A work sample test in which the applicant is asked to respond orally to hypothetical problems that might confront him while working on the job.

past behavior. The key differences between aptitude testing and skills testing are specificity and focus. Aptitude tests are generic and focus on abstract human attributes. Skill tests are specific and focus on concrete human behaviors. Aptitude tests tend to be purchased "off the rack" whereas skill tests are usually developed on site.

The key in skill testing is to develop tests that imitate or mimic the job in miniature form by *sampling* the specific behaviors the job requires. Because the behaviors tested are sampled from the job, these tests are often referred to as **work sample tests**. If the applicant cannot perform well on the "miniaturized job," it is unlikely that she will be able to perform well on the real job.

Work sample tests come in great variety. Look at Table 9-3, for example. This is a question from a **situational interview** test given to someone applying for a sales position in the Zales chain of jewelry stores. In the interview, the applicant must respond off the top of his head, and his response is scored for appropriateness on the scale shown in the table.

Another type of work sample test is the *business simulation*. In one well-known simulation, six applicants must work together as a group to operate a manufacturing company. This test calls for the job applicants to purchase raw materials, manufacture the product, develop a marketing plan, and then distribute and sell the product. IBM found that performance on this simulated manufacturing problem accurately predicted the number of promotions obtained by 94 middle managers three years into the future.[9]

There are also exercises called *in-basket tests* that confront the applicant with the kinds of problems she will encounter on the job. The term *in-basket* derives from the fact that the problems are often actual company memos or letters presented to the applicant as if they had just arrived in her "in" basket. As in the case of other tailored tests, it is assumed that if a job applicant can handle the simulated problem presented to her in a test, she will be able to handle similar problems on the job. Figure 9-3 shows an array of items confronting applicants in one in-basket test.

The most common way of validating a work sample test is to employ expert judgments about how well the test actually imitates the job. If experts agree that the content of the test accurately represents the content of the job, the test can be considered valid (this is content validity, as you may recall from Chapter 3), and we can use it to screen applicants.[10] Again, however, if the experts do not

---

[9] W. F. Cascio, *Managing Human Resources: Productivity, Quality of Worklife, Profits* (New York: McGraw-Hill, 1989), p. 211.

[10] G. F. Dreher and P. R. Sackett, "Some Problems with Applying Content Validity Evidence to Assessment Center Ratings," *Academy of Management Review* 6 (1981), 551–60.

T A B L E 9-3

A Question from a Zales Work Sample Test for Potential Jewelry Store Salespersons

A customer comes into the store to pick up a watch he left for repair. The repair was supposed to have been completed a week ago, but the watch is not back yet from the repair shop. The customer becomes very angry. How would you handle this situation?

1 • Tell the customer it isn't back yet and ask him or her to check back with you later.
2 • Apologize, tell the customer that you will check into the problem and call him or her back later.
3 • Put the customer at ease and call the repair shop while the customer waits.

Adapted from J. A. Weekley and J. A. Gier, Reliability and validity of the situational interview for a sales position. *Journal of Applied Psychology* 72 1987, pp. 484–87.

FIGURE 9-3

**Items from a Typical
In-Basket Test**

Source: N. Fredericksen, "Factors in In-Basket Performance," Psychological Monograph 76 (*1962*), *22–41.*

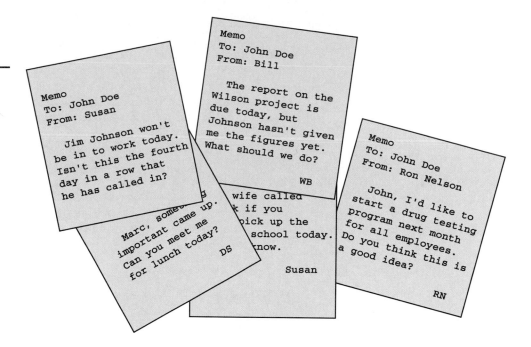

agree that our test samples the job in question accurately, we must reanalyze the job or design new tests.

APPRAISING PERFORMANCE BEHAVIORALLY

In Chapter 5, we discussed a number of barriers to perceptual accuracy. In fact, there are so many ways for bias to find its way into the subjective judgment process that many people question whether supervisors can evaluate their subordinates accurately. In one influential Supreme Court case, the court found that a General Motors foreman's judgments of workers' "ability, merit, and capacity" were too subjective to be fairly used in making promotion decisions. In other cases, supervisors' judgments of such qualities of their subordinates as leadership, resourcefulness, capacity for growth, loyalty, mental alertness, and personal conduct have been cited as "susceptible to partiality and to the personal taste, whim or fancy of the evaluator."[11]

If we cannot rely on subjective measures, what about objective measures? Sales volume, products produced per hour, customer repeat business, or departmental financial performance all seem at first glance like attractive alternatives to subjective judgments. A little scrutiny, however, usually reveals several very unattractive features in measures of this sort. The most serious problem is that many things that influence such seemingly objective indicators are not under the control of the employee.[12] An insurance agent's sales volume, for example, depends on the general level of the economy, the amount and nature of advertising, competitors' policies, territory served, and many other factors over which the

[11] R. D. Arvey and R. H. Faley, *Fairness in Selecting Employees* (Reading, Mass.: Addison-Wesley, 1988), p. 37.
[12] F. L. Landy and J. L. Farr, *The Measurement of Work Performance: Methods, Theory and Applications* (New York: Academic Press, 1983), p. 111.

salesperson has no control. Similarly, the number of products produced per hour can be influenced by such things as machinery breakdowns, quality of raw materials, and the quality of work performed on the product earlier on the assembly line.

One solution to the performance appraisal dilemma that originated out of theories of human perception is the behaviorally based appraisal. One such approach is the **behaviorally anchored rating scale (BARS).** The BARS attempts to take much of the subjectivity out of the performance appraisal process while still basing performance rating on things the employee can control.[13] Subjectivity is lessened somewhat by having the supervisor make simple, objective judgments about the kinds of behaviors the employee has exhibited. Focusing on behaviors also enhances perceptions of controllability. The worker has much more control over behaviors (e.g., how she treats a customer) than over the outcomes (e.g., sales volume) associated with most objective measures. Let's look next at the four-step development of a BARS (see also Figure 9-4).

behaviorally anchored rating scale (BARS) A method of performance appraisal in which each judgment point along the scale is illustrated with examples of concrete, on-the-job behaviors.

Identifying Behavioral Dimensions

In the first step, a group of experts, which may include supervisors, high-performing job holders, the company's owners, and some of the company's clients, are asked to *identify the important dimensions of performance* on the job in question. For example, in a hospital setting, an expert panel might decide that the important dimensions of a nurse's job are (a) demonstrating organizational ability, (b) showing compassion for patients, (c) working well with physicians, and (d) fulfilling technical responsibilities competently.

[13] H. J. Bernardin and P. C. Smith, "A Clarification of Some Issues Regarding the Development and Use of Behaviorally Anchored Rating Scales," *Journal of Applied Psychology* 66 (1981), 458–63.

FIGURE 9-4

Steps in Developing Behaviorally Anchored Rating Scales

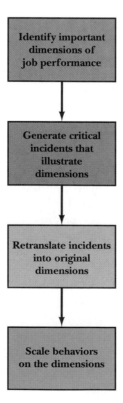

Identify important dimensions of job performance

Generate critical incidents that illustrate dimensions

Retranslate incidents into original dimensions

Scale behaviors on the dimensions

Generating Critical Behaviors

When the basic dimensions of the job in question have been established, a second group of experts is assembled to *generate behaviors that illustrate the performance dimensions*. It is this group's job to illustrate both effective and ineffective behaviors on the dimension with accounts of events that have actually occurred on the job. For example, for the dimension of organizational ability, this group may generate stories about effective nurses who "request early trays for patients who may take longer to eat," or "check medication orders for each day and arrange a schedule of distribution." Stories about ineffective nurses might include "make several trips to the supply closet to get a footboard" or "frequently leave important work undone in order to leave on time."

Retranslating Behaviors

When both the performance dimensions and the critical behaviors have been agreed on, a third group of job experts is convened (this group can be the same as the first one if there are few experts available). The job of this group is to *retranslate the behaviors back into the dimensions* they were chosen to represent. This process is called *retranslation*, because it is rather like translating one language into another. Here, one person translates from the original language to the second language, and then a different person translates that result back into the original language. If the original and the retranslation agree, one can conclude that everyone is "speaking the same language." Retranslation serves as a check on judges' accuracy. It is the basic reason for using multiple groups in the BARS development process.

For example, if one of the behaviors that was supposed to represent organizational ability is perceived by the retranslation group as representing working well with physicians, the description is eliminated from the scale for organizational ability. Conversely, if the retranslation group correctly identifies the behaviors, it is clear that everyone agrees.

Scaling Behaviors

In the last phase of the BARS building process, the behaviors that survive the retranslation process must be rated on a scale of effectiveness that ranges from 0, for completely ineffective, to 10, for very effective. In *scaling behaviors on a dimension*, we determine the mean, or average, value of each of the eleven ratings assigned to the scale by the members of a fourth group of experts (the second group if there are insufficient numbers of experts). Behaviors can also be dropped from the scale if there is substantial disagreement on rating—for example, if one person assigns a particular behavior a 2 on the scale but another assigns it an 8. This kind of disagreement suggests that the groups agree that the behavior reflects the dimension, but that the groups cannot agree on the extent to which the behavior is effective or ineffective.[14] Figure 9-5 shows what the final BARS might look like for the dimension of organizational ability in a nurse's position.

Research evidence has sometimes, though not always, found behaviorally anchored rating scales to generate more reliable ratings of performance than traditional measures. If too much time elapses between observation and rating, the BARS sometimes performs much like a subjective rating of personality char-

---

[14] R. Jacobs, D. Kafry and S. Zedeck, "Expectations of Behaviorally Anchored Rating Scales," *Personnel Psychology* 33 (1980), 595–640.

FIGURE 9-5

A Behaviorally Anchored Rating Scale for the Dimension of Organizational Ability for a Nursing Job

Raters are instructed to circle the number that best exemplifies the typical behavior of the person they are rating.

Reprinted from: J. Sheridan, "Measurement of Job Performance in Nursing Homes," report submitted to Health Resources Administration, 1980, p. 77.

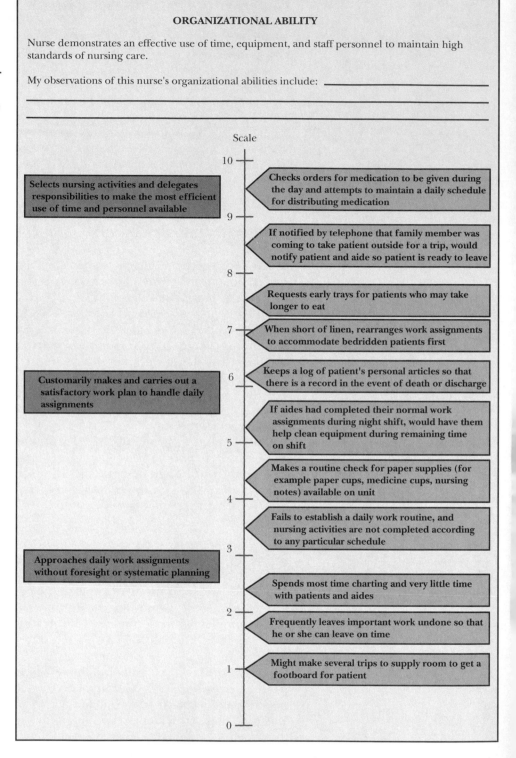

ORGANIZATIONAL ABILITY

Nurse demonstrates an effective use of time, equipment, and staff personnel to maintain high standards of nursing care.

My observations of this nurse's organizational abilities include: _____

_____

_____

Scale

Selects nursing activities and delegates responsibilities to make the most efficient use of time and personnel available

Checks orders for medication to be given during the day and attempts to maintain a daily schedule for distributing medication

If notified by telephone that family member was coming to take patient outside for a trip, would notify patient and aide so patient is ready to leave

Requests early trays for patients who may take longer to eat

When short of linen, rearranges work assignments to accommodate bedridden patients first

Customarily makes and carries out a satisfactory work plan to handle daily assignments

Keeps a log of patient's personal articles so that there is a record in the event of death or discharge

If aides had completed their normal work assignments during night shift, would have them help clean equipment during remaining time on shift

Makes a routine check for paper supplies (for example paper cups, medicine cups, nursing notes) available on unit

Fails to establish a daily work routine, and nursing activities are not completed according to any particular schedule

Approaches daily work assignments without foresight or systematic planning

Spends most time charting and very little time with patients and aides

Frequently leaves important work undone so that he or she can leave on time

Might make several trips to supply room to get a footboard for patient

acteristics.[15] Therefore, most experts agree that use of the BARS should be augmented with behavioral diaries (see Chapter 5 for a refresher on this).

The principal advantages of the BARS are that it is rooted in actual behaviors that are controlled by the employee, and that it requires relatively straightforward judgments of things the supervisor can observe directly. In addition, the common

[15] K. R. Murphy, C. Martin and M. Garcia, "Do Behavioral Observation Scales Measure Observation?" *Journal of Applied Psychology* 67 (1982), 562–67.

practice of involving subordinates in developing the scale increases their understanding of the process and hence their commitment to it and acceptance of it. Finally, the BARS provides a common frame of reference for supervisors and subordinates. It not only provides clear and specific feedback to poor performers but minimizes opportunities for disagreement and conflict.

AFFIRMATIVE ACTION PROGRAMS

In Chapter 6, on decision making, we noted that although there are a lot of pressures on organizations to make decisions rationally, many of the problems that confront decision makers are too complex to be solved by mathematical algorithms. One such problem that confronts most businesses today is managing affirmative action programs. These programs aim to increase the selection and promotion rates of employees who are members of various socially defined subgroups (for example, African-Americans, Hispanic-Americans, women, the elderly, the handicapped). Of the four factors prohibiting rational decision making discussed in that chapter, two stand out in the context of affirmative action planning: lack of goal consensus and bounded discretion. In the next two sections we will elaborate on the issues that complicate affirmative action programs, and show one widely used, but controversial solution.

Constraints on Decision Making and Actions

Managing affirmative action programs is characterized by *lack of goal consensus*. Planning in this context sometimes puts the goals of maximizing productivity and integrating the work force at odds with each other. It can also pit two American values against each other. The notion that people should be rewarded on the basis of achievement, or merit, can conflict with the notion of equal civil rights. The problem becomes, What is an organization to do when test scores or performance evaluations result in the selection or promotion of more white males than minority group members or women? This problem comes to the fore in two areas—tests of mental ability, which usually show large racial differences, and tests of certain physical abilities (like upper-body strength), which generate sex differences.[16] Should test scores or performance evaluations be ignored so that the work force can be integrated? Or should occupational segregation be ignored so as to promote those with the highest scores? In the United States, we have wrestled with this problem for years and still have not solved it.[17]

Managing affirmative action programs also involves the problem of *bounded discretion*, which means that the decision maker's list of alternatives is restricted by the social environment. In the context of affirmative action, bounds are often set for organizational decisions by social forces outside the organization itself.

In order to make personnel decisions, organizations must discriminate between employees on one basis or another every day. Yet laws like the Civil Rights Act of 1964, the Age Discrimination Act of 1967, and the Vocational Rehabilitation Act of 1978 prohibit discrimination if it relates to race, sex, religion, national origin, age, or handicapped status. Groups specified in this legislation are often referred to as **protected groups.**[18]

protected groups Groups of people defined in Civil Rights legislation who warrant special consideration in personnel selection, placement, and other procedures.

[16] Jenson, *Bias in Mental Testing*, p. 241; and Arvey and Faley, *Fairness in Selecting Employees*, p. 41.

[17] "Bigots in the Ivory Tower," *Time*, January 23, 1989, p. 22.

[18] K. J. McCulloch, *Selecting Employees Safely Under the Law* (Englewood Cliffs, N.J.: Prentice-Hall, 1981), p. 191.

disparate treatment An illegal practice in personnel selection wherein a person from one subgroup is asked to respond to questions, take tests, or display skills that are not asked of applicants from other groups.

disparate impact The tendency of a particular personnel selection practice to result in the hiring of a smaller percentage of the members of a particular group of job applicants than of other groups of applicants.

top-down selection within subgroups Personnel selection practice in which scores on a test are arrayed by subgroup and a flexible goal for representation from each group is decided upon. Selection proceeds from the highest to lowest score in each subgroup until all positions are filled and all subgroups are represented.

In 1990 President George Bush signed into law the Americans with Disabilities Act, which bars discrimination based on age, sex, religious, ethnic or racial origin, or physical or mental disability virtually across the board. Organizations throughout the United States in both the public and private sectors must henceforth hire without prejudice and must provide special facilities for the physically handicapped. Failure to comply with the new law may incur formal injunctions against violators and require back pay for victims of discrimination.
Source: Stephen A. Holmes, "House Approves Bill Establishing Broad Rights for Disabled People," The New York Times, May 23, 1990, p.1.

A review of the litigation in this area reveals that employers are bounded by two primary rules. First, it is illegal to engage in disparate treatment. **Disparate treatment** means that members of protected groups are subjected to employment practices that differ from those used with other groups. In a selection interview, a fire department manager cannot ask a woman, "Does your husband approve of your working?" unless he asks a man, "Does your wife approve of your working?" The apparent silliness of the latter question illustrates the sexist nature of the first question.

Second, any practice that, although it appears neutral, is shown to have adverse or disparate impact on any group must be shown to be a strict business necessity. **Disparate impact** is the harmful effect on the employment opportunities of a protected group of a particular practice, even if the practice is universally applied. For example, both male and female applicants for the job of firefighter may be subjected to a test of upper-body strength. This neutral-appearing practice usually results in the rejection of many more women than men. If this happens, the fire department must be able to prove that the test is a valid predictor of performance on the job. That is, it must establish job necessity.

Most people accept the arguments associated with the disparate-treatment restriction, yet there is quite a bit of controversy associated with the disparate-impact restriction. To crystallize this controversy for you, we will take the example of an employer who uses a validated test of general cognitive ability in managerial selection for both African-American and white applicants. Keep three facts in mind. First, roughly a tenth of the United States population is African-American. Second, because of cultural disadvantages and other factors, the scores of African-Americans on tests of cognitive ability are typically lower than those of whites. Third, across a wide variety of jobs, there is a weak but reliable relationship between general cognitive ability and performance. Clearly, if organizations are concerned only with hiring people who get the top scores on their tests, they will hire proportionately fewer minority applicants who, in general, achieve lower scores on such tests.

Top-Down Selection within Subgroups

One solution to the problem posed by affirmative action has been the development of the concept of top-down selection within subgroups.[19] To understand how this type of selection process works, let's look first at a process in which goal consensus maximizes performance and there are no bounds on decision making. This situation is often referred to as *pure top-down selection.*

Suppose we have 55 open positions and 20 applicants, and we are using a test of general cognitive ability for selection. The data could very well turn out as in Table 9-4. If we ignore the goal of integrating the work force, we can simply take each individual's score on our best-predictor-of-performance test, rank order the applicants, and hire the top scorers (those whose test scores are above the cutoff score). At this cutoff, however, almost all African-American applicants are rejected.

In a context where we place value on the goal of integrating the work force and equal civil rights, this outcome is unacceptable. The alternative, therefore, is **top-down selection within subgroups.**[20] With this method, one draws two separate cutoffs, one for each group (see Table 9-5). This way, the five jobs are filled with each group's top scorers (circled). In the example in Table 9-5, this

---

[19] L. J. Cronbach, E. Yalow, and G. Schaeffer, "A Mathematical Structure for Analyzing Fairness in Selection," *Personnel Psychology* 33 (1980), 692–703.
[20] Ibid., Cronbach et. al.

TABLE 9-4
Pure Top-Down Selection

APPLICANT NUMBER	TEST SCORE	
1	100	
2	98	
3	97	
4	94	Select
5	94	
-----	-----	*Cut-Off Point*
6	92	
7	90	Reject
8	89	
9	86	
10	85	
11	85	
12	85	
13	84	
14	81	
15	78	
16	74	
17	73	
18	68	
19	65	
20	57	

procedure would result in our hiring one minority member, one woman, and three other people.

Top-down selection is not the same thing as a quota. Quotas in personnel selection set aside a specific number of positions for protected group members irrespective of their standing on selection tests. Although top-down-within-subgroups strategy is a less controversial technique than the quota, many still object to its use because of its ability to put nonminority candidates at a disadvantage.

TABLE 9-5
Top-Down Selection within Subgroups

MINORITY GROUP NUMBERS		WOMEN		OTHERS	
Applicant No.	Test Score	Applicant No.	Test Score	Applicant No.	Test Score
⑦	90	⑧	89	①	100
11	85	10	85	②	98
13	84	15	78	③	97
14	81			4	94
				5	94
				6	92
				9	86
				12	85
				16	74
				17	73
				18	68
				19	65
				20	57

IN PRACTICE

Gearing Up for Workforce 2000

Consider the plight of Harold Epps, a plant manager at Digital Electronics Corporation in Boston. Epps has 350 workers in his plant assembling computer keyboards. These 350 people come from 11 different countries and speak 19 different languages. It is routine practice in this firm to issue plant announcements printed in English, Chinese, French, Spanish, Portuguese, Vietnamese, and Haitian Creole.

Workforce 2000 may sound like a futuristic, science fiction thriller to some, but for many managers like Epps, the future is now. *Workforce 2000* is actually the title of a study performed by the Hudson Institute on demographic changes in the United States and the implications of these changes for managing businesses in the years ahead. For employers the two most striking findings of this study are the type of work that will be required in the twenty-first century and who will be available to do it.

With respect to the second finding, it is clear that the work force will grow very slowly throughout the next decade, as ageing baby boomers begin to retire, and there are fewer workers available to take their places. Moreover, the workers who will be available will have more diverse backgrounds. Today, 47 percent of new entrants into the U.S. labor pool are native white males. In the year 2000, this group will constitute only 15 percent of new entrants.

As for the type of work to be done, it is also clear that new jobs in the year 2000 will demand much higher skill levels than the jobs of today. There will be few jobs for those who cannot read or perform basic mathematics. The trends in skill requirements, coupled with the trends in the nature of the work force, have made "managing diversity" a key issue.* Companies from Goodyear to Hewlett-Packard to Procter and Gamble are creating positions to handle this function—for example, "Diversity Manager" or "Vice President for Diversity." Jill Kanin-Lovers, vice-president at Towers Perrin, a management consulting firm, notes that "for the first time at many companies, human resources is a strategic issue." Companies are making a whole host of maneuvers to survive the population shifts that will confront them in the years ahead.

Some of the push comes in the area of recruiting. Procter and Gamble, for example, makes a concerted effort to recruit a higher percentage of women and minority engineers than we find with undergraduate degrees in engineering (10 percent for women and 15 percent for minorities). McDonald's provides summer corporate internships and year-round res-taurant management programs for minority college students. Xerox gives minority prospects reprints of an article in *Black Enterprise* magazine that rates the company as one of the best places for African-Americans to work. Hewlett-Packard employs the same strategy with a copy of *Working Women* that rates HP as one of the best places for women to work.

There is also a push to increase the general level of sensitivity to cultural differences in the work place. For example at the DEC keyboard plant in Boston, problems developed when a young man newly arrived from a foreign country tried to give a present to a female colleague who had come to the United States from a third country. In the man's culture, accepting such a gift signaled that the woman was romantically interested. The woman held no such feelings, however. Rather, in her culture, it was considered inappropriate ever to turn down a gift. Cultural clashes like this one can only be averted by training workers to recognize and understand the cultures of their coworkers.

Pushing in yet another direction, firms have begun to reach out and provide remedial training to workers who otherwise could not meet their qualifications. Word-processing jobs at Aetna Life Insurance, for example, require basic skills in reading and math. When applications for these jobs went down 40 percent, Aetna launched classes in inner-city areas teaching residents basic office skills in intensive 14-week courses. Aetna has hired all 47 graduates of this program and is delighted with their performance levels.

Finally, firms are also pushing to retain women and minority workers once they are hired and trained. Corning found, for example, that between 1980 and 1987, African-American and women professionals left the company at roughly twice the rate of white men. A diversity-training program for managers and professionals helped reduce attrition rates for both groups. Avon encourages employees to organize into African-American, Hispanic, and Asian networks by granting them official recognition and providing a senior mentor to act as an advisor to the group. The cosmetics company once had a similar network for women but disbanded it after the program achieved its objective (today women hold 79 percent of the management positions at Avon). Avon's chief of human resources told a reporter that "My objective is to create an organization where people don't feel a need for a black network, a Hispanic network, or an Asian network, just as women decided they didn't need their network."†

* J. Dreyfus, "Get Ready for the New Workforce," *Fortune*, April 23, 1990, p. 12.

† Ibid.

Another problem is that the technique has sometimes been used without informing those involved. For example, the United States Employment Service (USES) used this type of scoring procedure with its General Aptitude Test. The USES would give prospective employers applicants' scores that were adjusted for race without informing employers of the adjustment. When word was leaked to the press, officials at the Departments of Labor and Justice saw to it that the practice was stopped.

Interestingly, while the country vigorously debates affirmative action issues, large-scale changes in the nature of the U.S. labor pool are making such debates increasingly irrelevant. As the "In Practice" box shows, changes in the size and nature of the work force are giving "diversity" issues a level of urgency that affirmative action has never experienced.

DEVELOPING EQUITABLE PAY STRUCTURES

Most complex organizations employ many different people who have many different skills and perform many different jobs. Paying employees would be a simple matter if everyone were happy receiving the same pay. Unfortunately that is not the case. For many reasons, occupants of some jobs must be paid more than others. Some jobs may be more dangerous than others. Some jobs may require much more education and training. Some jobs require more of a person's time. Organizations are stuck with the problem of having to pay different wages for different jobs. **Pay structure** refers to the organization's hierarchical arrangement of jobs in terms of pay differentials.

The pay differentials created by the pay structure can pose a problem, however. Those who receive lower wages may perceive the differentials as unfair. As we made clear in our discussion of equity theory (see Chapter 7), the fact that some people are getting more rewards than others could have detrimental effects on the others' job performance and on their attitudes toward the company.

So developing a pay structure that determines the pay for each job relative to all other jobs is often a sensitive and problematic organizational task. As is clear from equity theory, differentials in pay will be tolerated only if there are perceived differentials in input as well. The solution to this problem for some firms is job evaluation.

In **job evaluation**, an organization investigates its jobs and the duties and responsibilities of each job in order to devise a hierarchy of value or worth on which a pay scale can be based. There are many ways of performing job evaluation, but the most widespread method is the point system. Although point plans vary, all involve three basic elements—determining compensable factors, rating jobs in terms of these factors, and using these ratings to determine the worth of each job relative to the others in the firm.

pay structure An organization's hierarchical arrangement of jobs expressed in terms of pay differentials.

job evaluation A process by which the pay differentials for jobs throughout the organization are established based on differences in job requirements.

San Antonio's USAA, an insurance and investment management company, gets high marks from clients for prompt and satisfactory settlement of claims. Under CEO Robert McDermott's leadership, the company has expanded its assets from $200 million to $19 billion over just two decades. With a 69-year record of no layoffs, a 4-day, 38-hour work week, and an extensive benefits program, the firm has significantly reduced turnover and absenteeism despite a pay structure that includes no fewer than 30 distinct pay grades. Employees are assessed both individually and as team members on such things as number of policies sold and pleasantness with clients, and every month, sales teams with the best scores are publicly commended.
Source: "Managing," Fortune, February 25, 1991.

Deriving Compensable Factors

compensable factors Those aspects of a job for which an organization is willing to pay a premium.

Compensable factors are those aspects of a job for which the organization is willing to pay a premium. They are dimensions that differentiate jobs and that are important enough to warrant differences in pay. In equity theory terms, these factors are the official "inputs" that can be used to justify pay differentials. There are several criteria for designating a compensable factor. It must be work related, it must be consistent with the organization's values, and it must be accepted by all parties involved. Let's look at some real-world examples of compensable factors.

The federal government is one of the nation's largest employers. Keeping government wages and salaries equitable is a major task, particularly because for many jobs—for example, the job of a federal judge—there are no direct analogs in the private sector. Table 9-6 describes the four compensable factors used by the government's *General Schedule System* to differentiate jobs for the purpose of devising pay scales. These factors are knowledge required, supervisory controls, job guidelines, and job complexity. Any pay differences between jobs in the federal government can be explained by reference to these four factors. A high-paying job, like that of a federal judge, requires more knowledge, has less supervisory control and fewer written guidelines and is more complex than a lower-paying job, like that of night watchman at a federal courthouse.

In the private sector, the *Hay system* is probably the most widely known method of job evaluation. It has been used in over 5,000 companies, including 130 of the nation's 500 largest corporations. Table 9-4 also describes this system's three compensable factors: know-how, problem solving, and accountability.[21] In the Hay system, higher-paying jobs are characterized as requiring more know-how, more problem solving, and more accountability than lower-paying jobs. A CEO of a major corporation will make more money under this system than a worker on the janitorial staff owing to these kinds of differences in their jobs.

[21] G. T. Milkovich and J. M. Newman, *Compensation* (Plano, Texas: Business Publications, 1987), p. 311.

T A B L E 9-6
Some Widely Used Compensable Factors

The United States Government's General Schedule System
1. Knowledge required—The nature and extent of information or facts that the worker must understand to do the work.
2. Supervisory controls—The extent of direct or indirect controls exercised by the supervisor and the level of responsibility on the part of the employee.
3. Job guidelines—The nature of the job guidelines and level of judgment needed to apply them.
4. Job complexity—The number, nature, variety, and intricacy of tasks performed; the difficulty of the job and the originality required.

The Hay System
1. Know-how—The sum total of every kind of skill required for acceptable job performance.
2. Problem solving—The original thinking required by the job in analyzing, evaluating, creating, reasoning, and reaching conclusions.
3. Accountability—Answerability for actions and for the consequences thereof; the effect or end results.

MANAGING INDIVIDUALS IN ORGANIZATIONS

Scaling Jobs and Weighting Compensable Factors

Once compensable factors have been chosen, we need to *scale,* or rate, them as they apply to a group of specific jobs and then weight the factors in terms of their relative importance in these jobs. Let's look at just two of the skills that might be required by the staff of a management consulting firm: mathematical skills and interpersonal skills. The first step is to determine the mathematic functions required by the jobs included in the analysis and order them in terms of complexity, or difficulty. Suppose we come up with the five levels of mathematical skill listed in Table 9-7, ranging from no math used at all to the use of fairly advanced techniques. We then rate these levels of skill from 1 to 5, as the table shows. By a similar process, we establish levels of interpersonal skills and rate those also from 1 to 5.

The next step in the point-plan method of job analysis is to weight the compensable factors by importance in the jobs under consideration. Sometimes this is done by means of a particular kind of statistical analysis, but it can also be done by having a committee make a collective judgment as to the factors' relative importance. Let's assume that a committee has decided that in the management consulting jobs we're analyzing, interpersonal skills are twice as important as mathematical skills. This means that in figuring points for different levels of math skills we must use a weight factor of 1 and for levels of interpersonal skills a weight factor of 2. As Table 9-7 shows, points for math skill levels are the same as the ratings for these levels, but for interpersonal skills, points are twice the ratings (because we multiply each of the latter ratings by 2 to get its point value).

T A B L E 9-7
Job-Evaluation Scaling Format for Two Skills: Mathematical and Interpersonal

MATHEMATICAL SKILLS

Points	Rating	Description
1	1	No mathematics used at all.
2	2	Simple arithmetic computations involving addition, subtraction, multiplication, or division.
3	3	Computations involving decimals, percentages, fractions, and/or basic statistics.
4	4	Computations involving algebra, (i.e., solving for an unknown) or geometry (i.e., calculating areas, volumes).
5	5	Computations involving the use of trigonometry, logarithms, exponents, or advanced statistics.

INTERPERSONAL SKILLS

Points	Rating	Description
2	1	No interactions with any other persons.
4	2	Interactions with others that involve providing or receiving information or documents.
6	3	Interactions with others that require explanation or interpretation of information.
8	4	Interactions that involve discussions with stakeholders on issues regarding policies or programs. Impact limited to one department.
10	5	Interactions that involve implementation decisions that will impact on the entire organization.

Now, to differentiate jobs in terms of the salary each merits, we need only to determine how much of each type of skill a particular job requires. Suppose that we rate the job of vice president for human resources 2 on math skills and 4 on interpersonal skills. This job would have a total point score of 10 (2 + 8). But the job of accountant-statistician, rated 4 on math skills and 2 on interpersonal skills, would have a total point score of only 8 (4 + 4). Thus even though each of these jobs requires one skill rated 2 and another skill rated 4, because the skills are weighted differently, one—the vice-president's job—will receive a higher salary. In the next section, we'll see how specific wages are determined.

Converting Points into Wages

Once we have a set of compensable factors that have been assigned points we need a way of translating these points into actual wages. Typically, organizations use benchmark jobs to help make this conversion. **Benchmark jobs** are jobs that are similar to jobs in other organizations. Because there is usually ample information on the going market rate for such jobs, it is a fairly easy task to determine the relationship between scores on compensable factors and market wages for particular jobs. In practice, as you can see from Figure 9-6, this relationship is depicted as a scatterplot.

Once the relationship between points and wages are known for benchmark jobs, pay rates for nonbenchmark jobs can be determined by using the figure's diagonal line that captures the relationship between total points and pay for benchmark jobs. We can simply locate the point on the horizontal axis that corresponds to the point value of the job in question, draw a line perpendicular to the horizontal that intersects the diagonal line, and then by drawing a line perpendicular to the vertical axis, locate the appropriate wage per hour on that axis. Thus in Figure 9-6, a job worth 30 points will be paid $6.85 an hour; a job worth 45 points will be paid $8.15 an hour.[22]

What job evaluation does, then, from an equity theory perspective, is to justify outcome differentials in pay by documenting input differentials in the form of compensable factors. Even though some employees are paid less than others, they feel equitably treated because it can be shown that these more highly paid others contribute more to the company.

benchmark jobs Common jobs for which market rates are readily available and which are used, along with point plans, to determine salaries for uncommon jobs.

[22] P. A. Katz, "Specific Job Evaluation Systems: White-Collar Jobs in the Federal Civil Service," in *Handbook of Wage and Salary Administration*, ed. M. Rock (New York: McGraw-Hill, 1984) pp. 14/1–14/10.

FIGURE 9-6

Determining Pay for Nonbenchmark Jobs Based on Pay and Points for Benchmark Jobs

In this graph, Xs represent benchmark jobs for which job evaluation points and market wage rates are known. The dashed line O_1 represents a nonbenchmark job whose 30 job evaluation points enable us to determine its wage of $6.85 per hour. The dashed line O_2 represents another nonbenchmark job, worth 45 job evaluation points, that merits a wage of $8.15 per hour.

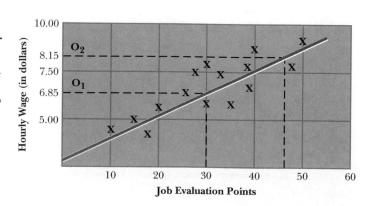

306

MANAGEMENT ISSUES
Comparable Worth Becomes a Reality in Ontario

It is well accepted throughout the United States and Canada that men and women should be paid equally for equal work. This is guaranteed in both countries by legislative acts. But what happens when men and women perform different jobs? In 1990, female workers earned only 65 cents for every dollar earned by male workers. Very little of this pay differential is caused by a difference in the pay of women and men working in the same jobs. Most of it is attributable to occupational segregation. Men hold "men's jobs" and women hold "women's jobs," and many argue that women's jobs pay less than they are worth. *Comparable worth* is a controversial remedy to this kind of discrimination. It refers to the practice of giving equal pay for work of comparable value when jobs are not the same.

For example, in Denver, Colorado, nurses (predominantly women) felt that their jobs were at least of equal value to the work performed by "tree trimmers" (predominantly men), yet they were paid significantly less. A study commissioned by the state of Washington showed that the jobs of truck driver (predominantly male) and laundry worker (predominantly female) were equal in skills, mental demand, accountability, and working conditions. Nevertheless, the drivers earned $1,574 a month compared to only $1,114 for the laundry workers. At the University of Washington, the predominantly female faculty of one department claimed that they were underpaid relative to faculty in departments that were predominantly male. These claims were all rebuffed by the courts. In the United States, the practice of paying market wages even where the result is pay discrimination against women appears legitimate.*

In Canada, on the other hand, the province of Ontario is moving full speed ahead with the notion of comparable worth. Because of a new Ontario law, employers in the province are struggling with the problem of how to compare jobs as diverse as secretary and warehouse worker, janitor and telephone operator, librarian and construction worker. Ontario is the first big jurisdiction anywhere to make private firms adopt comparable-worth plans. All businesses with more than 500 workers must do their own job evaluations to determine where pay discrimination is taking place. They must establish point values for each job and then pay a salary for that job that is based on the point values established.

At the Toronto Sun Publishing Corporation, for example, a job-evaluation system was put in place that rated jobs

on over 30 compensable factors (including working conditions, required education, and deadline pressures). This job-evaluation plan uncovered many disparities. The same number of points were given to the jobs of switchboard operator (held mostly by women) and night cleaning staffperson (held mostly by men), yet the operators were paid $25 a week less than the cleaners. To redress this disparity, the operators were given catch-up raises. Librarians got the biggest boost—almost $6 an hour—to make their pay comparable to that of entry-level engineers.

The law and the plans that it stimulates have triggered disputes, however. The Energy and Chemical Workers Union wanted Consumer's Gas Company to have one provincewide job-evaluation system. The alternative was one system for each different operating system in each different geographic region. A total provincewide plan would push wages in small towns up toward the high levels of wages in Toronto. The Pay Equity Commission, an administrative body set up to settle such disputes ruled against the union. It allowed Consumers Gas to adopt three different regional plans. Thus even in Ontario, prevailing markets, while not afforded the same weight as in the United States, are still given some deference.†

---

* G. T. Milkovich and J. M. Newman, *Compensation* (Homewood, Ill.: BPI/Irwin, 1990), p. 000.

† L. Kilpatrick, "In Ontario, 'Equal; Pay for Equal Work' Becomes a Reality, but Not Very Easily," *Wall Street Journal*, March 9, 1990, p. B1.

---

comparable worth Theory that sex differences in wages are attributable to discrimination and that such discrimination can be eliminated through job evaluation.

Some people have suggested that job evaluation might be used to fight pay discrimination against women. There is considerable debate on the notion of **comparable worth**—the idea that pay for jobs typically held by men (such as heavy equipment operator) and jobs typically held by women (such as kindergarten teacher) should be equalized. As the "Management Issues" box shows, this idea is more widely accepted in Canada than in the United States.

PAY-FOR-PERFORMANCE PROGRAMS

In theory, one of the least controversial statements one can make about work compensation is that it is important to tie pay to job performance, so that the better the worker performs, the higher he is paid. However, the actual implementation of programs to bring about such a relationship is often quite difficult. To get a feel for this difficulty, consider the following issues that arise when one tries to pay for performance.

Should pay increases be based on outcomes that occur at the individual level (worker performance) or the group level (work group or organizational performance)? At the individual level, the organization may create competition among co-workers, destroying team morale. At the group level, individuals may have a hard time seeing how their own performance relates to group performance and outcomes. In expectancy-theory terms, these kinds of conditions sever the performance-outcome relationship, or instrumentality (see Chapter 7).

If the firm decides to stay at the individual level, should the firm set up the rules for payment in advance, tying future pay to the eventual level of objective productivity? This sounds like a good idea, but the firm will be unable to forecast its labor costs. Moreover, because the price of the product sold or service rendered cannot be known in advance, the firm also cannot anticipate revenue. If the firm waits till the end of the year to see how much money is available for merit pay, people will not know how their performance relates to their pay. Moreover, if the firm, like most firms, engages in pay secrecy to protect people's privacy, how can anyone actually know how fair the merit system is?

If the firm decides to keep incentives at an organizational level, should they be based on cost savings and distributed yearly, or on profits and distributed on a deferred basis? The calculations and accounting procedures required by cost-savings plans are enormous and complex, but rewards are distributed quickly. Profit-sharing plans are much easier to handle from an accounting perspective. Because their rewards are distributed on a deferred basis, however, they are less motivating than cost-savings plans.

Asking all these questions illustrates the complexity inherent in putting into practice the seemingly simple concept of paying for performance. Covering all the complexities of these issues is well beyond the scope of this chapter. However, we will examine the distinguishing features of four different kinds of pay-for-performance programs: merit-based plans, incentive plans, cost-savings plans and profit-sharing plans.

Merit Pay and Incentive Systems

Individual pay-for-performance plans base pay, at least partially, on the accomplishments of individual workers. There are two types of individual programs, those based on merit and those based on incentives.

Merit-based pay plans are by far the easiest to administer and control. In these programs, performance is assessed at the end of the fiscal year by either subjective ratings or ratings on behaviorally based scales. Also at the end of the year, a fixed sum of money is allocated to wage increases. This sum is distributed to individuals in amounts proportional to their performance ratings.

In designing merit-based programs there are three major considerations. First, what will the average performer receive? Many firms try to make sure that average performers are at least able to keep up with inflation. As a result, the midpoint of the rating scales used is often tied to the yearly consumer price index (CPI).

merit-based pay plans Basing pay increases on subjective ratings of performance made at year end and allocating increases as a percentage of available funds based on these ratings.

Second, what will a poor performer receive? Companies rarely decrease an employee's wages because of performance deficiencies. In terms of buying power, however, raises that fail to cover the CPI are actually wage decreases. Is it in the best interest of the firm to hurt poor performers intentionally? If so, how much damage does the firm wish to inflict? How replaceable are these people if they are prompted to leave the firm?

Finally, how much will high performers receive? Will high performers at the top of a pay grade receive the same raise as those at the bottom? In discussing job evaluation, we noted that some jobs needed to be above other jobs in the pay hierarchy because of the different kinds of inputs that go into each. Paying for performance could cause top performers in a job lower in the hierarchy to surpass (through yearly raises) low performers in upper-level jobs. To prevent this kind of problem, most firms scale raises so that the raise level is a function of both performance and position in the pay grade for the job in question (see Table 9-8). A top performer at the top of a pay grade receives a smaller percentage raise than a top performer who is at the bottom of the grade. Another desirable outcome of scaling raises as a function of both performance and position in the pay grade is that the absolute dollar values of the raises for top performers are more equal. If those at the upper and lower ends of the grade were given the same percentage raise, the result would be a much greater dollar value for people at the top.

Although the performance ratings that determine merit pay have traditionally come from supervisors, this practice is starting to change. In the service sector of the economy, many companies trying to enhance customer service have eliminated the middle man (the supervisor). These companies tie merit pay raises to customer ratings obtained from surveys. For example, at GTE customer ratings are weighted 35 percent in annual merit pay decisions for certain managerial groups.[23]

incentive systems A process by which future pay is made contingent on individual performance based on objective performance indicators and using established quantitative rules.

Incentive systems differ from merit systems in two ways. First, incentive programs stipulate the rules by which payment will be made in advance, so that the worker can calculate exactly how much money she will earn if she achieves a certain level of performance. Second, rewards in an incentive program are based on objective measures of performance. Let's look at two plans: piece-work plans and standard-hour plans.

In simple *piece-work plans*, a standard of productivity per time interval is set, and any productivity beyond that standard is rewarded with a set amount per unit. This type of plan is easy for the worker to understand, and it creates an obvious performance-outcome expectancy. On the other hand, the standard must often be adjusted. If the standard is initially set too low, labor costs can get out

[23] S. Phillips, A. Dunkin, J. B. Treece, and K. H. Hammonds, "King Customer: At Companies That Listen Hard and Respond Fast, Bottom Lines Thrive," *Business Week*, March 12, 1990, pp. 88–94.

TABLE 9-8

Percent of Pay Increase as a Function of Both Performance and Position in a Job's Pay Range

POSITION IN RANGE	PERFORMANCE RATING				
	Unsatisfactory	Improvement Needed	Competent	Commendable	Superior
Fourth quartile	0%	0%	4%	5%	6%
Third quartile	0%	0%	5%	6%	7%
Second quartile	0%	0%	6%	7%	8%
First quartile	0%	2%	7%	8%	9%
Below minimum	0%	3%	8%	9%	10%

of hand. If it is set too high, workers will reject it when they find that even though they are trying harder, the standard cannot be reached (and pay is the same as before). But if the standard is flexible, gradual raises in the standard will be viewed as a management trick, and decreases will cause some workers to try to manipulate the system by lowering output. Furthermore, without built-in safeguards, these programs also lead workers to achieve quantity at the price of quality.[24]

The *standard-hour plan* stipulates normal time requirements and pay rates for certain tasks. For example, a heating and cooling company may tell its workers that the normal time required to remove an old furnace and replace it with a new one is six hours and that a worker will be paid $120 for this task. Highly skilled and motivated mechanics may be able to complete the job in less time, however. Standard-hour plans pay the worker the set amount even when the work takes less time than normal. If the skilled and hard-working mechanic can install two furnaces in eight hours, his pay for the day will be $240, compared to $120 for the novice or leisurely worker who can install only one furnace in eight hours. Standard-hour plans are more suitable than piece-work plans for complex, nonrepetitive tasks that require numerous skills for completion.[25]

Profit Sharing and Cost Savings

profit-sharing plans Fringe benefit programs in which profits are calculated at year end and distributed to employees, typically in a deferred fashion.

As the name suggests, **profit-sharing plans** distribute organizational profits to employees. According to recent estimates, some 20 percent of United States firms have such plans in place, and these plans are becoming increasingly popular. *Cash distribution plans* provide full payment soon after profits are determined (annually or quarterly). Because of tax advantages, however, most plans—indeed as many as 80 percent—are deferred.[26] In these plans, current profits accumulate in employee accounts, and a cash payment is made only when a worker becomes disabled, leaves the firm, retires, or dies. Of course, not all profits are redistributed. Research suggests that the percent of profits distributed may range from a low of 14 percent to a high of 33 percent.[27]

Employees often find it hard to see the connection between their activities and their company's profits. When multiple businesses are involved, they may find it even harder to see the link between their efforts and corporate profits. For this reason, some firms adopt **cost-saving plans**, that pay workers bonuses out of the money the company has saved as a result of the efficient performance of its workers. Workers often have more control over the costs of doing business than over profit making. Thus they can easily see the connection between their own work and cost reduction.

cost-saving plans Fringe benefit programs in which organizations pay workers year-end bonuses out of money saved through employee suggestions, increased efficiency, or increased productivity.

One type of cost-saving plan, called the *Scanlon Plan*, is designed to reduce labor costs. Incentives are calculated as a function of labor costs relative to the sales value of production (SVP). SVP is the revenue that would be obtained from sales of all the goods or services produced in a time unit. Say that in one year, $100,000 worth of labor is needed to generate $500,000 in goods and services. In the next year, however, that same amount of goods and services can be produced with $70,000 worth of labor. A portion of the $30,000 saved is distributed to the workers. A typical practice is to return 50 percent of such savings to the workers, retain 25 percent for the firm, and place 25 percent in a fund to cover future years where a "negative bonus" might occur.

[24] C. W. Hamner, "How to Ruin Motivation with Pay," *Compensation Review* 21 (1975), 88–98.
[25] R. I. Henderson, *Compensation Management* (Englewood Cliffs, N.J.: Prentice-Hall, 1984), p. 75.
[26] Bureau of National Affairs, "Incentive Pay Schemes Seen as a Result of Economic Employee Relation Change," *BNA Daily Report*, October 9, 1984, p. 1.
[27] R. McCaffery, *Managing the Employee Benefits Process* (New York: AMACOM, 1983), p. 17.

FIGURE 9-7

Deciding among Alternative
Pay-for-Performance Programs

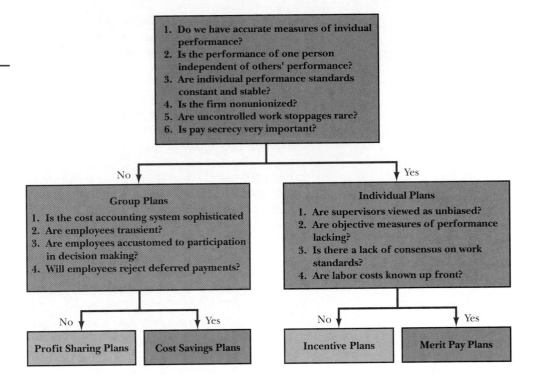

Although we have sampled only a few of the many pay-for-performance programs currently in use, by now you should have some feel for the kinds of issues raised by such programs. Figure 9-7 provides some guidance on choosing a suitable plan. It tells you under what circumstances an individual or a group plan is appropriate and in what situations specific individual or group plans are most effective.

TRAINING AND DISCIPLINE

New employees rarely know everything they need to know to perform a specific job in a specific context. Learning and applying what is learned to the job context lies at the core of all training programs. Although there are many kinds of training programs, we will focus on behavior modification inasmuch as it is a direct extension of the reinforcement theories of motivation we discussed in Chapter 7. Because modern behavior modification programs have their roots in B. F. Skinner's work on operant conditioning, they often emphasize positive reinforcement rather than punishment as a behavior change strategy. We will follow our discussion of behavior modification with an explanation of training that emphasizes punishment and discipline.

Behavior Modification

behavior modification
Application of contingent rewards in order to bring about behavioral change.

Behavior modification programs, though they vary slightly depending on the nature of the firm and the job, generally proceed in three distinct stages:

1. Identifying key behaviors
2. Monitoring key behaviors
3. Establishing positive contingencies between key behaviors and valued rewards

In the first stage we use job analysis to *identify a few critical behaviors* that should occur on the job in question. Only a few behaviors can be isolated because it would be impossible to monitor the hundreds that occur daily. At the same time, it is hoped that the 5-to-10 percent of all behaviors identified at this stage will actually represent 80-to-90 percent of the day-to-day activities that characterize the performance of the job in question. Other criteria for the behaviors selected are observability and ease of measurement.

This first step in identifying behaviors is important, because if anything, behavior modification can sometimes work too well. That is, any behavior that is critical to the job but not identified at this stage—and thus not monitored or rewarded—is likely to decrease in frequency. Unfortunately, supervisors do not always realize what they actually want until they start rewarding what they think they want. For example, a supervisor may think she wants productivity but may find that needed behaviors once taken for granted (like those dealing with quality, safety, teamwork, social relations, or general maintenance of facilities) start to disappear. Supervisors may also fall into the trap of selecting behaviors because they are easy to measure rather than because they are related to performance. These supervisors may then find themselves in a position of hoping for one thing while rewarding another.[28]

After the behaviors to be reinforced are selected, the next step is to *monitor the key behaviors*, that is, to observe the frequency with which these behaviors are already being exhibited. (This could be zero if the behavior desired has never been exhibited before.) Often tally sheets are developed to record observations, and behaviors are aggregated and displayed in a chart form. The degree to which the behavior occurs prior to the initiation of reinforcement is called baseline data.

Finally, after some period of collecting this baseline data, valued rewards are provided contingent upon the frequency with which workers display the critical behaviors. This step is referred to as *establishing positive contingencies*, and the nature of the rewards can vary. A reward may be money, time off from work, or simply praise from a supervisor. Following the application of these contingencies, critical behaviors (which are still being recorded) should increase in frequency relative to the baseline.

Behavior modification programs have been used in industry for some time. A substantial amount of evidence substantiates their effectiveness in a wide variety of jobs. Table 9-9 describes programs and results in five organizations.

[28] S. Kerr, "On the Folly of Rewarding A While Hoping for B," *Academy of Management Journal* 18 (1975), 769–83.

TABLE 9-9
Successful Applications of Behavior Modification Programs

COMPANY	NUMBER OF EMPLOYEES	BEHAVIOR TARGETED	REINFORCER USED	RESULT
Emery Air Freight	500	Low productivity and poor quality	Praise and recognition	Cost savings
Connecticut General Life Insurance	3,000	Absenteeism	Earned time off	Drastic reduction in absenteeism
City of Detroit garbage collectors	1,100	Poor productivity per man-hour	Pay bonus	Savings of $51.6 million
B. F. Goodrich Chemical Company	100	Failure to meet production schedules	Freedom to choose job activities	Production increases of 300%
ACDC Electronics	350	96% attendance	Praise	98% attendance

Behavior modification programs emphasize the positive rather than the negative control of behavior that is fueled by fear of punishment. (You may want to look at Chapter 7 for a refresher on the distinctions among punishment, negative reinforcement, positive reinforcement, and extinction.) Many behavior modification proponents believe that although punishment is often effective in reducing the frequency of an undesirable behavior, it does nothing to promote a desirable behavior. In addition, the punished employee often has negative emotional reactions to the person who punishes her and, by extension, to the firm itself. Let's look next at the use of punishment and disciplinary tactics in modern industry.

Punishment and Discipline Programs

There are several reasons why punishment is still widely practiced in many organizations despite the objections of behavior modification experts. First, not everyone is aware of the benefits of positive reinforcement. Managers and others need to become more knowledgeable about the methods we have just discussed. But also, there are some behaviors that are so damaging to the firm or to the employee himself that stopping them is crucial, even if it does nothing to promote positive behaviors. Moreover, failure to take immediate disciplinary action may sometimes imply acceptance or even approval of the offending behavior.

Several steps can be taken to improve the effectiveness of punishment programs. First, punishment should be *progressive*. It should proceed from a simple oral warning to a written formal notice to actual disciplinary action and, if the behavior persists, to termination of employment. Second, punishment should be *immediate*, rather than delayed. This maximizes the perceived contingency between the offending behavior and the punishment. It also minimizes any perceptions that the offending behavior is being used as a pretext to punish the person for something else. Third, punishment should be *consistent* so that no matter who commits the offense or in what circumstances, the punishment is the same. Fourth, punishment should be *impersonal* and directed at the offense itself, not at the person committing the offense. Fifth and last, punishment should be *documented*, so that a paper trail of evidence supports the fact that punishment was progressive, immediate, consistent, and impersonal. Figure 9-8 shows the sort of documentation that might support managerial action with respect to an employee's persistent absenteeism.

Sometimes an offense calls for a face-to-face meeting between supervisor and employee. Table 9-10 lists nine rules for conducting an effective *disciplinary meeting*.[29] When you are conducting a disciplinary meeting with a union member, a tenth rule must be observed. The offender has the right to have a witness at the meeting. Failure to allow a witness to be present has been interpreted by the Supreme Court as a violation of the National Labor Relations Act.[30]

Some firms that employ work teams try to get coworkers involved in disciplining their colleagues. According to Ralph Stoyer, CEO of Johnsonville Foods, discipline is best administered by the people who have to work with the individual. If you came to work late, which would you prefer, a lecture from your boss or protests from your seven coworkers who feel you let them down?[31]

Of course, the "capital punishment" of organizational life is *termination of employment*. Union workers are pretty well protected from this form of punishment,

[29] Cascio, *Managing Human Resources*, p. 55.
[30] D. Israel, "The Weingarten Case Sets Precedent for Co-Employee Representation," *Personnel Administrator* 28 (1983), 23–26.
[31] W. Kiechel, "How to Discipline in the Modern Age," *Fortune*, May 7, 1990, pp. 31–32.

FIGURE 9-8

A Written Reprimand
for a Worker Who Is
Repeatedly Absent

Memo
To: Jack Levitt
From: John Doe
Re: Absenteeism

　Friday, March 10th, 19X9 marked your
third absence in two weeks.

　I now find it necessary to tell you
in writing that this kind of absenteeism
will not be condoned.

　If you persist in this kind of action,
which is clearly a violation of Section 6 of
the work rules, I may be forced to take
disciplinary action, up to and including
dismissal.

John Doe

employment at will A provision
that either party in the
employment relationship can
terminate the relationship at any
time, even without reason.

except perhaps in the case of blatant and outrageous offenses. For many workers not represented by a union, however, termination is an ever-present danger. An **employment at will** doctrine is created whenever someone agrees to work for an employer for an unspecified length of time. Until recently, such an arrangement could be terminated at the whim of either party.

Increasingly, however, ex-employees are fighting back and suing for "wrongful discharge." Moreover, unlike discrimination cases involving age, sex, or race, in which employees can sue only for back wages, wrongful discharge suits can obtain punitive damages for plaintiffs as well. The fact that these cases are often

TABLE 9-10
Rules for Conducting an Effective Disciplinary Meeting

1. Conduct the interview in a quiet, private place.
2. Come prepared with the employee's personnel file to document past digressions or exemplary actions.
3. Do not aggressively prosecute the employee. Merely state facts in a straightforward fashion.
4. Clarify the exact work rule violated and its importance to the firm.
5. Allow the employee to defend or explain his or her actions without interruption.
6. Stay unemotional, and treat the employee with respect. Never use foul language, and never touch the employee.
7. If the problem was a result of a misunderstanding, simply admit it, and close the case.
8. If the problem was an honest mistake, take steps to prevent its reoccurrence, and communicate the expectation that it will not happen again.
9. Focus on the future. After discipline is administered, forget the past and express confidence in the employee's potential.

heard by a jury may explain why plaintiffs are so frequently vindicated. Juries tend to identify more readily with individual victims than with large, impersonal corporations, and welcome the chance to punish a company. Research indicates that juries find for the plaintiff in 75 percent of cases, awarding them, on average, over $500,000.[32]

In some instances, these cases are brought up under charges of fraud. For example, Ian Dowie, a former office-products executive at IBM, was lured to Exxon in 1979 with promises of a division presidency, an eventual $100,000-a-year contract, and hefty bonuses from a company profit-sharing plan. When none of these promises were honored and Dowie complained, he was fired. Dowie sued for fraud and breach of contract, and in 1986 a New York jury awarded him $10.1 million in damages—$9 million of which was to punish Exxon.[33]

Managers can take several steps to avoid problems of this sort. First, the rules we have laid out for discipline programs should be followed closely, especially the rules dealing with documentation. Second, in recruiting people for jobs, no promises of job security should be made unless one intends to keep them without exception. Third, employee handbooks or manuals should be developed that clearly spell out the rights and responsibilities of employees. These handbooks should specifically outline the disciplinary process and the actions or behaviors (drug use, theft, excessive absenteeism or tardiness) that will initiate disciplinary action. If these handbooks are distributed to people before they are hired, they are often treated as implied contracts. Indeed, in many cases where handbooks are not available, employees may actually demand written guarantees. Gerald Simmons, president of Handy Associates, an executive recruiting firm, notes: "People are holding out for letters specifying what they would get if the company lessens their responsibilities, moves them to another location, or uses another of the typical methods corporations use when they want to harass someone into resigning."[34]

Finally, employers must make frank performance appraisals if they are to assemble the documentation necessary to support a pattern of misbehavior or inadequate performance. A supervisor who inflates a subordinate's ratings for ten years in order to avoid conflict and then finally gets fed up and fires the person is going to have to do a lot of explaining to a jury.

CAREER DEVELOPMENT PROGRAMS

Cognitive appraisal theory deals with the process by which a person decides if his job conforms to his work-related values. As we discussed in Chapter 8, job dissatisfaction and a lack of organizational commitment stem from the perception that the rewards offered by one's work do not satisfy one's needs and values. Moreover, when a person is uncertain about whether he can ever make a job meet his needs, he experiences stress, which in turn increases the probability that he will resign.

Two things increase the difficulty of matching an individual's values to job rewards. First, different people have different values. Second, a person's values tend to change over time. As individuals' needs and values change, so do the needs of organizations, especially in these days of mergers, acquisitions, and downsizing. Organizations are trying to be "leaner and meaner" and, often, to

[32] Firing Line: Legal Challenges Force Firms to Revamp Ways They Dismiss Workers," *Wall Street Journal*, September 13, 1983, p. 1.

[33] M. Geyelin, "Fired Managers Winning More Lawsuits: Raising Stakes, Many Now Seek Punitive Awards," *Wall Street Journal*, September 7, 1989, p. 1.

[34] C. H. Deutsch, "When a Handshake Isn't Enough," *New York Times*, February 4, 1990, p. D29.

do more things with fewer people. In the highly competitive environment in which many organizations now operate, a firm can afford neither an excess of human resources nor an absence of required talent. At the same time, companies cannot dismiss all their old employees and hire new ones every time there is a shift in strategy or a shock wave in the economy. How can organizations maintain flexibility and adaptability while encouraging commitment among talented people? For some firms, career-development programs are the answer.

A *career* has been defined as an individually perceived sequence of attitudes and behaviors associated with work experiences over the span of a person's life.[35] A career typically unfolds in stages. A *career stage* is a period marked by a similarity of experiences that set one period apart from another. These experiences can be role transitions, crises, or other turning points. Figure 9-9 shows some of the major career stages that researchers have identified and the approximate ages at which they occur.

Career-development programs are created by organizations to help improve the fit between changing individual needs and values and changing organizational realities. Career-development activities in an organization attempt to provide for the effective, long-term utilization and development of human talent. Although each firm's career-development program may have idiosyncratic features, many include career counseling, mentoring, encouragement to women and minorities, and assistance to dual-career couples.

Career Counseling

Career counseling is designed to help individual employees understand and assess their own needs and values. It also helps them learn about opportunities in the firm that may help them satisfy these personal imperatives. In many companies, employees can participate in programs that focus on self-analysis. They can attend

[35] D. T. Hall, *Careers in Organizations* (Glenview, Ill.: Scott, Foresman, 1976), p. 112.

FIGURE 9-9

Major Career Stages in a Person's Life Span

In the stage of *exploration*, children and young people explore a wide range of jobs, seeking a personal identity. In the *trial* stage, the young adult may have a series of jobs and employers as he tries to match his identity with a work role. In the *establishment* stage, the person commits himself to one work role and develops as a specialized and involved worker. Negotiating the *midcareer transition*, the person reassesses the match between identity and work role, choosing to grow in the job, to maintain the same performance level, or to slow down. Finally, in the *exit* stage, the person becomes less involved in his work role, preparatory to eventual retirement.
Source: Adapted from D. T. Hall Careers in Organizations *(Glenview, Ill.: Scott, Foresman, 1976), 57.*

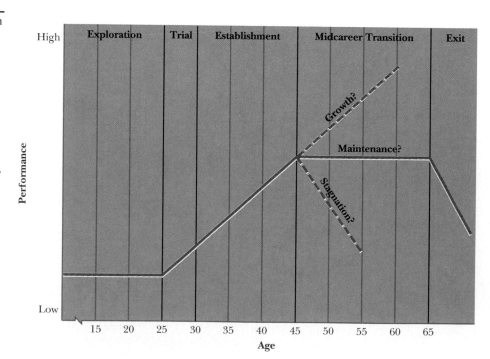

MANAGING INDIVIDUALS IN ORGANIZATIONS

BLACK

workshops on life and career planning or on interpersonal relationships. They can stop in at assessment centers for aptitude and interest evaluations.[36]

Mentor-Protégé Relationships

mentoring relationship A partnership between a senior and a junior colleague in which the senior partner promotes the development of the junior partner.

A **mentoring relationship** is a partnership between a senior and a junior colleague in which the senior partner promotes the development of the junior partner.[37] The senior partner might engage in *career advancement* activities such as coaching, providing visibility, protecting his protégé from threats, or providing her with challenging assignments. The mentor might also offer his protégé *personal support* by extending friendship, enhancing the junior person's confidence and self-concept.

It's not hard to see how these kinds of activities can help a younger person setting out on a career path. Perhaps it's less obvious just how these activities benefit the mentor. Typically, the mentor is established in her career and at the stage where she can experience growth, maintenance, or stagnation. Working with young, energetic junior people, who will be guiding the company long after the mentor is gone, is an excellent way of maintaining one's own motivation and desire for growth. At the same time, it allows one to pass on to a younger generation the unique knowledge about the firm and its business that can be achieved only by spending years in the trenches.

Organizations can promote mentoring relationships by providing opportunities for exchanges between senior and junior colleagues. They can provide training to mentors on how to handle these special interpersonal relationships. They can also reward managers who faithfully discharge their mentoring responsibilities, especially where they do so at some cost to their own careers.

Women and Minorities

Research shows that career-planning programs are especially needed for women and minority-group members, who generally have less access than white males to career-enhancing experiences.[38] Even in the 1990s, a majority of upper-level professional and managerial positions are still occupied by white males. Those

[36] J. W. Walker and T. G. Gutterridge, *Career Planning Practices* (New York: AMACOM, 1979), p. 36.

[37] K. E. Kram, *Mentoring at Work* (Glenview, Ill.: Scott, Foresman, 1984), p. 80.

[38] F. S. Hall and M. H. Albrecht, *The Management of Affirmative Action* (Santa Monica, Calif.: Goodyear, 1979), p. 101.

"He's an unlimited knowledge base," Jeffrey Parker, undergraduate student at Atlanta's Morehouse University, says of his mentor, Philip M. Butterfield. Butterfield, a Citibank vice-president, says he volunteered for the bank's Fellows Program because he felt mentoring was the best way to "make a change in someone's life." As a result of his mentoring relationship, which included two summer internships at Citibank, Parker has chosen a business major and plans to go on to law school after graduation. Source: Michel Marriott, "Matching Those Who Need Guidance with Those Who Have Been There," The New York Times, June 27, 1990.

executives tend to develop mentor-protégé relationships with other white males unless they are encouraged to do otherwise. Some organizations, such as Baxter Health Care Corporation and the Federal National Mortgage Association, go out of their way to make sure managers develop their female or minority employees. Both companies tie managerial bonuses to objective indicators of female and minority success. These programs achieve results. The Federal National Mortgage Association points to the fact that the representation of females at senior levels of management went from 4 percent to 25 percent between 1981 and 1990. Such programs fight stereotypical views about women and minorities in the hope that members of these groups will not be shunted into unchallenging, low-visibility, career-retarding job assignments.[39]

Finally, although managers are generally reluctant to give negative feedback to any subordinate, they are especially self-conscious about giving it to people who are unlike themselves for fear of being perceived as bigoted or sexist. Yet frank and open negative feedback is vital to new employees who are still learning the ropes and need proper guidance about the do's and don'ts of organizational life.

Organizational career-development programs have to overcome these obstacles by fostering good relations between minority protégés and non-minority mentors. That is the way to dispel stereotypes. Organizations also need to encourage company-wide networks of women and minority-group members so that they can exchange experiences and learn from each other. Moreover, if affirmative action programs do bring in women and minorities who might not otherwise have been hired, it is imperative to provide additional training and developmental experiences for these groups. Some organizations ignore scores on valid predictors of future job success to meet hiring quotas and provide no remedial training, then have trouble retaining "protected groups." Such companies have to consider whether they are helping or hurting the cause of integrating the work force.

Dual-Career Couples

Another issue addressed by career-development programs is the dual-career couple. If it is challenging to manage a single career, it can be exceedingly difficult to manage two careers in the same household at the same time. Almost invariably, the needs of one career will sometimes conflict with the needs of the other. For example, one person may be offered a desirable position in another geographical area, and the spouse may be forced to take a less desirable job in order to make the move. On top of this, if a dual-career couple have children, the role conflict (see Chapter 8) generated by the many competing demands on the couple, their family, and the organization may seem an almost unsurmountable obstacle.

Organizations can do several things to help meet this challenge. First, *flexible working arrangements* at least give the couple a fighting chance at managing the many demands on their time. For example, at Colgate Palmolive, some workers are on flexible hours, with a core time (10:00 AM–2:00 PM) when they must be at the office. The remaining part of their eight-hour day can be made up by coming in as early as 6:00 AM or staying as late as 7:00 PM.

Company-sponsored day care can help solve one of the major problems faced by dual-career couples. Indeed, the number of companies that offered some form of child-care assistance grew from 2,500 to 5,400 from 1986 to 1990 alone. The list of such companies includes some of the nation's most prestigious employers— IBM, Time-Warner, American Express, DuPont, Honeywell and Levi-Strauss.

[39] C. Trost, "Firms Heed Women Employee's Needs," *Wall Street Journal*, November 22, 1989, p. B1.

MANAGING INDIVIDUALS IN ORGANIZATIONS

Some companies, such as Stride Rite, even offer programs for employees' aging relatives. Care for the older generation is an increasing concern for baby-boomers.[40] Stride Rite spent $700,000 to convert 8,500 square feet of its head-quarters into an elder-care center. The company estimates that it costs $140 dollars a week to care for an ageing relative.

Company *relocation programs* that help find suitable employment for the spouse of a newly promoted or transferred employee are another useful resource. Finally, *minimizing travel requirements* can benefit dual-career couples. Today, with fax machines in most offices and the technology for holding conferences and seminars by satellite hook-up widely available, it is possible to cut down on business travel.

One controversial proposal is the development of separate career paths for employees who prefer to put family before work. These so-called mommy-tracks have been advocated by some who insist that women who are as committed to their families as to their careers should be given more flexible roles in the work-place, and eased off the "fast track."[41] Critics of these plans maintain that mommy tracks reinforce sexual stereotypes and assume that the burden of child-rearing responsibilities rests solely on women. Companies like Johnson and Johnson try to spare workers such devil's bargains by providing *family-care leaves*. Under these programs, workers can leave the job for one year with full benefits and guarantees of reemployment and career opportunities upon reinstatement.[42]

SUMMARY

There are eight areas of overlap between organizational behavior and human resource management. Employment testing programs, both *aptitude-based* and *skill-based*, are applications of theories of human attributes. Theories of perception and judgment inform the general process of performance appraisal as well as the specific development of *behaviorally anchored rating scales*. Affirmative action hiring and promotion programs make use of the administrative decision-making model. The *top-down-selection-within-subgroups* approach is one solution to the problem of integrating the work force when valid selection practices result in *disparate impact* on members of protected groups. Two theories of motivation, equity theory and expectancy theory, are useful in justifying pay differentials both across and within jobs. *Job evaluation* is a process for establishing equitable pay differentials across jobs. Merit and incentive systems are used to establish equitable pay differentials among employees working on the same job. *Profit-sharing plans* and *cost-saving plans* distribute rewards to all employees based on performance of the organization as a whole. Reinforcement theory offers potential solutions to problems regarding training and organizational discipline. Career-development programs offer many ways of enhancing employee commitment, satisfaction, and performance.

[40] C. Lawson, "Hope for the Working Parent: Company Care Plans Spread Slowly," *New York Times*, March 15, 1990, p. C1 and K. Teltsch, "For Younger and Older, Workplace Day Care," *New York Times*, March 10, 1990, p. A1.

[41] J. Solomon, "Schwartz of 'Mommy Track' Notoriety Prods Firms to Address Women's Needs," *Wall Street Journal*, December 11, 1989, p. B13.

[42] C. H. Deutsch, "Saying No to the 'Mommy Track': Some Companies Don't Require Part-Time Professional to Sacrifice Their Careers," *New York Times*, January 28, 1990, p. 29.

REVIEW QUESTIONS

1. Although employment tests are used to meet the needs of employers, why might the nature of tests selected be important to job applicants? That is, what does the type of selection instrument that a firm uses tell the applicant about the firm? What type of selection program, aptitude or skill, is likely to leave the best impression on the job applicant? Why?

2. Imagine two different pharmaceutical companies that employ the same job categories yet differ in their business strategy. One is trying to increase market share through innovation (developing new and better drugs). The other sticks to established products and tries to increase market share by lowering costs. Why might the two firms wind up with dramatically different pay structures even if both go through the process of job evaluation described in this chapter?

3. We discussed four types of pay-for-performance systems in this chapter: merit based, incentives, profit sharing, and cost saving. Compare each to the process used to develop a behavior modification program, and rank order the four in terms of how well each conforms to behavior modification principles.

4. Assume your organization wants to establish either an individually based or organizationally based pay-for-performance program. Which do you think would be most suitable and why? Assume further that your organization wants to use *both* individual and organizationally based rewards. Which pair (incentive + profit sharing, incentive + cost saving, merit + profit sharing, merit + cost saving) seems the best and the worst match in your opinion? Why?

5. We have drawn a distinction between line personnel and staff personnel. Many managers have the job of supervising staff personnel. In what way might this kind of task be more or less difficult than managing nonstaff personnel? Think about the task of managing human resource specialists in particular. In what way might this kind of task be more or less difficult than managing other types of staff personnel?

DIAGNOSTIC QUESTIONS

Few line managers and executives ever become specialists in personnel-human resources. Those with supervisory responsibilities, however, must have some working knowledge of the key issues to avoid costly mistakes. Moreover, this knowledge will facilitate communication and interaction between managers and P/HR specialists. This integration may be focused by concentrating on the following questions:

1. In this organization, who are the experts in P/HR? What is the best way to contact these people to discuss issues of mutual concern?

2. What are some of the major attributes of the important jobs in this organization? What kinds of aptitude tests might predict success in these jobs?

3. For what jobs in this organization could skill tests be developed? What kinds of work sample tests would be most appropriate for these jobs?

4. How free from bias are the subjective performance ratings of supervisors in this firm? If objective measures are used, how much control do employees have over the functions that these measures assess?

5. Are there any jobs in this firm for which a BARS might usefully be developed?

6. How does this firm manage the dual goals of selecting and promoting on the basis of merit and of integrating the work force?

7. What compensable factors does this organization value? How does the organization translate these factors into a pay structure that reflects job-based pay differentials?

8. How does the firm reward employees for their performance? If it uses pay as a reward, is a merit or incentive plan most appropriate?

9. How does the organization reward people for organizational performance? If it uses pay, would a cost-saving or a profit-sharing approach be most appropriate?

10. What are some of the critical behaviors that need to be displayed in a job? How might a behavior modification program be used to increase the frequency of the needed behaviors?

11. What are some damaging behaviors that occur on the job? How might a discipline program be developed to decrease the frequency of those behaviors?

12. What kinds of career-development programs might be helpful in creating a good fit between the changing needs of individuals and the changing needs of the organization?

LEARNING THROUGH EXPERIENCE

Although piecerate, commission, or other continuous reinforcement plans provide rewards to employees that are highly motivating, many organizations can only pay employees fixed salaries and make yearly salary adjustments. Thus an annual pay raise is about the only indicator the employees of such firms have of how the organization views their performance. Making salary decisions under these circumstances is a critically important but immensely difficult task. In this exercise you will get to experience the demands of this task first-hand.

STEP ONE: PRE-CLASS PREPARATION

Read the instructions to the "Employee Profile Sheet" below and then decide on a pay increase for each of the eight employees. Be prepared to explain your decisions in class.

STEP TWO: GROUP DISSCUSION

The class should divide into groups of four to six members each (if you have already formed permanent groups, reassemble in those same groups). Each member should share the recommendations he or she made in Step One and explain his or her reasons for them. After all members have reported, the group should analyze and try to explain differences among everyone's recommendations. The group should then develop a set of recommendations that it can agree on. A spokesperson should be appointed to present the group's recommendations to the class.

STEP THREE: CLASS DISCUSSION

Your instructor will reassemble the class so that group spokespersons can present their reports. As each group's recommendations are presented the instructor will record them on a blackboard, flipchart, or overhead projector. After the reports are completed, the class should look for similarities and differences among the recommendations of different groups and consider the following questions:

1. What kinds of differences could you detect among the eight managers described on the Employee Profile Sheet? Which of these differences served as factors that affected your pay raise decisions?

2. What were the reasons for basing pay raises on each of these factors? Why did you choose to concentrate on some differences among the eight supervisors and to ignore others?

3. If there are differences among the recommendations of different groups, how can you explain them? If there are similarities, what caused them?

4. What would probably happen if you implemented the recommendations made by your class? How would each of the managers react? How would these reactions affect the performance of the company?

CONCLUSION

Using rewards to motivate employees requires that the receipt of rewards be tied as closely as possible to instances of successful performance. Performance-reward contingency is certainly the strongest when piecerate or commission plans are implemented. If companies have no choice but to pay yearly salaries, a minimal degree of contingency can still be established if yearly raises are tied directly to employee performance.

As you have learned in this exercise, maintaining such a tight connection between employee performance and yearly raises can be more difficult than it sounds, sometimes requiring painful decisions. At some point in your future role as manager, it may be your job to make such decisions and to explain them to your subordinates. Base your decisions on sound information about employee performance, and make sure that your explanations are clearly understood.

* The Employee Profile Sheet is reprinted with the author's permission.

Employee Profile Sheet

You must make salary increase recommendations for eight managers whom you supervise. They have just completed their first year with the company and are now to be considered for their first annual raise. Keep in mind that you may be setting precedents that will shape future expectations and that you must stay within your salary budget. Otherwise, there are no formal company policies to restrict you as you decide how to allocate raises. Write the raise you would give each manager in the space to the left of each name. You have a total of $26,000 in your budget for pay raises.

$_____ A. J. Adams. Adams is not, as far as you can tell, a good performer. You have discussed your opinion with others and they agree completely. However, you know that Adams has one of the toughest work groups to manage. Adams' subordinates have low skill levels and the work is dirty and hard. If you lose Adams, you are not sure that you could find an adequate replacement. Current salary: $30,000.

$_____ B. K. Berger. Berger is single and seems to lead the life of a carefree swinger. In general, you feel that Berger's job performance is not up to par, and some of Berger's "goofs" are well known to other employees. Current salary: $33,750.

$_____ C. C. Carter. You consider Carter to be one of your best subordinates. However, it is quite apparent that other people don't agree. Carter has married into wealth and, as far as you know, doesn't need any more money. Current salary: $37,000.

$_____ D. Davis. You happen to know from your personal relationship that Davis badly needs more money because of certain personal problems. Davis also happens to be one of your best managers. For some reason, your enthusiasm is not shared by your other subordinates and you have heard them make joking remarks about Davis's performance. Current salary: $34,000.

$_____ E. J. Ellis. Your opinion is that Ellis just isn't cutting the mustard. Surprisingly enough, however, when you check with others to see how they feel you find that Ellis is very highly regarded. You also know that Ellis badly needs a raise. Ellis was recently divorced and is finding it extremely difficult to support a young family of four as a single parent. Current salary: $30,750.

$_____ F. M. Foster. Foster has turned out to be a very pleasant surprise, has done an excellent job, and is seen by peers as one of the best people in your group of managers. This surprises you because Foster is generally frivolous and doesn't seem to care very much about money or promotions. Current salary: $32,700.

$_____ G. K. Gomez. Gomez has been very successful so far. You are particularly impressed by this because Gomez's is one of the hardest jobs in your company. Gomez needs money more than many of your other subordinates and is respected for good performance. Current salary: $35,250.

$_____ H. A. Hunt. You know Hunt personally. This employee seems to squander money continually. Hunt has a fairly easy job assignment, and your own view is that Hunt doesn't do it especially well. You are thus surprised to find that several of the other new managers think that Hunt is the best of the new group. Current salary: $31,500.

DIAGNOSING ORGANIZATIONAL BEHAVIOR

CASE 9-1
DENVER DEPARTMENT STORES*
J. B. RITCHIE, *Brigham Young University*
PAUL H. THOMPSON, *Brigham Young University*

In the early spring of 1991 Jim Barton was evaluating the decline in sales volume experienced by the four departments he supervised in the main store of Denver Department Stores, a Colorado retail chain. Barton was at a loss as to how to improve sales. He attributed the slowdown in sales to the current economic downturn affecting the entire nation. However, Barton's supervisor, Mr. Cornwall, pointed out that some of the other departments in the store had experienced a 15 percent gain over the previous year. Cornwall added that Barton was expected to have his departments up to par with the others in a short period of time.

BACKGROUND

Jim Barton had been supervisor of the sporting goods, hardware, housewares, and toy departments in the main store of Denver Department Stores for three of the ten years he had worked for the chain. The four departments were situated adjacent to each other on the ground floor of the store. Each department had a head sales clerk who reported to Mr. Barton on merchandise storage and presentation, special orders, and general department upkeep. The head sales clerks were all full-time, long-term employees of Denver Department Stores, having an average of about eight years' experience with the chain. The head clerks were also expected to train the people in the department they supervised. The rest of the staff in each department was made up of part-time employees who lived in or near Denver. Most of the part-time people were students at nearby universities who worked to finance their education. In addition, there were two or three housewives who worked about ten hours a week in the evenings.

All sales personnel at Denver Department Stores were paid strictly on an hourly basis. Beginning pay was just slightly over the minimum wage and raises were given based on length of employment and work performance evaluations. The salespeople in the housewares and sporting goods departments were paid about forty cents an hour more than the clerks in the other departments because it was thought that more sales ability and experience were needed in dealing with the people who shopped for items found in those departments.

As a general rule the head sales clerk in each department did not actively sell, but kept the department well stocked and presentable, and trained and evaluated sales personnel. The part-time employees did most of the clerk and sales work. The role of the sales clerk was seen as one of answering customer questions and ringing up the sale rather than actively selling the merchandise except in the two departments previously mentioned where a little more active selling was done.

The sales clerks in Barton's departments seemed to get along well with each other. The four department heads usually ate lunch together. If business was brisk in one department and slow in another, the sales people in the slower area would assist in the busy department. Male clerks often helped female clerks unload heavy merchandise carts. Store procedure was that whenever a cash register was low on change a clerk would go to a master till in the stationery department to get more. Barton's departments, however, usually supplied each other with change, thus avoiding the longer walk to the master till.

Barton's immediate supervisor, Mr. Cornwall, had the reputation of being a skilled merchandiser and in the past had initiated many ideas to increase the sales volume of the store. Some of the longer-term employees said that Mr. Cornwall was very impatient and that he sometimes was rude to his subordinates while discussing merchandising problems with them.

The store manager, Mr. Blanding, had been with Denver Department Stores for twenty years and would be retiring in a few years. Earlier in his career Mr. Blanding had taken an active part in the merchandising aspect of the store, but recently he had delegated most of the merchandising and sales responsibilities to Mr. Cornwall.

SITUATION

Because of Mr. Cornwall's concern, Barton consulted with his department supervisors about the reason for the declining sales volume. The consensus reached was that the level of customer traffic had not been adequate to allow the departments to achieve a high sales volume. When Barton presented his problem to Mr. Cornwall, Cornwall concluded that since customer traffic could

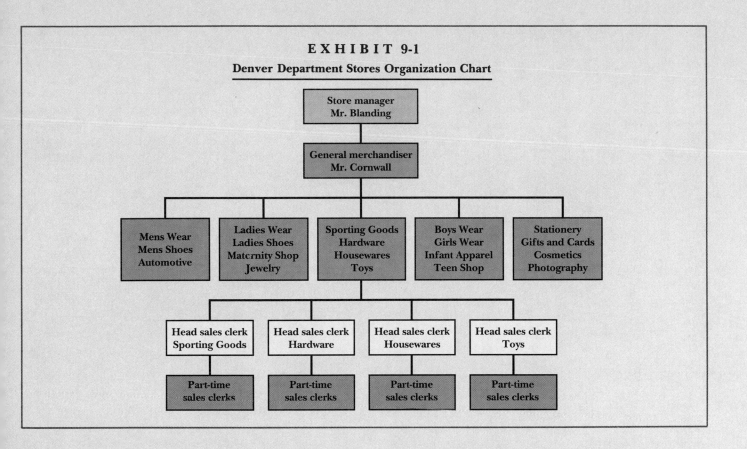

EXHIBIT 9-1

Denver Department Stores Organization Chart

Store manager
Mr. Blanding

General merchandiser
Mr. Cornwall

| Mens Wear Mens Shoes Automotive | Ladies Wear Ladies Shoes Maternity Shop Jewelry | Sporting Goods Hardware Housewares Toys | Boys Wear Girls Wear Infant Apparel Teen Shop | Stationery Gifts and Cards Cosmetics Photography |

Head sales clerk Sporting Goods — Head sales clerk Hardware — Head sales clerk Housewares — Head sales clerk Toys

Part-time sales clerks — Part-time sales clerks — Part-time sales clerks — Part-time sales clerks

not be controlled and since the departments had been adequately stocked throughout the year, the improvement in sales would have to be a result of increased effort on the part of the clerks in each department. Cornwall added that if sales didn't improve soon the hours of both the full- and part-time sales clerks would have to be cut back. Later Barton found out that Cornwall had sent a letter around to each department informing employees of the possibility of fewer hours if sales didn't improve.

A few days after Barton received the assignment to increase sales in his department, Mr. Cornwall called him into his office again and suggested that each sales person carry a personal tally card to record daily sales. Each clerk would record his or her sales and at the end of the day the personal sales tally card would be totaled. Cornwall said that by reviewing the cards over a period of time he would be able to determine who were the "deadwood" and who were the real producers. The clerks were to be told about the purpose of the tally card and that those clerks who had low sales tallies would have their hours cut back.

Barton told Cornwall he wanted to consider this program and also discuss it with the head salespeople before implementing it. He told Mr. Cornwall that the next day was his day off but that when he returned to work the day after he would discuss this proposal with the head sales clerks.

Upon returning to the store after his day off, Mr. Barton was surprised to see each of his salespeople carrying a daily tally sheet. When he asked Mr. Cornwall why the program had been adopted so quickly, Cornwall replied that when it came to improvement of sales, no delay could be tolerated. Barton wondered what effect the new program would have on the personnel in each of his departments.

When Mr. Cornwall issued the tally cards to Barton's salespeople, the head sales clerks failed to fill them out. Two of the head clerks had lost their tally cards when Cornwall came by later in the day to see how the program was progressing. Cornwall issued the two head clerks new cards and told them that if they didn't "shape up" he would see some "new faces" in the departments.

The part-time salespeople filled out the cards completely, writing down every sale. The rumor that those clerks who had low sales tallies would have their hours cut spread rapidly. Soon the clerks became much more active and aggressive in their sales efforts. Customers were often approached more than once by different clerks in each department. One elderly lady complained that while making her way to the restroom in the back of the hardware department she was asked by four clerks if she needed assistance in making a selection.

When Barton returned the day after the institution of the program, the head sales clerks asked him about the new program. Barton replied that they had no alternative but to follow Cornwall's orders or quit. Later that afternoon the head clerks were seen discussing the situation on their regular break. After the break the head clerks began waiting on customers and filling out their sales tally cards.

Not long after the adoption of the program, the stock rooms began to look cluttered. Unloaded carts lined the aisles of the stock room. The shelves on the sales floor were slowly emptied and remained poorly stocked. Sales of items that had a large retail value were especially sought after and the head sales clerks were often seen dusting and rearranging these more expensive items. The head clerks' tally sheets always had the greatest amount of sales when the clerks compared sheets at the end of each day. (Barton collected them daily and delivered them to Cornwall.) The friendly conversations among salespeople and between clerks and customers were shortened and sales were rung up on the cash register and completed in a much shorter time. Breaks were no longer taken as groups and when they were taken they seemed to be much shorter than before.

When sales activity was slow in one department, clerks would migrate to other departments where there were more customers. Sometimes conflicts between clerks arose because of competition for sales. In one instance the head clerk of the hardware department interrupted a part-time clerk from the toy department who was demonstrating a large and expensive table saw to a customer. The head clerk of the hardware department introduced himself as the hardware specialist and sent the toy clerk back to his own department.

Often customers asked for items which were not on the shelves of the sales floor. When the clerk looked for the item it was found on the carts which jammed the stock room aisles. Some customers were told the item they desired wasn't in stock and later the clerk would find it on a cart in the stock room.

When Barton reported his observations of the foregoing situations to Mr. Cornwall, he was told that it was a result of the clerks' adjusting to the new program and to not worry about it. Cornwall pointed out, however, that sales volume had still not improved. He further noted that the sum of all sales reported on the tally sheets was often $500 to $600 more than total department sales according to the cash register.

A few weeks after the instigation of the tally card system Cornwall walked through the hardware department and stopped beside three carts of merchandise left in the aisle of the stock room from the morning of the day before. He talked to the head clerk in an impatient tone and asked him why the carts weren't unloaded. The clerk replied that if Mr. Cornwall had any questions about the department he should ask Mr. Barton. Cornwall picked up the telephone and angrily dialed Barton's office. Barton told him that the handling of merchandise had been preempted by the emphasis on the tally card system of recording sales. Cornwall slammed down the receiver and stormed out of the department.

That afternoon, at Barton's request, Blanding, Cornwall, and Barton visited the four departments. After talking with some of the salespeople, Mr. Blanding sent a memo announcing that the tally card program would be discontinued immediately.

After the program had been terminated, sales clerks still took their breaks separately and conversations seemed to be limited to only the essential topics needed to run the department. Barton and the head sales clerk didn't talk as freely as they had before and some of the head clerks said that Mr. Barton had failed to represent their best interests to Cornwall. Some of the clerks said they thought the tally card system was Barton's idea. The part-time people resumed the major portion of the sales and clerking jobs and the head clerks returned to merchandising. Sales volume in the department didn't improve.

When you have read this case, look back at the chapter's diagnostic questions and choose the ones that apply to the case. Then use those questions with the ones that follow in your case analysis.

1. Do you agree with Mr. Cornwall that keeping sales records and terminating clerks who fail to perform acceptably should stimulate greater effort among the Denver department store's salesforce? Why? Or why not?

2. Describe the steps that the management of the Denver Department Stores should take to set up a more effective performance appraisal program than Mr. Cornwall's. Why would your program work better?

3. Suppose the Denver stores decided to implement a pay-for-performance program to motivate salesforce performance. What kind of program would you recommend? Why? Describe how you would implement your program.

CASE 9-2
CHANCELLOR STATE UNIVERSITY*
THOMAS R. MILLER, *Memphis State University*

THE SETTING

Chancellor State University is a large, urban university in the Midwest. Although the University had experienced rapid growth for several years, overall enrollment

* Copyright © 1985 by Thomas R. Miller. Reprinted with the author's permission.

had stabilized. The School of Business Administration, however, had continued to grow, drawing students away from programs in the School of Education and the College of Arts and Sciences as well as attracting new students concerned with future vocational opportunities. The faculty and administration of the business school were pleased to see the enrollment growth as it signaled acceptance of their degree programs, but the enrollment expansion also created strong pressure to expand the business faculty.

Under normal circumstances, faculty expansion would simply have meant an active recruitment effort by school administrators. But the situation at Chancellor State was representative of a national phenomenon of enrollment growth in business schools that had resulted in a strong demand for doctorally qualified faculty in the face of a relatively short supply. Thus, faculty recruitment at many business schools had become a priority activity, rather than merely one of the many administrative responsibilities of deans and department heads.

At Chancellor State, Fred Kennedy, Chairman of the Management Department, had been actively seeking new faculty members for his staff, which had the heaviest course load in the school. As is often customary in academia, the faculty in the Department of Management participated in recruitment, spending considerable time meeting with the faculty candidates in an effort to evaluate their candidacy for a faculty position. Faculty members could then make recommendations as to whether or not the prospect should be tendered an offer to join the staff.

THE CONFERENCE

It was late in February, and several prospective faculty members had visited Chancellor State for campus job interviews. Early one Friday morning, Kennedy was in his office reviewing the job files of prospective faculty members. He looked up as he heard the voice of Larry Gordon, an assistant professor of management who was now in his third year at Chancellor State.

"Good morning, Fred," said Larry, as he walked into the Department office. "Do you have a couple of minutes? I want to talk with you about something."

Fred gestured to him to come into his office.

"Sure, Larry, what's on your mind?"

After entering Fred's office, Larry closed the door, indicating to Fred that this was not to be just a casual, friendly conversation.

"Fred," Larry began, "I was wondering what you thought about the prospective faculty member we had in here for an interview last week. I've been talking with a couple other faculty members about him, and they're not really all that impressed. He seems to be OK, I guess, but we may be able to do better. Are we going to make him an offer? If we do, he's sure not worth top dollar in my opinion."

"Well, I've received some of the written evaluations back from the faculty, and they seem to be fairly positive," replied Fred. "They're not as favorable as they could be, but the other faculty seem to think that he would be acceptable and that he could work out pretty well on our staff. His academic credentials are not bad, and he has had some good experience. Given the state of the market for business faculty in his specialty, I expect that we'll extend an offer to him. By the way, I know that he already has a couple of offers in hand from our competition."

Fred could readily see that Larry was not pleased to hear all of this. From their earlier conversations, Fred could anticipate Larry's next comment.

"Yeah, O.K., I can see that we could use him, but what kind of money are we offering in these new positions?" questioned Larry. "I don't mean to pry into somebody else's business, but what sort of salary is the department offering our new faculty?"

Fred winced at this question. He had in the past made no secret about general salary ranges for new faculty members. In fact, this information was generally known throughout the school. But this had become a very sensitive issue in the last few years, given the rapid increases in starting salaries for new business faculty members.

"Well, Larry, I guess you know that we're paying competitively for our new faculty. With our enrollment increase we've got to increase our teaching staff, and to do that we're probably going to have to meet the market," Fred responded.

Larry was obviously not satisfied with this response and was becoming irritated with the conversation. "Fred, I assume that by 'meeting the market' you mean that we're going to offer this guy two or three thousand dollars more than some of us who have been here for several years are now making. This new guy has not yet finished his doctorate, has very little teaching experience, has no publications, and, in my opinion, is not as good as a lot of our current faculty. How much can you justify paying for an unknown quantity? I think it's just unfair to the present faculty to offer him more money than many of us are making. When is somebody going to do something for us? Fred, I'm not unhappy here in this department, but I'm sure going to keep my eyes open for other opportunities. I feel sure that I could move to another school at a higher rank and increase my salary significantly. You may think I'm wrong and maybe I shouldn't feel this way, but this situation is just not fair!"

Fred sighed and tried to calm Larry down. "Larry,

I know what you're concerned about, and I'm certainly sympathetic to the problem. After all, this salary compression issue affects me in the same way it does you. I can assure you that I have reservations about paying the kind of money we are for new faculty in light of our existing faculty salaries, but I don't believe that we can attract the kind of faculty we want by paying less than competitive rates. Although this seems to create some internal inequities, I hope that we'll have sufficient salary increase money to make some adjustments to reduce these discrepancies. Certainly I want to be able to reward and retain our productive people . . ."

Larry, feeling a little embarrassed by his earlier emotional statement, interjected: "I know you've got other problems, Fred, and I didn't mean to lash out at you. I know it's not really your fault, but a lot of the other faculty are talking about this salary issue. It surely doesn't help morale any when a new, inexperienced assistant professor is hired for more than some of the associate professors are making."

"Yes, I'm well aware of this, Larry, and I'm making the Dean aware of it as well. We're certainly going to do what we can to try to resolve this salary compression problem," Fred responded.

As Larry moved toward the door, he continued to make his point: "Well, I hope you can do something soon because it's most inequitable at the present time. People are pretty upset about it, and it's likely to cause the department some turnover problems in the future. No one likes to be treated unfairly. I'll see you later, Fred. I've got to run to class. Maybe we can talk about it again later."

As Larry walked out of his office Fred reflected on their conversation. It reminded him of other discussions he had had previously with several other faculty members. In fact, Larry had hinted at his dissatisfaction before, but had not been so outspoken about it. Yes, the salary compression problem was reaching a crisis. No longer was it a matter of the "new hires" nearing the salaries of some present faculty; it was a matter of their exceeding them. Never in his experience had Fred recalled a labor market for faculty that was this chaotic.

Fred had puzzled over this dilemma before, but he had not been able to come up with a solution for the problem. He wondered if, in fact, there was a solution that would enable him to hire the new personnel he wanted without offending some of the present staff. Maybe it's just one of those "no win" administrative

situations, he mused. Perhaps this was something that could be discussed with the other department chairmen and the Dean as some of them had basically the same problem. Maybe then, he would have a better idea of how to deal with the situation. He certainly hoped so!

When you have read this case, look back at the chapter's diagnostic questions and choose the ones that apply to the case. Then use those questions with the ones that follow in your case analysis.

1. How might a job analysis help Fred Kennedy restore equity to the pay structure of the management department at Chancellor State? How could he get the management faculty to cooperate?

2. What kind of pay-for-performance program is being used now in the department? Critique this program, pointing out specific strengths and weaknesses in Chancellor State's approach.

3. How do you think the department's current salary structure would affect faculty motivation? How could this situation be improved? What steps should Fred take to implement your suggestion?

CASE 9-3

THE SLAB YARD SLOWDOWN

Read Chapter 11's Case 11-2, "The Slab Yard Slowdown." Next, look back at Chapter 9's diagnostic questions and choose the ones that apply to that case. Then use those questions with the ones that follow in this analysis of the case.

1. What kind of pay-for-performance program is being used to determine the pay of Midland Steel's scarfers? Why isn't this program working out?

2. What steps would you take to modify the scarfers' practice of altering torch tips? Would punishment play a role in your approach? How? Why? What results would you expect from the steps you would implement?

3. If you suceeded in eliminating the scarfers' tip altering practice, do you think the company's pay-for-performance program would begin to work? What additional steps, if any, would the company have to take to make its program succeed?

CHAPTER 10

INTERPERSONAL PROCESSES AND COMMUNICATION

Some members of the Prentice Hall Management of Organizational Behavior *team. Left to right, standing: Martha Coffman, senior copywriter; Sandra M. Steiner, senior marketing manager; Lori Cowen, advertising manager; Robert Anderson, manufacturing buyer; Frances Russello, managing editor; Liz Robertson, scheduler; Trudy Pisciotti, pre-press buyer; Kris Ann Cappelluti, supplements production manager. Seated: Diane Peirano, editorial assistant; Alison Reeves, assistant vice president and executive editor; David Scholder, supplements editor; Esther S. Koehn, supervisory production editor; Virginia Otis Locke, senior editor; Ruta Kysilewskyj, senior advertising designer.*

People in organizations seldom work alone. It is more usual for them to interact with other people as they perform their jobs. For example, the book you are reading is the product of many people working together. The book's authors wrote initial drafts of each chapter and redrafted these chapters several times. A staff of market researchers at Prentice Hall, the book's publisher, gathered information about organizational behavior courses to guide the development of the book. A panel of reviewers—college instructors, like yours—offered opinions to help fine-tune the book's contents. A development editor analyzed reviewers' responses and made additional suggestions to make the book more readable. An art director engaged a designer to plan the book's layout and its cover. Photo researchers located the photographs that open each chapter and illustrate discussions. A pre-press buyer contracted with a compositor to set the book in type. A paper buyer purchased the quantities of paper required to print the desired number of copies. A manufacturing buyer contracted with a printer to do the actual printing of the book. A production manager worked with all of these people in overseeing the book's progress to completion.

At the same time, a marketing manager planned the sales and advertising campaigns for the book and informed the publisher's sales representatives about the book. The sales representatives brought the book to the attention of your instructor and helped to make sure that your bookstore stocked it in time for you to purchase it. Throughout the entire process, the executive editor who had contracted the authors initially coordinated activities at Prentice Hall and continued to keep in touch with the authors.

Group activities like the ones that produced this book are more the rule than the exception in organizational life. As we indicated in Chapter 2, organizations exist to produce goods and services that individuals working alone could not produce. So although it is important for managers to know how the individual-level characteristics we've discussed in Chapters 4–9 shape organizational behavior, they must also understand how group factors affect the way people behave on the job. Therefore, in this chapter we identify and explore key group processes. First we discuss several reasons why people band together and characterize the various types of interdependence that connect people. Then we examine the process of making and taking roles, in which people's behaviors are shaped by the expectations of others. Next we look at communication and the function it plays in linking people together. We conclude with a discussion of how socialization processes help shape and maintain relations among people at work.

DIAGNOSTIC ISSUES

Several diagnostic questions will guide us through this chapter. First, can we *describe* the various ways in which people come to depend on each other in work environments? What kinds of communication networks facilitate job performance and enhance job satisfaction? What *diagnostic* information can help us understand the situation in which a person develops a role for himself that goes beyond his written job description? Can we explain how some people become informal group leaders and amass power that exceeds the power of people higher up in the organizational hierarchy?

Can we *prescribe* how people should be socialized early in their employment so as to ensure successful performance and satisfaction? What can we tell a group to do when it must cope with an overwhelming amount of information? Finally, what *actions* can implement the most suitable communication medium—oral, written, nonverbal—for delivering a particular message? What can we do to ensure that organization members will conform to assigned work roles?

GROUP INTERACTION AND INTERDEPENDENCE

People in organizations have a rich variety of interconnections. Their work may require them to associate with each other as a regular part of job performance. They may belong to the same group in their organization's structure, although as the example that opened this chapter indicated, people form important interpersonal relationships not only with individuals in other departments but with people in outside organizations. People may band together to share resources, such as access to valuable equipment or pools of money. In addition, many employees may form friendships and get together away from work as well as on the job. Connections like these make interpersonal interactions a very important fact of organizational life.

Why Do People Interact with One Another?

Whether in organizations or in the societies that surround them, people form and maintain relations with others for many reasons. Let's look at five major forces that propel people into such relations—evolutionary adaptation, need satisfaction, interpersonal attraction, shared goals, and group activities (see Figure 10-1).

Evolutionary Adaptation. The tendency for people to associate with each other probably first arose from the benefits our ancestors derived from forming groups. Prehistoric humans undoubtedly discovered that living with others offered advantages for survival that were not available to the solitary individual. Banding together helped protect people from faster, physically stronger predators. People found they could hunt and farm more successfully together than alone. Gathering

FIGURE 10-1

Why People Form Groups

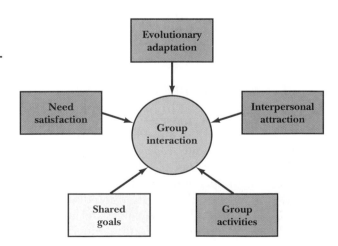

into groups also facilitated adaptive innovation. One person could pass his discovery on to others, who could refine it over time. Finally, mutual protection and nurturance sheltered reproduction and child-rearing activities. For all of these reasons, social behavior became adaptive and a part of what it is to be a human being.[1]

Need Satisfaction. Although it was the necessity of satisfying the lower-order needs such as food and safety that first promoted group formation, socializing eventually fulfilled other, higher-order needs as well. In particular, people now interact to fulfill needs for affiliation or social satisfaction. Furthermore, relations with others who are seen as prestigious can enhance a person's perceived self-worth. Thus other people can help fulfill one's desires for esteem and shape one's self-concept.[2]

Interpersonal Attraction. People may also be drawn to others by their attractiveness. Interpersonal attraction tends to be high when people have *similar attitudes and beliefs*. Interaction with others of like mind can reinforce one's own world views.[3] Interpersonal attraction can also be a function of the *dissimilarity of needs and abilities*. For instance, a person with a high need for power will tend to be attracted to people who have complementary, submissive needs. Finally, *proximity* plays an important part in determining the strength of interpersonal attraction (see Figure 10-2). Unless they are near one another, people generally do not have the opportunity to discover their similarities and dissimilarities.

Goal Pursuit. People may also band together to pursue mutual goals that they can achieve more effectively by working together. Mothers Against Drunk Driving (MADD) is a good example of a close-knit group of people who associate with each other to pursue a common goal—to protect society from the danger posed by drunk drivers. On the other hand, the members of a local school board may have very different goal-related reasons for associating with one another. One person may join the board because he is concerned about his children's education. Another may join out of her wish to control property tax rates. Many organizations—particularly business concerns—are held together by their members' interests in accomplishing specific economic goals. In a business, some members' goals may be shared and others may be quite distinctive. They may all advocate good wages and benefits, but some may be interested in power, and others may want to do a particular kind of work. Thus goals need not be shared for people

[1] F. L. Ruch and P. G. Zimbardo, *Psychology and Life* (Glenview, Ill.: Scott, Foresman, 1971), p. 32.

[2] R. Brown and J. Williams, "Group Identification: The Same Thing to All People?" *Human Relations* 43 (1984), 547–60.

[3] W. H. Whyte, *The Organization Man* (New York: Simon & Schuster, 1956), p. 55.

FIGURE 10-2

Bases of Interpersonal Attraction

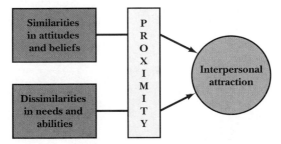

to band together. It is only necessary that the association helps people satisfy goals they value personally.

Attractive Activities. Finally, some people join groups to take part in activities that appeal to them. For example, some employees may form an organizational softball team because there is a mutual interest in playing this sport on nice spring days.

Types of Interdependence

As they work with each other, people form patterns of *interdependence*. They come to depend on each other for information, raw materials, social support, help in performing a task, and other equally important resources. This interdependence typically takes one of four forms: pooled, sequential, reciprocal, or team interdependence (see Figure 10-3).[4]

pooled interdependence A type of interaction where individuals draw off a common resource pool but do not interact with each other in any other way.

Pooled Interdependence. Pooled interdependence, as Figure 10-3A suggests, occurs among people who draw resources from a shared pool but have little else in common. For example, a college golf team is made up of individuals with pooled interdependence. The players share the course, the coach, and other resources, but when it comes to a match, they are on their own. One player cannot hit the ball for another, carry another's clubs, line up others' putts, or do much of anything to assist a teammate. In the end, the score for the team is simply the sum of the individual players' scores. Similarly, in an organization like Metropolitan Life Insurance, individual data-entry specialists draw off a common pool of work that needs to be entered into the firm's computers. Yet each data-entry person works alone in entering information. As with the golf team, the total amount of work accomplished by the group is simply the sum of all the individual accomplishments.

Pooled interdependence, the simplest form of interdependence, requires little or no interpersonal interaction. For example, although data-entry personnel

[4] J. D. Thompson, *Organizations in Action* (New York: McGraw-Hill, 1967), p. 41; and A. H. Van de Ven, A. L. Delbecq, and R. Koenig, Jr., "Determinants of Coordination Modes within Organizations," *American Sociological Review* 41 (1976), 322–38.

FIGURE 10-3

Types of Interdependence

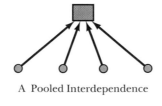

A Pooled Interdependence

B Sequential Interdependence

C Reciprocal Interdependence

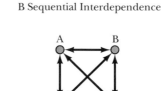

D Team Interdependence

at Metropolitan Life may be sitting right next to each other, there is no necessity for them to interact.

sequential interdependence A type of interaction in which individuals are arrayed in a chain of one-way links.

Sequential Interdependence. **Sequential interdependence** (see Figure 10-3B) is a chain of one-way interactions in which people later in the chain depend on those who precede them. People earlier in the chain, however, are independent of those who follow them. Thus sequentially interdependent relationships are said to be *asymmetric*. Some people depend on others who do not depend on them. People on an assembly line in a company like RCA or Navistar are connected by sequential interdependence. Workers earlier in the line produce partial assemblies that workers later in the line complete. By its nature, sequential interdependence prevents people at the end of the chain from performing their jobs unless people at the head of the chain have performed theirs. People at the head of the chain, however, can complete their tasks no matter what people at the end do.

Sequential interdependence usually involves some form of direct interaction. For example, people on an assembly line sometimes talk with each other to pass on information about work coming along the line. Although sequential interdependence is more complex than pooled interdependence, its one-way asymmetry makes it less complex than the types of interdependence we discuss next.

reciprocal interdependence A type of interaction in which there are two-way links among individuals.

Reciprocal Interdependence. In **reciprocal interdependence** (see Figure 10-3C), a network of two-way relationships tie a collection of people together. A good example of this kind of interdependence is the relationship between a sales force and a clerical staff. Sales representatives rely on clerks to complete invoices and process credit card receipts, and clerks depend on salespeople to generate sales. Reciprocal interdependence also occurs among the members of a hospital staff. Doctors depend on nurses to check patients periodically, administer medications, and report alarming symptoms. Nurses depend on doctors to prescribe medications and to specify what symptoms to look for.

Reciprocal interdependence always involves direct interaction of one sort or another, such as face-to-face communication, telephone conversations, or written instructions As a result, people who are reciprocally interdependent are more tightly interconnected than are individuals who are interconnected by either pooled or sequential interdependence. In addition, reciprocal interdependence is significantly more complex than either pooled or sequential interdependence. It incorporates symmetric, two-way interactions in which each person depends on the person who depends on her.

team interdependence A type of group interaction in which every group member depends on every other.

Team Interdependence. **Team interdependence**, depicted in Figure 10-3D, develops in a tight network of reciprocal interdependence. What makes team interdependence the most complex form of interdependence is that all members of the team or group are reciprocally interdependent on each other. As in reciprocal interdependence, people who depend on each other interact directly. In team interdependence, however, interactions tend to be more frequent, more intense, and of greater duration than in any other type of interdependence.

For example, in the brand-management groups that oversee the development of new products at firms like Colgate-Palmolive and Procter and Gamble, product designers, market researchers, production engineers, and sales representatives are linked by a completely connected network of two-way relationships. The product designers interact with the market researchers, product engineers, and sales representatives. The market researchers also interact with both the product engineers and sales staff, who in turn interact with each other. Similarly, the teams of engineers and scientists who design NASA spacecraft and satellites are linked by team interdependence.

The type of interdependence that characterizes the group has important managerial implications. First, there is a greater potential for conflict as the complexity of the interdependence increases from pooled to team situations. Second, turnover has more of an influence on the group when the group is characterized by team interdependence. One person's absence affects a large number of interactions. In some teams, the loss of a single player can make all the rest of the players perform below par. Third, teams tend to be more flexible and can adapt more quickly to changing environments than groups unified by less complex forms of interdependence.

ROLES AND GROUP INTERACTION

Within the networks of interdependence that characterize group interactions, people come to expect each other to behave in particular ways. Taxi drivers expect passengers to pay them when they reach their destinations. Instructors expect students to complete required assignments before coming to class. Spectators expect sports stars to exhibit skill and perseverance as they compete. Expectations such as these—and the behaviors they presuppose—make up roles that connect individuals interpersonally.

A **role** consists of the typical behaviors that characterize a person's position in a social context.[5] You'll recall that in Chapter 8 we discussed the concept of *organization role*, defining it as the set of behaviors that both the employee and the people with whom she regularly interacts expect her to perform in doing her job. We pointed out that in addition to the formal expectations of a jobholder, which are generally determined by a company's top management, many other, informal expectations evolve over time. Table 10-1 suggests some ways in which work roles extend beyond formal jobs.

According to Ilgen and Hollenbeck, work roles are comprised of two kinds of tasks.[6] First, there are the **established task elements** that make up the job. The job is a formal position and comes with a written statement of the tasks it entails. *Job descriptions* are generally prepared by managers or others at the upper levels of an organization's hierarchy. As a result, there is a fair amount of agreement at the outset as to what constitutes the established task elements of the job. Because job descriptions are prepared before the fact by people who do not

role The typical and expected behaviors that characterize an individual's position in some social context.

established task elements The components of work roles that are contained in written job descriptions and formally recognized in the organization.

[5] B. J. Biddle, *Role Theory: Expectations, Identities and Behaviors* (New York: Academic Press, 1979), p. 20.
[6] D. R. Ilgen and J. R. Hollenbeck, "The Structure of Work: Job Design and Roles," in *Handbook of Industrial/Organizational Psychology*, ed. M. Dunnette (Houston: Consulting Psychologist Press, in press.

TABLE 10-1
The Job versus Work Role Distinction

JOB	WORK ROLE
1. Created by the owners of the organization or their agents independently of the role occupant	1. Created by everyone who has a stake in how the role is performed, including the role incumbent
2. Has elements that are objective, formally documented, and about which there is considerable consensus	2. Has elements that are subjective, not formally documented, and open to negotiation
3. Static and relatively constant	3. Constantly changing and developing

In teaching, emergent task elements often seem to overwhelm established task elements. One school superintendent listed 52 nonacademic issues that his teachers must now deal with, ranging from day care to suicide prevention. At a 1990 conference, students, educators, business leaders, and politicians discussed ways that businesses can help overburdened schools. Here James Smith and Amanda Beliveau of New Hampshire's Thayer High School discuss needs with teacher Jean Kennedy and principal Dennis Littky. Typical of the programs discussed is the Arizona Business Coalition's task force, which has reshaped high school curricula, trained teachers, and provided technology, money, and employee volunteers to help students become productive members of the work force. Source: Nancy J. Perry, "Schools: Tackling the Tough Issues," Fortune, December 17, 1990, pp. 143–56.

emergent task elements The components of work roles that are not formally recognized by the organization but arise out of expectations held by others for the role incumbent.

actually perform the job they are usually incomplete. Job descriptions usually take no account of job incumbents or of the complex and dynamic environments in which jobs must be performed.

As a person begins to do a job, it becomes clear to her and all those around her that tasks never detailed in the written job description need to be performed for the role to be successfully played. These added-on tasks are referred to as **emergent task elements**. For example, secretarial workers are increasingly being called on nowadays to perform a variety of duties other than typing, filing, and answering telephones. As business has grown more complex and executives' time has become more precious, some secretaries have expanded their roles. "Today's executive secretaries have started to assume many of the burdens of middle management," according to Nancy Shuman, vice president of a New York placement firm called Career Blazers. For example, Kay Kilpatrick, assistant to Richard Smith, chairman of General Cinema Corporation, finds herself doing tasks that were never part of her job description. She runs the firm's employee matching gift program and charitable corporate gift program. She also evaluates stock portfolios and handles distributions from the company's corporate assets.[7]

As you can see from Figure 10-4, established and emergent task elements can combine in different ways. At one extreme is the *bureaucratic prototype*. This jobholder performs no duties other than those written in the job description. That is, his work role is made up entirely of established task elements. Many low-level jobs in automated, assembly-line factories are this type.

Almost completely opposite is the *loose-cannon prototype*, in which the few established elements are greatly outnumbered by emergent elements. For example, when General Motors hired the flamboyant Ross Perot, ex-CEO of Electronic Data Systems, as a general organizational trouble shooter, it gave Perot wide latitude in his role. He decided to tour GM plants and criticize what he thought were inefficient management practices. Eventually GM leadership tired of the role Perot developed and wound up paying over $7 million just to get rid of him. Similarly, ex-marine colonel Oliver North was pretty much allowed to do whatever he wanted in his role in President Reagan's National Security Council. One of the tasks he set for himself was the ill-fated "arms for hostages" deal with Iran, which generated a great deal of controversy in the final years of Reagan's presidency.

Finally, Figure 10-4C also shows the *job-similarity–role-difference prototype*. Here two individuals have the same job, but special characteristics of the incum-

[7] D. Fanning, "Calling on Secretaries to Fill in the Gaps," *New York Times*, March 11, 1990, p. A12.

FIGURE 10-4

Job versus Work Role:
Established and Emergent
Elements

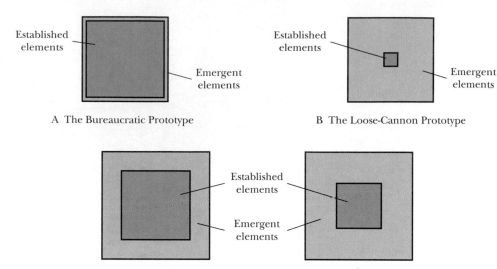

A The Bureaucratic Prototype

B The Loose-Cannon Prototype

C The Job-Similarity–Role-Difference Prototype

bents lead to the development of many emergent elements in one job but few in the other. On a football team, for example, an outside linebacker has established duties to contain the outside run and cover running backs in passing situations. A rookie linebacker will typically perform just those duties. An eight-year veteran, because of his experience, may have an expanded role with many emergent elements, such as serving as a team leader, calling defensive formations, and making decisions about whether to accept or decline penalties.

As Figure 10-4 suggests, a work role often includes a whole lot more than the job itself. It is important for managers to distinguish between jobs and more broadly defined work roles for several reasons. First, the manager must identify and reward individuals who are performing expanded roles to reinforce the behavior. At the same time, it is important to make sure that people do not expand their roles in directions that conflict with other people's formal responsibilities. Finally, when the established elements of a job are not well documented, it is critical that a manager anticipate the direction that a particular job applicant might take in the job before hiring him.

Dimensions of Role Specialization

Edger Schein has developed a conceptual framework that is particularly useful in understanding organizations as a set of interrelated roles.[8] Schein's model differentiates organizational roles from each other and from nonorganizational roles along three dimensions: functional, hierarchical, and inclusionary.

Functional. The *functional* dimension refers to the various tasks performed by members of the organization. Figure 10-5A shows the typical functional dimension of a conventional business organization: marketing, production, accounting, human resources, research and development, and finance. Similarly, the functional dimensions common to many universities are shown in Figure 10-5B. They include the schools of business, social sciences, arts and letters, medicine, engineering, and law. The roles performed in each of these dimensions are quite distinct because the jobholders are trying to accomplish different aspects of the organization's overall mission.

[8] E. H. Schein, *Organizational Psychology* (Englewood Cliffs, N.J.: Prentice Hall, 1970), pp. 111–33.

FIGURE 10-5

The Functional Dimension of Organizations

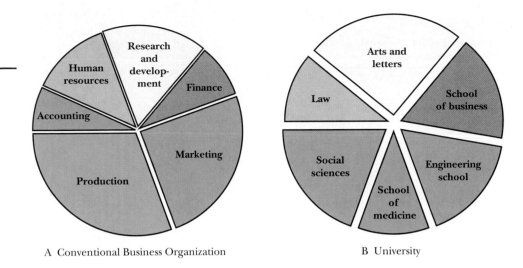

A Conventional Business Organization

B University

Hierarchical. Schein's *hierarchical* dimension concerns the distribution of rank, or the official lines of supervisory authority. As you will recall from Chapter 2, hierarchy has to do with who is officially responsible for the actions of whom. In traditional organizations, this dimension takes a triangular shape, in which the highest ranks are held by relatively few people. The roles performed by people higher in the pyramid differ from the roles of individuals lower in the pyramid largely in that the former have greater authority and power. In a highly centralized organization like the army, this triangle is often rather steep (see Figure 10-6A).

A decentralized organization has fewer levels of authority and looks like a flattened pyramid. Despite their militaristic nature, most city police departments

FIGURE 10-6

The Hierarchical Dimension of Organizations

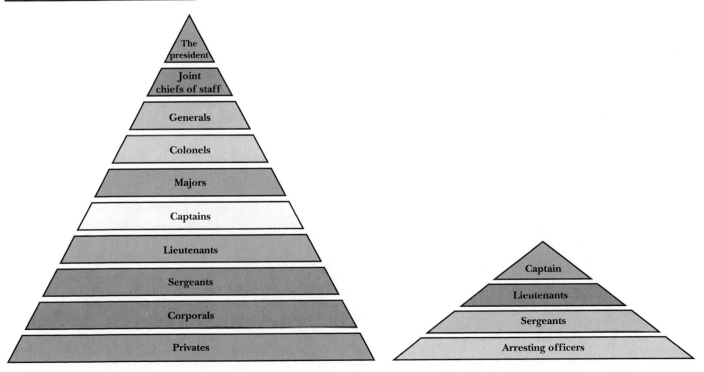

A Military Organization

B City Police Department

FIGURE 10-7

The Inclusionary Dimension
of Organizations

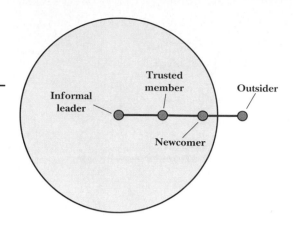

have fewer levels of hierarchy than the army. Most employees are arresting officers, the highest rank is captain, and there are only two genuine levels of hierarchy between the top and bottom (see Figure 10-6B).

Inclusionary. The third dimension of Schein's model, the *inclusionary* dimension, reflects the degree to which an employee of an organization finds herself at the center or on the periphery of things. As you can see from the circular diagram in Figure 10-7, a person may move from being an outsider, beyond the organization's periphery, to being an informal leader, at the center of the organization. A job applicant, or outsider, joins the organization and becomes a newcomer, just inside the periphery. To move further along the radial dimension shown in the figure the newcomer must become accepted by others as a full member of the organization. This move can be accomplished only by proving that one shares the same assumptions as others about what is important and what is not. Usually, newcomers must first be tested—formally or informally—as to their abilities, motives, and values before being granted inclusionary rights and privileges.

Putting all three of Schein's dimensions together lets us depict an organization as a three-dimensional inverted cone, as shown in Figure 10-8. The entire organization and all the individual roles that comprise it can be conceptualized in terms of the three dimensions of function, hierarchy and inclusion. This conception helps us integrate individual and organizational issues through the concept of role. Look first at Figure 10-8A. This represents a military operation, with its tall hierarchy and small number of functional units. As the "Management

FIGURE 10-8

The Inverted Cone, Three Dimensional Model of Organizational Roles

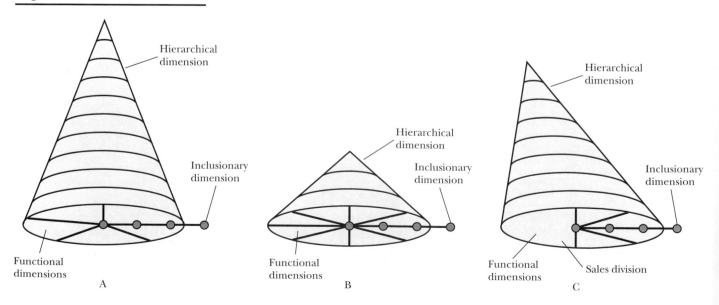

MANAGEMENT ISSUES

Too Many Chiefs and Not Enough Indians?

Many critics of American enterprise have suggested that organizations in this country have become top heavy. Richard Rosencrance, author of *America's Economic Resurgence: A Bold Strategy*, notes several disturbing statistics. First, more than half the employees of the modern American business corporation are not involved directly with production or service to consumers. For example, at General Motors, 77 percent of employees fill administrative and office positions, whereas only 23 percent handle operational, production jobs. The percentages of white-collar employees at Mobil, General Electric, and Du Pont all run over 50 percent. On the other hand, some more profitable companies, such as Ford, have only 37 percent administrative workers. Compare these data with the 8 to 10 percent administrative staff typical of similar large corporations in Japan.

This proclivity to generate too many chiefs and not enough Indians is not restricted to business ventures. Top heaviness is also present in the military and education sectors of the economy. For example, the number of senior military officers (three-star officers and full generals and admirals) is considerably greater now than it was at the peak of World War II, despite the fact that these officers command forces that are only a sixth as large as they were during that war. At both the high-school and college levels, administrators are now beginning to outnumber faculty. School districts in Los Angeles, New York, Philadelphia, and Denver all have more administrators and support staff than actual teachers.

To counter this trend, many have argued that corporate, government, military and educational bureaucracies need to be ruthlessly pruned. Executives in firms of the future need to be fewer in number but broader in talents. Workers need to be greater in number and also more willing to assume responsibility for decision making. In fact, in the future, the

very distinction between white- and blue-collar workers may disappear altogether. In the interim, the retraining of both those at the top and those at the bottom of the corporate ladder must be a high priority. Tall narrow cones are easily toppled. Shorter, wider cones are more resilient.

Source: R. Rosecrance, "Too Many Bosses, Too Few Workers," *New York Times*, July 15, 1990, p. 11.

Issues" box suggests, many critics of U.S. management practices feel that this military-style model is too common in American organizations.

In Figure 10-8B we see a research-and-development firm with a relatively flat hierarchy but a large number of functional departments. Finally, Figure 10-8C shows a real estate sales organization with a slightly skewed, or tilted, cone. The tilt of the cone indicates that the most important function of the firm is sales and that almost all positions at the top of the hierarchy are filled with people who moved up from the sales department. In this firm, a newcomer in the personnel department might be more of an outsider than a newcomer in sales. The probability that the former will ever rise to be CEO is almost zero given the role structure depicted in the figure.

Taking and Making Roles

Defining organizations as systems of roles highlights the fact that organizations are structured in terms of role behaviors, not in terms of the unique acts of specific individuals. Indeed, one of the strengths of formal organizations is their constancy under conditions of persistent turnover of personnel. For example, the New York Yankees are perceived to be a single, unified entity, despite the fact that within any two- to three-year period, 50 percent of the team members change. Thus roles are of crucial importance to organizations. The process by which they are developed is a central concern for the study of organizational behavior. In this section we will examine the model of the role-taking process shown in Figure 10-9.

The Role Set. A **role set** is a group of people who must interact with a role occupant either formally or informally. Typically a role set includes such people as an employee's supervisor and subordinates, other members of the employee's functional unit, and members of adjacent functional units that share tasks, clients, or customers.

Because they have something at stake in the role occupant's performance, members of the role set develop role expectations or **norms**. Norms are strong beliefs about how the role should be performed. There are norms for both the formal requirements of the job, or its established task elements, and its generally agreed upon informal rules, or emergent task elements.[9]

Norms may evolve out of a number of sources, as indicated in Table 10-2. Sometimes *precedents* that are established in early exchanges simply persist over time and become traditions. For example, students take certain seats on the first day of class and, even though the instructor establishes no formal seating arrangement, they tend over time to keep the same seats. Norms may also be *carryovers* from other situations. That is, people may generalize from what they have done in the past in other, similar situations. A person may stand when called on to make a presentation at a meeting because he was trained to stand in these circumstances. Sometimes norms reflect *explicit statements from others*. A part-time summer worker, for instance, may be told by more experienced workers to "slow down and save some work for tomorrow." Finally, some *critical historical event* may influence norms. Suppose, for example, that a secretary leaks important company secrets to a competitor. In response to this incident, an unwritten norm may evolve that requires that all sensitive information be typed personally, not delegated. In Chapter 11 we will discuss the different kinds of norms that often develop in organizations.

Of course, expectations and norms would have little effect on organizational behavior if they stayed inside the heads of role-set members. But they do not. As shown in Figure 10-9, norms, or role expectations, are "sent" to the role occupant. Some of the messages transmitted in *role sending* are informational and tell the focal person what is going on. Others are attempts to influence the role occupant in one way or the other (e.g., by letting her know what rewards or punishments will follow adherence to or disregard of particular norms). Some influence attempts may be directed toward accomplishing organizational objectives. Others may be unrelated to, or even contrary to, official requirements ("Don't

[9] J. R. Hackman, "Toward Understanding the Role of Tasks in Behavioral Research," *Acta Psychologica* 31 (1979), 97–128.

---

role set The entire group of individuals who have an interest in and expectations about the way a role occupant performs his job.

norms A strong set of expectations that members of a role set have for the role occupant.

FIGURE 10-9

The Role-Taking Process

Adapted from D. Katz and R. L. Kahn, The Social Psychology of Organizations (New York: John Wiley, 1978), p. 112.

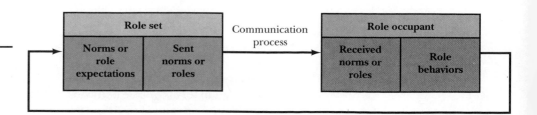

INTERPERSONAL PROCESSES AND COMMUNICATION

T A B L E 10-2
Sources of Group Norms

1. Precedents set by earlier interactions in a specific group
2. Carryovers from earlier interactions that group members had with people in other groups they belonged to
3. Explicit statements and agreements among group members
4. Critical events in the group's history

Source: Adapted from D. C. Feldman, "The Development and Enforcement of Group Norms," *Academy of Management Review* 9 (1984), 47–53.

waste your time filling out that form every time you have a complaint from a customer").

As long as the role occupant complies with the expectations of the role senders, the senders will attend to their own jobs. However, if the role occupant starts to deviate from the sent expectations, the role senders, their expectations, and their means of enforcing compliance will become quite visible. The part-time summer worker who fails to heed the warnings of more experienced personnel may soon become the victim of derision, practical jokes, or isolation.

As we will see in the next section of this chapter, communication can be a very complex process. Role sending is a form of communication and, as such, its success depends on a number of factors that we will examine shortly. For now, we need simply know that messages about role expectations may not always be transmitted as clearly as possible, and they may not always be accurately understood by recipients.

role occupant The current incumbent of an existing organizational work role.

The Role Occupant. Although it is through the sent role that the members of the organization communicate the do's and don'ts associated with a role, it is the "received" role that is the immediate influence on the behavior of a **role occupant**. As we will see, a number of factors may distort a message or cause it to be misunderstood. But even when messages are communicated effectively, senders' role expectations are often not met by role occupants. Several types of role conflict that we discussed in Chapter 8 can prevent a role receiver from meeting the expectations of a sender.

First of all, *inter-sender role conflict* may place competing, mutually exclusive demands on the role occupant. If the person meets one sender's expectations she may violate the expectations of another.

In addition, the role occupant may experience *person-role conflict*. He may have some ideas about how the role should be performed that conflict with role-sender demands. Finally, *inter-role conflict* can not only interfere with the performance of one or more roles (in Chapter 8 we contrasted the roles of parent and employee), it can in some cases lead an employee to flagrantly violate the expectations of his role set. For example, because news of the latest developments at Apple Computer was valuable currency in the social milieu of Silicon Valley, many Apple employees leaked sensitive information to friends. Clearly their desire to appear in the know conflicted with the organization's need for secrecy. To stop the practice, Apple came up with buttons for all employees that read, "I know a lot but I can keep a secret."[10]

After sorting through the various sent roles, the role occupant typically makes a decision about which role behaviors to perform. His reason for choosing one expectation over another affects both the stability of his behavior and the

[10] G. P. Zachary, "At Apple Computer Proper Office Attire Includes a Muzzle," *Wall Street Journal*, October 6, 1989, p. 1.

degree to which the role sender must monitor his behavior. Let us look at three primary reasons for conforming to sent role expectations—compliance, identification, and internalization.[11]

compliance Behaving in accord with norms out of fear of punishment or hope of reward.

In response to a role sender's communication, a role incumbent may choose **compliance** because the role sender has the power to reward or punish. Although this sounds like a good way of making sure that role behavior coincides with the sent role, as we will see, compliance is actually the least stable method of achieving conformity. To produce true compliance in a role occupant, a role sender must have three characteristics. First, she must be able to monitor the role occupant closely. Unless you know what a person is doing, you can hardly reward or punish him appropriately.

Second, the role sender must be able to deliver the rewards and punishments she has promised. If threats of punishments and pledges of rewards begin to be perceived as bluffs and empty promises, compliance will stop.

Third, the role sender's power must be stable. If there is a good chance that the role sender's power to reward and punish will soon diminish, compliance may not be the best means of achieving conformity. The moment the power balance changes, conformity will cease.

identification Behaving in accord with norms out of respect and admiration for one or more members of the role set.

A role incumbent may also conform to a role sender's expectations through **identification**. She may be attracted to the role sender; she may want to be like the role sender; and she may want the role sender's approval. Role behaviors are often a product of this kind of process. Role occupants may find someone they admire and then adopt the behaviors and attitudes of this person. Indeed, people whose actions and attitudes are imitated and adopted by others are referred to as *role models*.

Although more stable than compliance, identification is also hard to achieve over extended periods of time. First, role models are only human themselves. Often the more one learns about them, the less heroic or romantic they seem. When sordid details of the lives of the evangelical religious leaders Jimmy Swaggert and James Bakker became public, many of their followers were forced into some serious soul-searching. Second, as individuals develop, they often outgrow one role model and move on to another. Or they may stop modeling the behavior of others entirely, having developed a strong sense of their own roles.

internalization Behaving in accord with norms that are consistent with one's own value system.

Finally, a person may conform to a role sender's expectations because the sent role is consistent with the role occupant's own personal value system. Sometimes called **internalization**, this method of achieving conformity is also referred to as "winning the hearts and minds." Mary Kay Cosmetics, for example, which relies on a sales force that cannot be monitored, tries to equate selling success with personal growth and development. The company fosters the belief among its sales representatives that selling cosmetics will increase their interpersonal skills and their self-confidence. As a result, generating sales revenues is important to Mary Kay sales staff for more than financial reasons. (Just in case this pitch fails, the organization also provides sales commissions.) Theoretically, then, the sales representatives are motivated to perform their role because it leads to self-development and self-enhancement.

Because people's value systems are quite stable, (see Chapter 8), internalization is the most reliable method of achieving conformity. It also requires minimal monitoring, for role occupants come to monitor themselves. Indeed, some role behaviors, like a soldier's falling on a grenade to save his comrades, can be achieved only through internalization.

The Role Episode. A single iteration of the role expectation—sent roles—received role—roles behavior sequence is called a *role episode*. As Figure 10-9 shows,

---

[11] H. C. Kelman, "Processes of Opinion Change," *Public Opinion Quarterly* 25 (1961), 57–87.

the role-taking process is cyclical. The way the role occupant conforms to the role sender's expectations on a particular occasion will affect the role sender's expectations at a later point in time.

An initial influence attempt that results in conformity reinforces expectations. If the same initial influence attempt is met with a defensive counterattack, however, role senders may quickly modify their expectations. If the role occupant conforms partially when placed under a little pressure, the pressure may be increased in the next cycle. If the role occupant is obviously overwhelmed by the role, the role senders may agree to "lay off" until the person has developed a little further. Thus, when viewed as a system of roles, the organization is seen not as an immutable, objective entity but as a flexible, negotiated set of expectations and behaviors.

COMMUNICATION AND ROLES

We have suggested that an organization is best conceptualized as a system of negotiated roles in which both the organization and the roles are characterized by dimensions of function, rank, and inclusion. We have also suggested that at the heart of the role-taking process is the exchange of ideas between members of the role set (the role senders) and role occupants.

If roles are conceived of as the bricks of an organization, communication is the cement that holds those bricks together. **Communication** is the exchange of ideas through a common system of symbols. It is the only means by which people can transmit messages to one another about such things as role expectations and norms. We need to explore next how communication takes place and what factors may enhance or impede it.

communication The exchange of information between people through a common set of symbols.

The Communication Process

In Figure 10-9, we simply drew a straight line between the sent role and the received role to denote the transmission of ideas between members of the role set and the role occupant. Now we need to expand on that oversimplification. A much better model envisions the communication process in three stages:

1. Encoding information into a message
2. Transmitting the message by some medium
3. Decoding the information from the message[12]

encoding The process by which a communicator's abstract idea is translated into the symbols of language for transmission to someone else.

Encoding the Message. Encoding is the process by which a communicator's abstract idea is translated into the symbols of language and thus into a message that can be transmitted to someone else. The idea is subjective and known only to the communicator. The message, because it employs a common set of symbols, can be understood by other people who know the communicator's language.

Communication Media. The *medium* is the carrier of the message and is objectively observable. That is, it exists outside the communicator's mind and can be perceived by others. We can further characterize the media of organizational communication by the human senses they use. Oral speech uses hearing. Written

---

[12] C. Shannon and W. Weaver, *The Mathematical Theory of Communication*, (Urbana: University of Illinois Press, 1948), p. 17.

documentation uses vision or touch (Braille). Nonverbal communication may use at least four of the five basic senses.

Oral communication relies predominantly on the sense of hearing; its symbols are based on sounds. Face-to-face conversations, meetings, and telephone calls are the most commonly used forms of communication in organizations. Look back at Figure 2-10, where you will see that as much as 75 percent of a manager's time is devoted to meetings and telephone calls.[13] Oral communications are fast. One can encode information quickly, and the feedback cycle is rapid. If the receiver is unclear about the message, she can immediately ask for clarification. Presenting a proposal orally, for example, provides much more opportunity for clarifying questions than preparing a written report. Therefore, oral messages are generally efficient in handling the day-to-day problems that arise in organizations.

Although much oral communication in organizations takes place in meetings, the business meeting is generally perceived as an inefficient, unproductive activity. Can anything be done to overcome this problem? Yes, indeed. Many organizations have taken specific remedial steps. For example, Hercules, Inc., a chemical and synthetics manufacturer in Wilmington, Delaware mounts huge clocks at the back of every conference room to make it easier for meeting chairs to halt endless deliberations.[14] It is also a good idea to invite to a meeting only those people who have something to contribute or something at stake. Participants should know what the content of the meeting will be at least a day in advance, and an agenda and any required reading should be distributed before the meeting. Finally, the person leading the meeting should make sure that the shy get heard—even if this requires direct questioning—and that domineering people are held in check.

Sometimes *written communication* is preferred over oral communication. Although written messages are more slowly encoded, they allow the communicator to use more precise language. A sentence in a labor contract, for example, may be rewritten five or six times to make certain that everyone involved knows exactly what it means. The aim is to minimize the possibility of any future confusion or argument over interpretation. Written materials also provide a "hard copy" of the communication that can be stored and retrieved for later purposes. For example, a supervisor may write a formal memo to an employee informing her that she has been late for work 10 of the last 11 days and if she does not begin coming in on time she will be fired. If the behavior continues, the supervisor has documented evidence that the employee received fair warning.

Nonverbal communication covers a variety of transmission modes that rely on something other than the written and spoken word.[15] Table 10-3 describes several forms of nonverbal communication. It is easy to underestimate the impact that messages relayed this way have on others' perceptions, in part because this form of communication often reaches the listener at relatively low levels of awareness.

decoding The process by which a transmitted message is converted into an abstract idea in the mind of the person to which the communication is directed.

noise A collective term for a number of factors that can distort a message as it is transmitted from one person to another.

Decoding the Message. To complete the communication process, the message sent must be subjected to **decoding**, or translated in the mind of the receiver. When all works well, the resulting idea or mental image corresponds closely to the sender's idea or mental image.

Unfortunately, there is no shortage of things that can go wrong, making communication ineffective. The term **noise** refers to the factors that can distort a message. Noise can occur at any stage of the process. For example, a person may not encode exactly what he means to say. A surgeon may tell a nurse that "the patient has a cancerous tumor on his hand and it needs to be removed,"

---

[13] H. Mintzberg, *The Nature of Managerial Work* (New York: Harper & Row, 1973), p. 22.

[14] S. Hsu, "Dull Meeting? Turn the Tables," *Bergen Record*, July 30, 1990, p. C1.

[15] F. Williams, *The New Communications* (Belmont, Calif.: Wadsworth, 1989), p. 45.

TABLE 10-3
Forms of Nonverbal Communication

1. **Paralinguistics**   A form of language in which meaning is conveyed through variations in speech qualities, such as loudness, pitch, rate, and number of hesitations
2. **Kinesics**   The use of gestures, facial expressions, eye movements, and body postures in communicating emotions
3. **Haptics**   The use of touch in communicating, as in a handshake, a pat on the back, or an arm around the shoulder
4. **Chronemics**   Communicating status through the use of time. For example, making people wait or allowing some people to go ahead of others
5. **Iconics**   The use of physical objects or office designs to communicate status or culture, such as the display of trophies or diplomas
6. **Dress**   Communicating values and expectations through clothing and other dimensions of physical appearance

meaning that the tumor must be removed. The nurse, however, prepares the patient for an amputation of his hand.

Another communication error may lie in the selection of the medium for a message. Suppose you write a memo giving a colleague information about the date and time of an important meeting and a clear outline of the meeting agenda. You leave the memo in your colleague's mailbox. Unfortunately, your colleague, who is a sales representative, does not come into the office that day to collect her mail, so no communication takes place. A telephone call instead might have avoided this problem. Some executives feel the apparently growing need to communicate quickly with others, which explains the skyrocketing popularity of electronic telephone pagers.

Finally, problems can occur at the receiving end of communication. Because nonverbal language is as culture specific as any other form of language, you must choose your gestures and interpret others' gestures with caution. Putting your arm around an employee, for example, may be your way of saying, "We're all in this thing together, and we'll help one another out," but an employee may interpret your behavior as a sexual advance. In the next section, we will examine the great variety of noise factors that act as barriers to effective communication. We will use the role-taking model in Figure 10-9 to put these factors in a single framework.

Barriers to Effective Communication

Several organizational, interpersonal, and personal factors can either help or hinder communication within organizations, depending on how they are handled. These barriers need to be removed if effective communication is to take place. We will examine spatial arrangements of people and offices; characteristics of the communicators, both role sender and role occupant; and interpersonal differences in language and experience.

Organizational Factors: Spatial Arrangements.   The nature of the physical space occupied by jobholders inevitably affects patterns of communication. If an organization wants to promote the development of interpersonal relations, for example, it must place people in close physical proximity (although not too close, as we saw in Chapter 8). All else equal, people who work closely together have more opportunities to interact and are more likely to form lasting relationships than people who are physically distant. Apparently, whether you are a clerk, a

Partitions like these used at Xerox Corp. make it possible for people to exchange information directly with each other. But do they provide enough privacy and personal space? Do you think companies choose the type of arrangement pictured primarily to encourage worker interaction or to save money on costs of heating, air conditioning, and construction?

college professor, or a member of a bomber crew, the closer you work to other people, the more often you will communicate with them.[16]

Sometimes it is useful to distinguish between actual physical proximity and psychological proximity. For example, architectural arrangements can create psychological barriers to communication that can discourage interaction. On the other hand, arrangements that channel the flow of people who are moving about toward a common area, such as a reception area, a water fountain, and a bank of elevators, can create opportunities for spontaneous interaction. You'll remember that in Chapter 8 we discussed the open-office concept developed in an effort to increase the amount and quality of interaction among organizational members. As we learned, although this kind of design does increase interaction and communication, it does not always lead to greater job satisfaction. Indeed, offices can get too open, forcing people into too much interaction. People also have needs for privacy and personal space. Office designs that fail to recognize these needs may increase interaction and communication at the expense of satisfaction and productivity.

Role-Set Factors. Whether the purpose of the communication is to inform or persuade, the *credibility* of the source will largely determine whether the message is internalized by the role occupant. *Credibility* refers to the degree to which the information provided by the source is believable. Credibility is a function of two factors. The first factor is expertise, or the source's knowledge of the topic at hand. The second is trustworthiness, or the degree to which the recipient believes the communicator has no hidden motives. Thus a new manager may view an older, more experienced executive whose job is secure as a credible source of information and advice. The same manager, however, may take a skeptical view of advice from a fellow newcomer who may be competing with him for the same promotion six months down the road. The latter probably doesn't know any more than the former and may in fact have something to gain from his failure.

Protecting one's credibility is vital to one's long-term success in any company. If you lose your credibility you lose just about any influence you might have on others in your role set, and you may find yourself isolated and vulnerable. Much like the boy who cried wolf too often, organizational members who have lost credibility in the eyes of other role-set members may find themselves alone in

[16] J. T. Gullahorn, "Distance and Friendship as Factors in the Gross Interaction Matrix," *Sociometry* 15 (1952), 123–34.

confronting crisis situations. As the "In Practice" box shows, there is some evidence that employees' trust of top management has deteriorated recently. Many companies are going to great lengths to win back this trust.

A *power imbalance* between a role sender and a role occupant may also impede communication. Although we will discuss the concept of power at some length in Chapter 13, at this point we will consider just two kinds of power. One kind of power is based on legitimate authority, that is, the organizationally sanctioned ability of one person to reward or punish another. We will refer to the other kind of power as *status*, or the degree of prestige associated with a person's social position. Status is a function or both formal and informal authority.

The inverted-cone conception of organizations is useful in showing that communication can move in many directions. Legitimate authority affects the communication of messages that move along the vertical dimension of the inverted cone. A *downward communication* moves from a member of higher legitimate authority to a member of lower authority. Although today many successful executives do spend time on the shop floor talking with line workers, traditionally this type of communication has moved down the hierarchy one step at a time. The president of a large company would communicate with a vice-president, perhaps, who would speak to a line manager, who would issue directions to workers. As you may imagine, in this situation there are many opportunities for a mistranslation somewhere along the chain. It is a good idea for the initiator of a message to check the way it is being received.

Upward communication flows from people low in the organizational hierarchy to people above them. Because people at upper levels of the hierarchy have a great deal of power to reward and punish employees at lower levels, the latter are sometimes inhibited in their upward communication. Insecure lower-level workers may have a tendency to forget about the losses and exaggerate the wins when reporting information upward, leaving those at upper levels with a distorted sense of reality. Similarly, lower-level employees who are unsure about how to do their jobs may be reluctant to ask for assistance, fearing to appear unknowledgeable.[17] Here too, upper-level managers may get a distorted view of the competencies and capabilities of those who serve under them.

Finally, distortion can also occur in *radial communication*, which moves between a relatively peripheral member, say a newcomer, and a more central member, say an informal leader. As in the case of upward communication, the newcomer's reluctance to reveal ignorance to informal leaders may be a barrier to communication. Moreover, long-tenured, central members may share knowledge and language that newcomers find difficult to get a handle on, resulting in miscommunication and misunderstandings.

Role-Occupant Factors. As we saw in Chapter 5, people are bombarded with much more information than they can possibly attend to. Therefore, incoming information has to be filtered. The same thing holds true for communication. All the factors that affect perceptions affect communication as well.

A role occupant's *beliefs and values* will shape the way she interprets a message from a role sender. If she is anxious, for example, about how she is performing, she may place a great deal of weight on any message sent that reflects positive feedback. A person's strongly held beliefs can also affect his interpretation of messages sent. Perceivers tend to discount information that is not in accord with their beliefs. Messages that contradict those beliefs may not be correctly under-

---

[17] A. S. Tsui, "A Role Set Analysis of Managerial Reputation," *Organizational Behavior and Human Decision Processes* 34 (1984), 64–96.

Most top managers are quick to declare, "People are our most important asset." Yet all too often in recent years, this kind of declaration has been followed almost in the next breath with layoffs. Similarly, although many top managers stress the importance of quality, workers often see these same people as evaluating them solely in terms of the number of products pushed out the door. According to pollster Ilene Gochman of Opinion Research, "The days when management could say, 'Trust us, this is for your own good,' are over. Employees have seen that if the company steams off on some new strategic tack and it doesn't work, employees lose their jobs, not management."*

The credibility gap between what top managers say and what they do is matched by the gap in lifestyles between top managers and the rank-and-file employees. After Time, Inc., acquired Warner Communications, Time's CEO, J. Richard Munro stood to make $12 million on the deal. When asked about this, he responded, "That sounds like a lot of money unless you live in New York and live in the world I live in." Similarly, Citicorp chairman, John Reed, summarily dismissed an aide who had a problem with Reed's "Can't talk now—gotta meet [tennis star] Jimmy Connors." Finally, when asked if he ever shared his vision of the company's future with his employees, a head of an insurance company remarked in a surprised tone, "You mean, sit with them in little red plastic chairs and drink coffee out of styrofoam cups?" Comments like these have tended to dispel the myth that top managers and employees share something in the way of common goals or problems. The fact that top-executive salaries in the U.S. are commonly 100 times that of the average employee (this

* Based on A. Farnum. "The Trust Gap," *Fortune*, December 4, 1989, pp. 56–78.

Herb Kelleher, Southwest Airlines CEO, with some of the air carrier's staff.

rate is only 15 to 1 in Europe and Japan) adds fuel to this already raging fire.

Executives at many U.S. companies are working hard to close the credibility gap. Their efforts point to a number of positive, concrete behaviors that others could model to increase the perception of shared goals by the top and bottom halves of the organization.

One way to close the gap is to go through the bad times together as well as the good times. Herb Kelleher, CEO of Southwest Airlines, said, "If there's going to be a downside you should share it. When we were experiencing hard times two years ago, I went to the board and told them I wanted to

stood. Take the example of a sexist supervisor who believes that women are incapable of performing in managerial roles. He may distort or ignore messages that suggest a female manager is doing a good job but dutifully write down any evidence of her shortcomings.

The *frame of reference* of the receiver will also determine how well communication takes place. In Chapter 5, we noted that research by Tjosvold showed that the manager's frame of reference affects his decisions.[18] That is, managers made quite different decisions about the same situation depending on whether they interpreted the situation as a crisis or as a challenge. In this study, manager's interpretations also affected their communications. As shown in Table 10-4, when managers interpreted a situation as a crisis, they were less likely to ask questions, less knowledgeable about others' arguments, and less interested in hearing additional arguments. A crisis mentality appears to lead to a constriction of communication channels. The crisis frame of reference is particularly likely to crop up when communications must occur under heavy time pressures.

[18] D. Tjosvold, "Effects of Crisis Orientation on Managers' Approach to Controversy in Decision Making," *Academy of Management Journal* 27, 130–38.

cut my salary. I cut all the officers' bonuses 10 percent, mine 20 percent."

Herman Miller, one of the U.S.'s top furniture manufacturers makes sure that the ratio of executive salaries to that of the average worker never exceeds 20 to 1. Vermont ice-cream maker, Ben and Jerry's Homemade, goes even further, putting a cap on at a 5 to 1 ratio. Both these firms firmly believe that disproportionate top-management salaries disrupt teamwork.†

In addition to clamping down on salaries, some firms have moved away from executive perks, like country club memberships and chauffeurs. These so-called benefits create a psychological distance between the ranks and in doing so create more problems than they solve. For example, Union Carbide's headquarters on Park Avenue was at one time the most hierarchical, class-conscious office environment in New York City. When the firm moved its operations to Danbury, Connecticut, it took the move as the perfect opportunity to invoke change. According to Jim Barton, Carbide's director of general services, "In terms of amenities, everybody had the same stuff. It was an egalitarian approach: 2,350 private offices, all the same size. No executive parking. No executive dining room." These changes led to both increased productivity and satisfaction among employees.

There is no substitute in the pursuit of reduced psychological distance for reducing physical distance. Many top executives find that exposure to rank-and-file jobs promotes trust and understanding. For example, Darryl Hartley-Leonard, president of Hyatt Hotels, put his entire headquarters staff to work for a day changing sheets, pouring coffee, and running elevators. The president himself worked as a doorman alongside veteran porter Bill Kurvers. When asked what the president got from his experience other than tips, Kurvers noted quickly: "He got respect."

At Lincoln Electric, MBA's—even those from the most prestigious schools—spend eight weeks on a welding line. "We want them to understand the difficulty of the factory environment and have respect for people out there," says President Don Hastings. He adds, "These MBA's have got a big target on their backs. People have to see that they are not just traders coming in from the financial world."

Finally, although less dramatic, the use of regular employee surveys for increasing trust and cooperation should not be overlooked. For example, Preston Trucking, a Maryland-based carrier with nearly $600 million in yearly revenue, solicits its workers' ideas and opinions on a regular basis. By attending to workers' input and acting on it, the employees come to believe that management respects and trusts them.

This mutual respect can come in handy, especially during a crisis. Chuck Dunlop, manager at Preston's dock in Kearney, New Jersey, needed to save money by closing down the dock on the Friday before Christmas in 1988. However, a contract with the Teamsters stipulated that Friday was an official holiday. Dunlop could close the plant, but 35 workers would have to be paid anyway. Shop steward Carl Conoscenti told the drivers that they were entitled to the money, that no one would think less of them for taking it, and that no one would even know if they took it. None took it. Dunlop commented: "These are teamsters . . . This is *New Jersey.*" One wonders how employees working for Time's Munro or Citicorp's John Reed might have responded to such a crisis.

† J. Greenwald, Advice to Bosses: Try a Little Kindness. *Time,* September 11, 1989, p. 56

Differences in frames of reference often loom large in horizontal communication, or communication between functional departments of an organization. When such communications do occur, the radically different frames of reference adopted by members of each department can seriously complicate the communication process. For example, members of a sales department, who are close to consumers, may frame their communications in terms of revenue. Mem-

T A B L E 10-4
Framing a Problem as a Crisis or a Challenge: The Effect on Communication

	MEAN RESPONSE*	
	Crisis	Challenge
1. Number of questions asked	2.77	3.84
2. Knowledge of others' arguments	2.25	3.30
3. Interest in hearing more arguments	4.64	6.46

* Responses were measured on a scale that ranged from 1, "few" or "very little" to 7, "many" or "a great deal."

bers of a production group, on the other hand, who are closer to the manufacturing end, may frame messages in terms of costs. These different frames of reference cause each group to focus on different kinds of information and they may spend much of their time talking past each other.

Interpersonal Differences. Not only do different functional units have different frames of reference—they often speak different languages. Most specialized units develop their own **jargon**. Jargon is extremely useful. It maximizes information exchange with a minimum of time and symbols by taking advantage of the shared training and experience of its users. A coach of a football team, for example, may tell his quarterback to tell the team, "Left 41 out on three." This simple five-word message conveys a wealth of information. It provides detailed instructions to 11 people about complex behavioral sequences they are expected to perform. Jargon also may prevent others from understanding what is being communicated, which may be desirable. For example, a quarterback may have to change a play at the line of scrimmage in full earshot of the opposing players.

On the other hand, because jargon is likely to confuse anyone lacking the same training and experience, it can be a barrier to communication between groups. Often technical specialists get to the point where they use jargon unconsciously and indeed have a hard time expressing themselves in any other terms. This can become a permanent disability, greatly reducing people's career opportunities outside their own small groups.

jargon Idiosyncratic use of language that is often useful among specialists but that inhibits their ability to communicate with nonspecialists.

SOCIALIZATION, ROLES, AND COMMUNICATION

We have pointed out that people choose to work together to accomplish things they cannot accomplish alone. In so doing, they develop and take on specialized roles. We have also noted how these roles are formed and maintained. Group members develop communication processes so that they can exchange information. In the final section of this chapter, we will focus on two special facets of communication. Acknowledging that communication is part of all roles, we will examine some special roles in which communication is the key purpose of the role. We will also discuss a special kind of communication, called *socialization*, which takes place when a person first assumes a new role.

Communication Roles

Many problems can result from poor communication across roles. So it is not surprising that sometimes we create special roles whose sole purpose is to improve the effectiveness of communication. We will discuss three special communication roles in the organizational setting—gatekeeper, cosmopolitan, and opinion leader.[19]

Gatekeepers. One special communication role is that of the gatekeeper. The **gatekeeper**, as illustrated in Figure 10-10A, is responsible for controlling the messages sent through a particular communication channel. Gatekeepers are essential to prevent information overload from reducing the effectiveness of those in upper-level roles.

gatekeeper A person responsible for controlling messages sent through a particular communication channel.

[19] E. M. Rogers and R. A. Rogers, *Communications in Organizations* (New York: Free Press, 1978), p. 31.

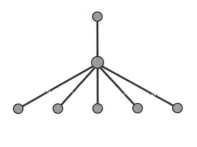

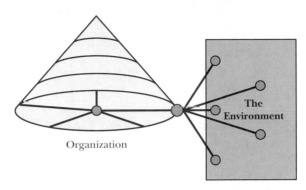

Organization

The Environment

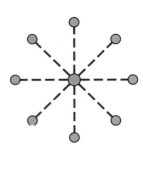

A Gatekeeper   B Cosmopolitan   C Opinion Leader

FIGURE 10-10
Special Communication Roles

For example, the role of chief of staff to the United States president is to shield the president from the multitude of people who want to influence him, seek his advice, or ask for favors. This gatekeeper must make important decisions regarding who will and will not have access to the president. Control over access to people in positions of power and authority gives a gatekeeper himself a great deal of power.

cosmopolitan A person who has many important contacts outside the organization and develops special knowledge from these contacts.

Cosmopolitans. **Cosmopolitans** are people with many contacts outside the organization who have special knowledge that the firm needs (see Figure 10-10B). Such people may be affiliated with professional groups that allow them to keep up to date on specific subjects, or they may have former associations that give them special expertise. For example, many defense contractors hire ex-Pentagon officials as consultants. The latter are very knowledgeable about the inner workings of defense contract decision processes and have a good understanding of the Pentagon's needs.

The ease with which some cosmopolitan workers move between organizational boundaries can sometimes be a problem. They develop a host of contacts outside the firm and many times decide to set up shop on their own. Rather than restrict their movement, some organizations have tried to give these employees their freedom in return for service. In fact, some companies trying to downsize set up consulting arrangements with departing employees. They are reducing the payroll and overhead while at the same time retaining the service of people who are familiar with the companies. Paul Kiczec, a systems analyst at Marine Midland Bank, developed a software program that helped commercial banks keep track of sales. The more he talked with people from other banks while developing the project, the more convinced he became that he had a marketable item on his hands. Kiczec got Marine Midland to give him the rights to the software in return for a royalty. Then he formed his own business. His biggest client right now? Marine Midland, although he hopes to reduce Marine's share to 10 to 20 percent in a few years.[20]

opinion leader A person who has special access to an organization's informal channels of communication and therefore has enhanced ability to influence others.

Opinion Leaders. A third communication role is that of the **opinion leader** (see Figure 10-10C). This person, has special access to an organization's informal channels of communication, often referred to as the grapevine. He has a greater than average ability to communicate with others in the organization and influence them. For example, an ex-foreman who was respected by both management and employees may still have many informal ties to both workers and management that enable him to shape organizational policies.

[20] C. H. Deutsch, "Turning a Boss into a Client," *New York Times*, July 8, 1990, p. 23.

Opinion leaders occupy a central position in the organization. For this reason they are closer both to the sources of legitimate authority and to opinion leaders in other functional units. The effective use of opinion leaders and their informal lines of communication is often what separates firms that are effectively integrated on all hierarchical and functional dimensions from firms in which these dimensions are poorly coordinated.

Socialization of New Group Members

organizational socialization The process by which a person acquires the social knowledge and skills necessary to assume an organizational role.

Just as there are certain situations in organizations in which a particular communication function is essential, there are certain occasions on which a very specific kind of communication seems especially critical. One of these is a person's entry into a new role within the organization. **Organizational socialization** is the process by which an individual acquires the social knowledge and skills necessary to assume an organizational role.[21] It is the process of learning the ropes and entails much more than simply learning the technical requirements associated with one's job. It deals with learning about the organization, its values, its culture, its past history, its potential, and where the newly admitted member fits in.

Socialization occurs any time an individual moves along any of the three dimensions of organizations (hierarchical, functional, or inclusionary). It is particularly intense when the target person is crossing all three organizational boundaries at once. When a person joins a new firm, she crosses the inclusionary boundary as she moves from nonmember to member status, and she crosses functional and hierarchical boundaries as she joins a particular function unit, such as the advertising department, at a specific hierarchical level, such as account executive. It is at this time that the organization has the most instructing and persuading to accomplish. It is also the time when a person is most susceptible to being taught and influenced. Being the new kid on the block typically causes a person to be anxious and self-conscious, and so the faster one can learn the ropes, the better.

custodianship A product of socialization in which a new group member adopts the means and ends associated with the role unquestioningly.

Desired Goals. Although instruction and persuasion are part of all socialization programs, different firms may seek different end goals in this process. Some organizations may pursue a **custodianship** response. Here the newcomer takes a caretaker's stance toward the means and ends associated with his role. He is not to question the status quo; he is merely to conform to it. A popular expression in the U.S. Marine Corps, paraphrased from Tennyson's "Charge of the Light Brigade," is "Ours is not to question why; ours is but to do or die."

role innovation A product of socialization in which a new group member is expected to improve on both the goals for her job and the means of achieving them.

When an organization hopes that the new member will change either the means by which her role is performed or the ends sought by the role, it may have as a goal **role innovation**. For example, in the medical community a subtle effort is being made—largely by health maintenance organizations, (HMOs)—to change the role of health-care provider. Instead of simply treating the sick, providers would promote physical and mental health and work to prevent illness. Of course, custodianship and role innovation are two ends of a continuum, and many firms seek something in the middle.

Socialization Tactics. Firms use several tactics in socializing new members. The chosen strategy will have a considerable impact on how the new recruit turns

[21] J. Van Maanen and E. H. Schein (1979). Toward a theory of organizational socialization. *Research in Organizational Behavior*. eds. B. Staw and E. L. Cummings, JAI Press: Greenwich, Conn., pp. 209–64.

out. There are four critical dimensions of socialization strategies: collective-individual, sequential-random, serial-disjunctive, and divestiture-investiture (see Figure 10-11). The first technique in each of these pairs indoctrinates the newcomer in the custodianship role. The second member of each pair leads the newcomer into role innovation.

In *collective socialization*, a group of new recruits may be put through a particular set of experiences together. This method is characteristic of army boot camps, fraternities, sororities, and management-training courses. In collective processes much of the socialization is accomplished by the recruits themselves. For example, Marine Corps recruits may abuse each other verbally or even physically, something the corps itself would not do.

In contrast, in *individual socialization*, recruits are taken one at a time and put through unique experiences. This treatment is characteristic of apprenticeship programs or on-the-job learning. It has much more variable results than collective socialization does and success depends a great deal on the qualities of the recruit herself.

The second dimension of socialization strategies is called *sequential socialization*. This technique takes recruits through a given sequence of discrete and identifiable steps leading to the target role. A physician's training, for example, includes several observable steps; the undergraduate premed program, medical school, an internship, and a residency. A person must complete all of these before taking specialist board examinations. Usually, in sequential processes, each stage builds on the prior stage. Moreover, there is a tendency on the part of those doing the socializing to suggest that all the other steps are easier than the current one. The algebra teacher socializing the student to the world of math notes that geometry will be easy if one understands algebra. The geometry teacher notes that trigonometry will be painless if one appreciates geometry. This type of presentation helps recruits keep focused on the current stage. It minimizes the discouragement that comes with the knowledge that they are a long way from where they need to be. Sometimes successful completion of a step is rewarded with a ceremony, such as a graduation, which reinforces the person's feeling of accomplishment.

At the other end of this dimension are *random socialization* processes, in which there is no rhyme or reason to learning experiences. The steps are unknown, ambiguous, or continually changing. Training for a general manager, for example, tends to be much less rigorously specified than that for a medical professional. Some managers rise from lower ranks, some come from other occupations, some come straight from MBA programs.

Socialization strategies also differ on the amount of help and guidance they give newcomers in learning their new roles. In *serial socialization*, experienced members of the organization teach the newcomers about the roles they are about to assume. These experienced members become role models or mentors for the new members. In police departments, for example, rookies are assigned as partners to older, veteran officers. Some observers have suggested that this practice creates a remarkable degree of inter-generational stability in the behaviors of

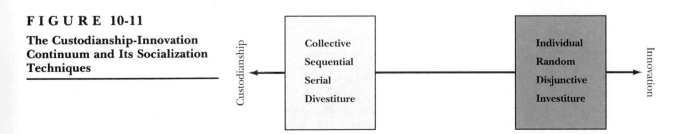

FIGURE 10-11

The Custodianship-Innovation Continuum and Its Socialization Techniques

Custodianship ←

Collective
Sequential
Serial
Divestiture

Individual
Random
Disjunctive
Investiture

→ Innovation

police officers. This method of socialization allows the recruit to see into the future in that he can expect to wind up much like the role model. This works well with the right role model. If, however, the picture of the future is not very flattering, the newcomer may never become committed to the organization.

In *disjunctive socialization*, on the other hand, a recruit must learn by herself how to handle a new role. For example, the first woman partner in a conservative law firm may find few people if any on the scene who have faced her unique problems. She may be completely on her own in coping with these problems. Disjunctive socialization is sometimes brought on by organizations who "clean house," that is, sweep out all the older members of the organization and replace them with new personnel. Such a shakeup causes almost all employees of the firm to relearn their role. Typically the organization hopes that the result will be more creativity in problem solving.

The fourth dimension of socialization deals with the degree to which a socialization process confirms or disconfirms the value of a newcomer's personal identity. *Divestiture socialization* ignores or denies the value of the newcomer's personal characteristics. The organization wants to tear the person down to nothing and then rebuild him as a completely new and different individual. Some organizations require either explicitly or implicitly that the recruit sever old relationships, undergo intense harassment from experienced members, and engage for long periods of time in doing the dirty work of the trade (work that is associated with low pay and low status). The organization promotes these ordeals in the belief that those who emerge from them will be strongly committed to the group's goal and identity.

In contrast, *investiture socialization* affirms the value to the organization of the recruit's particular personal characteristics. The organization says, in effect, "We like you just the way you are." It implies that rather than change the recruit, the firm hopes the recruit will change the organization. Under these conditions, the organization may try to make the recruit's transition process as smooth and painless as possible.

Designing Socialization Programs. The strategy you choose in designing your socialization program depends on your goal: custodianship or innovation. If you want to generate a custodianship response, you will want to use collective, sequential, serial, and divestiture socialization. In this way, you will give every recruit the same experiences in the same order. You will promote his acceptance of the status quo by replacing his own beliefs and values with those of experienced members. If, on the other hand, you want to promote innovation in the role, you will use just the opposite tactic. You will want a unique and individualized program for each recruit. The program must value and support the newcomer's particular personality characteristics and style. Figure 10-11 summarizes these two approaches.

By designing the appropriate socialization programs, organizations provide a link to the past and a blueprint for their future. The decisions reached about what new members will experience will profoundly affect the way the history and culture of an organization is preserved. Decisions should also promote innovation where necessary so that the organization can master the challenges of the future.

SUMMARY

Joining into groups allows individuals to accomplish goals and satisfy needs that could not be met if they acted alone. Individuals within groups become dependent upon each other in several different ways. The simplest type of relationship

INTERPERSONAL PROCESSES AND COMMUNICATION

involves *pooled interdependence*; the most complex form involves *team interdependence*. Interdependencies among individuals lead to the evolution of *roles*. These roles capture the expectations that members of a person's *role set* have for the person occupying a given work role. Roles can be differentiated on *functional*, *hierarchical* and *inclusionary* dimensions. Whereas roles are the building blocks of organizations, communication is the cement that hold these blocks together. *Communication* involves the encoding, transmission, and decoding of information sent from one person to another via any one of a number of media. There are several barriers to communication effectiveness such as spatial arrangements, status differentials and jargon. Special organizational roles such as those of *gatekeeper*, *cosmopolitan*, and *opinion leader* deal almost exclusively with communication issues. Certain recurring organizational problems, like *socialization* of new members, require special attention. In particular, depending upon the goal of one's socialization program, different communicators, using different tactics, might be required for different positions.

REVIEW QUESTIONS

1.   Of the four types of interdependence discussed in this chapter, which type do you think is most adversely affected by turnover among organizational members? Which type of interdependence is most adversely affected by turnover in group leadership? How might the nature of the turnover process affect the kind of interdependence one builds into groups?

2.   Two trends in organizations are a move toward more employee involvement (through employee ownership) and, at the same time, a move towards greater use of temporary workers. What is likely to be the strongest force affecting employee owners and temporary workers as far as compliance, identification, and internalization with group norms are concerned? If you specify different forces for these two groups, why might the use of both tactics be on the rise at the same time?

3.   Socialization refers to the impact that the group or organization has on the individual. We noted that this impact tends to be greatest when the individual is moving through more than one dimension at a time (e.g., functional and hierarchical). In contrast, when is the individual most likely to have the greatest impact on the organization? (Are there honeymoon periods? Do lame ducks have any influence?) How might your answer depend on the tactics of socialization employed when bringing the individual into the new group?

4.   What role do ceremonies play in the socialization process of someone crossing an important organizational boundary? If one looks at the three kinds of boundaries that one can traverse, where are ceremonies most frequently encountered, and why? What role do ceremonies play in the motivation of group members who are not crossing a boundary but are merely observers at the affair?

5.   In communication, it has been said that "the medium is the message." What are the factors that one should consider when choosing a medium for one's communication? Some of the greatest leaders of all time actually wrote very little. What might explain why people who are perceived as strong leaders avoid leaving a paper trail of writings? When might writing be used to enhance leadership?

DIAGNOSTIC QUESTIONS

When you are confronting problems of communication or socialization or attempting to deal with difficulties that arise out of interpersonal problems, the following questions may prove useful.

1.   What type of interdependence unites you with other employees? What sorts of problems might this interdependence cause?

2. What important components of your unique work role are not part of your job description?

3. What are some of the important functional, hierarchical and inclusionary dimensions in your organization? Sketch an inverted-cone diagram to represent these dimensions in your firm.

4. Who are the members of your role set? What are their expectations for the occupant of your role? How do they communicate these expectations to you?

5. What are your own expectations for your role? How do these expectations compare with your role set's expectations, and what should be done about any discrepancies?

6. What are the primary reasons that people in your organization conform to their role expectations—compliance, identification, or internalization? What do these choices imply for monitoring employees' behavior?

7. What means of communication (oral, written, or nonverbal) do you use for different organizational tasks? Are these the optimal choices for the purposes you seek to achieve? Why?

8. How would you characterize the communication network in your group? How does this network deal with or affect information overload, communication speed, and communication accuracy?

9. How do others in your group perceive your influence and credibility? How do these perceptions affect the communications others send you and the communications you send to them?

10. What are some of your major values, beliefs, and frames of reference? How might these affect the way you interpret communications you receive from others in the group?

11. Which people in your organization occupy communication roles (gate-keepers, cosmopolitans, opinion leaders)? How can their special expertise help you in the performance of your role?

12. What do you wish to accomplish when socializing new group members (custodianship or innovation)? How should your socialization program be designed to promote your goal?

EXERCISE 10-1
THE ADVERTISING FIRM: A GROUP FEEDBACK ACTIVITY*

JEANNE LINDHOLM, *College of William Mary*

Working successfully with others requires that people establish and maintain effective patterns of interdependence among each other. To develop such interdependence coworkers must be aware of how they work together, and they must take the time to figure out how to improve the way they do things. In this exercise you will learn how periodic feedback can help groups improve their effectiveness in performing a task. You will also develop a greater awareness of how you work with others.

STEP ONE: PRE-CLASS PREPARATION

Before class, read the entire exercise and familiarize yourself with the tasks described below.

STEP TWO: GROUP WORK—NAMING THE PRODUCT

The class should divide into groups of 4 to 6 members each (if you have formed permanent groups in an earlier exercise, reassemble in those same groups). Your group should then complete the following task:

> You and your fellow group members are a project team for an advertising firm. A candy company has just created a new candy bar made of chocolate, caramel, and pecans and has employed your advertising firm to *name the bar* and to *design a one-minute radio commercial* for it. In this step of the exercise your team will be given five minutes to name the new bar. Later you will spend about thirty minutes designing the radio commercial, and then presenting it to the class.

STEP THREE: PROCESS FEEDBACK— NAMING THE PRODUCT

Your instructor will terminate Step Two after five minutes and ask all group members to remain seated together. The instructor will then lead a class discussion in which the members of each group should respond to the following questions:

1. What name did the group come up with? How pleased are each of the group members with the group's final choice?

2. How was the final choice made? How pleased are each of the group members with the way this choice was made?

3. Is there anything the group might do differently to improve its effectiveness in its next task, of working on the radio commercial?

STEP FOUR: GROUP WORK— CREATING A COMMERCIAL

The class should resume working in groups and should now begin work on the radio commercial advertising the new candy bar. You will need to pace yourselves, keeping in mind that you will have about 30 minutes to complete this task.

After fifteen minutes the instructor will interrupt the groups and will ask you to discuss the following questions:

1. As you work on the radio commercial, to what extent are you using your greatest assets as a member of your group? How do you feel about this? What changes need to be made?

2. How satisfied are you with the way in which ideas are being shared in your group? How satisfied are you with the way in which the task is being completed? What improvements should be made?

3. In what ways are the members of your group encouraging one another to contribute? In what ways are you discouraging one another? Are these actions helping or hurting the performance of your group?

4. When you compare your group's work in Step Four with its work in Step Two, what improvements can you see? What improvements still need to be made?

5. In view of your answers to these questions, what will you do differently during the next 15 minutes as you complete the radio commercial?

Your instructor will guide all groups in discussing these questions openly and and will encourage you to consider each question carefully. Then all groups will return to the task of developing the radio commercial.

* Adapted from J. William Pfeiffer, *The 1988 Annual: Developing Human Resources* (San Diego, CA: University Associates, Inc., 1988). Used with permission.

STEP FIVE: GROUP PRESENTATIONS

After 15 minutes more the instructor will reconvene the class and will ask each group to present its commercial. After all of the commercials have been presented the instructor will lead the class in a discussion of the following questions:

1. How pleased are you with the quality of your group's commercial? How pleased are you with the quality of your group's presentation?

2. How did the group decide who would present the commercial? How pleased are you with the process that was used to make this decision?

3. On a scale of 1 = low to 10 = high, rate your group on the following dimensions of effective teamwork:
   _____ Participation (giving everyone the opportunity to contribute)
   _____ Sensitivity (taking one another's feelings into account)
   _____ Openness (being able to say what you really think)
   _____ Flexibility (being able to change and correct problems)
   _____ Commitment (feeling responsible for completing the group's task)
   _____ Risk taking (trying things out that might seem outlandish at first)
   In the light of your ratings, what can you say about the way your group works together? What changes still need to be made? What will you personally do in the future to improve the effectiveness of your group?

4. What have you learned about the role of periodic feedback in improving a group's effectiveness?

CONCLUSION

To work together effectively, interdependent individuals must receive periodic feedback that lets them know how they're doing and whether changes need to be made. In the absence of such feedback, people working together cannot tell whether they are fulfilling their roles effectively and may perform poorly. At present as you work with your classmates and throughout your managerial career, you should seek out periodic feedback and provide feedback in return to those with whom you are working.

DIAGNOSING ORGANIZATIONAL BEHAVIOR

CASE 10-1

NURSE ROSS*

WILLIAM M. FOX, *University of Florida*

The following situation was reported by Miss Jackson, who had known Miss Evelyn Ross for several years and had also worked in some of the same hospitals as Miss Ross on different occasions.

Miss Ross, a registered nurse, began working at Benton Hospital when she was 31 years old. This hospital was an industrial hospital in a fairly large city on the West Coast. The bed capacity of the hospital was about 150, but 50 to 100 patients received treatment daily through the hospital's clinic facilities. The hospital was built and operated by a large shipbuilding concern. All the employees of the company's shipyards and their dependents could receive medical care through the company's hospitalization plan.

The nursing staff was headed by a director of nurses who had two assistants. One was in charge of nursing services in the hospital, and the other was in charge of the clinic nursing services. However, the two departments operated as a coordinated unit, and personnel were exchanged between them in the event the work load became too heavy in either place.

The medical director of the hospital, Dr. Peake, was energetic and his manner was usually quite brusque. Although he was a stickler for discipline and efficiency, he was fair in his treatment of the staff and they respected him and cooperated well. Dr. Peake had many progressive ideas and had helped to build the hospital up from 75 to 150 beds. The new ideas he had were discussed in staff conferences. Any persons or heads of departments who might be affected by proposed changes participated in these conferences.

Miss Ross worked as a head nurse, both in the hospital and in the clinic, during her employment there. (Miss Jackson at that time was employed as assistant head nurse in the clinic.) Miss Ross resigned her position to enter the Army Nurse Corps as a first lieutenant. She served in the Army for two and a half years, most of which was duty in the South Pacific. During the time she was overseas, she was promoted to captain. She was transferred to reserve status upon leaving the corps. Shortly after this she took a three-month course in operating room supervision.

In the meantime, Miss Jackson had moved to the East Coast and was employed at Hughes Hospital, a large industrial hospital in a relatively small New England city. They had corresponded during this time and Miss Jackson wrote that the position of operating room supervisor would soon be open at the hospital and thought Miss Ross had a good chance of getting the position if she wanted to move to the East Coast. Miss Ross applied to the director of nursing at the hospital and was accepted for the position. She began working soon thereafter at Hughes.

Hughes Hospital was set up much like Benton Hospital. It took care of the medical needs of most of the community in addition to serving the employees of the Hughes Steel Company, the city's principal employer. It had clinic facilities for emergency and outpatient care. The bed capacity was 250 and the clinic staff treated well over 100 patients daily, although often a complete record of the number of patients was not kept.

The organization of the nursing department was quite similar to that of Benton Hospital with one important exception: the hospital department and the clinic department were operated as two completely separate units. The clinic was in a building separate from the hospital building; thus the problem of moving a stretcher case from the clinic to the hospital was an extreme ordeal. Besides the lack of proper equipment for moving patients, there was a shortage of male orderlies, and nurses' aides had to be utilized for this arduous task. This shortage of personnel and equipment was especially acute when emergency cases and accident victims came into the clinic and had to be moved to the hospital with a minimum loss of time and disturbance.

The director of nurses, Miss McHaffey, was about 45 years old; she had been at the hospital three years. Miss Linden had been the hospital supervisor for six months, and Miss Hartman had been employed as a clinic supervisor for over a year. There were 24 graduate nurses employed in the hospital wards, 30 aides, and 10 maids. The staff under Miss Hartman in the clinic consisted of five graduate nurses, four aides, and two maids. The orderly personnel numbered only six for all three shifts. One was utilized throughout the hospital on the evening shift, one on the night shift, and during the day shift one worked in the clinic, one in the operating room (O.R.), and one for each of the two men's wards in the hospital. Miss Ross, as supervisor of the O.R., had a staff of four nurses, three aides, and the one orderly. The nurses in the O.R. rotated turns, being "on call" each night for any emergency surgery cases.

Miss Ross found that the work was quite strenuous and often entailed long hours, but she was deeply interested in it and never seemed to object. She frequently stayed to help in emergency surgery cases, as a number of rather serious accidents occurred from time to time in the steel plants that the hospital served. Miss McHaffey praised her highly for increasing the efficiency and cleanliness in the operating rooms.

Dr. McMillan, the medical director of the hospital, was nearly 65 years old. He had been employed as a company doctor for the Hughes Steel Company for over 20 years. Dr. McMillan would usually arrive at his offices in the hospital about nine in the morning, would dictate answers to his correspondence, make sporadic rounds of some of the hospital wards (very rarely did he put in an appearance at the clinic), leave for lunch promptly at noon, and, only two or three times a week return to the hospital for a few hours after lunch. On his occasional ward rounds, he would stop at the floor nurse's desk, inquire if everything was going all right, then say, "Fine! Fine!" and go on his way.

When Dr. McMillan suffered a heart attack severe enough to prevent him from retaining his position at the hospital, a new medical director had to be found. The president of the steel company was familiar with the West-Coast shipbuilding concern and knew Dr. Peake had been at Benton. He contacted Dr. Peake to see if he would be interested in the position as the hospital medical director. Dr. Peake accepted. He entered the new situation with his usual brusque and energetic manner and made complete daily rounds in the clinic and hospital. He often spent considerable time talking to patients, nurses, aids, and the staff physicians.

After nearly a month of concentrated observation of the clinic and hospital routines, Dr. Peake had a conference with Miss McHaffey and the nursing supervisors. He criticized the "unprofessional attitude" of several of the nurses, and said he had had complaints from many of the patients about the care they were receiving. He asked why so many of the nurses seemed to be away from their wards when he made morning rounds. Miss McHaffey said the nurses were permitted to leave the wards at intervals between nine and eleven to have coffee in the hospital dining room. The time for this was not rigidly enforced. Dr. Peake also talked to Dr. Albright, the staff physician in charge of the clinic, and to the clinic nurses to ascertain why the clinic patients often had to wait so long to see a doctor in the clinic. (The gist of these conferences was given by Miss Jackson, who was assistant supervisor of the clinic.) The clinic staff agreed that there was definitely a "bottleneck" in the clinic, but they felt that it was due primarily to a shortage of personnel when needed most, the inconvenience of having to transport the patients the distance to the hospital, and the lack of satisfactory laboratory facilities in the clinic itself. Dr. Peake told the staff that the new additions being built onto the hospital were going to be utilized for clinic facilities. In the meantime, he said he would try to help them find some way to ease the situation.

During the second week of August of that year, Miss McHaffey asked Miss Ross to come into her office.

Miss McHaffey: Miss Ross, Dr. Peake tells me that you worked with him at Benton Hospital. I knew that he had been at Benton at one time, but didn't realize that it was during the same time you were there. He said that you are familiar with the clinic-hospital arrangement there and told me to relieve you of your present position so that you may help to co-ordinate the clinic and hospital units here.

Miss Ross: I'm sorry to hear that. I have been very happy with my present position. Will I be working in the clinic or in the hospital?

Miss McHaffey: Both. I want you to know that I consider Miss Linden a very capable supervisor and I don't want her to be hurt in this new arrangement. Also, I want to know everything that is going on down there. I expect you to report to me at least once a day. I don't know what Dr. Peake expects you to do that hasn't already been done. He should hire more people if he expects to make this a model hospital. He comes in here and all he does is criticize.

Miss Ross: I'll do the best I can. I am familiar with the setup that Dr. Peake had at Benton. Maybe I can help put it into operation here.

A few hours later Dr. Peake entered Miss Ross' office in the O.R. unit.

Dr. Peake: Hello, Rossie, I have a new job for you.

Miss Ross: Miss McHaffey has told me about it.

Dr. Peake: You know how things were at Benton. I want the units to be set up in exactly that way here. During the past few months I have arranged for another physician to help out in the clinic during their busy hours and we've hired a couple more aides, but there doesn't seem to be too much improvement. Maybe you can help me find out what

the trouble is there. Our new building program has been started and when it is finished I want the two units to be operating as one integrated unit. I don't like to take you away from the surgery—you've been doing a fine job here—but I feel you can help me get the clinic and hospital units functioning better together.

Miss Ross: I can try, Dr. Peake.

Dr. Peake: Good! Now I don't want you to go through anybody—if you have any problems, come right to me!

Miss Ross—knowing the strained relationship between Dr. Peake and Miss McHaffey—was especially dubious about bypassing her immediate supervisor, the director of nurses. She decided at that time it would be best to observe the regular channels of communications.

Miss Ross reported for her new job and discussed Dr. Peake's plans and ideas for integrating the two units with both Miss Linden and Miss Hartman. She also told them that the reason he picked her for the job was because she had worked at Benton under him. They had known that both she and Miss Jackson had worked at Benton for a time while Dr. Peake was there. Neither of the supervisors seemed very surprised. Miss Linden remarked that it sounded like another of Dr. Peake's "wild ideas." Both Miss Linden and Miss Hartman seemed concerned over the shortage of an adequate staff and said that any changes that would improve the situation would be welcomed.

Personnel problems were especially acute in the hospital at that time. Several staff members were off duty because of illness and there were more patients than usual. The clinic was open Saturday and Sunday for emergencies only. One nurse and two aides were on duty weekends but were not too busy. Miss Ross arranged to transfer the two aides to the hospital for the weekends. Miss Linden was elated with the additional help. On the following Wednesday, the clinic was far behind in its work because of an emergency that had arisen. Miss Ross went to Miss Linden to see if someone could go over for the afternoon to help. The following conversation ensued:

Miss Ross: Miss Hartman is swamped. She had an emergency to take care of and the other patients are not being seen. Have you anyone you can send to help?

Miss Linden: I am not going to send anyone to that clinic. They have enough help! We are too short here.

Miss Ross went over to one of the wards and found two of the aides in the ward kitchen drinking coffee. She asked if they were slack right then.

One of them said, "Oh, sure. We haven't had very much to do all afternoon."

Miss Ross returned to Miss Linden and told her of the episode. She asked that one of them be sent to help out in the clinic. Miss Linden complied reluctantly.

Shortly after this Miss Linden went on a vacation for two weeks. Miss McHaffey asked Miss Ross to take charge of the hospital unit until her return. Thus Miss Ross was faced with the problem of making out time schedules for all the nurses, aides, orderlies, and maids employed in the hospital unit. Dr. Peake had also asked her to initiate a study to determine the personnel needs in the various hospital wards and the clinic departments, and to help with the plans for the layout of new equipment in the building additions. During the two weeks of Miss Linden's absence, Miss Ross found that 1) one ward had more nurses than another one, although the work loads were the same, and 2) maids were not doing the cleaning assigned to them and some were not even aware of what their duties were. With the cooperation of Miss Hartman and the approval and permission of Miss McHaffey, Miss Ross arranged to reallocate the nursing personnel so that all wards would have equal coverage in relation to their work loads. She made out schedules to provide available clinic help as relief in the hospital on weekends and instructed the maids as to their duties.

There seemed to be a gradual improvement in the amount and quality of patient care and most of the employees seemed to be more satisfied when they were placed in jobs where they were kept busy and understood their duties. Several patients commented on the improved care they received after the changes had been made. Dr. Peake praised Miss Ross and Miss McHaffey for the success of the new program.

Two days after Miss Linden returned from her vacation Miss Ross was called the office of the director of nurses.

Miss McHaffey: Miss Ross, Miss Linden has requested a transfer to the operating room, because she doesn't think you and she will get along. She is doing a good job in the hospital and I don't want to lose her. Hereafter, you will not interfere with the operation of the hospital unit and its personnel. Miss Linden will take care of everything over there.

Miss Ross: I don't understand, Miss McHaffey. Do you mean that my job is finished?

Miss McHaffey: No. You are to continue working in the clinic and help set up new de-

partments there as the building program continues. I really don't know what made Dr. Peake think you would be able to do anything to improve the situation. He will just have to realize that we haven't sufficient personnel.

Miss Ross left the interview feeling very confused as to her exact status because she knew Dr. Peake would expect her to continue to try to coordinate the two units.

When you have read this case, look back at the chapter's diagnostic questions and choose the ones that apply to the case. Then use those questions with the ones that follow in your case analysis.

1. Why must Benton Hospital coordinate its hospital wards with its clinic? What kind of interdependence now links the hospital and the clinic and how has it affected relations between the units? How might this mode of interdependence be changed so as to coordinate the two units more effectively and improve the relations between them?

2. Examine the role that Dr. Peake expects Nurse Ross to play in linking the hospital with its clinic. What do other members of Nurse Ross's role set expect of her? Is it realistic to expect Nurse Ross to succeed in filling the role Dr. Peake has assigned her?

3. Describe the character and quality of the communication among the people involved in this case. Has it promoted mutual understanding or hindered it? Do all of the people in the case appear to be adequately socialized? What might Benton Hospital do to help Nurse Ross accomplish her task? How could it improve its communication networks and socialization procedures?

CASE 10-2

CAMERAN MUTUAL INSURANCE COMPANY

Review this case, which appears in Chapter 8. Next, look back at Chapter 10's diagnostic questions and choose the ones that apply to the case. Then use those questions with the ones that follow in your case analysis.

1. Describe the socialization process that Mrs. Kay went through as she began to work at Cameran Insurance. What are the strengths and weaknesses of this sort of socialization?

2. Many people believe that most interpersonal problems boil down to faulty communication. How

might improved communications affect the working relationship between Mrs. Kay and Mr. Landers? What good things might result? What negative outcomes might occur?

3. If you were asked to advise Cameran Insurance about how to manage the process of introducing new employees to the organization, what changes would you recommend? Why? What things would you want the company to keep doing the same way?

CASE 10-3

BETA BUREAU

Read Chapter 17's Case 17–2, "Beta Bureau." Next, look back at Chapter 10's diagnostic questions and choose the ones that apply to that case. Then use those questions with the ones that follow in this analysis of the case.

1. What type of interdependence would you expect to find in the modules formed in Beta Bureau? What kinds of problems does this type of interdependence stimulate? What are its strengths?

2. Suppose you were assigned the task of socializing new module members. What sort of program would you develop? What would be its aim? How successful would it be in achieving this aim?

3. Why did many supervisors at Beta Bureau react negatively to the changes caused by modularization? If you were responsible for making supervisory jobs more attractive to traditional managers, what would you do?

CHAPTER 11

GROUP FORMATION AND PERFORMANCE

GE's conversion of its Salisbury plant to team-based production, though ultimately highly successful, met with resistance at first. Some workers were reluctant to accept more responsibility and to move constantly from job to job and they quit, mirroring GE's own initial reluctance to commit itself to the teamwork concept. By 1989, however, nearly 20 percent of GE's 120,000 employees throughout the United States were members of work teams, and the corporation's goal was to raise that to 35 percent by the end of the year.
Source: John Hoerr, "The Payoff from Teamwork," Business Week, July 10, 1989, pp. 58–59.

If the United States is to become a world-class manufacturing nation, companies must be able to produce in small lots, customizing products to increasing demands. This calls for flexible work practices and workers who are willing to move from job to job. Teamwork makes this possible because the employees usually are cross-trained to perform all tasks. They can fill in for absent coworkers and respond quickly to changes in models and production runs. A General Electric Co. plant in Salisbury, N.C., typically changes product models a dozen times a day by using a team system to produce lighting panel-boards. This plant has increased productivity by 250 percent compared with GE plants that produced the same products in 1985. It combines teamwork with "flexible automation" [see Chapter 16] and other computerized systems.[1]

General Electric's experience at its Salisbury plant demonstrates that *teamwork* is today's watchword in many North American organizations. More than ever before, production teams are being used to increase efficiency in companies as well-known and diverse as Boeing Aircraft, Caterpillar Tractor, Ford, and Digital Equipment.[2] Companies throughout the United States and Canada have also begun to experiment with **participatory management** procedures. Teams of workers and managers work together to make such decisions as what products to produce, which raw materials to purchase, and what production processes to use. Growth in the use of teams and teamwork throughout North America was reflected in a 1987 survey by the United States General Accounting Office. This survey found that 70 percent of 476 large American companies had installed **quality circles**—committees charged with solving productivity problems. Current trends in the manufacturing and service sectors suggest that this growth will continue well into the twenty-first century.

In light of these trends, managing groups and group performance is becoming an increasingly critical part of the job of being a manager. Today's managers must be especially good at encouraging teamwork and productivity in groups of employees. Where group tasks involve decision making, contemporary managers must also know how to enhance the creativity, judgmental accuracy, and problem-solving abilities of groups. In this chapter, we will discuss the management of group performance. We will begin by identifying the different types of groups found in organizations and exploring the processes through which these groups form and develop. After laying this groundwork, we will identify several factors that can interfere with group productivity or enhance it. We will conclude by discussing the special challenges involved in using groups to make decisions or solve problems.

participatory management A management style in which managers and nonmanagers work together to make decisions about what products to produce, which raw materials to purchase, what production processes to use, and similar issues.

quality circles Committees charged with solving productivity problems. Typically, a participatory approach is used in such groups.

 ## Diagnostic Issues

Several questions come to mind when we apply our diagnostic model to problems of group formation and group performance. Can we *describe* stages of group development? How do such stages relate to group activity? How are group norms established and how do they affect group performance and satisfaction? Can we *diagnose* why some people in groups refuse to pull their

[1] John Hoerr, "The Payoff from Teamwork: The Gains in Quality Are Substantial—So Why Isn't It Spreading Faster?" *Business Week*, July 10, 1989, p. 58.
[2] Ibid., pp. 56–62.

own weight? Why do groups take risks that their individual members might want to avoid?

Can we *prescribe* which jobs should be performed by individual workers and which jobs by groups? Can we predict which groups will be productive and which won't? What *actions* can organizations take to facilitate the accuracy and creativity of group judgments? What can organizations do to promote group performance and member satisfaction?

GROUPS AND GROUP EFFECTIVENESS

What kinds of groups form in organizations? In what ways do they differ from one another? What purposes do they serve? Knowing the answers to these questions is the first step toward understanding how to manage groups. Let's begin answering them by defining a *group* as a collection of two or more persons who interact with one another in such a way that each person influences and is influenced by the others.[3] Group members draw important psychological distinctions between themselves and people who are not group members. People in a group generally

Define themselves as members
Are defined by others as members
Identify with one another
Engage in frequent interaction
Participate in a system of interlocking roles
Share common norms
Pursue shared, interdependent goals
Feel that their membership in the group is rewarding
Have a collective perception of unity
Stick together in any confrontation with other groups or other individuals.[4]

These distinctions provide the group with boundaries and a sense of permanence. They lend it a distinct identity and separate it from other people and other groups.

group effectiveness An assessment of the extent to which a group is accomplishing its task in the most productive and satisfactory manner.

Groups in organizations differ from one another in **group effectiveness**. Effectiveness is the ultimate aim of group activities and is assessed on the basis of three important criteria:

1. *Production output.* The product of the group's work must meet or exceed standards of quantity and quality defined by the organization. *Group productivity* is a measure of this product.

2. *Member satisfaction.* Membership in the group must provide people with short-term satisfaction and facilitate their long-term growth and development. If it does not, the group will cease to exist.

3. *Capacity for continued cooperation.* The interpersonal processes the group uses to complete a task should maintain or enhance members' capacity to work together. Groups that don't cooperate cannot remain viable.[5]

[3] George C. Homans, *The Human Group* (New York: Harcourt, Brace, Jovanovich, 1950), p. 1; Marvin E. Shaw, *Group Dynamics: The Psychology of Small Group Behavior* (New York: McGraw-Hill, 1981), p. 8; and Deborah L. Gladstein, "Groups in Context: A Model of Task Group Effectiveness," *Administrative Science Quarterly* 29 (1984), 499–517.

[4] Dorwin Cartwright and Alvin Zander, *Group Dynamics: Research and Theory* (New York: Harper & Row, 1968), pp. 46–48.

[5] David A. Nadler, J. Richard Hackman, and Edward E. Lawler III, *Managing Organizational Behavior* (Boston: Little, Brown, 1979), pp. 136–37.

Organizational groups have different purposes or reasons for being. As indicated in Table 11-1, some groups serve as reference groups that provide people a sense of identity. Others function as membership groups that fulfill various personal needs and organizational objectives.[6] We will look at varieties of each type of group in the next few sections.

Reference Groups

reference groups Groups of people with whom individuals compare themselves in order to assess their own personal attitudes or behavior.

Reference groups enable people to assess their own personal attitudes or behavior by comparing themselves with others whom they think have desirable characteristics. People may belong to such a group. For example, employees may assess their attitudes toward work by seeking their co-workers' opinions. One need not belong to a reference group, however, for the group to serve as an important point of reference. Lower-level managers, for instance, may adopt the norms and behaviors of top management in the hope of being invited to join top management themselves. A reference group can be an amalgam of people from different spheres of life. For example, in deciding whether to accept a promotion that requires relocation, an employee may solicit opinions from family members, co-workers, and friends.

Membership Groups

membership groups Formal and informal groups to which people belong.

In contrast to reference groups, **membership groups** are always groups to which people actually belong. There are two kind of membership groups in organizations: informal groups and formal groups.

informal groups Groups that satisfy personal needs of their members. *Friendship groups* form among people who like being with each other. *Interest groups* develop among people who want to achieve some mutually beneficial objective.

Informal Groups. Informal groups satisfy personal needs of their members. These groups are not intended to help accomplish organizational objectives. *Friendship groups*, for instance, form among people who gather together simply

[6] Linda S. Jewell and H. Joseph Reitz, *Group Effectiveness in Organizations* (Glenview, Ill.: Scott, Foresman, 1981), pp. 8–10.

TABLE 11-1
Types of Groups in Organizations

TYPE	FUNCTION
Reference groups	Provide points of reference for assessing attitudes and behaviors
Membership groups	Grant membership rights, obligations, and responsibilities
Informal groups	Satisfy members' personal needs
Friendship groups	Satisfy the members' social needs
Interest groups	Satisfy particular goals or purposes
Formal groups	Organize and direct task performance. Guided by official policies and procedures
Work groups	Perform day-to-day nonmanagerial work assignments
Management teams	Complete managerial work activities on a daily basis
Temporary groups	Work together to complete a specific assignment
Intermittent groups	Exchange work-related information on a regular basis to coordinate the activities of different work groups

because they like being with each other. Such groups exist to satisfy the social needs of their members. A group of co-workers may go out to dinner together after work. *Interest groups* (also coalitions or constituency groups; see Chapter 13), develop among people who want to achieve some mutually beneficial objective. For example, employees who want flexible working hours might band together to present a proposal to management. Or a group of salespeople might decide to pool their commissions to ensure that each receives a decent income each week.

formal groups Groups that serve specific organizational purposes. In *work groups* employees work together to produce their firm's goods or services. Higher-level managers and the managers they supervise work together in *management teams. Temporary groups* are formed to accomplish a specific task. *Intermittent groups* are composed of people who do not work with each other but meet regularly to exchange work-related information.

Formal Groups. Unlike informal groups, **formal groups** convene to serve specific organizational purposes. The most noticeable formal groups in a firm are *work groups*, composed of employees who work together to produce the firm's goods or services. Typically the members of such groups work in close proximity and share some degree of interdependence.[7] In addition, they usually report to a single supervisor. Examples of work groups are a group of employees running an assembly line, a sales force working in a car dealer's showroom, and the nurses on a particular hospital ward. As we discuss in the "International OB" box, the makeup of a work group may be influenced as much by characteristics of the surrounding society as by things like the work itself or the group's skills and abilities.

The *management team*, another kind of formal group, consists of a higher-level manager and the managers she supervises. For instance, a company's vice-president of sales and its regional sales managers form a sales management team. Unlike work groups, management team members may be separated by significant physical distance and may interact with each other infrequently. Regional sales managers may be scattered throughout the world and meet with their vice-president only occasionally to plan new-product introductions or get feedback on regional sales performance.

The *temporary group*, a third kind of formal group often found in organizations, is composed of people assigned to work together temporarily. As we will discuss in Chapter 15, temporary groups are sometimes used to solve specific problems and to link other groups together. In this guise they are often called *task forces*. For example, a group of engineers might be brought together to reduce

[7] Connie J. G. Gersick, "Marking Time: Predictable Transitions in Task Groups," *Academy of Management Journal* 32 (1989), 274–309.

Several formal work groups produced IBM's 1990 LaserPrinter, the company's challenger to the Hewlett-Packard LaserJet III. Design and manufacturing engineers simplified the design of the LaserPrinter without sacrificing quality. They figured out how to combine multiple components into a smaller total number of parts and how to substitute easy-to-handle snap-on fasteners for screws and bolts. They also discovered that it was cheaper and easier for a work group to put the printer together than to have robots do it.
Source: *"Manufacturing,"* Fortune, *May 21, 1990, p. 64.*

Putting car assembly employees into work groups is a straight-forward task, isn't it? Not really, if you consider that in two Volvo plants in Sweden, teams assemble large units of a car with little direct supervision. These teams may put together engines, transmissions, or even an entire car, as is the case at Volvo's new plant at Uddevalla. In contrast, the Japanese approach is to form groups along conventional lines. Members perform minutely subdivided tasks on American-style assembly lines without any sort of team work.* Why these differences?

The answer is that the appropriate way to cluster employees into work groups depends partly on a culture's definition of *group*. In the cultures of Scandinavian countries, the predominating values stress democracy, participation, and autonomy—in short, having a voice in how things are done. To be seen as functioning correctly, members of a work group must have the freedom to make decisions about what to do and how to do it. Automotive assembly groups are given large, complicated tasks and the freedom to decide how to break them into individual jobs. Much of the group's work involves the kind of decision making reserved for managers in other cultures.

In Japan, on the other hand, work groups arc often formed around relationships in which the junior members of a group owe allegiance to senior group members in much the same way that Japanese children are obligated to the elders

* John Hoerr, "The Payoff from Teamwork: The Gains in Quality Are Substantial—So Why Isn't It Spreading Faster?" *Business Week*, July 10, 1989, pp. 61–62.

Assembly line production of satellites in Japan.

of their family. Under such circumstances, obedience is more important than autonomy, and the Scandinavian approach of forming participatory work groups makes little sense. What *does* make sense, though, is to think of an entire assembly line as consisting of parents (supervisors) who give orders and siblings (employees) who must respect these orders as they work together to ensure the well-being of the family (assembly line). By applying the Japanese notion of "family" to the assembly line, Japanese automotive workers perceive themselves as a tightly knit group united by supervisory connections.

---

the cost of producing computer memory chips and then sent back to their original jobs after accomplishing their mission.

The members of a fourth kind of formal group, the *intermittent group*, do not normally work with each other but get together regularly to exchange work-related information. Common types of intermittent groups are the board of directors of a publicly owned corporation or the advisory board of a public service organization like the United Way. Both boards are policy-forming bodies that oversee the general direction of the organizations they serve. Another kind of intermittent group, the *standing committee*, consists of representatives from an organization's work groups and management teams who meet periodically to coordinate work among different groups (see Chapter 15). For example, representatives from college departments sometimes meet to ensure that the college's courses remain appropriately interrelated.

THE DEVELOPMENT OF GROUPS

Have you ever wondered about how groups form and develop? Although different types of groups are found in organizations, most of them originate, grow, and mature in about the same way. As groups develop, members design group tasks, clarify personal roles, and negotiate group norms. It is therefore important for you to understand the process of group development and be prepared to manage it from time to time in order to enhance group effectiveness.

Stages of Group Development

To understand the process of group development, you should know about the stages groups pass through as they form and grow. Current research suggests that groups usually progress through the four developmental stages outlined in Figure 11-1: formation, differentiation, integration, and maturity.[8]

formation The initial stage of group development, characterized by uncertainty and anxiety. People try to determine which behaviors will be appropriate and what contributions members should be expected to make to the group.

Formation. The initial stage of **formation** is characterized by uncertainty and anxiety. Potential members focus on getting to know each other's traits and abilities. They tend initially to discuss "safe" topics like the weather, local news, and sports that have little bearing on the group's purpose. As they become familiar with each other and more comfortable, discussion turns to general work issues and to each person's likely relationship to the group's task. Everyone concentrates on determining which behaviors should be considered appropriate and what sorts of contributions people should be expected to make to the group. As ideas are exchanged and discussed, people who have the option may decide whether to join or leave the group. Members may also try to choose someone to act as their leader.

Differentiation. When the group enters the **differentiation** stage of development, conflicts are likely to erupt as members try to reach agreement on the purpose, goals, and objectives of the group. Strong differences of opinion may also emerge as members try to achieve consensus on exactly how they will accomplish the group's task. Sorting out who will do what when, where, why, and how and what reward members will receive for their performances often proves to be extremely difficult. Sometimes disagreements about members' roles in the

differentiation The second stage of group development, characterized by conflicts that erupt as members seek agreement on the purpose, goals, and objectives of the group and the roles of its members.

[8] B. W. Tuckman, "Developmental Sequence in Small Groups," *Psychological Bulletin* 63 (1965), 384–99; Bernard M. Bass and Edward C. Ryterband, *Organizational Psychology*, 2nd ed. (Boston: Allyn & Bacon, 1979), pp. 252–4; John P. Wanous, Arnon E. Reichers, and S. Dolly Malik, "Organizational Socialization and Group Development: Toward an Integrative Perspective," *Academy of Management Review* 9 (1984), 670–83; Robert Albanese and David D. Van Fleet, *Organizational Behavior: A Managerial Viewpoint* (Hinsdale, Ill.: Dryden, 1983), p. 259; and Connie J. G. Gersick, "Time and Transition in Work Teams: Toward a New Model of Group Development, *Academy of Management Journal* 31 (1988), 9–41.

FIGURE 11-1

Stages in the Group-Development Process

As groups form and mature, they can cease to develop at any of the stages through which they progress. If this happens the group may disband. Or as shown by the dotted lines, it may return to an earlier stage if changes—in membership, the group's task, or the situation surrounding the group—make it important to redefine roles and relationships within the group.

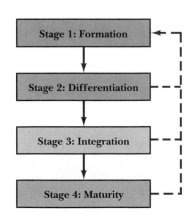

group become violent enough to threaten the group's very existence. If successful, though, differentiation creates a structure of roles and norms that allows the group to accomplish feats its members could not succeed at alone. For example, deciding that some members will wait on tables and others will cook enables a group to serve restaurant patrons in a timely manner.

integration The third stage of group development, which is focused on reestablishing the central purpose of the group in light of the structure of roles developed during differentiation.

Integration. Having weathered the differentiation stage, group members must resolve conflicts over other crucial issues in the **integration** stage of group development. Integration focuses on reestablishing the central purpose of the group in light of the structure of roles developed during differentiation. Among a group of restaurant employees, for instance, it may seem to waiters that the sole purpose of the group is to provide prompt, courteous service. Chefs, however, may argue that the group's true purpose is to dispense appetizing, well-prepared meals. Reaching a consensus about the group's purpose helps develop a sense of group identity among members and promotes cohesiveness within the group. It also provides the foundation for the development of additional rules, norms, and procedures that help coordinate interactions among members and facilitate the pursuit of group goals. If consensus cannot be attained, the group may either disintegrate or split into factions. If the latter happens, these subgroups of original group members must begin the process of development anew.

maturity The fourth and final stage of group development, in which members begin to fulfill their prescribed roles and work toward attaining group goals. Many of the agreements reached about goals, roles, and norms are formalized, or preserved in written documentation during this stage.

Maturity. In the final, **maturity** stage of group development, members begin to fulfill their prescribed roles and work toward attaining group goals. Many of the agreements reached about goals, roles, and norms are formalized by documenting them in writing. Formalizing these agreements helps to ensure that people joining the group at this stage will understand the group's purpose and way of functioning. Note, however, that even at this stage, the group may be confronted with new tasks or new requirements for performance. And changes in the group's environment or in its members may make it necessary to return to an earlier stage and resume the development process (see Figure 11-1).

Products of the Development Process

The four-stage process of group development yields three important products: group tasks, group roles, and group norms. Each of these has important effects on the productivity of a group and the satisfaction of its members.[9]

Group Tasks. Different group tasks have different performance requirements that affect the productivity and satisfaction of the members who perform them. Table 11-2 overviews the kinds of tasks that groups may undertake. As indicated in the table group tasks differ from one another in their *complexity*, ranging from simple tasks that involve physical demands but little mental effort to complex tasks that require significant mental effort and less physical exertion.[10] In all task situations, member satisfaction is affected most strongly by inclusion in successful task activities. Members feel most satisfied with their membership and task performance when they take part in activities that lead to task completion.[11]

[9] Briance Mascarenhas, "Strategic Group Dynamics," *Academy of Management Journal* 32 (1989), 333–52.

[10] John A Wagner III and Richard Z. Gooding, "Shared Influence and Organizational Behavior: A Meta-Analysis of Situational Factors Expected to Moderate Participation-Outcome Relationships," *Academy of Management Journal* 30 (1987), 524–41.

[11] John W. Thibaut and Harold H. Kelley, *The Social Psychology of Groups* (New York: John Wiley, 1959), p. 258.

TABLE 11-2
Types of Group Tasks

| | TASK COMPLEXITY | |
	Simple	Complex
Disjunctive	Physical demands predominate, and productivity is determined by the most able member	Mental demands predominate, and productivity is determined by the most able member
Conjunctive	Physical demands predominate, and productivity is constrained by the least able member	Mental demands predominate, and productivity is constrained by the least able member
Additive	Physical demands predominate, and all members contribute to productivity	Mental demands predominate, and all members contribute to productivity

Some people, however, are attracted primarily to physical activities. They are likely to get the most satisfaction from succeeding at simple, physical tasks such as planting trees or pouring concrete. In contrast, others find mental activities more appealing. They can be expected to derive greatest satisfaction from the completion of complex mental tasks like designing an office building or deciding how to display products in a convenience store.[12]

Besides differing in complexity, group tasks also differ in their *performance requirements*. Some tasks are **disjunctive tasks** that can be completed by having each group member work alone.[13] The productivity of a group performing such a task is determined by the ability of its most competent member. A "best-ball" team playing a hole of golf is an example of a group performing a simple disjunctive task. Two or more people play the hole, and the best player's score is recorded as the team's score. The most effective way to ensure group productivity on disjunctive tasks is to recruit and retain at least one highly competent member. Member satisfaction can be expected to vary in proportion to competence. Those members whose competence allows them to contribute to group performance will feel more satisfied than those whose lack of competence minimizes their contribution.

In contrast, productivity on a **conjunctive task** is determined by the performance of the group's *least* competent member.[14] A tug-of-war game is a simple conjunctive task, because every team member must help pull the rope but the weakest member constrains the team's likely success. Mountain climbing is also a relatively simple conjunctive task. Because climbers are tied together, they are forced to progress at the speed of the slowest climber. A group of advertising executives trying to generate as many prospective names as possible for a new product are performing a complex conjunctive task. The group's progress toward success is constrained by the inventiveness of the least creative individual. For a group to perform a conjunctive task effectively and with satisfaction, all members must be highly competent, and every group member must contribute fully to the group's efforts.

On an **additive task**, the accomplishments of each member are added to those of other members without regard for differences in competence.[15] For instance, for the simple additive task of shoveling snow, the amount of snow a

disjunctive task A group task that can be completed by single group members working alone.

conjunctive task A group task on which all group members must contribute to task performance.

additive task A group task on which the accomplishments of each member of the group are added to those of other members.

---

[12] J. Richard Hackman and Greg R. Oldham, *Work Redesign* (Reading, Mass.: Addison-Wesley, 1980), p. 85.

[13] Ivan D. Steiner, *Group Process and Productivity* (New York: Academic Press, 1972), p. 68.

[14] Ibid., p. 72.

[15] Ibid., p. 74.

group shovels equals the sum of the amounts shoveled by each group member. Similarly, the total number of documents that a group of people in a secretarial pool type equals the sum of the documents typed by each individual secretary. Gathering information about market trends is a complex additive task, because a larger group of people can collect and analyze more data than can a smaller group. To increase group performance on additive tasks, it is necessary to add more members. However, it is also important to keep in mind that every task has a ceiling on the number of people who can make useful contributions. We will return to this idea later when we discuss the notions of production blocking and process loss.

Group Roles. Another product of the group-development process is the set of group roles that people negotiate and fulfill. In order to maintain acceptably high levels of group productivity and member satisfaction, managers must see that group members assume task-oriented and maintenance roles and avoid individual roles.[16]

task-oriented roles Group roles that focus on making a contribution to successful task performance and accomplishing the group's task.

Task-oriented roles focus on making a contribution to successful task performance and accomplishing the group's task. *Initiators* offer new ideas or modifications of existing ways to perform the group's task. *Information seekers* try to clarify suggestions by acquiring information or data that can be used to judge their suitability. *Information givers* supply the information that the group uses to assess task performance and to weigh the appropriateness of alternative ways to improve it. *Coordinators* coordinate the work of other group members. They may also clarify relationships among different ideas and suggestions, pull different suggestions together, and combine pieces of information in different ways. *Evaluators* assess the quality of the ideas and information considered by the group. They also monitor the group's ultimate productivity.

maintenance roles Group roles that help ensure a group's continued existence by building and preserving strong interpersonal relations among its members.

Maintenance roles help ensure the group's continued existence by building and preserving strong interpersonal relations among its members. *Encouragers*

[16] K. Benne and P. Sheats, "Functional roles of group members," *Journal of Social Issues* 2 (1948), 42–47.

To improve its service to United Airlines' computer reservations system affiliate, known as COVIA, AT&T assembled a quality improvement team that cut across many divisions. Performing task-oriented roles, this team reviewed maintenance and report processes and identified the causes of specific problems. When the approaches developed by the team were put into effect, network availability for COVIA exceeded the goal set, and circuit trouble time dropped. The team received AT&T's Beacon of Quality award, and permanent COVIA/AT&T teams were formed to examine and further improve the processes.
Source: "A Celebration of the American Worker," (advertisement), Fortune, September 24, 1990.

enhance feelings of warmth and solidarity within the group by praising, agreeing with, and accepting the ideas of others. *Harmonizers* attempt to minimize the negative effects of conflicts among the group's members by resolving disagreements fairly, quickly, and openly and relieving interpersonal tension. *Standard setters* raise questions about group goals and goal attainment and set achievement standards with which group members can evaluate their performance. *Followers* passively agree with others' opinions and activities while serving as friends and colleagues. *Group observers* remain detached and monitor group performance from afar. If asked, they are usually able to provide performance feedback that is both unbiased and insightful.

individual roles In groups, roles that focus on the satisfaction of members' personal needs and interests even when they conflict with the well-being of the group.

Individual roles focus on the satisfaction of members' personal needs and interests even when they conflict with the well-being of the group. *Blockers* are negative, stubborn, and unreasonably resistant. *Recognition seekers* try to call attention to themselves, often by boasting, bragging, or acting superior. *Dominators* attempt to manipulate the group or its members by asserting authority or using flattery. They are also likely to interrupt or minimize others' contributions. *Avoiders* are passive resisters who try to insulate themselves from all group interaction.

Group Norms. The third major product of the group-development process, *group norms*, consists of shared standards that help guide member behavior and make it understandable (see Chapter 10).[17] Your class, for example, probably has a norm that directs students to sit down and wait for the instructor to begin the day's activities. Norms may also direct you to participate in class discussions and exercises and to contribute to group case discussions. Without norms, each class meeting would require your instructor to establish basic rules of behavior and an agenda for the day. As a result you would have much less time for the learning activities on the day's agenda. In fact, your class might find it impossible to accomplish anything at all.

pivotal norms Group norms for which adherence is an absolute requirement of continued group membership.

In all group situations, adherence to **pivotal norms** is an absolute requirement of continued group membership. Failure to adopt such norms threatens the survival of the group.[18] For example, the members of management teams are typically required to heed norms favoring free enterprise, capitalism, and the pursuit of profits. In a company like Levi Strauss, groups of managers must adhere to pivotal norms stressing product quality and durability. Social workers and other members of social-service organizations are required to follow norms that stress the importance of helping others. For example, employees of the State of Michigan's Division of Child and Family Services must adhere to strict norms of professional conduct that require them to report all cases of suspected neglect or abuse.

peripheral norms Group norms for which adherence is desirable but not essential.

In contrast, adherence to **peripheral norms** is desirable but not essential. For example, many business schools have dress codes that favor suits or jackets. As long as faculty members adhere to other pivotal norms, they can violate one or more peripheral norms—and, for example, wear jeans and sweaters—without being ousted from the group. Although such violations can threaten the character of the group, they do not jeopardize the group's existence.

Each group member's individual adjustment to pivotal and peripheral norms has an important effect on group productivity and thus has clear implications for the group's survival. As Table 11-3 indicates, *individual adjustment*, or the acceptance or rejection of these norms, leads to four basic behavior patterns: conformity, subversive rebellion, open revolution, and creative individualism. Let's look at each of these patterns of behavior.

[17] Daniel C. Feldman, "The Development and Enforcement of Group Norms," *Academy of Management Review* 9 (1984), 47–53.

[18] Edgar H. Schein, *Organizational Psychology*, 3rd ed. (Englewood Cliffs, N.J.: Prentice-Hall, 1980), p. 99.

TABLE 11-3
Norms and Group Behavior Patterns

		PIVOTAL NORMS	
		Accept	**Reject**
Peripheral Norms	Accept	Conformity	Subversive rebellion
	Reject	Creative individualism	Open revolution

Source: Edgar H. Schein, *Organization Psychology*, 3rd ed. (Englewood Cliffs, N.J.: Prentice Hall, 1980), p 100. Reprinted with permission of the publisher.

conformity Loyal but uncreative adherence by group members to both pivotal and peripheral norms.

When members choose to accept both pivotal and peripheral norms, their resulting **conformity** is marked by a tendency to try to fit in with the group in a loyal but uncreative way. People who conform to group norms are caretakers of the past. They tend to believe that things should be done in a particular way because they have always been done that way. So long as the group's task remains unchanged and the situation surrounding the group remains stable, conformity can facilitate group productivity. It can endanger a group's survival, however, if the group's task or surrounding situation changes significantly. A group that cannot adapt its task approach and procedures in the face of change is in trouble.

subversive rebellion Acceptance by group members of peripheral norms but rejection of pivotal ones.

When group members accept peripheral norms but reject pivotal ones, we have what is called **subversive rebellion**. People conceal their rejection of norms that are critical to group survival by acting in accordance with less important ones. This outward show of conformity may make it possible for rebellious members to stay in the group. If their number is large, however, their failure to adhere to important pivotal norms may jeopardize the group's survival.

open revolution Rejection by group members of both pivotal and peripheral norms.

Open revolution may break out if group members choose to reject both pivotal and peripheral norms. If only a few members revolt, they may be pressured to conform or asked to leave. However, a group dominated by open revolution may simply cease to exist.

creative individualism Acceptance by group members of pivotal norms but rejection of peripheral ones.

Finally, in **creative individualism**, group members accept pivotal norms but reject peripheral ones. This ensures continued productivity and group survival. It also opens the door to the individual creativity needed to develop new ways of doing things. Creative individualism is therefore especially desirable when a group faces change in its task or surrounding situation. Members have the freedom to invent new responses to changing conditions.

GROUP PRODUCTIVITY

The "In Practice" box suggests that employees can be more productive when working as teams than when working alone. But are groups always more productive than individuals? On the advice of both consultants and articles in business magazines like *Business Week*, *Fortune*, and *Forbes*, many managers believe that this is true.[19] In fact, however, a group of employees may sometimes be less productive than the same number of people working alone.[20] Knowing what can cause group productivity to decline and how to encourage strong group performance is thus an important part of every manager's job.

[19] For a discussion of several of the assumptions underlying this belief, see Gerald R. Ferris and John A. Wagner III, "Quality Circles in the United States: A Conceptual Reevaluation," *Journal of Applied Behavioral Science* 21 (1985), 155–67.

[20] G. W. Hill, "Group versus Individual Performance: Are N + 1 Heads Better Than One?" *Psychological Bulletin* 9 (1982), 517–39; Shaw, *Group Dynamics*, p. 78; and P. B. Smith, *Groups within Organizations* (London: Harper & Row, 1973), p. 17.

Teamwork Can Help Paper Pushers, Too

Although industrial firms like Ford, A. O. Smith, and General Electric typically serve as examples of successful teamwork, service organizations such as banks and insurance companies can also profit from the use of work teams. One example is the Aid Association for Lutherans (AAL), an 84-year-old fraternal society that operates an insurance business for its 1.5 million members. The AAL underwent a three-year reorganization in which cumbersome departments were replaced by all-purpose teams capable of operating without several layers of supervisors. Within a year, productivity increased by 20 percent, and the amount of time required to process insurance claims fell by as much as 75 percent.

What explains this sudden, impressive improvement in performance? Before the change, all life insurance claims had been handled by one section, health insurance by another, and support services (for example, billing and loans on policies) by still another. Because of this division of labor, complex claims often had to be routed from clerk to clerk within and between sections. Now, however, AAL's office work force is clustered into five groups, each serving clients in a different geographical region. Each group consists of three or four teams of 20 to 30 employees, who perform all of the 167 tasks that were formerly split among the three functional sections. No longer is it necessary to transfer paperwork throughout the firm. The result is savings in both time and effort.

Improved performance has not been without its costs. Many employees were forced to switch work groups, sometimes abruptly, causing feelings of uncertainty and many broken friendships. In addition, team members have had to learn how to manage themselves instead of waiting for direction from above, causing some people to report increased levels

Members of an AAL work team.

of stress. However, like one enthusiastic claims processor, most workers are coming to like the team approach: "The team idea lets you grow, and you don't always have a supervisor sitting over you."*

* John Hoerr, "Work Teams Can Rev Up Paper-Pushers, Too," *Business Week*, November 28, 1988, pp. 64–72.

In examining the products of group development—group tasks, roles, and norms—we have noted that each can have a significant effect on group performance. Consequently, managers can increase group productivity by assigning employees to groups on the basis of the match between their personal abilities and the performance requirements of group tasks. In addition, they can steer members toward the constructive behaviors of task and maintenance roles and away from the destructive actions of individual roles. Under stable work conditions, managers can reward conformity. Under changing conditions, they can encourage creative individualism.

Managers can also encourage group performance by reducing the negative effects of various obstacles to group productivity. In this section, we identify three such obstacles and consider several factors that can counteract their influence.

Major Obstacles to Group Productivity

Adding more people to a group increases the human resources that the group can put to productive use. Thus, as depicted in Figure 11-2, the *theoretical* productivity of a group rises in direct proportion to the size of the group. However,

FIGURE 11-2

Group Size and Process Loss

Process loss, represented by the shaded area, is the difference between potential and actual productivity. Theoretically, potential productivity rises as a group grows larger. Actual productivity, however, rises and then falls as a result of such obstacles to group performance as production blocking and social loafing. Thus, as you can see, process loss increases as group size increases.

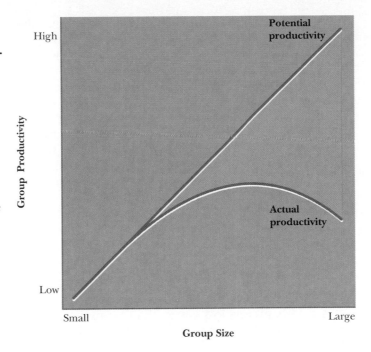

process loss The difference between what is produced by a group of individuals and what would be produced by the same people working alone.

production blocking The negative effect on productivity caused by people getting in each other's way as they try to perform a group task.

social loafing The choice by some group members to take advantage of others by doing less work, working more slowly, or in other ways contributing less to group productivity.

after an initial rise, the group's *actual* productivity falls as its size continues to increase. This difference between what a group actually produces and what it might theoretically produce is known as **process loss**.[21] It is caused by a variety of obstacles to group productivity, the most important of which are production blocking, group maintenance activities, and social loafing.

Production Blocking. **Production blocking** occurs when people get in each other's way as they try to perform a group task.[22] For example, production blocking occurs when one member of a moving-van crew is carrying a chair through a doorway and another member has to wait to carry a box of clothing through the same doorway. Similarly, in a classroom discussion, one student's comments will be blocked if others talk at the same time. Such interruptions can cause the student to forget important ideas. The result is process loss.

Group Maintenance Activities. The group maintenance roles that we've already discussed have both positive and negative features. Although *group maintenance activities* support and facilitate a group's continued functioning, they may also interfere with productive activity. For instance, members of a management team who are in conflict about a proposal must spend time not only on improving the proposal but also on managing the resolution of their conflict.

Group maintenance activities present us with a kind of catch-22. Without them, a group's existence may be seriously threatened. On the other hand, by diverting valuable time and effort to these activities, we reduce a group's productivity and thus contribute to process loss.

Social Loafing. Process loss can also be caused by **social loafing**, the choice by some members of a group to take advantage of others by doing less work, working

[21] Ivan D. Steiner, *Group Processes and Productivity* (New York: Academic Press, 1972). We use the term *process loss* somewhat more broadly than Steiner.
[22] Michael Diehl and Wolfgang Stroebe, "Productivity Loss in Brainstorming Groups: Toward the Solution of a Riddle," *Journal of Personality and Social Psychology* 53 (1987), 497–509.

more slowly, or in other ways decreasing their own contributions to group productivity.[23] According to economists, social loafing—also called *free riding*—makes sense from a loafer's perspective if the rewards his group receives for productivity are shared more or less equally among all group members.[24] A loafer can get the same rewards that everyone else gets but without having to expend personal effort.

Unless someone else in the group takes up the slack, the effect of even one person's loafing may be to lower the entire group's productivity. Consider a team of accountants performing an audit. If one takes a long lunch and misses an afternoon of counting inventory items, the others may be able to compensate by finishing their own work early and completing the inventory count themselves. However, if the other team members are so busy that they cannot take the time to count the inventory, the count will not be completed and process loss will occur.

Increasing Group Productivity

Is process loss inevitable? Or are there ways for managers to offset the negative effects of the factors we have discussed? There are indeed a number of things managers can do to maintain or improve productivity. They can adjust the sizes of groups. They can enhance group motivation. They can promote group cohesion and foster norms favoring high productivity. Finally, they can improve communication within groups.

Group Size. Decreasing *group size* can have a positive effect on productivity. On average, people working in smaller groups are more productive than people in larger groups.[25] As suggested by Figure 11-3, this relationship can be traced to several factors—physical constraints, social distractions, coordination requirements, behavioral masking, and diffusion of responsibility.

To begin with, small groups simply have fewer members to get in each other's way than large groups do. Clearly, production blocking caused by physical crowding is less likely to occur in small groups than in large ones. The effects of *physical constraints* are therefore lower in small groups.

In addition, group size influences productivity by affecting the amount of *social distraction* people experience when they work in a group. The smaller the group, the less likely it is that group members will distract one another and interrupt behavioral sequences that are important to the task. Production blocking traceable to distractions caused by others is therefore less likely to occur in small groups than in large ones.

Smaller groups also have lower *coordination requirements*. The fewer members a group has, the fewer the numbers of linkages between people and subtasks that must be formed and maintained (see also Chapter 15). In small groups, managers and group members need not devote a lot of time, energy, and other resources to group maintenance. As a result they have more time for productive work.

[23] Bibb Latané, Kipling Williams, and Stephen Harkins, "Many Hands Make Light Work: The Causes and Consequences of Social Loafing," *Journal of Personality and Social Psychology* 37 (1979), 822–32.

[24] Mancur Olson, *The Logic of Collective Action* (Cambridge, Mass.: Harvard University Press, 1965), p. 11. See also Robert Albanese and David D. Van Fleet, "Rational Behavior in Groups: The Free-Riding Tendency," *Academy of Management Review* 10 (1985), 244–55.

[25] Richard Z. Gooding and John A Wagner III, "A Meta-Analytic Review of the Relationship between Size and Performance: The Productivity and Efficiency of Organizations and Their Subunits," *Administrative Science Quarterly* 30 (1985), 462–81.

FIGURE 11-3

How Group Size Affects Group Productivity

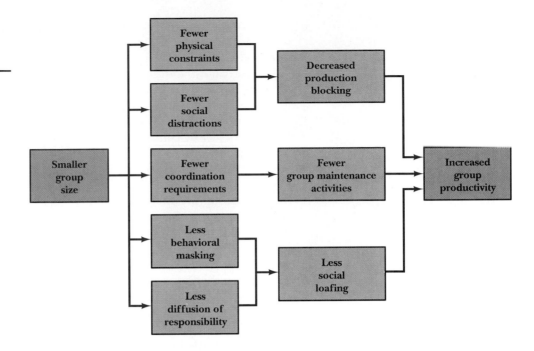

behavioral masking A phenomenon whereby the simple presence of other group members masks, or hides, the behaviors of one member.

diffusion of responsibility The sense among group members that responsibility is shared broadly rather than shouldered personally.

Group size is also related to the incidence of **behavioral masking**. The behaviors of a group member may be masked or hidden by the simple presence of other members.[26] The smaller the group, the easier it is to observe each member's behavior, and this visibility affects the incidence of such behaviors as social loafing.[27] If loafers can be easily detected, they can also be easily expelled from the group and lose their share of group rewards. In this setting, the role of social loafer may be rather unattractive.

Finally, group size influences the **diffusion of responsibility**, the sense that responsibility is shared broadly rather than shouldered personally. In general, the larger the group, the more likely it is that people will feel they share the responsibility for group tasks with others. Diffusion of responsibility tends to encourage social loafing, because it provides a ready excuse for loafing. In a large group, productivity is someone else's responsibility. In a small group, however, one is more apt to feel personally responsible for group performance and effectiveness.

Member Motivation. Member motivation is another important factor that affects group productivity and that can be managed to avoid or minimize process loss. As we saw in Chapter 7, motivation is a crucial factor in individual achievement, and it is just as crucial in the achievement of a group. Group members must be sufficiently motivated to reach the highest level of group productivity that their abilities permit. As we will see, goals and rewards can strengthen motivation in groups just as in individuals.

Research on individual motivation has repeatedly shown that setting specific, difficult personal goals has a strong positive effect on personal productivity (see Chapter 7). This effect is particularly strong when a person has the requisite abilities to perform the task and is committed to the goal. Studies of group

[26] John A. Fleishman, "Collective Action as Helping Behavior: Effects of Responsibility Diffusion on Contributions to a Public Good," *Journal of Personality and Social Psychology* 38 (1980), 629–37; Gareth R. Jones, "Task Visibility, Free Riding, and Shirking: Explaining the Effect of Structure and Technology on Employee Behavior," *Academy of Management Review* 9 (1984), 684–95.

[27] Kipling Williams, Stephen Harkins, and Bib Latane, "Identifiability as a Deterrent to Social Loafing: Two Cheering Experiments," *Journal of Personality and Social Psychology* 40 (1981), 303–11.

performance as well have substantiated that setting specific, difficult group goals has a strong positive effect on group productivity. In one early study, members of groups with clear, specific goals were compared with members of groups whose goals were vague and ambiguous. The results of this study indicated that the members of groups with specific goals were more attracted to their groups' tasks and conformed more to their groups' expectations. These factors enhanced group performance.[28] In another study of goal setting, researchers examined the effects of goal difficulty by comparing the outcomes of 149 United Way campaigns over a four-year period. Communities that set higher goals had better results than those that set lower goals.[29]

Other studies have also shown that group goals exert strong, persistent effects on group productivity. For instance, in a study of air force base personnel, researchers found that instituting a group goal setting and feedback program increased productivity by 75 percent.[30] Similarly, in a two-year study performed at Notre Dame, the university hockey team established goals for aggressive behavior. The result was an increase in the team's legal body checking (opponent-blocking). In the first playing season body checking increased by 82 percent and in the second season by 141 percent. In addition, the team posted winning records both years. These were the team's first winning seasons in five years.[31]

Recent research has also begun to highlight the specific processes through which group goals influence performance. One study in which students participated in a managerial simulation found that groups with specific, difficult goals outperformed groups with vague, "do-your-best" goals partially because of planning differences. The groups with specific and difficult goals were better than the other groups at planning how to meet those goals.[32]

Reflecting research on the importance of group goals, managers are currently paying more attention than ever before to the way groups set production goals. At the GM Saturn plant in Spring Hill, Tennessee, work is assigned to 165 teams, not individuals. These teams rather than their supervisors do much of the planning and goal setting. Each team of about ten members interviews and approves new hires and initiates problem solving and troubleshooting in production. It also has the responsibility for developing budgetary projections.[33] Recently, one team in Saturn's final assembly area even voted to reject some proposed pneumatic car assembly equipment offered by another GM division. Instead, the team bought electronic gear that its members believed to be safer from another supplier. Saturn's UAW coordinator Richard Hoalcraft said, "I don't know of a another UAW group who has ever decided on the purchase and installation of equipment."[34]

Rewards contingent on specific achievement also help to motivate groups. There are two fundamentally different types of rewards. **Cooperative group rewards** are distributed equally among the members of a group. That is, the

cooperative group rewards
Group rewards distributed in such a way that each member receives an equal reward in exchange for the successful performance of the group.

[28] B. H. Raven and J. Reitsema, "The Effects of Varied Clarity of Group Goals and Group Path on the Individual and His Relation to the Group," *Human Relations* 10 (1957), 29–44.

[29] Alvin Zander and Theodore Newcomb, "Group Level of Aspiration in United Fund Campaigns," *Journal of Personality and Social Psychology* 6 (1967), 157–62.

[30] R. D. Pritchard, S. D. Jones, P. L. Roth, J. Stuebing, and S. E. Ekeberg, "Effects of Group Feedback, Goal Setting, and Incentives on Organizational Productivity," *Journal of Applied Psychology* 73 (1988), 337–58.

[31] D. C. Anderson, C. R. Crowell, M. Doman, and G. S. Howard, "Performance Posting, Goal Setting, and Activity-Contingent Praise as Applied to a College Hockey Team," *Journal of Applied Psychology* 73 (1988), 87–95.

[32] Ken G. Smith, Edwin A. Locke, and David Berry, "Goal Setting, Planning and Organizational Performance: An Experimental Simulation," *Organizational Behavior and Human Decision Processes, 46* (1990), 118–34.

[33] J. Szczesny, "The Right Stuff," *Time* , October 29, 1990, pp. 74–82.

[34] Szczesny, "Right Stuff," p. 82.

group is rewarded *as a group* for its successful performance, and each member receives exactly the same reward.[35] This technique does not recognize individual differences in effort or performance but instead rewards employees' efforts to coordinate their work activities and to rely on one another. As a result, the cooperative reward system ignores the possibility that some members will make greater contributions to group task performance than others. As we saw in Chapter 7, the inequity caused by this type of reward distribution can demotivate group members who are high performers.

competitive group rewards
Group rewards distributed in such a way that members receive equitable rewards in exchange for successful performance as individuals in a group.

Under the **competitive group rewards** system, group members are rewarded for successful performance *as individuals in a group*. They receive *equitable* rewards that vary according to their individual performance. This system, which is based on the idea that high group performance requires all members to perform at their highest capacity, rewards those who do more than those who do not. As you can imagine, the system provides a strong incentive to individual effort and so it can enhance individual productivity. On the other hand, it can pit group members against each other in a struggle for greater personal rewards. If this happens, the cooperation and coordination needed to perform group tasks may never develop.

Which of these two approaches is likely to assure the highest group productivity? The answer is, it all depends on the degree of *task interdependence*.[36] Recall from Chapter 10 that high task interdependence—team, reciprocal, or sequential—requires that group members work together. For this reason, cooperative rewards, which encourage cooperation and coordination, promote group productivity when paired with high task interdependence. In contrast, low task interdependence, either complete independence or pooled interdependence, enables the members of a group to work independently. In this case, competitive rewards motivate high personal performance and lead to increased group productivity.

What happens if we switch reward systems? Pairing cooperative rewards with low interdependence will encourage unnecessary cooperation and may stifle personal performance. And as we've already suggested, coupling competitive rewards with high interdependence causes conflicts that undermine cooperation. Figure 11-4 summarizes the relations among type of group reward, task interdependence, and group productivity.

Research on group rewards has also affected operations in GM's Saturn plant. Instead of hourly pay, Saturn employees work for a salary that averages around $35,000 annually. Twenty percent of this salary is at risk, however. Saturn workers get this 20 percent only if measures of car quality, worker productivity, and company profits reach preset levels. The weight, or importance, of each goal varies over time. In the first year, the 20 percent depends largely on car quality. If the team produces fewer defects than the maximum level specified in the goal, team members receive 100 percent of their salary. If they perform even better, they are eligible for a bonus. Clearly, given the level of interdependence required to produce an automobile, these kinds of cooperative rewards are the key. A competitive plan that rewarded individual workers for their speed in installing one part in a car regardless of what anyone else did would clearly be inappropriate.

---

[35] Morton Deutsch, *The Resolution of Conflict: Constructive and Destructive Processes* (New Haven, Conn. Yale University Press, 1973), p. 325.

[36] L. K. Miller and R. L. Hamblin, "Interdependence, Differential Rewarding, and Productivity," *American Sociological Review* 28 (1963), 768–78; R. Slavin, "Classroom Reward Structure: Analytical and Practical Review," *Review of Educational Research* 47 (1977), 633–50; and John A Wagner III, Paul A. Rubin, and Thomas J. Callahan, "Incentive Payment and Nonmanagerial Productivity: An Interrupted Time Series Analysis of Magnitude and Trend," *Organizational Behavior and Human Decision Processes* 42 (1988), 47–74.

FIGURE 11-4

Effects of Task Interdependence and Type of Reward on Group Productivity

Cooperative rewards improve productivity when a task requires a high degree of cooperation and coordination. Conversely, competitive rewards improve productivity when low task interdependence makes it important for people to work productively as individuals.

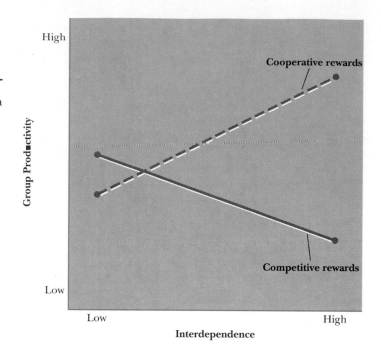

cohesiveness A measure of the interpersonal attraction among members of a group and their attraction to the group as a whole.

Cohesiveness and Productivity Norms. In addition to having the abilities and motivation required by their work, group members must also know what is expected of them on the job if their group is to be productive. Group norms provide this sort of knowledge, and group cohesiveness determines whether a mix of different norms will be found in a single group. Group norms and group cohesiveness thus combine to shape the performance expectations that influence member productivity.

A group's **cohesiveness** is measured by the degree to which a group sticks together. In a cohesive group, members feel attracted to one another and to the group as a whole.[37] A variety of factors encourage group cohesiveness. Among the most important are the following:

1. *Shared personal attitudes, values, or interests.* People who share the same attitudes, values, or interests are likely to be attracted to each other.

2. *Agreement on group goals.* Shared group goals encourage members to work together. When group members participate in determining their purpose and goals, they get to know and influence each other.

3. *Frequency of interaction.* Frequent interaction and the physical closeness this affords encourages group members to develop the mutual understandings and intimacy that characterize cohesiveness.

4. *Group size.* Smaller groups are more likely to be cohesive than larger groups, because physical proximity makes it easier for their members to interact.

5. *Group rewards.* Cooperative group rewards that encourage interaction can also stimulate cohesiveness, especially when group members are performing interdependent tasks.

6. *Favorable evaluation.* Recognition given a group for effective performance can reinforce feelings of pride in group membership and group performance.

[37] Shaw, *Group Dynamics*, p. 197; Dorwin Cartwright, "The Nature of Group Cohesiveness," in *Group Dynamics*, 3rd ed., ed. Dorwin Cartwright and Alvin Zander (New York: Harper & Row, 1968), pp. 91–109; Leon Festinger, Stanley Schachter, and Kurt Back, *Social Pressures in Informal Groups* (New York: Harper & Row, 1950), p. 164; and L. Libo, *Measuring Group Cohesiveness* (Ann Arbor: University of Michigan Press, 1953), p. 1.

7. *External threat.* Threats to a group's well-being that originate from outside the group can strengthen the group's cohesiveness by providing a common enemy that motivates a unified response. Conflict between groups can promote cohesion within groups.

8. *Isolation.* Being cut off from other groups can reinforce members' sense of sharing a common fate, again motivating a unified response.

The first six of the factors we have listed are clearly useful to managers in building group cohesiveness. It is not a good idea, however, to use intergroup conflict or isolation to encourage group cohesiveness. These approaches discourage the sort of cooperation among groups that is normally required to accomplish organizational goals.

If a group is really cohesive, shouldn't group productivity be enhanced? Possibly, but not necessarily. Cohesiveness *does* affect the degree to which the members of a group agree on productivity norms. The members of highly cohesive groups adopt the same norms, whereas the members of groups with low cohesiveness do not. In turn, the extent to which group members agree on norms interacts with the group's productivity norms to shape group productivity.[38] Therefore, if a highly cohesive group has adopted norms favoring high productivity, its productivity will be high because everyone agrees that working productively is the right thing to do (see the upper right cell in Figure 11-5). In stark contrast, the productivity of highly cohesive groups adopting norms that favor low productivity tends to be quite low because everyone agrees that working productively is *not* the thing to do (see lower right cell in Figure 11-5).

Once a manager has stimulated group cohesiveness, how can he ensure that the group will perform productively? He can persuade the group to adopt norms favoring high productivity. Our discussion of reinforcement theory in Chapter 7 would suggest that one way to guarantee that such norms emerge in a group

---

[38] Leonard Berkowitz, "Group Standards, Cohesiveness, and Productivity," *Human Relations* 7 (1954), 509–19; Stanley Schachter, N. Ellertson, D. McBride, and D. Gregory, "An Experimental Study of Cohesiveness and Productivity," *Human Relations* 4 (1951), 229–38; and Stanley E. Seashore, *Group Cohesiveness in the Industrial Work Group* (Ann Arbor, Mich.: Survey Research Center, Institute for Social Research, 1954), p. 80.

FIGURE 11-5

Cohesiveness and Productivity Norms Affect Group Productivity

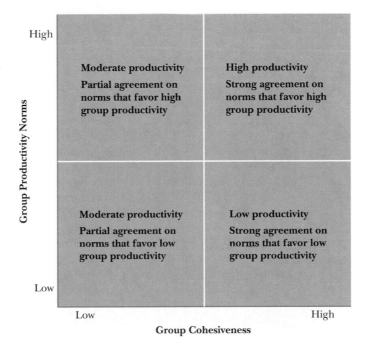

is to reward productivity whenever it occurs. Managers can use both material rewards and praise for this purpose. At the same time, they must avoid encouraging negative productivity norms by rewarding unacceptable performance or by punishing effective performers. Suppose, for example, that the management of an insurance company gives a group of salespeople $1,000 to split among themselves for every insurance policy a group member sells. Suppose further that the group sells more policies than expected and that the company then tightens the incentive system by reducing the group bonus to $500 per sale. As you can guess, the group will probably feel punished and may even decide to reduce its performance in the future.

What about the productivity of groups with low cohesiveness? As shown in both left cells in Figure 11-5, group productivity in situations of low cohesiveness fits between the two extremes described above because group members hold varying productivity norms. Some members of each group adopt high-productivity norms and work hard. Others adopt low-productivity norms and slack off or loaf. The aggregate result of this mix of norms is usually a moderate level of productivity.

Group Communication Structure. If the members of a group cannot exchange information about their work, the group cannot function effectively as a team. A viable **communication structure** is crucial to group productivity. For managers, two important questions are, What are the different kinds of group communication structures? and Which ones encourage the greatest productivity?

In response to the first question, five group communication structures have received considerable research attention. They are the wheel, Y, chain, circle, and completely connected communication networks (see Figure 11-6). The first three of these networks are the most centralized in that a central member can control information flows in the group. In the *Wheel*, one group member can communicate from a central hub with all the other members, but the others can communicate only with the member at the hub. The *Y* is a variation on this theme. It consists of three spokes, two of which are lengthened into two-person chains. Again, one group member serves as a central hub. A further modification produces the *Chain*, in which members are linked sequentially. A member in a chain network can communicate only with the two members who are immediately adjacent to him. Members at the ends of the chain can communicate only with one other person.

In contrast, in the decentralized circle and completely connected networks all members are equally able to send and receive messages. The *circle* allows each member to communicate with two others. The *completely connected* network puts every person in the circle in touch with every other.

These five communication networks differ in several important ways:

The *speed* at which information can be transmitted
The *accuracy* with which information is transmitted
Saturation, or the degree to which information is distributed evenly among the members of a group. Saturation is high when information is distributed evenly, low when distributed unevenly.
The *satisfaction* of members with communication processes and the group in general.[39]

Speed is linked to production quantity and accuracy to production quality. Saturation and satisfaction are closely related in that members who have access to

communication structure The pattern of interactions by which group members share information. In the *wheel*, a central hub member communicates with all other members, who communicate only with her. In the *Y*, the members of two pairs can communicate with each other and with the hub but the pairs cannot communicate directly. The *chain* links members sequentially so that some can communicate with two people but others with only one. In the *circle*, each member can communicate with two others. In the *completely connected network* each group member can communicate directly with every other.

---

[39] Alex Bavelas and D. Barrett, "An Experimental Approach to Organizational Communication," *Personnel* 27 (1951), 366–71.

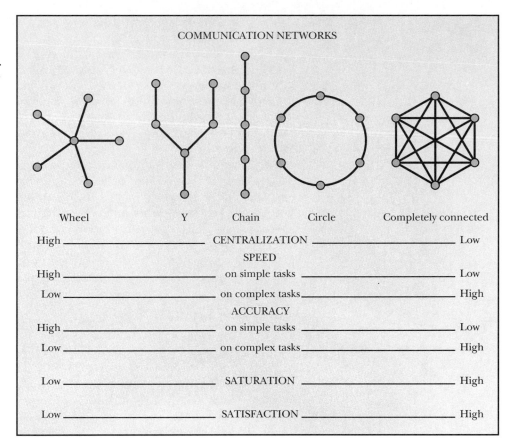

FIGURE 11-6

Group Communication Structures and Group Effectiveness

Based on information in Marvin E. Shaw, *Group Dynamics: The Psychology of Small Group Behavior* (New York: McGraw-Hill, 1976), pp. 262–314.

information are also the most satisfied with group communication processes. So both factors can have indirect effects on group productivity and effectiveness. Speed and accuracy of communication affect productivity directly.

As indicated in Figure 11-6, communication speed and accuracy in a group are influenced both by the nature of the group's communication network and by the relative complexity of the group's task. When a task is simple and communication networks are centralized, both speed and accuracy are higher. Centralization facilitates the minimal communication required to succeed at simple tasks. For instance, when a group is assigned the task of assembling boxes of food for a holiday donation program, little discussion is required to get the job done, and having a supervisor to coordinate activities makes the work go faster. When tasks are simple and communication networks are decentralized, however, speed and accuracy are lower because more people than need be are involved in communication. Turning 15 volunteers loose in a food bank without supervision is not likely to lead to the level of productivity achieved by a group working under common supervision.

In contrast, when tasks are relatively complex, centralized communication networks lower both speed and accuracy, because people serving as network hubs succumb to **information overload**. Suppose that a group of account managers are digesting information about competitors' advertising campaigns and designing a marketing response. If they have to get all their information from a central supervisor, the supervisor will be quickly overloaded, and the group's productivity will decrease. Overload and its effects are less likely in decentralized networks. More people can get involved in processing information and sorting out what is needed to perform specific tasks. Our entire group of account managers can

information overload A condition in which a person is presented with more information than he can possibly process.

share the complicated job of making sense of competitors' actions before they plot a response.

Both network saturation and member satisfaction are generally higher in decentralized networks. Everyone is informed and fully involved in the communication process and the task. Recall that involvement in all activities of a group is a criterion of individual satisfaction. (The only exception to this rule is that in centralized networks the one person at the hub of the network is usually very satisfied.) Task complexity does not appear to affect saturation or satisfaction in groups.

In sum, centralization increases the productivity of groups performing simple tasks that require little or no communication but generally reduces member satisfaction. For managers, this means that a group may perform a simple task efficiently but because members' satisfaction is low, the group is not totally effective. In contrast, decentralization not only increases the productivity of groups performing complex tasks that require a lot of communication but also increases member satisfaction. The decentralized network is therefore an efficient *and* an effective way of organizing communication when complex tasks are at hand.

GROUP JUDGMENT AND DECISION MAKING

Up to now we have been discussing productivity in group tasks that, whether they require physical or mental effort, result in a product or service that can be provided to a customer or client. Now we turn to a special kind of group task in which productivity is influenced by factors that are quite different from those we have discussed. **Group decision making**, or group judgment, is almost purely mental in character, and many of the factors that affect it are also mental in origin or effect. We'll begin by looking at several of these factors. Then we'll explore ways of lessening their effects through structuring patterns of group interactions.

group decision making   A group task in which the ultimate aim is to solve a problem or make a decision.

Decision-Making Errors

interactive group   A group whose members interact in unstructured, face-to-face relationships like those that take place during ordinary conversations.

In most everyday situations, decision-making tasks are performed by **interactive groups**—groups whose members work together in unstructured, face-to-face interactions like those that take place during ordinary conversations. If you analyze the cases in this book together with other students, you are probably working in an interactive group. In many organizations, a similar approach is used to conduct meetings. For example, a management team discussing the merits of adopting a new job-applicant screening program may meet as an interactive group. Steelworkers solving a problem with raw-material availability in what is called a quality circle (see Chapter 17) are also probably meeting as an interactive group.

Unfortunately, using interactive groups in decision-making tasks increases the likelihood that judgment errors will reduce the quantity, as well as the quality, of the judgments. Consequently, the group's productivity will be affected. Of these different judgment errors, three are quite likely to depress the performance of interactive groups: compliance, choice shift, and groupthink.

Compliance.   As we noted in Chapter 10, when people conform to others' expectations or behaviors in the hope of acquiring rewards or avoiding punishment, they are said to exhibit *compliance*. In a now classic series of laboratory experiments, Solomon Asch studied compliance in groups of people. He asked participants to compare three sets of lines and to judge which comparison line in each set was the same length as the standard line.[40] Without the knowledge of the participants, only one uncoached person was put in each group. All the others were actually accomplices of the experimenter. Asch instructed the accomplices to choose the appropriate comparison line in the first and second trials. In the third trial, however, they were all to choose the same, wrong comparison line. All group members were required to state their opinions aloud and the one authentic participant in each group was seated last so that he heard everyone else's "judgments" before he stated his own.

How did the genuine subjects react when asked to call out judgments on the third trial? About 40 percent refused to go along with the apparently unanimous but incorrect choice of the accomplices, making the correct judgment. Sixty percent, however, called out the incorrect response that the rest of the group had stated. After the experiment, many of the participants who had agreed with the group reported to the experimenter that they had known their responses were wrong but felt uncomfortable disagreeing. Asch's experiments thus demonstrated how the presence of other people can pressure individuals to conform to obviously incorrect group judgments.

This research offers a cautionary rule for managers. Members of a decision-making group may alter their private judgments if the group is not structured in a way that controls the effects of compliance. For instance, a group of brand managers in a consumer products company might accept overly optimistic sales projections for a new brand of detergent, even if they knew the projections were inflated, if at least some members of the group argued that the sales figures were valid. Structuring group interactions is therefore an important part of managing group decision making. We will return to this point later.

choice shift The tendency for groups to make decisions that appear more extreme than the decisions group members would make on their own. In *risky shift* group decisions appear more risky than decisions made by individuals, and in *cautious shift* group decisions appear more cautious than decisions made by individuals.

Choice Shift. Group judgment can also be affected by another judgment error. **Choice shift** is a tendency for groups to make decisions that appear more extreme than the decisions group members would make on their own.[41] Consider the following situation:

Martha works for a large consumer products corporation. She is assured a lifetime job with a modest, although adequate, salary and liberal pension benefits. It is unlikely, however, that her salary will ever increase much. While attending a conference, Martha is offered a job with a small, new company with an uncertain future. The new job would pay more to start and would offer the possibility of a share in ownership if the company survived the competition of larger firms. Imagine that you are advising Martha. What are the odds that the new company will stay in business? From the list that follows, check the lowest probability at which you would advise Martha to take the new job.

_____ The chances are 1 in 10 that the company will survive.

_____ The chances are 3 in 10 that the company will survive.

_____ The chances are 5 in 10 that the company will survive.

_____ The chances are 7 in 10 that the company will survive.

_____ The chances are 9 in 10 that the company will survive.

_____ Place a check here if you think Martha should not take the new job no matter what the odds.

[40] Asch, *Social Psychology* (Englewood Cliffs, N.J.: Prentice-Hall, 1952) pp. 451–501; "An Experimental Investigation of Group Influence," in *Symposium on Preventive and Social Psychiatry, Walter Reed Army Institute of Research* (Washington, D.C.: Government Printing Office, 1957), pp. 18–34; and "Studies of Independence and Conformity, I: A minority of One Against a Unanimous Majority," *Psychological Monographs* 70 (1956), 416–22.

[41] C. Fraser, C. Gouge, and M. Billig, "Risky Shifts, Cautious Shifts, and Group Polarization," *European Journal of Social Psychology* 1 (1971), 7–30; and R. E. Knox and R. K. Safford, "Group Caution at the Race Track," *Journal of Experimental Social Psychology* 12 (1976), 317–24.

Which probability would you check? When confronted with this choice and asked to make a decision alone, most people choose an alternative near the end of the list. Apparently they believe that Martha should not risk her economic security by taking the chancy job. When asked to make the decision in consultation with a group of other people, however, the same individuals choose from the longer odds, indicating that Martha should take a risk. Researchers have coined the term *risky shift* for this phenomenon.[42] They say that people make more risky decisions in groups than alone when the decisions involve tradeoffs among potential gains. Martha's choice between her current job and a more lucrative offer was such a tradeoff. Researchers have also found that groups shift toward more cautious judgments—the term is *cautious shift*—when they have to choose from among potential losses. Should a doctor treat a cancer patient with a combination of surgical removal, chemotherapy, and radiation treatments or should she use the simpler but less thorough procedure of chemotherapy alone?

Three explanations have been given for choice shift, whether risky or cautious. **Social comparison** proposes that people often voice opinions that are much less extreme than their private opinions—either less risky or less cautious. Apparently they are afraid that if they publicly advocate more extreme positions, they will be criticized and considered strange. In a group discussion, however, when they hear others voicing positions that are more extreme than the ones they have stated, they may move in the direction of the extreme positions they favored initially.[43] **Persuasive argumentation** suggests that choice shift occurs whenever group discussions uncover arguments favoring extreme positions. These arguments convince group members whose initial opinions, both public and private, were moderate, to switch to more extreme choices.[44] Finally, **decision bias** stems from the loss aversion threat to rational decision making we discussed in Chapter 6. According to decision bias, risky shift occurs when groups must choose between different potential gains such as Martha's present secure job and potential well-paying job.[45] The loss aversion bias makes individuals cautious, but it seems to have no effect on groups. When they select options that appear more risky than selected by individuals, they are actually behaving in a risk-neutral manner. Again according to decision bias, cautious shift occurs when people must choose between different potential losses. As in the case of risky shifts, groups exhibiting what appear to be cautious shifts are simply behaving in a risk-neutral manner.

social comparison The theory that when people in groups hear others voicing extreme positions they often abandon their cautious choices and revert to their initial extreme positions.

persuasive argumentation The theory that when group discussions uncover arguments favoring extreme positions, moderate group members may switch to more extreme choices.

decision bias The theory that group decisions are not affected by the loss aversion bias that affects individual decision making.

groupthink A threat to the effective performance of groups that develops in highly cohesive groups whenever strivings for harmony and unanimity override efforts to appraise group judgments realistically.

Groupthink. **Groupthink**, a common problem in group decision making, is a judgment error that develops in highly cohesive groups. Groupthink occurs whenever the desire for harmony and unanimity overrides members' efforts to ap-

[42] J. A. F. Stoner, "A Comparison of Individual and Group Decisions Involving Risk" (master's thesis, Massachusetts Institute of Technology, 1961); N. Kogan and M. A. Wallach, *Risk Taking: A Study in Cognition and Personality* (New York: Holt, Reinhart, & Winston, 1964); and D. Cartwright, "Risk Taking by Individuals and Groups: An Assessment of Research Employing Choice Dilemmas," *Journal of Personality and Social Psychology* 20 (1971), 361–78.

[43] R. S. Baron and G. Roper, "A Reaffirmation of a Social Comparison View of Choice Shifts, Averaging, and Extremity Effects in Autokinetic Situations," *Journal of Personality and Social Psychology* 20 (1976), 446–55; and G. S. Sanders and Baron, "Is Social Comparison Irrelevant for Producing Choice Shifts?" *Journal of Experimental Social Psychology* 13 (1977), 303–14.

[44] C. P. Morgan and J. D. Aram, "The Preponderance of Arguments in the Risky Shift Phenomenon," *Journal of Experimental Social Psychology* 11 (1975), 25–34; and E. B. Ebbesen and R. J. Bowers, "Proportion of Risky to Conservative Arguments in a Group Discussion and Choice Shift," *Journal of Personality and Social Psychology* 29 (1974), 316–27.

[45] Margaret A. Neale, Max H. Bazerman, Gregory B. Northcraft, and C. A. Alperson, "Choice Shift's Effects in Group Decisions: A Decision Bias Perspective," *International Journal of Small Group Research* 2 (1986), 33–42.

praise group judgments realistically.[46] The resulting overemphasis on consensus causes the group to follow a course of action that critical evaluation might have rejected.

Among the most shocking instances of groupthink is the Challenger space shuttle disaster of the early 1980s. Years of successful shuttle launches had lulled NASA (and the rest of North America, for that matter) into a sense of security and overconfidence. As a result, despite repeated warnings from engineers at the company that produced the shuttle's solid-fuel booster engines, NASA officials decided to launch the shuttle after a night of freezing temperatures. Seals on the shuttle's boosters failed because of cold-induced brittleness, and the shuttle exploded. Had NASA personnel given credence to the engineers' warnings, the shuttle disaster probably could have been avoided.[47] Unfortunately, it is a tragic example of the extremely harmful effects that cohesion-based groupthink can have on group decision making.

Groupthink has several distinctive characteristics:

1. A sense of *invulnerability* that encourages optimism and risk taking. Group members overemphasize the group's strengths and feel that it is beyond criticism or attack. This can lead the group to take risky actions that individual members would probably not take.

2. A belief in the group's *morality* so strong that group members disregard the ethical consequences of their judgments. Members feel that the group is right and above reproach. They feel no need to debate issues of ethics or morality.

3. *Rationalized* judgments that ignore warnings and disregard assumptions. Members explain away indications of impending disaster instead of taking them seriously and altering the group's actions.

4. A *stereotypic* view of outsiders as evil, weak, or stupid. Members do not examine the actions of outsiders realistically. Instead they tend to dismiss the stated goals or opinions of outside groups and their members.

5. *Self-censorship* that prevents members from voicing doubts about the wisdom of the group. Members decide to avoid communicating personal concerns to others for fear of disturbing group consensus and cohesiveness.

6. A shared sense of *unanimity* born out of self-censorship and the assumption that silence signifies agreement. Tests that might determine whether members truly agree are deemed inappropriate or unnecessary.

7. *Direct pressure* on group members not to argue against a group position lest they be considered disloyal. In the unlikely event that caution or concern is voiced, other members quickly respond by pressuring the deviant individual into conformity.

8. The emergence of *mindguards*, or members who protect the group from information that might interfere with the supposed unanimity of the group.[48]

As shown in Figure 11-7, these symptoms contribute to a variety of defects in the group judgment process that undermine the likelihood that the group will produce a reasonable decision.

Besides the Challenger disaster, there have been many other publicly aired instances of groupthink in the last 30 years. For example, President John F. Kennedy's decision to invade the Bay of Pigs, in Cuba, in the early 1960s is universally cited as the result of groupthink in Kennedy's cabinet. The Watergate

---

[46] Irving L. Janis, *Groupthink* (Boston: Houghton Mifflin, 1982), pp. 7–9.

[47] "Shuttle Probe Throws Shower of Sparks," *U. S. News and World Report*, March 3, 1986, pp. 6–7.

[48] Janis, *Groupthink*, pp. 174–75.

FIGURE 11-7

Symptoms and Consequences of Groupthink

Based on Irving L. Janis, *Groupthink*, 2nd ed. (Boston: Houghton Mifflin, 1982), pp. 243–48; and Irving L. Janis and Leon Mann, *Decision Making: A Psychological Analysis of Conflict, Choice, and Commitment* (New York: Free Press, 1977), pp. 180–87.

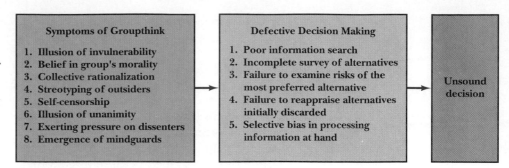

scandal, which led to President Richard M. Nixon's resignation in 1974, is usually interpreted as the result of groupthink among Nixon's top aides. The Soviets' mistaken attack on a Korean Airlines jet in the 1980s may also have been due to groupthink among top Russian military personnel. The effects of groupthink can be both pervasive and severe.

Overcoming Decision-Making Errors

Compliance, choice shift, and groupthink are all group errors and reflect the effects of social interaction on judgment processes. To determine how to counteract the effects of these errors, it helps to break the process of group judgment into two phases. *Idea generation* is the development of new ideas. *Idea evaluation* is the process through which the best ideas are winnowed out from the ones that have been generated.

Idea generation is a creative process intended to produce a large quantity of ideas no matter what their quality. An advertising group trying to come up with a name for a new cereal is involved in idea generation. So, too, are a group of research specialists searching for new ways to cook foods in microwave ovens. As suggested in Chapter 6, people must be able to take risks to succeed at idea generation. Sometimes they must even suggest alternatives that at first appear nonsensical or unworkable. Social interaction and the group judgment errors we have discussed present major threats to this phase of the judgment process. Working with others in a group can reduce the number of ideas that are generated. This is particularly likely when people are afraid to look silly in front of others, when undecided members are pressured to endorse premature judgments, and when unstated opinions imply agreement that does not really exist. It follows that idea generation should not be performed in unstructured, interactive groups.

In contrast, idea evaluation emphasizes quality. In evaluation, you choose the best idea from available alternatives. A group of classmates arguing about the best solution to a problem posed in a management case is engaged in idea evaluation. Similarly, a top-management group is evaluating ideas when it tries to decide the best location for a new production facility. Working in a group can be beneficial when making such judgments, because collaboration allows conflicting values and opinions to be aired. Considering different points of view can shed light on new ways of thinking about the various alternatives being evaluated. The result is a final evaluation that reflects a broad array of considerations instead of a narrow, restricted set of values, emotions, and opinions. Having people work together during idea evaluation also promotes long-term acceptance of the idea that is finally selected. This increases the likelihood that action will follow the judgment process. Idea evaluation clearly benefits from the social interaction of groups.

What can managers do to counteract or avoid the effects of group decision-making errors? Our distinction between idea generation and idea evaluation suggests a straightforward strategy. Managers should discourage social interaction so as to minimize its negative effects during idea generation, but encourage social interaction during idea evaluation so as to maximize the exchange of opinions. In practice, this strategy can be implemented, to a greater or lesser extent, using any of three different approaches: brainstorming, the Delphi technique, or the nomimal group technique.

Brainstorming. **Brainstorming** is a kind of idea-generation technique that attempts to minimize the negative effects of working with others in a group. A brainstorming group convenes, usually around a table, and the group leader reads a statement describing the sort of decision the group is to make. From this point on, the brainstorming group must follow a clearly stated set of rules in generating ideas:

brainstorming A group decision-making process based on a set of rules intended to encourage idea generation.

1. *Criticism is not allowed.* All evaluation of ideas, whether positive or negative, must be withheld until later.
2. *Free-wheeling is welcome.* The wilder the idea, the better. It is easier to tame down than to think up.
3. *Quantity is encouraged.* The more ideas generated, the more likely it is that there will be a number of useful ones.
4. *Combination and improvement are sought.* Group members are asked not only to contribute ideas of their own but to suggest how others' ideas might be improved or combined to make yet other ideas.[49]

Brainstorming calls for people with ideas to raise their hands and be recognized by the leader. As group members tell their ideas, the leader writes the ideas on a blackboard, flipchart, or overhead-projector transparency so that everybody can see the complete list as it evolves. In general, 30 to 45 minutes are allotted for an idea-generation session.

In a second session, either the original group or another group is convened to evaluate the ideas generated. Members review the ideas and discuss the various alternatives. No specific set of rules guides this discussion, although the leader again recognizes participants one at a time and keeps a written record of major discussion points. The session may conclude, like a meeting of an interactive group, with a majority vote or consensual decision.

[49] Alex F. Osborn, *Applied Imagination: Principles and Procedures of Creative Problem Solving*, 3rd ed. (New York: Scribner's, 1963), p. 156.

One of the newest ways to generate ideas is the electronic meeting, developed at the University of Arizona with IBM funding. In these meetings, people sit at personal computers (PCs) placed around a U-shaped table. Participants are silent during the meeting and make all their comments by typing them into their PCs. A local-area network (LAN) tracks and sorts sentences by topic and order of response, tallies votes, and displays all this material on a big screen. IBM and others say this approach, in which all responses are anonymous, brings people together who might have skirmished in other settings. How would you compare this system with the brainstorming, Delphi, *and* nominal *techniques?*
Source: Jim Bartimo, "At These Shouting Matches, No One Says a Word," Business Week, *June 11, 1990, p. 78.*

Delphi technique A group decision-making process in which the group never meets in person but instead corresponds with a central leader who initiates activities and receives all the resulting information.

nominal group technique A group decision-making process in which face-to-face interaction of group members is limited.

FIGURE 11-8

The Delphi Technique

Adapted with the authors' permission from Henry L. Tosi, John R. Rizzo, and Stephen J. Carroll, *Managing Organizational Behavior* (Marshfield, Mass.: Pitman, 1986), p. 458.

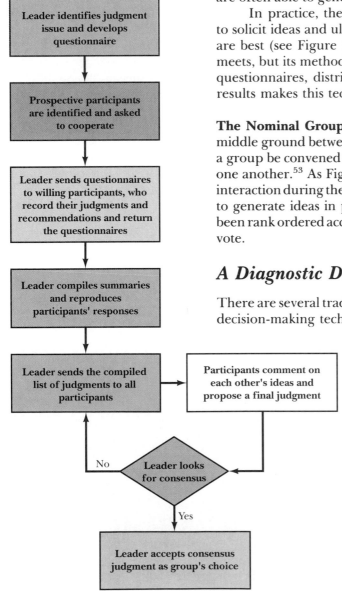

The success of a brainstorming session depends on how seriously participants take the rules of brainstorming. If criticism is truly avoided during idea generation, and if people genuinely lose their inhibitions and suggest whatever comes to mind, brainstorming can lead to more ideas than interactive groups produce.[50] Research has indicated, however, that in most cases, judgment errors and threats to group productivity still impede the generation of ideas in brainstorming groups.[51] Despite rules that support inventiveness and collaboration, the presence of others during idea generation usually leads to at least some of the conformity, polarization, and self-censure caused by compliance, choice shift, and groupthink. For this reason, an approach called the Delphi technique is sometimes used instead.

The Delphi Technique. Unlike the members of a brainstorming group, the participants in a Delphi group never communicate with each other or meet face to face. In fact, they may not even know each other's identities. Instead, they correspond by mail, computer networks, or other linking systems, with a central leader who initiates Delphi activities and receives all the resulting information.[52] By keeping participants apart, the **Delphi technique** eliminates the possibility that social interaction will affect the process of idea generation. Delphi groups are often able to generate a greater number of ideas than brainstorming groups.

In practice, the Delphi technique makes use of a series of questionnaires to solicit ideas and ultimately produces a consensus judgment about which ideas are best (see Figure 11-8). It avoids group pressures, because the group never meets, but its methodology is rather cumbersome. The time required to develop questionnaires, distribute them to participants, wait for responses, and collate results makes this technique quite slow.

The Nominal Group Technique. The **nominal group technique** represents a middle ground between brainstorming and the Delphi technique. It requires that a group be convened but limits the extent to which group members interact with one another.[53] As Figure 11-9 shows, the nominal group technique avoids social interaction during the strictly creative phase of the process by requiring individuals to generate ideas in private. Typically, it concludes after alternative ideas have been rank ordered according to judgments that participants have made in a private vote.

A Diagnostic Decision Tree

There are several tradeoffs among the brainstorming, Delphi, and nominal group decision-making techniques (see Table 11-4). For example, the nominal group

[50] Ibid., pp. 80–95.

[51] Michael Diehl and Wolfgang Stroebe, "Productivity Loss in Brainstorming Groups: Toward the Solution of a Riddle." *Journal of Personality and Social Psychology 53* (1987), 497–509.

[52] N. C. Dalkey, *The Delphi Method: An Experimental Study of Group Opinion* (Santa Monica, Calif.: Rand, 1969), p. 8; and Harold Sackman, *Delphi Critique* (Santa Monica, Calif.: Rand, 1975), pp. 8–10.

[53] Andre L. Delbecq, Andrew H. Van de Ven, and David H. Gustafson, *Group Techniques for Program Planning: A Guide to Nominal Group and Delphi Processes* (Glenview, Ill.: Scott, Foresman, 1975), p. 7; and Carl M. Moore, *Group Techniques for Idea Building* (Beverly Hills, Calif.: Sage, 1987), p. 24.

FIGURE 11-9

The Nominal Group Technique

Adapted with the authors' permission from Henry L. Tosi, John R. Rizzo, and Stephen J. Carroll, *Managing Organizational Behavior* (Marshfield, Mass.: Pitman, 1986), p. 456.

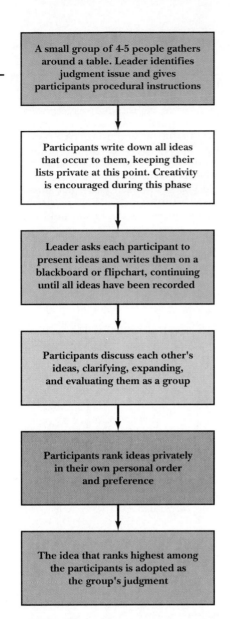

A small group of 4-5 people gathers around a table. Leader identifies judgment issue and gives participants procedural instructions

Participants write down all ideas that occur to them, keeping their lists private at this point. Creativity is encouraged during this phase

Leader asks each participant to present ideas and writes them on a blackboard or flipchart, continuing until all ideas have been recorded

Participants discuss each other's ideas, clarifying, expanding, and evaluating them as a group

Participants rank ideas privately in their own personal order and preference

The idea that ranks highest among the participants is adopted as the group's judgment

TABLE 11-4
A Comparison of Approaches to Group Decision Making

CHARACTERISTICS	INTERACTIVE	BRAINSTORM	DELPHI	NOMINAL
Number of ideas	Low	Moderate	High	High
Quality of ideas	Low	Moderate	High	High
Amount of social pressure	High	Low	Low	Moderate
Costs in time/money	Moderate	Low	High	Low
Potential for conflict	High	Low	Low	Moderate
Members' feelings of accomplishment	Varies	High	Moderate	High
Members' commitment to the solution	High	High*	Low	Moderate
Degree of group cohesiveness built	High	High	Low	Moderate

* If the brainstorming group is also responsible for choosing which alternative to select; otherwise, not applicable.

Source: Reprinted with the publisher's permission from J. Keith Murnighan, "Group Decision Making: What Strategies Should You Use?" *Management Review*, 70 (February 1981), 61. © 1981 American Management Association, New York. All rights reserved.

FIGURE 11-10

Selecting a Group Judgment Technique

Brainstorming (B), the Delphi technique (D), and the nominal group technique (N) are three techniques used to overcome group judgment errors. Groups performing these techniques can be composed of experts (E), who have special insights into the judgment issue, representatives (R), who embody the values and opinions of different organization groups, or coworkers (C), who work together every day. Group judgment processes can thus be performed by a brainstorming group of experts (E/B), representatives (R/B), or co-workers (C/B); a Delphi group of experts (E/D), representatives (R/D), or coworkers (C/D, an improbable combination not considered in this model); or a nominal group of experts (E/N), representatives (R/N), or co-workers (C/N). This decision tree poses six questions that help to determine which of these combinations should be used in each particular situation.
Stephen A. Stumpf, Dale E. Zand, and Richard D. Freedman, "Designing Groups for Judgmental Decisions," Academy of Management Review 4 (1979), 597. Reprinted with permission of the publisher.

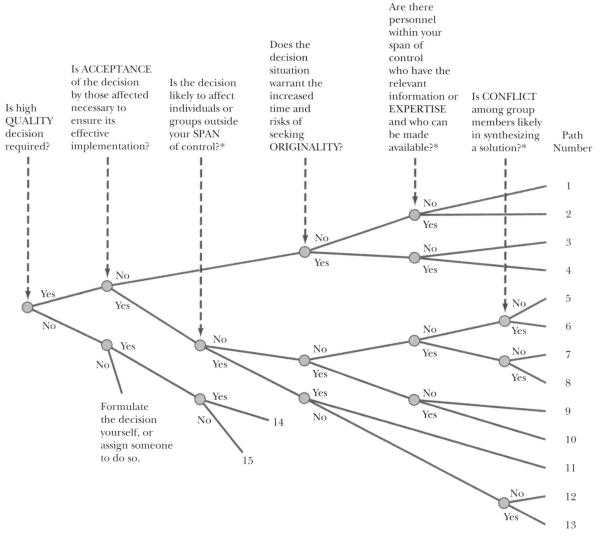

Path Number	Preferred Set	Path Number	Preferred Set	Path Number	Preferred Set
1	E/B, E/N, E/D	6	R/B	10	R/N, C/N
2	E/B, E/N, E/D, C/B,C/N	7 & 15	R/B,R/N, C/B, C/N	11	E/N, R/N
3	E/N, E/D	8	R/B, C/B,	12	E/B,E/N, R/B,R/N
4	E/N, E/D, C/N	9	R/N	13	E/B,R/B
5 & 14	R/B, R/N				

* The absence of a node means that the parameter is not relevant to that path.

and Delphi techniques generally generate a greater number of higher-quality ideas, but they forgo the possibility of building group effectiveness. And although the nominal group technique requires less time and money than the Delphi technique, it involves higher social pressure and a greater chance for interpersonal conflict.

If no one of these techniques consistently produces a large number of high-quality judgments, how can we choose among them? Indeed, *can* we choose one over the other? Yes we can, because one technique may work well in one situation whereas another may perform better in a different situation. As shown in the diagnostic decision tree in Figure 11-10, by asking a series of questions, you can determine whether to employ a brainstorming, nominal group, or Delphi approach. How important are quality, originality, and general acceptance of the results of a group's deliberation? How many people are likely to be affected by the decisions? How available is expertise to implement the decisions? And what is the likelihood that group members will come into conflict in arriving at a resolution?

SUMMARY

Organizations are composed of many different kinds of *groups*, ranging from the *reference groups* that shape the opinions of organization members to the *formal groups* in which members work. These groups develop in a four-stage process of *formation*, *differentiation*, *integration*, and *maturity* in which members discover similarities among themselves, determine who will do what, develop standards of behavior, and formalize the procedures needed to accomplish the group's purpose. This process creates several products—*tasks*, *roles*, and *norms*—that affect the group's productivity and effectiveness.

In general, as a result of *process loss*, groups are less productive than individuals working alone. Process loss can be traced, in turn, to the effects of *production blocking*, *group maintenance activities*, and *social loafing*. Factors that can be managed to reduce or eliminate the effects of process loss include group size, member motivation, group *cohesiveness* and norms, and the group's *communication structure*.

Productivity in the group judgment task is affected not only by process loss but by *conformity*, *choice shift*, and *groupthink*. *Brainstorming*, the *Delphi technique*, and the *nominal group technique* can reduce the effects of these three judgment errors and facilitate group decision making. Each of these techniques has particular strengths and weaknesses that make it suitable for use in some situations but not in others.

REVIEW QUESTIONS

1.   What are the three criteria of group effectiveness? Which one is the same as group productivity? Why is group effectiveness assessed in terms of all three of these criteria instead of being measured by group productivity alone?

2.   What abilities would you seek in group members who will be responsible for completing a disjunctive task? A conjunctive task? What would happen if you reassigned the first group to perform an additive task? What would happen if you reassigned the second group to the additive task?

3.   What is the difference between a pivotal norm and a peripheral norm? What kind of norm is embodied in the statement "Students should not cheat in college courses?"

4.   What is process loss? How do production blocking and social loafing con-

tribute to its presence? How does a group's size affect its productivity? What factors explain this relationship?

5. What influence do group goals have on member motivation? What effects do group rewards have on this motivation? What implications do your answers have for managers who must motivate individuals to perform productively in groups?

6. Explain why the statement "Highly cohesive groups are more productive than groups that are not cohesive" is not necessarily correct. What specific things might you do as a manager to ensure that high cohesion actually leads to high productivity?

7. Explain why centralized communication structures enhance the productivity of groups performing simple tasks but depress the performance of groups performing complex jobs. What sort of structure would you recommend for a group of accountants auditing the books of a large manufacturing firm? Why?

8. How does group decision making differ from other group tasks? What factors are especially likely to cause errors during the group judgment process? How would you structure this process to minimize errors if a judgment had to be made as soon as possible? Why?

DIAGNOSTIC QUESTIONS

Managing group effectiveness in general, and group productivity in particular, requires careful analysis. The following questions can help guide this analysis

1. In what stage of development is the group? Can ineffectiveness, such as poor productivity or member dissatisfaction, be traced to the group's current level of development?

2. What type of task is the group performing? What skill profile should characterize the group's members? Is this profile evident?

3. Does the group have the mix of task-oriented and maintenance roles required to work productively? Are the negative effects of individual roles controlled adequately?

4. Do group members demonstrate the adherence to pivotal norms necessary for group survival? If the group must cope with a changing work situation, is there evidence that it can adapt by selectively ignoring peripheral norms?

5. Have you evidence that the group suffers serious process loss? Is production blocking a problem? Are maintenance activities overwhelming productive resources? Is social loafing a problem?

6. Can group size be manipulated to solve productivity problems? If so, have you evidence that this manipulation will enhance productivity?

7. Can productivity problems be traced to poor group-member motivation? Does the group have specific and difficult individual *and* group performance goals? Are performance-contingent rewards used? Does the type of reward match the level of task interdependence?

8. Is the group cohesive? If so, do group norms support productive activities?

9. Can the group's communication structure cope with the information required to perform its task?

10. Is the group performing a decision-making task? If so, have you evidence that poor productivity is attributable to compliance, choice shift, or groupthink? Which technique—brainstorming, Delphi, or nominal group—seems most fitting given your diagnosis (use Figure 11-10) of the judgment situation?

EXERCISE 11-1
WILDERNESS SURVIVAL: A CONSENSUS-SEEKING TASK*

DONALD T. SIMPSON, *Eastman Kodak Company*

In *consensus acceptance*, all members of a group agree to support a group decision. Everyone in the group is actively involved in reaching consensus acceptance. Everyone discusses the issues, and all members' ideas are incorporated into the group's ultimate decision. This method of making a decision pools the knowledge and experience of all a group's members and gains each individual's personal support.

Consensus, however, is difficult to attain. Moreover, achieving it takes more time than other methods of decision making such as majority rule or autocratic imposition of one or only a few members. To achieve consensus agreement in a group, all members of the group must do the following:

1. Before meeting with the group they must consider and be ready to state their personal positions to the group. They must also keep in mind that the decision making process is incomplete until everyone has explained his own ideas and the group as a whole has reached a decision.

2. They must recognize their obligation to explain their own opinions fully, so that the group can benefit from each member's thinking.

3. They must accept the obligation to listen to the opinions of all other group members, and they must be able to modify their own positions on the basis of logic and improved understanding.

4. Realizing that differences of opinion are normal and helpful, they must not resort to conflict-reducing techniques like voting, compromising, or giving in to others. They must believe that in exploring differences, they will arrive at the best course of action.

In this exercise you will first work alone, deciding what you would do to survive in the wilderness. You will then join a group and reach a consensus about the best approach to wilderness survival. As you work together, remember that consensus is difficult to attain and that not every decision made during the wilderness survival task may meet with everyone's unqualified approval. However, there should be a general feeling of support from all members before a group decision is finalized. Take the time to listen, to consider *all* members' views, and to make your own view known. Be reasonable in arriving at a group decision.

STEP ONE: PRE-CLASS PREPARATION

Read the entire exercise, then fill in your answers to the questions on the Wilderness Survival Work Sheet in Exhibit 11-1. Be sure to bring your answers to class.

* Adapted from J. William Pfeiffer and John E. Jones (eds.), *The 1976 Annual Handbook for Group Facilitators* (San Diego, CA: University Associates, Inc., 1976). Used with permission.

EXHIBIT 11-1
Wilderness Survival Work Sheet

Here are twelve questions concerning personal survival in a wilderness situation. Your first task is *individually* to select the best of the three alternatives given for each item. Try to imagine yourself in the situation depicted. Assume that you are alone and have a minimum of equipment, except where specified. The season is fall. The days are warm and dry, but the nights are cold.

After you have completed this task individually,

you will again consider each question as a member of a small group. Your group will have the task of deciding, *by consensus*, the best alternative for each question. Do not change your individual answers, even if you change your mind in the group discussion. Both the individual and group solutions will later be compared with the answers provided by a group of experienced naturalists who conduct classes in woodland survival.

1. You have strayed from your party in trackless timber. You have no special signaling equipment. The best way to attempt to contact your friends is to:
   a. call "help" loudly but in a low register.
   b. yell or scream as loud as you can.
   c. whistle loudly and shrilly.

2. You are in "snake country." Your best action to avoid snakes is to:
   a. make a lot of noise with your feet.
   b. walk softly and quietly.
   c. travel at night.

3. You are hungry and lost in wild country. The best rule for determining which plants are safe to eat (those you do not recognize) is to:
   a. try anything you see the birds eat.
   b. eat anything except plants with bright red berries.
   c. put a bit of the plant on your lower lip for five minutes; if it seems all right, try a little.

4. The day becomes dry and hot. You have a full canteen of water (about one liter) with you. You should:
   a. ration it—about a cupful a day.
   b. not drink until you stop for the night, then drink what you think you need.
   c. drink as much as you think you need when you need it.

5. Your water is gone; you become very thirsty. You finally come to a dried-up watercourse. Your best chance of finding water is to:
   a. dig anywhere in the stream bed.
   b. dig up plant and tree roots near the bank.
   c. dig in the stream bed at the outside of a bend.

6. You decide to walk out of the wild country by following a series of ravines where a water supply is available. Night is coming on. The best place to make camp is:
   a. next to the water supply in the ravine.
   b. high on a ridge.
   c. midway up the slope.

7. Your flashlight glows dimly as you are about to make your way back to your campsite after a brief foraging trip. Darkness comes quickly in the woods and the surroundings seem unfamiliar. You should:
   a. head back at once, keeping the light on, hoping the light will glow enough for you to make out landmarks.
   b. put the batteries under your armpits to warm them, and then replace them in the flashlight.
   c. shine your light for a few seconds, try to get the scene in mind, move out in the darkness, and repeat the process.

8. An early snow confines you to your small tent. You doze with your small stove going. There is danger if the flame is:
   a. yellow.
   b. blue.
   c. red.

9. You must ford a river that has a strong current, large rocks, and some white water. After carefully selecting your crossing spot, you should:

a. leave your boots and pack on.
b. take your boots and pack off.
c. take off your pack, but leave your boots on.

10. In waist-deep water with a strong current, when crossing the stream, you should face: _____   _____
    a. upstream.
    b. across the stream.
    c. downstream.

11. You find yourself rimrocked: your only route is up. The way is mossy, slippery rock. You should try it: _____   _____
    a. barefoot.
    b. with boots on.
    c. in stocking feet.

12. Unarmed and unsuspecting, you surprise a large bear prowling around your campsite. As the bear rears up about ten meters from you, you should: _____   _____
    a. run.
    b. climb the nearest tree.
    c. freeze, but be ready to back away slowly.

STEP TWO: GROUP CONSENSUS SEEKING

The class should divide into groups of four to six members each (if you have formed permanent groups, reassemble in those groups). Your group should then seek consensus answers to each of the questions in the Wilderness Survival Work Sheet. You should appoint a spokesperson to report on the results of Steps One and Two to the entire class.

STEP THREE: CLASS DISCUSSION

Your instructor will reconvene the class, asking the members of each group to remain seated together. The instructor will then inform everyone of the right answers to the questions. Group members should then determine how many questions they answered correctly and give this information to their group spokesperson. The group spokesperson should also determine how many questions the group answered correctly.

Next, the instructor will call on each spokesperson and ask for the information needed to complete the tabulation below for each group:

After your instructor has completed this table on a blackboard, flipchart, or overhead projector, class members should discuss the consensus-seeking procedures they used in their groups and should consider the following questions:

1. What specific behaviors promoted productivity in your group? What behaviors hindered group productivity? What rules could be set up to encourage helpful behaviors and discourage harmful ones?

2. Did groups with wider ranges of individual scores have a harder time reaching consensus than groups whose individual scores were more similar? What effects, if any, did differences among the opinions of individual members have on your group's ability to reach consensus?

3. How might a group use socialization to improve its ability to reach group consensus? How might having clearly defined roles help the members of a group reach consensus more rapidly?

OUTCOME	GROUP 1	GROUP 2	GROUP 3 . . .
Range of individual scores (low-high)			
Average of individual scores			
Group score			

4. How might factors such as size, member motivation, cohesiveness, and the group's communication structure affect a group's ability to reach consensus? Could group judgment errors occur during the process of reaching consensus? What could be done to avoid these errors?

CONCLUSION

Requiring consensus acceptance increases the time it takes to make decisions and solve problems. However, it also enables every member to have an effect on the decisions that are made and encourages acceptance of those decisions. Whether consensus should be sought depends on a variety of factors. The need for speedy decisions will argue against it. If decision acceptance and commitment are important or if group members have uncommon abilities or insights that can be shared in consensus-building discussions, it would seem worthwhile to pursue consensus. The size and communication structure of the group will also affect the decision to seek consensus. Consensus can be very useful, but it can also be impractical.

DIAGNOSING ORGANIZATIONAL BEHAVIOR

CASE 11-1

HOVEY AND BEARD COMPANY*
GEORGE STRAUSS, *University of California, Berkeley*
ALEX BAVELAS, *Massachusetts Institute of Technology*

PART 1

The Hovey and Beard Company manufactured wooden toys of various kinds: wooden animals, pull toys, and the like. One part of the manufacturing process involved spraying paint on the partially assembled toys. The operation was staffed entirely by women.

The toys were cut, sanded, and partially assembled in the wood room. Then they were dipped into shellac, following which they were painted. The toys were predominantly two-colored; a few were made in more than two colors. Each color required an additional trip through the paint room.

For a number of years, production of these toys had been entirely handwork. However, to meet tremendously increased demand, the painting operation had recently been re-engineered so that the eight women who did the painting sat in a line by an endless chain of hooks. These hooks were in continuous motion, past the line of women and into a long horizontal oven. Each woman sat at her own painting booth, so designed as to carry away fumes and to backstop excess paint. She would take a toy from the tray beside her, position it in a jig inside the painting cubicle, spray on the color according to a pattern, then release the toy and hang it on the hook passing by. The rate at which the hooks moved had been calculated by the engineers so that each woman, when fully trained, would be able to hang a painted toy on each hook before it passed beyond her reach.

The women working in the paint room were on a group bonus plan. Since the operation was new to them, they were receiving a learning bonus which decreased by regular amounts each month. The learning bonus was scheduled to vanish in six months, by which time it was expected that they would be on their own— that is, able to meet the standard and to earn a group bonus when they exceeded it.

PART 2

By the second month of the training period, trouble had developed. The women learned more slowly than had been anticipated, and it began to look as though their production would stabilize far below what was planned for. Many of the hooks were going by empty. The women complained that the hooks were going by too fast, and that the time-study man had set the rates wrong. A few women quit and had to be replaced with new workers, which further aggravated the learning problem. The team spirit that the management had expected to develop automatically through the group bonus was not in evidence except as an expression of what the engineers called "resistance." One woman whom the group regarded as its leader (and the management regarded as the ringleader) was outspoken in making the various complaints of the group to the foreman: The job was a messy one, the hooks moved too fast, the incentive pay was not being correctly calculated, and it was too hot working so close to the drying oven.

* Exerpt from William Foote Whyte, *Money and Motivation* (New York: Harper & Row, Publishers, Inc., 1955). Reprinted by permission of the publisher.

PART 3

A consultant who was brought into this picture worked entirely with and through the foreman. After many conversations with him, the foreman felt that the first step should be to get the workers together for a general discussion of the working conditions. He took this step with some hesitation, but he took it on his own volition.

The first meeting, held immediately after the shift was over at 4:00 in the afternoon, was attended by all eight women. They voiced the same complaints again: The hooks went by too fast, the job was too dirty, the room was hot and poorly ventilated. For some reason, it was the last item that they complained of most. The foreman promised to discuss the problem of ventilation and temperature with the engineers, and he scheduled a second meeting to report back to the workers. In the next few days the foreman had several talks with the engineers. They and the superintendent felt that this was really a trumped-up complaint, and that the expense of any effective corrective measure would be prohibitively high.

The foreman came to the second meeting with some apprehension. The women, however, did not seem to be much put out, perhaps because they had a proposal of their own to make. They felt that if several large fans were set up so as to circulate the air around their feet, they would be much more comfortable. After some discussion, the foreman agreed that the idea might be tried out. The foreman and the consultant discussed the question of the fans with the superintendent, and three large propeller-type fans were purchased.

PART 4

The fans were brought in. The women were jubilant. For several days the fans were moved about in various positions until they were placed to the satisfaction of the group. The workers seemed completely satisfied with the results, and relations between them and the foreman improved visibly.

The foreman, after this encouraging episode, decided that further meetings might also be profitable. He asked the women if they would like to meet and discuss other aspects of the work situation. The women were eager to do this. The meeting was held, and the discussion quickly centered on the speed of the hooks. The women maintained that the time-study expert had set the hooks at an unreasonably fast speed and that they would never be able to reach the goal of filling enough of them to make a bonus.

The turning point of the discussion came when the group's leader frankly explained that the point wasn't that they couldn't work fast enough to keep up the hooks, but they couldn't work at that pace all day long. The foreman explored the point. The women were unanimous in their opinion that they could keep up with the belt for short periods if they wanted to. But they didn't want to because if they showed they could do this for short periods, they would be expected to do it all day long. The meeting ended with an unprecedented request: "Let us adjust the speed of the belt faster or slower, depending on how we feel." The foreman agreed to discuss this with the superintendent and the engineers.

The reaction of the engineers to the suggestion was negative. However, after several meetings, it was granted that there was some latitude within which variations in the speed of the hooks would not affect the finished product. After considerable argument with the engineers, it was agreed to try out the workers' ideas.

With misgivings, the foreman had a control with a dial marked "low, medium, fast" installed at the booth of the group leader; she could now adjust the speed of the belt anywhere between the lower and upper limits that the engineers had set.

PART 5

The women were delighted, and spent many lunch hours deciding how the speed of the belt should be varied from hour to hour throughout the day. Within a week the pattern had settled down to one in which the first half hour of the shift was run on what the women called medium speed (a dial setting slightly above the point marked "medium"). The next two and one-half hours were run at high speed; the half hour before lunch and the half hour after lunch were run at low speed. The rest of the afternoon was run at high speed with the exception of the last 45 minutes of the shift, which was run at medium.

In view of the women's reports of satisfaction and ease in their work, it is interesting to note that the constant speed at which the engineers had originally set the belt was slightly below medium on the dial of the control that had been given the women. The average speed at which the women were running the belt was on the high side of the dial. Few, if any, empty hooks entered the oven, and inspection showed no increase of rejects from the paint room.

Production increased, and within three weeks (some two months before the scheduled ending of the learning bonus) the women were operating at 30 to 50 percent above the level that had been expected under the original arrangement. They were collecting their base pay, a considerable piece-rate bonus, and the learning bonus which, it will be remembered, had been set to decrease with time and not as a function of current productivity. The women were earning more now than many skilled workers in other parts of the plant.

PART 6

Management was besieged by demands that this inequity be taken care of. With growing irritation between superintendent and foreman, engineers and foreman, superintendent and engineers, the situation came to a head when the superintendent revoked the learning bonus and returned the painting operation to its original status. The hooks moved again at their constant, time-studied designated speed; production dropped again; and within a month, all but two of the eight workers had quit. The foreman himself stayed on for several months but, feeling aggrieved, then left for another job.

When you have read this case, look back at the chapter's diagnostic questions and choose the ones that apply to the case. Then use those questions with the ones that follow in your case analysis.

1. At what stage of development was the group of toy painters at Hovey and Beard? What does this tell you about the group's roles and norms? What kind of task was the group performing? Did the group's members have the required abilities? How did the group's roles, norms, and task affect its performance?

2. Explain why the workers were upset with the line speed established by management but then established an average line speed that was even higher. Why did productivity drop when the line was returned to its original speed?

3. Why did most of the workers quit their jobs? What made the company take actions that had such dire consequences? Is there anything the company could have done that would have restored equity with other parts of the plant without precipitating dissatisfaction among the painters?

CASE 11-2

THE SLAB YARD SLOWDOWN*

HAL B. GREGERSEN, *Brigham Young University*
PAUL H. THOMPSON, *Brigham Young University*

Even the tremendous roar of the nearby open-hearth furnace would not have drowned out Bob Flint's

* J. B. Ritchie and Paul H. Thompson, *Organizations and People: Readings, Cases, and Exercises in Organizational Behavior*, 3rd ed. (St. Paul: West Publishing Company (1984), pp. 144–47. Reprinted with publisher's permission. All rights reserved.

screams when he was handed the latest slab yard payroll report. Flint, a division superintendent at Midland Steel's Dayton, Ohio plant, was outraged to discover that a crew of "scarfers" had reported a 410 percent incentive pay performance level on last week's day shift. To earn the $81 hourly wage reported by the scarfers would have required a physically impossible work pace.

THE OVERALL STEEL PRODUCTION PROCESS

Raw iron ore is melted down in large blast furnaces to form basic pig-iron soup. The soup is transported to open-hearth furnaces where certain alloys are added to produce a molten steel mixture of malleability and strength, tailored to unique specifications. This mixture is reheated, then poured into ingot molds and transported to a mill for further processing.

In the mill, the ingot molds are removed and the ingots rolled and chopped into steel slabs of predetermined dimensions. After the slabs cool to 1,000 degrees, jet streams of water are turned on them to further reduce their temperature. At this point, the scarfers mount the steel slabs and use their torches to burn off any cracks, scabs, or blemishes on the slab surface. When the scarfers have completed their work, the slabs are transferred to a rolling mill, reheated, and rolled into either plates or coils, depending on customer specifications.

THE SCARFING PROCESS

The scarfers were specifically responsible for burning all cuts, cracks, scabs, and blemishes off the surface of the steel slabs before they were reheated and rolled into plates or coils in the rolling mill. Their function was vital, since failure to remove defects in the steel slabs could have resulted in scrapping much of the metal during the rolling process. The defects could ruin the metal in two ways: (1) impurities could prevent the steel from reaching the required level of malleability during reheat, causing the metal to snap during the coiling process; or (2) even a small blemish could become greatly enlarged during the rolling process; e.g.; a two-inch-wide blemish on the surface of a six-inch-thick slab of steel would be stretched out over the face of over 100 feet of finished product when the slab was rolled into a plate one-tenth of an inch thick.

The scarfers' task was achieved by standing on top of the steel slabs in thick, wooden-soled boots and cutting paths along the steel surface with a heavy blowtorch. Obviously, the working conditions were not comfortable. The workers endured the discomfort of extreme heat, bulky clothing and protective goggles, moisture from the water jets used to cool the slabs, and an immediate environment full of acid fumes from molten steel.

This harsh environment dictated that a scarfer be in top physical condition. Some of the workers were very large physically while others were not. Regardless of his size, each scarfer was exceptionally strong. The majority of the scarfers were either junior high or high school dropouts. Most scarfers would spend their entire working lives in the slab yard, working until well into their sixties; consequently, many had worked together for years. Over time, they had developed good friendships and did many things together after work.

Added to the physical discomforts of the environment and the monotony of the task were the inherent dangers of working in an enclosed area among eight-foot stacks of hot steel slabs. The slab yard was the division with the highest accident rate in the corporation. According to the shift foremen, a high percentage of Midland's scarfers had died on the job from accidents or from heart attacks caused by overexertion.

THE CURRENT INCENTIVE PLAN

Because scarfing was one of the most difficult, dangerous, and dirty tasks at Midland Steel, the job was more financially attractive than others. Under the current incentive plan, scarfing had become the highest-paying blue-collar position in the steel plant. In fact, good scarfers would make over $80,000 a year; consequently, they were considered by themselves and others to be the "elite" of steelworkers. However, the large pay differential between scarfers and other blue-collar workers created tension between the two groups.

The scarfers' incentive system was based on measures of production output, i.e., actual number of slabs and amount of square inches scarfed. Measurement of square inches and slab counts were performed by inspectors who were also responsible for slab quality. Markers carried out another function, that of marking areas on the slabs that needed scarfing. Markers, as well as inspectors, received compensation based on the number of slabs scarfed.

In addition to the piece-rate incentive system, management provided scarfers with a base pay which was calculated by the dollar amount of rolled or coiled steel which would have been wasted in absence of the scarfing process. To increase their variable incentive pay, scarfers had often skipped their hourly heat breaks.

When the bargaining union had first negotiated the incentive plan in 1966, management had expected scarfers to average about 150 percent of their base pay, but scarfers saw the incentive plan as a much larger money-making opportunity. Throughout the twenty-five years of the plan's existence, scarfers had averaged 262 percent of base pay.

THE PROBLEM

Under Midland Steel's quantity-oriented incentive system, division superintendent Flint knew that the scarfers had been cheating for years by altering their blowtorch tips so that they could scarf more steel slabs per shift, thereby earning a higher wage. The workers would simply drill larger holes in the tip of their blowtorch so that the flame broadened, enabling them to burn a larger path with one pass of the torch over the steel slab. The larger torch path enabled the scarfer to finish more slabs during a shift, thereby increasing his income. However, by broadening the torch flame, the worker also decreased the flame's intensity such that the burn into the steel would not penetrate deeply enough to lift out the defects and blemishes from the steel. Rather, the weaker flame would simply cover the defect with molten steel, hiding it from the inspector's visual check. These hidden defects resulted in costly scrap in the final steel making process.

In addition, markers would often mark slabs for scarfing that did not need treatment in order to increase slab count and total square inches scarfed. Since quantity incentives were also offered to inspectors, they typically qualified inferior steel as acceptable in order to increase their own and scarfers' pay.

The only real contact between the scarfers and management was via the shift foremen. The shift foremen were thought of as the bridge between white- and blue-collar workers (each shift had two foremen—one in each slab yard). Their function was to ensure that the scarfers worked safely, kept on schedule, and did quality work. This was not an easy task considering the strong-willed and independent-minded attitudes of the scarfers.

The shift foremen also had the task of inspecting the blowtorches. Because some of the scarfers had altered their tips, a large number of defects had caused the rejection of significant quantities of finished steel products. In order to decrease their rejection rate, the shift foremen conducted periodic inspections to ensure that the tips met regulations. Managers at any level higher than the shift foremen were prohibited by union contract from conducting these inspections themselves.

THE RAID

Management, including the shift foremen, believed that greed was the motivating force behind the scarfers' altering their blowtorch tips. Management also thought that the incentive plan was a problem in that it rewarded output but not quality. The newer scarfers particularly were seen as guilty because they had been under pressure to keep up with older employees. The tip alteration problem had been going on for a long time, and the finished product rejection rate at the Dayton plant was twice the corporate rate. With the obvious abuse of the incentive plan (410 percent by one crew for one period), management felt that it was time to make an example of the violators and to correct the abuses.

Blowtorch tip checks had been conducted before on the initiative of the shift foremen to discover and replace altered torch tips and to mildly reprimand the men, but Flint felt the whole thing had gone too far this time. Now was the time for more drastic action. Flint felt that the recent 410 percent incentive pay performance level provided him with an opportunity to slow the scarfers who was boss. It would also serve as an excuse for him to implement changes in the types of torch tips the scarfers used and in their incentive system.

Consequently, Bob Flint ordered his shift foremen to conduct an immediate torch tip check on all scarfing crews, telling them that any workers found using altered tips were, in his words, "to be dealt with." When Dee Colton, the shift foreman at the time, conducted a jobsite tip check in the slab yard, he found 50 percent of the scarfers using altered tips. Following past procedure, he issued each guilty worker a reprimand requiring two days off without pay. When Colton reported his actions to Flint, however, Flint was incensed. He demanded that Colton fire the guilty men immediately and that he fire any other scarfers found cheating in the next two shifts. Despite the fact that the first shift had warned the next shift—swing shift—that a tip check was on, three men supposed that the action taken would not be any different from that of the usual inspections and therefore they did not bother to change their tips. They were subsequently fired. By the time the graveyard shift shuffled into the slab yard that night, the word had gotten around that top management had its hands in this crackdown. No altered tips were found during the graveyard shift.

Two days later the scarfers began a wildcat slow-down which created a bottleneck potentially costing the company millions of dollars.

When you have read this case, look back at the chapter's diagnostic questions and choose the ones that apply to the case. Then use those questions with the ones that follow in your case analysis.

1. Midland Steel's scarfers all seemed to produce at about the same rate. Can you explain this? What specific factors contributed to the level of productivity accepted by the scarfers as a "fair day's work"?

2. Why didn't the scarfers expect to be fired even if caught with an altered torch tip? What caused the wildcat slowdown? What steps should Midland Steel's management have taken to deal with the slowdown?

3. What long-term changes need to be made to maintain productivity in the slab yard? What must management do to get the group of scarfers to change the way they perform the slab yard work?

CASE 11-3

EXECUTIVE RETREAT: A CASE OF GROUP FAILURE

Review this case, which you read in Chapter 4. Next, look back at Chapter 11's diagnostic questions and choose the ones that apply to the case. Then use those questions with the ones that follow in your case analysis.

1. Through what stages of development did John Matthews' group progress during the fifteen days it spent together? Did the group's development affect its ability to perform effectively? How?

2. What kind of task was the group performing? What abilities does such a group task require? Did the group have these abilities?

3. Explain why the group failed to accomplish most of its goals. If it were to reconvene and try to accomplish the same goals again, what advice would you give the group to improve its chances for success?

C H A P T E R 12

LEADERSHIP

One of the most charismatic leaders in history, Martin Luther King, Jr. had a dream of what society could be, a dream that millions of Americans made their own. Winner of the Nobel Peace Prize in 1964, King dedicated his life to achieving rights for all citizens by nonviolent methods.

And so, in May 1941, Hitler stood master of Europe. It was an incredible achievement. Less than ten years before, he had tricked and blundered his way into the leadership of a penniless and disarmed nation. Now, from the Pyrenees to the Arctic Circle, from Brittany to Warsaw to Crete, this ex-corporal ruled virtually unchallenged over more of Europe than any man that had governed since the days of the Roman Empire. And his friends and allies ruled in Moscow, Tokyo, Rome, Madrid. His only remaining enemy, Britain, was badly mauled and begging the United States for supplies.[1]

From the mid-1950s until the late 1960s, Martin Luther King was the most important leader of a non-violent civil rights movement that transformed the politics of America and inspired oppressed people throughout the world. During this period, black Americans attained more progress than in the previous century. The system of *de jure* segregation was overturned in the South and essential legislation was enacted, enabling blacks to make significant strides toward resolving . . . the conflict between the nation's democratic ideals of freedom and equality and its practice of denying basic rights to black citizens.[2]

As we noted in Chapter 11, few important tasks or goals can be accomplished by one person working alone. It is for this reason that there are so many organizations in our society. On the other hand, few groups or organizations can accomplish much without the help of a single individual acting as a leader. Leadership is the force that energizes and directs groups. Some leaders, like Hitler, move groups in ways that greatly hinder their ultimate survival. Others, like Martin Luther King Jr., move groups in directions that vastly improve their ultimate welfare. Given the centrality of leadership to the behavior of people in groups and to organizational achievement, whether good or evil, it is of paramount importance that we understand how leaders emerge and what makes them effective.

DIAGNOSTIC ISSUES

Our diagnostic model highlights several important questions in the area of leadership. Can we *describe* the characteristics of people who develop into strong leaders? How do differences among groups affect the kinds of leaders who emerge? Can we *diagnose* different leadership styles? Can we explain why some people who are capable managers never become capable leaders? Can we *prescribe* which behaviors a leader should engage in to stimulate both productivity and satisfaction? Can we predict which kinds of situations will enhance the effectiveness of a particular style of leadership? Finally, what *actions* can organizations take to screen people for leadership positions? What sorts of abilities and personality characteristics should we look for? When should leaders use group decision-making processes and when should they make decisions on their own?

[1] "World War II: The Desperate Years," *Time*, September 4, 1989, p. 34.
[2] J. A. Colaiaco, *Martin Luther King, Jr.* (New York: St. Martin's Press, 1988), p. 37.

DEFINING LEADERSHIP

Supreme Court Justice Potter Stewart was once asked to define pornography so as to distinguish it from more conventional art. He replied that although he could not define pornography, he certainly knew what it was when he saw it. You get a similar feel for people's conceptions of leadership. Most people have a hard time explaining what they mean by it, and those who do offer definitions disagree on some of the major dimensions. At the same time, when people are asked to name strong leaders throughout history, they respond in a remarkably consistent way. Table 12-1 lists a number of people who are almost always cited as strong leaders.

Looking at the list in Table 12-1 may give you an idea of how difficult it is to come up with a definition of leadership that is specific enough to be useful yet broad enough to include people that differ so greatly from each other. Try to think of characteristics of these people or of their followers or of the situations they faced that were common to all. Thinking about each of these historic figures and the contexts within which they served as leaders will help dramatize the complexity of the leadership concept for you. As you study this chapter it will help you understand why there has been so little consensus among theories of leadership.

Components of Leadership

One concept that you may have found in common among the people listed in Table 12-1 is their *ability to influence* others. The notion of influence certainly should be paramount in any definition of leadership. Yet would we consider a mugger who enters a subway train and induces the group gathered there to hand over their personal belongings a leader? Most people would recognize this person's influence but they would not consider his act one of leadership.

A leader's influence must to some degree be *sanctioned by followers*. In some situations a person may be compelled by her followers to lead, and in other situations a leader may be merely tolerated for the time being. Still, the idea that followers voluntarily surrender control over their own behavior to someone else seems to be an integral part of any definition of leadership. Finally, a complete definition of leadership must include the nature of the context in which leadership occurs. Leadership occurs in *goal-oriented* group contexts.

Leadership versus Management

It is important to distinguish between leadership and management, two concepts that are frequently confused. To begin with, in Mintzberg's conception of management (see Table 2-8 in Chapter 2), the role of leader is just one of ten roles

---

T A B L E 12-1
Conventional Examples of Strong Leaders

Adolf Hitler	Martin Luther King, Jr.
Mahatma Gandhi	Napoleon Bonaparte
Mao Tse-Tung	Moses
Franklin D. Roosevelt	Abraham Lincoln
Winston Churchill	Golda Meir

As Chairman of the Joint Chiefs of Staff and leader of the country's military forces, General Colin Powell symbolizes the strength and purpose of the United States both to the men and women he leads and to the rest of the world.

leadership The use of noncoercive influence to direct and coordinate the activities of the members of an organized group toward the accomplishment of group objectives.

commonly ascribed to managers. Leadership, according to Mintzberg, deals explicitly with guiding and motivating employees.[3] From this point of view leadership is a managerial task, albeit one that many believe today's managers fulfill rather poorly.

The literature offers almost innumerable definitions of leadership. However, Arthur Jago's is the one that best captures the essence of the three components we have enumerated and that maintains the manager-leader distinction. Jago has defined **leadership** as the use of noncoercive influence to direct and coordinate the activities of the members of an organized group toward the accomplishment of group objectives.[4]

THE IMPORTANCE OF LEADERSHIP

Leaders perform several essential functions for the groups they serve.[5] They are responsible for generating and maintaining the required *level of effort* needed from individual group members. Leaders are also responsible for *directing the effort* of group members in ways that promote group survival and goal accomplishment. One important aspect of directing groups is ensuring the *coordination of effort* among group members. Finally, leaders *facilitate group membership* by attracting people to the group and its mission and by meeting the needs of group members. In sum, leaders help move a group in directions consistent with its mission and at the same time hold the group together.

In addition to these four goal-directed functions, leaders serve an important symbolic function for both group members and outsiders. It is virtually impossible for every employee in an organization to understand everything that goes on in the firm, especially one surrounded by a complex, dynamic environment. As we saw in Chapter 5, when the complexity of a stimulus exceeds a person's cognitive capacity, the person attempts to simplify the stimulus. In the organizational context, the leader provides the means for much of this simplification.

The leader offers a logically compelling and emotionally satisfying focal point for people who are trying to understand the causes and consequences of organized activity. Many of these causes and consequences of what organizations

---

[3] Henry Mintzberg, *The Nature of Managerial Work*. (New York: Harper and Row, 1973).

[4] A. Jago, "Leadership: Perspectives in Theory and Research," *Management Sciences 28* (1982), 315–36.

[5] D. Katz and R. Kahn, *The Social Psychology of Organizations* (New York: John Wiley, 1978), p. 125–37.

do are obscure, uncertain, and perhaps even objectionable. Focusing on the leader reduces these complexities to simple terms that people can easily understand and communicate. Sometimes, of course, this leads to misguided actions. For example, when a baseball team has a losing season, the owner and fans take comfort in firing the manager, even when what might truly be needed is to fire all the players. According to Meindl and Ehrlich, "As an explanatory concept, leadership has assumed a special status. Not merely a prosaic alternative that people dispassionately consider on an equal footing with other explanations, it has achieved a heroic, larger-than-life value."[6]

In this chapter we will put leadership into perspective. We will integrate the many theories and lines of research on leadership into a single unifying framework. With an appreciation of the major themes and the significant results of the work that has been done on leadership, you will be in a position to apply this knowledge in becoming an effective leader yourself.

THE TRANSACTIONAL MODEL: A DIAGNOSTIC FRAMEWORK

To make it easier for you to understand the dozen or so different theories of leadership we explore in this chapter, we will start with a conceptual framework that encompasses each theory. With this framework in place, we can examine each approach and fit it into the overall scheme. This single framework will also allow us, in the last section of the chapter, to build one integrated model of leadership that incorporates significant features of each theory we discuss.

Edward Hollander has convincingly suggested that the leadership process is best understood as the occurrence of *mutually satisfying transactions* among leaders and followers within a particular situational context.[7] As Figure 12-1 indicates, the *locus of leadership* is found where these three forces—*leaders*, *followers*, and *situations*—come together. In Hollander's view, one can understand leadership only by gaining an appreciation of the important characteristics of these three forces and of the ways in which they interact.

[6] J. R. Meindl and S. B. Ehrlich, "The Romance of Leadership and the Evaluation of Organizational Performance." *Academy of Management Journal 30* (1987), 91–109.

[7] Edward P. Hollander, *Leadership Dynamics* (New York: Free Press, 1978).

FIGURE 12-1

The Transactional Model of Leadership

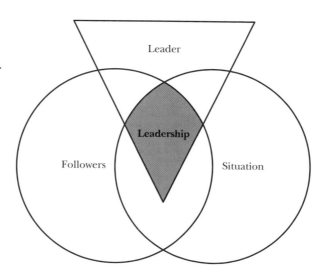

Leaders often recognize the important role played by their followers. At a 1936 speech in Nuremberg, for example, Hitler declared to 200,000 followers, "The wonder of this age is that you have found me—an unknown man among millions."[8] One nameless soldier-follower of Hitler's later remarked that "We, like the soldiers of other countries, were trained to obedience. We had not been brought up free to demonstrate our opposition under the protection of a liberal constitution. We had the same sensitivities that all humans have, but during a time of difficult decisions, we lacked political vision." The role of the follower has also been pointed to by Martin Luther King Jr.'s biographers. Ella Baker writes that "the movement made Martin rather than Martin making the movement."[9]

To appreciate the importance to a leader of followers, ask yourself the following questions. Could a person with Hitler's characteristics rise to power in a post-Vietnam war United States, where opposing almost any government act is close to a national pastime? Could King's peaceful, patient approach to civil rights have won the hearts of Shiite Muslims in Iran after the fall of the shah? Can anyone establish a position of leadership with people, such as a group of intellectuals, who reject the very idea that they need to be led?[10]

Turning to the characteristics of the situation, would Mahatma Gandhi's program of civil disobedience have been as successful had he been opposing the Nazis instead of the British? In 1989, could Tadeusz Mazowiecki have risen as the first non-Communist leader of Poland in forty years if the Polish economy had not been in total shambles? At Apple Computer, John Sculley reportedly believed in "borderline anarchy" and held that "a good company should constantly be stretching." Would Sculley's practice of almost annual reorganization in an industry where creativity is king have been effective if he had been the manager of a ball-bearing plant? These questions underline the complex nature of leadership and the important contribution to successful leadership of the three distinct elements of leader, follower, and situation.

Not all theoretical approaches to leadership emphasize the three-dimensional character of the leadership process proposed by Hollander. In fact, as we will see, universal approaches generally focus on one dimension, interaction approaches on two, and only a few, comprehensive approaches consider all three dimensions. We will examine each of these approaches in turn.

UNIVERSAL APPROACHES TO LEADERSHIP

Some of the earliest probes into the nature of leadership focused almost uniformly on leader characteristics. These *universal theories* emphasized personality traits, abilities, typical behaviors, and decision-making styles. These first approaches were followed by others that also focused on just one aspect of leadership—either the follower or the situation. Born out of the failure of leader-focused studies to explain the richness of the leadership process, these newer, anti-leadership theories discounted the leader almost entirely.

Qualities of the Leader

The earliest approaches to leadership, often referred to as the *great man theories of leadership*, held that leaders were born, not made. Sir Francis Galton, whose

---

[8] "World War II: Blitzkrieg," *Time*, August 28, 1989, p. 39.

[9] D. J. Garrow, *Bearing the Cross* (New York: Random House, 1986), p. 2.

[10] Hedley Donovan, "Managing Your Intellectuals," *Fortune*, October 29, 1989, pp. 177–80.

studies of individual differences we discussed in Chapter 4, argued in 1869 that the qualities found in great leaders were inherited. Later, researchers influenced by behavioral schools of thought discarded this idea, suggesting instead that the characteristics associated with successful leadership could be learned.

Physical and Mental Abilities. Studies of the physical characteristics of leaders have yielded rather weak but consistent relationships between a person's *energy level* and her ability to rise to a position of leadership.[11] Still weaker and less consistent results have been found for characteristics like height. Oddly, we tend to think of leaders as tall people even though many are not. Consider the leaders listed in Table 12-1. No more than half of them could have been considered tall or physically imposing people.

Research on mental abilities has produced few substantial predictors of leadership quality and effectiveness, although again some consistent findings have been reported. *General cognitive ability* (intelligence—see Chapter 4) seems to be one of the best overall predictors of leadership ability.[12] Specific *technical skills* or *knowledge about a group's task* also show modest relationships with success in leadership.[13]

Personality Characteristics. Researchers have related the development and effectiveness of leadership skills to almost all of the five classes of personality characteristics that we examined in Chapter 4. For example, there is evidence that leaders tend to exhibit the social trait of *dominance*, and that leadership potential is associated with the motives of *need for achievement* and *need for power*.[14] In addition, the personality dynamic of *self-esteem* (or self-confidence or self-assurance) seems to be related to leadership across a wide variety of situations and followers.[15]

These findings notwithstanding, for every personality characteristic that does appear to be related to leadership potential, skill, or effectiveness there are probably ten others for which no such evidence exists. As the "Management Issues" box indicates, even the basic moral character of the leader does not seem to relate in any simple manner to success. Moreover, the relations that have been found are modest at best. It was this failure to find significant relationships between leadership and individual personal qualities that led researchers to explore other approaches to understanding this important concept.

Leader Behaviors

University of Michigan Studies. In the late 1950s, Rensis Likert and other researchers at the University of Michigan began a series of leadership studies. They set out to identify aspects of leaders' behavior that might differentiate those who performed well from those who did not. Interviewing supervisors and clerical workers at the Prudential Insurance Company, these investigators concluded that there were two general classes of supervisory behavior.[16] **Employee-centered**

employee-centered behaviors
Leadership behaviors designed to meet the social and emotional needs of group members.

[11] G. Yukl, *Leadership in Organizations* (Englewood Cliffs, NJ: Prentice Hall, 1981), p. 71.

[12] R. M. Stodgill, *Handbook of Leadership* (New York: Free Press, 1974), p. 112.

[13] R. Katz, "Skills of an Effective Administrator," *Harvard Business Review 72* (1974), pp. 90–101.

[14] E. Constantini and K. H. Craik, "Personality and Politicians: California Party Leaders, 1960–1976," *Journal of Personality and Social Psychology 38* (1980), 641–61; and E. G. Ghiselli, *Explorations in Managerial Talent* (1966), p. 92.

[15] Jago, "Leadership," p. 319.

[16] Rensis Likert, *New Patterns of Management* (New York: McGraw-Hill, 1961), p. 36.

MANAGEMENT ISSUES

Managers and Moral Leadership: Is Pursuing Self-Interest Enough?

The predominant business ideology in the United States holds that when firms and individuals pursue their own self-interests, market forces bring about the most efficient use of resources and result in the greatest satisfaction of people's needs. Apparent breakdowns in this theory could be seen, for example, in the days of the Industrial Revolution when sweatshops employed ten-year-olds for seventy-hour work weeks. Although using cheap child labor was in a firm's self-interest, it was quite questionable whether this was in the best interests of society as a whole. Similar debates have appeared more recently on *greenmail, golden parachutes, downsizing, insider trading,* and *acid rain.** In each of these areas, one could argue that the interests of the few are at odds with the interests of the many.

Organizational leaders have to balance the needs of executives, employees, consumers, stockholders, suppliers, distributors, and the general public, all the while keeping their companies financially secure. With all this to manage, is it fair to ask them to be moral leaders of the nation and their communities as well? This is a volatile issue that is likely to generate considerable debate in the years ahead.

Clearly when one looks at contemporary business leaders it seems that what is traditionally defined as a strong moral character is neither a requisite of nor a deterrent to leadership success. Roy Vagelos is the CEO of Merck and Company, a large and highly successful pharmaceutical firm. Several years ago, Merck developed a drug named ivermectin that cured river blindness. River blindness is caused by the bite of a particular variety of fly that deposits a parasite in a person. The parasite can grow to two feet in length. If and when it reaches the victim's eye, blindness results. The disease has afflicted an estimated 40 million people in Africa, the Middle East, and Latin America. Unfortunately, the drug was expensive to produce, and most people who needed it could not afford to pay for it. Vagelos directed Merck to donate the drug to the World Health Organization (WHO) despite the substantial expense associated with this giveaway.†

James Burke, CEO of Johnson and Johnson has also been recognized as a moral business leader for his handling of the Tylenol tampering incident. In this incident, seven people died when an anonymous person placed cyanide in capsules that were already on store shelves. Even though Johnson and Johnson was clearly not responsible for the poisonings, Burke directed the company to recall all unused Tylenol, at a cost of over $100 million. Burke went on many television talk shows in a one man crusade to save Johnson and Johnson's image. Today, both Tylenol and Johnson and Johnson are stronger than ever, and Burke has become recognized as a business hero. In his own estimation, the reason the Tylenol rescue succeeded was "not that we did anything clever, but just that we are a company that tries to do the right thing."‡

Other business leaders have built financially successful enterprises despite being "at the margin" on ethical issues. For example, Thomas Jones, the longtime controversial CEO of Northrup, has been pursued almost constantly for potentially unethical or illegal activity. Northrup is a large aviation defense contractor that produces, among other things, the F-20 Tigershark fighter, the Stealth bomber, and the guidance system for the MX missile. In the 1960s Jones established a secret fund in Paris to launder illegal political contributions in the United States. In the early 1970s Northrup was again involved in scandal when it gave a bribe of $450,000 to two Saudi Arabian generals. Later, in 1974, Jones pleaded guilty to illegally contributing $150,000 to Richard Nixon's presidential campaign. Then, in 1983, Northrup was charged with influence peddling involving a bribe of $55 million made to a Korean official to help get his government to purchase a large number of F-20s. In 1988, Jones fought several suits brought by Northrup's own employees. They claimed that the company had billed the government $400 million in false labor charges for work supposedly done on the secret Stealth bomber.

Yet despite all this turbulence, Jones has engineered a successful financial performance for Northrup. One ex-Northrup executive commented, "Jones did a phenomenal job with the company. When I joined in 1963, the company had broken the $300 million mark. Now it sells more than $3 billion. I do think he tends to cut corners a bit ethically sometimes. . . . He'll do whatever is required for his company."§

Although one could debate forever the utility or disutility of a strong moral character as a requisite for leadership, what should not be overlooked in this debate is that leadership inherently involves moral philosophy. In the process of selecting and pursuing economic or social goals and policies, the leader of an organization is guided by his values and moral principles. Many times the values behind the leader's behavior are not even well thought out or articulated. Nevertheless, the leader's actions are value based. Moreover, these values are communicated, often subliminally, to followers and thus affect their behaviors. As one ethics scholar has commented, "The challenge for the manager is not whether to include ethical theory and criteria in strategic choice, but rather when and how."∥

---

* G. F. Cavanagh, *American Business Values* (Englewood Cliffs, NJ: Prentice Hall, 1990).
† M. Waldoz, "Merck to Donate Drug for "River Blindness," *The Wall Street Journal*, October 22, 1987, p. 38.

‡ L. Shames, *The Big Time: Harvard Business School's Most Successful Class and How It Shaped America* (New York: Mentor, 1986), p. 159.
§ R. Nader and W. Taylor, *The Big Boys* (New York: Pantheon Press, 1986), p 210.
∥ E. A. Murray, "Ethics and Corporate Strategy," in *Corporations and the Common Good,* ed. Robert B. Dickie and Leroy S. Rouner (Notre Dame: University of Notre Dame Press, 1986), p 115.

job-oriented behaviors
Leadership behaviors that focus on careful supervision of employees' work methods and performance level.

consideration leader behavior aimed at meeting the social and emotional needs of workers such as helping them, doing them favors, looking out for their best interests, and explaining decisions

initiating structure leader behaviors aimed at meeting the group's task requirements, such as getting workers to follow rules, monitoring performance standards, clarifying roles, and setting goals

The employee-centered, circular management structure initiated by Frances Hesselbein when she was executive director of the Girl Scouts of America does away with the traditional rising layers of management. According to Hesselbein, this type of management enables people to move "across" the organizational structure rather than up or down and fosters innovation and creativity.
Source: John A. Byrne, "Profiting from the Nonprofits," Business Week, March 26, 1990, pp. 66–74.

behavior aimed at meeting the social and emotional needs of group members. **Job-oriented behavior** focused on careful supervision of employees' work methods and task accomplishment. These two orientations were seen as mutually exclusive. A leader could display one pattern or the other but not both.

The first group of studies at Michigan indicated that work attitudes were better and productivity was higher in the groups led by supervisors who displayed employee-centered behaviors. These studies, however, measured both the independent and the dependent variables at the same time. As a result, we cannot tell whether supervisors' personal concern caused the high productivity and good attitudes or whether these positive employee behaviors attracted supervisory attention.

To clarify this point, Morse and Reimer undertook a follow-up field study in which they trained some supervisors to use job-centered behaviors and others to use employee-centered behaviors in interacting with employees.[17] The results of this study supported one of the earlier findings but not the other. Leaders' employee-centered behavior did appear to cause more positive attitudes among workers. However, productivity was higher among workers supervised by leaders who used a job-centered approach.

Ohio State University Studies. While Likert and his colleagues were exploring the effects of different leader behaviors, Edwin Fleishman was conducting similar research at Ohio State University. Analyzing workers' responses to a questionnaire by means of a sophisticated statistical procedure, the Ohio State group concluded that most supervisory behaviors could be assigned to either one of two dimensions: **consideration** or **initiating structure**.[18] Table 12-2 shows some items from the Leadership Behavior Description Questionnaire (LBDQ) that evolved out of the original Ohio State studies. As you can see, the consideration dimension resembles the Michigan group's employee-centered orientation. Both dimensions address individual and social needs of workers. Similarly, the initiating structure dimension is like the job-centered orientation identified by Likert and his associates. Both of these dimensions focus on issues of supervision and task accomplishment.

Despite their similarities, the Michigan and Ohio State conceptions differ in an important way. The former sees the two dimensions of leader behavior as mutually exclusive, whereas the latter sees these dimensions as coexisting. Thus, as Figure 12-2 suggests, a leader might be high on both consideration and initiating structure, high on one dimension and low on the other, low on both, moderately high on one and low on the other—or almost any combination of degrees on the two dimensions. Subsequent research with the scales has suggested that the relationship between the two dimensions is neither perfectly negative (as the Michigan studies imply) or perfectly zero (as the Ohio State studies imply). Rather, in roughly half the studies that used both sets of scales, a weak, positive relationship between the two was apparent.[19] In other words, there is a slight tendency for leaders who are considerate to initiate structure.

Initially it was thought that the most effective leader is one who engages in both consideration and initiating-structure types of behavior. Research at Navistar (formerly International Harvester) failed to indicate any clear pattern, however. Consideration seemed to relate positively to worker attitudes but not

---

[17] N. C. Morse and E. Reimer, "The Experimental Change of a Major Organizational Variable," *Journal of Abnormal and Social Psychology 52* (1956), 120–29.

[18] R. M. Stodgill and A. E. Coons, *Leader Behavior: Its Description and Measurement* (Columbus, OH: Ohio State University, Bureau of Business Research, 1957), p. 75.

[19] P. Weissenberg and M. H. Kavanaugh, "The Independence of Initiating Structure and Consideration: A Review of the Evidence, *Personnel Psychology 25* (1972), 119–30.

> **T A B L E 12-2**
> **Items Similar to Items in the Leader Behavior
> Description Questionnaire**

Consideration Items
1. Is easy to get along with
2. Puts ideas generated by the group into operation
3. Treats everyone the same
4. Lets followers know of upcoming changes
5. Explains actions to all group members

Initiation of Structure Items
1. Tells group members what is expected
2. Promotes the use of standardized procedures
3. Makes decisions about work methods
4. Clarifies role relationship among group members
5. Sets specific goals and monitors performance closely

to productivity. Initiating structure was not clearly related to either attitudes or productivity.[20]

The Leadership Grid®. Despite the conflicting results of the Michigan and Ohio State studies on the behavioral dimensions of leadership, Blake and Mouton developed the notion of the managerial grid, republished in 1991 as the **leadership grid figure** by Blake and McCanse.[21] Based on their own research, Blake and Mouton identified two attitudinal dimensions, as distinguished from the behavioral dimensions identified at Ohio and Michigan. As Figure 12-3 shows, the leadership grid proposes five different styles of leadership, based on the interaction between *concern for people* and *concern for production*. Each of these two dimensions is measured on a scale of 1 (low) to 9 (high). Blake and Mouton have

leadership grid figure A two-dimensional representation of leadership behaviors in which concern for people and concern for production combine to produce five behavioral styles.

[20] Stodgill and Coons, *Leader Behavior*, p. 112.

[21] R. Blake and J. S. Mouton, *The Managerial Grid III: The Key to Leadership Excellence* (Houston: Gulf Publishing Co., 1985); and R. Blake and A. A. McCanse, *Leadership Dilemmas—Grid Solutions* (Houston: Gulf Publishing Co, 1991).

F I G U R E 12-2

**Initiating Structure
and Consideration in the
Ohio State Studies**

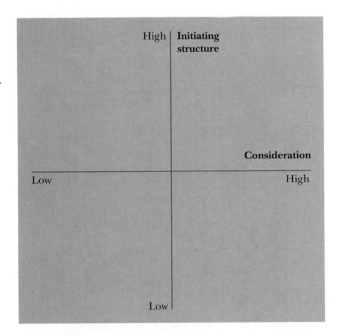

FIGURE 12-3

The Leadership Grid® Figure

Source: The Leadership Grid® Figure from Leadership Dilemmas—Grid Solutions, by Robert R. Blake and Anne Adams McCanse. Houston: Gulf Publishing Company, p. 29. Copyright © 1991, by Scientific Methods, Inc. Reproduced by permission of the owners.

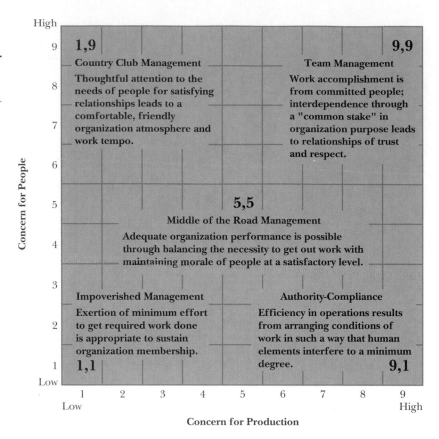

explicitly stated that the 9,9 Team Management style (see the upper righthand corner of the grid) is "the one best way" to lead, and they have developed an elaborate training program to move managers in that direction. Managers find the program appealing because it points to two specific sets of behaviors—consideration and initiating structure—that they can engage in to enhance the attitudes and performance of their group.

Despite its appeal, however, the managerial grid approach lacks empirical support from rigorous scientific studies, either in the lab or in the field. In fact, some investigators have gone so far as to label the whole 9,9 idea a myth.[22] In response to such criticisms, Blake and Mouton have offered only a conceptual defense, arguing that their theory *should* work.[23] In the absence of sound, supportive empirical data from independent researchers, it is hard to see the managerial grid as the final word on leadership effectiveness. Indeed, a good deal of research argues against the notion that there is any "one best way" of leading, irrespective of followers and situations.

Leaders' Decision-Making Styles

At the time of the Michigan and Ohio State studies, a third line of research on universal approaches to leadership was well under way under the direction of Kurt Lewin at the University of Iowa. The Iowa group studied the leader's manner

---

[22] L. L. Larson, J. G. Hunt, and R. Osburn, "The Great Hi-Hi Leader Myth: A Lesson from Occam's Razor," *Academy of Management Journal 19* (1976), 628–41.

[23] R. Blake and J. S. Mouton, "A Comparative Analysis of Situationalism and 9,9 Management by Principle," *Organizational Dynamics 24* (1982), 21.

LEADERSHIP

When Rosetta Riley took over the job of quality chief at Cadillac in 1985, customers were complaining that the company's cars were less powerful and smaller than they used to be. Using a democratic style of leadership, Riley worked with fellow executives and local dealers to create a new responsiveness to customers. She encouraged dealers to alert headquarters to problems and urged executives to begin calling recent buyers to ask how they liked their cars. Soon, market research reports were ranking Cadillac first among U.S. cars in terms of overall customer satisfaction.
Source: "Commissar of Quality," Fortune, *March 25, 1991, p. 131.*

authoritarian leader A leader who makes almost all decisions by herself, minimizing the input of subordinates.

democratic leader A leader who works to ensure that all subordinates have a voice in making decisions.

laissez-faire leader A leader who lets a group run itself, with minimal intervention from upper levels of the organizational hierarchy.

of making decisions and the effect that varying decision styles had on subordinates' rates of productivity and general satisfaction.

Lewin and his colleagues looked at three different decision-making styles: authoritarian, democratic, and laissez faire. The **authoritarian leader** made virtually all decisions by himself. The **democratic leader** worked with the group to help members come to their own decisions. The **laissez-faire leader** did just what this French term means—he left the group alone to do whatever it wanted.

The first Iowa study examined these leadership styles in groups of ten-year-old boys who were members of a hobby club. The investigators found that almost every group preferred a democratic leader best. Members of groups led by an authoritarian leader were either extremely submissive or extremely aggressive in interacting with each other. They were the most likely of any club members to quit the organization. Authoritarian groups were the most productive but only when members were closely supervised. When left alone, these groups tended to stop working. The results of this decision-style research were interesting and provocative. Like the personal characteristic and behavioral approaches discussed earlier, however, the Iowa studies revealed only rather modest relationships between leader style and follower behavior.

These three streams of early leadership research focused almost exclusively on the qualities of the leader. Although this early work has been abandoned, it continues to influence current theoretical and experimental work. Almost all of the comprehensive theories that we will discuss shortly include the three principal ways of characterizing a leader that we have explored: abilities and personal characteristics, behavioral styles, and decision-making styles (Figure 12-4). The value of this initial work lies also in its having pointed the way to the phenomena we look at next—the situation in which the leader finds himself and the followers who surround him.

Anti-Leadership Approaches

The primary problem of all three of the approaches we have discussed is that they specify one best way to lead regardless of the characteristics of followers and situations. Subsequent research has cast doubt on this notion. For example, although leadership requires intelligence, one study indicated that if a leader is far more intelligent than her followers, she may have difficulty communicating with them. As a result she may be less effective than a leader of more modest

FIGURE 12-4

Three Leadership Dimensions

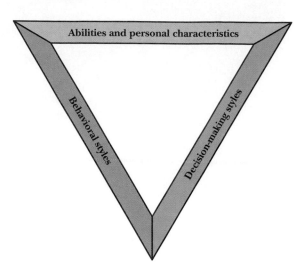

intelligence.[24] Another study that looked at decision-making styles among consumer-loan officers suggested that some followers actually prefer authoritarian leaders.[25] Finally, a number of studies indicate that initiating structure is more likely to be associated with increased productivity when tasks are complex than when they are relatively simple.[26] Findings like these led some to the conclusion that leadership per se did not really matter that much, and several *anti-leadership theories* began to take shape.

Situations and Leader Irrelevance. Jeffrey Pfeffer has argued that leadership is actually quite irrelevant to most organizational outcomes.[27] Pfeffer stresses a situation-based approach to understanding leadership. First, he says, *factors outside the leader's control* tend to affect profits and other critical elements in the business context more than anything a leader might do. Consider the recent plight of Lockheed Airlines. Much of this firm's revenue comes from defense contracts. When the federal government's 1990 budget slashed defense spending dramatically, CEO Daniel Tellep found himself almost powerless to prevent massive losses.

Second, even leaders at relatively high levels tend to have *unilateral control over only a few resource*s. Moreover, the capricious use of any set of resources is constrained by the leader's obligation to account for her behavior to other people both within and outside the organization. Even the CEO of a major corporation has to answer to shareholders, consumers, and government regulators.

Finally, the *selection process* through which all leaders must go filters people in such a way that those in leadership positions tend to act in similar ways. For example, the process used to select the president of the United States makes it impossible for some types of people (for example, illiterates, introverts, radicals of either the left or right, or people with past sexual indiscretions) to rise to that position. The people who make it through screening procedures of this kind tend to be alike in more ways than they are different. According to Pfeffer, "homogenizing" leaders in this way reduces the impact that any change in leadership has on an organization's outcomes. For all these reasons, Pfeffer has argued,

[24] Stodgill, *Handbook of Leadership*, p. 70.

[25] H. Tosi, "Effect of the Interaction of Leader Behavior and Subordinate Authoritarianism," Proceedings of the Annual Convention of the American Psychological Association, 1971, 473–74.

[26] A. K. Korman, "Consideration, Initiating Structure, and Organizational Criteria: A Review," *Personnel Psychology 19* (1966), 349–61.

[27] J. Pfeffer, "The Ambiguity of Leadership," *Academy of Management Review 2* (1977), 104–12.

situations are much more important determinants of events than leader characteristics.

Followers and Attribution Theory. Other anti-leader approaches emphasize follower perceptions as the key component of leadership. *Attribution theory* (see also Chapter 5) starts out with the relatively straightforward notion that people need to be able to make sense of the world around them. In particular, they need to be able to infer causes for important things that happen in their lives.[28]

In determining the causes of events, however, people have a built-in tendency to give too much credit to other people or to place too much blame on them.[29] Therefore, even though leaders may have little impact on their organizations, it is important for people both inside and outside the organization to think that the leader's impact is great. Attributing organizational outcomes to leaders makes the follower's world seem more predictable and manageable. For example, if the local economy is failing, people need to figure out why. In drawing conclusions about the causes of this situation, people are much more likely to direct their attention to the mayor's office than to esoteric notions of business cycles. People feel they can exercise some control over the mayor's actions because they can defeat him in the next election or even impeach him. They feel powerless, however, in the face of business cycles. People need heroes and scapegoats, and the leader, according to the attributional approach, fulfills this need.

In this framework, the successful leader is sensitive to the causal attributions of followers and can *manipulate followers' causal perceptions* in a favorable manner. Successful leaders can separate themselves from organizational failures and associate themselves with organizational successes. A president facing a large budget deficit might blame the shortfall on previous administrations and at the same time take credit for low unemployment rates, which could just as easily be attributed to past administrations.

Critique of Anti-Leadership Theories. Like the universal theories of leadership, the theories that emphasize either situations or followers seem overly simplistic. For example, in support of his leadership irrelevance conception, Pfeffer interpreted a study by Lieberson and O'Connor as concluding that "compared to other factors, administration had limited effects on organizational outcomes." If one examines this study closely, however, one finds that its authors actually concluded that "leadership influence on profit margins exceeds that for either industry or company effects."[30] It would seem that leadership can affect even bottom-line figures.

Although followers' perceptions are certainly central to leadership, even attributional models show how these perceptions are influenced from the very outset by leader behaviors. Each of the universal approaches we have discussed lays out an important part of the leadership transaction process—the characteristics of either the leader, the situation, or the follower. Because of their single-variable focus, however, none of these approaches is adequate.

Substitutes for Leadership. Kerr and Jermier's substitutes for leadership theory can be seen as a conservative version of the various anti-leadership approaches. Although this theory emphasizes characteristics of situations and followers, it

[28] B. J. Calder, "An Attribution Theory of Leadership," in *New Directions in Organizational Behavior*, ed. B. Staw and G. Salancik (Chicago: St. Clair Press, 1976).

[29] Fritz Heider, *The Psychology of Interpersonal Relations*. (New York: John Wiley, 1958), pp. 15–21.

[30] S. Leiberson, and J. F. O'Connor, "Leadership and Organizational Performance: A Study of Large Corporations," *American Sociological Review 37* (1972), 117–30.

Succession Planning: The Leader's Final Test

When Raymond Danner, founder and CEO of Shoney's, Inc., appointed J. Mitchell Boyd to succeed him, he took his successor into his office and showed him a plaque on the wall. Engraved there was the statement, "The final test of greatness in a CEO is how well he chooses a successor." Six months later, however, Danner and his associates on Shoney's board of directors pressured Boyd into resigning his new post. Shoney's stock dropped from $13\frac{1}{8}$ to $12\frac{1}{8}$ the day that Boyd resigned, and it appeared that Ray Danner was about to flunk that final test of greatness.

According to David K. Wachtel, president of Charley O's restaurant chain and former CEO of Shoney's, this was "the classic case of the founder not being able to get over his ego and let go." Clearly, Danner could not have been upset with the financial performance of Shoney's under Boyd's reign. With Boyd at the helm, the company experienced earnings of $115 million on sales of $680 million—$10 million more in profits than Danner himself had projected.

The problems with Boyd seemed to be over differences in corporate direction and personal style. Danner's focus was on day-to-day operations, holding down costs and sticking to Shoney's short but experience-tested menu. Danner, the son of a poor Louisville paperhanger, had a rough-and-ready leadership style—he often terrorized employees. For example, Danner once shoved a cook's arm into a large vat of soup to drive home the point that the soup was not hot enough to serve. Boyd on the other hand was smooth and polished, an intellectual with a prestigious MBA background. He spent much more money on marketing and advertising and was continuously experimenting with the restaurant's menu.*

Problems associated with leadership succession are hardly limited to Shoney's. Since Perry Ellis died in 1986, the fashion company that bears his name has faced nothing but adversity. After Ellis's death, the firm lost many key employees and went through several unsuccessful managerial changes. Despite attempts to restructure, the firm has struggled to maintain market share in the face of rising criticism that the clothes produced lack quality and appeal.

Although the importance of leadership-succession planning has long been recognized (in fact, no less a figure than God told Moses to instruct his successor, Joshua, on how to carry on after Moses left) there are built-in problems associated with shifting power that make it a difficult task nonetheless. To begin with, truly exceptional leaders are rare. As we have seen, legendary leaders are usually the result of a unique, one-time alignment of leader, follower, and situational characteristics. In addition, these kinds of leaders are rarely able to teach others the same vision or inspirational skills that made them so successful. In fact, they may shine so brightly and be so imposing that they drive away or stifle others who might otherwise be effective leaders.

Nowhere is this more evident than in entrepreneurial, family-run businesses. The child of such a family rarely feels free to be his own person. For example, Frederick Wang was never able to manage Wang Laboratories as successfully as his father, An Wang, the founder of the company. In fact, things got so bad that the father had to force his son to resign as president and CEO after the firm suffered a string of losses and problems in 1988.†

To avoid some of the pitfalls in succession, firms can

* W. Konrad, "Shoney's Needs a Recipe for Succession," *Business Week*, December 25, 1990, p. 52.

† G. Fuchsburg, "Loss of a Star Can Cast Shadow Over Firm," *The Wall Street Journal*, April 9, 1990, p. B1.

---

reintroduces leader behaviors to the process. In many ways, the substitutes approach solves many of the shortcomings of the other anti-leader approaches. It even borders on what we will classify later as comprehensive theories of leadership. For these reasons it will serve as a good bridge to the interactive and comprehensive approaches to leadership that we will discuss next.

substitute for leadership
Someone or something in the leader's environment that affects workers' attitudes, perceptions, or behaviors in such a way that the leader's role is made superfluous.

The **substitutes for leadership** theory argues that traditional leader behaviors such as initiating structure and consideration are often made irrelevant by certain characteristics of followers or situations.[31] According to the substitutes model, the success of a particular leadership behavior depends on characteristics of followers or of situations that can act to *substitute* for that particular behavior. Figure 12-5 illustrates the effect of a substitute. Here, consideration on the part of the leader leads to follower satisfaction when boring tasks must be performed. When tasks are intrinsically satisfying, however, leader consideration has no effect. It is not necessary because the satisfying nature of the task substitutes for the leader behavior.

[31] S. Kerr and J. M. Jermier, "Substitutes for Leadership: Their Meaning and Measurement" *Organizational Behavior and Human Decision Processes 22* (1978), 375–403.

take several steps. First, the leader should choose her successor long before the moment of transition. One advantage of this procedure is that the successor can acquire the kind of experience and knowledge that will be necessary when she takes hold of the reins. It also assures that succession takes place quickly and smoothly and reinforces the image that what is happening is not an unforseen emergency. Finally, it helps decrease some of the inevitable intragroup competition that can take place when power is suddenly up for grabs. In a battle for power, the firm is so gutted by strife and hard feelings that it is impossible for whoever emerges from the pack to lead effectively.

For example, Malcolm Forbes, Jr. held a press conference at Forbes headquarters the day after his father's death. Malcolm Jr., had already become president and deputy editor-in-chief at *Forbes* magazine, but he felt it necessary to assure financial writers at the conference that he was ready, willing, and able to guide Forbes through the next century.

Second, firms should explicitly remind both employees and the public at large that there is a lot more to their organization than just one person. This is true even at firms that have flaunted a strong leader in the past. For example, Fidelity Investments, Inc. always sold itself to investors by plugging the record of Peter Lynch—the stock analyzer who turned the firm's Magellan Fund into the nation's largest mutual fund. The day after Lynch made public his intention to leave Fidelity, the firm held a press conference. At this conference, they announced his successor, Morris Smith, and emphasized that Magellan made up only 11 percent of the firm's assets. Fidelity vice-president George Vanderheiden reassured investors that Fidelity "is a well-oiled machine,"—an analogy that explicitly depersonalized the reasons behind the firm's past success.‡

Third, while tempering the glorious history of the past leader, firms must also be careful to manage expectations about the new leader. The unique alignment of leader, follower, and situation that created the legendary leader may not be present for the new leader. The successor's credentials had better be able to speak for themselves, and excessive praise of the new leader at this point can often make matters worse. Lyman Wood, president of Brennan College Services, recalls, "My worst memory was having my predecessor trumpet my arrival out of all proportion—and there I was with no choice but to try to live up to these unrealistic expectations." Unrealistic expectations often wind up in anger and depression for both the new leader and the followers.§

Fourth, firms and ex-leaders should avoid making too many overly restrictive commitments that serve to bind the new leader. Confining her in this way will stifle her capacity for independent thought and action. It is natural for the ex-leader to hope that every small detail of his vision will continue indefinitely into the future—but that is unrealistic. The ex-leader's final acts are to groom a successor, develop a strong, multifaceted organization, and prepare the followers for the changeover. Then, all that is left is the hard part—getting out of the way.

‡ Ibid.
§ M. Feinberg, "Secrets of Successful Succession Planning," *The Wall Street Journal*, November 12, 1990, p. B1.

FIGURE 12-5

How a Situational Characteristic Can Substitute for Leader Behavior

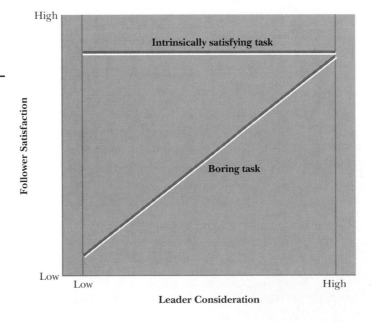

By far the most rigorous and comprehensive study of the substitutes concept has been conducted by Philip Podsokoff and his colleagues at Indiana University.[32] With a sample of over 600 people from three large firms, Podsokoff explored the degree to which 13 different variables moderated the relationship between seven different kinds of leader behaviors and eight possible outcomes. The comprehensiveness of this study is reflected in the fact that it allowed for a test of 728 (13 × 7 × 8) possible substitute effects.

Only 44 of the possible 728 interactions were statistically significant, and only 19 of these were in the predicted direction. Inasmuch as these numbers are close to what one would expect to find by chance, the results of this study cast doubt on the substitutes for leadership approach.

The substitutes for leadership theory did solve some of the problems with the universal approaches to leadership by incorporating the three components of leader, follower, and situation. It also rejected the narrow focus and the one-best-way philosophy. However, the substitutes approach has a major shortcoming in its lack of strong theoretical links explaining when and why various aspects of leadership and characteristics of followers or situation interact. The theories discussed in the next two sections retain many of the virtues of the substitutes approach—its broader scope and notion of contingency—but tighten the theory relating the leader to the situation and follower. Moreover, as the "In Practice" box on pages 422–23 shows, nothing can substitute completely for a leader. Leader replacement and succession are often difficult issues to manage, but they are critical to firms in a state of transition.

INTERACTION THEORIES OF LEADERSHIP

Interaction theories of leadership see the leadership process as evolving out of an interaction between two dimensions. For example, the influence of one dimension, such as leader behavior, may be contingent upon the nature of a second dimension, such as the situation. Although certainly more complex than the universal theories, these later approaches still neglect one major component of the transactional framework.

The Leadership Motivation Pattern

The theory behind the leadership motivation pattern grew out of David McClelland's research on characteristics of the leader.[33] McClelland has proposed that leaders must either have a high need for achievement (see Chapter 7) or display what he has called the **leadership motivation pattern (LMP)**. The leadership motivation pattern is a composite of three specific characteristics: a high need for power, a low need for affiliation with others, and a high degree of self-control.

McClelland also argues that there are two types of leadership situations. The *entrepreneurial situation* is found in small organizations or in small technical units in large organizations where a few key people do most of the work them-

leadership motivation pattern (LMP) A composite behavior pattern composed of a high need for power, a low need for affiliation, and a high degree of self control, that predicts success in bureaucratic leadership situations.

---

[32] P. M. Podsokoff, B. P. Niehoff, S. B. McKenzie, and M. L. Williams, *Organizational Behavior and Human Decision Processes*, in press.

[33] David McClelland, *Power: The Inner Experience* (New York: Irvington, 1975).

selves. The *bureaucratic situation* is found in the context of large, formalized, tightly structured organizations.

McClelland suggests that need for achievement is critical to leaders in entrepreneurial situations and that the leadership motivation pattern is essential for success in bureaucratic situations. According to McClelland, people high in need for achievement are primarily interested in their own progress and much less interested in influencing and encouraging others. As a result, although the need for achievement is useful in small groups or technical groups where one person's progress readily spills over into group progress, it is not that critical for leadership success in large organizations.

In large, bureaucratic organizations, the three-characteristic configuration of the leadership motivation pattern is much more useful. A person who has a strong need for power also has an interest in influencing and controlling others, a prerequisite for leading a group of people. A low need for affiliation enables a leader to make difficult decisions without worrying excessively about being unpopular. Finally, high self-control makes it possible for a person to use his power to get things done within the organizational rules of the game.

How do these predictions work out in the real world? One study of 246 AT&T managers, hired between 1956 and 1960 and followed up 16 years later, tested McClelland's theory.[34] The study predicted that high LMP scorers would be successful in nontechnical areas, which were generally bureaucratic in organizations, but not in technical ones, which tended to be more entrepreneurial. The results, plotted in Figure 12-6, show that this was exactly what happened. Nontechnical managers who had high LMP scores had a 75 percent rate of promotions. However, managers in technical units whose LMP scores were high had only a 25 percent promotion rate. The key to success for the latter managers was need for achievement. In fact, the correlation between need for achievement and success was twice as high in technical areas as in nontechnical ones.

These data strongly suggest that the effect of a set of leader characteristics on leaders' success depends on the situation in which the leader is performing. Entrepreneurial situations call for leaders high in need for achievement, but bureaucratic situations call for a leader high in LMP.

[34] David C. McClelland and R. E. Boyatzis, "Leadership Motive Patterns and Long-Term Success in Management," *Journal of Applied Psychology* 67 (1982), pp. 737–43.

FIGURE 12-6

Relation between LMP Scores and Success among AT&T Managers

Source: David C. McClelland and R. E. Boyatzis, "Leadership Motive Pattern and Long-Term Success in Management," Journal of Applied Psychology 67 *(1982), pp. 737-43.*

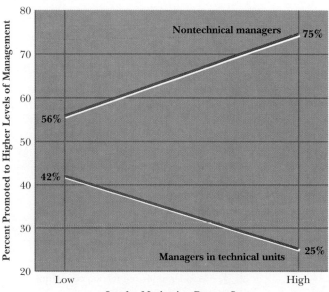

Vertical Dyad Linkage

vertical dyad Two persons who are related hierarchically, such as a supervisor-subordinate pair.

Another interaction approach to leadership examines the relations between the leader behavioral styles of consideration and initiating structure and certain follower characteristics. In George Graen's *vertical dyad linkage (VDL)* theory of leadership, a **vertical dyad** consists of two persons who are linked hierarchically, for example, a supervisor and a subordinate.[35] Most research based on the Ohio State studies measures leader consideration or initiating structure by averaging subordinates' ratings of leaders. VDL proponents, however, focus on the ratings of single followers. They argue that there is no such thing as an "average" leadership score. Instead, they insist, each supervisor-subordinate relationship is unique. A supervisor may be considerate toward one person but not another. Similarly, the leader may initiate structure for some workers but not others.

The importance of distinguishing dyadic from average scores has been supported by subsequent research. For example, Figure 12-7 compares correlations between (a) leader consideration and follower satisfaction and (b) leader initiating structure and follower role clarity as measured both by dyadic scores and average scores.[36] As you can see, the correlations obtained using dyadic scores were almost twice as high as those obtained with average scores. This suggests that leaders do behave differently with different subordinates and that these differences spill over into worker reactions.

The VDL approach also suggests that leaders tend to classify subordinates into in-group members and out-group members. According to Graen, *in-group members* are not only capable of doing more than the tasks outlined in a formal job description but are willing to do so. Once a leader has identified these people she generally gives them more and more latitude, authority, and consideration so that they become informal assistants. *Out-group members*, on the other hand, either cannot or will not expand their roles beyond formal requirements. Leaders assign these individuals more routine tasks, give them less consideration, and

[35] George Graen, "Role-Making Processes within Complex Organizations," in *Handbook of Industrial/ Organizational Psychology*, ed. M. D. Dunnette (Chicago: Rand McNally, 1976), pp. 1210–59.
[36] R. Katerberg and P. Hom, "Effects of Within-Group and Between-Groups Variation in Leadership," *Journal of Applied Psychology 66* (1981), 218–23.

FIGURE 12-7

Measuring the Relations between Leader Behaviors and Follower Outcomes by Dyadic Ratings and Average Group Ratings

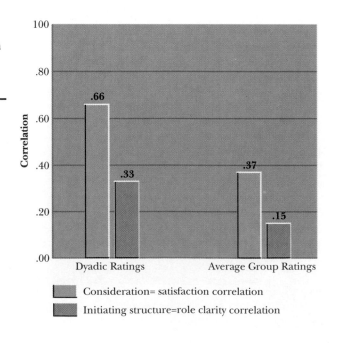

Consideration= satisfaction correlation

Initiating structure=role clarity correlation

426

communicate less often with them so that they become little more than hired hands. The Leader-Member Exchange Questionnaire, a self-report answered by subordinates, is often used to measure in-group versus out-group status.[37] Table 12-3 shows some items from this questionnaire.

Whether distinguishing among subordinates in this manner improves a leader's effectiveness depends on the leader's reasons for placing some people in the in group and others in the out group. Graen has suggested that a supervisor will "tend to select members who are compatible with him in terms of work competence and interpersonal skills . . . people he can trust to do the right thing."[38] This sounds like an effective leadership style. Graen has also noted, however, that "in some cases the selection probably is based upon the supervisor's prejudices concerning race, religion, or ethnic background."[39] Separating members into in groups and out groups based on information that is not related to performance could interfere with leader effectiveness. Highly competent and committed workers may differ from their supervisors but may excel if given in-group status and support. Unfortunately, the evidence suggests that in-group selections are often made capriciously. Demographic similarity and things like mutual interests outside of work have been found to predict in-group membership.[40]

Vertical dyad linkage theory suggests that as a potential leader you may find it worthwhile to behave in different ways with different followers. It also points out that you should base your distinctions among subordinates on their performance capabilities, not on the ways in which they are either similar to or different from you.

[37] G. Graen, R. Liden, and W. Hoel, "Role of Leadership in the Employee Withdrawal Process," *Journal of Applied Psychology 67* (1982), 868–72.

[38] Graen, "Role-making Processes," p. 1242.

[39] Graen, et al., "Role of Leadership," p. 869.

[40] D. Duchon, S. G. Green, and T. D. Taber, "Vertical Dyad Linkage: A Longitudinal Assessment of Antecedents, Measures, and Consequences," *Journal of Applied Psychology 71* (1986), 56–60; A. S. Tsui and C. A. O'Reilly, "Beyond Simple Demographic Effects: The Importance of Relational Demography in Superior-Subordinate Dyads," *Academy of Management Journal 32* (1989), 402–23; and A. Crouch and P. Yetton, "Manager-Subordinate Dyads: Relationships Among Task and Social Contract, Manager Friendliness and Subordinate Performance in Management Groups," *Organizational Behavior and Human Decision Processes 41* (1988), 65–82.

TABLE 12-3

Items That Assess Leader-Member Exchange

1. How flexible do you believe your supervisor is about evolving change in *your* job? 4 = Supervisor is enthused about change; 3 = Supervisor is lukewarm to change; 2 = Supervisor sees little need to change; 1 = Supervisor sees no need for change.

2. Regardless of how much formal organizational authority your supervisor has built into his/her position, what are the chances that he/she would be personally inclined to use his/her power to help you solve problems in your work? 4 = He certainly would; 3 = Probably would; 2 = Might or might not; 1 = No.

3. To what extent can *you* count on your supervisor to "bail you out," at his/her expense, when *you* really need him/her? 4 = Certainly would; 3 = Probably; 2 = Might or might not; 1 = No.

4. How often do you take suggestions regarding your work to your supervisor? 4 = Almost always; 3 = Usually; 2 = Seldom; 1 = Never.

5. How would *you* characterize *your* working relationship with your supervisor? 4 = Extremely effective; 3 = Better than average; 2 = About average; 1 = Less than average.

The five items are summed for each participant, resulting in a possible range of scores from 5 to 20.

Life Cycle Model

According to the *life cycle model* of Paul Hersey and Kenneth Blanchard, the effectiveness of a leader's decision style depends very largely on his followers' level of maturity, or their job experience and emotional maturity.[41] The life cycle model proposes two basic decision styles: *task orientation* and *relationship orientation*. As you might guess, these concepts were derived from the initiating structure and consideration dimensions of the early Ohio State studies.

The life cycle model suggests that there are four types of decision styles: telling, selling, participating, and delegating. In the *telling style*, which is characterized by high task orientation and low relationship orientation, the leader simply tells the follower what to do. In the *selling style*, characterized by both high task and high relationship orientations, the leader tries to sell his ideas to subordinates, to convince them that her decision is appropriate. The *participating style* is marked by a high relationship orientation but a low task orientation. The leader who uses this style of decision making includes subordinates in discussions so that decisions are made by consensus. Finally, in the *delegating style*, which is low on both task and relationship orientations, the leader actually turns things over to followers and lets them make their own decisions.

Like all interaction theories, the life cycle model proposes that there is more than one way to lead. The type of decision style that a leader should adopt depends on the level of maturity of his followers. By maturity is meant both job maturity,

[41] Paul Hersey and Kenneth Blanchard, *Management of Organizational Behavior* (Englewood Cliffs, NJ: Prentice Hall, 1977), p. 11–35.

FIGURE 12-8

The Life Cycle Model of Leadership in Four Dimensions

Three of this model's four dimensions are easily seen. *Relationship orientation* may be low (bottom half of the rectangular box model) or high (top half). *Task orientation* may also be low (left half of the model) or high (right half). *Follower maturity* ranges from very low (front of the model) to very high (back). The fourth dimension, *leader effectiveness*, is represented by the highlighted cell at each follower maturity level. For example, at the high maturity level, the highlighting of the cell for the participating leader style—which is high on relationship orientation and low on task orientation—indicates that at this level this style is the most effective.

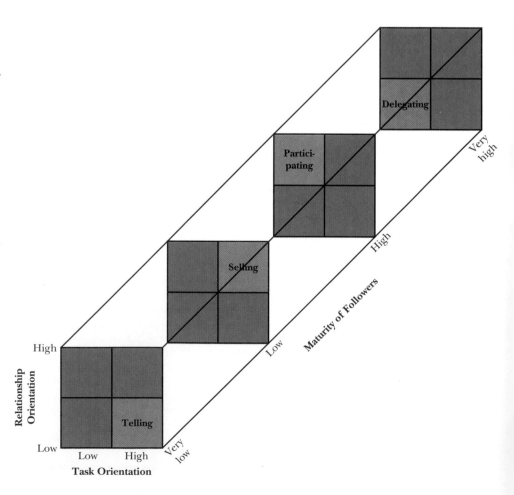

or task experience and skill, and psychological maturity, or feelings of self-worth and self-acceptance. As Graeff has correctly pointed out, the life cycle model has four dimensions: task orientation, relationship orientation, maturity, and effectiveness.[42] Figure 12-8 illustrates the four dimensions of this model.

As you can see, this model suggests that for followers at very low levels of maturity, telling is the most effective leadership decision style. As followers move from very low to moderately low levels of maturity, a selling style becomes more effective. When followers show a moderately high level of maturity, participating is the most effective style, and at the very highest levels of follower maturity, the delegating style leaves followers essentially on their own.

Like the managerial grid, the life cycle approach has been well received by practitioners because of its intuitive appeal. However, empirical research has not supported it. The most rigorous study of the approach to date suggests two conclusions, neither of which is encouraging. First, *satisfaction* with supervision is no higher in situations where leader style matches follower maturity level in the way the model prescribes than in situations where there is a mismatch. Second, the notion that *performance* will be higher in matched situations is supported at only one level of maturity, the lowest.[43] Thus, the most we can say at this point is that with workers at low levels of maturity, the telling style is slightly more effective in eliciting good performance than the other styles.

Comprehensive Theories of Leadership

Comprehensive leadership theories are interaction theories, like the ones we have just explored. Unlike the latter, however, comprehensive theories incorporate all three of the elements of the transactional approach to leadership—leader, follower, and situation. The three theories that we will examine next differ only in that each tends to focus on a particular leader characteristic—either a personal characteristic, a behavioral orientation, or a decision style.

Fiedler's Contingency Model

Think for a moment of someone with whom you have really had difficulty working. In fact, try to choose from all the people you have ever worked with the one you worked with least well. Now rate this person on the qualities listed in the *Least Preferred Coworker Scale* shown in Table 12-4. Put a checkmark in the blank that best represents your judgment of the person you have in mind. For example, 1 and 8 suggest *extremely* unpleasant or pleasant, 2 and 7 *quite* unpleasant or pleasant, 3 and 6 *moderately* unpleasant or pleasant, and 4 and 5 *somewhat* unpleasant or pleasant. Then total your answers to get a final score.

A low score on this scale (between 16 and 64) will indicate that you described your *least preferred coworker* in relatively harsh terms and that you would take a *task orientation* to leadership. Task oriented leaders, according to Fred Fiedler, the author of this theory, emphasize completing tasks successfully, even at the

---

[42] G. L. Graeff, "The Situational Leadership Theory: A Critical Review," *Academy of Management Review* 7 (1983), 285–91.

[43] R. P. Vecchio, "Situational Leadership Theory: An Examination of a Prescriptive Theory," *Journal of Applied Psychology* 72 (1988), 444–51.

TABLE 12-4
Items from the Least Preferred Coworker Scale

Pleasant	8	7	6	5	4	3	2	1	Unpleasant
Friendly	8	7	6	5	4	3	2	1	Unfriendly
Rejecting	1	2	3	4	5	6	7	8	Accepting
Helpful	8	7	6	5	4	3	2	1	Frustrating
Unenthusiastic	1	2	3	4	5	6	7	8	Enthusiastic
Tense	1	2	3	4	5	6	7	8	Relaxed
Distant	1	2	3	4	5	6	7	8	Close
Cold	1	2	3	4	5	6	7	8	Warm
Cooperative	8	7	6	5	4	3	2	1	Uncooperative
Supportive	8	7	6	5	4	3	2	1	Hostile
Boring	1	2	3	4	5	6	7	8	Interesting
Quarrelsome	1	2	3	4	5	6	7	8	Harmonious
Self-assured	8	7	6	5	4	3	2	1	Hesitant
Efficient	8	7	6	5	4	3	2	1	Inefficient
Gloomy	1	2	3	4	5	6	7	8	Cheerful
Open	8	7	6	5	4	3	2	1	Guarded

Note: LPC score is the sum of the answers to these 16 questions. High scores indicate a relationship orientation; low scores, a task orientation.
Source: From *Leadership and effective management* by Fred E. Fiedler and Martin M. Chomers. Copyright © 1974 by Scott, Foresman & Co. Reprinted by permission.

expense of interpersonal relations. A low score on the scale reflects a leader's inability to overlook the negative traits of a poorly performing subordinate.

On the other hand, a high score (between 80 and 128) will indicate that you described your least preferred coworker in relatively positive terms and that you would take a *relationship orientation* to leadership. Relationship-oriented leaders, according to Fiedler, are permissive, considerate leaders who can maintain good interpersonal relationships even with workers who are not contributing to group accomplishment. The leader's orientation toward either tasks or relationships is the central piece in the complex and controversial theory of leadership that Fiedler has proposed.

Fiedler's model is called a contingency theory of leadership because it holds that the effectiveness of a leader's orientation depends both on the leader's followers and on the situation in which she is functioning. A leadership context can be placed on a continuum of favorability, in which the interaction among three factors defines eight positions of varying favorability (see Figure 12-9). The three factors are leader-follower relations, task structure, and leader position power.

Leader-follower relations are good if followers trust and respect the leader and poor if they don't. Good relations are more favorable for leader effectiveness than poor relations. **Leader task structure** is high when a group has clear goals and clear means for achieving these goals. High task structure is more favorable

leader-follower relations A component of Fiedler's contingency theory that describes the level of trust and respect between leader and follower.

leader task structure A component of Fiedler's contingency theory that describes the clarity of goals and of means—end relationships in a group's task.

LEADERSHIP

FIGURE 12-9

How Situation Favorability Is Determined by Leader-Follower Relations, Leader Task Structure, and Leader Position Power

Source: Adapted from Fred E. Fiedler. A Theory of Leadership Effectiveness (New York: McGraw-Hill, 1967). Reprinted by permission.

Leader-follower relations	Good				Poor			
Leader task structure	High		Low		High		Low	
Leader position power	Strong	Weak	Strong	Weak	Strong	Weak	Strong	Weak
Situations	I	II	III	IV	V	VI	VII	VIII

Very favorable ⟵———⟶ Very unfavorable

leader position power A component of Fiedler's contingency theory that describes the degree to which the leader can administer significant rewards and punishments to followers.

for the leader than low task structure. Finally, **leader position power** is the ability to reward or punish subordinates for their behavior. Clearly, the more power a leader has, the more favorable the situation is from the leader's perspective.

As examples, Fiedler has suggested that the respected leader of a bomber crew might fit into situation I in Figure 12-9 (highly favorable); the disliked chairman of a volunteer committee asked to plan an office picnic on a nice Sunday afternoon might fit into situation VIII (very unfavorable); and the elected director of a food cooperative might fit into situation IV (moderately favorable).[44]

Fiedler's analysis of a number of studies that used the Least Preferred Coworker Scale suggested to him that task-oriented leaders are most effective in situations that are either extremely favorable or extremely unfavorable (I, II, III, and VIII in Figure 12-9). Relationship-oriented leaders, he found, were most successful in situations of moderate favorability (IV, V, VI, and VII in Figure 12-9).

Evidence for Validity. Over the last 25 years this theory has aroused considerable interest. One review described 24 studies that tested the model's predictions directly.[45] Figure 12-10 shows the empirical support for the model. For each of the eight situations described by the model, average correlations and the range of correlations between a leader's LPC score and his effectiveness are plotted.

These data suggest that the model works quite well at the extremes. For example, both the average correlation and the range of correlations between an LPC score and leader effectiveness are negative in situations I and VIII, as the model predicts. Similarly, in situations IV and V, the average correlation and the range of correlations are both positive, again as the model predicts. However, LPC scores fail to predict leader effectiveness in situations II, III, VI, and VII.

Leader Match Training. One offshoot of this theory is the leader training program called LEADER MATCH, which attempts to translate OB theory into managerial practice. Fiedler has commented that it is easier to change almost anything in the job situation than personality and leadership style, and this belief in the immutability of human beings is reflected in LEADER MATCH training.[46] This self-paced, programmed text tells leaders not to change their styles but instead to try to manipulate the situation. For example, if leader-follower relations are poor, the leader may try to raise morale by giving bonuses or time off. If a task is unstructured, a leader may break it down into simpler subtasks. If position

[44] Fred E. Fiedler, *A Theory of Leadership Effectiveness* (New York: McGraw-Hill, 1967), pp. 120–37.

[45] L. H. Peters, D. D. Hartke, J. T. Pohlmann, "Fiedler's Contingency Theory of Leadership: An Application of the Meta-analysis Procedures of Schmidt and Hunter," *Psychological Bulletin 97* (1985), 274–85.

[46] Fred E. Fiedler, "Engineering the Job to Fit the Manager," *Harvard Business Review 43* (1965) 115–22.

FIGURE 12-10

Evidence for Fiedler's
Contingency Theory of
Leadership

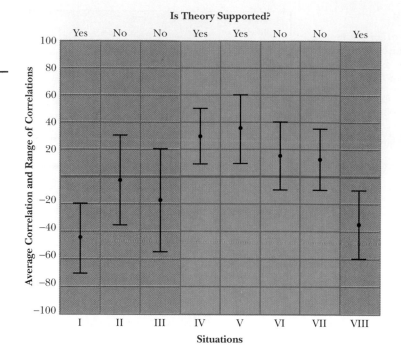

power is low, a leader may try to increase her authority by seeing that all information is channeled through her.

Critique of Fiedler's Model. Both the contingency theory and LEADER MATCH training have been subject to considerable criticism. The theory has been criticized as "too data driven." According to his critics, Fiedler started with a set of results that he tried to explain, rather than with a logical, deductive theory. Moreover, there is continuing controversy over why low LPC leaders should be best in situations that are either extremely good or extremely bad but not in situations of moderate favorability. It is somewhat disconcerting that a theory with a history as long as Fiedler's has not yet been able to specify why its predictions turn out to be correct. The LPC measure itself has aroused controversy. Critics have questioned what the scale actually measures and how well it measures this variable.[47]

LEADER MATCH training has been criticized for using questionable measures of performance and for failing to control for rater expectation biases (see Chapter 5) and the so-called Hawthorne effect (see Chapter 2).[48] In addition, some people have noted that the classifications of situations in the LEADER MATCH booklet are not what the original theory would predict.[49] Indeed, critics have suggested that mismatches could total 60 percent.[50] Finally, as Figure 12-10 shows, current evidence suggests for as many as half of the situations that

[47] A. K. Korman, "Contingency Approaches to Leadership: An Overview," in *Contingency Approaches to Leadership*, ed. J. G. Hunt and L. L. Larson (Carbondale: Southern Illinois Press, 1974), p. 24; and C. A. Schriesheim, B. D. Bannister, and W. H. Money, "Psychometric Properties of the LPC Scale: An Extension of Rice's Review," *Academy of Management Review 4* (1979), 287–90.

[48] B. Kabanoff, "A Critique of LEADER MATCH and Its Implications for Leadership Research," *Personnel Psychology* 34 (1981),749–64.

[49] A. G. Jago and J. W. Ragan, "The Trouble with LEADER MATCH Is That It Doesn't Match Fiedler's Contingency Model," *Journal of Applied Psychology* 71 (1986), 555–59.

[50] A. G. Jago and J. W. Ragan, "Some Assumptions Are More Troubling Than Others: Rejoinder to Chemers and Fiedler," *Journal of Applied Psychology* 71 (1986), 564–65.

might be encountered, LPC scores show no consistent relationship with performance.[51]

Despite all these problems, however, there certainly seem to be some situations (I, IV, V, and VIII) where the theory works quite well. In particular, assigning task oriented, low LPC leaders to groups in situations of extreme favorability or unfavorability seems to be a defendable prescription. Moreover, Fiedler's contribution and that of his followers cannot be denied. They proposed the first well developed leadership theory that includes all three aspects of the transactional model.

Vroom-Yetton Decision Tree Model

The first comprehensive model we looked at focused on personality characteristics of the leader. Now we will examine a model that centers on leader decision styles. The *decision tree model of leadership* originated by Victor Vroom and his colleagues emphasizes the fact that leaders achieve success through effective decision making. The model describes effective decisions as of *high quality*, *well-accepted* by followers, and made in a *timely* fashion.[52] According to this theory, leaders whose decisions do not meet all three criteria will ultimately fail.

Vroom recognizes four general classes of leadership style: *authoritarian*, *consultative*, *delegation*, and *group based*. He then breaks these down into seven specific decision styles. Three of these are appropriate to all decisions, two are appropriate only to decisions regarding individual followers, and two are appropriate only to decisions regarding an entire group of followers (see Table 12-5). We will focus our attention on the processes that involve groups.

Like all comprehensive theories of leadership, the decision-tree model proposes that the most effective leadership style depends on characteristics of both the situation and the followers. Specifically, the model asks eight questions—three about the situation and five about the followers—in order to determine which of the seven leadership styles outlined in Table 12-5 is best. The decision tree presented in Figure 12-11 on page 435 makes the question-and-answer process easy.[53] Responding to questions A through H will lead you to one of 18 answers, each of which identifies one or more decision styles that are appropriate to the problem you confront. To choose among two or more styles, the leader must decide whether she wishes to maximize the speed of decision making or the personal development of subordinates. Autocratic approaches favor speed, whereas consultative or group approaches favor employee growth.

Using the Decision Tree. The model may seem a little intimidating at first, but going through a few simple examples will show you that it is actually quite easy to follow. Suppose you are a camp counselor trying to get a dozen 12-year-olds to march two miles to a campsite. You have to decide between two routes. The marked path is four miles long, but if you go off the path—into the woods, over a large hill, and through rough terrain—the trek will be only one mile. How can you decide on a route? Let's try using the decision tree model in Figure 12-11.

---

[51] M. M. Chemers and F. E. Fiedler, "The Trouble with Assumptions: A Reply to Jago and Ragan," *Journal of Applied Psychology* 71 (1986), 560–663.

[52] Victor H. Vroom, "Leadership," in *Handbook of Industrial/Organizational Psychology*, ed. M.D. Dunnette (Chicago: Rand-McNally, 1976), p. 912.

[53] V. H. Vroom and A. G. Jago, "Decision Making as a Social Process: Normative and Descriptive Models of Leader Behavior," *Decision Sciences* 5 (1974), 743–69.

For All Problems

AI   You solve the problem or make the decision yourself, using information available to you at the time.

AII   You obtain any necessary information from subordinates, then decide on the solution to the problem yourself. You may or may not tell subordinates what the problem is, in getting the information from them. The role played by your subordinates in making the decision is clearly one of providing specific information which you request, rather than generating or evaluating solutions.

CI   You share the problem with the relevant subordinates individually, getting their ideas and suggestions without bringing them together as a group. Then *you* make the decision. This decision may or may not reflect your subordinates' influence.

For Individual Problems

GI   You share the problem with one of your subordinates and together you analyze the problem and arrive at a mutually satisfactory solution in an atmosphere of free and open exchange of information and ideas. You both contribute to the resolution of the problem with the relative contribution of each being dependent on knowledge rather than formal authority.

DI   You delegate the problem to one of your subordinates, providing him with any relevant information that you possess, but giving him responsibility for solving the problem by himself. Any solution which the person reaches will receive your support.

For Group Problems

CII   You share the problem with your subordinates in a group meeting. In this meeting you obtain their ideas and suggestions. Then, *you* make the decision which may or may not reflect your subordinates' influence.

GII   You share the problem with your subordinates as a group. Together you generate and evaluate alternatives and attempt to reach agreement (consensus) on a solution. Your role is much like that of chairman, coordinating the discussion, keeping it focused on the problem, and making sure that the critical issues are discussed. You do not try to influence the group to adopt "your" solution and are willing to accept and implement any solution which has the support of the entire group.

Note: A stands for *authoritarian*, C for *consultative*, D for *delegation*, and G for *group-based* decision styles.

Question A: Yes. If the children can follow the unmarked route, it is the shorter way.

Question B: No. You don't know the children's climbing skills.

Question C: Yes. What needs to be done going either way is clear, that is, you need to get the children home safely.

Question D: Yes. You must deliver all twelve children to the campsite, so refusal by even one is unacceptable.

Question E: Yes. You are older, more experienced, and the children respect you.

Question F: No. They would all be happy to stop and camp where they are.

You have now arrived at answer number 10. According to this model, a wholly group-based decision such as GII in Table 12-5 is out of the question. If it is getting dark and time is of the essence, the autocratic style of AII will be most appropriate. If it is early in the morning, however, and you want the children to learn from the experience, a more consultative style, like CII, may be appropriate.

Here's another example. A corporate vice president has just been given the responsibility for starting up a new plant in a developing country, and she must choose a plant manager. Should it be one of her five current and highly experienced plant managers? Should it be someone from outside the firm who has had experience working overseas? Should it be a citizen of the target country?

FIGURE 12-11

The Vroom-Yetton Decision Tree Model of Leadership

A. Is there a quality requirement such that one solution is likely to be more rational than another? (Situation)
B. Do I have sufficient information to make a high quality decision? (Situation)
C. Is the problem structured? (Situation)
D. Is acceptance of decision by subordinates critical to effective implementation? (Followers)
E. If I were to make the decision by myself, is it reasonably certain that it would be accepted by my subordinates? (Followers)
F. Do subordinates share the organizational goals to be attained in solving this problem? (Followers)
G. Is conflict among subordinates likely in preferred solutions? (This question is irrelevant to individual problems.) (Followers)
H. Do subordinates have sufficient information to make a high quality decision? (Followers)

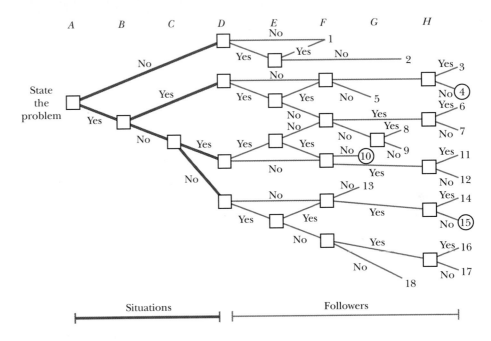

Answers and Appropriate Leadership Styles (see also Table 12-5)

Answer Number	Individual Problems	Group Problems	Answer Number	Individual Problems	Group Problems
1	AI, AII, CI, DI, GI	AI, AII, CI, CII, GII	10	AII, CI	AII, CI, CII
2	DI, GI	GII	11	AII, CI, DI, GI	AII, CI, CII, GII
3	AI, AII, CI, DI, GI	AI, AII, CI, GII, GII	12	AII, CI, GI	AII, CI, CII, GII
4	AI, AII, CI, GI	AI, AII, CI, CII, GII	13	CI	CII
5	AI, AII, CI	AI, AII, CI, CII	14	DI, CI, GI	CII, GII
6	DI, GI	GII	15	CI, GI	CII, GII
7	GI	GII	16	DI, GI	GII
8	CI, GI	CII	17	GI	GII
9	CI, GI	CI, CII	18	CI, GI	CII

The vice president might move through the decision tree as follows:

Question A: Yes. Some managers may be better suited than others.

Question B: No. The vice president may not know all the details of the candidates' personal lives, interests, or past experience that would be relevant to the assignment.

Question C: No. This is a new problem for the company, and thus there are no clear guidelines dictating what steps to take.

Question D: Yes. Any one of the vice president's current managers could find good jobs with other firms in their own country if they refused the overseas job.

Question E: No. The decision will have too large an impact on subordinates' lives.

Question F: Yes. They have been with the company a long time and are committed to the organization.

Question H: No. There are many details of the assignment that only the vice president knows.

The no response to question H leads to answer number 17. This answer, applied to a group problem, eliminates both autocratic and consultative styles, and recommends the GII, group-based decision style.

Evidence for Validity. Early studies of the model's usefulness asked managers to think about past decisions that were effective or ineffective and had them trace their decision processes back to see if they had followed the model's prescriptions. When the managers' decision processes were consistent with the model, 68 percent of decisions were effective, compared to only 22 percent when decisions violated the model.[54] Support for the model has also been obtained in studies that did not rely strictly on retrospective self-reports. In addition, when outside observers have been asked to rate decisions arrived at by groups following the model's rules, they have tended to rate these decisions as more effective than those taken by groups that violated the model's rules.[55]

Research also indicates that most managers' natural decision processes seem to violate the model's prescriptions. In particular, in both recalled and standardized problem sets, managers tend to overuse the group-based style CII and to underutilize the autocratic AI and group-based GII styles.[56] In addition, sex, experience, and organizational level may affect choice of style. Women tend to be more participative than men, students are more participative than experienced executives, and upper-level executives seem to be more participative than lower-level executives.[57]

Recent Extensions of the Model. Recently the decision tree model has been extended in several ways. First, it has become clear that the model should consider other leader characteristics besides decision style. One study, for example, has shown that using a group-based decision style when there is likely to be conflict among subordinates works only for managers who are skilled in conflict management. The study concludes that leaders who have trouble managing conflict should ignore model rules that dictate a group solution because they may not be able to manage the ensuing debate.[58]

The model has also been extended to include answers to questions that do not present simple yes or no choices. That is, the new model allows answers that are probability estimates or ratings on scales that include several numbers. This added complexity has been embedded in a computer software program that guides the manager through the decision-making process.[59] Evidence on the validity or

[54] V. H. Vroom and P. W. Yetton, *Leadership and Decision Making* (University of Pittsburgh Press, 1973), p. 12.

[55] R. H. Field, "A Test of the Vroom-Yetton Normative Model of Leadership," *Journal of Applied Psychology 67* (1982), 523–32.

[56] Vroom and Yetton, *Leadership*, p. 13.

[57] R. M. Steers, "Individual Differences in Participative Decision Making," *Human Relations 30* (1977), 837–47; A. G. Jago and V. H. Vroom, "Predicting Leader Behavior from a Measure of Behavioral Intent," *Academy of Management Journal 21* (1978), 715–21; and A. G. Jago, "Hierarchical Level Determinants of Participative Leader Behavior" (Ph.D. dissertation, Yale University, 1977).

[58] A. Crouch and P. Yetton, "Manager Behavior, Leadership Style, and Subordinate Performance: An Empirical Extension of the Vroom-Yetton Conflict Rule," *Organizational Behavior and Human Decision Processes 39* (1987), 384–96.

[59] V. H. Vroom and A. G. Jago, *The New Leadership: Cases and Manuals for Use in Leadership Training* (New Haven, Conn.: 1987). Authors retain all rights to decision trees, cases, and computer software.

batting average of the new model is unavailable, and many managers may be unwilling to turn their decision making over to a computer. As a result, it is hard to draw any conclusion about these extensions of the decision tree model.

Path Goal Theory

By far the most comprehensive theory of leadership to date and the one that best exemplifies all the aspects of the transactional model, is the *path-goal theory of leadership* originated by Martin Evans and Robert House.[60] At the core of this theory is the notion that the primary purpose of the leader is to motivate followers. Because they saw motivation as essential to the leader role, Evans and House built their theory on a base of expectancy theory. You will remember that we looked closely at expectancy theory in Chapter 7. Figure 12-12 is a condensed version of our treatment of that theory that emphasizes (a) followers' performance and satisfaction of followers as the primary outcomes of interest and (b) the five motivational variables that leaders may be able to influence through their behaviors or decision styles: valences, instrumentalities, expectancies, accuracy of role perceptions, and equity of rewards.

Manipulating Motivation. The job of the leader, according to path-goal theory, is to manipulate these five factors in desirable ways. The theory's proponents recommend that leaders

Manipulate follower valences by recognizing or arousing needs for outcomes that the leader can control

Manipulate follower instrumentalities by ensuring that high performance results in satisfying outcomes for followers

Manipulate follower expectancies by reducing frustrating barriers to performance

Manipulate the accuracy of role perceptions by making the paths to effective performance clear through coaching and direction

Manipulate equity of rewards by increasing the amount and types of rewards available when followers perform well.[61]

[60] Martin G. Evans, "The Effect of Supervisory Behavior on the Path-Goal Relationship," *Organizational Behavior and Human Decision Processes 5* (1970), 277–98; and R. J. House, "A Path-Goal Theory of Leadership Effectiveness," *Administrative Science Quarterly 16* (1971), 321–38.

[61] R. J. House and T. R. Mitchell, "Path-Goal Theory of Leadership," *Journal of Contemporary Business 3* (1974), 81–97.

FIGURE 12-12

A Condensed Version of Our Model of Motivation and Performance

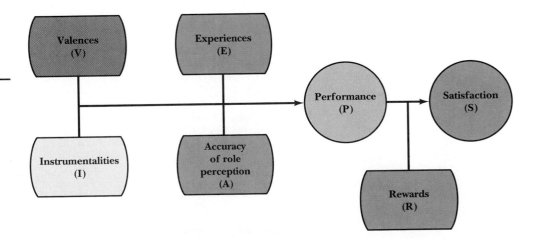

Behavioral Styles. Path-goal theory proposes four behavioral styles that can enable leaders to manipulate these five expectancy theory variables: directive, supportive, participative, and achievement-oriented leadership. As you can see from Table 12-6, these styles are composed of both behaviors, like initiating structure, and decision styles, like the authoritarian approach.

Note that the leader's effectiveness in each case will depend on follower and situation characteristics that may also affect these components. Much like the substitutes for leadership approach, path-goal theory recognizes that follower or situational characteristics may make leader behavior unnecessary or impossible.[62]

The full complexity of the path-goal model can be appreciated by looking at Figure 12-13, which combines Table 12-6 and Figures 12-1 and 12-12 to show how each one of the five aspects of motivation can be influenced by leader behavior styles, characteristics of the followers, and characteristics of the situation, as well as by interactions among variable across categories.

Evidence for Validity. Researchers have tested small parts of the path goal model. Some of their findings are as follows:

Leader participative behavior results in satisfaction in *situations* where the task is nonroutine but only for *followers* who are nonauthoritarian.[63]

Leader directive behavior produces high satisfaction and high performance but only among *followers* who have high needs for clarity.[64]

Leader supportive behavior results in follower satisfaction but only in *situations* where the task is highly structured.[65]

Leader achievement-oriented behavior results in improved performance but only when *followers* are committed to goals.[66]

---

[62] A. C. Filley, R. J. House, and S. Kerr, *Managerial Processes and Organizational Behavior* (Glenview, Ill.: Scott, Foresman, 1976), p. 91.

[63] R. T. Keller, "A Test of the Path-Goal Theory of Leadership with Need for Clarity as a Moderator in Research and Development Organizations," *Journal of Applied Psychology 74* (1989), 208–12.

[64] Ibid.

[65] J. E. Stinson and T. W. Johnson, "A Path-Goal Theory of Leadership: A Partial Test and Suggested Refinements," *Academy of Management Journal 18* (1975), 242–52.

[66] M. Erez and I. Zidon, "Effect of Goal Acceptance on the Relationship between Goal Difficulty and Performance," *Journal of Applied Psychology 69* (1984), 69–78.

T A B L E   12-6
Path-Goal Theory's Four Behavioral Styles

Directive leadership	The leader is authoritarian. Subordinates know exactly what is expected of them, and the leader gives specific directions. Subordinates do not participate in decision making.
Supportive leadership	The leader is friendly and approachable and shows a genuine concern for subordinates.
Participative leadership	The leader asks for and uses suggestions from subordinates but still makes the decisions.
Achievement-oriented leadership	The leader sets challenging goals for subordinates and shows confidence that they will attain these goals.

FIGURE 12-13

Path Goal Theory

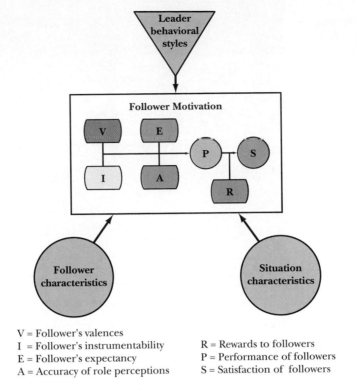

V = Follower's valences
I = Follower's instrumentability
E = Follower's expectancy
A = Accuracy of role perceptions

R = Rewards to followers
P = Performance of followers
S = Satisfaction of followers

Perhaps because the theory is so complex, no one has yet mounted a comprehensive study of path goal theory in which every variable is tested, like the Podsokoff study of substitutes for leadership theory. The theoretical framework provided by path-goal theory, however, is an excellent one for generating, testing, and understanding the complexities of the leadership process. Moreover, its tie to the expectancy theory of motivation makes it particularly suitable for leadership as conceptualized by Mintzberg, that is, the leader as a group motivator.

NEO-UNIVERSAL THEORIES

Although the increasing complexity of leadership theories presents an exciting challenge to theorists and researchers, it has left many people dissatisfied with what appears to be a lack of progress. In addition, it has created something of a backlash. Investigators have begun to propose what we may call *neo-universal theories of leadership* that, like some of the universal models, focus on a particular characteristic of the leader and exclude followers and situations.

Charismatic Leadership

charismatic leadership
Creating a new vision of an organization and getting group members to commit themselves enthusiastically to the new mission, structure, and culture embodied in the vision. Encouraging members to transcend self-interests on behalf of the organization as a whole.

For example, theories of **charismatic leadership** emphasize the ability of the leader to communicate new visions of an organization to followers.[67] Charismatic leaders or, as they are sometimes called, transformational leaders, raise followers' awareness of the importance and value of group goals, often getting people to

[67] J. M. Burns, *Leadership* (New York: Harper & Row, 1978), p. 52.

CEO Wayne Calloway had a vision that Pepsico could become the best consumer products company in the world. He envisioned a day when pizza, tacos, and chicken would be as convenient and easy to get as a bag of potato chips and set about changing the way the company's Pizza Hut, Taco Bell, and KFC (formerly Kentucky Fried Chicken) offered their services to the public. The company's delivery and carryout services are earning twice what the eat-in restaurants do, and already you can buy Pizza Hut's pizza from vendors at football stadiums and basketball arenas, in school cafeterias, and at airport shops.
Source: Patricia Sellers, "Pepsi Keeps on Going After No. 1," Fortune, March 11, 1991, pp. 62–70.

transcend their own interests. Charismatic leaders "raise the stakes" of organizational performance by convincing subordinates of the importance of the leader's vision. It is vision that distinguishes top performing managers from more ordinary managers.[68]

The demand for leaders with vision has never been higher. Stephen Garrison, chairman of Ward Howell International, an executive search firm, said in an interview, "In a third or a half of our searches these days, our client companies specify that they want a high level of vision."[69] Vision has become increasingly necessary since most businesses have finished (or are about to finish) major restructuring and now need to find new avenues to increased profitability. Visionaries are not just those who can predict or paint a picture of the future but those who can draw a map showing where the organization is now and where it should be in the imagined future. Vision is what distinguishes leaders from mere futurologists. Leaders like Apple Computer's Stephen Jobs, People's Express Airline's Donald Burr, and McDonald's Ray Kroc not only had vision—a computer in every home, no-frills air travel for everyone, inexpensive short-menu restaurants for every small town—but got others to help them make their vision reality.

Sometimes the leader whose vision created a successful enterprise has trouble relinquishing control of his creation to a successor. As the "In Practice" box suggests, there are a number of things a leader can do to ensure a smooth transition to a new leader and perhaps to new goals and new ways of achieving them.

Operant Model of Leadership

The *operant theory of leadership*, proposed by Judith Komacki and her colleagues at Purdue University, is also a throwback to universal approaches.[70] This approach, which is based on learning theory (see Chapter 7), focuses on specific leader behaviors: monitors and consequences. **Monitors** are behaviors associated with collecting performance information. For example, leaders may spotcheck subordinates' work or ask others to report on it. **Consequences** are behaviors in

monitors Leader behaviors that involve collecting performance information on subordinates.

consequences Leader behaviors that involve administering rewards and punishments contingent upon subordinate performance.

[68] J. J. Hater and B. M. Bass, "Superiors' Evaluations and Subordinates' Perceptions of Transformational Leadership," *Journal of Applied Psychology* 73 (1988), 695–702.

[69] W. Keichel, "A Hard Look at Executive Vision," *Fortune*, October 23, 1989, p. 44.

[70] J. L. Komacki and M. L. Desselles, *Supervision Reexamined: The Role of Monitors and Consequences* (Boston: Allyn & Bacon, in press).

440

which supervisors demonstrate their knowledge of employees' performance by taking action that responds to it. For example, a leader may give feedback on a worker's performance, praising a good job and criticizing a poor one; in short, he metes out rewards and punishment.

In several studies conducted by Komacki and her colleagues, the extent to which supervisors engage in these two types of behaviors has been found to relate to group performance.[71]

These neo-universal approaches have identified several important features of leader characteristics and behaviors. It seems likely, however, that they will ultimately have to incorporate qualities of followers and situations. No matter how charismatic the leader, a cynical audience may defeat his efforts to transform them. Similarly, overmonitoring a competent, high-self-esteem professional may engender little but resentment and dissatisfaction.

The Transactional Model Revisited

We started this chapter with a discussion of Mintzberg's and Hollander's conceptions of leadership. A relatively simple approach, Mintzberg's is defined in motivational terms. Hollander, on the other hand, sees leadership as a complex transaction involving characteristics of the leader, the followers, and the situation. These ideas provided a framework for our discussion of twelve theories and approaches to leadership that vary in the breadth of their view, or the number of variables they consider, and in the emphasis they place on different leader characteristics (see Figure 12-14).

The dynamic relationships among elements of these several theories as they fit together in an integrated *transactional model of leadership* are depicted in Figure 12-15. At the core of this model is the notion that leaders exist in order to meet the performance and satisfaction needs of individual group members. Through

[71] J. L. Komacki, M. L. Desselles, and E. D. Bowman, "Definitely Not a Breeze: Extending an Operant Model of Effective Supervision to Teams," *Journal of Applied Psychology* 74 (1989), 522–29.

FIGURE 12-14

Theories and Approaches to Leadership

		Leader Characteristics		
		Trait	Behavior	Decision Style
Breadth of Approach	Universal	Trait approaches	Ohio State & Michigan studies: Consideration & initiating structure	Iowa studies: Autocratic Democratic Laissez-faire
	Interactive	Trait and situation: Leadership motivation pattern	Behavior and follower: Vertical dyad linkage	Decision style and follower: Life cycle approach
	Comprehensive	Fiedler's contingency theory	Path-goal theory	Decision tree model

FIGURE 12-15

The Fully Articulated Transactional Model of Leadership

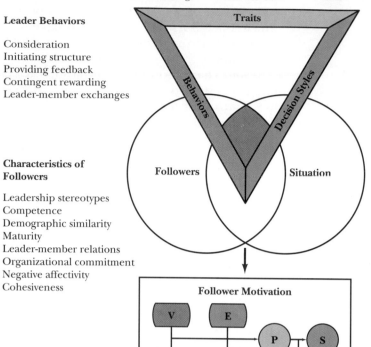

Leader Traits

Energy level	Supervisoty ability	Charisma
Cognitive ability	Dominance	LPC
Task knowledge	Self-confidence	LMP

Leader Behaviors

Consideration
Initiating structure
Providing feedback
Contingent rewarding
Leader-member exchanges

Leader Decision Styles

Autocratic
Laissez-faire
Participative
Delegative

Characteristics of Followers

Leadership stereotypes
Competence
Demographic similarity
Maturity
Leader-member relations
Organizational commitment
Negative affectivity
Cohesiveness

Characteristics of Situations

Economic conditions
Selection systems
Technical nature of tasks
Task structure
Position power
Contextual factors
Organizational formalizati
Spatial distance

their abilities and personality characteristics, their behaviors, and their decision styles, leaders must affect their followers' valences, instrumentalities, expectancies, role perceptions, and outcomes, or rewards.

At the same time, leaders must recognize that these phenomena do not exist in a vacuum and are affected by a variety of follower and situational characteristics. Thus a characteristic that works well with one unique configuration of situation and followers is unlikely to work well with another configuration. The initial match between the leader, the situation, and the follower is critical for leader emergence. The leader's ability to adapt to changing situations and followers will determine her staying power over time.

If our model looks complex, it is because the phenomenon it attempts to describe is complex. If leadership were easy, everyone would be doing it.

Summary

A great deal of theory and research has examined the topic of leadership. Leadership differs from management in that leading is one of the tasks of managerial work. The emergence and continued success of a *leader* is a complex function of his characteristics, characteristics of his *followers*, and characteristics of the *situation*.

Some of the more important personal characteristics of a leader seem to be high intelligence, need for power, energy level, and charisma and low need for affiliation. These characteristics are typically manifested in particular leader behaviors or decision styles.

The more important dimensions of leader behavior include *consideration* of employee needs, sometimes referred to as *relationship orientation* or concern for people; *initiating structure*, sometimes referred to as *task orientation*, or concern for production; and leader-member exchange behaviors that separate subordinates into in-groups and out-groups. Two other critical leader behaviors are *monitors*, or keeping track of employee performance, and *consequences*, or administering rewards and punishments contingent on performance.

Leader characteristics lead to different leader decision styles. Some *authoritarian* leaders make all decisions for their followers, whereas others take a *laissez faire* approach and leave followers to do as they please. Still others take a *democratic* approach, working actively with followers to ensure that all group members have a chance to contribute to a task. According to the *transactional model of leadership*, the effectiveness of these different behaviors and decision styles is contingent on characteristics of the followers and of the situation.

Followers differ along several important dimensions. They may be highly knowledgeable, mature, professional, and committed to the organization and its mission or they may be quite the opposite. Different leadership styles will be required to work effectively with followers with these different characteristics.

The situation in which leader and followers find themselves also affects the relationship between leader characteristics, behaviors, and decision styles on the one hand and leader effectiveness on the other. Where the leader has great *position power*, goals are clear, *leader task structure* is high, and *leader-follower relations* are characterized by trust and respect, one set of behaviors or decision styles may be required. In situations where the opposite conditions hold, a completely different kind of leader or leader style may be needed.

REVIEW QUESTIONS

1. Theories of leadership differ in terms of how adaptable they suggest the leader can be. Of the theories charted in Figure 12-14, choose two that suggest the leader is immutable and two that suggest the leader is readily adaptable. Which of these two conflicting perspectives seems most likely to be true? Are leaders born or are they made?

2. Most of the early research on leadership was done with leaders who were almost exclusively white and male. In the "Management Issues" box in Chapter 9 we discussed the report "Workforce 2000," which suggests that few of the new entrants in the labor force in the year 2000 will be white males. Which theories of leadership may need to be seriously reexamined because of this change, and which do you feel will generalize well to the new work force?

3. We discussed the Least Preferred Coworker Scale in this chapter. Although no such instrument exists, what if there were a Least Preferred Leader Scale? Who would be your least preferred leader, and why do you object so strongly to this person? Can you think of followers other than yourself, or situations other than the one you were in, where this person might be an excellent leader?

4. Although one can think of a few exceptions, in general people who achieve preeminence as leaders in business organizations do not achieve success as political leaders. What are some characteristics of leaders, followers, or situations that make this kind of transition difficult?

5. The list of often-cited leaders in Table 12-1 clearly includes both saints and sinners. Why is it that the general moral character of the leader apparently plays no consistent role in a leader's emergence or continuation in power?

DIAGNOSTIC QUESTIONS

We have attempted to develop and describe a model of the leadership process that will help you diagnose organizational problems attributed to poor leadership. The following questions should help you apply the transactional model in performing diagnostic analyses.

1. Compared to other aspects of managerial work, how important to you is the specific process of leadership?

2. Which of the five components of follower motivation—valence, instrumentality, expectancy, accuracy of role perceptions, or rewards—seems most lacking in your setting?

3. What abilities related to leadership (e.g., general cognitive ability, task knowledge, supervisory skills) do you or your managers have? How do these abilities relate to the five components of motivation?

4. What personality characteristics that are related to leadership (e.g., self-esteem, need for power, charisma) do you or your managers have? How do these characteristics relate to the five components of motivation?

5. How readily do you think your abilities and characteristics or the abilities and characteristics of your managers can be changed?

6. What leader behaviors (e.g., consideration, initiating structure, contingent rewarding and punishing) do you or you managers typically employ? How do these behaviors relate to the five components of motivation?

7. Do you and your managers tailor your behaviors to different followers?

8. How do you or your managers determine in-group versus out-group status for group members? For example, do you base your selection on competence or on demographic similarity?

9. What kind of decision styles (autocratic, participating, delegating) do you or your managers typically employ?

10. How should this decision style be tailored to your followers? Should you fit it to their level of maturity? their commitment to goals? or to the situation?

11. What are some of the major characteristics of the followers or of the situation you confront that might substitute for leader behaviors or neutralize them?

12. How favorable is the situation for the leader in terms of leader task structure, position power, and leader-member relations? What can be done to make this situation more favorable?

EXERCISE 12-1
EXECUTIVE PIE: SHARING LEADERSHIP*

STEPHAN H. PUTNAM, *University of North Carolina at Chapel Hill*

We tend to think of leaders as using their influence to help people achieve stated goals. Leaders, however, may choose to share their influence with others in pursuing a given mission or purpose. As you'll recall, in this chapter we discussed the Vroom-Yetton model, which proposed seven distinct leadership decision styles (see Table 12-5). From these seven styles we can distill four basic modes of handling influence and power in decision making. When a leader chooses the *autocratic* mode, she decides what to do without sharing any influence at all. If she chooses the *consultative* mode, she will share a modest amount of influence by asking others for their opinions before making a decision herself. If she chooses the *group-based* mode she will share her influence, encouraging others in the group to participate equally in the decision making. And if she chooses the *delegation* mode she will transfer all of her influence to others. This exercise will give you the opportunity to consider tradeoffs among these four leader decision styles as you decide which to use in dealing with a common management problem.

STEP ONE: PRE-CLASS PREPARATION

In the class before the one in which you will perform this exercise, your instructor will divide the class into groups of four to six people (if your class has formed permanent groups, you should reassemble in those groups). The instructor will then assign each group member the role of representative of one of six departments of a manufacturing business. Thus you will be a representative of sales and marketing, accounting and finance, manufacturing and operations, purchasing and legal affairs, research and development, or human resource management. Write the name of your role in the space provided in the "Task Role and Agenda" in Exhibit 12-1. Then read the task role and agenda description and prepare to follow it in the next class.

STEP TWO: GROUP DECISION MAKING

At the beginning of class, each group should meet and immediately elect or appoint a leader. In each group, every member should write his role on a piece of paper and place it in front of him so that everyone else will know what department he represents. When the groups have completed these tasks, the instructor will give each group leader a large paper circle. This "pie" represents all of the decision making power in the group, and it can be divided and distributed among the group's mem-

* Adapted from J. William Pfeiffer and John E. Jones, eds., *The 1977 Annual Handbook for Group Facilitators* (San Diego, Calif.: University Associates, Inc., 1977). Used with permission.

EXHIBIT 12-1
Task Role and Agenda Sheet

You are a member of a central steering committee composed of the heads of the departments in an industrial plant. The departments represented are sales and marketing, accounting and finance, manufacturing and operations, purchasing and legal affairs, research and development, and human resources management. Leadership of your committee rotates among the department representatives every six months.

Today's meeting has been called to allocate $100,000 which has come from company headquarters. This money must be spent within the next 60 days or be lost to taxes. The only restriction on your decision is that the money must be used to benefit the employees of your plant and to raise their morale. Your committee has 30 minutes to decide how the money will be spent.

You are the representative of the _____ department. Before the class in which your group will make its decision on this matter, you should think about your role and do whatever research is necessary to understand what functions are performed by departments like yours. You will be expected to fulfill your assigned role convincingly and with the expertise that one might expect of a department head.

bers as the leader sees fit. Once the leader gives the pie or any part of it to another person, power travels with that part by percentage. For instance, if the leader cuts the pie into four equal pieces and gives three to other individuals, keeping one for herself, each of those four members has equal decision-making power in the group and the remaining members have none.

After the pie has been distributed and everyone understands how decision making power is to be shared in this task, each group will have 30 minutes to reach the decision outlined in Exhibit 12-1. As group members work on the task, the group can further subdivide pieces of the pie if this seems desirable. A spokesperson should be appointed to keep a record of group activities and to report back to the class afterward.

STEP THREE: CLASS DISCUSSION

After 30 minutes the instructor should assemble the entire class, and spokespersons should report on the activities of their group. The class should then discuss its experience in allocating influence among the members of a group. Be sure to address the following questions:

1. For each group, which of Vroom's decision-making modes was the group's original choice? Which other mode(s) did the group try out subsequently? Which mode seemed to work the best? Which mode seemed least useful? Why?

2. Was it easy or difficult to move from one mode to another? How might rough transitions be smoothed?

3. If you had it to do over again, would you want your group to use the same decision-making modes? What changes, if any, would you make? Which things would you want to stay the same?

4. What aspects of a decision and the situation in which it must be made are most likely to influence the usefulness of a particular mode? Discuss your answer in the context of Vroom's model as it's described in this chapter.

5. In a real organization, what mechanisms might take the place of the "executive pie" in the regulating influence sharing? In your future job, how much say do you expect to have over who will have influence and who won't? Do you think you'll find this acceptable?

CONCLUSION

The process of sharing influence and reaching a decision is complicated and requires great managerial insight. Leading a group through decision-making procedures can involve as much attention to *how* to decide as to *what* to decide. No single mode of decision making is suitable for every situation. Instead, to perform effectively, managers must adopt the contingency approach, diagnosing each situation to determine which decision mode to employ.

DIAGNOSING ORGANIZATIONAL BEHAVIOR

In the spring of 1992 Sonia Harris was a financial analyst for Multinational Fiber Products, Inc., a multinational corporation based in San Francisco. Before enrolling in the Graduate Program in Management at Simmons College as a full-time student, Harris had been a computer programmer for eight years. In 1992 she was 30 years old.

Case Writer: What do you do as a financial analyst, Sonia?

S.H.: I'm in the earnings section of the financial reporting division within the comptroller's department. My group collects earnings information from all our regions worldwide and

CASE 12-1

SONIA HARRIS*

ARVA R. CLARK, *Simmons College*

compiles it for public reporting and government reporting.

When you collect this data, you have to be sure it's correct, so you're constantly checking and cross-checking. I'm the initial control person, in charge of seeing that all the earnings information comes in from all the regions I'm responsible for. I contact each of my regions every month and ask them for their net income—get a snapshot of what's going on. I also take care of any corporate adjustments to these numbers. Then I do an analysis of the numbers and prepare an explanation of changes over the last month or quarter or year.

After we get the numbers in, we as a group present worldwide earnings to the comptroller. I represent my regions in the presentations.

C.W.: How do you know the reasons for the monthly changes in your regions?

S.H.: The regions send in letters. If a letter is not complete I contact them. This process takes one day. My whole job is done in one day each month. The rest of the month is spent in preparing for that day, doing whatever comparisons and analyses can be done beforehand so that when the numbers come in, I'll be able to get everything done. Then, about 20 hours after the numbers actually come in, we make our presentation. It's a very tight time schedule.

At the end of each quarter, we put out a whole book of analyses. The book is solid numbers; there's much more data than at the end of the month. This usually takes three or four days to prepare and we work every night or an entire weekend. At year-end, we have ten times more data coming from the regions and we have to reconcile it all. That's really a panic time.

It's funny. We have a series of really tight time schedules that we know we're going to have. We know we're going to have a crisis every month, but I can't determine why. Why must all the monthly analysis be done within one day? Nobody knows, except that it's traditional. People get "up" for it. The adrenalin starts flowing. They like it. There's a sense of accomplishment, getting it done in such a short time. That's the biggest challenge we have. My theory is that these deadlines exist because they give people a sense of accomplishment.

C.W.: How is your earnings section structured?

S.H.: There are four of us—three women and one man—who report to the division leader, Pete Rinaldi. Another section, consisting of five people, does all the government reporting, and we often work with them. Then our two groups report to Aaron Rappaport, the head of the financial reporting division.

C.W.: How long have you been working in your present capacity?

S.H.: For a month. For five months before that I was an assistant to the woman who held my present job.

C.W.: Is that a typical way to come into the department?

S.H.: That's exactly the way it is done. It's considered a good way to see what's happening in the company. It's the most active section in the comptroller's department. Every month you get a snapshot of what the company is doing worldwide. It's considered excellent exposure.

C.W.: Have you worked in any other department in the company, or any other section in the comptroller's department?

S.H.: I was in the computer section within the comptroller's department for three months.

C.W.: Why did you leave?

S.H.: I wasn't happy there and I told people I wasn't happy. I never really had a boss there. The man in charge of that section and most of the rest of the staff travel constantly. So I had no direction.

C.W.: How did you let the company know you were unhappy there?

S.H.: I talked to a man from another department. I was doing a job for him but didn't report to him on a formal basis. He did talk to my boss and I assume he conveyed my discontent. After three months I was moved to the earnings reporting section.

C.W.: How did you choose this field, control?

S.H.: I was inclined towards the comptroller's area because it is operational. That means you get to know what a company is doing. We can call up anyone, anywhere in the company, and ask where the numbers come from. They have to explain—whether the markets have changed or expenses have gone up, whatever is going on. It's amazing the amount of information you can get from this position.

But, basically, all the comptroller's people do is collect numbers and reconcile them. If I stay in this area, I'll never get to use any finance, which I feel badly about. I love finance and did well in it at Simmons.

C.W.: Can you move from the comptroller's area to finance?

S.H.: I've asked about that. It's been done once, but it's very rare. Finance would be in the treasurer's department. They look at investments, the loan situation, the debt-equity situation, the purchasing of stock, taking care of stock options—things I'm interested in. I wasn't aware enough of the difference between the comptroller's department and the treasurer's department when I was interviewing for a job.

C.W.: What is the career progression for people in the comptroller's area?

S.H.: They go to the operating divisions. In corporate,

we get a surface picture. In the operational regions you actually have to deal with real-life problems. Usually, people relocate to different operational regions and move up the ladder in different areas. Then they'll get promoted to corporate to be group head, division head, department head, comptroller.

The company makes it very clear that you have to be free to relocate anywhere in the world. Virtually everyone on our floor has worked in South America, Africa, and Asia. They come back to corporate on higher levels after learning about different regions.

People relocate, move fast, climb up in the corporation. I see them as having no other lives except their careers. They've changed homes so many times that their nuclear families are the only thing they have to relate to except for the company. They are constantly moving. And they work very long hours. It's not clear to me *why* they work such long hours. That's another problem.

C.W.: Are long hours a part of the job as a way to show you're in earnest?

S.H.: Right. In my section, for example, I report to Claire Herzlinger, the supervisor who used to have my job, and to Pete Rinaldi, the head of the earnings section. Claire also reports to Pete Rinaldi. Claire is a workaholic. She gets in at 8 o'clock, an hour early, and works until 7 o'clock at night. Pete didn't always work that many hours but Claire told him he wasn't working hard enough. Since then he's been working longer hours. She really runs the whole floor.

C.W.: Does she expect long hours from you?

S.H.: Yes. For the last few weeks things have been really slow because we finally wrapped up our year-end report. When we're working on year-end, we work every night, every weekend, and we have no time off. I can understand that because we have a lot of work to do. But now people are still working late and there's not enough work to fill up my time during regular working hours. I've been putting in just regular working hours and Claire doesn't approve.

C.W.: How do you know that? Does she tell you?

S.H.: Once she told me. Otherwise she just glares. She works late every night. You know, you can always find something to do—material to read, people to talk to—if there isn't anything else to do.

Everyone watches to see what time you come in and when you leave. This morning I was fifteen minutes late and it was a mortal sin. In fact, it's a venial sin if you come in on time. If you come in a half hour early, then you're okay. And although you're supposed to come in early and stay late, it's okay to take a longer lunch hour than the alloted 45 minutes. It's perfectly okay to take an hour or an hour and a half. I don't understand that.

C.W.: What is your biggest problem here?

S.H.: Claire is my biggest problem. I'm terrified of her! I don't know anyone who isn't terrified of her.

C.W.: Both men and women?

S.H.: Even the comptroller! She has a terrible reputation.

C.W.: Why?

S.H.: She's so aggressive. Let me give you an example of what I'm going through right now. We're rewriting our instructions manual that tells the regions how to submit earnings reports. I was happy to see the improvements that were made. It looked great, a very professional job. So, since I report to Claire on things like that, I took it to her and said, "I'm reviewing the revised manual. They're revamped a lot of the troublesome areas. It really looks good. I want you to read it."

She came in the next morning and said, "Did you read this? This is awful! They tried to make these changes last year and I told them it wouldn't do! This is the same thing as last year!"

I guess some of the division people tried to make some changes last year and Claire absolutely forbade it. There was a lot of conflict between her and Francis McArthur, the person responsible for the manual, and they never revised it. So here I find I'm fighting her on the same issues. So I said, "Claire, what exactly don't you like about it?" She didn't like "this page" and "this page" and "this page." Finally, I said— trying to pin her down to something specific— "What is the thing you hate the most, Claire?" It was like handling fire. It's incredibly hard to get down to the nuts and bolts with her. She made me feel like I hadn't read the thing. She said, "Well, what do you *like* about it?" I went blank. I said, "I don't know anymore." She made me feel like dust, like dirt.

She does that to everybody. Francis McArthur, who did the revision, is a really strong man. He has very strong opinions. She made him back down in exactly the same way. She is very smart, and when she says something, she always has her back-up information. And she comes on so strong—her whole approach is overwhelming. She used to have my job, dealing with the regions, and she dealt with them in the same way. There were problems there.

C.W.: How much does she have to do with your career? Is she important for your promotions?

S.H.: I don't know. I think if she backs someone, that would carry a lot of weight. But if she puts someone down, that might not have as much weight because she's so offensive.

C.W.: Any other problems?

S.H.: Well, I came to this company with another woman from my class at Simmons, Marianna Perry, and we're as different as we can be. But because we went to Simmons together, we're thought of as twins. Our attitudes and our experiences and our abilities are completely different, but that doesn't matter. Marianna and Claire and I are the only professional women on this floor and we're all in the same section. We're all completely different, yet all of us are considered to be the same. We're not distinct. We're known as "Pete's harem."

C.W.: Is it usual or unusual to have that many women in one section?

S.H.: Unusual. This company has just started hiring women. I remember once I was issuing instructions to the regions and I signed my name as "Sonia A. Harris." One of the men in the department told me to sign "S. A. Harris," never to let the regions know I'm a woman.

Another problem is that when I came to this section, I think I was seen as somewhat uninterested in my job. Marianna and Claire really like the frenetic pace of the job. I would be happier if things would calm down and were better organized. Because I'm not like Claire or Marianna in that regard, some people saw me as uninterested.

C.W.: Who told you that—your boss, Pete Rinaldi?

S.H.: No, my peers. Claire and Marianna.

C.W.: How would you like people to see you?

S.H.: I would like to be seen as very competent and very organized, someone who can get the job done, someone who could take a situation where the energy might be frenetic and be able to calm it down. That's my personal goal, which is in tune with my personality.

C.W.: Are you saying that the company doesn't value that approach?

S.H.: Some people do, but not everyone. I was talking to a man from another section who told me about his experience as comptroller in our Chi-

cago office. He said that when he went there, people were running around, working late, but they couldn't get the work done. He went in, organized the work and stabilized the department. People didn't have to work overtime anymore and they weren't frantic at the end of every month. Then *his* boss came in and said, "What's wrong? This place used to be working overtime. People used to work all the time. What's wrong?" The comptroller said, "Well, I got it organized." His boss was critical; he didn't like the change. People in this department seem to lack perspective.

C.W.: Sonia, what about your future? If you want to move out of this department to the treasurer's department, who would you talk to about it?

S.H.: I've already talked to the personnel people about it, but they didn't like that at all. You're supposed to talk to your immediate boss. But I happen to know that there are some openings in the treasurer's department. I have some informal contracts over there.

C.W.: How do you know people in the treasurer's department?

S.H.: I have contacts all over the company. That's part of my job. They have to report earnings like everybody else.

C.W.: In general, how are you feeling about the company after nine months?

S.H.: I don't like it. I don't like the emphasis on long hours. I find that childish and unprofessional. I don't like the lack of challenge. The lack of direction on my first job—that was absolutely unacceptable. To go into a job and have no one to report to for three months—it's not the way to operate. They have no built-in procedure for taking care of new employees.

Let me tell you about the review procedure. They are supposed to review you once a year but they don't have to tell you about it. If they do tell you about it, they may or may not let you see the actual review papers. You're not allowed to express any differing opinions with your immediate supervisor on reviews. The type of savvy you're supposed to get, you have to get on your own and they'll respond to it by giving you promotions. But if you don't get a promotion, that's the only way you know that you're not doing well. It's very hard cornering managers to get a review. It's all up to the employee. You have to do it yourself. I don't like that at all.

I suspect I'm not ambitious enough to be at Multinational Fiber Products. When I was interviewing candidates for jobs here recently, one man in the department told me: "What we are looking for is people who are overachievers." You not only have to be brilliant—everybody here is brilliant—you have to be an overachiever. So you have all these brilliant overachievers doing their underchallenging jobs and what you end up with is an incredibly political situation because there is no place else to put your energy. I'd rather have something that is more intrinsically challenging because I'm no good at politics. So, frankly, I'm thinking of looking for a new job after I've been here for a year.

C.W.: Has this been a lost year for you then?

S.H.: Oh, no! This company has a fantastic reputation. Just to be hired by Multinational Fiber Products is desirable. It means you're a good person. They don't hire bad people; they're very picky. You really get a feeling for that when you're here and interviewing candidates.

C.W.: So how do you feel about this year?

S.H.: I've tried something new. This is entirely different from any other job I've had. It's what I wanted to do and I'm not at all disappointed that I tried it.

It's becoming clearer and clearer to me what I really want to do. As I think about this year and my past jobs, I realize that I'd really like to be a manager. The substance of the job isn't as important to me as the opportunity to manage people. Multinational Fiber wouldn't be so bad if I could see the prospect of being a manager somewhere down the road. I really don't care about job content when you come right down to it. If I could be a manager, I wouldn't care what the other responsibilities were.

If I can't be a manager, I'd like to get more into a financial area. A lot of people in San Francisco have their own tiny companies. I've run into some who need help in doing their books. That would be interesting. I'd be learning about people's businesses and they would be learning how to keep their books. I have the ability to teach people and it's really what I like to do, interacting with people. That's a possibility I'll be looking into.

When you have read this case, look back at the chapter's diagnostic questions and choose the ones that apply to the case. Then use those questions with the ones that follow in your case analysis.

1. What kind of a leader is Claire Herzlinger, Sonia Harris's supervisor? Do you think that other people at Multinational Fiber Products share Sonia's criticisms of Claire? What kinds of effects do leaders like Claire have on their subordinates' attitudes and performance? Is Claire affecting her subordinates in this way?

2. Do you agree with Sonia that the harried pace of work at Multinational is probably caused by the company's managers? May situational factors be contributing to the hectic work pace?

3. If Sonia achieves her goal of becoming a manager, what kind of a leader is she likely to be? Is her style of leadership likely to be consistent with the situational demands at Multinational? If she stays with the company, is Sonia likely to succeed as a manager and leader?

CASE 12-2

THE CASE OF DICK SPENCER*

MARGARET P. FENN, *University of Washington*

After the usual banter when old friends meet for cocktails, the conversion between a couple of university professors and Dick Spencer, a former student who was now a successful businessman, turned to Dick's life as a vice-president of a large manufacturing firm.

"I've made a lot of mistakes, most of which I could live with, but this one series of incidents was so frustrating that I could have cried at the time," Dick said in response to a question. "I really have to laugh at how ridiculous it is now, but at the time I blew my cork."

Spencer was plant manager of Modrow Company, a Canadian branch of the Tri-American Corporation. Tri-American was a major producer of primary aluminum, with integrated operations ranging from the mining of bauxite through the processing and fabrication of aluminum into a variety of products. The company also made and sold refractories and industrial chemicals. The parent company had wholly owned subsidiaries in five separate United States locations and had foreign affiliates in 15 different countries.

Tri-American mined bauxite in the Jamaican West Indies and shipped the raw material by commercial vessels to two plants in Louisiana where it was processed into alumina. The alumina was then shipped to reduction plants in one of three locations for conversion into primary aluminum. Most of the primary aluminum was then moved to the companies' fabricating plants for further processing. Fabricated aluminum items in-

---

* Reprinted with the author's permission.

cluded sheet, flat, coil, and corrugated products; siding; and roofing.

Tri-American employed approximately 22,000 employees in the total organization. The company was governed by a board of directors which included the chairman, vice-chairman, president, and twelve vice-presidents. However, each of the subsidiaries and branches functioned as independent units. The board set general policy, which was then interpreted and applied by the various plant managers. In a sense, the various plants competed with one another as though they were independent companies. This decentralization in organizational structure increased the freedom and authority of the plant managers, but also increased the pressure for profitability.

The Modrow branch was located in a border town in Canada. The total work force in Modrow was 1,000. This Canadian subsidiary was primarily a fabricating unit. Its main products were foil and building products such as roofing and siding. Aluminum products were gaining in importance in architectual plans, and increased sales were predicted for this branch. Its location and its stable work force were the most important advantages it possessed.

In anticipation of estimated increases in building product sales, Modrow had recently completed a modernization and expansion project. At the same time, their research and art departments combined talents in developing a series of twelve new patterns of siding which were being introduced to the market. Modernization and pattern development had been costly undertakings, but the expected return on investment made the project feasible. However, the plant manager, who was a Tri-American vice-president, had instituted a campaign to cut expenses wherever possible. In his introductory notice of the campaign, he emphasized that cost reduction would be the personal aim of every employee at Modrow.

Salesman

The plant manager of Modrow, Dick Spencer, was an American who had been transferred to this Canadian branch two years previously, after the start of the modernization plan. Dick had been with the Tri-American Company for 14 years, and his progress within the organization was considered spectacular by those who knew him well. Dick had received a Master's degree in Business Administration from a well-known university at the age of 22. Upon graduation he had accepted a job as salesman for Tri-American. During his first year as a salesman, he succeeded in landing a single, large contract which put him near the top of the sales-volume leaders. In discussing this phenomenal rise in the sales

volume, several of his fellow salesmen concluded that his looks, charm, and ability on the golf course contributed as much to his success as his knowledge of the business or his ability to sell the products.

The second year of his sales career, he continued to set a fast pace. Although his record set difficult goals for the other salesmen, he was considered a "regular guy" by them, and both he and they seemed to enjoy the few occasions when they socialized. However, by the end of the second year of constant traveling and selling, Dick began to experience some doubt about his future.

His constant involvement in business affairs disrupted his marital life, and his wife divorced him during the second year with Tri-American. Dick resented her action at first, but gradually seemed to recognize that his career at present depended on his freedom to travel unencumbered. During that second year, he ranged far and wide in his sales territory, and successfully closed several large contracts. None of them was as large as his first year's major sale, but in total volume he again was well up near the top of salesmen for the year. Dick's name became well known in the corporate headquarters, and he was spoken of as "the boy to watch."

Dick had met the president of Tri-American during his first year as a salesman at a company conference. After three days of golfing and socializing they developed a relaxed camaraderie considered unusual by those who observed the developing friendship. Although their contacts were infrequent after the conference, their easy relationship seemed to blossom the few times they did meet. Dick's friends kidded him about his ability to make use of his new friendship to promote himself in the company, but Dick brushed aside their jibes and insisted that he'd make it on his own abilities, not someone's coattail.

By the time he was 25, Dick began to suspect that he did not look forward to a life as a salesman for the rest of his career. He talked about his unrest with his friends, and they suggested that he groom himself for sales manager. "You won't make the kind of money you're making from commissions," he was told, "but you will have a foot in the door from an administrative standpoint, and you won't have to travel quite as much as you do now." Dick took their suggestions lightly, and continued to sell the product, but was aware that he felt dissatisfied and did not seem to get the satisfaction out of his job that he had once enjoyed.

By the end of his third year with the company, Dick was convinced that he wanted a change in direction. As usual, he and the president spent quite a bit of time on the golf course during the annual company sales conference. After their match one day, the president kidded Dick about his game. The conversion drifted back to business, and the president, who seemed to be in a jovial mood, started to kid Dick about his sales ability. In a joking way, he implied that anyone could sell a product as good as Tri-American's, but that it took real "guts and know-how" to make the products. The conversation drifted to other things, but the remark stuck with Dick.

Sometime later, Dick approached the president formally with a request for transfer out of the sales division. The president was surprised and hesitant about this change in career direction for Dick. He recognized the superior sales ability that Dick seemed to possess, but was unsure that Dick was willing or able to assume responsibility in any other division of the organization. Dick sensed the hesitancy, but continued to push his request. He later remarked that it seemed that the initial hesitancy of the president convinced Dick that he needed an opportunity to prove himself in a field other than sales.

Trouble-Shooter

Dick was finally transferred back to the home office of the organization and indoctrinated into production and administration roles in the company as a special assistant to the senior vice-president of production. As a special assistant, Dick was assigned several trouble-shooting jobs. He acquitted himself well in this role, but in the process succeeded in gaining a reputation as a ruthless head hunter among the branches where he had performed a series of amputations. His reputation as an amiable, genial, easy-going guy from the sales department was the antithesis of the reputation of a cold, calculating head hunter which he earned in his trouble-shooter role. The vice-president, who was Dick's boss, was aware of the reputation that Dick had earned but was pleased with the results that were obtained. The faltering departments that Dick had worked in seemed to bloom with new life and energy from Dick's recommended amputations. As a result, the vice president began to sing Dick's praises, and the president began to accept Dick in his new role in the company.

Management Responsibility

About three years after Dick's switch from sales, he was given an assignment as assistant plant manager of an English branch of the company. Dick, who had remarried, moved his wife and family to London, and they attempted to adapt to their new routine. The plant manager was English, as were most of the other employees. Dick and his family were accepted with reservations into the community life as well as into the plant life. The

difference between British and American philosophy and performance within the plant was marked for Dick who was imbued with modern managerial concepts and methods. Dick's directives from headquarters were to update and upgrade performance in this branch. However, his power and authority were less than those of his superior, so he constantly found himself in the position of having to soft pedal or withhold suggestions that he would have liked to make, or innovations that he would have liked to introduce. After a frustrating year and a half, Dick was suddenly made plant manager of an old British company which had just been purchased by Tri-American. He left his first English assignment with mixed feelings and moved from London to Birmingham.

As the new plant manager, Dick operated much as he had in his trouble-shooting job for the first couple of years of his change from sales to administration. Training and reeducation programs were instituted for all supervisors and managers who survived the initial purge. Methods were studies and simplified or redesigned whenever possible, and new attention was directed toward production which better met the needs of the sales organization. A strong controller helped to straighten out the profit picture through stringent cost control; and, by the end of the third year, the company showed a small profit for the first time in many years. Because he felt that this battle was won, Dick requested transfer back to the United States. This request was partially granted when nine months later he was awarded a junior vice president title, and was made manager of a subsidiary Canadian plant, Modrow.

Modrow Manager

Prior to Dick's appointment as plant manager at Modrow, extensive plans for plant expansion and improvement had been approved and started. Although he had not been in on the original discussions and plans, he inherited all the problems that accompany large-scale changes in any organization. Construction was slower in completion than originally planned, equipment arrived before the building was finished, employees were upset about the extent of change expected in their work routines with the installation of additional machinery and, in general, morale was at a low ebb.

Various versions of Dick's former activities had preceded him, and on his arrival he was viewed with dubious eyes. The first few months after his arrival were spent in a frenzy of catching up. This entailed constant conferences and meetings, volumes of reading of past reports, becoming acquainted with the civic leaders of the area, and a plethora of dispatches to and from the home office. Costs continued to climb unabated.

By the end of his first year at Modrow, the building program had been completed, although behind schedule, the new equipment had been installed, and some revamping of cost procedures had been incorporated. The financial picture at this time showed a substantial loss, but since it had been budgeted as a loss, this was not surprising. All managers of the various divisions had worked closely with their supervisors and accountants in planning the budget for the following year, and Dick began to emphasize his personal interest in cost reduction.

As he worked through his first year as plant manager, Dick developed the habit of strolling around the organization. He was apt to leave his office and appear anywhere on the plant floor, in the design office, at the desk of a purchasing agent or accountant, in the plant cafeteria rather than the executive dining room, or wherever there was activity concerned with Modrow. During his strolls he looked, listened, and became acquainted. If he observed activities which he wanted to talk about, or heard remarks that gave him clues to future action, he did not reveal these at the time. Rather he had a nod, a wave, a smile, for the people near him, but a mental note to talk to his supervisors, managers, and foremen in the future. At first his presence disturbed those who noted him coming and going, but after several exposures to him without any noticeable effect, the workers came to accept his presence and continue their usual activities. Supervisors, managers, and foremen, however, did not feel as comfortable when they saw him in the area.

Their feelings were aptly expressed by the manager of the siding department one day when he was talking to one of his foremen: "I wish to hell he'd stay up in the front office where he belongs. Whoever heard of a plant manager who had time to wander around the plant all the time? Why doesn't he tend to his paper work and let us tend to our business?"

"Don't let him get you down," joked the foreman. "Nothing ever comes of his visits. Maybe he's just lonesome and looking for a friend. You know how these Americans are."

"Well, you may feel that nothing ever comes of his visits, but I don't. I've been called into his office three separate items within the last two months. The heat must really be on from the head office. You know these conferences we have every month where he reviews our financial progress, our building progress, our design progress, etc? Well, we're not really progressing as fast as we should be. If you ask me we're in for continuing trouble."

In recalling his first year at Modrow, Dick had felt constantly pressured and badgered. He always sensed that the Canadians he worked with resented his presence since he was brought in over the heads of the operating staff. At the same time he felt this subtle resistance from his Canadian work force, he believed that the president and his friends in the home office were constantly on the alert, waiting for Dick to prove himself or fall flat on his face. Because of the constant pressures and demands of the work, he had literally dumped his family into a new community and had withdrawn into the plant. In the process, he built up a wall of resistance toward the demands of his wife and children who, in turn, felt as though he was abandoning them.

During the course of the conversation with his university friends, he began to recall a series of incidents that probably had resulted from the conflicting pressures. When describing some of these incidents, he continued to emphasize the fact that his attempt to be relaxed and casual had backfired. Laughingly, Dick said, "As you know, both human relations and accounting were my weakest subjects during the Master's program, and yet they are two fields I felt I needed the most at Modrow at this time." He described some of the cost procedures that he would have liked to incorporate. However, without the support and knowledge furnished by his former controller, he busied himself with details that were unnecessary. One day, as he described it, he overheard a conversation between two of the accounting staff members with whom he had been working very closely. One of them commented to the other, "For a guy who's a vice-president, he sure spends a lot of time breathing down our necks. Why doesn't he simply tell us the kind of systems he would like to try, and let us do the experiments and work out the budget?" Without commenting on the conversation he overheard, Dick then described himself as attempting to spend less time and be less directive in the accounting department.

Another incident he described which apparently had real meaning for him was one in which he had called a staff conference with his top-level managers. They had been going "hammer and tongs" for better than an hour in his private office, and in the process of heated conversation had loosened ties, taken off coats, and really rolled up their sleeves. Dick himself had slipped out of his shoes. In the midst of this, his secretary reminded him of an appointment with public officials. Dick had rapidly finished up his conference with his managers, straightened his tie, donned his coat, and had wandered out into the main office in his stocking feet.

Dick fully described several incidents when he had disappointed, frustrated, or confused his wife and family by forgetting birthdays, appointments, dinner engagements, etc. He seemed to be describing a pattern of behavior which resulted from continuing pressure and frustration. He was setting the scene to describe his baffling and humiliating position in the siding department. In looking back and recalling his activities during this first year, Dick commented on the fact that his frequent wanderings throughout the plant had resulted in a nodding acquaintance with the workers, but probably had also resulted in foremen and supervisors spending more time getting ready for his visits and reading meaning into them afterwards than attending to their specific duties. His attempts to know in detail the accounting procedures being used required long hours of concentration and detailed conversations with the accounting staff, which were time-consuming and very frustrating for him, as well as for them. His lack of attention to his family life resulted in continued pressure from both his wife and family.

The Siding Department Incident

Siding was the product which had been budgeted as a large profit item of Modrow. Aluminum siding was popular among both architects and builders because of its possibilities in both decorative and practical uses. Panel sheets of siding were shipped in standard sizes on order; large sheets of the coated siding were cut to specifications in the trim department, packed, and shipped. The trim shop was located near the loading platforms, and Dick often cut through the trim shop on his wanderings through the plant. On one of his frequent trips through the area, he suddenly became aware of the fact that several workers responsible for the disposal function were spending countless hours at high-speed saws cutting scraps into specified lengths to fit into scrap barrels. The narrow bands of scrap which resulted from the trim process varied in length from 7 to 27 feet and had to be reduced in size to fit into the disposal barrels. Dick, in his concentration on cost reduction, picked up one of the thin strips, bent it several times and fitted it into the barrel. He tried this with another piece and it bent very easily. After assuring himself that bending was possible, he walked over to a worker at the saw and asked why he was using the saw when material could easily be bent and fitted into the barrels, resulting in saving time and equipment. The worker's response was "We've never done it that way, sir. We've always cut it."

Following his plan of not commenting or discussing matters on the floor, but distressed by the reply, Dick returned to his office and asked the manager of the siding department if he could speak to the foreman of the scrap division. The manager said, "Of course, I'll send him up to you in just a minute."

After a short time, the foreman, very agitated at being called to the plant manager's office, appeared. Dick began questioning him about the scrap disposal process and received the standard answer: "We've always done it that way." Dick then proceeded to review cost-cutting objectives. He talked about the pliability of the strips of scrap. He called for a few pieces of scrap to demonstrate the ease with which it could be bent, and ended what he thought was a satisfactory conversation by requesting the foreman to order heavy-duty gloves for his workers and use the bending process for a trial period of two weeks to check the cost saving possibilities.

The foreman listened throughout the most of this hour's conference, offered several reasons why it wouldn't work, raised some questions about the record-keeping process for cost purposes, and finally left the office with the forced agreement to try the suggested new method of bending, rather than cutting, for disposal. Although he was immersed in many other problems, his request was forcibly brought home one day as he cut through the scrap area. The workers were using power saws to cut scraps. He called the manager of the siding department and questioned him about the process. The manager explained that each foreman was responsible for his own processes, and since Dick had already talked to the foreman, perhaps he had better talk to him again. When the foreman arrived, Dick began to question him. He received a series of excuses, and some explanations of the kind of problems they were meeting by attempting to bend the scrap metal. "I don't care what the problems are," Dick nearly shouted, "when I request a cost-reduction program instituted, I want to see it carried through."

Dick was furious. When the foreman left, he phoned the maintenance department and ordered the removal of the power saws from the scrap area immediately. A short time later the foreman of the scrap department knocked on Dick's door reporting his astonishment at having maintenance men step into his area and physically remove the saws. Dick reminded the foreman of his request for a trial at cost reduction to no avail, and ended the conversation by saying that the power saws were gone and would not be returned, and the foreman had damned well better learn to get along without them. After a stormy exit by the foreman, Dick congratulated himself on having solved a problem and turned his attention to other matters.

A few days later Dick cut through the trim department and literally stopped to stare. As he described it, he was completely nonplussed to discover gloved workmen using hand shears to cut each piece of scrap.

When you have read this case, look back at the chapter's diagnostic questions and choose the ones that apply to the case. Then use those questions with the ones that follow in your case analysis.

1. At the time Dick Spencer assumed his managerial job with the branch of Tri-American in Great Britain, what style of leadership did he exhibit? What kinds of outcomes did his leadership prompt?

2. What sort of a leader did Dick become when he took over the Modrow facility? How successful was he as a leader in the Canadian plant?

3. What does the siding department incident tell you about Dick's approach to leadership and management? Why didn't the foreman adopt his suggestions and direct subordinates to bend scrap pieces instead of cutting them? If you were Dick Spencer, what would you do when you discovered the workmen using shears to cut the scrap?

CASE 12-3

BOB COLLINS

Review this case, which you read in Chapter 6. Next, look back at Chapter 12's diagnostic questions and choose the ones that apply to the case. Then use those questions with the ones that follow in your case analysis.

1. What sort of a leader was Jim Douglas? Was he doing a good job of leading his subordinates, Bob Collins and Mark Douglas?

2. Why did Bob become upset with Jim? What could Jim have done differently to avoid the problems that were growing between the two men?

3. If you were asked to advise Jim on matters of leadership style, what advice would you give him? Could he follow your advice? Why? Why not?

CHAPTER 13

POWER, POLITICS, AND CONFLICT

In 1985, the leader of the 100-year-old Aluminum Company of America (Alcoa) undertook an unsuccessful program of diversification through acquiring companies in other industries. It took three years, nearly $500 million, and some power plays on the part of board members to convince the company that it should stick to the business it knew best—the production of aluminum.

Shareholders of Aluminum Company of America (Alcoa) can be excused if they missed the unveiling of the company's new strategic plan. It wasn't exactly a media event. But if they had read their recent annual reports closely, the change was right there. In his understated and direct style, Paul H. O'Neill, named Alcoa chairperson a year ago, simply told shareholders to forget what they had been hearing about diversification and acquisitions. Alcoa's future, he explained, lies in the aluminum business. Period.[1]

As suggested by this excerpt from a 1988 *Business Week* article, Alcoa's then-emerging strategy of refocusing its efforts on its original business—marketing aluminum—differed markedly from the plans of Charles W. Parry, Alcoa's chairperson prior to O'Neill. After spending nearly $500 million under Parry's direction to acquire twelve companies outside of the aluminum industry, Alcoa was going to sell off its nonaluminum businesses under O'Neill and return to its roots. What explained this sudden reversal in strategic direction? Answer: a well-hidden but nonetheless decisive political struggle which had occurred between Parry and Alcoa's board of directors.

Trouble had begun brewing early in 1985 following Parry's announcement of his intention to diversify half of Alcoa's business. Alcoa was then a century-old company steeped in conservatism, and the company's directors favored careful planning and familiar ways of doing things. In contrast, Parry's approach would require Alcoa to take a variety of precarious risks, seeking out unfamiliar businesses and embracing unexpected opportunities. Especially appealing, in Parry's view, were acquisitions in the aerospace industry. He bought the TRE Corporation, a Los Angeles-based defense manufacturer, and attempted to buy both LTV Aerospace, a division of the subsequently bankrupt LTV Corporation, and Goodyear Tire and Rubber Company's aerospace unit. The Goodyear business was subsequently purchased by Loral Corp. Parry was also attracted to various high-tech companies including Allen-Bradley Company, the factory automation specialist, which Parry tried to acquire but lost in a bidding war to Rockwell International Corp.

Fearing the perilousness of Parry's plans, several of Alcoa's directors began voicing personal concerns about the company's long-term security. Among them was W. H. Krome George, Alcoa's chief executive prior to Parry, who formed a coalition to press for Parry's resignation and search for a replacement. The coalition began its task by attempting to acquire Cummins Engine Company, a diesel engine manufacturer. The secret plan was to bring Cummins' CEO, Henry B. Schacht, into Alcoa as the firm's new head. The Cummins deal fell through, though, when an unsuspecting Parry concluded that Alcoa and Cummins shared little in common and rejected the merger. The board was forced to seek other options. In February 1987, the board quietly asked O'Neill, one of its own members, to take the chairperson's job. Several weeks later, the coalition called Parry to a meeting at Manhattan's River Club and abruptly demanded his resignation. O'Neill, who had been deputy director of the federal government's Office of Management and Budget during the 1970s and president of International Paper, was then publicly named Alcoa's chief executive officer.

As part of his severance settlement, Parry agreed to stay on for two years to facilitate the change of command. By 1989, O'Neill was completely in charge and Alcoa was again the world's largest producer of aluminum. Yet, with the coalition's victory over Parry, Alcoa became a captive of cyclical changes in

[1] Michael Schroeder, "The Quiet Coup at Alcoa: How the Board Rejected a New Vision for the Aluminum Giant," *Business Week*, June 27, 1988, p. 58.

world demand for aluminum. In the early 1990s, the market for aluminum declined substantially, and Alcoa's earnings fell with it.[2]

As shown by events at Alcoa, power and politics can gain some people jobs and force others aside. Power can also increase productivity and efficiency or reduce them substantially. Power, politics, and conflict can even decide the existence and strategic direction of entire organizations such as Alcoa. Rather than being the exception, Alcoa was one of many companies that experienced internal strife during the 1980s. Similar "palace revolts" ousted other top executives, such as Alegis/United Air Lines' Richard J. Ferris and Apple Computer's Steve Jobs. Political processes continue to influence business organizations in the 1990s. Current restructuring, often stimulated as much by internal politics as by external economic conditions, is prompting executives to search out new strategic directions for their firms. In the process, political considerations are altering the careers of thousands of managers and nonmanagers, creating opportunities for some but costing many others their jobs.[3]

Understanding power, politics, and conflict is therefore critical to managerial success—and survival—in today's organizations. For this reason, we begin Chapter 13 with a discussion of the nature, sources, and consequences of using power. Then, we will consider organizational politics, the process through which people acquire power and use it to pursue personal gains. Finally, we will explore conflict among groups, tracing through the origins, processes, and results of intergroup confrontation in organizations.

DIAGNOSTIC ISSUES

Our diagnostic model helps us raise a number of important questions about power, politics, and conflict. To begin with, can we *describe* different sources from which organization members derive power? In which situation is conflict a healthy sign and in which does it indicate severe problems within the organization? Can we *diagnose* how the aftermath of a conflict sets the stage for future conflicts? Can we explain why political decision making and negotiation sometimes take the place of more rational methods for making decisions?

Can we *prescribe* a plan of action to deal with conflict before it manifests itself? Can we prescribe how to manage interdependence that might otherwise cause destructive conflict? Finally, what managerial *actions* can be taken to prevent employees from engaging in destructive politics? If such politicking is inevitable, what actions can managers take to protect the organization?

POWER IN ORGANIZATIONS

power The ability to influence the conduct of others and resist unwanted influence in return.

If someone asked you to define **power**, how would you respond? Many people might think of a powerful person like Alcoa's Krome George and define power as the ability to influence the behaviors of others, getting them to do

---

[2] Jonathan P. Hicks, "Is That a Dark Cloud or a Silver Lining for Aluminum?" *The New York Times*, July 22, 1990, p. 12F.

[3] John A. Byrne, Wendy Zeller, and Scott Ticer, "Caught in the Middle: Six Managers Speak Out on Corporate Life," *Business Week*, September 12, 1988, 80–88.

460

POWER, POLITICS, AND CONFLICT

things they would otherwise avoid.[4] For other people, the image of a less powerful person like Alcoa's William Parry might come to mind, leading them to define power as the ability to avoid others' attempts to influence one's own behavior. In truth, both these views are correct because **power** can be formally defined as the ability to influence the conduct of others and resist unwanted influence in return.[5]

Why do people seek power over others? The work of David McClelland, a researcher interested in determining why some people succeed as managers while others do not, provides a clue.[6] McClelland deduced that people are driven to gain and use power by a need for power—*n Pow*—that develops during childhood and adolescence. McClelland thus suggested that experience teaches some people to seek and use power, contributing to the development of a high n Pow. Others, he said, learn to avoid its use and develop a low n Pow as a result. (See Chapter 7 for further discussion of McClelland's learned need theory).

The need for power can have several different effects on the way people behave. Generally speaking, people with high n Pow are competitive, aggressive, prestige conscious, action oriented, and prone to join groups. They are likely to be effective managers if, in addition to pursuing power, they also:

> Use power to accomplish organizational goals instead of using it to satisfy personal interests;
>
> Coach subordinates and use participatory management techniques rather than autocratic, authoritarian methods; and
>
> Remain aware of the importance of managing interpersonal relations but avoid developing close relationships with subordinates.[7]

According to McClelland, seeking power and using it to influence others are not activities in and of themselves to be shunned or avoided. In fact, the process of management *requires* that power be put to appropriate use—where appropriateness is determined on the basis of several competing ethical concerns (see the "Management Issues" box).

Interpersonal Sources of Power

If management requires the use of power, then how do people in organizations acquire the power needed to influence others' behaviors? That is, from where does a manager's power originate? In their pioneering work aimed at identifying different types of power in organizations, John French and Bertram Raven sought to answer such questions by identifying the major bases, or sources, of power in organizations.[8] The five sources and types of power they discovered are overviewed in Table 13-1.

---

[4] Robert A. Dahl, "The Concept of Power," *Behavioral Science*, 2 (1957), 201–15; Abraham Kaplan, "Power in Perspective," in *Power and Conflict in Organizations*, ed. Robert L. Kahn and Elise Boulding (London: Tavistock, 1964), pp. 11–32.

[5] V. V. McMurray, "Some Unanswered Questions on Organizational Conflict," *Organization and Administrative Sciences* 6 (1975), 35–53.

[6] David C. McClelland, *Power: The Inner Experience* (New York: Irvington Publishers, 1975) pp. 3–29; David C. McClelland and David H. Burnham, "Power Is the Great Motivator," *Harvard Business Review* 54 (1976), pp. 100–110.

[7] McClelland and Burnham, "Power is the Great Motivator."

[8] John R. P. French, Jr. and Bertram Raven, "The Bases of Social Power," *Studies in Social Power*, ed. Dorwin Cartwright (Ann Arbor: Institute for Social Research, University of Michigan, 1959), pp. 150–65.

MANAGEMENT ISSUES

The Ethics of Power

How should power holders determine whether the use of power is appropriate? One approach is to adopt the *utilitarianist* perspective and judge the appropriateness of the use of power in terms of the consequences of this use. Does using power provide the greatest good for the greatest number of people? If the answer to this question is yes, then, according to the utilitarian perspective, power is being used appropriately.

A second perspective, derived from the theory of *moral rights*, suggests that power is used appropriately only when no one's personal rights or freedoms are sacrificed. It is certainly possible for many people to derive great satisfaction from the use of power to accomplish some purpose, thus satisfying utilitarian criteria, and at the same for the rights of a few individuals to be abridged, an indication of inappropriateness according to the theory of moral rights. Power holders seeking to use their power appropriately must therefore respect the rights and interests of the minority as well as look after the well-being of the majority.

A third perspective, drawn from various theories of *social justice*, suggests that even having respect for the rights of everyone in an organization may not be enough to fully justify the use of power. In addition, those using power must treat people equitably, making sure that people who are similar in relevant respects are treated similarly and that people who are different in relevant respects are treated differently in proportion to the differences between them. Power holders must also be accountable for injuries caused by their use of power and must be prepared to provide compensation for these injuries in order for the use of power to be considered appropriate.

Obviously, the three perspectives offer conflicting criteria: there are no simple answers to questions concerning the appropriateness of using power.* Instead, power holders must seek a balance among concerns for efficiency, entitlement, and equity as they exercise influence over the behaviors of others.

* For an additional discussion of the three perspectives, see Gerald F. Cavanagh, Dennis Moberg, and Manuel Velasquez, "The Ethics of Organizational Politics," *Academy of Management Review,* 6 (1981), 363–74.

---

reward power Interpersonal power based on the ability to control how desirable outcomes are distributed.

Reward Power. The first type of power referred to in the table, **reward power**, is based on the ability to allocate rewarding outcomes—either the receipt of positive things or the elimination of negative things. If you are free to decide whether other people will receive rewarding outcomes, you can influence them by handing out rewards in return for their conformity to your demands. Praise, promotions, raises, desirable job assignments, and time off from work are outcomes that managers can often control. If they can control them, managers can use them to acquire and maintain reward power. Similarly, eliminating unwanted outcomes, such as unpleasant working conditions or mandatory overtime, can be used to reward employees. For instance, police officers given clerical support to help complete crime reports generally look at this reduction of paperwork as rewarding. Because company policies, union contracts, or similar constraints can

---

TABLE 13-1
Five Types of Power and Their Sources

TYPE OF POWER	SOURCE OF POWER
Reward	Control over rewarding outcomes
Coercive	Control over punishing outcomes
Legitimate	Occupation of legitimate position of authority
Referent	Attractiveness; charisma
Expert	Expertise, knowledge, talent

Source: Based on John R. P. French, Jr., and Bertram Raven, "The Bases of Social Power," in *Studies in Social Power,* ed. Dorwin Cartwright (Ann Arbor, MI: Institute for Social Research, University of Michigan, 1959), pp. 150–65.

sometimes abridge managers' ability to control the distribution of rewards, however, managers cannot always count on having reward power.

Coercive Power. While reward power involves the allocation of desirable outcomes, **coercive power** is based on the distribution of undesirable outcomes—either the receipt of something negative or the removal of something positive. People who control undesirable outcomes can get others to conform to their wishes by threatening to penalize them in some way. Coercive power exploits fear. An employee may be afraid that if she resists direction she will be punished. To influence subordinates' behaviors, managers may resort to punishments such as public scoldings, assignment of undesirable tasks, or loss of pay. Taken to the extreme, managers may threaten employees with layoffs, demotions, or dismissals.

coercive power Interpersonal power based on the ability to control the distribution of undesirable outcomes.

legitimate power Interpersonal power based on holding a position of formal authority.

Legitimate Power. **Legitimate power** is based on norms, values, and beliefs which teach that particular people have the legitimate right to govern or influence others. From childhood we learn to accept the commands of authority figures, first parents and then teachers. It is this well-learned lesson that gives people with authority the power to influence other people's attitudes and behaviors. In most organizations, authority is distributed in the form of a hierarchy (see Chapter 2). People who hold positions of hierarchical authority are accorded legitimate power by virtue of the fact that they are office holders. So, the vice-president of marketing at a firm like Coca-Cola or Scott Paper issues orders and expects people in subordinate positions to obey them because of the clout that being a vice-president affords.

referent power Interpersonal power based on the possession of attractive personal characteristics.

Referent Power. Have you ever admired a teacher, a student leader, or someone else whose personality, way of interacting with other people, values, goals, or other characteristics were exceptionally attractive? If so, you probably found yourself wanting to develop and maintain a close, continuing relationship with her. This desire can give her **referent power** over you. Because you hold her in such esteem, you are likely to be influenced by her attitudes and behaviors. In time you may identify with her to such an extent that you begin to think and act like her. Referent power is also called *charismatic power*.

Famous religious leaders and political figures often develop and use referent power. Mahatma Gandhi, John F. Kennedy, Martin Luther King, Jr., and Nelson Mandela are all examples of 20th-century people who have used personal charisma to profoundly influence the thoughts and behaviors of others. Referent power can also be put to more everyday use. Consider advertising's use of famous athletes and actors to help sell products. Athletic shoe manufacturers like Nike, Reebok and L.A. Gear, for example, employ sports celebrities like Michael Jordan of the Chicago Bulls basketball team and Joe Montana of the San Francisco Forty-Niners football team as spokespeople in an effort to influence consumers to buy their products. Similarly, movie makers try to ensure success of their films by getting stars like Jack Nicholson, Michelle Pfeiffer, and Tom Cruise to appear in them.

expert power Interpersonal power based on the possession of expertise, knowledge, and talent.

Expert Power. **Expert power** is based on the possession of expertise, knowledge, and talent. People who are seen as experts in a particular area can influence others in two ways. They can provide other people with knowledge that enables or causes them to change their attitudes or behavior, or they can demand conformity to their wishes as the price of the knowledge others need. Thus experts such as doctors, lawyers, and accountants provide advice that influences what their clients do. By expressing their own opinions, media critics shape people's attitudes about new books, movies, recordings, and television shows. Auto mechanics, plumbers, and electricians also exert a great deal of influence over customers who are not themselves talented craftspeople.

How People Respond to Interpersonal Power

How do employees respond when managers use the different kinds of power identified by French and Raven? According to Herbert Kelman, three distinctly different types of reactions are likely responses to attempts to influence behavior. As indicated in Chapter 10, these responses are compliance, identification, and internalization (see Table 13-2).[9]

Compliance. As you will recall from Chapter 10, compliance ensues when people conform to the wishes or directives of others to acquire favorable outcomes for themselves in return. They adopt new attitudes and behaviors not because the latter are agreeable or personally fulfilling but because they lead to specific rewards and approval or avoid specific punishments and disapproval. As indicated in Chapter 10, if people adopt attitudes and behaviors for these reasons, they are likely to continue to display them only as long as the receipt of favorable outcomes remains contingent on conformity.

Of the different types of power identified by French and Raven, which are most likely to stimulate compliance? The answer is reward and coercive power, which are based on linking employee performance with the receipt of positive or negative outcomes. Employees who work harder because a supervisor with reward power has promised them incentive payments are displaying compliance behavior. By choosing to work harder, they are essentially pursuing monetary rewards for their compliance with managerial desires for high productivity. They are likely to work harder only as long as incentive payments continue. Similarly, employees who work harder to avoid punishments administered by a supervisor with coercive power are likely to continue doing so only while the threat of punishment remains salient. In both of these examples, the same performance-outcome linkages that underlie reward and coercive power also encourage compliance, that is, conformity based on the receipt of rewards or the avoidance of punishments.

[9] Herbert C. Kelman, "Compliance, Identification, and Internalization: Three Processes of Attitude Change," *Journal of Conflict Resolution* 2 (1958), 51–60.

T A B L E 13-2
Three Responses to Interpersonal Power

LEVEL	DESCRIPTION
Compliance	Conformity based on desire to gain rewards or avoid punishment. Continues as long as rewards are received or punishment is withheld.
Identification	Conformity based on attractiveness of the influencer. Continues as long as a relationship with the influencer can be maintained.
Internalization	Conformity based on the intrinsically satisfying nature of adopted attitudes or behaviors. Continues as long as satisfaction continues.

Source: Based on Herbert C. Kelman, "Compliance, Identification, and Internalization: Three Processes of Attitude Change," *Journal of Conflict Resolution*, 2 (1958), 51–60.

Identification. Identification, you will recall from Chapter 10, takes place when people accept the direction or influence of other people because they want to establish or maintain satisfying relationships with these people. People come to believe in what they are doing because they identify with those who have asked them to do it, not necessarily because the specific nature of what they are asked to do is important to them. Referent power, discussed by French and Raven, is based on the same sort of personal attractiveness as identification. Consequently, referent power and identification are likely to be closely associated with each other. The use of referent power is likely to stimulate and be stimulated by identification. Charismatic leaders like Steven Jobs, now with Next Inc., or Chrysler's Lee Iacocca have power over others because of their own personal attractiveness. They are able to continue influencing other people's behaviors for as long as identification continues.

Internalization. Through internalization, people may adopt others' attitudes and behaviors because personal needs are satisfied or specific problems are solved. Another reason may be they find those attitudes and behaviors to be congruent with their own personal values. In either case, they accept the others' influence wholeheartedly. It follows that legitimate and expert power can stimulate internalization. Both forms of power rely on personal credibility—the extent to which a person is perceived as truly possessing authority or expertise. This credibility can be used to convince people of the intrinsic importance of the attitudes and behaviors they are being asked to adopt.

As we discussed in Chapter 10, internalization leads people to find newly adopted attitudes and behaviors personally rewarding and self-reinforcing. People who have internalized certain attitudes or behaviors will continue thinking or behaving in a particular way because they find these attitudes or behaviors satisfying in and of themselves. Therefore, a supervisor who can use her expertise to convince colleagues to use consultative leadership can expect the other managers to continue consulting with their subordinates long after she has withdrawn from the situation. In a related vein, a manager whose legitimate power lends credibility to the orders he issues can expect his subordinates to follow those orders even in the absence of rewards, punishments, or charismatic attraction.

A Model of Interpersonal Power: Assessment

French and Raven describe the different kinds of interpersonal power used in organizations, and Kelman's thoughts help identify how people respond to this use. Though valuable as a tool for understanding power and its consequences, the model summarizing their ideas, shown in Figure 13-1, is not entirely without fault. There is some question as to whether the five bases of power it describes are the separate, independent concepts that French and Raven propose or whether they are so closely interrelated as to be virtually indistinguishable from one another. The idea that reward, coercive, and legitimate power often derive from company policies and procedures has led some researchers to subsume these three types of power under **organizational power**. Because expert and referent power are based on personal expertise or charisma, they have sometimes been subsumed under **personal power**.

In fact, French and Raven's five bases of power may be even more closely interrelated than this categorization suggests. In their study of two paper mills, Charles Greene and Philip Podsakoff found that changing just one source of managerial power affected employees' perceptions of three other types of power.[10]

organizational power Types of interpersonal power (reward, coercive, and legitimate power) that often derive from company policies and procedures.

personal power Types of interpersonal power (expert and referent power) that are based on the possession of certain personal traits or characteristics.

[10] Charles N. Greene and Philip M. Podsakoff, "Effects of Withdrawal of a Performance-Contingent Reward on Supervisory Influence and Power," *Academy of Management Journal* 24 (1981), 527–42.

FIGURE 13-1

A Model of Interpersonal Power

Based on Herbert C. Kelman, "Compliance, Identification, and Internalization: Three Processes of Attitude Change," *Journal of Conflict Resolution* 2 (1958), 51–60; and Mario Sussmann and Robert P. Vecchio, "A Social Influence Interpretation of Worker Motivation," *Academy of Management Review* 7 (1982), 177–86.

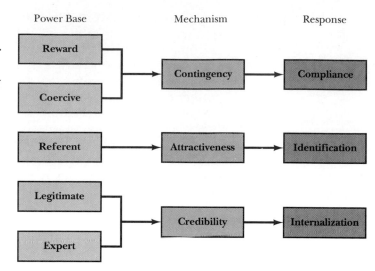

Initially, both paper mills used an incentive-payment plan in which employees' pay was determined by supervisors' monthly performance appraisals. At one mill, the incentive plan was changed to an hourly wage system in which seniority determined an employee's rate of pay. The existing incentive plan was left in place at the other mill. Following this change, the researchers found that employees at the first mill perceived their supervisors as having significantly less reward power—as we might expect—but they also saw significant changes in their supervisors' punishment, legitimate, and referent power. Specifically, they attributed a great deal more punishment power to their supervisors as well as a little less referent power and substantially less legitimate power (see Figure 13-2).

In contrast, employees in the second mill, where the incentive payment remained unchanged, reported no significant changes in their perceptions of their supervisors' reward, punishment, legitimate, and referent power. Because all other conditions were held constant in both mills, employees' changed per-

FIGURE 13-2

Effects of a Change in Method of Payment on Perceived Bases of Power

The change from incentive payment controlled by supervisory appraisals to hourly wages based on seniority eliminated supervisors' reward power and also affected subordinates' perceptions of their supervisor's legitimate, referent, and punishment power. Based on Charles N. Greene and Philip M. Podsakoff, "Effects of Withdrawal of a Performance-Contingent Reward on Supervisory Influence and Power," *Academy of Management Journal* 24 (1981), 527–42.

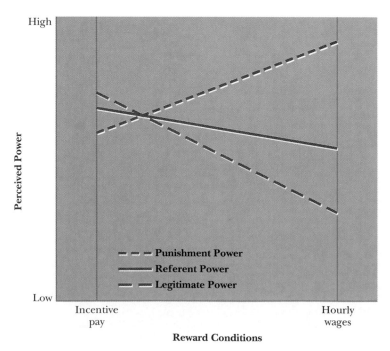

FIGURE 13-3

The Critical Contingencies Model of Group Power

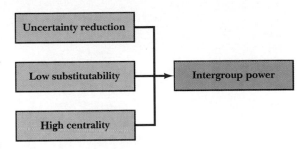

The ability to cope with uncertainty or to provide other critical contingencies combines with a group's centrality and substitutability to influence its power. For instance, a personnel department's ability to identify and hire skilled employees gives it power if other departments cannot attract employees on their own but know that the personnel department can do it for them. Based on David J. Hickson, C. Robin Hinings, Cynthia A. Lee, Rodney H. Schneck, and Johannes M. Pennings, "A Strategic Contingencies Theory of Intraorganizational Power," *Administrative Science Quarterly* 16 (1971), 216–229.

ceptions in the first mill could not be attributed to other unknown factors. Consequently, this study suggests that perceptions of reward, coercive, legitimate, and referent power are closely linked in the workplace. We can therefore conclude that four of the five types of power identified by French and Raven appear virtually indistinguishable to interested observers.[11] Despite its limitations, the model formed by joining French and Raven's classification scheme with Kelman's is useful in analyzing social influence and *interpersonal* power in organizations. Managers can use the model to help predict how subordinates will conform to directives based on a particular type of power. For example, how likely is it that the use of expertise will result in long-term changes in subordinates' behavior? Since the model shown previously in Figure 13-1 indicates that internalization is stimulated by the use of expert power, long-term behavioral changes are quite likely to occur. Alternatively, subordinates may find the model useful as a means of understanding—and perhaps influencing—the behaviors of their superiors. Can you explain why an employee interested in influencing his boss to permanently change her style of management is best advised to try using personal expertise?

Structural Sources of Power

In addition to the interpersonal sources discussed so far, power also originates in the *structure* of patterned work activities and flows of information found in every organization. In Chapter 15 we will examine the topic of organization structure in great detail, so we will limit our current discussion to those characteristics that shape power relations—uncertainty reduction, substitutability, and centrality. As depicted in Figure 13-3, these three variables combine to form the critical contingencies model of power.[12]

critical contingencies Events, activities, or objects that are required by an organization and its various parts to accomplish organizational goals and to ensure continued survival.

Uncertainty Reduction. Critical contingencies are things an organization and its various parts need in order to accomplish organizational goals and continue surviving. For example, the raw materials needed by a company to manufacture the goods it sells are critical contingencies. So, too, are the employees who make these goods, the customers who buy them, and the banks that provide loans to buy equipment. Information can also be a critical contingency. Consider the

[11] Another criticism of our model concerns problems with the measures and methods used to study the French and Raven classification scheme. For further information about these problems and their effects on power research see Gary A. Yukl, *Leadership in Organizations* (Englewood Cliffs, NJ: Prentice Hall, 1981), pp. 38–43; and Philip M. Podsakoff and Chester A. Schreisheim, "Field Studies of French and Raven's Bases of Power: Critique, Reanalysis, and Suggestions for Future Research," *Psychological Bulletin* 97 (1985), 387–411.

[12] David J. Hickson, C. Robin Hinings, Cynthia A. Lee, Rodney H. Schneck, and Johannes M. Pennings, "A Strategic Contingencies Theory of Intraorganizational Power," *Administrative Science Quarterly*, 16 (1971), 216–29; Jeffrey Pfeffer and Gerald R. Salancik, *The External Control of Organizations: A Resource Dependence Perspective* (New York: Harper & Row, 1978) p. 231; and Jeffrey Pfeffer, *Power in Organizations* (Marshfield, Mass.: Pitman, 1981), pp. 109–22.

The power of the Swedish furniture and housewares seller IKEA to control two crucial resources—its goods and its customers' good will—enabled it to nearly double its sales between 1987 and 1991. IKEA, which has stores in 22 countries including the United States, regularly undersells its competitors by 20 to 40 percent. It employs fewer salespeople, substituting a catalog of prices and specifications and plenty of space and time for customers to roam about, gather information, and decide on a purchase. The store's low prices and its relaxed atmosphere as well as its free babysitting services keep its customers very satisfied.
Source: Bill Saporito, "IKEA's Got 'Em Lining Up," Fortune, March 11, 1991, p. 72.

financial data used by banks to decide whether to grant loans, or the mailing lists required by catalog merchandisers to locate and attract prospective customers.

Uncertainty about the continued availability of such critical contingencies threatens organizational well-being. For example, if a purchasing manager cannot be certain she can buy raw materials at reasonable prices, her organization's ability to start or continue productive work is compromised. Similarly, when a marketing department reports shifting consumer tastes, its firm's ability to sell what it has produced is threatened. Thus, as explained by Jerry Salancik and Jeffrey Pfeffer, the critical contingencies model of power is based on the principle that "those [individuals or groups] most able to cope with [their] organization's critical problems and uncertainties acquire power."[13] In other words, individuals or groups that can reduce uncertainty on behalf either of other groups or of the whole organization may be able to exert influence by trading uncertainty reduction for whatever they want in return.

One way to reduce uncertainty is to gain *resource control*, that is, to acquire and maintain access to those resources that are otherwise difficult to get.[14] A personnel department may be able to reduce an important source of uncertainty in an organization that has had problems attracting qualified employees if it can hire and retain an acceptable work force. Similarly, a purchasing department that can negotiate discounts on raw materials can help reduce uncertainty as to whether the firm can afford to continue to produce its line of goods. Finally, a sales group that helps maintain market share by keeping key customers satisfied is preserving another very important resource, or critical contingency. Each of these groups, by delivering crucial resources and thereby reducing success-threatening uncertainty, gains power.[15]

Information control offers another way of reducing uncertainty in organizations. Providing information about critical contingencies is particularly useful when such information can be used to predict or prevent threats to organizational operations.[16] Suppose, for example, that a telecommunication company's legal department learns of impending legislation that will restrict the company's ability to buy additional television stations unless it divests stations it already owns. By

[13] Gerald R. Salancik and Jeffrey Pfeffer, "Who Gets Power and How They Hold On to It: A Strategic-Contingency Model of Power," *Organizational Dynamics* 5 (1977), 3–4.

[14] Rosabeth Moss Kanter, "Power Failures in Management Circuits," *Harvard Business Review*, 57 (1979), 65–75.

[15] Robert H. Miles, *Macro Organizational Behavior* (Santa Monica, Calif.: Goodyear, 1980), pp. 171–72.

[16] Ibid., p. 171.

alerting management and recommending ways to form subsidiary companies to allow continued growth, the firm's legal department may eliminate a lot of uncertainty for the firm. Or suppose an automobile manufacturer's market research group identifies an emerging consumer demand for safe cars. By providing important information about consumers' preferences, the market research department reduces uncertainty for the firm.

A third way to reduce uncertainty is to acquire *decision-making control*, that is, to have input into the initial decisions about what sorts of resources are going to be critical contingencies. At any time, events may conspire to give certain groups power over others, power that allows the former to determine the rules of the game or to decide such basic issues as what the company will produce, to whom it will market the product, and what kinds of materials, skills, and procedures are needed. In our opening story, Charles Parry apparently thought he had acquired decision-making control when he became Alcoa's chief executive. Since Alcoa's founding, the company's sole business had been the production and distribution of aluminum. Parry wanted to redefine Alcoa, however, as a company involved partly in the aluminum business but also in a variety of other business ventures. If the company had adopted this revised mission, aluminum production and marketing would have become less important. Other contingencies associated with conducting the new businesses would have emerged as critical sources of uncertainty.

Having the ability to create and impose definitions enables powerful groups to remain powerful. For instance, Alcoa's board members were knowledgeable about the aluminum industry and capable of reducing many of its critical uncertainties themselves. They retained power by imposing their definition of the company—"Alcoa is an aluminum business"—on Parry and other company officials. Having power can even enable those already in power to make the contingencies they manage more important to organizational well-being. Thus marketing research departments sometimes report the results of their research using advanced statistics that cannot be interpreted by other managers. Management therefore develops additional reliance on marketing researchers as interpreters of the reports they generate. In this manner, power can be used to acquire power of even greater magnitude—"the rich get richer."[17]

substitutability The extent to which other people or groups can grant access to the same critical contingencies provided by the focal person or group.

Substitutability. Whether individuals or groups gain power as a result of their success at reducing uncertainty depends partly on their **substitutability**. Simply put, if others can serve as substitutes and reduce the same sort of uncertainty, then individuals or departments who need help in coping with uncertainty can turn to a variety of sources and no single source is likely to acquire much power. For example, a personnel department's ability to attract potential employees does not help it gain power if other groups in the same organization are also able to bring in new workers. Similarly, a legal department's ability to interpret laws and regulations is unlikely to yield power for the department if legal specialists working in other departments can fulfill the same function. Owing to the presence of substitutes, other departments are able to ignore the pressures of any particular group, and so each group's ability to amass power is undermined.

If others, however, cannot get help in coping with uncertainty from any but the target person or group, this person or group is clearly in a position to bargain uncertainty reduction for desired outcomes. Alternatively, the person or group can withhold assistance as punishment for failure to conform. For example, a research and development group that is a company's sole source of new product ideas can threaten to reduce the flow of innovation if the firm does not provide

---

[17] Gerald R. Salancik and Jeffrey Pfeffer, "The Bases and Uses of Power in Organizational Decision Making," *Administrative Science Quarterly* 19 (1974), 470.

the resources it wants. Or a hospital's staff of physicians can raise or lower the number of patients it is willing to see depending on the treatment it receives from hospital administrators. As you can see, the less substitutability there is in a situation, the more likely it is that a particular person or group will be able to amass power.[18]

centrality The position of person or group within the flow of work in an organization.

Centrality. The ability of a person or a group to acquire power is also affected by its **centrality**, or its position within the flow of work in the organization. The ability to reduce uncertainty is not likely to affect a group's power if no one outside the group knows it has this ability and no one inside the group knows how important the ability is. Ignorance of both types is especially likely in the case of groups that (1) do not have a lot of connections with other groups and (2) have little or no effect on the flow of work through the firm. Thus, simply because few other people know of its existence, a clerical staff located on the periphery of a company is unlikely to be able to amass power even if its typing and filing activities bring it in direct contact with critically important information. Even when uncertainty emerges that the staff could help resolve, it is ignored because no one is aware of the knowledge and abilities the staff members possess.

The Critical Contingencies Model: Assessment

There is strong research support for the critical contingencies model's suggestion that power is a function of uncertainty reduction, substitutability, and centrality. For instance, an analysis of British manufacturing firms in business during the first half of the 20th century confirmed this idea. The analysis revealed that accounting departments dominated organizational decision making in the depression era preceding World War II because they kept costs down at a time when money was scarce.[19] Following the war, power shifted to purchasing departments as money became more readily available and strong consumer demand made access to plentiful supplies of raw materials more important. Then during the 1950s, demand dropped so precipitously that marketing became the most important problem facing British firms. As a result and as the model predicts, marketing and sales departments that succeeded in increasing company sales gained power over important decision making processes.

In another study, researchers examined 29 departments of the University of Illinois, looking at the departments' national reputations, teaching loads, and financial receipts from outside contracts and grants.[20] Results indicated that each department's ability to influence university decision making was directly related to its reputation, teaching load, and grant contributions. In addition, the amount of contract and grant money brought in from the outside had an especially strong effect on departmental power. Contracts and grants are sources of operating funds critical to the survival of a public institution like the University of Illinois. Thus, as predicted by the critical contingencies model, the power of each of the departments in the university was directly related to its ability to contribute to the management of critical contingencies.

An even more intriguing piece of evidence supporting the critical contingencies model was discovered by Michel Crozier, a French sociologist who studied

[18] Hickson et al., "A Strategic Contingencies Theory," p. 40.

[19] Henry A. Landsberger, "A Horizontal Dimension in Bureaucracy," *Administrative Science Quarterly*, 6 (1961), 299–332.

[20] Salancik and Pfeffer, "The Bases and Uses of Power." See also Jeffrey Pfeffer and Gerald R. Salancik, "Organizational Decision Making as a Political Process: The Case of a University Budget," *Administrative Science Quarterly* 19 (1974), 135–51.

470

a government-owned tobacco company located just outside of Paris.[21] As described by Crozier, maintenance mechanics in the tobacco company sought control over their working lives by refusing to share knowledge needed to repair crucial production equipment. The mechanics memorized repair manuals and threw them away so that no one else could refer to them. In addition, they refused to let production employees or supervisors watch as they repaired the company's machines. They also trained their replacements in a closely guarded apprenticeship process so that outsiders could not learn what they knew. Some mechanics even altered equipment so completely that the original manufacturer could not figure out how it worked. In this manner, the tobacco company's maintenance mechanics retained absolute control over the information and skill required to repair production equipment. Because mechanical problems were the most critical form of uncertainty threatening the tobacco plant's productivity, the mechanics' ability to control machine stoppages gave them power over production workers and their supervisors. In essence, maintenance personnel ran the production facility as a result of the information they alone possessed about its equipment.

Crozier's account of the tobacco factory mechanics illustrates the usefulness of the critical contingencies model in explaining why people who have hierarchical authority and formal power sometimes lack the influence needed to manage workplace activities. If subordinates have knowledge, skills, or abilities required to manage critical contingencies, thereby reducing troublesome uncertainties, they may gain the power to refuse to obey hierarchical superiors. Correspondingly, as long as superiors must depend on subordinates to manage such contingencies, it will be the subordinates and not the superiors who determine which orders will be followed and which will be ignored.[22]

In sum, the critical contingencies model appears to depict the structural bases of power quite accurately. Its utility for contemporary managers lies in the observation that the roots of power lie in the ability to solve crucial organizational problems. It is important for managers to know about these roots because such knowledge can help them acquire and hold on to the power needed to do their jobs. We will note several tactics that can be used for these purposes as we discuss politics and political processes in organizations.

politics Activities in which individuals or groups acquire power and use it to advance their own interests.

ORGANIZATIONAL POLITICS

Politics can be defined as activities in which individuals or groups acquire power and use it to advance their own interests. Politics is power in action.[23] In organizations, we can distinguish politics from other uses of power by emphasis on self-interest. Although political behavior may provide organizational benefit, often it is not intended to do so. Politics also differs from other uses of power in that it is often present outside the formally recognized network of

[21] Michel Crozier, *The Bureaucratic Phenomenon* (Chicago: University of Chicago Press, 1964), pp. 153–54.

[22] Chester I. Barnard, *The Functions of the Executive* (Cambridge, Mass.: Harvard University Press, 1938) p. 163; David Mechanic, "Sources of Power of Lower Participants in Complex Organizations," *Administrative Science Quarterly* 7 (1962), 349–64; Lyman W. Porter, Robert W. Allen, and H. L. Angle, "The Politics of Upward Influence in Organizations," in *Research in Organizational Behavior*, vol. 3, ed. Barry M. Staw and Larry L. Cummings (Greenwich, Conn: JAI Press, 1981) pp. 109–50; and Richard S. Blackburn, "Lower Participant Power: Toward a Conceptual Integration," *Academy of Management Review* 6 (1981), 127–31.

[23] Robert W. Allen, Dan L. Madison, Lyman W. Porter, Patricia A. Renwick, and Bronston T. Mayes, "Organizational Politics: Tactics and Characteristics of Its Actors," *California Management Review* 22 (1979), 77–83; Bronston T. Mayes and Robert W. Allen, "Toward a Definition of Organizational Politics," *Academy of Management Review* 2 (1977), 672–78; Victor Murray and Jeffrey Gandz, "Games Executives Play: Politics at Work," *Business Horizons* 23 (1980), 11–23; Pfeffer, *Power in Organizations*, p. 6.

hierarchical authority. It is the informal, unapproved face of power in organizations and may sometimes involve dishonesty or outright deception.

Political behavior is not necessarily bad. The unsanctioned, unanticipated changes wrought by political processes on outdated policies and procedures can, in fact, enhance organizational well-being. They do so by ridding companies of familiar but dysfunctional ways of doing things.[24] For instance, it was political in-fighting that led managers at Apple to reconsider an earlier decision to avoid any sort of compatibility with archrival IBM's personal computers. Subsequent hardware and software developments enabled Apple's Macintosh computers to read data files created by IBM PCs. Apple was then able to expand its market by convincing former IBM customers that they could convert to Macintosh machines without losing existing files.

Nonetheless, because politics has a negative connotation, political behavior is seldom discussed openly in organizations. Indeed, managers and employees may even deny that politics has any influence whatsoever on organizational activities. Research indicates, however, that politicking *does* occur and that it has measurable effects on organizational behavior.[25] We will now discuss many of the findings reported in research on politics and also introduce several of the management recommendations it suggests.

Personality and Politics

Why do people engage in politics? As with power in general, certain personal characteristics predispose people to exhibit political behaviors. For example, there is the need for power (n Pow) identified by McClelland and discussed previously. Just as n Pow drives people to seek out influence over others, it also motivates them to use this power for political gain. Other researchers have suggested that people who evidence the personality characteristic of Machiavellianism may also be inclined toward politics. **Machiavellianism** is defined as the tendency to seek to control other people through opportunistic, manipulative behaviors. Self-conscious people may be less likely than others to get involved in office politics because they fear being singled out as a focus of public attention and being evaluated

Machiavellianism A personality trait characterized by the tendency to seek to control other people through opportunistic, manipulative behaviors.

[24] Miles, *Macro Organizational Behavior*, p. 155.

[25] Allen et al., "Organizational Politics," p. 77; Murray and Gandz, "Games Executives Play;" and Abraham Zaleznik, "Power and Politics in Organizational Life," *Harvard Business Review* 48 (1970), 47–60.

According to several executive search firms, the 1990s will force CEOs to fulfill new assignments. Entrepreneurial skills will be less in demand, and the ability to raise capital and reduce debt will be at a premium. When he took over at General Dynamics in January 1991, William Anders declared that the defense industry faced a shrinking market and that it must become smaller, more productive, and focus more on profitability. Six months later he moved the company's headquarters from St. Louis to the Washington, D.C. area, clearly signaling the company's commitment to its principal customers at the Pentagon.
Source: Jennifer Reese, "CEOs: More Churn at the Top," Fortune, March 11, 1991, pp. 12–13; Richard W. Stevenson, "Mr. Anders Moves to Washington," The New York Times, June 23, 1991.

negatively for engaging in politics. This fear keeps them from seeking power and using it for personal gain.[26]

Antecedent Conditions and Politics

In addition to personality characteristics such as n Pow and Machiavellianism, certain antecedent conditions also encourage political activity in organizations (see Figure 13-4). One such antecedent condition is *uncertainty* of the sort that can be traced to ambiguity and change (see Table 13-3). Uncertainty reduces constraints on behaviors. If their behaviors are hidden or disguised by ambiguity and change, people find it possible to engage in self-interested activities that would otherwise be prohibited. Uncertainty also triggers political behavior because it gives people something to be political about. People want to find a way to reduce uncertainty and to benefit personally from its reduction.

As an example of how uncertainty can encourage politics, consider the following:

> In a budget presentation of all departments in a local community college, one head made a very pious and long presentation outlining the very deep cuts to be made in his area. The rest were moved by his presentation and a portion of his funds were restored. Following the meeting, the head asked for feedback on his "performance" from a small group of his staff who were also at the meeting. All were unanimous in awarding full marks for presentation, piety, general dishonesty, and success of the game plan. (Murray and Gandz "Games Executives Play" pp. 14–15)

In this example, uncertainty surrounding an important resource—the distribution of a community college's budget among its departments—provided the motivation for a department head to engage in politics. The head purposely deceived his colleagues to win a budget increase for himself and his department. Uncertainty surrounding budgetary matters also allowed the department head to keep information about his department's budget to himself and his staff. That enabled him to get away with his deception. Had the community college required that all departmental spending records be made public, others hearing the head's budgetary presentation, would have been aware of the deception and would probably have denied his appeals.

Besides uncertainty, some other antecedent conditions that may encourage political behavior are *organizational size, hierarchical level, membership heterogeneity,* and *decision importance.* Politicking is more prevalent in larger organizations than in smaller ones. The presence of a greater number of people is more likely to hide the behaviors of any one person, enabling him to engage in political behaviors with less fear of discovery. Politics is also more common among middle and upper

---

[26] David C. McClelland, "The Two Faces of Power," *Journal of International Affairs,* 24 (1970), 32–41; R. Christie and F. L. Geis, *Studies in Machiavellianism* (New York: Academic Press, 1970), pp. 1–9; and Gerald R. Ferris, Gail S. Russ, and Patricia M. Fandt, "Politics in Organizations," in *Impression Management in the Organization,* ed. R. A. Giacalone and P. Rosenfeld (Hillsdale, N.J.: Erlbaum, 1989), pp. 143–70.

FIGURE 13-4

A Model of the Emergence of Politics

Based on Gerald R. Ferris, Gail S. Russ, and Patricia M. Fandt, "Politics in organizations," in *Impression Management in the Organization* ed. R. A. Giacalone and P. Rosenfeld (Hillsdale, N.J.: Erlbaum 1989), pp. 143–70.

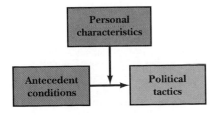

TABLE 13-3
Types of Uncertainty That Encourage Politics

1. Interruptions in the availability of critical resources or of information about these resources.
2. Ambiguity (no clear meaning) or equivocality (more than one possible meaning) in the information that is available.
3. Goals, objectives, work roles, or performance measures that are not well defined.
4. Unclear decision rules for such things as who should make decisions, how decisions should be reached, or when decision making should occur.
5. Change of any type; for example, reorganization, budgetary reallocations, or procedural modifications.
6. Dependence on other individuals or groups, especially when such dependence is accompanied by competitiveness or hostility.

Source: Based on Don R. Beman and Thomas W. Sharkey, "The Use and Abuse of Corporate Politics," *Business Horizons* 30 (1987), 26–30; Anthony Raia, "Power, Politics, and the Human Resource Professional," *Human Resource Planning* 8 (1985), 198–209; and John P. Kotter, "Power, Dependence, and Effective Management," *Harvard Business Review* 53 (1977), 125–36.

managers than at other levels of the organizational hierarchy. That is because the power required to engage in self-interested influence attempts is usually concentrated at upper hierarchical layers. In heterogenous organizations, members share few interests and values and therefore see things very differently. Under such circumstances, political processes are likely to emerge as members compete to decide whose interests will be satisfied and whose will not. Finally, important decisions stimulate more politics than unimportant decisions do simply because less important issues merit less interest and attention.

Political Tactics

When personal characteristics and antecedent conditions are favorable, a variety of political tactics may surface. Each tactic is intended to increase the power of one person or group relative to others. When power increases, so does the likelihood that the person or group will be able to seek out and acquire self-interested gains.[27]

coalition A group that forms to allow its members to combine their political strength in order to pursue interests they hold in common.

Acquiring Interpersonal Power: Forming Affiliations. Forming **coalitions** or political affiliations with each other is one important way for people to increase their power and pursue political gain.[28] By banding together, people can share any control they might have over rewards or punishments. They can also combine their expertise, legitimacy, and charisma. Pooling their power in this manner enables the members of a coalition to pursue mutually desirable outcomes that would be beyond their individual grasp. For instance, employees sometimes form unions to pursue economic rewards and improved working conditions. Collective bargaining enables union members to obtain wages and conditions far superior to those they could demand as individuals. On the other side of the coin, companies also form trade associations to exchange information about collective bargaining and union agreements. This enables employers to help each other bargain for affordable union contracts.

[27] Pfeffer, *Power in Organizations*; Richard L. Daft and Richard M. Steers, *Organizations: A Micro/Macro Approach* (Glenview, Ill.: Scott, Foresman and Company, 1986), pp. 488–89; and Allen et al., "Organizational Politics," pp. 77–83.

[28] William B. Stevenson, Jone B. Pearce, and Lyman W. Porter, "The Concept of Coalition in Organization Theory and Research," *Academy of Management Review* 10 (1985), 256–68.

POWER, POLITICS, AND CONFLICT

The Fine Art of Ingratiation

Suppose you want to improve your position with your boss. How do you do it? One way involves flattery, but through an indirect approach so as to be inconspicuous. Identify a co-worker of yours or a colleague of your boss who interacts with your boss on a regular basis, then praise your boss in front of this person. He or she will often pass your praise on. Another way to ingratiate yourself is to intentionally disagree with your boss, only to yield to your boss's persuasion at a later point in time. This approach enables you to avoid the stigma of looking like a yes man while still allowing you to gain your boss's trust by concurring with her way of seeing things. A third way is to present yourself as what you suspect is your boss's idea of a perfect employee. Being seen working late at the office—if your boss likes hard workers—is one way of managing the impression you make. *Not* being seen working late—if your boss likes employees who work smarter rather than harder—is another approach. In either case, impression management of this sort helps communicate the message that you accept the norms and values your boss espouses, thus, that you are worthy of your boss's respect and consideration.

Does "sucking up" of this sort pay off? Yes, according to several research studies. Employees who ingratiate themselves are more likely to have favored in-group status with those who can grant them power. They may be the recipients of important task assignments, delegated to them in order to prepare them for advancement. At the same time, ingratiators often come to believe in what they are doing, meaning that their attempts to play the role of perfect employee may, in fact, increase their sense of job commitment and improve their level of performance. A moderate amount of ingratiation may benefit everyone.*

* Edward E. Jones, *Ingratiation* (New York: Appleton-Century-Crofts, 1964); Camille B. Wortman and Joan A. W. Linsenmeier, "Interpersonal attraction and techniques of ingratiation in organizational settings," in *New Directions in Organizational Behavior*, eds. Barry M. Staw and Gerald R. Salancik, (Chicago: St. Clair Press, 1977), pp. 133–78; Rahul Jacob, "Sucking up pays off," *Fortune* December 18, 1989, p. 12.

As part of the process of forming political affiliations, doing favors for others is sometimes used to create a sense of indebtedness. Those receiving favors are obliged to reciprocate by doing favors in return. People who pursue this tactic can increase the dependence of others by building up a bank of favors that are owed them. In the U. S. Congress, for instance, members from industrial regions will vote for bills providing farm subsidies with the understanding that farm-state representatives will reciprocate by supporting bills that secure industrial assistance grants.

cooptation Making former adversaries into allies by involving them in planning and decision making-processes.

Besides exchanging favors, people engaging in politics sometimes use cooptation to preserve their interests in the face of adversity. In **cooptation** former adversaries are made into allies by involving them in planning and decision-making processes. Colleges and universities often use this tactic during periods of campus unrest, inviting student protestors to join university representatives on administrative committees. Making opponents part of the team often silences their objections. However, such a tactic risks major changes in plans and decisions.

ingratiation The use of praise and compliments to gain the favor or acceptance of others.

impression management Behaving in ways intended to build a positive public image.

Finally, ingratiation and impression management can be used to build and maintain political relationships. As described more fully in the "In Practice" box, **ingratiation** is the use of praise and compliments to gain the favor or acceptance of others. Similarly, **impression management** involves behaving in ways intended to build a positive image. Both ingratiation and impression management are used to increase personal attractiveness in order to increase the likelihood that others will seek a close relationship.

Acquiring Structural Power: Controlling Critical Resources. Another approach that can be used to amass power and further personal interests is to gain access to supplies of critical resources and control their distribution. As suggested by the critical contingencies model of organization power, controlling the supply of a critical resource gives people power over those whose success or survival depends on having access to that resource. A warehouse manager, for example, can decide which orders will be filled immediately and which will be delayed. He can acquire power by determining who will receive timely supplies of critical raw materials. As a political tool, power of this sort can be used to ensure that personal interests are satisfied.

Similarly, controlling access to information sources provides power over those who need information to reduce uncertainty. As part of this tactic, political players often attempt to control access to people who are sources of important information or expertise. It is not uncommon, for instance, for managers to shield from others in their firm staff specialists who advise them. Engineers working on new product development are often sequestered from other employees; cost accountants may be separated from others in a company's accounting department. Employees like these are an important resource because they possess critical information that is unavailable elsewhere.

To succeed as a political tactic, controlling access to important resources, information, or people, requires eliminating substitutes for these critical resources and discrediting alternative definitions of what is critical. The presence of substitutes counteracts attempts to win power by controlling critical resources because political efforts are neutralized. In addition, successful control of critical resources requires that people have at least the centrality needed to identify which resources are critical and which are not.

scapegoats People who are blamed, whether rightly or not, for the failures of groups or organizations.

Negative Politics. If all else fails, the political upper hand can sometimes be gained over others by attacking or blaming them. This strategy reduces the power they can wield in their own defense. Blaming others for negative outcomes and making them **scapegoats** for failures is one way political players attempt to triumph over adversaries. Another way is to denigrate or belittle others' accomplishments. Either approach involves a direct attack on the interpersonal sources of power others might possess in an attempt to weaken their political position. Such an attack could create doubt about their ability to control rewards and punishments or reduce their credibility, legitimacy, or attractiveness. Negative politicking can also provide reasons for creating substitute sources of critical resources or information or reducing the degree of centrality enjoyed by a person or group. After all, who would want an incompetent individual or group in charge of something that is critically important to organizational survival?

Managing Destructive Politics

You can imagine some of the consequences when people band together, hoard resources, or belittle each other for no other reason than to get their own way. Morale may suffer; battle lines between contending individuals or groups may impede important interactions; energy that should go into productive activities may instead be spent on planning attacks and counterattacks if politicking is left uncontrolled. For this reason, controlling political behavior is a big part of every manager's job.[29]

Set an Example. One way to manage destructive politics is to set an example. Managers who do not tolerate deceit and dirty tricks and refuse to engage in politics themselves make it clear that political tactics are inappropriate. Subordinates are thus discouraged from engaging in destructive political activities. In

[29] The political management techniques described in this section are based on discussions in Robert P. Vecchio, *Organizational Behavior* (Chicago, Dryden Press, 1988), pp. 270–72; and Gregory Moorhead and Ricky W. Griffin, *Organizational Behavior* (Boston: Houghton Mifflin, 1989), pp. 377–78.

contrast, managers who engage in politics—blaming their mistakes on others, keeping critical information from others—convey the message that politics are acceptable. It is little wonder that subordinates in such situations are themselves prone to politicking.

Communicate Openly. By sharing all relevant information with coworkers and colleagues you can alleviate destructive politics. Managers who communicate openly with their peers, superiors, and subordinates eliminate the political advantage of withholding information or blocking access to important people. Information that everyone already knows cannot be hoarded or hidden. In addition, open communication ensures that everyone understands and accepts resource allocations. Such understanding eliminates the attractiveness of political maneuvers intended to bias distribution procedures. Shrinking the potential benefits of destructive politicking acts to lessen the incidence of political behaviors.

Reduce Uncertainty. A third way to minimize destructive political behavior is to reduce uncertainty. Clarifying goals, tasks, and responsibilities makes it easier to assess people's behaviors and makes politics difficult to hide. Opening up decision making processes by consulting with subordinates or involving them in participatory decision processes (see Chapters 11 and 12) helps to make decisions understandable and discourages undercover politicking. In Chapter 14, we will discuss how explaining changes helps encourage people to accept them and reduces fears that can stimulate politics.

Manage Informal Coalitions and Cliques. Managing informal coalitions and cliques can also help reduce destructive politics. As you will see in Chapter 18, influencing the norms and beliefs that steer group behaviors can ensure that employees continue to serve organizational interests. When cliques resist less severe techniques, job reassignment becomes a viable option. Group politicking is abolished by eliminating the group.

Confront Political Game Players. A fifth approach to managing politics is to confront political game players. When people engage in politics despite initial attempts to discourage such activities, a private meeting between superior and subordinate may be enough to curb the subordinate's political pursuits. If not, it may be necessary to resort to disciplinary measures. Punishments such as a public reprimand or a period of layoff without pay ensure that the costs of politicking outweigh its benefits. If this does not work, managers having to cope with damaging politics may have no choice but to dismiss political game players.

Anticipate the Emergence of Damaging Politics. In any effort to control political behavior, awareness and anticipation are critical. If managers are aware that circumstances are conducive to politicking, they can try to prevent politics altogether. Detection of any of the personal characteristics or antecedent conditions discussed earlier should be interpreted as a signal indicating the need for management intervention *before* destructive politics crop up.

INTERGROUP CONFLICT

conflict A process of opposition and confrontation that can occur between either individuals or groups.

Conflict—a process of opposition and confrontation that can occur between either individuals or groups—is an inevitable feature of organizational life. As we pointed out in Chapter 8, in organizations we may see role conflicts *within people* that reflect differences between personal values and role expectations. In Chapter 10 we discussed the conflict *between people* that can arise out of contradictions among their varying role expectations. Now we turn to another important kind of conflict that occurs in organizations—conflict that occurs *between groups*.

Conflict between groups, or **intergroup conflict**, can be defined as a process of confrontation that occurs when one group obstructs the progress of one or more other groups.[30] Key to this definition is the idea that conflict between groups involves confrontation, that is, disputes among groups over clashing interests. Also important is the notion that conflict is a process—something that takes time to unfold, rather than an event that occurs in an instant and then disappears. Finally, to the extent that obstructing group progress threatens group effectiveness and organizational performance, our definition implies that group conflict is a problem that managers must be able to control. In this section, we will discuss the antecedent conditions that stimulate conflict and describe how conflict develops. We will also discuss how to manage conflict when it threatens group and organizational performance. Before considering these important points, though, we will first take a closer look at the basic nature of conflict.

intergroup conflict A process of confrontation that occurs when one group obstructs the progress of one or more other groups.

Is Conflict Necessarily Bad?

Intergroup conflict might seem inherently undesirable. In fact, many of the classic models of organization and management discussed in Chapter 2 support this view, suggesting that intergroup conflict is an indicator of failure or inadequacy in the formal design of an organization. Classic theorists often likened organizations to machines and therefore tended to see conflict as symptomatic of breakdown. Managers in the days of Henri Fayol and Frederick Taylor concerned themselves with discovering ways either to avoid conflict between groups or to suppress it as quickly and forcefully as possible.

Modern theorists, however, suggest that intergroup conflict is not necessarily bad.[31] To be sure, they say, *dysfunctional* intergroup conflict—confrontation between groups that hinders progress toward organizational goals—does occur. In the late 1980s, for example, a long period of labor-management conflict over wages at Hormel, a Minnesota meat packing firm, nearly caused the firm's failure. In 1989, a dispute between labor and management involving wages and working conditions helped push Eastern Airlines into bankruptcy.

Current research, however, suggests that intergroup conflict is sometimes *functional*, having positive effects such as the following:

1. Intergroup conflict can lessen social tensions, helping to stabilize and integrate relationships. If resolved in a way that allows the discussion and dissipation of disagreements between groups, it can serve as a safety valve that vents pressures built up over time.
2. It lets groups express rival claims and provides the opportunity to readjust inventories and allocations. Resource pools may thus be consumed more effectively due to conflict-induced changes.
3. It helps to maintain the level of stimulation or activation required to function innovatively. In so doing, intergroup conflict can serve as a source of motivation to seek adaptive change (see Chapter 14).
4. It supplies feedback about the state of interdependencies and power distributions that form the organization's structure. As a result, structural char-

[30] Miles, *Macro Organizational Behavior*, p. 122.

[31] Robert E. Quinn, *Beyond Rational Management: Mastering the Paradoxes and Competing Demands of High Performance* (San Francisco: Jossey-Bass, 1988), p. 2.

acteristics that promote coordinated effort are more visible and more readily understood (see Chapter 15).

5. Intergroup conflict can help provide a sense of group identity and purpose by clarifying differences and boundaries between groups. Outcomes of this sort are discussed in greater detail later in this chapter.[32]

At the very least, intergroup conflict can serve as a red flag or warning of the need for change. Believing that conflict can have positive effects, contemporary managers try to manage or resolve conflict, not simply avoid or suppress it.

Antecedent Conditions

In order for conflict to occur among groups, several antecedent conditions must be present—interdependence, political indeterminism, and diversity (see Figure 13-5).

Interdependence. Interdependence refers to relations among two or more groups in which the groups depend on each other for assistance, information, compliance, feedback, or other coordinative actions.[33] As you will recall from Chapter 10, four types of interdependence can link groups together—pooled, sequential, reciprocal, and team (see Figure 10-3). Any linkages between groups can become sources of conflict. For example, two groups that share a pooled source of funds may fight over who will receive money to buy new office furniture. Similarly, groups organized along a sequential assembly process may fight about the pace of work. In the absence of interdependence, however, groups have nothing to fight about and, in fact, may not even know of each other's existence.

Political Indeterminism. The emergence of intergroup conflict also requires that the political pecking order among groups be subject to question. If power relations among interdependent groups are unambiguous and stable and if they are accepted as valid by all, appeals to authority will replace conflict, and differences among groups then will be resolved in favor of the most powerful group. Only a group whose power is uncertain will gamble on getting its way through conflict rather than by using power and authority. For this reason, groups in a newly reorganized company are much more likely to engage in conflict than groups in an organization with a stable hierarchy of authority.

[32]Lewis Coser, *The Functions of Social Conflict* (New York: Free Press, 1956), p. 154; Miles, *Macro Organizational Behavior*, p. 123.

[33] Miles, *Macro Organizational Behavior*, p. 131.

FIGURE 13-5

Conditions that Stimulate Intergroup Conflict

Conflict among groups can occur only when groups differ among themselves but are dependent on one another and when lines of authority are obscured by uncertain power relations. For instance, conflict between an engineering department and a research and development department is likely when they must work together to develop new products but neither has the authority to tell the other what to do.

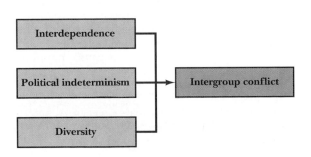

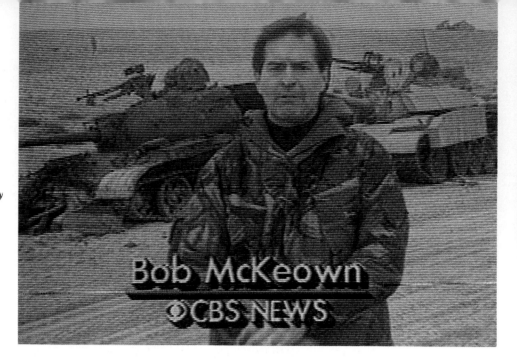

Diversity. Finally, in order for intergroup conflict to emerge there must be differences or disagreements among the groups that are worth fighting over. Let's look at some of the most common types of diversity that stimulate intergroup conflict.[34]

Owing to differences in the functions they perform, organizational groups may have varying *group goals*. Table 13-4 describes some differences in the goal orientations of marketing and manufacturing groups. As you can see, each group's approach reflects its particular orientation—marketing's focus on customer ser-

[34] Miles, Ibid., pp. 132–38; and John M. Ivancevich and Michael T. Matteson, *Organizational Behavior and Management*, 2nd ed. (Homewood, Ill.: BPI-Irwin, 1990), pp. 309–12.

TABLE 13-4
Differences in Goal Orientations: Marketing and Manufacturing

GOAL FOCUS	MARKETING APPROACH	MANUFACTURING APPROACH
Product variety	Customers demand variety.	Variety causes short, often uneconomical production runs.
Capacity limits	Manufacturing capacity limits productivity.	Inaccurate sales forecasts limit productivity.
Product quality	Reasonable quality should be achievable at a cost that is affordable to customers.	Offering options that are difficult to manufacture undermines quality.
New products	New products are the firm's life blood.	Unnecessary design changes are costly.
Cost control	High cost undermines the firm's competitive position.	Broad variety, fast delivery, high quality, and rapid responsiveness are not possible at low cost.

Source: Based on information presented in B. S. Shapiro, "Can Marketing and Manufacturing Coexist?" *Harvard Business Review*, 55, 5 (September-October 1977), 104–14.

---

vice, manufacturing's concern with smooth production runs. In such situations, conflicts may occur over whose goals to pursue and whose to ignore.

Groups also may have different *time orientations*. For example, tasks like making a sale to a regular customer require only short-term planning and can be initiated or altered quite easily. On the other hand, tasks like traditional assembly-line manufacturing operations necessitate a longer time frame because such activities require extensive preplanning and are not easy to change once they have begun. Certain tasks, such as the strategic planning activities that plot an organization's future, may even require time frames of several years. When differences between time orientations exist among groups in a firm, conflicts develop about which orientation should regulate task planning and performance.

Often, *resource allocations* among organizational groups are unequal. In state-supported universities, for example, business schools often receive more funding than liberal arts programs. Such differences usually stem from the fact that groups must compete with each other to get a share of their organization's resources. Generally someone wins and someone loses, laying the groundwork for additional rounds of conflict.

Another source of conflict may be the practices used to *evaluate* and *reward* groups and their members. Consider, for example, that manufacturing groups are often rewarded for efficiency, achieved by minimizing the quantity of raw materials consumed in production activities. Sales groups, on the other hand, are more likely to be rewarded for flexibility, which sacrifices efficiency. Conflict is likely to arise in such situations as each group tries to meet its own performance criteria or tries to force others to adopt the same criteria.

In addition, *status discrepancies* invite conflict over stature and position. Although a group's status is generally determined by its position in the organization's hierarchy of authority—groups higher in the hierarchy having higher status—sometimes other criteria also influence status.[35] A group might argue that its status should depend on the knowledge possessed by its members. Or a group might assert that status should be conferred on the basis of such factors as loyalty, seniority, or visibility.

Conflict can emerge in *jurisdictional disputes* when it is unclear who has responsibility for something. For example, if both the personnel and the employing departments interview a prospective employee, the two groups may get into a dispute over which has the ultimate right to offer employment and which must take the blame if mistakes are made.

Finally, groups can differ in the *values, assumptions*, and *general perceptions* that guide their performance. It is not unusual for a group to develop stereotypic perceptions of other groups that it deals with regularly. These perceptions *may* exaggerate otherwise minimal differences between groups in order to give each group a strong sense of identity. In turn, these exaggerated perceptions may cause conflict that centers on what might otherwise appear to be unimportant dissimilarities.

Stages of Conflict

As we mentioned previously, conflict is more appropriately thought of as a continuing process than as a discrete event. To simplify managerial analysis and action planning, the conflict process can be broken into the sequence of five developmental stages diagrammed in Figure 13-6.[36]

[35] David Ulrich and Jay B. Barney, "Perspectives on Organizations: Resource Dependence, Efficiency, and Population," *Academy of Management Review* 9 (1984), 471–81.

[36] Louis R. Pondy, "Organizational Conflict: Concepts and Models," *Administrative Science Quarterly* 12 (1967), 296–320.

FIGURE 13-6

A Model of the Conflict Process

Based on Louis R. Pondy,
"Organizational Conflict: Concepts
and Models," *Administrative Science
Quarterly* 12 (1967), 296–320.

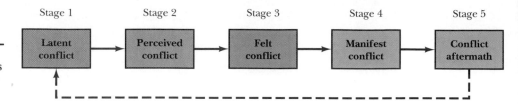

Latent Conflict. Conflict begins with antecedent conditions—interdependence, political indeterminism, and diversity—that provide the basis for argument, competition, and finally conflict. Sometimes these conditions stem from the aftermath of a preceding conflict. For example, managers in a firm such as Kodak may try tightening the linkages between the company's research and development group and its manufacturing group in an effort to deal with prior disagreements over the development of manufacturing techniques for new cameras. Unintentionally, though, tighter interdependence between the two groups may actually set the stage for additional episodes of intergroup conflict. At the stage of **latent conflict**, dissension is only suspected or at best dimly perceived. There is no open conflict at this stage.

latent conflict The stage of conflict development at which dissension is only suspected or at best dimly perceived.

Perceived Conflict. In the second stage, **perceived conflict**, problems are readily perceived and everyone involved in the conflict knows it exists. During this stage, groups sometimes choose to ignore the problem. If they decide to act, however, perceptions can often be changed, misunderstandings reconciled, and the conflict resolved before it progresses any further. Thus, if the conflict between Kodak's research and manufacturing groups evolves to this stage, the members of both groups are aware that a problem exists. They usually can sit down together and iron out differences without attacking each other or causing further misunderstanding.

perceived conflict The stage of conflict development at which problems are readily perceived and everyone involved in the conflict knows that it exists.

Felt Conflict. There is an important difference between perceived and **felt conflict**. When conflict is felt, people are not only aware of it but often feel tense, anxious, angry, or otherwise upset. These feelings emerge as group members involved in the developing conflict personalize the situation, internalizing and attempting to cope with the pressures building between their groups. Conflict can be defused at this stage only by providing a safety valve that allows conflictive feelings to be vented without detrimental effect. In the case of Kodak's research and manufacturing groups, the groups might be forced to confront each other in a carefully monitored meeting. Each group is allowed to verbally attack the other and react to the other's verbal attack in return. By letting groups work through their conflict verbally instead of confronting each other at work, meetings such as the intergroup mirroring intervention described in Chapter 14 help control the extent to which felt conflict undermines workplace performance.

felt conflict The stage of conflict development at which people are not only aware of the conflict but feel tense, anxious, angry, or otherwise upset.

Manifest Conflict. At the stage of **manifest conflict** people engage in behaviors that are clearly intended to frustrate or block their opponents. Such behaviors can range from refusals to cooperate to sabotage, verbal abuse, or even physical aggression. Kodak's research-and-development group might refuse to provide manufacturing personnel with the specifications needed to initiate trial production runs. In retaliation, the manufacturing group might sabotage the raw material inventories used by research-and-development scientists as they experiment with different ways of manufacturing cameras. At this stage, relations between conflicting groups are at greatest risk, and organizational performance is seriously

manifest conflict The stage of conflict development at which people engage in behaviors that are clearly intended to frustrate or block their opponents.

jeopardized. If manifest conflict is not resolved quickly, group and organizational productivity is likely to suffer.

conflict aftermath The stage of conflict development at which conflict sets the stage for later situations and events.

Conflict Aftermath. In the last stage of conflict, **conflict aftermath**, a conflict that has already occurred sets the stage for later situations and events. If the conflict is resolved, the basis for more cooperative relations may be established and the likelihood of recurrences of the conflict reduced. If the conflict is merely suppressed or smoothed over, however, even more serious episodes of conflict may develop. Discord may persist until either differences between conflicting groups are finally resolved or relations between the groups are dissolved. The seeds of future conflicts are often sown by current conflicts.

Effects of Intergroup Conflict

Conflict, especially when manifest, affects relationships within and between groups in several ways. We will look first at changes that typically occur within conflicting groups and then at the changes that occur in the relations between such groups.[37]

Changes Within Groups. Within groups engaged in manifest conflict, changes of four types are often observed. First, as we saw in Chapter 11, external threats such as intergroup conflict bring about *increased group cohesiveness*. As a result, groups engaged in intergroup conflict become more attractive and important to their members. Ongoing conflict also stimulates an *emphasis on task performance*. All efforts within each conflicting group are directed toward meeting the challenge posed by other groups, and concerns about individual members' satisfaction lose importance. A sense of urgency surrounds task performance; defeating the enemy becomes uppermost, and there is much less goofing off.

In addition, when a group faces conflict, its members will often submit to *autocratic leadership* to manage the crisis, perceiving participatory decision making as slow and weak. Strong, authoritarian leaders often emerge as a result of this shift. A group in such circumstances is also likely to place much more emphasis on standard procedures and centralized control. As a result, it becomes characterized by *structural rigidity*. By adhering to established rules and creating and strictly enforcing new ones, the group seeks to eliminate any conflicts that might exist among its members and ensure the repetition of task successes.

Changes Between Groups. In addition to these four changes within groups, four changes often occur in relations between conflicting groups. One such change concerns the *hostility* that conflict arouses between groups. Often this hostility surfaces in the form of hardened we-they attitudes. Each group sees itself as virtuous and other groups as enemies. Intense dislike often accompanies these negative attitudes. As attitudes within each group become more negative, group members develop *distorted perceptions* of other groups. They begin to emphasize negative traits and deemphasize positive ones. Negative stereotyping results, creating even greater differences between groups and further strengthening cohesiveness within each group.

[37] Muzafer Sherif and Carolyn W. Sherif, *Groups in Harmony and Tension* (New York: Harper, 1953) pp. 229–295; Andrew D. Szilagyi, Jr., and Marc J. Wallace, Jr., *Organizational Behavior and Performance*, 4th ed. (Glenview, Ill.: Scott, Foresman, 1987), p. 301; James L. Gibson, John M. Ivancevich, and James H. Donnelly, Jr., *Organizations: Behavior, Structure, Process* (Plano, Texas: Business Publications, 1988), pp. 314–16; Ivancevich and Matteson, *Organizational Behavior and Management*, pp. 313–15.

In time, negative attitudes and perceptions of group members are likely to fuel a *decrease in communication* among conflicting groups. The isolation that results only adds to the conflict, making resolution even more difficult. At the same time, however, conflicting groups often engage in *increased surveillance* intended to provide information about the attitudes, weaknesses, and likely behaviors of other groups. This covert monitoring of other groups' activities is considered essential to staying ahead of the others and winning the conflict. "Facts" that validate negative stereotypes are given preference to information that portrays intergroup relations in more accurate terms. Additional we-they thinking and further conflict are stimulated as a consequence.

Resolving Conflict through Restructuring or Bargaining and Negotiation

Situations in which conflict causes negative changes can be managed in a variety of ways. In general, conflict-management techniques can be clustered into the two categories shown in Figure 13-7. These are restructuring techniques that focus on changing the nature or meaning of relations among interdependent groups, and bargaining and negotiation procedures that are intended to reduce conflict-causing diversity among the interests of different groups.

Restructuring Intergroup Relations. Conflict requires interdependence. Thus it is possible to manage or resolve intergroup conflict by restructuring the connections that tie conflicting groups together.[38] One way to do so involves *developing superordinate goals*, that is, identifying and pursuing a set of performance targets that conflicting groups can achieve only by working together. By requiring conflicting groups to work together to succeed, superordinate goals tighten interdependence. In turn, sharing a common fate requires the groups to look beyond their differences and learn how to cooperate with each other. In the automobile industry, for instance, unions and management fearing plant closures have forgone adversarial relations in order to strengthen the competitiveness of their firms. Teamwork has replaced conflict in the pursuit of the superordinate goal of producing high quality products for today's world markets.

Another way to manage conflict by restructuring interdependence involves *clarifying hierarchical distinctions* and making the political position of each group readily apparent. If it is feasible, this political clarification affects interdependence between groups by strengthening the groups' understanding of how and why they are connected. This approach helps resolve conflict because it reduces the political indeterminism that must exist for conflict to occur. *Expanding the supply of critical resources* is yet a third way to restructure because it removes a major source of conflict between groups that draw from the same supply. Pools of critical

---

[38] Muzafer Sherif, "Superordinate Goals in the Reduction of Intergroup Conflict," *American Journal of Sociology* 63 (1958), 349–56; Jay R. Galbraith, "Organization Design: An Information Processing View," *Interfaces* 4 (1974), 28–36; and Pfeffer, *Power in Organizations*.

FIGURE 13-7

Conflict Resolution Techniques

Intergroup conflict can be resolved by managing interdependence or by managing diversity. Both these approaches seek to reduce or eliminate the negative antecedent effects of diversity, political indeterminism, or interdependence.

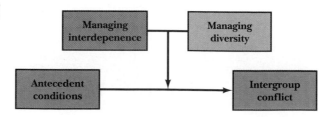

resources are not easily enlarged—which is what makes them critical to begin with. When this method is successful it decreases the amount of interdependence between groups by making groups compete less for available resources. For example, one way to eliminate interoffice conflicts over the availability of shared computers is to buy every department a network of personal computers. Therefore organizations, such as Ford Motor Company's Casting Division, purchase large quantities of used computers at reduced prices instead of a few new ones at full retail. Although the used machines may be slower and less powerful, they provide a greater number of employees with ready access to critical computer resources.

Conflicting groups can also be "decoupled," or separated from each other, by *implementing buffering devices*. In some coffee shops and restaurants, for example, you have probably seen a wheel or spindle on which waiters hang written food orders for the cooks. Eliminating direct communication between these two groups of employees substantially reduces the incidence of conflict.[39] Buffering devices like this one reduce interdependence substantially and they help to manage conflict.

A final approach to manipulate interdependence involves *designing self-contained groups*. Regrouping the members of conflicting groups into new groups that perform their work independently of others is effective. For instance, an engineering department and a computer-assisted drafting department may be involved in conflicts about responsibilities for setting deadlines, approving specifications, and so on. These departments can be reorganized into "cells" that consist of engineers and drafting technicians who complete the entire process of design and drafting without outside assistance. Interdependence between groups is completely eliminated by this approach.

Methods of conflict resolution like these are *structural* techniques because they affect the way an organization's work is divided into tasks and reintegrated into a meaningful whole. We will return to some of these techniques in Chapter 15, when we discuss the kinds of structural mechanisms that are used to coordinate intergroup relations.

Bargaining and Negotiation. In addition to employing structural techniques, managers attempting to resolve destructive conflict may try to work out the differences that generate conflicting interests and concerns. Bargaining and negotiation are two closely associated processes that are often used to accomplish this aim. **Bargaining** is a process that occurs between groups with conflicting interests in which offers, counteroffers, and concessions are exchanged as the groups search for some mutually acceptable resolution. **Negotiation**, in turn, is the process in which the groups decide what each will give and take in the exchange between them.[40]

In the business world, relations between management and labor are often the focus of bargaining and negotiation. Stories about negotiations between unions and local employers appear in newspapers and on news broadcasts on a regular basis. Usually unions are bargaining for better wages, working conditions, benefits, and job security, while management representatives are bargaining to hold down labor costs and ensure continued profitability. However, bargaining and negotiation also occur elsewhere in organizations as people and groups try to satisfy their own desires and control the extent to which they must sacrifice in order to satisfy others. In tight economies, groups of secretaries who are dependent on the same supply budget may have to bargain with each other to

bargaining A process in which offers, counteroffers, and concessions are exchanged as conflicting groups search for some mutually acceptable resolution.

negotiation A process in which groups with conflicting interests decide what each will give and take in the exchange between them.

---

[39] William Foote Whyte, *Human Relations in the Restaurant Industry* (New York: McGraw-Hill, 1948), pp. 67–70.

[40] J. Z. Rubin and B. R. Brown, *The Social Psychology of Bargaining and Negotiation* (New York: Academic Press, 1975), p. 3.

see who will get new computer equipment and who will have to make do with what is already available. A company's sales force may try to negotiate favorable delivery dates for their best clients by offering manufacturing personnel leeway in meeting deadlines for other customers' orders. Research-and-development specialists may offer to make their new discoveries easier to produce if only the manufacturing department will give them additional time.

In deciding whose conflicting interests will be satisfied and whose will not, groups engaged in bargaining and negotiation can choose the degree to which they will assert themselves and look after their own interests. They can also decide whether they will cooperate with their adversary and put its interests ahead of their own. As Figure 13-8 indicates, there are five general approaches to managing diverse interests that are characterized by different mixes of assertiveness and cooperativeness:[41]

competition A conflict management technique that involves attempts to overpower other groups in the conflict and to promote the concerns of one's own group at the expense of the other groups.

accommodation A conflict management technique that involves allowing other groups to satisfy their own concerns at the expense of one's own group.

avoidance A conflict management technique that involves staying neutral at all costs and refusing to take an active role in conflict resolution procedures.

collaboration A conflict management technique that involves attempting to satisfy the concerns of all conflicting groups by working through differences and seeking out optimal solutions in which everyone gains.

1. **Competition** (assertive, uncooperative). This involves overpowering other groups in the conflict and promoting the concerns of one's own group at the expense of the other groups. One way to accomplish this aim is by resorting to authority to satisfy the concerns of one's own group. Thus the head of a group of account executives may appeal to the Director of Advertising to protect the group's turf from the intrusions by other account execs.

2. **Accommodation** (unassertive, cooperative). This is allowing other groups to satisfy their own concerns at the expense of one's own group. Differences are smoothed over to maintain superficial harmony. A purchasing department that fails to meet budgetary guidelines because it overspends on raw materials to satisfy the demands of production groups is trying to use accommodation to cope with latent conflict.

3. **Avoidance** (unassertive, uncooperative). This approach requires staying neutral at all costs. Or it may be refusing to take an active role in conflict resolution procedures. The finance department that sticks its head in the sand and hopes that dissension about budgetary allocations will blow over is exhibiting avoidance.

4. **Collaboration** (assertive, cooperative). This involves attempting to satisfy the concerns of all of the groups by working through differences and seeking

[41] Kenneth W. Thomas, "Conflict and Conflict Management," *Handbook of Industrial and Organizational Psychology* ed. Marvin D. Dunnette (Chicago: Rand McNally, 1976), pp. 889–935; also see Kenneth W. Thomas, "Toward Multidimensional Values in Teaching: The Example of Conflict Behaviors," *Academy of Management Review* 2 (1977), 472–89.

FIGURE 13-8

Managing Diversity

Thomas L. Ruble and Kenneth Thomas, "Support for a Two-Dimensional Model of Conflict Behavior," *Organizational Behavior and Human Performance* 16 (1976), 143–55. Reprinted with permission.

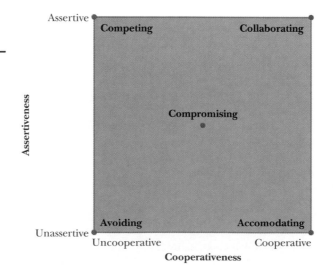

compromise A conflict management technique that involves seeking partial satisfaction of all conflicting groups through exchange and sacrifice.

solutions so that everyone gains as a result. A marketing department and a manufacturing department that meet on a regular basis to plan mutually acceptable production schedules are collaborating.

5. **Compromise** (mid-range assertiveness and cooperativeness). This approach seeks partial satisfaction of all groups through exchange and sacrifice, settling for acceptable rather than optimal resolution. Contract bargaining between union representatives and management typically involves significant compromise by both sides.

As indicated in Table 13-5, the appropriateness of each of these five approaches depends on the situation surrounding the conflict and, often, the time pressure for a negotiated settlement.

T A B L E 13-5
When Different Styles of Managing Diversity Should Be Applied

STYLE	APPLICATION
Competing	When quick, decisive action is required; to cope with crises. On important issues where unpopular solutions must be implemented, such as cost cutting or employee discipline. On issues vital to organizational welfare when your group is certain that its position is correct. Against groups who take advantage of noncompetitive behavior.
Accommodating	When your group is wrong and wants both to show reasonableness and to encourage the expression of a more appropriate view. When issues are more important to groups other than yours, to satisfy others and maintain cooperation. To build credits or bank favors for later issues. To minimize losses when your group is outmatched and losing. When harmony and stability are especially important.
Avoiding	When a conflict is trivial or more important conflicts are pressing. When there is no chance that your group will satisfy its own needs. When the costs of potential disruption outweigh the benefits of resolution. To let groups cool down and gain perspective. When others can resolve the conflict more effectively.
Collaborating	To find an integrative solution when conflicting concerns are too important to be compromised. When the most important objective is to learn. To combine the ideas of people with different perspectives. To gain commitment through the development of consensus. To work through conflicting feelings in individuals and between groups.
Compromising	When group concerns are important but not worth the disruption of more assertive styles. When equally powerful groups are committed to pursuing mutually exclusive concerns. To achieve temporary or transitional settlements. To arrive at expedient resolutions under time pressure. As a backup when neither competing nor problem-solving styles are successful.

Source: Adapted with permission from Kenneth W. Thomas, "Toward Multidimensional Values in Teaching: The Example of Conflict Behaviors," *Academy of Management Review*, 2 (1977), 487.

Beyond these styles of bargaining and negotiation, experts on organizational development have devised an assortment of conflict management techniques based on structured bargaining and negotiation. The next chapter describes several of these techniques in step-by-step detail (see Chapter 14's section on Intergroup Interventions).

SUMMARY

Power is the ability to influence others and to resist their influence in return. Compliance, identification, and internalization are outcomes that may result from the use of five types of interpersonal power—*reward, coercive, legitimate, referent,* or *expert*. In addition to interpersonal sources, power also grows out of uncertainty surrounding the continued availability of *critical contingencies*. It is thus based on the ability to reduce this uncertainty and is enhanced by low *substitutability* and high *centrality*.

Politics is a process in which power is acquired and used to advance self-interests. It is stimulated by a combination of personal characteristics and antecedent conditions and can involve a variety of tactics ranging from *controlling* supplies of critical *resources* to attacking or blaming others. There are several techniques to manage politicking. These include setting an example and confronting political game players.

Intergroup conflict is a process of opposition and confrontation that requires the presence of interdependence, political indeterminism, and diversity. It develops in a sequence of five stages—*latent conflict, perceived conflict, felt conflict, manifest conflict,* and *conflict aftermath*. Intergroup conflict can be resolved by restructuring intergroup relations or managed through bargaining and negotiation.

REVIEW QUESTIONS

1.   Is power being exercised when a manager orders a subordinate to do something the subordinate would do even without being ordered? When a subordinate successfully refuses to follow orders? When a manager's orders are followed despite the subordinate's reluctance?

2.   What is the difference between reward power and coercive power? What do these two types of power have in common? How are they similar to legitimate power? How do they differ from both expert and referent power?

3.   Why must uncertainty, centrality, and low substitutability *all* be present in order for power to be acquired. Explain how a group's power might be reduced by increasing substitutability.

4.   How does uncertainty encourage politics? What can managers do to control this antecedent condition?

5.   What is a coalition? What is gained by forming one? Explain how political tactics like impression management and doing favors for others can make forming a coalition easier.

6.   How can controlling information serve as a political tactic? What can managers do to guard against this tactic?

7.   Why does intergroup conflict require interdependence? How does political indeterminism influence whether this sort of conflict will occur? Based on your answers to these two questions, what can managers do to resolve intergroup conflicts without attempting to reduce diversity?

8.   Explain how one episode of conflict can set the stage for another. Based on what you know about the different stages of conflict, at which stage would you expect to find conflict the easiest to resolve? At which stage would you expect it to be most resistant to resolution?

9. Why is accommodation unlikely to succeed as a conflict management technique in most instances? Under what specific conditions is it most useful?

DIAGNOSTIC QUESTIONS

Considered together, power, politics, and conflict constitute a complex collection of political processes. If they take a dysfunctional turn, these processes can undermine the productivity and satisfaction of individuals and groups, jeopardizing organizational performance as a result. We suggest asking the following diagnostic questions to help manage the political face of organizations:

1. Do individuals and groups in the organization have the power required to function productively and interact effectively?

2. Which types of interpersonal power are currently in use? Are these types of interpersonal power likely to generate the compliance, identification, or internalization needed to energize appropriate behaviors? Might other types of interpersonal power be more effective?

3. If power inadequacies exist, are they traceable to limitations in the ability to reduce uncertainty? To high substitutability? To low centrality? What actions can be taken to correct these deficiencies?

4. Is politics undermining satisfaction or performance in the organization? Can antecedent conditions promoting politics be eliminated?

5. Are managers controlling politics by setting an example, encouraging open communications, managing coalitions, confronting game players, and anticipating future occurrences?

6. Do antecedent conditions—interdependence, political indeterminism, diversity—favor the emergence of intergroup conflict? Is there evidence that dysfunctional latent, perceived, or felt conflict is brewing? Can any of the antecedent conditions be modified to resolve the conflict before it manifests itself?

7. Is there evidence of manifest intergroup conflict? Do the dysfunctional, destructive effects of this conflict outweigh its functional benefits? Can any of the antecedent conditions be modified to resolve the conflict?

8. If interdependence or political indeterminism can be modified, which of the approaches to managing interdependence seems most suitable?

9. If diversity can be modified, which style of bargaining and negotiation best fits the conflict situation?

10. Is there evidence of conflict aftermath remaining from a previous episode that might encourage additional conflict? Can this aftermath be altered before destructive conflict reemerges?

EXERCISE 13-1
CONFLICT AND DISARMAMENT*
NORMAN BERKOWITZ, *Boston College*
HARVEY HORNSTEIN, *Columbia University*

Working in organizations means depending on others and having them depend on you. This interdependence can often stimulate conflict because individuals as well as organizational units have different needs and viewpoints. Although conflict is inescapable and sometimes harmful, you can learn to manage it. The purpose of this exercise is to give you a chance to observe and experience the feelings generated by conflict and confrontation and to examine strategies for developing collaboration among organizational units *before* conflicts arise.

STEP ONE: PRE-CLASS PREPARATION

To prepare for this exercise, label sixteen 3 × 5 index cards as follows:

1. On five of the cards, draw a large black "X" on one side only.
2. On three of the cards, write "Five Dollars" and "$5.00" on both sides.
3. On four of the cards, write "One Dollar" and "$1.00" on both sides.
4. On one of the cards, write "Fifty Cents" and "$.50" on both sides.
5. On two of the cards, write "Twenty Cents" and "$.20" on both sides.
6. On one of the cards, write "Ten Cents" and "$.10" on both sides.

In addition, familiarize yourself with the Disarmament Exercise Rules, described next, and briefly skim the rest of the exercise.

Disarmament Exercise Rules

The Disarmament Exercise is a game played by two teams. Each team can win money or lose it to a World Bank, which holds the funds for the game. Your objective, as a team member, will be to win as much money as you can. Each team will consist of 4 to 6 players. If there are more players on one team than the others, the extra players will assist the instructor and act as referees.

The Funds. Each player will distribute the $20 of "money" that he prepared before the exercise as follows:

1. He will put $15 in a team treasury. At the end of the game, or exercise, whatever is left in each team's treasury will be divided equally among the team members as a measure of the team's performance.
2. He will give $5 to the World Bank, which will be managed by a referee.

Your instructor will deposit an amount equal to the deposits of both teams in the World Bank. For example, for two teams of four players each, each team's treasury will contain $60 and the World Bank will hold $80 for that team—$20 from each team, plus a matching fund of $40 from the instructor.

Special Roles. At the start of Step Two, each team will have 15 minutes to review the instructions for the exercise and plan a team strategy. You must also select people to fill four special roles. No person can fill more than one role at the same time, and the roles can be reassigned at any time by a majority vote of the team. The roles are as follows:

1. Two *negotiators*: Their functions will be explained shortly.
2. A *team representative*: The representative will inform the referee of group decisions about such things as initiation and acceptance of negotiations, moves, and attacks. All such communications must be in writing. The referee will not acknowledge messages in any other form nor will he accept messages from any other team member.
3. One *recorder*: The recorder records team moves on the form provided in Exhibit 13-1. The record must include the action taken by the team in each move, and the team's weapon status at the end of each move. The recorder should also note who initiates decision making and how the team makes final decisions.

The Weapons. Members of each team should pool the cards they have marked with an "X" and then discard

* Adapted with the authors' permission from an exercise entitled "The Disarmament Game." This adaptation copyright © 1992 Prentice-Hall.

EXHIBIT 13-1

EXHIBIT 13-1
Record of Results

Move	SET 1 Actual Number of Armed Weapons	SET 1 Action Taken for This Move (Attack, Not Attack, Negotiate)	SET 2 Actual Number of Armed Weapons	SET 2 Action Taken for This Move (Attack, Not Attack, Negotiate)	SET 3 Actual Number of Armed Weapons	SET 3 Action Taken for This Move (Attack, Not Attack, Negotiate)	SET 4 Actual Number of Armed Weapons	SET 4 Action Taken for This Move (Attack, Not Attack, Negotiate)	SET 5 Actual Number of Armed Weapons	SET 5 Action Taken for This Move (Attack, Not Attack, Negotiate)	SET 6 Actual Number of Armed Weapons	SET 6 Action Taken for This Move (Attack, Not Attack, Negotiate)	
1.													
2.													
3.													
4.													
5.													
6.													
7.													
8.													
9.													
10.													
Ending no. of armed weapons of other team													Total of all sets
Line 1 $ paid to other team													
Line 2 $ paid to World Bank													
Line 3 $ received from other team													
Line 4 $ received from World Bank													
Total Results (Lines 3 + 4-1-2)													

all but 20. Each of the 20 remaining cards is a weapon: when the card is turned so that the "X" is visible, the weapon is armed; when the card is turned so that the blank side is visible, the weapon is unarmed. To begin the exercise, place all twenty of your team's weapons, in the armed condition ("X" side up), where all your team members can see them. During the course of the exercise, your own team's weapons should remain in your possession and out of sight of the other team.

Exercise Procedure. The exercise will consist of several sets of moves and negotiations, completed according to the following instructions:

1. Sets
   A. As many sets as possible will be completed in the time available. Payments will be made after each set.

B. Each set will consist of no more than ten moves for each team. An attack following any move ends a set. If there is no attack, the set ends after the tenth move. Each team has two minutes to make a move. At the end of two minutes, you must have moved two, one, or none of your team's weapons from "armed" to "unarmed" status. You may not rearm weapons that have been disarmed. If you fail to decide on a move in the allotted time, the status quo will be counted as your move. In addition, during each move you must decide whether you want to attack or negotiate (see "Negotiations"). You must communicate your decision to the referee within fifteen seconds of the end of the move.

C. Each team may announce an attack on the other team following any two-minute move period except for the third, sixth, and ninth periods. You may not attack during negotiations.

    D. Once a set ends, you should begin a new set immediately with all weapons armed. Continue with as many sets as time permits.

2. Negotiations

    A. Between moves your team will have the opportunity to communicate with the other team through negotiations.

    B. You may call for negotiations during the fifteen seconds between move periods. The other team may accept or reject your request to negotiate. Negotiations can last no longer than two minutes.

    C. Following negotiations, the next two-minute move period will start immediately after the negotiators have rejoined their teams.

    D. Negotiators may say whatever is necessary to most benefit their team.

    E. The team is not necessarily bound by agreements made by its negotiators.

    F. Negotiators *must* meet after the third, sixth, and ninth moves.

The Payoff. Teams will make payments or receive payoffs at the end of each set according to the following rules:

1. If there is an attack, the set ends immediately. The team with the greater number of armed weapons wins $.50 per member for each armed weapon it has *over and above* the number of armed weapons held by the other team. This is paid directly from the treasury of the losing team to the treasury of the winning team. If both teams have the same number of armed weapons when there is an attack, both teams pay the World Bank $.50 per member.

2. If there is no attack after ten moves, the set ends. If your team has more disarmed weapons than armed weapons, the World Bank should pay it $.20 per member for each surplus disarmed weapon. If your team has fewer disarmed weapons than armed weapons, it must pay the World Bank $.20 per member for each excess armed weapon.

Notes to Referee. While managing the exercise keep the following tips in mind:

1. Keep the pairs of teams separated, so that each team cannot hear the other's conversations. If possible, arrange for each team pair to be in a separate room.

2. To time the length of moves, use a watch with a second hand (your own or a classmate's). An alarm clock that will ring accurately at two-minute intervals would be helpful.

3. Be sure to permit the teams only the specified times. You may need to be forceful in directing the teams when to start and end moves in order to keep them on schedule.

4. You will be the sole manager of World Bank funds and should also check the accuracy of the teams' record keeping.

5. You must not assist either team.

STEP TWO: DISARMAMENT SETS

The class should divide into teams of four to six members each (if you have already formed permanent groups, reassemble in those groups). Your instructor will pair teams up and select extra members to serve as referees. Each pair of teams should then be assigned a referee and should immediately begin the Disarmament Exercise.

STEP THREE: CLASS DISCUSSION

Your instructor will notify all teams when the exercise is over. Each team should make sure its record of results (Exhibit 13-1) is complete and should calculate its profits or losses. A spokesperson should be elected to report briefly to the class on the team's activities. Funds remaining in the team's treasury should be divided equally among its members to further clarify the gains or losses of the team. The class should then reconvene and all team spokespersons should give their reports. Finally, the class should discuss the following questions:

1. What was each team's goal? Did the teams become aware of the need to collaborate with each other and the advantages of doing so? What part did trust between teams play in this exercise?

2. If you were to complete the exercise again, would you do anything differently?

3. If one of the "teams" in an analogous real-world situation were the manufacturing department and the other a sales department of an industrial company and the World Bank were the marketplace, what recommendations would you make to the two departments based on what you learned in this exercise?

CONCLUSION

As you have learned in this exercise, looking after the interests of one's own group and ignoring or even subverting the interests of another group can stimulate disagreements. These disagreements, when coupled with mistrust and opportunism, can ignite in intergroup conflict. Such conflict occurs when interdependent groups lack other means of resolving differences among themselves. It is thus important that groups who must work together develop trust and the ability to handle differences in constructive ways. You will learn more about how to accomplish these twin goals by completing the intergroup mirroring intervention in Exercise 14-1.

DIAGNOSING ORGANIZATIONAL BEHAVIOR

CASE 13-1
CITY NATIONAL BANK*

J. B. RITCHIE, *Brigham Young University*
PAUL H. THOMPSON, *Brigham Young University*

After having worked two months during the previous summer for City National Bank, I returned again this summer to work while on my break from school. Though I would only be there for four months, they hired me on as a full-time staff member replacing a woman who recently terminated. They also hired a woman just out of high school to help handle the extra work load our resort town gets throughout the vacation months. These additions brought our operations division up to seven women plus the assistant manager over our division (see Exhibit 13-2).

The same day I started, a new woman transferred up from a larger branch to our division to take over the note department. Marilyn, the new woman, was not very well liked by most of the workers in the branch because of some negative reports which had preceded her arrival and because her family "owned" the town we worked in.

City National Bank, like any other large bank with many branches, had standardized policies, procedures, and regulations. In order to protect customers, employees, and the corporation, these procedures have to be followed. The bank has auditors who come around periodically to check the books and operational procedures of the branches to assure maintenance of the high standards.

Our branch has relaxed several of the rules and has developed some policies unique to our branch. In part this stems from the informal and friendly relationships shared between customers and employees in our small town, where we know most of the customers on a first-name basis. Unlike our branch, the larger branch Marilyn previously worked in followed procedures strictly and supposedly did everything "according to the book." Marilyn let us know that we were inefficient and backward. Soon bad feelings developed and came to a head in the early part of August.

In August we were in the process of changing managers. Our assistant manager had also left on vacation, so we had a former auditor in management training and a newly promoted supervisor filling the management positions for two weeks. Their job was to sit in for people on vacations throughout our division until each was placed in his own branch. The new manager and assistant manager were upset with our lax attitude toward many rules, some of which we had never even heard of, and they set out to shape up our branch. Among the things we needed to reform were the opening and closing procedures, keeping our keys with us at *all* times, always locking our cash boxes, balancing procedures, check cashing policy, and several other regulations. Marilyn was happy with the new situation and told us "it was about time," but the rest of the branch was very defensive and uncooperative with the temporary management. During this time Marilyn changed several of her responsibilities with the temporary supervisor's permission, and when our assistant manager returned from vacation, there was a great deal of tension between them.

One afternoon while the assistant manager was out, Marilyn went around on her own and picked up three sets of keys that were lying on a table and turned them over to the other assistant manager, saying that the "women should be taught a lesson." This all occurred after the branch had closed, and there were some frantic minutes spent searching for the keys. Marilyn said nothing and we all kept looking until someone remembered seeing Marilyn in their work area. When confronted she merely told the women that Paul, the assistant manager, had the keys. When the whole story was put together, there was a lot of name-calling and derogatory comments, with Marilyn getting the silent treatment for almost a week.

Our management never took an official stand that was enforced. There was never a confrontation between the opposing sides. When Marilyn would approach them on a point, they would satisfy her by agreeing that she had a good point, and when the other side brought

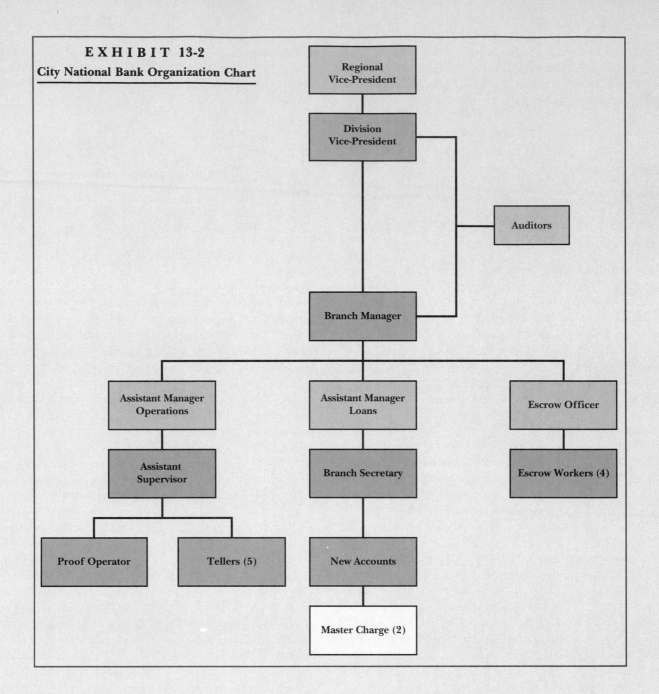

EXHIBIT 13-2
City National Bank Organization Chart

- Regional Vice-President
  - Division Vice-President
    - Auditors
    - Branch Manager
      - Assistant Manager Operations
        - Assistant Supervisor
          - Proof Operator
          - Tellers (5)
      - Assistant Manager Loans
        - Branch Secretary
          - New Accounts
            - Master Charge (2)
      - Escrow Officer
        - Escrow Workers (4)

up complaints, they would agree with them, too. A harmony between practices and policies was never reached. As the summer ended, many problems were compounded because there was no consistent authority and so many things "had changed" according to the original employees. We never knew what was expected. By Labor Day, I left to return to school and four other women had quit or transferred out of my hometown branch of City National Bank.

When you have read this case, look back at the chapter's diagnostic questions and choose the ones that apply to the case. Then use those questions with the ones that follow in your case analysis.

1. What sort of power were City National Bank's new manager and assistant manager using as they tried to reform the procedures followed by the employees at their branch? How did the employees react? Why did they react this way?

2. What should management have done to control Marilyn's political behavior? What was the effect of what they did do?

3. What stage of development had the conflict reached when the writer left the bank to return to school? What do you think is likely to happen in the future if management makes no effort to manage this conflict? What steps should management take to deal with this situation?

CASE 13-2

Rondell Data Corporation*

John A. Seeger, *Bentley College*

"God damn it, he's done it again!"

Frank Forbus threw the stack of prints and specifications down on his desk in disgust. The Model 802 wide-band modulator, released for production the previous Thursday, had just come back to Frank's Engineering Services Department with a caustic note that began, "This one can't be produced, either. . . ." It was the fourth time Production had kicked the design back.

Frank Forbus, director of engineering for Rondell Data Corp., was normally a quiet man. But the Model 802 was stretching his patience; it was beginning to look just like other new products that had hit delays and problems in the transition from design to production during the eight months Frank had worked for Rondell. These problems were nothing new at the sprawling old Rondell factory; Frank's predecessor in the engineering job had run afoul of them too, and had finally been fired for protesting too vehemently about the other departments. But the Model 802 should have been different. Frank had met two months before (July 3, 1988) with the firm's president, Bill Hunt, and with factory superintendent Dave Schwab to smooth the way for the new modulator design. He thought back to the meeting. . . .

"Now we all know there's a tight deadline on the 802," Bill Hunt said, "and Frank's done well to ask us to talk about its introduction. I'm counting on both of you to find any snags in the system, and to work together to get that first production run out by October second. Can you do it?"

"We can do it in Production if we get a clean design two weeks from now, as scheduled," answered Dave Schwab, the grizzled factory superintendent. "Frank and I have already talked about that, of course. I'm setting aside time in the card room and the machine shop, and we'll be ready. If the design goes over schedule, though, I'll have to fill in with other runs, and it will cost us a bundle to break in for the 802. How does it look in Engineering, Frank?"

"I've just reviewed the design for the second time," Frank replied. "If Ron Porter can keep the salesmen out of our hair, and avoid any more last minute changes, we've got a shot. I've pulled the draftsmen off three other overdue jobs to get this one out. But, Dave, that means we can't spring engineers loose to confer with

---

your production people on manufacturing problems."

"Well, Frank, most of those problems are caused by the engineers, and we need them to resolve the difficulties. We've all agreed that production bugs come from both of us bowing to sales pressure, and putting equipment into production before the designs are really ready. That's just what we're trying to avoid on the 802. But I can't have 500 people sitting on their hands waiting for an answer from your people. We'll have to have *some* engineering support."

Bill Hunt broke in, "So long as you two can talk calmly about the problem I'm confident you can resolve it. What a relief it is, Frank, to hear the way you're approaching this. With Kilmann (the previous director of engineering) this conversation would have been a shouting match. Right, Dave?" Dave nodded and smiled.

"Now there's one other thing you should both be aware of," Hunt continued. "Doc Reeves and I talked last night about a new filtering technique, one that might improve the signal-to-noise ratio of the 802 by a factor of two. There's a chance Doc can come up with it before the 802 reaches production, and if it's possible, I'd like to use the new filters. That would give us a real jump on the competition."

Four days after that meeting, Frank found that two of his key people on the 802 design had been called to Production for emergency consultation on a bug found in final assembly: two halves of a new data transmission interface wouldn't fit together because recent changes in the front end required a different chassis design for the back end.

Another week later, Doc Reeves walked into Frank's office, proud as a new parent, with the new filter design. "This won't affect the other modules of the 802 much," Doc had said, "Look, it takes three new cards, a few connectors, some changes in the wiring harness, and some new shielding, and that's all."

Frank had tried to resist the last-minute design changes, but Bill Hunt had stood firm. With a lot of overtime by the engineers and draftsmen, Engineering Services should still be able to finish the prints in time.

Two engineers and three draftsmen went onto 12-hour days to get the 802 ready, but the prints were still five days late reaching Dave Schwab. Two days later, the prints came back to Frank, heavily annotated in red. Schwab had worked all day Saturday to review the job, and had found more than a dozen discrepancies in the prints—most of them caused by the new filter design and insufficient checking time before release. Correction of those design faults had brought on a new generation of discrepancies; Schwab's cover note on the second return of the prints indicated he'd had to release the machine capacity he'd been holding for the 802. On the third iteration, Schwab committed his photo and plating capacity to another rush job. The 802 would be

---

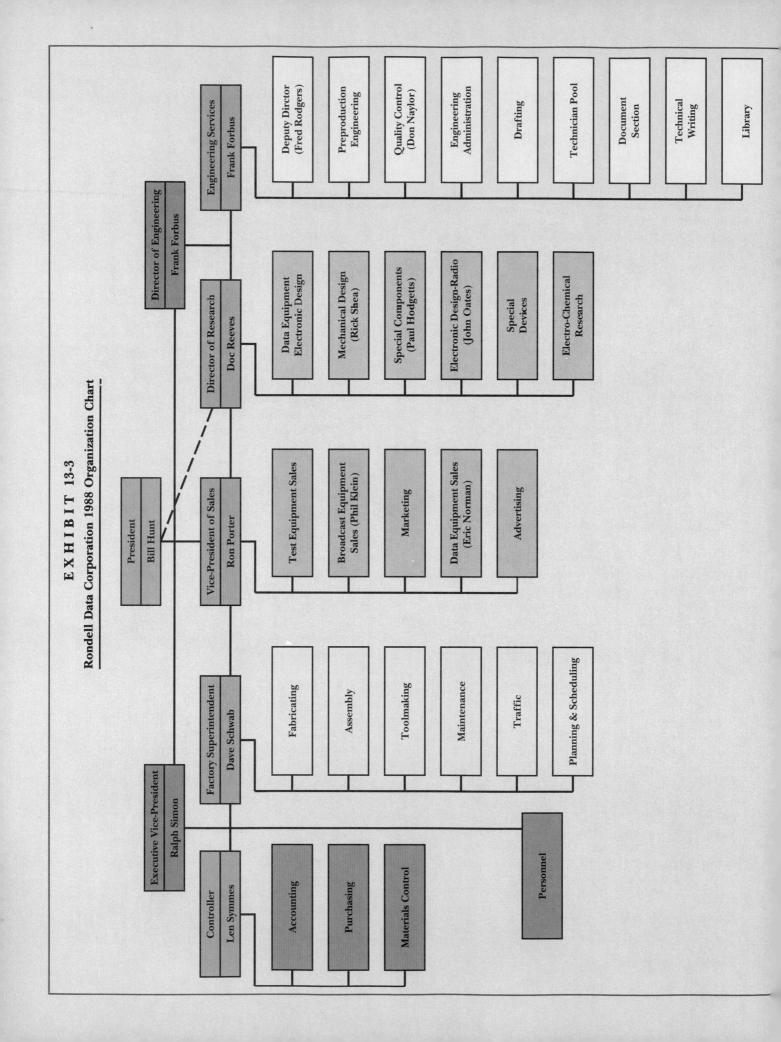

EXHIBIT 13-3

Rondell Data Corporation 1988 Organization Chart

at least one month late getting into production. Ron Porter, Vice President for Sales, was furious. His customer needed 100 units *NOW*, he said. Rondell was the customer's only late supplier.

"Here we go again," thought Frank Forbus.

COMPANY HISTORY

Rondell Data Corp. traced its lineage through several generations of electronics technology. Its original founder, Bob Rondell, had set the firm up in 1920 as "Rondell Equipment Co." to manufacture several electrical testing devices he had invented as an engineering faculty member at a large university. The firm branched into radio broadcasting equipment in 1947, and into data transmission equipment in the early 1960s. A well-established corps of direct sales people, mostly engineers, called on industrial, scientific, and government accounts, but concentrated heavily on original equipment manufacturers. In this market, Rondell had a long-standing reputation as a source of high-quality, innovative designs. The firm's salespeople fed a continual stream of challenging problems into the Engineering Department, where the creative genius of Ed "Doc" Reeves and several dozen other engineers "converted problems to solutions" (as the sales brochure bragged). Product design formed the spearhead of Rondell's growth.

By 1988, Rondell offered a wide range of products in its two major lines. Broadcast equipment sales had benefitted from the growth of UHF TV and FM radio; it now accounted for 35% of company sales. Data transmission had blossomed, and in this field an increasing number of orders called for unique specifications, ranging from specialized display panels to entirely untried designs.

The company had grown from 100 employees in 1947 to over 800 in 1988. (Exhibit 13-3 shows the current organization chart of key employees.) Bill Hunt, who had been a student of the company's founder, had presided over most of that growth, and took great pride in preserving the "family spirit" of the old organization. Informal relationships between Rondell's veteran employees formed the backbone of the firm's day-to-day operations; all the managers relied on personal contact, and Hunt often insisted that the absence of bureaucratic red tap was a key factor in recruiting outstanding engineering talent. The personal management approach extended throughout the factory. All exempt employees were paid on a straight salary plus a share of the profits. Rondell boasted an extremely loyal group of senior employees, and very low turnover in nearly all areas of the company.

The highest turnover job in the firm was Frank Forbus's. Frank had joined Rondell in January of 1988, replacing Jim Kilmann, who had been director of engineering for only 10 months. Kilmann, in turn, had replaced Tom MacLeod, a talented engineer who had made a promising start, but had taken to drink after a year in the job. MacLeod's predecessor had been a genial old timer who retired at 70 after 30 years in charge of engineering. (Doc Reeves had refused the directorship in each of the recent changes, saying, "Hell, that's no promotion for a bench man like me. I'm no administrator.")

For several years, the firm had experienced a steadily increasing number of disputes between research, engineering, sales, and production people—disputes generally centered on the problem of new product introduction. Quarrels between departments became more numerous under MacLeod, Kilmann, and Forbus. Some managers associated these disputes with the company's recent decline in profitability—a decline that, in spite of higher sales and gross revenues, was beginning to bother people in 1987. President Bill Hunt commented:

> Better cooperation, I'm sure, could increase our output by 5–10%. I'd hoped Kilmann could solve the problems, but pretty obviously he was too young, too arrogant. People like him—that conflict type of personality—bother me. I don't like strife, and with him it seemed I spent all my time smoothing out arguments. Kilmann tried to tell everyone else how to run their departments, without having his own house in order. That approach just wouldn't work, here at Rondell. Frank Forbus, now, seems much more in tune with our style of organization. I'm really hopeful now.
>
> Still, we have just as many problems now as we did last year. Maybe even more. I hope Frank can get a handle on Engineering Services soon. . .

THE ENGINEERING DEPARTMENT: RESEARCH

According to the organization chart (see Exhibit 13-3), Frank Forbus was in charge of both research (really the product development function) and engineering services (which provided engineering support). To Forbus, however, the relationship with research was not so clear-cut:

> Doc Reeves is one of the world's unique people, and none of us would have it any other way: He's a creative genius. Sure, the chart says he works for me, but we all know Doc does his own thing. He's not the least bit interested in management routines, and I can't count on him to take any responsibility in scheduling projects, or checking budgets, or what-have-

you. But as long as Doc is director of research, you can bet this company will keep on leading the field. He has more ideas per hour than most people have per year, and he keeps the whole engineering staff fired up. Everybody loves Doc—and you can count me in on that, too. In a way, he works for me, sure. But that's not what's important.

"Doc" Reeves—unhurried, contemplative, casual, and candid—tipped his stool back against the wall of his research cubicle and talked about what *was* important:

> Development engineering. That's where the company's future rests. Either we have it there, or we don't have it.
> There's no kidding ourselves that we're anything but a bunch of Rube Goldbergs here. But that's where the biggest kicks come from—from solving development problems, and dreaming up new ways of doing things. That's why I so look forward to the special contracts we get involved in. We accept them not for the revenue they represent, but because they subsidize the basic development work which goes into all our products.
> This is a fantastic place to work. I have a great crew and they can really deliver when the chips are down. Why, Bill Hunt and I (he gestured toward the neighboring cubicle, where the president's name hung over the door) are likely to find as many people here at work at ten P.M. as at three in the afternoon. The important thing here is the relationships between people; they're based on mutual respect, not on policies and procedures. Administrative red tape is a pain. It takes away from development time.
> Problems? Sure, there are problems now and then. There are power interests in production, where they sometimes resist change. But I'm not a fighting man; you know I suppose if I were, I might go in there and push my weight around a little. But I'm an engineer, and can do more for Rondell sitting right here, or working with my own people. That's what brings results.

Other members of the Research Department echoed Doc's views and added some additional sources of satisfaction with their work. They were proud of the personal contacts they had built up with customers' technical staffs—contacts that increasingly involved travel to the customers' factories to serve as expert advisors in preparation of overall system design specifications. The engineers were also delighted with the department's encouragement of their personal development, continuing education, and independence on the job.

But there were problems, too. Rick Shea, of the mechanical design section, noted,

> In the old days I really enjoyed the work—and the people I worked with. But now there's a lot of irritation. I don't like someone breathing down my neck. You can be hurried into jeopardizing the design.

John Oates, head of the radio electronic design section, was another designer with definite views:

> Production engineering is almost nonexistent in this company. Very little is done by the preproduction section in engineering services. Frank Forbus has been trying to get preproduction into the picture, but he won't succeed because you can't start from such an ambiguous position. There have been three directors of engineering in three years. Frank can't hold his own against the others in the company. Kilmann was too aggressive. Perhaps no amount of tact would have succeeded.

Paul Hodgetts was head of special components in the R & D department. Like the rest of the department he valued bench work. But he complained of engineering services.

> The services don't do things we want them to do. Instead, they tell us what they're going to do. I should probably go to Frank, but I don't get any decisions there. I know I should go through Frank, but this holds things up, so I often go direct.

THE ENGINEERING DEPARTMENT: ENGINERING SERVICES

The Engineering Services Department provided ancillary services to R & D, and served as liaison between engineering and the other Rondell departments. Among its main functions were drafting; management of the central technicians' pool; scheduling and expediting engineering products; documentation and publication of parts lists and engineering orders; preproduction engineering (consisting of the final integration of individual design components into mechanically compatible packages); and quality control (which included inspection of incoming parts and materials, and final inspection of subassemblies and finished equipment). Top management's description of the department included the line, "ESD is responsible for maintaining cooperation with other departments, providing services to the development engineers, and freeing more valuable people in R & D from essential activities which are diversions from and beneath their main competence."

Many of Frank Forbus's 75 employees were located in other departments. Quality control people were scattered through the manufacturing and receiving areas, and technicians worked primarily in the research area or the prototype fabrication room. The remaining ESD personnel were assigned to leftover nooks and crannies near production or engineering sections.

Frank Forbus described his position:

My biggest problem is getting acceptance from the people I work with. I've moved slowly rather than risk antagonism. I saw what happened to Kilmann, and I wanted to avoid that. But although his precipitate action had won over a few of the younger R & D people, he certainly didn't have the department's backing. Of course it was the resentment of other departments which eventually caused his discharge. People have been slow accepting me here. There's nothing really overt, but I get a negative reaction to my ideas.

My role in the company has never been well defined, really. It's complicated by Doc's unique position, of course, and also by the fact that ESD sort of grew by itself over the years, as the design engineers concentrated more and more on the creative parts of product development. I wish I could be more involved in the technical side. That's been my training, and it's a lot of fun. But in our setup, the technical side is the least necessary for me to be involved in.

Schwab (production head) is hard to get along with. Before I came and after Kilmann left, there were six months intervening when no one was really doing any scheduling. No work loads were figured, and unrealistic promises were made about releases. This puts us in an awkward position. We've been scheduling way beyond our capacity to manufacture or engineer.

Certain people within R & D, for instance John Oates, head of the radio electronic design section, understand scheduling well and meet project deadlines, but this is not generally true of the rest of the R & D department, especially the mechanical engineers who won't commit themselves. Most of the complaints come from sales and production department heads because items—like the 802—are going to production before they are fully developed, under pressure from sales to get out the unit, and this snags the whole process. Somehow, engineering services should be able to intervene and resolve these complaints, but I haven't made much headway so far.

I should be able to go to Hunt for help, but he's too busy most of the time, and his major interest is the design side of engineering, where he got his own start. Sometimes he talks as though he's the engineering director as well as president. I have to put my foot down; there are problems here that the front office just doesn't understand.

Sales people were often observed taking their problems directly to designers, while production frequently threw designs back at R & D, claiming they could not be produced and demanding the prompt attention of particular design engineers. The latter were frequently observed in conference with production supervisors on the assembly floor. Frank went on:

The designers seem to feel they're losing something when one of us tries to help. They feel it's a reflection on them to have someone take over what they've been doing. They seem to want to carry a project right through to the final stages, particularly the mechanical people. Consequently, engineering services

people are used below their capacity to contribute and our department is denied functions it should be performing. There's not as much use made of engineering services as there should be.

Frank Forbus's technician supervisor added his comments:

Production picks out the engineer who'll be the "bum of the month." They pick on every little detail instead of using their heads and making the minor changes that have to be made. The fifteen-to-twenty-year people shouldn't have to prove their ability any more, but they spend four hours defending themselves and four hours getting the job done. I have no one to go to when I need help. Frank Forbus is afraid. I'm trying to help him but he can't help me at this time. I'm responsible for fifty people and I've got to support them.

Fred Rodgers, whom Frank had brought with him to the company as an assistant, gave another view of the situation:

I try to get our people in preproduction to take responsibility but they're not used to it and people in other departments don't usually see them as best qualified to solve the problem. There's a real barrier for a newcomer here. Gaining people's confidence is hard. More and more, I'm wondering whether there really is a job for me here.

(Rodgers left Rondell a month later.) Another of Forbus's subordinates gave his view:

If Doc gets a new product idea you can't argue. But he's too optimistic. He judges that others can do what he does—but there's only one Doc Reeves. We've had 900 production change orders this year—they changed 2,500 drawings. If I were in Frank's shoes I'd put my foot down on all this new development. I'd look at the reworking we're doing and get production set up the way I wanted it. Kilmann was fired when he was doing a good job. He was getting some system in the company's operations. Of course, it hurt some people. There is no denying that Doc is the most important person in the company. What gets overlooked is that Hunt is a close second, not just politically but in terms of what he contributes technically and in customer relations.

This subordinate explained that he sometimes went out into the production department but that Schwab, the production head, resented this. Personnel in production said that Kilmann had failed to show respect for oldtimers and was always meddling in other departments' business. This was why he had been fired, they contended.

Don Taylor was in charge of quality control. He commented:

I am now much more concerned with administration and less with work. It is one of the evils you get into. There is tremendous detail in this job. I listen to everyone's opinion. Everybody is important. There shouldn't be distinctions—distinctions between people. I'm not sure whether Frank has to be a fireball like Kilmann. I think the real question is whether Frank is getting the job done. I know my job is essential. I want to supply service to the more talented people and give them information so they can do their jobs better.

The Sales Department

Ron Porter was angry. His job was supposed to be selling, he said, but instead it had turned into settling disputes inside the plant and making excuses to waiting customers. He jabbed a finger toward his desk:

You see that telephone? I'm actually afraid nowadays to hear it ring. Three times out of five, it will be a customer who's hurting because we've failed to deliver on schedule. The other two calls will be from production or ESD, telling me some schedule has slipped again.

The Model 802 is typical. Absolutely typical. We padded the delivery date by six weeks, to allow for contingencies. Within two months the slack had evaporated. Now it looks like we'll be lucky to ship it before Christmas. (It was now November 28.) We're ruining our reputation in the market. Why, just last week one of our best customers—people we've worked with for 15 years—tried to hang a penalty clause on their latest order.

We shouldn't have to be after the engineers all the time. They should be able to see what problems they create without our telling them.

Phil Klein, head of broadcast sales under Porter, noted that many sales decisions were made by top management. Sales was understaffed, he thought, and had never really been able to get on top of the job.

We have grown further and further away from engineering. The director of engineering does not pass on the information that we give him. We need better relationships there. It is very difficult for us to talk to customers about development problems without technical help. We need each other. The whole of engineering is now too isolated from the outside world. The morale of ESD is very low. They're in a bad spot—they're not well organized.

People don't take much to outsiders here. Much of this is because the expectation is built up by top management that jobs will be filled from the bottom. So it's really tough when an outsider like Frank comes in.

Eric Norman, order and pricing coordinator for data equipment, talked about his own relationships with the production department:

Actually, I get along with them fairly well. Oh, things could be better, of course, if they were more cooperative generally: They always seem to say, "It's my bat and my ball, and we're playing by my rules." People are afraid to make production mad; there's a lot of power in there. But you've got to understand that production has its own set of problems. And nobody in Rondell is working any harder than Dave Schwab to try to straighten things out.

The Production Department

Dave Schwab had joined Rondell just after the Korean War, in which he had seen combat duty (at the Yalu River) and intelligence duty at Pyong Yang. Both experiences had been useful in his first year of civilian employment at Rondell's: the wartime factory superintendent and several middle managers had been, apparently, indulging in highly questionable side deals with Rondell's suppliers. Dave Schwab had gathered evidence, revealed the situation to Bill Hunt, and had stood by the president in the ensuing unsavory situation. Seven months after joining the company, Dave was named Factory Superintendent.

His first move had been to replace the fallen managers with a new team from outside. This group did not share the traditional Rondell emphasis on informality and friendly personal relationships, and had worked long and hard to install systematic manufacturing methods and procedures. Before the reorganization, production had controlled purchasing, stock control, and final quality control (where final assembly of products in cabinets was accomplished). Because the wartime events, management decided on a check-and-balance system of organization and removed these three departments from production jurisdiction. The new production managers felt they had been unjustly penalized by this organization, particularly since they had uncovered the behavior that was detrimental to the company in the first place.

By 1988, the production department had grown to 500 employees, of whom 60% worked in the assembly area—an unusually pleasant environment that had been commended by Factory magazine for its colorful decoration, cleanliness, and low noise level. An additional 30% of the work force, mostly skilled machinists, staffed the finishing and fabrication department. About 60 others performed scheduling, supervisory, and maintenance duties. Production workers were nonunion, hourly-paid, and participated in both the liberal profit-sharing program and the stock purchase plan. Morale in production was traditionally high, and turnover was extremely low.

Dave Schwab commented:

To be efficient, production has to be a self-contained department. We have to control what comes into the department and what goes out. That's why purchasing, inventory control, and quality ought to run out of this office. We'd eliminate a lot of problems with better control there. Why, even Don Naylor in QC would rather work for me than for ESD; he's said so himself. We understand his problems better.

The other departments should be self-contained, too. That's why I always avoid the underlings, and go straight to the department heads with any questions. I always go down the line.

I have to protect my people from outside disturbances. Look what would happen if I let unfinished, half-baked designs in here—there'd be chaos. The bugs have to be found before the drawings go into the shop, and it seems I'm the one who has to find them. Look at the 802, for example. (Dave had spent most of Thanksgiving Day [it was now November 28] red-pencilling the latest set of prints.) ESD should have found every one of those discrepancies. They just don't check drawings properly. They change most of the things I flag, but then they fail to trace through the impact of those changes on the rest of the design. I shouldn't have to do that.

And those engineers are tolerance crazy. They want everything to a millionth of an inch. I'm the only one in the company who's had any experience with actually machining things to a millionth of an inch. We make sure that the things that engineers say on their drawings actually have to be that way and whether they're obtainable from the kind of raw material we buy.

That shouldn't be production's responsibility, but I have to do it. Accepting bad prints wouldn't let us ship the order any quicker. We'd only make a lot of junk that had to be reworked. And that would take even longer.

This way, I get to be known as the bad guy, but I guess that's just part of the job. (He paused with a wry smile.) Of course, what really gets them is that I don't even have a degree.

Dave had fewer bones to pick with the sales department because, he said, they trusted him.

When we give Ron Porter a shipping date, he knows the equipment will be shipped then.

You've got to recognize, though, that all of our new product problems stem from sales making absurd commitments on equipment that hasn't been fully developed. That always means trouble. Unfortunately, Hunt always backs sales up, even when they're wrong. He always favors them over us.

Ralph Simon, age 65, executive vice president of the company, had direct responsibility for Rondell's production department. He said:

There shouldn't really be a dividing of departments among top management in the company. The president should be czar over all. The production people ask me to do something for them, and I really can't do it. It creates bad feelings between engineering and production, this special attention that they (R & D) get from Bill. But then Hunt likes to dabble in design. Schwab feels that production is treated like a poor relation.

THE EXECUTIVE COMMITTEE

At the executive committee meeting of December 6, it was duly recorded that Dave Schwab had accepted the prints and specifications for the Model 802 modulator, and had set Friday, December 29, as the shipping date for the first 10 pieces. Bill Hunt, in the chairperson's role, shook his head and changed the subject quickly when Frank tried to open the agenda to a discussion of interdepartmental coordination.

The executive committee itself was a brainchild of Rondell's controller, Len Symmes, who was well aware of the disputes that plagued the company. Symmes had convinced Bill Hunt and Ralph Simon to meet every two weeks with their department heads, and the meetings were formalized with Hunt, Simon, Ron Porter, Dave Schwab, Frank Forbus, Doc Reeves, Symmes, and the personnel director attending. Symmes explained his intent and the results:

Doing things collectively and informally just doesn't work as well as it used to. Things have been gradually getting worse for at least two years now: We had to start thinking in terms of formal organization relationships. I did the first organization chart, and the executive committee was my idea too—but neither idea is contributing much help, I'm afraid. It takes top management to make an organization click. The rest of us can't act much differently until the top people see the need for us to change.

I had hoped the committee especially would help get the department managers into a constructive planning process. It hasn't worked out that way because Mr. Hunt really doesn't see the need for it. He uses the meetings as a place to pass on routine information.

MERRY CHRISTMAS

"Frank, I didn't know whether to tell you now, or after the holiday." It was Friday, December 22, and Frank Forbus was standing awkwardly in front of Bill Hunt's desk.

"But, I figured you'd work right through Christmas Day if we didn't have this talk, and that just wouldn't have been fair to you. I can't understand why we have such poor luck in the engineering director's job lately. And I don't think it's entirely your fault. But . . ."

Frank only heard half of Hunt's words, and said nothing in response. He'd be paid through February 28 . . . He should use the time for searching . . . Hunt would help all he could . . . Jim Kilmann was supposed to be doing well at his own new job, and might need more help . . .

Frank cleaned out his desk, and numbly started home. The electronic carillon near his house was playing a Christmas carol. Frank thought again of Hunt's rationale: conflict still plagued Rondell—and Frank had not made it go away. Maybe somebody else could do it.

"And what did Santa Claus bring you, Frankie?" he asked himself.

"The sack. Only the empty sack."

When you have read this case, look back at the chapter's diagnostic questions and choose the ones that apply to the case. Then use those questions with the ones that follow in your case analysis.

1. Why was Rondell Data unable to fill Frank Forbus's position successfully? What would you advise Frank to do to increase his chances of keeping his job?

2. What made Doc Reeves so powerful? What problems did Doc's power cause the rest of the company? What should be done to manage Doc and his relations with the rest of the engineering staff?

3. Describe the conflict between Rondell's departments. What is causing this conflict? How should it be managed? What specific steps would you advise Rondell's management to take?

CASE 13-3

NEWCOMER-WILLSON HOSPITAL

Read Chapter 16's Case 16-1, "Newcomer-Willson Hospital." Next, look back at Chapter 13's diagnostic questions and choose the ones that apply to that case. Then use those questions with the ones that follow in this first analysis of the case.

1. What is the source of the hospital's administrators' power? What is the source of the physicians' power? The source of the nurses' power? Which of these groups seems to have the most clout? The least?

2. What caused the conflict between the hospital administration and the staff doctors? Between the doctors and the staff nurses? Are these conflicts disruptive? In what ways?

3. How can the conflicts at Newcomer-Willson Hospital be resolved? Can a negotiated settlement be reached? Or are structural modifications needed?

C H A P T E R 14

MANAGING GROUP
AND INTERGROUP RELATIONS:
ORGANIZATION DEVELOPMENT I

NCR's new concurrent engineering *approach to product development, in which people in several different departments work side by side, offers both opportunities and challenges. Frequent exchange of information among team members keeps everyone better informed about the progress of work and can generate ideas about new ways of doing things. For example, a new product is a pen-and-tablet device intended to replace the keyboard on a personal computer. But the often intense interaction among team members can also lead to arguments and dissension, and managers using this approach need to be skilled in facilitating cooperation and in helping group members resolve conflicts.*

At its plant in Atlanta, NCR Corp. is trying a new approach to product development. Like most manufacturers, NCR used to develop products in a series of steps, starting with design and engineering, then letting contracts for various materials, parts, and services, then finally going into production. Each step was largely independent of the others, and changes made at any post-design stage caused major traumas. The late fixes would ripple back through a project, causing everything that had gone before to be reworked. That would delay the product and push costs through the ceiling. So NCR decided to test a new method. In 1988 it tore down the wall that separates most design and manufacturing departments. Now, all the plant's 100-odd engineers are located in a pool of identical cubicles, so the specialists involved in design, software, hardware, purchasing, manufacturing, and field support all work side by side and compare notes constantly. This makes for more synergy, curbs late fixes, and achieves what William R. Sprague, NCR's senior manufacturing engineer in Atlanta, calls the overriding factor—getting products out on time.[1]

NCR's new approach, called concurrent engineering, is catching on in companies in the United States and Canada and is being touted as a development that could help North America regain its competitive edge throughout the world.[2] Besides NCR, newly merged with American Telephone and Telegraph, John Deere and Company, Motorola, and Westinghouse's Electronic Systems Group are also using concurrent engineering to reduce the costs and time required to design new products and get them to the marketplace. These gains have their price, though. To work as planned, concurrent engineering requires intense cooperation within the teams formed to complete design assignments. Collaboration is also required between different design teams so that information about one team's innovations can filter outward to other teams and be used to reduce product-development times even further. Managers of concurrent engineering operations must therefore be experts in encouraging teamwork within and among groups.

Similar trends toward using teams at work are also noticeable in the manufacturing phase of company operations. For instance, in 1986 Caterpillar Inc., a United States manufacturer of tractors and other heavy equipment, adopted flexible manufacturing methods that made obsolete the old way of organizing work into individualized tasks. By 1990, many of the company's employees had been grouped into highly interdependent teams. Today, each of these teams operates a self-sufficient cell of robots and other computerized machinery that can be reconfigured quickly to adapt to new production requirements. This flexibility enables Caterpillar to be extremely responsive to changing customer demands.[3] However, it also requires that managers be adept at managing group and intergroup relations.

Just as NCR is not alone in its adoption of concurrent engineering, Caterpillar is but one of many companies that have turned to group manufacturing processes. Firms such as IBM, Procter and Gamble, and Monsanto have begun

[1] Reprinted from Otis Port, Zachary Schiller, and Resa W. King, "A Smarter Way to Manufacture," *Business Week*, April 30, 1990, p. 110.

[2] Ibid., pp. 110–17.

[3] Brian Bremmer, "Can Caterpillar Inch Its Way Back to Heftier Profits?" *Business Week*, September 25, 1989, pp. 75–78.

Like other manufacturers throughout the U.S. and Canada, General Motors has begun using the team concept to improve quality and productivity. To learn more about managing teams, in 1983 GM joined with Japan's Toyota Motor Company to form the New United Motor Manufacturing, Inc., or NUMMI. For GM, NUMMI is an experiment in abandoning the hundreds of job classifications often used in auto plants and substituting teams of multiskilled workers capable of performing a wide variety of tasks. As a result of such changes,

the NUMMI plant is able to produce more high-quality cars—NUMMI makes the Geo Prizm and many of Toyota's Corollas—at lower costs and with greater work-force satisfaction than most of GM's other facilities. What has GM learned from NUMMI and the Japanese? Simply put, that better management, not massive automation, is the key to efficient manufacturing.*

* Based on "This Team-Up Has It All—Except Sales," *Business Week*, August 14, 1989, p. 79.

to rely on the team approach.[4] General Motors has also experimented with team production at its NUMMI plant in California and is implementing what it has learned at its Saturn plant in Tennessee (see the "International OB" box). If this trend continues, by the beginning of the 21st century, most large companies in North America will employ team methods either to design or to manufacture their products. More than ever before, managers will have to be experts at helping employees as they form work teams, participate in group decision making, and cope with the transition from working alone to working closely with others. Managerial success will also require expertise in stabilizing groups and resolving occasional confrontations between group members or among groups.

As you know, we have already overviewed much of this expertise in the previous four chapters. By now you should be aware of the basic facts and theories you will need to function effectively as a manager of team operations. We have not spent much time, however, talking about specific actions managers can take and programs they can implement to manage relations in and among groups. In this chapter, we turn our attention to discussing such actions and programs in greater detail. As indicated in Chapter 1, it is the second of three chapters in this book that addresses what can actually be done to manage organizational behavior. We will explore the field of organization development, which is the study and practice of changing the way people interact in organizations. After defining the field of organization development, we will examine resistance to change and ways to overcome it. In the process, we will talk about factors that can act as forces for and against change in organizations. We will also discuss what it means to be a *change agent* charged with overseeing an organization-development intervention. We will conclude by describing a variety of such interventions that managers can use to change and manage interpersonal, group, and intergroup relations on the job.

DIAGNOSTIC ISSUES

Our diagnostic model points to several important issues in organization development and change. How do we *describe* an organization's current situation and the kinds of problems we are having with group and intergroup relations? Can we distinguish the forces or groups within the organ-

[4] James G. Ellis, "Monsanto Is Teaching Old Workers New Tricks." *Business Week*, August 21, 1989, p. 67.

ization that will favor change from those that will resist it? What *diagnostic* procedures can we use to decide which changes to make and how to make them? How can we distinguish the situation in which organization development efforts will lead to permanent change from the situation in which the effects of such efforts will not last?

How can we *prescribe* the most effective method for overcoming resistance to change? Can we predict whether the changes we need to make will be best achieved by someone inside the organization or by an outside consultant? Finally, in putting organization development plans into *action*, how do we decide who should evaluate the effectiveness of these plans? Who should have access to this information?

WHAT IS ORGANIZATION DEVELOPMENT?

organization development A planned approach to interpersonal, group, intergroup, and organization-wide change that is comprehensive and long term and under the guidance of a change agent.

intervention A particular organization development technique, such as counseling or team building, that is used to stimulate change in organizations.

Organization development, often referred to as *OD*, is a process of planning, implementing, and stabilizing the results of change in organizations. OD is also a field of research that specializes in developing and assessing specific **interventions** or change techniques.[5] As both a management process and a field of research, OD is characterized by five important features:

1. *Emphasis on planned change.* The field of organization development evolved out of the need for a systematic, planned approach to managing change in organizations. It is OD's emphasis on *planning* that distinguishes it from other kinds of organizational changes that are more spontaneous or less methodical.

2. *A social-psychological focus.* OD interventions can stimulate change at many different levels—interpersonal, group, intergroup, or organization wide. The field of OD is thus neither purely psychological (focused solely on individuals) nor purely sociological (focused solely on organizations) but instead incorporates a mixture of both orientations.

3. *Attention to comprehensive change.* Although every OD intervention focuses on a specific organizational target, planners also keep in mind the effects of change on the *total system.* No OD intervention is designed and implemented without considering its effects on the rest of the organization.

4. *Long-range orientation.* OD experts emphasize that change is a continuing process that can sometimes take months—or even years—to produce desired results. Although managers often face pressures for quick, short-term gains, the OD process is not intended to yield stopgap solutions.

change agent A person who manages the OD process, serving both as a catalyst for change and as a source of information about OD.

5. *Guidance by a change agent.* OD interventions are designed, implemented, and assessed with the help of a **change agent**, who serves both as a catalyst for change and as a source of information about the OD process. Successful organization development does not grow out of an unguided, do-it-yourself approach to organizational change.[6]

---

[5] Gordon L. Lippitt, Petter Longseth, and Jack Mossop, *Implementing Organizational Change* (San Francisco: Jossey-Bass, 1985), p. 3; and Ellen Fagenson and W. Warner Burke, "The Current Activities and Skills of Organization Development Practitioners," *Academy of Management Proceedings*, August 13–16, 1989, 251.

[6] Alan C. Filley, Robert J. House, and Steven Kerr, *Managerial Process and Organizational Behavior*, 2nd ed. (Glenview, Ill.: Scott, Foresman, 1976), pp. 488–90; and Wendell L. French and Cecil H. Bell, Jr., *Organization Development: Behavioral Science Interventions for Organizational Improvement*, 4th ed. (Englewood Cliffs, N.J.: Prentice Hall, 1990), pp. 21–22.

Together, these five features suggest the following definition: Organization development is a planned approach to interpersonal, group, intergroup, and organization wide change that is comprehensive, long-term, and under the guidance of a change agent.

The Change Agent

As indicated in our definition of OD, a change agent is a person who takes responsibility for overseeing the process of organization development. Such a person might be from outside the **client organization**—the organization undergoing development. An **external change agent** of this sort may be the employee of a consulting firm such as Arthur Andersen, she may be a specialist who is also a university professor, or she may be a full-time independent consultant. In any case, she probably has one or more graduate degrees in specialties that focus on individual and group behavior in organizations—organization development, organizational behavior, management, industrial/organizational psychology, or related fields of social science. This background, combined with an outsider's somewhat greater objectivity, supports a professional perspective that enables the external change agent to manage the change process in an unbiased manner. On the downside, the external change agent is unlikely to know as much about organizational policies, practices, and politics as someone from inside the firm.

Sometimes the change agent may already work for the client organization. Often, but not always, this person will be an employee of the firm's human resource management department or, in large companies like General Motors or IBM, of a separate training-and-development group. Being employed by the organization gives the **internal change agent** insight into the details of day-to-day events and procedures.[7] The internal change agent, however, may not always have the training of an external consultant, and his objectivity may be considerably less than that of an outside observer.

As you can see, choosing between external and internal change agents involves tradeoffs between professional expertise and objectivity, on the one hand, and insider familiarity and insight, on the other.[8] Sometimes an organization can seek a middle road, combining professional objectivity with insider familiarity by using a team of external and internal change agents. Although this seems like a very sensible approach, it is not used often now, partly because it is quite expensive. It seems likely, however, that as the emphasis on group production methods and intergroup collaboration continues to grow, the external-internal change agent team may become more common.

Resistance to Change

Change, often both the impetus and the product of OD efforts, involves modifying the ways the people and groups in an organization normally work together. Table 14-1 outlines the three types of change that take place in organizations—adaptive, innovative, and revolutionary. Whenever we attempt to set any one of these kinds of changes in motion we can expect resistance, for people tend to resist what they perceive as a threat to the established way of doing things. Eliminating or greatly decreasing this resistance is critical to the success of all OD interventions or other change-oriented processes.

---

[7] Stephen C. Harper, "The Manager as Change Agent: 'Hell No' to the Status Quo," *Industrial Management* 3 (1989), 8–11.

[8] Manuel London, *Change Agents* (San Francisco: Jossey-Bass, 1988), p. 194.

Margin glossary:

client organization An organization involved in the process of organization development.

external change agent An OD change agent who is not a member of the client organization.

internal change agent An OD change agent who is a member of the client organization.

508

MANAGING GROUP AND INTERGROUP RELATIONS: ORGANIZATION DEVELOPMENT I

T A B L E 14-1
Types of Organizational Change

TYPE OF CHANGE	DESCRIPTION	EXAMPLE IN THE RETAIL SALES INDUSTRY	COMPLEXITY, COST, AND UNCERTAINTY	POTENTIAL RESISTANCE
Adaptive	Reintroducing a familiar practice—one used previously or used elsewhere in the organization	Adoption of longer business hours during holiday shopping season	Lowest	Lowest
Innovative	Introducing a practice that is new to the organization but used elsewhere in the industry	Use of point-of-sale computers connected to cash registers to keep running account of inventory	Moderate	Moderate
Revolutionary	Introducing a practice that is new to the organization and new to the industry	Use of automated salesclerk machines that allow customers to complete an entire sales transaction without human assistance	Highest	Highest

Source: Based on Paul C. Nutt, "Tactics of Implementation," *Academy of Management Journal* 29 (1986), 230–61; and Manuel London and John Paul Mac-Duffie, "Technical Innovations: Case Examples and Guidelines," *Personnel* (1987), 26–38.

Sources of Resistance. Resistance to change may take different forms. It may be physical, intellectual, or emotional. Some of the most common sources of this resistance are individual self-interest, fear of the unknown, general mistrust, fear of failure, differing perceptions and goals, possible loss of status, social disruption, pressure from peers, managerial tactlessness, poor timing in introducing changes, personality conflicts, and bureaucratic inertia.[9]

Change can threaten *self interest*. People may fear that change will make it difficult or impossible for them to continue to satisfy personal needs and desires at work. For example, employees accustomed to working alone may feel that a change to team operations costs them the autonomy to decide how to do their own jobs. Conversely, employees used to working on teams may mourn the loss of social interaction if new job assignments require them to work alone.

Uncertainty about what to expect, or *fear of the unknown*, can arouse anxiety and create resistance. Especially when innovative or radically different ideas are introduced without warning, employees likely to be affected become fearful of the implications of change. Consider how you would react if it were suddenly announced that your college was going to change from semesters to quarters (or vice versa). Most likely, your first response would be to resist this change. You would worry about how credits obtained under the old system would transfer into the new system, about the courses taught in the new system, and about whether you would still be able to graduate on time.

When people mistrust others' intentions and behavior, they are particularly apt to be suspicious of impending change. *General mistrust* encourages secrecy or even deception, either of which creates further doubts about the intentions underlying change. At Eastern Airlines during the period of Frank Lorenzo's ownership, mechanics kept secret diaries detailing alleged rushed repairs and unsafe working conditions. Later they turned the diaries over to union representatives

---

[9] Paul R. Lawrence, "How to Deal with Resistance to Change," in *Organizational Change and Development*, ed. G. W. Dalton, P. R. Lawrence, and L. E. Greiner, (Homewood, Ill.: Irwin-Dorsey, 1970), pp. 181–97; Rino J. Patty, "Organizational Resistance to Change: The View from Below," *Social Service Review* 48 (1974), 371–72; Gerald Zaltman and Robert Duncan, *Strategies for Planned Change* (New York: Wiley-Interscience, 1977), pp. 98–121; and Joseph Stanislao and Bettie C. Stanislao, "Dealing with Resistance to Change," *Business Horizons*, 26 (1983), 74–78.

and government officials. One of the reasons for the mechanics' secret activities was their mistrust of Lorenzo. He had a history of trying to eliminate unions in the companies he owned. The mechanics' activities, along with similar actions by pilots, cabin attendants, and other airline employees, eventually undermined cost-saving changes that Lorenzo was trying to implement and pushed Eastern into bankruptcy. Mistrust can thus doom to failure an otherwise well-conceived change program.

The challenge posed by change may cause some members of an organization to doubt their personal competence. The *fear of failure* stimulated by this self-doubt may increase peoples' reluctance to support efforts to change familiar practices. General Motors employees throughout the Midwest who were invited to move to the new Saturn plant in Tennessee in the late 1980s sometimes voiced personal concerns about their ability to succeed in Saturn's new, high-tech assembly operations. Many refused to move even though they faced likely layoffs if they remained in their old jobs.

Because individuals and groups have *differing perceptions and goals*, what is good for one group may sometimes be bad for another. Members of different groups may often have legitimate disagreements about whether a particular change is necessary or about how it may affect them. For example, a company's accounting department may expect to gain through the adoption of a new computerized information system. They know it will provide up-to-the-minute information on work in progress, making bookkeeping and auditing activities easier to perform. Employees in the company's manufacturing department, however, may anticipate being hurt by the system, because it will require them to take time out from their production activities to enter data into remote computer terminals. Groups that do not benefit from a given change may choose to resist it. In our example, manufacturing employees would probably be resistant to attempts to implement the new computerized system.

Organizational change often threatens existing power distributions and may require the elimination of jobs. The *prospective loss of status* that such change may pose can build strong resistance among the individuals and groups affected. For instance, managers in a company moving toward participatory decision making may be apprehensive about their loss of power over subordinates if employees are allowed to make decisions for themselves. Or the members of a company's human resource management department may resist attempts to automate staffing and selection procedures because they are concerned that their own importance will be diminished.

Change often causes *social disruption*; that is, it disturbs existing traditions or relationships within and between groups. The threat that interpersonal and group dynamics will be thrown into disequilibrium can stimulate resistance. A seemingly harmless attempt to combine research specialists and product engineers in a new-product-development group may unintentionally stimulate extreme resistance within the company's existing research and engineering departments. In highly cohesive groups, people are likely to resist change simply out of fear that it will break the group apart.

Peer pressure may cause employees who are not directly affected by a particular change to resist it nevertheless, to protect the interests of friends or co-workers. For example, employees are sometimes laid off when automation enables fewer individuals to produce more. In such cases, workers facing possible layoff may pressure their colleagues to resist automation, despite the fact that most employees will remain on the job and perform the same basic tasks as before. Even people who might otherwise support change may be pressured into resistance. Secretaries already familiar with a new word processing program may resist its introduction if the other secretaries in their office voice strong opposition.

People may resist change that is introduced at an inopportune time or in an insensitive manner. *Tactlessness and poor timing* can undermine routine acceptance. Awarding executive bonuses at the same time that hourly wages are being cut exemplifies the sort of tactlessness that has got companies like GM into trouble from time to time. Choosing the December holiday season as the time to announce that plant closings will require employees to move their families from one location to another is another example of how poor timing can ruin what might otherwise be seen as a positive change.

Resistance can evolve out of *personality conflicts* between those who advocate change and the individuals and groups directly affected by a proposed change. Imagine yourself in the position of working for a boss you don't especially like. Are you more likely to follow your boss's lead and accept change, or might you instead resist your boss in order to assert your personal feelings? Indeed, not getting along with others in the organization can substantially limit an individual's ability to encourage successful change.

Finally, resistance may be built into the very structure of the organization in the form of *bureaucratic inertia*. Managers of large, bureaucratic organizations like Exxon, General Dynamics Corporation, or the Chase Manhattan Bank often complain that their employees lack initiative and flexibility. Yet when inflexible, bureaucratic rules and rigid, standardized procedures are used to manage organizational behavior, is it any wonder that flexible, adaptive behavior is rare?

Forces for Change. Opposing these sources of resistance to change are a number of forces that favor or promote change. These forces are found both within the firm and outside of it.

External pressures for change come from a number of different sources—changes in international markets, shifts in national business and industry, shifting economic conditions, new governmental laws and regulations, changing population trends, and technological advances.[10]

Engaging in *international trade* for the first time opens up new problems and opportunities for a company. Dealing with different national cultures, economies, and organizing styles often highlights limitations in the way things have been done in the firm and provides the initial impetus for change. For instance, when American car manufacturers decided to enter the domestic Japanese market they had to learn how to conduct the door-to-door visits that Japanese automobile salespeople make. The purpose of the visits is to form close relationships with their customers and cultivate long-term loyalty.

Changing customer tastes, the entry of new competitors, and the introduction of new goods and services that may replace or substitute for established products all may cause *industry shifts*, that is, changes in the pattern of interfirm relationships within an industry. In turn, they usually require internal changes in the way each firm in the industry does business. For example, yogurt makers' introduction of frozen yogurt into the ice cream market influenced the sales of ice-cream manufacturers, who responded by introducing their own frozen yogurt desserts.

Changes in interest rates, inflation, labor markets, and other *economic conditions* can affect a company's ability to do business. Thus it can strengthen the drive to change the way things are done in the organization. Just-in-time inventorying procedures, which substantially reduce the amount of inventory maintained by a company, were adopted by American manufacturers during the early 1980s. The aim was to counteract the effects of growing inventory costs. Firms

[10] Andrew D. Szilagyi, Jr., and Marc J. Wallace, Jr., *Organizational Behavior and Performance*, 4th ed. (Glenview, Ill.: Scott, Foresman, 1987), pp. 635–36.

Though unusual, war is an environmental force that can have a very sudden and intense impact on the activities within a firm. During the Persian Gulf war, production of General Dynamics' M-1 Abrams tank was high. The war ended early in 1991, and more than 300 assemblers stood to lose their jobs by the middle of the year. The company, its new CEO William Anders, and others began efforts to convince the U.S. government that it should not close down the country's tank industry and at the same time began trying to sell the tank on the international market. Source: Bill Saporito, "This War Doesn't Mean a Windfall: General Dynamics," Fortune, February 25, 1991, pp. 40–42.

throughout the U.S. and Canada also sought out energy-efficient production equipment and manufacturing methods to counteract the soaring costs of petroleum products and electricity.

Changes in *government regulations* or laws that regulate business practices, such as antitrust regulations, employment laws, safety codes, and tax acts, are an important external force favoring change within a company. For instance, deregulation in the air transportation industry in the early 1980s led to the emergence of several "super carriers," such as Northwest and U.S. Air. Their growth by merger stimulated a multitude of changes in company operations.

Changing birthrates and lifespans are among the *population trends* that affect societal age groups and consequently, the different pools from which an organization draws employees and customers. Having to meet changing employee demands, consumer preferences, and client needs mandates new ways of doing business and thus organizational change. For example, as the baby-boom generation grows older, hospitals are putting more emphasis on geriatric medicine and less on other specialties.

Changes in *technology*—the machines, procedures, and know-how used to create goods and services—create new products, industries, and ways of organizing work. For instance, food processors who failed to redesign canned or frozen items for convenient use in microwave ovens saw their market position shrink considerably during the 1980s. To keep up with spreading technological change or to create their own new technologies, firms must emphasize innovation and successful adaptation.

In addition to external, environmental forces, internal pressures within an organization also act as forces for change. Among the most important internal forces promoting change are organizational crises such as shortages of raw materials, increased understanding of the need for change, a drop in production quality or quantity, changing viewpoints of organization members, and a gut feeling that change is needed.[11]

More than anything else, the sense of emergency produced by an *organizational crisis* can stimulate support for change. For example, companies that suddenly face shortages of critical tools or materials may be forced to find substitutes: Milk producers turned to plastic crates when metal ones became too

[11] Edgar Huse and James Bowditch, *Behavior in Organizations: A Systems Approach to Managing* (Reading, Mass.: Addison-Wesley, 1973), p. 391.

expensive to be affordable. The United States Mint began to manufacture copper-centered coins when the high price of silver made it impossible to produce solid dimes, quarters, and half dollars.

Increased knowledge about a problem motivates people to attempt to solve it by changing the way things are done. For instance, Chrysler employees willingly participated in a wage-reduction program during the early 1980s after learning that their company was on the verge of declaring bankruptcy. Since then, wage reduction has become fairly common among United States firms as a way to cope with adverse economic conditions and foreign competition.

A significant decrease in the *quality or quantity of production*, resulting in fewer saleable goods or services, will stimulate concerns about long-term survival and make people more receptive to the idea of change. Having fewer customers is likely to make restaurant employees more open to changes in the firm's menu and pricing habits. Similarly, losing the business of a long-standing industrial buyer is likely to make the employees of an electronic-components manufacturer like Motorola more receptive to designing products faster and manufacturing them more efficiently.

New information, education, or additional experience can bring about *changes in management or work-force viewpoints*. With changing perceptions may also come an increased desire to change the way things are done in the firm. For example, companies that fund continuing education programs typically find it necessary to make jobs more interesting and challenging, because better-educated people demand more stimulating work.

Finally, change is sometimes supported simply by the feeling that it is needed. No specific factor may underlie or explain the *felt need for change*. People may just feel that things have been the same for too long. A senior employee's gut instinct, developed through years of experience, may be the only clue that a problem exists.

forcefield analysis A diagnostic method that depicts the array of forces for and against a particular change in a graphic analysis; often used as a component of the OD process.

Overcoming Resistance through Forcefield Analysis. Setting change in motion requires identifying and overcoming sources of resistance, on the one hand, and encouraging and strengthening sources of support, on the other. **Forcefield analysis** is a diagnostic method that depicts the array of forces for and against a particular change in a graphic analysis. It is a useful tool for managers and change agents who are attempting to envision the situation surrounding a prospective change. As Figure 14-1 shows, in a forcefield analysis, two lines are drawn, one representing the organization's present situation (the solid horizontal line) and the other the organization after the desired change has been put into effect (the dashed horizontal line). Next, forces identified as supporting change are depicted as arrows pushing in the direction of the desired change. Forces resisting change are drawn as arrows pushing in the opposite direction. The length of each arrow indicates the perceived strength of the force represented by the arrow relative to the other forces in the forcefield.

There is no universal, fail-safe way to overcome the resistant factors identified in a forcefield analysis. Of the many available options, the six that are used most often include:

1. *Education and communication.* Disseminating information about the need and rationale for a prospective change through one-on-one discussions, group meetings, and written memos or reports. This approach is best used where change is being undermined by a lack of information or where available information is inaccurate. Its strength is that once persuaded through education, people will often help with the implementation of change. Its primary weakness is that it can be quite time consuming if many people must be involved.

FIGURE 14-1

Forcefield Analysis

During the middle 1980s, IBM, Compaq, and other U.S. manufacturers faced the task of introducing a new line of computers to maintain position in an increasingly competitive world market for personal computers. Forces resisting this change included the following: (1) differing perceptions among the management of American companies about the need for new products (as opposed to modest improvements of existing lines), (2) employee concerns about the social disruption likely to occur as old work groups disbanded to staff new production facilities, (3) bureaucratic inertia stemming from the rules and procedures used to coordinate existing ways of doing things, and (4) employee fears about not being able to cope with the demands of new production technologies. Opposing these forces were others supporting change. Those forces included the following: (1) growing competition from Asian computer manufacturers, (2) a drive in American computer firms to introduce greater factory automation to cut costs and increase quality, (3) and a general sense of impending crisis throughout the American computer industry. In the end, forces supporting change won out with the introduction of IBM's micro-channel series and Compaq's Desqpro personal computers. Both lines proved to be quite successful in the marketplace.

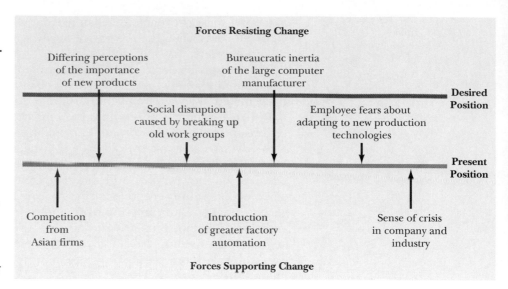

2. *Participation and involvement.* Involving those to be affected by a change in its design and implementation. Employees meet in special committees or task forces to participate in the decision making. There are two situations where this option is most effective. It works well when information required to manage change is dispersed among many people and where employees who have considerable power are likely to resist change if not involved themselves. It facilitates information exchange among people and breeds commitment among the people involved, but it can slow down the process if participants design an inappropriate change or stray from the task at hand.

3. *Facilitation and support.* Providing job training and emotional support through instructional meetings and counseling sessions for employees affected by a change. This method is most useful when people are resisting change because of problems with personal adjustment. No other method works as well with adjustment problems, but it can consume significant amounts of time and money and still fail.

4. *Bargaining and negotiation.* Working with resistant employees through bargaining and tradeoffs to provide them with incentives to change their minds. This technique is sometimes used if an individual or group with the power to block a change is likely to lose out if the change takes place. Negotiation can be a relatively easy way to avoid such resistance but can prove costly if it alerts other individuals and groups that they might be able to negotiate additional gains for themselves.

5. *Hidden persuasion.* Using covert efforts and providing information on a selective basis to get people to support desired changes. This approach is sometimes used when other tactics will not work or are too expensive. It can be a quick and inexpensive way to dissolve resistance. However, it can lead to future problems if people feel manipulated.

6. *Explicit and implicit coercion.* Using power and threats of negative consequences to change the minds of resistant individuals. It tends to be used when speed is essential and where those initiating change possess considerable power. It can overcome virtually any kind of resistance. Its weakness is that it can be risky if it leaves people angry.[12]

[12] John P. Kotter and Leonard A. Schlesinger, "Choosing Strategies for Change," *Harvard Business Review* 57 (1979), 102–21; and John M. Ivancevich and Michael T. Matteson, *Organizational Behavior and Management*, 2nd ed. (Homewood, Ill.: BPI-Irwin, 1990), pp. 621–22.

Values That Guide Change

When set in motion by organization-development processes, organizational change is guided by a set of fundamental values. These values direct the way OD interventions influence relations among people and groups and include the following:

1. *The needs and aspirations of human beings are the reasons for organized effort in society.* Out of this value grows a strong concern with enhancing the personal development and satisfaction of all the members of an organization. This concern then creates a self-fulfilling prophesy. The belief that you can grow and develop in personal and organizational competence tends to produce conditions conducive to such growth and development. When managers at American Steel and Wire Company, formerly a unit of USX, became concerned about the personal development of their employees, they began involving all employees in strategic-planning processes. They found that the resulting exchange of information created a team feeling that led to even greater employee involvement in carrying out strategic objectives. Today, American Steel is among the lowest cost, highest-quality wire and rod producers in the U.S., while retaining strong loyalty and a sense of enhanced personal worth among its employees (for more information about how American Steel encourages teamwork, see the "In Practice" box later in this chapter).[13]

2. *Openness is essential to working together effectively.* This value holds that work and life can be more worthwhile and organized effort more effective and enjoyable if people openly express their feelings and sentiments to each other. Openness is sometimes hazardous for employees, though, as might be the case if a subordinate were to be openly critical of her boss without receiving protection from possible retribution. It is also naive to expect two groups engaged in conflict to trust each other enough to communicate openly without the help of a neutral party or procedure. So it is unrealistic to believe that openness will develop in the workplace without first eliminating the negative effects of hierarchical and political barriers.

3. *Commitment to both action and research is required.* It is possible to get so caught up in the action of implementing change that instituting the careful design, controls, and other necessary elements of formal research go by the board. However, research into the nature of change processes and the effectiveness of different interventions is an indispensable part of the OD process. If we don't use scientific methods (see Chapter 3) to study what we do as we manage organizational change, we will never know why something works when it does or why it doesn't work when it fails.

4. *Democratization, or power sharing, in organizations is a valued outcome of the OD process.* Placing a high value on humanizing the workplace and building a participatory atmosphere does not mean that we want to reduce or neutralize the power of owners and managers. The goal of organization development is to increase everyone's power by encouraging the development of both technical and human relations competence in all employees.[14]

When put into practice, these four values promote the assumptions summarized in Table 14-2. As you can see from these assumptions, the OD framework emphasizes the necessity for organizations to help facilitate the personal growth of their members. Equally, it emphasizes the importance of employees' contributions to the continued well-being of the organization. All change stimulated

---

[13] Joan E. Rigdon, "Team Builders Shine in Perilous Waters," *Wall Street Journal*, October 29, 1990, p. B1.
[14] French and Bell, *Organization Development*, pp. 49–50.

T A B L E 14-2
Assumptions Underlying the Practice of Organization Development

People
    Have inherent needs for personal growth and development.
    Want to contribute more to their organization than unchanged conditions often allow.
    Desire to be accepted and interact cooperatively in at least one small group of peers.
    Look to their work group as an important reference group that helps them form personal beliefs, values, and norms.

In groups
    Members must assist each other with effective leadership and membership behaviors. Formal leaders cannot be expected to do all that is required to keep groups performing effectively.
    Suppressed feelings and attitudes reduce problem solving, personal growth, and satisfaction.
    The level of interpersonal trust, support, and cooperation is typically much lower than is either necessary or desirable.
    Solutions to problems are only likely to succeed if all members alter their mutual relationships; doing things alone will not help.

In organizations
    Groups linked together by work activities affect the attitudes and beliefs of each other's members.
    Conflicts between people and groups in which one party wins and the other loses do not provide long-term solutions to organizational problems.
    Changes stimulated by OD interventions must be reinforced and sustained by appropriate changes in the human resource management system—performance appraisal, compensation, training, staffing, task and communication processes and procedures.
    Members place a high value on collaboration and cooperation, and seek to avoid exploitation or manipulation.

Source: Based on Wendell L. French and Cecil H. Bell, Jr., *Organization Development: Behavioral Science Interventions for Organizational Improvement*, 4th ed. (Englewood Cliffs, N.J.: Prentice Hall, 1990), pp. 44–51.

by OD is thus seen as having the dual goals of human fulfillment and organizational accomplishment.

THE ORGANIZATION-DEVELOPMENT PROCESS

Regardless of the type of change being pursued, organization development follows a multiple-step process. We can gain insight into the way the process of OD is conducted from the Lewin development model, the planned change model, and the action research model.

The Lewin Development Model

Lewin development model A three-step model of the development process that is followed in every successful OD intervention.

The **Lewin development model**, named for its creator, the social scientist Kurt Lewin, is a three-step model of the development process that takes place during every successful OD intervention. According to this model, OD progresses through stages of unfreezing, transforming, and refreezing.[15]

[15] Kurt Lewin, *Field Theory in Social Science* (New York: Harper & Row, 1951), pp. 228–29. See also Marvin W. Weisbord, *Productive Workplaces: Organizing and Managing for Dignity, Meaning, and Community* (San Francisco: Jossey-Bass, 1987), pp. 14–23.

How to Institutionalize Teamwork

To institutionalize the results of change means to stabilize them and make them permanent. Suppose you have completed a group intervention that resulted in a good team spirit and an ability to work together effectively. Now you want to institutionalize the outcome. What do you do? Tom Tyrrell, president of American Steel and Wire Company, has several answers. First you don't lay off employees if the economy slows down. Instead, you make what cuts you can through attrition, leaving the jobs of newly retired employees unfilled. You keep the rest of your employees busy rebuilding machinery and doing maintenance chores that have to be ignored during busier times. In so doing, you are helping to maintain the teams and team relations you have worked so hard to build. Second, you treat all your employees with the same sense of fairness. All employees at American Steel and Wire receive the same vacations and benefits and share the same formula for profit sharing. In this way, inequity that might otherwise undermine teamwork is avoided. Third, you give your em-

ployees greater control over their work and working lives. Process managers (foremen) at American Wire once made virtually every day-to-day decision about production activities, but today lower-level employees now make many of these decisions. In addition, they are encouraged to look beyond daily activities and to think about long-term cost cutting and quality assurance. This way, employees have the feeling that teams and team tasks are *their* creations instead of something forced on them by a distant management. Fourth, you hold social get-togethers to give employees the chance to relax and enjoy each other's company. American Steel and Wire recently had international dinner costing $25,000, but it was worth much more, according to Tyrrell. Getting everyone together gives people the chance to overcome anxieties and build camaraderie. Team effectiveness improves even more as a result.

Joan E. Rigdon, "Team Builders Shine in Perilous Waters," *Wall Street Journal*, October 29, 1990, p. B1.

---

unfreezing The first step in the Lewin development model; the step in which one tries to weaken old attitudes, values, and behaviors and to get people ready for change.

Unfreezing. Unfreezing is a preparatory step in which one tries to weaken old attitudes, values, and behaviors and get people ready for change. New and different experiences or information that challenges routine perceptions facilitate this unfreezing process. The forcefield analysis procedure described earlier can be especially helpful at this stage, because it clarifies which forces and perceptions must be weakened and which should be encouraged.

To stimulate unfreezing, change agents use various OD interventions, for instance, the counseling, team building, and intergroup mirroring techniques described later in this chapter. Their purpose is to increase people's awareness of challenging information and encourage employees to question current behaviors and attitudes. This questioning can lead to greater readiness for change, because the less satisfied people are with the status quo, the more likely they are to feel that change is necessary.

transforming The second step in the Lewin development model; the step in which change actually occurs.

Transforming. Transforming is the step in which change actually occurs. It takes place as organization members first identify with the change agent. They begin to internalize the values of organization development and to adopt new attitudes and behaviors at work. This process often requires (1) facilitation, in which the change agent helps members understand why change is necessary; and (2) training, in which employees learn how they will be affected by the change and what will be expected of them after the change has taken place. These techniques are an integral part of all OD interventions and help dispel most remaining resistance to change.

refreezing The third step in the Lewin development model; the change that took place during the transforming step becomes stable and permanent.

Refreezing. Refreezing focuses on institutionalizing change. In this step, the change that took place during the transforming step becomes stable and permanent. During refreezing, new attitudes, values, and behaviors are integrated into everyday organizational processes and procedures. For example, leaders become less directive as subordinates assume newly developed decision-making roles. Reward systems change so that they reinforce cooperation instead of competition. Managers and their subordinates meet regularly to encourage greater communication (see the "In Practice" box for additional examples). Refreezing does not imply rigidity or resistance to future change. Indeed, because of their experience with successful organization development, the members of an organization learn not to fear change but to welcome it instead.

The Planned Change Model

planned change model A model of the OD process that is an expansion of the Lewin development model. Tells how OD proceeds when an off-the-shelf intervention is implemented.

According to the Lewin model, we must prepare for organizational change and monitor its progress if we are to expect an OD intervention to produce lasting results. The **planned change model** is an expansion of Lewin's approach in which the basic steps of unfreezing, transforming, and refreezing have been elaborated to produce an organization-development action guide.[16] As Figure 14-2 shows, in this expanded model, Lewin's three steps have become seven stages.

Scouting. During the first stage of the planned change model, a change agent and the management of a client organization jointly explore a particular orga-

[16] R. Lippitt, J. Watson, and B. Westley, *The Dynamics of Planned Change* (New York: Harcourt, Brace, & World, 1958) pp. 129–44; and D. A. Kolb and A. H. Frohman, "An Organization Development Approach to Consulting," *Sloan Management Review* 12 (1970), 51–65.

FIGURE 14-2

The Planned Change Model Compared to the Lewin Development Model

From Edgar F. Huse, Organization Development and Change, *2nd ed. (St. Paul, Minn.: West, 1980), p. 87. Reprinted with permission of the publisher.*

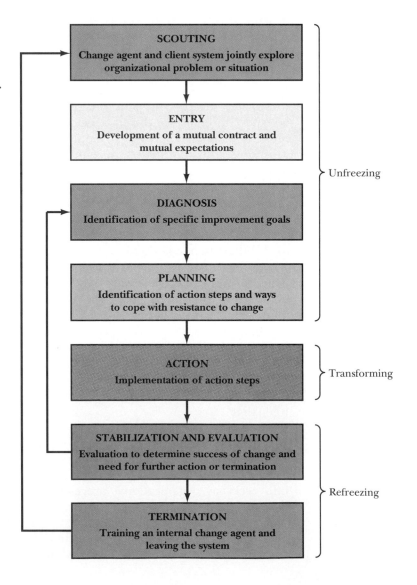

nizational problem or situation. If an external change agent has been called in, it is at this stage that she decides whether to become involved. Meanwhile, management checks out her expertise and ability. If an internal change agent is involved, scouting is an exercise in employee selection (see Chapter 9).

Entry. Together, the change agent and the client organization develop a contract and expectations as to how stages three to seven will be carried out. If an external change agent is involved, the contract may specify how long she will work with the client organization and whether she will train an internal agent to take over after her departure. The contract may also specify what results the client organization wants. An honest contract, however, will *not* guarantee these results. Just as medical doctors cannot guarantee successful treatment and lawyers cannot guarantee success in the courtroom, OD change agents cannot guarantee successful change.

Diagnosis. The change agent and the client identify general goals for improvement, specific problems to be addressed, and indicators of success to be used during postaction evaluation. They boil down the general expectations that were identified during the entry stage and turn them into concrete problem statements. Also they look for various off-the-shelf OD interventions that have been used to solve similar problems in other organizational settings.

Planning. The change agent and representatives of the client organization jointly develop a plan of action, including specific ways of dealing with potential resistance to planned change. They select for use in the client organization one of the OD interventions identified during diagnosis and make preparations for its implementation.

Action. The change agent oversees implementation of the plan of action. Members of the client organization participate in an OD intervention that leads them through the process of determining what specific changes to make and how to make them. Then they implement these changes.

Stabilization and Evaluation. The change agent and representatives of the client organization work together to assess the accomplishments of the intervention, using the success indicators identified during the diagnosis stage. If further action is required, the planned change process returns to the diagnosis stage. If not, the process moves on to the termination stage.

Termination. Termination ends the change agent-client organization relationship. If an external change agent is involved and contractual agreements specify it, the change agent trains others in the organization to maintain the change. Then she either leaves the organization or moves on to another assignment in the firm. If an internal change agent is involved, she will be assigned new duties.

The Action Research Model

action research model A model of the OD process that permits the development and assessment of original, innovative interventions.

The **action research model** is a bit more complicated than the planned change model, incorporating a recurrent cycle of data-based action planning (see Figure 14-3). Organization-development programs based on the planned change model usually involve the implementation of standard off-the-shelf interventions that

FIGURE 14-3

The Action Research Model

*Based on Wendell French,
"Organization Development:
Objectives, Assumptions, and
Strategies,"* California Management
Review *12 (1969), 26.*

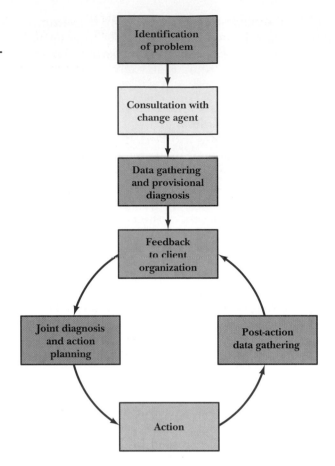

have been used before. The action research model, however, permits the development and assessment of original, innovative procedures.

Problem Identification. In the initial stage of action research, someone in an organization, often a top manager, perceives problems that might be solved with the assistance of an organization-development change agent. Specific problem statements can usually be formulated at this stage. Sometimes, though, problem identification cannot progress beyond an uneasy feeling that something is wrong. Consultation with a change agent may then be required to crystallize the problems.

Consultation. In the second stage, the manager and a change agent clarify the perceived problems and consider ways of dealing with them. During this discussion, they assess the degree of fit between the organization's needs and the change agent's expertise. For example, if the organization is troubled by poor interpersonal relations, does the change agent know how to help people interrelate? Or if the organization is having problems with intergroup conflict, does the change agent have experience in conflict management? If the agent fits the situation, action research progresses to the next stage. If not, another change agent is called in and consultation begins anew.

Data Gathering and Provisional Diagnosis. The change agent initiates the diagnostic process by gathering data about the organization and its perceived problems. He observes, interviews, and questions employees and analyzes performance records. If an external change agent is employed, a member of the organization may assist during this process, facilitating the agent's entry into the firm and providing access to a significant amount of otherwise hidden or unavailable data. The agent concludes this stage by examining the data and performing a provisional analysis and diagnosis of the situation.

Feedback to the Client Organization. Next, the data and provisional diagnosis are submitted to the client organization's top management group. Informing top management early on of the OD process under way is absolutely necessary to secure the managerial support that any OD effort must have to succeed. The change agent is careful, during this presentation, to preserve the anonymity of people serving as sources of information. Identifying them could jeopardize their willingness to cooperate later on.

Joint Diagnosis and Action Planning. During the fifth stage of the action research model, the change agent and the top management group discuss the meaning of the data, their implications for organizational functioning, and any need for further data gathering and diagnosis. At this point, other people throughout the organization may also become involved in the diagnostic process. Sometimes employees meet in feedback groups and react to the results of top management's diagnostic activities. At other times, work groups elect representatives, who then get together to exchange views and report back to their coworkers. If the firm is unionized, union representatives may also be consulted. No matter which members of the organization are specifically involved in the change process, however, the important point to remember is that in action research, the change agent does not impose interventions on the client organization. Instead, members of the organization deliberate jointly with the change agent and work as a team to develop wholly new interventions and plan specific action steps.

Action. Next, the company puts plan into motion and executes its action steps. In addition to implementing the jointly designed intervention, action may involve such activities as additional data gathering, further analysis of the problem situation, and supplementary action planning.

Postaction Data Gathering and Evaluation. Because action research is a cyclical process, data are also gathered after actions have been taken. The purpose is to monitor and assess the effectiveness of an intervention. In evaluating the intervention, groups in the client organization review the data and decide whether they need to rediagnose the situation, perform further analyses of the situation, and develop new interventions. The change agent's role during this process is to serve as an expert on research methods as applied to the process of development and evaluation. In filling this role, he will probably perform data analyses, summarize the results of these analyses, guide subsequent rediagnoses, and position the organization for further intervention.

Managing Organization Development

What do the three models we have just described have to say about managing the process of organization development? The Lewin development model highlights the fact that successful OD efforts require adequate preparation and careful stabilization. The planned change model shows how problems can sometimes be solved with existing OD interventions like the ones we describe next. The action research model summarizes the process of inventing, implementing, and evaluating new OD interventions. Each of these models thus provides a working framework for change agents. Guided by a set of basic values, they can manage OD programs intended to bring about significant changes in organizational behavior.

ORGANIZATION-DEVELOPMENT INTERVENTIONS

You now know about the role of change agent and the values that underlie the field of organization development. You also understand the process of OD and how it incorporates existing interventions or leads to the creation of new ones. However, you have yet to learn about the kind of actions involved in working through a specific OD intervention. We turn our attention next to this final topic.

A Matrix of Interventions

There are a large number—perhaps hundreds—of different OD interventions. Many of these interventions are widely known and employed often by change agents pursuing the planned change approach. Some of them also serve as a source of ideas for change agents who are following the action research approach to create and evaluate new interventions. In this section, we examine nine well-known interventions that, as Table 14-3 shows, differ in terms of two principal factors—depth and target.

depth The degree or intensity of change that an organization development intervention is designed to stimulate.

Depth. The **depth** of an intervention is the degree or intensity of change that the intervention is designed to stimulate.[17] A *shallow* intervention is intended mainly to provide people with information or facilitate communication. Interpersonal counseling interventions, for instance, often involve little more than acquainting individuals with ideas they might not otherwise consider. This sort of exposure to new knowledge can trigger a modest amount of cognitive or behavioral change but is not intended to alter deeply held feelings or opinions. Little personal risk is involved in interventions of this sort.

[17] Roger Harrison, "Choosing the Depth of Organizational Intervention," *Journal of Applied Behavioral Science* 6 (1970), 181–202.

T A B L E 14-3
Organization-Development Interventions

TARGET	FOCAL PROBLEM	DEPTH		
		Shallow	Moderate	Deep
Interpersonal relations	Problem fitting in with others	Counseling	Role analysis technique	Sensitivity training
Group relations and leadership	Problem with working as a group	Process consultation	Team building	Team development
Intergroup relations	Problem with relations between groups	Third-party peacemaking	Intergroup mirroring	Intergroup team building
Organization-wide relations	Problem with functioning effectively	Interventions described in Chapter 18		

In sharp contrast, a *deep* intervention is intended to effect massive psychological and behavioral change. An intervention of this type and the OD change agent guiding it both attack basic beliefs, values, and norms in an attempt to bring about fundamental changes in the way people think, feel, and behave. Taken to the extreme, a deep intervention, such as interpersonal sensitivity training, can even resemble a session of brainwashing in which participants risk exposure to extreme psychological injury. Therefore, deep interventions must be approached with great caution and require the guidance of an expert change agent.

Between these two extremes, interventions of *moderate* depth seek to challenge existing attitudes and bring about changes in people's points of view without precipitating major psychological change. Often, interventions of this sort involve getting people with differing viewpoints together to discuss the way they perceive each other and the organization. For instance, the role analysis technique described below is a structured procedure of moderate depth that enables colleagues to trade opinions about each other's role responsibilities. They exchange more than the simple information of a shallow intervention, because participants in a role analysis session bargain with each other about personal roles and argue about interpersonal expectations. The sort of behavioral change caused by role analysis, however, falls far short of the more extreme psychological change aimed for in deeper interventions.

target The specific focus of an OD intervention's change efforts.

Target. The **target** is what an intervention focuses on. In Chapter 9, we discussed the individual-level target of human resource management (career planning and development, employee mentoring, and so on.) In addition, interpersonal, group, intergroup, and organization-wide relations can serve as targets of OD interventions. We will wait until Chapter 18 to discuss organization-wide interventions, because we have not yet described the types of organizational problems that such interventions can solve. For now, we will concentrate on interventions aimed at solving the kinds of interpersonal, group, and intergroup problems discussed in Chapters 10–13.

Some business leaders like Max DePree believe that organization development interventions must take on a spiritual nature. DePree, who heads Herman Miller, a leading furniture design and manufacturing firm, says that businesses must offer workers the community and psychological sustenance that churches, families, and neighborhoods no longer provide. DePree proposes a "covenant" between company and employee as the basis for superior management.
Source: "Should Your Company Save Your Soul?" Fortune, January 14, 1991, p. 31.

Interpersonal Interventions

Interpersonal interventions focus on solving several of the problems that people sometimes have in fitting in with others at work. We highlighted some of those problems in Chapter 10. Depending on the particular intervention, attempts may be made to define personal roles, clarify social expectations, or strengthen sensitivity to others' needs and interests.

counseling A shallow interpersonal OD intervention in which a change agent meets, either one on one or in small groups, to provide helpful information to people who are having trouble relating with others.

Counseling. **Counseling** is a shallow interpersonal intervention in which an OD change agent meets, either one on one or in small groups, with people who are having trouble relating with others. In these meetings, the change agent's role is to suggest alternative ways of looking at things and provide information that otherwise might not be considered.[18] In the process, the change agent may act as a coach who encourages troubled people to find out how others see their behavior and also how others expect them to behave. In fulfilling the roles of coach and counselor, the change agent is as nondirective as possible. Changes and improvements in behavior, if any, are decided upon and implemented after counseling has run its course. The change agent neither advocates nor supervises any particular type of change.

realistic previewing A technique sometimes used during counseling interventions to help people form sensible expectations about workplace relationships.

During the counseling process, a technique called **realistic previewing** is sometimes used to help people form sensible expectations about workplace relationships. Realistic previewing was initially developed as an employee selection and socialization technique.[19] It was intended to reduce turnover by acquainting prospective employees with both the positive and negative aspects of a job prior to their decision to work for a company (see Chapter 9). This was in contrast to the positive-only orientations that new employees often received. It is now also used as an intervention aimed at solving interpersonal problems. In a realistic previewing intervention of this type, a counselor provides employees with information that they might not otherwise have about interpersonal relations. The counselor might talk about coworkers' opinions of their boss and her management style or about forming informal friendships on the job or even about off-the-job activities, such as company picnics or bowling leagues. In addition to the counselor, a group of coworkers are sometimes assembled to provide their own comments about working conditions and interpersonal relations. This kind of intervention helps employees form realistic impressions about their coworkers. Consequently, it can reduce the likelihood that unreasonable expectations will undermine interpersonal relations as they develop.

role analysis technique An interpersonal OD intervention of moderate depth intended to help people form and maintain effective working relationships by clarifying role expectations.

Role Analysis Technique. The **role analysis technique** (RAT), an interpersonal intervention of moderate depth, is also intended to help people form and maintain effective working relationships.[20] As we saw in Chapter 10, people at work fill specialized *roles* in which they are expected to engage in specific sorts of behavior. Often, however, employees lack a clear idea of what their roles entail, or they are overburdened by role demands. RAT, outlined in Figure 14-4, is designed to help reduce role ambiguity and conflict by clarifying interpersonal expectations and responsibilities.

To initiate a RAT intervention, the occupant of a troublesome role contacts a change agent about her problem and receives instruction from the agent on

[18] Edgar H. Schein, *Process Consultation: Its Role in Organization Development* (Reading, Mass.: Addison-Wesley, 1969), p. 115.

[19] John P. Wanous, *Organizational Entry: Recruitment, Selection, and Socialization of Newcomers* (Reading, Mass.: Addison-Wesley, 1980), p. 43.

[20] Ishwar Dayal and John M. Thomas, "Operation KPE: Developing a New Organization," *Journal of Applied Behavioral Science* 4 (1968), 473–506.

FIGURE 14-4

Steps in the Role Analysis
Technique

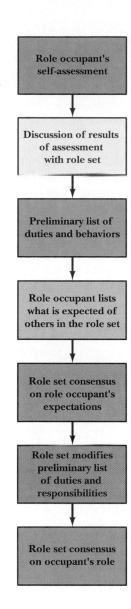

the RAT procedure. Next, she works alone to analyze the rationale for the role as well as its place in the organizational network of interpersonal relations. She tries to learn how to use her role in meeting personal, group, and organizational goals. Then she discusses the results of her analysis in a meeting attended by everyone whose work is directly affected by her role. During this discussion, the change agent lists on a blackboard or flipchart the specific duties and behaviors of the role as identified by the role occupant. The rest of the group suggest corrections to this list. Behaviors are added or deleted until the role occupant is satisfied that the role as she performs it is defined accurately and completely.

Next, the change agent directs attention to the role occupant's expectations of others. To begin this step, the role occupant lists her expectations of the roles that are connected with her own. The group then discusses and modifies these expectations until everyone agrees on them. After this, all participants have the opportunity to modify their expectations about the person's role, in response to her expectations of them. So, as you can see, RAT is a process of negotiation. The person who is the focus of the intervention can ask others to do things for her, and others can ask her to do something for them.

In the final step of role analysis technique, the subject writes a summary or profile of her role as it has been defined. This profile specifies which behaviors are absolutely required and which are discretionary. It thereby constitutes a clearly defined listing of the role-related activities to be performed by the role occupant. The meeting continues, focusing on the roles of the other RAT participants, until all relevant interpersonal relationships have received adequate clarification.

sensitivity training A deep interpersonal OD intervention that focuses on developing greater sensitivity to oneself, to others, and to one's relations with others through an intense, leaderless group experience.

Sensitivity Training. As a deep interpersonal intervention, **sensitivity training** focuses on developing greater sensitivity to oneself, to others, and to one's relations with others.[21] Designed to promote emotional growth and development, sensitivity training typically takes place in a closed session away from work. It may involve a collection of people who do not know each other, a group of people who are well acquainted, or a combination of both. A sensitivity-training session may last for as little as half a day or may go on for several days. It is begun by a change agent, who announces that his role is to serve solely as a nondirective resource. He then lapses into silence, leaving the participants with neither a leader nor an agenda to guide interpersonal activities. The purpose of putting people in such an ambiguous situation is to force them to structure relationships among themselves and, in the process, question long-held assumptions about themselves, about each other, and about interpersonal relations.[22]

Sensitivity-training participants take part in an intense exchange of ideas, opinions, beliefs, and personal philosophies as they struggle with the process of structuring interpersonal relations. Here is a description of one four-day session.

> The first evening discussion began with a rather neutral opening process which very soon led to strongly emotional expression of concern. . . . By the second day the participants had begun to express their feelings toward each other quite directly and frankly, something they had rarely done in their daily work. As the discussion progressed it became easier for them to accept criticism without becoming angry or wanting to strike back. As they began to express long-suppressed hostilities and anxieties the "unfreezing" of old attitudes, old values, and old approaches began. From the second day onward the discussion was spontaneous and uninhibited. From early morning to long past midnight the process of self-examination and confrontation continued. They raised questions they had never felt free to ask before. Politeness and superficiality yielded to openness and emotional expression and then to more objective analysis of themselves and their relationships at work. They faced up to many conflicts and spoke of their differences. There were tense moments, as suspicion, distrust, and personal antagonisms were aired, but more issues were worked out without acrimony.[23]

By completing this process, people learn more about their own personal feelings, inclinations, and prejudices and about what other people think of them.

A word of warning: Sensitivity training is a deep intervention that can initiate profound psychological change. It is not uncommon for participants to engage in intensely critical assessments of themselves and others that can be both difficult and painful. Therefore, the change agent overseeing sensitivity training *must* be a trained professional who can help participants deal with criticism in a con-

---

[21] John P. Campbell and Marvin D. Dunnette, "Effectiveness of T-Group Experiences in Managerial Training and Development," *Psychological Bulletin* 65 (1968), 73–104.

[22] Elliot Aronson, "Communication in Sensitivity Training Groups," in *Organization Development: Theory, Practice, and Research*, ed. Wendell L. French, Cecil H. Bell, Jr., and Robert A. Zawacki (Plano, Texas: Business Publications, 1983), pp. 249–53.

[23] G. David, "Building Cooperation and Trust," in *Management by Participation*, ed. A. J. Marrow, D. G. Bowers, and S. E. Seashore (New York: Harper & Row, 1967), pp. 99–100.

structive manner. In the absence of expert help, participants could risk serious psychological trauma.[24]

Group Interventions

Group interventions are designed to solve many of the problems with group performance and leadership identified in Chapters 11 and 12. In general, such interventions focus on helping the members of a group learn how to work together to fulfill the group's task and maintenance requirements.

process consultation A shallow group-level OD intervention in which a change agent meets with a work group and helps its members examine group processes such as communication, leadership and followership, problem solving, and cooperation.

team diagnostic session A group OD intervention of moderate depth in which a change agent and a work group critique the group's performance and look for ways to improve it.

At The New England, an insurance company founded in 1835, management attempts to monitor changes in the economic environment and to help the company's associates respond to these changes. Here a group meets in a "process improvement" session, focusing on the ways insurance agents, agencies, and the home office can work together to generate new business. (Left to right) James Medeiros, Judith Precourt, Christopher Frachette, Linda Collins, Bonnie Mallin, Patrick Hanlon (standing), Karen Rosser, and Scott Andrews.
Source: "A Celebration of the American Worker," Fortune, September 24, 1990.

Process Consultation. **Process consultation** is a relatively shallow, group-level OD intervention. In a process consultation intervention, a change agent meets with a work group and helps its members examine group processes such as communication, leadership and followership, problem solving, and cooperation. The specific approach taken during this exploration, which varies from one situation to another, may include:

1. Stimulus questions asked by the change agent that direct attention to relationships among group members. Ensuing discussions between group members may focus on ways to improve these relationships and on how such relationships can influence group productivity and effectiveness.

2. A process analysis session, during which the change agent watches the group as it works, followed by feedback sessions in which the change agent discusses his observations about how the group maintains itself and how it performs its task. There may also be supplementary feedback sessions to allow the change agent to clarify the events of earlier sessions for individual group members.

3. Suggestions made by the change agent, which may pertain to group membership, communication, and interaction patterns and the allocation of work duties, responsibilities, and authority.[25]

Whatever the change agent's approach in a given situation, his primary focus in process consultation is on making a group more effective by getting its members to pay more attention to important *process* issues. He wants them to focus on *how* things are done in the group, rather than on the issues of *what* is to be done which normally dominate a group's attention. The ultimate goal of process consultation is to help the group improve its ability to solve its own problems by increasing the ability of members to identify and correct faulty group processes.[26]

Team Diagnostic Sessions. A **team diagnostic session** is a group intervention of moderate depth that normally takes place outside the work setting and may last from four to eight hours. In a team diagnostic session, a change agent and a work group critique the group's performance. During the session, each member of the group has the opportunity to exchange personal perceptions about group problems with every other member. Group members prepare separately for the

[24] Carl A. Bramlette and Jeffrey H. Tucker, "Encounter Groups: Positive Change or Deterioration," *Human Relations* 34 (1981), 303–14.
[25] Schein, *Process Consultation*, pp. 102–3; and Christian F. Paul and Albert C. Gross, "Increasing Productivity and Morale in a Municipality: Effects of Organization Development," *Journal of Applied Behavioral Science* 17 (1981), 59–78.
[26] Schein, *Process Consultation*, p. 135.

session by asking themselves such questions as, Where are we going? How are we doing? What opportunities should we take advantage of? and What problems do we have that we should work on? When the group assembles, the change agent uses one of the following techniques to make personal perceptions public:[27]

1. A whole-group discussion, in which every member makes personal contributions.
2. Subgroup discussions, in which the larger group is broken down into smaller groups for intensive explorations. Members then report the results of subgroup discussion back to the total group.
3. Pair discussions, in which two people discuss their ideas with each other and report the results back to the total group.

After group members have described their personal perceptions to the larger group, the session progresses through the third, fourth, fifth, and sixth steps shown in Figure 14-5. First, the group discusses the issues uncovered in the first two steps and tries to categorize them; for example, goal difficulty problems, role ambiguity problems, or leadership problems. Next, the group enters into an action planning phase in which each problem category is assigned to a subgroup, which develops a solution strategy. Subgroups then report their strategies back to the larger group, and the group decides whether to accept or reject recommended strategies.

[27] French and Bell, *Organization Development*, p. 129.

FIGURE 14-5

Steps in a Team Diagnostic Session

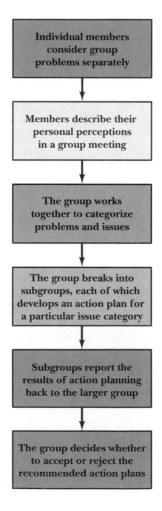

Individual members consider group problems separately

Members describe their personal perceptions in a group meeting

The group works together to categorize problems and issues

The group breaks into subgroups, each of which develops an action plan for a particular issue category

Subgroups report the results of action planning back to the larger group

The group decides whether to accept or reject the recommended action plans

Depending upon the strategies they accept, group members may move on to other interventions. For instance, they may enter into an RAT intervention as part of a strategy developed to counteract role ambiguity. Or they may undertake a team-development session (discussed next) to help overcome problems with leadership and group functioning.

team development A deep group-level extension of interpersonal sensitivity training in which a group of people who work together on a daily basis meet over an extended period to assess and modify group processes.

Team Development. Team development is a deep, group-level extension of interpersonal sensitivity training. In a team-development intervention, a group of people who work together on a daily basis meet over an extended period of time to assess and modify group processes.[28] Throughout these meetings, participants focus their effort on achieving a balance of such basic components of teamwork as:

1. An understanding of, and commitment to, common goals
2. Involvement of as many group members as possible, in order to take advantage of the complete range of skills and abilities available to the group
3. Analysis and review of group processes on a regular basis to ensure that there are sufficient maintenance activities
4. Trust and openness in communication and relationships
5. A strong sense of belonging on the part of all members[29]

To begin team development, the group first engages in a lengthy diagnostic meeting in which a change agent helps members identify group problems and map out possible solutions. The change agent asks them to observe interpersonal and group processes and to be prepared to comment on what they see. Thus the group works on two basic issues. They look for solutions to problems of everyday functioning that have come up in the group, and they observe the way group members interact with each other during the meeting.

Based on the results of these efforts, team development then proceeds in two specific directions. First, the change agent and group implement the interventions chosen during diagnosis, to solve the problems the group is able to identify. Second, the change agent initiates group sensitivity training to uncover additional problems that might otherwise resist detection:

> As the group fails to get [the change agent] to occupy the traditional roles of teacher, seminar leader, or therapist, it will redouble its efforts until in desperation it will disown him and seek other leaders. When they too fail, they too will be disowned, often brutally. The group will then use its own brutality to try to get the [change agent] to change his task by eliciting his sympathy and care for those it has handled so roughly. If this manoeuver fails, and it never completely fails, the group will tend to throw up other leaders to express its concern for its members and project its brutality onto the consultant. As rival leaders emerge it is the job of the consultant, so far as he is able, to identify what the group is trying to do and explain it. His leadership is in task performance, and the task is to understand what the group is doing "now" and to explain why it is doing it.[30]

As you can see, group sensitivity training is really an interpersonal sensitivity training intervention conducted with an intact work group. It enables coworkers to critique and adjust interpersonal relations problems that are inevitable during the workday.

[28] Robert T. Golembiewski, *Approaches to Planned Change, Part 1: Orienting Perspectives and Micro-Level Interventions* (New York: Marcel Dekker, 1979), p. 301.
[29] Gordon L. Lippitt, *Organization Renewal* (New York: Appleton-Century-Crofts, 1969), pp. 107–13.
[30] A. K. Rice, *Learning for Leadership* (London: Tavistock Publications, 1965), pp. 65–66.

Intergroup Interventions

Intergroup interventions focus on solving the types of intergroup problems identified in Chapter 13. In general, these problems concern politicking, conflict, and associated breakdowns in intergroup coordination. Thus OD interventions developed to manage intergroup relations involve various open communication techniques and conflict resolution methods.

third party peacemaking A shallow OD intervention in which a change agent seeks to resolve intergroup misunderstandings by encouraging communication between or among groups.

Third-Party Peacemaking. Third-party peacemaking is a relatively shallow intervention in which a change agent seeks to resolve intergroup misunderstandings by encouraging communication between or among groups. The change agent, who is not herself a member of any of the groups and is referred to as a third party, guides a meeting between the groups. To be productive, the meeting must be characterized by the following attributes:

1. *Motivation*: All groups must be motivated to try to resolve their differences.
2. *Power*: A stable balance of power must be established between the groups.
3. *Timing*: Confrontations must be synchronized so that no one group can gain an information advantage over another.
4. *Emotional release*: People must be given the time to work through the negative thoughts and feelings that have built up between the groups. They need to recognize and express their positive feelings as well.
5. *Openness*: Conditions must favor openness in communication and mutual understanding.
6. *Stress*: There should be enough stress, enough pressure on group members to motivate them to give serious attention to the problem but not so much that the problem appears insoluble.[31]

The change agent facilitates communication between the groups both directly and indirectly. In a direct fashion, she may interview group members before an intergroup meeting, help to put together a meeting agenda, monitor the pace of communication between groups during the meeting, or actually referee the interaction. Acting in a more subtle, indirect way, she may schedule the meeting at a neutral site or establish time limits for intergroup interaction. The whole process can be as short as an afternoon but more likely as long as several months of weekly sessions. As the result of actions like these, the group members begin to learn things about each other and their relationship that can help them focus on common interests and begin to overcome conflictive tendencies.

intergroup mirroring An OD intervention of moderate depth in which representatives from several groups tell the members of a particular group with whom they interact how the people they represent perceive the host group.

host group A group that is experiencing difficulties in working with other groups and asks them to send representatives to an intergroup mirroring intervention.

Intergroup Mirroring. Intergroup mirroring is an intervention of moderate depth in which representatives from several groups tell the members of another group with whom they all interact how the people they represent perceive this other group.[32] This other group is the **host group**—a group that is having difficulty in working with the rest of the groups. To begin a mirroring intervention, the host group asks key members of the other groups to come to a meeting. Next, as Figure 14-6 indicates, a change agent interviews the people who will attend the meeting and gets a sense of the problems between the groups.

The mirroring meeting begins with a feedback session in which the change agent reports on the results of premeeting interviews. Following this session, the representatives from all groups except the host group break into small groups

---

[31] Richard E. Walton, *Interpersonal Peacemaking: Confrontation and Third Party Consultation* (Reading, Mass.: Addison-Wesley, 1969), pp. 94–115.

[32] French and Bell, *Organization Development*, pp. 147–48.

FIGURE 14-6

Steps in an Intergroup Mirroring
Intervention

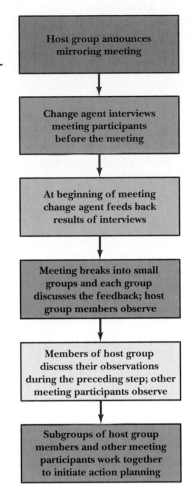

and discuss in greater detail the data provided by the change agent. During these discussions, members of the host group sit around the perimeter of each discussion group, forming a "fishbowl." They observe what goes on in order to learn about the other groups' feelings and perceptions. Next, the host group reconvenes and its members discuss what they have observed. This time, the representatives of the other groups form a fishbowl around the discussion and provide clarification as needed. They want to make sure the host group clearly understands how it is perceived.

The informational stage of the mirroring intervention ends at this point. Small groups composed of host- and other-group members begin to work on the key problems uncovered during the two fishbowl discussions, and on developing strategies to solve them. When they have finished, the larger group reconvenes to make a master list. This list then serves as the basis of an action plan that is devised to help the host group improve relations with the other groups. Once the action plan has been established, people are assigned to specific tasks, and target dates are set for task completion. At a follow-up meeting, held later, the large group assesses progress toward completion of the action plan and allows for the correction of faulty aspects of the plan.

intergroup team building A deep OD intervention intended to improve communication and interaction between work-related groups.

Intergroup Team Building. Intergroup team building is a deep intervention that has three primary aims. They are (1) to improve communication and interaction between work-related groups, (2) to decrease counterproductive competition between the groups, and (3) to replace group-centered perspectives with an orientation that recognizes the necessity for various groups to work together.[33] As indicated in Figure 14-7, during the first step of intergroup team building, two groups (or their leaders) meet with an OD change agent and discuss whether relations between the groups can be improved. If both groups agree that improvement is possible, the change agent asks the two groups to commit themselves to searching for ways of improving their relationship. Once they do so, they move to the second step. The two groups meet in separate rooms, and each makes two lists. The group's perceptions, thoughts, and attitudes toward the other group are on one list. Their thoughts about what the other group is likely to say about them are on the other. In the third step, the two groups reconvene and compare their lists. Each group can compare its view of the other group with the way the other group expects to be seen. Discrepancies uncovered during this comparison are discussed during the fourth step, when the groups meet separately. Each one reacts to what it has learned about itself and the other group. Then each group makes a list of important issues that need to be resolved between the two groups.

[33] Robert R. Blake, H. A. Shepard, and Jane S. Mouton, *Managing Intergroup Conflict in Industry* (Houston: Gulf, 1965), pp. 36–100; and Richard Beckhard, *Organization Development: Strategies and Models* (Reading, Mass.: Addison-Wesley, 1969), pp. 33–35.

FIGURE 14-7

Steps in an Intergroup Team-Building Intervention

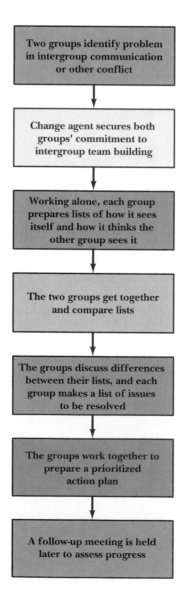

Two groups identify problem in intergroup communication or other conflict

Change agent secures both groups' commitment to intergroup team building

Working alone, each group prepares lists of how it sees itself and how it thinks the other group sees it

The two groups get together and compare lists

The groups discuss differences between their lists, and each group makes a list of issues to be resolved

The groups work together to prepare a prioritized action plan

A follow-up meeting is held later to assess progress

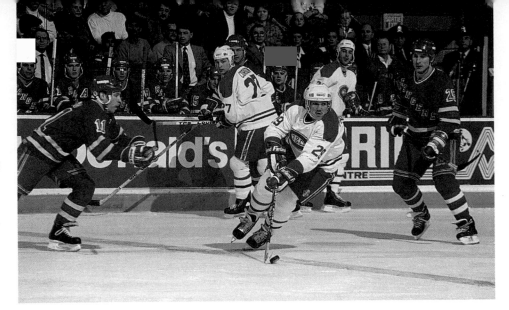

You may not think of the NHL's hockey teams as needing to engage in intergroup team building—as needing to improve their communication and develop a joint perspective. That is just what they must do, however, if the League is to expand its present 21 teams to 28 and make hockey as popular in the U.S. South as it is in Canada. To get the TV exposure necessary to such nationwide popularity the entire NHL will need to cooperate to get more large cities to offer homes to teams. Source: Bill Saporito, "The Hockey Puck as Globalizer," Fortune, January 14, 1991.

The two groups come back together during the fifth step and compare the lists of issues, setting priorities. Then they work together on a plan of action to resolve the issues in order of their priority. They assign individual responsibilities and target dates for completion. The final step is a follow-up meeting held later on to assess progress. At that time, additional actions are planned as required to make sure that intergroup cooperation will continue over the long run.

EVALUATING DEVELOPMENT AND CHANGE

No matter which organization-development intervention you decide to use, the concluding stage of the OD process always consists of an evaluation of effectiveness. Based on the results of this evaluation, efforts may be devoted to ensuring the permanence of newly developed attitudes, values, and behaviors. Alternatively, OD may begin anew, and additional interventions may be initiated to stimulate further change. Table 14-4 contains a checklist of questions that can be useful in deciding what criteria to use and how to measure them when evaluating the effectiveness of organization development.

As suggested by the checklist, resources are expended to acquire the outcomes generated by the OD process. So OD's effectiveness must be judged partly

TABLE 14-4	
Criteria for Evaluating Change Efforts	
CRITERION	**SUGGESTED QUESTIONS**
Overall Results	
Desired outcomes	1. What were the intended outcomes of the intervention? How do they compare with the outcomes actually realized?
Guiding assumptions	2. How explicit were the assumptions that guided the intervention? Did experience prove them to be both valid and appropriate? Did everyone understand and agree with the intervention's purpose as a result?
	3. How consistent with current theories of OB and OD are these assumptions? Was everything currently known with regard to the intervention's focus and purpose incorporated in the intervention?

TABLE 14-4   Cont'd.

CRITERION	SUGGESTED QUESTIONS
Phase of intervention	
Initiation	4. What was the reason for starting the intervention? Who was initially involved? Was the intervention initiated because of a broadly felt need or a narrow set of special interests?
Entry	5. What activities were there at the start of the intervention process? Who was involved in them? Was the intervention implemented prematurely, without adequate diagnosis? Did unnecessary resistance arise as a result?
Diagnosis	6. What specific diagnostic activities took place? Were they carried out fully and effectively? What aspects of the organization were diagnosed to determine the target and depth of the intervention that was implemented?
Planning	7. How was the intervention planned, and who planned it? How were resources used in this effort? How explicit and detailed were the plans that resulted?
Action	8. What was actually done? When was it done? Who did it? How do the answers to these questions compare with the action plan as initially developed?
Evaluation	9. Was evaluation included from the outset as part of the intervention? Were deficiencies identified during evaluation corrected through a careful, planned modification to the intervention or its action plan?
External factors	
Work-force traits	10. Were the results of the intervention affected, either positively or negatively, by work-force characteristics, e.g., age, gender, education, unemployment level?
Economy	11. What was the state of the economy and the firm's market at the time of the intervention? Did economic factors affect the success of the intervention?
Environment	12. How much did the organization's environment change over the course of the intervention? Are the intended results of the intervention still desirable given the organization's current environment?
Internal factors	
Size	13. How large is the organization? Did its size permit access to the resources required for the intervention to succeed?
Technology	14. What is the organization's primary product, and what sort of technology is used to make it? Do the results of the intervention fit in or conflict with the requirements of this technology?
Structure	15. How mechanistic or organic is the organization's structure? Do the results of the intervention fit in or conflict with this structure?
Culture	16. What are the organization's prevailing norms and values concerning change? Concerning involvement in OD interventions?

Source: Based on Noel Tichy and Jay N. Nisberg, "When Does Work Restructuring Work? Organizational Innovations at Volvo and GM," *Organizational Dynamics*, (1976), 13–36; and Wendell L. French, "A Checklist for Organizing and Implementing an OD Effort," in *Organization Development: Theory, Practice, and Research*, rev. ed., ed. Wendell L. French, Cecil H. Bell, Jr., and Robert A. Zawacki (Plano, Texas: Business Publications, 1983) pp. 451–59.

in terms of its outcomes. In addition, measuring its effectiveness requires remembering why it was undertaken to begin with and assessing what took place during each stage of the OD process. This procedure guarantees that an OD effort labeled "effective" not only accomplished its intended purpose but did so in a manner that left everyone more informed about the process of change and how to manage it. Finally, the effects of external and internal factors—whether positive or negative—on the OD process must be examined and cataloged for subsequent reference. That way, the factors that support change can be called into play when needed again in the future, and the ones that are resistant can be anticipated and neutralized.

SUMMARY

Organization development is both a field of research and a collection of *interventions* intended to stimulate planned change in organizations. Associated with OD is a concern about managing resistance to change and strengthening forces that favor change. *Forcefield analysis* is a technique that can be used to aid in the pursuit of these complementary goals.

OD is based on a set of underlying values and assumptions that stress the importance of encouraging human growth and development in organizations. *External* or *internal change agents* are guided by these values and assumptions as they guide the process of implementing OD interventions. When already established interventions are used, the properly managed OD process unfolds as described by the *planned change model*. When new interventions are being invented and assessed for the first time, they follow the *action research model*.

OD interventions differ from each other in the *depth* of change they are intended to stimulate and the types of organizational behavior that are their *target*. No matter which intervention is used, all OD efforts should conclude with an evaluation of program effectiveness.

REVIEW QUESTIONS

1. What differences are there between organization development and other approaches to change in organizations? Are these differences important? Why or why not?

2. What is an external change agent? What is an internal change agent? What are the major advantages and disadvantages of each type of change agent? Why don't more companies use teams composed of both types?

3. Suppose you were given the assignment of developing a new grading system for your OB class. Draw a forcefield analysis showing the major forces for and against change that you would probably encounter while implementing your new grading system. What would you do to weaken the forces against change? How would you strengthen the forces for change? Is it likely that your change intervention would succeed?

4. In what ways is the Lewin development model similar to the planned change model? How do the two models differ from one another? What does the action research model tell you about OD that is not discussed in the other two?

5. Why is it important to avoid using an intervention that is deeper than needed to stimulate the required amount of change? How can you increase the likelihood that the intervention is focused on the appropriate target?

6. Which off-the-shelf intervention would you choose for each of the following situations: two groups that strongly disagree about both groups' task responsibilities; a person who understands her role in a group but can't seem to get along with her coworkers; a group of people who get along with each other but fail to be as productive as expected.

7. Why is it always important to evaluate the results of an OD intervention? What kinds of information should you collect and consider during an evaluation?

Diagnostic Questions

Organization development is a source of action steps that you can use to solve many of the interpersonal, group, and intergroup problems identified in this part of the book. The following diagnostic questions offer practical guidance as you go through this process.

1.   What sort of change is being contemplated? What sources of resistance to this change exist in the organization? What might you do to overcome this resistance? How successful are you likely to be?

2.   What are the forces in the organization that favor the change? How can you strengthen them? How strong can they be made?

3.   Based on a forcefield analysis, what is the likely combined effect of the forces for and against change? Is it realistic to attempt to institute change, or should the status quo be accepted instead?

4.   If change is a realistic goal, do cost, availability, expertise, and similar considerations favor using an external change agent? An internal change agent? A team of external and internal change agents?

5.   Once chosen, does the change agent behave in accordance with the basic values and assumptions of OD? If the aim is to use an existing OD intervention to solve an organizational problem, is the change agent adhering to the planned change model of OD? If the aim is to develop and assess a new type of intervention, do change agent behaviors conform to the action research model?

6.   Do the depth and target of the OD intervention being implemented seem to match the problem? Note that the shallowest intervention likely to stimulate the required amount of change is the one that should be selected for implementation.

7.   Is evaluation an integral part of the OD effort? As evaluation criteria and procedures are established, are serious attempts made to guard against bias and distortion?

8.   How likely is it that positive change will persist after the OD effort has ended? What can be done to ensure lasting change?

LEARNING THROUGH EXPERIENCE

Intergroup mirroring is an organization development intervention used to help bring to the surface the root causes of conflict between two groups. This technique is also designed to create conditions under which a win-win attitude can prevail and mutual problem solving can occur. The mirroring process involves three major phases:

1. *Imagery*. Each group develops images of itself and of the other group. This first step elicits stereotypes and untested assumptions about "them" and "us." Often just correcting misperceptions of each other can bring groups closer together.

2. *Confrontation*. Each group acknowledges its uniqueness and its differences from the other group. The aim here is to specify differences that are accepted as valid but that are causing conflict. Without this clarification and labeling of just what is in conflict, meaningful resolution is unlikely. Smoothing over or avoiding the conflict is more apt to occur.

3. *Bonding*. Groups experiencing conflict that is apparently unreconcilable begin to collaborate and address problems mutually. They become more alike in their perceptions of the necessity of working together and of understanding one another.

In order to succeed, intergroup mirroring must occur between groups that are both motivated to improve the situation and relatively equal in the power they can bring to bear. If one group favors the current situation, it is rational for that group to avoid the changes otherwise stimulated by intergroup mirroring. And if one group can force the other to do things it wouldn't otherwise consider doing, true collaboration is unlikely.

Anyone who wants to use intergroup mirroring must understand some basic assumptions underlying its design. First, the technique assumes that both groups in conflict are acting with integrity and good intentions. If you believe that groups actually wish to harm, punish, or humiliate one another there can be no resolution of differences. Second, the intervention assumes that both groups are responsible for the conflict between them. This responsibility may be unequal, but it must be shared.

STEP ONE: PRE-CLASS PREPARATION

The upcoming class session will give you the opportunity to experience a mirroring intervention for yourself. Prepare for it by reading the entire exercise before coming to class.

STEP TWO: GENERATING IMAGES— HOMOGENOUS GROUPS

The class should divide into the same pairs of groups that completed the Disarmament Exercise in Exercise 13-1. If the class has not yet completed Exercise 13-1 it should do so before proceeding further.

To begin Step Two, each group should meet by itself and list as many responses as possible to the three statements that follow. In filling in the blanks with as many words or phrases as you can, think about your own group and the group that is paired with yours.

1. How we see the other group: "We see the other group as _____."

2. How we see ourselves: "We see ourselves as _____."

3. How we think the other group sees us: "The other group sees us as _____."

Brainstorming or going around the group at first will help elicit ideas. As ideas are presented they should be listed on a chalkboard or flipchart so that everyone in the group can see them. Try to reach a consensus on whatever you decide to include in your group's lists. If opinion is clearly split on an item, note this next to the item. A spokesperson should be appointed to prepare a presentation for Step Three.

STEP THREE: SHARING IMAGES— HETEROGENOUS GROUPS

Each pair of groups should form one discussion group. Spokespersons for each group should begin this step

* Adapted with the authors' permission from Mark S. Plovnick, Ronald E. Fry, and W. Warner Burke, *Organization Development: Exercises, Cases, and Readings* (Boston: Little, Brown, 1982), pp. 89–93. Copyright © 1982 by Mark S. Plovnick, Ronald E. Fry, and W. Warner Burke.

by reporting the results of Step Two. During these reports, listeners may ask for information providing further clarification or understanding, but they may not debate any aspect of either report.

STEP FOUR: IDENTIFYING DISCREPANCIES—HOMOGENOUS GROUPS

All groups should reform, and each group should examine what it said about itself and what was said about it. Make a list that everyone can see of as many discrepancies as you can identify between how the group views itself, how the other group views it, and how it thought the other group would view it.

STEP FIVE: SHARING AND PRIORITIZING DISCREPANCIES— HETEROGENOUS GROUPS

In this step each pair of groups should get together again and group spokespersons should report on the results of Step Four. Similarities in the discrepancies identified by the two groups should be noted and combined. Then each pair of groups should decide on two to four discrepancies that the pair would like to work on.

STEP SIX: PROBLEM-SOLVING— HETEROGENOUS SUBGROUPS

Mixed subgroups made up of members from each of the groups in the pairing should discuss how to manage, neutralize, or eliminate the two to four discrepancies identified at the end of Step Five. Each subgroup should then prepare some recommendations to be considered by the class as a whole in Step Seven. A spokesperson should be appointed to report on the discrepancies examined and actions recommended by the subgroup.

STEP SEVEN: CLASS DISCUSSION

The entire class should assemble, and all spokespersons should give their reports. As actions are recommended, class members should discuss each action's practicality and likelihood of success. A master list of discrepancies and ways of overcoming their effects should then be created. The last part of the class should be devoted to discussing the usefulness of intergroup mirroring and should focus on the following questions:

1. Knowing what you do now, what would you do differently if you were required to complete the Disarmament Exercise again? Would you change any of your answers to the questions at the end of Exercise 13-1?

2. When would you recommend an intergroup mirroring intervention? When would you *not* recommend one?

3. How might intergroup mirroring help interdependent task groups (such as manufacturing employees and sales personnel) set realistic performance goals? What other benefits would mirroring provide such groups?

CONCLUSION

Intergroup mirroring can be especially helpful in eliciting and exploring general attitudes and feelings groups hold toward one another. Mirroring can also be useful for getting at specific procedural problems that have arisen between groups who need each other to get their work done. As you may have discovered during this exercise, it is usually easier to generate perceptions and even to identify discrepancies than to agree on how to change them. This is why an intervention like intergroup mirroring is an invaluable aid to managers who must cope with intergroup conflict and build a sense of intergroup team spirit.

DIAGNOSING ORGANIZATIONAL BEHAVIOR

It all started so positively. Three days after graduating with his degree in business administration, Mike Wilson started his first day at a prestigious insurance company—Consolidated Life. He worked in the Policy Issue Department. The work of the department was mostly

CASE 14-1
THE CONSOLIDATED LIFE CASE: CAUGHT BETWEEN CORPORATE CULTURES*

JOSEPH WEISS, *Bentley College*
MARK WAHLSTROM, *Bentley College*
EDWARD MARSHALL, *Bentley College*

* Reprinted by permission of the publisher from *The Journal of Management Case Studies*, 2, 238–43. Copyright © 1986 by Elsevier Science Publishing Co., Inc.

clerical and did not require a high degree of technical knowledge. Given the repetitive and mundane nature of the work, the successful worker had to be consistent and willing to grind out paperwork.

Rick Belkner was the division's vice-president, "the man in charge" at the time, an actuary by training and a technical professional described in the division as "the mirror of whomever was the strongest personality around him." It was also common knowledge that Belkner made $60,000 a year while he spent his time doing crossword puzzles.

Mike was hired as a management trainee and promised a supervisory assignment within a year. However, because of a management reorganization, it was only six weeks before he was placed in charge of an eight-person unit. The reorganization was intended to streamline workflow, upgrade and combine the clerical jobs, and make greater use of the computer system. It was a drastic departure from the old way of doing things and created a great deal of animosity and anxiety among the clerical staff.

Management realized that a flexible supervisory style was necessary to pull off the reorganization without immense turnover, so the firm gave its supervisors a free hand to run their units as they saw fit. Mike used this latitude to implement group meetings and training classes in his unit. In addition, he assured all members raises if they worked hard to attain them. By working long hours, participating in the mundane tasks with his unit, and being flexible in his management style, he was able to increase productivity, reduce errors, and reduce lost time. Things improved so dramatically that he was noticed by upper management and earned a reputation as a "superstar" despite being viewed as free-spirited and unorthodox. The feeling was that his loose, people-oriented management style could be tolerated because his results were excellent.

After a year, Mike received an offer from a different Consolidated Life division located across town. Mike was asked to manage an office in the marketing area. The pay was excellent and it offered an opportunity to turn around an office in disarray. The reorganization in his present division at Consolidated was almost complete, and most of his mentors and friends in management had moved on to other jobs. Mike decided to accept the offer. In his exit interview, he was assured that if he ever wanted to return, a position would be made for him. It was clear that he was held in high regard by management and staff alike. A huge party was thrown to send him off.

The new job was satisfying for a short time, but it became apparent to Mike that it did not have the long-term potential he was promised. After bringing on a new staff, computerizing the office, and auditing the books, he began looking for a position that would both challenge him and give him the autonomy he needed to be successful.

Eventually, word got back to Rick Belkner that Mike was looking for another job. Rick offered Mike a position with the same pay he was now receiving and control over a 14-person unit in his old division. After considering other options, Mike decided to return to his old division, feeling that he would be able to progress steadily over the next several years.

Upon his return to Consolidated Like, Mike became aware of several changes that had taken place in the six months since his departure. The most important change was the hiring of a new divisional senior vice-president, Jack Greely. Greely had been given total authority to run the division. Rick Belkner now reported to Jack.

Belkner's reputation was now that he was tough but fair. It was necessary for people in Jack's division to do things his way and "get the work out." Mike also found himself reporting to one of his former peers, Kathy Miller, who had been promoted to manager during the reorganization. Mike had always "hit it off" with Miller and foresaw no problems in working with her.

After a week, Mike realized the extent of the changes that had occurred. Gone was the loose, casual atmosphere that had marked his first tour in the division. Now, a stricter, task-oriented management doctrine was practiced. Morale of the supervisory staff had decreased to an alarming level. Jack Greely was the major topic of conversation in and around the division. People joked that MBO now meant management by "oppression," not by "objectives."

Mike was greeted back with comments like "Welcome to prison" and "Why would you come back here? You must be desperate!" It seemed as if everyone was looking for new jobs or transfers. Their lack of desire was reflected in the poor quality of work being done.

Mike felt that a change in the management style of his boss was necessary in order to improve a frustrating situation. Realizing that it would be difficult to affect Greely's style directly, Mike requested permission from Belkner to form a Supervisors' Forum for all the managers on Mike's level in the division. Mike explained that the purpose would be to enhance the existing management-training program. The Forum would include weekly meetings, guest speakers, and discussions of topics relevant to the division and the industry. Mike thought the Forum would show Greely that he was serious about both his job and improving morale in the division. Belkner gave the O.K. for an initial meeting.

The meeting took place, and ten supervisors who were Mike's peers in the company eagerly took the opportunity to "Blue Sky" it. There was a euphoric attitude about the group as they drafted their statement of intent. It read as follows:

TO: Rick Belkner
FROM: New Issue Services Supervisors
SUBJECT: Supervisors' Forum

On Thursday, June 11, the Supervisors' Forum held its first meeting. The objective of the meeting was to identify common areas of concern among us and to determine topics that we might be interested in pursuing.

The first area addressed was the void that we perceived exists in the management-training program. As a result of conditions beyond anyone's control, many of us over the past year have held supervisory duties without the benefit of formal training or proper experience. Therefore, what we propose is that we utilize the Supervisors' Forum as a vehicle with which to enhance the existing management-training program. The areas that we hope to affect with this supplemental training are: (a) morale/job satisfaction, (b) quality of work and service, (c) productivity, and (d) management expertise as it relates to the life insurance industry. With these objectives in mind, we have outlined below a list of possible activities that we would like to pursue.

1. Further utilization of the existing "in-house" training programs provided for manager trainees and supervisors, i.e., Introduction to Supervision, E.E.O., and Coaching and Counseling.

2. A series of speakers from various sections in the company. This would help expose us to the technical aspects of their departments and their managerial style.

3. Invitations to outside speakers to address the Forum on management topics such as management development, organizational structure and behavior, business policy, and the insurance industry. Suggested speakers could be area college professors, consultants, and state insurance officials.

4. Outside training and visits to the field. This could include attendance at seminars concerning management theory and development relative to the insurance industry. Attached is a representative sample of a program we would like to have considered in the future.

In conclusion, we hope that this memo clearly illustrates what we are attempting to accomplish with this program. It is our hope that the above outline will be able to give the Forum credibility and establish it as an effective tool for all levels of management within New Issue. By supplementing our on-the-job training with a series of speakers and classes, we aim to develop prospective management's role in it. Also, we would like to extend an invitation to the underwriters to attend any programs at which the topic of the speaker might be of interest to them.

cc: J. Greely
    Managers

The group felt the memo accurately and diplomatically stated their dissatisfaction with the current situation. However, they pondered what the results of their actions would be and what else they could have done.

Shortly after the memo had been issued, an emergency management meeting was called by Rick Belkner at Jack Greely's request to address the "union" being formed by the supervisors. Four general managers, Rick Belkner, and Jack Greely were at that meeting. During the meeting, it was suggested the Forum be disbanded to "put them in their place." However, Rick Belkner felt that if "guided" in the proper direction the Forum could die from the lack of interest. His stance was adopted, but it was common knowledge that Jack Greely was strongly opposed to the group and wanted its founders dealt with. His comment was "It's not a democracy and they're not a union. If they don't like it here, then they can leave." A campaign was directed by the managers to determine who the main authors of the memo were so they could be dealt with.

About this time, Mike's unit had made a mistake on a case, which Jack Greely was embarrassed to admit to his boss. This embarrassment was more than Jack Greely cared to take from Mike Wilson. At the managers' staff meeting that day, Greely stormed in and declared that the next supervisor to "screw up" was out the door. He would permit no more embarrassments of his division and repeated his earlier statement about "people leaving if they didn't like it here." It was clear to Mike and everyone else present that Mike Wilson was a marked man.

Mike had always been a loose, amiable supervisor. The major reason his units had been successful was the attention he paid to each individual and how they interacted with the group. He had a reputation for fairness, was seen as an excellent judge of personnel for new positions, and was noted for his ability to turn around people who had been in trouble. He motivated people through a dynamic, personable style and was noted for his general lack of regard for rules. He treated rules as obstacles to management and usually used his own discretion as to what was important. His office had a sign saying "Any fool can manage by rules. It takes an uncommon man to manage without any." It was an approach that flew in the face of company policy, but it had been overlooked in the past because of his results. However, because of Mike's actions with the Supervisors' Forum, he was now regarded as a thorn in the side, not a superstar, and his oddball style only made things worse.

Faced with the fact that he was rumored to be out the door, Mike sat down to appraise the situation.

When you have read this case, look back at the chapter's diagnostic questions and choose the ones that apply to the case. Then use those questions with the ones that follow in your case analysis.

1. Why was Mike Wilson so successful in his first managerial position at Consolidated Life? Evaluate his approach in managing the animosity and anxiety that the company's reorganization had created among his subordinates.

2. Was the Supervisors' Forum a success? Why or why not? What was it intended to accomplish? What forces favored its success? What forces stood in its way? Is there anything that Mike and the other managers could have done to increase top management's acceptance of the forum?

3. Describe Jack Greely's attitude toward change. Given Greely's stance and Mike's situation after the forum, what would you advise Mike to do?

CASE 14-2
L. J. SUMMERS COMPANY*

J. B. RITCHIE, *Brigham Young University*
PAUL H. THOMPSON, *Brigham Young University*

Jon Reese couldn't think of a time in the history of L. J. Summers Company when there had been as much anti-company sentiment among the workers as had emerged in the past few weeks. He knew that Mr. Summers would place the blame on him for the problems with the production workers because Jon was supposed to be helping Mr. Summer's son, Blaine, to become oriented to his new position. Blaine had only recently taken over as production manager of the company (see Exhibit 14-1). Blaine was unpopular with most of the workers, but the events of the past weeks had caused him to be resented even more. This resentment had

* Reprinted with the publisher's permission from pages 344–48 of *Organizations and People: Readings, Cases, and Exercises in Organizational Behavior*, 4th ed. by J. B. Ritchie and Paul H. Thompson, copyright © 1988 by West Publishing Company. All rights reserved.

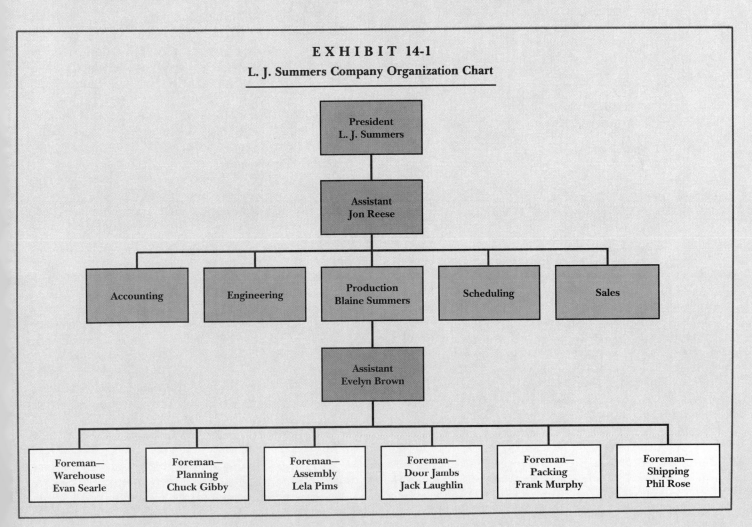

EXHIBIT 14-1
L. J. Summers Company Organization Chart

President
L. J. Summers

Assistant
Jon Reese

Accounting — Engineering — Production Blaine Summers — Scheduling — Sales

Assistant
Evelyn Brown

Foreman— Warehouse Evan Searle | Foreman— Planning Chuck Gibby | Foreman— Assembly Lela Pims | Foreman— Door Jambs Jack Laughlin | Foreman— Packing Frank Murphy | Foreman— Shipping Phil Rose increased to the point that several of the male workers had quit and all the women in the assembly department had refused to work.

The programs that had caused the resentment among the workers were instituted by Blaine to reduce waste and lower production costs, but they had produced completely opposite results. Jon knew that on Monday morning he would have to explain to Mr. Summers why the workers had reacted as they did and that he would have to present a plan to resolve the employee problems, reduce waste, and decrease production costs.

COMPANY HISTORY

L. J. Summers Company manufactured large sliding doors made of many narrow aluminum panels held together by thick rubber strips, which allowed the door to collapse as it was opened. Some of the doors were as high as 18 feet and were used in buildings to section off large areas. The company had grown rapidly in its early years due mainly to the expansion of the building program of the firm's major customer, which accounted for nearly 90 percent of Summers' business.

When L. J. Summers began the business, his was the only firm that manufactured the large sliding doors. Recently, however, several other firms had begun to market similar doors. One firm in particular had been bidding to obtain business from Summers' major customer. Fearing that the competitor might be able to underbid his company, Mr. Summers began urging his assistant, Jon, to increase efficiency and cut production costs.

CONDITIONS BEFORE THE COST REDUCTION PROGRAMS

A family-type atmosphere had existed at Summers before the cost reduction programs were instituted. There was little direct supervision of the workers from the front office, and no pressure was put on them to meet production standards. Several of the employees worked overtime regularly without supervision. The foremen and workers often played cards together during lunchtime, and company parties after work were common and popular. Mr. Summers was generally on friendly terms with all the employees, although he was known to get angry if something displeased him. He also participated freely in the daily operations of the company.

As Mr. Summers's assistant, Jon was responsible for seeing to it that the company achieved the goals established by Mr. Summers. Jon was considered hard-working and persuasive by most of the employees and

had a reputation of not giving in easily to employee complaints.

Blaine Summers had only recently become the production manager of Summers. He was in his early 20s, married, and had a good build. Several of the workers commented that Blaine liked to show off his strength in front of others. He was known to be very meticulous about keeping the shop orderly and neat, even to the point of making sure that packing crates were stacked "his way." It was often commented among the other employees how Blaine seemed to be trying to impress his father. Many workers voiced the opinion that the only reason Blaine was production manager was that his father owned the company. They also resented his using company employees and materials to build a swing set for his children and to repair his camper.

Blaine, commenting to Jon one day that the major problem with production was the workers, added that people of such caliber as the Summers' employees did not understand how important cost reduction was and that they would rather sit around and talk all day than work. Blaine rarely spoke to the workers but left most of the reprimanding and firing up to his assistant, Evelyn Brown.

Summers employed about 70 people to perform the warehousing, assembly, and door-jamb building, as well as the packing and shipping operations done on the doors. Each operation was supervised by a foreman, and crews ranged from 3 men in warehousing to 25 women in the assembly department. The foremen were usually employees with the most seniority and were responsible for quality and on-time production output. Most of the foremen had good relationships with the workers.

The majority of the work done at Summers consisted of repetitive assembly tasks requiring very little skill or training; for example, in the pinning department the workers operated a punch press, which made holes in the panels. The job consisted of punching the hole and then inserting a metal pin into it. Workers commented that it was very tiring and boring to stand at the press during the whole shift without frequent breaks.

Wages at Summers were considered to be low for the area. The workers griped about the low pay but said that they tried to compensate by taking frequent breaks, working overtime, and "taking small items home at night." Most of the workers who worked overtime were in the door-jamb department, the operation requiring the most skill. Several of these workers either worked very little or slept during overtime hours they reportedly worked.

The majority of the male employees were in their mid-20s; about half of them were unmarried. There was a great turnover among the unmarried male work-

MANAGING GROUP AND INTERGROUP RELATIONS: ORGANIZATION DEVELOPMENT I ers. The female employees were either young and single or older married women. The 25 women who worked in production were all in the assembly department under Lela Pims.

THE COST REDUCTION PROGRAMS

Shortly after Mr. Summers began stressing the need to reduce waste and increase production, Blaine called the foremen together and told them that they would be responsible for stricter discipline among the employees. Unless each foreman could reduce waste and improve production in his department, he would either be replaced or receive no pay increases.

The efforts of the foremen to make the workers eliminate wasteful activities and increase output brought immediate resistance and resentment. The employees' reactions were typified by the following comment: "What has gotten into Chuck lately? He's been chewing us out for the same old things we've always done. All he thinks about now is increasing production." Several of the foremen commented that they didn't like the front office making them the "bad guys" in the eyes of the workers. The workers didn't change their work habits as a result of the pressure put on them by the foremen, but a growing spirit of antagonism between the workers and the foremen was apparent.

After several weeks of no improvement in production, Jon called a meeting with the workers to announce that the plant would go on a 4-day, 10-hour-a-day work week in order to reduce operating costs. He stressed that the workers would enjoy having a three-day weekend. This was greeted with enthusiasm by some of the younger employees, but several of the older women complained that the schedule would be too tiring for them and that they would rather work five days a week. The proposal was voted on and passed by a two-to-one margin. Next Jon stated that there would be no more unsupervised overtime and that all overtime had to be approved in advance by Blaine. Overtime would be allowed only if some specific job had to be finished. Those who had been working overtime protested vigorously, saying that this would only result in lagging behind schedule, but Jon remained firm on this new rule.

Shortly after the meeting, several workers in the door-jamb department made plans to stage a work slowdown so that the department would fall behind schedule and they would have to work overtime to catch up. One of the workers, who had previously been the hardest working in the department said, "We will tell them that we are working as fast as possible and that we just can't do as much as we used to in a five-day week. The only thing they could do would be to fire us, and they would

never do that." Similar tactics were devised by workers in other departments. Some workers said that if they couldn't have overtime they would find a better paying job elsewhere.

Blaine, observing what was going on, told Jon, "They think I can't tell that they are staging a slowdown. Well, I simply won't approve any overtime, and after Jack's department gets way behind I'll let him have it for fouling up scheduling."

After a few weeks of continued slowdown, Blaine drew up a set of specific rules, which were posted on the company bulletin board early one Monday morning (see Exhibit 14-2). This brought immediate criticism from the workers. During the next week they continued to deliberately violate the posted rules. On Friday two of the male employees quit because they were penalized for arriving late to work and for "lounging around" during working hours. As they left they said they would be waiting for their foreman after work to get even with him for turning them in.

EXHIBIT 14-2

Production Shop Regulations

1. Anyone reporting late to work will lose one half hour's pay for each five minutes of lateness. The same applies to punching in after lunch.
2. No one is to leave the machine or post without the permission of the supervisor.
3. Anyone observed not working will be noted, and if sufficient occurrences are counted the employee will be dismissed.

That same day the entire assembly department (all women) staged a stoppage to protest an action taken against Myrtle King, an employee of the company since the beginning. The action resulted from a run-in she had with Lela Pims, foreman of the assembly department. Myrtle was about 60 years old and had been turned in by Lela for resting too much. She became furious, saying she couldn't work 10 hours a day. Several of her friends had organized the work stoppage after Myrtle had been sent home without pay credit for the day. The stoppage was also inspired by some talk among the workers of forming a union. The women seemed to favor this idea more than the men.

When Blaine found out about the incident he tried joking with the women and in jest threatened to fire them if they did not begin working again. When he saw he was getting nowhere he returned to the front office. One of the workers commented, "He thinks he can send us home and push us around and then all he has to do is tell us to go back to work and we will. Well, this place can't operate without us."

Jon soon appeared and called Lela into his office and began talking with her. Later he persuaded the women to go back to work and told them that there would be a meeting with all the female employees on Monday morning.

Jon wondered what steps he should take to solve the problems at L. J. Summers Company. The efforts of management to increase efficiency and reduce production costs had definitely caused resentment among the workers. Even more disappointing was the fact that the company accountant had just announced that waste and costs had increased since the new programs had been instituted, and the company scheduler reported that Summers was farther behind on shipments than ever before.

When you have read this case, look back at the chapter's diagnostic questions and choose the ones that apply to the case. Then use those questions with the ones that follow in your case analysis.

1. Critique Blaine Summers's behavior as a change agent. Why did the L. J. Summers Company's employees resent his actions? What should he do to curb this resentment?

2. Why did the door-jamb department employees stage a work slowdown? What do you think about Blaine's reaction to this slowdown? What would you advise Blaine to do instead?

3. What would you advise Jon Reese to do in order to correct the situation at Summers? What intervention would you implement if hired as an organization development change agent? What results would you expect this intervention to yield?

CASE 14-3

SONIA HARRIS

Review this case, which appears at the end of Chapter 12. Next, look back at Chapter 14's diagnostic questions and choose the ones that apply to the case. Then use those questions with the ones that follow in your case analysis.

1. Might Sonia Harris benefit from a counseling intervention? What would you expect such an intervention to accomplish? What benefits would it have for the Multinational Fiber Company?

2. What kind of an organization development intervention would you recommend to improve relations between Claire Herzlinger and Multinational Fiber's other employees? What is the purpose of an intervention of this type? How would it improve interpersonal relations?

3. If you were given the job of revising the company's instruction manual and getting management and workers to accept the revision, how would you go about this task?

CHAPTER 15

STRUCTURING THE ORGANIZATION

In 1987 John Sculley undertook a second reorganization of Apple Computer Inc., but by 1990 the company was in trouble again. Its domestic market share and rate of growth had declined, and its income had leveled off. According to Sculley, the firm was confused about where it was going. Dissension between the two largely autonomous divisions of marketing and product development kept both from being in touch with the market. For example, this structural problem may have caused Apple to miss a rare opportunity. Microsoft's OS/2, introduced in 1987 to give IBM PCs graphics capability, wasn't selling. Apple could have attracted frustrated OS/2 customers with lower-priced Macintoshes, but it elected to keep its prices high. Late in 1990 Apple's new Chief Operating Officer, Michael Spindler, announced detailed plans for regaining market share, while Sculley took over the research and development work on computers for the 21st century.

Hightigh on the list of Apple Computer's proficiencies is "event marketing"—turning corporate announcements into spectacles that reap extensive press coverage. Lately though, the press has been reporting events that the Cupertino, California, company would prefer not to publicize at all. From the end of May to the middle of June, Apple reorganized in a rush, fired 20 percent of its work force, and relieved Steven P. Jobs, Apple's 30-year-old cofounder and chairman, of all operating duty. John Sculley, 46, president and chief executive, noted with regret that Apple's moves were attracting as much attention as a popular television soap opera.

These changes are part of an overhaul Sculley has been working on since being wooed away from the presidency of Pepsi-Cola USA. From the beginning Sculley's mission was to improve Apple's responsiveness to retailers and customers. That required merging the company's nine highly decentralized divisions, most of which had broad responsibility for a product line, into an organization structured according to such business functions as engineering, manufacturing, and marketing.

Transforming Apple was more challenging than Sculley first imagined. Under Jobs the company had acquired a single-minded focus on products. The former chairman had often electrified Apple's employees with talk of "insanely great" new computers. But Sculley managed to consolidate Apple's divisions into just three—a sales division for all products, a division for the Apple II family of products, and one with the Macintosh as its focus.[1]

Shortly after this mid-1985 reorganization described in *Fortune* magazine, Apple's president, John Sculley, further transformed the firm by merging the Apple II and Macintosh divisions into a single department for product development and manufacturing. Sales and marketing remained combined in a second department. Sculley also implemented strict financial controls and formal reporting procedures within the scaled-down, streamlined version of Apple, Inc., increasing the efficiency of the firm's operations. In addition, the authority to make major decisions was taken away from middle management and pushed upward to the top of the organization. What remained after these changes bore little resemblance to the sprawling patchwork of nine loosely connected, autonomous divisions that Steve Jobs and Apple's other founder, Steve Wozniak, had created.[2]

Apple's transformation involved changes in the way the firm's employees were organized. Employees formerly grouped together according to the specific type of computer they produced and sold (Apple II, Lisa, Macintosh, among others) were regrouped according to the kind of work they performed (research and development, manufacturing, sales and marketing, and so on). The new methods of coordination—Sculley's formal procedures and controls—served to keep everyone in Apple's different groups working together toward the firm's overall objectives. In addition, there were changes in the hierarchical network of connections among the groups in Apple. Formerly each of the nine original divisions had been largely self-sufficient and able to succeed by working alone.

[1] Based on Bro Uttal, "Behind the Fall of Steve Jobs," *Fortune*, August 5, 1985, pp. 20–21.
[2] Katherine M. Hafner and Geoff Lewis, "Apple's Comeback," *Business Week*, January 19, 1987, pp. 84–89; Deborah C. Wise, "Can John Sculley Clean up the Mess at Apple?" *Business Week*, July 29, 1985, pp. 70–71; and Uttal, "Fall of Steve Jobs," pp. 20–24.

The groups created by Sculley's reorganization scheme became extremely interdependent and had to learn how to work together. Finally, Apple's reorganization involved critical modifications in decision-making procedures. By confining decision making to top management, Sculley gave himself and other top managers the authority to personally coordinate intergroup relations at Apple.

These changes constituted major modifications to Apple's *structure*. The composition of Apple's basic groups, the methods used to coordinate activities within those groups, the mechanisms used to link the groups together, and the distribution of decision making throughout the firm were all new. Like the steel framework of a building or the skeletal system of the human body, the structure of an organization like Apple separates its different parts from each other and also helps keep those parts interconnected. Specifically, an organization's structure groups its members together and separates the resulting groups from one another. In so doing, the structure also creates relationships of interdependence or interconnectedness within and among these groups. It is the structure of an organization that gives shape to the various interpersonal, group, and intergroup processes examined in Chapters 10–14. It defines the context that surrounds and influences the individual-level processes discussed in Chapters 4–9.

For this reason, an organization's structure has widespread effects on behavior and productivity within the firm. Managers like Apple's John Sculley must know how to structure their organizations in different ways. They must also know about the strengths and weaknesses of the different ways of structuring. In this chapter, we will examine the basic elements of an organization's structure—how the organization's work is divided and allocated among groups and the linking and coordinating mechanisms that facilitate the smooth flow of that work.

DIAGNOSTIC ISSUES

Our diagnostic model highlights several important questions about organization structure. What are some of the major dimensions that *describe* the way firms are structured? What different ways of coordinating work are used in different kinds of structures? How can we *diagnose* whether an organization's structure will promote efficiency or flexibility and adaptability? Can we explain the reason why employees in an organization are grouped into structural units?

Can we *prescribe* how to link the units in an organization together? Can we specify an adequate balance in a firm between hierarchical control and the need to keep work flowing? Finally, what kinds of *actions* should managers take to devise ways of coordinating work in the organization? What corresponding adjustments should they make to the way jobs are designed and responsibilities are assigned?

WHAT IS ORGANIZATION STRUCTURE?

As you learned in Chapter 2, all organizations consist of people performing tasks that when combined, create goods or services whose production lies beyond the abilities of people working alone. Whether as well known as Apple or as anonymous as a locally owned convenience store, every organization is characterized by a pattern of interrelated tasks that are essential to its efficient functioning. This identifiable **organization structure** consists of a relatively stable

organization structure The relatively stable network of interconnections or interdependencies among the people and tasks that make up an organization.

network of interconnections or interdependencies among the people and tasks that make up an organization.[3]

An organization's structure serves as a framework that both integrates the individuals and groups that constitute the organization and differentiates them from each other. Typically, the structure of an organization takes the form of a hierarchy such as the one diagrammed in the organization chart shown in Figure 2-1. Balancing structural *integration* and *differentiation* within structural hierarchies is an important challenge facing managers.[4] The ability to sense a workable balance and arrange an organization's structure accordingly can have a major effect on the firm's productivity.

FORMING AND COORDINATING STRUCTURAL UNITS

Managers first strive to balance integration and differentiation by determining the most effective way to group employees. This process is one of seeking acceptable answers to questions such as, "Who should work with whom?" "What mechanisms should be used to coordinate activities in each group?" and "How large should each group be?"

Unit Grouping

unit grouping The process of grouping the members of an organization into work groups or units.

Answering the first question, Who should work with whom? is neither simple nor straightforward. In general, however, the people in an organization are placed in work groups or units according to similarities either in what they do or in what they produce.[5] To illustrate these two types of **unit grouping**, let us imagine a company that makes wooden desks, bookshelves, and chairs. To produce each of these products, four basic activities are required. A receiver must unpack and stock the raw materials required for the product. A fabricator must shape and assemble the raw materials into a partially completed product. A finisher must complete the assembly operation by painting and packaging the product. Finally, a shipper must dispatch the finished products to the organization's customers. In summary, the manufacturing work force of the company consists of 12 employees organized into three assembly lines consisting of four employees each.

functional grouping People are grouped into units according to similarities in the functions they perform. Grouping word-processing typists into a word-processing pool is an example.

market grouping People are grouped into units according to similarities in the products they make or markets they serve. Grouping the members of an automobile assembly line into an assembly unit is an example.

What the management of this company must decide is whether to group its 12 employees by the tasks they perform, called **functional grouping**, or by the products they produce or markets they serve, **market grouping**. As you will see, each method has both advantages and disadvantages, so the choice presents managers with a tradeoff. Let's start by considering what functional grouping, or grouping by the means of production, will do for the firm. The upper panel of Figure 15-1 shows how the four tasks from each assembly line can be grouped together so that the four resulting work units consist of people with the same sets of abilities, knowledge, and skills. The receivers, the fabricators, the finishers, and the shippers thus form four *functional* work units.

[3] James G. March and Herbert A. Simon, *Organizations* (New York: John Wiley 1958) p. 4; James D. Thompson, *Organizations in Action* (New York: McGraw-Hill, 1967), p. 51; W. Richard Scott, *Organizations: Rational, Natural, and Open Systems*, 2nd ed. (Englewood Cliffs, N.J.: Prentice Hall, 1987), p. 15.

[4] Paul R. Lawrence and Jay W. Lorsch, "Differentiation and Integration in Complex Organizations," *Administrative Science Quarterly* 12 (1967), 1–47; and Lawrence and Lorsch, *Organization and Environment* (Homewood, Ill.: Richard D. Irwin, 1967), p. 7.

[5] Henry Mintzberg, *The Structuring of Organizations* (Englewood Cliffs, N.J.: Prentice Hall, 1979), pp. 108–29.

FIGURE 15-1

Unit Grouping

People are put into work units according to similarities in what they do or what they produce. The upper diagram shows an organization with its units formed around similarities in what their members do, that is, functional similarities. The lower diagram shows the same organization with its units formed around similarities in what their members produce, in other words, market similarities.

Unit Grouping by Functional Similarities

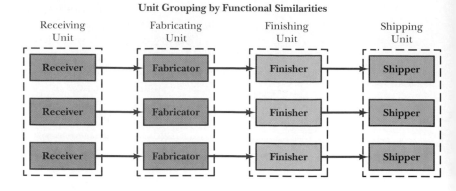

Unit Grouping by Market Similarities

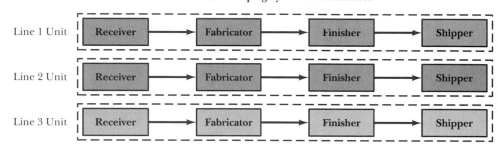

Functional work units help integrate and coordinate employees who perform the same sorts of tasks. Employees in such units can exchange information about task procedures, sharpening their knowledge and skills. They can also help each other out when necessary. This sort of cooperation can greatly enhance unit productivity.

Functional grouping can also allow the organization to take advantage of certain other cost savings. Suppose that in our example, receivers for all three of the assembly lines typically need only five hours a day to complete their work and are idle for the remaining three hours. If receiving is handled in a single work unit, the firm can economize by employing two receivers instead of three. In a full eight-hour day, these two people should be able to complete the unit's work (3 workers × 5 hours each = 15 hours; 2 workers × 8 hours each = 16 hours), minimizing idle time and improving the firm's economic efficiency.

Functional grouping, however, separates people performing different tasks along the same work flow. This differentiation can encourage slowdowns that block the flow, reducing productivity as a result. For instance, suppose the finisher on the desk-assembly line has nothing to do and wants the desk fabricator to speed up in order to provide more work. Because of functional grouping, the two people are in different units, and there is no simple way for them to communicate with each other directly. Instead, the desk finisher must rely on hierarchical communication linkages between the fabricating and finishing units. The finisher must tell the supervisor of the finishing unit about the problem. The finishing supervisor must notify the superintendent overseeing all manufacturing operations. The manufacturing superintendent must talk with the supervisor of the fabricating unit. And the fabricating supervisor must tell the desk fabricator to work faster. Meanwhile, productivity suffers owing to the absence of direct communication along the flow of work.

Now let's consider what happens if the firm decides to create *market-based* work units. Such units can be formed on the basis of similarities in products, in customer groups, or in geographic regions served. We will assume that our company decides to create units based on its three product lines of desks, bookshelves, and chairs. The lower panel of Figure 15-1 illustrates this option. Now the company is grouped into three work units, and each unit completely contains one of the firm's product-assembly lines.

One of the primary strengths of market grouping is that it integrates activities along the flow of work. Each separate work flow is completely enclosed within a single unit. If employees who fill different functions along the assembly line need to coordinate with each other to maintain the flow of work, they can do so without difficulty. As you can imagine, in an organization grouped by market similarities, work tends to flow very smoothly.

Owing to its encouragement of work-flow integration, market grouping also enhances the organization's adaptability. Operations on any of the firm's three assembly lines can be halted or stopped without affecting the rest of the company. For example, suppose the desk-assembly line in the company is shut down because of poor sales. To simulate this situation, cover the upper assembly line in the bottom panel of Figure 15-1 with a piece of paper. You can see that neither of the remaining two units will be affected in any major way. Work on the bookcase and chair lines can continue without interruption. Under functional grouping, however, the firm would not have the same degree of flexibility. If you cover the upper assembly line in the top panel of Figure 15-1, you will note that all four of the units created by functional grouping would be affected if desk production were interrupted. Complete reorganization would be required by any long-term disturbance. Thus the adaptability allowed by the relative independence of different work flows in an organization grouped according to market similarities is not available to companies composed of functionally grouped units.

Despite its strengths, however, market grouping does not permit the scale economies offered by functional grouping. Under the market grouping arrangement, people who perform the same function (e.g., receiving) cannot help or substitute for one another. In addition, at times they will inevitably duplicate one another's work, adding to the firm's overall costs. Moreover, it becomes very difficult for people who perform the same task to trade information about such things as more efficient work procedures and how to improve task skills. So just as functional grouping does not allow the adaptability of market grouping, market grouping does not incorporate the economic efficiency of functional grouping.

Unit Coordination Mechanisms

Deciding how an organization's employees should be grouped is one of the most important structural decisions a manager can make. Assigning people to work units helps establish physically close relationships among the members of each unit, making it easier for them to engage in face-to-face communications. Grouping workers can also make it easier to carry out superior-subordinate interactions. Furthermore, people who work close together are more likely to develop common norms and behaviors. These similarities can make it easier to establish standardized work processes and outputs. All these outcomes encourage greater coordination.

Coordination is a process in which otherwise disorganized actions are integrated so as to produce a desired result. Different parts of our bodies, for example, work together to produce complex, coordinated behaviors. Your hands follow a trajectory plotted by your eyes in order to catch a ball. Your hands also manipulate your car's steering wheel at the same time that your foot depresses the accelerator pedal. It would be very difficult, if not impossible, to catch the ball if you could not see it. It would be dangerous to accelerate or even to move the car if you could not control its direction.

unit coordination mechanism A mechanism that sustains structural interconnections in structural units by helping to mesh interdependent task activities.

In similar fashion, the members of an organization by working together can accomplish outcomes that would be beyond the abilities of any one person working alone. By helping to mesh interdependent task activities, three **unit coordination mechanisms** sustain the structural interconnections in the units of an organization. These mechanisms are mutual adjustment, direct supervision, and standardization. As the primary means by which organizational activities are integrated, they are the glue that holds the organization together.[6]

Mutual Adjustment. By **mutual adjustment**, we mean coordination accomplished through interpersonal communication in which coworkers who occupy positions of similar hierarchical authority share job-related information.[7] Mutual adjustment, the simplest of the three unit coordination mechanisms, is the face-to-face exchange of information about how a job should be done and who should do it. A group of factory-maintenance mechanics who are examining service manuals and discussing how to fix a broken conveyor belt are coordinating by means of mutual adjustment.

mutual adjustment A unit coordination mechanism in which coordination is accomplished via face-to-face communications. Coworkers who occupy positions of similar hierarchical authority exchange information about how a job should be done and who should do it.

Note that in mutual adjustment, information is exchanged by people who can exercise at least partial control over the tasks they perform. Clearly, unless the people doing the communicating possess this control, they cannot coordinate their activities in this way.

direct supervision A unit coordination mechanism in which one person takes responsibility for the work of a group of others. She determines which tasks need to be performed, who will perform them, and how they will be linked together to produce the desired end result.

Direct Supervision. In **direct supervision**, one person takes responsibility for the work of a group of others.[8] As part of their responsibilities, direct supervisors may determine which tasks need to be performed, who will perform them, and how they will be linked together to produce the desired end result. They may then issue orders to subordinates under their jurisdiction, check to see that these orders have been executed, and redirect subordinates as needed to fulfill additional work responsibilities. The owner of a grocery store is functioning as a direct supervisor when having instructed an employee to restock the shelves, he finds that the clerk has completed the job and directs her next to change the signs advertising the week's specials. A shop-floor supervisor overseeing a potato chip production line is also coordinating by direct supervision when she orders workers to stop the line to adjust the heat in its drying oven.

standardization A unit coordination mechanism in which work is coordinated by providing employees with carefully worked out standards and procedures that guide the performance of their tasks. It is coordination achieved on the drawing board, before the work is actually undertaken, and may involve standardization of work processes and behaviors, outputs, skills, or norms.

Standardization. **Standardization** coordinates work by providing employees with carefully worked out standards and procedures that guide the performance of their tasks. This kind of coordination is achieved on the drawing board, before the work to be performed is actually undertaken.[9] So long as drawing-board plans are followed and the work situation remains essentially unchanged, interdependence is maintained.

There are four types of standardization—standardization of work processes, or behaviors, and standardization of outputs, skills, and norms. As you will see from the brief descriptions that follow, each kind of standardization draws on procedures discussed in other parts of the book. For example, work process standardization can grow out of the process of job design examined in Chapter 17. Output standardization can incorporate the sort of goal setting discussed in Chapter 7. Skill standardization can be based on human resource training pro-

[6] Ibid., pp. 2–3; March and Simon, *Organizations*, p. 160; and Jay R. Galbraith, *Designing Complex Organizations* (Reading, Mass.: Addison-Wesley, 1973), p. 4.

[7] Thompson, *Organizations in Action*, p. 62.

[8] Mintzberg, *Structuring of Organizations*, pp. 3–4. See also the discussion in Chapter 2 of Henri Fayol's management principles.

[9] Mintzberg, *Structuring of Organizations*, p. 5.

cedures identified in Chapter 9. And norm standardization can grow out of the interpersonal socialization described in Chapter 10.

Work process standardization is sometimes called *behavioral standardization*. It involves specifying the precise behaviors or actions employees must perform to accomplish their assigned tasks. Specified behaviors are a part of the process, or behavioral standards, for a particular job. They link that job with other jobs in the organization. For instance, the behavioral specifications for the worker who is responsible for filling soda-pop bottles may include step-by-step instructions for controlling the flow of the soda, checking for cracked bottles, positioning the bottles for filling, and placing filled bottles on a conveyor line. The behavioral specifications for the worker who is responsible for capping the bottles may include step-by-step instructions for checking that all bottles on the conveyor line have been filled, that none have cracked during filling and capping, that all caps are tightly secured, and that all properly capped bottles move forward along the line to the shipping department. In this example, the two people are connected by the conveyor line and are able to work together without any further coordination.

Output standardization is the formal designation of output targets, or performance goals. For example, a sales representative of a publishing company might be assigned the goal of getting university English departments to adopt 1,000 copies of a new English grammar textbook within a 12-month period. Alternatively, workers on an assembly line in a baseball glove manufacturer might be given the goal of producing 25 gloves per hour. Unlike employees working under behavioral standardization, people coordinated by output standardization are free to decide for themselves how to attain their goals. So long as everyone accomplishes his goal, work continues, unchanged, and no one needs to engage in further coordination.

Skill standardization involves specifying in advance the skills, knowledge, or abilities that people must have to perform a task competently. Because skill standardization is aimed at regulating characteristics of people rather than jobs, it is used most often in situations where neither work process standards nor output targets can be easily specified.

For example, few experts agree on the precise behaviors that high-school teachers should engage in while teaching. Moreover, there is a general consensus that the *output indicators* for the job of teaching, such as course grades and standardized test scores, have little validity as measures of teaching success. (Grades can be artificially inflated, and test scores can be undermined by pretest coaching.) On the other hand, almost all community school districts mandate that their teachers be certified by an agency of the state, and such certification often requires that teachers not only hold certain educational degrees but give evidence of having acquired specific knowledge and skills. Thus all teachers hired by a school district that requires state certification should possess a more or less standardized set of job qualifications or skills.

Skilled employees seldom need to communicate with each other to figure out what to do and can usually predict with reasonable accuracy what other similarly skilled employees will do on the job. Consequently, on jobs staffed by specially skilled employees, there may be much less need to coordinate work behaviors in other ways.

As you will recall from Chapters 10 and 11, norms describe desirable and expected forms of behavior. They are statements of what people should or should not do. For example, a norm often found in work organizations is that people should arrive at their jobs on time and should not leave before the end of the normal workday. *Norm standardization* is present when the members of a unit or organization share a set of beliefs about the acceptability of particular types of behavior and so tend to behave in ways that are generally approved. For instance, Ford Motor employees who believe that "quality is job one" work in ways that enhance product quality. They do not need to discuss the merits of this philosophy with each other or to be directed by a supervisor to produce quality products. Similarly, the employees of United Parcel Service who share a belief in the importance of on-time delivery tend to make their deliveries promptly or to see that their subordinates do so.

Choosing among the Mechanisms. Managers charged with designing an organization structure continually confront choices among the three unit coordination mechanisms we have discussed (these mechanisms are reviewed in Table 15-1). Most of the time, two or more of these mechanisms are used concurrently to integrate work activities in organizational units. In such instances, one of them serves as the primary mechanism used to solve most coordination problems. The others (if present) serve as secondary mechanisms that supplement the primary mechanism, backing it up in case it fails to provide enough integration. It is up to managers to determine which mechanism will serve as the primary means of coordination and which ones (if any) will act as secondary mechanisms. Besides cultural tendencies (see the "International OB" box), two factors govern such choices—first, the number of people whose efforts must be coordinated in order to ensure the successful performance of interdependent tasks; second, the relative stability of the situation in which the tasks to be coordinated must be performed.[10]

In small groups, of about 12 people or fewer, coordination is often accomplished by everyone's doing what comes naturally. Employees communicate face to face, using mutual adjustment to fit individual task behaviors into the group's overall network of interdependence. No other coordination mechanisms are needed, and none are used. Family farms and specialty restaurants are often organized around this type of coordination. Similarly, students working together on textbook exercises or case analyses often coordinate among themselves using mutual adjustment alone.

Suppose a group is made up of many more than 12 people—as many as 30, 40, or even 50. Now face-to-face mutual adjustment may fail to sustain purposeful interdependence. It may need to be replaced by some other unit coor-

---

[10] Mintzberg, *Structuring of Organizations*, pp. 7–9; and Mintzberg, "The Structuring of Organizations," in *The Strategy Process: Concepts, Contexts, and Cases*, ed. James Brian Quinn, Henry Mintzberg, and Robert M. James (Englewood Cliffs, N.J.: Prentice Hall, 1988), pp. 276–304.

T A B L E 15-1
Unit-Coordination Mechanisms

MECHANISM	DEFINITION
Mutual Adjustment	Face-to-face communication in which hierarchical equals exchange information about work procedures
Direct Supervision	The direction and coordination of the work of a unit by one person who issues direct orders to the unit's members
Standardization	The planning and implementation of standards and procedures that regulate work performance
Work process/behavior standardization	The specification of sequences of task behaviors
Output standardization	Establishment of goals or desired end results of task performance
Skill standardization	Specification of the abilities, knowledge, and skills required by a particular task
Norm standardization	Inculcation of attitudes and beliefs that lead to specific desired behaviors

Effects of National Cultures on Organization Structures

Research has revealed four dimensions along which national cultures can be differentiated (see Chapter 19). Two of these dimensions, uncertainty avoidance and power distance, affect the emergence of different unit coordination mechanisms.*

The first dimension, uncertainty avoidance, concerns the extent to which people are comfortable with ambiguous situations and an unknown future. In national cultures with strong uncertainty avoidance, people try to make the present more comfortable by developing extensive rules and regulations to standardize behavior. There are far fewer rules in national cultures characterized by weak uncertainty avoidance.

The second dimension, power distance, is the degree to which people feel that power differences should be minimized and political equality encouraged. In national cultures characterized by small power distance, participatory processes are preferred over hierarchical procedures. In cultures with tendencies toward large power distance, the opposite is true, and hierarchy is the preferred way of coordinating activities.

What effects do these two international dimensions have on the choice of unit coordination mechanisms? In countries with strong tendencies toward uncertainty avoidance (Greece, Japan, France), rules and regulations developed to cope with uncertainty also push toward the emergence of standardization even before information-processing requirements make it necessary. In countries with weak uncertainty avoidance (U.S., Canada, Sweden), firms turn to standardization only when other methods of unit coordination fail to perform appropriately. In countries favoring large power distance (Mexico, India, Hong Kong), direct supervision appears early and dominates unit coordination even after the emergence of extensive standardization. In countries with small power distance (Israel, Sweden, Great Britain), mutual adjustment may be used even when process loss would seem to necessitate its

* Geert Hofstede, *Culture's Consequences: International Differences in Work Related Values* (Beverly Hills, Calif.: Sage, 1980).

replacement. Thus, although the same unit coordination mechanisms are used in organizations throughout the world, cultural tendencies can alter the specific point at which one type of unit coordination mechanism is replaced by another.

---

dination mechanism. As you can see from Figure 15-2, the reason mutual adjustment alone cannot effect coordination among large numbers of people is that the number of needed communication links rises geometrically as the number of individuals rises arithmetically. Clearly, the members of larger groups would have to spend so much time communicating with each other that they would have very little time to actually complete their tasks. Process loss (see Chapter 11) would substantially undermine the group's productivity.

Thus, in larger groups, direct supervision takes the place of mutual adjustment as the primary means of coordinating group activities. Direct supervision reduces the number of linkages needed to coordinate tasks to one superior-subordinate linkage for each employee. In communicating information to her subordinates, the direct supervisor acts as a proxy for the group as a whole. To use an analogy, the direct supervisor functions like the sort of automated switching facility that routes telephone messages from callers to receivers. She originates direct orders and collects performance feedback while channeling information from one interdependent group member to another. In such situations, however,

FIGURE 15-2

Group Size and Mutual Adjustment Links

For each person added to a group, the number of links needed to coordinate through mutual adjustment rises geometrically. Thus, although 2 people need only 1 link, 3 people need 3, and 6 people need 15. In an organization of 30 people, how many links would be required?

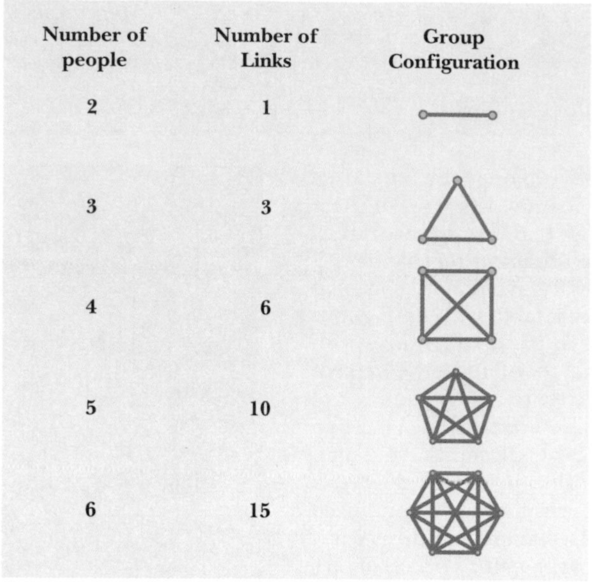

Number of people	Number of Links	Group Configuration
2	1	
3	3	
4	6	
5	10	
6	15	

mutual adjustment still continues as a supplementary coordination mechanism. When the direct supervisor is unavailable or does not know how to solve a particular problem, employees resort to face-to-face communication among themselves to try to figure out what to do.

Besides clarifying how direct supervision functions as a unit coordination mechanism, the telephone-switching analogy also helps to explain the failure of even direct supervision to coordinate the activities of members in very large groups. Just as a switching facility can be overloaded by an avalanche of telephone calls, in successively larger groups the direct supervisor is increasingly burdened by the need to obtain information and channel it to the right people. Ultimately, the direct supervisor must succumb to information overload. She is unable to keep up with the demands for coordination made by her subordinates.

At this point, the third unit coordination mechanism, standardization, replaces direct supervision as the primary means of sustaining coordinated task interdependence. As long as the conditions on which established standards have been based continue to prevail, coordination by standardization can prevent information overload. That is because it greatly reduces or eliminates the amount of communication needed for effective coordination. Workers are performing prespecified task behaviors, producing prespecified task outputs, using prespecified task skills, or conforming to prespecified workplace norms. Therefore, members of very large groups can complete complex, interdependent networks of task activities with little or no need for further coordination.

Where standardization is the primary means of coordination, direct supervision and mutual adjustment are still available for use as secondary coordination mechanisms. Direct supervision may be used to make sure that workers on the assembly line adhere to standards. Mutual adjustment may also be used on the assembly line to cope with machine breakdowns, power outages, or other temporary situations in which standard operating procedures lose effectiveness. In this example, the secondary mechanisms of direct supervision and mutual adjustment supplement the primary mechanism of standardization, filling in the holes left by momentary failures in the primary mechanism.

Standardization requires stability. If the conditions envisioned during the planning of a particular standardization program change, the usefulness of that program may be destroyed. For example, behavioral specifications that detail computerized check-in procedures are likely to be of little use to hotel-registration personnel facing a long line of guests and a dead computer screen. Similarly, output specifications requiring the sale of 50 pairs of denim jeans per day provide no useful guidance if denim goes out of fashion.

When changing conditions completely undermine coordination via standardization, mutual adjustment sometimes reemerges as the primary unit coordination device. When large groups or organizations face rapidly changing conditions that make standardization impossible, they rely heavily on face-to-face communication. The process loss associated with mutual adjustment in these situations is simply tolerated as a necessary cost of staying in business.

The three means of coordination, then, form a continuum, from mutual adjustment at one extreme, through direct supervision and standardization in the middle ranges, and back to mutual adjustment at the other extreme.[11] This continuum is depicted in Figure 15-3. It is important to remember that as coordination needs progress from left to right along the continuum, mechanisms to the left are not completely abandoned. So at the point represented all the way to the right of the continuum, standardization, direct supervision, and secondary mutual adjustment are available to supplement the mutual adjustment that serves as the primary means of coordination.

When you are choosing among coordination mechanisms, you must keep in mind that there is a critical tradeoff between the *costs* of using a particular mechanism and the *flexibility* it permits. The simplest coordination mechanism, mutual adjustment, requires neither extensive preplanning nor preexisting hierarchical differentiation. Therefore, it affords a high degree of flexibility. Changing circumstances can be readily accommodated. The links forged by mutual adjustment, however, cannot usually be banked for future use. Instead, each time mutual adjustment is used, it generates new coordination costs. These costs may take the form of time, effort, and similar resources that must be diverted away from task-related activities and directed toward face-to-face communications. The costs of each instance of mutual adjustment tend to be modest, but over time they add up and become quite significant.

In contrast, the initial costs of standardization are quite high. Planning standards and procedures often means contracting with specialists, and otherwise productive resources must be diverted to the planning process. Yet once a program of standardization has been designed and implemented, it no longer consumes resources of major significance. The coordination costs associated with standardization can therefore be amortized or spread over long periods of time and across long production runs. The result will be an extremely low coordination cost per unit of goods or services produced. Standardization is thus less costly than mutual adjustment. As mentioned earlier, however, standardization requires that the work situation remain essentially unchanged—changing conditions would render existing standards obsolete. So it lacks the flexibility of mutual adjustment.

The flexibility of direct supervision lies between the extremes of mutual adjustment and standardization. Because it presupposes a hierarchy of authority,

FIGURE 15-3

A Continuum of Coordination Mechanisms

The three basic means of coordinating unit activities—mutual adjustment, direct supervision, and standardization—fulfill increasingly demanding needs for coordination and come into use at varying points along a continuum of unit size and complexity.

[11] Mintzberg, *Structuring of Organizations*, p. 7.

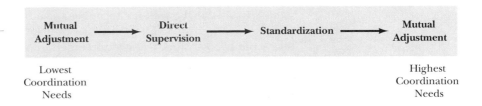

it lacks the spontaneity and fluidity of mutual adjustment. Yet because direct supervision requires much less planning than standardization, it is more flexible. Not surprisingly, the coordination costs of direct supervision also fall between those of mutual adjustment and standardization. Although supervision requires fewer costly communication links than mutual adjustment, new coordination costs are generated each time a supervisory action is taken.

Unit Size

unit size The number of people who belong to a structural unit.

span of control Another name for unit size; the number of people under the supervision of a single direct supervisor.

Besides having major effects on the costs and quality of coordination, the different coordination devices used in a group also determine the appropriate **unit size**, or **span of control**, of the group. As we have implied, mutual adjustment is most effective in small units of about 2 to 12 people in which each member is able to talk with everyone else. In contrast, large units of 50 or more people can be coordinated effectively by means of standardization, which requires minimal face-to-face communication. Groups of moderate size can be handled by direct supervision, which requires less communication than mutual adjustment but more than standardization.

The optimal size of a particular work unit is also a function of the kinds of tasks its members and supervisor perform. Homogeneity of tasks reduces the variety of problems likely to arise and makes it easier for the unit's supervisor and members to solve the ones that do come up. For example, coping with the work problems of a group of 12 computer operators is easier than overseeing a group of 6 computer operators and 6 computer programmers. All 12 operators are likely to require help only with operating problems (following directions found in computer manuals, dealing with machine breakdowns, deciding the priority of different computer jobs). In the programmers' group, half will have one kind of problem, while the other half are likely to need help with a whole set of entirely different problems (plotting the basic logic of programs yet to be written, finding errors in newly written programs, determining how to update older programs). Consequently, the more similar the tasks performed by a group's members, the larger the group can be without overloading the supervisor or requiring extensive mutual adjustment.

In addition, optimal unit size depends on the extent to which employees in the unit must consult with the supervisor in order to perform their work. Although the demands on the supervisor's time in a small group can be reasonable, they may prove overwhelming in a larger group. The manageability of a particular unit size may also reflect the number of nonsupervisory duties the supervisor must perform. Such duties will reduce the time she has available to manage group activities.

To some degree, the size of a work unit is determined by its hierarchical position. Typically, groups found lower in a firm's hierarchy are larger than groups at higher levels. This tendency is generally due to the fact that the work performed at lower levels tends to be relatively less complex, therefore, less difficult to standardize and supervise than work performed at higher levels. It may also be caused by attempts to reduce distortion in the flow of information traveling up and down the hierarchy. As shown in Figure 15-4, increasing the size of groups at the bottom of an organization's hierarchy reduces the number of lower-level groups. Therefore, it can also reduce the number of hierarchical levels required to link the groups together. In turn, because fewer people are involved in the firm's vertical communication channels, cutting down on hierarchical levels lessens the chance that information transferred along vertical communication channels will be distorted.

FIGURE 15-4

Unit Size and Vertical Information Flow

Increasing the size of units at the bottom of an organization's hierarchy can decrease the number of levels in the hierarchy. The result is reduced distortion in information flowing up and down the hicrarchy.

A Units of 3 with 3 Hierarchical Levels

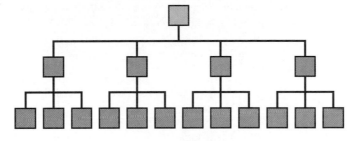

B 1 Unit of 12 with 2 Hierarchical Levels

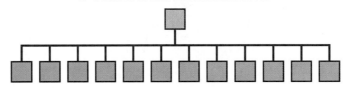

You can see that there is no magic number of members that will guarantee unit effectiveness. Instead, the size that is most appropriate for a particular group depends on the factors we have just mentioned. It is management's responsibility to assess these factors and adjust the group's size accordingly.

STRUCTURAL CORRELATES OF STANDARDIZATION

Besides affecting the type of coordination mechanism used to integrate activities within structural units, the decision to coordinate by standardization affects the nature of two other structural characteristics—formalization and specialization. They are *correlates* of standardization, meaning that they change in association with changes in standardization. We will discuss them more fully in this section.

Formalization

formalization The process of planning the regulations that control organizational behavior; also the written documentation produced by the planning process. Jobs, work flows, or general rules may be formalized.

Formalization is the process of planning the regulations that control organizational behavior. It also refers to the written documentation produced by the planning process. As you can see, there is a clear relationship between formalization and standardization. Formalization gives concrete form to the behavioral, output, skill, and norm standards used to coordinate by standardization. Thus you are likely to find extensive formalization only in organizations that make use of standardization as a coordination mechanism. In organizations that make little use of standardization, formalization will be almost nonexistent. Figure 15-5 shows a few items from an instrument that is useful in assessing the amount of formalization in a firm.[12]

---

[12] D. S. Pugh, D. J. Hickson, C. R. Hinings, and C. Turner, "Dimensions of Organization Structure," *Administrative Science Quarterly*, 13 (1968), 65–91; J. H. K. Inkson, Pugh, and Hickson, "Organization, Context, and Structure: An Abbreviated Replication," *Administrative Science Quarterly* 15 (1970), 318–29; and John Child, "Organization, Structure, and Strategies of Control: A Replication of the Aston Study," *Administrative Science Quarterly* 17 (1972), 163–77.

FIGURE 15-5

A Questionnaire Measure
of Formalization

Circle your response to each of the following items as they apply to the organization in question.

1. Written job descriptions are available for
   a. operative employees only.
   b. operative employees and first-line supervisors only.
   c. operative, first-line supervisory, and middle management personnel.
   d. operative, first-line supervisory, middle and upper-middle management personnel.
   e. all employees, including senior management.

2. Where written job descriptions exist, how closely are employees supervised to ensure compliance with standards set in the job description?
   a. very loose
   b. loose
   c. moderately close
   d. close
   e. very close

3. How much latitude are employees allowed from the standards?
   a. a great deal
   b. a large amount
   c. a moderate amount
   d. very little
   e. none

4. What percentage of nonmanagerial employees are given written operating instructions or procedures for their jobs?
   a. 0–20%
   b. 21–40%
   c. 41–60%
   d. 61–80%
   e. 81–100%

5. Of those nonmanagerial employees given written instructions or procedures, to what extent are they followed?
   a. none
   b. little
   c. some
   d. a great deal
   e. a very great deal

6. To what extent are supervisors and middle managers free from rules, procedures, and policies when they make decisions?
   a. a very great deal
   b. a great deal
   c. some
   d. little
   e. none

7. What percentage of all the rules and procedures that exist within the organization are in writing?
   a. 1–20%
   b. 21–40%
   c. 41–60%
   d. 61–80%
   e. 81–100%

Scoring: For all items, a = 1, b = 2, c = 3, d = 4, e = 5. Add up the score for all seven items. The sum of the item scores is the degree of formalization (out of a possible 35).

Types of Formalization. There are three types of formalization—formalization by job, by work flow, and by rules (see Table 15-2). *Formalization by job* is used to set up coordination by work process standardization. It is the process of planning and documenting the sequence of steps employees must take to perform their jobs. For example, a fast-food restaurant may prepare procedures manuals that specify how long employees should cook each type of food they serve, what condiments they should use to flavor it, and how they should package it for the customer. Likewise, a bank may develop detailed job descriptions that specify steps tellers must follow to cash checks, deposit funds, accept loan payments, and so forth.

Formalization by workflow is the process of establishing standards, or goals, for the flow of work in a firm. It provides the underpinnings for output standardization. An example is the posted monthly sales goals that insurance sales representatives are expected to achieve. Another example would be a set of standards for display-screen brightness, keyboard responsiveness, and exterior appearance prepared for workers assembling laptop personal computers. They can use these standards to assess the quality of their output.

TABLE 15-2
The Three Types of Formalization

TYPES OF FORMALIZATION	DEFINITION
Formalization by job	Planning and documentation of the details of task performance, such as the specific steps to be taken and the sequence of those steps
Formalization by work flow	Planning and documentation of work-flow standards, such as quality specifications and daily output goals
Formalization by rule	Planning and documentation of general workplace rules and procedures

In *formalization by rules*, general rules and procedures are planned and documented to govern all the members of an organization irrespective of the specific jobs they perform. For instance, everyone in an organization might be subject to the rule that lunch breaks are to be taken between noon and 1:00 P.M. You can find other examples of this type of formalization in the work-rules sections of collective-bargaining contracts or in the policy manuals that many organizations prepare to guide employees' conduct.

Formalization by rules is closely associated with both work flow and output standardization. Because they help restrict the range of activities likely to occur in the workplace, general rules streamline the task of specifying appropriate task behaviors or outputs.

Problems and Substitutes. Despite the fact that formalization contributes to the reduction of coordination costs by making standardization possible, it can also lessen efficiency in several ways. For one thing, the very existence of rules can encourage the practice of following them to the letter. Some employees may interpret rules that were intended to describe *minimally* acceptable levels of performance as describing the *maximum* level of performance for which they should aim. As a result, their performance may suffer. For example, the rule that tables in a self-serve restaurant must be wiped clean at least once every hour may have the unintended consequence of curbing more frequent cleaning.

In addition, rigid adherence to rules and regulations can discourage initiative and creativity among workers, and the organization can lose its ability to adapt to new or changing conditions. For instance, rules requiring lengthy approval reviews for even minor design changes limited the ability of American firms to improve existing products or introduce new ones in the consumer-electronics market of the 1980s. As a result, American companies like General Electric and Sunbeam are no longer major manufacturers in markets for everything from hair-curling irons to stereo receivers.

Formalization can also undermine performance by narrowing the scope of workplace activities to the point where employees become bored. If boredom is unrelieved, it can lead to dissatisfaction and rebelliousness. Groups of workers may develop informal social structures in which low productivity is the norm. Employees may even turn to dangerous horseplay or costly sabotage to break up the monotony or to get even with a company they perceive as insensitive and uncaring.

Formalization can become an instrument of political maneuver. That is, it can be used to develop rules, regulations, and standards that favor the interests of some groups over others, thus maintaining the power of the favored groups. The individuals or groups who make an organization's rules can write rules that assure their power. They can require the continued use of resources or knowledge

In an effort to build sales and market share, Burger King CEO Barry Gibbons streamlined the chain's management structure and changed the formal rules by which employees do their jobs—that is, the way they prepare and serve their customers. Responding to consumer demand for more nutritional foods, Gibbons changed some ingredients—french fries are now cooked in 100% vegetable oil—and created new dishes—a broiled-chicken sandwich. Source: Gail deGeorge, "Can Barry Gibbons Put the Sizzle Back in Burger King?" Business Week, October 22, 1990.

561

that only they themselves can provide. Moreover, they can develop regulations that force the organization as a whole to move in the direction they prefer. To the extent that this kind of gamesmanship detracts from productivity, organizational efficiency is impaired.

There are several substitute measures that managers can take to avoid problems like the foregoing and yet coordinate by means of standardization. Those measures are professionalization, training, and socialization, all of which concern the possession of specific skills (see Table 15-3). In **professionalization**, managers hire people to perform certain work for which useful written specifications do not exist and in some cases cannot be prepared.[13] Such **professionals** are people who develop work-related knowledge, skills, and abilities in training programs conducted outside an employing organization. For example, teachers learn how to teach in schools of education, and medical doctors acquire their skills in medical schools. Similarly, business professionals develop their expertise in business programs in colleges and universities.

Professional skills are both portable and nonsubstitutable. That is, they can be employed in a variety of different organizational circumstances to perform tasks that lie beyond the abilities of people who are not themselves professionals. Professional skills can form the basis for the coordination of work, specifically by means of skill standardization. Because the professional learns the rules and standards of conduct needed to perform her job during the professional-training process, further formalization may not be required.

When the knowledge and skills needed to perform the work of an organization can be acquired within the organization itself, **training** (see Chapter 9) may be an effective substitute for formalization. Such training, provided by the employing organization, is purposely organization specific and often job specific. No attempt is made to teach the trainee the sort of generalized code of conduct that professionals learn. When training can be conducted on the job rather than in a formal program of instruction, it often does not require the use of written documentation. As with professionalization, training enables us to coordinate by means of skill standardization but without formalization by job, work flow, or rules.

Finally, organizations can use *socialization* (see Chapter 10) to teach employees, particularly newcomers, the norms of the organization. To the extent that these norms regulate behavior and activities required to coordinate the flow of work, coordination by norm standardization can be enacted without formalized written rules and procedures.

professionalization The use of professionals to perform work for which useful written specifications do not exist and in some cases, cannot be prepared.

professionals People who develop work-related knowledge, skills, and abilities in training programs conducted outside an employing organization. Examples include teachers, lawyers, doctors, and managers trained in schools of business.

training The process of teaching organization-specific and, often, job-specific skills on the job or in a formal program sponsored by the employing organization.

[13] Richard H. Hall, "Professionalism and Bureaucratization," *American Sociological Review* 33 (1968), 92–104; and Jerald Hage and Michael Aiken, "Relationship of Centralization to Other Structural Properties," *Administrative Science Quarterly* 12 (1967), 72–91.

TABLE 15-3
Substitutes for Formalization

SUBSTITUTE	DEFINITION
Professionalization	The use of professionally trained people whose abilities, knowledge, and skills equip them to perform work for which written specifications have not been developed
Training	Teaching an organization's employees skills needed to perform specific jobs within the organization
Socialization	Teaching new employees the norms of the organization

At Singapore Airlines, one of the world's youngest and most profitable air carriers, learning how to deal with emergencies is an important part of cabin attendants' skills training. Source: Louis Kraar, "Ten to Watch Outside Japan," Fortune, March 25, 1991, p. 26.

Specialization

specialization The division of an organization's work into specialist jobs of narrow scope and limited variability.

Just as formalization (or the substitutes discussed above) precedes standardization, **specialization** usually follows from its use. Specialization refers to the way an organization's work is divided into individualized tasks. In some organizations, everyone performs the same sort of *generalized* tasks. In others, employees perform *specialized* tasks that differ from each other in significant ways. The questionnaire measure shown in Figure 15-6 captures this distinction, asking you to indicate which functions in an organization are carried out by specialists.

Specialization can be seen in the scope or variety of activities included in the employees' jobs. The higher the degree of specialization, the narrower the scope of each job's activities.[14] Assembly-line work is extremely specialized, because each worker is responsible for only a small task—attaching a chrome strip to the door of a car, placing the label on a bottle of liquid detergent, putting an assembled calculator in a shipping box. At the opposite extreme, being the owner and sole employee of a small company is not a specialized task because the same

[14] Mintzberg, *Structuring of Organizations*, p. 69.

FIGURE 15-6

A Questionnaire Measure of Specialization

Check each of the following activities that is carried out by at least one full time person in your organization.

a ____	Accounts	l ____	Strategic planning
b ____	Financial control	m ____	Production planning
c ____	Sales	n ____	Inspection/quality control
d ____	Market research	o ____	Buying
e ____	Advertising	p ____	Inventory control
f ____	Public relations	q ____	Research and development
g ____	Personnel	r ____	Maintenance
h ____	Training	s ____	Computing
i ____	Industrial relations	t ____	Transport
j ____	Medical and welfare	u ____	Industrial engineering
k ____	Legal	v ____	Operations research

Scoring: For all items, a blank = 0, a check = 1. Add up the score for all 22 items. The sum of the item scores is the degree of specialization (out of a possible 22).

horizontal specialization The type of specialization in which the work performed at a given hierarchical level is divided into specialized jobs. An example is to divide secretarial work into the jobs of typist, receptionist, and file clerk.

person is responsible for doing all the buying, bookkeeping, selling, and other jobs required to keep the company in business.

Types of Specialization. There are two types of specialization—horizontal and vertical. **Horizontal specialization** refers to the way the work to be performed in each hierarchical level (see Chapter 2), or horizontal "slice," of an organization is divided into discrete, individualized jobs. At one extreme, or in *low horizontal specialization*, the work at a particular hierarchical level is distributed among workers as generalist jobs. The first panel of Figure 15-7 depicts an office arrangement in which filing, typing, and telephone-answering duties are distributed equally among three generalist secretaries. All three secretarial jobs are virtually identical, and each person performing one of these jobs can readily substitute for any of the others.

In contrast, at the other extreme, or in *high horizontal specialization*, the work within a hierarchical level is distributed in the form of specialist jobs. This form of specialization is shown in the second panel of Figure 15-7, where each of three employees—a typist, a file clerk, and a receptionist who answers the phone—has entirely separate duties.

Although the same type of work can be performed in both situations depicted in Figure 15-7, higher horizontal specialization has the potential to produce greater productivity.[15] First, people performing horizontally specialized jobs complete the same task activities again and again. This repetition enables them to learn their jobs thoroughly and, over time, to sharpen job-related knowledge and skills. Second, high horizontal specialization substantially reduces the amount of time lost in switching from one task activity to another, because such specialized jobs consist of a limited number of different activities. Third, because it is easier to identify and analyze a smaller number of critical task activities, high horizontal specialization makes it easier to develop new methods and new equipment. It is the potential for high productivity associated with these three benefits that makes horizontal specialization attractive to managers.

vertical specialization The type of specialization in which the management of work is separated from the performance of that work. It establishes the number of levels of hierarchy in an organization.

The other type of specialization, **vertical specialization**, describes the division of an organization into hierarchical levels. As you can see in Figure 15-8, the higher the degree of specialization, the more vertical layers an organization's hierarchy of authority contains—and the greater the separation of the management of a task from its performance. The upper panel of Figure 15-8 illustrates low vertical specialization. With only a single managerial layer, much of the actual management of the organization's tasks rests with those who perform them. For instance, workers on the shop floor of a company like Whirlpool or Gaines Pet Food may design their own jobs and decide who will do them. They may also order their own raw materials, set their own work hours, and even hire and fire coworkers. In the second hierarchy shown in Figure 15-8, higher vertical specialization has produced several managerial layers. Here, hierarchical superiors rather than the people who actually perform the work generally handle man-

[15] For further support of this statement see the discussion of Adam Smith's ideas in Chapter 2.

FIGURE 15-7

Horizontal Specialization

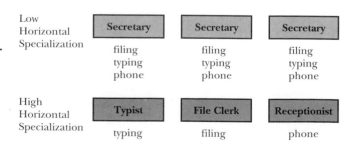

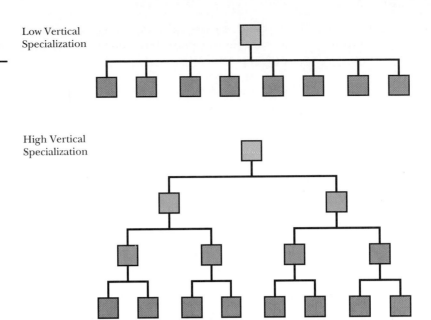

FIGURE 15-8
Vertical Specialization

Low Vertical Specialization

High Vertical Specialization

agement activities. Thus decision making about work methods, job assignments, hours of work, and such is taken away from shop-floor employees and made the task of management.

Problems with Specialization. As the level of horizontal specialization rises in an organization, so does the degree of vertical specialization. That is because the more specialized each job is, the less easily an employee working at the base of the company can see the big picture required to coordinate with others, let alone manage the organization as a whole. A first managerial level is added above specialized workers to handle coordination and management tasks. If this new level becomes so specialized that it can no longer develop and pursue organizational goals, a second, third, fourth, and perhaps even fifth managerial level may be added. You can see that achieving productivity through horizontal specialization incurs significant costs in the form of higher management payroll expenses.

Specialization also increases the costs of management in other significant ways. Vertical specialization increases the number of managers, who must then spend increasing amounts of time coordinating with each other to oversee organizational activities. This additional coordination raises costs. Furthermore, horizontal specialization increases task interdependence, because it creates networks of tasks that must be performed together in order to accomplish the desired end result. For example, the typist, file clerk, and telephone receptionist envisioned in Figure 15-7 must cooperate closely in order to complete the same work that any one of the three secretaries in the same figure could complete alone.

Specialization can also force an organization to pay for specialists who may be idle at a given moment but who are expected to be needed at some future time. These carrying costs can add up. Imagine a small hospital that must offer full-time employment to a highly skilled cardiovascular surgeon so that he will be available to perform the three or four operations per month that the hospital requires. The hospital has a choice. Either it must bear the costs of carrying an idle specialist or it must reduce the scope of the services it can offer its patients.

Finally, specialization can sometimes simplify an organization's jobs to the point that they become tiresome and unchallenging. If such oversimplification happens, it can contribute to serious problems of work-force motivation and, as a consequence, poor performance.[16] We will explore this problem in some depth in Chapter 17.

So specialization can have important drawbacks. It is up to managers to keep these drawbacks in mind as they balance the benefits of standardization with the costs of specialization. Finding that level of standardization which generates no more than an acceptable amount of specialization is a difficult but necessary process of trial and error.

METHODS OF INTERUNIT COORDINATION

Although unit grouping draws the members of each unit closer together, it increases or accentuates the distance separating different units from one another. For instance, say we put the three fabricators in our furniture manufacturer (see Figure 15-1) into one work unit. Then the interdependencies between each one of these people and the receiver, finisher, and shipper who work on the same assembly line fall outside unit boundaries and cannot be easily maintained. Similarly, suppose we form separate desk, bookcase, and chair units. People fulfilling the same functions—receiving, fabricating, finishing, or shipping—for the different product lines will now find it hard to confer with one another. As suggested by these examples, the distance between units created by unit grouping makes it difficult to coordinate interunit linkages with the same types of mutual adjustment, direct supervision, and standardization used to coordinate activities within units. So although grouping people into units can facilitate coordination within the units, it decreases the ability to coordinate interdependencies among units.

Departmentation

departmentation The process of grouping structural units into larger clusters. In functional departmentation, units are grouped into departments according to functional similarities—similarities in the work they do. In divisional departmentation, units are grouped into divisions according to market similarities—similarities in their products or in customers or geographical areas they serve.

In an effort to cope with interunit coordination problems, managers apply some of the same principles to the job of designing the overall structure of an organization that are also applied to the task of grouping units together. The result is two different types of **departmentation** schemes, each of which corresponds to one of the kinds of unit grouping described earlier.[17]

To understand them, let's consider an organization that consists of four functional areas—marketing, research, manufacturing, and accounting—and three product lines—automobiles, trucks, and small gasoline engines. Figure 15-9 shows the departmentation in this firm. Each box represents one of the four functions, and each of the horizontal work flow depicts one of the three product lines. The first type of departmentation, *functional departmentation*, is the equivalent of performing functional grouping at the top of the firm. All marketing tasks are combined into a single marketing department, all research tasks are combined into a single research department, and so forth. As with functional unit grouping, the result is a form of departmentation that is economically efficient but relatively inflexible.

In contrast, the second type of departmentation, *divisional departmentation*, is the same as using market unit grouping at the top of the organization. Instead

---

[16] Glenn R. Carroll, "The Specialist Strategy," *California Management Review* 26 (1984), 126–37.

[17] Pradip N. Khandwalla, *The Design of Organizations* (New York: Harcourt, Brace, Jovanovich, 1977), pp. 489–97; and A. Walker and Jay Lorsch, "Organizational Choice: Product versus Function," *Harvard Business Review* 46 (1968), 129–38.

FIGURE 15-9

Types of Departmentation

A comparison between the diagrams in this figure and the ones shown in Figure 15-1 shows how unit grouping and departmentation involve the same sort of logic applied at different organizational levels.

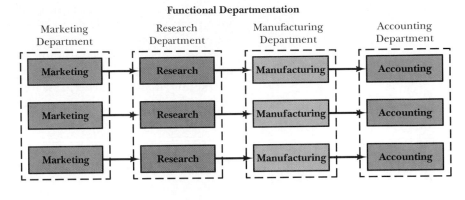

Functional Departmentation

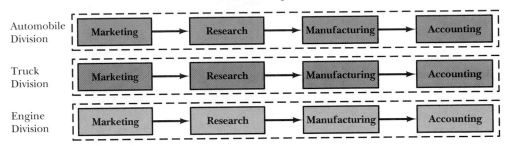

Divisional Departmentation

of being clustered into marketing, manufacturing, research, and accounting departments, the organization's activities are grouped into product divisions—an automobile division, a truck division, and a gasoline engine division. When an organization's clients differ more than its products, the organization's work may be grouped according to differences in the clients served. For instance, there might be a military contracts division, a wholesale distribution division, and an aftermarket parts division. In a third alternative, when an organization's operations are spread throughout the world, its parts may be geographically grouped into a North American division, an Asian division, and a European division. In any of these forms, the organization possesses division-by-division flexibility. Each division can tailor its response to the particular demands of its own market. For example, Ford's Lincoln-Mercury division can decide to redesign its luxury market automobiles to be more Mercedes-like without having to worry about Ford products and markets. The economic efficiency of functional departmentation is sacrificed, however, because effort is duplicated across the organization's three product lines. Lincoln-Mercury's product design studios duplicate Ford's, but the two divisions' studios cannot be consolidated without losing divisional flexibility. So as with unit grouping, managers making departmentation decisions must grapple with a tradeoff between economy and flexibility.

By clustering related groups together, departmentation accentuates similarities that facilitate the management of intergroup relations. Specifically, in an organization structured around functional departmentation, groups in the same department share the same specialized knowledge, language, and ways of looking at the company's business. For instance, all the members of a marketing department share the same general marketing know-how. They talk about things like market segmentation and market share and generally agree that the best way to ensure their company's success is by appealing to customer needs. A manager charged with coordinating different units in the marketing department can base her actions on this common knowledge, language, and viewpoint despite the fact that she is dealing with several different groups of employees. She can manage the different groups using the same basic management approach.

Similarly, in an organization structured around divisional departmentation, groups in the same division share interests in the same basic line of business. Thus all employees in the truck division of a company like General Motors or Ford are concerned about doing well in the truck industry. This commonality allows the manager of a division to treat groups performing different functions—marketing, manufacturing, research, and so forth—in much the same way. He doesn't have to tailor management practices to the functional specialty of each particular group.

Hierarchy and Centralization

By grouping units together, divisionalization creates clusters of units and a layer of managers having responsibility for the activities of particular clusters. Hierarchy (see Chapter 2) can then be used to control intergroup relations. Specifically, a manager having hierarchical authority over a particular cluster of units can use this authority to issue orders that, when followed, will help coordinate activities among those units. For instance, the manager having hierarchical authority over all the manufacturing operations of the furniture factory in Figure 15-1 can use that authority to smooth the flow of work among units if functional grouping is used to form them. Alternatively, the manufacturing manager can help facilitate communication among employees performing similar functions on different lines if market grouping is used. In turn, interdependencies that span different clusters of units can be coordinated by managers higher in the organization's hierarchy. For example, problems between the manufacturing department of our furniture company and other departments, such as sales, accounting, or personnel, can be dealt with by the executive responsible for overseeing the various department managers. Hierarchical authority, then, can be used to coordinate intergroup relations among units in much the same way that direct supervision is used to coordinate interpersonal relations within units.

The use of hierarchy as an intergroup coordination mechanism differs from one organization to the next as to the level of managers—top, middle, or supervisory—who have the ultimate authority to make the decisions and issue the orders that coordinate intergroup activities and direct the organization's overall progress. Left to their own devices, many top managers in the United States favor **centralization**, the concentration of authority and decision making at the top of a firm.[18] Centralization affords top managers a high degree of certainty. Because they alone make the decisions in centralized firms, they can be sure not only that decisions are made but that they are made in accordance with their own wishes. In addition, centralization can minimize the time needed to make decisions. That is because only an extremely limited number of people are involved in the decision-making processes. In Figure 15-10, a questionnaire measure of centralization illustrates the kind of authority and decision making that can be centralized. This measure can be used to assess the amount of centralization in an organization.

Despite centralization's appeal to top management, **decentralization**, is increasingly common in modern organizations (see the "In Practice" box). In decentralization, authority and decision making are dispersed downward and outward through the hierarchy. Several factors push otherwise reluctant top

centralization The concentration of authority and decision making at the top of an organization; the opposite of decentralization.

decentralization The dispersion of authority and decision making downward and outward through the hierarchy of an organization; the opposite of centralization.

[18]Pugh et al., "Dimensions of Organization Structure," p. 72; J. Hage and M. Aiken, "Relationship of Centralization to Other Structural Properties" *Administrative Science Quarterly* 12 (1967), 72–92; Peter Blau, "Decentralization in Bureaucracies," in *Power in Organizations*, ed. Mayer N. Zald (Nashville, Tenn.: Vanderbilt University Press, 1970), pp. 42–81; N. M. Carter and J.B. Cullen, "A Comparison of Centralization/Decentralization of Decision Making Concepts and Measures," *Journal of Management* 10 (1984), 259–68; and Roger Mansfield, "Bureaucracy and Centralization: An Examination of Organizational Structure," *Administrative Science Quarterly* 18 (1973), 477–78.

FIGURE 15-10

A Questionnaire Measure of Centralization

Circle your response to each of the following items as they apply to the organization in question.

1. How much direct involvement does top management have in gathering the information input that they will use in making decisions?
   a. none
   b. little
   c. some
   d. a great deal
   e. a very great deal

2. To what degree does top management participate in the interpretation of the information input?
   a. 0–20%
   b. 21–40%
   c. 41–60%
   d. 61–80%
   e. 81–100%

3. To what degree does top management directly control the execution of the decision?
   a. 0–20%
   b. 21–40%
   c. 41–60%
   d. 61–80%
   e. 81–100%

For questions 4 through 10, use the following responses:
   a. very great
   b. great
   c. some
   d. little
   e. none

4–10. How much discretion does the typical first-line supervisor have over
   4. Establishing his or her unit's budget?
   5. Determining how his or her unit's performance will be evaluated?
   6. Hiring and firing personnel?
   7. Personnel rewards (i.e., salary increases, promotions)?
   8. Purchasing of equipment and supplies?
   9. Establishing a new project or program?
   10. How work exceptions are to be handled?

Scoring: For all items, a = 1, b = 2, c = 3, d = 4, e = 5. Add up the score for all ten items. The sum of the item scores is the degree of centralization (out of a possible 50).

managers toward its implementation. First, some decisions require top managers to consider a great deal of information. The managers may become overloaded by the task of processing all this information and therefore find it useful to involve more people in the decision-making process. Second, decentralization may be stimulated by a need for flexibility. If local conditions require that different parts of an organization respond differently, managers of those organizational units must be empowered to make their own decisions. Third, decentralization may be useful in dealing with employee motivation problems if those problems can be solved by according employees control over workplace practices and conditions (we will discuss this further in Chapter 17). In any of these cases, the failure to decentralize can undermine attempts to coordinate intergroup relations.

Intergroup Coordination Mechanisms

Even when an organization is suitably centralized or decentralized, sometimes it is impossible to coordinate all the interdependencies among an organization's units by means of departmentation and hierarchy alone. One way of dealing with the need for additional coordination among units is to reduce it. Decoupling mechanisms accomplish this by severing connections between groups. When the number of connections cannot be reduced, unit-linking mechanisms can be used instead to promote the exchange of information among interdependent work units.[19] Table 15-4 previews the mechanisms that we will discuss next.

[19] Galbraith, *Designing Complex Organizations*, 14–18.

Changes at IBM

Apple was not the only computer company to restructure itself during the 1980s. IBM, the world's leading computer manufacturer, also reorganized its 387,000 employees. Unlike Apple, however, IBM moved toward decentralization.

What triggered this change? IBM had lost sight of computer customers and their changing tastes. Where large mainframe computers—IBM's specialty—had once dominated the industry, business customers now wanted networks of smaller, more powerful desktop models. Sales were soaring in personal computers, a market segment IBM had joined only as a reluctant latecomer. The company had not even tried to develop leading products in the laptop and work-station markets, two areas of high future growth.

John Akers, IBM's chief executive officer, recognized that their problems arose from a common source, the company's tendency to make all important decisions in its Armonk, New York, corporate office. There, a corporate management board of 18 senior executives relied on experience and consensus to decide about everything from advertising campaigns to new directions in product development. This centralization blinded the company to many important changes in the computer industry. It also created a tendency to respond to those few changes the management board did learn about by in-

sisting on doing things "the IBM way"—which meant remaining the same mainframe-producing giant.

In IBM's new structure, the firm is now composed of nearly autonomous business divisions. Each year, division managers negotiate business plans with Akers and the board and then go off to run their divisions. Where managers once took conflicts between divisions to the board, now they meet among themselves to solve interdivisional problems. Problems that resist resolution are referred only one level up. Peer negotiation has replaced direct orders. Moreover, the customer now has the company's undivided attention, and divisions can respond to customer demands without referring up the hierarchy to top management. As a result, the corporate management board is spending two-thirds less time with month-to-month management issues (leaving more time for the sort of long-term strategic management we will discuss in Chapter 18). Customers are once again getting products and services that meet their needs.* IBM is again returning to its former position of prominence.

* Joel Dreyfuss, "Reinventing IBM," *Fortune*, August 14, 1989, pp. 30–39.

TABLE 15-4
Intergroup Coordination Mechanisms

MECHANISM	ACTION
Decoupling Mechanisms	
Slack resources	Lessen the ability of one unit to affect the activities of another interdependent unit by creating buffer inventories.
Self-contained tasks	Redesign work formerly performed by two or more interdependent units and assign it to new groups composed of representatives from all the original units.
Unit-linking mechanisms	
Vertical information systems	Facilitate the transfer and processing of large amounts of information throughout an organization's hierarchy of authority.
Lateral linkage devices	Facilitate the use of unit-coordination mechanisms in handling intergroup dependencies.
Liaison positions	Make one individual responsible for ensuring that communications flow freely and directly between interdependent groups.
Representative groups	Create task force or standing committee in which representatives from interdependent groups coordinate by means of mutual adjustment.
Integrating managers	Create a managerial position that spans interdependent groups and has the authority to issue orders and expect obedience.
Matrix structure	Combine functional and divisional departmentation; use only as a last resort.

decoupling mechanisms
Mechanisms that regulate intergroup coordination by making work units less dependent on each other. The use of decoupling mechanisms involves making adjustments to the relationships formed among units during departmentation.

slack resources The type of decoupling mechanism in which groups are separated from each other by buffer inventories.

self-contained tasks The type of decoupling mechanism formed by combining the work of two or more interdependent units and assigning their work to several independent work units. Those units are then staffed by people drawn from each of the original units.

unit-linking mechanisms
Mechanisms that regulate intergroup coordination by linking interdependent units more closely together.

Decoupling Mechanisms. Two **decoupling mechanisms**—slack resources and self-contained tasks—regulate intergroup coordination by making work units less dependent on each other. Both these approaches involve adjustments to the relationships formed among units during departmentation.

Slack resources help to decouple otherwise interconnected groups by creating buffers that lessen the ability of one group to affect the activities of another. For example, suppose one group assembles telephone handsets, and another group connects finished handsets to telephone bodies to form fully assembled units. The two groups are sequentially interdependent, because the second group's ability to perform its work is contingent on the first group's ability to complete its task (see Chapter 10 for a more complete definition of sequential interdependence). Work in the second group comes to a halt if the handset-assembly group stops producing. If, however, we create a buffer inventory—a supply of finished handsets—that the second group can draw on when the handset-assembly group is not producing anything, we have at least temporarily decoupled the two work groups. There are various ways to create and replenish this inventory: (1) delay the second group's startup, (2) have the handset-assembly group work extra hours, (3) form an additional group of handset assemblers from time to time, or (4) buy extra handsets from another source.

Another way of reducing interdependence among groups is to create **self-contained tasks** by combining the work of two or more interdependent units and assigning this work to several independent work units. Typically, such self-contained units are staffed by employees drawn from each of the original interdependent units. For example, engineering and drafting units might have problems coordinating engineering specifications and the drawings produced by the drafting unit. These two units might be regrouped into several independent engineering-drafting units. Each one can produce product specifications and drawings without outside assistance. After this regrouping, the original two units would no longer exist. Similarly, a marketing research unit and a sales unit might be merged into a single marketing unit to coordinate information about a firm's market more effectively. In both these examples, key interdependencies that lie outside the original units are contained within redesigned units. They can then be handled by one or more of the unit coordination mechanisms we have already discussed.

Unit-Linking Mechanisms. Sometimes concerns about minimizing inventory costs rule out the use of slack resources. Among U.S. manufacturers, for instance, the cost of carrying excessive inventory is a growing concern and has stimulated

IBM used to store its parts and equipment in some 21 warehouses of its own, but in 1989 it worked out an arrangement with Federal Express that is a good example of a **self-contained task**. *Now Federal Express stores all IBM's materials, and an IBM employee can call just one telephone number rather than several in order to locate the part she needs. This consolidation has reduced the need for workflow coordination without endangering crucial inventory levels.*
Source: Thomas A. Stewart, "There Are No Products—Only Services," Fortune, January 14, 1991, p. 32.

increasing interest in just-in-time (JIT) procedures. Using JIT, items are produced for use only when needed, eliminating the cost of having unused inventory lying around. In addition, work often cannot be divided into self-contained tasks. For example, the task of producing the parts required to make a car and assembling them into a final product is so immense that many groups (in fact, many companies) must be involved. In such cases, intergroup interdependencies can be coordinated instead by means of various **unit-linking mechanisms**. Vertical information systems facilitate information transmission among different hierarchical levels, and lateral linkage devices foster direct communication between interdependent units.

Vertical information systems usually consist of mainframe computers with remote terminals or networks of personal computers that can be used to input and exchange information about organizational performance. If you have taken courses in computer science, you have probably had experience with a computer network similar to those used in businesses as vertical information systems. Managers use such systems to communicate among themselves and store information for later review. These systems facilitate the transfer of large amounts of information up and down an organization's hierarchy of authority. They also make it easier to process this information centrally without overloading normal supervisory processes. Thus these systems make it possible for managers at higher levels of a firm's hierarchy to coordinate intergroup relations. Just as a direct supervisor issues orders to subordinates in order to coordinate activities within a work unit, so hierarchical supervisors of two or more units can use vertical information systems to issue orders and gather the performance feedback needed to coordinate activities among those units. The fact that many organizations have recently added the corporate position of chief information officer (CIO) reflects the growing use of vertical information systems to coordinate organizational activities.

There are times when decoupling mechanisms cannot be used, and centralized information processing is undermined by either the absence or overabundance of timely, relevant information. Even then, managers can use **lateral linkage devices** to foster direct communication between interdependent units. For example, an employee may be assigned a **liaison position** in which he is responsible for seeing that communications flow directly and freely between interdependent units. The liaison position is an alternative to hierarchical communication channels. It reduces both the time needed to communicate between units and the amount of information distortion likely to occur. The person occupying a liaison position has no authority to issue direct orders decreeing coordination but relies instead on negotiation, bargaining, and persuasion. He may also mediate between units in conflict, resolving differences and moving the units toward voluntary intergroup coordination.

The liaison position is the least costly of the lateral linkage devices. Because one person handles the task of coordination, a minimum of a firm's resources are diverted from the primary task of production. Moreover, because the position has no formal authority, it is also the least disruptive of normal hierarchical relationships.

Sometimes a liaison position is not strong enough to solve interunit coordination problems. Managers then have the option of turning to a second unit linking mechanism, **representative groups**, to coordinate activities among interdependent units. Representative groups consist of representatives from the interdependent units who meet to coordinate intergroup activities. There are two kinds of representative groups. One, called a **task force**, is formed to complete a specific task or project and is then disbanded. By encompassing intergroup

---

vertical information system The type of unit-linking mechanism in which computer networks are used to facilitate managerial communication and information processing. Managers can deal with more coordination information than would otherwise be possible.

lateral linkage devices The types of unit-linking mechanism in which hierarchical links between interdependent units are supplemented by various avenues of mutual adjustment or direct supervision.

liaison position The type of unit-linking mechanism in which one person is made responsible for seeing that communication flows directly and freely between interdependent units. A liaison position has no authority, so its occupant must rely on negotiation, bargaining, and persuasion to move interdependent units toward voluntary coordination.

representative groups The type of unit-linking mechanism in which representatives of interdependent units meet to coordinate intergroup activities.

task force The type of representative group formed to complete a specific task or project and then disbanded.

interdependencies, the task force transforms intergroup coordination problems into intragroup problems so that the mechanism of mutual adjustment can be used temporarily. Companies like Colgate-Palmolive or Procter and Gamble form product task groups. They draw members from advertising, marketing, manufacturing, and product research departments to identify consumer needs, design new products that respond to these needs, and manage their market introduction. Once a new product is successfully launched, the task force responsible for its introduction is dissolved, and its members return to their former units.

standing committee The type of representative group formed to meet on a regular basis to discuss and resolve intergroup coordination problems. A standing committee has no specific task, nor is it expected to disband at any particular time.

The other type of representative group is a more-or-less permanent one. Like the members of the task force, the members of this group, called the **standing committee**, represent interdependent work units, but they meet on a regular basis to discuss and resolve intergroup coordination problems. No specific task is assigned to the standing committee, nor is the committee expected to disband at any particular time. An example of a standing committee is a factory's Monday morning production meeting. At that meeting, representatives from production control, purchasing, quality assurance, shipping, and the company's different assembly groups overview the week's production schedule and try to anticipate coordination problems.

Like task forces, standing committees make it possible to use intragroup mutual adjustment to coordinate intergroup relations. Despite their usefulness in this regard, both these linkage devices are more costly than the liaison position. The reason is that through process loss, group meetings inevitably consume otherwise productive resources. In addition, because representative groups (especially task forces) are sometimes designed to operate outside customary hierarchal channels, they can prove quite disruptive to normal operations.

Occasionally, neither liaison positions nor representative groups are enough to solve interunit coordination problems. The *integrating manager* is a third type of lateral linkage device. Like the liaison officer, the integrating manager mediates between interdependent units, but unlike the liaison officer, the integrating manager has the formal authority to issue orders and expect obedience. He can tell interdependent groups what to do to coordinate their work. Project managers at companies like Rockwell International and Lockheed fill the role of integrating manager. They oversee the progress of a project by making sure that the various planning, designing, assembling, and testing groups work together successfully.

Normally, an integrating manager issues orders only to the supervisors of the units she is coordinating. Giving orders to the people who report to these supervisors would violate the principle of unity of command (see Chapter 2) and would confuse employees. They would feel they were being asked to report to two supervisors. Because an integrating manager disrupts normal hierarchical relationships, shortcircuiting the relationship between unit supervisors and their usual superior, this device is used much less often than either the liaison position or representative groups.

matrix organization structure The type of lateral linkage mechanism that is an organization structure incorporating both functional and divisional departmentation.

Once in a while, even integrating managers cannot provide the guidance needed to coordinate activities among units. In these rare instances, a fourth type of lateral linkage device, called the **matrix organization structure**, is sometimes employed. Matrix structures are the most complicated of the mechanisms used to coordinate intergroup relations and are extremely costly to sustain. They incorporate both functional and divisional departmentation and coordinate intergroup linkages through a complex network of mutual adjustment. We will discuss the matrix organization structure in greater detail in Chapter 16, because it is both a coordination mechanism and a specific type of organization structure. Now we will just say that matrix structures are appropriate only when all other intergroup coordination mechanisms have proven ineffective.

SUMMARY

An *organization's structure* is a relatively stable network of interdependencies among the people and tasks that make up the organization. It is created, first, by the process of *unit grouping* in which the organization's members are grouped together into structural units on the basis of similarities in what they perform, called *functional grouping*, or similarities in the products they produce or markets they serve, called *market grouping*. Within these units, the *unit coordination mechanisms* of *mutual adjustment, direct supervision,* or *standardization* are used to manage interdependence. Along with several other factors, the type of coordination mechanism used in a unit affects the optimum size of the unit.

Using standardization to coordinate within units encourages the emergence of two other structural characteristics, *formalization* and *specialization*. Professionalization, training, or socialization sometimes substitute for formalization. Organizations are also structured by mechanisms that coordinate relations among units. Those are *departmentation* (either functional or divisional), *centralization*, and various *decoupling mechanisms* or *unit-linking mechanisms*.

REVIEW QUESTIONS

1.   Given that an organization's structure integrates and differentiates activities in the organization, tell which of the following structural characteristics provide integration and which produce differentiation: unit grouping, unit coordination mechanisms, formalization, specialization, departmentation, hierarchy and centralization.

2.   With respect to unit grouping, why is market grouping more flexible than functional grouping? If your company sold pencils, pens, and notebook paper, which type of unit grouping would provide the greatest benefit? Why?

3.   Explain why standardization requires stability. Why is mutual adjustment so much more flexible? How does direct supervision fit between the two extremes? What mechanism(s) would you use to coordinate a television-assembly unit of 50 employees? Six custom jewelry makers? A dozen door-to-door magazine salespeople? Why?

4.   Suppose you want to increase the size of a work unit that is already having coordination problems. What can you do to ensure that the larger group will be adequately coordinated?

5.   Draw and explain a diagram showing how standardization, formalization, and specialization are interrelated. If an organization decided to institute participatory decision making, thereby replacing standardization with mutual adjustment, what effects does your diagram suggest this plan would have on the organization's structure?

6.   Explain how professionalization, training, and socialization can act as supplements or substitutes for formalization. Name some other purposes these three processes serve in organizations.

7.   What kinds of departmentation can be used to cluster structural units together? How do departmentation and hierarchy work together to resolve coordination problems among structural units?

8.   How do decoupling mechanisms reduce interunit coordination problems? How does this approach differ from that of unit-linking mechanisms?

DIAGNOSTIC QUESTIONS

You can use what you have learned in this chapter to identify the specific characteristics of an organization's structure and to gain insight into the probable strengths and weaknesses of that structure. The following questions are provided to assist this diagnostic process.

1. Are structural units grouped according to functional or market similarities? What does that tell you about the relative emphasis placed by the firm on efficiency? On adaptability?

2. Which of the three unit coordination mechanisms are used in the organization's units? Which is used as the primary means of coordination, and what does that tell you about the importance the firm accords to efficiency? To flexibility?

3. What secondary coordination mechanisms back up the primary mechanisms used throughout the firm? Are unit activities coordinated adequately?

4. Are the sizes of unit groups consistent with the types of unit coordination mechanisms being used? With the tasks of unit members and supervisors? With the units' positions in the organizational hierarchy? With needs for undistorted vertical information flow?

5. If standardization is present, is the appropriate type of formalization or substitute for formalization—professionalization, training, socialization—also present?

6. If standardization and formalization are evident in the firm, are jobs horizontally specialized? Is vertical specialization also present? Does each type of specialization seem balanced in relation to the other?

7. Is the firm's structure based on functional or divisional departmentation? What does that tell you about the probable balance between efficiency and adaptability in the organization?

8. Are intergroup relations adequately coordinated by hierarchy and centralization, or are additional intergroup coordination mechanisms needed?

9. If additional coordination is needed, is decoupling feasible? If not, which unit-linking mechanism or mechanisms should be employed?

10. Across the array of structural characteristics that you have identified does a general profile stressing efficiency emerge or does a profile stressing flexibility and adaptability appear instead?

RESTRUCTURING A UNIVERSITY*

ERIC PANITZ, *University of Detroit*

How to group units into departments or divisions is a key issue facing managers as they structure an organization. As we have discussed in this chapter, such grouping is accomplished by combining units together according to either what they do or what they produce.

Concerns about administrative overhead can also influence choices about how to form units and combine them together. Administrative overhead is the cost of supervising the units and departments or divisions in a firm. It consists largely of the salaries paid to managers employed as supervisors. Sometimes it is possible to group units together in such a way that fewer managers are needed.

Like other organizations, universities have structures that consist of units (called departments) grouped together into large clusters (called colleges). Administrators who manage educational institutions like yours must choose what sorts of groups to form. In the process, they must often consider tradeoffs affecting administrative overhead, asking themselves which sort of grouping will minimize the number of people needed to manage organizational activities. In this exercise, you will experience some of the problems and make some of the decisions that the management of an educational institution must make in this process.

STEP ONE: PRE-CLASS PREPARATION

In class you will work with other class members to restructure a university. In preparation for this exercise, session, read the following description of Midwestern State University and then familiarize yourself with the rest of the exercise. Next, list two or more structural modifications that could be made to help the university save money:

1. _____

2. _____

3. _____

4. _____

5. _____

Be prepared to explain your suggestions and describe their benefits.

Midwestern State University has a student population of 14,500 undergraduates and 1,500 graduate students, divided among the university's colleges as shown in the table at the bottom of the page.

The university must reduce its budget. All of the "easy" actions such as eliminating travel budgets, leaving open positions unfilled, and trimming operating expenses have been implemented. Now the Vice President for Academic Affairs is considering restructuring the organization to save money. However, the Board of Regents which governs the university has made the following stipulations:

1. The number of currently employed teaching faculty must not be reduced.
2. No increases can be made in the number of administrative personnel or staff members.
3. No employee can be terminated, but employees' positions and responsibilities may be changed.

* Adapted with the author's permission from an exercise entitled "Restructuring the University—An Experiential Exercise." This adaptation copyright © 1992 Prentice Hall.

COLLEGE	UNDERGRADUATE STUDENTS	MASTERS STUDENTS	DOCTORAL STUDENTS
Business Administration	4500	600	29
Natural Sciences and Mathematics	1500	125	38
Humanities and Social Sciences	1750	25	25
Law Enforcement	2000	65	0
Allied Health and Nursing	750	40	3
Education	2800	405	42
Health and Recreation	1200	85	18

4. No existing undergraduate program may be modified so extensively that it would be put in a position of losing its accreditation.

5. Graduate programs are not to be considered during reorganization; they will be integrated into whatever organization results from restructuring the undergraduate programs.

The current structure of the university is shown in Exhibit 15-1. We will describe three colleges—the Colleges of Business Administration, Allied Health, and Natural Sciences—in some detail shortly. In addition to these three colleges, the university has a College of Humanities and Social Sciences, a College of Education, a College of Health and Recreation, a College of Law Enforcement (which also offers first aid courses) and a separate Graduate School. The latter school advises graduate students, approves theses and dissertations, and manages associated paperwork. Graduate courses are taught by faculty housed in the university's seven colleges.

Every college (including the Graduate School) is headed by a Dean who receives a salary of $90,000–$150,000 depending on seniority, job responsibilities, scholarly reputation, and other factors. Each college consists of several departments, and every department is headed by a chairperson. Department chairs receive a 20 percent salary supplement (added to the salary they would normally receive as members of the teaching faculty). In addition, to give them the time they need for their managerial duties, they are relieved of all teaching responsibilities. All department chairs are former faculty members who can return to teaching when their services as chairperson are no longer required.

The College of Business Administration

As shown in Exhibit 15-2, the College of Business Administration consists of 5 departments and 13 programs. These programs are summarized next. Not only business majors but many students in the Colleges of Allied Health and Natural Sciences take several business courses as part of their major or minor programs. For example, Health Record Administration majors must take the Principles of Management course.

Department of Business Administration and Marketing. This department includes the management, marketing, general business, and coal mining administration programs. There are a total of 17 faculty, 4 in management, 4 in marketing, 6 in general business, and 3 in coal mining administration.

Management offers three majors: Business Administration trains students to become mid-level managers. Industrial Relations develops skills in human resource management, organization development, and labor relations. Operations Management develops skills in production management, quality control, inventory administration, and operations research.

Marketing offers two majors: Marketing prepares students for positions in sales and sales management,

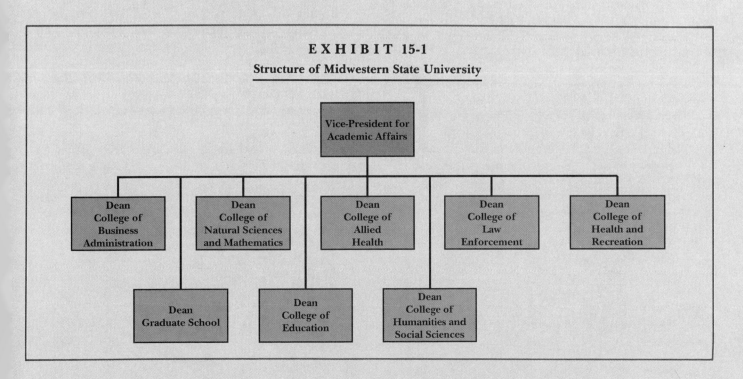

EXHIBIT 15-1

Structure of Midwestern State University

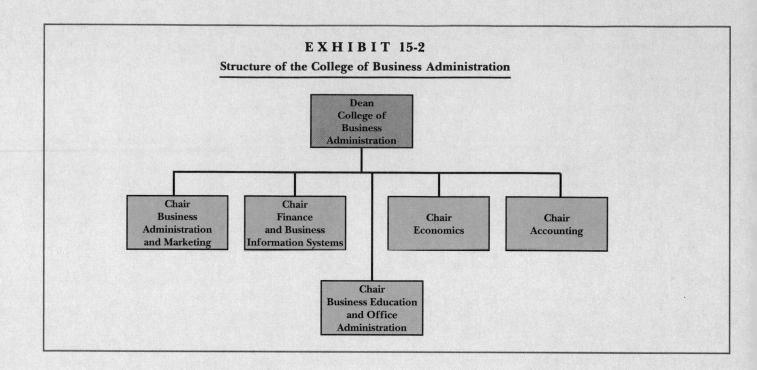

EXHIBIT 15-2

Structure of the College of Business Administration

Dean
College of
Business
Administration

Chair
Business
Administration
and Marketing

Chair
Finance
and Business
Information Systems

Chair
Economics

Chair
Accounting

Chair
Business Education
and Office
Administration

retailing, market research, promotion, and advertising. Transportation qualifies students for jobs in the field of transportation and physical distribution.

General Business offers courses in law, the capstone policy course, and courses in small business administration. There is also a major in general business for students planning to attend professional or graduate schools.

Finally, *Coal Mining Administration* qualifies students to enter managerial positions in the coal industry such as mine supervision and occupational safety administration. This program reflects the importance of the mining industry in the state.

Department of Finance and Business Information Systems. This department houses 16 faculty members, 4 in each of 4 majors. Management Information Systems and Programming trains students in computer programming for business applications and in management information system development and management. Finance gives students the tools for financial decision making to needed for careers in corporate finance, banking, or investment. Insurance provides students with the background needed for careers in the insurance industry. Real Estate develops students' capabilities in real estate management, marketing, appraisal, and property development.

Department of Economics. The Economics Department has 11 faculty members who teach primarily in-

troductory economics and business statistics courses. Advanced courses are offered to all majors in the College of Business Administration. Economics majors are offered through both the College of Business and the College of Humanities.

Department of Accounting. The Accounting Department includes 11 faculty members who teach the introductory accounting course to all business majors as well as business minors from other colleges. Two majors are offered through the department. Accounting prepares students to seek CPA certification and accountancy positions in government or industry. Health Care Administration offers specific training for positions in hospital administration. This is a cooperative program that includes faculty from the College of Allied Health.

Department of Business Education and Office Administration. This department has 8 faculty members who teach business communications courses for all majors and office management, secretarial, and business education courses to students with the following majors. Office Administration provides the skills required to fill positions as executive secretaries and administrative assistants. Secretarial Training is a two-year degree program that trains legal, medical, and other specialized secretaries in office services. Business Education prepares students to teach business subjects at the high school level.

The College of Natural Sciences and Mathematics

The College of Natural Sciences and Mathematics, diagrammed in Exhibit 15-3, has 6 departments that offer 13 programs. Many of this college's courses are general education requirements that must be completed by all students in the university. In addition, many courses in the biology and chemistry departments serve as preparatory courses for students in the allied health programs (nursing, medical technology, environmental health).

Department of Biology. This department has 17 faculty members and offers 5 majors. General Biology provides an overview of the biological sciences and the component fields of ecology, botany, physiology, biostatistics, entomology, vertebrate and invertebrate biology, and cell biology. Microbiology emphasizes the study of pathogenic and nonpathogenic bacteria, fungi, virology, and parasitology in clinical and nonclinical settings. Wildlife Biology focuses on the management and health of terrestrial wildlife and its environments. Aquatic and Fisheries Biology concerns the management of fisheries and their habitats, including pollution control and other aspects of marine biology. Environmental Resources Biology offers a broad view of economic and environmental aspects of biological resources.

Department of Chemistry. This department has 10 faculty members who offer 2 majors. Chemistry contains coursework in analytical, physical, and organic chemistry and biochemistry. Chemical Technology is a two-year program that prepares students for positions as laboratory technicians.

Department of Geology. This department has 8 faculty members and offers 3 majors designed to prepare students for careers in the petroleum, coal mining, and other related industries, and for teaching assignments at the secondary level. The majors offered are Geology, Earth Science, and a two-year program in Geological Engineering.

Department of Mathematics and Computer Science. This is a 12-member department offering majors in Computer Science, Mathematics, and Statistics. Most of the courses in this department are part of the general education requirement that all students must fulfill. The department has few math majors and is trying to cope with the effects of the specialized courses in statistics offered by other colleges such as Business and Law Enforcement.

Department of Natural Resources. The Department of Natural Resources has 6 faculty members and offers science courses for non-majors who must take science to fulfill general education requirements. These courses

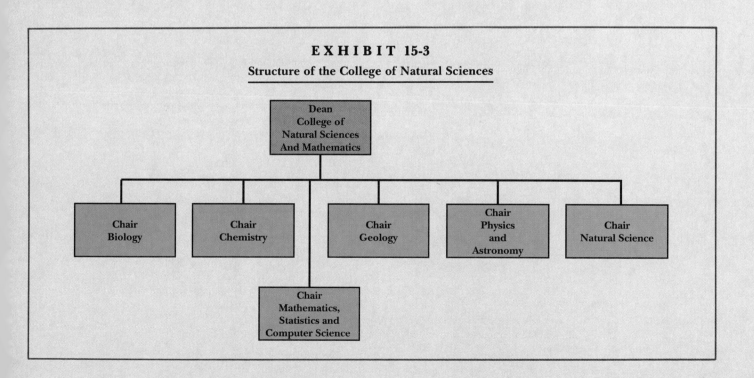

EXHIBIT 15-3

Structure of the College of Natural Sciences

emphasize the historical development of scientific knowledge and its effects on present-day life.

Department of Physics and Astronomy. This 6-member department offers a physics major and teaches courses on physics and astronomy that are listed as general education requirements.

The College of Allied Health and Nursing

The College of Allied Health and Nursing, shown in Exhibit 15-4, has 37 faculty members and offers 14 programs in the departments of emergency medical technology, environmental health, health records administration, medical technology, occupational therapy, and nursing.

Department of Emergency Medical Technology (EMT). This three-member department offers one-year programs leading to certification in EMT and advanced EMT, and a two-year program leading to an EMT Services Management degree. Students are trained in techniques and management of ambulance services and accident management. Similar courses are offered in the College of Law Enforcement, but the Law program does not include a certification or degree program in this area.

Department of Environmental Health. The Department of Environmental Health has three full-time and one part-time faculty member. It offers a program in applied biology and chemistry with emphasis on public health aspects of pollution control, disease transmission, and waste disposal. Students are trained to manage related types of public health problems.

Department of Health Records Administration. This department has 3 faculty members and offers 4 programs from a one-year certification in medical transcription through a four-year degree in health record administration. The program is designed to train students in the effective management, storage, and retrieval of hospital records.

Department of Medical Technology. This department's seven faculty members offer a 2-year medical assistant degree and 4-year degrees in medical technology and medical laboratory technology. These programs are designed to train students to perform the medical testing required to support physician decision making, and to prepare students to attain the certification needed to work in hospital laboratories, clinics, or medical testing facilities. Areas of study are hematology, clinical chemistry, clinical microbiology, parasitology, and similar subjects.

Department of Occupational Therapy. The Department of Occupational Therapy offers a 4-year training program in physical therapy and has 7 faculty members.

Department of Nursing. The Department of Nursing is the largest department in the college, offering 2 pro-

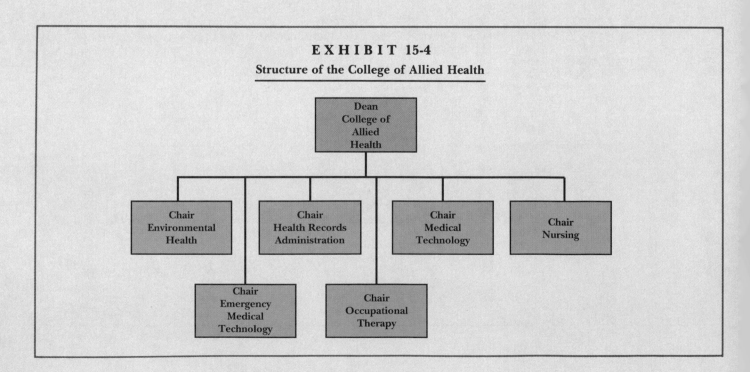

EXHIBIT 15-4
Structure of the College of Allied Health

STRUCTURING THE ORGANIZATION

grams leading to 2-year or 4-year nursing degrees along with state RN (registered nurse) or LPN (licensed practical nurse) certification.

Step Two: Sharing Suggestions

The class should divide into groups of about 4 to 6 members each. If your class has already formed permanent groups, these groups should reconvene. In each group, members should describe and explain their reasons for the structural modifications they recommend to solve Midwestern State's fiscal problems. If you think of additional modifications during these discussions, you should work together to describe them. Each group should combine all of the modifications it has thought of into a single list.

Step Three: Designing a New Structure

After the group has listed all proposed modifications, members should work together to find the combination that will create a structure that saves as much money as possible yet remains consistent with the requirements of the Board of Regents. You should redraw Exhibits 15-1 through 15-4 as necessary to show the changes your group is suggesting. One group member should be appointed spokesperson to explain the group's proposal to the rest of the class.

Step Four: Group Reports and Discussion

Each group spokesperson should summarize the results of the group's design efforts in a five-minute presentation to the rest of the class. The list of modifications considered by the group as well as its revised structural diagrams should be presented on a chalkboard, flipchart, or overhead transparencies.

Step Five: Class Discussion of the Restructuring Process

The class should review the lists of modifications and structures developed by the groups, looking for similarities and differences among the ideas of different groups. If time permits, the class should try to reach consensus on one combination of modifications that will be consistent with the Regents' guidelines and achieve the greatest budget reduction. The class may discuss questions like the following during this process.

1. Which modifications seemed obvious at first but later proved to be inappropriate?
2. Which modifications came to the surface only after further consideration?
3. Which modifications, if any, conflicted with others? In the event of such conflicts, how did you decide which modification to choose?
4. In what ways is Midwestern State University similar to your school or educational program? What sort of structural modifications might the administrators of your school or program make if required to reduce costs?
5. In general, what should you do to an organization's structure to economize on administrative overhead?

Conclusion

Forming structural units and combining them into departments or divisions involves tradeoffs between the economy of functional grouping and the flexibility of divisional groupings. The costs of administrative overhead may also enter into decisions about how to form units and cluster them together. Subtle changes in structure can sometimes save an organization a lot of money without affecting its ability to accomplish its mission and goals.

DIAGNOSING ORGANIZATIONAL BEHAVIOR

CASE 15-1

O Canada*

Bonnie J. Lovelace, *University of Alberta*
Royston Greenwood, *University of Alberta*

The Public Service Commission of Canada (PSC) is responsible for the provision of a comprehensive human resources management service to the fifty-two departments and agencies of the federal public service. Initially, the commission operated through six branches.

* Reprinted with the author's permission.

One of these, the Staff Development Branch (SDB), is the focus of the present case. The case examines the SDB subsequently as it began to experience problems of financial restraint. The SDB was responsible for the provision of:

1. regularly scheduled courses in a variety of professional, technical, and general subjects;
2. regular and special courses for senior and executive managers;
3. specialized, custom-designed courses on a consulting basis as needed;
4. a research and development service on federal adult educational needs.

Since its creation, the SDB had grown steadily. Its members were highly qualified professionals in their specific fields, and the SDB provided them with extensive training in adult education methods. The SDB served the federal government on a cost-recoverable basis. That is, it had to market courses and cover *all* of its costs, including overhead. Courses were sold to client departments at prices comparable to those charged for similar programs available on the open market. Before this case was written, SDB had enjoyed more business than it could handle. It had an excellent reputation, and there had been no lack of funds within departmental training budgets.

In prior years, the SDB had about 250 members and was organized as shown in Exhibit 15-5. Each of the five directorates was a cost center, responsible for forecasting its own revenues and costs. Although the SDB technically operated on a "branch break-even" basis, each directorate operated on the assumption that it should cover costs.

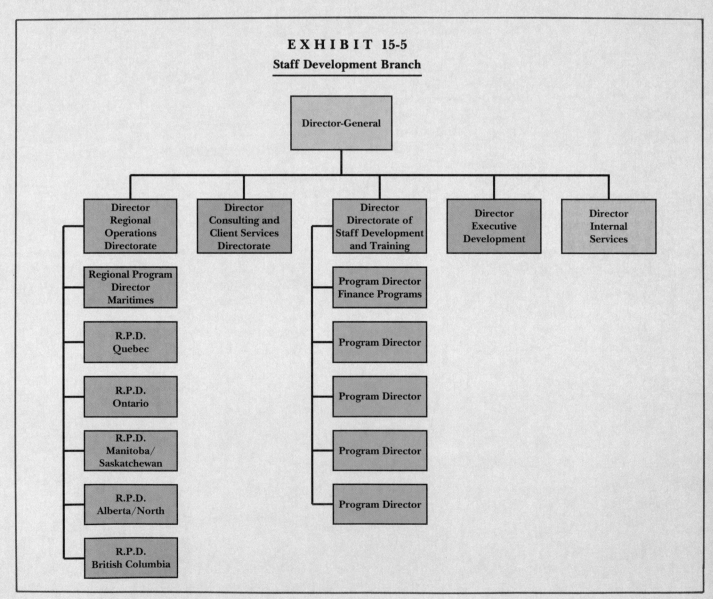

E X H I B I T   15-5

Staff Development Branch

The two largest directorates within the branch were the Directorate of Staff Development and Training (DSDT) and the Regional Operations Directorate (ROD). These provided the bulk of the regularly scheduled courses offered by the branch. The primary division of responsibility between the DSDT and the ROD was that the DSDT serviced the Ottawa region, where the vast bulk of the public service was located, and the ROD serviced the rest of Canada. The six regional units of the ROD and the DSDT operated the same courses, but in different locations.

DIRECTORATE OF STAFF DEVELOPMENT AND TRAINING

The DSDT was organized in terms of *six programs*, each headed by a program manager and staffed by up to fourteen people (including two clerks). Each program had its special field and provided a full range of courses within that field. Trainers within a program did most of their own course design and teaching and would hire outside consultants only for very special courses offered on a limited basis.

The client group of the DSDT included any public servant in the Ottawa region who was not a senior manager or an executive. The latter groups were serviced through the Executive Education Directorate. The DSDT trainers worked singly or in teams, depending on the course and their experience. Each trainer generally was responsible for one or two courses that would be taught ten to fifteen times a year.

Consulting and custom design work in the Ottawa region was not handled by the DSDT. Such work would be handled through the Consulting and Client Services Directorate (CCSD). If a client department wanted a regular course to be run in-house and for itself alone (as opposed to sending participants to the DSDT's courses), the DSDT would "sell" an appropriate trainer to the Consulting Directorate. Regional units of the ROD also could use (and be charged for) DSDT trainers.

Marketing and registration for Ottawa courses were handled through the Internal Services Directorate. Program units within the DSDT concentrated on the provision of high-quality, regularly scheduled courses in Ottawa, leasing out trainers to consulting or to regional operations when time permitted and as need demanded.

Essentially, the task facing the DSDT was reasonably straightforward: develop and teach courses in one city for a very large population. The directorate was large and operated through four levels of management providing a heavy schedule of repeated courses. Each of these levels of management had controls and pressures that affected the next.

REGIONAL OPERATIONS DIVISION

The ROD had a small headquarters group in Ottawa, headed by the director. The six regional offices were located in Halifax, Montreal, Toronto, Winnipeg, Edmonton, and Vancouver. Each regional office was headed by a regional program director and staffed by two or three full-time trainers, supported by a secretary, a registry clerk, and a student from Waterloo University who administered the Open Learning Systems Correspondence courses.

Regional offices catered to federal public servants in the regions and handled most SDB business within their area. The basic role of the ROD was to provide the same spectrum of courses for the regions as was offered in Ottawa by the DSDT. However, because of the lower volume of demand, regional trainers were generalists and were required to teach and manage a variety of courses that in Ottawa were divided between the six program areas. The regional trainers were responsible for all administrative support services. They would design and advertise courses, prepare necessary materials, set up the classroom, teach, and assess the course. In addition, the regional trainers would administer, but not teach, a wide range of other courses. These courses would be taught by local consultants or Ottawa trainers (from DSDT) hired by the regional trainer.

The director and the trainers in the regions spent a considerable amount of time visiting clients, advertising programs, and putting out newsletters. The registry clerk spent most of her time contacting departmental training officers, looking for course participants. She also ensured that administrative letters and details were put out on time by the trainers. In addition, the trainers and director actively sought out consulting work, which they set up and discharged themselves.

The regions carried high overhead and travel expenses and had smaller clients with smaller budgets. The trainers were conscious that every penny counted. At the same time, quality had to be maintained. In times of trouble, most rules were set aside, and people within the regional offices worked together to generate new ideas for courses. The regional offices were small enough to encourage considerable face-to-face interaction.

Relationships between the DSDT and the regional offices of ROD had always been good. Many of the regional people had worked in the DSDT earlier in their careers. Two regional directors had worked through the ranks of the Ottawa division. Minor skirmishes had often occurred over the years, generally relating to problems with a few DSDT trainers who tended to head for the regions and demand that everyone from the director down should cater to their every whim. These few were well known, however, and avoided when possible. The

Regional Operations Directorate, however, deliberately sought persons who preferred smaller working groups, diverse tasks, and a great deal of autonomy. The DSDT tended more towards individuals who had a particular specialty and taught it, leaving their senior managers to handle the "paperwork." There was no question that Ottawa trainers felt strong ownership of "their" courses and, given the opportunity, wanted a say in the regions. The regional people taught "everyone's" courses, depending on the schedule, and were just as happy to find local people who could do the others with a little guidance.

FROM BOOM TO BUST

In prior years, the SDB had enjoyed a booming business. There was no lack of funding in departmental training budgets, and the branch had all the business it could handle. Although the economy seemed to be slumping, it did not appear serious. Rumors, however, were circulating about cutbacks as the full force of the economic downturn began to make itself felt. The Treasury Board demanded thorough reviews of departmental budgets, and one of the first areas cut by most departments was training. The SDB, on full cost recovery, found its market suddenly less affluent.

In June, the regional directors were in Halifax for their semi-annual meeting. They usually met in one of the regions during September for a general meeting and again in January in Ottawa for a budget meeting. This year, however, they were meeting in June because a major educational conference was taking place for two days at Dalhousie University at which some of the top experts in the field were featured speakers. The regional directors had agreed with their boss, George Hudson, that they would work Sunday through Wednesday to handle regular business, leaving Thursday and Friday for the conference.

On Tuesday afternoon, the group was discussing what the ensuing months might hold. . . .

"I'm worried," mused Herb Aiken of Halifax. "My registrations are dropping off, and we're looking at cancelling courses. You know what that means; trainers sitting around on the overhead with nothing to do."

Sarah Wilson from Edmonton concurred. She had just received a telex from her office informing her that a three-day course set to start the next day had just suffered seven last-minute cancellations.

"That only leaves eight people; we can't do it, financially or pedagogically. And we've sunk training time and administrative costs into it. I'm going to have to call and tell my staff to contact the other participants and try to postpone. This is very bad for business, though, and we can't keep it up."

She left to make her call. Thomas Russell from Vancouver picked up the ball:

"The funny thing is, our clients are willing to lose the one third late cancellation penalty, rather than pay the whole course fee. Forecasting revenues is becoming impossible, and we're barely keeping our heads above water. Where is this taking us?"

George Hudson tried to soothe everyone's fears, saying everyone in Ottawa was still doing okay and was optimistic. The directors looked at one another, each silently thinking that it was always the regions that got hit first. It was easier for the Ottawa mandarins to make cuts where the pain wasn't staring them in the face every morning. At that moment, Sarah returned and told George there was an urgent phone call for him. He left, and the others continued to discuss the future. Hudson returned about ten minutes later, his face grim.

"There's very bad news," he said flatly. "Treasury Board issued a directive this morning stating that all nonessential training is to be reviewed and cancelled whenever possible. The phones are ringing off the wall and everything on our books is on hold until October or November."

The situation worsened during the summer. Regional trainers were out visiting their clients constantly, trying desperately to drum up business, selling a day's consulting here, working on a problem there. It was difficult. Many clients were in offices located significant distances from the regional centers. Regional directors, however, were on the rampage over travel costs and telephone bills. But, as one Toronto trainer said to her boss one day:

"A letter a day just won't do it! We need to talk to them, get them to spend whatever money they've got on our courses, rather than buying on the private market."

Alice Waters knew this was true, but she *had* to keep costs trimmed to the bone. The Treasury Board had told departments to trim training costs. Given their smaller budgets, many departments preferred to provide their own training or use consultants.

By late summer, a few courses were beginning to pick up registrants as people began to sort out their budgets. Some Ottawa courses were rescheduled, but there was still a lot of slack.

One morning, Sam Wisler of Winnipeg called Vancouver.

"I just had a long talk with Mike White, the Financial Management Program manager. He wants to negotiate with us about having his trainers do all the resourcing on our regional financial courses from now on. Did a lot of talking about how we should be saving branch funds by keeping the money inside wherever possible."

Thomas Russell, listening carefully, said:

"Well, in the past, we could never get their trainers, unless somebody wanted to visit his relatives and made a deal with us. All the regions hire local consultants for courses we don't teach ourselves. Saves all those travel costs. However, it's worth thinking about. What did you tell him?"

Wisler replied:

"Just that. We should all think about it. The way I see it, things are getting better, but we may never see those good times again. If we can get Programs to do some of our courses (which are the same ones being done in Ottawa), and for less than our local consultants can do it, we'll be helping each other. They've got a lot of trainers with expensive time on their hands, and we've got courses our own staff can't do, especially in EDP, Finance, and Personnel. Maybe we can help each other. I think I should talk it over with Hudson, and see about putting out a telex to all regions on it. We can discuss it on our next teleconference."

By November, both Ottawa and the regions had managed to reschedule most of their courses, but at drastically reduced registration levels. This meant costs were more or less the same, but revenues were way down. Even though the branch had an official policy that break-even was calculated on the branch level, everyone knew that cost centers losing money were vulnerable. And each program, each region, was a cost center. They closed ranks. People who had worked well together for years with colleagues in the other directorate suddenly discovered negative characteristics of which they had previously been unaware. ROD jealously defended its right to hire local resources; the DSDT stubbornly insisted that course manuals were their property. Each group saw the other as untrustworthy, and open communication virtually ended. This was on everyone's mind as the regional directors held a conference by phone one morning. George Hudson opened the discussion:

"I've been getting feedback from all of you by telex on progress with Programs. My assessment so far is that they want to sell you their trainers' time to cut their overhead, and you're willing to buy it as long as charges are comparable to what it costs when you resource these programs locally. However, it appears that what they want to charge exceeds your local costs. Not only that, but each of you is negotiating separate agreements."

Thomas Russell broke in angrily:

"You can say that again. Mike White wants to send me two trainers to do the four-day "Fundamentals of Budget Formulation and Control" course, and he wants a total of nineteen days of time plus travel costs to do it. But he offered to do it for Sarah with one trainer and fewer days of time. What's going on here?"

Sarah's reply was consistent with what everyone had been experiencing.

"The month my course is scheduled is one where most of Mike's trainers are booked. He gave me whatever time was left. It seems that they want to dump all their excess time on us. Well, our budgets won't take it."

Evelyn D'anjou in Montreal continued:

"We've got to negotiate standard charges. And they must be reasonable ones, or we'll go to local, as we've always done when we had to rely on ourselves."

George Hudson, sensing that feelings were heating up and deciding a teleconference was not the best medium for this discussion, told everyone to sit back. He promised to meet with the DSDT Director, Bob Smythe, and talk things over as soon as possible.

The next day a furious Alice Waters was on the phone to George Hudson.

"Things are getting totally out of hand. I phoned Mike this morning to tell him we couldn't accept the charges he wants for our next financial course, so I had hired the Jameson people to do it. He tells me that's just fine, but all those new regulations for budgeting are being worked into the course, and his people are the only ones who can do it. And he refuses to release the new course manual because he claims it's not in its final form. George, you know we can't do outdated courses in the regions. I have to have that course book. Those manuals are branch property, not DSDT property! The Programs develop them because that's part of their responsibility, but it's policy that they must be made available to the regions, because we have to offer the same course out here. Mike as much as hinted that we will all be having trouble getting manuals for the Programs from now on. He says when things were slack over the summer, they revamped many of our courses, but the changes are still being tested. We're being blackmailed!"

Alice stopped, having run out of breath. George questioned her, giving her time to cool off a bit, but he was concerned. Alice was one of his best managers, a skilled trainer herself, and one who was more than able to negotiate solid agreements with her colleagues. If her problem-solving skills were not helping, they were in trouble.

"Have you considered training some of your own staff to do the more specialized courses, Alice? Maybe we can reduce our dependence on the Programs that way."

Alice was not mollified:

"George, you know what our trainers do. Everything . . . teach, administer, market, consult, clean up classrooms, weekends in airports. They just don't have time for more. Besides, why train them to do a course that's only offered twice a year in their own region. . . . We have others that run frequently both on our regular schedule and on an in-house basis. But the Ottawa trainers only have their one or two little courses to think about. No marketing, no consulting. Even big training centers with everything done for them! They walk out of our classrooms on Friday night and don't clean up a thing! They say that's our job, not theirs. Well, we don't have big staffs catering to our small offices, and it's our weekend, too. But I'm getting off the topic. . . . What about those course books? I've already telexed the other regions to warn them about what's happening."

Inwardly, Hudson groaned. Every one of his directors would be up in arms by the end of the day. He promised Alice he'd go to Bob Smythe, the director of DSDT, to talk matters over, and hung up. Glancing at his telephone, he could see the lights coming on; it was starting already. Thankful it was Friday, he told his clerk to hold the calls and left to find Bob Smythe.

A half hour later, Hudson returned, and dictated a telex: everyone was to sit tight. Smythe was meeting with his managers Monday morning to discuss the matter.

The following Tuesday, Hudson picked up the teleconference phone to address his regions. He wondered how much he'd get through before the protests began.

"I just had a meeting with Bob Smythe. His managers claim we're doing outdated courses and that they should be given control of course content. They also believe we should hire their resources before any consultants, to help minimize branch downtime. Smythe agrees with them, and they're tabling the matter with the Director General at the next management committee meeting."

There was silence as the six listeners digested this news, each realizing the potential consequences. Then Sam Wisler in Winnipeg spoke angrily:

"This is incredible. They want to make money at our expense! Are we working for the same place or aren't we? What the hell is going on here? We won't let those bastards get away with this!"

Herb Aiken's language was much stronger, but the message was the same. Hudson listened to the chorus of angry voices for a while and then asked for everything in the way of financial ammunition, details of travel costs, local costs, and Programs changes. Then he ended the call.

The SDB Management Committee came to the conclusion that branch resources should be used whenever possible to teach branch courses. The regions and the Programs were instructed to work out standard charges to be used in the January budget exercise for the upcoming fiscal year. The point was noted that the regions had to provide up-to-date courses and, if that involved using the DSDT resources, that was the way things had to be.

In January, two of the regional directors came to Ottawa to meet two representatives from the DSDT. The objective was to settle standard charges for all courses. Preparation time, teaching time, travel time, and administrative responsibilities would be fixed. Ratios were to be agreed upon and used as formulas for all courses in the future. Alice Waters and Sarah Wilson had convassed the other regional directors on acceptable alternatives and had full authority from them to act. They had requested that the two DSDT representatives come with the same authority, as time was running out. The group met for a full day on the Monday and, by the end of it, the two regional directors were exhausted and frustrated. The DSDT representatives were demanding costly ratios, were not giving an inch, and had to take back any proposals to their own director for his approval. And he was away until Wednesday.

That night Alice and Sarah paid a late night visit to Hudson, venting their anger openly. The regions could not survive the charges being imposed by DSDT. It seemed that the SDB had some fundamental decisions to make about its internal affairs, decisions that were beyond the authority of Wilson and Waters. Those decisions had to be made before the new budgets were drafted.

Despite meeting again on Tuesday and Wednesday, the DSDT and ROD representatives failed to agree on standard charges. The matter was again put to the Management Committee. The committee reiterated its position that in-house resources had to be used and decided that the regions would have to live with the Program demands.

In March, the Regional Operations Directorate tabled its budget for the upcoming fiscal year. It showed a substantial projected loss. The DSDT tabled its budget, showing a substantial projected profit.

When you have read this case, look back at the chapter's diagnostic questions and choose the ones that apply to the case. Then use those questions with the ones that follow in your case analysis.

1. What type of unit grouping was used to form the directorates that make up the Public Service Commission's Staff Development Branch? What are the strengths and weaknesses of this type of structure?

2. What sorts of coordination mechanisms are being used to coordinate activities in the SDB's unit groups? Given the apparent importance of controlling costs in the SDB, how suitable do you think these mechanisms are? What are the costs and benefits of structuring an organization in this manner?

3. What triggered the breakdown between the Regional Operations Directorate and the Directorate of Staff Development and Training? What interunit mechanisms should the SBD consider implementing in order to deal with this situation? Prepare a diagram that shows how the SBD's structure would look after implementing your suggestions.

CASE 15-2

RONDELL DATA CORPORATION

Review this case, which appears in Chapter 13. Next, look back at Chapter 15's diagnostic questions and choose the ones that apply to the case. Then use those questions with the ones that follow in your case analysis.

1. What type of unit grouping was used to form the departments in the Rondell Data Corporation? What are the strengths and weaknesses of this approach?

2. How are Rondell's research and engineering departments interconnected? What relations do these departments have with the company's sales and production departments? What triggered the breakdown in coordination among Rondell's departments? What interunit mechanisms should Rondell's management consider implementing in order to improve matters? Draw a diagram of the kind of structure the company would have if it implemented your suggestions.

3. Did Frank Forbus fail because of personal deficiencies? Given Rondell's current structure, could someone else have performed his job successfully?

CASE 15-3

DUMAS PUBLIC LIBRARY

Read Chapter 18's Case 18-2, "Dumas Public Library." Next, look back at Chapter 15's diagnostic questions and choose the ones that apply to that case. Then use those questions with the ones that follow to begin your analysis of the case.

1. How were the unit groups formed in the city government of Kimball, New Mexico? What are the benefits of this method of unit grouping? What are its weaknesses?

2. What mechanisms were used to coordinate activities within the units of the Kimball government structure? Between or among these units? Do these mechanisms seem appropriate? What changes would you recommend?

3. Is the conflict between Debra Dickenson and Helen Hendricks simply a matter of incompatible personalities? Are the coordinating mechanisms used in the city government contributing to this conflict? If they are, what modifications would you make in order to resolve the conflict?

CHAPTER 16

ORGANIZATION DESIGN

When Roger Smith, former CEO of General Motors, reorganized the huge company in 1984, GM had already announced its design of the Saturn and its intention to create a separate company to produce it. As we go to press in mid-1991, the Saturn has yet to prove itself in the marketplace. But the company's employees seem to agree that two of Saturn's most important achievements are the new design of the organization that is producing it and the new roles that design has created for managers, workers, and union representatives.

At an upcoming meeting in New York, Roger B. Smith, chairman of General Motors Corporation, will ask the GM board of directors to approve a plan to reduce the company's five car divisions—Chevrolet, Pontiac, Oldsmobile, Buick and Cadillac—to two. The new Chevrolet-Pontiac division will produce and sell only GM's smaller cars, and the Buick-Oldsmobile-Cadillac division will handle the larger models. Beyond merging nameplates, Smith's plan will change General Motors in other important ways. From the company's beginning, design, engineering, and marketing activities have been directed by central staffs at the top corporate level. Under the new plan, these activities will be handled by separate staffs at the two divisions. In charge of these divisions will be two new executive vice presidents who will be strictly accountable for divisional profit and performance to GM's top management.[1]

The 1984 meeting announced in *Business Week* had been in the making for quite some time. Like Apple's John Sculley, the management of General Motors Corporation had struggled, beginning in the late 1960s, with the task of streamlining a sprawling corporation and controlling the costs of its operations. In an attempt to reduce the duplication of effort that was then increasing the cost of production, GM's top management had consolidated many of the assembly operations of the firm's five automotive divisions—Chevrolet, Pontiac, Buick, Oldsmobile, and Cadillac—into a single unit, the General Motors Assembly Division. Responsibility for major purchasing, product design, and engineering decisions had also migrated from the "nameplate" automotive divisions to GM's Detroit headquarters. By the early 1970s General Motors had moved toward a structure that resembled, in many important respects, the structure of Sculley's reorganized Apple (described at the beginning of Chapter 15).[2]

Unfortunately, however, whereas Sculley's Apple flourished, the centralized General Motors failed to perform as expected. Publicly, GM's management blamed this failure on conflicts over product development that erupted between the newly consolidated assembly division and the remnants of the five nameplate divisions which continued to handle product distribution.[3] Privately, detractors also suggested that the restructuring reduced GM's sensitivity to changes in the preferences of American car buyers, leading the company to produce cars that nobody wanted to purchase.[4] Whatever the cause, Roger Smith reacted by proposing his two-division reorganization plan in early 1984, and GM's board of directors gave its approval. Restructuring began later that year.

Why did the same kind of structural changes that put Apple back on its feet in the 1980s prove to be inappropriate for GM in the 1970s? Was it due to differences between the two firms' products—Apple's computers versus GM's cars? Or differences between the sizes of the two companies—the large Apple versus the mammoth General Motors? Or yet other differences? Without guidance, managers like Apple's Sculley and GM's Smith are unlikely to know the

[1] Tom Nicholson, James C. Jones, and Erik Ipsen, "GM Plans a Great Divide," *Business Week*, January 9, 1984, p. 68.

[2] Ibid., pp. 68–69.

[3] "Can GM Solve Its Identity Crisis?" *Business Week*, January 23, 1984, pp. 32–33; and William J. Hampton and James R. Norman, "General Motors: What Went Wrong?" *Business Week*, March 16, 1987, pp. 102–110.

[4] J. Patrick Wright, *On A Clear Day You Can See General Motors* (Grosse Pointe, Mich: Wright Enterprises, 1979), pp. 219–20.

answers to questions like these. Organizational well-being may be threatened as a result. Contemporary managers, whether they are maintaining existing structures or devising new ones, therefore need to know about various structural alternatives and their effects on performance. For this reason, in this chapter we will consider the several different types of contemporary organizational structure. We will look especially at how the structural characteristics discussed in Chapter 15—unit grouping and coordination mechanisms, formalization, specialization, interunit coordination mechanisms—combine to determine the strengths and weaknesses of each structural type. We will then examine the factors that influence the effectiveness of each type of structure and show how a particular structure's strengths and weaknesses make it appropriate for some situations but not others. In so doing, we will present a contingency model of organization design that provides guidance to managers engaged in structuring modern organizations.

DIAGNOSTIC ISSUES

Our diagnostic model highlights many critical questions in the area of organization design. For starters, we need to *describe* the structure of an organization and determine whether it is performing effectively. We must also be able to characterize the situation in which the organization must do its work. How do we *diagnose* what kind of technology is used by the firm and what its effects are on the firm's structure? How do we assess the environment surrounding an organization and determine whether the organization is suitably structured?

How do we *prescribe* the right type of coordinating mechanism for a particular type of environment? How can we determine what structure an organization should have in light of the organization's age and maturity? Finally, what *actions* can managers take to match structure to an organization's technology? What steps can managers take to improve the fit between an organization's structure and its environment?

A CONTINGENCY MODEL OF ORGANIZATION DESIGN

Is there a single *best* form of organizational structure? Our quick comparison between GM and Apple suggests that no one type of structure is suitable for all organizations. Instead, each type of organization structure has unique strengths and weaknesses that make it more appropriate for some situations than for others. Structuring an organization involves choices among various alternatives.

organization design The process of diagnosing the situation that confronts a particular organization and selecting and putting in place the organization structure most appropriate for that situation.

Organization design is the process of making these choices. That is, management diagnoses the situation confronting a particular organization and selects and puts in place the structure that seems most appropriate. It is guided by the contingency perspective, described in Chapter 1, that no single management approach—or structure—is useful in every situation and that the usefulness of a particular approach depends on the situation being managed. Organization design is thus based on the principle that the degree to which a particular type of *structure* will contribute to the *effectiveness* of an organization depends on *contingency factors* that impinge on the organization (see Figure 16-1).

FIGURE 16-1

The Contingency Model of Organization Design

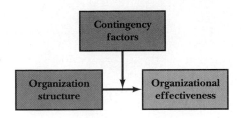

Organizational Effectiveness

organizational effectiveness The degree to which an organization is successful in achieving its goals and objectives while at the same time ensuring its continued survival by satisfying the demands of interested parties, such as suppliers and customers.

Organizational effectiveness, the ultimate aim of organization design, is a measure of an organization's success in achieving its goals and objectives. In an effective organization, employee behaviors, group and intergroup processes, and organizational factors all contribute toward accomplishing the goals and objectives that serve as the firm's purpose. You will recall from Chapter 2 that goals and objectives of this sort might include targets pertaining to profitability, growth, market share, product quality, efficiency, stability, or similar outcomes.[5] An organization that fails to accomplish such goals is ineffective because it is not fulfilling its purpose.

constituency groups Groups such as employees, customers, and suppliers upon whom the survival of an organization depends. Constituency groups make demands that they expect will be fulfilled in return for their support of the organization.

An effective organization must also satisfy the demands of the various **constituency groups** that provide it with the resources it needs to survive. For example, as Figure 16-2 suggests, if a company satisfies customers' demands for desirable goods or services, it will probably continue to enjoy its customers' pa-

[5] James L. Price, "The Study of Organizational Effectiveness," *Sociological Quarterly* 13 (1972), 3–15; Stephen Strasser, J. D. Eveland, Gaylord Cummings, O. Lynn Deniston, and John H. Romani, "Conceptualizing the Goal and System Models of Organizational Effectiveness—Implications for Comparative Evaluative Research," *Journal of Management Studies* 18 (1981), 321–40; and Y. K. Shetty, "New Look at Corporate Goals," *California Management Review* 22 (1979), 71–79.

FIGURE 16-2

Types of Constituency Groups and Their Demands

Circles surrounding the central organization in this figure represent a few of the many constituency groups whose demands must be satisfied to ensure continued organizational survival. Arrows pointing toward the center indicate the sorts of demands that the constituency groups make on the organization. Arrows pointing outward indicate the kinds of responses that an effective organization might make in return.

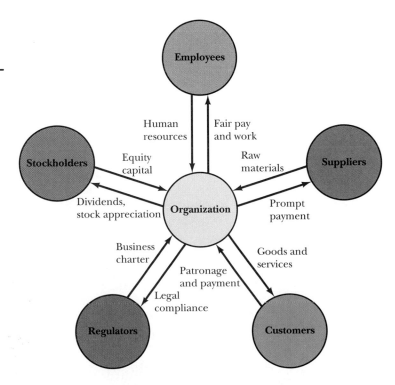

Constituency groups *in an organization's environment often influence organizational behavior. For example, increasing fire from environmental protection groups has led Procter & Gamble to develop a disposable diaper that will break down wholly into compost and to push local governments to construct more facilities for solid waste composting. P&G also hopes to remove some of the guilt they think customers feel about using a product that has been contributing to environmental problems. Although the 15% increase in P&G's worldwide sales of Pampers and Luvs between 1989 and 1990 suggested that the company's customers were still satisfied with P&G's product, the company decided to get a jump on an issue that could cause it trouble down the line. Source: Zachary Schiller, "Turning Pampers into Plant Food?" Business Week, October 22, 1990.*

organizational productivity The amount of goods or services produced by an organization. Higher productivity means that more goods or services are produced.

organizational efficiency The ratio of outputs produced per unit of inputs consumed; minimizing the raw materials and energy consumed by the production of goods and services.

tronage. If it satisfies its suppliers' demands for payment in a timely manner, the suppliers will probably continue to provide it with needed raw materials. If it satisfies its employees' demands for fair pay and satisfying work, it will probably be able to retain its workers and recruit new employees. If it satisfies stockholder demands for profitability, it will probably have continued access to equity funding.[6] If a firm fails to satisfy any one of these demands, however, its effectiveness will be weakened, because the potential loss of needed resources, such as customers or employees, threatens its survival.

Effectiveness is not the same thing as **organizational productivity**. The latter concept does not take into account whether a firm is producing the *right* goods or services.[7] A modern company producing more buggy whips than ever before is certainly productive, but it is also ineffective, because few people need buggy whips in today's society. Effectiveness is not efficiency, either. **Organizational efficiency** means minimizing the raw materials and energy consumed by the production of goods and services. It is usually measured as the ratio of outputs produced per unit of inputs consumed.[8] Thus efficiency means *doing the job right*, whereas effectiveness means *doing the right job*—determining whether a company is producing what it ought to produce in light of the goals, objectives, and constituency demands that influence its performance and are its reason for being.

Structural Alternatives

The extent to which an organization is effective is strongly influenced by its structure. One type of structure enhances the ability to attain goals and satisfy constituencies, while others are likely to detract from these pursuits. In general, organization structures differ from one another along a dimension ranging from *mechanistic* to *organic*.[9]

---

[6] Constituency models of effectiveness and other examples of constituencies and their interests are discussed by Paul S. Goodman, Johannes M. Pennings and Associates, *New Perspectives on Organizational Effectiveness* (San Francisco: Jossey-Bass, 1977); John A Wagner III and Benjamin Schneider, "Legal Regulation and the Constraint of Constituent Satisfaction," *Journal of Management Studies* 24 (1987), 189–200; and Raymond F. Zammuto, "A Comparison of Multiple Constituency Models of Organizational Effectiveness," *Academy of Management Review* 9 (1984), 606–16.

[7] Richard Z. Gooding and John A Wagner III, "A Meta-Analytic Review of the Relationship between Size and Performance: The Productivity and Efficiency of Organizations and Their Subunits," *Administrative Science Quarterly* 30 (1985), 462–81.

[8] Ibid.

[9] Tom Burns and G. M. Stalker, *The Management of Innovation* (London: Tavistock Publications, 1961), pp. 119–22.

ORGANIZATION DESIGN

TABLE 16-1
Comparison of Mechanistic and Organic Structures

CHARACTERISTICS OF MECHANISTIC STRUCTURES	CHARACTERISTICS OF ORGANIC STRUCTURES
Tasks are highly specialized. It is often not clear to members how their tasks contribute to accomplishing organizational objectives.	Tasks are broad and interdependent. Relation of task performance to attainment of organizational objectives is emphasized.
Tasks remain rigidly defined unless formally altered by top management.	Tasks are continually modified and redefined by means of mutual adjustment among task holders.
Specific roles (rights, duties, technical methods) are defined for each member.	Generalized roles (acceptance of the responsibility for overall task accomplishment) are defined for each member.
Control and authority relationships are structured in a vertical hierarchy.	Control and authority relationships are structured in a network of both vertical and horizontal connections.
Communication is primarily vertical, between superiors and subordinates.	Communication is both vertical and horizontal depending on where needed information resides.
Communication is mainly in the form of instructions and decisions issued by superiors, performance feedback, and requests for decisions sent from subordinates.	Communication takes the form of information and advice.
Loyalty to the organization and obedience to superiors are insisted upon.	Commitment to organizational goals is more highly valued than loyalty or obedience.

Source: Based in part on Tom Burns and G. M. Stalker, *The Management of Innovation* (London: Tavistock Publications, 1961), pp. 120–122.

mechanistic structures Machine-like organization structures designed to enhance efficiency; characterized by large amounts of formalization, standardization, specialization, and centralization.

organic structures Organism-like organization structures designed to enhance flexibility and innovation; characterized by large amounts of mutual adjustment and decentralization.

structural contingency factors Characteristics of an organization and its surrounding circumstances that influence whether its structure will contribute to organizational effectiveness.

Wholly **mechanistic structures** are machinelike. They permit workers to complete routine, narrowly defined tasks in an efficient manner, but they lack flexibility. As Table 16-1 indicates, they are characterized by large amounts of formalization, standardization, and specialization. Therefore, they are much the same as the *bureaucratic* form of organization described by Max Weber nearly a century ago (see Chapter 2). Mechanistic structures are centralized and usually have *tall hierarchies* of vertical authority and communication relationships such as the one depicted in the upper panel of Figure 16-3.

Highly **organic structures** are more like living organisms in that they are innovative and can adapt to changing conditions. Owing to their flexibility, however, organic structures lack the stability or constancy that enables more mechanistic structures to perform routine work efficiently. Organizations with organic structures rely more on mutual adjustment than on formalization, standardization, and specialization. Their divisions, departments, and people are connected by a decentralized network. Often, though not always, this network takes the form of a *flat hierarchy*, such as the one shown in the lower panel of Figure 16-3. Its emphasis on horizontal relationships can help reduce the number of vertical layers required to process information and manage activities.

A particular organization's structure may fit at any point along the mechanistic-organic dimension. The more mechanistic the structure, the more efficient but less flexible it will be. The more organic the structure, the more flexible but less efficient it will be. These differences in efficiency and flexibility can be traced to the mechanisms used to coordinate work activities. As you will remember from Chapter 15, standardization embodies low long-term coordination costs and is thus the basis of mechanistic efficiency. Mutual adjustment, on the other hand, is quite flexible and is therefore the source of organic flexibility.

Structural Contingencies

Whether mechanistic efficiency or organic flexibility will lead to greater organizational effectiveness depends on the influence of a variety of factors. **Structural**

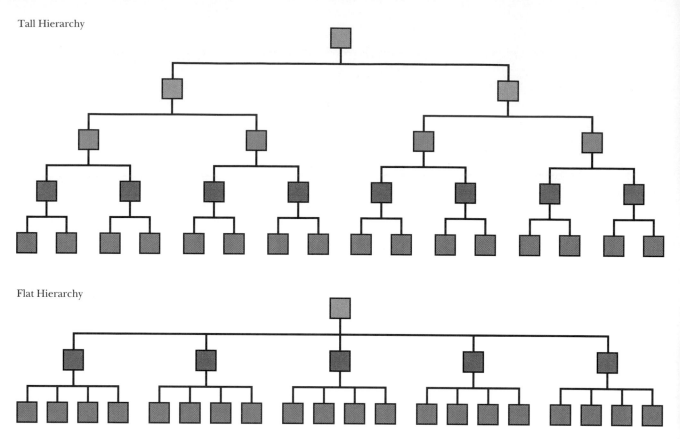

Tall Hierarchy

Flat Hierarchy

FIGURE 16-3

Tall and Flat Organizational Hierarchies

closed system contingencies
Structural contingency factors that are characteristics of the organization. Size and technology are the most dominant of these factors.

open system contingencies
Structural contingency factors that are characteristics of the environment surrounding an organization.

contingency factors such as characteristics of an organization and the surrounding situation shape or constrain the firm's work. Two perspectives on organizational design—the closed system perspective and the open system perspective—help to identify several contingency factors that can influence the success of different organization structures.

The *closed system perspective* focuses on enhancing the efficiency of activities within organizations but tends to ignore the effects of outside factors.[10] So **closed system contingencies** are factors within the organization. Of these contingencies, the two most noteworthy ones are the organization's *size* and the *core technology* it employs to produce its goods or services. Closely related to the size of an organization are two additional contingencies, the firm's *age* and its stage of *life-cycle* development.

In contrast, you may recall from Chapter 2 that the *open system perspective* recognizes that organizations are shaped by the circumstances that surround them. To remain viable, companies must acquire energy, materials, and other resources from the external environment and offer finished goods or services in return.[11] **Open system contingencies** thus consist of features of the *environment* surrounding a firm.

Considered together, closed and open system contingencies constitute the situation that managers must diagnose correctly to design a structure that promotes organizational effectiveness. Later in this chapter, we will examine the contingency factors of size, core technology, and environment in greater detail and discuss their effects on organization design. First, however, we turn to an overview of the specific types of structures found in contemporary organizations.

[10] James D. Thompson, *Organizations in Action* (New York: McGraw-Hill, 1967), p. 4.

[11] Thompson, *Organizations in Action*; Daniel Katz and Robert L. Kahn, *The Social Psychology of Organizations*, 2nd ed. (New York: John Wiley, 1978), p. 3.

ORGANIZATION DESIGN

TYPES OF ORGANIZATION STRUCTURE

How do the various structural characteristics discussed in Chapter 15 combine to form fully developed organization structures? What kinds of structures are formed as a result? Which of these structures are more mechanistic and efficient, and which are more organic and flexible? The answers to questions like these are found in the "menu" of alternative structures overviewed next.

Simple Structures

As suggested by their name, **simple structures** are the least complicated form of structure used in today's organizations. Their simplicity stems from their reliance on the relatively uncomplicated coordination mechanisms of mutual adjustment or direct supervision to integrate work activities. There are two types of simple structures—simple undifferentiated and simple differentiated structures.

Simple Undifferentiated Structure. In a **simple undifferentiated structure**, coordination is accomplished solely by mutual adjustment. As you will recall from Chapter 15, mutual adjustment is a process in which coworkers talk with each other to determine how to coordinate work among themselves. Because talking with other people is natural for most of us, mutual adjustment is easy to initiate and relatively simple to sustain. Thus simple undifferentiated structures can often be established and perpetuated fairly easily.

As Figure 16-4 suggests, there is no hierarchy of authority in a simple undifferentiated structure. Such a structure is nothing more than an organization of people who decide what to do by talking with each other as they work. No single individual has the authority to issue orders, and there are few if any written procedures to guide performance. A group of friends who decide to open a small restaurant, gift shop, or similar sort of business might, at the outset, adopt this type of structure for the business. Similarly, the kind of classroom discussion group you might form to analyze the cases or do the exercises in this book could be thought of as a small organization with a simple undifferentiated structure.

The primary strengths of simple undifferentiated structures are their simplicity and extreme flexibility. Networks of face-to-face conversations occur spontaneously and can be reconfigured almost instantly. For instance, adding another member to a small classroom discussion group is likely to cause only a momentary lapse in the group's activities. A major weakness of these structures, however, is their limitation to small organizations. Suppose you were a manager in an advertising firm composed of 25 or 30 people. Could you rely solely on mutual adjustment to ensure that the firm's accounts were properly handled? Probably you could not, because as you'll recall from Chapter 11, process loss undermines the usefulness of face-to-face coordination when it is applied to groups much larger than 12 people. Mutual adjustment requires so many links between people in large groups that valuable time and effort are lost in the exchange of needed

simple structure An uncomplicated type of organization structure that relies on mutual adjustment or direct supervision to achieve coordination.

simple undifferentiated structure A type of simple organization structure in which coordination is achieved solely by means of mutual adjustment.

FIGURE 16-4

The Simple Undifferentiated Structure

The simple undifferentiated structure is the simplest of all structures, relying only on face-to-face mutual adjustment to coordinate work.

Employee 1   Employee 2   Employee 3   Employee 4

information. As a result, only a very small organization can function effectively with a simple undifferentiated structure.

Another important—and related—weakness is that simple undifferentiated structures cannot provide the coordination needed to accomplish complex tasks. It is difficult to imagine 12 or so people being able to assemble cars, but simple undifferentiated structures cannot coordinate the efforts of larger groups of people in an efficient manner. Complicated work requires a more complicated form of organization structure.

Simple Differentiated Structure. In the second type of organizational structure, the **simple differentiated structure**, direct supervision replaces mutual adjustment as the primary unit coordination mechanism. You probably encounter organizations with simple differentiated structures every day—a bookstore or clothing shop on your campus or the family-owned grocery store or gas station in your neighborhood. Look at the diagram of a simple differentiated structure in Figure 16-5. The relatively flat hierarchy pictured in this figure contains small but significant amounts of *vertical specialization* and *centralization*. One person (usually the firm's owner or the owner's management representative) retains the hierarchical authority needed to coordinate work activities by means of *direct supervision*. As a secondary mechanism, mutual adjustment is used to deal with coordination problems that direct supervision cannot resolve. For example, while the owner of a small insurance office is at the post office getting the morning mail, clerks in the insurance office may talk among themselves to decide who will answer the telephone and who will process paperwork until she returns.

The simple differentiated structure can coordinate larger numbers of people than can the simple differentiated structure. The reason is that, as indicated in Chapter 15, shifting to direct supervision eliminates much of the process loss associated with reliance on mutual adjustment alone. In addition, because its decision-making powers are centralized in the hands of single person, a simple differentiated structure can respond rapidly to changing conditions. At the same time, this structure retains a good deal of flexibility, because it avoids standardization. Its weaknesses, however, are its inability to coordinate the activities of more than about 50 people and its failure to provide the integration needed to accomplish complex tasks. It is just as unlikely that a group of people could organize themselves to produce cars by using a combination of direct supervision and mutual adjustment as it is that they might organize themselves for such a task using mutual adjustment alone. A single direct supervisor would soon be overwhelmed by the vast amount of information required to know which sort of cars to produce, what parts to order, whom to order them from, how to assemble them properly, and so forth.

Complex Structures

Both kinds of simple structures are overwhelmed by the coordination requirements of complicated tasks. Standardization—of processes, outputs, skills, or

FIGURE 16-5

The Simple Differentiated Structure

The emergence of hierarchical, superior-subordinate differentiation distinguishes the simple differentiated structure from the simple undifferentiated structure.

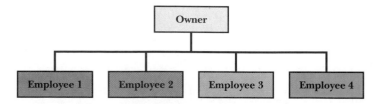

complex structure A type of organization structure that relies on standardization to achieve coordination; a complex structure is therefore characterized by noticeable formalization and specialization.

norms—becomes useful in this situation. It greatly reduces the amount of information that must be exchanged and the number of decisions that must be made as work is being performed. Such standardization is the hallmark of **complex structures**. In these structures, direct supervision and mutual adjustment are retained as secondary mechanisms that kick in when standardization fails to meet all coordination needs. This combination of unit coordination mechanisms allows organizations with complex structures to integrate the variety of jobs needed to perform complicated, demanding work. There are three major kinds of complex structures—functional structures, divisional structures, and matrix structures.

functional structure An efficient but inflexible type of complex structure characterized by functional departmentation and centralization.

Functional Structure. **Functional structures** are characterized by four key attributes. First, because they are complex structures, functional structures are based on coordination by *standardization*. As you'll recall from Chapter 15, standardization is preceded by *formalization* and contributes to *specialization*. So both of these characteristics are also features of functional structures. Second, functional structures are *centralized*. Most if not all important decisions are made by one or a few people at the tops of firms with functional structures—for instance, decisions leading to the formation of organizational goals, objectives, and mission statements. Third, owing to their centralization, functional structures require a great deal of vertical communication and tend to have *tall hierarchies*. Fourth, these structures are characterized by *functional departmentation*. That is, units within them are grouped into departments that are named for the functions their members perform, such as marketing, manufacturing, or accounting.

As Figure 16-6 suggests, one of the easiest ways to determine whether a particular firm has a functional structure is to examine the titles held by its vice-presidents. If the firm has a complex structure, and all of its vice-presidents have titles that indicate what their subordinates do—for example, vice president of manufacturing, vice president of marketing, vice president of research and development—the firm has a functional structure. If one or more vice-presidents have other sorts of titles, however, for instance, vice president of the consumer finance division or vice president of European operations—the firm has another type of structure.

Organizations like credit unions and locally owned banks, car dealerships, department stores, and many junior colleges, colleges, and universities have functional structures. The primary strength of this type of structure is its economic efficiency. Standardization minimizes the long-term cost of coordination. In addition, centralization makes it possible for workers to focus their attention on their work rather than having to take time out to make needed decisions. Functional structures, however, have a critical weakness. They lack flexibility. The standardization that provides so much efficiency not only takes lengthy planning and documentation (formalization) to set in place but requires that the same standards be followed again and again. This inflexibility reduces the functional structure's ability to cope with instability or change. Functional departmentation adds to this rigidity, because as you will recall from Chapter 15, changes to any work flow in a company organized by functional departmentation also affect the other work flows in the organization.

A functional structure can coordinate the work of an organization effectively if the firm limits itself to one type of product, produces this product in a single geographic location, and sells to only one general type of client. Many organizations produce more than one product, however, or do business in several different locations or seek to serve a variety of clients. Such diversity of products, locations, or clients injects variety into the information a firm needs to make managerial decisions. This variety overloads the centralized decision-making processes on which the functional structure is based. Let's look next at the kind of

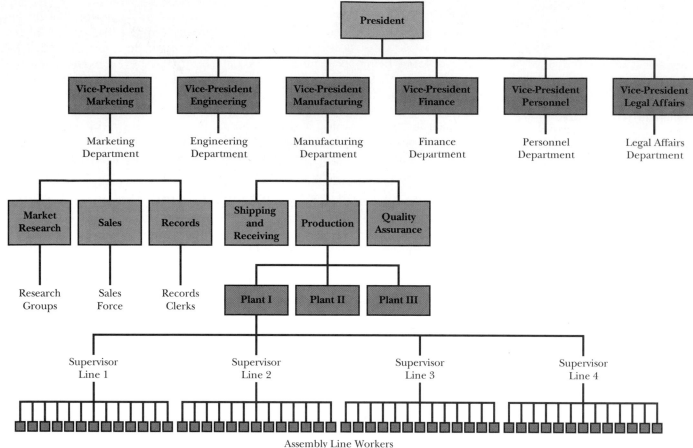

FIGURE 16-6

The Functional Structure

The functional structure uses a combination of functional grouping, centralization, and standardization to organize work activities. The marketing and manufacturing departments are shown in some detail to illustrate how the departments of a functional structure are composed of smaller units that facilitate coordination among employees who must work closely with each other.

divisional structure A flexible but inefficient type of complex structure characterized by divisional departmentation and moderate decentralization.

product structure A type of divisional structure formed by grouping units according to similarities in the products they make and sell.

geographic structure A type of divisional structure formed by grouping units according to similarities in their geographic location.

market structure A type of divisional structure formed by grouping units according to similarities in the clients or customers they serve.

structure that enables an organization to cope with this sort of diversity—the divisional structure.

Divisional Structure. Like functional structures, **divisional structures** are complex structures characterized by *standardization*, and, therefore, by *formalization* and *specialization*. Unlike functional structures, however, divisional structures are moderately *decentralized*. Decision making is pushed downward one or two hierarchical layers, so a company's vice-presidents and sometimes their immediate subordinates share in the process of digesting information and making key decisions. *Divisional departmentation* is another notable feature that distinguishes divisional structures from functional structures. Units in divisional structures are grouped together according to similarities in products, geographic locations, or clients. For this reason, divisional structures are also sometimes called **product structures**, **geographic structures**, or **market structures**.

Look at Figure 16-7, which depicts several different divisional structures. Can you see how they differ from the functional structure diagrammed in Figure 16-6? You're right: In each of the structures in Figure 16-7, vice-presidential titles include product, geographic, or client names. Note, though, that in these

A Product Structure

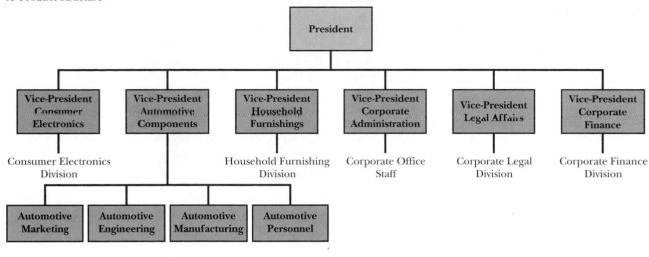

B Geographic Structure

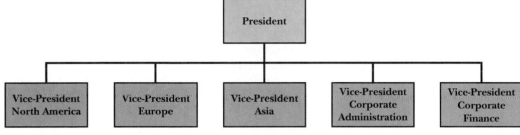

C Client Structure

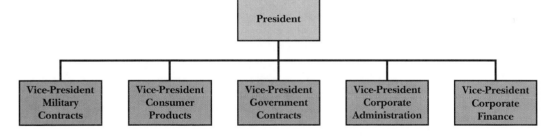

FIGURE 16-7

Divisional Structures

The divisional structure incorporates decentralization, standardization, and divisional departmentation. The diagram shows three divisional structures in which departmentation is based on (a) product similarities, (b) geographic similarities, and (c) client similarities. Note how the lower groupings of the automotive-components division shown in panel A resemble a small functional structure.

divisional structures, vice-presidents of *staff* units have titles that sound like functions; for example, vice-president of legal affairs and vice-president of corporate finance. (If you don't remember what staff means, review the discussion in Chapter 9 of the line-versus-staff distinction).

The divisional structure's departmentation and moderate decentralization give it a degree of adaptability not found in the functional structure. Each unit, or division, of such a structure can react to issues concerning its own product, geographic region, or client group fairly independently of other units. It must not, however, lose sight of the overall organization's goals and objectives. For example, the vice-president of consumer electronics, shown in the upper panel of Figure 16-7, can make decisions affecting the production and sales of clock radios and steam irons without consulting with the company's president or other vice-presidents. This degree of independence even allows a division to stop doing business without seriously interrupting the operations of the organization's other units. For example, the division of TRW that fulfills NASA space contracts could discontinue doing business without affecting work in the firm's credit information division. Remember, though, that each division in a divisional structure is itself organized like a functional structure—take another look at the product structure shown in Figure 16-7. As a result, a particular division cannot change products, locations, or clients without serious interruption to its own internal operations. For example, the decision at TRW to reduce reliance on military contracts would require that the division servicing such contracts be substantially reorganized.

The adaptability that is the main strength of divisional structures comes at the price of increased costs because of duplication of effort across divisions. For example, every division is likely to have separate sales forces even though that means that salespeople from several different divisions may repeatedly visit the same customer. So the primary weakness of divisional structures is the fact that they are, at best, only moderately efficient.

matrix structure An extremely flexible but also extremely costly type of complex structure characterized by both functional and divisional departmentation as well as high decentralization. Also called the simultaneous structure.

Matrix Structure. **Matrix structures**, like divisional structures, are adopted by organizations that must integrate work with a variety of products, locations, or customers. Firms that have matrix structures, however, need even more flexibility than divisional structures allow. They try to achieve this flexibility by reintegrating functional specialists across different product, location, or customer lines. Because matrix structures use functional and divisional departmentation *simultaneously* to group structural units together, they are also called *simultaneous structures*.

Figure 16-8 illustrates the matrix structure of a firm that has three divisions, each of which manufactures and sells a distinct product line. Each box, or cell, in the matrix is a distinct group composed of a small hierarchy of supervisors and one or more structural units having both functional and divisional responsibilities. For example, cell 1 in the figure is a consumer-electronics-marketing group composed of units that market televisions, radios, cellular telephones, and other electronic merchandise. Cell 2 is the automotive-components-engineering group consisting of engineering units that design automobile engines, suspensions, steering assemblies, and other such items. Cell 3 is a household-products-manufacturing group made up of facilities that produce furniture polish, floor wax, window cleaner, and other household supplies. Note that the figure also indicates that staff units in a matrix structure are often excluded from the matrix itself. The three staff departments shown in the diagram—personnel, finance,

F I G U R E 16-8

The Matrix Structure

The matrix structures increase the flexibility of a large organization by incorporating both functional departmentation (shown horizontally in the diagram) and divisional departmentation (shown vertically). The groupings represented by each cell perform functional duties related to a particular type of product.

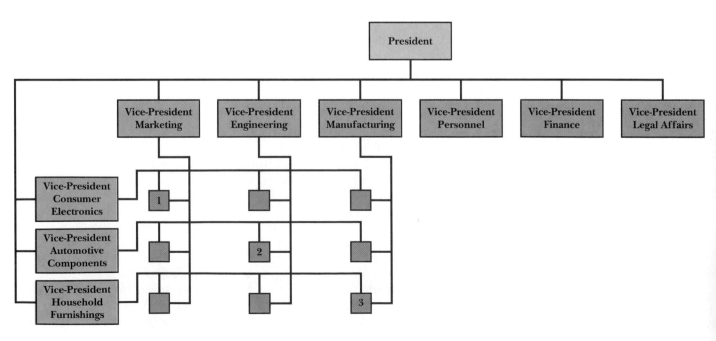

and legal affairs—provide advice to top management but are not part of the matrix.

You will recall from Chapter 15 that the matrix is both a structure and a lateral linkage device used to interconnect the units in a firm. *Mutual adjustment* is the primary means of coordination within the upper layers of a matrix structure, and decision making is *decentralized* among matrix managers. Both these characteristics allow top managers to reconfigure relationships among the cells in the matrix, promoting extreme flexibility. Because of their dual responsibilities, each matrix cell has two bosses—a functional boss and a divisional boss. This arrangement violates Fayol's principle of unity of command (see Chapter 2). Thus mutual adjustment must also be used in the upper layer of each cell to cope with conflicting orders from above.

Beneath the upper layer of each cell, however, formalization, standardization, and specialization are used to integrate work activities. Both direct supervision and lower-level mutual adjustment serve as supplementary mechanisms that coordinate cell activities. For instance, once managers at the top of the matrix structure shown in Figure 16-8 have decided to manufacture a new kind of floor wax, formalization is used to develop new standards. Standardization is then used to coordinate activities in the units in the household-products-manufacturing cell that make this new product. Direct supervisors help employees learn the new standards and also work to correct deficiencies in the standards as they become apparent. In addition, employees engage in mutual adjustment to cope with problems that their supervisor cannot resolve. Thus a matrix structure basically consists of a simple structure designed into the upper layers of a complex structure. The simple structure injects mutual adjustment to encourage communication, coordination, and flexibility among the managers who oversee organizational operations. Beneath this simple structure is a *tall hierarchy* of cells, cell supervisors, and nonsupervisory employees.

The primary strength of matrix structures is their extreme flexibility. They can adjust to changes that would overwhelm other complex structures. Why do you suppose, then, that matrix structures are extremely rare? The reason is that they have one primary and very crucial weakness. They are extremely costly to operate. In part, this costliness stems from the proliferation of managers in matrix firms. They need two complete sets of vice-presidents. Matrix structures also incorporate the same sort of duplication of effort—multiple sales forces, for instance—that make divisional structures so expensive to operate. Moreover, because employees near the top must deal with two bosses and often conflicting orders, working in a matrix is a stressful situation. It can lead to absenteeism, turnover, and ultimately to lowered productivity and higher human resource costs.

More important, however, matrix structures are economically inefficient, because they rely on mutual adjustment as their primary coordination mechanism despite extremely costly levels of process loss. Matrix structuring thus represents the decision to put up with costly coordination in order to secure high flexibility. Firms that choose matrix structures and function effectively thereafter are generally those that face radical change that would destroy them if they could not easily adapt to such change. Those firms include the Monsanto Company, Prudential Insurance, and the Chase Manhattan Bank. In effect, they are choosing the lesser of two evils—the inefficiency of a matrix rather than dissolution. Firms that try matrix organization but later abandon it do not face the degree of change required to justify the costs of the matrix approach. Among those firms have been Phillips Petroleum and Texas Instruments.

strategic business unit structure An extremely complex structure consisting of two or more autonomous strategic business units (SBUs), which themselves have complete organization structures.

Strategic Business Unit Structure. **Strategic business unit (SBU) structures** are a recent invention that offer an attractive alternative to matrix structuring. These structures encourage adaptability by *deintegrating* divisions of a large organization rather than by integrating functional and divisional elements, as the matrix structure does. SBU structures redefine divisions as autonomous, fully independent structures, called strategic business units, or SBUs. They allow divisions to fend for themselves with little or no interference from the rest of the firm. (Note that *SBU structure* refers to a complete organization structure while *SBU* refers to a single business entity within an SBU structure.) Thus an SBU structure is actually a "structure of structures." Each SBU has its own relatively complete organization structure, and its chief reports to an upper-level manager in the hierarchy of the parent corporation. An SBU may have a simple or functional structure. or even a divisional structure if its parent is a very large organization. Divisional SBUs can be created by combining several divisions from the parent structure into the same strategic business unit.

Figure 16-9 shows an SBU structure. Such structures are quite *decentralized*. SBU managers three or four levels below the parent firm's CEO may have broad decision-making authority. At the same time, SBU structures are coordinated through *standardization*. Thus they are characterized by high degrees of bureaucratic *formalization* and *specialization*. They have extremely *tall hierarchies* and are organized around *divisional departmentation*. As we've already noted, however, each of an SBU structure's "divisions" is actually a self-sufficient business concern.

A major strength of SBU structures is their ability to provide the coordination required to integrate large or extremely large organizations without incurring the inefficiency of matrix structuring. Thus, prior to its mid-1980s breakup, Beatrice had an SBU structure. General Electric still does and is experimenting with ways to improve it. A weakness of SBU structures, however, is the requirement that top managers give up control over day-to-day operations within each SBU. They retain only the ability to sell laggard SBUs or to buy attractive ones from other companies. Although this might sound like a small price to pay for needed flexibility, it has discouraged the adoption of SBU structures in many instances. Another deterrent to the use of this type of organization is the fact that even SBU structures have some degree of inefficiency inasmuch as their divisional departmentation means substantial duplication of effort. A final drawback is that SBU structures are not useful when strong links are needed between the different parts of an organization. For example, it is difficult to imagine organizing a hospital as an SBU structure. Too many transfers are required among the units of a hospital to allow any of them to have the autonomy of an SBU.

FIGURE 16-9

The Strategic Business Unit (SBU) Structure

The SBU structure resembles a divisional structure in which each "division"—an SBU—is itself an autonomous firm with a functional, divisional, or matrix structure.

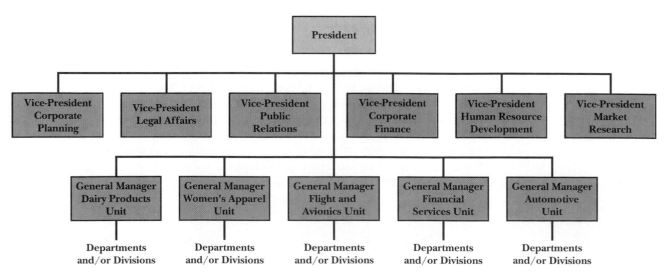

ORGANIZATION DESIGN

TABLE 16-2
Diagnostic Design Chart I: Organizational Structure

Structural Type	COORDINATION MECHANISMS			BUREAUCRATIC CORRELATES		OTHER CHARACTERISTICS			OUTCOMES	
	Mutual Adjustment	Direct Supervision	Standardization	Formalization	Specialization	Centralization	Hierarchy	Departmentation Scheme	Efficiency	Flexibility
Simple undifferentiated	Primary	None	None	Absent	Absent	Low	Flat	None	Low-high*	High
Simple differentiated	Secondary	Primary	None	Absent	Absent	High	Flat	None	Low-high*	High
Functional	Secondary	Secondary	Primary	Present	Present	High	Tall	Functional	High	Low
Divisional	Secondary	Secondary	Primary	Present	Present	Moderate	Tall	Divisional	Moderate	Moderate
Matrix	Primary and Secondary	Secondary	Secondary	Present	Present	Low	Tall	Simultaneous	Extremely low	High
SBU	Secondary	Secondary	Primary	Present	Present	Low	Tall	Divisional	Low	High

* Note: Simple structures are highly efficient at handling simple work but inefficient when complex work must be performed.

Diagnostic Design Chart I

Table 16-2 reviews the six organizational structures we have described, indicating how the different structural characteristics explained in Chapter 15 fit together to form each structural type. We said earlier that organizational structures vary along a scale ranging from mechanistic to organic. Which of these six structural types do you think is the most mechanistic? Which is the most organic? Where do the others fit into the mechanistic-organic dimension we have proposed?

The most straightforward way to address these questions is to look at Table 16-2 and review the type of coordination used in each of the six structures. Bear in mind that mechanistic structures rely mainly on standardization, while organic structures are based primarily on mutual adjustment.[12] Centralization is also a useful indicator, because mechanistic structures tend to be more centralized than organic ones. Let's review the different structural types in the order in which they appear on the continuum in Figure 16-10, moving from the most mechanistic—the functional structure—to the most organic—the simple undifferentiated structure.

> *Functional* structures are the most mechanistic, because they are highly centralized and use standardization as their primary mechanism of unit coordination.
> *Divisional* structures, which also use standardization as their primary unit

[12] Henry Mintzberg, *The Structuring of Organizations* (Englewood Cliffs, N.J.: Prentice-Hall, 1979), p. 86.

FIGURE 16-10
A Continuum of Organization Structures

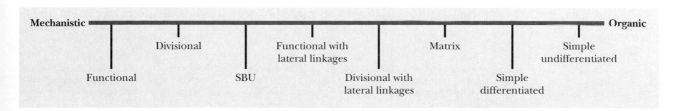

coordination mechanism, are basically mechanistic, but they are slightly more organic than functional structures because they are less centralized.

SBU structures are somewhat mechanistic, because they are based primarily on standardization. But because they are highly decentralized, they are more organic than divisional structures.

Matrix structures rely on mechanistic standardization beneath their upper layers. They are no more decentralized than SBU structures, but they are more organic, because they use mutual adjustment to coordinate activities at the top.

Simple differentiated structures are more organic than matrix structures because they do not use standardization. On the other hand, because they are centralized, they are not completely organic.

Simple undifferentiated structures are the most organic of all, because they rely solely on mutual adjustment and are completely decentralized.

Functional and divisional structures can be made more organic with the use of *lateral linkage devices* that coordinate interunit relations through mutual adjustment or direct supervision (these devices are discussed in Chapter 15). As shown in Figure 16-10, these modified structures then fit between the SBU and matrix structures on our continuum, yielding a total of eight structural alternatives. These eight alternatives form a menu of possibilities available for consideration during the process of organization design.

CONTINGENCY FACTORS

We turn our attention now to the three contingency factors that have the greatest influence on whether a particular form of structure will contribute to organizational effectiveness. They are organization size, core technology, and the external environment. We will begin by discussing the effects of organization size and, in the process, will also examine the related effects of the age of an organization and its stage of life-cycle development.

Organization Size

organization size The number of members in an organization; its volume of sales, clients, or profits; its physical capacity (e.g., a hospital's number of beds or a hotel's number of rooms); or the total financial assets that it controls.

Organization size can be defined as the number of members in an organization; its volume of sales, clients, or profits; its physical capacity (e.g., a hospital's number of beds or a hotel's number of rooms); or the total financial assets it controls.[13] In keeping with our focus on structural coordination, we will adopt the first definition. We will consider *size* to be the number of members or employees within the organization and thus the number of people whose activities must be integrated and coordinated.

The size of an organization affects its structure mainly by determining which of the three coordination mechanisms that we discussed in Chapter 15 is most appropriate as the primary means of unit coordination in the organization. The three mechanisms, you will recall, are mutual adjustment, direct supervision, and standardization. (Size also has direct effects on organizational performance. See the "In Practice" box.) In extremely small organizations of 12 or fewer people, mutual adjustment alone can provide adequate coordination without incurring

---

[13] John R. Kimberly, "Organizational Size and the Structuralist Perspective: A Review, Critique, and Proposal," *Administrative Science Quarterly* 21 (1976), 571–97; Patricia Yancy Martin, "Size in Residential Service Organizations," *Sociological Quarterly* 20 (1979), 569–79; and Gooding and Wagner, "A Meta-Analytic Review," p. 463.

IN PRACTICE

Organization Size and Performance: Is Bigger Better?

When it comes to organizations, what size is "just right?" Experience at AT&T seems to suggest that smaller is better. The telephone company has downsized significantly in the last six years, shrinking by 92,000 to its current size of 281,000. Though still enormous, AT&T's smaller size has enabled its fewer remaining employees to make more decisions themselves and react more quickly to customer needs. Customer response appears positive. Other once-giant firms, ranging from Johnson & Johnson to Hewlett-Packard Company have similarly downsized or reorganized into smaller groups to foster flexibility and innovation.*

However, the success of other companies seems to suggest that bigger is better. The Illinois Tool Works, a manufacturer of nuts, bolts, nails, and screws, succeeds precisely because of its largeness. By reducing prices and maintaining high production volumes, the firm blocks other potential competitors from entering its midwestern fastener market.† More generally, the 500 largest companies in the United States ac-

count for one-third of the nation's gross national product and employ three-quarters of the scientists and engineers who work in industry (encouraging creativity and innovation). Companies like General Motors, USX, and General Electric have the resources to do things that smaller firms can't—incubating new-product ideas for years, surviving through periods of temporary adversity, rewarding successful employees with career promotions.‡

Although current trends seem to favor downsizing, research actually indicates that larger organizations produce more goods or services than smaller organizations. At the same time, though, they are *not* any more efficient than smaller firms. It takes 100 employees to do 100 employees' worth of work, regardless of the overall size of the organization. Thus, from the standpoint of overall performance, bigger appears to be better, but managers who expect some net gain in efficiency from size changes of any sort are likely to be disappointed.§

* Claudia H. Deutsch, "Less Is Becoming More at AT&T," *New York Times*, June 3, 1990, 25.

† Ronald Henkoff, "The Ultimate Nuts and Bolts Company," *Fortune*, July 16, 1990, pp. 70–73.

‡ John A. Byrne, "Is Your Company Too Big?" *Business Week*, March 27, 1989, pp. 84–94.

§ Gooding and Wagner, "A Meta-Analytic Review," p. 478.

---

overwhelming process loss. Thus small organizations of this sort can have simple undifferentiated structures and survive without additional structural mechanisms.

If more than about a dozen people try to coordinate by means of mutual adjustment alone, however, so much time, energy, and other resources are diverted away from productive activities and into coordination procedures that performance declines substantially. As we noted in Chapter 15, the activities of larger numbers of people—30, 40, or even 50—can be coordinated instead by direct supervision. This reduces the amount of time and effort that must be devoted to coordination. Simple differentiated structures are ideally suited for this slightly larger organization.

What happens when an organization exceeds 50 people? As you might guess, both simple undifferentiated structures and simple differentiated structures are

The U.S. Postal Service is such a huge organization—it has nearly 700,000 employees—that **standardization** *has to be its primary mode of coordination. Yet technological-environmental changes demand constant flexibility, something this highly bureaucratic organization does not have. Repeated raises in rates have led many large mailers to desert the Postal Service for lower-priced delivery services. But the powerful American Postal Workers Union has so far prevented the elimination of many jobs that new technology could replace. What do you think the postal service can do to improve its efficiency, cut costs, and keep its workers motivated and happy?*
Source: Susan B. Garland and Mark Lewyn, "Can Tony Frank Get Postal Workers to Cut Him Some Slack?" Business Week, *August 27, 1990.*

overwhelmed by coordination requirements. As the primary means of unit coordination, mutual adjustment becomes extremely expensive, and direct supervision is bogged down by growing information-processing needs. Standardization thus assumes the role of primary unit coordination mechanism, and the organization takes on a complex form of structure. Whether the most effective structure for a company will be a functional or divisional structure depends on the effects of the other contingency factors, which we will discuss below.

Finally, in extremely large organizations of thousands of employees, standardization sometimes proves inadequate as the primary means of unit coordination. The reason is the difficulty of formalizing the wide variety of activities that must go on during the normal course of business. In such "super organizations," standardization may be replaced by the mutual adjustment of matrix structuring if business activities have to remain integrated across different functions and markets. Alternatively, SBU structuring may be used to decouple parts of an extremely large organization, creating several smaller, more easily managed, strategic business units.

life-cycle model A model that proposes that organizational growth progresses through a series of stages, each of which has its own structural requirements.

Organization Age. Closely related to the size of an organization is its age. Increasing age tends to be positively related to greater size. Thus, a firm may require different structures as it grows older. This process of growing out of one structure and into another is captured quite explicitly in life-cycle models such as the one described next.

Organization Life Cycle. As proposed in the **life cycle model** developed by Robert Quinn and Kim Cameron, organizational growth progresses through a series of stages, each of which has its own structural requirements. In the *entrepreneur stage*, one person or a small group of people create an organization and identify the firm's initial purpose. As commitment to this purpose develops, initial planning and implementation bring the firm to life. There is little, if any, formal coordination. Usually mutual adjustment or direct supervision suffices as the primary means of unit coordination. So, at this stage, the firm can be organized as a *simple undifferentiated* or *simple differentiated structure*.

An organization experiences rapid growth in the *collectivity stage*. To cope with changes stemming from the growth of their firm and provide stability, members begin to routinize activities. At the same time, members spend long hours at work and develop a strong sense of identification with the organization and its mission. Communication and structural relations remain informal, and the organization may retain a simple structure, but the newly developing rules and procedures indicate the beginning of formalization.

The *formalization stage* is characterized by the division of work into different functional areas, the development of systematic evaluation and reward procedures, and formal planning and goal setting to determine the organization's direction. Professional managers may replace the firm's owners as the day-to-day bosses who run the company. Management emphasizes efficiency and stability, and work becomes even more routine. In the process, the organization adopts a *functional structure*.

To adapt to changing conditions and to pursue continued growth, a firm in the *elaboration stage* may seek out new product, location, or client opportunities. As the company's business diversifies, its functional structure loses the ability to coordinate work activities, and there is a need for divisional departmentation and greater decentralization. The organization may then adopt a *divisional structure*. If the firm continues to mature even further, continued growth and diversification may require additional structural elaboration. The company may then adopt a *matrix* or *SBU structure* to cope with its greater size or with its need for greater flexibility.

608

Diagnostic Design Chart II

As you can see, the larger an organization becomes, the more likely it is to develop increasingly complex structures. As it ages, then, it tends to become more formalized, standardized, and specialized. Age pushes firms toward the adoption of functional, divisional, matrix, or SBU structures. Youth may allow companies to perform effectively with simple undifferentiated or simple differentiated structures. The chart in Table 16-3 reviews the stages of development described in the Quinn-Cameron model. It puts into life-cycle terms the influence of changes in organizational size and age.

Core Technology

technology The knowledge, procedures, and equipment used in an organization to transform unprocessed resources into finished goods or services.

core technology The dominant technology used in performing work at the base of the organization.

An organization's **technology** consists of the *knowledge*, *procedures*, and *equipment* used to transform unprocessed resources into finished goods or services.[14] **Core technology** is a more specific term, pertaining to the dominant technology used in performing work at the base of the organization. You can find core technologies in the assembly lines on which cars are manufactured at GM, Ford, and Chrysler; in the kitchens where fast foods are prepared at McDonald's, Burger King, and Wendy's; in the offices in state employment agencies and job-training centers where job applicants are processed and in the reactor buildings where electricity is generated at nuclear power plants. In this section, we introduce two contingency models—the *Woodward manufacturing model* and the *Thompson service model*. They propose that core technology influences the effectiveness of an organization by placing certain coordination requirements on its structure.

Woodward's Manufacturing Technologies. Joan Woodward, a British researcher who started studying organizations in the early 1950s, was one of the

[14] Charles Perrow, "A Framework for the Comparative Analysis of Organizations," *American Sociological Review* 32 (1967), 194–208; and Denise Rousseau, "Assessment of Technology in Organizations: Closed versus Open System Approaches," *Academy of Management Review* 4 (1979), 531–42.

TABLE 16-3
Diagnostic Design Chart II: Stages in the Structural Life Cycle

STAGE	PRIMARY CHARACTERISTICS	STRUCTURAL TYPES
Entrepreneur	Determination of firm's purpose Growth of commitment Initial planning and implementation Reliance on mutual adjustment	Simple undifferentiated Simple differentiated
Collectivity	Rapid growth and change Development of routine activities Appearance of rules and procedures	Simple undifferentiated Simple differentiated
Formalization	Division of work into functions Systematic evaluation and rewards Formal planning and goal setting Entry of professional management Emphasis on efficiency, stability	Functional
Elaboration	Search for new opportunities Diversification, decentralization Maturation and continued growth	Divisional Matrix SBU structure

Source: Based on Robert E. Quinn and Kim Cameron, "Organizational Life Cycles and Shifting Criteria of Effectiveness: Some Preliminary Evidence," *Management Science* 29 (1983), 29–34.

first proponents of the view that an organization's technology can have tremendous impact on structural effectiveness.[15] She began her work by studying 100 British manufacturing firms, examining their organizational structures and their relative efficiency and success in the marketplace. Analyzing her data, she discovered that not all companies that had the same type of structure were equally effective. Hypothesizing that these differences in effectiveness might be traced to differences in core technologies, Woodward devised a classification scheme of three basic types of manufacturing technology—*small-batch production*, *mass production*, and *continuous process production*. When she tested her theory by reanalyzing data from the 100 firms she found evidence to support it.

small-batch production A type of manufacturing technology that involves the production of one-of-a-kind items or small quantities of goods designed to meet unique customer specifications. Also called unit production.

SMALL-BATCH PRODUCTION **Small-batch production** (also called *unit production*) is a technology that involves the manufacture of one-of-a-kind items or small quantities of goods designed to meet unique customer specifications. Such items range from specialized electronic instruments, weather satellites, and space shuttles to custom-tailored clothing and custom-made leather sandals. To make this kind of product, craftspeople work alone or in small, close-knit groups. Because customer specifications often change from one order to another, it is almost impossible to predict what will be required on the next job. Thus the work in firms using small-batch technologies varies in an unpredictable way.

It is this unpredictability that fuels the effect of small-batch technologies on organizational structures and effectiveness. Unpredictability impedes advance planning and therefore makes it difficult to coordinate by means of standardization. It is impossible to plan legitimate standards for use in a future that cannot be foreseen. Instead, employees must decide for themselves how to perform their jobs. When employees work alone, they are guided by their own skills and expertise and by customer specifications. When employees work in groups, they coordinate with one another by means of mutual adjustment.

Woodward found that the important role played by mutual adjustment in coordinating small-batch production was pivotal. Her research showed that among organizations using this type of technology, firms with organic structures were significantly more likely to be successful than companies with mechanistic structures. This suggests that an organization employing small-batch technology would be wise to adopt one of the structures found on the right side of the continuum in Figure 16-10. A simple, matrix, or laterally linked functional or divisional structure may help a company with small-batch production technology be more effective. Similarly, because every SBU in an SBU structure is itself an organization with its own structure and technology, each SBU using small-batch technology should opt for an organic form of structure—again, one of the types found on the right side of Figure 16-10.

mass production A type of manufacturing technology in which the same product is produced repeatedly, either in large batches or in long production runs. Also called large-batch production.

MASS PRODUCTION In **mass production** (also referred to as *large-batch production*), the same product is produced repeatedly, either in large batches or in long production runs. For instance, rather than producing a few copies of this book each time an order was received, Prentice Hall initially printed thousands of copies at the same time and warehoused them to fill incoming orders. Other examples of mass production range from word-processing pools in which midterm examinations are consolidated and typed in large batches to car-manufacturing operations in which hundreds of thousands of Ford Escorts are made on an assembly line that remains virtually unchanged for years at a time.

As these examples suggest, work in mass production technologies is intentionally repetitive and remains so over the course of extended periods of time.

---

[15] Joan Woodward, *Management and Technology* (London: Her Majesty's Stationery Office, 1958). See also Woodward's *Industrial Organization: Theory and Practice* (London: Oxford University Press, 1975).

Employees perform the same jobs over and over. They know that the work they'll do tomorrow will be the same as the work done today. This stability and routineness facilitates planning and formalization. As a result, a company is likely to use standardization to reduce the long-term costs of coordination. Woodward's research thus revealed that mass-production firms with mechanistic structures were far more likely to be effective than those with organic structures. Therefore, structures on the left side of our continuum—functional or divisional structures—are more apt to enhance the effectiveness of firms or SBUs employing mass production than are structures on the right side of the continuum.

continuous process production
A type of manufacturing technology in which automated equipment makes the same product in the same way for an indefinite period of time.

CONTINUOUS PROCESS PRODUCTION In **continuous process production**, automated equipment makes the same product in the same way for an indefinite period of time. For example, at Phillips Petroleum, one refinery makes nothing but gasoline, another refines motor oil, and a third produces only diesel fuel. The equipment used in this type of technology is designed to produce one product and cannot readily be used for any other. Moreover, there is no starting and stopping once the equipment has been installed. Machines in continuous process facilities perform the same tasks without interruption.

Of the three types of technology discussed so far, continuous process production involves the most routine work. Few changes, if any, occur in production processes even over the course of many years. You might expect, then, that organizations using continuous process production would be most effective if structured along mechanistic lines. Interestingly, however, closer examination reveals that few, if any, of the people involved in continuous process production perform routine, repetitive jobs. Machines perform these jobs instead. The people are technicians, who monitor production equipment—watching dials and gauges, checking machinery, inspecting finished goods—and who deal with the problems that arise when this equipment fails to function properly. Although some of these problems occur again and again and can be planned for in advance, a significant number are emergencies that have never happened before and cannot be anticipated. Some of the most critical work performed by people in continuous process production technologies is therefore highly unpredictable, and as a result, standardization is not feasible. Mutual adjustment, sometimes in conjunction with direct supervision, is the dominant mode of coordination. Technicians who oversee production equipment manage unusual events by conferring with each other and devising solutions to emergencies as they arise.

Therefore, Woodward's finding that firms using continuous process production technologies were most effective when structured organically is not surprising. We can conclude that structures on the right side of the continuum shown in Figure 16-10—simple, matrix, or laterally linked functional or divisional structures—are the ones most likely to encourage effectiveness in organizations or SBUs that use continuous process production.

flexible cell production A type of manufacturing technology in which a cell of computer-controlled production machines are connected together by a flexible network of conveyors that can be rapidly reconfigured for different production tasks.

FLEXIBLE CELL PRODUCTION: A RECENT DEVELOPMENT Since Woodward's studies, advances in computers, robotics, and automation have helped create another type of manufacturing technology, **flexible cell production**. In this system, a group, or cell, of computer-controlled production machines are connected by a flexible network of conveyors. These conveyors can be rapidly reconfigured to adapt the cell for different production tasks. This technology is used mainly to produce a wide variety of machined metal parts—pistons for car engines, hinges for the passenger entries of jet planes, parts for the lock on the front door of your house or apartment. Conceivably, though, it could be used to make virtually any kind of product.

As in continuous process production, work in flexible cells is performed by automated equipment. The only people involved are technicians who monitor the equipment and handle problems. But while continuous process production facilities can make only a single product, flexible cells can make many different things. In this respect, flexible cell production resembles small-batch production. It is an efficient method of producing one-of-a-kind items or small quantities of similar items built to satisfy unique customer specifications.

Inasmuch as Woodward found mutual adjustment the most effective co-ordination mechanism for both continuous process and small-batch production technologies, an organic structure would seem most suitable for a firm using flexible cell production. Indeed, a study of 110 manufacturing firms in New Jersey revealed a significant positive relationship between organic structuring and the effectiveness of organizations with flexible cells.[16] We can use this information to update Woodward's research. Referring to Figure 16-10, we will suggest that companies or SBUs employing flexible cell technologies are likely to be more effective if they adopt simple, matrix, or laterally linked functional or divisional structures.

Thompson's Service Technologies. Because Woodward focused her research solely on manufacturing firms, her contingency model is applicable only to technologies used to produce tangible goods. Today, however, firms that provide services—telephone communications, appliance repair, vacation planning—make up an increasingly critical element of the United States economy as well as the economies of other nations. Thus another contingency model, developed by James D. Thompson, is also quite useful, because it examines technologies often employed in service organizations. These technologies, diagrammed in Figure 16-11, are mediating technology, long-linked technology, and intensive technology.[17]

[16] Frank M. Hull and Paul D. Collins, "High Technology Batch Production Systems: Woodward's Missing Type," *Academy of Management Journal* 30 (1987), 786–97.

[17] Thompson, *Organizations in Action, pp. 15–18.*

FIGURE 16-11

Thompson's Service Technologies

This figure depicts the three service technologies identified by Thompson. Rectangles represent work groups or organizations, circles represent employees, and arrows represent work flows. These diagrams form a measure of core technology if preceded by instructions to respondents to choose the picture that best illustrates the way work is performed in their organizations.

A Mediating Technology

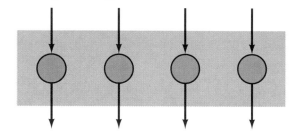

B Long-Linked Technology

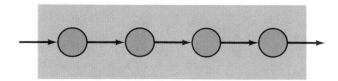

C Intensive Technology

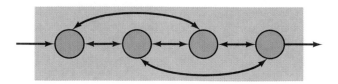

MEDIATING TECHNOLOGY A mediating technology provides services that link clients together. For example, banks connect depositors who have money to invest with borrowers who need loans; insurance companies enable their clients to pool risks, permitting one person's losses to be covered by joint investments; and telephone companies provide the equipment and technical assistance people need to talk with each other from separate locations.

When mediating technology is used to provide a service, employees usually serve each client individually. For instance, bank tellers serve customers one at a time. Consequently, as depicted in Figure 16-11A, bank tellers and workers in other mediating technologies normally perform their jobs without assistance from others in their organization. Assuming adequate training, a single bank teller can handle a deposit or withdrawal without requiring help from other tellers. She and other workers, however, may share equipment, such as the central computer that keeps track of all bank transactions.

Although in the service organization individual employees work independently, many perform the same job. Coordination in such firms is needed to make sure that workers provide a consistently high quality of service and offer the same basic service to each client. Thus managers in service firms develop lists of the different types of clients their organization is likely to serve and devise a particular standard operating procedure to be followed while serving each type of client. For example, a bank teller will follow one procedure while serving a client who is making a savings account deposit, another procedure when waiting on a client who is making a loan payment, and yet a third when helping a client open a new checking account. This standardization of work processes or behaviors means that firms or SBUs using mediating technologies to coordinate worker-client relationships are most likely to be effective when structured mechanistically. Going back to our continuum in Figure 16-10, it would appear that either functional or divisional structures would be most suitable for such firms or SBUs.

LONG-LINKED TECHNOLOGY Thompson's long-linked technology is analogous to Woodward's mass production technology. Both refer to sequential chains of simplified tasks. A service-sector example of this type of technology is the state employment agency that requires all clients to follow the same lock-step procedures. Each client moves along an "assembly line" starting with registration and progressing through assessment, counseling, training, and placement activities. Another example of long-linked technology in a service organization consists of the in-person registration procedures used at some universities. If you haven't experienced this sort of registration yourself, imagine moving along a line of tables, picking up courses at one, having identification pictures taken at another, buying meal passes at a third, and making tuition payments at a fourth. The sort of sequential movement—from one table or station to the next—that characterizes long-linked technology is diagrammed in Figure 16-11B.

Like firms that use mass-production technology, those that use long-linked technology coordinate by means of standardization. According to Thompson, the effectiveness of a firm using long-linked technology is likely to be enhanced by mechanistic structuring. Our continuum suggests, therefore, that long-linked technology will be most effectively paired with functional or divisional structures.

INTENSIVE TECHNOLOGY Intensive technology consists of work processes whose configuration may change as employees receive feedback from the clients they serve. The specific assortment of services to be rendered to a particular patient in a hospital, for example, depends on the symptoms this particular patient exhibits. A patient entering the hospital's emergency room complaining of chest pains may be rushed to an operating room and then to a cardiac-care unit. A patient with a broken arm may be shuttled from the emergency room to the radiology lab for an x ray and then back to the emergency room for splinting. A third patient with uncertain symptoms may be checked into a room for further observation and testing (see Figure 16-11C).

To fit itself to the needs of each client, a firm using intensive technology must be able to reorganize itself again and again. So above all, it must have flexibility. And because the needs of future clients cannot be foretold, the work of such a firm is too unpredictable to be successfully formalized. Both flexibility and unpredictability require the use of mutual adjustment as a coordinating mechanism. Thus firms using intensive technology will be best suited by structures located toward the right side of our continuum. They will require simple or matrix structures or else, laterally linked functional or divisional structures.

Diagnostic Decision Chart III

The Woodward and Thompson technology models we have discussed will be important to you as a manager. They help to identify which organization structure is most likely to enhance the effectiveness of a firm using a specific type of technology. The main points of these models are summarized in the diagnostic design chart shown in Table 16-4. As indicated in this table, standardization and mechanistic structuring generally enhance the effectiveness of firms using technologies that are suited to more-routine work—mass production, mediating, and long-linked technologies. Mutual adjustment, on the other hand, promotes effectiveness in firms that use technologies suited to unpredictable, often rapidly changing requirements—small batch, continuous process, flexible cell and intensive technologies.[18] As we would expect, and as Table 16-4 shows, the first group of technologies tend to be best served by the mechanistic type of structure (found on the left side of our Figure 16-10 continuum), the second group by the organic structural type (found on the right side of the continuum).

[18] Charles Perrow, "A Framework for the Comparative Analysis of Organizations," *American Sociological Review* 32 (1967), 194–208; Raymond G. Hunt, "Technology and Organization," *Academy of Management Journal* 13 (1970), 235–52; and William H. Starbuck, "Organizational Growth and Development," in *Handbook of Organizations*, ed. J. G. March (New York: Rand McNally, 1965), Chapter 11.

TABLE 16-4
Diagnostic Design Chart III: Technological Contingencies

| INDUSTRY TYPE | TECHNOLOGY | STRUCTURAL TYPE | SIZE | |
			SMALLER STRUCTURE	LARGER STRUCTURE
Manufacturing	Small batch	Organic	Simple*	Matrix
			Laterally linked functional	Laterally linked divisional
	Mass	Mechanistic	Functional	Divisional
	Continuous process	Organic	Simple*	Matrix
			Laterally linked functional	Laterally linked divisional
	Flexible Cell	Organic	Simple*	Matrix
			Laterally linked functional	Laterally linked divisional
Service	Mediating	Mechanistic	Functional	Divisional
	Long Linked	Mechanistic	Functional	Divisional
	Intensive	Organic	Simple*	Matrix
			Laterally linked functional	Laterally linked divisional

* Note: Simple structures may be either simple undifferentiated or simple differentiated.

The External Environment

environment The context surrounding an organization, consisting of economic, geographic, and political conditions that impinge on the firm.

An organization's **environment** consists of everything outside the organization. Suppliers, customers, and competitors are part of an organization's environment as are the governmental bodies that regulate its business, the financial institutions and stockholders that supply it with funding, and the labor market that provides it with employees. In addition, general factors such as the economic, geographic, and political conditions that impinge on the firm are part of its environment. Central to this definition is the idea that the term *environment* refers to things external to the firm. The internal "environment" of a firm, more appropriately called the company's culture, will be discussed in Chapter 18.

As a structural contingency factor, an organization's environment influences the effectiveness of its structure by placing certain coordination and information-processing requirements on the firm. Five specific environmental characteristics influence structural effectiveness—environmental change, complexity, uncertainty, hostility, and diversity.

environmental change An environmental characteristic concerning the extent to which conditions in an organization's environment change unpredictably.

Environmental Change. **Environmental change** concerns the extent to which conditions in an organization's environment change unpredictably. At one extreme, an environment is stable if it does not change at all or if it changes only in a cyclical, predictable way. An example of such a stable environment is the one that surrounds many of the small firms in Amish communities throughout the midwestern United States. Amish religious beliefs require the rejection of modern conveniences, such as automobiles, televisions, and automated farm equipment. So Amish blacksmiths, dry-goods merchants, and livestock breeders have conducted business in much the same way for generations. Another stable environment is that surrounding firms that sell Christmas trees. The retail market for cut evergreen trees is predictably strong in November and December but absent at other times of the year.

At the other extreme, an environment is dynamic when it changes over time in an unpredictable manner. Because the style of dress changes so frequently in societies like ours, the environment surrounding companies in the fashion industry is quite dynamic. Similarly, the environment surrounding companies in the consumer-electronics industry has changed dramatically. New products, such as projection television, videotape machines, and Walkman radios, have created entirely new markets. Older products have been redesigned to incorporate computer microchips, digital displays, infrared remote controls, and similar technological breakthroughs.

Environmental change affects the structure of an organization by influencing the predictability of the firm's work and, therefore, the method of coordination

Videoconferencing may become an increasingly important way of coordinating an organization's workflow as firms continue to establish departments, divisions, and subsidiaries in locations far from headquarters offices. PictureTel of Peabody, Massachusetts, has developed a video system that can accommodate the starts, stops, and interruptions of normal conversation, even when people seem to be talking all at once. In addition, a "windowing feature" lets people see themselves as they appear to conference participants at the other end of the line.
Source: "Videoconferencing Gets Cheaper," Fortune, March 11, 1991, p. 76.

used to integrate work activities.[19] Stability allows managers to complete the planning needed to formalize organizational activities. One can predict and plan for variation when it is cyclical in nature. Firms operating in stable environments can use standardization as their primary coordination mechanism and will typically elect to do so to reduce long-term coordination costs. Mechanistic structures are the most likely to prove effective in such instances.

In addition, as with the technological contingencies discussed earlier, each SBU in an SBU structure has its own environment and should therefore be structured in accordance with that environment. Thus an SBU dealing with a stable environment should have a mechanistic structure.

In a dynamic environment, it is difficult to establish formal rules and procedures. In fact, it is useless for managers to try to plan for a future they cannot foresee. Members of an organization or SBU facing a dynamic environment must adapt to changing conditions instead of relying on inflexible, standardized operating procedures. Dynamism in the environment leaves management with little choice but to rely on mutual adjustment as a primary coordination mechanism. Organic structuring is therefore appropriate.

environmental complexity An environmental characteristic referring to the degree to which an organization's environment is complicated and therefore difficult to understand.

Environmental Complexity. **Environmental complexity** is the degree to which an organization's environment is complicated and therefore difficult to understand. A simple environment is composed of relatively few component parts—for example, suppliers, competitors, types of customers. So there is not much that can affect organizational performance. A local Amoco gas station does business in a relatively simple environment. It orders most of its supplies from a single petroleum distributor, does business almost exclusively with customers who want to buy gasoline or oil for their cars, and can limit its attention on the competitive activities of a fairly small number of nearby stations. On the other hand, a complex environment consists of a large number of component parts. The environments of aviation firms like Boeing and McDonnell Douglas are extremely complex, including an enormous number of suppliers, many different types of customers, and scores of foreign and domestic competitors.

Complexity influences structural effectiveness by affecting the amount of knowledge and information people must process to understand the environment and cope with its demands.[20] Consider an inexpensive digital watch. If you took this watch apart, you would probably not have much trouble putting it back together again, because it has very few parts—a computer chip programmed to keep time, a digital liquid-crystal face, a battery, and a case. With only a few minutes of practice or simple instructions, you could quickly learn to assemble this watch. Now suppose you had the pieces of a Rolex watch spread out before you. Could you reassemble the watch? Probably not, because it is made up of hundreds of springs, screws, gears, and other parts. Learning to assemble a Rolex properly would require intensive training.

Similarly, the organization facing a simple environment—one with few "parts"—can understand environmental events and meet the challenges they pose using a minimal amount of knowledge and processing little new information. For instance, a local lawn-care firm that is losing business can determine the reason for its plight simply by telephoning a few former customers and asking

---

[19] Burns and Stalker, *The Management of Innovation*; C. R. Hinings, D. J. Hickson, J. M. Pennings, and R. E. Schneck, "Structural Conditions of Intraorganizational Power," *Administrative Science Quarterly* 19 (1974), 22–44; Robert B. Duncan, "Multiple Decision-Making Structures in Adapting to Environmental Uncertainty: The Impact of Organizational Effectiveness," *Human Relations* 26 (1973), 273–91.

[20] Robert B. Duncan, "Characteristics of Organizational Environments and Perceived Environmental Uncertainty," *Administrative Science Quarterly* 17 (1972), 313–27; and Jay R. Galbraith, *Designing Complex Organizations* (Reading, Mass.: Addison-Wesley, 1973), pp. 4–6.

them why they stopped using the company's service. However, organizations in complex environments—environments with many "parts"—must draw on a considerable store of knowledge and process an overwhelming amount of information to understand environmental events. To find the reason for their loss of market share in the early 1980s and again in the late 1980s, Chrysler Corporation analyzed competitors' marketing strategies and performed extensive market studies of consumer preferences. To recapture market share, Chrysler also worked with hundreds of suppliers to increase the quality and reduce the cost of the parts used to produce its cars.

How does environmental complexity affect organizational structures? Simply stated, environmental complexity influences the suitability of centralization as an interunit coordination mechanism. As you will recall from Chapter 15, in centralization, decision making is limited to a select group of top managers. Centralization thus minimizes the number of people available to digest information and determine its meaning. Because simple environments require little information processing, organizations operating in such environments can be centralized and function quite effectively. However, because environmental complexity requires the ability to process and understand large amounts of information, centralized organizations in complex environments can suffer the effects of information overload. One way to cope with this information overload is to involve more individuals in information-processing activities. Thus organizations like Chrysler that are attempting to cope with complex environments often decentralize decision making. That way, they include more people—more brains—in the process of digesting and interpreting information.

environmental uncertainty An environmental characteristic formed by the combination of change and complexity that reflects the absence of information about environmental factors, activities, and events.

Environmental Uncertainty. In addition to pointing out distinctive environmental differences, the two environmental dimensions of change and complexity also combine to define yet another important environmental characteristic—**environmental uncertainty** (see Figure 16-12). Uncertainty reflects the absence of information about environmental factors, activities, and events.[21] It undermines

[21] Jay R. Galbraith, *Organization Design* (Reading, Mass.: Addison-Wesley, 1977), p. 4.

FIGURE 16-12

Environmental Uncertainty as a Function of Change and Complexity

The amount of change and complexity in an organization's environment affects the degree to which executives perceive the environment as uncertain. As this figure shows, greater change and increasing complexity contribute to higher levels of perceived uncertainty.
Based on Robert B. Duncan, "Characteristics of Perceived Environments and Perceived Environmental Uncertainty," Administrative Science Quarterly *17 (1972), 313–27.*

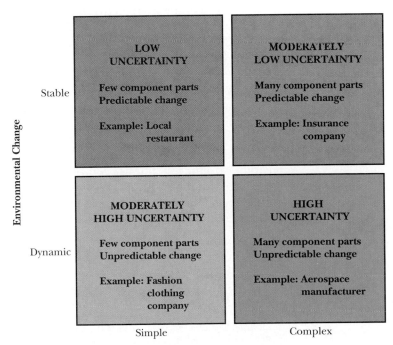

boundary spanner A member or unit of an organization that interacts with individuals or firms in the organization's environment.

an organization's ability to manage current circumstances and plan for the future. To cope with uncertainty, organizations try to find better ways of acquiring information about the environment. This effort often involves the creation of boundary-spanning positions that can strengthen the information linkage between an organization and its environment.

A **boundary spanner** is a member or unit of an organization that interacts with people or firms in the organization's environment.[22] Salespeople, who have contact with customers, purchasing departments that deal with suppliers of raw materials, and top managers who in their figurehead roles represent the company to outsiders are all boundary spanners. In boundary-spanning roles, employees or units

Monitor the environment for information that is relevant to the organization

Serve as gatekeepers, simplifying incoming information and ensuring that it is routed to the appropriate people in the firm

Warn the organization of environmental threats and initiate activities that protect it from them

Represent the organization to other individuals or firms in its environment, providing them with information about the organization

Negotiate with other organizations to acquire raw materials and sell finished goods or services

Coordinate any other activities that require the cooperation of two or more firms.[23]

These activities enable boundary spanners to provide the organization with information about its environment that can help make change and complexity more understandable. As a result, the organization can adapt to its environment instead of being overwhelmed by unexpected environmental events.

environmental receptivity The degree to which an organization's environment supports the organization's progress toward fulfilling its purpose.

Environmental Receptivity. **Environmental receptivity** is the degree to which an organization's environment supports the organization's progress toward fulfilling its purpose. In a munificent environment, a firm is able to acquire the raw materials, employees, technology, and capital resources needed to perform productively. In such an environment, the firm finds a receptive market for its products. Its competitors, if any, do not threaten its existence. Regulatory bodies do not try to impede its progress. Thus, for example, the environment surrounding the McDonald's fast-food chain at the time of its founding was munificent. Few other fast-food franchises existed, labor was fairly plentiful in the post-Korean war era, and a convenience-minded middle class was emerging throughout North America. Organizations involved in military contracting enjoyed this same munificent environment during the Reagan presidency.

In a hostile environment, the opposite situation obtains. An organization may have great difficulty acquiring, or may be unable to acquire, needed resources, employees, knowledge, or money. The firm's future may also be threatened by customer disinterest, intense competition, or severe regulation. During the early 1980s, for example, American auto producers faced an intensely hostile environment as U.S. consumers shunned Fords, Chryslers, and Chevys in favor of fuel-efficient Toyotas, Hondas, and Nissans. The Phillip-Morris Company and

[22] J. Stacy Adams, The Structure and Dynamics of Behavior in Organization Boundary Roles," in *Handbook of Industrial and Organizational Psychology*, ed. M. D. Dunnette (Chicago: Rand McNally, 1976), pp. 1175–99.

[23] Howard Aldrich and Diane Herker, "Boundary Spanning Roles and Organization Structure," *Academy of Management Review* 2 (1977), 217–39; Robert Miles, *Macro Organizational Behavior* (Santa Monica, Calif.: Goodyear, 1979), pp. 320–39; and Richard L. Daft and Richard M. Steers, *Organizations: A Micro/Macro Approach* (Glenview, Ill.: Scott, Foresman, 1986), p. 299.

Although organizations are influenced by their environments, the opposite is equally true. Organizations often attempt to influence their environments. For example:

Facing increasing public resistance and threatened anti-smoking legislation in many states and communities, Phillip-Morris began a series of advertisements extolling the importance of constitutional rights. The implicit message of these advertisements, printed and televised in 1989 and 1990, was that smoking is a personal choice with which government agencies should not interfere.
The savings and loan (S&L) bailout of the 1990s resulted from the deregulation of the 1980s. This deregulation developed as the S&L industry lobbied congressional regulation committees to allow S&Ls greater leeway in making loans to real estate partnerships and other speculative business ventures. The same industry supposedly controlled by federal regulations had a strong hand in developing those regulations.

Are activities of this sort right or wrong? Why? Are all attempts by organizations to influence the surrounding environment necessarily good or bad? How might society determine which (if any) of such activities are improper and guard against them? What is sacrificed when it becomes necessary to be on guard?

The same environment that created S&L failures also caused trouble in the general banking industry.

other members of the tobacco industry had to cope with extreme hostility later in the same decade. C. Everett Koop, then surgeon general of the United States, set a goal of eliminating smoking throughout North America by the year 2000 (see the "Management Issues" box for a related discussion).

Environmental hostility, though normally temporary, represents a crisis that must be dealt with quickly and effectively if the firm is to survive. An organization facing such hostility either finds a way to deal with it—for example, by substituting one raw material for another, marketing a new product, or lobbying against threatening regulations—or it ceases to exist. Thus American automobile manufacturers quickly designed smaller, higher-efficiency cars, such as the Ford Escort and Plymouth Reliant, and began to market them in the mid-1980s. Phillip-Morris in 1989 began a massive advertising campaign centered on the U.S. Constitution and "the freedom to choose."

To deal with the crisis of a hostile environment, firms that are normally decentralized because of environmental complexity will centralize decision making for a limited period of time.[24] This temporary centralization facilitates crisis management. Because it reduces the number of people who must be consulted to make a decision the organization can respond to threatening conditions more quickly. It is important to emphasize that centralization established in response to a hostile environment should remain in effect only so long as the hostility persists. When munificence reappears, a firm dealing with a complex environment will perform effectively only if it reinstates decentralized decision making.

[24] Mintzberg, *Structuring of Organizations*, p. 281.

environmental diversity The degree to which an organization's environment is varied or heterogeneous in nature.

environmental domain A part or segment of the environment in which an organization does business.

Environmental Diversity. **Environmental diversity** refers to the number of distinct **environmental domains** served by an organization. A firm in a uniform environment serves a single type of customer, provides a single kind of product, and conducts its business in a single geographic location. Thus it serves only a single domain. A campus nightclub, for example, that caters to the entertainment needs of local college students operates in a uniform environment. So does a building-materials firm whose sole product is concrete, which it sells only to local contractors. In contrast, an organization in a *diverse* environment produces an assortment of products, serves various types of customers, or has offices or other facilities in several geographic locations. It does business in several different domains. IBM, for instance, sells computers to businesses, universities, and the general public. General Electric handles consumer electronics, financial services, jet engines, and diesel locomotives. Ford Motor Company markets cars in North America, South America, and Europe.

Environmental diversity affects an organization by influencing the amount of diversity that must be built into its structure.[25] In organizations with uniform environments managers can use *functional* departmentation to group units together. Because firms in uniform environments face only a single domain, they need concern themselves only with information about a single kind of environment, and they need react to only a single set of environmental events. Functional departmentation, which facilitates this sort of unified information processing and response, is therefore sufficient in such situations. The absence of environmental diversity permits the firms to operate effectively without significant internal diversification.

In organizations with diverse environments, however, management must use divisional departmentation so as to gather work associated with each product, customer, or location into its own self-contained division. Companies in diverse environments face a number of distinct domains and must acquire information about each in order to cope with its particular demands. Divisional departmentation allows these firms to keep track of each domain separately and respond to the demands of one domain independently of others. If managers didn't structure the firm this way, work on one product could get in the way of work on other products, services rendered to one type of customer could detract from services provided to other types of customers, or operations at one location could impede operations at other locations.

Environmental uniformity, then, favors functional departmentation, therefore a functional structure. Environmental diversity requires divisional departmentation and either a divisional, matrix, or SBU structure, depending on other contingency factors. It is important to note that organizational size affects the likelihood that a firm will have to deal with appreciable environmental diversity. It's only when an organization has grown from a relatively small firm into a larger organization that it begins to evidence product, customer, or location diversity. Moreover, because a small firm has a simple structure and uses neither functional nor divisional departmentation, environmental diversity is not an issue for such an organization.

Diagnostic Design Chart IV

Environments have five distinct characteristics—change, complexity, uncertainty, receptivity, and diversity. Therefore, diagnosing the nature of a firm's environment during the process of organization design requires that managers do five environmental analyses more or less simultaneously. To help you perform this

[25] Thompson, *Organizations in Action*, pp. 25–38.

sort of diagnosis, we've devised the *decision tree* shown in Figure 16-13. If you trace through the branches of this tree as you answer each of the four questions we suggest, you will be led to the most suitable organizational structure for the environment you are diagnosing.

Each question deals with one of the environmental characteristics we have just examined. Note that we need not ask a separate question about uncertainty. Because it is a combination of change and complexity, uncertainty is assessed by the answers to questions 1 and 2 (see Figure 16-12).

1. *Is the environment stable or dynamic?* The answer to this question identifies the amount of change in the environment and helps to determine whether standardization or mutual adjustment is likely to be the more effective co-ordination mechanism for the firm under analysis. Stable environments either do not change or change in a predictable, cyclical manner and thus allow the use of standardization. Dynamic environments change in unpredictable ways and require mutual adjustment as a result.

2. *Is the environment simple or complex?* Here the answer will be an assessment of environmental complexity and will indicate whether centralization or decentralization is more appropriate for the firm. Simple environments are easy to figure out and allow centralization. Complex environments require

FIGURE 16-13

Diagnostic Decision Chart IV: Environmental Contingencies

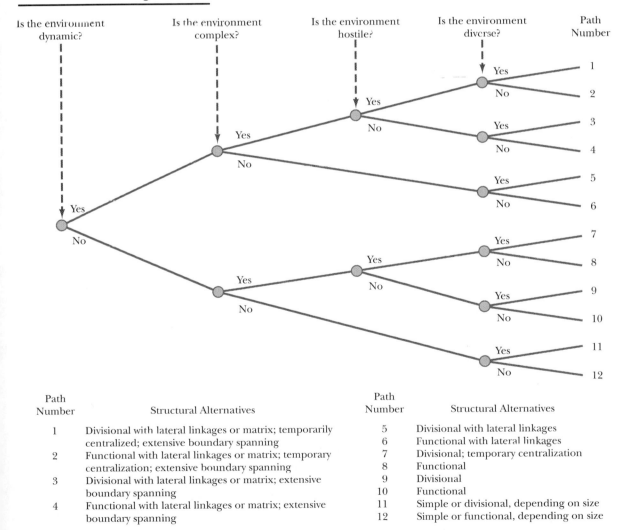

Path Number	Structural Alternatives	Path Number	Structural Alternatives
1	Divisional with lateral linkages or matrix; temporarily centralized; extensive boundary spanning	5	Divisional with lateral linkages
		6	Functional with lateral linkages
2	Functional with lateral linkages or matrix; temporary centralization; extensive boundary spanning	7	Divisional; temporary centralization
		8	Functional
3	Divisional with lateral linkages or matrix; extensive boundary spanning	9	Divisional
		10	Functional
4	Functional with lateral linkages or matrix; extensive boundary spanning	11	Simple or divisional, depending on size
		12	Simple or functional, depending on size

a great deal of information processing and therefore exert pressure toward decentralization.

3. *Is the environment munificent or hostile?* This question is relevant only if an organization has a complex environment and is thus decentralized. How it is answered gauges environmental receptivity and indicates whether temporary centralization is necessary. Munificent environments are resource rich and allow continued decentralization, but hostile environments are resource poor and stimulate crises that mandate temporary centralization.

4. *Is the environment uniform or diverse?* In response to this question, a manager must evaluate environmental diversity so as to determine what form of departmentation to use. Environmental uniformity allows the structural uniformity of functional departmentation. Environmental diversity requires the structural diversity of divisional departmentation.

SUMMARY

Organization design is the process of structuring an organization so as to enhance *organizational effectiveness* in the light of the *contingency factors* it faces. *Functional* and *divisional* structures are *mechanistic. Matrix, simple differentiated,* and *simple undifferentiated* structures are *organic. Strategic business unit* structures can combine both mechanistic and organic parts.

Whether an organization should have a mechanistic structure or an organic structure depends on the effects of *closed system contingency* factors within the organization, and on the influence of *open system contingency* factors outside of it.

One closed system contingency, the *size* of an organization in terms of the number of members it has, influences the amount of coordination and information exchange needed to integrate work activities and thus the likely effectiveness of different coordination mechanisms. Size is often related to two other contingency factors, *life-cycle stage* and *age*. Organizations usually grow larger as they grow older and progress from earlier stages of development to later ones.

An additional closed system contingency factor, *technology*, affects the degree to which an organization's work is more or less routine and thus, again, the appropriateness of different coordination mechanisms. More routine technologies such as *mass production, mediating technology,* and *long-linked technology* can be coordinated with standardization. Less routine technologies such as *small-batch production, continuous process production, flexible cell production,* and *intensive technology* require the use of mutual adjustment. The organization's *environment* is an open system contingency factor that places coordination and information-processing requirements on the firm. These requirements stem from environmental *change, complexity, uncertainty, receptivity,* and *diversity*. In turn, these requirements influence the coordination, decision-making, boundary-spanning, and departmentation processes that give rise to the organization's structure.

REVIEW QUESTIONS

1. Name a specific business organization in your community and identify three of its most important constituency groups. What interests do each of the constituency groups expect the organization to fulfill? How does the organization's structure affect its ability to satisfy these interests? Is the company effective?

2. In what major way do simple undifferentiated structures differ from simple differentiated structures? What is the importance of this difference? What strengths do both kinds of simple structure share? What are the major weaknesses of each one?

3.   How do complex structures differ from simple structures? Which complex structure is the most mechanistic? Why? Which is the most organic? Why? Compare the strengths and weaknesses of these two types of complex structure.

4.   What typical effect does the age of an organization have on its size? According to the Quinn-Cameron life-cycle model, how does growing older and larger affect organizational structure?

5.   In which of Woodward's and Thompson's technologies is work routine and predictable? In which of them is work nonroutine and unpredictable? What kinds of structures are most fitting for each of the two clusters of technologies you have identified? In general terms, how does the routineness and predictability of an organization's technology affect the appropriateness of different types of structure?

6.   Explain why environmental change impedes an organization's ability to coordinate by means of standardization. What sort of coordination is used instead? Why does environmental complexity push toward decentralization? Given that environmental uncertainty is a combination of change and complexity, what effects besides increased boundary spanning would you expect it to have on the way an organization is structured?

7.   Why is environmental receptivity an issue only for organizations facing complex environments? Under conditions of environmental complexity, why should the centralization stimulated by hostility be eliminated as the environment becomes munificent?

8.   After reviewing the story that opened this chapter, use the concept of environmental diversity to explain the failure of General Motors' attempted use of functional departmentation to group its assembly units together. What had GM's management hoped to gain by using functional grouping? Why didn't things work out as expected?

Diagnostic Questions

The following questions should help you during the process of designing or redesigning an organization's structure by guiding you through the diagnosis of the contingency factors we have discussed.

1.   What kind of structure does the organization currently have? What is its primary means of coordination? Do the titles of its line vice-presidents provide evidence of one particular form of structure?

2.   Is the organization's current structure the one dictated by its size? If the organization has a simple undifferentiated structure, does it have no more than about 12 employees? If the organization has a simple differentiated structure, does it have no more than about 50 employees? If the organization has a complex structure, is it substantially larger?

3.   Is the organization's current structure the one suggested by the firm's life-cycle stage and age? If the firm is young and in the entrepreneur or collectivity stage, does it have a smaller, simple structure? If it is older and in the formalization or elaboration stage, does it have a larger, complex structure?

4.   Does the organization have an SBU structure? If so, perform separate technology and environment analyses. That is, answer the rest of the diagnostic questions for each SBU as though it were a separate organization.

5.   Is the organization's primary purpose to manufacture a tangible product? Does it use small-batch production, continuous process production, or flexible cell production? If it uses one of these, does the organization have an organic structure? Is it simple or matrix, functional, or divisional with lateral linkages? Or does it use mass production? Does the organization have a mechanistic structure? Is it functional or divisional?

6.   Is the organization's primary purpose instead to provide a service? Does it use intensive technology? If so, does the organization have one of the organic

structures named above? Or does it use mediating technology or long-linked technology? If one of these, does the organization have one of the mechanistic structures named above?

7. Is the organization's external environment stable or dynamic? Does the organization's primary mode of coordination match the amount of change in its environment? Is the environment simple or complex? Does the degree of decentralization in the organization's structure match the amount of complexity in its environment?

8. Is the organization's external environment uncertain? If so, is there evidence of significant boundary-spanning activities? Is the environment munificent or hostile? If hostility exists and the environment is also complex, is the organization temporarily centralized? Is the environment uniform or diverse? Does the type of departmentation used to structure the firm match the diversity of its environment?

9. Do the various contingencies seem to mandate the same type of structure? If not, and if there is no evidence of recent changes that might serve as an explanation, look for faulty diagnosis in one or more of your contingency analyses.

10. If the different contingencies *do* seem to point toward the same type of structure, is this structure the same as the one the organization has now? If not, the structure recommended by your analysis should be implemented; structural redesign is needed. If, however, the current structure is the one recommended by your analysis, structural deficiencies are not the cause of the organization's problems. Look for individual or group-level problems instead.

EXERCISE 16-1
OPEN SYSTEM PLANNING*
MARK S. PLOVNICK, *University of the Pacific*
RONALD E. FRY, *Case Western Reserve University*
W. WARNER BURKE, *Columbia University*

Open system planning (OSP) is a technique that can be used to clarify an organization's mission and plan how to achieve it in the face of demands and expectations originating in the environment. These demands come from such constituency groups as employees, customers, and raw material suppliers. OSP is an integral part of the process of strategic planning and a useful way to improve an organization's understanding of its environment (see Chapter 18).

An open system planning intervention begins with a discussion of the organization's basic goals, mission, and reason for being. The participants in an initial OSP session then identify the constituency groups that can have an impact on the organization's accomplishment of its goals and mission. Participants describe the current relations between the organization and each of its constituency groups. They assess these relations, deciding whether they satisfy both the organization and the constituency group. If assessment uncovers dissatisfaction, participants determine how relations ought to be to achieve a good balance between organizational effectiveness and constituency satisfaction.

OSP participants then assess the organization's current response to each constituency group by answering several questions. What does this type of constituency want from us? What are we currently doing in response to this demand? Is our current response moving us closer to where we want to be in relation to our organization's goals and purpose? Finally, OSP participants decide what actions, if any, must be taken to redirect the organization toward the desired state of affairs.

This exercise will give you the opportunity to experience the process of open system planning first-hand as you work with other class members to assess the environment and constituency groups of a real organization.

STEP ONE: PRE-CLASS PREPARATION

In class you will perform parts of each phase of the open system planning process. The focal organization will be the school or education program in which you are enrolled (unless your instructor specifies another organization instead). In preparation for class, read the entire exercise. Then think about what the basic mission

or purpose of the organization should be and write a mission statement here:

_____

_____

_____

Finally, identify five constituency groups that expect the organization to do something for them. List these groups and their demands here:

1. _____

2. _____

3. _____

4. _____

5. _____

STEP TWO: DEFINING A MISSION

The class should divide into planning groups of four to six members each. If you have already established permanent groups, reassemble in those groups. In each group, members should share the mission statements they developed before class and reach a consensus about the organization's mission. Next, your instructor will lead the entire class in developing a mission statement to be used for the rest of the exercise.

STEP THREE: IDENTIFYING CONSTITUENCY GROUPS

The class as a whole should agree on the key constituency groups in the environment that create demands on the organization. If the organization you have decided to focus on is your school, examples of these

* Source: Mark S. Plovnick, Ronald E. Fry, and W. Warner Burke, *Organization Development: Exercises, Cases, and Readings* (Boston: Little, Brown and Company, 1982), pp. 67–73. Copyright © 1982 by Mark S. Plovnick, Ronald E. Fry, and W. Warner Burke.

groups might include students, faculty, alumni, and employees. Each planning group should be assigned one constituency group to consider in the next step of this exercise (every group should be assigned a different constituency).

STEP FOUR: OPEN SYSTEM PLANNING IN GROUPS

In order to experience the OSP process, each planning group should complete the remaining phases of the process, focusing only on the constituency group assigned to it. Following is a description of the five phases you should complete.

1. *Identification of current demands.* What does the constituency group currently expect from or demand of the organization? (estimated time: 15 minutes)
2. *Current response.* For the one or two most important of these demands, what is the organization's current response? Is it a response of action or inaction? (estimated time: 10 minutes)
3. *Future demands.* Considering the current response and whatever changes or trends you think are likely to occur over the next two years, what are the key demands from your constituency group going to be two years from now? (estimated time: 10 minutes)
4. *Ideal state.* Imagine two years from now. What kinds of expectations or demands would the organization like to see coming from the constituency group you are analyzing? (estimated time: 10 minutes)
5. *Identifying gaps and planning action.* Compare and contrast the results of phases 3 and 4. What gaps exist between anticipated and ideal demands? Choose one of these gaps and suggest what the organization should do to alter its current course. (estimated time: 15 minutes)

Note that you have one hour to complete these five phases. You will have to manage your time carefully. A spokesperson should be ready to present a summary of the group's work in Step Five.

STEP FIVE: PLANNING GROUP REPORTS AND DISCUSSION

A spokesperson from each group should take no more than five minutes to summarize what the group discovered, discussed, and concluded about the constituency group it examined. Any suggestions for action should be listed on a chalkboard, overhead transparency, or flipchart.

STEP SIX: CLASS DISCUSSION OF THE OSP PROCESS

The class as a whole should now review the OSP process just completed and discuss the following questions:

1. Do the planning group reports reveal any potential conflicts between satisfying different constituency groups' demands? That is, will satisfying one constituency make it difficult to satisfy another? How might such conflicts be resolved?
2. Do the actions proposed by the planning groups fit together into a meaningful action plan? If so, describe the plan. If not, how can they be made to do so?
3. What changes, if any, would you recommend in the mission statement developed in Step Two? How does knowledge about an organization's environment affect perceptions of its mission?
4. How would you expect OSP as conducted in real organizations to differ from the process you have completed in class? In what ways might it be more complicated? Less complicated?
5. What kinds of organizations or situations do you see as likely candidates for OSP? Which ones should probably not use it?

CONCLUSION

Open system planning is not a panacea for all organizations. A significant investment of time and energy is required. In addition, the OSP process may involve a great deal of ambiguity and stress. However, OSP can enable organizations to manage their responses to important but often conflicting environmental demands. OSP can also be used as a method to help the members of organizations achieve consensus about organizational missions and goals. The resulting consensus can provide the coherent sense of direction needed to function effectively in complex, changing environments.

CASE 16-1

NEWCOMER-WILLSON HOSPITAL*
SAMUEL M. WILSON, *Temple University*

The administrative process in a hospital is complex. There are not many organizations with such cumbersome structures that still succeed. The administrative task is neither clear, definite, nor clean cut at any time. If it were, the doctors would not want it to be. So, we have to set up an elaborate framework of communications, especially with committee structures, in order to keep things moving.

This is the view of how hospitals are organized and run held by Mr. William Baker, the professionally trained and experienced hospital Director (administrator) of the Newcomer-Willson Hospital.

THE HOSPITAL BUSINESS— BACKGROUND AND CURRENT STATUS

In medieval Europe, hospitals were lodging places for travelers and were supported primarily by religious organizations. Later these places started taking care of old people and the homeless. Originally they were not institutions for the care and recovery of the sick. These charitable institutions provided for the needy, and doctors did provide some medical care mostly as a benevolence. Until about 1850 hospitals were usually very poor substitutes for home care. Living standards, the evolution of modern medicine, along with many scientific and technological developments associated with the detection and treatment of illnesses, have caused hospitals to become important centers for medical care and training of doctors and nurses. Today doctors usually have a primary interest in the establishment and operation of hospitals because their chief professional interest is medical care, i.e., the same objective as that of hospital management.

The purpose of all hospitals is to provide medical care. Most hospitals provide this care on a "nonprofit" basis from an accounting point of view. However, hospitals are business organizations and must conduct their long-run activities in such a manner that total revenue from all sources equals total expenditures, i.e., they must break even.

HOSPITAL ADMINISTRATION

The growth of hospitals in size and numbers during the first part of the twentieth century ushered in a new era in hospital administration. Traditionally hospital administrators were either doctors or nurses who devoted whatever time was needed to the administrative matters of the organization. In small hospitals, this was not a particularly time-consuming job especially when a full-time clerical assistant was used. The growth of hospitals (size and numbers) challenged this arrangement. Doctors and nurses were taken from their respective professional fields too much of the time, and they did not have the training or experience necessary for successful managers. As far back as 1938 the University of Chicago established the first program designed especially for hospital administration. Since that time many other universities have initiated such programs while many Schools of Business Administration feel that they prepare graduates who are qualified for this type of work.

THE NEWCOMER-WILLSON HOSPITAL

The Newcomer-Willson Hospital is located in a growing and prosperous suburban community. It has grown rapidly in the last 15 years, and with its recent expansion a total of 285 beds, 45 bassinets, and 700 rooms for different purposes are provided. It has a good rate (85%) of bed utilization as compared to the national average. There are 700 full-time employees, 400 medical staff members (of which 270 are courtesy members), and a nursing school of 160 students.

The policies and organization of the hospital were reviewed two years ago by Cresap, McCormick and Paget, Management Consultants. The Consultant's report covered all areas of the hospital in a rather broad way. It was generally favorable. It noted that over the past several years prime attention had been given to organization for administration, but that there were some problem areas needing additional attention.

AUTHORITY STRUCTURE AT NEWCOMER-WILLSON HOSPITAL: TOP MANAGEMENT

Exhibit 16-1 reveals the top and middle management organization at Newcomer-Willson. The top corporate body is the Board of Trustees, which is composed of

* Reprinted with the author's permission.

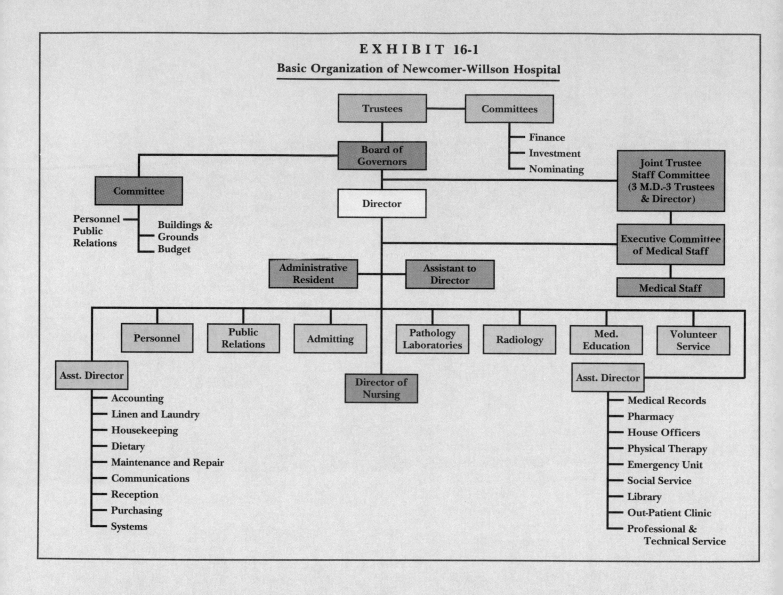

EXHIBIT 16-1
Basic Organization of Newcomer-Willson Hospital

about 70 Volunteers (nonmedical) from a variety of fields. Most of the trustees are local citizens of some standing in the community.

The most important body in the administrative process which deals with top level considerations and problems is the Board of Governors. This Board includes the four corporate officers from the Board of Trustees and nine elected trustees. The Board of Governors is responsible for the general administration of the organization, and it appoints all members of the Medical Staff and all other key people of the hospital.

The Medical Staff organization is headed by an Executive Committee. This committee operates within the framework of the By-laws of the Corporation and more specifically within its own By-laws which were approved by the Board of Governors. This committee may report to either the Director, Mr. Baker, or to the Joint Trustee Medical Staff Committee, depending on a variety of situations. In the past there has been a deliberate attempt at times to override the Director because of the

nature of the problems. This has not usually been achieved, however, because the Director is a member of the Joint Committee.

The medical staff is composed of doctors who have private practice in the surrounding community. They use the hospital when the need arises. They serve on committees of various types (see committees on Exhibit 16-2. These staff members are highly trained in their individual professional fields of medicine, and their primary concern is for their particular patients who are in the hospital. In fact, this concern causes some problems for Mr. Baker, the nursing staff, and others in supervisory positions because the hospital staff must think in terms of all of the patients, not just one or a few.

The chief full-time administrative position is that of the Director, currently held by Mr. Baker. Mr. Baker has been with the hospital for several years. He is a Fellow in hospital administration and has a great deal of administrative experience in several different positions of various organizations. He has been a prime

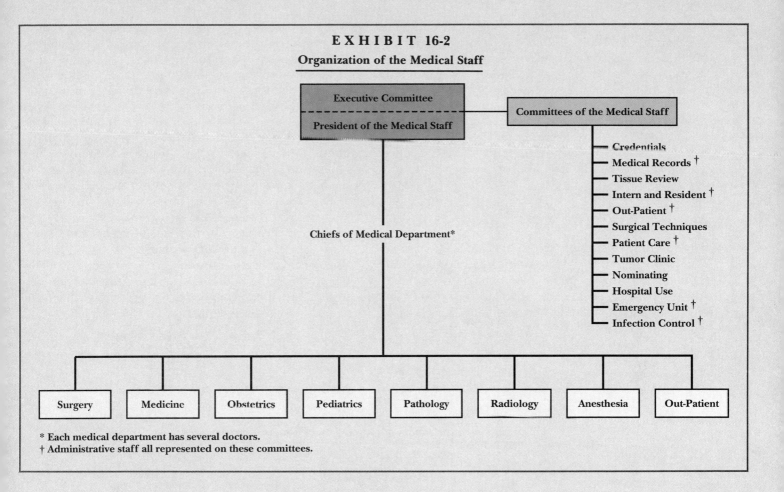

EXHIBIT 16-2
Organization of the Medical Staff

Executive Committee
President of the Medical Staff

Committees of the Medical Staff

- Credentials
- Medical Records [†]
- Tissue Review
- Intern and Resident [†]
- Out-Patient [†]
- Surgical Techniques
- Patient Care [†]
- Tumor Clinic
- Nominating
- Hospital Use
- Emergency Unit [†]
- Infection Control [†]

Chiefs of Medical Department*

| Surgery | Medicine | Obstetrics | Pediatrics | Pathology | Radiology | Anesthesia | Out-Patient |

* Each medical department has several doctors.
† Administrative staff all represented on these committees.

mover in establishing an improved administrative organization with the establishment of committees, by-laws for the medical staff, and written descriptions of duties and responsibilities for all managers and committees. He has an excellent rapport with the medical staff doctors, the members of the Board of Governors, and his subordinates. Although the administrative process seems to bog down at times, the network of communications through the organization and committee structure ultimately yields satisfactory results. Mr. Baker is a member of most of the administrative committees of the hospital and spends a great deal of time with committee meetings.

Mr. Baker emphasizes the fact that the administrator's job involves many problems and believes a study made by Charles Prall is reasonably representative. This study shows the percentage of administrators (by type) who reported one or more problems in several given categories. The summary report is presented in Exhibit 16-3.

EXHIBIT 16-3
Percentage of Hospital Administrators Reporting One or More Problems in Specific Categories—By Type of Administrator

PROBLEM AREAS	PERCENTAGE REPORTING ONE OR MORE PROBLEMS BY AREA		
	LAYMEN	DOCTORS	NURSES
Working with doctors	40	41	71
Improvement of Medical Care	50	63	90
Business and Finance	61	40	43
Public Relations	50	50	50
Physical Plant	33	25	50

Mr. Baker looks upon the extensive committee structure at the Trustee, Board of Governors, and top medical staff level with mixed feelings. On the one hand, they are release valves for troublesome issues and represent the democratic process which keeps everyone informed. On the other hand, they are very numerous, slow-acting, time-consuming, and reach few decisions which would not have been reached on a more timely basis by the Director working directly with the Executive Committee of the Medical Staff or the Board of Governors.

MIDDLE MANAGEMENT ORGANIZATION

The full-time operations of the hospital are organized and conducted under the supervision of 12 persons who report directly to Mr. Baker (see Exhibit 16-1).

Nursing activities are divided into two main groups; namely, Nursing Services and the School of Nursing. Exhibit 16-4 shows the internal organization for conducting these nursing activities. The School of Nursing has its own autonomy to a great extent because of its educational mission. Along with the medical staff, Nursing Services constitutes the very heart of hospital operations. The members of the Nursing staff are specialized and perform their duties on a round-the-clock basis every day of the year (by shifts) in such departments as Medicine, Surgery, Obstetrics, Pediatrics, and Operating Room. Theoretically each nurse has an immediate superior (Head Nurse) but during a normal work period she may be involved in taking instructions from several different persons. This is especially the case when dealing with the individual doctors of her various patients. Her work seems to run smoothly until "outsiders" create confusion and frustration by telling her to do things which do not constitute her job, interfere with her primary duties, or things which are against the rules or regulations of the hospital.

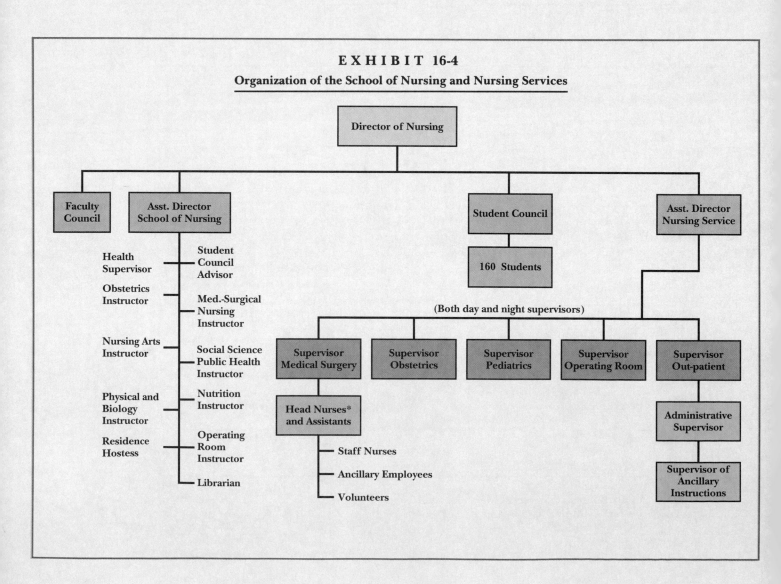

EXHIBIT 16-4

Organization of the School of Nursing and Nursing Services

The Medical Staff Organization includes the doctors who are associated with the hospital. (See Exhibit 16-2 for the internal organization of the Medical staff.) The hospital's existence depends on the requirements for patient care as determined by the individual medical staff members. Sometimes the individual doctors do not fully realize the "public utility"nature of the hospital. While the doctor is concerned with his patient, the hospital personnel are concerned with all patients. This leads to some difficulties in such activities as scheduling of operating rooms, proper use of precautionary methods, and administering the rules and regulations established by the Board of Governors and outside agencies.

ADMINISTRATIVE AND MEDICAL STAFF CONFLICT

Until about 15 tears ago, Newcomer-Willson had a doctor administrator. After a brief experience with a layman administrator, it went back to a doctor. About nine years ago it decided again to employ a nonmedical professional administrator. Since then, strides have been made in the administrative activities of the hospital. Basic problems do arise, however, which seem to indicate the need for further improvement in the organizational arrangement and/or the administrative processes. For example, the Head (physician) of one of the full-time departments recently demanded "individual professional status" which he thought the medical staff members had and which he did not have. The problem became so serious that the physician threatened to resign if he did not get the status desired. After considerable discussions with various people and in several committee meetings, the Board of Governors decided that the current status would not be changed substantially and the issue seemed to have been settled—with no resignations. A by-product of this action was the clear evidence that the Board of Governors is the "governing" body of the hospital.

Another incident reflects the type of problems which Mr. Baker and the administrative supervisors face. Only recently a patient had been placed on "precaution" by her doctor. Her physician, accompanied by several resident doctors, came into the patient's room without observing the precautionary rules. The staff nurse reported this incident immediately to her supervisor. The supervisor ordered all the doctors from the room, explaining the reasons to them. The physician took the patient off "precaution" on the spot and remained in the room. This upset the nursing staff; however, the next morning the physician placed the patient back on precaution. After discussing the problem with the Director of Nursing and the physician, Mr. Baker

had to decide what must be done in this instance and also in the future to reduce or eliminate such situations.

Mr. Baker said: "I suppose our problem is that the nature of hosptial operations makes it necessary to violate some of the essential characteristics of good organization which authorities like Urwick emphasized. Maybe Emerson was right when he said poor organization is the 'hook-worm disease' of industry. It is a disease we haven't completely cured. Everyone seems to have too many bosses, but somehow we do get the job done."

When you have read this case, look back at the chapter's diagnostic questions and choose the ones that apply to the case. Then use those questions with the ones that follow in your case analysis.

1. What constituencies must be satisfied if Newcomer-Willson Hospital is to operate effectively? What demands are made by these constituencies? How well is the hospital satisfying them?

2. What kind of structure does the hospital have now? What are the strengths and weaknesses of this type of structure? How does the hospital's structure affect its effectiveness?

3. What contingency factors have an impact on the hospital's effectiveness? In view of these factors, what sort of structure should the hospital have? What modifications must be made to the current structure?

CASE 16-2
CORRECTIONS CORPORATION OF AMERICA*

WINTHROP KNOWLTON, KENNEDY SCHOOL OF GOVERNMENT, *Harvard University*

Thomas W. Beasley and Doctor R. Crants, Jr., first met at West Point. After graduating in 1966, they served together in Vietnam where Beasley received the silver star and two bronze stars for valor.

The turn of the decade found both men back in school, Beasley at Vanderbilt University's School of Law and Crants enrolled in a joint Law and Business School program at Harvard.

After receiving his law degree in 1973, Beasley returned to his hometown of Dickson Falls, Tennessee, and began his own law practice. One observer said:

He's really a country boy who likes farming. But he got bored with the practice of law and turned his attention to politics. He'd gotten a taste of that at Vanderbilt and in 1974 he ran Lamar Alexander's losing

* Reprinted with the author's permission.

campaign for the Tennessee governorship. Lamar lost bad, and from 1974 to 1978 the Democrats controlled the House, the Senate, and the State House. Tom became chairman of the Republican Party. Over the next four years he represented the party in all the important debates; he learned how to handle the press; and he developed a certain expertise under fire.

"Doc" Crants came to Tennessee in 1974 at the urging of his old friend Beasley and another West Point classmate then practicing law in Nashville. While Beasley operated in the world of politics, Crants pursued a career in real estate development, banking, and financial consulting. "Somewhere along the line," he says, "I became aware of the value of franchises—nursing homes and radio and television stations, for example. I discovered that the process of applying for licenses was exceedingly cumbersome—dealing with all that bureaucratic red tape—and not many people were willing to put up with it. I *was*. I didn't mind doing the dirty work, and occasionally I found that at the end of the process, I was the only bidder for a valuable property."

In 1978 Beasley ran Lamar Alexander's second, and successful, campaign for the governorship. Afterwards, he was charged with helping find candidates for the governor's cabinet. One job seemed unfillable: that of State Commissioner of Corrections. Beasley said:

> It was the one area where you couldn't find anyone with a good reputation. People would have a good reputation *for awhile* but they always seemed to lose it and get fired. There weren't any exceptions. It's a very difficult job to begin with, of course, but it always gets worse. The prison population grows, and legislatures are unwilling to provide money. So the institutions become more crowded. Indeed, they become inhumane. There are scandals and lawsuits. Many of our state correctional systems have been declared unconstitutional under the cruel and inhumane treatment of prisoners provision of the Constitution. The commissioner is the one who takes the rap.

While the new governor eventually filled the position, the new commissioner did not last, and during Alexander's first term Beasley kept wondering whether the public sector was really capable of running a decent corrections system. By 1982, with the Republicans in power in Washington, there was much talk in the air of reducing the activities of government in general and providing the private sector with a greater role in solving societal problems. It seemed to Beasley that the corrections area was one where this might be possible. He began taking small groups of Nashville businessmen to dinner at the Bellemeade Country Club to see if they could be persuaded to put money in a new venture that would try to run prisons for a profit. One businessman

who was interested was his old West Point classmate, "Doc" Crants.

Not long after the two men agreed, late in 1982, to go into business together, they enjoyed two remarkable strokes of good fortune. It turned out that several other Nashville businessmen were considering the same kind of proposition. Jack Massey, the founder of American Hospital Supply of America, and his young colleague, Lucius E. Burch III, had formed a new venture-capital firm, Massey Burch, in June 1981, to provide a formal vehicle for venture-capital investments for a very limited number of large outside clients. Already highly successful in the privatization of hospitals, already committed to the concept of building strong franchises (as in the case of at least one other extraordinarily successful investment, Kentucky Fried Chicken Corporation), Massey Burch was now considering starting a company called Prisons Corporations of America. Hearing of Beasley's and Crants's efforts to launch a similar concern, Burch set up a meeting of the parties, and a deal was quickly struck. For an investment of $500,000 Massey Burch would obtain a 50 percent interest in the Beasley/Crants venture. It would be called Corrections Corporation of America. Beasley would be president and chairman of the Board of Directors; Crants, secretary, treasurer, and vice chairman; and Burch would become a director and senior adviser.

The second lucky stroke came in the form of T. Don Hutto, an experienced corrections professional who had just been replaced as head of Virginia's corrections system as a result of the election of a new governor, Democrat Charles Robb. Hutto was the chairman-elect of the American Correctional Association (the ACA), the watchdog trade association that had been struggling since 1977 to formulate humane operating standards for American prisons. The ACA was planning to hold its next convention in Nashville in early 1983. Beasley, Crants, and Hutto met, and Hutto was brought aboard as executive vice-president of the new firm.

THE U.S. DETENTION AND CORRECTIONS SYSTEM

The American prison system consist of two broad types of institutions (although, as indicated below, the two sometimes overlap): facilities for detention and for correction.

The most widespread of the former are local jails where individuals are held awaiting trial or, having been convicted, are held awaiting sentencing to a corrections institution. The most common corrections institutions are penal farms and workhouses, where individuals are sent to serve terms of less than six years and penitentiaries (state and federal) where they serve longer terms for more serious crimes. Because corrections institutions are often overcrowded, some prisoners who would ordinarily be sent to the latter are kept instead in local jails serving out their terms alongside other individuals who have yet to be found guilty of any crime or who have been convicted of relatively minor offenses. Sometimes individuals are "detained" in penal farms and workhouses, so that these serve both as "detention" and "corrections" facilities. In addition, there are a number of specialized institutions where illegal immigrants or juveniles are held for a variety of purposes.

Describing U.S. jails in a 1981 report, the ACA wrote:

> Since the first jail built in the Jamestown Colony, Virginia, in 1608, American society has caged human beings like animals with the expectation that they would return to the community and become law-abiding citizens. Traditional jail procedures have changed very little since the beginning of the 17th century, continuing to reflect a punitive "lock 'em up" approach in facilities. Prisoners often languish in idleness and boredom, under primitive conditions. Jails were primarily designed then, and still are, to enable a small number of staff to confine securely a comparatively large number of prisoners.
>
> From the small to the large, today's detention facilities are poorly equipped to handle their diverse populations ranging from homeless drunks and the mentally ill to individuals accused of every conceivable crime. When such human beings are imprisoned with little regard for individual needs and rights their further deterioration is virtually assured. At detention facilities, the intake point in the criminal justice system, petty offenders comingle with hard-core criminals. Contempt for the law as well as knowledge and skills for future criminal careers are readily available to the young and first offenders. Their exposure to and acceptance of such opportunity is reflected by their high rates of failure and recidivism.
>
> Despite decades of failure and criticism, most jails have remained unchanged, continuing to function as human warehouses. The reasons for this phenomenon can be any combination of such factors as limited local financing, public indifference and apathy, emphasis on restraint, and public ambivalence regarding concepts of punishment and treatment. Jails are the least studied and least understood of all penal institutions and are often held in low esteem by the public and its officials. Supporting jail reform has become a politically unpopular cause, and the tendency to minimize the importance of detention facilities and their impact on society is growing. The rare existence of sound operational standards for detention facilities and the failure of the many states to enforce those that do exist further depress the situation.[1]

Justice Department data released in the spring of 1985 indicated:

- In 1974, the United States prison population in federal and state penal institutions totaled approximately 229,000. By 1984, this number had doubled to 464,000. Between 1980 and 1984 the prison population increased by more than 40 percent. These increases were spurred in part by the arrival at the prison-prone ages (20–29 years) of the "baby boom" generation.

- In addition to state and federal prison systems, there are approximately 3,400 local jails within the United States. On an given day, there are approximately 300,000 people residing in these jails. In 1984, a total of 11,500 sentenced prisoners were held in local jails because of state prison overcrowding, an increase of more than 40 percent over the previous year.

- The number of prison admissions from court for every 100 serious crimes reported to the police declined from 6.3 in 1960 to 2.3 in 1970. The ratio began to increase in 1981, reaching 4.0 in 1983. If the 1960 rate of prison admissions relative to crime had prevailed in 1983, the number of offenders sentenced that year would have been about 100,000 higher than the 173,000 who were actually incarcerated.

- The strain placed on prison systems by the rapid influx of prisoners in recent years has been accompanied by a series of court interventions charging that individual prisons or whole state systems are violating the constitutional provision prohibiting "cruel and unusual treatment" of prisoners. In 1984 the entire prison systems in eight states were operating under court order or consent decree. Thirty-three state correctional systems had been declared unconstitutional, either in whole or in part, by the federal courts or were currently defending litigation in that regard.

- Despite substantial increases in expenditures for new prison capacity in recent years, both federal and state systems were operating at over-capacity occupancy rates in 1984: federal institutions at 110–137 percent of capacity and states at 105–116 percent (depending on how capacity is measured). One in 10 prisoners was housed in a facility built before 1875, half of all prisoners in facilities 40 or more years old.[2]

Experts predict that inmate populations will level off from about 1985 to 1990 when they are again expected to increase. These projections are based on expected population age groupings and the fact that young people are the high-risk group and commit most crimes.

The Immigration and Naturalization Service (INS) reports that they arrested 1.2 million illegal aliens

[1] *Standard for Adult Local Detention Facilities*, 2nd ed. American Correctional Association, 1981.

[2] *Prisoners in 1984*, Bureau of Justice Statistics Bulletin.

in 1983. Because of jail overcrowding and despite the fact that INS operates over 3,000 beds, INS finds itself without places to detail aliens once they are arrested. It is not uncommon for local district offices to stop arresting aliens as early as 9 A.M. each day because there is no further place to detain them.

It is expected that the illegal alien problem will worsen over the next 10 years and that the need for detention of aliens will increase. Even if Congress passes a reform bill, most observers believe that this will increase the numbers in detention. This is based on the premise that declaring amnesty for present aliens within this country will only serve to encourage other aliens to enter illegally in the future.

CCA's Operating Strategy

The Company's managers and owners believed that the state of the nation's detention and corrections system provided it with a unique commercial opportunity. As Lucius Burch put it, in an early memorandum on CCA:

> It is evident that change in the corrections industry is necessary and imminent. Public entities clearly are not managing the prison systems effectively.
>
> While the American public has taken a "hard-line" attitude in regard to the suppression of crime, this attitude has not translated itself into support for tax initiatives to build additional facilities to handle the increased population. There is no political constituency for building and housing criminals. It is a low budget priority and will not receive proper attention absent private intervention.
>
> Further, as public treasuries grow leaner in the years ahead, experts believe that the role of private enterprise in criminal justice will increase.
>
> Prisons in the United States are aging and are in need of repair or replacement. Private entities can relieve municipalities (and ultimately taxpayers) from the burden of additional capital outlays and high operating expenses for these facilities. In fact, a corrections corporation is a tax-paying entity and will provide additional capital through payment of state and federal taxes.
>
> Most importantly, however, a private entity can manage correctional facilities more economically and efficiently than the governmental entities. A private entity can be competitive in its costs relative to governmental operations for several reasons:

- Personal economies can be achieved through careful attention to the design of the facility. In a twenty-four (24) hour operation, such economies are of major importance.
- Further economies can be achieved through mass purchasing, an advantage not available to small single jail operations.
- Private entities are not required to operate under cumbersome bureaucratic purchasing regulations which, inevitably,

increase the cost of supplies and materials. As a result, a private operation can trim an estimated 10–25 percent off the cost of running conventional facilities. The bidding procedures designed to maintain honesty, while resulting in low bids for the government, usually do not result in low prices.

With solid financial backing from Massey Burch, with a small cadre of managers experienced in politics (Beasley), business (Crants), and corrections management (Hutto), CCA determined that it would attempt to contract with local, state, and federal governmental bodies for the detention of persons for whom a minimum to medium level of security was required and who presented, in the management's opinion, "a relatively low risk of violence or other untoward behavior." The company would build, own (or lease), staff, and manage such correctional and detention facilities. It would contract with government bodies to "detain or incarcerate, provide food and other necessities for, and supervise persons in the correctional and detention facilities owned by government bodies."

Although this statement of purpose seemed relatively straightforward, the leaders of the company knew that implementation would be no simple matter. They understood that the process of "selling" their concept to local elective officials (sheriffs, county executives, and county commissions) would be time-consuming and difficult. Many local officials had a stake in the existing system. For them, employment opportunities in county jails represented a source of patronage. At the state and federal level there would be legislative oversight committees to deal with as well as elective and appointive officials in the executive branches. How would these public bodies feel about turning over the administration of corrections facilities to a for-profit body?

What standards would need to be established so that the public sector would feel at home delegating these kinds of responsibilities to private concerns? The ACA had recently set a standard of 70 square feet of cell space for each prisoner. The federal standard was 60 square feet. But it was estimated that only 1 percent of all facilities met these levels. There were numerous instances, in fact, where four prisoners were crowded into cells of less than 60 square feet, where there were no outdoor recreation areas, and where health, sanitation, and hygiene facilities were lamentable. Indeed, it was the public sector's inability or unwillingness to provide these standards that created the opportunity that CCA wished now to exploit. Should CCA strive to build and run facilities that met the ACA standards or some less stringent test that would still substantially improve upon existing practice?

There were a number of other questions on CCA's

managers' minds in 1983 as it began formulating its first bids:

- What role, if any, would public sector officials play in monitoring what went on inside a prison once CCA "owned" or managed it?
- How much competition did CCA want? It was important that the public sector have more than one firm bidding for this kind of business. On the other hand, nothing would damage the privatization concept faster than fly-by-night operators who failed to make good on their promises. Was there any way CCA could influence the competitive environment in which it operated? Should it even attempt to do so?
- What liabilities would the company be exposing itself to in the management of detention and corrections facilities? And how could these be contained?
- How would the company meet its staffing requirements—both for its own management and for the staff required within the facilities it operated—given the poor reputation of the public officials now in the business.
- What would the media make of all this? And the liberal academic intelligentsia? And how could *they* be "managed"? Or should the company even try?

THE FIRST CONTRACT

The company submitted its first proposal and bid to manage a detention facility on August 26, 1983, to the Immigration and Naturalization Service for the operation of an approximately 67,600-square-foot, 350-bed detention facility for illegal aliens in Houston, Texas. On October 6, 1983, the company received notification from the INS that its proposal and bid to operate the facility had been accepted and that the INS contract was effective from that date. On October 11, 1983, the company purchased an approximately 5.84-acre site in Houston for construction of the facility for a price of approximately $763,000. On October 21, 1983, the company entered into a construction contract with Trimble & Stephens Co. of Houston, Texas, for the construction of the facility. Construction commenced on October 26, 1983, and was completed on April 20, 1984. The company also incurred architectural and engineering fees in connection with the construction.

The initial term of the INS contract terminated on September 30, 1984. The INS renewed the INS contract to September 30, 1985 and subsequently sent the company a letter of intent to renew the contract until September 30, 1986. The INS had the option to renew the INS contract for three consecutive one-year periods with adjustments in the amounts paid by the INS to the company during such renewal periods. These adjustments were designed, in part, to offset inflation. Unless the company operated the facility for at least five years, the company would likely lose a substantial amount of money on the project. The company was to receive $25.74 per day per person from the INS through September 1985.

When you have read this case, look back at the chapter's diagnostic questions and choose the ones that apply to the case. Then use those questions with the ones that follow in your case analysis.

1. What major constituencies are likely to make demands on the Corrections Corporation of America as it opens prison facilities throughout the United States? What demands are these constituencies apt to make? Do you believe that CCA will be able to satisfy these demands?
2. At what life-cycle stage is CCA? What type of structure should it have? Does it appear that the company does in fact have this type of structure?
3. How will CCA's expected growth affect its structure? What structural changes will have to be made as the company grows larger? What should CCA's current management do to prepare the company for these changes?

C A S E 16-3

DUMAS PUBLIC LIBRARY

Read Chapter 18's Case 18-1, "Dumas Public Library," or review it if you have read it for Case 15-3. Next, look back at Chapter 16's diagnostic questions and choose the ones that apply to that case. Then use those questions with the ones that follow in your analysis of the case.

1. What constituency groups are making demands on the city government of Kimball, New Mexico? What are their demands? How successful has the city been in its efforts to meet those demands?
2. What kind of structure does the city government have? How has this structure contributed to the conflict between Debra Dickenson and Helen Hendricks? What structural changes should be made to minimize the reoccurrence of similar conflicts in future?
3. Diagram what you think would be the most effective structure for Kimball's city government. Where do the library board and city council belong in your diagram?

CHAPTER 17

JOB DESIGN

At National Bevpak, a bottling and canning plant that is a subsidiary of the National Beverage Corp., this worker spends his day checking the flow of bottles along the conveyor belt. How can a company keep employees who perform boring jobs like this motivated and satisfied? It could teach workers other tasks, such as packing the bottles in boxes, so they could rotate from one job to another. Or it could try to invent a machine to do these simple, highly repetitive tasks. What other approaches might an employer take?

I stand in one spot, about a two- or three-feet area, all night. . . . We do about thirty-two [welding] jobs per car, per unit. Forty-eight units an hour, eight hours a day. Thirty-two times forty-eight times eight. Figure it out. That's how many times I push that button. . . . You dream, you think of things you've done. I drift back continuously to when I was a kid and what me and my brothers did. . . . [Y]ou're nothing more than a machine. They give better care to that machine than they will to you. They'll have more respect, give more attention to that machine. . . . Somehow you get the feeling that the machine is better than you are.[1]

*****

The other day when I was proofreading [insurance policy] endorsements I noticed some guy had insured his store for $165,000 against vandalism and $5,000 against fire. Now that's bound to be a mistake. They probably got it backwards. . . . I was just about to show it to [my supervisor] when I figured, wait a minute! I'm not supposed to read these forms. I'm just supposed to check one column against another. And they do check. . . . They don't explain this stuff to me. I'm not supposed to understand it. I'm just supposed to check one column against the other. . . . If they're gonna give me a robot's job to do, I'm gonna do it like a robot! Anyway, it just lowers my production record to get up and point out someone else's error.[2]

It's easy to understand why workers who perform monotonous, unchallenging jobs like these feel bored and frustrated. Yet almost all such jobs are the result of conscious, deliberate planning. Why do managers intentionally design jobs that are so unappealing? What do they expect to gain by simplifying work so drastically? Can anything be done to counteract the negative effects of oversimplifying work—effects like the welder's detached daydreaming and the insurance clerk's decision to overlook an obvious error? Or, can oversimplification be avoided altogether?

job design The process of deciding what specific tasks each job holder should perform in the context of the overall work that an organization must accomplish.

We will seek answers to questions such as these in this chapter as we examine theories and methods of **job design**, the process of deciding what specific tasks each jobholder should perform in the context of the overall work of an organization. In Chapters 15 and 16, we focused on the structural characteristics that help coordinate tasks and integrate the work of an organization. Here, we will consider the opposite side of the coin, so to speak, as we see how an organization's work is divided into jobs that can be performed by individual workers.

We will begin by overviewing one approach to job design, the efficiency perspective, which originated in work on scientific management discussed in Chapter 2. Today, it belongs to the field of industrial engineering. Next, we will turn our attention to another approach, the satisfaction perspective, which arose largely in reaction to problems with the efficiency perspective. It is based on ideas about motivation, satisfaction, and performance like those we have already discussed in Chapters 7 and 8. We will conclude by describing several recent developments that are changing the way work is organized and accomplished in modern organizations.

[1] Studs Terkel, *Working* (New York: Avon Books, 1972), pp. 221–23.
[2] Barbara Garson, *All the Livelong Day: The Meaning and Demeaning of Routine Work* (New York: Penguin Books, 1977), p. 171.

DIAGNOSTIC ISSUES

Before we start our discussion of job design, let's consider some issues our diagnostic model raises. To begin with, can we *describe* how the organization's work is divided into jobs and the effects of this division of labor on employees? In designing its jobs, is the organization primarily concerned with efficiency or with satisfaction? Can we *diagnose* whether a job needs to be simplified? What signals might indicate instead that a job has been made too simple?

On what basis do we *prescribe* that a job be redesigned? How can we predict who will react positively to enriched jobs and who won't? Finally, what *actions* can managers take to make jobs more challenging and rewarding? What can be done if such actions "overstretch" the work force?

THE EFFICIENCY PERSPECTIVE ON JOB DESIGN

To achieve *efficiency*, companies minimize the resources that are consumed providing a product or service. The **efficiency perspective** on job design is concerned with creating jobs that economize on time, human energy, raw materials, and other productive resources. It is the basis for the field of **industrial engineering**, which focuses on maximizing the efficiency of the methods, facilities, and materials used to produce commercial products. Industrial engineers design products—whether tangible goods or intangible services—in a way that simplifies production processes. They also develop standard procedures and materials to cut production costs, design and test production machinery to ensure proficient operation, and devise inspection procedures to guarantee product quality. Among the pioneers of this approach was Frederick Winslow Taylor (1856–1915), whose studies of efficiency in the workplace gave rise to the field of scientific management.

efficiency perspective An approach to job design that focuses on the creation of jobs that economize on time, human energy, raw materials, and other productive resources.

industrial engineering A branch of engineering that concerns itself with how to maximize the efficiency of the methods, facilities, and materials used to produce commercial products.

Scientific Management

As he rose from laborer to chief engineer at the Midvale Steel Company, Taylor formulated a set of principles of scientific management that today's managers continue to consult in designing and managing jobs in organizations (see Table 2-2). To illustrate the potential benefits of following these principles, Taylor often told a story about a worker named Schmidt who loaded pig iron, or ingots of iron, into railroad cars for the Bethlehem Steel Company. At Bethlehem, before Taylor analyzed the job of loading iron, each employee would pick up a pig of iron that weighed 92 pounds, carry it up a ramp to the door of a railroad car, and drop it into the car. In this manner, a worker could load about $12\frac{1}{2}$ long tons in a day (2,240 pounds = 1 long ton). Taylor set out to improve this rate of productivity by selecting a worker, Schmidt, and offering him $1.85 per day rather than the usual $1.15 per day to do the job of loading pig iron exactly as Taylor instructed. Following Taylor's directions (which involved loading each pig at a prescribed pace and taking periodic rest breaks to allow muscle recuperation), Schmidt was able to load $47\frac{1}{2}$ long tons per day. Considering wages paid and tons of pig iron loaded, Taylor's approach yielded a cost per ton of 3.9 cents versus the old way's cost of 9.2 cents.

Doubt surrounds the authenticity of many of the details recounted in Taylor's pig iron story, suggesting that it be interpreted more as an illustrative allegory rather than as a factual account.[3] But whether allegory or fact, it shows that besides Taylor's trademark concern with efficiency and orderliness, an important feature of his approach was the idea of gainsharing—the sharing by both employers and employees of the economic gains that resulted from applying the principles of scientific management. In Taylor's era, this idea was considered a threat to the well-being of both unions and employers. Unions often used employees' wage dissatisfaction to gain support for unionization. Employers did not want to give up their claim to their firms' profits. Despite this initial resistance, Taylor's approach caught on, aided by the publicity he gained when he appeared before the United States House of Representatives to defend his principles. Others built on his ideas about engineering jobs and the methods used to perform them.

Methods Engineering

methods engineering An area of industrial engineering that attempts to improve the methods used to perform work.

One of the most important descendants of Taylor's pioneering work, **methods engineering**, is an area of industrial engineering that attempts to improve the methods used to perform work. It incorporates two related endeavors—process engineering and human factors engineering.

process engineering A type of methods engineering in which specialists study the sequence of tasks required to produce a particular good or service and examine how these tasks fit together into an integrated job.

Process Engineering. Process engineering studies the sequence of tasks required to produce a particular good or service and examines the way these tasks fit together into an integrated job. It also analyzes tasks to see which should be performed by human beings and which by machines and tries to determine how workers can perform their jobs most efficiently. Process engineers examine the good or service to be produced and decide what function, if any, human beings should serve in its production. They also determine the need for some employees to serve as managers, to direct and control the flow of work (see Chapter 2), and they differentiate the resulting managerial jobs from those of nonmanagerial workers. They specify the procedures for employees to follow, the equipment they should use, and the physical layout of offices, work stations, and materials-storage facilities.

Consider the task of selling a sweater. The process chart in Figure 17-1 details the original job design. To sell one sweater, clerks regularly performed 46 different work activities and walked a distance of 318 feet. To redesign the job of selling sweaters, process engineers analyzed the salespersons' movements and actions guided by questions like the following:

1. Should all the work activities now included in the job actually be in this one job?
2. Does the job holder currently perform some of the work activities in the job in a random fashion when order and consistency might promote greater efficiency?
3. Can some of the work activities be batched, that is, performed in groups for several transactions, rather than separately for each one?
4. Can instructions for managing work activities be standardized?
5. Does the layout of the workplace (including equipment and supplies) facilitate the completion of work activities?

[3] See Charles D. Wrenge and Amedeo G. Perroni, "Taylor's Pig-Tale: A Historical Analysis of Frederick W. Taylor's Pig-Iron Experiments," *Academy of Management Journal* 17 (1974), 6–27.

FIGURE 17-1

Process Chart of Sweater Sale, Original Method

This chart depicts a method of selling a sweater before process engineering. The large circles denote operations performed at a fixed location. The small circles indicate movements by which the clerk moves toward an object or changes the location of an object. The inverted triangles signify delays during which the clerk is motionless. Thus the original process consists of 26 activities, 14 movements, and 6 delays and requires the clerk to walk a distance of 318 feet.
From Marvin E. Mundel, Motion and Time Study: Improving Productivity, *6th ed. (Englewood Cliffs, N.J.: Prentice Hall, 1985), pp. 591–92. Reprinted with the publisher's permission.*

		BASIC CHART FORM		
Process chart-man	Type of chart		383-#138	Department
Original	Original or proposed		S.W.	Chart by
Sweater sale	Subject charted		9/14	Date charted

DIST.	SYMBOL	EXPLANATION
	▽	Waits to greet customer (from counter)
	◉	Greets customer, inquires and shows black cardigan
	◉	Gets black pullover from display case
	◉	Shows to customer
	◉	Puts cardigan on to display; too small for customer
	◉	Takes cardigan off
	◉	Replaces cardigan in display case
90'	○	Walks to stock room
5'	○	Climbs ladder (splintery and unsafe)
	◉	Gets box
	◉	Takes out 1 cardigan of larger size
5'	○	Climbs down ladder
90'	○	Returns to customer
	◉	Shows cardigan to customer
12'	○	Walks around counter
	○	Gets whisk broom
12'	◉	Returns to customer
	◉	Brushes lint off sweater
	◉	Hands brush to customer at customers request
	▽	Waits while customer brushes sweater
	◉	Accepts brush; lays brush on counter
	▽	Customer agrees to buy
	◉	Asks if "charge or cash" (charge)
12'	○	Walks to end of sales counter
	◉	Gets sales book
12'	○	Returns to customer
10'	○	Walks to shelf

6. Is the time and effort consumed by a particular work activity so great that it should be broken into a sequence of smaller activities?

7. Can some of these smaller work activities be eliminated by physical rearrangement of the workplace or by the use of different equipment (calculators rather than adding machines, word processors instead of typewriters)?

8. If some of the smaller work activities were performed in a different sequence, could any of them be eliminated or combined?

9. Could overall productivity be increased by redistributing work activities among a group of workers?[4]

---

[4] Adapted from Marvin E. Mundel, *Motion and Time Study: Improving Productivity*, 6th ed. (Englewood Cliffs, N.J.: Prentice Hall, 1985), p. 115.

	●	Looks for another cardigan (not there)
10'	○	Returns to customer
	●	Writes sales check and enters on book index
	●	Hands ballpen to customer
	▽	Waits while customer signs
	●	Takes ballpen; turns book around
	●	Tears out sales check set; picks up charge card
15'	○	Walks to charge verifier
	●	Enters charge card number
	▽	Waits for response
	●	Enters response on sales check
	●	Separates sales check set; puts original in box
15'	○	Returns to customer
	●	Picks up cardigan
15'	○	Walks with customer (for box for cardigan)
	●	Lays sweater with sales check on wrap desk
	●	Thanks the customer
15'	○	Returns to counter
	▽	Waits for next customer

SUMMARY

Dist. walked, 318'

●	26
○	14
▽	6

human factors engineering A type of methods engineering in which experts design machines, operations, and work environments so that they match human capacities and limitations.

ergonomics Another name for human factors engineering, a type of methods engineering that focuses on designing machines to match human capacities and limitations.

Now look at Figure 17-2. As you can see, the improved method that the process engineers devised reduced the job of selling sweaters by 16 activities and saved clerks 264 feet of walking.

Human Factors Engineering. In **human factors engineering**, sometimes called **ergonomics**, experts design machines, operations, and work environments so that they match human capacities and limitations. Table 17-1 lists some of the concerns of human factors engineering. Note that this area of methods engineering differs noticeably from process engineering. Process engineers fit people to jobs; human factors engineers fit jobs to people.

When people make mistakes at work, human factors engineers ask, Is the

F I G U R E 17-2

Process Chart of Sweater Sale, Improved Method

This chart indicates the correct method of selling a sweater, determined by process engineering. Note that it consists of five fewer activities, ten fewer movements, and one less delay than the original method. In addition, the distance walked by the sales clerk is shortened by 264 feet (83 percent).
From Marvin E. Mundel, Motion and Time Study: Improving Productivity, *6th ed. (Englewood Cliffs, N.J.: Prentice Hall, 1985), pp. 593–94. Reprinted with the publisher's permission.*

BASIC CHART FORM

Process chart-man — Type of chart	383-#138 — Department
Original — Original or proposed	S.W. — Chart by
Sweater sale — Subject charted	9/14 — Date charted

DIST.	SYMBOL	EXPLANATION
	▽	Waits to greet customer (from counter)
	◯	Greets customer, inquires, and shows black cardigan
	◯	Gets black pullover from case
	◯	Shows to customer
	◯	Puts on black cardigan to display
	◯	Takes off cardigan
	◯	Puts cardigan back into case
	◯	Takes out larger size black cardigan
	◯	Displays to customer
	▽	Customer agrees to buy
	◯	Asks if "charge or cash" (charge)
12'	○	Walks to end of sales counter
	◯	Gets sales book
12'	○	Returns to customer
	◯	Writes sales check and enters on book index
	◯	Hands ballpen to customer
	▽	Waits for customer to sign
	◯	Takes ballpen; turns book around
	◯	Tears out sales check set; picks up charge card
15'	○	Walks to charge verifier
	◯	Enters charge card number
	▽	Waits for response
	◯	Enters response on sales check
	◯	Separates sales check set; puts original in box
	◯	Gets box and bag from under counter
15'	○	Returns to customer
	◯	Picks up cardigan
	◯	Puts cardigan in box; box in bag
	◯	Hands to customer and thanks the customer
	▽	Waits for next customer

SUMMARY

Category	Original	Proposed	Saved
Distance walked	318'	54'	264'
◯	26	21	5
○	14	4	10
▽	6	5	1

TABLE 17-1
Areas of Study in Human Factors Engineering

AREA OF STUDY	EXAMPLES
Physical aspects of the user-machine interface	Size, shape, color, texture, and method of operation of displays and controls for such things as cars, home appliances, and industrial and commercial equipment.
Cognitive aspects of the user-machine interface	Understanding of instructions and other information; style of dialogue between computer and user
Workplace design and workspace lay-out	Layout of offices, factories, home kitchens, and other places in which people work; detailed relationships between furniture and equipment and between different equipment components
Physical environment	Effects of climate, noise and vibration, illumination, and chemical/biological contaminants on human performance and health

Source: Adapted with the publisher's permission from I. A. R. Galer, *Applied Ergonomics Handbook* (London: Butterworth, 1987), p. 6.

equipment being used partially to blame for these mistakes? Are mistakes made when certain kinds of equipment are used rather than others? Is it possible to redesign equipment so as to minimize or even eliminate human error? More often than not, the effects of human fallibility and carelessness can be substantially decreased by minimizing error-provoking features of jobs and equipment. For example, shape-coded controls like those shown in Figure 17-3 can be used to reduce aircraft accidents caused by reaching for the wrong control.

Work Measurement: Motion and Time Studies

Besides engineering the methods used to perform jobs, industrial engineers sometimes also examine the motions and time required to complete each job. Such work can be traced to Frederick Winslow Taylor's principles of scientific management but is more directly the product of research by Frank and Lillian Gilbreth, who set out to find the "one best way" to do any job (see also Chapter 2). In the course of this pursuit, the Gilbreths developed motion study, a procedure that reduces jobs to their most basic movements. As you will recall from Chapter 2,

FIGURE 17-3

Shape-Coding to Reduce Flying Errors

The knobs shown in this figure are intended to help pilots differentiate among control levers without looking at them. Two general rules were followed during the design process: (1) The shape of a control should suggest its purpose, and (2) the shape should be distinguishable even when gloves are worn.
Adapted from C. T. Morgan, J. S. Cook, A. Chapanis, and M. W. Lund, Human Engineering Guide to Equipment Design (New York: McGraw-Hill Book Company, 1963), p. 25. Reprinted with permission of McGraw-Hill, Inc.

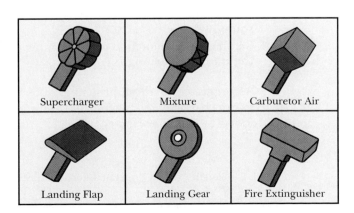

Supercharger	Mixture	Carburetor Air
Landing Flap	Landing Gear	Fire Extinguisher

each of these basic movements is called a therblig (a near reversal of *Gilbreth*) and consists of motions such as "search," "grasp," and "assemble." The Gilbreths also developed procedures to determine the time required by each of the movements needed to perform a job. Time-and-motion analysis was thus invented.

Like Taylor, the Gilbreths were fanatics about efficiency in all aspects of their lives. For example, through a lengthy analysis, Frank determined that 12 was the number of children that allowed the most efficient use of a family's resources, so the Gilbreths had 12 children. Among other projects aimed at increasing the efficiency of everyday living, they attempted to simplify the English alphabet, the typewriter, and spelling. Frank even went so far as to apply time-and-motion experimentation to the task of shaving:

> For a while he tried shaving with two razors, but finally gave it up. "I can save forty-four seconds," he grumbled, "but I wasted two minutes this morning putting a bandage on my throat." It wasn't the [nicked] throat that really bothered him. It was the two minutes.[5]

The Gilbreths developed their methods to eliminate unnecessary motion and effort and to set accurate job standards, or expected levels of job performance. These procedures constituted an indispensable addition to the efficiency perspective on job design. They gave rise to **work measurement**, an area of industrial engineering concerned with measuring the amount of work accomplished and developing standards for performing work of an acceptable quantity and quality. Work measurement includes micromotion analysis, memomotion analysis, and time study procedures.

work measurement An area of industrial engineering concerned with measuring the amount of work accomplished and developing standards for performing work of an acceptable quantity and quality.

micromotion analysis A type of work measurement in which industrial engineers analyze the hand and body movements required to do a job.

Micromotion Analysis. In **micromotion analysis**, industrial engineers analyze the hand and body movements required to do a job. This technique is a direct descendant of the motion study methods devised by the Gilbreths. Their therbligs continue to be used in current micromotion procedures. Industrial engineers usually perform micromotion analysis by using a slow-speed film or videotape of a person performing her job. They analyze the movements involved in the task and try to improve performance efficiency by means of principles like the following:

1. Try to have both hands doing the same thing at the same time or to balance the work of the two hands.
2. Try to avoid using the hands simply for holding. Use specialized jigs, vises, or clamps instead.
3. Keep all work inside a work area bounded by the worker's reach.
4. Relieve the hands of work wherever possible.
5. Eliminate as many therbligs or as much of a therblig as possible and combine therbligs when possible.
6. Arrange therbligs in the most convenient order. Each therblig should flow smoothly into the next.
7. Standardize the method of performing the job in the manner that promotes the quickest learning.[6]

As suggested by these principles, jobs designed by means of micromotion analysis are characterized by great economy of motion. The technique, of course, is intended to promote efficiency.

---

[5] Frank B. Gilbreth, Jr., and Ernestine Gilbreth Carey, *Cheaper by the Dozen* (New York: Thomas Y. Crowell, 1948), p. 2.
[6] Adapted from Mundel, *Motion and Time Study*, p. 309.

JOB DESIGN

memomotion analysis A type of work measurement in which industrial engineers examine longer activity sequences by using slow speed to film or videotape a person at work and then playing back the resulting film or tape at normal speed.

Memomotion Analysis. Memomotion analysis is used to analyze jobs that are less repetitive than most assembly-line jobs and that have longer activity sequences. This time, the analyst uses a slow speed to film or videotape a person at work and then plays back the resulting film or tape at normal speed. As you can imagine, job activities are sped up—one hour of activity may be viewed in as little as four minutes—and the analyst is able to identify and observe gross movements that normally occur over long periods of time.

The type of movements identified in this sort of analysis and some of its potential benefits are illustrated in Figure 17-4, which shows two alternative layouts of a dentist's office. In the left diagram, a memomotion analysis has captured the travel paths of the dentist and an assistant during a typical patient visit. In the right diagram, the analyst has again traced the travel paths of the dentist and his assistant during a similar patient visit but after the dentist's office has been rearranged in accordance with the recommendations of the memomotion analyst. You don't have to look very hard to see that many fewer motions are shown in the lower diagram and that they stretch over a smaller area in space.

Time-Study Techniques. Time-study techniques are generally used to measure the time consumed by job performance, but they are sometimes used also to specify the time that a particular job should take to complete. In **stopwatch time analysis**, an analyst uses a stopwatch to time the sequence of motions needed to complete a job. In **standard time analysis**, the analyst matches the results of micromotion analysis with standard time charts to determine the average time that should be required to perform a job. When combined with micromotion analyses, the results of either type of time analysis can be used to create job element descriptions such as the one shown in Figure 17-5.

stopwatch time analysis A time study technique in which an analyst uses a stopwatch to time the sequence of motions needed to complete a job.

standard time analysis A time study technique in which an analyst matches the results of micromotion analysis with standard time charts to determine the average time that should be required to perform a job.

FIGURE 17-4

Memomotion Analysis of a Dentist's Office

Initial film viewings showed the travel paths sketched in (a). Memomotion analysis led to the redesigned office and resulting travel paths shown in (b).

From Marvin E. Mundel, Motion and Time Study: Improving Productivity, *6th ed. (Englewood Cliffs, N.J.: Prentice Hall, 1985), pp. 320–21. Reprinted with the publisher's permission.*

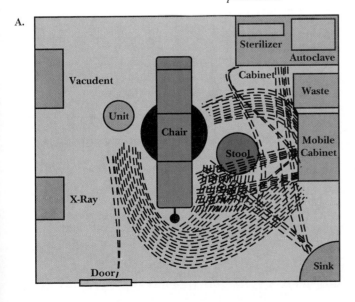

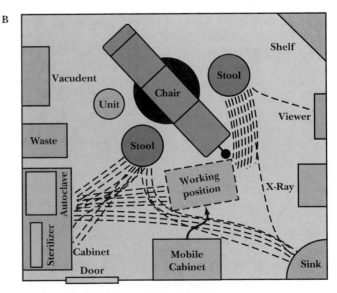

PRODUCTION STANDARD- - JOB SUMMARY SHEET

C.O.00.1120.0

Page No. __1__ Of __3__ Dept. __Process Ham__ Study Date __2-16-__ Study No. __3-6-111__

Operation __Bone 4½-5½ S.S. Picnics-Skin On__ Job __Bone Picnics__

Backing ‾ ‾ ‾ ‾ ‾ ‾ Machine No. ‾ ‾ ‾ ‾ ‾ ‾ Ave. Equip. __Job Symbol 150-h__

No.	DETAILED DESCRIPTION OF JOB ELEMENTS		Std. Allowed Time/Unit
	LEFT HAND	**RIGHT HAND**	
1.	Grasp picnic from conveyer or from pile at side of operator. Slide picnic on cutting board to position in front of operator - face side up.	Hold knife.	.0371
2.	Pick up steel from cutting board - Hold steel - aside steel to cutting board.	Slide knife blade across steel. (3 strokes)	.0408
3.	Smooth out skin around shank end - pull up on skin during cut - use skin as handle to roll picnic over so skin side is up. Roll picnic back so face side is up - aside skin to conveyer.	Slit skin on shank end - cut skin away from skin side of picnic complete skinning by cutting away skin from shank end on face side.	.2786
4.	Hold picnic down on cutting board.	Make horizontal cut at side of picnic length of the arm bone to the area in the center of the picnic near the bone.	.1390
5.	Hold picnic - grasp and hold bone at center area. Hold bone at blade end, until bone is free of picnic.	Guide knife along contour of arm bone, around center area of bone until entire center area is free of picnic. Cut away meat at blade end of arm bone. Cut away meat from shank end of arm bone until bone is completely free of picnic.	.5877
6.	Aside bone to top conveyer - hit counter on return motion to record number of picnics boned.	Aside picnic to bottom conveyer.	.0370

Converted to		Cwt.	Std. Allowed Time Min/Unit		1.1762
Basis Unit	Wt. Per Piece	4.83 Lbs.	Std. mos/ 100 Units		1.9603
Std. Allowed Time Min/Unit		.2435	Units/Mos.		51.0
Std. was 100/Units		.4058	Approved by	A.D.	
Units/Mos.		246.4	Approved by		

FIGURE 17-5

Summary of the Job of Preparing Hams

This description summarizes the hand movements and time required to process a picnic ham. It brings together the results of micromotion analysis and standard time analysis.

From Marvin E. Mundel, Motion and Time Study: Improving Productivity, *6th ed. (Englewood Cliffs, N.J.: Prentice Hall, 1985), p. 502. Reprinted with permission of Patrick Cudahy, Inc.*

Besides reducing satisfaction, oversimplified, repetitive tasks can also depress employee health. According to government sources, repetitive motion disorders accounted for 147,000 instances of job-related illness in 1989.* Such disorders result from repeating the same motions with arms and hands throughout the day. Also called cumulative trauma injuries, repetitive motion disorders include carpal tunnel syndrome, a painful wrist ailment found among people who use typewriter keyboards for extended periods of time, and white finger, an injury common among operators of pneumatic drills that is caused by intense vibration.

To combat the health effects of repetition, the U.S. Department of Labor's Occupational Safety and Health Administration (OSHA) has warned employers of the negative health effects of repetition and has developed plans with some to reduce the presence of repetitive tasks. For example, Chrysler Corporation has hired experts to study jobs at five of the company's assembly plants. It has also begun to rotate workers among tasks to break up repetition over the course of each working day. Working with human factors engineers, Chrysler has redesigned many jobs and developed special tools to reduce or eliminate repetitive motions at work. In this manner, the company expects to begin to bring the problem under control within three years.†

* "Repetitive Motion Disorders Lead Increase in Job Illnesses," *New York Times*, November 16, 1990, p. D7.

† "Chrysler Agrees to Curtail Repetitive Tasks for Workers," *Lansing State Journal*, November 3, 1989, p. 4B.

Evaluating Industrial Engineering and the Efficiency Perspective

Consistent with the efficiency perspective that serves as their foundation, all the industrial engineering methods we have described attempt to enhance productivity by simplifying jobs. Often, industrial engineers using these methods can improve productivity dramatically. There is, however, a danger that simplification will be carried too far, leading to the creation of oversimplified jobs like those of the welder and clerk described at the beginning of this chapter. This danger looms particularly large in bureaucratic organizations, because the common use in such firms of standardization and formalization increases the pressure to simplify work (see Chapter 15).

Why worry about oversimplification? As we said in Chapters 7 and 8, workers performing oversimplified, routine jobs may become bored, resentful, and dissatisfied. They may even engage in sabotage because of the absence of challenge and interest in their work. Oversimplified work may also lead employees to be absent a lot of the time or to start looking for other jobs. Oversimplification can even have dire health consequences, as discussed in the "In Practice" box. So the same simplification intended to enhance the efficiency of work processes may actually reduce that efficiency if carried to an extreme.

THE SATISFACTION PERSPECTIVE ON JOB DESIGN

satisfaction perspective An approach to job design that suggests that fitting the characteristics of jobs to the needs and interests of the people who perform them provides the opportunity for satisfaction at work.

What can be done to counteract the effects of oversimplification or to make sure that jobs are not oversimplified to begin with? The answer to this question, offered initially by Lillian Gilbreth, is that jobs should be designed in such a way that performing them creates feelings of fulfillment in their holders.[7] This idea is the central tenet of the **satisfaction perspective**

[7] Lillian M. Gilbreth, *The Psychology of Management* (New York: MacMillan, 1921), p. 19.

T A B L E 17-2
Two Perspectives on Job Design

EFFICIENCY PERSPECTIVE	SATISFACTION PERSPECTIVE
Tasks are shaped mainly by technology and organizational needs.	Tasks are shaped at least partly by workers' personal needs.
Tasks are repetitive and narrow.	Tasks are varied and complex.
Tasks require little or no skill and are easy to learn and perform.	Tasks require well developed skills and are difficult to learn and perform.
The management and performance of work are separated into different jobs.	The management and performance of work are merged in the same job.
It is assumed that there is only one best way to do each job. Tools and methods are developed by staff specialists.	It is assumed that each job can be performed in several ways. Tools and methods are often developed by the people who use them.
Workers are an extension of their equipment and perform according to its requirements. Work is often machine paced.	Workers use equipment but are not regulated by it. The pace of work is set by people rather than machines.
Primarily extrinsic rewards (incentive wages) are used to motivate performance.	Intrinsic rewards (task achievements) are used with extrinsic rewards to motivate performance.
Social interaction is limited or discouraged.	Social interaction is encouraged, in some cases required.
Efficiency and productivity are the ultimate goals of job design.	Satisfaction and fulfillment are the ultimate goals of job design.

horizontal job enlargement A type of job design based on the idea that increasing the number of tasks a job holder performs will reduce the repetitive nature of the job and thus eliminate worker boredom.

job range The number of tasks a job holder performs to complete the job.

job extension A type of horizontal job enlargement in which several simplified jobs are combined to form a single new job.

One way to make workers proud of their work and customers happy with their purchases is to produce a unique product every time. At Matsushita's National Bicycle Industrial Co., employees work with computers and robots to make customized bicycles, each one tailored to the specifications of an individual customer. The 20-worker plant can produce any of 11,231,862 variations on 18 models of racing, road, and mountain bikes in 199 color patterns and about as many sizes as there are people. Source: Susan Moffat, "Japan's New Personalized Production," Fortune, October 22, 1990.

on job design. The satisfaction perspective suggests that fitting the characteristics of jobs to the needs and interests of the people who perform them provides the opportunity for satisfaction at work.[8] Table 17-2 contrasts this approach with the efficiency perspective discussed in the last section. Among the methods of job design developed with the satisfaction perspective in mind are horizontal job enlargement, vertical job enrichment, comprehensive job enrichment, and sociotechnical enrichment.

Horizontal Job Enlargement

To counteract oversimplification, managers sometimes attempt to boost the complexity of work by increasing the number of task activities a job entails. This approach, called **horizontal job enlargement**, is based on the idea that increasing **job range**, or the number of tasks a jobholder performs, will reduce the repetitive nature of the job and thus eliminate worker boredom.[9] Increasing job range in this manner is *horizontal* enlargement, because the job is created out of tasks from the same horizontal "slice" of an organization's hierarchy.

Job Extension. Some horizontal job enlargement programs involve **job extension**, an approach in which several simplified jobs are combined to form a single new job. For example, the job of our insurance company clerk, which consists solely of proofreading, might be extended by adding filing and telephone-an-

[8] Gerald R. Salancik and Jeffrey Pfeffer, "An Examination of Need-Satisfaction Models of Job Attitudes," *Administrative Science Quarterly* 22 (1977), 427–56.

[9] The classic piece on this approach to counteracting oversimplification is Charles R. Walker and Robert H. Guest, *The Man on the Assembly Line* (Cambridge, Mass.: Harvard University Press, 1952).

swering tasks. Similarly, the welder's job might be extended by adding other assembly operations to it.

Organizations as diverse as Maytag, AT&T, and the U.S. Civil Service have implemented job extension in one form or another. However, especially when a number of simple, easy-to-master tasks are combined, it is easy for workers to view job extension as giving them more of the same routine, boring work to do. Thus, although initial tests seemed promising, most research has suggested that job extension rarely succeeds in reversing oversimplification sufficiently to strengthen employee motivation and satisfaction.[10]

Job Rotation. In **job rotation**, workers are rotated among several jobs in a structured, predefined manner. Rotation of this sort creates horizontal enlargement without combining or otherwise redesigning a firm's jobs. For instance, a supermarket employee might run a checkout lane for a specific period of time and then, switching jobs with another employee, restock shelves for another set period of time.

job rotation A type of horizontal job enlargement in which workers are rotated among several jobs in a structured, predefined manner.

As workers rotate, they perform a wider variety of tasks than they would if limited to a single job. Again, though, critics have observed that job rotation often achieves little more than having people perform several boring, routine jobs rather than one. As a result, although companies including Ford Motor Company and Western Electric have tried job rotation, it has generally failed to improve worker motivation or satisfaction.[11]

Vertical Job Enrichment: Herzberg's Two-Factor Theory

The failure of horizontal job enlargement to successfully counteract the undesirable effects of oversimplification has led many managers to try other approaches instead. Many such trials involve attempts to increase **job depth**, that is, the amount of discretion a jobholder has to choose job activities and outcomes. This approach, called **vertical job enrichment**, is based on the work of Frederick Herzberg, an industrial psychologist who studied the causes of employee satisfaction and dissatisfaction at work.[12]

job depth The amount of discretion a job holder has to choose job activities and outcomes.

vertical job enrichment A type of job design based on the idea that giving job holders the discretion to choose job activities and outcomes will improve their satisfaction.

Herzberg, who began his research in the mid-1950s, started out by interviewing 200 engineers and accountants in nine companies, asking them to describe incidents at work that had made them feel "exceptionally good" or "exceptionally bad" about their jobs. From these interviews, Herzberg concluded that satisfaction, or feeling good, and dissatisfaction, or feeling bad, should be thought of as independent concepts, not opposites on a single continuum, as traditional views had held. What this suggests is that a person might feel more satisfied with her job without feeling less dissatisfied, more dissatisfied without feeling less satisfied, and so forth. Figure 17-6 contrasts Herzberg's two-factor view with the traditional single-factor view of satisfaction in which higher satisfaction always accompanies lower dissatisfaction and vice versa.

As he dug further into his interview data, Herzberg also found that certain characteristics of the work situation seemed almost always to affect employee satisfaction. Quite different work characteristics appeared to be associated with employee dissatisfaction. **Motivator factors**, such as achievement or recognition,

motivator factors Characteristics of the job that according to Frederick Herzberg, influence the amount of satisfaction experienced at work.

---

[10] J. D. Kilbridge, "Reduced Costs through Job Enlargement: A Case," *Journal of Business* 33 (1960), 357–62; J. F. Biggane and P. A. Stewart, "Job Enlargement: A Case Study," in *Design of Jobs*, ed. Louis E. Davis and James C. Taylor, (New York: Penguin, 1972), pp. 264–76; and Gerald E. Susman, "Job Enlargement: Effects of Culture on Worker Responses," *Industrial Relations* 12 (1973), 1–15.

[11] Ricky W. Griffin, *Task Design: An Integrative Approach* (Glenview, Ill.: Scott, Foresman, 1982), p. 25.

[12] Frederick Herzberg, Bernard Mausner, and Barbara Bloch Snyderman, *The Motivation to Work* (New York: John Wiley, 1959).

FIGURE 17-6

Contrasting Views of Satisfaction and Dissatisfaction

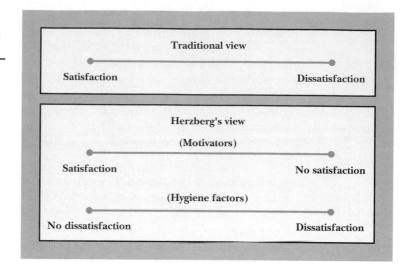

Traditional view

Satisfaction •————————————————• Dissatisfaction

Herzberg's view

(Motivators)

Satisfaction •————————————————• No satisfaction

(Hygiene factors)

No dissatisfaction •————————————————• Dissatisfaction

hygiene factors Characteristics of the job that according to Frederick Herzberg, influence the amount of dissatisfaction experienced at work.

increased satisfaction. Their absence produced a lack of satisfaction but not active dissatisfaction. On the other hand, **hygiene factors**, such as company policy or employees' relationships with their supervisors, usually led to serious dissatisfaction and rarely contributed to a gain in satisfaction.

Armed with this distinction, Herzberg then noticed that only the motivator factors identified in his research seemed able to increase the incentive to work. Hygiene factors, he said, could help to maintain motivation but would more often contribute to a decrease in motivation. If you examine Figure 17-7, you will see that many of Herzberg's hygiene factors are the very job characteristics emphasized by the efficiency perspective on job design. You can undoubtedly anticipate Herzberg's argument. In fact, he contended that following the principles advocated by Taylor, the Gilbreths, and later specialists in industrial engineering would create oversimplified jobs that could only dissatisfy and demotivate workers. Thus, he suggested, managers should pay less attention to things like working conditions and salary and instead design jobs that incorporate opportunities for such positive outcomes as growth, achievement, and recognition.

Over the years, many critics have attacked Herzberg's ideas.[13] Among the most serious criticisms are the following:

1. The *critical-incident technique* that Herzberg used, in which he asked people to recall earlier feelings and experiences, is a questionable research method subject to errors in perception or memory and to subconscious biases. Thus the validity of his conclusions is questionable.

2. Herzberg's interviewees, engineers and accountants, were all members of professional, white-collar occupational groups and male (few women were engineers or accountants in Herzberg's day). Women, minorities, and members of other occupational groups, such as salespeople or industrial laborers, could be expected to answer Herzberg's questions differently.

[13] For example, see Robert. J. House and Lawrence A. Wigdor, "Herzberg's Dual-Factor Theory of Job Satisfaction and Motivation: A Review of the Empirical Evidence and a Criticism," *Personnel Psychology* 20 (1967), 369–89; Marvin D. Dunnette, John P. Campbell, and Milton D. Hakel, "Factors Contributing to Job Dissatisfaction in Six Occupational Groups," *Organizational Behavior and Human Performance* 2 (1967), 146–64; Joseph Schneider and Edwin A. Locke, "A Critique of Herzberg's Classification System and a Suggested Revision," *Organizational Behavior and Human Performance* 6 (1971), 441–58; Donald P. Schwab and Larry L. Cummings, "Theories of Performance and Satisfaction: A Review," *Industrial Relations* 9 (1970), 408–30; and Richard J. Caston and Rita Braito, "A Specification Issue in Job Satisfaction Research," *Sociological Perspectives* 28 (1985), 175–97.

FIGURE 17-7

Herzberg's Motivator Factors
and Hygiene Factors

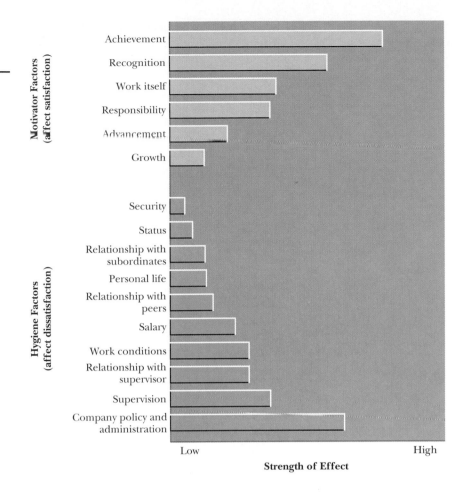

3. Other studies have failed to replicate Herzberg's results. You will recall from Chapter 3 that such failure casts grave doubts on the merits of research findings.

4. Job design programs based on Herzberg's model almost always fail to stimulate work-force satisfaction of lasting significance.

Despite these criticisms, Herzberg's theory is widely known among managers and continues to stimulate interest in questions of motivation, satisfaction, and job design. In addition, it has influenced more recent approaches to job design by highlighting the importance of designing jobs that satisfy human desires for growth, achievement, and recognition. Owing to questions about its validity, however, Herzberg's two-factor theory is not a useful guide for managerial actions.[14]

Comprehensive Job Enrichment: The Hackman-Oldham Job Characteristics Model

Although neither the horizontal loading of job enlargement nor the vertical loading of Herzberg's job enrichment is able to counteract oversimplification when used separately, **comprehensive job enrichment** programs that combine

comprehensive job enrichment A type of job design that combines both horizontal and vertical improvements to stimulate employee motivation and satisfaction.

[14] Griffin, *Task Design*; also see J. Richard Hackman, "On the Coming Demise of Job Enrichment," in *Man and Work in Society*, ed. Eugene Louis Cass and Frederick G. Zimmer (New York: Van Nostrand, 1975), pp. 45–63

THE SATISFACTION PERSPECTIVE ON JOB DESIGN

both horizontal and vertical improvements are usually quite successful in stimulating motivation and satisfaction. Many such programs are based on the model of job design developed by J. Richard Hackman and Greg Oldham, which is shown in Figure 17–8.[15]

As the figure suggests, Hackman and Oldham proposed that five core job characteristics influence workers' experience of three critical psychological states. These critical states, they said, lead to a variety of work and personal outcomes. This process is affected by certain moderating factors, so that the model works as expected under some circumstances but not others. Let's look at the Hackman-Oldham model in greater detail.

Core Job Characteristics. According to Hackman and Oldham, jobs that in and of themselves are likely to motivate performance and contribute to employee satisfaction exhibit the following five **core job characteristics:**

1. *Skill variety.* The degree to which a job holder must carry out a variety of different activities and use a number of different personal skills in performing the job.
2. *Task identity.* The degree to which performing a job results in the completion of a whole and identifiable piece of work and a visible outcome that can be recognized as the result of personal performance.
3. *Task significance.* The degree to which a job has a significant impact on the lives of other people, whether those people are coworkers in the same firm or other individuals in the surrounding environment.
4. *Autonomy.* The degree to which the job holder has the freedom, independence, and discretion necessary to schedule work and to decide what procedures to use in carrying it out.

core job characteristics Job characteristics identified in the Hackman-Oldham model that lead their holders to experience certain critical psychological states.

---

[15] Hackman and Oldham, "Motivation through the Design of Work: Test of a Theory," *Organizational Behavior and Human Performance* 16 (1976), 250–79; Hackman and Oldham, *Work Redesign* (Reading, Mass.: Addison-Wesley, 1980); Karlene H. Roberts and William H. Glick, "The Job Characteristics Approach to Task Design: A Critical Review," *Journal of Applied Psychology* 86 (1981), 193–217; and Ramon J. Aldag, Steve H. Barr, and Arthur P. Brief, "Measurement of Perceived Task Characteristics," *Psychological Bulletin* 99 (1981), 415–31.

FIGURE 17-8

The Hackman-Oldham Job Characteristics Model

Adapted with the publisher's permission from J. Richard Hackman and Greg R. Oldham, "Motivation through the Design of Work: Test of a Theory," Organizational Behavior and Human Performance 16 (1976), 256.

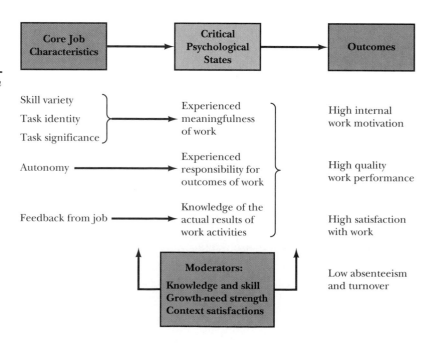

5. *Feedback*. The degree to which performing the activities required by the job provides the worker with direct and clear information about the effectiveness of her performance.

Critical Psychological States. These five core job characteristics, in turn, influence the extent to which employees experience three **critical psychological states**:

1. *Experienced meaningfulness of work.* The degree to which a worker experiences her job as having an outcome that is useful and valuable to her, the company, and the surrounding environment.
2. *Experienced responsibility for work outcomes.* The degree to which the worker feels personally accountable and responsible for the results of her work.
3. *Knowledge of results.* The degree to which the worker maintains an awareness of the effectiveness of her work.[16]

As Figure 17-8 shows, each of the job characteristics influences one particular psychological state. Specifically, *skill variety*, *task identity*, and *task significance* are seen as affecting the *experienced meaningfulness of work*. Thus jobholders should experience their jobs as meaningful if they must use a variety of activities and skills to produce an identifiable piece of work that influences the lives of others. *Autonomy*, on the other hand, influences the job holder's *experienced responsibility for work outcomes*. This means that workers who have the discretion to determine work procedures and outcomes should feel responsible for the results of their work. Finally, *feedback* determines whether a worker will have *knowledge of the results of work*. Through information about performance effectiveness that comes from the job itself, the jobholder can maintain an awareness of how effectively she is performing.

Work and Personal Outcomes. According to the Hackman-Oldham model, if workers experience these three psychological states, several work and personal outcomes may result. First, workers may view their jobs as interesting, challenging, and important and may be motivated to perform them simply because they are so stimulating, challenging, and enjoyable. *High internal work motivation*, or being "turned on" to job performance by its personal consequences, is thus one possible outcome. Second, experiencing the three critical psychological states and the internal, or intrinsic, motivation they arouse can encourage *high-quality work performance* (and sometimes greater production quantity).[17] Third, workers who experience the three psychological states do so because their work allows them opportunities for personal learning, growth, and development. As we saw in Chapter 8, these kinds of experiences generally promote *high satisfaction with work*. Fourth, work that includes these kinds of experiences also tends to be associated with *lower absenteeism* and *turnover*.

Moderating Factors. The Hackman-Oldham model proposes several moderating factors. They determine whether its core job characteristics will indeed trigger the critical psychological states leading to the work and personal outcomes we have identified. The first of these moderators is the worker's *knowledge and skill*.

---

[16] Hackman and Oldham, "Design of Work," pp. 256–57.
[17] Raymond A. Katzell, Penny Bienstock, and Paul H. Faerstein, *A Guide to Worker Productivity Experiments in the United States 1971-1975* (New York: New York University Press, 1977) p. 14; Edwin A. Locke, Dena B. Feren, Vickie M. McCaleb, Karyll N. Shaw, and Anne T. Denny, "The Relative Effectiveness of Four Methods of Motivating Employee Performance," in *Changes in Working Life*, ed. K. D. Duncan, Michael M. Gruneberg, and D. Wallis (London: John Wiley, 1980), pp. 363–88; and Richard E. Kopelman, "Job Redesign and Productivity: A Review of the Evidence," *National Productivity Review* 4 (1985), 237–55.

To succeed on a job with the five core job characteristics, a worker must have the knowledge and skill required to perform the job successfully. People who cannot perform a job because they lack the necessary knowledge or skill will only feel frustrated by their failure. The motivational aims of job enrichment will be thwarted.

Growth-need strength, the strength of a worker's need for personal growth, is the second factor that affects the operation of the Hackman-Oldham model. Workers who have strong growth needs are attracted to enriched work because it offers the opportunity for growth. On the other hand, workers whose need for growth is weak are likely to feel overburdened by the opportunities offered them. Therefore they will try to avoid enriched work.

Finally, certain *context satisfactions* can act as moderator factors that influence the Hackman-Oldham model's applicability. Hackman and Oldham identified them as satisfaction with pay, with job security, with coworkers, and with supervisors. Workers who feel exploited and dissatisfied because they are poorly paid, feel insecure about their jobs, or have abusive coworkers or unfair supervision are likely to view job enrichment as just one more type of exploitation. Context dissatisfaction can thus negate the expected benefits of Hackman-Oldham job enrichment.

Job Diagnostic Survey A questionnaire that measures workers' perceptions of core job characteristics, critical psychological states, and different moderating factors.

The Job Diagnostic Survey. To put their model to use, Hackman and Oldham developed a questionnaire, the **Job Diagnostic Survey** (JDS), that measures workers' perceptions of the five core job characteristics, the three critical psychological states, and different moderating factors. (The Task Diagnostic Questionnaire that appears in Exercise 17-1 is based on many of the questions that appear in the JDS and can be substituted for it in the following procedure.) Figure 17-9 shows two ways to use the data on core job characteristics acquired with the JDS. On the left side of the figure, JDS scores on each of the five characteristics have been plotted for two jobs. As you can see, Job A rates well across the five characteristics, but Job B rates poorly overall. Its reasonably high level of task significance and moderate levels of skill variety and task identity are offset by rather poor feedback and very little autonomy. Clearly, enrichment of Job B will require changes in four of the five core job characteristics.

FIGURE 17-9

JDS Profiles and MPS Comparison

From J. R. Hackman, "Work Design," in Improving Life at Work: Behavioral Science Approaches to Organizational Change, *ed. J. R. Hackman and J. L. Suttle (Santa Monica, Calif.: Goodyear Publishing Co., 1977), p. 135. Reprinted with the authors' permission.*

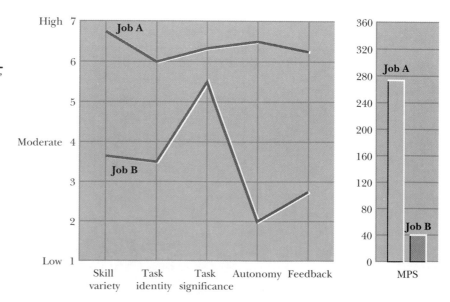

On the right side of Figure 17-9, a bar chart reflects the calculation for each of the two jobs of a **motivating potential score** (MPS), entering the JDS scores into the following formula:

$$\text{MPS} = \frac{(\text{Variety} + \text{Identity} + \text{Significance})}{3} \times \text{Autonomy} \times \text{Feedback}$$

This formula reflects the Hackman-Oldham model's conception of skill variety, task identity, and task significance as exerting a joint effect on experienced meaningfulness. These three characteristics are averaged before being combined with autonomy and feedback scores. (If you perform Exercise 17-1 you will use this same formula to compute a motivational summary score or MSS.) Some investigators are beginning to use a simpler additive formula to perform this combination instead of the multiplicative one suggested by Hackman and Oldham. Which one will ultimately prove to be the most useful is currently unclear.[18]

Examination of the bar chart suggests that the MPS facilitates gross comparisons among jobs and can help managers locate trouble spots quickly even if a large number of different jobs must be scrutinized. A lower MPS means a job needs enrichment while a higher MPS indicates that the job doesn't. However, the MPS does not tell managers how to enrich a particular job. To learn that, they must construct profiles like the ones in the left-hand part of Figure 17-9, which reveal a job's specific strengths and weaknesses.

There are a number of ways of correcting the deficiencies identified by a JDS analysis. To enhance skill variety and task identity, oversimplified jobs can be *combined* to form enlarged modules of work. For example, the production of a toaster could be redesigned so that the entire appliance is constructed by a single employee working alone rather than by a dozen people working on an assembly line. *Natural units of work* can be formed by clustering similar tasks into logical or inherently meaningful groups. For example, a data-entry clerk who formerly selected work orders randomly from a stack might be given sole responsibility for the work of an entire department or division. This intervention might strengthen both task identity and task significance for the clerk.

In an effort to increase task variety, autonomy, and feedback, a firm can give workers the responsibility for *establishing* and *managing client relationships*. In several General Motors plants, assembly workers can telephone people who have recently purchased a GM car to ask for feedback about product quality. Or to increase autonomy, managerial duties can be designed into a particular job through *vertical loading*. Finally, to increase feedback, *feedback channels* can be opened by adding to a job such things as quality-control duties and computerized feedback mechanisms.

Sociotechnical Enrichment: The Tavistock Model

The Hackman-Oldham model focuses on jobs as individualized units of work, each performed by a single employee. It is therefore not appropriate for jobs performed by closely interacting groups of workers. How can managers counteract

---

[18] Hugh J. Arnold and Robert J. House, "Methodological and Substantive Extensions of the Job Characteristics Model of Motivation," *Organizational Behavior and Human Performance* 25 (1980), 161–83; Arthur P. Brief, Marc J. Wallace, Jr., and Ramon J. Aldag, "Linear vs. Non-Linear Models of the Formation of Affective Reactions: The Case of Job Enlargement," *Decision Sciences* 7 (1976), 1–9; Gerald R. Ferris and David C. Gilmore, "A Methodological Note on Job Complexity Indices," *Journal of Applied Psychology* 70 (1985), 225–27; and Denis D. Umstot, Cecil H. Bell, Jr., and Terrence R. Mitchell, "Effects of Job Enrichment and Task Goals on Satisfaction and Productivity: Implications for Task Design," *Journal of Applied Psychology* 61 (1976), 379–94.

sociotechnical enrichment A type of job design that recognizes the importance of satisfying the needs of employees within the technical requirements of an organization's production system.

the negative effects of oversimplified *group* work? Answer: They can make use of some form of **sociotechnical enrichment**, an approach to designing group jobs that recognizes the importance of satisfying employees' personnel needs.

Sociotechnical Principles. Sociotechnical enrichment originated in the early 1950s when researchers from England's Tavistock Institute set out to correct faults in the processes used to mine coal in Great Britain.[19] Historically, coal had been mined by teams of miners working closely with each other to pool efforts, coordinate activities, and cope with the physical threats of mining. With the advent of powered coal-digging equipment in the 1930s and 1940s, however, coal mining changed drastically. Teams were split up, and miners often found themselves working alone along the long walls of exposed coal created by the equipment. Mining, normally a hazardous, physically demanding occupation anyway, grew even more unbearable owing to changes stimulated by the new technology. Miners expressed their dissatisfaction with these circumstances through disobedience, absence, and occasional violence.

The Tavistock researchers soon realized that the roots of the miners' dissatisfaction lay in the loss of the social interaction that mining teams had provided and that had made the dangerous, demanding job of mining more tolerable. It appeared to the researchers that technology had been allowed to supersede important social factors and that performance in the mine could be improved only if this balance were redressed.

Indeed, after small teams were formed to operate and provide support for clusters of powered equipment, production rose substantially. This experience led the Tavistock researchers to suggest that work-force productivity could be hurt when either social or technical factors alone were allowed to shape work processes. They further suggested that job designs that balanced social (socio) and technological (technical) factors—*sociotechnical designs*—encourage both performance and satisfaction.

In other words, employees should work in groups that allow them to talk with each other about their work as they do it. Those work groups should include the people whose frequent interaction is required by the production technology being used. For instance, salespeople, register clerks, and stock clerks who must often interact with each other to serve customers in a department store should be grouped together to facilitate communication about work. Salespeople and clerks from other departments should not be included in the group, because they do not share job-related interdependencies with the group's members.

In the course of performing their research, the Tavistock sociotechnical researchers identified the following psychological requirements as critical to worker motivation and satisfaction:

1. The content of each job must be reasonably demanding or challenging and provide some variety, although not necessarily novelty.
2. Performing the job must have perceivable, desirable consequences. Workers should be able to identify the products of their efforts.
3. Workers should be able to see how the lives of other people are affected by the production processes they use and the things they produce.
4. Workers must have decision-making authority in some areas.
5. Workers must be able to learn from the job and go on learning. This implies appropriate performance standards and adequate feedback.

[19] Eric L. Trist and K. W. Bamforth, "Some Social and Psychological Consequences of the Longwall Method of Coal-Getting," *Human Relations* 4 (1951), 3–38.

6. Workers need the opportunity to give and receive help and to have their work recognized by others in the work place.[20]

The Tavistock group, who worked mainly in England and Norway, developed this list of required job characteristics independently of Hackman and Oldham, who worked only in the United States. But as you can see, items 1 through 5 correspond loosely with the five core job characteristics of the Hackman-Oldham model. Item 6 highlights the emphasis placed by sociotechnical enrichment on interpersonal relations and social satisfaction in the workplace.

semiautonomous groups Groups that are subject to the management direction needed to ensure adherence to organizational policies but are otherwise responsible for managing themselves.

Semiautonomous Groups. Contemporary sociotechnical designs normally involve **semiautonomous groups**. These groups are subject to the management direction needed to ensure adherence to organizational policies but are otherwise responsible for managing group activities. Within each such group

> Individuals must move about within the group spontaneously and without being ordered to do so, because it is necessary to the efficient functioning of the [group]. . . . If we observe the group in action, we will see movements of individuals between different jobs. When an especially heavy load materializes at one work station and another is clear for the moment, we will see the person at the latter spontaneously move to help out at the former. . . . It is a natural and continuous give and take within a group of people, the object being to attain an established production target. . . . The group members are not merely carrying out a certain number of tasks. They are also working together, on a continuing basis, to coordinate different tasks, bearing responsibility, and taking whatever measures are necessary to cope with the work of the entire unit.[21]

As they work together in this manner, the members of a semiautonomous group are able to (1) rotate in and out of tasks to enhance skill variety; (2) work together on a group product that is a whole, identifiable piece of work; (3) influence the lives of other members of the group and the lives of those who consume the group's output; (4) decide as a group who will belong to the group and what tasks group members will perform; (5) obtain feedback from group members about task performance; and (6) count on the help and support of other group members if it is needed.

Shop-Floor Implications. Figure 17-10 contrasts a traditional assembly line with semiautonomous groups. As you can see, the decision to adopt sociotechnical design principles has important implications for shop-floor operations. In both panels of the figure, workers are assembling truck engines. In panel A, each worker performs a simplified job in which he takes a part from a storage bin and attaches it to a partially completed truck engine as it moves along a conveyor. In panel B, however, workers are grouped into semiautonomous groups, each of which removes a bare engine block from a conveyor loop, assembles a complete truck engine from parts in surrounding storage bins, and returns the finished engines to the conveyor loop for transportation to other truck-assembly operations. As suggested by this example, sociotechnical job designs normally eliminate traditional assembly-line operations. The "International OB" box describes another example of how the sociotechnical approach can affect shop-floor layout.

---

[20] Adapted from Fred Emery and Einar Thorsrud, *Democracy at Work: The Report of the Norwegian Industrial Democracy Program* (Leiden, The Netherlands: H. E. Stenfert Kroese, 1976), p. 14.

[21] David Jenkins, trans., *Job Reform in Sweden: Conclusions from 500 Shop Floor Projects* (Stockholm: Swedish Employers' Confederation, 1975), pp. 63–64.

F I G U R E   17-10

Comparison of an Assembly Line and Semiautonomous Groups

Adapted with the publisher's permission from Jan-Peder Norstedt and Stefan Aguren, The Saab-Scania Report *(Stockholm: Swedish Employers' Confederation, 1973), pp. 35, 37.*

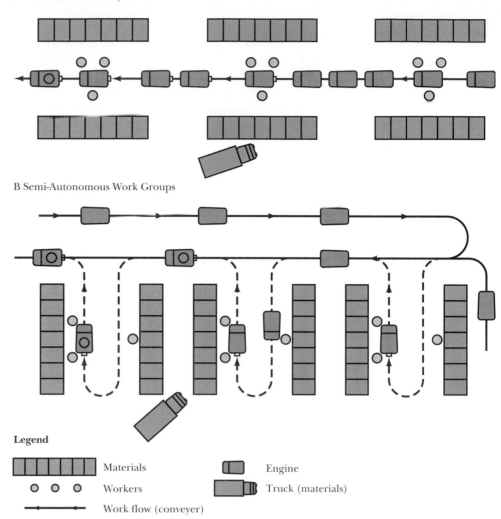

A Traditional Assembly Line

B Semi-Autonomous Work Groups

Legend

Materials

Workers

Work flow (conveyer)

Engine

Truck (materials)

Evaluating Job Enrichment and the Satisfaction Perspective

Consistent with the satisfaction perspective that serves as their foundation, all enlargement and enrichment techniques are aimed at designing jobs that satisfy the needs and interests of their holders. As we have already indicated, methods that consist solely of horizontal enlargement or vertical enrichment have largely failed to achieve this goal. However, methods of job design that incorporate *both* horizontal enlargement and vertical enrichment have proven effective in stimulating work-force motivation and satisfaction in a wide variety of situations.

Research on the Hackman-Oldham model has sometimes failed to verify the existence of five distinct job characteristics.[22] It is also unclear whether JDS

[22] Studies that have confirmed the existence of five distinct characteristics include Ralph Katz, "Job Longevity as a Situational Factor in Job Satisfaction," *Administrative Science Quarterly* 23 (1978), 204–23; and R. Lee and A. R. Klein, "Structure of the Job Diagnostic Survey for Public Service Organizations," *Journal of Applied Psychology* 67 (1982), 515–19. Studies that have failed to reveal confirmatory evidence include Randall B. Dunham, "The Measurement and Dimensionality of Job Characteristics," *Journal of Applied Psychology* 61 (1976), 404–9; Jeannie Gaines and John M. Jermier, "Functional Exhaustion in a High Stress Organization," *Academy of Management Journal* 26 (1983), 567–86; Jon L. Pierce and Randall B. Dunham, "The Measurement of Perceived Job Characteristics: The Job Diagnostic Survey vs. the Job Characteristics Inventory," *Academy of Management Journal* 21 (1978),

INTERNATIONAL OB

The Sociotechnical Layout of Volvo's E Plant

One example of how sociotechnical job design can affect the physical layout of the workplace is depicted in Figure 17-11. In Volvo's E-shaped plant in Skovde, Sweden, the work of several semiautonomous groups is combined to produce one completed product. In the four "arms" of the plant, semi-autonomous groups complete machining operations that produce parts for gasoline engines. Assembly is done in the main plant, located in the body of the *E*. Besides assembly operations, the main plant also houses several groups that perform final quality inspections. The building is intended to separate the machining groups to give each its own identity, yet facilitate interactions among groups that occur as work flows from one group to another.

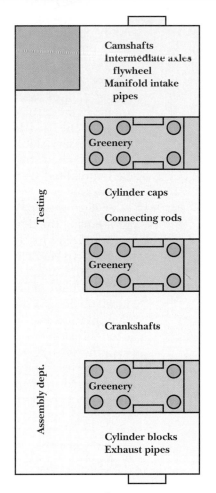

FIGURE 17-11

The Volvo Skovde Plant

From Stefan Aguren and Jan Edgren, New Factories: Job Design through Factory Planning in Sweden *(Stockholm: Swedish Employers' Confederation, 1980), p. 92. Reprinted with the publisher's permission.*

questionnaire items measure objective, stable job characteristics or only subjective, changing worker opinions.[23] Some researchers have even questioned whether job characteristics like those identified by Hackman and Oldham truly influence motivation and satisfaction. They suggest instead that employees' feelings about themselves and their work might be affected more by the opinions of others in

123–28; and Denise M. Rousseau, "Technological Differences in Job Characteristics, Job Satisfaction, and Motivation: A Synthesis of Job Design Research and Sociotechnical Systems Theory," *Organizational Behavior and Human Performance* 19 (1977), 18–42.

[23] Objectivity is suggested by studies such as Rickey W. Griffin, "A Longitudinal Investigation of Task Characteristics Relationships," *Academy of Management Journal* 42 (1981), 99–113; Eugene F. Stone and Lyman W. Porter, "Job Characteristics and Job Attitudes: A Multivariate Study," *Journal of Applied Psychology* 60 (1975), 57–64; and Carol T. Kulik, Greg R. Oldham, and Paul H. Langner, "Measurement

the surrounding social context.[24] We will return to this idea and discuss it in detail as we talk about *social information processing* and organizational culture in Chapter 18. Finally, some disagreement exists as to whether the moderators identified by Hackman and Oldham actually influence the model's applicability.[25]

Nonetheless, the Hackman-Oldham model has served as the basis of successful job design programs at Texas Instruments, AT&T, Motorola, Xerox, and many other firms of similar size and reputation. Such programs are not without their drawbacks. They are usually incompatible with assembly-line production processes. To enrich jobs using the Hackman-Oldham approach, a firm must almost always abandon the sort of simplified, repetitive tasks that serve as the foundation of assembly lines. Consequently, companies with substantial investments in modernized assembly lines are often reluctant to try Hackman-Oldham enrichment. In addition, because some 5 to 15 percent of the work force lack the necessary skills, growth needs, or context satisfactions, they are likely to be "overstretched" by enriched work. Therefore, a cluster of unenriched jobs must be maintained if the firm wants to avoid losing a significant number of its employees.

Turning to sociotechnical enrichment, this approach started out in Europe, influencing the design of jobs in firms such as Norsk Hydro, Volvo, Saab-Scania, and the Orrefors Glass Works. Now American companies such as Xerox, Cummins Engine, IBM, Polaroid, and General Electric have begun to experiment with sociotechnical job design.[26] Virtually the same outcomes stimulated by the Hackman-Oldham method are produced by the sociotechnical approach. Sociotechnical job designs do not always improve productivity, but most evidence indicates that they increase motivation and satisfaction and decrease absenteeism and turnover.[27] In addition, as is true for programs based on the Hackman-Oldham model, experience suggests that a small but significant number of workers are likely to resist sociotechnical enrichment. Consequently, either a few jobs must be left unchanged or managers must be prepared to deal with a small but significant amount of "overstretching."

EMERGING METHODS

Within the last two decades, several additional approaches to job design have emerged as researchers and managers have sought new ways to improve workplace productivity and satisfaction. Of these emerging methods, quality circles, alternative work schedules, and automation and robotics have had the greatest effects on the way work is now designed.

---

of Job Characteristics: Comparison of the Original and the Revised Job Diagnostic Survey," *Journal of Applied Psychology* 73 (1988), 462–66. Other studies that seem to support the subjectivity side of the argument include Arthur P. Brief and Ramon J. Aldag, "The Job Characteristic Inventory: An Examination," *Academy of Management Journal* 21 (1978), 659–70; and Philip H. Birnbaum, Jiing-Lih Farh, and Gilbert Y. Y. Wong, "The Job Characteristics Model in Hong Kong," *Journal of Applied Psychology* 71 (1986), 598–605.

[24] Gerald R. Salancik and Jeffrey Pfeffer, "A Social Information Processing Approach to Job Attitudes and Task Design," *Administrative Science Quarterly* 23 (1978), 224–53.

[25] Arthur P. Brief and Raymon J. Aldag, "Employee Reactions to Job Characteristics: A Constructive Replication," *Journal of Applied Psychology* 60 (1975), 182–86; and Henry P. Sims and Andrew D. Szilagyi, "Job Characteristic Relationships: Individual and Structural Moderators," *Organizational Behavior and Human Performance* 17 (1976), 211–30.

[26] Richard E. Walton, "From Control to Commitment in the Workplace," *Harvard Business Review* 63 (1985), 76–84.

[27] For instance, see Thomas G. Cummings and Edmond S. Molloy, *Strategies for Improving Productivity and the Quality of Work Life* (New York: Praeger, 1977), pp. 38–49.

Quality Circles

quality circles Small groups of employees who meet on company time to identify and resolve job-related problems.

Many companies suffer the negative consequences of job oversimplification. They are unable or unwilling, however, to modify production equipment or methods to the extent required by the Hackman-Oldham and sociotechnical models. In some of these firms, managers are trying to use **quality circles** to counteract oversimplification.

Quality circles (QCs) are small groups of employees, ranging in size from about 3 to 30 members, who meet on company time to identify and resolve job-related problems. Although usually thought of as a Japanese management technique, QCs were actually invented in the United States and exported to Japan by American quality experts Edward Demming and J. M. Juran in the years following World War II.[28] In North America, companies such as Lockheed, Westinghouse, Eastman Kodak, Procter and Gamble, General Motors, Ford, and Chrysler have implemented quality circles. Sometimes they call them quality teams, work teams, or productivity teams. The objectives of all such groups include:

> Reducing assembly errors and enhancing product quality
> Inspiring more effective teamwork and cooperation in everyday work groups
> Promoting a greater sense of job involvement and commitment
> Increasing employee motivation
> Creating greater decision-making capacity
> Substituting problem prevention for problem solving
> Improving communication in and between work groups
> Developing harmonious relations between management and employees
> Promoting leadership development among nonmanagerial employees[29]

Ordinarily, QC membership is voluntary and stable over time. The amount of time spent in QC activities may range from an hour a month to a few hours every week. Topics of discussion may include quality control, cost reduction, improvement of production techniques, production planning, and even long-term product design.[30] Over the course of many meetings, the activities of a typical QC proceed through a series of steps:

1. Initially, members of the QC identify concerns they have about their work and workplace in a group discussion coordinated by their supervisor or a specially trained facilitator. Often, the facilitator is an internal change agent with expertise in many of the group-level organization-development interventions described in Chapter 14.

2. QC members next examine their concerns and look for ways to collapse or integrate them into specific projects. For instance, concerns about production speed and raw-material quality may be grouped together in a production-methods project. Concerns about workplace safety and worker health may be put into a work environment project.

3. Members perform initial analyses of their QC's projects using various group decision-making techniques and tools, including data gathering, graphs, checklists, or charts.

4. The QC then reaches consensus decisions about the feasibility and impor-

---

[28] William L. Mohr and Harriet Mohr, *Quality Circles: Changing Images of People at Work* (Reading, Mass.: Addison-Wesley, 1983), p. 13.

[29] Donald L. Dewar, *The Quality Circle Handbook* (Red Bluff, Calif.: Quality Circle Institute, 1980), pp. 17–104.

[30] Gerald R. Ferris and John A Wagner III, "Quality Circles in the United States: A Conceptual Reevaluation," *Journal of Applied Behavioral Science* 21 (1985), 155–167.

tance of different projects, deciding which ones to abandon and which ones to pursue.

5. Representatives from the QC make a presentation or recommendation to management that summarizes the work of their group.

6. Management reviews the recommendation and makes a decision. Often, the decision is that QC members will have the opportunity to implement their own recommendations.[31]

QCs fight oversimplification by giving employees the opportunity to participate in the management of their jobs rather than by modifying existing work technologies. For example, employees who work on an assembly line for 39 hours each week might meet as a QC group during the last hour to evaluate the assembly line's performance and prepare for the following week's work. They might also meet in an extended session once a month to discuss more-complicated issues and resolve more-difficult problems. These monthly sessions offer an opportunity for more managerial activity, group autonomy, and information exchange than the regular QC meetings allow. To the extent that QC meetings focus workers' attention on the outputs of the whole assembly line, they may reinforce task identity and task significance.

Research evidence on the effects of QCs as a form of job enrichment is sketchy. What information we do have suggests that QCs have little effect on productivity but can enhance feelings of satisfaction and involvement significantly.[32] The magnitude of such effects is usually smaller than from job enrichment programs based on the Hackman-Oldham model or the Tavistock sociotechnical model. That is understandable, because workers who participate in QCs must still perform unenriched jobs during most of the time spent at work.

Alternative Work Schedules

Besides reshaping jobs themselves, concerns about employee satisfaction have also led managers and OB specialists to reshape the way work is scheduled. This reshaping leads to such innovations as flexible-hour programs, compressed work weeks, and job sharing. Virtually all such plans are intended to stimulate satisfaction by helping employees balance the time and scheduling demands of their work with those of their nonworking lives.

flexible-hour programs
Alternative work schedules that specify a block of core hours during which everyone must be on the job but allow each employee to choose when to start work and when to go home. Also called flextime.

Some firms offer employees the chance to participate in **flexible-hour programs**, also known as *flextime*. These programs generally specify a block of core hours during which everyone must be on the job but allow each employee to choose when she will start and quit work. Core hours are generally the period between 10:00 A.M. and 3:00 P.M. One employee might choose to come to work as late as 10:00 A.M. and remain until 6:00 P.M. Another might arrive at 7:00 A.M. and leave at 3:00 P.M. Flexible-hour programs make it easier for employees to coordinate work responsibilities with nonwork obligations. They allow parents to start work later in the morning if child care is unavailable earlier, for instance. Consequently, flextime can help decrease absenteeism and turnover.[33]

[31] Barbara Rae Lee, "Organization Development and Group Perceptions: A Study of Quality Circles," Ph.D. dissertation, University of Minnesota, 1982; and Mike Robson, *Quality Circles: A Practical Guide*, 2nd ed. (Hants, England: Gower, 1988), pp. 47–62.

[32] Robert P. Steel and Russell F. Lloyd, "Cognitive, Affective, and Behavioral Outcomes of Participation in Quality Circles: Conceptual and Empirical Findings," *Journal of Applied Behavioral Science* 24 (1988), 1–17; Howard H. Greenbaum, Ira T. Kaplan, and William Metlay, "Evaluation of Problem Solving Groups: The Case of Quality Circle Programs," *Group and Organization Studies* 13 (1988), 133–47; and Kimberly Buch and Raymond Spangler, "The Effects of Quality Circles on Performance and Promotions," *Human Relations* 43 (1990), 573–82.

[33] Robert Golembiewski and Carl W. Proehl, Jr., "A Survey of the Empirical Literature on Flexible Workhours: Character and Consequences of a Major Innovation," *Academy of Management Review* 3 (1978), 837–55.

compressed work week An alternative work schedule that allows employees to work a 40-hour week in fewer than the normal five days.

Some firms also offer a work schedule known as the **compressed work week**, enabling employees to work a 40-hour week in fewer than the normal five days. Most programs of this sort are based on the 4/40 work week in which employees work for ten hours on each of four days. Nearly 2000 organizations, ranging from IBM to the U.S. Army Corps of Engineers, have experimented with 4/40 scheduling. Many have reported that it has helped reduce costs, improve efficiency, reduce absenteeism, and improve satisfaction.[34]

Job sharing is another scheduling innovation in which companies attempt to reconcile the desire of employees to work part time with the organization's need to staff jobs on a full-time basis. Two or more part-time employees are allowed to share a full-time job. For example, one worker might perform a job from 8:00 A.M. to noon, and another might perform the same job from 1:00 P.M. to 5:00 P.M. Job sharing can be beneficial to both companies and employees, because it allows firms to employ capable people who might otherwise be unable to work. However, the effects of this type of alternative work schedule on such outcomes as productivity, satisfaction, and absenteeism have yet to be carefully documented.

job sharing An alternative work schedule in which two or more part-time employees are allowed to share a full-time job.

Automation and Robotics

Automation offers managers who are designing jobs yet another alternative. For years, automation in the form of assembly-line manufacturing created many of the most oversimplified, demotivating, dissatisfying jobs in industry. Today, however, with the invention of automated technologies that can totally replace people in production processes, automation is sometimes an attractive option.

In some firms, much of a traditional assembly operation is left unchanged, but the most repetitive or physically demanding tasks are turned over to automated equipment. Frequently, this equipment consists of **industrial robots**, or machines that can be programmed to repeat the same sequence of work movements over and over again. Robots have been introduced throughout the automotive industry, taking over various painting and installation jobs. In fact, the welding job described at the beginning of this chapter is currently performed by robots on many North American auto-assembly lines.

industrial robots Machines that can be programmed to repeat the same sequence of work movements over and over again.

Robots are not without their flaws. At General Motors, for example, employees regularly tell stories of one robot busily smashing windshields installed

[34] Paul Dickson, *The Future of the Workplace* (New York: Weybright and Talley, 1975), p. 219.

by another or of a group of robots painting each other instead of the cars passing them by on the assembly line. Proper programming is obviously an essential aspect of introducing robots into the workplace. Careful planning, implementation, and adjustment is thus essential. Experience has also shown that building a robot capable of performing anything more than the simplest of jobs is often cost prohibitive. Consequently, the American population of robots is not the hundreds of thousands once predicted but about 37,000, according to the Robotic Industries Association of Ann Arbor, Michigan. Nonetheless, robots are an effective way to cope with many repetitive jobs that people don't want or are not very good at.[35]

Computer-integrated manufacturing in the form of *flexible manufacturing cells* is another type of automated technology but one that focuses primary attention on adaptability instead of robotic repetitiveness (see Chapter 16). Products made in such cells include gear boxes, cylinder heads, brake components, and similar machined-metal components used in the automotive, aviation, and construction-equipment industries. Companies throughout Europe, Japan, and North America are also experimenting with using flexible manufacturing cells to manufacture items out of sheet metal.[36]

Each flexible manufacturing cell consists of a collection of automated production machines that cut, shape, drill, and fasten metal components together. These machines are connected with each other by convertible conveyor grids that allow quick rerouting to accommodate changes from one product to another. It is possible, for instance, to produce a small batch of automotive door locks, then switch over to machine and finish a separate batch of crankshafts for automotive-air-conditioner compressors. It is simply a matter of turning some machines on and others off, then activating those conveyors that interconnect the machines that are in use. In this manner, the same collection of machines can make more than 100 different products without having to alter the cell substantially.[37]

Workers in a flexible manufacturing cell need never touch the product being produced, nor do they perform simple, repetitive production tasks. Instead, their jobs consist of the surveillance and decision making required to change the cell from one product configuration to another and to oversee equipment operations. Often, a cell's work force forms a semiautonomous group to accommodate the sizeable amount of mutual adjustment that must occur to keep production flowing smoothly. Employees in a flexible manufacturing cell thus exercise expertise in teamwork, problem solving, and self-management as they work.[38]

At its core, automation of this sort represents a return to the efficiency perspective of industrial engineering. Some jobs resist enrichment, and it is more effective to turn them over to machines than attempt to convert them into interesting, enjoyable work. But with the efficiency perspective, the danger that human satisfaction will be ignored also returns. So once workplace automation is established, managers must find a way to ensure that the worker-held jobs that remain offer each person the opportunity to experience sufficient levels of motivation and satisfaction.

[35] Peter T. Kilborn, "Brave New World Seen for Robots Appears Stalled by Quirks and Costs," *New York Times*, July 1, 1990, p. C7.

[36] Robert B. Kurtz, *Toward a New Era in U. S. Manufacturing* (Washington, D.C.: National Academy Press, 1986), p. 3.

[37] Ramchandran Jaikumar, "Postindustrial manufacturing," *Harvard Business Review* 44 (1986), 69–76.

[38] Peter Senker, *Towards the Automatic Factory: The Need for Training* (New York: Springer-Verlag, 1986), pp. 27–43.

SUMMARY

Contemporary *job design* began with Frederick Taylor's pioneering work on scientific management. Other experts, notably Frank and Lillian Gilbreth, refined Taylor's ideas and founded the field of *industrial engineering*. Frederick Herzberg differentiated between *motivator* and *hygiene factors*, and joined other specialists in introducing early models of *horizontal job enlargement* and *vertical job enrichment*. Eventually, two perspectives on job design emerged—the *efficiency perspective* and the *satisfaction perspective*.

Today's industrial engineering methods continue to reflect the efficiency perspective. *Methods engineering* attempts to improve the methods used to perform work. *Work measurement* examines the motions and time required to complete each job. *Comprehensive job enrichment* programs are guided by the *Job Diagnostic Survey* and, like *sociotechnical job enrichment* methods, are based on the satisfaction perspective. Other methods of designing jobs that have evolved in recent years include *quality circles, flexible-hour programs, job sharing*, and *robotics*.

REVIEW QUESTIONS

1.   Explain how following Taylor's principles of scientific management can simplify the jobs in an organization. What are some of the positive effects of this simplification? What negative effects might occur?

2.   What do the fields of process engineering and human factors engineering share in common? How do they differ from one another? Are they more likely to enhance satisfaction or efficiency? Why?

3.   What effects do motion and time studies have on the design of jobs? What type of work measurement would you use to analyze the job of installing engines on an automobile assembly line? What type would you use to analyze the job of sorting and shelving library books?

4.   Why do horizontal job-enlargement programs like job extension and job rotation often fail to stimulate employee satisfaction?

5.   How do job design programs based on the Hackman-Oldham job characteristics model differ from programs based on Herzberg's motivator-hygiene model? Of the two types of programs, which are most likely to lead to significant improvements in employee motivation and satisfaction?

6.   In what ways is the sociotechnical model of job design similar to the Hackman-Oldham model? In what ways do the two models differ? Which would you use if you were designing the job of a postal carrier? Which would you use to design the job of a surgical team?

7.   Which of the following job design methods are products of the efficiency perspective, and which are products of the satisfaction perspective—quality circles, alternative work schedules, automation and robotics. Which of these approaches would you select to enrich jobs in a newly built assembly line? Which would you use to design jobs that resist all attempts at enrichment?

DIAGNOSTIC QUESTIONS

The number of different job design methods available today invites confusion. They require managers to consider carefully which of the various methods to use in solving the specific job design problems faced by their organizations. To help alleviate this confusion, the following diagnostic questions are provided.

1.   Does the design of the organization's current jobs seem to reflect the effi-

ciency or the satisfaction perspective? Are most jobs simplified, or have attempts been made to alter job range or depth?

2. If the efficiency perspective appears dominant, do productivity and satisfaction data support the idea that jobs have not been oversimplified? Or does faltering productivity and conspicuous dissatisfaction indicate that oversimplification may be a problem?

3. Can the firm's current technology be changed to the degree required by job enrichment methods? Are jobs mainly individualized, indicating the appropriateness of Hackman-Oldham enrichment? Or are jobs often performed by groups of people working together closely, suggesting the sociotechnical approach?

4. If technological considerations prohibit job enrichment, might quality circles provide enough relief to restore motivation and satisfaction? If not, can you eliminate the troublesome jobs through automation?

5. If the satisfaction perspective appears dominant, do productivity and satisfaction data suggest that jobs have been enriched without creating work that is overdemanding? Or do falling productivity and satisfaction indicate that workers are being "overstretched" and asked to do more than they can?

6. If you are facing an overenrichment problem, do the results of work measurement procedures suggest ways to simplify jobs enough to facilitate successful performance while still retaining opportunities for growth, achievement, and recognition?

7. If work measurement fails to reveal a remedy, can methods engineering be used to create new jobs that are both doable and capable of adequate enrichment? If not, can you eliminate the troublesome jobs through automation?

EXERCISE 17-1
REDESIGNING A SIMPLIFIED JOB*

MARK S. PLOVNICK, *University of the Pacific*
RONALD E. FRY, *Case Western Reserve University*
W. WARNER BURKE, *Columbia University*

The drive toward efficiency in modern organizations sometimes results in the creation of oversimplified jobs that fail to challenge or involve the worker. People in these jobs often express strong dissatisfaction as product quality falls and both absenteeism and turnover increase. Comprehensive job enrichment is intended to counteract this situation. This technique changes job content in several ways. It combines tasks and forms natural work units so as to increase skill variety, task identity, and task significance. It gives each worker more autonomy on the job. And it opens up channels for immediate feedback to the worker. In this exercise you will diagnose a job and suggest how it might be enriched, thus experiencing for yourself the initial steps of job redesign.

STEP ONE: PRE-CLASS PREPARATION

In Step Two of this exercise you will work in groups to diagnose one of the following jobs:

1. A job your group has observed and discussed before class. If your instructor assigns you this option you should meet as a group, decide what job you want to observe, verify with your instructor that your choice is appropriate, and meet on site and observe the jobholder as he performs the job for _____. Be sure to take notes to refresh your memory as you perform the rest of the exercise.
2. A job that has been performed by a member of your class. If your instructor assigns you this option, he or she will ask for volunteers from class to serve as interviewees. In this role, they will describe in depth a job they have performed. Depending on the number of volunteers, each group may have a volunteer to interview, several groups may have to combine together to interview the same volunteer, or the class as a whole may be required to conduct a single interview. Depending on your instructor's preference, interviews may be conducted before or at the beginning of class.
3. A videotaped job. If your instructor assigns this option he or she will show a videotape of a job being performed and you will diagnose the job based on what you see. Your instructor will supply the videotape and will show it at the beginning of class.

Now read the remainder of the exercise and prepare for the next step as you need to, depending on the option your instructor has chosen.

STEP TWO: COMPLETING THE TASK DIAGNOSTIC QUESTIONNAIRE (TDQ)

The class should divide into groups of four to six members each. If you have already formed permanent groups, you should reassemble in those groups. If your instructor has assigned you the task of observing a job before coming to class, the groups you form for this step of the exercise should be the same as the ones you formed to observe the job. The members of each group should work together to fill out the Task Diagnostic Questionnaire (TDQ) shown in Exhibit 17-1. The group should reach consensus on its response to each item. Any significant disagreements should be noted next to the relevant item on the TDQ.

STEP THREE: SCORING AND DISCUSSING THE TDQ

Here is how you score your group's evaluations, on the Task Diagnostic Questionnaire, of the job you're examining:

1. For items 2, 4, 6, 8, 10, and 12, subtract the number you circled from 8. The result is your score for each of these items. For items 1, 3, 5, 7, 9, 11, 13, 14, and 15, the number you circled is the correct score.
2. Add your scores for items 1, 4, and 13, divide by 3, and write the result here: _____. This is the job's score on *skill variety*.
3. Add your scores for items 2, 7, and 12, divide by 3, and write the result here: _____. This is the jobs's score on *task identity*.
4. Add your scores for items 5, 10, and 14, divide by

* Exercise adapted with the authors' permission from Mark S. Plovnick, Ronald E. Fry, and W. Warner Burke, *Organization Development: Exercises, Cases, and Readings* (Boston: Little, Brown, 1982), pp. 94–105. Copyright © 1982 by Mark S. Plovnick, Ronald E. Fry, and W. Warner Burke. Questionnaire adapted with the authors' permission from the Job Diagnostic Survey developed by J. Richard Hackman and Greg R. Oldham.

EXHIBIT 17-1
Task Diagnostic Questionnaire

This questionnaire contains statements with which you may agree or disagree. It is intended to reveal how people perceive different kinds of jobs. It is not intended to measure how much someone likes or dislikes a job but to elicit as accurate and objective a description as possible. To be useful, the questionnaire must be answered honestly.

In the blank next to each statement, write the number that represents how accurate you think the statement is in describing the job: 1 = very inaccurate, 2 = mostly inaccurate, 3 = slightly inaccurate, 4 = uncertain, 5 = slightly accurate, 6 = mostly accurate, 7 = very accurate.

_____ 1. The job requires the worker to use a number of complex, high-level skills.

_____ 2. The way the job is structured, the worker does not have the opportunity to do a complete piece of work from beginning to end.

_____ 3. Just doing the job provides the worker with many chances to figure out how well she is doing.

_____ 4. The job is quite simple and repetitive.

_____ 5. In this job, a lot of other people can be affected by how well the work is done.

_____ 6. The job does not give the worker any chance to use his personal initiative or judgment in carrying out the work.

_____ 7. The job allows the worker to completely finish every piece of work she begins.

_____ 8. The job itself provides very few clues about whether the worker is performing well.

_____ 9. The job gives the worker considerable independence and freedom in the way he does the work.

_____ 10. The job is not very significant or important in the overall work of the organization.

_____ 11. The job permits the worker to decide for herself what needs to be done.

_____ 12. The job is only a small part of an overall piece of work that is finished by other people or by automated machines.

_____ 13. The job requires the worker to do many different things, using a variety of skills and talents.

_____ 14. The results of the job have a significant effect on the lives and well-being of other people.

_____ 15. The job itself provides clues about how well the worker is doing; feedback from coworkers or supervisors is not needed.

3, and write the result here: _____. This is the job's score on *task significance*.

5. Add your scores for items 6, 9, and 11, divide by 3, and write the result here: _____. This is the job's score on *autonomy*.

6. Add your scores for items 3, 8, and 15, divide by 3, and write the result here: _____. This is the job's score on *feedback*.

Next, using these group consensus scores, draw a job profile for your job like the one shown in Figure 17-9 in this chapter. Then calculate a motivational summary score, or MSS (similar to the motivation potential score discussed in this chapter), using the formula that follows.

MSS

$$= \frac{\text{(Skill Variety + Task Identity + Task Significance)}}{3}$$

$$\times \text{Autonomy} \times \text{Feedback}$$

Your group should discuss the meaning of the scores it has derived and the results of its diagnosis. Then appoint a spokesperson to present a report to the class. The report should include information about what kind of job the group diagnosed, the group's scores on each of the five dimensions, significant disagreements among group members, and the MSS calculated by the group. The spokesperson should also show a diagram of the job profile developed by the group on a blackboard, flipchart, or overhead transparency.

STEP FOUR: DEVELOPING COMPREHENSIVE JOB ENRICHMENT STRATEGIES

The class should convene and all spokespersons should give their reports. After discussing the different jobs the class has analyzed, members should return to their groups and each group should develop a strategy to enrich the job it has diagnosed. The following points should be considered during this step:

1. Which specific job characteristics need enrichment? Which, if any, are good enough as is? What specific actions should be taken to enrich the job along the dimensions that need further help?

2. Who in the organization will be responsible for developing the strategy if additional refinement is needed? Who will be responsible for implementing it? How will the effectiveness of the implementation be measured? Who will perform this evaluation?

3. Before redesigning the job, what additional data should be collected? From whom? By whom? To whom should the data be fed back? What will this person or persons do with it?

4. What are some likely sources of resistance to the strategy you have developed? How should they be dealt with?

The group spokesperson should prepare an overview of the group's strategy for presentation to the class.

STEP FIVE: STRATEGY REPORTS AND CLASS DISCUSSION

The class should reconvene and each spokesperson should report on the results of Step Four. Class members should ask questions of clarification as needed to understand each strategic plan. The total class should then compare, contrast, and critique the strategies developed by the groups, being sure to address the following points.

1. To what extent did each strategy emphasize employee involvement? Changes in the job itself? Changes in the context surrounding the job? Does the strategy appear workable?

2. What consequences would the strategy have for the structure of the organization? For current policies? For the distribution of power in the firm?

3. For each strategy, what positive and negative indirect effects might it have on those individuals who are not directly involved in it? How might these individuals act as forces for or against change?

CONCLUSION

This exercise has introduced you to some of the factors underlying the nature of work and to the complexity of issues involved in trying to redesign jobs. Job redesign programs can be applied to jobs in the consumer products industry, jobs in service industries, white collar jobs, blue collar jobs—any place where work has been oversimplified to the point of reducing worker satisfaction and productivity.

DIAGNOSING ORGANIZATIONAL BEHAVIOR

CASE 17-1
THE LORDSTOWN PLANT OF GENERAL MOTORS*
HAK-CHONG LEE, YONSEI UNIVERSITY†

Although the events we're about to describe took place more than twenty years ago, this case remains a classic example of certain kinds of problems that managers and employees face in modern industrial workplaces. Today, companies throughout the United States wrestle with exactly the same predicaments as those that confronted General Motors in its Lordstown plant in the early 1970s.

INTRODUCTION

In December 1971, the management of the Lordstown Plant was very much concerned with an unusually high rate of defective Vegas coming off the assembly line.

For the previous several weeks, the lot with a capacity of 2,000 cars had been filled with Vegas which were waiting for rework before they could be shipped out to the dealers around the country.

The management was particularly disturbed by the fact that many of the defects were not the kinds of quality deficiency normally expected in an assembly production of automobiles. There was a countless number of Vegas with their windshields broken, upholstery

* Reprinted with the author's permission.

† This case was developed for instructional purposes from published sources and interviews with the General Motors Assembly Division officials in Warren, Michigan and Lordstown, Ohio. The Public Relations Office of GMAD read the case and made minor corrections in it. However, the author is solely responsible for the content of the case. The author appreciates the cooperation of General Motors.

slashed, ignition keys broken, signal levers bent, rear-view mirrors broken, or carburetors clogged with washers. There were cases in which, as the Plant Manager put it, "the whole engine blocks passed by 40 men without any work done on them."

Since then, the incident in the Lordstown Plant has been much publicized in news media, drawing public interest. It has also been frequently discussed in the classroom and in the academic circles. While some people viewed the event as "young worker revolt," others reacted to it as a simple "labor problem." Some viewed it as "worker sabotage," and others called it "industrial Woodstock."

This case describes some background and important incidents leading to this much publicized and discussed industrial event.

The General Motors Corporation is the nation's largest manufacturer. The Company is a leading example among many industrial organizations which have achieved organizational growth and success through decentralization. The philosophy of decentralization has been one of the most valued traditions in General Motors from the days of Alfred Sloan in the 1930s through Charles Wilson and Harlow Curtice in the 1950s and up to recent years.

Under decentralized management, each of the company's car divisions, Cadillac, Buick, Oldsmobile, Pontiac and Chevrolet, was given maximum autonomy in the management of its manufacturing and marketing operations. The assembly operations were no exception, each division managing its own assembly work. The car bodies built by Fisher Body were assembled in various locations under maximum control and coordination between Fisher Body and each car division.

In the mid-1960s, however, the decentralization in divisional assembly operations was subject to a critical review. At the divisional level, the company was experiencing serious problems of worker absenteeism and increasing cost with declines in quality and productivity. They were reflected in the overall profit margins which were declining from 10% to 7% in the late 1960s. The autonomy in the divided management in body manufacturing and assembly operations, in separate locations in many cases, became questionable under the declining profit situation.

In light of these developments, General Motors began to consolidate in some instances the divided management of body and chassis assembly operations into a single management under the already existing General Motors Assembly Division (GMAD) in order to better coordinate the two operations. The GMAD was given an overall responsibility to integrate the two operations in these instances and see that the numerous parts and components going into car assembly got to the right places in the right amounts at the right times.

THE GENERAL MOTORS ASSEMBLY DIVISION (GMAD)

The GMAD was originally established in the mid 1930s, when the company needed an additional assembly plant to meet the increasing demands for Buick, Oldsmobile, and Pontiac automobiles. The demand for these cars was growing so much beyond the available capacity at the time that the company began, for the first time, to build an assembly plant on the west coast which could turn out all three lines of cars rather than an individual line. As this novel approach became successful, similar plants turning out a multiple line of cars were built in seven other locations in the east, south and midwest. In the 1960s, the demand for Chevrolet production also increased, and some Buick-Oldsmobile-Pontiac plants began to assemble Chevrolet products. Accordingly, the name of the division was changed to GMAD in 1965.

In order to improve quality and productivity, the GMAD increased its control over the operations of body manufacturing and assembly. It reorganized jobs, launched programs to improve efficiency, and reduced the causes of defects which required repairs and rework. With many positive results attained under the GMAD management, the company extended the single management concept to six more assembly locations in 1968 which had been run by the Fisher Body and Chevrolet Divisions. In 1971, GM further extended the concept to four additional Chevrolet-Fisher Body assembly facilities, consolidating the separate management under which the body and chassis assembly had been operating. One of these plants was the Lordstown Plant.

The series of consolidations brought to eighteen the number of assembly plants operated by the GMAD. In terms of total production, they were producing about 75% of all cars and 67% of trucks built by GM. Also in 1971, one of the plants under the GMAD administration began building certain Cadillac models, thus involving GMAD in production of automobiles for each of the GM's five domestic car divisions as well as trucks for Chevrolet, GMC truck, and GM's Coach Division.

THE LORDSTOWN COMPLEX

The Lordstown complex is located in Trumbull County in Ohio, about 15 miles west of Youngstown and 30 miles east of Akron. It consists of the Vega assembly plant, the van-truck assembly plant, and Fisher Body metal fabricating plant, occupying about 1,000 acres of land. GMAD, which operates the Vega and van-truck assembly plants, is also located in the Lordstown complex. The three plants are in the heart of the heavy industrial triangle of Youngstown, Akron and Cleveland. With Youngstown as a center of steel production,

Akron the home of rubber industries, and Cleveland as a major center for heavy manufacturing, the Lordstown complex commands a good strategic and logistic location for automobile assembly.

The original assembly plant was built in 1964–1966 to assembly Chevrolet Impalas. But in 1970 it was converted into Vega assembly through extensive redesign. The van-truck assembly plant was constructed in 1969, and the Fisher Body metal fabricating plant was further added in 1970 to carry out stamping operations to produce sheet metal components used in Vega and van assemblies. In October 1971, the Chevrolet Vega and van-assembly plants and Fisher Body Vega assembly plants which had been operating under separate management were merged into a single jurisdiction of the GMAD.

WORK FORCE AT THE LORDSTOWN PLANT

There are over 11,400 employees working in the Lordstown Plant (as of 1973). Approximately 6,000 people, of whom 5,500 are on hourly payroll, work in the Vega assembly plant. About 2,600 workers, 2,100 of them paid hourly, work in van-truck assembly. As members of the United Auto Workers Union, Local 1112, the workers command good wages and benefits. They start out on the line at about $5.00 an hour, get a 10¢ an hour increase within 30 days, and another 10¢ after 90 days. Benefits come to $2.50 an hour. The supplemental unemployment benefits virtually guarantee the worker's wages throughout the year. If the worker is laid off, he gets more than 90% of his wages for 52 weeks. He is also eligible for up to six weeks for holidays, excused absence or bereavement, and up to four weeks vacation.

The work force at the plant is almost entirely made up of local people with 92% coming from the immediate area of a 20-mile radius. Lordstown itself is a small rural town of about 500 residents. A sizable city closest to the plant is Warren, 5 miles away, which together with Youngstown supplies about two-thirds of the work force. The majority of the workers (57.5%) are married, 7.6% are home owners, and 20.2% are buying their homes. Of those who do not own their homes (72%), over one-half are still living with their parents. The rest live in rented houses or apartments.

The workers in the plant are generally young. Although various news media reported the average worker age as 24 years old, and in some parts of the plant as 22 years, the company records show that the overall average worker age was somewhat above 29 years as of 1971–72. The national average is 42. The work force at Lordstown is the second youngest among GM's 25 assembly plants around the country. The fact that the Lordstown plant is GM's newest assembly plant may partly explain the relatively young work force.

The educational profile of the Lordstown workers indicates that only 22.2% have less than a high school education. Nearly two-thirds or 62% are high school graduates, and 16% are either college graduates or have attended college. Another 26% have attended trade school. The average education of 13.2 years makes the Lordstown workers among the best educated in GM's assembly plants.

THE VEGA ASSEMBLY LINE

Conceived as a major competitive product against the increasing influx of foreign cars which were being produced at as low as one-fourth the labor rate in this country, the Vega was specifically designed with a maximum production efficiency and economy in mind. From the initial stages of planning, the Vega was designed by a special task team with most sophisticated techniques, using computers in designing the outer skin of the car and making the tapes that form the dies. Computers were also used to match up parts, measure the stack tolerances, measure safety performance under head-on collision, and make all necessary corrections before the first 1971 model car was ever built. The 2300-cubic-centimeter all-aluminum, 4-cylinder engine, was designed to give gas economy comparable to the foreign imports.

The Vega was also designed with the plant and the people in mind. As the GM's newest plant, the Vega assembly plant was known as the "super plant" with the most modern and sophisticated designs to maximize efficiency. It featured the newest engineering techniques and a variety of new power tools and automatic devices to eliminate much of the heavy lifting and physical labor. The line gave the workers an easier access to the car body, reducing the amount of bending and crawling in and out, as in other plants around the country. The unitized body in large components like prefab housing made the assembly easier and lighter with greater body integrity. Most difficult and tedious tasks were eliminated or simplified, on-line variations of the job were minimized, and the most modern tooling and mechanization was used to the highest possible degree of reliability.

It was also the fastest moving assembly line in the industry. The average time per assembly job was 36 seconds with a maximum of 100 cars rolling off the assembly line per hour for a daily production of 1,600 cars from two shift operations. The time cycle per job in other assembly plants averaged about 55 seconds. Although the high speed of the line did not necessarily imply greater work load or job requirement, it was a part of GM's attempt to maximize economy in Vega assembly. The fact that the Vega was designed to have 43% fewer parts than a full-size car also helped the high-speed line and economy.

IMPACT OF GMAD AND REORGANIZATION IN THE LORDSTOWN PLANT

As stated previously, the assembly operations at Lordstown had originally been run by Fisher Body and Chevrolet as two plants. There were two organizations, two plant managers, two unions, and two service organizations. The consolidation of the two organizations into a single operating system under the GMAD in October 1971 required a difficult task of reorganization and dealing with the consequences of manpower reduction such as a work slowdown, worker discipline, grievances, etc.

As duplicate units such as production, maintenance, inspection, and personnel were consolidated, there was a problem of selecting the personnel to manage the new organization. There were chief inspectors, personnel directors and production superintendents as well as production and service workers to be displaced or reassigned. Unions which had been representing their respective plants also had to go through reorganization. Union elections were held to merge the separate union committees at Fisher Body and Chevrolet in a single union bargaining committee. This eliminated one full local union shop committee.

At the same time, GMAD launched an effort to improve production efficiency more in line with that in other assembly plants. It included increasing job efficiency through reorganization and better coordination between the body and chassis assembly, and improving controls over product quality and worker absenteeism. This effort coincided with adjustments in line balance and work methods. Like other assembly plants, the Vega assembly plant was going through an initial period of diseconomy caused by suboptimal operations, imbalance in the assembly line, and a somewhat redundant work force. According to management, line adjustment and work changes were a normal process in accelerating the assembly operation to the peak performance the plant had been designed for after the initial break-in and start-up period.

As for job efficiency, the GMAD initiated changes in those work sequences and work methods which were not well coordinated under the divided managements of body and chassis assembly. For example, previous to the GMAD, Fisher Body had been delivering the car body complete with interior trim to the final assembly lines, where oftentimes the workers soiled the front seats as they did further assembly operations. GMAD changed this practice so that the seats were installed as one of the last operations in building the car. Fisher Body also had been delivering the car body with complete panel instrument frame which made it extremely difficult for the assembly workers to reach behind the frame in installing the instrument panels. The GMAD improved the job method so that the box containing the entire instrument panel was installed on the assembly line. Such improvements in job sequences and job methods resulted in savings in time and the number of workers required. Consequently, there were some jobs where the assembly time was cut down and/or the number of workers was reduced.

GMAD also put more strict control over worker absenteeism and the causes for defective work; the reduction in absenteeism was expected to require fewer relief men, and the improvement in quality and less repair work were to require fewer repairmen. In implementing these changes, the GMAD instituted a strong policy of dealing with worker slowdowns via strict disciplinary measures including dismissal. It was rumored that the inspectors and foremen passing defective cars would be fired on the spot.

Many workers were laid off as a result of the reorganization and job changes. The union was claiming that as many as 700 workers were laid off. Management, on the other hand, put the layoff figure at 375 to which the union later conceded. Although management claimed that the changes in job sequence and method in some assembly work did not bring a substantial change in the overall speed or pace of the assembly line, the workers perceived the job change as "tightening" the assembly line. The union charged that the GMAD brought a return of an old-fashioned line speedup and a "sweatshop style" of management reminiscent of the 1930s, making the men do more work at the same pay. The workers were blaming the "tightened" assembly line for the drastic increase in quality defects. As one worker commented, "That's the fastest line in the world. We have about 40 seconds to do our job. The company adds one more thing and it can kill us. We can't get the stuff done on time and a car goes by. The company then blames us for sabotage and shoddy work."

The number of worker grievances also increased drastically. Before GMAD took over, there were about 100 grievances in the plant. After GMAD's entry, grievances increased to 5,000, 1,000 of which were related to the charge that too much work had been added to each job. Worker resentment was particularly great in the "towveyor" assembly and seat sub-assembly areas. The "towveyor" is the area where engines and transmissions are assembled. Like seat sub-assembly there is a large concentration of workers working together in close proximity. Also, these jobs are typically performed by beginning assemblers who are younger and better educated.

The workers in the plant were particularly resentful of the company's strict policy in implementing the changes. They stated that the tougher the company became, the more they would stiffen their resistance even though other jobs were scarce in the market. One worker said, "In some of the other plants where the GMAD did the same thing, the workers were older and they took this. But, I've got 25 years ahead of me in this plant." Another worker commented, "I saw a woman running to keep pace with the fast line. I'm not going to run for anybody. There ain't anyone in that plant that is going to tell me to run." One foreman said, "The problem with the workers here is not so much that they don't want to work, but that they just don't want to take orders. They don't believe in any kind of authority."

While the workers were resisting management orders, there were some indications that the first-line supervisors had not been adequately trained to perform satisfactory supervisory roles. The average supervisor at the time had less than 3 years of experience, and 20% of the supervisors had less than 1 year's experience. Typically, they were young, somewhat lacking in knowledge of the provisions of the union contract and other supervisory duties, and less than adequately trained to handle the workers in the threatening and hostile environment which was developing.

Another significant fact was that the strong reactions of the workers were not entirely from the organizational and job changes brought about by the GMAD alone. Management felt that the intense resentment was particularly due to the nature of the work force in Lordstown. The plant was not only made up of young people, but also the work force reflected the characteristics of "tough labor" in steel, coal and rubber industries in the surrounding communities. Many of the workers in fact came from families who made their living working in these industries. Management also noted that the worker resistance had been much greater in the Lordstown Plant than in other plants where similar changes had been made.

A good part of the young workers' resentment also seemed to be related to the unskilled and repetitive nature of the assembly work. One management official admitted that the company was facing a difficult task in getting workers to "take pride" in the product they were assembling. Many of them were participating in the company's tuition assistance plan which was supporting their college education in the evening. With this educated background, obviously assembly work was not fulfilling their high work expectations. Also, the job market was tight at the time, and they could neither find any meaningful jobs elsewhere nor, even if found, they could not afford to give up the good money and fringe benefits they were earning on their assembly-line jobs. This frustrated them, according to company officials.

Many industrial engineers were questioning whether management could continue simplifying assembly line work. As the jobs became easier, simpler, and repetitive, requiring less physical effort, there were fewer and fewer traces of skill and increased monotony. Worker unrest indicated that employees not only wanted to go back to the work pace prior to the "speedup" (pre-October pace), but also wanted the company to do something about the boring and meaningless assembly work. One worker commented, "The company has got to do something to change the job so that a guy can take an interest in the job. A guy can't do the same thing 8 hours a day year after year. And it's got to be more than the company just saying to a guy, 'Okay, instead of 6 spots on the weld, you'll do 5 spots.'"

As the worker resentment mounted, the UAW Local 1112 decided in early January 1972 to consider possible authorization for a strike against the Lordstown Plant in a fight against the job changes. In the meantime, the union and management bargaining teams worked hard on worker grievances; they reduced the number of grievances from 5,000 to a few hundred; management even indicated that it would restore some of the eliminated jobs. However, the bargaining failed to produce accord on the issues of seniority rights and shift preference, which were related to wider issues of job changes and layoff.

A vote was held in early February 1972. Nearly 90% of the workers came out to vote in the heaviest turnout in the history of the Local. With 97% of the votes supporting, the workers went out on strike in early March.

In March 1972, with the strike in effect, the management of the Lordstown Plant was assessing the impact of the GMAD and the resultant strike in the Plant. It was estimated that the work disruption because of the worker resentment and slowdown had already cost the company 12,000 Vegas and 4,000 trucks amounting to $45 million. There had been repeated closedowns of assembly lines since December 1971, because of the worker slowdowns and the cars passing down the line without all necessary operations performed on them. The car lot was full with 2,000 cars waiting for repair work.

There had also been an amazing number of complaints from Chevrolet dealers, 6,000 complaints in November alone, about the quality of the Vegas shipped to them. This was more than the combined complaints from the other assembly plants.

The strike in the Lordstown Plant was expected to affect other plants. The plants at Tonawanda, New York and Buffalo, New York were supplying parts for

Vega. Despite the costly impact of the worker resistance and the strike, management felt that the job changes and cost reductions were essential if the Vega were to return a profit to the company. The plant had to be operating at about 90% capacity to break even because its highly automated features cost twice as much as had been estimated.

While the company had to do something to increase the production efficiency in the Lordstown Plant, the management was wondering whether it couldn't have planned and implemented the organizational and job changes differently in view of the costly disruption of operations that the Plant had been experiencing.

When you have read this case, look back at the chapter's diagnostic questions and choose the ones that apply to the case. Then use those questions with the ones that follow in your case analysis.

1. What kinds of jobs are performed in the General Motors Lordstown plant? Would further simplification reduce workers' complaints? Should the jobs be enriched instead?
2. Does it make sense to recommend that major changes be made to Lordstown's assembly lines? Why, or why not?
3. Which job design approach seems best suited to the situation at Lordstown? What steps should be taken to implement this approach? How successful is it likely to be in improving workforce attitudes throughout the Lordstown plant?

C A S E 17-2

BETA BUREAU*
DONALD AUSTIN WOOLF, UNIVERSITY OF OKLAHOMA

PART A

The Sigma Agency is a large division of the Epsilon Department, a cabinet-level department of the federal government. It has primary responsibility for the administration of a law providing a variety of services to a large number of citizens. In general terms, the Agency is organized in terms of operating bureaus, an administrative and staff services bureau, and a bureau providing support services. Each of the operating bureaus administers or assists in administering a separate portion of the law. Beta Bureau operates regional claims processing centers for the Sigma Agency.

Claims are filed by applicants at widely dispersed branch offices which are administered by a branch office bureau. Those claims which are strictly routine in nature

* Copyright (©) 1981 by Donald Austin Woolf. Reprinted with the author's permission.

may be authorized by representatives at the branch offices. All others—about half of the total work load—are forwarded to Beta Bureau processing centers along with the record of actions taken on those claims authorized at the branch office. The processing center reviews all actions taken at the branch level, processes initial claims not authorized by branches, reviews or authorizes changes in eligibility of existing claimants (post-entitlement), and initiates recovery action in cases where claimants have received services in excess of that permitted by law, rule, or regulation. Claim files are physically maintained at and by the processing centers. Finally, information on all actions taken is transmitted to the central data storage and retrieval system, located at Headquarters near Washington, D.C. Central Data operates as a separate, service bureau, and provides this service to all operating bureaus. Each of the Centers employs about 2,000 people.

Most of the bureaus—including Beta Bureau—have been organized along "functional" lines, that is, relatively large sections of people in which all do the same or very similar work. Accordingly, processing centers have had an intake unit, which receives and sends correspondence, records, claims, and files, a records unit, and two kinds of claims units, each constituting several sections, which are devoted to initial claims and post-entitlement claims, respectively. Records assembles various documents relating to a given case, places them in a folder, and routes the folder to the appropriate section. Accordingly, queueing occurs at records, and at each of the subsequent sections to which the file is sent. Because of the magnitude of records, they formerly were moved from place to place in large canvas "tubs" mounted on casters, with about 11,000 folders in each tub. Folders frequently failed to have all information necessary to complete processing, so were rerouted to other sections or even other centers, where queueing occurred again. In the past, it has taken from one to two weeks for a given case to move through a queue. As queues multiplied, the time necessary for processing sometimes extended to several months.

Authorizers processing initial claims held the most prestigious professional jobs, post-entitlement authorizers holding a lesser grade and pay status. The sections were relatively large, having as many as sixty kinds of cases. This specialization was formal in some instances and informal in others. Since all authorizers were evaluated in terms of number of cases processed and the accuracy thereof, there was a tendency for difficult cases to be rerouted, ostensibly for more documentation, or because another authorizer was deemed to have superior expertise in the problem associated with the case. Given the queueing phenomenon associated with functional organization, Beta Bureau experienced a chronic problem with aged cases. Unsurprisingly, claimants were likely to file complaints, sometimes with Sigma Agency, frequently with Congressmen, and occasionally with the Executive Office of the President. Sigma Agency maintained a special headquarters unit to process these complaints and to continue communication with the claimant, the elected official referring the complaint, and the bureau responsible for the claim. Meanwhile, the claim, most likely in transit, could prove exceedingly difficult to track down. Accordingly, processing centers developed "freeze lists" of aged claims. All claims on the freeze list were to be assigned highest priority until located and processed.

By the late 1980s processing time, error rates, employee morale, turnover, and service to clients had reached unacceptable levels. Documentation of cases became critical in several areas, especially in "unassociated material," i.e., documents needed to complete a claims case which, for one reason or another, never found their way to the claims folder for that case.

Efforts were made to improve the existing system through upgrading the data storage and retrieval system, and through tightening controls. A somewhat higher proportion of new claims were authorized at the branch office, enabling the same official to follow through from start to finish on a new claim. Numerous additional changes in equipment and procedure were authorized to expedite processing and to improve control. Although there is little hard evidence to suggest that firmer discipline was exercised, awards for exceptional service were increased and publicized.

Results of these efforts were disappointing, serving mainly to slow the decline in service, rather than to reverse it. Accordingly, bureau top management decided that the basic structure itself would have to be revised. A special staff was authorized to design and experiment with organizational structures to identify a system which would enhance service to the clientele and improve case control as well as productivity. Among things to be considered were job enlargement and enrichment, physical layout, composition of the work group and supervision.

PART B

Becaused of increasing problems of administration under the existing structure, top management of Beta Bureau of the Sigma Agency initiated a study of alternative forms of organization utilizing its in-house special staff. After initial research and planning at headquarters, special staff conducted field research at a processing center. Interviews and meetings were held with all levels of management, professional and support personnel, and union representatives. Results of the research indicated that it would be appropriate to conduct a pilot study to determine further the feasibility of work units organized along lines different from the traditional functional organization.

The Bureau Director, working with special staff and relevant line managers, proposed a concept of a "processing center within a processing center." Accordingly, the kinds of work to be done in such a unit, optimum size, positions, support staff, equipment, and facilities had to be determined as well as the appropriate grade and pay for new positions created. After some discussion, it was decided to call the new type of work group a "module," and the concept, "modular organization."

A number of combinations and variations in size, composition, workflow support equipment, span of control, chain of command, and support services were tried. Experimentation with and evaluation of two pilot work units over a period of two years produced a viable structure, although not one considered by staff to be "optimum." Top management determined that the problems leading to the experimentation were of such urgency that further study and experimentation were precluded. Also, in the interim, a number of new buildings had been built to house existing centers and it was felt that moving from existing facilities to the new ones could be combined with the change in organizational structure.

Matters were further complicated by a number of major, new amendments to the law relating to the programs being administered. New positions were created, necessitating authorization by the Civil Service Commission, which proved more difficult than had been anticipated. All of these events placed a massive burden on the existing training staff as well as on management from the first-line level to the top. Rank-and-file employees were also obviously affected by the rapid rate of change. Concurrent adoption of new technologies of case handling further complicated matters. The result was a kind of "future shock" felt by all concerned. Finally, during the latter stages of phasing in modularization, a massive reorganization of top management took place following the retirement of the bureau director who had initiated the original study.

Interviews with employees produced responses such as, "I wish the world would just stop for about six months so I could catch up," and, "We might just be able to do a workmanlike job on this program if Congress would quit making special exceptions for left-handed Eskimo veterans of the Korean War," or, "If management *really* knew what it was doing, we wouldn't have procedural changes every fifteen minutes."

Modules which emerged from this process contained about fifty employees each, supervised by a module manager and two assistant managers. A technical adviser served as a resource for professionals in the module. The latter position tended to be of a "rotating" nature in some locations, i.e., different rank-and-file professionals were temporarily assigned to the position rather than having it as a permanent assignment. Case records were specifically assigned to and physically located in each module. Accordingly, at the time a case was assigned an identification number it was determined which of the over two hundred modules would have virtually absolute responsibility for any future claim related to the case. Each time a folder was moved, information as to location change was fed to a central computer through a network terminal. For the most part, individual authorizers followed through on a single case until it was completed. Queueing was reduced to a minimum.

Two years after initial installation, a "faculty fellow" from a state university was assigned to attempt evaluation. Most of his efforts were directed toward job satisfaction. Initially, productivity was determined to be extremely difficult to measure because of the massive changes in the law, increased mechanization of some activities, difficulty in evaluating increased complexities in the program and resulting impact on processing, and a number of changes in data bases. Realignment of the work load between branch offices, processing centers and headquarters combined to make precise evaluation of productivity unobtainable. Nevertheless, some useful base data were obtained.

Two years later, a follow-up study was commissioned almost immediately after the conversion to modular organization was completed. In addition to job satisfaction, aggregate measures of productivity, turnover, absenteeism, processing time, control and relative cost were obtained. From the initiation of modular organization, massive change was a continuous phenomenon. In addition to the change in the form of organization, substantial revision of relevant legislation was passed, creating a number of new programs. In general, the new laws tended to make all but purely routine cases more difficult to process. Estimates of the level of increased difficulty ranged around fifteen percent. During the second study, the bureau was engaged in a project to upgrade data processing equipment such that each module had complete access to the master data file at headquarters. Accordingly, given the variety of changes, it was difficult to measure the precise impact of reorganization.

Nevertheless, a variety of findings were demonstrable. In comparison with other operating bureaus doing comparable work both absenteeism and turnover declined. Cost of administration as a proportion of total cost declined. "Freeze lists" declined by 85 percent or more demonstrating a marked improvement in control. Average processing time declined slightly where the new remote terminals had not been installed, and declined markedly where they were installed. Job satisfaction for the modules studied improved in four out of five categories measured; however, there were significant differences in perceived job satisfaction among different classes of employees. In general, lower-level clericals liked the change to modular organization, while professionals and first-line supervisors exhibited considerable variance in their opinion. Of the total number surveyed, about 80 percent preferred modules to functional organization. Few, if any, changes in quality control were demonstrated, but a decline attributable to the massive change in procedures as well as the law would not have been unexpected. Such a decline did not take place.

In the early stages, union representatives expressed substantial reservations about the proposed reorganization. This initial reluctance declined in most of the processing centers, although one local continued to maintain an official attitude of opposition. The attitude change was attributable in part to a modest net increase in pay-grade level resulting from the reorganization.

Summing up results of the studies, there appear to be few, if any, problems with the structural configuration of modules. They will work in this kind of service operation. Nevertheless, problems still remain with the operation of the centers as a whole. A few of these are structural, but most appear procedural or managerial.

In the process of abolishing sections of people all of whom were doing about the same thing and substituting modules of people doing different things, a number of one-of-a-kind positions were created. For example, some of the specialized sections merged into modules had only a couple of dozen people in them. This resulted in each module having only a single specialist in that category after reorganization. Accordingly, if the incumbent were promoted or left the job, the function served went uncovered. Although other professionals could be temporarily assigned to the function, they did not like it, and such occurrences were disruptive. Meanwhile, support functions such as recruiting and training were geared to the old-style sections, and would allow vacancies to accumulate in substantial numbers before selecting new candidates.

Job enlargement has been found also to be a mixed blessing. Professionals, and indeed, entire sections had tended to specialize in particular kinds of cases under the functional pattern of organization. With modularization, it became necessary to become proficient in all kinds. This latter kind of problem was intensified for module managers. Previously, they needed only to have detailed technical knowledge about a single phase of the processing operation, and how it interfaced with other parts; under the new scheme of organization it became necessary to be familiar with all parts of it.

Among the most visible results of the latter observation was a substantial exodus of former section heads destined to become—or who had become—module managers. Although headway was being made, the highest proportionate number of vacancies in modules was at the managerial level, with up to one-third of the modules, system-wide, operating either with "acting" (temporary) managers or without the usual complement of a manager and two assistant managers in each module. Estimates are that up to one-third of the former supervisors retired or transferred to other jobs in the federal government. On a brighter note, the remaining managers plus a number of newer appointees appear to be more flexible, more knowledgeable, and to consider the new position more of a challenge.

A continuing problem is that of substantial variation in productivity between individuals and between modules. Moreover, marginal personnel are at least benignly tolerated to the effect that an employee could be producing up to four times the amount of his neighbor doing the same work, and getting identical pay. The result of this amounted to rewarding poor performance rather than excellence. Predictably, a lack of consistent application of policy appeared because of relatively poor intermodular communication in some instances. In viewing the physical arrangement of modules, it was noteworthy that barriers, such as files, tables, and coatracks were placed so as to impede movement between the modules. In part, this was done so that anyone entering or leaving a module would have to pass in view of the manager, a form of control. On the other hand, it discouraged professionals and others from seeking counsel from their fellows in other modules. Professionals also aired complaints about inequitable distribution of the work load.

A substantial minority of professionals perceived a loss of status in that they were physically located with lower-level personnel. By contrast, the overwhelming majority of all personnel approved of the opportunity to observe all phases of the work as well as the integration of it. Good producers were very pleased with the increased accountability found in the modules, but not as pleased with what they viewed as inadequate management response to poor work.

In summation, the movement of an organization of this size from a traditional, functional mode to a form not previously tried on a large scale in service organizations during a period marked by a new construction, new law, and new procedures was an accomplishment of considerable magnitude in itself. Improvements in relative cost, case control, processing time (which means improved service to clientele), absenteeism, turnover,

and job satisfaction were observed. Remaining problems include interfacing staff support and service to the modular structure, intermodular communication, consistency of application of policy, and improving performance of some low producers. These would not appear to be insurmountable.

When you have read this case, look back at the chapter's diagnostic questions and choose the ones that apply to the case. Then use those questions with the ones that follow in your case analysis.

1. What kinds of jobs were being performed in the Beta Bureau processing centers during the time period covered in Part A of this case? How did employees react to these jobs? What other effects of the design of Beta Bureau's jobs were evident? What do you think caused employees' reactions and the other effects of job design in the bureau's processing centers?

2. What kind of job design approach did management take in creating the jobs described in Part B of the case? Was this approach successful? What effects did it have?

3. What problems were caused by the job redesign program at Beta Bureau? How would you deal with these problems?

CASE 17-3

THE PRODUCTION DEPARTMENT AT KCDE-TV

Review this case, which appears in Chapter 7. Next, look back at Chapter 17's diagnostic questions and choose the ones that apply to the case. Then use those questions with the ones that follow in your case analysis.

1. How did the employees of KCDE's production department feel about their jobs? What effects did these attitudes have on job performance?

2. How might jobs in the production department be redesigned to improve employee attitudes and performance? What specific approach to job design should be used?

3. What steps should the management of KCDE-TV take to implement your program of job redesign? To what extent should employees be involved in the process of designing and implementing job changes at KCDE?

CHAPTER 18

MANAGING THE ORGANIZATION: STRATEGY, CULTURE, AND ORGANIZATION DEVELOPMENT II

In February of 1991, just 19 months after he became chairman of USX, Charles Corry succeeded in defusing two of the steel and energy giant's major problems. Satisfying the demands of investors, Corry issued a new class of stock representing the firm's steel assets but kept the steel unit within the organization, thus retaining this highly profitable business. At the same time, Corry negotiated a tentative labor settlement in bargaining that United Steel Workers union president Lynn Williams called "open, communicative, and realistic."
Source: Clare Ansberry, "USX Posts Rise of 9% in Profit for 4th Quarter," The Wall Street Journal, *January 30, 1991, p. A9; Michael Schroeder, "How Charles Corry Became a Dragon Slayer at USX,"* Business Week, *February 18, 1991, p. 35.*

When Charles A. Corry was named chief of USX Corp. in June, some Wall Streeters wondered if he could fill the shoes of his charismatic predecessor, David M. Roderick. But on October 2, Corry made it clear that he aims to put his own mark on USX. Repudiating Roderick's troubled, $3 billion purchase of natural gas producer Texas Oil and Gas Corp. (TXO), Corry announced that he's putting TXO's energy reserves up for sale.

USX says it plans to use any proceeds to buy back stock and pay off debt. Analysts expect the bulk of the $1.5 billion to $2 billion raised from the sale of reserves will go to a massive stock buyback. And, ultimately, observers and former USX executives who know Corry well expect him to proceed with delayed plans to spin off at least 20% of the $5.8 billion steel unit to the public. That would still leave USX with its giant Marathon Oil Co. unit, which accounts for 53% of sales.[1]

As you know from reading this 1989 report, USX is a dominant player in the international petroleum industry. What you may not know, though, is that USX was once called U.S. Steel and until the early 1980s was the largest steel company in the world. What could possibly explain the company's metamorphosis from steel producer to petroleum refiner? Answer: from 1982 onward, USX's top managers intentionally redirected the firm into the increasingly profitable petroleum industry and out of the weakening world market for steel.

U.S. Steel—the world's first billion-dollar business—was born in 1901 when J. P. Morgan merged ten steel companies to overtake a competing steel empire owned by Andrew Carnegie. From then until the early 1980s, the firm maintained a leading role in the North American steel industry, serving as a major supplier for the automotive and heavy manufacturing industries. All that changed in 1982, however, when David M. Roderick, U.S. Steel's chair at the time, acquired Marathon Oil Company for $5.9 billion and began to transform it into a business that was more oil producer than steel manufacturer. Later in the same decade, the company changed its name to USX and strengthened its position in the petroleum industry by acquiring Husky Oil in 1984 and Texas Oil and Gas Corporation in 1985.[2]

As U.S. Steel ventured out of steel and into petroleum, the firm's business situation changed radically. From the relatively simple, stable steel industry where up to the end of the 1970s, it had held a comfortable position, the company now found itself moving into the more complex, dynamic environment of the petroleum industry of the 1980s. With this move came changes in the company's jobs and technology, away from the routine work and large-batch techniques of its foundry operations toward the nonroutine tasks and continuous process methods of its oil refineries. All these new conditions required that flexibility replace bureaucracy and that members of the firm learn to cope with change. USX managers thus found themselves wrestling with the task of refocusing the beliefs,

---

[1] Gregory L. Miles and Mark Ivey, "A New Iron Man Recasts USX," *Business Week*, October 16, 1989, p. 37.

[2] William C. Symonds, Gregory L. Miles, Mark Ivey, and Steven Prokesch, "The Toughest Job in Business: How They're Remaking U.S. Steel," *Business Week*, February 25, 1985, p. 50–56; Miles, Cheryl Debes, Richard A. Melcher, and James R. Norman, "It's USX vs. Everybody: Even If the Raiders Back Off, the Company Must Restructure Drastically," *Business Week*, October 6, 1986, pp. 26–27; and Miles and Ivey, "Iron Man Recasts USX."

values, and norms that had guided the company since the early 1900s. It was necessary to deemphasize norms and values that supported adherence to time-tested procedures and encourage creativity and innovation.[3] By the time Charles Corry replaced Roderick in 1989, USX was primarily an oil company and was struggling to separate itself from its bureaucratic past.

You will recall from Chapter 1 that this chapter is the last of three in our book (the others are Chapters 9 and 14) that focus attention on application issues—things that managers *do* to manage organizational behavior. It addresses the task of managing the organization as a whole. As is evident from our brief analysis of USX, managing the organizational context is an extremely complex task. Managers must plot the strategic direction of their firm. They must also design an organization structure of interdependent jobs to meet the demands of their company's work. In addition, they must shape the norms, values, and ways of thinking that influence behavior throughout the organization. In other words, managing the organizational context involves the management of *strategy*, *structure* and *job design*, and *culture*.

In keeping with what we have learned by examining management activities at USX, we will discuss the topics of strategy and culture in this chapter. Continuing the discussion begun in Chapter 14, we will also examine several organization-development interventions that can be used to manage organization-wide changes such as those that took place in USX throughout the 1980s. In addition, we will note how strategy, culture, and change at the organization level are related to the topics of structure and job design discussed in Chapters 15–17. After completing this chapter, you will be familiar with the broad range of activities involved in managing the organization as a whole.

DIAGNOSTIC ISSUES

When we talk about managing the entire organization, applying our diagnostic model raises some critical questions. Can we *describe* an organization's strengths and weaknesses and the way they affect its ability to survive? Can we identify the competitive forces arrayed against a firm? Can we *diagnose* and understand a situation in which an organizational culture persists in spite of the need for change? How can we *prescribe* which technique to use to overcome such resistance and stimulate needed change? Can we prescribe whether a business should grow and how fast? Finally, what *actions* can managers take to define the mission and strategy of their firm? What can they do to encourage changes that will enhance organizational effectiveness?

STRATEGIC MANAGEMENT AND THE FORMAL ORGANIZATION

strategy A plan of action that states an organization's goals and outlines the resources and activities required to achieve them.

strategic management A process of setting organizational goals and directing the organization toward goal achievement.

A strategy is a plan of action that states an organization's goals and outlines the resources and activities required to achieve them.[4] **Strategic management** is thus a process of setting organizational goals and directing the organization toward goal achievement. During the process of strategic management, managers make decisions and implement changes that shape the **formal**

---

[3] Symonds et al. "Toughest Job in Business."

[4] Roger Evered, "So What *Is* Strategy?" *Long Range Planning* 16 (1983), 57–72; and Ari Ginsberg, "Operationalizing Organizational Strategy: Toward an Integrative Framework," *Academy of Management Review* 9 (1984), 548–57.

formal organization Those aspects of an organization that are officially sanctioned, including intentionally designed structures and jobs.

organization of intentionally designed structures and jobs. New jobs are created, old jobs are eliminated, and structural arrangements are altered to fit the demands of the organization's strategy.

For example, in our opening story, David Roderick and his colleagues at U.S. Steel were engaged in strategic management as they formulated the strategy of diversifying into the oil industry. They were also performing strategic management as they put their strategy into action by acquiring Marathon Oil and other petroleum companies. With this change in U.S. Steel's business came new markets and technologies, therefore, pressures to create a new organization structure and new jobs. The formal organization moved toward change in response to the needs of the company's strategy. Later, Charles Corry and his staff were involved in strategic management when they sold off many of the assets acquired under Roderick's leadership. Again, as the company's business changed, pressure mounted to redesign its structure and the jobs performed by its employees. In the case of U.S. Steel, later USX, strategic management and the formal organization proved to be closely interrelated.

The Strategic Management Process

What do managers like Roderick and Corry do to develop and manage the strategy of a company? As shown in Figure 18-1, the process of strategic management involves five key phases—defining the organization's mission and strategic goals, analyzing its current situation, formulating a strategic plan, implementing the plan, and evaluating strategic performance.

Defining the Mission and Goals of the Organization. Strategic management begins with the definition of the mission of the firm. As you will recall from Chapter 2, an organization's mission is its purpose, or reason for being. Often the mission of a company can be expressed in the form of a statement that identifies the primary goods or services the company produces and the markets it hopes to serve. In conjunction with the mission, managers also identify strategic goals to be achieved as the organization progresses toward accomplishing its mission. Such goals might include gaining control over 20 percent of the market served by the company or doubling the company's level of profitability in five years. Together, the mission and goals developed during the initial phase of strategic management provide the organization with a sense of direction and serve as an indication of what must be accomplished for the organization to function successfully.

Performing a Situation Analysis. The aim of any strategy is to capitalize on what the organization does well and avoid what the organization does poorly. Thus the second phase of the strategic management process involves a careful

FIGURE 18-1

The Strategic Management Process

Feedback from evaluation

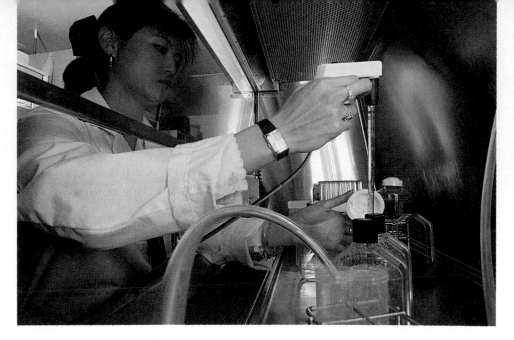

In 1980, Robert A. Swanson founded Genentech Inc. with a mission of building an independent pharmaceutical company that would do research in genetic engineering and develop products that would cure cancer, heart disease, and other major illnesses. But its first major product, the heart-attack drug known as TPA (tissue plasminogen activator), produced only half the sales the company had projected, and it became increasingly difficult to plow enough money back into research to keep the company's many projects going. In 1990 Swanson sold a controlling interest in the company to Roche Holding Ltd., the Swiss parent of Hoffmann-La Roche Co. Genentech's mission could change further if Roche takes over, as its stock options would allow it to do.
Source: Joan C. Hamilton et al., "Why Genentech Ditched the Dream of Independence," Business Week, February 19, 1990, pp. 36–37.

situation analysis An analysis of internal strengths and weaknesses and external opportunities and threats that is performed during the process of strategic planning.

situation analysis (see Figure 18-1).[5] To perform a situation analysis, top management begins by looking at the company's *strengths*, which are characteristics of the company that can help it achieve its strategic goals. Examples of such strengths include the United Parcel Service's reputation for providing fast, dependable delivery and IBM's reputation for providing some of the best client services of any computer manufacturer. In both these instances, the company's reputation is a strength that helps attract customers. Other strengths might include having experienced, knowledgeable managers and a skilled work force, holding extensive financial reserves, and owning the rights to important information or equipment.

Next is an assessment of the company's *weaknesses*. Those are the characteristics of the company that can block its progress toward goal achievement. Lacking a clear strategic direction is a notable weakness, as are operating out of obsolete facilities, failing to perform adequate research and development, and lacking essential managerial talent.

The situation analysis then focuses on conditions outside the organization. Managers first assess *opportunities* or characteristics of the environment surrounding the company that might help it meet or exceed its strategic goals. A healthy economy, readily available raw materials, and an expanding market are all environmental opportunities. The situation analysis concludes with an examination of *threats*. These threats are environmental factors that may prevent the organization from attaining its strategic goals. Examples are adverse government policies, growing competitive pressures, scarce labor resources, and changing consumer tastes.

Formulating A Strategic Plan. During the third phase of strategic management, managers work to develop a strategic plan that will take advantage of the strengths and opportunities uncovered during situation analysis and minimize the negative effects of weaknesses and threats. Strategies formulated during this phase are of the three types depicted in Figure 18-2—corporate, business, and functional.[6]

[5] Arthur A. Thompson, Jr., and A. J. Strickland III, *Strategic Management: Concepts and Cases*, 4th ed. (Plano, Texas: Business Publications, 1987), p. 97.
[6] Dan E. Schendel and Charles Hofer, eds., *Strategic Management: A New View of Business Policy and Planning* (Boston: Little, Brown, 1979), pp. 11–14; Milton Leontiades, *Strategies for Diversification and Change* (Boston: Little, Brown, 1980), p. 63; and Robert H. Hayes and Steven C. Wheelwright, *Restoring Our Competitive Edge: Competing through Manufacturing* (New York: John Wiley, 1984), p. 28.

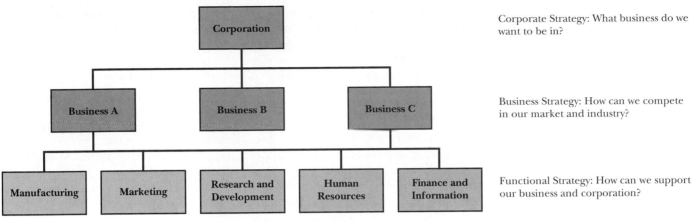

FIGURE 18-2

Three Types of Strategies

Organizations consist of a corporate body often made up of several different businesses, each of which is composed of a number of functional units. *Corporate* strategies concern the mix of businesses constituting the organization. *Business* strategies specify the goals and actions of each business. *Functional* strategies indicate how each of the functions in a particular business will contribute to the success of the business and the company that owns it.

They specify the *means* or procedures to be used to accomplish the *ends* or objectives that are in the organization's strategic goals. Later in this chapter, following a description of the strategic management process, we will examine the three types of strategies shown in Figure 18-2.

Implementing the Strategic Plan. Implementation involves putting the strategy into place and getting individuals and groups in the organization to execute their part of the strategic plan. It focuses on activities such as

> Developing an organization structure capable of coordinating the jobs that must be performed to fulfill the company's mission
>
> Formulating budgets and resource allocation procedures that will help the company attain strategic goals
>
> Inspiring employee commitment to the company's strategy and mission
>
> Linking employee motivation and the organization's reward system to the achievement of strategic goals
>
> Creating a culture of norms and values that supports the strategic mission and successful goal attainment
>
> Developing an information system to track and control the process of strategic implementation
>
> Exerting the leadership needed to drive strategic implementation forward and to stimulate continual improvement in the execution of the company's strategy.[7]

Implementing an organization's strategy means evaluating and sometimes changing a firm's structure, technology, information flows, and leadership patterns to achieve the strategic goals of the firm. Management must examine the formal organization to determine what strategy-supporting features are required and then do what must be done to put these features in place.

[7] Thompson and Strickland, *Strategic Management*, p. 11.

Evaluating Strategic Performance. The final phase of the process of strategic management is an evaluation of the organization's performance to determine whether strategic goals are being met. It is not unusual for evaluation procedures to uncover operational shortcomings or changing conditions that require adjusting the strategic implementation or even the strategic plan itself. For instance, strategic adjustments may be required by changes in the internal strengths and weaknesses of the company that occur as some employees leave and others take their place. Or external opportunities and threats may shift as new competitors enter the market or technological breakthroughs influence the industry. Simply building up experience in executing a strategy can pinpoint what works and what doesn't. It stimulates additional planning and a change in strategic direction. As shown in Figure 18-1, evaluation feeds back to earlier phases of strategic management, influencing future missions and goals, situation analyses, strategic plans, and implementation efforts.

Types of Strategies

The direction ultimately pursued by an organization is the product of several types of strategies: (1) a corporate strategy that determines what businesses the firm is in, (2) different business strategies that influence the direction of each of the businesses in the firm, and (3) various functional strategies that help coordinate the activities of the different functional areas in each of the firm's businesses. Let's take a closer look at these three types of strategies.

corporate strategy A strategic plan that specifies the desired mix of businesses in a firm and how resources should be allocated among them.

Corporate Strategies. **Corporate strategies** address the question, *What business or businesses do we want to be in?* When a firm is involved in only a single business, the answer to this question may seem relatively obvious. For instance, the managers of a college bookstore probably have little difficulty determining that the business of their firm is selling college texts and that because there is a continuing demand for textbooks from one term to the next, they want to stay in that business.

When a company is involved in several different businesses, however, top management may find it hard to answer questions about the firm's present and prospective composition. The company's businesses may be as diverse as fashion apparel, consumer electronics, and petroleum production. To visualize the task of managing a firm consisting of several businesses, take a look at the **BCG Matrix** diagrammed in Figure 18-3. This matrix, developed by the Boston Consulting Group (BCG), is a tool that can be used to track the **portfolio** of businesses owned by an organization.[8]

BCG Matrix A management tool that depicts the mix of businesses owned by a firm.

portfolio The mix of different businesses owned by an organization.

Businesses that appear in the upper left-hand quadrant of the BCG Matrix are called *stars*, because they are the most desirable of all the businesses in the matrix. Stars are very valuable, because each controls a large share of the market in a growing industry. Firms normally try to hold on to the stars they already own as they try to find new stars for their portfolios.

In the lower-left-hand quadrant of the BCG Matrix, *cash cows* control large market shares of stagnant, less desirable industries. Cash cows generate a lot of money because of their market position. Management, however, has little reason to spend this money on developing them further, because their industries are so weak. Instead, they become sources of funds for maintaining existing stars or developing new ones.

[8] Bruce D. Henderson, *The Experience Curve Reviewed, IV* (Boston: Boston Consulting Group, 1973), p. 3; and Barry Hedley, "A Fundamental Approach to Strategic Development," *Long Range Planning*, 9 (1976), 2–11.

FIGURE 18-3

The BCG Matrix

The vertical axis of the BCG Matrix maps industry growth rates for all businesses in the firm's portfolio. The horizontal axis charts each business's market share. Each business is represented by a circle whose size indicates the percentage of corporate revenues that business generates. The position of each circle within the matrix indicates the market share that the business it represents holds as well as the growth rate of the industry in which the business functions.

Based on Bruce D. Henderson, The Experience Curve Reviewed, IV: The Growth Share Matrix of the Product Portfolio (*Boston: Boston Consulting Group, 1973) p. 3; and Barry Hedley, "Strategy and the Business Portfolio,"* Long Range Planning 10 (*1977*), 2–11.

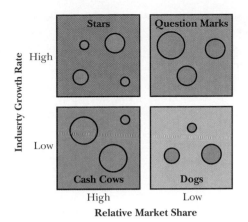

convergent growth strategies A class of corporate strategies that involve starting, acquiring, or maintaining businesses in the market and industry already served by the firm. Included in this class are the concentration strategy and the horizontal integration strategy.

evolutionary growth strategies A class of corporate strategies in which the firm develops products, markets, or businesses that are similar though not identical to the ones already associated with the company. Product development, market development, and concentric diversification are all evolutionary growth strategies.

Businesses in the upper-right-hand quadrant of the BCG Matrix are called *question marks*. The future of a question mark, which has only a small market share in a healthy, growing industry, is uncertain. If its market position cannot be improved, such a business may consume more resources than it produces and become a costly burden to its owner. On the other hand, by reallocating money from a cash cow or even a star, it may be possible to transform a question mark into a star for less money than it would cost to start a successful business from scratch or to buy one from another company.

Businesses in the lower-right-hand quadrant of the BCG Matrix, called *dogs*, occupy small market positions in stagnant industries and are the least desirable type of business to own. A firm will usually try to sell the dogs in its portfolio. If it cannot find buyers, the firm may choose to close the dogs and absorb the resulting short-term loss rather than endure a long-term drain on company resources.

The BCG Matrix demonstrates that managing a company's portfolio involves the acquisition of desirable businesses, the spin off of undesirable businesses, and the transfer of resources from lucrative businesses to those in need of additional support. Let's look next at some of the corporate strategies (see Table 18-1) that companies follow in performing these activities.[9]

A company uses **convergent growth strategies** to start, acquire, or maintain businesses in the market and industry it already serves. In the strategy known as *concentration*, a firm attempts to strengthen the market position of a business it already owns by using the firm's resources to sell the business's product more effectively in its current market. For example, in 1991 Apple Computer initiated a concentration strategy by introducing lower-priced versions of its most popular products and kicking off an aggressive marketing campaign. In *horizontal integration*, a firm tries to increase its market share by starting or acquiring other businesses that make the same product it produces itself. For instance, in 1990 GM opened its new Saturn division, reflecting the pursuit of a strategy of horizontal integration in the automotive industry.

Using **evolutionary growth strategies**, an organization may develop products, markets, or businesses that are similar though not identical to the ones already associated with the company. In *product development*, a firm tries to strengthen its position by selling a new product in its current market. For example, during the 1980s, Anheuser-Busch introduced a line of low-alcohol beverages to

[9] The strategies discussed in this section are based on a typology presented in Richard Z. Gooding, "Structuring Strategic Problems: Antecedents and Consequences of Alternative Decision Frames" (Ph.D. dissertation, Michigan State University, 1989). See also J. A. Pearce and R. B. Robinson, Jr., *Strategic Management: Strategy Formulation and Implementation* (Homewood, Ill.: Richard D. Irwin, 1985); and Thompson and Strickland, *Strategic Management*.

TABLE 18-1
Types of Corporate Strategies

STRATEGIC GOAL	DESCRIPTION	SPECIFIC STRATEGIES
Convergent growth	Acquisition or maintenance of businesses in the firm's current market and industry	Concentration Horizontal integration
Evolutionary growth	Acquisition of businesses in markets and industries that are similar but not identical to those currently served by the firm	Product development Market development Concentric diversification
Revolutionary growth	Acquisition of businesses in markets and industries that differ from those currently served by the firm	Forward integration Backward integration Conglomerate diversification
Adaptive decline	Downsizing, or elimination of some of the firm's current businesses	Retrenchment Divestiture Liquidation

take further advantage of the distribution network of supermarkets and convenience stores that the firm's brewery business had already established. Following a strategy of *market development*, a firm sells its current product to new markets. The decision of CBS Records to start a mail-order club to sell CDs and tapes exemplifies the market-development strategy, because it enabled the firm to branch out beyond the network of retailers that normally sell sound recordings. In *concentric diversification*, an organization establishes a business that is similar but not identical to its current businesses in products, markets, and technologies. This sort of strategy is exemplified by Boeing Aircraft's decision to enter the market for civilian aircraft when orders for military planes and armament declined at the end of World War II.

As their name suggests, **revolutionary growth strategies** call for a firm to develop or acquire businesses that are quite different from businesses it already owns. In *forward integration*, a company grows by acquiring one or more businesses in the distribution channel that connects it with the final consumers of its products. For example, Benetton, a manufacturer of sweaters and other clothing, acquired warehousing facilities and retail stores so that it could retail its own products. Conversely, in *backward integration*, a firm acquires businesses in the channels that connect it with the raw materials it needs. For instance, the Goodyear Tire and Rubber Company owns plantations throughout the world that it bought to ensure an uninterrupted supply of rubber for its tires and other products. In *conglomerate diversification*, a company establishes businesses in areas totally unrelated to its current undertakings. General Electric's move into financial services, including consumer credit operations and venture capital financing, exemplifies this strategy.

When none of the corporate growth strategies we have discussed are successful in improving or at least maintaining the profitability of an organization's portfolio of businesses, the organization may be forced to choose an **adaptive decline strategy**. It either downsizes or eliminates one or more businesses. Sometimes a firm will cut back on the operating levels of a business to reduce current costs. By such temporary *retrenchment*, the firm hopes to give the business a chance to deal with its problems and reemerge in a stronger position. American Motors attempted to survive in the mid-1980s by scaling back other products and focusing on the production and sales of Jeeps. When its retrenchment strategy failed to

revolutionary growth strategies A class of corporate strategies in which the firm develops or acquires businesses that are quite different from businesses it already owns. Included in this class are forward integration, backward integration, and conglomerate diversification.

adaptive decline strategies A class of corporate strategies in which the firm reduces its size by either downsizing or eliminating one or more businesses. Retrenchment, divestiture, and liquidation are all adaptive decline strategies.

Some managers argue that employees should be the last to know the details about a pending sale of their business unit. What they don't know won't hurt their productivity or morale. Other managers argue just the opposite, suggesting that employees who are let in on the news from the beginning are more able to cope with the changes that occur once the sale actually takes place. Consider the following story as you think about which position you agree with.

In December 1989, the Chrysler Corporation publicized its plan to sell its Gulfstream Aerospace subsidiary. Within a day, Allen E. Paulson, Gulfstream's founder and chief executive, announced that he would attempt to buy the company back from Chrysler. Why was Paulson so quick to act?

In 1985, the year Paulson had sold Gulfstream to Chrysler, the company was healthy and productive. "We were working hard, everyone had a piece of the action, we all felt good," recalled James Swindells, Gulfstream's director of completion center operations. Then came the announcement that the company was up for sale. One rumor (false) had it that Paulson was leaving Gulfstream. Another (false) was that layoffs were just ahead. A third (true) was that the new owner knew little about aerospace. "Everyone was insecure, handing his résumé to anyone who came in to have an airplane serviced," Swindells said. Things got even worse when employees discovered that Chrysler was going to be the new owner. "Workers were wor-

rying they'd be moved to Detroit or asked to build cars in Savannah, and managers were worrying if they'd have jobs at all," said Preston Blackwelder, Gulfstream's director of personnel.

This experience taught Paulson that keeping employees in the dark about the sale of their business can do more harm than good. It is certainly true that publicizing a pending sale can stimulate a bidding war that undermines the original buyer's position and can create a sense of worrisome uncertainty among employees. Keeping things out in the open, however, gives management the chance to deal with prospective issues before they turn into problems. In the Gulfstream of 1989, managers held weekly meetings to field employee questions and dispel rumors. One particularly troublesome rumor was that Mitsubishi was negotiating for the company. Management responded immediately by posting a notice that Mitsubishi was looking to buy one of Chrysler's auto plants, not Gulfstream. Workers clearly appreciated such responses. Unlike five years ago, no one quit for fear of ownership. "I've faced uncertainties in aviation before, and I've always made calls right away," says service mechanic Kenneth Farris. "This time I'm waiting patiently."*

* Claudia H. Deutsch, "Letting Employees in on The News," *New York Times*, March 4, 1990, p. F37.

---

work, however, the company was purchased by Chrysler. Sometimes reduction becomes permanent elimination. In *divestiture* a firm sells its entire interest in one of its businesses to another firm, as exemplified by Chrysler's sale of its military tank and armament business to General Dynamics in the early 1980s. In *liquidation*, a firm breaks up a failing business, salvaging whatever it can by selling one or more parts of the otherwise unsaleable business or merging parts of the failed business with other businesses it owns. Texas Instruments liquidated its personal-computer division in the mid-1980s after IBM became the dominant player in the personal-computer industry.

Decline strategies present the special problem of managing workers who face the prospect of losing their jobs. Should the managers of the business that is about to be divested tell employees about upcoming changes? Or should management keep news about the sale to itself? The "Management Issues" box considers some of the problems for employees when a business is put up for sale.

Business Strategies. For each business in the corporate portfolio, management formulates a **business strategy** in an attempt to ensure the business's successful performance. Business strategies address the question, How can we compete most effectively in our market and industry? In searching for an answer, managers assess the effects of five competitive forces. Those forces are the business's current rivals in the marketplace, its potential rivals in the form of new entrants into the market, firms that make products that might substitute for the business's own, the business's suppliers of raw materials, and the business's customers (see Figure 18-4). On the basis of this assessment, managers typically choose one of three

business strategy A strategic plan that specifies the way a business plans to compete in its market and industry. Overall cost leadership, differentiation, and focus are all business strategies.

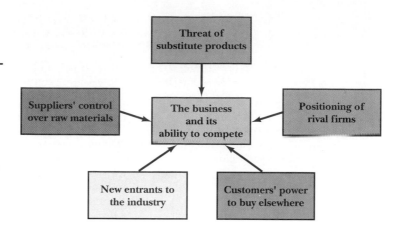

*The Campbell Soup Co., facing
declining profits, attempted to move
into other product lines but stretched
its resources too thin. When David
Johnson took over as CEO in 1990
he concluded that the company had
failed to capitalize on its strongest
product. Campbell soups continue to
command almost two-thirds of the
U.S. market for soup. In a*
differentiation strategy, *the
company brought out a new and
unique version of its current product:
a line of soups just for children. In a
further effort to reinforce brand
loyalty, the company brought back its
famous "Campbell Kids," featuring
them, with new friends, on the labels
of the new product.*
Source: *"From Soup to Nuts and Back
to Soup,"* Business Week, *November
5, 1990, p. 114.*

types of competitive strategies—overall cost leadership, differentiation, or focus.[10]

The competitive thrust in the strategy of *overall cost leadership* is on cutting operating costs and selling at prices below those of competitors. In the retailing industry, for example, Wal-Mart has used this strategy to compete with K Mart, Woolco, and other discount chains. Clearly, in order to sell goods at the lowest market prices, a firm must organize with the utmost efficiency. It must be able to exert tight control over the costs of research and development, production, sales, and similar functional activities as well as over general overhead expenses. Careful cost accounting, close financial control, and investment in labor-saving equipment are all hallmarks of the cost-leadership strategy.

Cost leadership not only helps a business compete on the basis of price. It enables the business to defend itself against price-war conditions and earn acceptable profits in markets dominated by price competition. This strategy also makes it easy to use price cutting as a defense against new entrants into the market as well as against companies that offer substitute products. A highly efficient operation can absorb increasing costs of raw materials without forcing a significant rise in selling prices. Of course, building a reputation for consistently offering goods or services at lower prices than any competitor's also goes a long way toward ensuring customer loyalty.

Using the strategy of *differentiation*, a firm tries to distinguish its product or service. It creates something that differs in important ways from other competitive products—something that will be perceived as unique. Differentiation can be accomplished in many ways. Mercedes Benz and BMW, for example, use a com-

[10] Michael E. Porter, *Competitive Strategy: Techniques for Analyzing Industries and Competitors* (New York: Free Press, 1980), p. 35.

bination of design innovations and upscale advertising to build images of exceptional quality, durability, and luxury. Sony Electronics and Compaq Computer set themselves apart from competitors by staying on the cutting edge of technological advance. Caterpillar Tractor plays up its extensive dealer and service network as distinguishing it from its competitors.

The purpose of the differentiation strategy, however it is accomplished, is to create brand loyalty among a business's customers and in that way, insulate the business from the rivalry of both current and potential competitors. Brand loyalty, in turn, can provide something of a cushion in a situation where the firm is forced to raise selling prices. The loyalty stimulated by differentiation may reduce customers' sensitivity to price. Differentiation also allows the increased profit margins needed for protection against increasing raw materials costs.

In the *focus* business strategy, a firm decides to concentrate on serving a particular, or target, market. This strategic decision enables the firm to contain costs by limiting the scope of its research and development, advertising, marketing, and sales efforts. By tailoring its product to the special needs of its target group of customers, the firm can more easily differentiate itself from competitors. It does not have to meet the needs of a broad array of potential customers. Consider the strategy of the Fort Howard Paper Company, which targets industrial suppliers of paper goods and avoids the retail market. To these suppliers of factories, schools, government offices, and similar facilities, Fort Howard sells washroom paper products at prices that competitors like Kimberly-Clark or Scott Paper — which serve a wide consumer market—cannot beat. As you can see, the focus strategy lets a firm use elements of both the overall cost leadership and the differentiation strategies. It can maintain low costs by limiting itself to a specific market segment and distinguish itself from other competitors by focusing on that segment alone.

Functional Strategies

functional strategy A strategic plan that specifies how a functional unit will contribute to the attainment of corporate and business goals.

As you will recall from Chapters 15 and 16, businesses are organized in structural units responsible for specific *functions*. Some such units that are common to many firms are the departments for manufacturing, marketing, materials management, research and development, human resources, and financial-information systems.[11] **Functional strategies** address the question, How can we support our firm's corporate and business strategies most effectively? They help ensure that unit activities play a role in meeting corporate and business goals. Such strategies can not only build new strengths in a firm; they can also turn a company's weaknesses into strengths. For instance, in the 1970s, various food-processing businesses overhauled their manufacturing and marketing operations and then introduced generic food products. This move transformed money-losing products into profitable lines of overall cost leadership. A decade later, the Nippon Electric Company engaged in aggressive research and development and added a unique product—laptop computers—to an aging line of desktop computers. The company then initiated a new and successful differentiation strategy.

How Strategy Shapes the Formal Organization

The three types of strategies we have described exert strong influence over one another. Successful functional strategies increase the likelihood of success in

[11] Charles W. L. Hill and Gareth R. Jones, *Strategic Management: An Integrated Approach* (Boston: Houghton Mifflin, 1989), p. 230.

business operations, and successful business strategies improve the position of the corporation as a whole. Conversely, an effective corporate strategy also improves the resource positions of the firm's businesses, and a successful business strategy underwrites continued activity in the business's functional units.

In addition, as we said at the beginning of this chapter, strategic management influences a firm's formal organization of intentionally designed jobs and structural arrangements. One way it does so is by affecting the contingencies that determine structural effectiveness.[12] Consider the following points:

1. The environmental diversity surrounding a firm depends largely on whether the firm chooses to concentrate on a single business or develop a portfolio of different businesses. As long as an organization consists of a single business, it will probably face a uniform environment. If, however, it has a portfolio of different businesses, its management can expect to encounter significant environmental diversity.

2. The levels of complexity, stability, uncertainty, and hostility of the firm's environment are also affected by strategic decisions as to which businesses to acquire, which to keep, and which to sell. For instance, when Honeywell Bull acquired Zenith Data Systems, it left the relative stability of the mainframe computer industry for the much more volatile personal-computer market. Similarly, when R. J. Reynolds acquired Nabisco, the firm encountered a less hostile environment in the prepared-foods industry than the one it had previously dealt with as a tobacco manufacturer.

3. The size of a firm is a direct consequence of strategic choice. Adding additional businesses to the corporate portfolio and pursuing growth strategies in existing businesses increases organizational size. In contrast, reducing the size of the corporate portfolio or pursuing adaptive decline strategies reduces the size of an organization.

4. The technology employed in a business is often the consequence of choosing one business strategy over another. For instance, choosing to pursue an overall cost leadership strategy in a manufacturing firm pushes toward the adoption of an efficient technology—most often, mass production or continuous operations. In contrast, a differentiation strategy may necessitate the custom-building adaptability of unit or flexible-cell technologies.[13]

Strategy also influences the formal organization by affecting the design of jobs. Just as a strategy of overall cost leadership favors the adoption of efficient technologies, it calls for efficiency-oriented approaches to job design, such as work measurement and job simplification. American automobile companies often compete on the basis of cost, as shown by the countless rebates and discount programs they have offered. And their assembly lines consist of simplified jobs, such as the welding task described at the beginning of Chapter 17. On the other hand, a differentiation strategy that emphasizes product quality may favor the adoption of job enrichment methods. Experiences at Volvo and Saab indicate that the comprehensive enrichment afforded by sociotechnical job design can have a substantial positive effect on product quality.

In sum, the process of strategic management creates many of the contingencies and conditions that influence managers as they design organizational structures and the jobs within them. In turn, the structures and jobs that managers design define the nature of the organizations, businesses, and functional units that are the focus of further strategic management activities. Strategic management is therefore an integral part of the process of managing the formal organization.

[12] Alfred D. Chandler, Jr., *Strategy and Structure* (Garden City, N.Y.: Anchor Books, 1966), pp. 7–17; and Danny Miller, "Relating Porter's Business Strategies to Environment and Structure: Analysis and Performance Implications," *Academy of Management Journal* 31 (1988), 280–308.

[13] Porter, *Competitive Strategy*, pp. 35–40.

ORGANIZATIONAL CULTURE
AND THE INFORMAL ORGANIZATION

Beneath every formal organization of official jobs and structural relationships lies an **informal organization** of unofficial rules, procedures, and interconnections that develops as employees make spontaneous, unauthorized changes in the way things are done. An important part of the informal organization is the **grapevine**, an unofficial communication network through which employees trade gossip and rumors about their jobs, their coworkers, and the organization. In many organizations, hearing from the grapevine that the company's business is off often precedes formal management announcements of layoffs or other cutbacks. Similarly, it is not uncommon for rumors that a favorite boss is about to retire to predate the formal announcement by several weeks. Although the information transmitted in a company's grapevine lacks official authorization, it does not necessarily lack validity.

The workings of the informal organization are also illustrated by the employee-created performance quotas that sometimes take the place of formal production goals. When employees perceive official standards as unfair or overly demanding, they may develop unofficial, lower standards of productivity. They may also develop a complex social structure of informal rewards and punishments around these standards. If employees catch peers working too hard, they may subject them to verbal threats, social isolation, and even physical abuse.[14]

In both these examples, the informal organization arises as day-to-day adjustments to the formal way of doing things create a **culture** of attitudes and understandings that are shared among coworkers. An organization's culture is

> A pattern of basic assumptions—invented, discovered, or developed [by a firm's members] to cope with problems of external adaptation and internal integration—that has worked well enough to be considered valid and, therefore, to be taught to new members as the correct way to perceive, think, and feel in relation to those problems.[15]

Culture is thus an informal, shared way of perceiving life and membership in an organization that binds members together and influences what they think about themselves and their work.

In the process of helping to create a mutual understanding of organizational life, organizational culture fulfills four basic functions:

1. It gives members an organizational identity. Sharing norms, values, and perceptions gives people a sense of togetherness that helps promote a feeling of common purpose.

2. It facilitates collective commitment. The common purpose that grows out of a shared culture tends to elicit strong commitment from all those who accept the culture as their own.

3. It promotes system stability. By encouraging a shared sense of identity and commitment, culture encourages lasting integration and cooperation among the members of an organization.

4. It shapes behavior by helping members make sense of their surroundings. An organization's culture serves as a source of shared meanings that explain why things occur the way they do.[16]

informal organization The unofficial rules, procedures, and interconnections that develop as employees make spontaneous, unauthorized changes in the way things are done.

grapevine The unofficial communication network within the informal organization through which employees trade gossip and rumors about their jobs, their coworkers, and the organization.

culture The shared attitudes and perceptions in an organization that are based on a set of fundamental norms and values and help members understand the organization.

[14] Fritz J. Roethlisberger and William J. Dickson, *Management and the Worker* (Cambridge, Mass.: Harvard University Press, 1939), p. 523.

[15] Edgar H. Schein, *Organizational Culture and Leadership* (San Francisco: Jossey-Bass, 1985), p. 9.

[16] Robert Kreitner and Angelo Kinicki, *Organizational Behavior* (Homewood, Ill.: BPI-Irwin, 1989), pp. 649–50. See also Linda Smircich, "Concepts of Culture and Organizational Analysis," *Administrative Science Quarterly* 28 (1983), 339–58.

By fulfilling these four basic functions, the culture of an organization serves as a sort of social glue that helps reinforce persistent, coordinated behaviors at work.

Elements of Organizational Culture

Deep within the culture of every organization are a collection of fundamental norms and values that shape members' behaviors and help them understand the surrounding organization. In some companies, for example, Polaroid, 3M, and DuPont Chemical, cultural norms and values emphasize the importance of discovering new materials or technologies and developing them into new products. In other companies, such as AT&T and Maytag Appliances, cultural norms and values focus on high product quality.[17] Fundamental norms and values like these are the ultimate source of the shared perceptions, thoughts, and feelings that constitute the culture of an organization.

How are these fundamental norms and values expressed? How are they passed from one person to another? Certain surface elements of the culture help employees interpret everyday events in the organization and are the principal means by which cultural norms and values are communicated from one person to another. *Ceremonies*, *rites*, and *rituals* reinforce particular norms and values by demonstrating their worth through special events. *Stories* and *myths* exemplify norms and values by encompassing them in memorable narratives. In the exploits of *heroes* and *superstars*, organization members see the fruits of adhering to the firm's norms and values. *Symbols* and special *language* are constant reminders of important norms and values (see Table 18-2).

[17] Terrence E. Deal and Allan A. Kennedy, *Corporate Cultures: The Rites and Rituals of Corporate Life* (Reading, Mass.: Addison-Wesley, 1982), p. 15.

TABLE 18-2
Surface Elements of Organization Cultures

ELEMENT	DESCRIPTION
Ceremonies	Special events in which organization members celebrate the myths, heroes, and symbols of their firm
Rites	Ceremonial activities meant to communicate specific ideas or accomplish particular purposes
Rituals	Actions that are repeated regularly to reinforce cultural norms and values
Stories	Accounts of past events that illustrate and transmit deeper cultural norms and values
Myths	Fictional stories that help explain activities or events that might otherwise be puzzling
Heroes	Successful people who embody the values and character of the organization and its culture
Superstars	Extraordinary individuals who personify the upper limits of attainment in the organization and its culture
Symbols	Objects, actions, or events that have special meanings and enable organization members to exchange complex ideas and emotional messages
Language	A collection of verbal symbols that often reflect the organization's particular culture

ceremonies Special events in which the members of an organization celebrate the myths, heroes, and symbols of their culture.

rite A ceremonial activity meant to communicate particular messages or accomplish specific purposes.

Ceremonies, Rites, and Rituals. Ceremonies are special events in which the members of a company celebrate the myths, heros, and symbols of their culture.[18] Ceremonies thus exemplify and reinforce important cultural norms and values. In sales organizations like Mary Kay or Amway, annual ceremonies are held to recognize and reward outstanding sales representatives. Part of the reason for holding these ceremonies is to inspire sales representatives who have been less effective to adopt the norms and values of their successful colleagues. In personifying the "Mary Kay approach" and the "Amway philosophy," the people who are recognized and rewarded in these ceremonies greatly enhance the attractiveness of their companies' special philosophies.

Often, organizational ceremonies incorporate various **rites**—ceremonial activities meant to send particular messages or accomplish specific purposes. Let's look next at some of the most common kinds of organizational rites.[19]

Rites of passage are used to initiate new members and can convey important aspects of the culture to them. An elaborate example of this phenomenon is military boot camp. The entire experience is designed to inculcate a particular military culture into recruits. In some business firms, new recruits are required to spend considerable time talking with veteran employees and learning about cultural norms and values by listening to stories about their experiences at work. In other companies, however, the rite of passage is merely a brief talk about company rules and regulations delivered by a human resources staff member to newcomers during their first day at work. It is little more than a formal welcoming and doesn't really help newcomers learn about the culture of the firm.

When employees are transferred, demoted, or fired because of low productivity, incompatible values, or other personal failings, *rites of degradation* may draw the attention of others to the limits of acceptable behavior. Today, rites of degradation are generally deemphasized, involving little more than quiet reassignment, but they have on occasion been quite dramatic. In the early days of NCR, executives would learn that they had lost their jobs by discovering their desks burning on the lawn in front of corporate headquarters.

Rites of enhancement also emphasize the limits of appropriate behavior but in a positive way. They recognize increasing status or position in a firm and may range from simple promotion announcements to intricate recognition ceremonies, such as the Mary Kay and Amway ceremonies we have already described.

In *rites of integration*, members of an organization become aware of the common feelings that bond them together. Often in rites of this sort, official titles and hierarchical differences are intentionally ignored so that members can get to know each other as people rather than as managers, staff specialists, clerks, or laborers. At Tandem Computer, for example, a Friday "TGIF" is held each week, giving employees the opportunity to chat informally over pizza and drinks. Company picnics, golf outings, softball games, and holiday parties can also serve as rites of integration.

ritual A ceremonial event that occurs repeatedly and continues to reinforce key norms and values.

A rite that is repeated on a regular basis becomes a **ritual**, a ceremonial event that continually reinforces key norms and values. The morning coffee break is a ritual that strengthens important workplace relationships. So, too, is the annual stockholder meeting held by management to convey cultural norms and values to company shareholders. Just as routine coffee breaks enable coworkers to gossip among themselves and reaffirm important interpersonal relationships, annual stockholder meetings give the company the opportunity to strengthen connections between it and people who would otherwise have little more than a limited financial interest in its continued well-being.

[18] Deal and Kennedy, *Corporate Cultures*, p. 63.
[19] Janice M. Beyer and Harrison M. Trice, "How an Organization's Rites Reveal Its Culture," *Organizational Dynamics* 15 (1987), 3–21.

CEO Robert Paluck believes that Convex Computer's annual summer picnic inspires enthusiasm among his employees. For this rite of integration in 1990 the company had 200 tons of sand trucked in to its headquarters in Richardson, Texas, and, at the suggestion of the company's 1200 employees, filled a pool with 72 gallons of iced raspberry Jell-O. Five vice presidents followed Paluck himself in splashing down into the goo. Paluck uses other rites and rituals to reinforce team spirit and feels it pays off. In 1989, the company's earnings on its supercomputers, which sell for up to $2.5 million each, rose by 93%. Source: Mark M. Colodny, "High-Tech CEO Splashes Down," Fortune, August 27, 1990, p. 104.

story An account of past events that all employees are familiar with and that serves as a reminder of cultural understandings.

myth A story that provides a fictional but plausible explanation for something that might otherwise seem puzzling.

Stories and Myths. Stories are accounts of past events that all employees are familiar with and that serve as reminders of cultural values.

> Bill Hewlett and Dave Packard are "legends in their own time" to the employees of Hewlett-Packard. New employees learn from a slide presentation shown when they first arrive that "Bill and Dave" started the company in Bill's garage and made some of the first products using the Hewlett kitchen oven. They hear informally from many employees stories about how Bill and Dave expect employees to address them by their first names. Stories emphasize and legitimate the management philosophy to avoid long-term debt and . . . layoffs. Stories also help define, in a way mere statements can't, what the "HP way" is.[20]

As organization members tell stories and think about the messages the stories convey, concrete examples facilitate their later recall of the concepts presented. It is easier, for instance, to remember that Bill and Dave want to be called by their first names than to memorize an abstract rule stating that undue formality is discouraged at Hewlett-Packard. Stories also provide information about historical events in the development of a company that can improve employees' understanding of the present.

> In one organization, employees tell a story about how the company avoided a mass layoff when almost every other company in the industry . . . felt forced to lay off employees in large numbers. The company . . . managed to avoid a layoff of 10% of their employees by having everyone in the company take a 10% cut in salary and come to work only 9 out of 10 days. This company experience is thus called the "nine day fortnight."[21]

The story of the nine-day fortnight vividly captures the cultural value that looking after employees' well-being is the right thing to do. Present-day employees continue to tell the story among themselves as a reminder that the company will avoid layoffs as much as possible during economic downturns.

A **myth** is a special type of story that provides a fictional but likely explanation for an event or thing that might otherwise seem puzzling or mysterious. Ancient civilizations often invented myths involving gods and other supernatural forces

---

[20] Alan L. Wilkins, "Organizational Stories as Symbols Which Control the Organization," in *Organizational Symbolism*, ed. Louis R. Pondy, Peter J. Frost, Gareth Morgan, and Thomas C. Dandridge (Greenwich, Conn.: JAI Press, 1983), pp. 81–92.

[21] Ibid.

to explain natural occurrences such as the rising and setting of the sun, the phases of the moon, and the formation of thunderstorms. Similarly, the members of an organization sometimes develop fictionalized accounts of the company's founders, origins, or historical development to provide a framework for explaining current activities in their firm. In many instances, organizational myths actually contain at least a grain of truth. For example, myths told throughout General Motors about the management prowess of Alfred P. Sloan, one of the company's earliest chief executives, are based in part on a study of GM's structure and procedures that Sloan performed in 1919–20. It is this bit of truthful information that make myths sound completely true.

Heroes and Superstars. Heroes are people who embody the values of an organization and its culture. They serve as role models, illustrating personal performance that is not only desirable but attainable.

> Richard A. Drew, a banjo-playing college dropout working in 3M's research lab during the 1920s, [helped] some colleagues solve a problem they had with masking tape. Soon thereafter, DuPont came out with cellophane. Drew decided he could go DuPont one better and coated the cellophane with a colorless adhesive to bind things together—and Scotch tape was born. In the 3M tradition, Drew carried the ball himself by managing the development and initial production of his invention. Moving up through the ranks, he went on to become technical director of the company and showed other employees just how they could succeed in similar fashion at 3M.[22]

The deeds of heroes are out of the ordinary but not so far out as to be beyond the capabilities of other employees. In contrast, organizational **superstars** are so extraordinary that they rise above their peers and sometimes even become symbols for an entire industry. For example, in the early 1900s, Thomas Edison personified the then astounding advance of commercial electricity. More recently, Drexel Burnham Lambert's Michael Milken has become a symbol—a negative one—of the excesses of the investment industry of the late 1980s.

Symbols and Language. Symbols are objects, actions, or events to which people have assigned special meanings. Company logos, flags, and trade names are symbols that come readily to mind. Mercedes's three-point star logo is synonymous with quality in most people's minds, and even the youngest children know that the McDonald's golden arches mark the locations of certain fast-food restaurants. In organizations, symbols may also include official titles, such as chief operating officer. Or special eating facilities, official automobiles, or airplanes may be given symbolic status. Sometimes even the size of an employee's office or its placement or furnishings have special symbolic value.[23]

Symbols mean more than might seem immediately apparent. For instance, despite the fact that a reserved parking space is just a few square feet of asphalt, it may symbolize its holder's superior hierarchical status or clout. It is the ability to convey a complex message in the efficient, economical manner that makes symbols so useful and important.

> When two people shake hands, the action symbolizes their coming together. The handshake may also be rich in other kinds of symbolic significance. Between free-masons it reaffirms a bond of brotherhood, and loyalty to the order to which they belong. Between politicians it is often used to symbolize an intention to cooperate and work together. To members of the counter-culture of the 1960s and early 1970s, their special hand clasp and a cry of "Right On!" affirmed a set

heroes People who embody the values of an organization's culture and serve as role models for other members in the organization.

superstars Cultural figures who are so extraordinary that they rise above their peers and sometimes even become symbols for an entire industry.

symbol An object, action, or event to which people have assigned special meaning.

[22] Deal and Kennedy, *Corporate Cultures*, pp. 40–41.

[23] Jeffrey Pfeffer, *Power in Organizations* (Marshfield, Mass.: Pitman, 1981), p. 50.

of divergent values and opposition to the system. The handshake is more than just a shaking of hands. It symbolizes a particular kind of relationship between those involved.[24]

Clearly, we need symbols. They are able to convey complex ideas in a simple manner, and they enable people to convey emotional messages that cannot easily be put into words. Without symbols, many of the fundamental norms and values of an organization's culture could not be communicated among the members.

Language, too, is a means for sharing cultural ideas and understandings. In many organizations, the language members use is itself a reflection of the organization's particular culture. At Microsoft, for example, a young-techie vocabulary has developed, largely because of the youth of the firms' founder, Bill Gates (mid-30s) and its work force (median age, about 31). A confusing situation is called random. Bandwidth refers to the amount of information one can absorb. Things that go right are labeled radical, cool, or super.[25] Whatever the source of a common vocabulary, the fact that such a vocabulary exists attests to the presence and acceptance of a shared set of norms and values.

language A system of shared symbols that the members of an organization use to communicate cultural ideas and understandings.

Managing Organizational Culture

Organizational culture grows out of the informal organization of unofficial ways of doing things. It influences the formal organization by shaping the way employees perceive and react to formally defined jobs and structural arrangements. Put another way, cultural norms and values provide **social information** that helps employees determine the meaning of their work and the organization around them. For example, in a company that promotes the "Protestant work ethic"—the idea that working hard is the way to get ahead in life—employees are led to view their jobs as critical to personal success and therefore as important, interesting, challenging, and in other ways worthwhile. By encouraging employees to perceive success as something to be valued and pursued, these norms also encourage the development of a need for achievement (see Chapter 7) and motivate hard work and high productivity. As Figure 18-5 indicates, cultural norms and

social information Information growing out of cultural norms, values, and shared opinions that shapes the way people perceive themselves, their jobs, and the organization.

[24] Gareth Morgan, Peter J. Frost, and Louis R. Pondy, "Organizational Symbolism," in *Organizational Symbolism*, pp. 3–38.

[25] Richard Brandt, "The Billion-Dollar Whiz Kid," *Business Week*, April 13, 1987, pp. 68–76.

F I G U R E 18-5

Cultural Elements as Social Information

Cultural norms and values are a source of basic social information that influences how members perceive the formal organization, their own needs and interests, and their work. Work behaviors that are based on these perceptions can stimulate cultural change.
Based on Gerald R. Salancik and Jeffrey Pfeffer, "A Social Information Processing Approach to Job Attitudes and Task Design," Administrative Science Quarterly 23 *(1978), 224–53.*

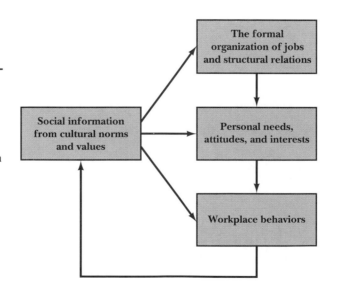

values convey social information that can influence the way people choose to behave on the job. They do so by affecting the way employees perceive themselves, their work, and the organization.

Can organizational culture be managed? You might be tempted to answer no to this question for the following reasons:

1. Cultures are so spontaneous, elusive, and hidden that they cannot be accurately diagnosed or intentionally changed.

2. Considerable experience and deep personal insight are required to truly understand an organization's culture, making cultural management infeasible in most instances.

3. There may be several subcultures in a single organizational culture, complicating the task of managing organizational culture to the point where it becomes impossible to accomplish.

4. Cultures provide organization members with continuity and stability. Therefore, members are likely to resist even modest efforts at cultural management or change because of concerns about discontinuity and instability.[26]

Most management experts disagree with these arguments, however, and suggest that organizational cultures can be managed by using the two approaches we discuss next.

symbolic management A process in which managers attempt to influence deep cultural norms and values by shaping the surface cultural elements that organization members use to express and transmit cultural understandings.

Symbolic Management. In **symbolic management**, managers attempt to influence deep cultural norms and values by shaping the surface cultural elements—such as symbols, stories, and ceremonies—that people use to express and transmit cultural understandings.[27] Managers can accomplish shaping of this sort in a number of ways. They can issue public statements about their vision for the future of the company. They can recount stories about themselves and the company. They can use and enrich the shared company language. In this way, managers not only communicate the company's central norms and key values but devise new ways of expressing them.

Managers who practice symbolic management realize that every managerial behavior broadcasts a symbolic message to employees about the norms and values of the organization. They consciously choose to do specific things that will symbolize and strengthen a desirable culture. For example, deciding to promote from within and avoid hiring people from outside the firm sends employees the message that strong performance is rewarded by career advancement. This message reinforces cultural norms and values that favor hard work. Filling positions by hiring from other organizations gives precisely the opposite message—hard work may *not* be rewarded by promotion—and undermines cultural norms and values that suggest otherwise.

The fact that symbolic management involves the manipulation of symbols is apt to lead some managers to play down its importance. Telling stories, performing ceremonies, and anointing heros might seem soft-headed or a waste of time to managers who do not understand the importance of managing cultural understandings. However, underestimating the importance of symbolic management can have disastrous consequences. A good illustration was the failure by Kraft Foods to identify and manage cultural inconsistencies between itself and Celestial Seasonings, a producer of specialty teas that it acquired in the mid-1980s

[26] John B. Miner, *Organizational Behavior: Performance and Productivity* (New York: Random House, 1988), p. 571. See also Harrison M. Trice and Janice M. Beyer, "Using Six Organizational Rites to Change Culture," in *Gaining Control of the Corporate Culture*, ed. R. H. Kilmann, M. J. Saxon, and R. Serpa (San Francisco: Jossey-Bass, 1985), pp. 370–99.

[27] Jeffrey Pfeffer, "Management as Symbolic Action: The Creation and Maintenance of Organizational Paradigms," in *Research in Organizational Behavior*, vol. 3, ed. L. L. Cummings and B. M. Staw (Greenwich, Conn.: JAI Press, 1981), pp. 1–52.

Celestial Seasonings Wasn't Kraft's Cup of Tea

Bicycling is an article of faith at Celestial Seasonings, Inc., the herbal tea company based in Boulder, Colorado. The sport appeals to the same sort of health-conscious consumers who are likely to be herbal tea drinkers. Celestial thus hosts a top pro cycle race, the Red Zinger, named after one of its teas. To drive home the company's feelings, President Barnet M. Feinblum often pedals a racer of his own.

No wonder trouble started brewing when Celestial's corporate owner, Kraft, Inc., ordered the company to cut its ties with cycling. Instead, Feinblum signed a deal with bicycling legend Greg LeMond to ride on Celestial's team. Relations between Kraft's board-room executives and the more casual Feinblum deteriorated further when Kraft, responding to anonymous letters charging drug use at Celestial, slipped an undercover agent into the company.

Such culture clashes helped push Kraft to put Celestial up for sale. Certainly the tea producer was quirky to the point of having trouble fitting into any large, bureaucratic firm. However, Kraft, too, was at fault. In its effort to create a mass market for herbal teas, Kraft lost sight of Celestial's wholesome image and frolicsome spirit. Celestial will certainly miss Kraft's deep pockets: New-product development and marketing may prove increasingly difficult without Kraft's resources. However, Feinblum believes he wrested his company away from Kraft in the nick of time. On the eve of Celestial's parting, Philip Morris bought Kraft. "It was bad enough being part of Velveeta's company," says Feinblum. "Can you imagine Celestial Seasonings being owned by a tobacco company?"*

* Based on Sandra D. Atchison, "Why Celestial Seasonings Wasn't Kraft's Cup of Tea," *Business Week*, May 8, 1989, p. 76.

(see the "In Practice" box). Managers at companies ranging from Disney to DuPont agree that managing symbols is a critical part of their job.[28]

Organization Development. Another way of managing the culture of an organization is to use organization-development interventions like those discussed in Chapter 14 and also later in this chapter. OD interventions can contribute to cultural management by helping the members of an organization progress through the following steps:

1. *Identifying current norms and values.* OD interventions typically require people to list the norms and values that guide their attitudes and behaviors at work. This kind of list gives members insight into the organization culture.

2. *Plotting new directions.* OD interventions often make it possible for the members of an organization to evaluate present personal, group, and organization goals and consider whether these goals represent the objectives they really want to achieve. Evaluation of this sort often points out the need to plot new directions.

3. *Identifying new norms and values.* Those OD interventions that stimulate think-

[28] Brian Dumaine, "Creating a New Company Culture," *Fortune*, January 15, 1990, 127–31.

ing about new directions also provide organization members with the opportunity to develop new norms and values that will promote a move toward new goals.

4. *Identifying culture gaps.* To the extent that current (step 1) and desired (step 3) norms and values are articulated, the OD process enables organization members to identify as culture gaps the differences between the current and the desired.

5. *Closing culture gaps.* OD gives people the opportunity to forge agreements that new norms and values replace old ones and that every employee will take responsibility for managing and reinforcing these changes.[29]

When people engage in behaviors that are consistent with the new norms and values developed in an OD intervention, they reduce culture gaps and, in effect, change the organization's culture.

CHANGING THE ORGANIZATIONAL CONTEXT: ORGANIZATION DEVELOPMENT II

B esides the interpersonal, group, and intergroup interventions discussed in Chapter 14, OD experts have also designed a variety of organization-level interventions. As you will recall from Chapter 14, the general purpose of any OD intervention is to provide a planned, systematic way of introducing and managing long-term change in organizations. The purpose of organization-level OD interventions is thus to introduce and manage planned change throughout the entire organization.

Organization-Level Change

What sorts of organization-wide change might be stimulated by organization-level OD interventions? Four of the most important kinds of change are (1) shaping the informal organization, (2) redesigning the formal organization, (3) improving the fit between the informal and formal organizations, and (4) planning and implementing strategies.

Shaping Culture and the Informal Organization. Suppose you are David Roderick, chair of U.S. Steel during the firm's transformation into USX. You are the head of a company with a culture that stresses risk avoidance, stability, and originality. Changes underway in your company's business, however, make it imperative for your employees to adopt a culture of norms and values that favor creativity, innovation, and flexibility. What do you do?

Managers in this predicament often turn to organization-level OD interventions owing to the ability of these interventions to shape the informal organization. As is true for any OD intervention, the ones aimed at organization-wide change can help create an awareness of existing norms and values, facilitate evaluation and redirection of the organization and its culture, and encourage efforts to identify and eliminate cultural gaps. Compared to less-expansive OD techniques, organization-level interventions have the added advantage of stimulating change that pervades the entire organization. Such interventions are therefore especially useful when broad-based cultural change is the goal.

[29] Miner, *Organizational Behavior*, pp. 574–75. See also Ralph H. Kilmann, *Beyond the Quick Fix* (San Francisco: Jossey-Bass, 1984), pp. 105–23.

Redesigning Structures, Jobs, and the Formal Organization. Managers who must alter the formal organization to match contingency conditions face the daunting task of actually implementing structural change. Imagine, for instance, the job of dividing a centralized, functionally structured firm into a decentralized company of several divisions. That chore, you will recall from Chapter 15, was precisely what Roger Smith undertook at General Motors during the 1980s. How does one decide which specific structural relations to change and which to preserve? What jobs should be redesigned, and which approach to job design should be used? How can employees' views on structural change and job modification be collected and assessed? Is there any way to stimulate acceptance of such sweeping, eventful changes?

Organization-level interventions, like every other type of OD intervention, have a grounding in the developmental process described in Chapter 14. So they are of use to managers who want to initiate participatory diagnosis and problem-solving procedures. As we noted in Chapter 14, such procedures give employees input into the change process and stimulate employee acceptance of the changes. Consequently, organization-level OD interventions are quite useful in obtaining opinions from every part of an organization, involving all employees in design procedures, and obtaining total commitment to the structural changes and job modifications that result.

Improving the Informal-Formal Fit. Sometimes the informal organization and its culture of norms and values support the formal organization of structural relations and jobs. You will find that kind of support, for instance, at Next Computer, where norms and values favoring creativity and flexibility flourish in an adaptable, organic organization structure. Frequently, though, the informal and formal organizations do not fit together that well. Recall that David Roderick faced both cultural rigidity and the need for structural flexibility at U.S. Steel in the early 1980s. What can be done in such cases to improve the degree of fit?

Here, too, organization-level OD provides a way of dealing with an important organizational problem. Through it, the company can make employees aware of the organization's formal structural arrangements, goals, and strategic direction. Such awareness can help them develop, and become committed to, a culture of norms and values consistent with the formal organization. Conversely, organization-level OD interventions can also improve the fit between the informal and formal organizations by calling attention to existing norms and values and strengthening employee commitment to supportive structural relations.

Planning and Implementing Strategies. Finally, organization-level OD interventions can play a major role in strategic planning and implementation. If they are used during strategic planning, their participatory nature can help inspire widespread commitment to the mission and strategic goals of the firm. In addition, they can prove helpful in initiating the development of norms and values that reinforce the strategy of the firm. Such interventions can also make the task of fitting the firm's structure and jobs to its strategy more manageable. OD does this by lowering resistance to change and encouraging employee involvement throughout the process of structural and job redesign.

Organization-Level OD Interventions

What specific organization-level OD interventions can be used for the purposes just described? To answer this question, we will now look at three OD interventions that differ in depth but have the same target of organization-wide change. They are survey feedback, organizational confrontation, and open system planning. Notably, these three interventions fit within the unfilled cells of the matrix of OD interventions shown in Table 14-3. To conclude our overview of organization-level OD, we will discuss how several interventions are sometimes combined to form comprehensive programs intended to enhance the quality of working life.

survey feedback A shallow organization-level OD intervention intended to stimulate information sharing throughout the entire organization.

Survey Feedback. The main purpose of **survey feedback** is to stimulate information sharing throughout the entire organization. Planning and implementing change are of secondary importance. It is, then, a relatively shallow organization-level intervention. The survey feedback procedure normally proceeds in four stages.[30] First, under the guidance of a trained change agent, top management engages in preliminary planning, deciding such questions as who should be surveyed and what questions should be asked. Other organization members may also participate in this first stage if their expertise or opinions are needed. Second, the change agent and his staff administer the survey questionnaire to all organization members. Depending on the kinds of questions to be asked and issues to be probed, any of the questionnaire items we have included in this book may be included in the survey questionnaire. Third, the change agent categorizes and summarizes the data. After presenting it to management he holds group meetings to let everyone who responded to the questionnaire know the results. Fourth, the groups that received the feedback information hold meetings to discuss the survey. The group leaders—perhaps a foreman or an assistant vice-president—take the groups through an interpretation of the data, helping them to diagnose the results and identify specific problems, make plans for constructive changes, and prepare to report on the data and proposed changes with groups at the next lower hierarchical level. The change agent usually acts as a process consultant during these discussions so as to ensure that all group members get to contribute their opinions.

Survey feedback, as you can see from Figure 18-6, is very different from the traditional questionnaire method of gathering information. In survey feed-

[30] Floyd C. Mann, "Studying and Creating Change," in *The Planning of Change*, ed. W. G. Bennis, K. D. Benne, and R. Chin (New York: Holt, Rinehart & Winston, 1961), pp. 605–13.

FIGURE 18-6

Two Approaches to Data Collection by Questionnaire

Survey feedback differs from more traditional uses of questionnaires in its emphasis on influence sharing and participatory decision making. During a survey feedback intervention, all organization members likely to be affected by subsequent changes are involved in providing and analyzing data. *Adapted with the publisher's permission from Wendell L. French and Cecil H. Bell, Jr.,* Organization Development: Behavioral Science Interventions for Organization Improvement, *4th ed. (Englewood Cliffs, N.J.: Prentice Hall, 1990), p. 170.*

	Traditional Approach	Survey Feedback or OD Approach
Data collected from:	Workers and maybe foreman	Everyone in the system or subsystem
Data reported to:	Top management, department heads, and perhaps to employees through newspaper	Everyone who participated
Implications of data are worked on by:	Top management (maybe)	Everyone in work teams, with workshops starting at the top (all superiors with their subordinates)
Third-party intervention strategy:	Design and administration of questionnaire, development of report	Obtaining concurrence on total strategy, design and administration of questionnaire, design of workshops, appropriate interventions in workshops
Action planning done by:	Top management only	Teams at all levels
Probable extent of change and improvement:	Low	High

back, not only are data collected from everyone, from the highest to the lowest level of the hierarchy, but everyone in the organization participates in analyzing the data and in planning appropriate actions. These key characteristics of survey feedback reflect OD's basic values, which stress the critical importance of participation as a means of encouraging commitment to the organization's goals and stimulating personal growth and development.

organizational confrontation An organization-level OD intervention of moderate depth that enables managers to assess the internal workings of the organization and plan corrective actions as needed.

Organizational Confrontation. Organizational confrontation is an organization-level OD intervention of moderate depth. Its purpose is to provide a setting in which the managers of a firm can assess the internal workings of the company and plan corrective actions as needed. To conduct organizational confrontation, a management meeting is called. The organization's top manager—sometimes with the help of a change agent—guides the group through the six-step process shown in Figure 18-7.[31]

In the first step, *climate setting*, the manager states the goals of the confrontation. She stresses the need for free and open discussion of issues and problems and pledges that participants will not be punished for voicing their opinions. The change agent, if included in the meeting, may give a brief presentation on the importance of open communication and cooperative problem solving.

[31] Richard Beckhard, "The Confrontation Meeting," *Harvard Business Review* 45 (1967), 149–55.

FIGURE 18-7

Steps in an Organization Confrontation Intervention

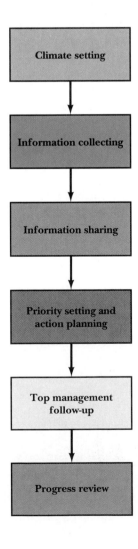

Climate setting

Information collecting

Information sharing

Priority setting and action planning

Top management follow-up

Progress review

The meeting then breaks up into small, heterogeneous groups of managers from different functional areas and hierarchical levels, reflecting a cross-section of problems and interests. In this *information-collecting* step, superiors are not put in the same group with direct subordinates, and top managers meet as a separate group. All groups are instructed as follows:

> Think of yourself as an individual with needs and goals. Also think as a person concerned about the total organization. What are the obstacles, "demotivators," poor procedures or policies, unclear goals, or poor attitudes that exist today? What different conditions, if any, would make the organization more effective and make life in the organization better?[32]

The groups work on this task for about an hour, and in each group a spokesperson records the results of the discussions.

In the third step, of *information sharing*, the groups reassemble into the larger group, and each spokesperson reports his group's findings to the meeting. As they are presented, these findings are listed on a blackboard, flipchart, or similar display. After everyone has completed his presentation, the resulting list of items is categorized into a few major topics. These topics reflect different types of problems (communication, motivation problems, job design problems), relationships (union-management relations, hierarchical connections, coworker affiliations), and functional matters (personnel management issues, accounting problems, marketing matters).

To get started on *priority setting and action planning*, the fourth step, the meeting coordinator reviews the list of categories and items. Then participants form functional work teams reflecting the way they are normally organized, for example, accountants in one group and salespeople in another. Each group is headed by its manager, and all groups are asked to do four things: (1) identify and prioritize problems that seem related to work in the group's functional area, (2) plan preliminary action steps to solve these problems, (3) identify any remaining problems and priority issues that require top management's attention, and (4) determine how to communicate the results of the confrontation meeting to their subordinates.

In the fifth step, *top management follow-up*, the top-management group meets alone to review the action plans developed in the fourth step by the functional teams and determine what additional actions, if any, should be taken. The resulting follow-up action plan is communicated to all managers within a few days.

The sixth and last step is a *progress review*—an appraisal session in which all confrontation participants meet four to six weeks later to review progress and, where necessary, develop supplementary action plans. This step is crucial for top management because it must demonstrate its commitment to follow through on suggestions made during the confrontation meeting.

The six steps of organizational confrontation provide a forum allowing the quick, accurate diagnosis of organizational problems and the development of constructive solutions. The intervention enhances hierarchical communication, increases involvement, and encourages managerial commitment throughout the organization.

open system planning A deep organization-level intervention that helps the members of an organization devise ways to accomplish the mission of their firm in light of the demands of environmental constituency groups.

Open System Planning. Open system planning is a fairly deep organization-level intervention. It is distinguished by its focus on the organization as a system open to its surrounding environment. That is, it sees the organization as a configuration of work processes that depend for their good function on external situations and events that impinge on them. The primary purpose of open system

[32] Beckhard, "Confrontation Meeting," p. 154.

planning is to help the members of an organization devise ways to accomplish the mission of their firm in the light of demands and constraints that originate with constituency groups in the organization's environment. These groups include raw-material suppliers, potential employees, and customers (see Chapter 16). The intervention consists of the following five steps (see Figure 18-8):

1. *Identification of core mission or purpose.* The members of the organization meet and, through open discussion, define the firm's basic goals, purpose, and reason for being.
2. *Identification of important constituency groups.* Then participants identify the environmental constituencies that can affect the firm's ability to accomplish its goals and purpose.
3. *"Is" and "ought" planning.* Next, participants describe current relations between the organization and its constituencies. They consider each constituency separately, focusing on the importance and duration of the relationship. Other factors are the frequency with which the parties are in contact and the organization's ability to sense and react to changes in the constituency group. Then participants determine how satisfactory the relationship *is* to both organization and constituency. If this assessment uncovers deficiencies, participants then specify what the relationship *ought* to be to be satisfactory to both sides.
4. *Current responses to constituency groups.* Participants then assess the organization's current response to each constituency group by answering these questions: What does this constituency want from us? What are we currently doing in response to this demand? Is our current response moving us closer to where we want to be in relation to our company's goals and purpose?
5. *Action planning.* If the current situation is not what it ought to be, and if the organization's current response to its constituency groups is not adequate, participants face the final task of deciding how to redirect the firm's behavior. In planning corrective action, firm members usually consider these questions: What actions should be taken, and who should take them? What

FIGURE 18-8

Steps in an Open System Planning Intervention

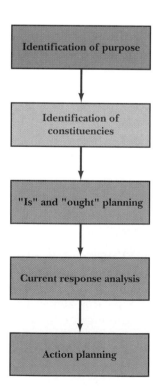

resource allocations are necessary? What time table? When should each action start and finish? Who will prepare a progress report, and when will it be due? How will actions be evaluated to ensure progress in the desired direction?[33]

Unlike other OD interventions, open system planning directs primary attention to factors *outside* the organization that can influence organizational performance. It is especially useful during strategic planning, providing a structured yet participatory way to establish a firm's mission and set the strategic goals required to accomplish this mission. Open system planning can also help identify critical environmental contingencies during the process of organization design. Identifying them encourages the development of a better fit between an organization's structure and its environment.

quality of work life The degree to which work and membership in an organization facilitates the satisfaction of important personal needs and interests.

Quality-of-Work-Life Programs. Quality-of-work-life (QWL) programs often use one or more of the organization development techniques we have discussed to improve the "degree to which members of a work organization are able to satisfy important personal needs through their experiences in the organization."[34] In addition, QWL programs incorporate changes contributing to (1) adequate and fair compensation, (2) a safe and healthy work environment, (3) the immediate opportunity to use and develop human capacities, (4) future opportunities for continued growth and security, and (5) social integration in the work organization.[35] Such changes often involve the introduction of participatory decision making, payment according to skill development, and various work-environment improvements.

Improving the quality of working life became a major concern in the United States in the early 1970s in response to the publication of *Work in America*, a government report. It claimed that American workers were overwhelmingly dissatisfied with their jobs and employers. Although much of this report was subsequently discredited, it aroused considerable interest in improving the working lives of employees throughout North America.[36] It is this interest, combined with a growing concern about the competitiveness of American industry in the world marketplace, that continues to focus managerial attention on the importance of managing the organizational context in a way that enhances both productivity and satisfaction.

SUMMARY

Strategic management is a process of setting organizational goals and directing progress toward goal attainment. It consists of five steps: defining the mission and goals of the organization, performing a *situation analysis*, formulating a stra-

---

[33] William G. Dyer, *Strategies for Managing Change* (Reading, Mass.: Addison-Wesley, 1984), pp. 149–50.

[34] J. Lloyd Suttle, "Improving Life at Work—Problems and Perspectives," in *Improving Life at Work: Behavioral Science Approaches to Organizational Change*, J. Richard Hackman and J. Lloyd Suttle (Santa Monica, Calif.: Goodyear Press, 1976), p. 4.

[35] Richard E. Walton, "Quality of Working Life—What Is It?" *Sloan Management Review* 15 (1973), 11–21.

[36] James O'Toole, Elizabeth Hansot, William Herman, Neal Herrick, Elliot Liebow, Bruce Lusignan, Harold Richman, Harold Sheppard, Ben Stephansky, and James Wright, *Work in America: Report of a Special Task Force to the Secretary of Health, Education, and Welfare* (Cambridge, Mass.: MIT Press, 1973). For another point of view, see John B. Miner, *Theories of Organizational Behavior* (Hinsdale, Ill.: Dryden Press, 1980), p. 263.

tegic plan, implementing the plan, and evaluating the resulting performance. The direction pursued by the company is a function of three types of strategies: first a *corporate strategy* of *convergent growth, evolutionary growth, revolutionary growth,* or *adaptive decline*; second, one or more *business strategies* of overall cost leadership, differentiation, or focus; and third, various *functional strategies* that support the organization's corporate and business strategies. Strategic management influences the process of designing an organization's structure and jobs by influencing environmental, organizational, and technological contingencies. Thus strategic management is inseparable from the structure and design issues discussed in Chapters 15–17.

Besides the *formal organization* of structures and jobs, every firm also has an *informal organization* of deep-seated cultural norms and values as well as surface expressions of these norms and values. The latter include *ceremonies, rites, rituals, stories, myths, heroes, superstars, symbols,* and *special language.* A firm's *culture* is a cohesive force that also influences the way the firm's members perceive the formal organization, their behaviors, and themselves. *Symbolic management* and OD interventions can be used to manage the culture of an organization.

Organization-level OD interventions can also help manage change in the formal organization and integrate the formal and informal aspects of a firm. One organization-level intervention, *survey feedback,* is a questionnaire-based technique used to gather and analyze organization-wide opinions and data. Another intervention, *organizational confrontation,* helps management examine and improve the organization as a whole. *Open system planning,* a third technique, directs attention to the organization's environment and is especially helpful during strategic planning and structural contingency analyses. *Quality-of-working-life* programs integrate such techniques with the aim of improving employee development and satisfaction.

REVIEW QUESTIONS

1.   Why do managers perform strategic management? What would happen to a firm if the process of strategic management were not performed? What would happen if strategic plans were ignored? If the results of strategic implementation were not evaluated?

2.   What is the difference between a strength and an opportunity? Between a threat and a weakness? Why are both internal and external conditions assessed during a situation analysis?

3.   How does a company's corporate strategy affect the business strategies it pursues? What effects do its business strategies have on the firm's corporate strategy? How are the organization's business and functional strategies interrelated?

4.   As a manager, you face the task of reversing cultural norms that currently favor low performance. What do you do to accomplish this task? What role do the surface elements of culture play in your plan?

5.   How do cultural norms and values act as social information? What effects does this information have on organizational behavior? Why is it important for managers to take social information into account when designing jobs and structuring the organization?

6.   How are the strategies, structure and jobs, and culture of an organization interrelated? Explain how organization-level OD can be used to manage these interrelationships.

DIAGNOSTIC QUESTIONS

Managing the organization context—devising strategies, shaping cultures, and fitting the formal and informal organizations together—means asking a lot of questions and gathering a lot of data. The diagnostic questions that follow will get you started on this challenging task.

1. What are the organization's current strengths and weaknesses? What opportunities and threats are present in the environment? What might be done to capitalize on current strengths and opportunities? How might current weaknesses and threats be avoided or even converted into strengths and opportunities?

2. What business or businesses comprise the organization? If the organization owns more than one business, which should be kept and which should be sold? Should the firm grow by moving into new businesses? Should it instead consider adaptive decline? How should resources be distributed among the firm's businesses to ensure overall success?

3. For each business, what competitive forces—existing market rivals, potential new entrants, suppliers, sources of substitute products, customers—threaten continued success? Should the business pursue cost leadership? Differentiation? Focus?

4. What functional needs are stimulated by the firm's corporate and business strategies? What functional strategies are required to ensure that these needs can be satisfied?

5. What cultural norms and values guide behaviors and understandings in the firm? Do surface elements reinforce these deeper elements? Do differences between surface elements and cultural norms and values suggest ongoing cultural change? Is this change desirable?

6. Does the culture help hold the organization together in a way that supports the formal organization? Does it provide social information that is consistent with the firm's purpose, strategic direction, and general well-being?

7. Do organization-wide problems suggest a need for organization-level OD? Would the information sharing of survey feedback provide adequate help? Do management problems seem to require the more intensive analysis of organizational confrontation? Or do problems with the organization's environment mandate the outward orientation of open system planning?

EXERCISE 18-1
THINKING ABOUT ORGANIZATION CLIMATES*
BENJAMIN SCHNEIDER, *University of Maryland*

An *organization climate* is the general perception that people have of the organization in which they work. In this chapter we have defined organizational culture as the collection of norms and values that shape the behavior of people in an organization. Climate is the "feel" of the organization that grows out of its culture. The ebb and flow of everyday activities, events, practices, and procedures make up an organization's climate.

How do we assess the climate of an organization? We can have employees answer a series of questions about their personal impressions. Or we can have employees engage in a group discussion and keep track of what they say. You will have the opportunity to experience both of these approaches in this exercise as you examine the climate of your classroom and your educational institution.

STEP ONE: PRE-CLASS PREPARATION

To prepare for class, read the entire exercise. Next, thinking about your classroom as an organization, complete the Organization Climate Questionnaire shown in Exhibit 18-1.

STEP TWO: STRATEGIC PLANNING IN GROUPS

The class should divide into groups of 4 to 6 members each (if you have formed permanent groups, reassemble in those groups). In each group, members should share their responses to each questionnaire item and arrive at a group consensus. You should note significant disagreements, and the group should try to determine the reasons for such disagreements. After the group has reached agreement on its answers, members should examine any gaps the group has uncovered between the way things actually occur in the classroom and the way they would occur in an ideal situation. For each gap, the group should develop a strategy that could reduce the difference between actual and ideal circumstances. Each strategy should specify the actions to take, who should take them and when, and how to identify successful change. A spokesperson should be appointed to report to the class on the group's discussion and strategic plan.

STEP THREE: ACTION PLANNING

Group spokespersons should report the results of Step Two to the class. As presentations are made, the class should look for similarities in the gaps identified by different groups and in the strategies developed to deal with them. After all spokespersons have completed their reports the class should develop an action plan for implementing the strategies it feels are the most likely to have a positive impact on the classroom climate. The instructor should list relevant action steps on a blackboard, overhead transparency, or flipchart, and specific class members should be assigned responsibility for overseeing their implementation.

STEP FOUR: GROUP DISCUSSION

The class should break into the same small groups. Each group's members should then describe the "dos" and "don'ts" that create the climate experienced by students at your school. It helps to recall your days as a new student and to think about what you had to learn to "fit in" to the activities around you. A spokesperson should prepare a brief presentation to be given to the class.

STEP FIVE: CLASS DISCUSSION

Spokespersons should present their reports. The class should then develop a comprehensive listing of the cultural norms it has identified and consider the following questions:

1. In what ways has the climate of your educational institution influenced the climate of your classroom? What aspects of your classroom's climate

* Adapted with the author's permission. The questionnaire appearing in this exercise was developed by Benjamin Schneider and C. J. Bartlett and is reprinted with permission. Those interested in a version useful for research should contact Benjamin Schneider, Department of Psychology, University of Maryland, College Park, MD 20742.

EXHIBIT 18-1
Organization Climate Questionnaire

Using the spaces in the left-hand column, describe the ideal practices and procedures you would like to see in this organization (your classroom). Next, using the spaces in the right-hand column, describe what you believe actually happens now in this organization. To record your answers, use the following scale: 1 = almost never, 2 = infrequently, 3 = sometimes, 4 = frequently, 5 = very frequently.

Ideal   Actual

1. This organization takes care of the people who work in it.
2. Members keep up with current events outside the organization.
3. People in this organization ask each other how they are doing in reaching their goals.
4. Management effectively balances people problems and production problems.
5. There are definite "in" and "out" groups in the organization.
6. This organization encourages employees to exercise their own initiative.
7. This organization takes an active interest in the progress of its members.
8. Members of this organization have a wide range of interests.
9. More experienced members of this organization take time to help newer members.
10. Neither people problems nor production problems receive undue management attention.
11. Members of this organization always have complaints no matter what is done to correct them.
12. This organization willingly accepts members' ideas for change.
13. This organization recognizes that its life depends upon its members.
14. Members keep themselves informed on many topics besides their immediate job-related activities.
15. People in this organization speak openly about each other's shortcomings.
16. There is a sense of purpose and direction in this organization.
17. Members are prone to overstate and exaggerate their accomplishments.
18. Management does not exercise unnecessary control over members' activities.

To complete pre-class preparation, score your responses using the following guide:

SCALE	ADD ITEMS	IDEAL TOTAL	ACTUAL TOTAL	GAP (IDEAL —ACTUAL)
Support	1, 7, 13			
Quality	2, 8, 14			
Openness	3, 9, 15			
Leadership	4, 10, 16			
Conflict	5, 11, 17			
Autonomy	6, 12, 18			

seem unaffected by the surrounding institution? Can you think of any ways in which your classroom's climate might affect the climate of your school?

2. How easy would it be to implement the action plan you developed in Step Three? How likely is it that your plan would have lasting effects on the climate of your classroom? What could you do to increase this likelihood?

3. Suppose you were asked to develop an action plan to change the climate of your educational institution. What additional complications would you have to deal with? How does the size of the organization affect the ability of its management to identify and modify features of its climate?

4. How are an organization's climate and culture interrelated? How do the two differ? How might managing the climate of an organization affect the organization's culture? How might managing the culture affect the climate?

CONCLUSION

Climate is an umbrella concept that summarizes numerous detailed perceptions in a small number of general dimensions. It describes how people think and feel about the organizations around them, and how they react to the norms and beliefs they encounter in these organizations. As you have probably discovered in this exercise, climates are difficult to measure—people in an organization often differ in their perceptions of what the organization is all about—and hard to change. Nevertheless, managers need to be aware of an organization's climate and must be able to intercede if it appears likely to threaten the effectiveness of the firm.

DIAGNOSING ORGANIZATIONAL BEHAVIOR

CASE 18-1
HARVARD UNIVERSITY STAFF SURVEY*

HILLARY BALLANTYNE, Boston University
FRED K. FOULKES, Boston University

INTRODUCTION

Daniel D. Cantor was in his ninth year as Director of Personnel for Harvard University. Cantor had joined the university in 1976 after many years of personnel work in industry and in the Peace Corps.

Cantor viewed the decade of his tenure as an eventful and productive one for the personnel function. Of the programs enacted under his leadership, he thought the recently conducted 1985 attitude survey was one of his significant accomplishments. Although attitude surveys were common tools of the personnel trade in corporations, among universities only Stanford was known to have conducted a staff survey when Cantor had introduced the idea in 1984. In addition, Harvard had been experiencing a unionization drive, which subjected any move on the administration's part to scrutiny. As Cantor faced the difficult administrative task of collecting, assimilating and acting on the results of the attitude survey in an organization that was highly decentralized, he, nevertheless, was optimistic about the work that needed to be done in the weeks and months ahead.

STRUCTURE OF HARVARD UNIVERSITY

Founded sixteen years after the arrival of the Pilgrims at Plymouth, Harvard University had grown from twelve students with a single master to an enrollment of some 16,000 degree candidates. This included students in the undergraduate college, in ten graduate and professional schools, and in an extension school, taught by a faculty of over 3,000.

The university had two governing boards. The Harvard Corporation, consisting of the president and Fellows of Harvard College, was the university's executive board. This seven-member board was responsible for the day-to-day management of the university's finances and business affairs. Significant matters of educational and institutional policy were also brought before the president and Fellows.

The Board of Overseers consisted of thirty members who were elected at large by graduates of Harvard. Through standing and visiting committees, the overseers learned about educational and administrative policies and practices of the university, provided advice to the corporation, and approved important actions of that body. Both the corporation and overseers had to approve major teaching and administrative appointments.

The expression "every tub on its own bottom" was often used to describe the decentralized organization and financial arrangement of the ten faculties overseeing Harvard's separate schools and colleges. Each faculty was headed by a dean, appointed by the president,

* Copyright © 1988 by the Human Resources Policy Institute, School of Management, Boston University. Reprinted with permission.

and approved by the board of overseers and Harvard Corporation. Each was directly responsible for its own academic programs, finances and organization. President Derek Bok directly controlled approximately 10% of the university's $700 million annual budget. Reporting to President Bok were five vice presidents (Administration, Finance, General Counsel, Development, and Government, Public and Community Affairs) and ten Deans.

Harvard's endowment and other funds were valued at more than $2.8 billion in 1985. Strong alumni support, through the recently completed Harvard Campaign, enabled the Faculty of Arts and Sciences, which is responsible for the education of more than half of Harvard's students, to renovate classroom buildings and the residential houses, strengthen the excellence of its faculty, and maintain its commitment to provide adequate financial aid for qualified students.

The university encompassed over 400 buildings spread across a radius of several miles. While most of Harvard was located in Cambridge, both the medically oriented schools and the business school were located in Boston. The business school was just across the Charles River from Harvard College, the undergraduate houses, and the Kennedy School of Government and the other schools and administrative offices. The schools of medicine, public health and dental medicine, however, were in Boston, approximately three miles from the main campus.

THE HARVARD STAFF

In 1985, Harvard employed nearly 12,000 people, 9,000 of whom held staff positions. The fifth largest employer in the Commonwealth of Massachusetts, Harvard employed 10% of the people working in the city of Cambridge, Massachusetts. The staff was occupied in a wide variety of jobs, from grounds maintenance to skilled laboratory work to clerical, library and administrative positions.

Fourteen hundred of Harvard's staff belonged to seven unions. The unionized employees had jobs in food and custodial services, skilled trades, security, the print shop and the cogeneration plant. Of the 7,500 non-union staff employees, about one quarter were occupied in unskilled or semi-skilled work. Another quarter made up the bulk of the technical, secretarial and clerical workforce that supported the teaching, research, professional and administrative functions at the university. Approximately 82% of these non-exempt employees were women. Roughly 3,500 exempt professional and administrative positions made up the rest of Harvard's staff. The exempt staff included all supervisors and managers who were not faculty members.

THE PERSONNEL FUNCTION

Harvard's central personnel function in 1985 consisted of six department heads and eighty staff, half of whom were professionals. Each of the schools at Harvard had its own personnel officer who reported to the administrative dean with "dotted line" responsibility to the central organization.

The relationships between central personnel and the school's personnel offices varied, according to Dan Cantor, from "close and comfortable to we-don't-need-you!" Benefits were administered entirely by central personnel, from distribution of information to medical form processing. Central personnel issued wage guidelines by job grade to the schools. Posting for all open positions at the university was also done centrally, although actual recruitment was done both centrally and by the schools themselves.

UNION ORGANIZATION CAMPAIGN

In 1984 Dan Cantor had been aware of the potential results to be gleaned from employee surveys, and for years had felt that such a project would be beneficial for Harvard. But two major obstacles existed: the union organizing campaign and the decentralized structure of the university. Cantor described these dilemmas:

> The idea of doing an attitude survey was long thought of. We were so spread out in terms of how we govern that there was no coordinated way of getting feedback from staff. The union organizing efforts impacted the project both positively and negatively. It increased concern about how people feel but also hindered a survey project that might have been construed as an unfair labor practice.

Organizing efforts among technical and clerical workers had been going on since the mid-seventies, focused on the three schools in the medical area. But staff members there had voted against bargaining units twice in the past eight years. In 1984 the National Labor Relations Board handed down a decision requiring the union to treat the entire Harvard technical and clerical force as a single potential bargaining unit, forcing the organizing to go campus-wide.

BACKGROUND OF HARVARD'S STAFF MEMBER SURVEY

Dan Cantor felt that the 1984 NLRB decision enlarging the bargaining unit to the entire university created an opportunity for conducting an attitude survey among staff. He introduced the idea at that time to the Personnel Policy Council, a group that consisted of nine administrative deans and three of Harvard's vice presidents. Although Stanford was the only university known to have surveyed its people, the council favored the idea. Cantor had suggested a 100% sample of one-third of the schools every three years. To take the project forward, during the summer of 1984, the council appointed a committee headed by Robert Scott, Vice President of Administration. Scott was seen as best suited to chair the committee because of his extensive administrative responsibilities and his knowledge of computers and data analysis.

The committee was composed of administrators and personnel officers representing a cross-section of the university. They met more than a half dozen times over five months beginning in the fall. Dan Cantor also consulted with faculty experts from the School of Education and the Business School about how best to proceed.

The committee received proposals for developing the survey from three consulting firms. The criteria used to make the selection were:

- The consultants' willingness and ability to understand the unique nature of Harvard's project
- The availability of a large database and the ability to use it
- Price
- Competence in developing and using data

The committee ultimately chose Opinion Research Corporation (ORC), a division of Arthur D. Little, to conduct the survey, although ORC's bid was not the lowest.

The allocation of the survey's cost was an issue because of Harvard's decentralized organization. The committee decided that the cost of the survey would be charged to each of the "tubs" on a per capita basis. The charge was higher for the units of the central organization than for the schools, but averaged under $10 per staff member. The decision was also made to survey the entire university rather than one-third at a time.

ORC developed a 24-page survey of over 100 items that varied in the number and type of possible responses. The main subjects of inquiry were compensation, performance evaluation, working conditions, career development and training, communications, and productivity. The survey was intended for the approximately 7,000 Harvard staff members, which excluded the faculty and members of bargaining units.

After the committee and other concerned individuals and groups had reviewed and approved the survey, it was mailed to employees at their homes in April 1985, seven weeks after the arrival of a letter to each employee from President Bok advising them of the survey and asking for their cooperation.

The questionnaire was sent to employees, with the covering letter signed by a vice president of ORC. All questionnaires were to be returned by April 19. So that ORC could analyze the results of the survey by various groupings of employees, respondents were asked to check off the Harvard unit where they worked; whether they were in academic/research, administration, or the library, the number of years they had worked for the university; the number of positions they had held at Harvard; their age, sex, and race; whether their immediate supervisor was a faculty member or a non-faculty member; their level of education; and whether their employment status was full or part time. Respondents were asked not to sign their names and they were assured that ". . . there are always enough people in any [employee] grouping so that no individual can be identified" and that if there were not 10 people in a group, the results of that group would not be released but instead would be combined with another group of employees.

Fifty-nine percent of the administrative/professional staff and 46% of the support staff completed the survey, which represented an overall response rate of 55% of Harvard staff members. During May and June ORC prepared a report that contained the principal results of the survey. ORC also prepared reports for each of Harvard's principal units. ORC delivered the results of the survey during the early part of the summer. Only President Bok and Messrs. Steiner and Cantor would see the complete results, including a comparison of responses by school.

With both President Bok and Mr. Steiner on vacation, Dan Cantor studied the results carefully. He was scheduled to go on vacation in a week, and the beginning of the fall term was just six weeks away. Cantor knew, however, that a well thought out action plan was needed by the end of August or, at the latest, immediately after the Labor Day weekend. Cantor also recalled that in President Bok's February 21 letter to each Harvard staff member, he had pledged that ". . . you will receive results from the survey, and an opportunity to discuss the results."

When you have read this case, look back at the chapter's diagnostic questions and choose the ones that apply to the case. Then use those questions with the ones that follow in your case analysis.

1. What type of organization development intervention does Harvard's employee attitude survey represent? Why did the university decide to undertake this survey? What benefits did Dan Cantor and the committee headed by Robert Scott expect the survey to yield? Do you agree with the committee's criteria for selecting the consultants who conducted the survey? Why or why not?

2. Do you think the committee will invite employees to participate in interpreting the results of the survey? Should they? What are the strengths of the survey approach? The weaknesses?

3. Who should be involved in deciding how to deal with problems identified by the survey? How participatory should this process be? Why?

CASE 18-2

DUMAS PUBLIC LIBRARY*

MARK HAMMER, *University of San Diego*
GARY WHITNEY, *University of San Deigo*

It came as a surprise when Jeff Mallet learned of the conflict between Debra Dickenson and Helen Hendricks because he knew them both personally and regarded them both as competent administrators. Debra Dickenson, 38, was the youngest mayor in the state when she was elected three years ago, and was the first female mayor in Kimball's history. She was widely recognized for her high levels of energy and dedication. Helen Hendricks, 62, had been the head librarian at Dumas Public Library for 15 years and was widely acknowledged among Kimball citizens as being primarily responsible for the high quality of the library services to the community.

Dumas Public Library serves the citizens of Kimball, New Mexico, a town of 20,000 people in rural Eastern New Mexico State. Kimball is dominated by the 16,000-student state university located there and this university presence creates a rather unique clientele for the public library. The library has enjoyed a history of solid citizen support and has until recently benefitted from cordial relations between the library staff and the city's administration.

The library is housed in a modern, air-conditioned structure with carpeted floors and attractive furnishings. Approximately 35,000 volumes are on the shelves. The 1988 budget, including payroll, acquisition of new books, and building maintenance, was $195,000.

The library has no formal organization. Helen Hendricks has reporting to her five fulltime employees, three of whom are professional librarians. Completing the staff are ten halftime permanent employees, ten to twelve unpaid volunteers, and an occasional intern from the university.

The city is governed by an elected city council and mayor. Day-to-day administration is the responsibility of Ralph Riesen, the City Supervisor, who is a permanent employee of the city.

Jeff Mallet, Professor of Management, first learned about the existence of strained relationships between the library and the city administration from Linda Turner, Adult Services Librarian. According to Linda, feelings of distrust and animosity toward City Hall had been growing recently among the library staff. Linda was concerned about the unhealthy climate that this hostility was creating at the library.

Several weeks later Jeff had an opportunity to talk with Debra Dickenson and Ralph Riesen. Jeff said he had heard that relations between City Hall and the library were not good. Debra and Ralph confirmed that relations between the two groups had reached an intolerably low level, and they agreed something would have to be done about it. Debra and Ralph expressed bewilderment about what could be done to improve the situation. "If you have any ideas or suggestions. I'd certainly like to hear them," Debra said.

Jeff suggested that it might prove helpful to have an outsider interview members of both groups to provide some independent perspective. He volunteered his services for this purpose. Debra and Ralph readily agreed to Jeff's offer.

The next day Jeff was talking to Paul Everest, a fellow business faculty member and consultant, about the situation at the library. Jeff invited Paul to join him on the case and Paul accepted.

Next week Jeff made a series of personal visits and phone calls to the key staff members from City Hall and the library. An agreement was reached to have Jeff and Paul interview both groups and make recommendations. Appointments were made for an interview with Debra Dickenson and Ralph Riesen at City Hall, followed by one with Helen Hendricks, Linda Turner, and Maude Richardson [Children's Librarian] at the library.

THE VIEW FROM CITY HALL

Debra: I'm really concerned about the way things have developed between us here at City Hall and the library staff. There is animosity between these two groups, and the situation has been worse over the past few months. There's not nearly the level of cooperation that there should be.

I'll be eager to consider any suggestions that you (professors) might have for how to improve the situation. I know that something has to be done, and I'm willing to devote some time and effort to working on it.

The problem at the library is that I no longer have administrative control over their operations. In the past the library has reported to the mayor through the city supervisor and that has worked reasonably well. Recently however, we discovered that legislation passed back in the 1930's makes it very clear that the Library Board of Trustees has the legal authority for the conduct of the day-to-day operations of the library.

My concern is that since the library is a part of the city administration, the city is legally responsible for its operations. I'm talking specifically about legal liability for such things as personnel selection, equal employment opportunity regulations, purchasing guidelines, and budgeting procedures set down by the state. In the case of lawsuits and budget overruns it seems clear to me that the city will be liable and hence we need to have administrative control over these matters. Also it just makes good common sense for us to coordinate certain administrative functions from City Hall, such as personnel selection and budgeting. Basically the library staff agrees with us on this, and we have been doing many of these functions at City Hall.

One of the things that irks me most about Helen Hendricks (Head Librarian) and her staff is that they continue to insist on politicizing the budget making process, even when they know or should know that this is an extremely disruptive and unfair practice. I have made it pretty clear to all the department heads within the city that the budget making process should be one where budget requests are submitted to the city administration and to the City Council along with the implications of funding increases or decreases. Based on that input, the City Council then decides on the services that it wants in a non-emotional manner. The City Council represents the citizens and that is a perfectly democratic procedure.

Prior to the recent budget preparation period the City Council gave budget directives to all city departments. The Library Board chose to ignore these directives and submitted their own budget. Subsequently the library staff started a big political campaign to pack the council chambers at all the budget hearings with patrons of the library and other citizens who supported the library's request for more funding.

I have tried to point out to Helen how disruptive and unfair this is. The fact is that almost every city department serves some consistency and could if they were so inclined rally citizen support from among their clients or constituents to bring political pressure to bear on the City Council and other members of the city administration to fund their individual projects. It seems obvious to me that this is a chaotic way to try to prepare a city budget. Special interest politics has no place in the preparation of the city budget which is fair to all parties concerned. Only people who have looked at the entire city budget and have considered the total revenues available to the city and the cost and benefit trade-offs made by each one of the city departments are in any position to judge whether any particular department is reasonably funded or not. The fact is that there are prime financial needs in all of the city departments and the library is not alone.

I support the library wholeheartedly; we all do. I'm just not one bit impressed when the librarians campaign to have a flock of citizens pack the council chambers to stand there and tell us that they support the library. That is not a helpful input to the budget making process. Everybody supports the library.

Following one occurrence of inappropriate political lobbying last fall, I expressed my annoyance to Walter Roy [chairperson of the Library Board of Trustees]. Subsequently Helen was told by the Board to cease her lobbying activities. I think she got the message, but I know the lobbying did not stop. That tells me that the Trustees do not have control over the library staff.

Don't get me wrong. Helen Hendricks has done a marvelous job down there at the library, but things just haven't been the same since her husband died unexpectedly two years ago. She seems to have retreated into a womb or something. I think she uses the library staff as a personal support group. I don't know who is running the library anymore, but it certainly isn't Helen. I think the staff is running the library to tell you the truth.

Ralph: I too have noticed the worsening relations between us and the library staff. Part of the problem may be the physical isolation of the library and the fact that they don't interact much with other city personnel. [The library is three blocks from City Hall.]

If you ask me I think there is a case of paranoia down there at the library. Some of them seem to believe that I'm out to get them. In fact, I have a definite feeling that several of the library staff members think that I'm some sort of an ogre.

I think many of the problems that the library staff think they have are more imaginary than real. I remember once I talked to Helen and she was complaining about some things. I asked her to make me a list of grievances that they had, ways in which they had less money or things that weren't satisfactory. Do you know, I've never gotten any list from Helen. I really don't think they have any substantial problems that aren't of their own making.

Debra: I get the impression that the library staff feels that they are picked on and mistreated. The fact is that the library has the best working conditions of almost any other department in the city. Not only are their working conditions congenial and agreeable, but the clientele they serve are all happy and supportive of the library. It's a totally positive environment. That's quite a bit different from the city engineer's department where they have to talk to irate contractors and home owners, or the police who have to deal with drug offenders and unhappy traffic violators.

I'm still very confused about the proper roles of

the library administration, the Library Board of Trustees, and the city administration.

Ralph: Lynn King [the city finance director] is another player in this scenario. Lynn probably has more interaction with the library staff on a day-to-day basis than anybody else here in City Hall. She deals with them on matters of auditing, purchasing procedures, and employee selection procedures. There have been disagreements and friction generated over a number of these issues. Lynn really distrusts Helen as an administrator.

Debra: I really would like to hear from the library staff on their perceptions of what our problems are. I don't really know what they think.

One of the areas that Helen and I have had disagreements about has been that of Helen's classification within the city administrative system. Helen seems to think that she should be classified as a department director. The trouble is that Helen's responsibilities are simply not equivalent to those of other department directors within the city. Each of the other directors has at least two major administrative functions reporting to him or her. For example, the Director of Public Safety has both Police and Fire reporting to him.

When we reorganized the city administration recently, we changed it so that Helen was reporting to the mayor through the director of public services, Jack Feldner. Helen got all bent out of shape that she wasn't reporting directly to the mayor and that she had to report through someone else. She made such a fuss about it that we finally agreed to her request and Ralph issued a memo of understanding to Helen to the effect that she still had direct access to us here at City Hall and that we would interact with her on a direct basis.

One of the City Council members introduced a proposal to classify Helen as a department head recently, but this proposal was withdrawn at my request. I'm afraid that as a result some people are getting the impression that I am not really supportive of the library. I really am, but my concern in this matter is with equity— all the other department directors have considerably more administrative responsibility than Helen does and they wouldn't consider it fair to have Helen classified as a department director.

Ralph: Helen keeps raising the issue of her salary level. I'm convinced that Helen is fairly paid in relation to other city employees. The trouble is that all city employees are underpaid compared to university salaries and we're *never* going to catch up. Dissatisfaction with pay is just one of those things that we have to accept and live with.

Despite what Helen says, I don't think salary is that big a problem. I remember from the supervision class that you (Jeff) taught that according to Herzberg, pay is a hygiene factor. I don't think that we're going to solve any big problems down at the library by working on hygiene factors.

Debra: An incident that happened recently will illustrate what I consider to be totally unprofessional conduct on the part of the library staff. As you know, I recently refused to reappoint Cecil Hockman to the Library Board of Trustees after his first term expired. Now as the mayor, I have the duty and obligation to the citizens of Kimball to appoint people to boards that I think are best qualified to do the jobs. I had my reasons for not reappointing Cecil; reasons which I consider to be good. Because we are making agreements with the Trustees about the administration of the library I want trustees who will work with us to try to reach a compromise. Cecil has never agreed to any compromise action and would stop library cooperative efforts.

What happened was that somebody down at the library called a reporter and told them about my refusal to reappoint Cecil Hockman. They apparently said that I had a vendetta going against Cecil and that a reporter should look into this. The reporter did check with Mr. Hockman and got a bunch of quotes from him concerning my nonsupport for library programs. Then the reporter called me and asked me if I wanted to respond to the charges. *I was furious.* I told her, "No, I do not want to respond." I did explain my duties and responsibilities as mayor to the reporter and she subsequently decided that there was no story.

Sometimes I feel like calling Helen up here on the carpet and telling her to shape up her act or get out. It becomes clearer to me all the time that, whatever else she is, Helen is not a competent administrator.

If the problems we're having with administration at the library can't be solved we are going to be forced to look at the issue of regionalization of this library, that is, having the city library join the county system along with the library in Morton. However, it is apparent to me that the idea of regionalization is extremely threatening to everybody down at the library. This showed up recently when the Capital Expenditures Committee recommended, among other things in its report to City Council, that the feasibility of regionalization of the city's library, cemetery, and health care facilities be studied. You wouldn't believe how upset the librarians became over that recommendation. They got a City Council member to make a motion that the recommendation be deleted from the Committee's report, and unfortunately it passed. The librarians clearly didn't even want the issue studied!

THE VIEW FROM THE LIBRARY

Helen: I'm surprised and delighted to hear you (professors) report that Debra Dickenson and Ralph Riesen are really interested in improving relations with us here at the library. I feel that we have been wasting a lot of time down here because of the poor relations we have with City Hall, and I wasn't at all sure how concerned they felt about it up there.

One of the main problems that I see between us and the city administration is their general resentment toward anything involving political pressure. I sense that Debra and Ralph get upset when the community voices opinions which are contrary to their views. I sometimes get the feeling that they would like to run the city without interference from citizens. However, that's the very nature of the political process. The mayor's job is inherently a political one. You shouldn't be in that position and expect to be immune from public pressure. So, I don't think it's appropriate that Debra gets upset when the citizens rally to support a program that they want.

During the recent budget hearings we have had lots of good people come to our defense. The Library Board of Trustees have been very supportive. The AAUW (American Association of University Women) has several members who have been strong supporters. These friends have been instrumental in helping us make the case to the mayor and the City Council that the community really supports a quality program here at the library.

Linda: We don't seem to have any problems of misunderstanding or nonsupport from either the Library of Board of Trustees or the City Council. I feel good about our relations with both of these groups. When we have gone to the City Council with our recommendations and proposals, they have been sympathetic and supportive. In the budget hearings both the Library Board and the City Council supported our proposed budget over the objections of Debra and Ralph. In effect, we bypassed the city administration and we came out better than if we had gone to them first, as they apparently wanted us to do.

One example of a way in which we have felt "under attack" by City Hall has been the way they have acted in regard to the appointment of members of the Library Board of Trustees.

Helen: That's right. You probably heard that just recently Debra refused to reappoint Cecil Hockman to the Board for a second term. Now Cecil has been a strong, energetic supporter of the library. He has given a great deal of his time and dedication to public service on the Library Board. Mr. Hockman's first term on the Board has just recently expired, and for no apparent reason Debra has declined to reappoint him, even though it has been customary in the past that members serve for two terms. So, Cecil Hockman is not only eligible for reappointment, but he has demonstrated in his first term that he is a dedicated and concerned public citizen.

It seems apparent to us that Debra resents anyone who supports the library as strongly as Cecil Hockman did. You see, Cecil initiated some legal research which determined that the Library Board of Trustees has the ultimate legislative authority for the administration of the library. Furthermore, Cecil Hockman took the initiative to argue our budget proposals before the City Council. Debra did not appreciate either of these, I am sure, and now it seems that she is out to get him.

In the past, I have always participated with the mayor when selecting candidates for the Library Board. The mayor has always been glad to have my input and opinion on which citizens would be good for the Library Board. None of that consultation has gone on between Debra and me recently; I just find out about her Board appointments by reading the newspaper.

Linda: Another way that we have felt attacked by the city administration has been the way we were treated in the recent reorganization of the city administrative hierarchy.

Helen: What they did was to demote the library by changing the reporting patterns so that instead of reporting directly to the city supervisor, I was directed to report through Jack Feldner, the director of public services.

This reassignment of the library was a serious downgrading of our status within the city. I was really upset when I learned that they expected me to report *through* Jack Feldner. Why, I have more education than Jack does. I have longer service to the City of Kimball than he does, and I supervise a *lot* of people here at the library. The very idea that the library with its staff of professionals should be considered subordinate to someone whose main concern is parks and recreation was an appalling idea to us over here. You see, that demotes us from one of the major functional units within the city administration to merely one of the concerns of the Parks and Recreation Department. I don't have anything against Jack Feldner, but I don't think it's right to have the city library subordinate to him and his department.

I was told that in the reorganization of the city administration I was not considered an administrator (Department Director level) because I supervise so few people. However, Lynn King [Finance Director] only supervises a few people, and she doesn't have the education I do either.

Maude: I don't think that they regard us as professionals over here, but we *are* professionals. Each one of us has had five years of college plus additional professional training, and yet we continually get treated as if we were mere clerks.

Linda: An incident which illustrates the library's diminished status was City Hall's insistence that Helen could not retain the title of "Library Director." The title

"Library Director" is common among librarians having similar jobs to Helen's. Among the staff here at the library, it seems the logical choice of position titles. And yet the city administration insisted that Helen could not be called a "Director." So they suggested that we call her the "Library Supervisor." Of course, "supervisor" denotes someone just above the clerical level; someone who is supervising a bunch of clerks. That seems natural to them, but the idea is appalling over here. We hassled back and forth over different possible titles for Helen's position and finally settled on "City Librarian." This title is less descriptive than "Library Director" and reflects Helen's lowered status in the city.

Maude: I don't think Helen is regarded as an administrator by the city administration. I don't think they really know how many people she has reporting to her, or how much leadership it takes to coordinate all the volunteer help we have. Helen has a substantial administrative job to keep this library running smoothly.

Helen: Going along with that is their resistance to paying me a salary reflecting my abilities and contribution. My salary is simply not in line with the requirements of this job, my education, and the experience I have with the City of Kimball. I know that I'm paid less than many other people in the city who have less education and less experience than I do. The city administration simply refuses to recognize the importance of my job.

Jeff: How would your salary compare, Helen, to other library directors having similar jobs around the state?

Helen: Well, I would have to say that my salary today reflects some very significant adjustments upward which were made during the 1960s. At that time the university was under heavy pressure to equalize the salaries of its female professionals, and the City of Kimball also upgraded their women's salaries at the same time. So I shared with some other women in some impressive gains during the 1960's.

If you looked just at the figures, my salary wouldn't look that far off relative to other city librarians. However, the figures don't reflect the quality of education I have received, the length of my service to the City of Kimball, and the contributions that I have made to the development of this library today.

Jeff: Could you give us an example or two of specific ways that the library's effectiveness has been impaired by the actions of members of the city administration?

Helen: Certainly. One good example would be the copier incident. That's a long story. Sometime ago we experienced an equipment failure with the copier which we had for patrons to use. Therefore, I asked permission from the Board of Trustees to allocate Kimball Fund [donated] money to purchase a new copier, and they approved. I went ahead with procedures to order a new copier. The next thing that I learned was that Debra had disallowed the purchase. She said that I should have checked with her first.

I was flabbergasted. I had never felt that I had to check with the mayor on decisions like that. Furthermore, I was angry because she had ruled on the decision without checking into what the reasons for it were. I felt "zapped" by Debra, like I have in several other situations.

It seems to me that I did the right thing by checking with my Board of Trustees on the decision I made. As you know, by legislation they have the responsibility for the administrative functions of the library. When they have approved a decision like this, what basis does the mayor have for interfering in our decision?

Another way that Debra has demonstrated her lack of support for the library is by advancing the idea that the library should be regionalized to become a part of the county system. Anybody who knows anything about the library regards this as a preposterous idea.

In the first place, to seriously consider the idea of regionalization you would have to undertake a rather comprehensive study of the consequences. That in itself would be a major, expensive undertaking, which I don't think Debra is ready to shoulder. It is clear to me if such a study were done, the result would overwhelmingly favor the present organizational arrangement. We have very little in common with the Morton Library, and nothing at all to be gained by being put in the county system. Kimball is a unique community with citizens who have very different expectations from those in the remainder of the county, which is largely rural. The whole idea of regionalization is so preposterous that it seems to me to be irresponsible to even advance the idea.

I get the feeling that Debra is accumulating a check-list against me. I have had a fear for sometime now that Debra could at any time try to have me fired. I get the feeling in talking to them that I'm not getting straight messages from them.

At least there's one thing to be grateful for—I just passed my sixty-second birthday and can't be deprived of my pension if I am fired or forced to resign. I would like to stay on until I am sixty-five, but the way things are going between Debra and me I never know.

I get to feeling sad and hopeless and despairing when I think about the way I'm regarded at City Hall. I think it's tragic when someone like me has given many dedicated years of service and has made major contributions to building a strong program, and then finds themselves spending their last few years in an atmosphere of distrust and unappreciation. I think I deserve better.

Linda: The distrust in our relationship shows itself

practically every time we have an interaction. Recently I have taken on the duties of Adult Services Librarian and have been out visiting members of other city departments discussing ways that the library could be of service to them. I have had really warm and friendly receptions from everybody I have visited, with the exception of Ralph Riesen. When I talked to him in the same way that I had the other people, I felt like I got a cold shoulder. He seemed very uninterested. What I would most like would be to talk straight to Debra and Ralph and get straight answers in return.

Helen: We shouldn't overlook the fact that there have been some positive developments recently. For example, the new personnel officer, Joyce Gardner, came down and visited us last week. She was very understanding and very sympathetic about our problems. I am rather optimistic that many of our problems concerning selection, advertising, and interviewing will be better now that Joyce is here.

Linda: The recent hiring of two part-time people with Joyce's advice and help is an example of how well things *can* be done and how we and the city administration can work together. We should find more ways to use our separate expertise cooperatively!

Helen: Also, I am encouraged by the cooperation I have been getting from Jack Feldner. He recently responded favorably to my request for a crew to come over here and help with moving books away from an area where we had a leaking roof. I haven't always felt that I've had Jack's complete support and cooperation, but lately I've been feeling better about that.

One example of an item I'll bet is on Debra's checklist against me is the fact that the library is over its budget this year. Now the reason for this is that since the budgeting processes have been centralized in City Hall, I simply haven't had access to the kind of information I need to keep track of the budget. I'm afraid that I'm going to be unjustifiably blamed for this situation. This is an example of the kind of information I should not have to ask for—they should automatically give it to me.

Linda: I *am* concerned about the way that these crises with the city affect our morale and productivity. I have observed that when these crises come up we of the staff cease to care about our work as much, we spend *much* time rehashing incidents to reassure ourselves, and we do not do as good a job because we do not feel secure or appreciated. I am amazed to see myself doing this, as I like my job, but I do find myself lowering the quality of my work when I feel threatened, and I see others doing it too. So, continued bad feelings are counterproductive and inefficient.

Maude: One indicator of the kind of relationship which Debra has with us down here in the library is the reaction she gets when she comes down here. I remember a time when she was down here recently. We were

all very nervous and very alert. It was like we all suspected that she was up to no good being down here, and we had to watch her every step.

Initial Meetings

After reviewing what they had learned in the meetings with City Hall and the library staff, Jeff and Paul decided to recommend a series of four two-hour meetings. They formulated tentative meeting agendas and sent copies to each of the five prospective participants. After informal checks had established the agreement of each of the five to the proposed meetings, the consultants sent a confirming memo to each, announcing the time and place for each of the four meetings.

Meeting 1, March 19

The agenda presented by the consultants for the first meeting included a brief introduction by the consultants, an expectations check, a sharing appreciations exercise, and a closing process check.

Following the introduction, the participants were asked to participate in an expectations check. For the first half of this exercise each person was asked to write on two separate sheets of paper 1) their hopes, and 2) their fears for the upcoming series of meetings. In the second half of the exercise these hopes and fears were shared, posted on newsprint, and discussed. This exercise activity took about 40 minutes.

The "sharing appreciations" exercise contained four steps. In the first step each of the participants were given 3 × 5 cards and asked to write appreciation messages to other participants. Each message was to be addressed to another person on a separate card and was to be unsigned. A format suggested was, "I appreciate _____ about you." Each person was asked to write at least one such message to each of the other four participants present.

In step two of the appreciations exercise the cards were collected and sorted and then read by one facilitator while the other wrote the appreciations on newsprint. The result was one large newsprint sheet of appreciation messages for each of the five participants.

In step three each person was instructed to add to their individual sheets other things for which they would like to be appreciated, or for which they felt they deserved appreciation.

Step four consisted of a series of one-on-one conferences where each participant met individually with each of the other four participants for five minutes each. During these conferences each member of the pair was asked to *acknowledge* to the other person the appreciations which had been contributed by other participants, and further to acknowledge the appreciations which he or she had contributed or agreed with.

The sharing appreciations exercise took about 30 minutes.

The final activity for Meeting 1 was a process check, where participants were invited to share their feelings about the activities of the first meeting and about the upcoming meetings.

The expectations check generated a list of hopes and fears which was posted on two large sheets of newsprint. The main themes reflected in the "hopes" list included desires to improve working relations and communications between the library and the city, to clarify reporting patterns, to know others as individuals, to develop a more relaxed atmosphere among group members, to confront differences, to reduce felt threats, and to restore library staff confidence.

The list of fears included the following: that the library would become even more committed to single issue political activity; that the meetings would result in "unpleasant repercussions" for some; that information shared in the meetings would get out and be damaging or embarrassing; that the meetings would be a waste of time; that the library would move further away from the rest of the city and become more entrenched; and that Debra and Ralph would become too busy to attend one or more of the meetings.

The general mood during the meeting was one of cautiousness. Jeff and Paul noted that the appreciations shared were quite general and that some uneasiness was sensed during the appreciation sharing exercise. The process check at the end of the meeting revealed mildly positive reactions. Ralph seemed cool and reserved; he said that there were no dramatic gains but that he was willing to continue. Linda seconded Ralph's sentiment. Debra and Maude seemed to be more positive and appeared to feel reassured. Helen appeared to have very positive feelings about the meeting; she expressed reduced apprehensions about the meetings and increased comfort with the other participants.

Meeting 2, March 21

The meeting began with a brief introduction to the planned activities by Paul. He also apologized for having to leave early that day. Instructions were then given for the first phase of an "image exchange" exercise. Participants were told that each group was to meet in a separate room and prepare two lists. The first list was to summarize their own group's images of the other group, including thoughts, attitudes, feelings, perceptions, and behavior. The second list was to predict what the other group's images recorded in their first list would be.

After approximately 30 minutes of list preparation time, the two groups were reconvened to share the lists. During the list-sharing period a ground rule was enforced with disallowed debate and discussion but which allowed questions for clarification.

The librarians were invited to share their list of images of the city administration first. As they did so Jeff (Paul had gone) summarized the entries on newsprint. Next the city administration's images of the library were shared and posted. Time was allowed for clarification questions after each list had been aired.

Next the two groups shared their predictions of the other group's list with the librarians again going first. The time required for the sharing of the four lists was approximately 40 minutes. These four lists are reproduced in Exhibit 18-2.

Following the image exchange period the groups were again sent to separate rooms. This time each group was instructed to create a prioritized list of issues needing resolution. Twenty minutes was allocated for this activity.

The final activity for Meeting 2 was the sharing of the two lists of priority issues. Exhibit 18-3 shows the priority issues which were generated in this activity. This sharing and posting used up the remainder of the meeting time available.

At the conclusion of the meeting, Jeff's impression was that there was a general sense of tension relief that this long-repressed animosity was finally out in the open. Debra appeared to feel particularly good about the meeting when she left. Jeff was impressed by the casualness and informality with which Ralph engaged in musing conversation concerning the meeting with the three librarians for fifteen minutes after the meeting. This was the first time that Jeff could remember Ralph's being relaxed and at ease in any of the meetings concerning the library. Jeff guessed that Ralph might have felt good that some real progress had been made during this meeting.

Two days after this meeting, Linda reported to Jeff that the librarians left the meeting feeling quite discouraged.

Consultants' Meeting, March 22

Jeff Mallet and Paul Everest met at Paul's house to compare notes on the progress of the meetings so far, and to discuss strategy for the upcoming meetings.

When Paul saw the two priority lists of issues for resolution which had been generated by the two groups, he had an immediate reaction. Paul noted that the items listed by the librarians appeared to reflect a willingness to compromise, collaborate or negotiate; whereas, those

EXHIBIT 18-2

Image Exchange Data From Second Meeting of City Hall and Library Administration

I. Library Administration views of City Hall
   1. They are suspicious of the library.
   2. They are well-intentioned but inept.
   3. They are uninterested in the library program.
   4. They are protective of their own power.
   5. They are unfriendly.
   6. They want the library to accept administrative changes from City Hall, but are unwilling to accept administrative changes made by the Library Board.
   7. They don't really want public input.
   8. They are very willing to put library staff (esp. Helen) between power play of City Hall and the Library Board.
   9. They are personally against Helen.

II. City Hall views of Library Administration
   1. They have limited or no respect for the administrative abilities of City Hall.
   2. "Massive paranoia" exists among the library staff.
   3. The librarians have been operating a propaganda organ:
      • Internally with library staff
      • Externally with City Council and the public
   4. The library staff has used the Library Board as a separate political support group.
   5. There has been a concerted program by the librarians to establish a separate political base and become invulnerable.
   6. Library personnel operate a tight "clique."
   7. Library personnel distrust (and dislike and despise . . .) City Hall.
   8. Library personnel wish to do their own thing without coordination.
   9. Library personnel don't readily accept administrative assistance.

III. Library Administration's predictions of City Hall views of Library Administration
   1. They think we are paranoid.
   2. They think we are snobbish & isolated.
   3. They think we are spreading our views of the problem among staff & public.
   4. They think we are overprotective of the library.
   5. They think we are inappropriately political.
   6. They think we are encouraging the Library Board to move away from City Hall.

IV. City Hall's predictions of Library views of City Hall
   1. They think that we believe the library is not a critical service; it is dispensable, or first to go in a crunch.
   2. They think we are non-supportive of the library.
   3. They think we discriminate against the library.
   4. They think we impose unreasonable guidelines.
   5. They think we have a vendetta against the library.
   6. They think we are uncaring and unhelpful.
   7. They think that the library gets the short end of resource allocations.
   8. They think that we are fast to control and restrict, but seldom volunteer assistance.

items listed by Debra and Ralph appeared to reflect the expectation that it was the library which should do the changing. Jeff and Paul wondered if this was a pattern. They recalled other times when they had vague feelings that perhaps Debra or Ralph or both regarded the meetings as an opportunity to get the library to shape up. Following the meeting, Jeff had the feeling that the three librarians had seemed to take the instructions and the sessions more seriously than did Debra and Ralph. Jeff had hoped that the period for sharing the four lists would leave everyone in an introspective mood. This seemed to take place for the librarians, but not for Debra and Ralph.

After reflecting on the outcomes from Meeting 2,

EXHIBIT 18-3

Priority Issues for Resolution: Second Meeting, City Hall and Library Administration

I. Priorities of Library Staff
    1. Clarify the role of the Library Board of Trustees:
        a) State-wide
        b) City-wide
        c) Vis-a-vis the library staff
    2. Clarify the roles of the library staff, library administration, and City Hall.
    3. Reach agreement regarding appropriate political activity for the library,
    4. Develop mutual respect for one anothers' administrative abilities.

II. Priorities of City Hall
    1. (Debra) Inappropriate political activity.
    2. (Ralph) Resolve the perception that City Hall is doing something "bad" to Helen, i.e., perceived vendetta.
    3. Library's impression that City Hall is uninterested in the library program.
    4. Library's impression that members of City Hall are being protective of their own power.

Jeff reported feeling overwhelmed by the pervasiveness of the issue concerning appropriate political activity. His review had led him to the conclusion that this issue was so fundamental to all the problems being experienced between the library and City Hall that it was likely to be futile to work on any specific issues before addressing this major one.

As Jeff saw it, there were two major questions which needed to be resolved. First, what is the relationship of the Library Board of Trustees to City Hall? And secondly, how are the diametrically opposed views expressed by the library and City Hall concerning appropriate political activity going to be resolved? It seemed to Jeff that neither of these issues could be settled by the group which had been meeting with Jeff and Paul. Instead, it seemed more plausible that these issued needed to be referred to either the Library Board or to the City Council.

Paul agreed that there were no instant solutions in sight, and that the appropriate strategy for where to go with the present group was not at all apparent.

After some discussion, Paul and Jeff agreed on the prognosis that until the overriding issue of political activity was dealt with, administrative issues would probably be resistant to solution. They further agreed that it seemed unlikely that solutions to the political activity question could be generated from within the present group, and that action strategies to address this issue probably would have to come from the City Council or the Library Board.

Concerning strategy for Meeting 3, Paul and Jeff agreed to begin it by reviewing for the participants the consultants' interpretations of the outcome of Meeting 2 and to invite them to join in a problem-solving session

concerning appropriate action strategies. Paul and Jeff could think of two strategies which might prove fruitful:

1. Refer the issue of appropriateness of political activity to the City Council with a request for a definitive guideline on what activities are appropriate.

2. Have Debra and Helen get together, with or without a process consultant, to work out an agreement concerning political activity.

Jeff and Paul discussed whether the issue of the newspaper reporter being called should be brought up and dealt with at the next meeting. They agreed that Debra had stored up much resentment over this issue, and that if it came out it could be a "heavy" confrontation. Jeff and Paul were very uncertain about whether the issue could be constructively dealt with in one meeting. The uncertainties concerning the outcome of such a confrontation led Paul and Jeff to agree that they should probably try to avoid confronting this issue at the next meeting.

FURTHER DISCUSSIONS

Meeting 3, March 24

As Jeff and Paul arrived at the Savings Bank Community Room for Meeting 3, they exchanged the sentiment, "God knows what's going to happen today!"

As participants entered the meeting room, they were given a three-page handout summarizing the previous meeting's outcomes. This handout contained the data generated in Meeting 2 from the image exchange exercise and the priority issues for resolution list (Exhibits 18-3 and 18-4).

Jeff began by sharing some of his and Paul's reflections concerning the pervasiveness of the political issue. He raised the question about whether administration concerns could be addressed while the political issue remained unsolved. He further voiced some skepticism concerning whether the present group was the appropriate one to settle the political issue, or whether it could.

At this time, Jeff spent some time reflecting on the nature of the conflict over political activities. He tried to summarize the position of each of the two parties to the conflict. In doing this Jeff emphasized his understanding that each of the parties had a position which was logically defensible, internally consistent, and supportable by others.

Jeff concluded by inviting the group members to comment on the consultants' diagnosis of the problem, and to join in a problem-solving session to identify reasonable options which could be taken. The remainder of the meeting time was used for unstructured discussion, with the exception of a brief process check at the end of the meeting.

Paul served in a process observation role during this meeting. During the time that Jeff was giving an overview of the problem situation, Paul noted the reactions of the five participants. Linda, Helen, and Ralph all seemed quite attentive. Debra and Maude were observed to be staring intently at their handouts for long periods of time. This was particularly true for Maude who hardly shifted her gaze from her handout for al-

---

EXHIBIT 18-4
City Hall and Library Administration Action List

ISSUE	ACTION
• Calling reporter anonymously	• Announcement at staff meeting (Helen will do. OK to break confidentially.)
• Offer by Debra to spend time in library	• Helen will schedule with staff and Debra.

• Reporting relations	• Helen will draft memo to Library Board by May 2 asking them for direction or clarification on the following issues:
	  • Legal liability; errors & omissions
	  • Property
	  • Maintenance
	  • Reporting relations
	  • Political activity
	  • Debra and Ralph will review memo
	• Ralph and Helen will attend May 2 meeting of Library Board.

• Maintaining good relations	• Debra, Ralph, Helen, Linda, and Maude will meet for brown bag luncheons. • First luncheon: Tuesday, Apr. 24 12:00 to 1:00 in Ralph's office; Linda will facilitate. Participants to begin with "check-in" concerning problem issues and good news. • Facilitator and location will rotate for subsequent luncheons. • Brown bag discussion item: exchanging of staff people
• Perception that City Hall is going to do something bad to Helen	• Brown bag luncheon "check-in" item
• Perception that City Hall is "inept" • Perception that library staff is "incompetent"	• All such evaluative stereotypes were declared inoperative by Jeff, who banned their use in thought and speech.

most twenty minutes. Paul noted that Maude looked dejected, and that she was avoiding eye contact with others present. Because the meeting room was chilly, Maude (along with most of the others) was feeling physically cold. Maude had also mentioned that she was coming down with a cold.

After Jeff had finished his introductory remarks. Debra abruptly initiated a discussion of political activity on the part of the library staff. Debra's remarks may be paraphrased as follows:

> Politics is a fact of life now. The library staff has started something that will be very hard to stop. They have politicized the budgeting process and it will be very hard to go back to a non-political procedure. What I need to know from the library staff is whether these activities are going to continue. If they are, there are going to be unpleasant repercussions which the library staff should understand.
>
> There are two things that are really bothering me; first, the fact that someone from the library called a newspaper reporter to ask that my "vendetta" against Cecil Hockman and the library be investigated. When I got that telephone call from the reporter, I felt 'angry, betrayed, and nonplussed.' Second is the issue of political activity by library staff members aimed at packing the City Council chambers with citizens supporting the library. That represents a clear violation of instructions from the Library Board, and leads me to wonder, "Who's running the library, anyway?"

When Debra made the point that the library staff had disregarded instructions concerning political activity, Helen pointed out that the library staff did not perceive that they had received any such instructions. Following Helen's point, discussion proceeded in another direction, with no overt evidence that Helen's comment was heard or understood.

Following Debra's expression of her feelings about the telephone call, Helen and Linda expressed consternation that the telephone call had been made. Both made it very clear that they thought such a telephone call was inappropriate. Linda said, "I didn't realize we had sunk to that low a level," and Helen seconded Linda's sentiment. During this conversation Maude was noticeably quite, and was avoiding eye contact.

Ralph said, "When I come in the library, I feel hostility all around me." When Ralph had said this, Paul intervened and asked Ralph to focus on his personal feelings when he was in this situation. Ralph's responses generally depicted his impressions of library staff members' attitudes. Paul pursued the issue by asking Ralph two more times to focus on and report his own feelings in this situation. After Ralph's responses again did not describe his own feelings, Jeff probed him by asking if he might have been feeling hurt, or disliked, or disrespected. In response to this prompting Ralph acknowledged that some of these guesses were accurate.

At this point Paul intervened with a few observations designed to set the stage for the librarians to air some of their feelings. With a few minor exceptions, the librarians did not divulge their feelings on issues.

At one point in the conversation Debra offered "to spend a week working in the library," if that would help to resolve some of the problems. Helen responded to this offer with apparent guardedness, citing the difficulties of time scheduling and the requirements of attending the human understanding workshops currently being conducted for all city employees. Debra seemed annoyed that Helen's reaction to her offer was not totally positive. At this point Maude made a pointed observation to Debra: "I have to tell you that there are some people in the library who will be pretty hostile toward you."

The question of whether the library should regionalize by joining the Morton County system was raised. Debra expressed dismay that the Library staff, the Library Board of Trustees, and several others had reacted so vehemently to the proposal that regionalization should be studied. The librarians responded to Debra's sentiment by assertively pointing out that the proposal [which had been part of a report to the City Council by the Capital Expenditures Committee] did not call for a study but called for *implementation* which was to occur by January 1, 1990. Both Debra and Ralph replied that they were sure that the wording of the Capital Expenditures Committee report was that the January 1, 1990 date was the deadline for *completion of a study*. The librarians were equally certain that their interpretation of the report was correct. Members of both groups vowed to get a copy of the committee report to bring to the next meeting.

Discussion of the regionalization issue continued. Helen referred to a previous study concerning regionalization which had been conducted by the League of Women Voters. This study had gathered some utilization data. Helen felt that the study supported her opinion that regionalization would be most unwise. Debra said that she had not seen or heard of the League study, and was very interested: "That's the kind of information I need to know."

At this point one of the librarians volunteered that they had prepared a "fact sheet" concerning the regionalization issue. Debra expressed surprise at hearing about the fact sheet. Paul noted that Debra seemed annoyed about learning about the fact sheet, and that Ralph gave the librarians a dirty look during this time.

The librarians at this point explained that the fact sheet was prepared in response to a request by an individual City Council member.

Lively discussion of substantive issues was continuing when Jeff interrupted at a few minutes before the end of the meeting time to ask for a process check. During this check the general sentiment expressed was, "Whew! we really got into it today!" Linda said that she thought a lot had been accomplished, and nods of agreement from other participants were noted. Ralph acknowledged some real accomplishment for the first time. Paul and Jeff shared both surprise and relief that the issue concerning the reporter had been successfully dealt with and largely defused. In fact, they expressed the view that the whole issue of political activity had been defused at least somewhat.

Meeting 4, March 25

The meeting began with Paul and Jeff suggesting a review of the "Priority Issues for Resolution" list generated in Meeting 2. The consultants suggested that the group make an "action/no action" decision for each of the priority issues. This was to provide some closure for this last of four scheduled meetings.

During the last half of the meeting Paul started an action list on newsprint, and he and Jeff pressed the participants for specific action commitments as the discussion approached agreement.

The last ten minutes of the meeting were spent reviewing the list of hopes and fears generated at the beginning of Meeting 1.

The action list that Paul constructed on newsprint during the last half of the meeting is shown in Exhibit 18-4. The last issue on the action list, i.e., the perceptions of "ineptness" and "incompetence," still had not been discussed as the end of the meeting time approached. Jeff called attention to the issue, and shared the perception of the consultants that the range of specific behaviors which each group found upsetting in the other group seemed quite small, too small to support the "inept" or "incompetent" generalizations. He pointed out that feedback on specific behaviors had been constructively shared during the four meetings, but that feedback on broad evaluative generalization was hard to respond to constructively. Jeff urged each participant to consciously avoid lapsing into the use of such evaluative stereotypes, and instead to concentrate on specific behaviors.

During the review of the hopes and fears lists the general feeling was that most of the hopes had been either partially or fully realized, and that most of the fears had dissipated. Concerning the fear that the meetings might prove to be a waste of time, Ralph said, "that remains to be seen." Concerning the hope that better working relations would be developed, all participants seemed to agree that this had been accomplished.

FOLLOW-UP

A survey instrument called the Intergroup Profile was used by the consultants to measure the climate existing between City Hall and the library staff. This instrument has eight Likert-type questions concerning relationships existing between two groups. Measurements were taken in March before the first intergroup meeting, and in May, six weeks after the last meeting. Parallel measurements were obtained from nine separate control organizations.

Data analysis revealed that the Library/City Hall climate prior to the meetings was considerably worse than that existing in any of the nine control organizations ($p < .0001$). Following the meetings the Library/City Hall climate scores had improved substantially ($p = .001$), but were still lower than the scores of any control organization.

In early August, four months after meeting four, a two-page written evaluation form was filled out by each of the five meeting participants. Their responses reflected general agreement that, as a result of the meetings, the climate between City Hall and the library had improved, but not dramatically.

Ralph Riesen commented, "We achieved a better understanding of positions, but no real resolution of conflicts. The conflicts that exist are political rather than personal."

Debra Dickenson noted that the meetings had provided ". . . a good chance to share concerns," and that they resulted in ". . . better feelings for the individuals involved." She continued,

> There is a period of transition that is required—just plain time to see how we all deal with the next 'challenge to authority.' Political changes have an effect. I don't feel the library personnel understand the scope of City demands and needs any better than before. In my opinion they just feel we are being nicer to them. Their anxieties are relieved a bit so the climate is improved. There is a value to that without a doubt.

Helen Hendricks noted three specific changes which had resulted from the meetings:

1. The Librarian is aware that her personal situation cannot improve but she is not threatened by further deterioration of her position.
2. The administrative reporting pattern between Library Administration, Library Board, and City Supervisor has improved.
3. The Library Staff are more united and supportive than ever.

Additional comments made by Helen included the following:

I believe the Library's fears and concerns were substantiated by the meetings but it was good to bring them into the open. The Librarian's and City Supervisor's personal contacts are slightly improved.

The problems at the Library stemmed from the City Administration decision to regroup the City program with the resultant down-grading of the library service and personal demotion of the Librarian—the view of the Library. The City Administration did not recognize this as the cause.

Linda Turner reported that the meetings ". . . relieved the Mayor's mind by allowing her a chance to 'let off steam.' Coming from the library, I [now] feel more relaxed in talking with the Mayor and City Supervisor—though not totally relaxed. The City Librarian and City Supervisor can now talk to each other—this is by far the most important result."

Maude Richardson concurred with Linda and Helen that the relationship between the City Librarian and the City Supervisor was much more comfortable. She also observed that "foul-ups at City Hall are no longer seen as personally directed at the library."

When you have read this case, look back at the chapter's diagnostic questions and choose the ones that apply to the case. Then use those questions with the ones that follow in your case analysis.

1. What kinds of problems in the Dumas library and the Kimball city government did Jeff Mallet and Paul Everest uncover in their interviews? What expectations did they create by their interviewing process? Were these expectations fulfilled by later actions and events?

2. What kind of organization development intervention did Jeff and Paul implement? Why did they choose this particular type of intervention? Did they implement it properly? Was it the best choice, or should they have used another intervention instead?

3. Critique Jeff's and Paul's overall effectiveness as OD change agents. What would you have done differently? Would you hire them to manage change in your organization?

CASE 18-3

O CANADA

Review this case, which appears in Chapter 15. Next, look back at Chapter 18's diagnostic questions and choose the ones that apply to the case. Then use those questions with the ones that follow in your case analysis.

1. What organization development interventions could the Public Service Commission use to identify and diagnose the problems confronting the Directorate of Staff Development and Training and the Regional Operations Directorate? Which intervention would probably work best? Why? What steps should be taken to implement this intervention?

2. What OD interventions could be used to deal with the kinds of problems likely to be identified by your initial intervention? Describe a specific program of interventions and implementation steps that you would recommend.

3. How would your program benefit the Public Service Commission and its divisions? What obstacles might it encounter? How would you overcome such resistance?

CHAPTER 19

INTERNATIONAL DIMENSIONS: ORGANIZATIONAL BEHAVIOR ABROAD

THE GRADUATION CEREMONY OF INTERNATIONAL UNIVERSITY OF JAPAN

国際大学大学院修了式

With help from Dartmouth College's Amos Tuck School of Business, the International University of Japan opened its International Management MBA Program in 1988 and graduated its first class two years later. Students in the initial program, most of whom were supported by their companies, found the "giant" textbooks somewhat daunting and the pressure to offer their opinions in class disconcerting, particularly because all instruction in the new program is offered in English. The students liked their U.S. professors' openness to them, however, and even learned to evaluate them at the end of the term. One student said that he had never asked "Why?" in his business career but was now very quick to ask this question. His wife was worried, however, lest he be "kicked out [of his firm] for insulting the existing way of doing things."
Source: Patricia A. Langan, "Trying to Clone U.S.-Style MBAs," Fortune, October 8, 1990.

Backed in most cases by corporate cash and charged with the mission of deciphering the often inscrutable American culture, Japanese "salarymen" are coming to America. They have attended American business schools in small numbers since the 1960s, even though corporate leaders in Japan have preferred to teach business the old-fashioned way—on the job. But Japanese students now account for more than five percent of the total enrollment at America's top business schools. To them, the MBA has come to mean Mastering Being in America.

More than three fourths of Japanese business students in the United States are sponsored by their employers, and many of them expect to manage Japanese subsidiaries in the U.S. someday. Naoki Yamamori is typical. Formerly a bank branch manager for Dai-Ichi Kangyo in Tokyo, he came to MIT's Sloan School of Management nearly two years ago. Though he hopes to learn more about finance, Yamamori's foremost goals are "to have an American friend and understand how they think." Jinei Yamaguchi, a Mitsubishi Bank employee attending Sloan, echoes that notion. "Business school is more to learn about America," he says, "than to learn about net present value." Yamaguchi says his experience at Sloan should pay off later if he has to communicate with branch managers of Mitsubishi's American subsidiaries.[1]

In the world economy of the 1990s, it is becoming increasingly difficult to find a company that doesn't conduct business across national boundaries. Indeed, "American" companies like McDonald's, Coca-Cola, and General Motors and "Japanese" companies like Sony, Honda, and Mitsubishi do so much business outside their original homelands that they are more accurately described as global enterprises. As discussed in the "In Practice" box, multinational companies and stateless corporations spanning several countries are quite common in today's business world.

How seriously must the managers of such organizations take differences in nationality? How significantly do international differences affect the management of organizational behavior? In response to these questions, consider that Japanese companies are paying top dollar for younger salarymen (managers) to learn about the American way of life so that the Japanese approach to management can be fitted to the task of managing American employees. As suggested by the actions of the Japanese—who have amassed a strong record of success in multinational management—contemporary managers *must* take international differences seriously and adapt familiar management practices to compensate for these differences. Otherwise, they risk losing out in today's competitive world markets.[2]

The purpose of this chapter is to discuss important international differences. How do we fit the management practices we have examined in this book—practices that are overwhelmingly American in origin and focus—to the job of managing people and organizations in other national cultures? We will begin by examining the ways the cultures of nations differ from one another, identifying four dimensions that delineate key international differences. Next, we will take a closer look at how these differences affect organizations and organizational behavior.

[1] Todd Barrett, "Mastering Being in America: Japanese Are Flocking to U.S. Business Schools," *Newsweek*, February 5, 1990, p. 64.

[2] For a discussion of how the Japanese have adapted familiar management practices for use abroad, see Peter B. Smith, "The Effectiveness of Japanese Styles of Management: A Review and Critique," *Journal of Occupational Psychology* 57 (1984), 121–36.

Today, dozens of American industrial companies, including IBM, Gillette, Xerox, Dow Chemical, and Hewlett-Packard sell more of their products outside the U.S. than they do at home, and American service firms such as McDonald's, Time-Warner, Disney, and American Express do at least 20 percent of their business in foreign markets. Many of these companies are *multinationals*—globe-spanning organizations that treat foreign operations as outposts that produce products designed and engineered back home. Others, however, are *stateless corporations*, or firms that customize products to regional tastes and are totally localized in the many sites they own.

Stateless is a relatively new strategy. How is it working out? Otis Elevator's decision to design its newest high-speed elevator in five different countries—systems integration in the U.S., motor drives in Japan, door systems in France, electronics in Germany, and gear components in Spain—saved more than $10 million in design costs and two years of product-devel-

opment time. Canada's Northern Telecom Ltd. moved many of its operations into the U.S. and became eligible to bid for Japanese contracts as an American company. This eligibility is critical to Northern Telecom. Japan now favors U.S. telecommunications companies over Canadian firms because of the politically sensitive U.S.-Japanese trade gap. Honda Motor Company is able to circumvent anti-Japanese trade barriers in Israel, Taiwan, and South Korea by shipping American-made Accords and Civics to these destinations. Statelessness thus appears to offer important competitive advantages to companies that are doing business in the international markets of the 1990s.

Adapted from William J. Holstein, Stanley Reed, Jonathan Kapstein, Todd Vogel, and Joseph Weber, "The Stateless Corporation: Forget Multinationals—Today's Giants Are Really Leaping Boundaries," *Business Week*, May 14, 1990, pp. 98–105.

We will narrow our focus to two of the four dimensions as we compare management practices in Scandinavian, Japanese, and Israeli kibbutz organizations. We will conclude by discussing the task of adapting familiar management techniques to the demands of different national cultures.

DIAGNOSTIC ISSUES

In this final chapter, we will again use our diagnostic model to call attention to several important considerations. In examining the international context we need to ask how we can *describe* how nations and their cultures differ from one another. What dimensions can we use to capture and understand such differences? How do specific countries differ on these dimensions? How can we *diagnose* whether a particular theory we have discussed will apply in a particular national culture? Is there any way to assess whether a management practice developed in one nation's culture will work in another?

Can we *prescribe* what sorts of structure, jobs, and leadership will work best in a particular country? Can we predict what sorts of efforts to increase motivation will be appropriate? Finally, what *actions* can managers take to adapt management practices that work in one country for use in another? How can managers adapt their own behavioral styles to living and working overseas?

NATIONAL CULTURES AND ORGANIZATIONAL BEHAVIOR

national culture The collection of societal norms and values in the environment surrounding an organization.

We have seen that organizational behavior is influenced by social information that originates in the organization's culture of norms and values (Chapter 18). Behavior in organizations is also shaped by social information residing in the **national culture** of societal norms and values that is part of the organization's environment. Sometimes the norms and values in an

Changing an organization's culture can be a very difficult task, but turning around an entire nation's norms and values is a job of overwhelming proportions. The Soviet Union's new efforts at entrepreneurism have touched only a very small percent of society. Because the new ventures have not yet become fully and legally independent of the state, other organizations may not want to follow the same path, and the fledgling companies themselves may not survive. Meanwhile, many workers like these Russian women still labor for low pay on state-owned collectives.
Source: Richard I. Kirkland Jr., "Can Capitalism Save Perestroika?" Fortune, July 30, 1990.

organization's culture seem not only to mirror but to actually intensify characteristics of the surrounding national culture.[3] For example, promptness, which is viewed favorably in the U.S. national culture, is valued so highly in some American firms that missing a deadline by an insignificant amount of time is considered grounds for dismissal. In other instances, norms and values from the national culture can even overwhelm those residing in the organization's culture. Whistle blowing—in which one person reports organizational wrongdoing to others in authority—is an example. A whistle blower must violate organizational values favoring loyalty or secrecy to honor societal values that endorse honesty and truthfulness.

Frequently, however, the norms and values of an organization's culture are imported directly from, and are therefore consistent with, the national culture. For example, norms in American organizations assert that "a fair day's work should receive a fair day's pay." Those norms are based on societal norms of fairness and reciprocity that lie at the core of the American culture. Similarly, the value placed on deferring to hierarchical superiors in Japanese organizations is based on societal values that emphasize the importance of obedience and harmony. In cases like these, societal norms and values are themselves sources of social information that have direct effects on organizational behavior.

DIMENSIONS OF CROSS-CULTURAL DIFFERENCES

How do societal norms and values differ from one national culture to another? In what ways are the cultures of different countries similar? What effects do these similarities and differences have on people's attitudes and behaviors? Geert Hofstede set out to answer these questions by surveying employees of IBM offices located in 40 countries throughout the world. As he examined the data from 116,000 questionnaires, Hofstede discovered that most differences among national cultures were described by four dimensions— *uncertainty avoidance*, *masculinity-femininity*, *individualism-collectivism*, and *power distance*.[4]

---

[3] Andre Laurant, "The Cultural Diversity of Western Conceptions of Management," *International Studies of Management and Organization* 13 (1983), 75–96.

[4] Hofstede, "Motivation, Leadership, and Organization: Do American Theories Apply Abroad?" *Organizational Dynamics* 9 (1980), 42–63; and *Culture's Consequences: International Differences in Work-Related Values* (Beverly Hills, Calif.: Sage, 1984), pp. 153–212.

Uncertainty Avoidance

uncertainty avoidance A cross-cultural dimension that refers to the degree to which people are comfortable with ambiguous situations and with the inability to predict future events with assurance.

Uncertainty avoidance concerns the degree to which people are comfortable with ambiguous situations and with the inability to predict future events with assurance. People with weak uncertainty avoidance feel comfortable even though they are unsure about current activities or future events. Their attitudes are expressed in the following statements:

> Life is inherently uncertain and is most easily dealt with if taken one day at a time.
> It is appropriate to take risks in life.
> Deviation from the norm is not threatening; tolerance of differences is essential.
> Conflict and competition can be managed and used constructively.
> There should be as few rules as possible, and rules that cannot be kept should be changed or eliminated.[5]

In contrast, people characterized by strong uncertainty avoidance are uncomfortable when they are unsure what to expect. Their attitudes about uncertainty and associated issues can be stated as follows:

> The uncertainty inherent in life is threatening and must be fought continually.
> Having a stable, secure life is extremely important.
> Deviant persons and ideas are dangerous; neither should be tolerated.
> Conflict and competition can unleash aggression and must be avoided.
> There is a need for written rules and regulations; if people do not adhere to them it is because of human frailty, not defects in the rules and regulations themselves.[6]

In cultures characterized by high uncertainty avoidance, behavior is motivated at least partly by people's fear of the unknown and their need to cope with this fear. In addition, people in such cultures try to reduce or avoid uncertainty by establishing extensive formal rules. For instance, having extensive laws about marriage and divorce reduces uncertainty about the structure and longevity of family relationships. If uncertainty proves unavoidable, people with a cultural aversion to uncertainty may instead engage in *ritualistic* activities that help them cope with the anxiety that uncertainty arouses. Such activities may include the development of extensive planning systems that are designed to speculate about the future and make it seem more understandable and predictable. They dispel some of the anxiety even if the resulting plans prove to be completely useless when put into action. Seeking to cope with uncertainty, people may also hire "experts" who seem to have the ability to apply knowledge, insight, or skill to the task of making something uncertain into something understandable. Like the sorcerers or witch doctors of primitive cultures, these experts need not actually accomplish anything so long as they are perceived as understanding what others do not.

Masculinity-Femininity

Hofstede used the term masculinity to refer to the degree to which a culture is founded on values that emphasize independence, aggressiveness, dominance,

[5] Hofstede, "Motivation, Leadership, and Organization," p. 47.
[6] Ibid.

and physical strength. According to Hofstede, people in a national culture tilted toward masculinity hold beliefs such as the following:

> Sex roles in society should be clearly differentiated; men are intended to lead and women to follow.
> Independent performance and visible accomplishments are what counts in life.
> People live in order to work.
> Ambition and assertiveness provide the motivation behind behavior.
> People admire the successful achiever.[7]

Femininity, according to Hofstede, describes a society's tendency to favor such values as interdependence, compassion, empathy, and emotional openness. People in a national culture oriented toward femininity hold such beliefs as the following:

> Sex roles in society should be fluid and flexible; sexual equality is desirable.
> The quality of life is more important than personal performance and visible accomplishments.
> People work in order to live.
> Helping others provides the motivation behind behavior.
> People sympathize with the unfortunate victim.[8]

masculinity-femininity A cross-cultural dimension that refers to the degree to which a culture is founded on values that emphasize independence, aggressiveness, dominance, and physical strength, on the one hand, or interdependence, compassion, empathy, and emotional openness, on the other.

Together, masculinity and femininity form the dimension of **masculinity-femininity** in Hofstede's model of cross-cultural differences. One important effect of the differences mapped by this dimension is the way a nation's work is divided into jobs and distributed among its citizens. In masculine national cultures, women are forced to work at lower-level jobs. Managerial work is seen as the province of men who have the ambition and independence of thought required to succeed at decision making and problem solving. Women also receive less pay and recognition for their work than their male counterparts. Only in "feminine" occupations—teacher or nurse or supporting roles such as secretary or clerk—are women allowed to manage themselves. Even then, female supervisors are often required to imitate their male bosses in order to be accepted as managers.

In contrast, equality between the sexes is the norm in national cultures labeled feminine. Neither men nor women are considered to be better managers, and no particular occupation is seen as masculine or feminine. Both sexes are equally recognized for their work, and neither is required to mimic the behaviors of the other for the sake of acceptance in the workplace.

Individualism-Collectivism

individualism-collectivism A cross-cultural dimension that refers to two opposing points of view on the norms and values of a national culture—whether they should place greater emphasis on satisfying personal interests or on looking after group needs.

Individualism-collectivism, according to Hofstede, is the tendency of a culture's norms and values to emphasize either satisfying personal needs or looking after the needs of the group. From the point of view of individualism, pursuing personal interests is more important, and succeeding in the pursuit of these interests is critical to both personal and societal well-being. If each person takes care of personal interests, then everyone will be well off. Consistent with this perspective, the members of individualistic national cultures espouse the following attitudes:

> "I" is more important than "we."
> People are identified by their personal traits.

[7] Ibid. p. 49.

[8] Ibid.

Success is a personal achievement. People function most productively when working alone.

People should be free to seek autonomy, pleasure, and security through their own personal efforts.

Every member of society should take care of his personal well being and the well being of immediate family members.[9]

In contrast, the collectivist perspective emphasizes that group welfare is more important than personal interests. If you hold this view, you believe that only by belonging to a group and looking after its interests can people secure their own well-being and that of the broader society. The members of collectivistic national cultures are thus inclined to make personal sacrifices for the sake of their groups—ensuring group well-being even if personal hardships must be endured occasionally. They agree that:

"We" is more important than "I."

People are identified by the characteristics of the groups they belong to.

Success is a group achievement. People contribute to group performance, but groups alone function productively.

People can achieve order and security and fulfill their duty to society only through group membership.

Every member of society should belong to a group that will secure members' well being in exchange for loyalty and occasional self-sacrifice.[10]

How do these two very different views of the individual in society affect people's attitudes and behaviors? Principally, they determine the degree to which people feel independent, on the one hand, or interdependent, on the other. In individualistic national cultures, membership in a group is something that can be initiated and terminated whenever convenient. The individualist does not necessarily have a strong feeling of commitment to any of the groups to which she belongs. In collectivistic national cultures, however, changes in membership status can be traumatic. Joining and leaving a group can be like finding and then losing one's sense of identity. The collectivist feels a very strong sense of commitment to his group.

Power Distance

power distance A cross-cultural dimension that refers to the degree to which the members of a society accept differences in power and status among themselves.

Power distance refers to the degree to which the members of a society accept differences in power and status among themselves. In national cultures that tolerate only a small degree of power distance, norms and values specify that power differences should be minimal and political equality encouraged. People in these cultures show a strong preference for participatory decision making, and tend to distrust autocratic, hierarchical types of governance. Such people hold the following beliefs:

Superiors should consider subordinates "people just like me," and subordinates should regard superiors in the same way.

Superiors should be readily accessible to subordinates.

Using power is neither inherently good nor inherently evil; whether power is good or evil depends on the purposes for, and consequences of, its use.

Everyone in a society has equal rights, and these rights should be universally enforced.[11]

[9] Ibid., p. 48.
[10] Ibid.
[11] Ibid., p. 46.

In contrast, national cultures characterized by a large degree of power distance are based on norms and values that stipulate that power should be distributed hierarchically. People in these cultures advocate the use of autocratic authority and supervision to coordinate individual efforts. They hold the following beliefs:

> Superiors and subordinates should consider each other to be different kinds of people.
> Superiors should be inaccessible to subordinates.
> Power is a basic fact of society; notions of good and evil are irrelevant.
> Power holders are entitled to special rights and privileges.[12]

Power distance affects attitudes and behaviors by affecting the integration of a society's various parts. When only a small degree of power distance is favored, government hierarchies are noticeably flatter, and societal decision making tends to be decentralized and participatory. In contrast, where societal norms and values favor larger power distance, decision making tends to be centralized, and governmental hierarchies are taller. Authoritarian, autocratic government is the hallmark of larger power distance.

THREE CULTURAL EXAMPLES

Hofstede's four-dimensional model is not without its critics. For instance, a study that used the same four dimensions to assess the societal values of American, Japanese, and Taiwanese managers in Taiwan revealed problems with measurement validity and reliability (see Chapter 3 for a discussion of these kinds of problems).[13] Nonetheless, the Hofstede model is the most comprehensive cross-cultural framework currently available, and it provides useful insights into key international differences. Table 19-1 summarizes the results of Hofstede's analysis, indicating average scores on the four dimensions for each of the 40 countries included in the study.

What effects do the differences found by Hofstede's research have on the management of organizational behavior? To answer this question, let's look at two of Hofstede's dimensions—individualism-collectivism and power distance. We will examine the ways these two dimensions of international differences influence the management of structure, motivation, leadership, and job design.

The United States national culture is extremely individualistic. It is also oriented toward larger degrees of power distance than many of the other cultures included in Hofstede's study (see Table 19-1). As a result, the American models and practices described throughout this book are attuned to individualism and large power distance. How would the models and practices described in this book look if shaped instead by a national culture of individualism and small power distance? We will answer this question shortly when we look at how things are done in the Scandinavian countries of Norway and Sweden. As Table 19-1 shows, the cultures of both these countries are individualistic (though not to the same extreme as the U.S. culture) and oriented toward relatively small power distance.

How would the models and practices we have described in this book appear if attuned instead to collectivism and a large level of power distance? We will address this second question by analyzing the workings of Japanese organizations. As shown in Table 19-1, Japan's national culture is fairly similar to that of the United States in terms of power distance but is noticeably more collectivistic.

---

[12] Ibid.

[13] Rhysong Yeh, "Values of American, Japanese, and Taiwanese Managers in Taiwan: A Test of Hofstede's Framework," *Academy of Management Proceedings 1988*, pp. 106–110.

TABLE 19-1
A Comparison of Cultural Characteristics

NATIONAL CULTURE	UNCERTAINTY AVOIDANCE	MASCULINITY-FEMININITY	INDIVIDUALISM-COLLECTIVISM	POWER DISTANCE
Argentina	86	56	46	49
Australia	51	61	90	36
Austria	70	79	55	11
Belgium	94	54	75	65
Brazil	76	49	38	69
Canada	48	52	80	39
Chile	86	28	23	63
Colombia	80	64	13	67
Denmark	23	16	74	18
Finland	59	26	63	33
France	86	43	71	68
Great Britain	35	66	89	35
Germany	65	66	67	35
Greece	112	57	35	60
Hong Kong	29	57	25	68
India	40	56	48	77
Iran	59	43	41	58
Ireland	35	68	70	28
Israel	**81**	**47**	**54**	**13**
Italy	75	70	76	50
Japan	**92**	**95**	**46**	**54**
Mexico	82	69	30	81
Netherlands	53	14	80	38
Norway	**50**	**8**	**69**	**31**
New Zealand	49	58	79	22
Pakistan	70	50	14	55
Peru	87	42	16	64
Philippines	44	64	32	94
Portugal	104	31	27	63
South Africa	49	63	65	49
Singapore	8	48	20	74
Spain	86	42	51	57
Sweden	**29**	**5**	**71**	**31**
Switzerland	58	70	68	34
Taiwan	69	45	17	58
Thailand	64	34	20	64
Turkey	85	45	37	66
United States	46	62	91	40
Venezuela	76	73	12	81
Yugoslavia	88	21	27	76

Note: Larger numbers signify greater amounts of uncertainty avoidance, masculinity, individualism, and power distance.
Source: Based on Geert Hofstede, "Motivation, Leadership, and Organization: Do American Theories Apply Abroad?" *Organizational Dynamics* 9 (1980), 42-63.

How would the models and practices described in this book look if fitted to a culture that is characterized by collectivism and small power distance—a culture exactly opposite to the U.S. national culture? We will approach this third question by looking at practices in Israeli kibbutz organizations. The Israeli national culture is characterized by collectivism and very small power distance, and kibbutz work organizations are even more collectivistic than the Israeli norm shown in Table 19-1.

To summarize, we will begin by describing structure, motivation, leadership, and job design in Scandinavian, Japanese, and Israeli kibbutz organizations. That will give us an idea of how cross-cultural differences in individualism-collectivism and power distance affect organizational behavior. We will then conclude by comparing these descriptions with some of the ideas about management and organizational behavior that we introduced in earlier chapters.

Scandinavian Industrial Democracies

industrial democracies
Industrial organizations that are required by law to permit their members to govern themselves.

In Norway and Sweden, companies like Volvo, Saab, Hunsfos Paper, and Norsk Hydro include many participatory features in their management practices. Most Scandinavian firms are **industrial democracies**, organizations required by law to permit their members to govern themselves. In Norway, the first companies to become industrial democracies were government-owned firms. That was in the mid-1930s, after the formal establishment of national labor-management relationships. In the 1970s, many private firms followed suit and began to experiment with various types of shop-floor participation.[14] The movement began even earlier in Sweden, where labor-management cooperation was mandated by the government in 1928. Later laws led to the creation of works councils in many Swedish industrial firms. Those councils soon became participatory forums in which organizational policies related to working conditions, productivity, employee facilities, training, and corporate expansion programs could be developed through negotiations between labor and management representatives. Various types of shop-floor participation grew out of the policies formulated by these works councils.[15]

Structure. Because of their emphasis on worker participation, Norwegian and Swedish industrial democracies are structured differently than the typical American industrial firm. An American organization is usually built around a single, more-or-less bureaucratic hierarchy. Scandinavian firms, on the other hand, often incorporate a **collateral structure**—a second hierarchy of groups and committees that parallels and sometimes takes the place of the primary managerial hierarchy.[16] This collateral structure, a portion of which is shown in Figure 19-1, is made of three types of groups—works councils, special-interest committees, and semiautonomous work groups.[17] Let's look for a moment at what these groups do.

collateral structure A second hierarchy of groups and committees that parallels and sometimes takes the place of the primary managerial hierarchy in Scandinavian industrial democracies.

works council A committee of worker representatives who are elected by their peers and management representatives who are appointed by top management. It oversees policy formulation in Scandinavian industrial democracies.

The **works council** is composed of worker representatives who are elected by their peers and management representatives who are appointed by top management. There is usually only one works council in an organization. It is the council's responsibility to develop overall organizational policies and procedures.

[14] Fred E. Emery and Einar Thorsrud, *Form and Content in Industrial Democracy* (London: Tavistock, 1964), p. 24; *Democracy at Work* (Leiden, the Netherlands: Kroese, 1976), p. 46; and Bjorn Gustavson and Gerry Hunnius, *New Patterns of Work Reform: The Case of Norway* (Oslo: Universitetsforlaget, 1981), p. 37.

[15] *Job Reform in Sweden* (Stockholm: Swedish Employers' Confederation [SAF], 1975), p. 6.

[16] Dale E. Zand, "Collateral Organization: A New Change Strategy," *Journal of Applied Behavioral Science* 10 (1974), 63–89.

[17] H. Lindestadt and G. Rosander, *The Scan Vast Report* (Stockholm: Swedish Employers' Confederation [SAF], 1977), pp. 3–12; Fred E. Emery and Einar Thorsrud, *Democracy at Work* (Leiden, the Netherlands: Kroese, 1976), pp. 27–32; and Joep F. Bolweg, *Job Design and Industrial Democracy: The Case of Norway* (Leiden, the Netherlands: Martinus Nijhoff, 1976), pp. 98–109.

FIGURE 19-1

The Structure of Advisory Committees in a Scandinavian Firm

The collateral structure of Kockums, Malmo, a shipbuilder, has two layers—general advisory committees clustered around the company's works council and special advisory committees charged with providing input about specific topics and issues. *Adapted with the publisher's permission from H. G. Jones,* Planning and Productivity in Sweden *(London: Croom Helm, 1976), p. 111.*

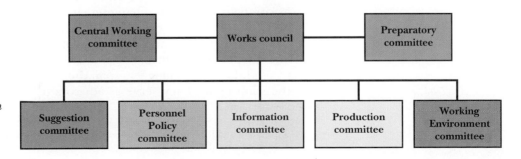

Works councils have little or no direct decision-making power, but they provide a forum in which worker representatives can express their opinions and thereby be instrumental in shaping the mission and strategic direction of the firm.

Special-interest committees, which are also composed of worker and manager representatives, provide the works council with advice on specific issues, such as job design, plant sanitation, personnel practices, and environmental safety. These committees combine with middle management to produce yearly reports that assist works councils with the task of formulating company policies. Such reports might include an analysis of water and air pollution caused by the company, a set of guidelines for curbing absenteeism, or a proposal about how to reduce the amount of inventory kept on hand.

Semiautonomous work groups consist of groups of employees who are given the responsibility for completing a particular job. As described in Chapter 17, in each group members negotiate the breakdown of work responsibilities into individualized tasks and decide who will perform these tasks. They may also have a say in hiring and firing decisions affecting group membership.

In addition to these three types of groups, works councils are typically supported by several general advisory committees located lower in the organization hierarchy. Such advisory groups may include suggestion committees, personnel-policy committees, or information committees. As a whole, the collateral system shown in Figure 19-1 provides a structure in which employees and management can work together to influence company policies and procedures.

Motivation. In Scandinavian industrial democracies, national welfare programs meet most lower-order needs for food, clothing, shelter, and health care. Methods of motivating employees, therefore, are aimed at satisfying higher-order needs for autonomy, growth, and development. The semiautonomous work groups we have just described are a good example of this approach, for these groups give employees the opportunity to control their own working lives—to manage themselves. Scandinavian managers consider semiautonomous groups an important means of encouraging productivity as well as combating turnover and absenteeism.

In most Scandinavian firms, wages consist of a base payment designed to further ensure employees' basic welfare, an incentive payment based on the productivity of the semiautonomous work group an employee interacts with, and a second incentive payment based on the number of job skills a worker has.[18] This system of payment reflects and reinforces the group-oriented structure of the Scandinavian industrial firm and also encourages continued personal development.

Leadership. As you might expect, Scandinavian managers often do not supervise employees directly, nor are they always required to issue direct orders to coordinate work activities. Instead, they usually function as boundary spanners who facilitate relations within and between groups while allowing employees to handle many coordination responsibilities themselves. Top managers span organizational boundaries. They gather information about the organization's environment, such as competitors' actions, changing customer tastes, and raw-material availability, and relay it to the works council. Then, with input from the company works council, top management charts the long-term policies that establish the direction and purpose of the firm.

Middle-level managers span the boundaries between top management and the shop floor. They serve as advisors to special interest groups or join these

---

[18] *Pay Reform in Sweden* (Stockholm: Swedish Employers' Confederation [SAF], 1977) p. 18; and H. Lindestadt and J. P. Norstedt, *Autonomous Groups and Payment by Result* (Stockholm: Swedish Employers' Confederation [SAF], 1973).

groups as managerial representatives. Lower-level managers span boundaries between semiautonomous work groups. They coordinate intergroup relations on the shop floor by helping to distribute raw materials and forward completed work. They also serve as interpersonal facilitators within semiautonomous groups, resolving conflicts and helping group members interact in the course of participatory decision making.

Job Design. In Scandinavian industrial democracies, jobs are frequently designed according to the sociotechnical approach described in Chapter 17. You will recall that this approach is based on the notion that individualized, standardized, simplified jobs not only prevent workers from satisfying social, esteem, and actualization needs but subject them to boring and repetitive work.[19] In an effort to guard against these negative effects of job simplification, Scandinavian industrial democracies divide work to be done into job clusters that are distributed to the semiautonomous work groups we've described. Group members then have the freedom to determine task assignments, work procedures, and personnel policies in their own groups.[20]

Large Japanese Corporations

Unlike Scandinavian industrial democracies, large Japanese corporations are based on hierarchical management procedures. However, they also support and depend on close interpersonal relations.[21] The Japanese organization is a product of many influences. Most important was the cultural seclusion of the country between 1634 and 1868 and the feudal and kinship traditions that developed during this era. The period of seclusion encouraged the development of a homogeneous culture based on feudal master-servant obligations that permeated the life of the family as well as societal life. These obligations created a kind of permanent state of dependence within families and between families and their feudal lords. Children were obligated to follow the wishes of their parents, who were required to obey their feudal master. Feudal *zaibatsu* organizations were built around these chains of vertical obligation, passing from children through father to master. The *zaibatsu* were large companies spanning many businesses and owned by wealthy, powerful clans.

The period of Allied occupation that followed World War II also had a profound influence on Japanese organizations. During the occupation, in an effort to westernize Japanese businesses, American military commanders forcibly disbanded the *zaibatsu* and required companies to permit the formation of workers' unions. In addition, massive capital restoration programs funded by the U.S. and its allies enabled the Japanese to build modern, sophisticated production facilities. Subsequently, Japanese businesses reorganized into six industrial conglomerates (Mitsui, Mitsubishi, Sumitomo, Fuyo, Sanwa, and Dai-Ichi Kangyo) and a number of independent firms, such as Nissan, Toyota, and Sony. The six conglomerates were essentially the original *zaibatsu*, now centered in banks rather than feudal clans. In addition, a collection of smaller, "satellite" companies developed to supply the large corporations with raw materials, parts, and supplementary labor. These companies often started out under the management of a retiree from one of the large organizations.

[19] P. G. Herbst, *Alternatives to Hierarchies* (Leiden, the Netherlands: Kroese, 1976); and G. I. Susman, *Autonomy at Work: A Sociotechnical Analysis of Participative Management* (New York: Praeger, 1976).

[20] Ulla Ressner and Evy Gunnarsson, *Group Organised Work in the Automated Office* (Brookfield, Vt.: Gower, 1986).

[21] Peter B. Smith, "The Effectiveness of Japanese Styles of Management: A Review and Critique," *Journal of Occupational Psychology* 57 (1984), 121–36.

Structure. Outwardly, the structures of most large Japanese corporations resemble the functional or divisional structures of large American companies. In fact, Japanese organization charts often display the same hierarchy of vertical relations that characterize an American firm's organization chart. In Japanese firms, however, these vertical relationships are often patterned after the parent-child (*oyabun-kobun*) relations of traditional Japanese families. In the organizational *oyabun-kobun* relationship, a subordinate is encouraged to feel loyal and obligated to his superior as well as dependent on him. This feeling of dependence in turn encourages—in fact, requires—acquiescence to autocratic, hierarchy-bound management policies and practices.[22]

Subordinates' loyalty and dependence is tested regularly by *ringi* decision making. In this process, decision making is initiated by subordinates, and possible decisions are circulated upward for superiors' approval. (The Japanese word *ringi* derives from *ringiseido*, which means "a system of reverential inquiry about a superior's intentions.") Though seemingly participatory, this form of decision making is often little more than an exercise in anticipating superiors' wishes. Subordinates try to make only those suggestions that their superiors will approve in order to avoid embarrassment.[23] Japanese aversion to standing out in a crowd and concerns about saving face would make such embarrassment intolerable.

Although at first glance, Japanese and American organization charts look quite similar, there is a critical difference between the Japanese and American approaches to structuring large organizations. In American organizations, the vertical lines of command that appear in organization charts are meant to be the only formal channels of communication. To communicate with someone at the same horizontal level, an employee is expected to pass a message up the hierarchy to a superior who then sends it downward to the final recipient. In Japanese corporations, however, whether they are conglomerates or independents, certain formally designated *horizontal* relationships are accorded the same degree of importance as the vertical relationships depicted in the organization chart. These horizontal relationships, which allow communication to flow across the hierarchy rather than having to go up and down, connect managers who entered the company at the same time and are encouraged by several socialization processes.

More specifically, the managerial hierarchy in most large Japanese firms is discontinuous. Lower-level managers are recruited from the ranks of shop-floor workers but cannot rise above the rank of foreman. Middle-level managers are recruited from Japanese universities and are able to rise to the top of their company. When they first join a large Japanese firm, candidates for middle-management positions are trained in groups, and throughout their careers with the company, they are encouraged to maintain contact with other members of their "entering class." Most white-collar employees in large corporations remain with the same firm from college graduation until retirement. During the period of training, a Japanese manager rotates from one functional area to another, often becoming more of a generalist than a specialist and cultivating a collection of horizontal linkages that unite him with management peers across functional boundaries.[24]

latticework hierarchy The structure of vertical and horizontal relationships found in many large Japanese corporations.

This **latticework hierarchy** of vertical and horizontal relationships, which connects Japanese superiors and subordinates in a single managerial unit, is

---

[22] Ronald Dore, *British Factory—Japanese Factory* (Berkeley: University of California Press, 1973); Peter F. Drucker, *Management* (New York: Harper & Row, 1974); and Nina Hatvany and C. V. Pucik, "Japanese Management Practices and Productivity," *Organizational Dynamics* 9 (1981), 5–21.

[23] For further discussion on this topic see S. Prakash Sethi, Nobuaki Namiki, and Carl L. Swanson, *The False Promise of the Japanese Miracle: Illusions and Realities of the Japanese Management System* (Boston: Pitman, 1984), pp. 34–41.

[24] Robert E. Cole, *Japanese Blue Collar* (Berkeley: University of California Press, 1971) p. 122; and R. J. Samuels, "Looking behind Japan Inc.," *Technology Review* 83 (1981), 43–46.

analogous to a comprehensive lateral linkage mechanism. Continuing relations among management peers from different functional areas, such as marketing and manufacturing, help stimulate harmony and coordination between functional groups. Do you think, then, that the Japanese latticework structure resembles the American matrix structure? Both types of structure involve simultaneous functional and divisional grouping. Note, however, that the latticework structure falls short of being a true matrix, because in large Japanese firms, decision-making authority remains highly centralized. Thus the Japanese latticework structure is unique.

Motivation. Managing motivation in large Japanese corporations is primarily a matter of reinforcing each employee's sense of loyalty, obligation, and dependence on superiors and coworkers. The widespread practice among Japanese firms of offering lifetime employment (to age 56) to their permanent employees goes a long way toward encouraging workers' loyalty. Japanese employees find it difficult to behave disloyally toward a firm that is willing to commit itself to them up to their retirement.[25]

nenko system A Japanese system of payment in which the pay an employee receives is determined by a basic wage plus merit supplements and job-level allowances.

Loyalty is also encouraged by the **nenko system** of wage payment that is used throughout Japan. Under the *nenko* system, the employee's pay is composed of a basic wage plus merit supplements and job-level allowances. The basic wage, which constitutes about 55 percent of total pay, consists of the employee's starting wage plus yearly increases. Those increases are determined (in order of importance) by seniority, or length of service with the company; age; and supervisory ratings on such qualities as seriousness, attendance, performance, and cooperativeness.[26]

Merit supplements make up an additional 15 percent of the employee's pay and are based on supervisory assessments of specific job behaviors. They are meant, in principle, to reward exemplary performance. In fact, merit supplements are heavily influenced by seniority, because they are calculated as a percentage of the basic wage. Moreover, junior employees' performance is typically rated below senior employees' work regardless of real differences between the two.[27] Clearly, Japanese merit supplements reward loyalty and longevity with the company.

Job-level allowances, which account for about 30 percent of each worker's total pay, are based on the importance of each worker's job in relation to the other jobs in the organization. Job-level allowances may sound similar to pay increments that result from American job-evaluation procedures. In Japan, however, each employee's position in the hierarchy of jobs—which affects his job-level allowance—is more directly influenced by seniority than by skill.[28]

Thus, as you can see, seniority is the single most important factor in determining a Japanese worker's compensation. It affects the basic wage, it affects merit supplements, and it affects the job-level allowances. The large Japanese firm is like a family in the sense that its employees spend their lives in a stable social setting and receive positions of increasing importance as they grow older.[29] Along with the *nenko* method of compensation, this familylike system rewards its members for loyalty to the company over everything else. Employees' decisions

[25] Cole, *Japanese Blue Collar*, pp. 72–100; and Dore, *British Factory—Japanese Factory*, pp. 74–113. It is important to note that *nenko* employment occurs only in large firms and applies to no more than a third of Japan's labor force; for further information, see T. K. Oh, "Japanese Management: A Critical Review," *Academy of Management Review* 1 (1976), 14–25.

[26] Cole, *Japanese Blue Collar*, p. 75.

[27] Dore, *British Factory—Japanese Factory*, p. 112.

[28] Cole, *Japanese Blue Collar*, p. 79; and Dore, *British Factory—Japanese Factory*, p. 390. Review Chapter 9 for further information on job evaluation in the United States.

[29] Rodney Clark, *The Japanese Company* (New Haven, Conn.: Yale University Press, 1979), p. 38.

to attend work and to perform productively grow out of this sense of loyalty and obligation to the familylike firm.

Leadership. The primary leadership task in large Japanese corporations is to guarantee the continued existence of vertical dependence—the acceptance of hierarchical relationships and obedience to superiors. At the lowest levels of management, shop-floor foremen (Japanese supervisors are still virtually all male) wear two hats. By day, they perform the same types of jobs as their subordinates. Indeed, to the casual observer, superior and subordinate seem almost indistinguishable at work. Away from work, however, foremen inquire at the homes of sick employees about their health and the welfare of their families. From time to time, they also do such things as giving subordinates small gifts and hosting social events for them and their families. In return, subordinates are led, by their sense of *giri*, or "obligation," to perform as their supervisors direct. Subordinates cannot fully repay their obligations by returning visits, reciprocating gift giving, helping sponsor social events, or even following orders. Japanese *giri* requires unending obedience. Lower-level management's primary leadership function, then, is to maintain subordinates' followership. This system enables management in large Japanese firms to operate autocratically.[30]

Leaders in middle and upper management ensure similar followership among their subordinates by immersing them in a program of intensive socialization during organizational entry. Initially, groups of new members learn the history of the organization, its mission, and its values. Then, as we have indicated, these "entering classes" spend several years together rotating among functional departments to develop horizontal ties and acquire a generalist's understanding of the organization. During this period, management leaders emphasize vertical relations by teaching and repeatedly encouraging the use of the *ringi* decision-making process that we have already discussed. By the time they have completed the process of socialization, managerial employees have learned the importance of followership, called *tsukiai*, and typically behave accordingly.[31]

Job Design. In the United States, jobs are usually individualized and allocated among the members of an organization on a one-to-one basis. Because many Japanese corporations adopted American industrial engineering practices during the postwar occupation, Japanese assembly lines today are often composed of similarly individualized tasks.[32] However, the interpretation of such jobs is de-

[30] Dore, *British Factory—Japanese Factory*, p. 228.

[31] Reiko Atsumi, "Tsukiai—Obligatory Personal Relationships of Japanese White-Collar Company Employees," *Human Organization* 38 (1979), 63–70.

[32] Koji Matsumoto, *Organizing for Higher Productivity: An Analysis of Japanese Systems and Practices* (Tokyo: Asian Productivity Organization, 1982), pp. 27–31.

In 1990 the Japanese Ministry of International Trade and Industry (MITI) issued an industrial policy paper in which, against tradition, it put human concerns before strictly business issues. MITI came out strongly for longer vacations for employees and better child-care facilities for them. One result was the establishment in Tokyo of a combined nursery school and home for the aged. Some of the older people help to care for the young ones, and all gain from companionship with the children. There are a number of such combined facilities in the United States, but formal child or elder care has lagged in Japan largely because families in which both parents work outside the home are rare and the extended family system usually provides such care.
Source: "Looking Ahead," Fortune, September 24, 1990.

cidedly Japanese. Japanese workers consider the tasks they perform parts of a larger, group job. Consistent with this interpretation, they do not wish to be publicly recognized for good personal performance, and they prefer to share the blame for poor productivity with others, regardless of personal fault.[33] Although the tasks themselves may be individualized, task performance is seen as a group activity.

Away from assembly lines, work is more often divided into group tasks and assigned to groups of employees. Quality Circles (QCs), which we discussed in Chapter 17, are representative of the kinds of groups often formed among shop-floor employees to encourage working together. On the surface, a QC might seem similar to a semiautonomous work group formed by the sociotechnical method of job design employed in Scandinavian industrial democracies. However, semiautonomous groups in Scandinavian firms are formed by means of participatory decision making in works councils and other advisory committees, whereas groups in Japanese corporations are formed by edict from above. Furthermore, Scandinavian groups are intended to allow workers to participate directly in managing their working lives. Participation of this type is rare in Japanese work groups. In Japan, the family, or parent-child, model rules the work group as it does the larger society, and superiors retain control over subordinates' actions at all times.

Israeli Kibbutz Industries

Israeli kibbutzim combine the member commitment found in large Japanese corporations with the participatory aspect of Scandinavian industrial democracies. The **kibbutz** (*kibbutzim* is the plural form) is a close-knit community of people organized on the principles of collective ownership and direct participation in self-governance. The kibbutzim, which range in size from 40 to 2,000 members, were started early in the 20th century by young European Jews who moved to Palestine to escape anti-Semitic persecution. Consistent with the philosophies of the European youth movements of the day, kibbutz settlers favored Marxist economics and a rural, naturalistic lifestyle. These beliefs led them to establish a number of small agricultural communities in which they shared everything from basic foodstuffs to civic obligations.

Newly formed kibbutzim were immediately threatened by Arab neighbors, who held conflicting religious beliefs and whose lifestyles were based on open-land herding. In addition, most *kibbutzniks* (kibbutz members) had little farming experience and were quite poor. In order to survive, members had to share the few possessions they had brought with them as well as the wages they received for working outside the kibbutz. Of course, that fit in with their Marxist beliefs. After several years of hardship, the success that followed reinforced kibbutzniks' belief in the importance of sharing and helping each other out. Consequently, contemporary kibbutzim are still organized around principles that stress sharing both work responsibilities and the material results.[34]

Structure. In most kibbutzim, even clothing is owned collectively, and it is cleaned, mended, and distributed in central facilities. Children spend time with their parents each day but are raised in communal quarters. Individuals and families alike eat many of their meals in central dining halls. Kibbutzniks are

kibbutz A close-knit community of people located in Israel and organized on the principles of collective ownership and direct participation in self-governance.

[33] William G. Ouchi, *Theory Z: How American Business Can Meet the Japanese Challenge* (Reading, Mass.: Addison-Wesley, 1981), pp. 48–49.

[34] H. Darin-Drabkin, *The Other Society* (Harcourt, Brace, & World, 1963) pp. 66–70.

allowed only a limited number of personal possessions, most of which are received as gifts from nonkibbutz relatives.[35] Because the material goods of each kibbutz are collectively owned, decisions about their acquisition and distribution must be reached through public consensus. Thus weekly assembly meetings are held in which voting members participate in determining kibbutz policies and procedures.

In these meetings, interested parties raise issues that need to be decided, and after open discussion, participants are polled and the decision is made. The secretariat—an administrative board consisting of elected officials—is empowered only to implement policies approved by the kibbutz assembly. No official is permitted to act outside assembly mandates. Thus, as Figure 19-2 shows, the structure of an Israeli kibbutz is inverted, unlike the structures of American, Scandinavian, and Japanese firms. The officers of the kibbutz occupy positions of lower status than the assembly, which consists of the kibbutz membership as a whole.

The kibbutz depicted in Figure 19-2, like many kibbutzim, operates one business—a farm. Some kibbutzim, however, have added industrial branches to supplement their agricultural activities. These branches are organized around industrial assemblies and internal governance processes that reflect those of the larger kibbutz. Each industrial branch's officials are elected by its work force and are charged with implementing decisions reached by the branch's assembly. Decisions that might affect the larger kibbutz—major decisions about industrial operations, for example—are taken by the full kibbutz assembly. Officials of the kibbutz secretariat oversee industrial operations to make sure they conform with

---

[35] Melford Spiro, *Kibbutz: Venture in Utopia* (Cambridge, Mass.: Harvard University Press, 1958), p. 207; Yosef Criden and Saadia Gelb, *The Kibbutz Experience: Dialogue in Kfar Blum* (New York: Herzl, 1974), p. 100; Joseph Blasi, *The Communal Experience of the Kibbutz* (New Brunswick, N.J.: Transaction Books, 1986).

FIGURE 19-2

The Structure of an Agricultural Kibbutz

Amitai Etzioni, *The Organizational Structure of the Kibbutz* (New York: Arno Press, 1980), p. 266. Reprinted with the author's permission.

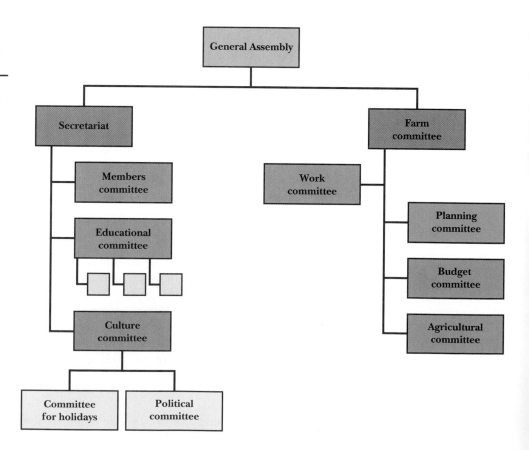

INTERNATIONAL DIMENSIONS: ORGANIZATIONAL BEHAVIOR ABROAD

kibbutz policies. Nevertheless, kibbutz industrial branches are the most decentralized, participatory form of industrial organization in the world.[36]

Motivation. Kibbutzniks are motivated by concerns about the security of their community and by values that encourage hard work. The founders of the first kibbutzim believed that people realized their true worth only by working hard, and motivation in the kibbutz has continued to derive from the notion that physical labor is an intrinsically important endeavor. Simcha Ronen compared the job satisfaction of workers in a kibbutz industrial branch with the satisfaction of industrial employees in Israel's private sector. Ronen found that kibbutzniks' satisfaction was strongly influenced by the tasks they performed. In contrast, private-sector workers in Ronen's study based job satisfaction on such things as power, prestige, and wealth. Their degree of satisfaction was strongly related to the wages and benefits they received, not to the tasks they performed.[37]

Kibbutznik motivation also grows out of concerns for community well-being. Within the kibbutz, every member derives equal benefit from kibbutz resources. For example, everyone gets the same amount and kind of food, everyone gets the same clothing to wear, everyone lives in a similar kind of structure. This system of wageless compensation based on egalitarian sharing—except for cash allowances for travel outside the kibbutz and small amounts of pocket money for miscellaneous purposes—guarantees the well-being of all kibbutz members. Because members need not concern themselves with personal welfare, they are free to direct their full attention to improving the state of the kibbutz as a whole. Kibbutzniks identify this freedom from concern for personal security a valuable reward of kibbutz membership. Desires to preserve this freedom are an important motivational force underlying kibbutznik performance.[38]

Leadership. Leadership is shared by all members of each kibbutz, being vested in the kibbutz assembly rather than in the hands of a small management group. Kibbutz officials, as we have already noted, occupy positions *beneath* the general assembly in the inverted kibbutz hierarchy. They are elected by the assembly, serve fixed terms of office, and cannot hold the same office for more than one consecutive term. As a result, the ability of any officeholder to amass the power needed to function as an autonomous leader is strictly limited. On occasion, a small number of members may rotate among the various kibbutz offices, allowing the possible emergence of a dominant group. However, since participation in the kibbutz assembly is nearly universal—all members who are kibbutz-born and 19 or older or who have completed a one-year naturalization program can vote in assembly meetings—officials are under the watchful eyes of every other member. It is virtually impossible to try to usurp the assembly's power without being caught.

Similarly, leadership in kibbutz industrial branches is vested in branch assemblies. Officials in each branch are elected by the branch's assembly and are required to rotate out of office after completing their term. As in the wider kibbutz, ethical codes and member sentiment both oppose the emergence of officeholder-leaders.[39]

[36] A. S. Tannenbaum, B. Kavcic, M. Rosner, M. Vianello, and G. Weiser, *Hierarchy in Organizations* (San Francisco: Jossey-Bass, 1974), p. 34.

[37] Ronen, "Personal Values: A Basis for Work Motivational Set and Work Attitudes," *Organizational Behavior and Human Performance* 21 (1978) 80–107.

[38] Criden and Gelb, *The Kibbutz Experience*, p. 33.

[39] Criden and Gelb, *The Kibbutz Experience*, pp. 37–57; and Blasi, *The Communal Experience of the Kibbutz*, p. 112.

Job Design. All kibbutz jobs are shared, and all kibbutzniks work at them from childhood onward. Adult members of the kibbutz feel that introduction to the community's work at a young age is tremendously important, because it teaches children about the relationship between personal productivity and the well-being of the overall community.[40] Reflecting this primary concern with the welfare of the kibbutz, jobs are designed and assigned so as to enhance the society's welfare. Personal abilities and interests are not often given much attention. In practice, if a kibbutz member has skills that qualify her for a particular job, and if that job is open, she will be assigned to it. However, members who fail to make such a match are assigned to a general labor pool and may be drafted into any kibbutz branch that is short of workers.

Jobs are assigned by branch officials operating according to assembly mandates. All workers rotate in and out of less desirable jobs so as to share the burden of disagreeable work. For example, the lowest-level kitchen jobs are filled in this manner, although a permanent staff of kitchen workers is also maintained. So although kibbutz jobs are designed and assigned as individualized tasks, because members rotate among jobs and never get attached to any one, they tend to see their jobs as just a small part of the overall work of the community.

A CROSS-CULTURAL COMPARISON

We have briefly described several important features of Scandinavian industrial democracies, large Japanese businesses, and Israeli kibbutz industries. How do these three kinds of organizations compare with one another and with the models and practices described throughout this book? What cultural effects are uncovered by such comparisons?

To respond to these questions, recall how most American business firms are structured. They are hierarchies in which coordination is achieved mainly by standardization implemented from above and secondarily by direct supervision (Chapter 15). Employee attendance and performance are motivated by rewards that satisfy personal needs and are received in proportion to personal performance (Chapter 7). Leadership in American firms is largely a task of coordinating the work of individuals and looking after their personal well-being (Chapter 12). Jobs in the United States are designed and assigned as individualized tasks (Chapter 17).

These features of American business firms would seem to reflect the individualism and large power distance of the American national culture. Let's isolate the effects of individualism by looking for similarities in the way things are done in U.S. business firms and Scandinavian industrial democracies. In both, people are motivated to do their jobs by the desire to satisfy personal needs, and achievement on the job is seen as attributable to individual effort. In Scandinavian countries, however, specific tasks and procedures are often performed by groups and group incentives are sometimes used to motivate a high level of performance.

To examine some of the effects of collectivism on organizational behavior, let's look for similarities in the workings of large Japanese businesses and Israeli kibbutzim, both are surrounded by collectivistic national cultures. One similarity is that work motivation grows out of a sense of loyalty and a concern for the well-being of everyone in the organization. Another similarity is that both Japanese and Israeli employees view job performance as something people can accomplish only by working together.

Based on these comparisons, it appears that the amount of individualism or collectivism in the national culture has major effects on employee motivation

[40] Milford Spiro, *Children of the Kibbutz* (Cambridge, Mass.: Harvard University Press, 1975), p. 266.

FIGURE 19-3

A Two-Dimensional Comparative Analysis

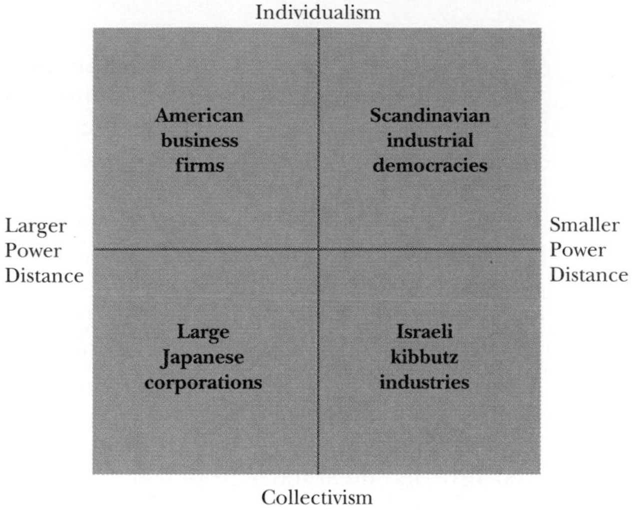

Individualism

| American business firms | Scandinavian industrial democracies |

Larger Power Distance — Smaller Power Distance

| Large Japanese corporations | Israeli kibbutz industries |

Collectivism

and job design. Cultural individualism focuses attention on the performance and satisfaction of the individual. Cultural collectivism directs attention to the performance and satisfaction of the group.

What about the effects of power distance? Let's begin by examining the workings of American business organizations and large Japanese businesses, both of which are located in national cultures oriented toward large power distance. Structurally, these firms strongly emphasize coordination processes that are based on a combination of rules, procedures, and direct orders issued by hierarchical superiors. They use direction rather than participation to integrate work activities. Leadership activities reflect this directive orientation, focusing on supervising subordinates and making sure that superiors' orders are carried out.

However, in Scandinavian industrial democracies and Israeli kibbutz industries, both of which are surrounded by national cultures with small power distance, structural relationships are far more participatory. People who occupy positions lower in the structural hierarchy are able to advise hierarchical superiors or even become directly involved in decision making. Leadership is more a process of facilitating communication and mutual adjustment than one of ensuring that subordinates follow the directives of superiors.

From this pattern, we can conclude that the power distance of the surrounding national culture has strong effects on organizational structure and leadership processes. Large power distance stimulates directive structural relationships and leadership that is focused on supervision. Small power distance supports participatory structural relationships and leadership that concentrates on interpersonal facilitation.

In sum, the cross-cultural comparison depicted in Figure 19-3 suggests that features of the surrounding national culture can have significant effects on the characteristics of an organization and on the management of organizational behavior. With this in mind, we will now see how to fit management procedures to the demands of different national cultures.

MANAGING IN A MULTICULTURAL WORLD

Although the cross-cultural differences we have discussed are still very much in evidence, it is sometimes suggested that management practices throughout the world are becoming more alike as nations grow modern and prosperous.[41] Consistent with this suggestion, practices developed in one culture are occasionally borrowed for use in another. For instance, sociotechnical interventions patterned after Scandinavian programs and quality circles resembling Japanese QC groups are so prevalent in contemporary American companies that they are considered part of the U.S. approach to job design. You will recall that we discussed both of these interventions in Chapter 17.

convergence hypothesis A theoretical assertion that organizations and management practices throughout the world are growing more alike.

Instances of cross-cultural borrowing like these seem to support the **convergence hypothesis**, that organizations and management practices throughout the world are growing more alike.[42] In a review of studies that have examined this hypothesis, John Child found some evidence for convergence but also some evidence for divergence, or continued cross-cultural differences. Interestingly, Child found that the studies that supported convergence typically focused on organizational variables, such as structure and technology, whereas the studies that revealed divergence in practices usually concerned employee attitudes, beliefs, and behaviors.[43] He concluded that organizations themselves may be becoming more alike throughout the world but that people in these organizations are maintaining their cultural distinctiveness. Therefore, the cultural convergence hypothesis is not entirely valid: management in a multicultural world currently requires an understanding of cultural differences and will continue to do so for quite some time.

Understanding Behavior in Other Cultures

How can the information in this chapter help managers understand cultural differences? You can find out by putting yourself into the managerial role and applying the Hofstede model to diagnose several intercultural differences. In the following examples, try using the four dimensions of the model to explain the differences described.

1. *Feelings about progress.* Being modern and future oriented is highly valued in many of today's national cultures. In others, tradition, the status quo, and the past are highly revered. From the modernist perspective, something that has been around for a while may seem old-fashioned or obsolete. To a traditionalist, the same thing may be perceived as trustworthy, proven, and worthwhile.

2. *Tendencies toward confrontation or consensus.* In some national cultures, it is important to smooth over differences to preserve agreement. Emphasis is placed on building consensus among coworkers and avoiding personal confrontation. In other national cultures, conflict and confrontation are accepted or even encouraged. In such cultures, conflict is often perceived as a signal of the need for change.

3. *Locus of control.* Some national cultures instill a sense of personal responsibility for the outcomes of individual behaviors. Others focus on external, social causes to explain similar outcomes. Although rewarding people for personal performance is logical in a culture that values personal respon-

---

[41] Clark Kerr, John T. Dunlop, Frederick H. Harbison, and Charles A. Meyers, *Industrialism and Industrial Man* (Cambridge, Mass.: Harvard University Press, 1960), pp. 282–88; John Kenneth Galbraith, *The New Industrial State* (Boston: Houghton Mifflin, 1967), pp. 11–21; and F. Harbison, "Management in Japan," in *Management in the Industrial World: An International Analysis*, ed. F. Harbison and C. A. Meyers (New York: McGraw-Hill, 1959), pp. 249–64.

[42] Peter J. Dowling and Randall S. Schuler, *International Dimensions of Human Resource Management* (Boston: PWS-Kent, 1990), pp. 163–64.

[43] Child, "Culture, Contingency, and Capitalism in the Cross-National Study of Organizations," in *Research in Organizational Behavior*, ed. Larry L. Cummings and Barry M. Staw (Greenwich, Conn.: JAI Press, 1981), pp. 303–56.

sibility, it may not be understood in a culture that believes that behaviors are caused by outside forces.

4. *Status and social position.* In some national cultures, status is accorded on the basis of family, class, ethnicity, or even accent. High-status people in such cultures are often allowed to impose their will on people of lower status even when such people are as knowledgeable and competent as they. In other cultures, where status is earned through personal achievement, shared governance—majority rule or participatory decision making—is more apt to be valued over personal fiat. In such cultures, expertise usually outranks social position in determining who will be involved in decision-making procedures.[44]

Were you able to explain the first example? As you probably figured out, differing feelings about progress are produced by cross-cultural differences in uncertainty avoidance. Cultures with aversion to uncertainty honor tradition and feel threatened by new ways of doing things. Cultures with tolerance for uncertainty more readily embrace modern ways.

The second example focuses on conflict avoidance, a cultural tendency that is also closely associated with uncertainty avoidance. Simply put, conflict creates uncertainty, and cultures that cannot deal with uncertainty cannot handle the competition and aggression that conflict unleashes. In contrast, cultures that can tolerate uncertainty are also able to cope with conflict.

The third example concerns locus of control, and as you have probably surmised, arises out of cross-cultural differences in individualism and collectivism. On the one hand, the sense of personal responsibility stimulated by believing that the locus of control for personal behavior lies inside the individual is consistent with the norms and values of an individualistic national culture. On the other hand, the focus on social causes for behaviors that is prompted by an external locus of control is compatible with cultural collectivism.

The fourth example shows how cultural differences in power distance can show up as differences in the way status and social position are accorded and perceived. Cultures in which status and position are birthrights—the special-privilege approach—also tend to be oriented toward large power distance. In contrast, cultures in which status and position are awarded according to personal abilities—the equal opportunity approach—are more inclined toward smaller power distance.

Managing Cross-Cultural Differences

Understanding international differences such as the ones depicted in our four cross-cultural examples is important for managers. It can help them determine whether they need to alter familiar management practices before using them abroad. Looking beyond our four examples, a glance back at Table 19-1 indicates that the national cultures of the United States and Canada are approximately equal in terms of power distance, uncertainty avoidance, masculinity, and individualism. Owing to this similarity, U.S. managers can expect to succeed in Canada and Canadian managers can anticipate working effectively in the United States without making major adjustments to customary management practices.

According to Hofstede's findings, however, the level of uncertainty avoidance in Denmark is about half that found in the United States and Canada. Therefore, American managers are likely to find it necessary to tailor their normal way of doing things if required to work in Denmark. More generally, managers

---

[44] For additional examples, see Leonard Sayles, "A 'Primer' on Cultural Dimensions," *Issues and Observations of the Center for Creative Leadership* 9 (1989), 8–9.

MANAGEMENT ISSUES

How Ugly Are Today's Americans?

The year 1958 marked the publication of *The Ugly American*, a novel in which William J. Lederer and Eugene Burdick criticized the United States foreign policy in Southeast Asia. The late 1950s were a time of unrest throughout the area as the French fought Communist armies in Vietnam and Russian agents spread Communist doctrine in the neighboring countries of Laos, Cambodia, and Burma. Through a sequence of stories about events in the fictional country of Sarkhan, Lederer and Burdick described how the Russians learned the local language, traveled the countryside, and provided basic necessities that made the lives of farming peasants somewhat easier. In contrast, according to Lederer and Burdick, American ambassadors assigned to duty in Southeast Asia often refused to learn the language, rarely if ever ventured out of their embassy compounds, and were interested only in building highways and dams that had high political visibility but lacked useful function. It was thus no wonder that the Russians were more successful in winning the hearts and minds of the local population. By bringing in American ways and expecting the locals to adapt, the Americans were devaluing the surrounding national culture and offending the very people they had been sent to assist.

Lederer and Burdick's book was a huge success in the U.S. and the term *ugly American* was soon applied to anyone who went abroad and refused to respect and abide by local customs. Discussions in schools, businesses, and churches focused on the importance of developing greater sensitivity and respect for the many different cultures throughout the world. Americans agonized over their cultural "ugliness" and sought ways to eliminate it.

More than three decades later, late in 1990, a military coalition that included a large contingent of American soldiers was gathering in Saudi Arabia to shield against an Iraqi attack from neighboring Kuwait. The dominant religion in Saudi Arabia, Wahhabism (a puritanical strain of Sunni Islam), forbade women to drive, to travel unaccompanied, or to expose anything other than their hands and eyes in public. At the request of Saudi officials, American military commanders instructed all female soldiers to wear long sleeves (despite the desert heat), refrain from driving in Saudi towns, and travel in groups that included men.*

* William Dowell, Dean Fischer, and Christopher Ogden, "Lifting the Veil: A Secretive and Deeply Conservative Realm, Saudi Arabia Suddenly Finds Itself on the Sword Edge of Change," *Time*, September 24, 1990, pp. 38–44.

These instructions caused an immediate uproar in the U.S. In speeches before Congress, representatives likened the Saudi's treatment of women to the treatment of blacks under South Africa's system of apartheid. Women's-rights organizations roundly criticized Saudi practices and the American military's hasty compliance. Breaking ranks with the military, some female soldiers even complained during television interviews that the restrictions were unfair.

The controversy in Saudi Arabia grew out of a clash between the norms and values of the increasingly feminine U.S. national culture and those of the strongly masculine Saudi national culture. Who was right in this situation—those Americans who argued that ugliness should be avoided and that female soldiers should observe local customs, or those Americans who argued instead that treating women differently from men can never be justified and that Saudi traditions should be overturned? If you had been the military commander charged with deciding what to do, what decision would you have made? What facts or opinions would you use to justify your decision? Would you be an ugly American?

---

working in national cultures characterized by *weaker uncertainty avoidance* must learn to cope with higher levels of anxiety and stress while reducing their reliance on planning, rule making, and other familiar ways of absorbing uncertainty. How to deal with this sort of situation? One way is to develop off-the-job interests and activities. You can take weekend trips to places of historical interest, study the culture's art and music, participate in sports activities. On the other side of the coin are managers working in cultures with *stronger uncertainty avoidance* than they are accustomed to. They must learn not only to accept but to participate in the development of seemingly meaningless rules and unnecessary planning in order to help other organization members cope with stressful uncertainty. Rituals that at first glance might appear useless or even irrational may serve the very important function of diminishing what is perceived to be an otherwise intolerable level of uncertainty.

Let us next look at the dimension of masculinity-femininity. Female managers working in cultures that display *more cultural masculinity* than their own face the prospect of receiving less respect at work than they feel they deserve (see the "Management Issues" box for a related discussion). To cope with gender discrimination of this sort, a female manager may have to seek out male mentors in senior management to secure her place in the organization. Conversely, male managers in national cultures that display *more cultural femininity* than their own must control aggressive tendencies and learn to treat members of both sexes with equal dignity and respect. Acting as mentors, female managers can help men accomplish transformations of this sort by demonstrating that women are as adept at their jobs as men.

The next dimension is individualism-collectivism. Managers who must work in national cultures that are more *individualistic* than their own must first learn to cope with the sense of rootlessness that comes from the absence of close-knit group relationships. They must also learn not to be embarrassed by personal compliments, despite their belief that success stems from group effort. At work, they must develop an appreciation of the importance of rewarding individuals equitably and must adjust to the idea that organizational membership is impermanent. Conversely, managers attempting to work in cultures that are more *collectivistic* than their own must learn to deal with demands for self-sacrifice in support of group well-being. They must also learn to accept equal sharing in lieu of equity and exchange at work. Consequently, they must refrain from paying individual employees compliments and instead praise group performance. Managers adjusting to collectivistic national cultures must also learn to understand that belonging to an organization in such cultures is more than just a temporary association. It is an important basis of each employee's personal identity.

Finally, managers working in cultures that favor *less power distance* must cope with initial discomfort stemming from an unfamiliar decentralization of authority and from feeling less in control. They must also learn to be less autocratic and more participatory in their work with others. On the other hand, managers facing cultural tendencies toward *more power distance* must accept the role that centralization and tall hierarchies play in maintaining what is deemed to be an acceptable level of control. They must also adopt a more authoritarian, autocratic style of management, and they may even find that subordinates, if asked to participate in decision making, will refuse on the grounds that decision making is management's rightful job.

SUMMARY

Whether comparisons are made within a single *national culture* or across different national cultures, no two organizations are exactly alike. And no two people in the world hold exactly the same beliefs and values. Thus our discussions in this chapter have necessarily involved generalization. Not every Japanese organization has a fully developed *latticework hierarchy*, and not every kibbutznik is completely collectivistic. Nevertheless, firms in a particular national culture are more like each other than they are like organizations in other national cultures. Moreover, people in the same national culture tend to think and act more similarly than people from different cultures. Cross-cultural differences exist and can have significant effects on the management of organizational behavior.

Many of these cross-cultural differences are captured by four dimensions: *uncertainty avoidance*, *masculinity-femininity*, *individualism-collectivism*, and *power distance*. The latter two of these dimensions explain many of the differences between American, Scandinavian, Japanese, and Israeli *kibbutz* management practices. Compared to American firms Scandinavian companies are far more participatory, Japanese organizations involve stronger feelings of obligation and dependence, and Israeli kibbutzim require greater member commitment to community well-being. Considered together, the four dimensions are helpful in understanding why people in a particular national culture behave the way they do and can be useful to managers as they adapt familiar management practices for use in unfamiliar cultures.

REVIEW QUESTIONS

1. Compared to the national culture of Sweden, what level of uncertainty avoidance characterizes the national culture of the United States? Of the two countries, in which one would you expect to find greater evidence of ritualistic behavior? Why? How would your answers to these questions change if you were asked to compare the U.S. with Greece?

2. Hofstede's findings indicate that the U.S. national culture at the time of his research was more masculine than many of the other national cultures he examined. In your opinion, is the American culture still as masculine as Hofstede's research suggests? Why?

3. According to Hofstede's research, the three most individualistic national cultures are found in the United States, Australia, and Great Britain. Can you think of a reason why these three countries share this cultural characteristic? Does your answer also explain the relatively strong individualism of the Canadian national culture?

4. Would you expect the structures of organizations in Denmark to be taller or flatter than those of organizations in the United States? Why? How are organization structures in Mexico likely to compare to those in Denmark and the U.S.?

5. Comparing U.S. business firms with Scandinavian industrial democracies, large Japanese businesses, and Israeli kibbutz industries, which of the four has the most equitable payment system? Which has the most egalitarian payment system? What explains this difference?

6. If you had to adapt the theories and models described in this book for use in Chile, what kinds of changes would you think about making? Explain your answer using Hofstede's four-dimensional model.

DIAGNOSTIC QUESTIONS

As we have shown, national cultures can have major effects on organizations and the behaviors of their members. Thus it is critical that you, as a manager, are able to assess the characteristics of the national culture surrounding your organization and understand the effects of that culture on organizational behavior. The following diagnostic questions are provided to facilitate this process.

1. What are the characteristics of your own national culture? Is it more individualistic or collectivistic? Are its values consistent with more or less power distance? Is it characterized more by masculinity or femininity? Does it favor strong or weak uncertainty avoidance?

2. What are the characteristics of the national culture surrounding your or-

ganization? How do they compare with the characteristics of your own national culture?

3. Based on your diagnosis of cultural differences, what adjustments should you make to familiar management practices to fit them to the current cultural situation?

4. Are there colleagues in the organization who can help you with the necessary adaptation? Should others outside the organization be asked to help instead?

5. Might other new entrants in the future benefit from what you learn as you cope with cultural adjustment in the present? Will informal mentoring provide future entrants with enough guidance? Should a formal adjustment program be designed and implemented instead?

EXERCISE 19-1

DEGREES OF CULTURAL CONSISTENCY: SOCIETAL AND ORGANIZATIONAL*

JOHN E. OLIVER, *Valdosta State College*
GARY B. ROBERTS, *Kennesaw College*

The cultures of organizations and the societies that surround them consist of fundamental norms and values that are manifested in many ways such as taking part in ceremonies, telling stories about people and events, and honoring heroes. In both organizations and societies, norms and values are shared among members and give rise to common attitudes and understandings. Culture is thus a source of similarity and commonality that helps people communicate with one another and make sense of their world.

Can a society's culture affect the cultures of its organizations? Can the norms and values in an organization's societal environment shape the norms and values that influence what its employees think and do at work? After reading Chapters 18 and 19 you probably realize that the answer to both of these questions is yes. However, you have yet to examine first-hand how one cultural domain can affect another. This exercise gives you the opportunity to examine differing degrees of cultural consistency and to explore their potential consequences.

STEP ONE: PRE-CLASS PREPARATION

If your class completed Exercise 4-1 earlier this term, you should review your answers to the Personality Dimensions Questionnaire (Exhibit 4-1). If your class did *not* complete Exercise 4-1, you should fill out its questionnaire now and score your answers according to the instructions in Step One of Exercise 4-1. When you have either reviewed your earlier answers or completed the questionnaire, you should read the rest of this exercise to prepare for class activities.

STEP TWO: FORMING HOMOGENOUS GROUPS

If your class completed Exercise 4-1 earlier you should reassemble in the same homogenous groups you formed for Step Two of that exercise. When each group gets together it should review its notes from the discussions that took place during Exercise 4-1.

If your class did not complete Exercise 4-1 you should instead divide into groups as directed in Step Two of that exercise (if you have been assembling in

permanent groups throughout this term you should *not* do so this time). Once you have formed groups you should briefly discuss the two questions in Step Two of Exercise 4-1 and be sure that everyone in your group understands the nature and potential effects of the similarities shared among group members.

STEP THREE: EXAMINING CULTURAL CONSISTENCIES

After groups have formed and considered their similarities, everyone should read the Organization Culture Profiles shown in Exhibit 19-1. Next, each group should discuss the following issues and arrive at a consensus on the group's response:

1. Which organization profile is most consistent with the attitudes and interests that are shared among the members of your group? Explain your choice.
2. What inconsistencies can you find between each of the remaining three profiles and the "culture" of your group? What effects might these inconsistencies have on the attitudes and behaviors of people like you?
3. Which of the societal cultures listed in Table 19-1 in this chapter resemble your group in terms of their most pronounced characteristic? How would you expect people in these societal cultures to think and behave?
4. What kind of culture would you expect to find in organizations located in the societal cultures you have identified? Why? Which organizational culture would you be least likely to find? Why?

STEP FOUR: HETEROGENOUS GROUP DISCUSSIONS

Next the class should divide into groups consisting of one individual from each of the four kinds of homogenous groups. Members of these new heterogenous

* Adapted with the authors' permission from an exercise entitled "Personality Traits and Organizational Cultures: Two One-Hour Experiential Learning Exercises." The organization culture profiles included in this exercise are based on information presented in Terrence E. Deal and Allen A. Kennedy, *Corporate Cultures: The Rites and Rituals of Corporate Life* (Reading, MA: Addison-Wesley, 1982).

EXHIBIT 19-1
Organizational Culture Profiles

	TYPE OF CULTURE			
	COMPETITIVE	ENTHUSIASTIC	PROFICIENT	METHODICAL
Type of risks assumed	High	Low	High	Low
Type of feedback from decisions	Fast	Fast	Slow	Slow
The ways survivors and heroes behave in this culture	They have a tough attitude. They are individualistic. They can tolerate all-or-nothing risks.	They are super sales-people. They often are friendly, hail-fellow-well-met types. They use a team approach to problem solving. They are nonsuperstititious.	They can endure long-term ambiguity. They always double check their decisions. They are technically competent. They have a strong respect for authority.	They are very cautious and protective of their own flank. They are orderly and punctual. They are good at attending to detail. They always follow established procedures.
Strengths of the people who best match this culture	They can get things done in short order.	They are able to produce a high volume of work quickly.	They can generate high quality inventions and major scientific breakthroughs.	They bring order and system to the workplace.
Weaknesses of the people who best match this culture	They do not learn from past mistakes. Everything tends to be short-term in orientation. The virtues of cooperation are ignored.	They look for quick-fix solutions. They have a short-term time perspective. They are more committed to action than to problem solving.	They are extremely slow in getting things done. Their organizations are vulnerable to short-term economic fluctuations. Their organizations often face cash-flow problems.	There is lots of red tape. Initiative is down-played. They work long hours.

groups should share the results of Step Three with one another and work to develop a diagram or table that matches the four dimensions (uncertainty avoidance, empathy-aggression, individualism-collectivism, power distance) with the four types of organizational culture. This diagram or table should also indicate which societal cultures reflect dominant amounts of each of the four dimensions. Note: there need not necessarily be a one-to-one correspondence between the four dimensions and the four cultures. Each group should appoint a spokesperson to report to the class on the results of its discussion.

STEP FIVE: CLASS DISCUSSION

As the group spokespersons give their report the rest of the class should ask whatever questions are needed to clarify each presentation. The instructor should summarize the presentations on a blackboard, flipchart, or overhead transparency, and the class should look for similarities and differences among the different group reports. All differences should be discussed and resolved by consensus and the class should consider the following questions:

1. With which of the four dimensions is each organizational culture most compatible? Least compatible? What does this imply about the relations between societal cultures and organizational cultures?

2. What kind of organizational culture seems most compatible with the Mexican societal culture? Why? With the Greek societal culture? Why?

3. What implications do the results of this exercise have for the task of international management? Why can't managers working outside their native culture simply ignore cultural differences?

CONCLUSION

Seldom do people or organizations fall neatly into any one category. Organizational and societal cultures are similarly difficult to categorize. Every organizational culture exhibits some of the characteristics of each of the cultural profiles shown in Exhibit 19-1. Moreover, members of the same societal culture may differ from one another almost as much as they differ from the members of other cultures. Overgeneralization is thus unwise and can artificially simplify what is actually quite complex. Nevertheless, limited use of the dimensions and profiles we have examined can help managers reduce complexity to a tolerable level and perform effectively in a variety of different cultures and contexts.

DIAGNOSING ORGANIZATIONAL BEHAVIOR

CASE 19-1
LANGLEY INTERNATIONAL GROWERS, INC.*
RAE ANDRE, *Northeastern University*

David Langley is the 58-year-old president of Langley International Growers, Inc., a Connecticut-based firm with annual sales close to $4 million. Like his father and grandfather before him, Langley grows flowers for distribution to wholesale markets along the eastern coast of the United States. Domestically, he runs about 12 acres of greenhouses, putting the company among the top ten greenhouse operations in the United States. In 1980, Langley started a subsidiary in Santa Nueva, an island republic in the Caribbean. The following account is based on discussions with Langley in December of 1982.

PART I

We first became interested in going abroad when we heard about Santa Nueva from one of our competitors. Because of the fuel situation we had decided it might be a good idea to hedge our bets and move to a climate where there's no fuel requirement. So we went down to Santa Nueva to see the competitor's operation, and we thought he was doing a good job. Sixty percent of the flowers used in the United States today are imported. Those flowers are grown with labor that costs $2 a day, versus what we have to pay at minimum wage, around $4.25 per hour. We thought there was money in it.

But establishing yourself in a foreign country is not easy. There are pitfalls. The laws of these governments look like they welcome business coming in. It's all on the books. The laws are there to help you. The government itself wants you there in a lot of these countries. What they spend nationally on oil alone exceeds the money they get from exports, which constantly puts them in the doghouse internationally. They can't buy anything outside, so they're constantly in a state of devaluation relative to everybody else. In addition to that, they have an enormous birthrate which constantly keeps their poverty in place. (You go down there with the idea you're going to help them out from that standpoint—

forget it, because they're not going to let you do it.) There's a lot of money to be made if you know how. You go down there and start spending your money and then you find out that the laws have to be administered by people, and the people are where the hangups come because they don't obey the law. They circumvent it to their own benefit. In other words, they make it difficult for you for various reasons. The political aims start to disappear in the bureaucracy.

For example, we have to import a lot of things into the country because they don't have them. Well, they can let that stuff sit down at that dock until some guy clears it. They let our crates of greenhouses sit there for two to three *months*. It threw us way back, cost us thousands of dollars. We had importers down there who knew their business. All the paperwork was right, but all the guy says is "I don't think this is right," and it gets kicked back and forth. One problem is that a lot of the government income is taxes on imports, so they're very strict, particularly if it's an American company that's shipping. This holdup means that everybody's benefiting except the poor guy who has to cut the flowers, because they've made work for the guy who's pushing that paper all around, they've made work for the guy down at the dock, they've made work for the phone operator. You're constantly checking, checking, checking. It's a make-work scheme, in any sense of the word, and they're masters at it. A lot of these foreign countries, they don't operate, they make work.

For example, down where we are, the bureaucracy has increased 50 percent in four years—50 percent more government employees. Going through the airports, there's a guy who puts the tag on your thing and there's a guy who takes it off, five feet away. You can tell them your problem, but they don't understand the problem of business having to get that money moving that's sitting there. They don't realize that they have to collect their taxes and build their country from business. I wanted a land map. It took us three hours to get that

* Reprinted with the author's permission.

map and it had to go through three different people, and I had to sign a paper that I would get my lawyer to state the reason I wanted that map. Even answering the phone: the conversations are long, the conversations are flowery. They don't get to the point, and this, of course, is frustrating if you're not used to it. And especially if you're paying for a long distance phone call. It takes them a half hour to say good morning!

Back about six months ago, we needed this particular type of spreader for an insecticide and I wanted to make sure it was there. We wanted it the following morning and I wanted it delivered that day. And my secretary is on the phone talking to this guy twenty-five miles away. He kept saying, *"Mañana"* ("tomorrow"), and I kept saying, *"Ayer"* ("yesterday"). The secretary kept saying, *"Mañana"* and I kept saying, *"Ayer."* Finally, with negotiations back and forth, I got it.

So you have to tighten things. They don't respect you if they know they're getting away with it, because everybody's watching everybody else. We made that mistake. We were too easy. Of course, these people are very hungry. Their unemployment rate is tremendous. The established rate is 40 percent, but they don't count everybody. If they counted everybody, its around 80 percent. You learn as you go, and you learn from talking to people. They don't respect softness and, yet, they don't respect anybody who's going around shouting and yelling either. You've got to have them understand who's boss. We had a guy who was coming in late all the time, so we gave him a written notice. After you hire him for three months, the government says you own him: it costs you money to let him go. If he's there three months, you might have to give him another three months. After a year, you might have to give him another six months. The guy was late. We gave him the notice. He still was late, so we had to let him go. It didn't cost us anything. See, if he breaks the company rules and they're allowable rules according to the law, then you can get rid of him without any pay. But we had to get tougher and tougher and tougher. It's so easy to be easy because the labor's cheap. But you have to realize that any time you're not making money, it's coming out of capital, so labor's not cheap then.

We weren't knowledgeable about the culture. We assumed that they're like us—sort of like us—if you have the language. That's the mistake you make. You can hire a Neuvan to run the place if you've got the language yourself, but you have to know the language so well that you get the innuendoes, and that's something none of us have. Very few Americans have that. You could hire a Cuban, Mexican, or a Puerto Rican, but even they do not think like we do. They're more apt to identify with the person instead of identifying with the problem. They identify with their emotions and they think, "Well, poor guy." We hadn't taken one dime out of there yet,

and we were asked for a raise. They'll say, "Look at these poor people here. Don't you think they ought to be given hope?" Well, we hired them and they had 60 percent unemployment in the town, and yet I didn't give them hope?

They're big on expectations and poor on execution down there. You have to have an American boss, period. All those guys underneath can be Nuevans, but you gotta have an American boss because you have to teach those Nuevans how you want it. If you go down there and take their way of doing it, you've lost everything you've ever had.

When we went into the village there the only means of transportation was the truck that we had bought. Now, almost everybody rides up in a new Honda motorcycle. The standard of living has gone up.

There was a lot of petty thievery when we built the place. A bar down the end of the street was built in the last year since we built. The owner didn't have a thing before. He's the guy that plowed our property and worked the field before we put our greenhouses up. Right after we built, he was able to build himself a bar and a dancehall from similar materials that were used to construct Langley Greenhouses. I call it Langley's bar. It's right at the end of our road. I often stop in for a *cerveza* ("beer").

All the foreigners do better than we Americans do. Number one, they can bribe the governments. We put strings on our businessmen that are absolutely abominable and then holler that we can't export anything. Another thing is the gringo approach. The Japanese are a new face in there and they operate a little differently than we do. They always say, "Yes." We say, "No," but they say "Yes" and don't mean it, so it doesn't hurt as much. It's a different approach and they've sold one hell of a lot of cars. In fact, I have never driven an American car down there. If you want to go buy an American truck, just forget it. We have a little two-cylinder Japanese truck that's running up and down those hills for fifty kilometers per gallon.

PART II

Our manager there came originally from Puerto Rico. I hired him when he was fifteen or sixteen years old. He's worked for me for seventeen years. We usually have about 75 percent Puerto Ricans working for us up North. I am like a father to him. He had a child and named it after me.

I sent him down and he's been as happy as a lark, but that's Jorge. That's not everybody. You can't generalize on Jorge. He's doing a good job. Of course, he lost his first wife because she thought the girls were a little too loose in Santa Nueva. She wan't wrong. She walked out on him. I don't know whether he got divorced, but he got married again. To give you just a brief insight into it, we won't allow him to hire any woman under forty. We don't want him to be passing his favors out. There's another reason for that. They'll come and work for you, but if they get pregnant, you have to give them at least a month off with pay. Sure enough, they'll come when they're already pregnant. First thing you know, you have five young ladies pregnant, nobody to do the work and you're paying for it. We hired the first secretary, thought she could speak English, took me nine months to get rid of her. I fired her. She couldn't speak a word of English. "Yes," or "No." She had the books all fouled up. Pregnant, too. She lied to us about it. She came back and had the kid here. Now he's an American citizen.

We have three managers and twenty employees. We have an office manager, a pack and ship manager, and an overall manager. These people can all speak Spanish. Then we have about twelve men and eight women. The women do the bunching. The men do the cutting, are night watchmen, and all kinds of things. You look in that packing shed down there and it's probably identical to this one up here, only there are no conveyers. I won't put a conveyer down there because it'll only work about three hours. And that's when I'm working. The more we check up on them, the more controls we put on them in equipment, the more apt they are to say, "This doesn't work now." It's so simple to break a computer. You spit at it or push the wrong damn buttons and it's done. We sent down one of the finest little power mowers you can buy. We started it up before it went down. It worked perfectly. It was eight or nine months later and three mechanical overhauls before we got that thing working. Last year I arrived and found ten or fifteen men cutting the fields with machetes. I'm still not sure that isn't the cheapest. If you hire them for $2 a day, they're telling you something. They really are telling you something. You can hire their people, on certain jobs anyway, cheaper than you can use the damned equipment. You won't see a lot of bookkeeping machines in Santa Nueva. They use people and they'll get it right. They'll have a calculator, but that's about the extent of it. You might in a very big American company, but not generally.

We have parameters for the manager: checklists for his rounds, a checklist for his maintenance, a checklist for his nightman. You must be specific. You don't just walk out and say "clean." You've got to say, "Clean this table, clean that table, clean this." Write it down and give it to him. If you don't do that some of it will be forgotten, some of it just won't be done. And then you can't come in and holler, because the guy will say he didn't hear you. They're really sharp this way. You have to be specific. You have to draw it step by step or

they just won't do it. If they have a package of cigarettes, the empty packs will go onto the floor, until you tell them, "The next time you do that. . . . out. We are not going to have that. This is not the way we're going to be." You go to the company next door to ours where he never enforced these things and it's a dump. Not that he doesn't make money, but it's a dump, a literal dump. It's terrible.

We have the manager take videotape pictures around the plant every week so we see what the plants look like, see what the surroundings look like, see what the housekeeping looks like. We also have him send all the bills, the bank balances, and the payroll up each week.

We have a problem with visitors, too. We have to keep them out. They'll just drop in and say, "Can I see the place?" and they'll take up the manager's time and they'll take up the office time. When they get to talking, they'll talk about their grandfather, their father, their brothers, their sisters, and it's on your time. So we had to discourage that. We had to fence the place to keep the horses out, the cows out, and the people out. Just so you can keep control of the flowers. I don't know if we stopped it. If you have a fence, you have to say, "Don't crawl over the fence."

A lot of growers don't do things the way we do them, even up North. I like it written down. I hate verbal orders, unless it's just a day order. If it's a long-term deal it should be written down and put in the policy. "This is what we do in this way at this particular time." We're known to have the best place in Santa Nueva and there are a lot of flower growers. In the town, we're known as operating a very tight ship.

PART III

The hotels are owned by the government and they're rented from the government. It's amazing. These beautiful hotels rent for two or three hundred dollars a month. And you should see the way they keep it. Terrible. You can't swim in the swimming pool. It's green. It's a beautiful swimming pool and I know how to tell them to keep it, but they won't. If I were going to be down there a lot, I'd take my own chlorine and fix it. It would only cost $100 to use the pool the whole time I was there. Probably, they'd give me free drinks out of it, they'd make it up. They just don't know how to do things. They fool around.

When I was robbed at the hotel, I went to the police station and gave them a list just because I wanted it for the insurance company. Nothing happened. Nobody found anything. I didn't eat in that hotel for the next two months, the next two times I was there. I wouldn't go in their dining room, because I knew those guys knew who did it. I was there alone. Somebody had to be watching and the town is too small not to know the thief and I knew the police knew. I found out the hotel was responsible, but you can't get blood out of a stone, so I said "All right, I want a 10 percent discount rate until this is paid off on my hotel room," which they went along with. After that, they put a guard on me. Every night I have a guard—a private guard. They give him a peso. He's sitting right outside my door. I've never felt physically afraid.

I went down to town one night trying to negotiate for this land. Downtown at night looks like a country road. The house lights are on, but there are no street lights. I went down there negotiating with this family right in their house. (The guy who said that he owned the land really made me mad. I had it all negotiated and later found out we couldn't get a clear title.) Anyway, I'm sitting there in this house with this family. Nobody can speak English, and I can't speak Spanish, but we're negotiating. It was this guy and his son, who could speak English a little, and the whole family—his wife, and relatives. They all come in to look at me. Everybody was just staring. All of a sudden, I started to wiggle my ears, and I'll tell you, they had a hilarious time. My wife was up in the hotel. She was worried I'd disappeared in the middle of the night down in a strange country. I didn't get home till one or two o'clock in the morning.

But it's gorgeous. It's a paradise. You couldn't believe it until you see it. Everything grows. You can have a terrific amount of flowers; I love to go there. I'm getting homesick for it. I would say they've treated us very well. After all, it's their country. It's not up to them to change . . . we're trying to take a profit out of it.

PART IV

The United States has rules, too. It's just a new ballgame and you should detail it right from the beginning. We should have had notebooks, which was my fault. We should have had everything detailed—the duties, the laws of the country, the work rules. If I were to do it now, I would have all this stuff researched and if we ever expand again, we'll know what we're doing. And there'll be no problem. I spent quite a bit of time down there last June when we were planting, but I should have spent two months down there. I did spend practically that much time down there off and on, but I should have been right there and taken over the job of doing it. It's not the Nuevans' fault at all. I might lose it if I don't get down there more. If I were going to do it over again, I wouldn't invest down there, but if I had to do it, I'd still pick that country. I didn't make a mistake in the country. We did not do that. It's probably the best of the lot. They're more democratic than most. The problem is that poverty does strange things. Poverty will turn those people into almost anything if they don't get it straightened out. That birth rate should be zero right now, but the population is going to double in the next ten years. It takes somebody to say you can't have any more children or to teach them birth control. You have to instill that over three or four generations. And this is where we've lost them. We get insurance against that. Our government insures us if we're taken over down there because of riot or insurrection or government acquisition. Otherwise, you couldn't get any loans. You'll see people with jobs there and you wouldn't believe it. Take the waiters in the hotels. You'll go down there today and five years from now and they're practically working for nothing. There's nobody in the hotels from one day to the next. Yet, they'll be there. They have no place to go. There's no place to go except the United States and there are 500,000 Nuevans working in the United States. You literally can't get a plane reservation back to the States during the first two weeks of January.

When you have read this case, look back at the chapter's diagnostic questions and choose the ones that apply to the case. Then use those questions with the ones that follow in your case analysis.

1. Using Hofstede's dimensions, characterize the societal culture of Santa Nueva. What kinds of adaptations would a manager trained in United States methods have to make to succeed in this culture? Has David Langley made any of these adaptations? Is Langley an "ugly American"?

2. How did Langley learn about the culture of Santa Nueva? You're read his account of his experiences, and you now know something about managing organizational behavior in the United States and in other cultures. If you had to start doing business in Santa Nueva and learn first-hand about Santa Nuevan ways, would you take Langley's approach? Why or why not?

3. How likely is it that Langley's company will be successful in the long run? What lessons does this case teach about the task of managing in another culture?

CASE 19-2

WORLD INTERNATIONAL AIRLINES

Review this case, which appears in Chapter 5. Next, look back at Chapter 19's diagnostic questions and choose the ones that apply to the case. Then use those questions with the ones that follow in your case analysis.

1. On the basis of Hofstede's dimensions and the fact that Stephen Esterant is Spanish, how would you

expect Stephen to behave toward subordinates? Does he behave in the manner you would predict?

2. What are the cultural differences between Stephen's native Spain and the United States location of World International Airlines? Do these differences explain any of the problems that Stephen is having with his American subordinates?

3. If you had to train Stephen in how to interact with American employees, how would you do it? Would he be likely to follow your advice? Describe specific steps you would consider taking to increase this likelihood.

C A S E 19-3

PRECISION MACHINE TOOL

Review this case, which appears in Chapter 6. Next, look back at Chapter 19's diagnostic questions and choose the ones that apply to the case. Then use those questions with the ones that follow in your case analysis.

1. What cultural differences existed between the American managers of Precision Machine Tool and Ako Wang, a Japanese businessman? How did these differences affect the deliberations described in the case?

2. If you were a consultant hired by John Garner and Tom Avery, what would you do to make them aware of how cultural factors are affecting their decision making? What modifications would you suggest they make?

3. What sort of response do you expect John and Tom to communicate to Ako Wang? Why? Would this be your response if you were in John's and Tom's position?

GLOSSARY

accommodation A conflict management technique that involves allowing other groups to satisfy their own concerns at the expense of one's own group (*p. 486*).

action The diagnostic model step in which one stipulates the specific actions needed to implement a prescribed solution (*p. 13*).

action research model A model of the organization development process that permits the development and assessment of original, innovative interventions (*p. 519*).

adaptive decline strategies A class of corporate strategies in which the firm reduces its size by either downsizing or eliminating one or more businesses. Retrenchment, divestiture, and liquidation are all adaptive decline strategies (*p. 690*).

additive task A group task in which the accomplishments of each member of the group are added to those of other members (*p. 374*).

administrative decision-making model A model in which decisions pursuant to negotiated goals are made based on satisficing rather than maximizing outcomes, through a sequential consideration of alternatives (*p. 178*).

administrative principles school The school of management thought that deals with streamlining administrative procedures in order to encourage internal stability and efficiency (*p. 30*).

advanced beginner The stage of skill development in which people learn to base behaviors on an expanded set of rules that include both the elementary rules of novices and circumstantial rules discovered through experience (*p. 9*).

aptitude testing Measuring broad, general abilities of job applicants (*p. 291*).

assimilation effect The tendency for present judgments to be biased in the direction of past judgments (*p. 147*).

attention stage The stage in the information processing cycle in which the individual decides what will be processed and what will be ignored (*p. 130*).

attribution The process whereby observers decide what caused the behavior of another person (*p. 140*).

authoritarianism A set of personality characteristics that include ethnocentrism and strong tendencies to overvalue authority, to stereotype others, and to be suspicious and distrustful of people in general (*p. 99*).

authoritarian leader A leader who makes almost all decisions by herself, minimizing the input of subordinates (*p. 418*).

automatic processing A type of information processing in which the perceiver is not aware that he is processing information (*p. 129*).

availability bias The tendency in decision makers to judge the likelihood that something will happen by the ease with which they can recall examples of it (*p. 169*).

avoidance A conflict management technique that involves staying neutral at all costs and refusing to take an active role in conflict resolution procedures (*p. 486*).

bargaining A process in which offers, counteroffers, and concessions are exchanged as conflicting groups search for some mutually acceptable resolution (*p. 485*).

base rate bias The tendency in decision makers to ignore the underlying objective probability, or base rate, that a particular outcome will follow a particular course of action (*p. 171*).

BCG Matrix A management tool that depicts the mix of businesses owned by a firm (*p. 688*).

behavior modification Application of contingent rewards in order to bring about behavioral change (*p. 311*).

behavioral masking A phenomenon whereby the simple presence of other group members masks, or hides, the behaviors of one member (*p. 381*).

behaviorally anchored rating scale (BARS) A method of performance appraisal in which each judgment point along the scale is illustrated with examples of concrete, on-the-job behaviors (*p. 296*).

benchmark jobs Common jobs for which market rates are readily available and which are used, along with point plans, to determine salaries for uncommon jobs (*p. 306*).

benign reappraisal A response to stress in which the person reassesses an apparently threatening environmental demand and modifies his original perception of it (*p. 249*).

biofeedback A technique that uses machines to monitor bodily functions thought to be involuntary, such as heart beat and blood pressure, so that a person can learn to regulate these functions (*p. 272*).

boundary spanner A member or unit of an organization that interacts with individuals or firms in the organization's environment (*p. 618*).

bounded discretion The recognition that the alternatives available to a decision maker are bounded by social, legal, moral, and organizational restrictions (*p. 176*).

brainstorming A group decision-making process based on a set of rules intended to encourage idea generation (*p. 393*).

buffering The notion that certain positive factors in the person's environment can limit the capacity of other factors to create dissatisfaction and stress (*p. 260*).

bureaucracy An idealized description of an efficient organization based on clearly defined authority, formal record keeping, and standardized procedures (*p. 32*).

business strategy A strategic plan that specifies the way a business plans to compete in its market and industry. Overall cost leadership, differentiation, and focus are all business strategies (*p. 691*).

centrality The position of a person or group within the flow of work in an organization (*p. 470*).

centralization The concentration of authority and decision making at the top of an organization; the opposite of decentralization (*p. 568*).

ceremonies Special events in which the members of an organization celebrate the myths, heroes, and symbols of their culture (*p. 697*).

change agent A person who manages the organization development process, serving both as a catalyst for change and as a source of information about OD (*p. 507*).

charismatic leadership Creating a new vision of an organization and getting group members to commit themselves enthusiastically to the new mission, structure, and culture embodied in the vision. Encouraging them to transcend self-interests on behalf of the organization as a whole (*p. 439*).

choice shift The tendency for groups to make decisions that appear more extreme than the decisions group members would make on their own. In *risky shift* group decisions appear more risky than decisions made by individuals, and in *cautious shift* group decisions appear more cautious than decisions made by individuals (*p. 389*).

classical conditioning Learning that occurs when a neutral stimulus, through repeated pairing with a stimulus that elicits a specific response, comes to elicit that same response (*p. 211*).

client organization An organization involved in the process of organization development (*p. 508*).

closed system contingencies Structural contingency factors that are characteristics of the organization. Size and technology are the most dominant of these factors (*p. 596*).

coalition A group that forms to allow its members to combine their political strength in order to pursue interests they hold in common (*p. 474*).

coercive power Interpersonal power based on the ability to control the distribution of undesirable outcomes (*p. 463*).

cohesiveness A measure of the interpersonal attraction among members of a group and their attraction to the group as a whole (*p. 384*).

collaboration A conflict management technique that involves attempting to satisfy the concerns of all conflicting groups by working through differences and seeking out optimal solutions in which everyone gains (*p. 486*).

collateral structure A second hierarchy of groups and committees that parallels and sometimes takes the place of the primary managerial hierarchy in Scandinavian industrial democracies (*p. 741*).

communication The exchange of information between people through a common set of symbols (*p. 345*).

communication structure The pattern of interactions by which group members share information. In the *wheel*, a central hub member communicates with all other members, who communicate only with her. In the *Y*, the members of two pairs can communicate with each other and with the hub but the pairs cannot communicate directly. The *chain* links members sequentially so that some can communicate with two people but others with only one. In the *circle*, each member can communicate with two others. In the *completely connected network* each group member can communicate directly with every other (*p. 386*).

comparable worth Theory that sex differences in wages are attributable to discrimination and that such discrimination can be eliminated through job evaluation (*p. 307*).

compensable factors Those aspects of a job for which an organization is willing to pay a premium (*p. 304*).

competence The stage of skill development in which people replace basic rules with advanced rules of thumb that can be altered to fit a wide range of circumstances (*p. 9*).

competition A conflict management technique that involves attempts to overpower other groups in the conflict and to promote the concerns of one's own group at the expense of the other groups (*p. 486*).

competitive group rewards Group rewards distributed in such a way that members receive equitable rewards in exchange for successful performance as individuals in a group (*p. 383*).

complex structure A type of organization structure that relies on standardization to achieve coordination. A complex structure is therefore characterized by noticeable formalization and specialization (*p. 599*).

compliance Behaving in accord with norms out of fear of punishment or hope of reward (*p. 344*).

comprehensive job enrichment A type of job design that combines both horizontal and vertical improvements to stimulate employee motivation and satisfaction (*p. 653*).

compressed work week An alternative work schedule that allows employees to work a 40-hour week in fewer than the normal five days (*p. 665*).

compromise A conflict management technique that involves seeking partial satisfaction of all conflicting groups through exchange and sacrifice (*p. 487*).

conceptual skills Management skills involving the ability to perceive an organization or organizational unit as a whole, to understand how its labor is divided into tasks and reintegrated by the pursuit of common goals or objectives, and to recognize important relationships between the organization or unit and its environment (*p. 44*).

conditioned stimulus A stimulus that is initially neutral but when repeatedly paired with an unconditioned stimulus, elicits the response associated with the latter stimulus (*p. 211*).

confirmation bias The tendency for raters to seek out information that supports and reaffirms their earlier judgments (*p. 148*).

conflict A process of opposition and confrontation that can occur between either individuals or groups (*p. 477*).

conflict aftermath The stage of conflict development at which conflict sets the stage for later situations and events (*p. 483*).

conformity Loyal but uncreative adherence by group members to both pivotal and peripheral norms (*p. 377*).

conjunctive task A group task in which all group members must contribute to task performance (*p. 374*).

consequences Leader behaviors that involve administering rewards and punishments contingent upon subordinate performance (*p. 440*).

consideration Leader behavior aimed at meeting the social and emotional needs of workers such as helping them, doing them favors, looking out for their best interests, and explaining decisions (*p. 416*).

constituency groups Groups such as employees, customers, and suppliers upon whom the survival of an organization depends. Constituency groups make demands that they expect will be fulfilled in return for their support of the organization (*p. 593*).

construct validation Establishing validity by showing that a measure of a concept is congruent with the theory and data that support the concept (*p. 62*).

content theories Theories of motivation that attempt to specify what sorts of events or outcomes motivate behavior (*p. 200*).

content validation Establishing validity by showing that, according to expert judges, the measure samples the appropriate material (*p. 62*).

contingency perspective The view that no single theory, procedure, or set of rules is useful in every situation and that each situation determines the usefulness of different management approaches (*p. 14*).

continuous process production A type of manufacturing technology in which automated equipment makes the same product in the same way for an indefinite period of time (*p. 611*).

controlled processing A manner of information processing in which the perceiver is aware that he is processing information (*p. 129*).

controlling The management function of evaluating the performance of an organization or organizational unit to determine whether it is progressing in the desired direction (*p. 27*).

convergence hypothesis A theoretical assertion that organizations and management practices throughout the world are growing more alike (*p. 752*).

convergent growth strategies A class of corporate strategies that involve starting, acquiring, or maintaining businesses in the market and industry already served by the firm. Included in this class are the concentration strategy and the horizontal integration strategy (*p. 689*).

cooperative group rewards Group rewards distributed in such a way that each member receives an equal reward in exchange for the successful performance of the group (*p. 382*).

cooptation Making former adversaries into allies by involving them in planning and decision-making processes (*p. 475*).

core job characteristics Job characteristics identified in the Hackman-Oldham model that lead their holders to experience certain critical psychological states (*p. 654*).

core technology The dominant technology used in performing the organization's basic work (*p. 609*).

corporate strategy A strategic plan that specifies the desired mix of businesses in a firm and the way resources should be allocated among them (*p. 688*).

correlation coefficient A statistic that assesses the degree of relationship between two variables (*p. 64*).

cosmopolitan A person who has many important contacts outside the organization and develops special knowledge from these contacts (*p. 353*).

cost-saving plans Fringe benefit programs in which organizations pay workers year-end bonuses out of money saved through employee suggestions, increased efficiency, or increased productivity (*p. 310*).

counseling A shallow, interpersonal organization development intervention in which a change agent meets either one-on-one or small groups to provide helpful information to people who are having trouble relating with others (*p. 524*).

covariation The degree to which two variables are associated with each other; the degree to which changes in one are related to changes in the other (*p. 63*).

creative individualism Acceptance by group members of pivotal norms and rejection of peripheral ones (*p. 377*).

criterion-related validation Establishing validity by showing that a measure predicts some variable that, based on theory, it should predict (*p. 62*).

critical contingencies Events, activities, or objects that are required by by an organization and its various parts to accomplish organizational goals and to ensure continued survival (*p. 467*).

critical psychological states Mental conditions identified in the Hackman-Oldham model as being triggered by the presence of certain core job characteristics (*p. 655*).

culture The shared attitudes and perceptions in an organization that are based on a set of fundamental norms and values and that help members understand the organization (*p. 695*).

custodianship A product of socialization in which a new group member adopts the means and ends associated with the role unquestioningly (*p. 354*).

decentralization The dispersion of authority and decision making downward and outward through the hierarchy of an organization; the opposite of centralization (*p. 568*).

decision bias The theory that group decisions are not affected by the loss aversion bias that affects individual decision making (*p. 390*).

decoding The process by which a transmitted message is converted into an abstract idea in the mind of the person to whom the communication is directed (*p. 346*).

decoupling mechanisms Mechanisms that regulate intergroup coordination by making work units less dependent on each other. The use of decoupling mechanisms involves making adjustments to the relationships formed among units during departmentation (*p. 571*).

deductive ability An individual's capacity to use logic and to evaluate the implications of various arguments (*p. 89*).

defense mechanism In Freudian psychology, a kind of mental operation by which individuals rechannel the energies linked to socially unacceptable urges (*p. 93*).

Delphi technique A group decision-making process in which the group never meets in person but instead corresponds with a central leader who initiates activities and receives all the resulting information (*p. 394*).

democratic leader A leader who works to ensure that all subordinates have a voice in making decisions (*p. 419*).

departmentation The process of grouping structural units into larger clusters. In functional departmentation units are grouped into departments according to functional similarities—similarities in the work they do. In divisional departmentation, units are grouped into divisions according to market similarities—similarities in their products, their customers, or the geographical areas they serve (*p. 566*).

depth In organization development, the degree or intensity of change that an intervention is designed to stimulate (*p. 522*).

description The diagnostic model step in which information about a situation without attempting to explain either the cause of the situation or the motives of the people involved in it (*p. 10*).

diagnosis The diagnostic model step in which one looks for the causes of a troublesome situation and summarizes them in a problem statement (*p. 11*).

diagnostic model A four-step model that describes how managers perceive and solve problems. The model is both a learning tool and an on-the-job guide (*p. 10*).

differential accuracy The extent to which a rater's assessment of one individual, on one single dimension, is reflective of the person's true standing on that one dimension (*p. 128*).

differential elevation accuracy The extent to which a rater's assessment of one individual, across a number of dimensions, reflects that person's true standing on those dimensions (*p. 127*).

differentiation The second stage of group development, characterized by conflicts that erupt as members seek agreement on the purpose, goals, and objectives of the group and the roles of its members (*p. 372*).

diffusion of responsibility The sense among group members that responsibility is shared broadly rather than shouldered personally (*p. 381*).

directing The management function of encouraging and guiding employees' efforts toward the attainment of organizational goals and objectives (*p. 26*).

direct supervision A unit coordination mechanism in which one person takes responsibility for the work of a group of others. She determines which tasks need to be performed, who will perform them, and how they will be linked together to produce the desired end result (*p. 552*).

discretion An area of latitude wherein the decision maker can use her own judgment in developing and deciding among alternative decisions (*p. 180*).

disjunctive task A group task that can be completed by single group members working alone (*p. 374*).

disparate impact The tendency of a particular personnel selection practice to result in the hiring of a smaller percentage of the members of a particular group of job applicants than of other groups of applicants (*p. 300*).

disparate treatment An illegal practice in personnel selection wherein a person from one subgroup is asked to respond to questions, take tests, or display skills that are not asked of applicants from other groups (*p. 300*).

distributive justice An individual's perception of the fairness of his reward in comparison with the rewards given others (*p. 162*).

divisional structure A flexible but inefficient type of complex structure characterized by divisional departmentation and moderate decentralization (*p. 600*).

division of labor The process and result of breaking difficult work into smaller tasks (*p. 23*).

economic rationality The belief underlying rational decision-making models that people attempt to maximize their individual economic outcomes (*p. 163*).

efficiency perspective An approach to job design that focuses on the creation of jobs that economize on time, human energy, raw materials, and other productive resources (*p. 640*).

elevation accuracy The degree to which a rater's assessment of an entire group of people, across a number of different dimensions, reflects the group's true standing on those dimensions (*p. 125*).

emergent task elements The components of work roles that are not formally recognized by the organization but arise out of expectations held by others for the role incumbent (*p. 337*).

emotional adjustment A class of personality variables that deal with the extent to which a person experiences affective distress or engages in socially unacceptable behaviors (*p. 99*).

employee-centered behaviors Leadership behaviors designed to meet the social and emotional needs of group members (*p. 414*).

employment at will A provision that either party in the employment relationship can terminate the relationship at any time, even without reason (*p. 314*).

encoding The process by which a communicator's abstract idea is translated into the symbols of language for transmission to someone else (*p. 345*).

entity attraction Satisfaction with other persons in the workplace that comes about because these people share one's fundamental values, attitudes or philosophy (*p. 259*).

environment The context surrounding an organization, consisting of economic, geographic, and political conditions that impinge on the firm (*p. 615*).

environmental change A measure of the extent to which conditions in an organization's environment change unpredictably (*p. 615*).

environmental complexity A measure of the degree to which an organization's environment is complicated and therefore difficult to understand (*p. 616*).

environmental diversity A measure of the degree to which an organization's environment is varied or heterogeneous in nature (*p. 620*).

environmental domain A part or segment of the environment in which an organization does business (*p. 620*).

environmental receptivity The degree to which an organization's environment supports the organization's progress toward fulfilling its purpose (*p. 618*).

environmental uncertainty An environmental characteristic formed by the combination of change and complexity that reflects the absence of information about environmental factors, activities, and events (*p. 617*).

equity theory A theory of motivation originated by Adams that suggests that behavior is motivated by the desire to reduce guilt or anger associated with social exchanges that are perceived to be unfair (*p. 224*).

ERG theory A theory of motivation developed by Alderfer that suggests that behavior is driven by the urge to fulfill three essential needs: existence, relatedness, and growth (*p. 207*).

ergonomics Another name for human factors engineering, a type of methods engineering that focuses on designing machines to match human capacities and limitations (*p. 643*).

escalation of commitment Investing additional resources in failing courses of action that are not justified by any foreseeable payoff (*p. 173*).

established task elements The components of work roles that are contained in written job descriptions and formally recognized in the organization (*p. 336*).

eustress A particular kind of stress created when an individual is confronted with an opportunity (*p. 247*).

evolutionary growth strategies A class of corporate strategies in which the firm develops products, markets, or businesses that are similar though not identical to the ones already associated with the company. Product development, market development, and concentric diversification are all evolutionary growth strategies (*p. 689*).

expectancy A person's beliefs regarding the link between his efforts and his performance (*p. 203*).

expectancy theory A broad, cognitive, process theory of motivation that explains behavior as a function of expectancies, instrumentalities, and valences (*p. 201*).

expected value The projected value of an outcome that has less than a 100 percent probability of occurring. The expected value is derived mathematically by multiplying each possible outcome of a particular course of action by the probability that that outcome will occur (*p. 166*).

expertise The stage of skill development in which individuals develop the ability to act intuitively in a wide variety of situations, rarely needing to deliberate consciously (*p. 10*).

expert power Interpersonal power based on the possession of expertise, knowledge, and talent (*p. 463*).

explicit theories Internally consistent, formal theories that are subject to empirical test (*p. 60*).

external change agent An organization development change agent who is not a member of the client organization (*p. 508*).

extinction The gradual disappearance of a response that occurs after the cessation of positive reinforcement (*p. 212*).

felt conflict The stage of conflict development at which people are not only aware of the conflict but feel tense, anxious, angry, or otherwise upset (*p. 482*).

fight or flight response A response to stress in which a person confronts and overcomes a stressful demand or escapes it by leaving the scene (*p. 249*).

flexible cell production A type of manufacturing technology in which computer-controlled production machines are connected together in a group, or cell, by a flexible network of conveyors that can be rapidly reconfigured for different production tasks (*p. 611*).

flexible-hour programs Alternative work schedules that specify a block of core hours during which everyone must be on the job but allow each employee to choose when to start and quit work. Also called flextime (*p. 664*).

forcefield analysis A diagnostic method that depicts the array of forces for and against a particular change in a graphic analysis; often used as a component of the OD process (*p. 513*).

formal groups Groups that serve specific organizational purposes. In *work groups* employees work together to produce their firm's goods or services. Higher-level managers and the managers they supervise work together in *management teams*. *Temporary groups* are formed to accomplish a specific task. *Intermittent groups* are composed of people who do not work with each other but meet regularly to exchange work-related information (*p. 370*).

formal organization Those aspects of an organization that are officially sanctioned, including intentionally designed structures and jobs (*p. 685*).

formalization The process of planning the regulations that control organizational behavior; also the written documentation produced by the planning process. Jobs, work flows, or general rules may be formalized (*p. 559*).

formation The initial stage of group development, characterized by uncertainty and anxiety. People try to determine which behaviors will be appropriate and what contributions members should be expected to make to the group (*p. 372*).

functional attraction Satisfaction with other persons in the workplace that comes about because these other people help one attain valued work outcomes (*p. 259*).

functional grouping People are grouped into units according to similarities in the functions they perform. Grouping word-processing typists into a word-processing pool is an example (*p. 549*).

functional strategy A strategic plan that specifies how a functional unit will contribute to the attainment of corporate and business goals (*p. 693*).

functional structure An efficient but inflexible type of complex structure characterized by functional departmentation and centralization (*p. 599*).

gatekeeper A person responsible for controlling messages sent through a particular communication channel (*p. 352*).

general adaptation syndrome The theory developed by Hans Selye that the body's response to stress occurs in three distinct stages: alarm, resistance and exhaustion (*p. 250*).

general cognitive ability The totality of an individual's mental capacity, summing across specific mental abilities such as verbal comprehension, quantitative aptitude, reasoning ability, and deductive ability (*p. 88*).

generalizability The degree to which the result of a study conducted in one sample-setting-time configuration can be replicated in other sample-setting-time configurations (*p. 73*).

geographic structure A type of divisional structure formed by grouping units according to similarities in their geographic location (*p. 600*).

goal commitment A person's willingness to put forth effort in accomplishing goals and unwillingness to lower or abandon goals (*p. 220*).

goal-setting theory A theory of motivation originated by Locke that suggests that behavior is driven by goals and aspirations, such that specific and difficult goals lead to higher levels of achievement (*p. 219*).

grapevine The unofficial communication network within the informal organization through which employees trade gossip and rumors about their jobs, their coworkers, and the organization (*p. 695*).

group decision making A group task in which the ultimate aim is to solve a problem or make a decision (*p. 388*).

group effectiveness An assessment of the extent to which a group is accomplishing its task in the most productive and satisfactory manner (*p. 368*).

groupthink A threat to the effective performance of groups that develops in highly cohesive groups whenever strivings for harmony and unanimity override efforts to appraise group judgments realistically (*p. 390*).

halo error A rating error wherein a rater's judgment about a specific behavior is colored by her overall evaluation of the person she is rating (*p. 137*).

hedonism The belief that human beings generally behave so as to maximize pleasure and minimize pain (*p. 211*).

heroes People who embody the values of an organization's culture and serve as role models for other members in the organization (*p. 699*).

hierarchy of authority A pyramidal distribution of authority in which managers higher in the pyramid can tell managers in lower positions what to do (*p. 23*).

historical decision model A method of generating alternatives for current decisions by reviewing processes that were used in the past (*p. 165*).

history threat A threat to validity created when some important variable other than the one manipulated experimentally changes during an experiment (*p. 69*).

horizontal job enlargement A type of job design based on the idea that increasing the number of tasks a job holder performs will reduce the repetitive nature of the job and thus eliminate worker boredom (*p. 650*).

horizontal specialization The type of specialization in which the work performed at a given hierarchical level is divided into specialized jobs. An example is to divide secretarial work into the jobs of typist, receptionist, and file clerk (*p. 564*).

host group A group that is experiencing difficulties in working with other groups and that asks those groups to send representatives to an intergroup mirroring intervention (*p. 530*).

human factors engineering A type of methods engineering in which experts design machines, operations, and work environments so that they match human capacities and limitations (*p. 643*).

human relations school The school of management thought that emphasizes increasing employee growth, development, and satisfaction (*p. 36*).

human resource management A domain of organizational research that focuses on devising practical, effective ways to manage employee behaviors (*p. 15*).

human skills Management skills involving the ability to work effectively as a group member and to build cooperation among the members of an organization or unit (*p. 44*).

hygiene factors Characteristics of the job that according to Frederick Herzberg, influence the amount of dissatisfaction experienced at work (*p. 652*).

hypothesis A specific, testable prediction, derived typically from a theory, about the relationship between two variables (*p. 59*).

identification Behaving in accord with norms out of respect and admiration for one or more members of the role set (*p. 344*).

implicit theories Loose, informal theories about phenomena that people rarely test in a rigorous, empirical fashion (*p. 59*).

impression management Behaving in ways intended to build a positive public image (*p. 475*).

incentive systems A process by which future pay is made contingent on individual performance based on objective performance indicators and using established quantitative rules (*p. 309*).

incubation A stage in the creative decision-making process in which the person apparently stops attending to the problem at hand (*p. 183*).

individualism-collectivism A cross-cultural dimension that refers to two opposing points of view on the norms and values of a national culture—whether they should place greater emphasis on satisfying personal interests or on looking after group needs (*p. 737*).

individual roles In groups, roles that focus on the satisfaction of members' personal needs and interests even when they conflict with the well-being of the group (*p. 376*).

industrial democracies Industrial organizations, common in Scandinavian countries, that are required by law to permit their members to govern themselves (*p. 741*).

industrial engineering A branch of engineering that concerns itself with how to maximize the efficiency of the methods, facilities, and materials used to produce commercial products (*p. 640*).

industrial robots Machines that can be programmed to repeat the same sequence of work movements over and over again (*p. 665*).

informal groups Groups that satisfy personal needs of their members. *Friendship groups* form among people who like being with each other. *Interest groups* develop among people who want to achieve some mutually beneficial objective (*p. 369*).

informal organization The unofficial rules, procedures, and interconnections that develop as employees make spontaneous, unauthorized changes in the way things are done. (*p. 695*).

information overload A condition in which a person is presented with more information than he can possibly process (*p. 387*).

ingratiation The use of praise and compliments to gain the favor or acceptance of others (*p. 475*).

initiating structure Leader behaviors aimed at meeting the group's task requirements, such as getting workers to follow rules, monitoring performance standards, clarifying roles, and setting goals (*p. 416*).

insight A stage in the creative decision-making process in which the solution to a problem manifests itself in a flash of inspiration (*p. 184*).

instrumentality A person's subjective belief about the relationship between performing a behavior and receiving an outcome (*p. 202*).

instrumentation threat A threat to validity created by artificial changes in the measurement device used to assess an experimental effect (*p. 69*).

integration The third stage of group development, which is focused on reestablishing the central purpose of the group in light of the structure of roles developed during differentiation (*p. 373*).

interaction An experimental outcome in which the relationship between two variables changes depending on the presence or absence of some third variable (*p. 72*).

interactive group A group whose members interact in unstructured, face-to-face relationships like those that take place during ordinary conversations (*p. 388*).

intergroup conflict A process of confrontation that occurs when one group obstructs the progress of one or more other groups (*p. 478*).

intergroup mirroring An organization development intervention of moderate depth in which representatives from several groups tell the members of a particular group with whom they interact how the people they represent perceive the host group (*p. 530*).

intergroup team building A deep OD intervention intended to improve communication and interaction between work-related groups (*p. 531*).

internal change agent An OD change agent who is a member of the client organization (*p. 508*).

internalization Behaving in accord with norms that are consistent with one's own value system (*p. 344*).

interpretation stage The stage in the information processing cycle in which meaning is attached to the relation among abstract concepts (*p. 139*).

intervention An organization development technique, such as counseling or team building, that is used to stimulate change in organizations (*p. 507*).

jargon Idiosyncratic use of language that is often useful among specialists but that inhibits their ability to communicate with nonspecialists (*p. 352*).

job burnout A condition of emotional, physical, and mental exhaustion resulting from prolonged exposure to intense, job-related stress (*p. 251*).

job depth The amount of discretion a jobholder has to choose job activities and outcomes (*p. 651*).

job design The process of deciding what specific tasks each jobholder should perform in the context of the overall work that an organization must accomplish (*p. 639*).

Job Diagnostic Survey A questionnaire that measures workers' perceptions of core job characteristics, critical psychological states, and different moderating factors (*p. 656*).

job evaluation A process by which the pay differentials for jobs throughout the organization are established based on differences in job requirements (*p. 303*).

job extension A type of horizontal job enlargement in which several simplified jobs are combined to form a single new job (*p. 650*).

job-oriented behaviors Leadership behaviors that focus on careful supervision of employees' work methods and performance level (*p. 416*).

job range The number of tasks a jobholder performs to complete the job (*p. 650*).

job rotation The process by which employees are moved periodically from one type of job to another in order to increase their job satisfaction. In formal job rotation programs, workers are rotated among specific jobs in a systematic fashion (*pp. 273, 651*).

job satisfaction The perception that one's job enables one to fulfill important job values (*p. 244*).

job sharing An alternative work schedule in which two or more part-time employees are allowed to share a full-time job (*p. 665*).

judgment stage The stage of the information processing cycle in which recalled information is weighted and aggregated to come up with a single overall judgment (*p. 146*).

kibbutz A close-knit community of people located in Israel and organized on the principles of collective ownership and direct participation in self-governance (*p. 747*).

laissez-faire leader   A leader who lets a group run itself, with minimal intervention from upper levels of the organizational hierarchy (*p. 419*).

language   A system of shared symbols that the members of an organization use to communicate cultural ideas and understandings (*p. 700*).

latent conflict   The stage of conflict development at which dissension is only suspected or at best dimly perceived (*p. 482*).

lateral linkage devices   The types of unit-linking mechanism in which hierarchical links between interdependent units are supplemented by various avenues of mutual adjustment (*p. 572*).

latticework hierarchy   The structure of vertical and horizontal relationships found in many large Japanese corporations (*p. 744*).

leader-follower relations   A component of Fiedler's contingency theory that describes the level of trust and respect between leader and follower (*p. 430*).

leader position power   A component of Fiedler's contingency theory that describes the degree to which the leader can administer significant rewards and punishments to followers (*p. 430*).

leadership   The use of noncoercive influence to direct and coordinate the activities of the members of an organized group toward the accomplishment of group objectives (*p. 411*).

leadership grid figure   A two-dimensional representation of leadership behaviors in which concern for people and concern for production combine to produce five behavioral styles (*p. 417*).

leadership motivation pattern (LMP)   A composite behavior pattern composed of a high need for power, a low need for affiliation, and a high degree of self control, that predicts success in bureaucratic leadership situations (*p. 424*).

leader task structure   A component of Fiedler's contingency theory that describes the clarity of goals and of means-end relationships in a group's task (*p. 430*).

legitimate power   Interpersonal power based on holding a position of formal authority (*p. 463*).

level of analysis   A dimension that classifies the five areas of organizational research according to whether their primary focus is on the behaviors of individuals, of groups, or of organizations (*p. 16*).

Lewin development model   A three-step model of the development process that is followed in every successful OD intervention (*p. 516*).

liaison position   The type of unit-linking mechanism in which one person is made responsible for seeing that communication flows directly and freely between interdependent units. A liaison position has no authority, so its occupant must rely on negotiation, bargaining, and persuasion to move interdependent units toward voluntary coordination (*p. 572*).

life-cycle model   A model that proposes that organizational growth progresses through a series of stages, each of which has its own structural requirements (*p. 608*).

locus of control   The extent to which an individual believes that his own actions influence the environment (*p. 98*).

loosely coupling   Managing interrelatedness across different functional areas by not allowing the actions or decisions of one functional unit to have an overly large or immediate impact on the actions or decisions of other functional units (*p. 181*).

loss aversion bias   The tendency of most decision makers to weigh losses more heavily than gains, even when the absolute value of each is equal (*p. 169*).

Machiavellianism   A personality trait characterized by the tendency to seek to control other people through opportunistic, manipulative behaviors (*p. 472*).

macro organizational behavior   The subfield of organizational behavior that focuses on understanding the actions of a group or an organization as a whole (*p. 15*).

maintenance roles   Group roles that help ensure a group's continued existence by building and preserving strong interpersonal relations among its members (*p. 375*).

management   A process of planning, organizing, directing, and controlling organizational behaviors in order to accomplish a mission through the division of labor (*p. 24*).

manager   A person who is responsible for planning, organizing, directing, and controlling behavior in organizations. *Top managers* are responsible for the entire firm; *middle managers* manage an organizational unit; *supervisory managers* manage the employees who do the firm's basic work (*p. 41*).

managerial role   Behaviors expected of managers in performing their jobs. Managers promote good interpersonal relations in the *interpersonal* role, receive and send information to others in the *informational* role, and determine the firm's direction in the *decisional* role (*p. 45*).

manifest conflict   The stage of conflict development at which people engage in behaviors that are clearly intended to frustrate or block their opponents (*p. 482*).

market grouping   A grouping of people into units according to similarities in the products they make or markets they serve. Grouping the members of an automobile assembly line into an assembly unit is an example (*p. 549*).

market structure   A type of divisional structure formed by grouping units according to similarities in the clients or customers they serve (*p. 600*).

masculinity-femininity   A cross-cultural dimension that refers to the degree to which a culture is founded on values that emphasize independence, aggressiveness, dominance, and physical strength, on the one hand, or interdependence, compassion, empathy, and emotional openness, on the other (*p. 737*).

Maslow's need theory   A theory of motivation that suggests that behavior is driven by the urge to fulfill five fundamental needs: physiological and safety needs love, esteem, and self-actualization (*p. 205*).

mass production   A type of manufacturing technology in which the same product is produced repeatedly, either in large batches or in long production runs. Also called large-batch production (*p. 610*).

matrix organization structure   The type of lateral linkage mechanism that has an organization structure incorporating both functional and divisional departmentation. It is a complex network of mutual adjustment through which intergroup relations are coordinated (*p. 573*).

matrix structure   An extremely flexible but also extremely costly type of complex structure characterized by both functional and divisional departmentation as well as high decentralization. Also called the simultaneous structure (*p. 602*).

maturity   The fourth and final stage of group development, in which members begin to fulfill their prescribed roles and work toward attaining group goals. Many of the agreements reached about goals, roles, and norms are formalized, or preserved in written documentation during this stage (*p. 373*).

mechanistic structures   Machine like organization structures designed to enhance efficiency; characterized by large amounts of formalization, standardization, specialization, and centralization (*p. 595*).

membership groups   Formal and informal groups to which people belong. (*p. 369*).

memomotion analysis   A type of work measurement in which industrial engineers examine longer activity sequences by using slow speed to film or videotape a person at work and then playing back the resulting film or tape at normal speed (*p. 647*).

mentoring relationship   A partnership between a senior and a junior colleague in which the senior partner promotes the development of the junior partner (*p. 317*).

merit-based pay plans   Basing pay increases on subjective ratings of performance made at year end and allocating increases as a percentage of available funds based on these ratings (*p. 308*).

methods engineering   An area of industrial engineering that attempts to improve the methods used to perform work (*p. 641*).

micromotion analysis   A type of work measurement in which industrial engineers analyze the hand and body movements required to do a job (*p. 646*).

micro organizational behavior   The subfield of organizational behavior concerned with understanding the behaviors of individuals working alone or in small groups (*p. 14*).

mirror image fallacy   The false belief that all people are alike or that others share one's own abilities, beliefs, motives, or predispositions (*p. 83*).

mission   An organization's purpose or reason for being (*p. 22*).

monitors   Leader behaviors that involve collecting performance information on subordinates (*p. 440*).

mortality threat A threat to validity created when subjects who drop out of an experimental group differ on some significant characteristic or characteristics from those who drop out of the control group (*p. 68*).

motivating potential score A summary score calculated from data obtained with the Job Diagnostic Survey (*p. 657*).

motivation The factors that initiate, direct, and sustain human behavior over time (*p. 200*).

motivator factors Characteristics of the job that according to Frederick Herzberg, influence the amount of satisfaction experienced at work (*p. 651*).

motive A reflection of an individual's underlying drives, needs, and values (*p. 97*).

mutual adjustment A unit coordination mechanism in which coordination is accomplished via face-to-face communications. Coworkers who occupy positions of similar hierarchical authority exchange information about how a job should be done and who should do it (*p. 552*).

myth A story that provides a fictional but plausible explanation for something that might otherwise seem puzzling (*p. 698*).

national culture The collection of societal norms and values in the environment surrounding an organization (*p. 734*).

negative affectivity A person's tendency to often experience feelings of subjective distress such as anger, contempt, disgust, guilt, fear, and nervousness (*p. 261*).

negative reinforcement The increase in a response that occurs when engaging in the response leads to the removal of an aversive stimulus (*p. 212*).

negotiation A process in which groups with conflicting interests decide what each will give and take in the exchange between them (*p. 485*).

nenko system A Japanese system of payment in which the pay an employee receives is determined by a basic wage plus merit supplements and job-level allowances (*p. 745*).

noise A collective term for a number of factors that can distort a message as it is transmitted from one person to another (*p. 346*).

nominal group technique A group decision-making process in which face-to-face interaction of group members is limited (*p. 394*).

norms A strong set of expectations that members of a role set have for the role occupant (*p. 342*).

nova technique A method of generating alternatives by seeking new and innovative solutions (*p. 166*).

novice The stage of skill development in which people learn elementary rules and procedures that, followed mechanically, result in actions resembling skilled behaviors (*p. 8*).

objectivity In science, the degree to which a set of scientific findings are independent of any one person's opinion about them (*p. 56*).

off-the-shelf decision model A method of generating alternatives for current decisions by consulting agents external to the organization that have standardized, ready-made alternatives (*p. 165*).

open-office plan A physical work environment that minimizes interior walls and partitions (*p. 261*).

open revolution Rejection by group members of both pivotal and peripheral norms (*p. 377*).

open system contingencies Structural contingency factors that are characteristics of the environment surrounding an organization (*p. 596*).

open system planning A deep organization-level intervention that helps the members of an organization devise ways to accomplish the mission of their firm in light of the demands of environmental constituency groups (*p. 707*).

open systems school The school of management thought that characterizes every organization as a system that is open to the influence of the surrounding environment (*p. 38*).

opinion leader A person who has special access to an organization's informal channels of communication and therefore has enhanced ability to influence others (*p. 353*).

organic structures Organism-like organization structures designed to enhance flexibility and innovation; characterized by large amounts of mutual adjustment and decentralization (*p. 595*).

organization An assembly of people and materials brought together to accomplish a purpose that would be beyond the means of individuals working alone (*p. 22*).

organization design The process of diagnosing the situation that confronts a particular organization and selecting and putting in place the organization structure most appropriate for that situation (*p. 592*).

organization development (OD) A planned approach to interpersonal, group, intergroup, and organization-wide change that is comprehensive and long term and that is guided by a change agent. Organization development research develops techniques to encourage cooperation and to manage change (*pp. 15, 507*).

organization role The total set of expectations that people who interact with an organizational member have for that person and his performance of his job (*p. 260*).

organization size The number of members in an organization; its volume of sales, clients, or profits; its physical capacity (e.g.,a hospital's number of beds or a hotel's number of rooms); or the total financial assets that it controls (*p. 606*).

organization stage The stage in the information processing cycle in which many discrete bits of information are chunked into higher-level, abstract concepts (*p. 134*).

organization structure The relatively stable network of interconnections or interdependencies among the people and tasks that make up an organization (*p. 548*).

organizational behavior (OB) A field of study that endeavors to understand, explain, predict, and change human behavior as it occurs in the organizational context (*p. 7*).

organizational commitment Identification with one's employer that includes the willingness to work hard on behalf of the organization and the intention to remain with the organization for an extended period of time (*p. 254*).

organizational confrontation An organization-level OD intervention of moderate depth that enables managers to assess the internal workings of the organization and plan corrective actions as needed (*p. 706*).

organizational effectiveness The degree to which an organization is successful in achieving its goals and objectives while at the same time ensuring its continued survival by satisfying the demands of interested parties, such as suppliers and customers (*p. 593*).

organizational efficiency The ratio of outputs produced per unit of inputs consumed; minimizing the raw materials and energy consumed by the production of goods and services (*p. 594*).

organizational power Types of interpersonal power (reward, coercive, and legitimate power) that often derive from company policies and procedures (*p. 465*).

organizational productivity The amount of goods or services produced by an organization. Higher productivity means that more goods or services are produced (*p. 594*).

organizational socialization The process by which a person acquires the social knowledge and skills necessary to assume an organizational role (*p. 354*).

organizational unit A recognizable group of employees responsible for completing its own particular functional and/or operational objectives (*p. 26*).

organizing The management function of developing a structure of interrelated tasks and allocating people and resources within this structure (*p. 25*).

participatory management A management style in which managers and nonmanagers work together to make decisions about what products to produce, which raw materials to purchase, what production processes to use, and similar issues (*p. 367*).

pay structure An organization's hierarchical arrangement of jobs expressed in terms of pay differentials (*p. 303*).

perceived conflict The stage of conflict development at which problems are readily perceived and everyone involved in the conflict knows that it exists (*p. 482*).

perceptual ability An individual's capacity to quickly and accurately recognize visual details (*p. 89*).

perceptual defense The process by which an individual avoids processing information that is potentially threatening (*p. 132*).

performance programs Scripts that detail exactly what actions are to be taken by a job incumbent when confronted with a standard problem or situation (*p. 180*).

peripheral norms Group norms for which adherence is desirable but not essential (*p. 376*).

personal conceptions A person's thoughts, attitudes, and beliefs about his social and physical environment (*p. 98*).

personal power Types of interpersonal power (expert and referent power) that are based on the possession of certain personal traits or characteristics (*p. 465*).

personality dynamics A class of personality characteristics that deal with the integration and organization of traits, motives, personal conceptions, and adjustment (*p. 100*).

personnel placement The process by which an organization assigns new employees to specific jobs (*p. 85*).

personnel selection The process by which an organization decides who will and who will not be allowed to work for an organization (*p. 84*).

persuasive argumentation The theory that when group discussions uncover arguments favoring extreme positions, moderate group members may switch to more extreme choices (*p. 390*).

phenomenal absolutism The belief that one's perceptions reflect reality perfectly (*p. 121*).

physical ability Ability to perform a task involving body movement, strength, endurance, dexterity, force, or speed (*p. 85*).

pivotal norms Group norms for which adherence is an absolute requirement of continued group membership (*p. 376*).

planned change model A model of the organization development process that is an expansion of the Lewin development model and that describes the implementation of an off-the-shelf intervention (*p. 518*).

planning The management function of deciding what to do in the future; setting goals and establishing the means to attain them (*p. 25*).

politics Activities in which individuals or groups acquire power and use it to advance their own interests (*p. 471*).

pooled interdependence A type of interaction where individuals draw off a common resource pool but do not interact with each other in any other way (*p. 334*).

portfolio The mix of different businesses owned by an organization (*p. 688*).

positive reinforcement The increase in a response that occurs when engaging in the response leads to obtaining a pleasurable stimulus (*p. 212*).

power The ability to influence the conduct of others and resist unwanted influence in return (*p. 460*).

power distance A cross-cultural dimension that refers to the degree to which the members of a society accept differences in power and status among themselves (*p. 738*).

preparation A stage in the creative decision-making process in which the person accumulates information needed to solve a problem (*p. 182*).

prepotency The notion arising from Maslow's theory that higher-order needs can influence motivation only if lower-order needs are largely satisfied (*p. 205*).

prescription The diagnostic model step of developing a solution to a problem statement that has been identified through diagnosis (*p. 12*).

primary appraisal In cognitive appraisal theory, the first stage in one's assessment of the environment in which one judges whether some object in the environment is good or bad, beneficial or harmful, an opportunity or a threat (*p. 248*).

primary orientation A dimension that classifies the five areas of organizational research according to whether their main focus is on abstract theories or practical techniques (*p. 16*).

priming Forcing raters to recall a specific set of events so that subsequent judgments will be biased by what is recalled (*p. 147*).

privacy The freedom to work unobserved by others and without undue interruption (*p. 261*).

procedural justice Perceived fairness of the process by which reward allocations have been made (*p. 162*).

process consultation A shallow group-level OD intervention in which a change agent meets with a work group and helps its members examine group processes such as communication, leadership and followership, problem solving, and cooperation (*p. 527*).

process engineering A type of methods engineering in which specialists study the sequence of tasks required to produce a particular good or service and examine how these tasks fit together into an integrated job (*p. 641*).

process loss The difference between what is produced by a group of individuals and what would be produced by the same people working alone (*p. 379*).

process theories Theories of motivation that attempt to specify how different kinds of events or outcomes motivate behavior (*p. 201*).

product structure A type of divisional structure formed by grouping units according to similarities in the products they make and sell (*p. 600*).

production blocking The negative effect on productivity caused by people getting in each other's way as they try to perform a group task (*p. 379*).

professionalization The use of professionals to perform work for which useful written specifications do not exist and in some cases, cannot be prepared (*p. 562*).

professionals People who develop work-related knowledge, skills, and abilities in training programs conducted outside an employing organization. Examples include teachers, lawyers, doctors, and managers trained in schools of business (*p. 562*).

proficiency The stage of skill development in which people learn how to read situations instinctively and respond to familiar circumstances intuitively, deliberating consciously only in unusual situations (*p. 9*).

profit-sharing plans Fringe benefit programs in which profits are calculated at year end and distributed to employees, typically in a deferred fashion (*p. 310*).

projection A bias in the interpretation of information wherein the perceiver assumes that his own motivations explain the behaviors of others (*p. 140*).

projective test A measure of personality in which individuals are asked to assign meaning to an ambiguous stimulus. Unconscious aspects of the personality are inferred from the person's responses (*p. 103*).

protected groups Groups of people defined in Civil Rights legislation who warrant special consideration in personnel selection, placement, and other procedures (*p. 299*).

prototype One type of schema that involves a unified configuration of personal characteristics that are used to classify persons into "types" (*p. 136*).

psychomotor ability Ability to perform a task involving coordination between physical and mental functions (*p. 86*).

punishment A decrease in a response that occurs when engaging in the response leads to receiving an aversive stimulus (*p. 212*).

quality circles Committees or small groups of employees charged with identifying and solving productivity problems on the job. Quality circles typically use a participatory approach (*pp. 367, 663*).

quality of work life The degree to which work and membership in an organization facilitates the satisfaction of important personal needs and interests (*p. 709*).

quantitative ability A specific form of cognitive ability that deals with the understanding and application of mathematical rules and operations (*p. 89*).

random assignment A method of increasing the validity of a study by ensuring that each subject has an equal probability of being assigned to any one experimental condition. Random assignment eliminates the *selection threat* (*p. 71*).

rational decision-making model A model in which decisions are made systematically and based consistently on the principle of economic rationality (*p. 163*).

realistic previewing A technique sometimes used during counseling interventions to help people form sensible expectations about workplace relationships (*p. 524*).

reasoning ability An individual's capacity to invent solutions to many different types of problems (*p. 89*).

reciprocal interdependence A type of interaction in which there are two-way links among individuals (*p. 335*).

reference groups Groups of people with whom individuals compare themselves in order to assess their own personal attitudes or behavior (*p. 369*).

referent power Interpersonal power based on the possession of attractive personal characteristics (*p. 463*).

refreezing The third step in the Lewin development model in which the change that took place during the transforming step becomes stable and permanent (*p. 517*).

regression toward the mean The phenomenon whereby in a series of events that is influenced by complex factors, any single extraordinary event is almost sure to be followed by a more ordinary event (*p. 172*).

reinforcement theory A theory of motivation that suggests that people are motivated to engage in or avoid certain behaviors because of past rewards and punishments associated with those behaviors (*p. 212*).

reliability The degree to which a measure of an individual, group, organizational, or environmental attribute is free from random error and thus replicable (*p. 61*).

representative groups The type of unit-linking mechanism in which representatives of interdependent units meet to coordinate intergroup activities (*p. 572*).

retrieval stage The stage of the information processing cycle in which the observer tries to recall information about past events (*p. 144*).

revolutionary growth strategies A class of corporate strategies in which the firm develops or acquires businesses that are quite different from businesses it already owns. Included in this class are forward integration, backward integration, and conglomerate diversification (*p. 690*).

reward power Interpersonal power based on the ability to control how desirable outcomes are distributed (*p. 462*).

rite A ceremonial activity meant to communicate particular messages or accomplish specific purposes (*p. 697*).

ritual A ceremonial event that occurs repeatedly and continues to reinforce key norms and values (*p. 697*).

role The typical and expected behaviors that characterize an individual's position in some social context (*p. 336*).

role ambiguity Lack of clarity about the expectations of a person's role in an organization (*p. 267*).

role analysis technique An interpersonal OD intervention of moderate depth intended to help people form and maintain effective working relationships by clarifying role expectations (*p. 524*).

role conflict Conflict or incompatibility between the demands facing a person who occupies a particular role (*p. 267*).

role innovation A product of socialization in which a new group member is expected to improve on both the goals for her job and the means of achieving them (*p. 354*).

role occupant The current incumbent of an existing organizational work role (*p. 343*).

role scope The total number of expectations that exist for the person occupying a particular role (*p. 267*).

role set The entire group of individuals who have an interest in and expectations about the way a role occupant performs his job (*p. 342*).

satisfaction perspective An approach to job design that suggests that fitting the characteristics of jobs to the needs and interests of the people who perform them provides the opportunity for satisfaction at work (*p. 649*).

satisficing Settling for a decision alternative that meets some minimum level of acceptability, as opposed to trying to maximize utility by considering all possible alternatives (*p. 178*).

scapegoats People who are blamed, whether rightly or not, for the failures of groups or organizations (*p. 476*).

schema Cognitive structures that group discrete bits of perceptual information in an organized fashion. (The term *schema* is used for both singular and plural forms) (*p. 135*).

scientific management school The school of management thought that focuses on increasing the efficiency of production processes in order to enhance organizational profitability (*p. 28*).

scientific method An objective method of expanding knowledge characterized by an endless cycle of theory building, hypothesis formation, data collection, empirical hypothesis testing, and theoretical modification (*p. 56*).

script A schema that involves well-known sequences of action (*p. 135*).

secondary appraisal In cognitive appraisal theory, the second stage in a person's assessment of the environment in which he judges his capacity to cope with perceived threats or opportunities in the environment (*p. 248*).

selection threat A threat to validity created when experimental and control groups differ from each other before an experimental manipulation (*p. 68*).

self-contained tasks The type of decoupling mechanism formed by combining the work of two or more interdependent units and assigning their work to several independent work units. Those units are then staffed by people drawn from each of the original units (*p. 571*).

self-efficacy The judgments people make about their ability to execute courses of action required to deal with prospective situations (*p. 216*).

self-esteem The degree to which a person believes that she is a worthwhile and deserving individual (*p. 100*).

self-inventory A measure of personality characteristics that asks the individual to describe herself by means of standardized responses to questionnaire items (*p. 101*).

semiautonomous groups Groups that are subject to the management direction needed to ensure adherence to organizational policies but are otherwise responsible for managing group activities (*p. 659*).

sensitivity training A deep interpersonal OD intervention that focuses on developing greater sensitivity to oneself, to others, and to one's relations with others through an intense, leaderless group experience (*p. 526*).

sequential interdependence A type of interaction in which individuals are arrayed in a chain of one-way links (*p. 335*).

shaping Bringing about a desired behavior by rewarding successive approximations to that behavior (*p. 214*).

simple differentiated structure A type of simple structure in which coordination is achieved by means of direct supervision (*p. 598*).

simple structure An uncomplicated type of organization structure that relies on mutual adjustment or direct supervision to achieve coordination (*p. 597*).

simple undifferentiated structure A type of simple organization structure in which coordination is achieved solely by means of mutual adjustment (*p. 597*).

situation analysis An analysis of internal strengths and weaknesses and external opportunities and threats that is performed during the process of strategic planning (*p. 686*).

situational interview A work sample test in which the applicant is asked to respond orally to hypothetical problems that might confront him while working on the job (*p. 294*).

skill-acquisition model A five-stage model of the process of developing expertise in a particular behavior (*p. 8*).

skill testing Measuring narrow, job-specific abilities of job applicants (*p. 293*).

slack resources The type of decoupling mechanism in which groups are separated from each other by buffer inventories (*p. 571*).

small-batch production A type of manufacturing technology that involves the production of one-of-a-kind items or small quantities of goods designed to meet unique customer specifications. Also called unit production (*p. 610*).

social comparison The theory that when people in groups hear others voicing extreme positions they often abandon their cautious choices and revert to their initial extreme positions (*p. 390*).

social density An index of crowding, typically calculated as the number of people occupying an area divided by the number of square feet in that area (*p. 261*).

social desirability bias The tendency for individuals responding to self-inventories to describe themselves in socially flattering ways (*p. 102*).

social information Information growing out of cultural norms, values, and shared opinions that shapes the way people perceive themselves, their jobs, and the organization (*p. 700*).

social-learning theory A theory of motivation originated by Bandura that suggests that behavior is often driven by the desire of an observer to model the behavior of some other person (*p. 214*).

social loafing The choice by some group members to take advantage of others by doing less work, working more slowly, or in other ways contributing less to group productivity (*p. 379*).

social support　A surrounding environment in which people are sympathetic and caring (*p. 260*).

social traits　Behavior patterns that an individual typically displays when interacting with others in social contexts (*p. 95*).

sociotechnical enrichment　A type of job design that recognizes the importance of satisfying the needs of employees within the technical requirements of an organization's production system (*p. 658*).

solution verification　A stage in the creative decision-making process wherein the person tests the efficacy of a proposed novel solution (*p. 184*).

span of control　Another name for unit size; the number of people under the supervision of a single direct supervisor (*p. 558*).

spatial visualization　An individual's capacity to mentally manipulate objects in space and time (*p. 89*).

special-interest committees　Committees in Scandinavian industrial democracies composed of worker and manager representatives. They combine with middle management to produce yearly reports that assist works councils with the task of formulating company policies (*p. 742*).

specialization　The division of an organization's work into specialist jobs of narrow scope and limited variability (*p. 563*).

standard time analysis　A time study technique in which an analyst matches the results of micromotion analysis with standard time charts to determine the average time that should be required to perform a job (*p. 647*).

standardization　In scientific measurement, the practice of ensuring that all people measure the same variables with the same instruments applied in the same manner. In structural design, a unit coordination mechanism in which work is coordinated by providing employees with carefully worked out standards and procedures that guide the performance of their tasks. It is coordination achieved on the drawing board, before the work is actually undertaken, and may involve standardization of work processes and behaviors, outputs, skills, or norms. (*p. 552*).

standing committee　The type of representative group formed to meet on a regular basis to discuss and resolve intergroup coordination problems. A standing committee has no specific task, nor is it expected to disband at any particular time (*p. 573*).

statistical significance　A numerical index of the probability that a relationship detected between two variables could be explained by luck or chance (*p. 65*).

stereotype accuracy　The extent to which a rater's assessment of a group of people, on a single dimension, reflects the group's true standing on that dimension (*p. 127*).

stopwatch time analysis　A time study technique in which an analyst uses a stopwatch to time the sequence of motions needed to complete a job (*p. 647*).

story　An account of past events that all employees are familiar with and that serves as a reminder of cultural understandings (*p. 698*).

strategic business unit structure　An extremely complex structure consisting of two or more autonomous strategic business units (SBUs), which themselves have complete organization structures (*p. 603*).

strategic management　A process of setting organizational goals and directing the organization toward goal achievement. Strategic management research is concerned with defining an organization's purpose and planning how to achieve organizational objectives (*pp. 16, 684*).

strategy　A plan of action that states an organization's goals and outlines the resources and activities required to achieve them (*p. 684*).

stress　An unpleasurable emotional state resulting from the perception that a situational demand exceeds one's capacity and that it is very important to meet the demand (*p. 246*).

structural contingency factors　Characteristics of an organization and its surrounding circumstances that influence whether its structure will contribute to organizational effectiveness (*p. 595*).

subliminal perception　Information that is encoded by a perceiver without his or her awareness (*p. 130*).

substitutability　The extent to which other people or groups can grant access to the same critical contingencies provided by the focal person or group (*p. 469*).

substitute for leadership　Someone or something in the leader's environment that affects workers' attitudes, perceptions, or behaviors in such a way that the leader's role is made superfluous (*p. 422*).

subversive rebellion　Acceptance by group members of peripheral norms but rejection of pivotal ones (*p. 377*).

superstars　Cultural figures who are so extraordinary that they rise above their peers and sometimes even become symbols for an entire industry (*p. 699*).

survey feedback　A shallow organization-level OD intervention intended to stimulate information sharing throughout the entire organization (*p. 705*).

symbol　An object, action, or event to which people have assigned special meaning (*p. 699*).

symbolic management　A process in which managers attempt to influence deep cultural norms and values by shaping the surface cultural elements that organization members use to express and transmit cultural understandings (*p. 701*).

target　The specific focus of an OD intervention's change efforts (*p. 523*).

task force　A type of representative group that is formed to complete a specific task or project and then disbanded (*p. 572*).

task-oriented roles　Group roles that focus on making a contribution to successful task performance and accomplishing the group's task (*p. 375*).

team development　A deep group-level extension of interpersonal sensitivity training in which a group of people who work together on a daily basis meet over an extended period to assess and modify group processes (*p. 529*).

team diagnostic session　A group OD intervention of moderate depth in which a change agent and a work group critique the group's performance and look for ways to improve it (*p. 527*).

team interdependence　A type of group interaction in which every group member depends on every other (*p. 335*).

technical skills　Management skills involving an understanding of the specific knowledge, procedures, and tools used to make the goods or services produced by an organization or unit (*p. 45*).

technology　The knowledge, procedures, and equipment used in an organization to transform unprocessed resources into finished goods or services (*p. 609*).

temporal precedence　The degree to which any measured cause actually precedes an effect in time (*p. 63*).

theory　A set of interrelated constructs, definitions, and propositions that present a systematic view of phenomena by specifying relations among variables (*p. 59*).

Theory X　A managerial point of view that assumes that nonmanagerial employees have little interest in attaining organizational goals and must therefore be motivated to fit the needs of the organization (*p. 36*).

Theory Y　A managerial point of view that assumes that nonmanagerial employees will readily direct behavior toward organizational goals if given the opportunity to do so (*p. 36*).

third party peacemaking　A shallow OD intervention in which a change agent seeks to resolve intergroup misunderstandings by encouraging communication between or among groups (*p. 530*).

top-down selection within subgroups　Personnel selection practice in which scores on a test are arrayed by subgroup and a flexible goal for representation from each group is decided upon. Selection proceeds from the highest to lowest score in each subgroup until all positions are filled and all subgroups are represented (*p. 300*).

training　The process of teaching organization-specific and, often, job-specific skills on the job or in a formal program sponsored by the employing organization (*p. 562*).

transforming　In the Lewin development model, the step in which change actually occurs (*p. 517*).

Type A behavior pattern　A set of personality characteristics that include aggressiveness, competitiveness, and the tendency to work under self-induced time pressures (*p. 99*).

uncertainty avoidance　A cross-cultural dimension that refers to the degree to which people are comfortable with ambiguous situations and with the inability to predict future events with assurance (*p. 736*).

unconditioned stimulus A stimulus that naturally and invariably produces a given response (*p. 211*).

unfreezing In the Lewin development model, the step in which one tries to weaken old attitudes, values, and behaviors and to get people ready for change (*p. 517*).

unit coordination mechanism A mechanism that sustains structural interconnections in structural units by helping to mesh interdependent task activities (*p. 552*).

unit grouping The process of grouping the members of an organization into work groups or units (*p. 549*).

unit linking mechanisms Mechanisms that regulate intergroup coordination by linking interdependent units more closely together (*p. 571*).

unit size The number of people who belong to a structural unit (*p. 558*).

utility maximization A process by which a decision maker selects the one alternative that leads to the highest possible payoff (*p. 166*).

valence The amount of satisfaction an individual anticipates receiving from a particular outcome (*p. 202*).

validity The degree to which a measure of an individual, group, organizational, or environmental attribute does what it is intended to do (*p. 62*).

verbal ability A specific type of cognitive ability that deals with the comprehension and use of language (*p. 89*).

verification A stage in the scientific process in which scientists assess the degree to which hypotheses based on theories match empirical data (*p. 59*).

vertical dyad Two persons who are related hierarchically, such as a supervisor-subordinate pair (*p. 426*).

vertical information system The type of unit linking mechanism in which computer networks are used to facilitate managerial communication and information processing. Managers can deal with more coordination information than would otherwise be possible (*p. 572*).

vertical job enrichment A type of job design based on the idea that giving job holders the discretion to choose job activities and outcomes will improve their satisfaction. (*p. 651*).

vertical specialization The type of specialization in which the management of work is separated from the performance of that work. It establishes the number of levels of hierarchy in an organization (*p. 564*).

voice The formal opportunity to complain to the organization about one's work situation (*p. 271*).

work measurement An area of industrial engineering concerned with measuring the amount of work accomplished and developing standards for performing work of an acceptable quantity and quality (*p. 646*).

work sample tests Tests that present job applicants with realistic simulations of actual job problems and ask them to indicate how they would handle them (*p. 294*).

works council A committee of worker representatives who are elected by their peers and management representatives who are appointed by top management. It oversees policy formulation in Scandinavian industrial democracies (*p. 741*).

INDEXES

NAME

COMPANY

Deprivation-domination hypothesis, 207
Depth, of interventions, 522–23
Description, as purpose of science, 57
Description step, diagnostic model, 10–11, 78, 124, 161, 200
Descriptive information, 10
Design, organization (see Organization design; Structure, organization)
Designs, research, 69–73
Desire, in motivation, 203–4, 216 (see also Needs)
Diagnosis stage, and OD, 519
Diagnosis step, diagnostic model, 11–12, 78, 124, 161, 200
Diagnostic model or approach, 10–14, 78
  and change, 506–7
  and communication, 331–32
  and conflict, 460
  and contingency perspective, 14
  and decision making, 161
  definition, 10
  ethical implications, 13
  and groups, 331–32, 367–68
  and international management, 734
  issues, 83
  and job design, 640, 684
  and leadership, 409
  and motivation, 200, 204
  observation in, 10
  and organization design, 592
  and organization development, 506–7
  and perception, 124–25
  and personnel duties, 291
  and politics, 460
  and power, 460
  problem statement, 11–12
  steps, 10–13, 17
  and stress, 244
  and structure, 548, 684
  using, 13
Differential accuracy, 128
Differential Aptitude Test, 293
Differential elevation accuracy, 127
Differentiation, and structure (see Structure, organization)
Differentiation stage, of group development, 372–73
Differentiation strategy, 692–94
Diffusion of responsibility, 381
Dimensions, cognitive ability (see Cognitive abilities)
Direct interaction, 335
Direct supervision, and structure, 552, 555–58, 598–99, 603, 606–8, 611, 750
Directing:
  definition, 26
  as part of management process, 24, 26–27, 43–44
Disciplinary meeting rules, 313–14
Discipline (see also Punishment):
  as a principle of management, 31n
  programs, 313–15
  progressive, 313
  in work teams, 313
Discretion, in decision making, 180
Disparate impact, 300
Disparate treatment, 300
Dissatisfaction, job (see Satisfaction, job)
Disseminator, role of, 45–46
Distinctiveness, in attributions, 143
Distress (see Stress)
Distributive justice, 162
Disturbance handler, role of, 45–46
Disturbed reactive environment, 39
Diversity:
  and intergroup conflict, 480–81
  internal, 187
  training, 302
  in workforce, 302
Divestiture strategy, 691
Division, as type of organizational unit, 26
Division of labor, 23, 31, 32, 44
Division of work, principle of management, 31n
Divisional departmentation, 566–68, 600, 602, 606, 620 (see also Divisional structure)
Divisional objectives, 25
Divisional structure, 600–602, 604, 606, 608, 611, 613–14, 744 (see also Divisional departmentation)
Documents, written, 11, 32
Dog, and BCG Matrix, 689
Dominance, and leadership, 414
Domination, and management, 27
Dominators, as type of individual role, 376
Dress, as form of nonverbal communication, 347n

Drive (see Instincts, Motive; Needs)
Dual-career couples, 318–19

Economic maximization, 163
Economic rationality, 163
Economic rewards, 36
Economic sanctions, 36
Economics, 15
Effectiveness:
  goals and objectives, 25
  organizational, 593–94, 596, 614
Efficacy-based futility, 216
Efficiency:
  and administrative principles school, 30
  and bureaucracy, 33
  and division of labor, 23
  and Hawthorne studies, 34–36
  and job design, 639–49, 665–66
  organizational, 594–95, 599, 603–4
  and principles of scientific management, 28–29, 40, 639
  with standardized measures, 62
  and Theory X assumptions, 36
Effort (see also Motivation):
  in motivation, 203–4, 216, 218–20
  and performance, 223
Ego, as defense mechanisms, 93–94
Elaboration stage, in organization life cycle, 608
Elevation accuracy, 125–27
Emergent task elements, 337
Emotional adjustment, personality characteristic, 99–100
Emotional release, and OD, 530
Employee Aptitude Survey, 293
Employee assistance programs, 257
Employee-centered behavior, of leaders, 414, 416
Employee ownership, 36
Employee Polygraph Protection Act, 97
Employee relations index, 53
Employee reliability scale, 96
Employee Retirement Income Securities Act, 253
Employees:
  growth and development, 36
  motivation of, 3, 36 (see also Motivation)
Employment at will doctrine, 314
Encoding stage, in communication, 345
Encouragers, as type of maintenance role, 375–76
Engineering, and job design, 640–46
Enriched model, in decision making, 165
Entity attraction, 259
Entrepreneur, role of, 45–46
Entrepreneur stage, of organization life cycle, 608
Entrepreneurial situation, and leadership, 424–25
Entry stage, and OD, 519
Environment (see also Climate; Culture; Hawthorne studies; Physical environment; Social environment; Structure, organization)
  adapting to, 38–40
  and buffering, 260
  and change, 615–16
  characteristics, 620
  complexity, 616–17, 621
  in decision making, 174, 177–78, 180, 182
  demands, 249
  diversity, 620
  domains, 620
  dynamic, 615–16, 621
  external, 615
  hostility, 618–19, 622
  internal, 615 (see also Culture)
  monitoring, 46, 742
  munificent, 618, 622
  open systems school, 38–40
  physical-technological, 258–59
  receptivity, 618–19
  simple, 621
  social, 259–61, 658
  and social support, 260, 273
  stable, 615–16, 621
  and stress, 246, 249
  and structure, 596, 615–20
  types, 39
  uncertainty, 617–18
  uniformity, 620
Equalization component, 227
Equating groups, 72
Equity:
  principle of management, 31n
  of rewards, 437

Equity theory, 224–28, 303
  and compensable factors, 304, 306
  negative inequity, 225
  over-compensation effect, 225
  positive inequity, 225
  responses to inequity, 225–28
  and satisfaction, 228
  under-compensation effect, 225
Equivocal feedback, 175
ERG theory, of motivation, 207–8
Ergonomics, 643–45
ERISA (see Employment Retirement Income Securities Act)
Escalation of commitment, as threat to decision making, 173–74
Esprit de corps, principle of management, 31n
Established task elements, 336
Esteem, in need hierarchy, 205–6
Ethical issues:
  and environmental influences, 619n
  in honesty testing, 97
  and power, 462n
  in problem resolution, 12–13
  in research, 74
Eustress, 247
Evaluating OD, 533–35
Evaluators, as type of task-oriented role, 375
Evolution, theory of, 85
Evolutionary adaptation, in group formation, 332–33
Evolutionary growth strategies, 689–90
Example setting, and politics, 476–77
Excellence, principles of, 53–54
Executive celebrities, 21
Exercise, and stress, 272
Exhaustion stage, in General adaptation syndrome, 250–51
Existence needs, 207
Expectancy, 201, 203, 205, 216, 219, 309, 437 (see also Expectancy theory)
Expectancy theory, 201–3, 205, 308, 437, 442 (see also Expectancy; Instrumentality; Valence)
Expectation effects, 291
Expectations (see also Norms):
  conforming to, 344–45
  internal factor in attention stage, 131
  and organization role, 266–67
  of workers, 336
Expected values, in decision making, 166, 168
Experience, job, 91
  and job knowledge, 110
  as moderator, 93
Experiential exercises, definition, 8
Experiment, and generalizability, 73–76
Experimental group, 71
Experimental psychology, 14
Expert judgments, in test validation, 294–95
Expert power, 463–64, 466–67 (see also Power)
Expertise stage, management skills learning, 8, 10
Explanation:
  building into research, 72
  in causal inference, 68
  as purpose of science, 57
Explicit statements, in norm formation, 342
Explicit theories, and scientific process, 59–60
External factors, in attention stage, 130–31
Extinction, 212–13, 229

Faces Scale, 245–47
Faulty designs, 70–71
Fear of failure, and change, 510
Feedback:
  channels, 657
  in decision making, 167, 175
  in goal setting, 220
  in job design, 655, 657
  loops, in motivation, 228–29
Feedback stage, and OD, 521
Femininity dimension, of culture, 736–37, 753, 755
Fiedler's contingency model of leadership, 429–33
Fight response to stress, 249
Figurehead, role of, 45–56
Fixed interval schedule of reinforcement, 214
Fixed ratio schedule of reinforcement, 213
Flexible cell production, and technology, 611–12 (see also Flexible manufacturing cells)
Flexible-hour programs, and job design, 664
Flexible manufacturing, 505
Flexible manufacturing cells, 666
Flextime, 664
Flight response to stress, 249, 255, 273
Focus strategy, 693

Followers, as type of maintenance role, 376
Forcefield analysis, and change, 513–14, 517
Formal groups, 370–71
Formal organization, 684–85
Formalization, and structure, 559–62, 595, 599, 600, 603–4, 609, 649
Formalization stage, in organization life cycle, 608
Formation stage of group development, 372
Forward integration strategy, 690
Frame of reference in communication, 350–52
Free riding, 380
Frequency, external factor in attention stage, 131
Frequency of data collection, 69–73
Friendship groups, 369–70
Functional attraction, 259
Functional departmentation, 566–67, 599, 602, 620 (*see also* Functional grouping; Functional structure)
Functional dimension, of organizations, 338, 354
Functional grouping, and structure, 549–50
Functional objectives, 25
Functional principle of organization, 33
Functional strategies, 693–94
Functional structure, 549–51, 599–600, 604, 606, 608, 611, 613–14, 744 (*see also* Functional departmentation)

Gainsharing, 641
Gantt chart, 30
Gatekeeper, as communication role, 352
Gender discrimination, 755
General adaptation syndrome, 249–51, 273
General Aptitude Test, 302
General intelligence (*see* Intelligence)
General Schedule System, for pay scales, 304
Generalizability, of research, 73–76
Geographic structures (*see* Divisional structure)
GMAT, 293
Goal commitment, 220
    and need for achievement, 221
Goal consensus:
    in affirmative action, 299
    in decision making, 174–75
Goal origin, 221
Goal-setting theory, 219–23
Goals (*see also* Objectives):
    and abilities, 223
    assigned, 221
    as benchmarks, 25
    challenging, 3
    and change, 510
    and conflict, 484
    in decision making, 174–75
    definition, 220
    difficult, 219–20, 222
    and group formation, 333–34
    and industrial democracy, 34
    means-ends relationship, 223–24
    organizational, 733
    as part of planning, 25
    and performance, 222, 381–82
    personal, 37
    private, 220–21
    public, 220–21
    research, 76
    of science, 57–58
    self-set, 221
    setting, 46, 76, 100
    shared, 174
    simple, 220, 222
    specific, 219–20, 222
    strategic goals, 25
    and strategy, 222, 684, 685
    and structure, 560
    superordinate, 484
    and task complexity, 222
    understanding, as scientific goal, 78
    vague, 220
Government regulations, and change, 512
Graduate Management Admissions Test, 293
Grapevine, 695 (*see also* Communication)
Gratification-activation hypothesis, 207
Group (*see also* Intergroup conflict; Intergroup coordination mechanism; Intergroup interventions; Intergroup mirroring; Intergroup team building; Satisfaction, of group members; Team development; Team interdependence; Teams; Teamwork; Work group):
    characteristics of, 368
    cohesiveness, 373, 384–86, 390–91, 483, 510

communication structure, 386–88
    and conflict, 485
    consensus, 373
    constituency, 593–94
    control, in research, 71
    cultural differences, 371n
    decision making, 388–97
    definition, 368
    development of, 371–77
    effectiveness, 368
    equating, in research, 72
    experimental, in research, 71
    goals, 373
    homogeneous, 72
    interaction, 332–45, 388
    interventions, and OD, 527–29
    maintenance activities, 379
    matching of, 72
    motivation, 381
    norms, 35, 373, 376–77, 385
    and organizational behavior, 7
    participation, 37
    productivity, 368, 375, 386–88
    products of development, 373–77
    purposes, 369–71
    random assignment, 71–72
    and research designs, 70–73
    rewards, 382–83
    roles, 375–76
    self-contained, 485
    semiautonomous groups, 659, 666, 742–43, 747
    size, 380–81
    stages of development, 372–73
    and structure, organization, 549
    tasks, 373–75
    and threats to validity, 68–69
    types, 369–71
    why groups form, 332–34
Group observers, as type of maintenance role, 376
Groupthink, in decision making, 390–92
Growth:
    of employees, 36
    of organizations, 38
Growth needs, 207, 742
Growth need strength, 656

Hackman-Oldham Job Characteristics Model, 653–57, 659, 662, 664
Halo error:
    in organization stage of perceptual process, 137–39
    in retrieval stage of perceptual process, 146
Haptics, as form of nonverbal communication, 347n
Harmonizers, as type of maintenance role, 376
Hawthorne:
    effect, 432
    environment, 36
    studies, 34–36, 258
    work situation, 36
Hay system, in job evaluation, 304
Health, and job design, 649n
Health plans, 253
Hedonism, 211
Heroes, organizational, and culture, 699
Herzberg's Two-Factor Theory, 651–53
Heterogeneity, and power, 473–74
Hierarchy:
    of authority, 23, 28, 32, 42–43, 481, 558, 564, 572, 597, 603–4
    as coordination mechanism, 568–69
    of goals and objectives, 25–26
    latticework, 744–45
    organizational, 24, 339
    and power, 473–74
    and scalar chain, 31, 33
    and structure, 558
    and unity of command principle, 31n, 573, 603
Hiring decision, 74, 105
Historical decision model, 165
History threat to validity, 68, 70
Homogeneous groups, 72, 75
Honesty tests, 97
Horizontal integration strategy, 689
Horizontal job enlargement, 650–51, 660
Horizontal specialization, 564
Host group, in intergroup interventions and OD, 530
Human behavior:
    and Hawthorne studies, 34–36
    and Theory X, 36–37
Human factors engineering, 643–45

Human relations school:
    assumptions, 36–37, 40–41
    definition, 36
    Hawthorne studies, 34–36
    Mary Parker Follett, 34
    scientific methods, 34
Human resource management (*see also* Personnel):
    definition, 15, 18
    and micro OB, 15
Human skills, 44–45
Human Subjects Committee, 74
Humor as coping mechanism, 274
Hygiene factors, 652
Hypothesis and scientific process, 59

Iconics as form of nonverbal communication, 347n
Idea evaluation in decision making, 392
Idea generation in decision making, 392
Identification:
    as response to power, 465
    and role conforming, 344
Illumination, Hawthorne studies, 34
Illusion (*see* Perception)
Imitation in learning, 215
Implicit theories, and scientific process, 59–60
Impression management, and power, 475
In Search of Excellence, 53–54
In-basket tests, 294
Incentive, in motivation, 203
Incentive payment:
    and Hawthorne studies, 35
    and locus of control, 98
    programs, 15, 227, 308
Incentive systems, 309–10
Inclusionary dimension of organizations, 339, 354
Incremental adjustments of time, 48
Incubation stage in creative decision making process, 183–84
Individual adjustment to norms, 376
Individual differences (*see also* Abilities; Personality; Selection), 94, 110
    in communication, 348, 352
    in hiring, 82
    and mirror image fallacy, 84
    social traits, 95, 105, 110
    study of, 85
Individual roles, 376
Individual versus general interests, principle of management, 31n
Individualism-collectivism dimension, of culture, 737–39, 750–51, 753, 755
Induction (*see* Scientific process)
Industrial democracy, 34, 741
Industrial engineering, 28, 640–43, 646, 649
Industrial psychology, 14
Industrial revolution:
    and management practices, 28
Industrial robots, 665
Inequity (*see* Equity theory)
Informal groups, 369–70
Informal organization, 695–703
Information:
    acquisition of, 10–11, 13
    and environment, 39
    evaluating, 27
    inputs, and open systems, 39
    methods of acquiring, 10–11
    networks, 46
    overload, 387, 617
    social, 700
    upward, 42
Information, social, 700, 734
Information-collecting step, and OD, 707
Information givers as type of task-oriented role, 375
Information seekers as type of task-oriented role, 375
Information sharing step, and OD, 707
Informational roles, 45–46
Informed consent in research, 74
Ingratiation, and power, 475
In-group members:
    and leadership, 426–27
    and power, 475n
Initiating structure, 416–17, 426
Initiative principle of management, 31n
Initiators as type of task-oriented role, 375
Innovation in decision making, 182, 185
Inputs and open systems, 38
Insight stage in creative decision-making process, 184
Instincts, 93–94

Machiavellianism, 472
Macro organizational behavior, 14–15, 18
  journals, 77n
  research, 77–78
Maintenance roles, in groups, 375–76
Management (see also Leader; Leadership;
    Managers):
  and contingency framework, 14, 40
  delegation by top mangement, 42
  definition, 22, 24
  and domination, 27
  functions of, 24–28, 30, 33, 41–44
  intuition in, 13, 32
  and Hawthorne studies, 34–36
  participative (see Participative management)
  principles, 28, 33
  process, 24
  skill acquisition model, 7–8
  skill acquisition stages, 8–10
  skill types, 44–45
  theories, 28–39
  Theory X assumptions, 36–37
  Theory Y assumptions, 37
Management team, as type of formal group, 370
Management thought, schools of, 28–41
Manager (see Management; Managers)
Managerial authority, 24
Managerial grid, 417
Managerial roles, 45–47, 410–11
Managerial skills, 44–45
Managers (see also Leader; Leadership;
    Management):
  as sources of attitudes, 259
  charisma, 27
  definition, 41
  influence, 27
  learning of, 7–10
  line, 289
  and personnel tasks, 290
  problem solving, 10–13
  roles, 45–57, 410–11
  skills, 44–45
  staff, 289
  time spent, 48
  types, 41–44
Market:
  development, 690
  futures, 76
  and organizational environments, 39
Market structure (see Divisional structure)
Masculinity-femininity dimension of culture,
    736–37, 753, 755
Maslow's need theory, 205–7
Mass production, and technology, 610–11
Matching subjects, 72
Matrix organization structure, 573, 602–3, 606,
    608, 614
Maturity and leadership, 428–29
Maturity stage of group development, 373
McClelland's theory of achievement motivation,
    209–10
Mean differences, test of, 63–64
Measurement (see also Test):
  designs, 70–73
  instruments, validity threat, 69
  of locus of control, 98
  of motives, 97–98
  observational, 102
  of physical abilities, 86
  projective, 103
  timing, 70–73
Mechanistic structure, 594–95, 605–6, 610–11,
    613–14, 616 (see also Bureaucracy)
Mediating technology, 612–13
Meditation, 272
Medium, stage in communication, 345–46
Membership groups, 369–71
Memomotion analysis, 647
Memory, as cognitive ability, 89–90
Memory decay, 144
Mental tests (see Abilities; Cognitive abilities)
Mentor-protege relationships, 317–18
Mentoring relationship, 317
Merit-based pay plans, 308–9
Methods engineering, 641
Micro organizational behavior, 14, 18
  journals, 77n
  research, 77–78
Micromotion analysis, 646
Middle Ages, 59
Minnesota Importance Questionnaire (MIQ),
    97–98
Minnesota Multiphasic Personality Inventory
    (MMPI), 100

Minnesota Satisfaction Questionnaire, 246
Mirror image fallacy, 83–84, 121
Mission of organization:
  definition, 22, 685
  and industrial democracy, 34
  and managers, 41
  statement of, 22
Model of bureaucracy, 32
Modeling, 214
Monitor, role of, 45–46
Morale (see Satisfaction; job)
Mortality threat, to validity, 68, 71
Motion study, 29
Motivating potential score, and JDS, 657
Motivation (see also Effort):
  Alderfer's ERG theory, 207–8
  and cognition, 201
  cognitive theories, 201
  and compensation, 6, 308
  content theories, 200–201
  and culture, 742, 745–46, 749–50
  and decentralization, 569
  definition, 200
  equity theory, 224–28
  expectancy theory, 201–3, 437
  and goal setting, 3, 219 (see also Goals)
  of groups, 381–83
  and job design, 3, 651–56, 658, 661–63, 666
  and leadership, 437
  learning theories, 210–15
  by managers, 46
  manipulating, 437
  Maslow's need hierarchy, 205–7
  McClelland's theory of achievement
      motivation, 209–10
  Murray's theory of manifest needs, 208–9
  and organization development, 530
  and participation, 6
  and performance, 4, 5, 106–10, 199, 204
  process theories, 201
  and rewards, 224, 229
  and specialization, 566
  Theory X assumptions, 36–37
  VIE theory, 201
Motivator factors, 651–52
Motive:
  for behavior, 199
  as a personality characteristic, 97–98
Motor skills (see Psychomotor ability)
Multinational organization, 734n
Multiple perspectives in retrieval stage of
    perceptual process, 146
Murray's theory of manifest needs, 208–9
Mutual adjustment, 552, 554, 556–58, 573, 595,
    597–99, 603, 605–8, 610–12, 613–14, 616,
    621, 666, 751
Myth, organizational, and culture, 698–99

National culture, 734–35 (see also Culture)
National differences (see Culture)
National Labor Relations Act, 313
Natural selection, theory of, 85
Need for achievement, 209–10, 221, 414, 424–25
Need for affiliation, 424–25
Need for change, 513, 515
Need for power, 414, 424–25, 461, 472
Need prepotency, 205
Need satisfaction in group formation, 333
Need theories of motivation, 200, 203, 205–10,
    216
Needs (see also Motivation):
  and career counseling, 316
  and change, 509, 515
  definition, 245
  general, 315, 742
  and group formation, 333
  as internal factor in attention stage, 132
  Maslow's hierarchy, 205–7
  in motivation, 205, 217, 750
Negative affectivity, 261–63
Negative feedback and open systems, 39
Negative politics, 476
Negative reinforcement, 212–13
Negative relationship, 65
Negotiation:
  and change, 514
  and conflict, 485
Negotiator, role of, 45–46
Nenko system, 745
Neo-universal theories of leadership, 439–41
Noise in communication, 346
Noisy environments in decision making, 177–78
Nominal group technique, 394

Nonprogrammed decision, 176
Norms (see also Culture; Expectations):
  and change, 522, 684
  and culture, 695–97, 700–704, 733–35,
      737–39, 753, 754n
  in decision making, 176–77
  definition, 553
  formation of, 342
  group, 376–77, 385
  in Hawthorne studies, 35
  and legitimate power, 463
  peripheral, 376
  pivotal, 376
  and politics, 477
  in roles, 342
  standardization, 553–54, 599
  and structure, 551
North America, productivity, 3
Nova technique, 166
Novelty, external factor in attention stage, 131
Novice stage, management skills learning, 8

Objectives (see also Goals):
  as benchmarks, 25
  divisional, 25, 43
  functional, 25, 43
  and managerial level, 41–44
  operational, 25, 43
  setting, 25, 30, 43
  types of, 25
Objectivity:
  defined, 56
  in standardized measures, 62
Observation:
  in diagnostic model or approach, 10–11
  in measuring personality, 102
  as source of self-efficacy, 218
Occupation:
  and personal styles, 96
  and self-esteem, 101
Occupational Reinforcer Pattern (ORP), 98
Occupational Safety and Health Act, 252, 266
OD (see Organization development)
Off-the-shelf decision model, 165–66
Ohio State University studies on leadership,
    416–17, 426
One-group before-after research design, 70
Open-office plan, 261
Open revolution and norms, 377
Open system planning, as OD intervention, 707–9
Open systems school, 37–41
Operant conditioning, 211–12 (see also
    Reinforcement)
Operational objectives, 25
Opinion leader, as communication role, 352
Opportunity:
  in decision making, 164
  and situation analysis, 686
  and stress, 247
Oral communication, 346
Order, principle of management, 31n
Organic structure, 594–95, 605–6, 610–12, 614,
    616, 704
Organization:
  attributes of, 22–23
  definition, 22
  division of labor, 23
  hierarchy of authority, 23
  mission, 22
  principles of, 33
Organization characteristics and structure, 606–8
Organization chart:
  Briggs-Stratton, 24
  and structure, 549, 744
Organization design (see also Structure,
    organization):
  and constituency groups, 593–94
  contingency model, 592–96
  definition, 592
  and organizational effectiveness, 593–94, 596
  and structure, 594–95
Organization development (see also Change,
    organizational; Change agent):
  action research model, 519–21
  and culture, 702–3
  definition, 15–16, 18, 506–8
  evaluation of, 533–35
  features of, 507
  general, 507–35
  group interventions, 527–29
  intergroup interventions, 530–33
  interpersonal interventions, 524–27
  interventions, 522–33